THE WESTMINSTER
DICTIONARY
OF
CHRISTIAN ETHICS

THE WESTMINSTER DICTIONARY OF CHRISTIAN ETHICS

EDITED BY
JAMES F. CHILDRESS
AND
JOHN MACQUARRIE

THE WESTMINSTER PRESS
PHILADELPHIA

Published by The Westminster Press®
Philadelphia, Pennsylvania

PRINTED IN THE UNITED STATES OF AMERICA
6   8   9   7

Library of Congress Cataloging-in-Publication Data

Main entry under title:

The Westminster dictionary of Christian ethics.

 Rev. ed. of: A dictionary of Christian ethics /
edited by John Macquarrie. 1967.
  Bibliography: p.
  Includes index.
  1. Christian ethics—Dictionaries. 2. Ethics—
Dictionaries. I. Childress, James F. II. Macquarrie,
John. III. Dictionary of Christian ethics.
BJ1199.W47 1986   241′.03′21   85-22539
ISBN 0-664-20940-8

PREFACE

The first edition of the *Dictionary of Christian Ethics,* which was prepared by John Macquarrie and published in 1967, has been a valuable and durable reference work. Any dictionary bears the imprint of its time and place, as well as its editor's predilections, in its organization, selection of topics, and allocation of space to various topics, as well as in the content of its entries. Thus, even though this new edition has been built on Macquarrie's foundation, it reflects several major changes in the methods, content, and context of Christian ethics.

The field of Christian ethics has expanded greatly in the last twenty years. For example, in 1967 the American Society of Christian Ethics had only 245 members, but in 1984 the renamed Society of Christian Ethics had 682 members. Similar developments have occurred in the United Kingdom. The list of contributors to this dictionary has more than doubled since the first edition. Still drawn mainly from the United States and the United Kingdom, with a few from Australia and Canada, these authors are nevertheless a more diverse group. In the post–Vatican II era, Christian ethics and moral theology have become more genuinely ecumenical, and this ecumenical spirit is reflected in both the topics and the contributors. We are fortunate to have had the cooperation of such a wide range of scholars from Protestant, Anglican, Roman Catholic, Orthodox, and Jewish backgrounds. The institutional context of scholarship in Christian ethics has also been enlarged, as scholars now often teach in secular colleges and universities as well as in religious institutions, seminaries, and divinity schools. This new context is reflected in the concerns, methods, and style of a number of articles.

The area of applied or practical ethics has also undergone remarkable transformation and expansion since the late 1960s, as theologians have been joined by philosophers—who for many years were interested primarily in metaethics—and by physicians, lawyers, and other professionals, in reflecting on major developments and problems in science, medicine, and health care, among other areas. This dramatic change can be seen in the large number of articles in applied or practical ethics, particularly in the addition of several topics in bioethics or biomedical ethics. Other topics and problems that received little or no attention earlier are now central in Christian ethical reflection. For example, in the first edition there were articles on "Peace and War" and "Just War," but now there are several articles on this range of topics and problems, including nuclear warfare and deterrence. And, among other topics and problems that are featured here, the environment, world hunger, and liberation are also central.

Following the general lines of John Macquarrie's conception of the dictionary, but expanding it, this volume includes several subject areas: (1) Basic ethical concepts, such as "duty," "goodness," "rights," and "conscience," often analyzed by philosophers. (2) Biblical ethics, including overview articles on Old Testament ethics and New Testament ethics, as well as articles on major strands and concepts of biblical ethics and on the use of the Bible in Christian ethics. (3) Theological ethics, including major ethical categories, such as conscience, natural law, and orders; theological concepts, such as faith, grace, and sin; and major theological ethical systems or perspectives, such as Augustinian ethics, Thomistic ethics, and Lutheran ethics. (4) Philosophical traditions in ethics, such as Aristotelian ethics, Kantian ethics, and Utilitarianism. (5) Major non-Christian religious traditions in ethics, such as Islamic ethics and Buddhist ethics. (6) Psychological, sociological, political, and other concepts that are important for Christian ethics. (7) Substantial ethical problems, such as abortion, war, and unemployment, usually including relevant factual information along with an indication of major options in Christian ethical debate.

The main criterion for inclusion was the importance of the topic for Christian ethical reflection, and, in general, the contributors wrote to highlight this importance. Even when not indicated in the title or subtitle (for example, "Stoic Ethics" or "Paul, Ethical Teaching of"), each article is intended to examine ethical issues. For example, an article on "Liberation Theology," "Political Theology," or "Pragmatism" in this dictionary should be assumed to be focused on its ethical presuppositions and implications.

The earlier book included articles on individual thinkers, such as Aristotle, Augustine, and Calvin. These have been replaced by articles on major traditions, movements, or themes that may have been decisively formulated by an individual thinker (for example, "Aristotelian Ethics," "Augustinian Ethics," and "Calvinist Ethics"). Individual thinkers are discussed in that context; in addition, there is an index of names so that the reader can ascertain whether a thinker's position is also discussed elsewhere.

As befits a dictionary, most entries can only provide bare essentials about their topics. They are intended to be both concise and authoritative. Cross references—by asterisks after key words or by explicit reference to other entries, either within or at the end of the discussion—have been used extensively to direct the reader to other articles for further treatment of the same or related issues. In addition, bibliographies with most major entries direct the reader to other resources. Because of the increased number of topics and contributors, some themes are discussed in more than one place; some overlap was tolerated in order to gain comprehensiveness and diversity of perspective. The dictionary is designed to indicate what is controversial as well as what is settled in Christian ethical reflection.

When The Westminster Press persuaded me to undertake the preparation of a new edition of the *Dictionary of Christian Ethics* on the basis of John Macquarrie's earlier one, I greatly underestimated how much time and energy it would consume and also how much I would enjoy the project, especially because of what I have learned, despite its various tedious activities. The enjoyment was enhanced by the cooperation of many people—particularly John Macquarrie and Ronald Preston—who recommended topics and authors and contributed articles. John Bowden, of SCM Press, first had the vision of what might be accomplished by a new edition and developed an initial list of topics, which formed the basis of my work. I was also greatly aided by suggestions from James Heaney and Max Stackhouse. In addition, John Macquarrie and Ronald Preston read most of the articles and offered valuable suggestions for revision. I am deeply indebted to both of them. Of course, preparing this edition was made much easier by the solid foundation originally laid by John Macquarrie.

The editors of The Westminster Press were helpful and patient, especially in the final stages of the project. Several research assistants at the University of Virginia—Steve DalleMura, Courtney Campbell, William Boley, and James Tubbs—provided valuable assistance, as did Valerie Piper, an intern at the Wilson Center. Albert Franklin Childress helped greatly in the final stages, and Courtney Campbell prepared the name index. I am also grateful to Wanda Proffitt, LaRea Frazier, and Dawn Reynolds of the Department of Religious Studies at the University of Virginia for their excellent secretarial assistance.

As a fellow at the Woodrow Wilson International Center for Scholars in Washington, D.C.—with additional support from the Guggenheim Foundation—I was able to put the finishing touches on this dictionary in that comfortable and stimulating environment. I deeply appreciate the support from the Wilson Center and the Guggenheim Foundation; of course, they are in no way responsible for the content.

The value of this dictionary rests finally on the quality of the individual entries, and I am grateful to the many authors in the United States, the United Kingdom, Australia, and Canada who responded so graciously to my request for contributions. Approximately 40 percent of the entries have been retained from the first edition. When possible, the authors of the retained articles were invited to revise them, and I am delighted that most were able and willing to do so. In other cases, I made revisions where required to update the entries. To all of the authors who contributed to this volume I express my deepest gratitude.

JAMES F. CHILDRESS

Charlottesville, Virginia

CONTRIBUTORS

James Luther Adams, *Edward Mallinckrodt, Jr. Professor of Divinity Emeritus, Harvard Divinity School.* Voluntary Associations

Joseph L. Allen, *Professor of Ethics, Perkins School of Theology, Southern Methodist University, Dallas.* Covenant; Democracy; Personal Ethics; Social Ethics

Terence R. Anderson, *Professor of Social Ethics, Vancouver School of Theology, Vancouver, B.C., Canada.* Environmental Ethics

Dick Anthony, *Private Practice in Transpersonal Psychotherapy, Berkeley, California.* Deprogramming

Sherwin Bailey†, *formerly Chancellor of Wells Cathedral.* Lesbianism; Sodomy

Sydney D. Bailey, *Friends House, London.* Collective Security; Disarmament; Internationalism; Security; World Government

Hugh Barbour, *Professor of Religion, Earlham College and Earlham School of Religion, Richmond, Indiana.* Quaker Ethics

William Barclay†, *formerly Lecturer in the University of Glasgow.* Cynics, Ethics of the; Cyrenaics, Ethics of the; Epicureanism, Ethics of; Essenes; Skeptics; Stoic Ethics

Robert Benne, *Jordan-Trexler Professor of Religion, Roanoke College, Salem, Virginia.* Capitalism

John C. Bennett, *President Emeritus and Reinhold Niebuhr Professor of Social Ethics Emeritus, Union Theological Seminary, New York.* Freedom; State

William H. Boley, *Department of Religious Studies, University of Virginia.* Wesleyan Ethics

Richard Bondi, *Research Assistant Professor of Christian Ethics, Candler School of Theology, Emory University, Atlanta.* Character; Children; Family; Parenthood

Eugene B. Borowitz, *Professor of Education and Jewish Religious Thought, Hebrew Union College—Jewish Institute of Religion, New York.* Jewish Ethics

Vernon J. Bourke, *Professor Emeritus, Philosophy, St. Louis University.* Medieval Ethics; Thomistic Ethics

Roy Branson, *Senior Research Fellow, Kennedy Institute of Ethics, Georgetown University, Washington, D.C.* Refugees

Paul Brett, *Director for Social Responsibility, Diocese of Chelmsford.* Automation; Computers; Robots

R. E. C. Browne†, *formerly Canon of Manchester.* Accidie; Hybris

Don S. Browning, *Alexander Campbell Professor of Religion and Psychological Studies, The Divinity School, University of Chicago.* Counseling, Ethical Problems in; Psychoanalysis; Psychology and Ethics

John Burnaby, *Professor Emeritus, University of Cambridge.* Love

Lisa Sowle Cahill, *Associate Professor of Theology, Boston College.* Abortion; Excommunication; Sexual Ethics

Paul F. Camenisch, *Professor of Religious Studies, DePaul University, Chicago.* Gratitude

Alastair V. Campbell, *Senior Lecturer, Department of Christian Ethics, University of Edinburgh.* Persons and Personality

James F. Childress, *Edwin B. Kyle Professor of Christian Studies and Professor of Medical Education, University of Virginia, Charlottesville.* Adiaphora; Amnesty; Anthropology and Ethics; Applied Ethics; Aristotelian Ethics; Autonomy; Axiology; Bioethics; Blessedness/Blessed; Care; Charity; Civil Disobedience; Civil Rights; Coercion; Compassion; Conscientious Objection; Conscription; Consent; Consequentialism; Contracts; Cost-Benefit Analysis; Covetousness; Cruelty; Dilemma; Dirty Hands; Discrimination; Dissent; Divine Right of Kings; Envy; Ethicist, Ethician; Exploitation; Fairness/Fair Play; Fetal Research; Formalism; Gluttony; Harm; Hatred; Health Care, Right to; Honor; Hypocrisy; Image of God; I-Thou Relationship; Jealousy; Justification, Moral; Liberalism; Life, Quality of; Lust; Magnanimity; Malice; Masturbation; Medical Ethics; Meekness; Mercy; Militarism; Moralism; Motives and Motivation; Mutual Aid; Necessity; Nonmaleficence; Norms; Obligation; Order; Organ Transplantation; Pacifism; Paternalism; Platonic Ethics; Privacy; Promise; Proportionality, Principle of; Public Policy; Rationalization; Realism; Remorse; Repentance; Resistance; Righteousness; Risk; Sanction; Secrecy; Secularization; Seven Deadly Sins; Shame; Sin; Situation Ethics; Social Service of the Church; Superior Orders; Teleological Ethics; Temperance; Theodicy; Tobacco, Use of; Trust; Tyrannicide; Vice; Wedge Argument, Slippery Slope Argument, etc.; Whistle-blowing; Zeal

Drew Christiansen, S.J., *Assistant Professor of Social Ethics, Jesuit School of Theology at Berkeley, California.* Aged, Care of the

Henry B. Clark II, *Professor of Social Ethics, University of Southern California, Los Angeles.* Civilization; Community; Culture; Social Class; Society

Harvey G. Cox, Jr., *Victor S. Thomas Professor of Divinity, Harvard Divinity School.* Power

Antonio S. Cua, *Professor of Philosophy, The Catholic University of America, Washington, D.C.* Confucian Ethics; Taoist Ethics

Charles E. Curran, *Professor of Moral Theology, The Catholic University of America, Washington, D.C.* Counter-Reformation Moral Theology; Modern Roman Catholic Moral Theology; Official Roman Catholic Social Teaching; Subsidiarity, Principle of

Thomas E. Davitt, S.J.†, *formerly Professor, Marquette University, Milwaukee.* Law

V. A. Demant†, *formerly Professor in the University of Oxford.* Good Works; Mixed Motives

Valerie DeMarinis, *Assistant Professor of Theology and Psychology, United Theological Seminary of the Twin Cities, New Brighton, Minnesota.* Procreation

Mark J. Dresden, *Emeritus Professor of Iranian Languages, University of Pennsylvania.* Zoroastrian Ethics

G. R. Dunstan, *Professor Emeritus of Moral and Social Theology, University of London.* Conventions

Arthur J. Dyck, *Mary B. Saltonstall Professor of Population Ethics, Harvard School of Public Health, and Member, Faculty of Divinity, Harvard University.* Population Policy; Procreation

Craig Dykstra, *Thomas W. Synnott Professor of Christian Education, Princeton Theological Seminary.* Education, Christian Moral; Moral Development

Charles Elliott, *Director, Christian Aid, British Council of Churches.* Economic Development

Dorothy Emmet, *Emeritus Professor of Philosophy, University of Manchester.* Evolutionary Ethics; Professional Ethics

H. Tristram Engelhardt, Jr., *Professor, Departments of Medicine and Community Medicine, Baylor College of Medicine, Houston.* Alcoholism; Circumcision; Drug Addiction; Health and Disease, Values in Defining; Libertarianism

A. C. Ewing†, *formerly of the University of Cambridge.* Categorical Imperative; Choice; Conflict of Duties; Heteronomy; Kantian Ethics; Kingdom of Ends; Naturalistic Ethics; Practical Reason

Alan D. Falconer, *Lecturer in Systematic Theology, Irish School of Ecumenics, Dublin.* Dehumanization; Human Dignity, Humanitarianism

Margaret A. Farley, *Professor of Christian Ethics, Yale Divinity School.* Feminist Ethics

John C. Fletcher, *Assistant for Bioethics, National Institutes of Health, Washington, D.C.* Genetics; Reproductive Technologies

Joseph Fletcher, *Visiting Scholar, School of Medicine, University of Virginia.* Hippocratic Oath

Duncan Baillie Forrester, *Professor of Christian Ethics and Practical Theology, New College, University of Edinburgh.* Socialism

William K. Frankena, *Emeritus Professor of Philosophy, University of Michigan.* Morality and Religion, Relations of

E. Clinton Gardner, *Professor of Christian Ethics, Emory University, Atlanta.* Eschatological Ethics; New Testament Ethics; Temptations of Jesus

Alan Geyer, *Executive Director, Churches' Center for Theology and Public Policy, Washington, D.C.* National Sovereignty; Nationalism; Patriotism

Robin Gill, *Lecturer in Christian Ethics and the Sociology of Religion, University of Edinburgh.* Sociology of Ethics

Glenn C. Graber, *Professor of Philosophy, University of Tennessee.* Divine Command Morality

Ronald M. Green, *John Phillips Professor of Religion, Dartmouth College, Hanover, New Hampshire.* Future Generations, Obligations to

Kenneth G. Greet, *Secretary of the British Methodist Conference.* Temperance

Graeme M. Griffin, *Professor of Church and Community, Uniting Church Theological Hall, Melbourne, Australia.* Anger; Conviction of Sin; Defense Mechanisms; Ego; Emotion; Empathy; Enthusiasm; Guilt; Habit; Id; Inhibition; Repression; Superego; Sympathy; Unconscious

Jon P. Gunnemann, *Associate Professor of Social Ethics, Candler School of Theology, Emory University, Atlanta.* Business Ethics; Revolution

James M. Gustafson, *University Professor of Theological Ethics, University of Chicago.* Christian Ethics

John Stapylton Habgood, *Archbishop of York.* Brainwashing; Indoctrination; Science and Ethics

Robert T. Handy, *Henry Sloane Coffin Professor of Church History, Union Theological Seminary, New York.* New England Transcendentalism; Pragmatism; Social Gospel

Stanley S. Harakas, *Professor of Orthodox Christian Ethics, Holy Cross Greek Orthodox School of Theology, Brookline, Massachusetts.* Eastern Orthodox Christian Ethics

E. R. Hardy†, *formerly Professor, Berkeley Divinity School, New Haven, Connecticut.* Abstinence; Asceticism; Celibacy; Chastity; Fasting; Monastic Ethics; Mortification; Poverty; Self-Denial; Virginity

Richard M. Hare, *White's Professor of Moral Philosophy Emeritus, University of Oxford.* Conventional Morality; Decision; Deliberation; Descriptivism; Emotivism; Ethics; Intention; Prescriptivism; Relativism; Right and Wrong; Subjectivism, Ethical; Universalizability of Moral Judgments; Utilitarianism

Walter Harrelson, *Distinguished Professor of Old Testament, Vanderbilt University Divinity School, Nashville.* Decalogue; Mosaic Law; Prophetic Ethics; Wisdom Literature, Ethics in

Beverly Wildung Harrison, *Professor of Christian Ethics, Union Theological Seminary, New York.* Sex Discrimination; Women, Status of

Julian N. Hartt, *Kenan Professor of Religious Studies Emeritus, University of Virginia.* Faith

Stanley Hauerwas, *Professor of Theological Ethics, The Divinity School, Duke University, Durham, North Carolina.* Virtue

Roger Hazelton, *Abbot Professor of Christian Theology Emeritus, Andover Newton Theological School, Newton Centre, Massachusetts.* Courage; Humanistic Ethics

Brian Hebblethwaite, *Dean of Chapel, Queens' College, and University Lecturer in Divinity, Cambridge.* Dialectic; Meaning/Meaninglessness; Transcendence

Martin J. Heinecken, *Professor Emeritus, Systematic Theology, The Lutheran Theological Seminary at Philadelphia.* Justification by Faith; Law and Gospel; Pietism

Ian Henderson†, *formerly Professor in the University of Glasgow.* Innocence; Original Sin; Self-Love; Temptation; Total Depravity

Carl F. H. Henry, *Lecturer at Large, World Vision International, Monrovia, California.* Evangelical Ethics; Fundamentalist Ethics

Seward Hiltner†, *formerly Professor of Theology and Personality, Princeton Theological Seminary.* Anxiety

Simon Holdaway, *Lecturer in Sociology, The University of Sheffield.* Crime; Juvenile Delinquency

J. L. Houlden, *Lecturer in New Testament Studies, King's College, London.* Jesus, Ethical Teaching of; Johannine Ethics; Kingdom of God; Neighbor; Parenesis; Paul, Ethical Teaching of

Gerard J. Hughes, S.J., *Head of Department of Philosophy, Heythrop College, University of London.* Ignorance; Natural Law; Self-Deception; Totality, Principle of; Weakness, Moral

T. E. Jessop†, *formerly Professor in the University of Hull.* Chivalry; Mean, Doctrine of the; Nihilism; Perfectionism; Renaissance, The; Romanticism

James Turner Johnson, *Professor of Religion, Rutgers University, New Brunswick, New Jersey.* Crusade; Deterrence; Just War; Nuclear Warfare; Peace; Puritan Ethics; War

Penelope Johnstone, *Oriental Institute, Oxford.* Islamic Ethics

Albert R. Jonsen, *Professor of Ethics in Medicine, School of Medicine, University of California, San Francisco.* Casuistry; *Epikeia;* Experimentation with Human Subjects; Responsibility

Charles W. Kegley, *Outstanding Professor of Philosophy, California State University, Bakersfield.* Meliorism; Optimism; Pessimism; Progress, Belief in

Walter Klaassen, *Professor of History, Conrad Grebel College, University of Waterloo, Waterloo, Ontario, Canada.* Anabaptist Ethics; Mennonite Ethics

S. J. Knox, *Minister of Old Church, Port Seton, East Lothian.* Nonconformist Conscience

James Kuhn, *Courtney Brown Professor of Corporate Relations and Labor, Columbia University, New York.* Industrial Relations

John P. Langan, S.J., *Senior Fellow, Woodstock Theological Center, Georgetown University, Washington, D.C.* Cardinal Virtues; Common Good; Metaethics; Prudence

James N. Lapsley, Jr., *Carl and Helen Egner Professor of Pastoral Theology, Princeton Theological Seminary.* Environment and Heredity; Instincts or Drives; Scrupulosity

William H. Lazareth, *Pastor, Holy Trinity Lutheran Church, New York.* Lutheran Ethics; Orders; Two Realms

Robert Lee, *President, Enfield Resources, Inc., Vancouver, B.C., Canada.* Anomie

Paul Lehmann, *Charles A. Briggs Professor of Systematic Theology Emeritus, Union Theological Seminary, New York.* Forgiveness

Andrew Linzey, *Anglican Chaplain to the University of Essex.* Animals

David Little, *Professor of Religious Studies, University of Virginia.* Comparative Religious Ethics; Human Rights; Natural Rights

Paul A. Lombardo, *Attorney-at-law, Sacramento, California.* Eugenics

Edward LeRoy Long, Jr., *James W. Pearsall Professor of Christian Ethics and Theology of Culture, The Theological School, Drew University, Madison, New Jersey.* Modern Protestant Ethics; Technology

Robin W. Lovin, *Associate Professor of Ethics and Society, The Divinity School, University of Chicago.* Anarchism; Ethos; Genocide

Harvey K. McArthur, *Professor Emeritus, Hartford Seminary, Hartford, Connecticut.* Golden Rule; Household Codes; Mammon

Dennis P. McCann, *Associate Professor Religious Studies, DePaul University, Chicago.* Conscientization; Liberation Theology; Utopian Thought

McCormick, Richard A., S.J., *Rose F. Kennedy Professor of Christian Ethics, Kennedy Institute of Ethics, Georgetown University, Washington, D.C.* Double Effect, Principle of; Finality; Magisterium

William McKane, *Professor of Hebrew and Oriental Languages, University of St. Andrews.* Babylonian Ethics; Egyptian Ethics, Ancient

Henry McKeating, *Senior Lecturer in Theology, University of Nottingham.* Old Testament Ethics

Donald MacKenzie MacKinnon, *Norris-Hulse Professor Emeritus of Divinity, University of Cambridge.* Happiness; Intuition; Pleasure; Socratic Ethics; Sophists

John Macquarrie, *Lady Margaret Professor of Divinity and Canon of Christ Church, University of Oxford.* Abandonment; Abjuration; Absolution; Accidents; Act, Action, Agent; Addiction; Adoption; Affinity; Affirmation; Alienation; Altruism; Amusements; Anarchy; Antinomianism; Appetites; Aristocracy; Aspiration; Authenticity; Authority; Beneficence; Benevolence; Boycott; Canon Law;

Censure; Compensationism; Confession; Conservatism; Contemplation; Contrition; Counsels; Deontology; Destiny; Discipline; Dispensation; Egoism; Endogamy; Erastianism; Eudaemonism; Excellence; Exogamy; Exposition; Fornication; Free Will and Determinism; Hedonism; Interim Ethic; *Koinonia;* Laicity; Legalism; Manichean Ethics; Merit; Monogamy; Moral Argument; Otherworldliness; Penance; Polygamy; Quietism; Restitution; Ritschlian Ethics; Scandal; Self-Examination; Seven Gifts of the Holy Spirit; Simony; Social Contract; Suffering; Sumptuary Laws; Supererogation, Works of; Synderesis; Synergism; Theocracy; Theological Virtues; Will

Daniel C. Maguire, *Professor of Moral Theology, Marquette University, Milwaukee.* Cooperation with Evil; Omission, Sin of

John Mahoney, S.J., *Lecturer in Moral and Pastoral Theology, Heythrop College, University of London.* Ascetical Theology; Blasphemy; Holiness; Reverence; Sacrilege

William F. May, *Carey M. Maguire University Professor in Ethics, Southern Methodist University, Dallas.* Philanthropy

David L. Mealand, *Lecturer in New Testament, University of Edinburgh.* Poverty; Wealth

Stewart Mechie, *formerly Lecturer in the University of Glasgow.* Industrial Revolution

Kenneth N. Medhurst, *Professor of Political Studies, University of Stirling.* Dictatorship; Political Parties

Gilbert Meilaender, *Associate Professor of Religion, Oberlin College, Oberlin, Ohio.* Friendship

Carl Michalson†, *formerly of Drew University, Madison, New Jersey.* Existentialist Ethics; Secularism

Basil Mitchell, *Nolloth Professor of the Philosophy of the Christian Religion Emeritus, University of Oxford.* Morality, Legal Enforcement of

Elizabeth R. Moberly, *Psychologist, Theologian, and Criminologist, Clare College, Cambridge.* Concupiscence; Incest; Pederasty; Penology; Rape; Retribution; Transsexualism

R. C. Mortimer†, *formerly Bishop of Exeter.* Formalism; Ignorance; Moral Theology; Oaths; Vows

Walter G. Muelder, *Dean Emeritus and Lecturer in Social Ethics, Boston University School of Theology.* Personalism

Philip A. Muntzel, *Associate Professor of Theology, King's College, Wilkes-Barre, Pennsylvania.* Hope

James B. Nelson, *Professor of Christian Ethics, United Theological Seminary of the Twin Cities, New Brighton, Minnesota.* Homosexuality; Prostitution

Robert C. Neville, *Professor of Religious Studies and Philosophy, State University of New York at Stony Brook.* Behavior Control

John T. Noonan, Jr., *Professor of Law, University of California, Berkeley.* Bribery; Contraception

Richard A. Norris, Jr., *Professor of Church History, Union Theological Seminary, New York.* Neoplatonism; Patristic Ethics

Oliver O'Donovan, *Regius Professor of Moral and Pastoral Theology, University of Oxford.* Augustinian Ethics; Reconciliation

Thomas W. Ogletree, *Dean, The Theological School, Drew University, Madison, New Jersey.* Interpretation

Helen Oppenheimer, *Member of the Inter-Anglican Doctrinal and Theological Commission.* Desire; Divorce; Humility; Marriage; Obedience; Pride; Saintliness; Sanctification; Sloth

Gene Outka, *Dwight Professor of Philosophy and Christian Ethics, Yale University.* Kierkegaardian Ethics; Love; Respect for Persons; Self-Realization

Huw Parri Owen, *Emeritus Professor of Christian Doctrine, King's College, London.* Evil; Goodness

Barrie Paskins, *Lecturer in War Studies, King's College, London.* Imperialism; International Order; Terrorism; Torture

Terry Pinkard, *Kennedy Institute of Ethics, Georgetown University, Washington, D.C.* Hegelian Ethics

Raymond Plant, *Professor of Politics, University of Southampton.* Ideology; Pluralism; Politics

Ronald H. Preston, *Emeritus Professor of Social and Pastoral Theology, University of Manchester.* Capital Punishment; Collective Bargaining; Compromise; Conscience; Corporal Punishment; Equality; False Witness; Honesty; Labor Movements; Lying; Middle Axioms; Slander; Strikes; Trade Unions and Professional Associations; Truthfulness; Unemployment; Vocation; Wages and Salaries; Welfare State; Work, Doctrine of

Warren T. Reich, *Professor of Bioethics and Director, Division of Health and Humanities, School of Medicine, Georgetown University, Washington, D.C.* Handicapped, Care of the; Life, Prolongation of

Thomas L. Robbins, *Associate Editor, Sociological Analysis.* Deprogramming

Brian Rodgers, *formerly Senior Lecturer in the University of Manchester.* Almsgiving; Orphans; Widows

Edward Rogers, *formerly of the Department of Christian Citizenship, The Methodist Church in Great Britain.* Gambling

Cicely Saunders, *Medical Director, St. Christopher's Hospice, Sydenham, London.* Hospice.

Roger L. Shinn, *Reinhold Niebuhr Professor Emeritus of Social Ethics, Union Theological Seminary, New York.* Anti-Semitism; Apartheid; Collectivism; Individualism; Segregation; Slavery

Donald W. Shriver, Jr., *President of Faculty and William E. Dodge Professor of Applied Christianity, Union Theological Seminary, New York.* Hunger, World

Roger C. Sider, *Associate Professor and Associate Chairman, Department of Psychiatry, University of Rochester School of Medicine and Dentistry.* Involuntary Hospitalization; Mental Health; Mental Illness

Ulrich Simon, *Lecturer in the University of London.* Heaven; Hell; Rewards and Punishments

John Frederick Sleeman, *Senior Research Fellow in Political Economy, University of Glasgow.* Advertising; Just Price and Just Wage; Laissez-faire; Usury and Interest

William A. Smalley, *Professor of Linguistics, Bethel College, St. Paul, Minnesota.* Custom; Primitive Ethics; Taboo

Ninian Smart, *Professor of Religious Studies, University of Lancaster, and University of California, Santa Barbara.* Buddhist Ethics; Fate and Fatalism; Hindu Ethics; Relativism in Ethics

David H. Smith, *Professor of Religious Studies and Director, The Poynter Center, Indiana University.* Fidelity; Hospitality; Loyalty; Sick, Care of the

John E. Smith, *Clark Professor of Philosophy, Yale University.* Absolutes, Ethical; Autonomy of Ethics; Duty; Rights; Values and Value Judgment

Ronald Gregor Smith†, *formerly Professor in the University of Glasgow.* Enlightenment; Worldliness

A. Brendan Soane, *Lecturer in Moral Theology, Allen Hall, London.* Insurance; Property; Theft

William C. Spohn, S.J., *Assistant Professor of Theological Ethics, Jesuit School of Theology at Berkeley, California.* Discernment

Max L. Stackhouse, *Professor of Christian Social Ethics, Andover Newton Theological School, Newton Centre, Massachusetts.* Aggression; Church; Cursing/Swearing; Ecclesiology and Ethics; Institution/Institutionalization; Sect; Urbanization

The Rt. Hon. David Steel, M.P., *Leader of the Liberal Party, London.* Liberalism

Jeffrey Stout, *Associate Professor of Religion, Princeton University.* Behaviorism; Idealist Ethics; Positivism; Tradition in Ethics

Douglas Sturm, *Professor of Religion and Political Science, Bucknell University, Lewisburg, Pennsylvania.* Political Theology

John Tinsley, *formerly Bishop of Bristol.* Imitation of Christ; Media, Ethical Issues in; Mysticism and Ethics; Propaganda; Public Opinion

Steven M. Tipton, *Associate Professor of Sociology of Religion, Candler School of Theology, Emory University, Atlanta.* Cults

James B. Tubbs, Jr., *Adjunct Instructor in Philosophy, Virginia Commonwealth University.* Aristotelian Ethics; Energy; Platonic Ethics

Robert M. Veatch, *Professor of Medical Ethics, Kennedy Institute of Ethics, Georgetown University, Washington, D.C.* Codes of Ethics; Death, Determination of

Allen Verhey, *Associate Professor of Religion, Hope College, Holland, Michigan.* Bible in Christian Ethics

Dan O. Via, *Professor of New Testament, The Divinity School, Duke University, Durham, North Carolina.* Sermon on the Mount

Alec R. Vidler, *Honorary Fellow of King's College, Cambridge.* Church and State

Herbert Waddams†, formerly *Canon of Canterbury.* Adultery; Bigamy; Concubinage; Illegitimacy; Nullity

LeRoy Walters, *Director, Center for Bioethics, Kennedy Institute of Ethics, Georgetown University, Washington, D.C.* Confidentiality; Sterilization

Theodore R. Weber, *Professor of Social Ethics, Candler School of Theology, Emory University, Atlanta.* Collective Responsibility

William Werpehowski, *Assistant Professor of Christian Living, Villanova University, Villanova, Pennsylvania.* Justice

Charles C. West, *Stephen Colwell Professor of Christian Ethics, Princeton Theological Seminary.* Communism, Ethics of; Ecumenical Movement, Ethics in the; Marxist Ethics

Alan R. White, *Ferens Professor of Philosophy, University of Hull.* Negligence

James Aitken Whyte, *Professor of Practical Theology and Christian Ethics, University of Saint Andrews.* Calvinist Ethics; Censorship; Continence; Ends and Means; Sabbatarianism; Sunday Observance; Voluntarism

Daniel Day Williams†, *formerly Professor, Union Theological Seminary, New York.* Grace

Preston N. Williams, *Houghton Professor of Theology and Contemporary Change, The Divinity School, Harvard University.* Afro-American Religious Ethics; Colonialism; Prejudice; Race Relations; Racism

Gerald R. Winslow, *Professor of Religion, Walla Walla College, College Place, Washington.* Triage; Vegetarianism

Gibson Winter, *Maxwell M. Upson Professor of Christianity and Society, Princeton Theological Seminary.* Oppression; Phenomenology

Frederik Wisse, *Associate Professor of New Testament, McGill University, Montreal.* Gnosticism, Ethics of

J. Philip Wogaman, *Professor of Christian Social Ethics, Wesley Theological Seminary, Washington, D.C.* Commercialism; Persecution and Toleration

Thomas Wood, *Department of Theology and Religious Studies, St. David's University College, University of Wales.* Anglican Moral Theology/Ethics; Equiprobabilism; Euthanasia; Homicide; Infanticide; Life, Sacredness of; Probabiliorism; Probabilism; Suicide; Tutiorism

Jonathan R. C. Wright, *Tutorial Fellow and University Lecturer, Christ Church College, Oxford.* Fascism; Totalitarian State

Richard M. Zaner, *Ann Geddes Stahlman Professor of Medical Ethics, Vanderbilt University, Nashville.* Body; Embodiment

ABBREVIATIONS

ANET	J. B. Pritchard, *Ancient Near Eastern Texts Relating to the Old Testament,* ²1955
ASV	American Standard Version
AV	Authorized Version (King James Version)
CD	Karl Barth, *Church Dogmatics*
DME	*Dictionary of Medical Ethics,* ed. A. S. Duncan, G. R. Dunstan, and R. B. Welbourn, new rev. ed. 1981
EB	*Encyclopedia of Bioethics,* ed. W. T. Reich, 1978
EP	*The Encyclopedia of Philosophy,* ed. P. Edwards, 1967
ET	English translation
HCR	*Hastings Center Report*
HERE	J. Hastings (ed.), *Encyclopaedia of Religion and Ethics,* 1908–27
IDB	*Interpreter's Dictionary of the Bible,* ed. G. Buttrick, 1962; Supplementary volume, ed. K. Crim, 1976
JME	*Journal of Medical Ethics*
JRE	*Journal of Religious Ethics*
LCC	Library of Christian Classics
NEB	New English Bible
NT	New Testament
OED	Oxford English Dictionary
OT	Old Testament
PL	*Patrologia Latina,* ed. J. P. Migne
RGG	*Die Religion in Geschichte und Gegenwart*
RSV	Revised Standard Version
ST	Thomas Aquinas, *Summa Theologiae*
TDNT	*Theological Dictionary of the New Testament,* ed. G. Kittel and G. Friedrich; tr. and ed. G. W. Bromiley, 1964 76
UK	United Kingdom
UN	United Nations
USA	United States of America
USSR	Union of Soviet Socialist Republics
WA	*Weimarer Ausgabe* (standard edition of Luther's works; Weimar, 1883–)
WCC	World Council of Churches

* An asterisk denotes a reference to another article in the *Dictionary.*

The Index of Names begins on page 671.

Abandonment

The word has been used in at least three senses that have ethical implications.

1. Abandonment to God is a form of spirituality, given classic expression by Jean-Pierre de Caussade in the writing *Self-Abandonment to Divine Providence* (published in French in 1861, over a century after his death; ET 1959). The central idea of this teaching is that the Christian should surrender his or her will entirely to the will of God. It implies a strong doctrine of providence; whatever is going on in the world around us flows from the will of God. The duty of the Christian is to acquiesce in this will and respond to the duties that present themselves in each moment. One is to forget oneself completely and become "as a thing sold and delivered to the purchaser." This, however, is not mere quietism or passivity. It needs an openness and sensitivity to God in each situation, and a willingness to obey his command. Something like a secular equivalent of abandonment is found in Heidegger's idea of *Gelassenheit,* with a meaning ranging from "serenity" to "detachment" (this last point may be compared with what is said below on the Radical Reformers).

During the 16th century, several Radical Reformers (George Williams's designation) gave the term *Gelassenheit*— often translated as abandonment, resignation, or yieldedness —strong ethical and social significance. For example, it expressed the religious motivation for Hutterite communism, which was a way to achieve abandonment to God (*see* **Anabaptist Ethics**). As Ulrich Stadler wrote about the sharing of goods: "It is true abandon to yield and dispose oneself with goods and chattels in the service of the saints. It is also the way of love."

2. Some atheistic existentialists (*see* **Existentialist Ethics**) have used the expression "abandonment" in a sense that is just about exactly opposite to the first one discussed. They see human beings abandoned to themselves in a godless world. This calls for complete moral autonomy* on the part of the human being. There are no eternal values and no divine commands to guide human life, so we each have the responsibility of deciding our own values and pursuing them in our own strength.

3. In a very different sense, the word "abandonment" is used for the practice of deserting infants and leaving them to their fate. This practice, also called "exposition"* of infants, was used in the ancient world as a crude and primitive method of family limitation. It was opposed by the early church as cruel and barbarous, and from about the 5th century the church was making provision for abandoned children. Children are sometimes abandoned at the present day, but although this practice is dangerous and irresponsible, it is not usually deliberately cruel. The intention is not to let the child die, but to let it be found and tended, because the parents are inadequate or unwilling to care for it themselves.

G. H. Williams (ed.), *Spiritual and Anabaptist Writers,* LCC, 1957.

JOHN MACQUARRIE

Abjuration

A solemn and formal act of renunciation. The term is chiefly used nowadays for the renunciation of a false opinion. For a discussion of the moral characteristics of such solemn declarations, *see* **Oaths; Vows.**

JOHN MACQUARRIE

Abnormality

see **Handicapped, Care of the**

Abortion

The ethics of abortion turns on several central factors: (1) *procreation** as a potential outcome of sexual activity; (2) the status, value, or rights of *unborn human life;* (3) the welfare of pregnant *women,* including self-determination of reproductive capacity and protection from physical, mental, and social harm; and (4) the interests of *others,* such as the father, the family, and the religious and civil communities in the numbers, timing, and outcomes of pregnancies and births. Few deny that each factor represents a value to be respected, all other things being equal. The moral dilemma of abortion arises in precisely those situations in which not all values can be given equal support, or in which support of one precludes another. Disagreements about the morality of abortion arise from differing evaluations of the relative priority of these values in conflict cases.

To generalize, the Christian tradition brings to the question of abortion not only respect for the lives of all human individuals but also an extreme caution (if not absolute prohibition) regarding the killing of innocent persons. Abortion has never been seen as in itself a good, or even as morally neutral. However, Christians throughout their history have not been unanimous in determining exactly from what point in the process of conception, gestation, and birth the unborn offspring of human parents deserve the full respect and protection due "innocent persons"; nor on the circumstances which could morally justify a resort to abortion either early or late in pregnancy. Much less have they been unanimous in recognizing for pregnant women a right to self-determination or a sphere of well-being substantially distinct from that of the family and *paterfamilias.*

Biblical and historical resources. Scriptural references to abortion are all but nonexistent. The Old Testament (Hebrew Bible) stipulates merely that if men quarreling cause a woman to miscarry, the guilty one shall pay a fine to the woman's husband. If the woman herself be killed, then the attacker must "give life for life" (Ex. 21:22–23). (The Septuagint introduces into the text a distinction between the "formed" and "unformed" fetus not present in the Hebrew original.) Other texts, which do not mention abortion, demonstrate the ancient Israelite reverence for God's intimate formation of every life (Gen. 4:1; Job 31:15; Isa. 44:24; 49:1, 5; Jer. 1:5) and hope for descendants (Gen. 15:5; Deut. 7:12–14; Pss. 127:3; 128:1–3). A positive valuation of life in the womb in view of God's involvement with it also is to be found in the New Testament infancy narratives (Matt. 1:18; Luke 1:40, 42). The New Testament makes no specific reference to abortion but does reject evil drugs or potions (*pharmakeia*), which may include abortifacients (Gal. 5:20; cf. Rev. 9:21; 18:23; 21:8; 22:5). Explicit condemnations of abortion and infanticide* occur in two contemporaneous but noncanonical catechetical writings: the *Didache,* or *Teaching of the Twelve Apostles,* and the *Epistle of Pseudo-Barnabas.*

Condemnation of abortion is prevalent in the early church and focuses particularly on the integrity of the reproductive process and its place within marriage, the inviolability of life *in utero,* and the duties of love toward offspring. Clement of Alexandria associates abortion with sexual immorality and prohibits abortifacient drugs (the *Pedagogue*). Tertullian of Carthage also repudiates abortion to hide pregnancy (the *Veiling of Virgins*), and counters a charge of infanticide made

against Christians by pointing out that they even regard it as wrong to kill what has been conceived in the womb (the *Apology*). In one ambiguous passage, Tertullian does refer to abortion to save a woman's life as a "necessary cruelty," but his primary aim in the text is to show that the fetus is alive before birth (*On the Soul*).

Though they all disapprove of abortion, Tertullian, Jerome, and Augustine distinguish between the formed and unformed, and the ensouled and unensouled, fetus. These and some later writers take the view that the body is not formed into a "man" until sometime after conception, and at least entertain the possibility that the soul is not infused by God until the body is formed. If not, then abortion before ensoulment would not be the sin of homicide, though still seriously sinful. For instance, Augustine says that the fetus is animated (ensouled) at 46 days, but condemns the killing of both formed and unformed fetus, as well as contraception, even in marriage (*On Marriage and Concupiscence*). One reason for the lack of clear distinction in patristic and medieval writing between the immorality of contraception* and that of abortion is rudimentary biological information regarding reproduction. It was commonly believed that the semen itself was formed into the fetus, or that the semen contained the "man" in miniature (the *homunculus*), which grew in the woman's womb as in a nest. On the basis of notions such as these, the wasting of male seed would be the moral equivalent at least of destruction of the unformed fetus.

Thomas Aquinas did not hold that ensoulment occurs at conception, but, following Aristotle's estimates of time of formation, at 40 days for the male and 90 for the female (*Commentary on Book III of the Sentences of Peter Lombard*). Aquinas says that one who causes an abortion by striking a pregnant woman commits the sin of homicide* only if the fetus is formed. Placing the lives of mother and fetus on a par, he rejects killing the mother in order to baptize the fetus, even though its eternal life may be at stake (*Summa Theologiae* III).

The distinction between animated and unanimated fetus continues to be influential in Catholic discussions until the 18th century. Theologians debate whether countervailing considerations might override the value of fetal life, particularly before ensoulment. Preservation of the life of the mother is the reason most frequently put forward, although protection of her health and reputation also are considered. In the 18th century the teaching of the church shifts significantly toward the position that the human fetus deserves from conception the care due the human person which it at least has the potential to become. By the late 19th century, the Catholic Church had limited even "life against life" abortions to those few in which the procedure is physically "indirect," that is, one which does not destroy the fetus directly, being aimed instead at relief of a condition of the mother, and resulting only secondarily in the death of her offspring. The two most frequently cited cases of "indirect" abortion are removal of a cancerous but pregnant uterus and excision of a fallopian tube in which exists an ectopic pregnancy (*see also* **Double Effect**).

The Protestant Reformers follow the tradition in seeing procreation as an important natural and divinely mandated purpose of sexual activity. They are interested in the status of the fetus mainly in relation to God's creation of the soul and predestination, with Luther and Calvin holding that both soul and body exist immediately at conception, and Melanchthon that the soul is given by God only after the body has been formed. Although Martin Luther speaks of the child in the womb as having a soul ("Interventions in the Theological Disputation of Peter Herzog, *De homini*"), he does not appear to have discussed abortion. In his *Commentaries,* at Gen. 38:10 John Calvin calls abortion "an inexpiable crime," and in response to Ex. 21:22 he adds that "the fetus enclosed in its mother's womb already is a man." Seventeenth-century Anglican and Puritan authors shared in condemning abortion, usually associating it with sexual immorality, and sometimes reviving the distinction between the formed and the unformed fetus.

Current discussion. Twentieth-century perspectives on abortion are significantly different from biblical and traditional ones, due to changed understandings of the values in conflict which lead to abortion. First, procreation is no longer understood to be the sole or primary purpose of sexual activity, which is now seen to be directed at least equally to affective communication between sexual partners. Second, as women gain moral and social autonomy, claims are made on behalf of their right to decide whether or not to bear children. Some see access to abortion as a necessary guarantee of reproductive self-determination. Third, controversies over the status of fetal life at various stages continue, but with the added dimension of more detailed and accurate information about embryonic and fetal development. Fourth, the capacity to predict congenital abnormalities through genetic evaluation of the parents or testing of the fetus *in utero* makes it possible to abort offspring in whom abnormality is anticipated (*see* **Genetics**). Such abortions are asserted to be in the interests of the abnormal individuals themselves, of their families, or of the larger social groups who stand to bear the eventual costs of support. Arguments for abortion on "fetal indications" in particular raise the question whether the same arguments are logically extendable to infanticide, and if not, then the question of what are the morally significant differences between the fetus and the infant.

The status of the fetus. One of the most fundamental and perplexing issues in abortion is the status, value, or "rights" of the life taken. While information about fetal development is widely available, this in itself does not settle the question of fetal status at any particular phase. Few doubt that there exists from conception some form of "human life" in the literal sense; the crucial question is whether from conception or at any subsequent time during pregnancy that life deserves the same respect and protection due an infant. Each claim that at a particular point during gestation the fetus acquires a new or decisive standing in the human community entails an implicit or explicit claim about the minimum characteristics necessary to constitute what could be called, e.g., "human life in the full sense," a "person," or a "child." Some suggested "lines" are conception, nidation and implantation, "quickening," viability, the presence of major organ systems or of electrically recordable brain waves. The associated characteristics are, respectively, human genotype, determinate individuality, movement perceptible to the mother, ability to live outside the womb, presence of the physiological substrata necessary for integrated physical functioning or for consciousness. Further, the development of any particular characteristic subsequent to the genotype will be gradual and variable in individual fetuses, and, in the case of viability, relative to the state of medical practice. Because it has proven exceedingly difficult to reach a consensus that any one line or characteristic is decisive for "full humanity," some philosophers and theologians have taken what might be called simply a "developmental" or "incremental" view of fetal status, holding that it increases as pregnancy progresses. It must be noted, finally, that the question of fetal status and protection is not a specifically or exclusively "religious" issue, since evaluation of fetal life does not depend on and is not derivable in any direct or simple way from assertions that God creates life or forbids the murder of the innocent. The debated question is whether the fetus is in fact in a morally decisive sense "innocent human life."

Feminism and abortion. The feminist critique of Christianity begins from women's experience of oppression and exclusion from power within the history of Christianity and the patriarchal institutions which it has supported. A central target is the subordination of women within the family and the confinement of female influence to the domestic sphere. Women's role has long been defined primarily in terms of motherhood, and women have had limited freedom in deciding whether or not to fill this role. Christian feminists aim for shared male and female responsibility within domestic, economic, political, religious, and ecclesiastical spheres. As a precondition, many view it as necessary to enhance the autonomy* of women in matters of reproduction, freeing them from the burden of unplanned or unwanted pregnancy. This burden is particularly acute when it presents a grave threat to life or health or when it results from rape or incest. However, the "pro-choice" claim that abortion must be available to every woman at her own decision has a political basis which goes beyond ensuring protection of women in extreme conflicts of maternal and fetal rights. Indeed, feminist authors argue that construals of abortion situations as "conflicts of rights*" are too narrow, focusing on individuals at the expense of adequate attention to the social contexts within which individual decisions occur. Those who are sympathetic to the feminist critique but who also view the fetus as worthy of protection may observe that, in view of the fact that most women who choose

abortion do so regretfully and as a "last resort," the enhancement of women's freedom in childbearing might better be served by providing more effective social support for those in difficult circumstances of pregnancy and parenthood (*see* **Feminist Ethics; Women, Status of**).

Abortion and the law. Restrictive or permissive public policies on abortion fall under the rubric of social ethics. The key ethical issues in the legalization of abortion are: (1) whether and when the fetus has a valid moral claim on social protection; (2) whether and when the pregnant woman has a legally protectable claim to decide to abort and to be guaranteed that the competence of abortion practitioners will be supervised; (3) whether certain laws regarding abortion are enforceable and nondiscriminatory and prevent more harm than their alternatives. Those who minimize fetal in favor of maternal rights see abortion as a "private decision" which should not be curtailed by law; those who see the rights of the fetus as equivalent to or approaching those of its mother refuse to accept policies which make its destiny wholly subordinate to its mother's decision (*see* **Morality, Legal Enforcement of**). Suffice it to say that to the degree that battles over abortion policy continue to inflame national politics, they represent the absence of consensus on fetal status, the relative weight of maternal and fetal rights, and the measures warranted in pursuit of equality for women.

Abortion and religion. Views of abortion vary greatly among Christian communities. Although the weighing of fetal, maternal, familial, and social goods does not depend on specifically religious premises, Christianity's doctrines of creation and redemption sustain biases in favor both of preserving human life and of enhancing its quality. The symbols of sin, cross, forgiveness, and reconciliation provide a perspective on moral decisions in which are recognized also human finitude, the "brokenness" of the human condition, and the need to make difficult choices which achieve at best the "lesser evil." Eastern Orthodox Christianity has followed the church fathers in viewing all life, including prenatal life, as the image of God. Following Basil, the distinction of formation is discounted, but the moral legitimacy of direct abortion to save the mother's life is not entirely ruled out.

Roman Catholic Christians generally tend to place a high value on the unborn, even early in pregnancy, but show increasing sensitivity to the difficulties which pregnancy can cause for women and families. The mainstream Protestant traditions diverge sharply from the Catholic by placing more weight on the unique circumstances of each abortion decision and on the responsibility to decide of those involved, especially the woman. Often the conflict inherent in abortion is acknowledged by calling abortion tragic and ambiguous, even when morally warranted.

To summarize: The Christian tradition yields a generally negative view of abortion, but contemporary Christians are divided on whether it can be justified in some exceptional cases, and if so, what those cases are. Abortion as an option receives broader support when the pregnancy has resulted from a clear injustice to the mother (e.g., rape* or incest*), when it gravely threatens her physical or mental health, or when the fetus is seriously abnormal; and when the abortion can be performed early in pregnancy. There are continuing questions as to the precise moral status of the fetus, the importance of its rights in relation to those of its mother, and the degree and kind of injury to the mother or of abnormality in the child necessary to justify abortion.

See also **Adoption; Eugenics; Parenthood; Persons and Personality; Population Policy; Reproductive Technologies; Sexual Ethics.**

E. Batchelor (ed.), *Abortion: The Moral Issues,* 1982; W. B. Bondeson, H. T. Engelhardt, Jr., S. F. Spicker, and D. H. Winship (eds.), *Abortion and the Status of the Fetus,* 1983; J. T. Burtchaell (ed.), *Abortion Parley,* 1980; D. Callahan, *Abortion: Law, Choice, and Morality,* 1970; S. Callahan and D. Callahan (eds.), *Abortion: Understanding Differences,* 1984; J. Connery, *Abortion: The Development of the Roman Catholic Perspective,* 1977; J. Feinberg (ed.), *The Problem of Abortion,* 1973; R. F. R. Gardiner, *Abortion,* 1972; G. Grisez, *Abortion: The Myths, the Realities, and the Arguments,* 1970; B. W. Harrison, *Our Right to Choose: Toward a New Ethic of Abortion,* 1983; S. Nicholson, *Abortion and the Roman Catholic Church,* 1978; J. T. Noonan (ed.), *The Morality of Abortion: Legal and Historical Perspectives,* 1970.

LISA SOWLE CAHILL

Absolutes, Ethical

By an "absolute" value or good is meant one that maintains its validity under any and every circumstance, no matter what. Thus the ancient maxim of the Stoics "Let justice be done though the heavens fall" is a dramatic way of expressing the absolute validity of justice as a principle. For the moral theologians of the Middle Ages the general principle "Follow the good and avoid the evil" was regarded as a major or ultimate premise carrying with it absolute validity. In modern philosophy the ethics of Immanuel Kant furnishes the best example of an ethical absolute. The good will, which Kant defined as the will that acts out of respect for the moral law, has absolute validity; it is good in any context and has a worth that cannot be calculated because it surpasses all values in exchange (*see* **Kantian Ethics**).

Ethical absolutes have come under attack from at least three distinct points of view. From the standpoint of some forms of subjectivism* in ethics there can be no absolutes because moral judgments have neither objectivity nor universality and there is not sufficient constancy in human nature to guarantee for any good or value a place of absolute validity. It is important to notice that not all forms of subjectivism are thus relativistic, but only those positions according to which human nature has no universal structure. The second and more powerful source of relativism* in ethics stems from anthropological and cultural analyses that make paramount the great variety of customs and practices to be found in different cultures. From this vantage point ethical absolutes are ruled out because there cannot possibly be a universal agreement or consensus of opinion with regard to any standard or norm. Each set of values is "relative" to a geographical time and place and we have no way of transcending this situation and of establishing any one set of norms as *the* final criterion (*see also* **Anthropology and Ethics; Sociology of Ethics**).

Ethical absolutes have been attacked from a third source, this time in the name of a religious standpoint. Kierkegaard, for example, in his famous "teleological suspension of the ethical" was calling attention to the problems that arise when the ethical standpoint is absolutized and becomes free of any critical vantage point beyond itself. If the ethical becomes absolute, then legalism* and moralism* result. The ethical must be limited by the mercy and forgiveness of the religious, and if it is not, the ethical will absolutize itself with evil consequences. A similar point about absolutizing the ethical is made from the standpoint of dialectical theology so-called; the counsels* of perfection stemming from the teaching of Jesus are not meant to apply absolutely and literally to the world of actual existence but rather are said to define the ideal standard in terms of which humanity and the world are judged. As absolute, the Christian ethic is said to be an "impossible ideal," and yet it retains its relevance for historical life.

See also **Norms; Situation Ethics.**

J. M. Gustafson, *Ethics from a Theocentric Perspective,* vol. 1, 1981; G. Hunsinger (ed. and tr.), *Karl Barth and Radical Politics,* 1976; S. Kierkegaard, *Fear and Trembling* (1844), tr. W. Lowrie, 1954; R. Niebuhr, *An Interpretation of Christian Ethics,* 1935; G. Outka and P. Ramsey (eds.), *Norm and Context in Christian Ethics,* 1968; P. Tillich, *Morality and Beyond,* 1963.

JOHN E. SMITH

Absolution

The act of freeing or loosing from sin and its penalties. When Jesus said to the paralytic, "My son, your sins are forgiven," he was accused of blasphemy, and it was argued that God alone can forgive sins (Mark 2:5–7). However, the NT makes clear the belief of the early church that the power to remit sins belonged not only to Jesus but had also been committed by him to the church's officers. This is made explicit in such passages as Matt. 16:19 and John 20:23. In the NT, remission of sins is closely associated with healing and exorcism.

The conditions for receiving absolution are that offenders have repented of their sin, have made a full confession of it, and are willing to make reparation for it. Absolution may be given in various forms, and three of these may be distinguished in the *Book of Common Prayer.* (1) The *indicative* form, ". . . by his authority committed to me, I absolve thee from all thy sins," is used on hearing a private confession, as in the Order for the Visitation of the Sick. (2) In the context of the eucharist, the *precatory* form, "Almighty God . . . have mercy upon you, pardon and

deliver you from all your sins," is used after the general confession. (3) In the orders for matins and evensong, a *declaratory* form is used: "Almighty God . . . hath given power and commandment to his ministers, to declare and pronounce to his people, being penitent, the absolution and remission of their sins."

See **Confession; Penance.**

JOHN MACQUARRIE

Abstinence

The term may be used in various senses. Thus one may speak of abstinence from sexual intercourse, temporary (cf. 1 Cor. 7:5) or permanent; or total abstinence from alcoholic beverages, the form which the temperance movement has taken among many Protestants since the 1820s. Its most technical use is for a lesser form of fasting* that reduces the quality of food, though not necessarily the quantity. In the 2nd century some Montanists and other rigorists added periods of abstinence (*xerophagiae,* "dry meals") to the fasts commonly observed in the church. Later abstinence from flesh meat, assumed on fast days, came to be the common observance of the less solemn fasts. The early Middle Ages discussed whether this should also exclude fish and meat products (*lacticinia*) such as cheese and eggs. The Eastern Orthodox Church still assumes that it should. Benedict directed his monks to abstain from the "flesh of quadrupeds" except when sick (*Rule,* ch. 39), perhaps in the interest of simplicity as much as that of asceticism*. But the Middle Ages commonly assumed that strict monastic asceticism demanded perpetual abstinence from flesh; this is still practiced by the stricter monks of the Eastern church, as on Mt. Athos, and by the Cistercians of Strict Observance (Trappists). The Protestant Reformers generally opposed compulsory abstinence as legalistic—the first formal act of protest at Zurich was a secret supper of sausages in Lent of 1522. But in England the custom not only continued on Fridays and in Lent, but was increased by civil days of abstinence (under Elizabeth I called "Cecil's fasts") ordered to encourage fisheries for the benefit of the navy.

Abstinence may be undertaken for various reasons. Many Orientals and some Westerners practice vegetarianism*, either as an expression of reverence for life or out of conviction that meat is unhealthy and unnecessary. The dietary laws of the OT may be partly based on sanitary grounds, partly on the association of certain kinds of food with pagan sacrifices. For whatever reason adopted, abstinence often becomes a formal badge of religious profession—Hindus generally abstain from beef, Jews and Muslims from pork, Catholics traditionally from meat on Friday, many Protestants from alcohol and tobacco, some Mennonite sects from forms of dress associated with worldly display, Mormons from hot drinks of all kinds.

E. R. HARDY

Accidents

Accidents are events which have not been foreseen and have not been consciously intended to happen. The term "accidents" is used especially when these events cause loss, damage, injury, or death. Although accidents are often said to happen "by chance," they are as much a part of the causal network as any other events. They arise when two or more separate series of events unexpectedly converge or coincide (e.g., a mountaineer is caught in a storm), or when through human negligence* or misjudgment an expected event fails to happen (e.g., a driver goes through a red light), or through a combination of such circumstances. Accidents are as old as human history—some people have always been falling off cliffs or getting drowned in rivers. But with industrialization and the multiplication of equipment, the variety and incidence of accidents has enormously increased. Accidents ranked fourth among the leading causes of death in the USA in 1981.

Transportation accounts nowadays for the largest number of accidents. By far the greatest number arise from the use of motor vehicles on the roads. In the early days of railroads, there were many accidents, but this form of transport is now so strictly regulated that serious accidents are uncommon; in any case, very few people now use this form of transportation. Aviation is also subject to strict regulation and is relatively safe, though when accidents do happen they often involve large numbers of people. Shipping is also subject to strict safety regulations, but these vary in different countries, and anxiety has been caused by a series of accidental oil spillages from tankers flying so-called "flags of convenience." Even if these spillages have not directly resulted in death or injury, the long-term threat to the environment is serious. Accidents at work have tended to decline in industrial countries as machinery has been made safer. Even in the home one is not secure against accidents, sometimes due to carelessness, sometimes to dangerous appliances or even unsafe toys. Sport is another area which is productive of accidents. They occur also in the course of medical care, and indeed all human activities seem to be open to the possibility of accidents.

It would seem that human life cannot be entirely protected from the bad effects of accidents. We have in fact become tolerant of accidents as a feature of modern society. In the USA (and something similar could be said about other countries), the occurrence of 50,000 deaths each year on the roads, together with a much larger number of serious injuries, has come to be regarded as a tolerable price to pay for the conveniences of the motor vehicle. Many wars have produced far fewer casualties.

Many events that we call accidents are undoubtedly preventable. They are traceable to lack of due care, unwillingness to spend time and money in producing safe equipment and maintaining it in good condition, lack of consideration for other people, or other causes that are morally culpable and could be removed. Although much has been done and is being done to reduce the number of accidents, the advance of technology keeps bringing new dangers. The most obvious of these at the present moment is the increasing use of atomic energy as a source of power. This introduces the possibility of accidents on an unprecedented scale.

The duty to prevent accidents as far as is humanly possible makes both personal and social moral demands. On the personal level, there must be the avoidance of acts that are dangerous to oneself or others. For instance, it is morally wrong to drink alcoholic beverages before driving an automobile (alcohol is said to be a contributory factor in one third of all road accidents in the UK) and morally wrong to go mountain climbing in bad weather. The first of these instances is an offense punishable by law; the second is not, although it frequently endangers many lives among rescue teams. This brings us to the social obligation. Each society has the duty to legislate in the interests of the safety of its citizens. This ought to be done, even if the legislators find themselves unpopular because of higher prices to consumers or lower profits to manufacturers.

No matter how much is done in the way of prevention, some accidents will still happen. While the primary moral duty is to prevent accidents, responsibility does not end there. Allowing that some accidents will still happen, we have a further duty to minimize the evils that will arise from them. One of the most obvious ways of doing this is through insurance*. The law requires employers, drivers, and others to carry such insurance as will give some compensation (often inadequate) to persons accidentally injured by their operations; and, more generally, there is a personal obligation to insure against unforeseen happenings, especially any that would be damaging to one's dependents.

See **Risk;** *see also* **Cost-Benefit Analysis; Negligence; Welfare State.**

JOHN MACQUARRIE

Accidie

Accidie (or acedia) is a state of sad heaviness in which the mind is stagnant and the flesh a burden. It is said to be particularly bad at midday. In the past monks used the psalmist's words to describe it as "the sickness that destroyeth in the noon-day."

See **Sloth.**

R. E. C. BROWNE

Accountability *see* Responsibility

Act, Action, Agent

These words are all derived from the Latin *agere,* "to do," and are commonly used in ethics. The "act" is the deed done; the "action" is the doing of it; and the "agent" is the doer. While some moral philosophers (e.g., Sir W. D. Ross) have distinguished rather carefully between "act" and "action," the distinction is difficult to maintain and is not observed by many other writers. An act, as what is done, need not be overt behavior. An act of mental prayer, let us say, is certainly something done by an agent, but it is not an observable occurrence. If the distinction between "act" and "action" has value, then it would seem to be that it draws attention to two aspects of ethical behavior, which may be considered as appropriate or inappropriate ("right" or "wrong") in the context in which it is done,

or which may be considered good or bad with reference to the end which the agent had in view in the doing of the deed.

A first step toward delimiting the meaning of "act" or "action" is to distinguish it from mere process or happening. A leaf falling to the ground is a mere happening or occurrence, not an act. What is distinctive in a human act is that there is both an outside and an inside to it, so to speak. Normally, there is an outside, that is to say, an observable occurrence in the world, though we have conceded that in exceptional cases an act may be entirely internal to the agent. But what differentiates the observable occurrences of human conduct from the falling of a leaf is that in the former case there is a whole complex of mental events associated with the occurrence and, we believe, initiating it—events that we call by such names as decision*, choice*, responsibility*, deliberation*, intention*, motivation*. These internal concomitants of overt human behavior are, however, not always all of them present, or not always present to the same extent. Thus not all human behavior can be reckoned as "action" that would be of interest to ethics. Acts that are done in abnormal states of mind, or again, "reflex acts" over which we have no conscious control, are not reckoned "acts" or "actions" having moral significance. Whereas descriptive sciences such as psychology and sociology are interested in all human behavior, ethics is concerned only with the kind of behavior that is sufficiently differentiated from mere happening to show at least some of the characteristics mentioned above; and ethics is further concerned with the problem of how such behavior can be thought capable of being evaluated, as right or wrong, or good or bad.

Obviously there are borderline cases, and our language for talking about action and its characteristics is far from precise. However, we may try to set down what seem to be the conditions that must obtain if we are to talk of "acts" or "action" in an ethical sense and recognize these as the doings of an "agent."

1. To qualify as an "act," what is done must be done freely, that is to say, not because of any compulsion, external or internal. Words like "decision" and "choice" point to this experience of freedom*. Needless to say, the freedom is always a matter of degree, and choices are always limited,

sometimes severely so. Yet it would seem that the notion of action presupposes some area of free choice (see **Free Will and Determinism**).

2. Closely connected with the idea of freedom is that of knowledge. The agent must be aware of what he or she is doing. Different kinds of knowledge are involved here. Some of this knowledge is factual—knowledge of the circumstances of the act, knowledge of the persons affected by it, and so on. There is also the question of knowing what is right in the particular situation, or knowing what are the ends at which one ought to aim. Our knowledge both of facts and of ethical values is bound to be more or less deficient in every situation, so that all ethical action would seem to imply an element of risk, inseparable from our human finitude. But some basic minimum of knowledge there must be before we can talk of "action" or recognize anyone as the responsible "agent" of a deed (see **Ignorance; Responsibility**).

3. An act is intentional, that is to say, it is directed upon some definite state of affairs (sometimes called the "object" of the act) which the act seeks to realize. Because of the limitations of our knowledge, we often do things unintentionally. What we have done might still be an act with moral quality if, for instance, we had acted with negligence*. The typical act, however, from an ethical point of view, is one that is done with definite intention. If we think of the intention as relating to some limited, well-defined situation, this enables us to distinguish it from the fourth condition, the end or purpose of the act.

4. Action is purposive. My immediate intention may be to catch a train, but the end or purpose of this act is, let us say, to attend a meeting to forward some cause in which I am interested. Thus acts cluster together in policies of action, and the unifying factor is some long-range end or some overarching commitment. Here again we have to notice that it is impossible to draw hard and fast lines. In any particular case, it is likely that we act from "mixed motives."* Some motives may become dominant, and their dominance sets up patterns of action which, in turn, form a recognizable character*. Specially discussed in ethics and moral theology are the ulterior or ultimate ends of human action—self-love, love of humankind, love of God.

See **Conscience; Ethics; Motives and Motivation; Right and Wrong**.

Thomas Aquinas, *Summa Theologiae* I-II. 6–17; J. Macmurray, *The Self as Agent,* 1957.
                                                JOHN MACQUARRIE

Addiction
The state of being given over to the habitual use of alcohol or other drugs.

See **Drug Addiction;** see also **Abstinence; Alcoholism; Temperance**.
                                                JOHN MACQUARRIE

Adiaphora
The term "adiaphora" (plural of the Greek *adiaphoron*) denotes things or acts that are indifferent. It was used by the Cynics* and later by the Stoics*. Although early Christians considered several matters to be morally or religiously indifferent, "adiaphora" was not applied to Christian liberty in the NT, but was first used by the church fathers. The presumption about adiaphora differs greatly, some holding that what is not specifically allowed by scripture is prohibited, others holding that what is not expressly prohibited by scripture is permitted. For the Reformer John Calvin (*Institutes* 3.19.7–12), there are three parts of Christian liberty, freedom from law righteousness, willful and joyful obedience to God's will, and freedom to use or not to use outward things that are themselves "indifferent." But following Paul (1 Cor. 10:23–24), Calvin notes that "nothing is plainer than this rule: that we should use our freedom if it results in the edification of our neighbor, but if it does not help our neighbor, then we should forgo it."

In a 16th-century controversy, the Adiaphorists were Melanchthon's followers who held that some Catholic practices, such as the veneration of saints, were "adiaphora" and could be accepted for the sake of peace and order, while others repudiated them as a restoration of "popery." In the second Adiaphoristic controversy, in the 17th century, the Pietists (see **Pietism**) held that secular amusements, such as the opera, were excluded by the Christian life, while their opponents contended that they were adiaphora, or indifferent matters. Schleiermacher later rejected the concept of adiaphora in view of the unity and continuity of the Christian life, but also held that ordinary, secular amusements could be obligatory as well as permissible.

Emphasizing that "the life of the Christian is a whole, and . . . is not composed of different isolated segments," Emil Brunner (*The Divine Imperative,* ET 1937) contends that "both these statements are true: there are *no* 'Adiaphora,' and—everything is 'adiaphoron'—save love. *Dilige et fac quod vis* [Love, and do what you will—Augustine]." Everything is neutral, and yet everything is connected with the whole which God directs. Thus, "there are no moral holidays."

Most ethical theories concentrate on the determination of obligatory and prohibited, right and wrong, actions, sometimes also identifying praiseworthy actions, such as works of supererogation*. Even if they do not explicitly identify and specify indifferent acts, they recognize them, at least implicitly. Such acts are optional and are thus within the agent's discretion, as long as they do not harm, injure, or offend others.

JAMES F. CHILDRESS

Adoption

Adoption is the procedure whereby a child who is for some reason not able to live with its natural parents is taken into the home of other persons who become the legal parents of the child. The practice is ancient and sometimes rulers, being childless, would adopt a child to carry on the dynasty. In such cases, adoption was seen as benefiting the adoptive parent, while nowadays we are more concerned with the welfare of the child and a couple seeking a child for adoption would be carefully screened for suitability. In fact, however, both the child and the adopting parents benefit from the arrangement. If the parents would otherwise have been childless, adoption gives them the satisfaction as well as the responsibility of parenthood. A couple should not be deterred from adopting a child because they expect such satisfaction. It would be wrong to demand that their motives should be entirely altruistic, for in such cases motives will always be mixed. It is in the actual living out of the relationship that a true parent-child bond will be established. Christians will normally think of adoption as commendable and to be encouraged. It does, however, raise some moral questions. What is the position of the natural parents? Once the adoption has taken place, these natural parents have surrendered both their responsibility and their privileges with respect to the child. The important thing then is to let the new relationship between the child and the adopting parents flourish, and any influence which might hinder this flourishing should be removed. Recently, however, there has been considerable controversy about whether adopted children should be able to learn the identity of their biological parents. Questions arise too about the relation of adoption to other ways of meeting the problem of childlessness, such as artificial insemination by husband or donor, test-tube techniques, surrogate mothers, etc. (*see* **Reproductive Technologies**). Some of these are morally dubious, and there is a strong case for the traditional practice of adoption, especially as at any time there are many children already alive and in need of a home.

See **Children; Orphans; Parenthood.**

JOHN MACQUARRIE

Adultery

Sexual intercourse between a man or woman who is married and someone other than the marriage partner. Its prohibition as a moral offense among Christians derives from the OT, where it is specifically forbidden in the Seventh Commandment (Ex. 20:14), though the Ten Commandments are concerned with more than the external act, as can be seen from the Tenth Commandment: "You shall not covet your neighbor's wife" (Ex. 20:17).

In his Sermon on the Mount Jesus does nothing to lessen this moral offense of adultery, but points the attention of his hearers to the springs from which a desire to commit adultery rises (Matt. 5:27–31; the Greek word *porneia* in this passage is probably a general term referring to the sins of the flesh). The teaching of Jesus in this, as in other matters, does not deal with the outward offense, which he assumes to be wrong, but concentrates attention on the inner thoughts and desires, implying that it is here that the moral offense has its origin, and that therefore this is the point where action needs to be taken.

Christians have allowed divorce* for adultery, even when they have forbidden it for any other reason, on the basis of the passage from Matthew's Gospel (5:31–32).

In the early days of the Christian church the effect of Christian attitudes on the practices of the time was one of moderation. Severe penalties for adultery were in force in the ancient world, including the death sentence and mutilation. The discipline of the church itself was more rigorous in the early days, when the end of the world was regarded as imminent, than in later times.

Roman Catholic teaching holds that adultery is a sin against the threefold good of marriage*, and that the consent of the other marriage partner in no way diminishes its evil.

In recent years it has been suggested that artificial insemination by donor (AID), that is, from the semen of an unknown man, may be considered as an act of adultery and that legislation should be framed accordingly. It would, however, seem clearer to discuss and legislate for AID without using terms derived from different concepts (see also **Reproductive Technologies**).

Adultery from a moral point of view is damaging to the good of the family and is a direct betrayal of the most sacred human relationships. It has certainly increased during the last seventy-five years owing to greater facilities for divorce and to the availability of contraceptives. The atmosphere that is created by easy divorce facilities weakens the resistance of many men and women when temptation to be unfaithful to their marriage vows assails them, and this, together with the availability of contraceptives, has assisted the growth of adultery.

See also **Sexual Ethics.**

HERBERT WADDAMS

Advertising

Advertising has become an essential part of modern market economies because business firms, having undertaken the investment necessary to produce a new product, must ensure that there is a market for it. In practice there is no clear distinction between informing the public of a means of satisfying existing wants and creating new wants. It is claimed that advertising, by making possible larger markets, leads to greater economies of scale and hence to lower costs and prices. This is true in part, but much advertising by large combines, e.g., by the manufacturers of cosmetics, detergents, or cigarettes, tends to be purely competitive, to protect the market against rival firms. It is also claimed that advertising enriches our lives, by making us aware of new forms of satisfaction. This is also true in part, but Christians cannot be happy about the types of satisfaction often encouraged, about the general encourage-

ment of acquisitiveness and "getting on" as the most important things in life, or about the doubtful claims often made about the goods advertised. Christians must accept advertising as being part and parcel of modern life, but they must be alert against its dangers and abuses.

See **Business Ethics; Commercialism.**

W. S. Cormanor and T. A. Wilson, *Advertising and Market Power,* 1974; K. Cowling et al., *Advertising and Economic Behaviour,* 1975; V. Packard, *The Hidden Persuaders,* 1957.

JOHN F. SLEEMAN

Affection, Affectivity, Affects
see **Emotion**

Affinity
The word used to denote those relationships arising from marriage, as distinct from those dependent on birth and parentage. Certain degrees of affinity constitute an impediment to marriage after the death of a spouse. Regulations vary somewhat from country to country and from one Christian communion to another. For the Church of England, see "A Table of Kindred and Affinity" in the *Book of Common Prayer.*

See **Marriage.**

JOHN MACQUARRIE

Affirmation
A solemn declaration of truth, made before a magistrate or other officer. It is equivalent to an oath, and may be made by those who have conscientious objections to oaths (cf. Matt. 5:34). The right to affirm was originally provided for Quakers, but has been extended to other groups, including atheists.

See **Oaths.**

JOHN MACQUARRIE

Affluence
see **Mammon; Poverty; Wealth**

Afro-American Religious Ethics
Afro-American religious ethics has been developed by Americans of African descent. Its origins lie in blacks' African heritage, their appropriation of Christian beliefs and norms, and their rejection of the assertion by America's dominant groups that they were inferior or not even members of the moral universe. Though the policy of moral exclusion was

never fully implemented, a civil war, a division of Christianity along racial lines, and a black-led revolt against legal segregation* and discrimination* were necessary before blacks were in principle included in the Western moral universe. The Afro-American religious ethic continues as an effort to correct the tendency of American society to use its material superiorities to determine moral rules and practices.

The Afro-American moral perspective makes central the belief in the common origin and humanity of individuals and thus their sacredness and equality* (*see* **Human Dignity; Image of God**). This belief is based upon the Afro-American's understanding of the Christian faith as well as the ideals expressed in the Declaration of Independence and the US Constitution. The African roots of this moral belief cannot be positively stated because of the lack of clear written sources and the pervasive contacts with Western culture. Since most white Americans apparently denied the full equality of all people and established the USA as a slave nation, it is not improper to suppose that the African roots of the black Americans played an important role in their assertion of the inclusiveness of the moral universe and the equality of all individuals. The experience of slavery was an experience of gross injustice, even as defined by the norms of justice of the dominant system, and this experience of injustice was in part responsible for black efforts to enlarge the moral vision of the white West, particularly by calling attention to its hypocrisy*. Slavery also weakened some traditional moral bonds, such as family ties. Following slavery*, legal segregation and discrimination deprived Afro-Americans of many educational and employment opportunities open to whites. As a result, the Afro-American religious ethic, rooted in the life of black churches, stressed moral improvement, along with other improvements, within the Afro-American group itself. This morality was often conventional and customary, provided norms of good citizenship, and emphasized benevolence toward fellow blacks, including Africans elsewhere. It did not, however, deny common humanity or universal moral norms and expected love to be displayed even toward white oppressors. The theodicy* connected to the experience of oppression* held that God favored the incessant striving of the people for freedom, equal-

ity, and justice while condemning the failure of the people to improve themselves morally. The black churches and other institutions were structured to implement this morality.

Many individuals have contributed to the formation of this ethical perspective, including David Walker, Richard Allen, Frederick Douglass, Sojourner Truth, Harriet Tubman, Alexander Crummell, and W. E. B. Du Bois. During the three hundred years that Africans have been in America, this perspective has undergone several changes, but its main features have remained essentially the same even when reinterpreted by such black nationalists as Marcus Garvey or such integrationists as Father Divine. In the late 1950s some major changes resulted from the thought of Martin Luther King, Jr., and his colleagues, as well as the response of the American society to the civil rights struggle. In particular, King reformulated the traditional belief of the community in nonviolent persuasion through moral education, legal action, political protest, and economic coercion. As a theologian and pastor, King appealed to love* as the supreme moral norm and defined justice as a form of love correcting all that stands against love. Mohandas K. Gandhi's campaigns of nonviolent resistance* offered a model for making love relevant to social problems. King's nonviolent direct action required masses of people to translate their moral convictions about justice into actions involving sacrifice and suffering that could be redemptive by transforming both themselves and their society. A significant number of black and white Americans responded to King's message, particularly its emphasis on the worth and dignity of the individual and the inclusiveness of the human family. But nonviolent direct action also created tensions within the white and black communities. White resentment of black progress resulted in violence and brutality against protesters, sorely testing the commitment to love and redemptive suffering. Some blacks rejected King's themes and methods, accepting violence and any means that might be effective, and condoning or even requiring hatred of the white oppressor. Malcolm X was the chief exponent of these views in the black Islamic community, and James Cone in the Christian community. Malcolm X taught that whites were utterly depraved and repudiated the idea of one humanity and moral universe; Cone denied the humanity of white oppressors and nonmilitant Afro-Americans. Both subsequently modified their views, and the secular black power and nationalist movements to which they appealed lost much of their popularity in the black community. More recently Cone has attempted to subsume his black theology under the Third World liberation theologies and their American counterparts, which incorporate Marxist social analysis (*see* **Liberation Theology**).

The main norms of the Afro-American religious ethic have not been fundamentally altered, despite various tensions and different emphases in interpretation and application at different times. King highlighted ethical universalism, an inclusive community, and the worth and dignity of persons, as well as the goal of a just political, economic, and social system. His method of nonviolent direct action has proved too demanding and also unnecessary in view of increased black opportunities and power. Thus, the main moral influence of black Americans will probably be through various social and political structures. Some themes in the Afro-American religious ethic need further development—for example, the equality of women and international relations, including war and peace. Concern about these matters has been present in the moral tradition since the 1840s, but they have not yet achieved clarity and force. Furthermore, the growing class differentiation within the black community needs attention.

The Afro-American religious ethic involves reflection on the historical experience of blacks in America and elsewhere in the light of religious, mainly but not exclusively Christian, beliefs and norms. It has also directed activities by blacks, including their efforts to transform both themselves and the larger society. As long as consciousness about race persists, the Afro-American religious ethic may have a significant role, particularly in its call for an inclusive moral community.

See **Equality; Freedom; Race Relations; Racism.**

J. H. Cone, *Black Theology and Black Power,* 1969; *Black Theology of Liberation,* 1970; and *God of the Oppressed,* 1975; M. L. King, Jr., *Stride Toward Freedom,* 1958; and *Where Do We Go From Here? Chaos or Community,* 1967; Malcolm X, *Autobiography of Malcolm X,* 1965; C. West, *Prophesy Deliverance! An Afro-American Revolutionary Christianity,* 1982; G. S. Wilmore, *Black Religion and Black Radicalism: An Interpretation of the Religious History of Afro-American People,* 2nd rev. and enl. ed., 1983; G. S. Wilmore and J. H. Cone (eds.), *Black Theology: A Documentary History, 1966–1979,* 1979.

PRESTON N. WILLIAMS

Agape *see* **Charity; Love; Neighbor**

Agathology

From the Greek *agathos* (good) and *logos* (discourse), agathology is the science or theory of the good.

See **Axiology; Teleological Ethics.**

Aged, Care of the

In 1980, one in ten younger households in the USA was involved in giving care or support to enfeebled older relatives. Twice as many old people were cared for at home as were found in nursing homes. Greater numbers received assistance from family members in their homes and apartments. Thus, the family remained the chief support of the elderly infirm. Long-term care facilities were populated disproportionately by unmarried persons, people without children, and the extreme elderly whose needs had grown too extensive for their adult children, who were themselves old. The situation in the UK is similar, though the greater availability of health and welfare services extends the possibility of independent living for Britons as compared to Americans. The greater availability of services also reduces the care-giving burden of late-middle-aged children.

Theological background.

Scripture. Though the Hebrew scriptures record a diversity of conditions among the elderly, old age is frequently pictured as a time of insecurity. The elderly fear the vulnerability and resourcelessness that comes with advanced age (Ps. 71:9–10; Ecclus. [Sirach] 3:12–16; 41:2). The biblical authors also show an aversion to dependence (e.g., Ecclus. 33:20–21). At the same time, they enjoin respect and care for parents (Ex. 20: 12; Deut. 5:16; Ecclus. 3:1–18).

"Honor your father and your mother." The command of the Decalogue* "Honor* your father and your mother" requires a reverence* akin to religious awe. The analogy

between the parent-child relationship and the bond between Yahweh and Israel is a commonplace, especially in the prophets. This kind of filial piety is reflected in Thomas Aquinas's classification of filial piety alongside religion as a primordial virtue (*ST* II-II.101), and by Karl Barth's designation of parents as "the ambassadors of God" (*Church Dogmatics* III/4, ET 1961, p. 256). The other warrants for respecting parents are many and diverse: eschatological blessing (Deut. 5:16; Ecclus. 3:6), divine decree (Ecclus. 3:2), atonement for sins (vs. 14–15), intergenerational reciprocity (vs. 8–9), and divine condemnation (v. 16).

Reverence for parents preeminently entails caring for them in their old age (Gen. 45: 9–11; Ecclus. 3:12–16), and their abandonment is considered blasphemy* (Ecclus. 3: 16). Particular consideration is required of those whose parents are feebleminded. "Even if he is lacking in understanding, show forbearance; in all your strength do not despise him" (v.13).

Widowhood in the early church. The NT assumes Israelite norms of filial piety, particularly the requirement that children support their parents in need (1 Tim. 5:3–4). Widowhood as an established order in the early church, however, represented a significant development in the care of the elderly. Widows* had benefited from almsgiving* in ancient Israel, but on the death of their husbands they usually fell outside the normal structures of family support. The institution of widowhood in the early church provided secure material support for familyless older women. In addition, widowhood conferred status on older women (vs. 9–11).

Theological warrants of care-giving. One central theological motif consistent with the insecurity of old age is the biblical affirmation of the dependability of God as the Creator. This Christian belief affirms God's goodness and the goodness of creation. As God's creatures we are brought into existence and sustained by the one ultimately reliable power, who wills our good as the good of all he creates. Aged dependency itself takes on a kindly face because it reflects our ultimate dependence on the Source of all life. The dependability of family care-givers sustains the basic trust of old people at a time when they have much to fear. Thus, care-giving becomes a sign of God's unfailing goodness.

Related to the Creation motif is gratitude*. Gratitude is a central affection of the Christian life. Care of aged parents might also be warranted, therefore, on grounds that it shows gratitude for God's special providence for us. Grateful service of parents replicates the joyful giving by which God creates, sustains, and redeems the world (Matt. 5:45).

A normative ethics of care-giving to the elderly. Normative foundations for the familial dependence of the elderly are difficult to formulate in modern society because of the high valence assigned to individual liberty*. For it appears incompatible with the dependent condition of the elderly infirm. Yet care-giving within families and between generations is extensive. What normative pattern could reconcile the priority of liberty with the familial dependence of the elderly?

One proposal is that liberty is only one component in a set of essential values whose relative weight changes with the advance of infirmity in old age. The core value is human dignity*. In terms of biblical theology, one might talk of this core value as God's love for each man and woman. Another classic theological formulation of this affirmation is to found human dignity on "the image of God* in the human person." If human dignity is the central value, then respect for liberty would be subordinate to the affirmation of personal worth.

The basic norms of care-giving to the elderly derive, then, from a tripartite division of human dignity into liberty, welfare, and family membership. Due to the infirmity and dependence of the elderly and the demands placed on the care-giver, there is a conditional priority to welfare. Welfare is a convoy concept embracing many different goods: e.g., financial support, bathing and grooming, provision of food, supervision of medication, assistance with movement. Of particular importance are continuity and regularity of care. Welfare would also entail prohibitions of neglect and abuse.

The liberty of the elderly is still to be respected. Dependence will reduce the reach of autonomy*, but it continues to retain its primacy in key decisions affecting the dependent elder's life: the decision to enter into a clearly dependent relationship like conjoint living, or to terminate one; changes in that status, such as home nursing care or institutionalization; major medical decisions and choices about the end of life (e.g., living wills). While accommodation required by familial dependence may reduce the range of a parent's effective preferences, children need to be alert to how the fulfillment of those preferences enhances an old person's sense of well-being and therefore shows respect for his or her own worth as a person.

The contexts of care. Contextual questions are a part of ethical analysis because abstract norms seldom capture the complexities of moral responsibility. Knowing the particularities of a case helps in assessing the appropriateness of applying a norm to a given situation, in making a justified exception or excusation, and in resolving conflicts of obligations.

The primacy of the family context. Caregiving, as opposed to medical treatment, is a properly familial duty (*see* **Family**). Obligations to care for the elderly fall chiefly on two groups. The first is family members; the second is health professionals. In long-term care of the elderly, health professionals may be regarded either as extension of the family network or as family surrogates.

The family care-giving context. For families involved in care-giving, there is seldom a need to make once-for-all decisions. Family involvement is usually an incremental affair with choices and adjustments to be made at each stage: e.g., cross-household support, shared living arrangements, long-term or hospice care. Since the changes in situation affect the elder's basic life plan, as a rule he or she should retain freedom with respect to entering on a new arrangement or not. Dependency does not entail paternalism*.

On the side of the care-giver, possible limits on family care might include other family problems, the excessive needs of the elder or lack of capacity on the part of the child, and personality disorders or long-standing family alienation. The decision to institutionalize an elderly relative, ending immediate involvement in care-giving, is often warranted by the prolonged stress of chronic care and the difficulty in coping with the increasing debilitation of the patient.

Institutional care-givers. The first responsibility of institutional care-givers is to ensure the quality of nursing care. But, since the majority of nursing home patients are familyless, it is also important that the institutional staff function as a surrogate family, showing the kind of personal interest in patients that might be found in the family. In addition, because the losses of old age can be so threatening, personal involvement is required in order to assist the infirm elder with the life tasks of the senior: accepting one's own worth, interpreting the significance of one's life, and coming to terms with frailty and mortality.

The role of the state.* Government bears three responsibilities in the care of the elderly. Under its police powers, it has the duty to protect the elderly from abuse and neglect. In virtue of its role in upholding general welfare, it has the duty to provide support for old people who have no near relatives to care for them. Finally, as the arbiter of social welfare, it may provide an array of programs to assist the elderly and their care-givers alike. While the basic protections provided by the British welfare state are more extensive than those provided in the USA, the latter has made significant progress in reducing poverty among the aged and in making provision for their medical care. Because of the great increase in the number of elderly, both governments face major pressures to reduce and to control the costs of care for the elderly.

See **Children; Family; Gratitude; Health Care, Right to; Honor; Life, Prolongation of; Parenthood; Sick, Care of the; Social Service of the Church; Welfare State.**

On social gerontology, see P. Regan (ed.), *Aging Parents,* 1980; E. Shanas, P. Townsend, et al., *Old People in Three Industrial Societies,* 1968; U.S. Department of Health and Human Services, Social Security Administration, ". . . *Thy Father and Thy Mother . . .*": *A Second Look at Filial Responsibility and Family Policy,* by Alvin Schorr (SSA Publication No. 13-11953), 1980.

On biblical and theological warrants for care-giving, see W. Harrelson, *The Ten Commandments and Human Rights,* 1980, pp. 92–105; W. Clements (ed.), *Ministry with the Aging,* 1981; D. Christiansen, "The Elderly and Their Families: The Problems of Dependence," *New Catholic World* 223, no. 1335, 1980, pp. 100–104.

On the normative ethics of aging, see D. Christiansen, "Aging: Ethical Implications"; and E. Young, "Health Care and Research in the Aged," both in *EB,* 1978; S. F. Spicker et al., *Aging and the Elderly: Humanistic Perspectives in Gerontology,* 1978.

DREW CHRISTIANSEN, S.J.

Aggression

Aggression is a pugnacious behavior in which the threat or use of violence initiates conflict or destruction. It may be directed against persons, objects, groups, nation-states, or meaning systems (some examples are cursing, ridicule, book burning).

Aggression usually connotes either uncontrollably ferocious reaction to stress or unprovoked combativeness in an attempt to obtain territory, resources, or dominance over others. It may be contrasted with "aggressiveness" insofar as the latter connotes an admired characteristic in controlled situations such as legal advocacy, some aspects of business life, sports, and many forms of leadership. In these areas, "aggressiveness" implies energetic initiative and willingness to take risks in performing legitimate tasks well.

Modern usages of the term "aggression" tend to cluster in four bodies of literature: bioethology, social psychology, international politics, and religious ethics. Most studies treat aggression as an "evil" and seek means to eliminate, control, or channel it into "aggressiveness."

In bioethology, aggression is often attributed to genetic, endocrinological, or "instinctual" factors, although it is also argued that aggression is, at least in part, a learned behavior by which various patterns—territorial; (rank, species, or sexual) dominance; or predatory—are transmitted over generations. The importance of these discussions for ethics depends on how much continuity is assumed between beasts and humans, specifically regarding the relative importance of "culture" as a cause of aggression. K. Lorenz's view that humans are more prone to aggression than other species because culture releases humans from nature's harmonies is now widely repudiated, as is E. O. Wilson's contention that aggression is an adaptive, genetically controlled, ecologically influenced trait necessary to increase the survival and reproductive performance of species, with culture supplying only incidental channels for the carrying out of aggression.

In social psychology, the main debate is whether aggression is due to innate aspects of the human personality or whether aggression arises from socially induced causes. Freud's theory of a "death impulse" and Adler's understanding of the "will to power" focus on what is innate in humans, while Malinowski, Dollard, and Maslow focus on the socio-cultural, environmental, or interactive situations that may produce aggression. At stake in these debates are several questions of importance for ethics: To what degree are the causes of aggression malleable to therapeutic control? If they are, to what degree must persons change before social forms of aggression can be limited? Or must social patterns first be altered to reduce the frustrations that induce aggression?

In this area, one widely held view seems to have been laid to rest, namely, that it is "healthy" to vent aggressions to prevent a psychological implosion or an uncontainable viciousness toward scapegoats. Contemporary evidence suggests that "therapeutic" legitimations of aggression increase the probability of subsequent violence.

In international politics, "aggression" has become a technical term for the illegal initiation of offensive, armed attack on a sovereign power. This usage is found in the League of Nations Covenant (1919), the Geneva Protocol (1924), and the Charter of the United Nations (1945). The last states that "armed force shall not be used save in the common interest . . . to maintain international peace and security, and to . . . [suppress] acts of aggression" (Art. 1). These usages imply that it is possible and necessary to distinguish between legitimate and illegitimate use of force by political authority.

Recent debates have broadened this usage to condemn (a) "economic aggression" in the senses of exploitation, oppression, and neocolonialism; (b) "psychological aggression" as in slanderous or pornographic portrayals of minorities and in "genocidal" propaganda against peoples, cultures, or subcultures; and (c) the manufacture and deployment of "offensive" weapons which, whether used or not, threaten destabilization of international balances. These uses are not, at present, internationally justiciable.

In Christian social ethics (and some cross-cultural religious studies) all of the above ways of treating aggression can be found, but two other issues are also raised. One is theological: If God is thought to be vengeful or to require militant compliance, are not believers given license for immoral aggression in the form of holy wars, crusades, or inquisitions? And does such an affect ethically discredit the piety, the theology, or the God worshiped? The second issue is anthropological: How much should the evidence from the human sciences shape our ethical reflections and actions? Christian understandings of sin presume that what people study empirically is "fallen." Thus, aggression is unlikely to be utterly eliminated from the human heart or human affairs in this world. The Christian understanding of redemption, however, suggests that even now aggression can be constrained and limited by reconciliation with God and neighbor, and by the obedient establishment of those relatively just, peaceful, and righteous relationships possible in history by God's grace.

See also **Just War; Militarism; War.**

L. Berkowitz, *Aggression,* 1962; J. Dollard, *Frustration and Aggression,* 1939; K. Lorenz, *On Aggression,* ET 1966; M. L. Stackhouse, *The Ethics of Necropolis,* 1971; E. O. Wilson, *On Human Nature,* 1978, ch. 5; Q. Wright, *A Study of War,* ²1964.

                                        MAX L. STACKHOUSE

Akrasia

A Greek term for moral weakness. *See* **Weakness, Moral; Will.**

Alcoholism

The problems associated with characterizing and treating alcoholism reveal the extent to which the significance of such phenomena depend on particular social structures and the values and explanatory frameworks they employ. For centuries excessive alcohol consumption has been seen as a problem for religion, morality, and the law. It has been regarded as a sin*, a vice*, and a crime*. In the latter part of the 18th century, it was brought within the province of medicine as a form of disease. In 1784 Dr. Benjamin Rush, one of the signers of the American Declaration of Independence, published *An Inquiry Into the Effects of Ardent Spirits on the Human Body and Mind.* He was followed in 1788 by Thomas Trotter, who published a dissertation that was later translated in 1804 as *An Essay, Medical, Philosophical, and Chemical, on Drunkenness, and Its Effects on the Human Body.* In this work Trotter attempted to place the problems associated with alcoholism within a medical language, accenting the adverse health consequences of excessive alcohol consumption.

In the 19th century medical interest in the disease of alcoholism was combined with the growing American temperance movement and the development of asylums for the care and treatment of inebriates. The choice to medicalize alcoholism was based on the medical consequences of excessive drinking, as well as the hope that medicine would in fact be able to treat and cure alcoholics. In addition, there was the beginning of the attempt generally to medicalize vices. It was at this same time that masturbation came to be seen not just as a vice, but as a disease as well. In the 20th century the emphasis on alcoholism as a disease was further developed and has been tied to an attempt to relieve alcoholics of the religious and ethical disapproval of excessive drink, so as to encourage an effective use of the sick role. This translation of alcoholism from a vice into a disease does not relieve the alcoholic of an adverse social judgment because, all things being equal, being diseased is disvalued. To judge an individual as diseased is to find that the individual fails to live up to a physiological or psychological norm. Excessive alcohol consumption was thus moved to a new matrix of values but did not take on a value-neutral character (*see* **Health and Disease, Values in Defining**).

Such medicalizations of social and moral problems have not been without their critics. It has been held that the medicalization of problems such as alcoholism and drug addiction overextends the gamut of medical interventions and undermines individual responsibility*. The shift from the language of sin and moral failing to the language of disease and illness is seen by such critics to be fraught with its own social dangers, as evidenced by countries such as the USSR where political dissent is at times regarded as a disease. Even with the medicalization of alcoholism, many of the "treatments" maintain a moral and religious character. One might think of Alcoholics Anonymous, which argues that alcoholics must cooperate in their own treatment and must recognize their helplessness, their need of the group and the "Higher Power." Despite the attempt to medicalize the problems of excessive drinking, a single medical account of its etiology has not emerged. Instead, accounts have been provided in terms of transactional analysis, psychoanalytic theory, learning theory, and family dynamics, in addition to the medical model, which was elaborated by E. M. Jellinek and others. There have also been attempts to find genetic bases for alcoholism, but none of these has been thoroughly convincing, though there do appear to be some genetically determined differences in the response of individuals to ethanol. Problems with alcohol abuse and dependence are listed as disorders in the *Diagnostic and Statistical Manual of Mental Disorders* (³1980) of the American Psychiatric Association.

Excessive alcohol consumption continues to be regarded within different theoretical frameworks. Religious groups continue to impute some level of responsibility to individuals who develop such an expression of the vice of gluttony*. Nor has excessive alcohol consumption been decriminalized. The move to develop more stringent penalties for driving while under the influence of alcohol is but one expression of the law's continuing relationship to the control of alcohol abuse. This approach accents individual culpability and responsibility. Moreover, within medicine, alcoholism tends to be treated both in terms of various psychologically oriented therapeutic approaches, as well as in terms of therapeutic approaches based on a medical model. This variety of approaches reflects not only the various theoretical understandings of alcoholism but also the complexity of problems with drinking, which involve at least fifteen million individuals and over one fifth of all households in the USA. The widespread character of problems with drinking suggests that an account of the difficulties will not be fully forthcoming within any one theoretical framework.

See also **Autonomy; Drug Addiction; Involuntary Hospitalization; Mental Health; Mental Illness; Morality, Legal Enforcement of; Paternalism; Responsibility; Sick, Care of the; Temperance.**

H. TRISTRAM ENGELHARDT, JR.

Alienation

The word "alienation" has been used in a number of senses in different disciplines. Literally, alienation is the process of becoming other, or the state of being other, and it is used of a person or a group that feels itself cut off from some larger whole.

The concept of alienation was developed through the 19th century. Whereas Hegel taught that the absolute Spirit becomes other than itself by going out into the finite and knowing itself through the finite, Feuerbach turned this view upside down and claimed that it is human beings that project their own spiritual aspirations on the fiction that they call God. In this way, humanity becomes alienated from what is best in human nature, for all that is good has been attributed to God, and human beings are deemed sinful and corrupt. Thus Feuerbach saw religion as essentially alienating. Marx agreed with Feuerbach that in religion the human being revolves around a false sun and must rather put humanity itself in the center. But for Marx, religion is not the source of alienation but only a symptom. The basic alienation lies in the fact that workers have been separated from the product of their work; indeed, their very labor has been turned into a commodity to be bought and sold. Marx believed that workers must affirm themselves in their work, and that when prevented from doing this they are denied fulfillment as human beings, and so "alienated" (*see* **Marxist Ethics**). Later in the century, Nietzsche returned to the theme that God alienates us from our own nature and frustrates our human transcendence, but whereas Nietzsche, like Feuerbach, hoped that the abolition of God would bring an end to alienation, Sartre in the 20th century depicts the human condition as both without God and thoroughly alienated in itself.

Alienation occurs on a number of levels. We have already noted the phenomenon of alienation from one's own nature, the sense of not having fulfilled one's human potentiality. Then there is alienation from other human beings, which may be experienced either by individuals or by minority groups within a society. There is also a deeper ontological alienation from the whole scheme of things, found, for instance, among the ancient Gnostics or among some modern existentialists (*see* **Existentialist Ethics**). Christian theologians, e.g., Tillich, have been too quick in claiming that there is a correlation among these levels, so that where there is alienation from God (which he identifies with sin) there is also alienation from self and from one's fellows. There is no convincing evidence that the correlation is quite so definite.

It must be added that alienation is not always to be judged as bad. It has an ambiguous character. The early Christians were alienated from Roman society and suffered various kinds of discrimination, but this was partly by their own choice, as they sought to preserve their own distinctness and to keep themselves clear of paganism. In more recent times, the Jews of Europe and the blacks of the USA have been alienated from the mainstream of society, but while this has been the result of unjust discrimination, these groups have also resisted total integration and have tried to maintain a distinct cultural identity.

F. Johnson (ed.), *Alienation: Concept, Term, and Meanings,* 1973; P. Masterson, *Atheism and Alienation,* 1971.

JOHN MACQUARRIE

Almsgiving

Though giving to the poor has been a part of the Hebraic tradition, the word "alms" does not appear in the OT. In this form the concept is Christian and is highly commended in the NT, where it is regarded as an act of virtue*. Until modern times, almsgiving has been one of the most important of "transfer payments." This persisted while there was no established machinery for giving regular aid to the poor, and royal families and the great nobles would often appoint "almoners" who would distribute largesse for them. In England the Queen's High Almoner is the bishop of St. Albans. The monasteries would also appoint almoners, but though it should have been possible for them to develop into something like social workers, this did not happen. Almsgiving was an essential part of the social system, and many would have starved to death without the alms that were given to them. Almsgiving suffered from three defects: (1) it created in many a monetary calculus of virtue, (2) it created a relationship of subordination and superordination between people, (3) it resulted in the growth of professional begging. During the 19th century a considerable opposition developed to almsgiving on the part of those who wanted to suppress professional begging and in some measure on the part of some socialists who wanted aid to be given to the poor as a right*, and not as an act of virtue on the part of others.

When the first social worker was introduced into the Royal Free Hospital in London in 1894, she was given the title of "almoner"; since then that word in England has come to mean a medical social worker.

With the growth of social services and the reduction of poverty*, direct almsgiving has tended to decline, and the very large numbers of those who give money away do so by subscribing to charities and voluntary social service organizations. Almsgiving has become a vicarious act.

See **Charity; Mutual Aid; Philanthropy; Social Service of the Church; Welfare State.**

R. M. Grant, *Early Christianity and Society,* 1977, ch. 6; D. Owen, *English Philanthropy,* 1965.

BRIAN RODGERS

Altruism

Conduct aimed at the good of other persons (Latin *alter,* "the other"). Christians are commanded by the NT to love their neighbor as themselves, and even to love their enemies. Other religions likewise teach an altruistic ethic. Some exponents of a naturalistic ethic* (e.g., Sir Charles Sherrington) have argued that since cooperation has proved more successful than competition in the evolutionary process, altruistic conduct has its basis in the way things are. However, altruism usually runs so counter to human self-regarding tendencies that it might seem almost unnatural. Many philosophers have argued that altruistic actions are at bottom self-regarding, and are done to win esteem or to enjoy the gratitude of the person benefited or to bask in the feeling of having done "the right thing." No doubt there is some truth in this, but it would surely be cynical to suppose that all altruistic conduct is a disguised egoism; and it is in fact possible to point to many deeds that have been done for the sake of others and that could not possibly have benefited the agent even in the most subtle ways. On the other hand, it must be acknowledged that purely altruistic acts are probably very rare, and that when we leave the sphere of individual ethics and think of social ethics or international order, pure altruism is presumably never found at all. Reinhold Niebuhr has remarked: "The new life in Christ represents the perfection of complete and heedless self-giving which obscures the contrary impulse of self-regard. It is a moral ideal scarcely possible for the individual, and certainly not relevant to the morality of self-regarding nations" (*Man's Nature and His Communities,* 1965, p. 42).

See **Egoism; Philanthropy.**

JOHN MACQUARRIE

Ambiguity *see* **Conflict of Duties; Dilemma; Dirty Hands; Norms; Situation Ethics**

Ambition

see **Honor; Magnanimity; Pride; Self-Love; Sloth**

Amnesty

In amnesty a government overlooks or pardons past offenses. Whether to punish various legal offenses, such as civil disobedience*, draft evasion, or desertion, is never simply a legal question, for it also involves moral and political arguments about whether legal penalties and associated civil disabilities should be imposed on certain classes of offenders. The terms "amnesty" and "pardon" are sometimes used interchangeably, but they can be distinguished in the following way: Pardon usually involves the remission of the punishment (*see* **Penology**) of a named individual or individuals, while amnesty overlooks the offenses of a class of persons whose names and individual circumstances may not be specified. Furthermore, pardon usually applies to postconviction remission of punishment, but amnesty may be granted before or after conviction. Often amnesties play an important role in reconciliation after serious social conflicts, such as mass protests, rebellion, or civil war—for example, the amnesties in the USA during the Civil War and Reconstruction. Remitting punishment and removing civil disabilities (e.g., restoring the right to vote, to hold public office, and to be admitted to the professions) can close the books on a conflict for the sake of the community as a whole, as well as the individuals involved. As Hannah Arendt noted, both punishment and forgiveness "have in common that they attempt to put an end to something that without interference could go on endlessly." Critical questions emerged in the USA during and after the war in Vietnam about what a policy of amnesty, subsequently adopted, would symbolize about the government's involvement in the war and about those who were involved in civil disobedience, violent acts, draft evasion, or desertion, often on grounds of just war* criteria or pacifism*. Considerations of justice* are also important for choosing between a policy of punishment and a policy of amnesty, as well as the conditions and scope of either policy.

JAMES F. CHILDRESS

Amusements

Activities that divert us from the everyday routine of life. They include games and sports, spectacles and entertainments, hobbies and leisure-time activities. From the earliest times, people have had some amusements. What is common to such activities is their nonserious character. They are play, and play has a legitimate place in human life (as perhaps also in animal life). Play serves as a relaxation from work, and indeed only if people have periods of relaxation can they work effectively. There is nothing in the Christian religion that should be considered hostile to legitimate amusements, and only puritanical distortions of Christianity have frowned upon play activities. Even if this puritanical prejudice against enjoyments is today much rarer than it has sometimes been, it lingers on in the superstition that somehow amusements ought to be edifying or educative if Christians are to give them wholehearted approval. Many amusements do in fact increase skills, and are therefore useful; but there is nothing whatever wrong with amusements that are entirely frivolous and do not aim at being useful or edifying in some kind of oblique way. Moreover, Christian ethics should not allow itself to get involved in questions of taste, especially where these are usually dictated by middle-class and middle-aged preferences. Listening to Beethoven has no merit, from an ethical point of view, over listening to the Beatles. On the other hand, amusements are not exempt from the ethical standards that apply in our more serious activities. Cruel spectacles, dangerous sports, lewd shows—in short, any amusements that are detrimental to the well-being of participants or spectators, must be condemned by the Christian. There are many borderline cases. The question to be asked is whether an amusement excites states of mind that are either sinful in themselves or predispose to sinful acts. For the question of cruel sports, *see* **Animals;** for the question of a conflict between ethical and aesthetic interests, *see* **Censorship.**

JOHN MACQUARRIE

Anabaptist Ethics

Anabaptists were a collection of religious dissenters in Europe between 1525 and 1600 who separated from both Catholicism and Protestantism. Beginning in Zurich in 1524, under the leadership of Conrad Grebel, they often called themselves "Christian Brethren," but they were called Anabaptists, or rebaptizers, by their opponents because of their practice of adult, believer's baptism. They denied the charge that they were "rebaptizers" because they repudiated infant baptism as invalid. Many Anabaptist beliefs and practices continue among the Mennonites, Amish, and Hutterian Brethren.

Anabaptists always insisted that ethics and theology, deeds and creeds, could not be separated from each other. It was not possible to consider faith and works separately, and they vehemently criticized Catholics and Protestants for doing so. Believing in Jesus Christ as the Son of God would, they argued, be of no avail before God unless one did what Jesus commanded. Justification by faith*, a belief they shared with Protestants, therefore included for them both *credo* and *oboedio*. The one was as necessary as the other to salvation. This frankly synergistic view (*see* **Synergism**) bore more resemblance to the late medieval view on faith and works than to that of the Reformers.

Anabaptists were biblicists in the sense that they used the Bible and especially the New Testament exclusively as a blueprint for both theology and ethics. The ethical injunctions of the prophets, Jesus, and the apostles constituted for them a pattern for living. They attempted with some success to read the Bible directly rather than through the ancient premises of Christendom. The result was an ethical radicalism whose closest relative was medieval monasticism (*see* **Monastic Ethics**). The difference was their belief that the counsels* of perfection and the precepts of Christ were not a vocational but a universal obligation for Christians (*see* **Vocation**).

They saw ethics, therefore, not in terms of principles but in terms of specific injunctions governing all personal and social relationships. Ideally, the context of ethical decision-making was the disciplined community of faith in which mutual aid* also included assistance in finding any right course of action. They regarded common obedience to specific ethical mandates rather than common confession as the basis of Christian unity.

Anabaptists rejected the doctrines of special predestination and bondage of the will. Each person therefore had to be free to believe or not. Hence they espoused religious liberty and rejected all coercion in matters of faith. And since governments in the sixteenth century everywhere regarded the maintenance of the unity of faith as an important part of magisterial function, they rejected any participation in government for themselves. Since, in their view, the church was not territorial, they rejected the oath of loyalty to city or principality. Because for them force and killing not only were incompatible with the clear words of scripture but also constituted abridgment of freedom for others, they refused military service (*see* **Pacifism**). There were a few early exceptions to these generalizations. According to the Schleitheim Confession of Faith (1527), the sword was ordained by God but "outside the perfection of Christ."

They took a much freer view of marriage* than most of their contemporaries. If, as happened frequently, conflicting claims to loyalty demanded a choice between Christ and the spouse, separation or divorce* were allowed. Finally, they rejected the notion of private property* as the exclusive right to possession. What one had was ideally always available to whoever needed it. All commercial activity for the sake of gain was condemned, as was the charging of interest. The Hutterite Anabaptists instituted total community of goods in 1533, allowing for no private property. It was based on the NT, but also on the old classical view that greed was the original sin.

See also **Ecclesiology and Ethics; Mennonite Ethics; Persecution and Toleration.**

W. Klaassen, *Anabaptism in Outline: Selected Primary Sources,* 1981; J. M. Stayer, *Anabaptists and the Sword,* 1978; G. H. Williams, *The Radical Reformation,* 1962.

WALTER KLAASSEN

Anarchism

A political movement and social philosophy that urges the elimination of government and seeks the good human life in communities of persons living in free cooperation. Historians sometimes locate the origins of this movement in the radical Christian communities of the Reformation, which often rejected participation in secular government. Others find the origins of anarchism in the English Levellers, who extended the religious claim of equality before God to include political and economic equality and freedom from arbitrary authority. Systematic philosophical expressions of anarchism, however, first appear as an extension of the libertarian ideals of the French Revolution. Pierre-Joseph Proudhon (1809–1865) is identified as the founder of modern anarchism, which usually calls for communal sharing of goods and rejects organized religion along with government. Anarchism today is more important as a philosophical expression of the ideal of uncoerced community* than as a practical political program.

See **Anarchy; Libertarianism; State.**

ROBIN W. LOVIN

Anarchy

The absence of government. Such a state of affairs is indeed advocated by a few small extremist revolutionary groups. The Christian attitude to anarchy is perhaps best stated by Calvin. He acknowledges that in an ideal world (that is, where humankind had not fallen into sin) the restraints of civil government would be unnecessary; but in our actual world, he argues that even a bad government is better than none at all.

See **Anarchism.**

JOHN MACQUARRIE

Anger

Anger is one of the basic emotions*. For the most part it is unpleasant in its feeling tone, creates a great deal of physical tension which seeks release in action, and tends to engender both impulsiveness and a sense of power and self-assurance. It has a wide variety of causes. Its destructive potential is well known, both when it is turned outward toward others (especially when it results in violent or aggressive behavior) and also when it is turned inward (as in bitterness, resentment, guilt, or depression). Theologically, anger has traditionally been regarded as one of the seven deadly sins, and there are many biblical passages which acknowledge its dangers and the difficulties it creates in human affairs (e.g., Gen. 4:4–8; Matt. 5:22; Gal. 5:20–21). Both Platonism and Stoicism saw anger as an irrational, and therefore unworthy, passion.

The negative view of anger in Western Christian piety is currently undergoing reappraisal. In part this is a response to developing psychological awareness of the creative as well as the destructive possibilities of anger and of its importance both to survival and to quality of life. In part also the reappraisal reflects changing theological emphases, especially in process theology, liberation theol-

ogy*, and feminist theology (see **Feminist Ethics**). These have acknowledged the role of anger as a motivating power for justice* and have seen its intimate relationship to love*. As understandings of God have broadened to include renewed awareness of the divine anger (or wrath), so more attention is now being given to the significance of the undoubted place of anger in the life and actions of Jesus. Pastoral care has recognized the importance of acknowledging what anger we have (including any we may feel toward God) and learning how to express it appropriately —for the sake of minimizing its destructive potential and of enhancing its creative possibilities.

Anger is a fact of human life and in itself ethically neutral. Ethical issues may be raised, however, by whatever it is that makes us angry and by what we do with our anger. These factors also reflect our personal temperament and history and our culture and its values. Much of our everyday anger is petty and selfishly oriented, but if we had no capacity for anger we would equally have no capacity for genuine love and little or no motivation to attack what is evil and false in our own lives or in the life of our world. Anger is an emotion which commonly only arises when we care sufficiently about someone or something and we see that person or thing under threat. The ethical ambiguities surrounding anger are neatly summed up in Eph. 4:26: "Be angry, but do not sin."

See **Meekness.**

B. W. Harrison, "The Power of Anger in the Work of Love," *Union Seminary Quarterly Review* 36, Suppl., 1981; C. Tavris, *Anger: The Misunderstood Emotion,* 1982.

GRAEME M. GRIFFIN

Anglican Moral Theology/Ethics

There is no generally accepted body of moral teaching that permits one to speak of "Anglican moral theology" in the same way as one can speak of "Roman Catholic moral theology"; and there is no single dominant figure in Anglicanism, like Luther or Calvin, so that one cannot point to a coherent body of "Anglican ethics" comparable to "Lutheran ethics" or "Calvinist ethics." The purpose of this article, therefore, is not to present a type of ethical thinking which is exclusively Anglican, but rather to recall a number of important contributions made by individuals, groups, or movements all confessedly Anglican in allegiance though sometimes differing widely in approach and emphasis.

We may note four early intimations of the lines along which the post-Reformation Anglican moral tradition was expected to move. (1) The Catechism of 1549, as enlarged in 1604, contained an exposition of the Decalogue flanked on one side by the Creed and on the other by the Lord's Prayer and the sacraments. (2) In 1552 a rehearsal of the Commandments was introduced into the Communion rite after the Collect for Purity. (3) In 1571, the seventh of the Thirty-nine Articles reaffirmed the long-familiar distinction: "Although the Law given from God by Moses, as touching Ceremonies and Rites, do not bind Christian men, nor the Civil precepts thereof ought of necessity to be received in any commonwealth; yet . . . no Christian man whatsoever is free from the obedience of the Commandments which are called Moral." (4) In 1603–1604 appeared the revised Canon Law, modest in scope yet comprehensive in intention. Thus was right living declared to be inseparable from true belief; the Decalogue was acknowledged as summarizing the chief requirements of the natural law and as finding its complete unfolding and fulfillment in the teaching and person of Christ; moral obedience was perceived to be not the cause but the consequence of a right relationship with God, sustained by prayer and worship; and the church's institutional structures were justified by the need to provide for the pastoral care of the faithful and for the extension of the kingdom through its ministry toward society at large.

Pointers in the same direction came from Richard Hooker (c. 1554–1600) in his *Treatise of the Laws of Ecclesiastical Polity* (published in four installments, 1594–1662), which tried to resolve the issues raised in his controversy with those who wished to reform the English church on the Geneva pattern. Rejecting "scripture only," Hooker appealed to reason, scripture, and tradition as complementary authoritative guides in morals as in belief and worship. The key to his teaching lies in his theory of law* which, with minor modifications, follows closely the *De Legibus* of Aquinas (*ST* I-II.90–108). All the laws of the universe are grounded in the eternal law of God's own being. Human beings participate in this eternal law and perceive their chief moral duties by the law of reason (natural law*). This is amplified and interpreted by divine positive law made known in the Old and New Testaments, without which sinful humans cannot attain to their supernatural end.

Here was a firm foundation for the Caroline moral theology—an inexact but convenient term to denote the works on moral theology published in England during the seventeenth century, when the subject was highly esteemed by church people of all persuasions. After the upheavals of the Reformation the provision of a moral theology appropriate to the needs of a reformed Church of England had been delayed, primarily because those who were best qualified to give a lead had been immersed in doctrinal controversies. A few modest contributions appeared during the Elizabethan period, but the first notable volume was William Perkins's *The Whole Treatise of the Cases of Conscience* (posthumously published in 1606). Other works of major importance included: William Ames's *De Conscientia et Eius Jure vel Casibus* (1630); Robert Sanderson's *De Juramenti Promissorii Obligatione* (1647) and *De Obligatione Conscientiae* (1660); Joseph Hall's *Resolutions and Decisions of Divers Practical Cases of Conscience* (1649); Jeremy Taylor's *The Rule and Exercises of Holy Living* (1650) and *Ductor Dubitantium* (1660); Richard Baxter's *A Christian Directory* (1673); John Sharp's *A Discourse Concerning Conscience* (1683) and *The Case of a Doubting Conscience* (1684). Among these authors were famous leaders of the "Puritan wing" (*see* **Puritan Ethics**) of the Church of England as well as bishops. Further contributions were made by them and many others in treatises and monographs, popular handbooks, lectures, occasional discourses, letters, devotional works, and sermons. The total relevant literature is enormous. Moral theology* (or "practical" or "casuistical" divinity, as they called it) was not regarded as a priestly pursuit alone nor identified mainly with the confessional (*see* **Casuistry**). The English moralists wrote in English, or their works were quickly translated from Latin, for the benefit of all who could read them; and, though the need of personal direction was never minimized, they wished to assist people as far as possible to resolve their own moral problems with confidence and safety. They were ready to learn from their medieval predecessors and Roman contemporaries, _dialogical_

but quick to criticize and reject whatever they believed to be inconsistent with "right reason," scripture, and early Christian teaching—though some required a weightier scriptural reference than others. Much of the terminology and many of the categories and distinctions employed by medieval moralists reappeared in their pages, and in their expositions of conscience and law they were largely Thomistic. Accordingly, they sought to demonstrate by the range of their studies that no area of human life, public or private, lies outside the orbit of Christian moral principles. But they reacted adversely to certain elements in contemporary Roman moral theology, and were inclined to pillory whatever might be labeled "Jesuitry." It was not simply a matter of Jesuit political theory or of devices like verbal equivocation and mental reservation. They dismissed probabilism* and defended probabiliorism* as the correct method to determine most cases of conscientious doubt. They rejected the distinction of mortal and venial sin as commonly taught. Dissatisfied with a doctrine of repentance that seemed to be inseparably linked with the sacrament of penance, they insisted that only a sorrow for sin that is properly contrition (not "attrition") will suffice for absolution, and emphasized the scriptural concept of repentance as a radical conversion to the life of obedient sonship. Their tendency toward rigorism was partly a reaction to the alleged laxity of many continental Roman casuists, but was also related to their own conception of the nature and function of moral theology. They saw it as a comprehensive science adequate to lead a heedful society in the ways of justice and the individual Christian in the path of holiness*: as including not only casuistry and the resolution of difficult cases of conscience, but also the whole range of what is sometimes thought of separately as ascetic theology: not a legalistic system but a body of teaching, commended within a pastoral setting, that would help persons in all the circumstances of life to grow in grace and "guide them safely in their walk with God, to life eternal" (Baxter). (See H. R. McAdoo, _The Structure of Caroline Moral Theology_, 1949; Thomas Wood, _English Casuistical Divinity During the Seventeenth Century_, 1952.)

A consensus of the kind that the Caroline moral theologians envisaged was not forthcoming. Their many contributions, though often of great value and widely read, remained fragmentary, and too often there was a tendency only to repeat traditional teaching on the social, political, and economic order, instead of an attempt to present a creative reinterpretation of it in a century of great upheaval and rapid social change. It is a permissible exaggeration to say that the latter part of the 17th and the opening years of the 18th century saw a slide from moral theology into moralism*. There was a marked drop in spiritual temperature as the mysterious harmony of belief, worship, and conduct succumbed to a rationalistic presentation of a codified morality of joyless common sense. The Tillotsonian sermon, so admirable in composition but so platitudinous in moral content became the model for 18th-century clergymen, and _The Whole Duty of Man_ (anon., 1657), torn from its original ascetical context, reached its 28th edition by 1790.

This was the background to the most notable contribution made to the century's ethical studies by an English churchman, namely, the _Fifteen Sermons_ (1726) and the _Dissertation on the Nature of Virtue_ (1736) by Joseph Butler (1692–1752), successively bishop of Bristol and Durham. In these short masterpieces he spoke of general moral principles in a way that enhanced the natural law tradition, yet revealed an empirical strain which recognized the complexity of the moral life. He propounded a doctrine of the sovereignty of conscience* which nevertheless permitted him to commend virtue on prudential grounds. Though often prescribed reading for ordinands during the 19th century, these were less exercises in theological ethics than discourses in moral philosophy. They remind us that, supportive of the Anglican moral tradition, there has been an honorable line of moral philosophers extending backward to the Cambridge Platonists and represented nearer our own day by men like Hastings Rashdall (_The Theory of Good and Evil_, 1907), W. R. Sorley (_Moral Values and the Idea of God_, 1918), and A. E. Taylor (_The Faith of a Moralist_, 1930).

Those pressing social questions which the 18th-century Establishment would scarcely acknowledge were bravely tackled by some of the Anglican Evangelicals, and more especially by a group nicknamed "the Clapham Sect." They included William Wilberforce, the redoubtable advocate of the abolition of the slave trade, who persuasively enunciated their ideals in his _Practical View of the Pre-_

vailing Religious Systems of Christians . . .
(1791). Their ethical teaching was expressed
in terms of a scriptural Christianity of a well-
nigh fundamentalist kind. With a profound
belief in the efficacy of Christ's atoning work
and the need of personal conversion, they
stressed the individual's dutiful fulfillment of
his or her calling in daily life and work. They
were conservative in their approach to the
social order, but moved by a powerful if
somewhat paternalistic humanitarian concern. Thus it was not to a radical criticism of
the prevailing political and economic structures that their energies were directed, but
rather to a relentless campaigning for specific
social reforms and industrial legislation that
would ameliorate the hardships and injustices of the deprived and oppressed. This biblical evangelicalism, which later stirred men
like Lord Shaftesbury (1801–1885) to work
for social reforms and factory acts that would
still further improve the conditions of the
working class, has persisted to our own day
as a firm strand in the varied texture of the
Anglican moral tradition.

One might have expected the quest for a
distinctively Anglican moral theology to
have been resumed by the Oxford Movement,
but this was not so. Indeed, in this respect the
Tractarians might be thought to have done
the English church a disservice; for, while
admiring their Caroline predecessors and
republishing many of their works, they were
content to use contemporary Roman Catholic manuals and make the priestly ministry of
reconciliation* a close imitation of that
church's interpretation of the sacrament of
penance*. This can now be seen to have done
much to foster among later generations of
Anglicans the mistaken notion that the study
of moral theology is an exclusive pursuit for
"high churchmen" and is inseparably connected with "the confessional."

In 1851 William Whewell published an an-
notated edition of Sanderson's *De Obligatione Conscientiae;* and in 1877 a revised English version, *Bishop Sanderson's Lectures on
Conscience and Law,* was provided by Bishop
Christopher Wordsworth as a set book for
ordinands in the Lincoln diocese. But in 1919
Kenneth E. Kirk (1886–1954; bishop of Oxford from 1937) noted that in the preceding
fifty years only three important Anglican
studies of moral theology had appeared, two
in America, J. J. Elmendorf's *Elements of
Moral Theology* (1892) and W. W. Webb's

The Cure of Souls (1892), and one in England, James Skinner's *Synopsis of Moral and
Ascetical Theology* (1882). It was to the
rehabilitation of this discipline within Anglicanism that Kirk addressed himself in four
substantial volumes which combine an aston-
ishing breadth of biblical and historical
scholarship with a pastoral sensitivity of rare
depth. For him the Oxford Professorship of
Pastoral Theology, founded 1842, was renamed the Chair of Moral and Pastoral Theology in 1932. Like Skinner, he endorsed the
Caroline view that ascetic theology is part of
moral theology's total content. Accordingly,
in *Some Principles of Moral Theology and
Their Application* (1920) he expounded traditional principles and terminology relating to
conscience, law, casuistry, and sin in the
wider setting of discourses on Christian character, penitence and the treatment of sin, the
healing of the soul, its education and spiritual
progress. He then turned to the perennial
need in the institutional church of a reconciliation of law and liberty sufficient to avert
the twin dangers of authoritarianism and
lawlessness. With this in mind he undertook,
in *Ignorance, Faith and Conformity* (1925), a
historical study of the notions of "invincible
ignorance" and "conscientious nonconformity," and concluded that the wide tolerance
within Anglicanism was a legitimate development of the catholic principles of Western
Christendom. A theme confined to one chapter of *Some Principles* received full treatment
in *Conscience and Its Problems* (1927). Here,
a thorough study of the meaning of conscience and of the necessity, dangers, and history of casuistry prepared the way for an
attempt to articulate sound procedures for
the resolution of difficult cases of conscientious error, doubt, and perplexity. But moral
theology must treat of all the minutiae of
human conduct only because its overriding
purpose is to assist every Christian to reach
the final goal of human life which is to know
God and enjoy him for ever. Appropriately,
Kirk's longest (and greatest) book, *The Vision of God* (1931), was an exhaustive exploration of this single but all-embracing theme:
"The highest prerogative of the Christian is
the activity of worship; and nowhere except
in this activity will he find the key to his
ethical problems."

As a moral theologian, Kirk has had no
Anglican successor of comparable stature,
but the work of three later writers should be

noted. *The Elements of Moral Theology* (1947), by R. C. Mortimer (d. 1976), who had the Oxford chair before becoming bishop of Exeter, is a tightly written book, heavily dependent on Aquinas, with five principal themes: the end of man, law, human actions, conscience, and the seven virtues. *A New Introduction to Moral Theology* (1964), by H. M. Waddams (d. 1972), is a useful middle-weight volume, simpler and less technically exact than Mortimer's but more comprehensive: it has a section on sin, examines briefly a wide range of contemporary moral problems, and repudiates the allegation that moral theology is necessarily legalistic. *An Outline of Anglican Moral Theology* (1968), by Lindsay Dewar (d. 1976), reaffirmed much that we found to be characteristic of Caroline moral theology and emphasized that the Anglican approach, while adopting many of the well-proven traditional principles, categories, and distinctions, is less systematic and authoritarian than the Roman, that on many questions there is no official Anglican position, and that educating conscience is not a matter of spoon-feeding. Dewar observed that for these reasons "perhaps the time will never come when an Anglican text book of moral theology can be adequately written." Certainly no further attempt has yet been made.

Not as an essential part of the formation of a comprehensive moral theology (as the Carolines would have expected), but almost as a distinct and unplanned enterprise, there was amassed after the 1840s a not unimpressive collection of Anglican social teaching of a kind more radical and positive than anything earlier envisaged by the Evangelicals. It began with the tentative Christian Socialism of 1848–1854. Its founder was J. M. Ludlow (1821–1911), a layman familiar with the Social Catholics in France. Its theologian and prophet was F. D. Maurice (1805–1872), whose rejection of the literalist view of endless punishment in hell cost him his chair at King's College, London. Its popular interpreter was Charles Kingsley (1819–1875), who was greatly influenced by Coleridge and Carlyle. While the official church tolerated utilitarian laissez-faire doctrines and seemed indifferent to the iniquitous social conditions and mounting discontent consequent upon the Industrial Revolution*, this group sympathized with the aspirations of the unenfranchised working class which had been voiced in the People's Charter of 1838. They propounded no precise economic doctrine. For them Socialism meant "the science of partnership," and Christianity entailed a form of society in which people could work together. Competition was blasphemous. The Fatherhood of God, the incarnation, and Christ's teaching about the kingdom mean that human brotherhood is not a distant ideal but a present fact to be recognized and acted upon. It is the church's task to help people to see and become what they already are. The group pleaded for social justice in the spirit of a crusade, meeting regularly for prayer and Bible study under Maurice, whose *The Kingdom of Christ* (1838) contained his social teaching in embryo. God's kingdom, the universal community of Christ, was already "the great practical existing reality which is to renew the earth." Socialism* meant "the assertion of God's order" and therefore demanded something more radical and all-embracing than a display of benevolence toward the less fortunate. Their periodical *Politics for the People* (1848) was followed by *Tracts on Christian Socialism* (1850) and *The Christian Socialist* (1850–51). In 1850 Kingsley published two didactic novels, *Yeast* and *Alton Locke,* and a blistering denunciation of "the political economy of mammon" in *Cheap Clothes and Nasty.* The majority of church people continued to be either apathetic or hostile to the movement, but on the long view it was not a failure: it initiated the Provident and Friendly Societies Act of 1852, exercised a formative influence on the Cooperative Movement, and encouraged the infant trade unions.

The seeds which had been sown continued to grow. In 1877 S. D. Headlam (1847–1924) founded the Guild of St. Matthew, which combined the theological outlook of Maurice with the high churchmanship of the Tractarians. In 1899 the Christian Social Union was formed, a larger body devoted to a more protracted study and interpretation of fundamental Christian social principles. Bishop Westcott (1825–1901) was its first president, and its leaders included Henry Scott Holland (1847–1918) and Charles Gore (1853–1932). The momentum was now so increasing that by the turn of the century one could speak not simply of the Christian Socialists of the Anglican Church but of the Christian Social Movement of England as a whole. By 1911 it was possible for representative Anglicans,

Roman Catholics, and Nonconformists to meet at Birmingham under the chairmanship of Bishop Gore to form the Interdenominational Conference of Social Service Unions. Something of Gore's independent mind, prophetic spirit, and resolve to bring to bear on social questions the principles implicit in an incarnational theology is evident in his introductions to two volumes of essays by various writers, *Property, Its Duties and Rights* (1913) and *The Return of Christendom* (1922), and in his own *Christ and Society* (1928).

This growing corpus of Anglican social teaching was augmented between 1930 and 1950 by the writings of the strongly Anglo-Catholic "Christendom Group," which shared the basic concern of the Christian Socialists while following an independent political line. It coined the phrase "Christian sociology" to indicate its determination to propound an informed critical judgment upon the structure of society itself and not only upon the behavior of persons within society; and it designated its journal *Christendom* to symbolize the inspiration it derived from the medieval synthesis when articulating its own hope of a renewed Christian ethical guidance in the secular spheres of the 20th century. Its members included M. B. Reckitt (*A Christian Sociology for Today,* 1934; *From Maurice to Temple,* 1947), V. A. Demant, for twenty-two years Professor of Moral and Pastoral Theology at Oxford (*God, Man and Society,* 1933; *Theology and Society,* 1947; *Religion and the Decline of Capitalism,* 1952), W. G. Peck, P. E. T. Widdrington, and Ruth Kenyon; and perhaps the best introduction to its teaching is Reckitt's *Prospect for Christendom* (1945).

In this area the mantle of Gore fell upon William Temple (1881–1944), bishop of Manchester from 1921, archbishop of York from 1929, and of Canterbury from 1942. His theology, resting upon a profound devotion to scripture and a deep respect for reason, conscience, and the achievements of science and philosophy, was unified by a conviction that the incarnational and sacramental teaching of Christianity "invested the material with worth and overcame the separation between spirit and matter—so the Christian must be concerned in realizing his faith in the daily life of the world, its economics and its politics" (J. Macquarrie). It was in the challenging aftermath of the First World War

that he presided at the interdenominational Conference on Christian Politics, Economics, and Citizenship (COPEC) in Birmingham in 1924. The enormous amount of preparatory research provided material for a series of twelve reports. In 1927 Temple published *Essays in Christian Politics and Kindred Subjects,* and in 1928, *Christianity and the State.* In January 1941, in the dark days of the Second World War, he presided over the Anglican conference at Malvern on "The Life of the Church and the Order of Society," which analyzed the crisis facing civilization and declared that continued private ownership of the industrial resources of the country may be incompatible with the Christian doctrine of man. Its papers were published in *Malvern 1941* (1941), and it was here that Temple expressed the need of "middle axioms": "We lack what one school of Greek moralists called the 'middle axioms'* which connect the ultimate (moral) principles with the complexities of the actual historical situation in which action has to take place." This was the setting of his *Citizen and Churchman* (1941) and of *Christianity and the Social Order* (1942), which, it has been said, together with his widely publicized speeches, helped to prepare public opinion for the extensive social legislation of the postwar period.

Since 1920 Anglican thinking on ethical questions has been enriched by reports emanating from the central councils of the English "Church Assembly" and its successor (since 1970), the General Synod, and from comparable bodies in all the major autonomous provinces of the Anglican communion. It has benefited from projects and publications sponsored by the World Council of Churches, and has been fed once a decade by the advisory reports and resolutions of the Lambeth Conferences. Indeed, Bishop I. T. Ramsey of Durham (d. 1972) held that the report on *The Family in Contemporary Society,* prepared for the 1958 Conference, marked the beginning of a new era in Christian moral thinking by the way in which the interdisciplinary team which produced it combined, in their corporate evaluation, the insights of traditional moral theology and the experts' professional understanding of the empirical data (*Church Quarterly,* January 1970).

Yet the last quarter of a century has been for Anglicans a period of ethical uncertainty.

In England, in 1958, J. A. T. Robinson (after-wards bishop of Woolwich, d. 1983) asked whether anyone of academic standing would be prepared to teach for the morals paper of the General Ordination Examination (*Theology,* December 1958); and, almost before the question had been put, Christian ethics was withdrawn from that examination and not restored until 1965. It has also been a period of confusion and controversy associated with that "Storm Over Ethics" which provided the title of a symposium published in the USA in 1967. At the edge of the storm was a process of revaluation of concepts and terminology like natural law, conscience, duty, and God's will, as in *Christian Ethics and Contemporary Philosophy,* edited by I. T. Ramsey (1966). But at its center was the challenge to Christian decision-making of "situation ethics."* All Christians would say that they should make a loving response to each new situation. But what constitutes a loving response? Moral theology has always been "situational" inasmuch as its casuistry has tried to interpret the generally accepted principles or norms, according to the circumstances of any particular case, in a manner consistent with love* (agape), which is itself the fulfillment of the moral law. The "situationist," however, not only stresses the uniqueness of every situation but also holds that love itself is the *only* norm, that the end justifies the means, and that love's decisions are made entirely situationally and not prescriptively (Joseph Fletcher, *Situation Ethics,* 1966). The new teaching, with all its ambiguities and imprecision, provoked a tortuous debate recorded in *Deeds and Rules in Christian Ethics,* by Paul Ramsey (1967), and *Norm and Context in Christian Ethics,* edited by Gene H. Outka and Paul Ramsey (1968). It has been seen by some as a welcome simplification of the tradition, and by others as its threatened disintegration. In the event it has simply added one more to the possible ethical approaches available to Anglicans. Now, however, in ethics as in doctrine, there is an increasing tendency to regard these varying stances and emphases not so much as a series of options containable within Anglicanism itself but rather as differences which cross denominational boundaries. Thus it is hardly surprising to find that, on nearly all the major ethical issues of today, Anglicans are deeply divided.

THOMAS WOOD

Animals

After years of apparent neglect, human treatment of animals has become an issue of moral concern. This has been inspired in part by moral philosophers who have taken questions of duty to animals with renewed seriousness. Peter Singer begins *Animal Liberation* (1976), "This book is about the tyranny of human over nonhuman animals." Recent interest can be traced to the publication of *Animals, Men and Morals* (S. and R. Godlovitch and J. Harris, eds.), assembled by three Oxford philosophy students in 1971. Since then there has been a flood of publications, a symposium on Animals' Rights at Cambridge in 1977, and seminal works by Stephen Clark, Tom Regan, and Mary Midgley.

Some philosophers question the Judeo-Christian tradition for apparently legitimizing the tyranny of human beings over animals. Man's dominion in Genesis is seen as "benevolent despotism" with animals "delivered into his hands" (*Animal Liberation*). Aquinas, who objected to animal cruelty on the basis that it made humans more liable to commit acts of human cruelty, is dismissed as revealing "the essence of speciesism." Even Francis of Assisi, who is otherwise thought of as an exception, is regarded as speciesist for holding that the sun shines for man. But it is with Descartes and his denial of sentience in animals that the Christian tradition is seen to reach its lowest point. Animals are perceived as automata devoid of consciousness and their pain is compared to the creaking of machinery. Pope Pius IX is charged with having forbidden an animal protection office in Rome on the basis that this would imply that humans have duties to animals. The denial of rationality, theologically justified by the Thomist conviction that animals are not possessed of immortal souls, has led to what Midgley describes as the "absolute dismissal" by post-Enlightenment philosophy (*Animals and Why They Matter,* 1983).

The idea that animals have some claim to moral treatment independent of their value to humanity is comparatively new for moralists and theologians. It would be a mistake, however, to take past indifference as wholly characterizing Christian attitudes. The English SPCA (later to become the RSPCA) was able to record in its first minute book in 1832 that "the proceedings of this Society are entirely based on the Christian Faith, and on

Christian principles." Much in the theological tradition on closer inspection supports some regard for animals and our responsibilities toward them.

The OT comprises a variety of attitudes: as created by God, animals have worth and value to him; they are blessed, i.e., given the authorization to be and to reproduce themselves (Gen. 1:22). Animals are part of God's covenant and exist in a symbiotic relationship with humans (9:10). This means that they share both the Noachic judgment and the hope of renewal (8:1). Their life is a gift and belongs to the mystery and fullness of God's creative work which humans often fail to perceive (Job 38–41). The prerogatives of human beings develop ambivalently. They have been given power over animals as expressed by the concept of dominion (Gen. 1:28) and the naming of them (2:19). But dominion did not initially extend to the right to kill (1:29), and only after the Flood did God's command include the taking of animals for food (9:3). The right to take animal flesh as food appears as a concession to human sinfulness and hence arose the continuing hope of final peace and harmony among creation (e.g., Hos. 2:18; Isa. 11:6f.; Ezek. 34:25f.). Until that day beasts share with humanity the ability to praise God (Isa. 43:20–21) but also the same burden and judgment (see, e.g., Hos. 4:3; Jer. 7:20; Isa. 50:2). Humans must have regard for animals (Prov. 12:10) and should care for the land (Gen. 2:15). Even the cattle of Nineveh were of account to the Lord (Jonah 4:11). It is sometimes suggested that dominion gives humans a license to use animals as they wish. Recent scholarship, however, places this idea within the theology of kingship, i.e., the responsible and accountable use of privilege in accordance with God's will. "In both the Old Testament creation stories we have the picture of man, the ideal king, God's perfect viceregent, under whom nature is fertile and peaceful and all she was meant to be" (J. A. Baker, in *Man and Nature*, ed. H. Montefiore, 1975). Further, it cannot be said that animals were made for humankind. This is shown in the limitation about the taking of blood (Gen. 9:4), for blood contains the life (*nephesh*) of the animal, and humans should not appropriate it for their own purposes. In this sense we may understand the otherwise puzzling practice of animal sacrifice. Such a practice appears inconsistent with respect for life, but it

is likely that the ritual was understood as the freeing of the animal to be with God rather than its gratuitous destruction. We should, however, note the protest that accompanies it (e.g., Isa. 1:15; Ps. 50:9f.). Also note the many humane provisions of Hebrew law (e.g., Deut. 25:4; Ex. 23:4–5).

The NT has few direct references to the status of animals, but it speaks of the value of sparrows (Matt. 10:29; Luke 12:6), the care of oxen (1 Cor. 9:9), and the cleanness of animal food (Acts 10:9f.; cf. Mark 7:15). Jesus accepts God's providential care of animals and all creation (Matt. 6: 26; Luke 12: 24). But its development of new covenant theology has a crucial, if indirect, bearing on animal questions. The sacrificial system is replaced by the sacrifice of Christ (Heb. 10:12); creation is seen as groaning under the weight of bondage, awaiting deliverance (Rom. 8: 28); the hope of renewal is developed Christologically into the promise of cosmic redemption for all that lives (e.g., Col. 1:20; Eph. 1:10). Perhaps most important, the self-costly love* of Jesus is seen as the moral exemplar and there is the hint that this ethic extends to the outcast and least of all (Matt. 25:40).

It is possible to offer a theological understanding of animals which takes account of the many positive elements within the tradition. Briefly: (*a*) animals as created beings share the gift of creaturely existence with humanity; (*b*) they too are valuable in the Lord's eyes and give him praise; (*c*) they are designed to live in symbiotic harmony with humans—a situation only changed after the Fall; (*d*) God's covenant* includes and enfolds all animals even to the extent that they are his companions, sojourners, and even forerunners; (*e*) humans are placed among animals in a privileged position of power that they must exercise responsibly according to the will of God; and (*f*) the redeeming purposes of God in Christ extend in principle to the entire created order of which animals form a part. Nevertheless, theologians have given scant attention to the doctrine of the nonhuman. Many classical writers (Aquinas, Luther, Calvin) have simply accepted a subordinate relationship and failed to ascribe any other purpose to animals than that of serving humanity. "For by divine providence they are intended for man's use in the natural order. Hence it is not wrong for man to make use of them, either by killing or in any way whatever" (Aquinas, *Summa Contra Gentiles* III.112). Karl Barth also appears to regard nonhuman beings as doctrinally peripheral. "In practice the doctrine of creation means anthropology—the doctrine of man" (*Church Dogmatics* III/2, ET 1960, p. 3). This self-confessed "anthropocentricity" stems from a high doctrine of man and in particular a Christologically informed anthropology. But has the special place given to humanity in doctrine led to the neglect of the nonhuman? While it is possible, for example, to interpret incarnational theology in an anthropocentric sense, i.e., as God's sole concern with the human creation, this is not a necessary implication. It is possible to interpret incarnation as God's "yes" to creation, as reaffirming the value of the whole. Paul Tillich writes, "Man cannot claim that the infinite has entered the finite to overcome its existential estrangement in man alone" (*Systematic Theology,* vol. 2, 1957, p. 96).

Christian ethics have been overwhelmingly concerned with human problems of right conduct, motivation, and duty to other humans. This has made discussion of animal questions appear peripheral and incidental. "Brutes are things in our regard. . . . They exist for us, not for themselves" (J. Rickaby, *Moral Philosophy,* 1888, pp. 244f.). The effects of abuse on the human abuser are often regarded as the primary matter of concern. Such a view, rationalist as well as Christian, excludes animals as objects of moral concern in their own right, and hence recent philosophical literature has been concerned with questions of the individual animal's interests or rights*. Here the problem is deciding by what standard we know these claims and by which criteria we judge them. The most influential view is that which takes consciousness, sense perception, and the ability to feel pain as the basis for interests or rights. Like Bentham they argue: "The question is not, Can they *reason?* nor, Can they *talk?* but, Can they *suffer?*" (*Principles of Morals and Legislation,* 1789, p. 310 n.). Hence it is argued that all sentient animals should have rights analogous to those of humans. Does this mean that all sentient beings should be regarded as of equal worth? Not necessarily. The point here is the claim to equality* of treatment, all circumstances being equal. And how do we judge these competing claims? Some degree of utilitarian calculation

as with other moral questions seems inevitable.

Can Christians accept talk of animal rights as theologically proper? One recent critic claims that acceptance has now reached such a point that it amounts to a "deeply felt, philosophical orthodoxy on rights, animals and vegetarianism" (R. G. Frey, *Interests and Rights: The Case Against Animals,* 1980). Can such terminology bear much relation to the biblical language of obligation and responsibility? Can rights cohere with the doctrine of creation as gift? Are concepts of value* and duty* better starting points than talk of objective rights*? Even the granting of rights still leaves open the further question of how humans resolve conflicts between one set of right holders and another.

Such objections may not meet the new concern. Behind every reforming movement lies the question of changed perceptions, and our perception of animals has vastly altered. Ethology has immeasurably reformed our view of animals as automata. Few scientists doubt the existence of consciousness, sentiency, and rudiments of rationality in the higher mammals. The thoughts of Darwin and Wallace have fueled a moral revolution. These discoveries have encouraged the recognition of the intrinsic value of other species. This has led to a renewed sense of moral obligation and the desire to establish moral limits. Hence it is plausible to see the claiming of rights for animals as part of a new sense of kinship with and duty toward them. If Christians are to incorporate rights within their ethical systems, it is difficult to see how some acceptance of animal rights can be avoided. Perhaps theologically, however, if we wish to speak of animal rights, it would be more accurate to do so in terms of humans "Having no right," or of God's right to have his creation treated with respect.

There are two basic issues: (1) To what extent, if at all, have humans the right to kill? (2) To what extent, if at all, have humans the right to cause pain, suffering, or stress?

1. Killing. We need to distinguish between sentient and nonsentient life. Most philosophers accept a distinction between the justifiability of killing sentient beings, i.e., conscious beings with a capacity for pain, and the justifiability of killing other beings. Some Christians still doubt whether the killing of sentients is a moral matter. Their view has been based on a distinction between the morality of killing and that of causing pain. Such a position is reflected in English law, where it is illegal (under some circumstances) to cause an animal pain, whereas it is not illegal to kill it. The precise grounds for this view are obscure. Presumably it relates to the accepted justification for killing animals for food. But as Godlovitch has pointed out (*Animals, Men and Morals*), it is difficult to see how we can place a value on the suffering* of an animal without logically implying the value of the life itself. If we accept the value of creation and arguably the special value of sentient life, it must follow that its destruction without good cause is wrong. The problem is deciding what constitutes "necessary" and therefore justifiable killing.

For food. Humans have assumed the right and the necessity of killing for food. But this has recently been challenged by the increased awareness that humans can achieve a nutritionally adequate diet provided there are a sufficient variety of plant foods available. How far humans can relieve themselves of dependence upon animal food is debatable. In certain parts of the world (e.g., Alaska), people are heavily dependent upon animal protein, so it is not clear that vegetarian agricultural systems could work on a large scale. However, because a vegetarian diet is now a feasible option, philosophers radically question the human right to kill for food. Clark is emphatic: "Vegetarianism is now as necessary a pledge of moral devotion as was the refusal of emperor-worship in the early Church. . . . Those who still eat flesh when they could do otherwise have no claim to be serious moralists" (*The Moral Status of Animals,* 1977). Other Christians argue that meat-eating is a concession given by God and that flesh may be taken on the understanding that the full kingdom of peace and righteousness has yet to dawn. Barth, for example, judges that vegetarianism "represents a wanton anticipation of . . . existence in the new aeon for which we hope." But he also judges that "animal protection, care and friendship are quite indispensable" (*Church Dogmatics* III/4, ET 1961). Other Christians will defend their practice on the grounds that Jesus, as recorded, ate fish and possibly meat. But whatever necessities, cultural or agricultural, existed in the past, it seems

that Christians will need to think afresh their moral ground in this matter (*see* **Vegetarianism**).

Is it possible to live without some use of animal products or by-products? Even vegans, who do not eat dairy produce or eggs, have problems about plastic shoes whose toxicity has been tested through animal experimentation. It does appear that, in the interdependent world God has created, no line of absolute consistency is possible, for we are all involved at some stage in utilizing some beneficial results of animal exploitation*. Nevertheless, it may be that Christian "care and friendship" requires a preparedness to forgo use of animals where there are alternatives available.

For sport. The traditional sports of cockfighting, cock-throwing, bearbaiting, and bullfighting are outlawed in many Western countries but fox, deer, and hare hunting, including hare coursing, are still legal. Shooting and angling have many thousands of adherents in Britain and America. Can the killing of animals for sport be justified? Arguments for justification are usually threefold: (i) the benefit and enjoyment to the humans involved; (ii) the need to control pests; and (iii) the contribution that hunters and fishers make to conservation and the upkeep of the countryside. (i) It is difficult to see how human pleasure* can justify the death of sentient beings (*see* **Amusements**). On any utilitarian calculus the balance of interest must lie with the animal, which has more to lose. Sport may be judged morally neutral, but when it has as its inherent and necessary ingredient the destruction of animals, it must be morally questionable if we are to take the value of creation and human responsibility* seriously. We need to distinguish between human wants and moral necessity. (ii) The question of control will be discussed below. But arguments for hunting cannot easily be turned into arguments for control of animal populations unless this can be shown to be the hunter's main or primary intention. (iii) The third argument is the weakest. It would need to be shown that there is a necessary connection between animal sport and altruistic conservation. Many sportspeople are involved in conservation for the purpose of maintaining the abundance of game. There is evidence to suggest that the hunting of the otter in Britain and the subsequent disruption of its habitat has been one of the main reasons for introducing legal measures to protect dwindling populations.

For control. Competition is thought to be at its fiercest when it comes to sharing food and habitation. But how real is this competition? "Crop pests of all kinds—not just insects, but rodents, birds, even deer, baboons and elephants—*must* be killed, if only by starvation, by people who mean to survive" (*Animals and Why They Matter*). We face a double problem of interpreting the evidence and disentangling territorial rights. It would be a mistake to assume that there are never any real conflicts of interest and that humans are not sometimes right in judging their interests to be primary. Agriculture must involve some control of environmental life, and the interests of locusts must be subordinated to those of growing food. Perhaps this needs to be accepted with the theological proviso that as humans we need to keep before us the recognition that the earthly habitat is not solely ours. We share the gift of dry land with other sentient animals. There must be some cognizance of God's right to let the species he has created exist for his own sake as well. Clark's line is worth remembering: "It is *we* that steal their land for cattle, and for roads, and industry, and then complain that they come poaching" (*The Moral Status of Animals*).

2. Causing pain, suffering or stress. There are two main areas:

In intensive farming. Economic pressures during the last thirty years have forced farmers to adopt procedures which increase livestock numbers and specialize in one form of production. Many of the systems used are termed "intensive" because of the standardization of buildings, machinery, and techniques which are designed to maximize efficiency and profit. Since Ruth Harrison's *Animal Machines* (1964), considerable unease has been felt about the welfare of animals reared under such conditions. Among objectionable features are "around forty-five million laying-hens kept in crowded battery cages, unable to spread even one wing and standing permanently on sloping wire mesh; around half a million sows kept in narrow stalls in which they are unable to turn around . . . and some tens of thousands of young calves . . . kept in slatted-floored crates unable to turn round, unable to lie down freely or even to groom themselves" (E. Carpenter,

Animals and Ethics, 1980). Some mutilations (e.g., de-beaking of chickens and tail-docking of pigs) are necessary to prevent cannibalism. Do animals suffer under these conditions? It is exceedingly difficult to gauge in each situation what degree of suffering may be experienced. M. S. Dawkins's *Animal Suffering: The Science of Animal Welfare* (1980) has shown how some objective assessment may be possible by taking a number of factors into account: physical health, physiological measurements, and abnormal behavior patterns. One hopeful method of determining the welfare of hens was to try to discover their own preferences. But all these have failed to provide a moral rule of thumb. How then can we judge the morality of these systems? One way recommended by *Animals and Ethics* was that basic guidelines should govern the management of farm animals, and that "no husbandry system should deny the environmental requirements of their basic behavioral needs." These include: freedom to move, association with other animals, provision of food and water, ability to perform natural activites, and satisfaction of minimal spatial requirements. These guidelines, minimal as they may appear, would at least prevent unacceptable stress and possible suffering. It does seem that whenever humans take over the life of an animal to the extent of substantially modifying its natural environment, there should be some moral and legal framework to protect it. Since the use of animals to provide a rich and varied diet goes far beyond the most generous interpretation of need, especially in Western countries, humans can afford to be more generous in their rearing of food animals than is often the case.

In animal experimentation. Procedures in Britain and America include poisoning, burning, freezing, mutilations, use of electric shocks, and environmental deprivations of all kinds. Experiments broadly fall into three categories: (i) in educational settings for the acquisition of manual skill and expertise; (ii) in the testing of new products for their toxicological effects; and (iii) in scientific research. Many Christians have accepted the justification for experimentation and have felt that the moral claims of animals should be subordinated to the cause of medical progress. Renewed concern, however, has been caused by the numbers involved, and by the nature and degree of pain inflicted. *Victims of Science* (1975) by Richard Ryder in Britain and *Painful Experiments on Animals* (1976) by Dallas Pratt in America have significantly affected opinion. How is it possible to assess the morality of these experiments? Research with animals has brought considerable benefits, and it would be a mistake to underestimate the indispensability of animals in many areas. But the problem is compounded by the use of animals for apparently trivial purposes. The first two categories mentioned are especially vulnerable. (i) It is difficult to justify harming animals for the routine passing on of knowledge to students where other educational methods may be effective. (ii) A whole range of products which may be toxic are tried on animals in LD50 and other tests which often involve considerable pain. Can the development of new kinds of paints, skin fresheners, hair shampoos, bleaches, crayons, and antifreeze chemicals justify pain and death? Many theologians would now doubt that the ends justified the means. (iii) What of experiments which are pursued in the hope of alleviating human pain or conquering disease? Broadly, there are three moral responses: the primacy of human interests view; the animal utilitarian view; and the animal rights view. The first holds that where there is any conceivable human interest at stake, however negligible or hypothetical, animals should be used. The second holds that animal and human interests need to be evaluated according to their consequences. Pain and death to many animals may not justify negligible gain to humans. But negligible pain to animals may be worth serious human gain. Some utilitarians (*see* **Utilitarianism**), like Singer, while eager to see reform of animal experimentation, hold that "if one, or even a dozen animals had to suffer experiments in order to save thousands, I would think it right in accordance with equal consideration of interests that they should do so" (*Practical Ethics,* 1979). The third view holds that the rights of individual animals are not expendable. Like the rights of individual humans they may sometimes be overridden, but in the case of experimentation it is unjust to coerce animals to suffer risks for the sake of hypothetical good for humans. Risks* cannot, therefore, be morally transferred to those beings who do not voluntarily choose them. Regan is the leading exponent of this view: "To treat them *as if* their value were reducible to their utility for human interests, even important human interests, is to treat

them unjustly" (*The Case for Animal Rights,* 1983).

Arguably, the last two views have more convincing theological support. While it cannot be doubted that humans hold a high place in creation, it does not follow that their own estimation of their welfare can be the sole guide in determining their relations with other creatures. Animals cannot possess absolute rights, but humans have no absolute rights over creation either. The recognition of the value of animals must place some limit on human demands. It could be argued that in the light of the moral exemplar of Jesus, Christians have a positive duty to work for the welfare of creation and its lesser inhabitants. Perhaps Christians who have a vision of human responsibility to creation can argue that there are some risks which humans ought to bear for themselves rather than inflict them on animals.

See **Environmental Ethics; Image of God; Vegetarianism.**

S. R. L. Clark, *The Nature of the Beast: Are Animals Moral?* 1982; A. Linzey, *Animal Rights: A Christian Assessment of Man's Treatment of Animals,* 1976; M. Midgley, *Beast and Man,* 1979; H. Montefiore (ed.), *Man and Nature,* 1975; D. Paterson and R. D. Ryder (eds.), *Animals' Rights—A Symposium,* 1979.

ANDREW LINZEY

Anomie

From its Greek roots, anomie (or anomy or anomia) may be defined as "broken limits." The concept of anomie was initially developed by Emile Durkheim to refer to a condition of relative normlessness in a society or group. In his study of suicide* Durkheim noted that anomic suicide is common among individuals who lack self-identity with a system of norms or values. Anomie refers to the absence of guiding or governing norms*, the state of rulelessness, or deregulation, or of social anarchy*. By extension, the term is now applied to individuals, as the theme of uprooted persons in quest of self-identity and community* has become prevalent in our time.

The anomic person is spiritually sterile and responsible to no one. Anomie conceived sociologically refers to the strain toward normlessness occurring when there is a disjunction or malintegration between cultural goals and the capacity of people to act in accord with these goals. Anomie is a useful concept for understanding deviant behavior. Social chaos, moral confusion, and disintegration of value systems are marks of an anomic society.

See **Alienation.**

E. Durkheim, *Suicide* (1930), ET 1951; R. K. Merton, *Social Theory and Social Structure,* 1957; D. Riesman, N. Glazer, and R. Denney, *The Lonely Crowd,* 1950.

ROBERT LEE

Antenatal Diagnosis
see **Abortion; Genetics**

Anthropology and Ethics
As the study of mankind, or humankind, anthropology could encompass many studies that ordinarily fall under some other academic discipline. In theological discourse, anthropology often refers to the doctrine of man, or human beings, as created, fallen, and redeemed. Such a theological anthropology is very important for Christian ethics (*see* e.g., **Realism; Sin(s); Free Will and Determinism**). Most often, however, anthropology designates several related but distinguishable academic disciplines or subdisciplines. The following divisions, largely pragmatic in nature, have been particularly prominent: physical anthropology, cultural and social anthropology, archaeology, linguistics, and applied anthropology. Whether there is a significant distinction between cultural and social anthropology will depend on whether it is possible to separate culture and social structure for purposes of study. (As a matter of emphasis, cultural anthropology tends to be favored in the USA, and social anthropology in the UK.) According to many interpreters, the fundamental division is between physical anthropology and sociocultural study. In much of the world, anthropology corresponds to physical anthropology, and ethnology designates the sociocultural study of humankind. Within social and cultural anthropology there are several theoretical debates, for example, among the functionalists, the structuralists, the symbolic theorists, and theorists influenced by Marxist perspectives. An even more fundamental matter is whether anthropology is more humanistic in its perspectives and methods—e.g., "a form of art" (E.

Leach) or "interpretive" (C. Geertz)—or more scientific in the tradition of the natural sciences.

Historically, anthropologists have usually concentrated on primitive or preliterate peoples; only since the 1930s have they turned to literate societies and modern urban, industrial societies. Sometimes the distinctions between anthropology and sociology are difficult to detect, especially when both consider modern industrial societies, particular communities, or such areas as medicine (e.g., Charles Bosk, *Forgive and Remember: Managing Medical Failure,* 1979). Nevertheless, in general, anthropologists tend to emphasize fieldwork, holistic perspectives, and comparative approaches—tendencies that are less pronounced in most sociological theory and practice. Some of the categories developed in the study of primitive societies have also been used to illuminate modern societies—for example, Mary Douglas and Aaron Wildavsky, *Risk and Culture: An Essay on the Selection of Technological and Environmental Dangers* (1982).

Anthropology has contributed significantly to the understanding of humankind by describing and explaining similarities and differences among human groups. It has also illuminated the meaning of human actions in their sociocultural contexts. As William Smalley noted in *DCE* (1967), "The suicide of an elderly Eskimo compelled by his sense of the importance of preserving the meagre stock of food for the young and the fit, the self-immolation of the Buddhist priest [in protest of government policy], the hara-kiri of the Japanese officer who has lost face, and the plunge of the neurotic young man who steps from the fortieth floor of a New York building have vastly different meanings because they stem from vastly different sets of assumptions and attitudes, as well as custom."

Many anthropologists have significantly illuminated religious phenomena by their field studies or theories—for example, E. Durkheim, B. Malinowski, A. R. Radcliffe-Brown, E. E. Evans-Pritchard, E. Leach, C. Lévi-Strauss, R. Firth, C. Geertz, M. Douglas, and V. Turner. Religion has remained a major subject of interest, receiving more and clearer attention than morality or ethics, though the relation of religious beliefs, myths, rituals, and values in a social context has been important (*see* **Comparative Reli-**

gious Ethics; Custom; Primitive Ethics; Sociology of Ethics; Taboo).

By its very nature anthropology tends to emphasize diversity, and such an emphasis often goes hand in hand with relativism*. Although some anthropologists have been interested in determining whether there are cross-cultural constants or universals, most of the plausible candidates, such as the regulation of violence and sexual activity, are so general as to permit great variations in the way human groups structure, interpret, and justify their modes of existence. In his powerful book *The Mountain People* (1972), Colin Turnbull shows how one African tribe deteriorated in such a way as to call into question whether some important human values are universal.

Some ethical issues in the conduct of fieldwork in anthropology have become more prominent in recent years. The first ethical question is that of risk-benefit analysis (*see* **Risk; Experimentation with Human Subjects**). In fieldwork the main risk is the violation of privacy* and confidentiality*, though there may also be other harms to the community when the research is itself an intervention and when the knowledge that is gained is used against the community's interests. However, as Joan Cassell notes, the harms are "less immediate, measurable, and serious than the harms associated with other research modes." The main benefit is the generation of knowledge, since the research subjects themselves do not usually benefit directly. The consent* or assent of the community is another ethical issue.

In addition to books and articles by anthropologists mentioned above, see the several articles on anthropology in the *International Encyclopedia of the Social Sciences,* ed. D. L. Sells, 1968; see also T. L. Beauchamp et al. (eds.), *Ethical Issues in Social Science Research,* 1982.

JAMES F. CHILDRESS

Antinomianism

The view that, for the Christian, faith has abolished the law so that one is no longer subject to it. The extreme antinomian point of view, which leads into licentious conduct, is condemned both in the NT and by the Reformers. Yet both the NT and the Reformers were clear that the gospel rules out any legalistic ethic. The place of law in Christian ethics is still being discussed.

See **Law; Law and Gospel; Legalism; Justification by Faith; Natural Law; Norms; Situation Ethics.**

JOHN MACQUARRIE

Anti-Semitism

Anti-Semitism, in everyday usage, refers to attitudes and acts of prejudice* against the Jewish people, ranging from violent persecution* to tacit discrimination*. Strictly speaking, Semites include the peoples in several linguistic groups of Southwest Asia and North Africa (Hebrews and Arabs among modern peoples; Assyrians, Phoenicians, and Babylonians among ancient peoples). Thus it is a contradiction to speak, for example, of Arab anti-Semitism. But the word has come to refer to hostility to Jews, whether among Semites or among other peoples.

Anti-Semitism is a problem of special concern to Christian ethics, because of the unique relations between Christians and Jews. "Spiritually we are all Semites," said Pope Pius XI (1938). But from early times hostility has been common between Christians and Jews. The indications appear even in the NT. Christians appeared to Jews as heretics, and Jews appeared to Christians as recalcitrant unbelievers. As Christianity grew in numbers and power, Christians subjected Jews to many forms of discrimination, sometimes to outright persecution with fratricidal fury. Some Christians attacked Jews as "Christ-killers," guilty of deicide. In the Middle Ages the Jews in Europe were generally consigned to ghettos and regarded as aliens within the feudal order. Yet Christians could not, without denying their own scriptures, deny the covenant* of God with Israel. Sometimes Christians, with a utilitarian cynicism, encouraged Jews to undertake financial activities that were regarded as unethical but necessary to society. Martin Luther, launching the Protestant Reformation, was at first conciliatory toward the Jews, but then turned his fury against them. Precisely speaking, he was anti-Jewish rather than anti-Semitic, since his complaints were against Jewish beliefs, not Jewish ethnicity.

Anti-Semitism has sometimes erupted in organized massacres of Jews, as in the pogroms of Czarist Russia. It has entered deeply into the ethos of modern European-

American civilization. Modern democratic movements led to the emancipation of Jews and their admission to full political rights in the late 18th and early 19th centuries. But the rationalism of the Enlightenment, while rejecting many traditional prejudices, did not know what to do with a people of distinctive history and customs, and thereby fostered new forms of anti-Semitism. The neopaganism of Nazism brought in the 20th century the most bitter, systematic anti-Semitism in all history, with the deliberate extermination of some six million Jews (*see* **Genocide**).

Latent and sometimes explicit anti-Semitism persists in modern civilization. Some votes against Israel in organizations of the United Nations appear to be a combination of normal political conflicts with anti-Semitism. The USSR harasses Jews and makes their emigration difficult. The USA, by establishing the Holocaust Memorial Council in 1981, made at least a gesture of expiation for past indifference, but illegal anti-Semitic acts persist.

The Christian church has formally renounced anti-Semitism on almost all levels of its organized life. The First Assembly of the World Council of Churches (1948) denounced anti-Semitism as "sin against God and man." The Third Assembly (1961) specifically insisted that "the historic events which led to the Crucifixion should not be so presented as to fasten upon the Jewish people of today responsibilities which belong to our corporate humanity and not to one race or community." After a series of papal declarations against anti-Semitism over a period of many years, Vatican Council II declared that "the Jews should not be presented as repudiated or cursed by God, as if such views followed from the holy Scriptures." The Council further deplored "hatred, persecutions, and displays of anti-Semitism directed against the Jews at any time and from any source" (Declaration on the Relationship of the Church to Non-Christian Religions, 1965). Christian theology increasingly emphasizes that the covenant of God with Israel is not revoked by the "new covenant" with the church. But this conviction does not entail uncritical support for policies and actions by the state of Israel.

E. B. Borowitz, *Contemporary Christologies: A Jewish Response,* 1980; A. Hertzberg, *The French Enlightenment and the Jews,* 1968; J. Isaac, *The Teaching of Contempt: Christian Roots of Anti-Semitism,* 1964; J. Maritain, *A Christian Looks at the Jewish Question,* 1939; D. S. Wyman, *The Abandonment of the Jews: America and the Holocaust, 1941–45,* 1984.

ROGER L. SHINN

Anxiety

Anxiety connotes, in common speech, a certain kind of feeling, ranging from jitteriness to terror. In several areas of knowledge it is used precisely but not always with the same meaning. In theology, Augustine made the first considerable use of it. It entered modern theology through Kierkegaard, who regarded anxiety as intimately related to freedom*. When we confront all the undetermined choices yet to be made in our lives (our freedom), we properly become dizzy (or anxious). The anxiety is painful but necessary. If we react only to its pain, we draw back, and thus never quite become human. But if we see the worth of the freedom despite the pain, anxiety becomes a kind of tutor as we become human, use our creative powers, and confront life as it is. Among modern theologians, Reinhold Niebuhr presents substantially the same view as Kierkegaard. Paul Tillich, in partial contrast, distinguishes between ontological anxiety (like Kierkegaard) and pathological anxiety, but believes both are forms of the same phenomenon. Most Continental theologians speak of anxiety sparingly, regarding it as mainly a subjective phenomenon not a proper topic for theology. In earlier American evangelicalism, "anxious inquirers" were persons seriously concerned about the gospel but not yet committed to it.

Several modern fields of study have contributed to the understanding of anxiety including its pathologies. The seminal work from a psychological and psychiatric point of view was done by Freud (*see* **Psychoanalysis**). First identifying anxiety with the tensions produced by frustrated excitation within, and hence as a kind of feeling, he later set forth an understanding that roots anxiety in the process whereby we send and receive signals of danger or challenge. Thus the normative function of anxiety is to ring the alarm when there is peril or possibility. If the signal is properly heard and heeded, then the ego or person examines, identifies, and protects itself against the peril; and the unpleasant feeling is dissipated. When the person is unable to mobilize himself or herself relevantly, then pathologies appear, beginning with a continuing unease or jitteriness, extending in more severe cases to phobias (like fear of horses), and finally to symptoms that keep the alarm signal from producing pain but at the cost of adaptation to the situation. The danger about which anxiety rings the alarm may be small or large, may come from outside or inside. But in all cases, it is the ego or person who must interpret and mobilize to meet it. When its source is properly identified, then the feeling that persists until action has been taken is fear. Thus the primary phenomenon is anxiety, while fear is an aspect of it.

Authorities disagree on the extent to which there is a single phenomenon of anxiety, of which everything spoken of as anxiety is derivative, or whether there are two or three central phenomena all identified as anxiety in different contexts.

If anxiety is used to refer only to phenomena already judged pathological, then it would have a place in psychiatry and psychology but perhaps not in theology and philosophy. If it were used only as a kind of cognitive confrontation, for instance, of God, then it might be regarded suspiciously by psychiatrists who need some word to describe the painful feelings of some patients. Freud's theory of the signal offers a bridge.

The statement is often made that creativity depends on anxiety, as if uncertainty or discomfort were the soil of creativity. This seems to be false. But if anxiety is understood in the sense of either Freud or Kierkegaard, then the capacity to experience its signals, interpret them aright, and act relevantly upon them, would indeed be closely related to capacity for creativity.

Ethics is concerned with anxiety as a motive (see **Motives and Motivation**) for decision* and action, or as a deterrent. Discriminating capacity to feel danger or challenge signals is an indispensable condition for relevant ethical decision. Conversely, if anxiety as affect or feeling is too strong, it paralyzes all decision and action. Thus, the reduction of capacity to deal with anxiety decreases initiative in moral decision; while an intact anxiety signaling system, although neither making nor guaranteeing moral deci-

sions, is nevertheless a necessary base for them.

See **Counseling; Mental Health; Persons and Personality.**

R. May, *The Meaning of Anxiety,* rev. ed. 1977; K. Menninger and S. Hiltner (eds.), *Constructive Aspects of Anxiety,* 1963.

SEWARD HILTNER

Apartheid

Apartheid (literally "apartness") designates the rigorous form of racial segregation* and white supremacy in the Republic of South Africa. The word, introduced when the Nationalist Party came into power in 1948, stood for intensification of the traditionally racial policies of the white minority, seeking to perpetuate political and economic control. The population of South Africa is approximately 67 percent black, 19 percent white, 11 percent "colored" or mixed, 3 percent Asian.

The Group Areas Act of 1950 established forcible separation of races. About 13 percent of the land has been set aside as "homelands" for the black people. Over the past two decades 3.5 million blacks have been resettled from ancestral lands into these crowded, impoverished areas where they are permitted limited local self-government, subject to approval of the national government. Their former settlements have been destroyed. Those who are allowed to remain and hold jobs in the white-dominated areas have few legal rights. They must carry passbooks; they usually must live apart from their families; their movements and occupations are controlled; and they are subject to expulsion.

Enforcement of apartheid has led to harshly repressive acts. The government may detain persons without trial for renewable periods of 90 days. It may forbid publications and political meetings. It has punished opponents of apartheid for "sabotage" or furthering "communism." It has halted peaceful demonstrations by violence, most notably at Sharpeville in 1960, where 69 persons were killed and 186 wounded. More recently demonstrations have repeatedly been put down by police.

World opposition has embarrassed but not softened government policies. The Nobel Peace Prize has twice gone to African leaders who opposed apartheid: in 1960 to Chief A. J. Luthuli and in 1984 to Bishop Desmond

Tutu. The United Nations has repeatedly urged the end of apartheid. The General Assembly has asked UN members to break diplomatic and trade relations, and the Security Council has asked for a cessation of shipment of arms to South Africa. But increasing foreign investments have contributed to the prosperity of the dominant groups in the nation. The corporations argue that they bring economic advancement to black employees, but they are required to operate within the legal confines of apartheid.

The government has substituted the phrase "separate development" for apartheid. It promises eventual "political independence" to the Africans in their "homelands," but it assures its white constituency of "domination," "control," and "supremacy." In 1984 it introduced a new form of parliament, with separate houses of virtually no power for Asians and colored, but no representation for the black majority. The action was resisted by white traditionalists as an erosion of their power; it was criticized by nonwhites as a token effort to give legitimacy to a racially oppressive system.

Apartheid has posed a grave problem for the Christian conscience in South Africa. The dominant Dutch Reformed Church traditionally offered biblical and theological arguments for apartheid, sometimes making analogies between the Israelites and the Dutch, the Canaanites and the black Africans. Theologians are increasingly abandoning that position, but its ingrained power remains strong.

Churches other than the Dutch Reformed (Roman Catholic, Anglican, Methodist, Lutheran, and Congregational) have spoken against apartheid, as has The Christian Institute. In 1960 at the Cottesloe Consultation, officials of the World Council of Churches met with representatives of South African churches. A resulting declaration—that churches may not exclude Christians on grounds of race and that the state may not interfere with the church's proclamation of the gospel—led to counterstatements from Dutch Reformed officials and to withdrawal from the WCC of the three Dutch Reformed Synods that had been members. Grants to freedom movements from the WCC's Programme to Combat Racism have led to further antagonism from the dominant churches. In August 1984 the World Alliance of Reformed Churches suspended from its membership the two white Dutch Reformed Churches that defended apartheid, with the suspension to continue until they reject apartheid and end segregated Communion and worship. Some Dutch Reformed theologians have opposed apartheid, sometimes at the cost of heresy trial and conviction or removal from their pastoral or professorial posts.

See **Race Relations; Racism; Ecumenical Movement, Ethics in the.**

A. Boesak, *Farewell to Innocence,* 1977; J. W. de Gruchy and C. Villa-Vicencio (eds.), *Apartheid Is a Heresy,* 1983; L. A. Hewson (ed.), *Cottlesloe Consultation, The Report,* 1961; T. Huddleston, *Naught for Your Comfort,* 1956; J. C. G. Kotzé, *Principle and Practice in Race Relations According to Scripture,* ET 1961; D. Tutu, *Crying in the Wilderness,* 1982.

ROGER L. SHINN

Apocalyptic *see* Eschatological Ethics

Appetites

The basic human desires and needs. The word has become somewhat old-fashioned in ethics, modern writers preferring to speak of drives or instincts*.

JOHN MACQUARRIE

Applied Ethics

The terms "applied ethics" and "practical ethics" are used interchangeably to indicate the application of ethics to special arenas of human activity, such as business, politics, and medicine, and to particular problems, such as abortion. In some respects applied ethics is close to casuistry even though it does not entail a formal system of casuistry*. Christian theologians and ethicists have long focused on practical problems in the light of their moral principles and religious beliefs, but many philosophers, especially during the 1950s and 1960s, retreated from practical problems to concentrate on metaethics* before returning again to applied ethics in the 1970s and 1980s. The term "practical ethics" has a longer history than "applied ethics," which became common in the last fifteen years. There is a danger that applied ethics will be viewed as analogous to engineering, with ethics being reduced to solving problems. But ethical considerations set problems as well as solve them and also include such matters as character* and virtue*.

See **Bioethics; Business Ethics; Medical Ethics; Professional Ethics.**

P. Singer, *Practical Ethics,* 1979.

JAMES F. CHILDRESS

Arbitration *see* **Collective Bargaining; Industrial Relations; Labor Movements; Strikes**

Aristocracy

In the strict sense, aristocracy means government by the best element in the people. The best-known, though imaginary, example of such an aristocracy is provided in the *Republic* of Plato. More commonly, an aristocracy is a country where the power lies with a class enjoying hereditary privileges, such as ownership of the land. The political power of a landowning aristocracy has long ceased to be a problem in industrialized countries, but it remains a factor to be reckoned with in the so-called "underdeveloped countries." The church has frequently been allied with aristocracy, but there is now a strong movement, for example in Latin America, to throw the weight of the church behind those seeking social reform (*see* **Liberation Theology**).

JOHN MACQUARRIE

Aristotelian Ethics

The Greek philosopher Aristotle (384–322 B.C.) at age seventeen entered Plato's Academy in Athens, where he remained, as a student and then a teacher, until Plato's death in 347 B.C. Later he served for several years as tutor to young Alexander of Macedon (Alexander the Great) and then in about 335 founded his own school, the Lyceum, in Athens.

Most of what we have of Aristotle's works are thought to consist of summaries of his lectures on various subjects; they have probably been revised several times by Aristotle himself, his students, or later editors. The scope of his investigations is truly catholic. Whereas Plato stressed the unity and interdependence of all branches of knowledge, Aristotle was more concerned to differentiate the various branches and to elucidate the particular science of each.

Ethics is, in Aristotle's view, a branch of political or social science, for that is the science which studies the good for human beings. The individual's good and the state's good are the same, but the state's attainment of the good is "greater and more perfect" inasmuch as it means securing the good for the many. Aristotle's most comprehensive and influential treatises on ethics and political theory are the *Nicomachean Ethics* (named for its presumed editor, Aristotle's son Nicomachus) and the *Politics.* Full appreciation of those works requires some preliminary grounding in Aristotle's understanding of both the natural world and the human soul.

Nature, physics, and metaphysics. Aristotle's science of physics is concerned with the study of nature, and it attempts to account for the dynamics of change, motion, or development which we apprehend in the world. Rejecting Plato's explanation of Reality as involving unchanging Forms projected in the phenomenal world, Aristotle explains the "real" in terms of substrates to which varying qualities could attach. His explanation of change involves three ingredients: substrate, or matter, which persists through change; form, which appears in the process of change; and privation, or the absence of a (particular) form. The "causes" of change in any thing include its form (formal cause) and matter (material cause), and also what Aristotle calls "final" and "efficient" causes. For example, the causes of a marble block's transition into a statue are its matter (marble), its form (the finished statue's shape), its efficient cause (the sculptor's craft), and its final cause (the end or purpose for which the change was commenced). Further, since every change involves matter's transition from not-being (privation of a form) to being (having the quality of that form), Aristotle accounts for the state of transition by distinguishing *potential* and *actual* form. Potential form can mean either a quality being realized (e.g., an acorn has the potential form of an oak tree) or a quality possessed and not expressed (e.g., a builder who is not now building but could choose to do so at any time). Actual form denotes a quality both realized and expressed.

In the realm of living things, the formal, final, and efficient causes may all coincide; so Aristotle often refers to biological entities in shorthand terms of form and matter alone. His view of nature is inherently teleological: Nature produces nothing without a purpose. More specifically, his view is that the purpose of every object is to be itself in the fullest sense, to realize and express its own internal finality*. The study of the final purpose of natural objects is also, then, the study of their forms. Aristotle's acceptance of natural teleology informs his normative views on proper or "natural" human life.

The soul. Aristotle's account of the soul (*psychē*) diverges markedly from Plato's dualistic notion of immaterial *psychē* trapped in a phenomenal body. In his treatise on the soul (*De Anima*) Aristotle claims that every living thing possesses *psychē* as its vital principle. The soul is as "form" to the body, which is in turn as "matter" to the soul. So the soul is the body's entelechy (that is, its internal orientation toward its proper purpose, or *telos*); it actualizes the body's "potentiality of life." The souls of plants, the lowest form of life, actualize their potential for nutrition and reproduction. The souls of animals provide also the capacities of sense-perception, desire, locomotion, and in some cases memory. Human souls possess, in addition to these lower powers, the gift of intelligence (*nous*) which is capable of both scientific thought (which has as its object truth per se) and deliberative thought (aimed at practical and prudential truths).

The human soul's capacity for sense-perception and desire has an ambiguous status in Aristotle's psychology. Desire is a faculty of the irrational soul inasmuch as it "fights and resists the guidance of reason," but it also seems to "partake of reason" in that it can comply with reason and accept its leadership. Aristotle points to our commonplace assumption that admonition, rebuke, and exhortation are indeed appropriate as evidence of our belief that rational control of desire must be possible. Such control is the normative state of the truly human animal and is the basis for the virtue of "self-control."

Virtue and happiness. Aristotle's ethical theory presupposes his natural teleology and his psychology of the soul and its functions, for his central moral category is that of virtue* (*aretē*), which is defined as excellence* in fulfilling one's proper task or purpose. Now, what is peculiar to human animals is the soul's capacity for reason, both theoretical and deliberative; so human excellence refers to the fullest development of this most human capacity. "Intellectual virtues" are excellences of the theoretical or scientific rea-

son; "moral virtues" are excellences of the deliberative reason in its control of desires (*see* **Deliberation; Desire**). Further, Aristotle accepts as given the assumptions that all things by nature seek their own good, and that everyone would agree that man's final good is happiness* (*eudaimonia,* or "living well"; *see* **Eudaemonism**). He defines happiness, then, as a life of activity in accordance with reason—i.e., in accordance with the intellectual and moral virtues. This definition conflates the meanings of "a good man" and "the good man seeks."

Having indicated the province of moral virtue as rational control of desires, Aristotle goes on to describe virtuous actions as proceeding from choice*—i.e., they are actions which involve a deliberate desire to properly fulfill our human purpose and which are performed voluntarily and with awareness of the unchosen alternatives. Moral virtues themselves are defined, rather circularly, as settled habits or dispositions (*hexeis*) to choose to act according to that norm or principle by which a virtuous person would choose. While we all have natural capacities for virtue (or vice*), these capacities must be developed as habits* through practice. In other words, we become virtuous by doing virtuous things: we begin by doing objectively virtuous acts because they are taught to us or commanded of us, without any interior intention and reasoning toward the good in our choices; later, through education and habituation, we come to understand our virtuous actions as "right" in themselves. Aristotle admits that it makes "all the difference" whether a particular virtue is inculcated in us from early childhood, and he places great emphasis on training in virtue by parents, teachers, and the state. But he gives no ground to behavioral determinism.

In describing the object of virtuous actions, Aristotle points to the centrality of *proportion,* for action is a response to desire, and an individual's response to desire may be either excessive or deficient (in terms of both emotion and act-execution). The virtuous response follows a "mean" between these vicious extremes. The virtue of generosity, for example, represents a mean between the twin vices of extravagance and stinginess, and gentleness the mean between short temper and apathy. Aristotle's doctrine of the mean does not involve fixed or arithmetical determinations; rather, moral virtue involves a dispositional mean "relatively to us." For we have different natural inclinations which reason must guide and correct, and thus what would seem excessive for one person may be deficient for another (*see* **Mean, Doctrine of the**). (For a discussion of the virtue of justice, *see* **Justice**.)

In books 8 and 9 of the *Ethics* Aristotle analyzes friendship* as one of the "prime necessities of life." Carefully distinguishing several types of friendship, Aristotle attempts to reconcile self-love with other-regard by suggesting that in true friendships the friend appears as "another self" to whom the agent's own self-interest extends.

The final topic of the *Ethics* is the ideal life of the human being. Having argued that happiness is activity in accord with virtue, and that the highest virtue is that of pure theoretical wisdom, Aristotle concludes that perfect happiness is in the exercise of the contemplative faculty. Of course, a life of pure contemplation* would be "more than human"; but we should try nevertheless to live in accordance with what is highest in us and thus "become immortal as far as that is possible." Aristotle seems to make the moral life subsidiary to the intellectual, but he does not work out the relation between them in any detail. Moreover, the vast bulk of his ethical and political writings is concerned explicitly with the good life as activity in accordance with moral virtue.

Politics. Man, or the human being, is in Aristotle's view "a political animal." Humans are destined by nature to be social, as is evidenced by their natural gift of speech, and the complete form of social life is that of the *polis* (for which Aristotle's model is the Greek city-state). Only in the *polis* can humans live the good life in its fullest sense; it is the community of all smaller communities and shares with them the single end of *eudaimonia* for its citizens. The isolated person who is self-sufficient and not part of the *polis* must be "either a beast or a god." The *polis* should be large enough, in both citizenry and territory, to be self-sufficient but small enough to be governed effectively. For Aristotle, the ideal form of government is monarchy, followed by aristocracy*, but it is difficult to realize either of them. Democracy is opposed because it aims at private interests rather than the common interest.

Aristotle's idea of the *polis* is, of course, fundamentally different from modern liberal notions of the state*: The *polis* exists for the positive advancement of commonly shared ideals of virtue and happiness, while the liberal state presupposes a plurality of personal values and protects individual liberties (*see* **Liberalism; Pluralism**). Specific contrasts in political operation must remain theoretical, however, for the ideal Aristotelian *polis* has never been realized historically. The classical era of the city-state did not long survive Aristotle himself.

Aristotle's influence. Aristotle's published dialogues now exist only in fragments quoted by others, and his technical treatises were not published by the Lyceum until about 70 B.C. While both Platonic and Stoic thought influenced early Christianity, including its ethics, Aristotelian thought was not widely appropriated until the Middle Ages when Aristotle's writings reached the West (the 12th century) and were translated into Latin (the 13th century). Influential in both Islam and Judaism, Aristotelian thought was synthesized with Christian beliefs, which were already shaped in part by Platonic philosophy. The most remarkable synthesis was achieved by Thomas Aquinas in the 13th century (*see* **Medieval Ethics; Thomistic Ethics**). As Copleston notes, the Thomistic synthesis was "unified by the application of fundamental Aristotelian principles." The authority* of Aristotle as expressed in Scholasticism was sharply rejected by humanists in the Renaissance* and by the Protestant Reformers, but it endured in Roman Catholic theology. The Thomistic application of Aristotelianism gained official sanction in 1879 when Pope Leo XIII recognized it as the framework for Catholic theological reflection. In this century, particularly since Vatican Council II, moral theologians have experimented with other philosophical perspectives, such as existentialism and phenomenology (*see* **Modern Roman Catholic Moral Theology**). Outside Roman Catholicism, Aristotelian perspectives have appeared in efforts to revive natural law* and teleological ethics* (see, for example, Henry Veatch). Other philosophers, such as Philippa Foot, Alasdair MacIntyre, and James Wallace, and Protestant ethicists, such as Stanley Hauerwas, have drawn on Aristotelian perspectives in their revival of the virtues*. Even philosophers who repudiate Aristotelianism frequently find Aristotle's analysis of human action, deliberation*, ignorance*, intention*, etc., to be illuminating (*see also* **Responsibility**).

J. M. Cooper, *Reason and Human Good in Aristotle,* 1975; F. C. Copleston, *A History of Philosophy,* vol. 1, 1946; W. F. R. Hardie, *Aristotle's Ethical Theory,* 1968; A. Kenny, *The Aristotelian Ethics,* 1978; G. B. Kerferd, "Aristotle," *EP,* 1967; A. MacIntyre, *After Virtue,* 1981; A. O. Rorty, *Essays on Aristotle's Ethics,* 1981; W. D. Ross (ed.), *The Works of Aristotle Translated Into English,* 12 vols., 1908–52.

JAMES B. TUBBS, JR./JAMES F. CHILDRESS

Armaments *see* **Deterrence; Disarmament; War**

Arms Race *see* **Deterrence; Disarmament; War**

Artificial Insemination *see* **Population Policy; Procreation; Reproductive Technologies**

Ascetical Theology

As a branch of theology given its fullest precision in 17th-century Roman Catholicism, ascetical theology has been broadly defined as the science concerned with the Christian striving for perfection in the spiritual life. Throughout the Middle Ages the Neoplatonist *Mystical Theology* of the 6th-century Pseudo-Dionysius had provided a framework for the life of the spirit by identifying within it a possible progression through the stages of purgation and illumination to culminate in union with the Divine in mystical contemplation* (*see* **Mysticism and Ethics**). From the 13th century this attractive triad was also taken to correspond to that popularized by Aquinas (*ST* II-II.24.9), influenced by Augustine and Gregory the Great, in which he distinguished within the growth of supernatural charity in the soul three stages, corresponding to beginners, those making progress, and those who had reached a certain perfection. Not necessarily mutually exclusive in the history of the individual, these three stages of "spiritual freedom" (*ST* II-II.183.4) were nevertheless characterized by particular concerns, first to distance oneself from sin and wrong inclinations, secondly to

advance in the cultivation of the virtues, and finally to rest in loving union with God.

With the controversies engendered in the Roman Catholic Church after the Reformation by quietist and illuminist tendencies which tended to denigrate personal effort, the traditional term "mystical theology," which had hitherto applied to the whole ascent of the Christian spiritual life to culminate in perfection, came to refer only to its highest peaks, and the term "ascetical theology" was introduced to identify and concentrate upon the spiritual stages preparatory to such perfection. In modern times it is standard to refer to the whole science as "spiritual theology," and within that to distinguish between, on the one hand, mystical theology as the study of the prayer of "infused contemplation" and other mystical experiences and phenomena, and, on the other hand, ascetical theology as systematically concentrating on the more "active" elements of the spiritual life, including asceticism, "acquired contemplation," and what the influential Spanish Jesuit Alfonso Rodriguez typically titled *The Practice of Perfection and Christian Virtues* (1609).

From the viewpoint of Christian ethics, ascetical theology as so understood occasions reflections that may be considered in turn as social, psychological, theological, and disciplinary. With its stress on the progress of the Christian through various stages of his or her "spiritual life," ascetical theology, at least in some of its more popular expositions and practices, has incurred charges of spiritual and liturgical individualism and elitism. Concentration of attention on interior individual perfection was stimulated and justified by Counter-Reformation insistence that at justification an ontological change is effected in the soul, and by the recovery, after years of decadent Scholasticism, of the Thomist analysis of the effects and potentialities for development in the soul of the "sanctifying grace" thus created. The corrective, however, for such preoccupations lies neither in liturgical collectivism and spiritual egalitarianism nor in a neonominalism that disregards the transforming effects of love, but in a more socially conscious theology of grace* and in the renewed self-awareness of the Christian community. Varied in its individual gifts, the church is also called in its entirety to holiness, and thus to what the Second Vatican Council described as "the fullness of the

Christian life and the perfection of charity" which would, in turn, promote "a more human way of life" (Dogmatic Constitution on the Church, par. 40).

It is, however, the apparently inhuman, and even antihuman, nature of much that has passed for Christian asceticism* which has done much to arouse misgivings and hostility toward systematic ascetical theology, particularly in a world grown more sensitive to the possible varieties of religious and psychic pathology. And concentration upon such traditional terms as "mortification,"* "self-abnegation," and "self-denial,"* particularly when associated with physical austerities and penitential practices undertaken voluntarily or under "spiritual direction," can lend weight to charges of an obsessively negative and dualistic attitude to "the flesh," underlying the Pseudo-Dionysian *via purgativa* (see **Body; Embodiment**). The principle needs continual restatement that Christian asceticism is only part of a process of gradual spiritual development, which is less concerned with acquiring Stoic *apatheia* (peace and tranquillity) than with removing obstacles to the pervasive influence of divine grace, and less with gaining ethical self-mastery than with achieving interior freedom to respond with loving facility to the call of Christ. Early Christianity viewed martyrdom as the paradigm of perfect discipleship, and with the advent of social acceptance Christians were at pains to find other means, not simply of leaving "the world," but of "being with Christ" (Phil. 1:23), whether in virginity and celibacy or in the desert, the monastery, or the convent. At times such a mentality would invite the prescribing of forceful contraries to one's besetting faults or human weaknesses, in a medical analogy going back beyond Cassian to pre-Christian Egypt; and it is here particularly that ascetical theology does well today to maintain a continual dialogue with such humane sciences as psychology, history, and social anthropology. And yet no Christian ethics can gainsay the importance ascribed by Jesus and Paul to *askēsis*, or spiritual effort and exercise, in the Christian life, in which the personal choice and cultural appropriateness of means are of only secondary, if still important, consideration. To an ethics rightly grown more humanist in its respect not only for human values but above all for the personal subject and its fulfillment, what a balanced ascetical the-

ology can continually bear at least cautionary witness to is the judgment of "Christ crucified" upon all such human endeavors.

It is the underlying theological presuppositions of ascetical theology, of course, which find Catholic and Protestant tradition most sharply divided, although perhaps, in principle and in retrospect, unnecessarily so. The whole Reformation reaction to the imposition, proliferation, and mathematics of pious and penitential practices was a taking of theological offense at a theology of "good works."* And a theology that systematically stressed personal effort could easily appear no more than a Pelagian program of self-perfection. And yet Calvin could give eloquent witness to the need for radical denial of the self in the Christian life and also acknowledge the possibility of daily progress in personal goodness (*Institutes* 3.6–8). And at its best, the Catholic tradition would stress that the entire striving for, and achievement of, spiritual progress takes place always within the brackets of divine saving initiative and love. While *sola fide* (by faith alone) and *sola gratia* (by grace alone), and even *soli Deo* (to God alone), can rightly point to an emptying of the self before and for Christ, they can never require an annihilation of the free self which is God's handiwork. Nor, indeed, may these axioms be claimed to support a univocal view of divine and human causation as engaged in some form of border dispute over created reality which would make nonsense of the Augustinian and Catholic belief that the merits of human beings are at the same time the gifts of God (cf. *Epistle* 194.5, *PL* 33.880). As God's kingship graciously expands within our lives, and as God's light is imparted to us in the *via illuminativa*, we are so to let our light shine before others that they may indeed see our good works, but give the glory only to our heavenly Father (cf. Matt. 5:16).

Finally, it must be noted that the discipline of ascetical theology as it has developed, occupied with daily growth in the supernatural life of grace and the virtues, and directed at exploring the evangelical counsels* as an invitation to holiness extended by Christ only to some of his followers, could do so only alongside a negative and impoverished moral theology, which concentrated on salvation and the minimal obligations required for it, and which was concerned not with growth in sanctifying grace but with its absence or presence in the soul through "mortal" sins and their sacramental absolution. With the renewal of moral theology and its difficult adoption of a more positive function in Christian living, the challenge to ascetical theology is to rediscover a role for itself in identifying a contemporary theology of holiness—less in terms of renunciation and more in terms of integration, with its own struggles and sacrifices for the individual, whether within the self, or with the created environment, or within the ecclesial and human community, all of which is "in travail" (Rom. 8:22–23) toward "the stature of the fulness of Christ" (Eph. 4:13).

See **Asceticism; Good Works; Holiness; Modern Roman Catholic Moral Theology; Perfectionism.**

J. de Guibert, *The Theology of the Spiritual Life,* ET 1954.

J. MAHONEY

Asceticism

The Greek word *askēsis* has as one of its meanings practice or discipline, and therefore came to be used for the disciplined way of life inculcated by Stoics and other philosophers. Greco-Roman observers called Judaism a "barbarian philosophy," with reference as much to its rules of life as to its doctrines —and passed a similar judgment on the Brahmins of India. The community made known to us through the Dead Sea Scrolls was an outstanding example of Jewish asceticism; other instances are described by Philo and Josephus, and in the Gospel accounts of John the Baptist. Asceticism may be considered as spiritual athletics; Paul uses the figure in describing the Christian life as a race (or even a prizefight) for the eternal prize (1 Cor. 9:24–27). But the charter of Christian asceticism is to be found even higher, in the teaching and example of Jesus. He was both humanist and ascetic, who "came eating and drinking" (Luke 7:34), but called on his followers to deny themselves and take up the cross after him (Mark 8:34, etc.).

In the early centuries of the church the threat of persecution and the pressure of surrounding paganism gave the whole Christian community an ascetic character. One can see this in the writings of Christian humanists such as Clement of Alexandria as well as those of rigorists like Tertullian. However, in addition to the common standard, dedication

to virginity, whether by men or women, was a special ascetic renunciation (cf. 1 Cor. 7:8). In the early 4th century Methodius of Olympus, in his *Banquet of the Ten Virgins,* extols virginity as the perfect way of life. But "Origen's rash act," the literal following of Matt. 19:12, was an extreme practice finally condemned by the church (Canon 1 of the Council of Nicaea, 325). After the time of Constantine the church came closer to the world, for good or ill, and those who wished to leave all for Christ fled into the desert, or its equivalent, as monks or hermits (*see* **Monastic Ethics**). Many carried poverty to the greatest possible extreme and engaged in competition in self-denial. A striking type were the stylites ("pillar saints") who settled on pillars (*stylai*), where their simple needs were met by admiring pilgrims. Early monastic writers discuss whether the greater renunciation is that of the hermits who fight alone with the powers of evil, or that of the cenobites who renounce their own will in obedience to their abbot; the asceticism of the former was more visibly heroic, that of the latter perhaps more profound. Meanwhile devout Christians living "in the world" were still expected to live up to a fairly ascetic discipline. Leo the Great (bishop of Rome 440–461) in his Lenten sermons expounds ascetic principles in terms of the three "notable good works" of Matt. 6— prayer raises the mind to God, fasting disciplines the will, almsgiving expresses love of neighbor. In the next century Benedict may be described as a humanist ascetic. The external regimen envisaged in his monastic *Rule* did not differ greatly from the life of devout laypeople of moderate means—ascetic discipline was found in the common life of prayer, study, and work under obedience.

In the early Middle Ages, perhaps due to the rapid spread of the church in northern Europe, there was an increasing difference between the minimum standard expected of the laity and the ascetic practice of monks— though disciplinary literature such as the Celtic Penitentials shows that strict standards were still held up at least in theory. But the laity often sank into the position of spectators in the life of the church, while clergy performed their sacred rites and monastics accepted more intense obligations. A visible sign of this development was the decline of Communion among the laity, for whom the Fourth Lateran Council in 1215 was obliged to lay down a minimum rule of annual reception (Canon 21). Since monasticism itself could become worldly and comfortable, religious revivals took the form of a return to greater simplicity and austerity in the cloister. And the clergy generally adopted some features of monastic asceticism, such as celibacy (in the Eastern church only for bishops) and rules of daily prayer.

The coming of the friars began to bridge the gap between secular and ascetic Christians. Francis of Assisi challenged the standards of the world while still remaining closely connected with it; however, in his *Rule* the friars are bound to live in poverty, chastity, and obedience, the three "evangelical counsels" of traditional asceticism, which in previous monastic rules are implied rather than formally stated. Rather than being organized by them, the "third orders" of lay associates forced themselves on the friars as a result of their preaching. Their members combined a semimonastic discipline with life in the world, still responsible for property, family, and personal rights, thus beginning to bring asceticism out of the cloister into the home and the marketplace. Laypeople as well as monks and clerics often lived strict and devout lives in the later Middle Ages—a famous example is Sir Thomas More, in England on the eve of the Reformation. On the other hand the older monastic orders were often stagnant if not actually corrupt. Humanists like Erasmus, as well as the Reformers, accused their members of falsely claiming superior merit before God for purely formal religious practices.

The Reformers generally attacked the traditional forms of asceticism—not that the call to a life of discipline and self-sacrifice was abandoned, but that it was proclaimed as something expected of all Christians, and as the result rather than the cause of their justification before God. Luther tended to leave this to the work of grace in the believer. The Reformed tradition, especially in its Calvinist form, aimed to enforce generally what Ernst Troeltsch described as *innerweltliche Askese,* that is, an ascetic life within the common orders of society. In its Anglo-American form we know this as the Puritan ideal, which aims to bring the whole social order into obedience to the law of Christ. Protestant asceticism faces the same problem as that of its Catholic precursor—the strict ideal will appeal only to an elite, which will either try to dominate the church and the world, or will flee from worldliness into isolation. As Catholicism produced new ascetic orders, so Protestantism has produced ascetic sects, a tendency illustrated in different ways by such groups as the Mennonites, the Quakers, the Moravians, and the Salvation Army (*see* **Mennonite Ethics; Quaker Ethics**).

Parallel to the Protestant development is a similar urge within the Catholic tradition to bring the devout life out of the monastery into the world. In 17th-century France this is illustrated by the devout humanism of Francis de Sales (and the active ministry of Vincent de Paul), in 18th-century England by the work of William Law (with his influence on the Wesleys), in 19th-century Russia by the surprisingly down-to-earth spiritual guidance given by the monastic elders (*startsi*). In modern Catholic writing ascetical theology means the systematic discussion of the life of prayer and personal discipline, intermediate between the treatment of ethical duties in moral theology and that of intense forms of spiritual experience in mystical theology.

There is always in the Christian life some expression of the paradox of the cross. We are called to joy and to suffering, to freedom and to discipline, to love the world which God loves and yet to be ready to renounce everything, even our own selves (cf. the apparent contrast of John 3:16 and 1 John 2:15ff.). With our contemporary concern for the outreach of the gospel into the common life it has been suggested that the modern form of *innerweltliche Askese* is a call to "holy worldliness." A 20th-century form of ascetic is the Christian who answers a call to witness at the peril of fortune or life for a social cause—against war, for instance, or for racial equality. The Reformers rightly opposed the dangerous idea of a more meritorious way of life which could be undertaken optionally. But some of their followers have forgotten the principle of varying vocations (cf. 1 Cor. 7:7b), some of which are in external appearance more heroic than others. And wisdom is justified by all her children (Luke 7:35).

Two classical studies of the history of Christian asceticism are E. Troeltsch, *The Social Teaching of the Christian Churches* (1912), ET 1931, repr. 1960; and K. E. Kirk, *The Vision of God: The Christian Doctrine of the Summum Bonum,* 1931. In its own immense literature cf. the works of John Cassian, *Institutes* and *Conferences;* Martin Luther, *The Freedom of a Christian Man;* Francis de Sales, *Introduction to the Devout Life,* tr. and ed. J. K. Ryan, 1953; William Law, *A Serious Call to a Devout and Holy Life,* ed. J. Meister et al., 1955; O. Chadwick (tr.), *Western Asceticism,* LCC, 1958; T. Tappert (ed.), *Luther: Letters of Spiritual Counsel,* LCC, 1955.

E. R. HARDY

Aspiration

The desire to realize an ideal. Sometimes a "morality of aspiration," that is, one motivated by pursuit of the good, is contrasted with a "morality of obligation," that is, one that proceeds from a sense of duty.

JOHN MACQUARRIE

Association, Right of *see* Church and State; Democracy; Industrial Relations; Liberalism; Pluralism; Rights; State; Trade Unions and Professional Associations; Voluntary Associations

Asylum *see* Refugees

Ataraxia

A Greek term for tranquillity of mind. *See* Skeptics.

Atomic Weapons *see* Deterrence; Disarmament; Just War; Nuclear Warfare; Pacifism; War

Attrition

Roman Catholic theologians view attrition as imperfect sorrow for sin because it arises from fear—in contrast to contrition*, which arises from the love of God. There is debate about whether attrition in conjunction with penance* is sufficient to secure God's forgiveness*.

Augustinian Ethics

Augustine of Hippo (354–430) has been a seminal influence permeating every branch and every period of Western Christian ethics. An account of his thought is necessarily selective; the following topics are chosen in the light of contemporary discussions that most often invoke Augustine's name.

Happiness and the good. Following the Peripatetic tradition Augustine asserts that all human action arises from a quest for happiness* (*Confessions* 10.20ff.). God alone can make human beings happy, and happiness cannot be reached by solitary individuals or under the conditions of earthly existence: these are the grounds for a Christian critique of classical ethics. The way to happiness lies through faith in the Mediator and obedience to his commands. Augustinian eudaemonism*, then, is not a teleological ethic in the modern sense, but a teleological metaphysical framework that serves to give intelligibility to ethics that are in substance command-based (*see* **Teleological Ethics**).

The identity of God with happiness is not established inductively, by tracing the inherent *telos* of human action as we know it, but deductively, through an account of being and the good which is heavily dependent on Plotinus (*see* **Neoplatonism**). God is absolute being and absolute good; created being depends upon him both for its being and for its goodness. That God is our happiness, then, is not determined by an arbitrary "change of taste" on the part of human beings (as K. Holl alleged), but on the ontological fact that God is good in himself while we are good only in dependence upon him.

Moral agents must distinguish the uncreated good in which their quest will reach its end from the multitude of created goods by which they are surrounded. They must "refer" these to the pursuit of the highest good. Augustine described this referral as "use," and contrasted it with the "enjoyment" appropriate only in relation to God himself (a contrast that had extensive influence in the Middle Ages through its adoption by Lombard). Initially Augustine was inclined to think that human beings, like other created things, were to be "used" (*On Christian Doctrine* 1); but he later held that community of the saints was itself an aspect of final happiness, and spoke of "a communal enjoyment of God and of one another in God" (*City of God* 19). This change of emphasis indicates (as Burnaby argued) an increasing distance between Augustine and the Plotinian ideal of a solitary mystical experience of God, and a distinctively Christian reinterpretation of the quest in terms of history and eschatology. At the same time Augustine's polemic against Manichean dualism stressed the real goodness of the material universe; so that the use-relation was not purely instrumental, but cognitive, and the use-object was properly respected by being subordinated to higher objects of love (*see* **Manichean Ethics**).

Theory of love. The motivation of any act or attitude is love (most commonly *dilectio*), which is a metaphysical dynamism at the heart of all cosmic movement. Right and wrong loves are distinguished by the appropriateness of their object, and virtue is the conformity of love to the structure of reality. This use of love* as an all-embracing category of ethics corresponds to the unprecedented centrality assigned to Matt. 22:39 and parallels; Gal. 5:14; and Rom. 13:9 in Augustine's interpretation of NT ethics. Despite the popularity of his aphorism "Love and do what you will" (*On the Epistle of John* 7) among modern contextualists, Augustine did not derive from these texts any devaluation of moral laws, and indeed gave recognizably "absolutist" interpretations of the prohibitions of lying (*Against Lying*) and suicide (*CG* 1).

Love must always be subject to norms, since it follows the *cognitive* recognition of the structure of reality. A. Nygren was thus correct to contrast Augustine's conception of love with his own conception of an *agapē* that "creates value in its object." Augustine's love could never do that—but not, as Nygren thought, because of its compromise with an aspiring *erōs*, but because of its relation to the goods of creation. No possible object of love is without value, since it is always possible to recognize created goodness, even in the midst of its corruption. And God's love, too, does not create value absolutely *de novo*, but recognizes "what he himself has made" in distinction from "what we have made of ourselves."

Marriage. The defense of created goods is the key to Augustine's conception of marriage*. Historically his treatment of the subject arose in response to controversies elsewhere, and represents an attempt to modify excessive claims made by such champions of the ascetic life as Jerome. Augustine took over from Ambrose what was to become the classic Western Catholic view of marriage and celibacy*, distinguishing between "commands" and "counsels* of perfection"—while remembering that commands have priority, so that a humble wife is better than a proud virgin (*On Holy Virginity*). The depreciation of marriage to a kind of tolerated failing struck Augustine as dangerously reminiscent of Manichean "self-hatred," and, discounting the apparent significance of Gen. 4:1, he argued that Adam and Eve might in principle have had sexual relations before their expulsion from the garden (*CG* 14).

From past church tradition Augustine inherited a justification of marriage in terms of its procreative importance, which did not entirely satisfy him as it stood, since the church (unlike patriarchal Israel) recruits its members not by physical generation but by baptismal regeneration. His own doctrine of the goods of marriage, based on close attention to 1 Cor. 7 and Eph. 5, was more comprehensive. Marriage served three ends: "progeny," "pledge," and "sacrament" (*On the Good of Marriage*). To the traditional good of procreation is added the mutual "pledge" of sexual fidelity, directed to the sanctification of each partner; and the third is the sacramental permanence conferred upon marriages of the baptized, which reflects the permanence of Christ's union with his church. Augustine's belief in the proportioning of love to reason made him distrust the spontaneity of sexual emotion as a sign of irrational passion. Passion is not *any* emotion* that affects the soul —for emotion is essential to the joy of the saints—but only emotion that defies rational self-possession and control. Thus he believed that an act of sexual intercourse which is not rationally required for the purpose of procreation is sinful—though only venially so, and only on the part of the incontinent partner. In the context of anti-Pelagian polemics Augustine makes great use of the thought that sexual desire as we know it *post lapsum* is disturbed by a "concupiscence"* that was not original to it. The disorderly rebellion of the body against the mind is a fitting punishment for the disorderly self-assertion of the soul against God. Its association with the process of generation is symbolically appropriate, and is even thought of as the causal link by which our racial solidarity with Adam's sin is communicated (*see* **Original Sin**). This view has attracted sharp criticism in the modern period; but it can also claim to be the precursor of much modern sexual psychology.

Political thought. Augustine's influence on political thinkers is disproportionate to the limited discussion of political questions in his writings. His ideas have been represented in contrasting ways, but contemporary interpreters have agreed in regarding *CG* 19 as the key to them.

In this book Augustine reformulates his teaching about the good in terms of peace*. Every person and community loves some form of peace. On its pilgrimage to its final peace in the enjoyment of God, the City of God (the community of the elect) intermingles with the earthly city, which, seeking its own "unequal peace" rather than true peace, is destined for destruction. But the City of God "makes use of the peace of Babylon . . . the temporal peace of the meantime, shared by good and bad alike." Thus, like other Christian political conceptions of the period, Augustine's ideas are fashioned by a Christian sense of history and eschatology. A century earlier, apologists for the Constantinian regime interpreted the Christian Roman Empire as the triumph of God's saving purposes in history. The separatist Donatists, on the other hand, understood the political situation in terms of the radical eschatological separation between church and world. Augustine differs from both: on the one hand detaching himself from a theology of the Christian empire; and on the other conceiving of a "meantime," a space characterized by ambiguity, from which the ultimate significance of history as judgment on good and evil is providentially held in abeyance. He finds an OT parallel in the life of Israel in Babylon, commanded to seek the peace of the city of its exile for seventy years (Jer. 29). Thus Augustine can be seen as the first theologian of the secular (Markus), the area of public abstraction in which provisional goods may be pursued in common, without prejudice to the contrasting final destinies of two irreconcilable moral communities.

Rome, as Augustine saw it, was the natural successor to "Babylon" (the ancient Mesopotamian empires as a whole), an imperial power grown great through sinful love of glory. But because even such a corrupt peace was a defective form of good, the pursuit of it evoked virtues, for which God had rewarded Rome with earthly success. Yet these virtues were not *true* virtue, which is built on the love of God above all. Consequently, the Roman polity could not claim to stand for "right" (*ius*). Generalizing, Augustine offers a definition of political community (*populus*) that involves no mention of "right": "A people is the association of a multitude of rational beings united by a common agreement on the objects of their love." It was at this point that Aquinas sharply diverged from the Augustinian tradition to reestablish the connection, carefully severed by Augustine, between earthly politics and humanity's final good (*see* **Thomistic Ethics**). At this point, too, the early modern contractarians took their lead from the Augustinian tradition, seizing on the hint of voluntarism in the "citizens' agreement in the matter of giving and obeying commands," limited to "matters of mortal existence" (*see* **Social Contract**). But underlying Augustine's conception, and distancing him from contractarian voluntarism, is the notion that all order is given by God, and that true order is based on the worship of God; so that the limited *compositio voluntatum*, however useful to the City of God, is never more than the Babylonian corruption of a providential gift.

Dominion ("giving and obeying commands") is the essence of government, and coercion ("punishment and vengeance") its necessary mode of practice. Consequently it is understood as a discipline upon a fallen race; in created nature humans were intended to exercise dominion only over animals. When Christians undertake governmental responsibilities (which they should be willing to do out of love for their neighbors), they do so with a restraint born of repugnance, for they understand the inherent tragedy in the need for coercive justice. This modifies their severity and makes them seek opportunities for constructive love to the offender: emperors take vengeance only for unarguable reasons of state (*CG* 5); warriors are peacemakers even at war (*Letter* 189); judges are tormented by the limitations of their ignorance; slaveowners make themselves the servants of those they appear to command. Augustine disliked the death penalty because it left no room for repentance and mercy. Yet these distinctively Christian approaches to the administration of justice should not be described (H. R. Niebuhr) as "transforming" earthly institutions, for they do not anticipate the eschatological kingdom but assert the created order of loving equality as the context in which juridical coercion should be interpreted. In the final peace of God itself there will be no human dominion.

Works of Augustine of Hippo: *Confessions; On Christian Doctrine; The City of God* (*CG*),

On the Epistle of John; Against Lying; On Holy Virginity; On the Good of Marriage; Letters.

Translations will be found in P. Schaff and H. Wace (eds.), *Nicene and Post-Nicene Fathers,* series 2, 1890–1900, vols. 1–7; also in *The Confessions of St. Augustine,* tr. F. J. Sheed, 1944; *On Christian Doctrine,* tr. D. W. Robertson, 1958; *City of God,* tr. H. Bettenson, 1972.

Studies: J. Burnaby, *Amor Dei,* 1938; R. Holte, *Béatitude et sagesse,* 1962; R. A. Markus, *Saeculum,* 1970; O. O'Donovan, *The Problem of Self-Love in St. Augustine,* 1980; E. Schmitt, *Le mariage Chrétien dans l'oeuvre de S. Augustin,* 1983.

OLIVER O'DONOVAN

Authenticity

Authenticity, in the terminology of many existentialist writers, denotes a quality of existence in which the existent has become genuinely himself or herself. It is assumed that most people for most of the time simply follow the conventional paths laid down by the society in which they live. Only rarely do they go against the stream and decide a matter in the light of their own intelligence, conscience, and integrity. The English word "authentic" is derived from the Greek, where it referred to the actual doer of a deed. "Authenticity" is used to translate the German *Eigentlichkeit,* from the word *eigen,* "own." To be authentic is thus to be one's own self, acting independently of extraneous influences.

Strictly speaking, authenticity is not a moral conception in the usual sense. It has nothing to do with conforming to moral rules or even with realizing some universal ideal of humanity, but rather is opposed to such ideas. Nevertheless, authenticity does acquire something of a moral connotation in existentialist ethics*, or perhaps one should say that it is regarded as supramoral, in the sense that it makes demands that override those of conventional morality*. Authentic existents are precisely the persons who do not take refuge in rules or ready-made ideals, but accept themselves as unique persons who have to realize the possibilities that belong peculiarly to them. From this point of view, it is the freedom and even the intensity of an action that gives it worth, not its conformity to what is commonly held to be right. A classic example is discussed by Kierkegaard.

Abraham, in response to the command of God, sets aside (or "suspends") ethical considerations and is prepared to sacrifice his son. Although God appears in this incident, the decision is really Abraham's. It was Abraham who decided that this was indeed God's command to him, and, according to Kierkegaard, the decision to sacrifice Isaac for God's sake was "absolutely identical" with doing it for his own sake (*see* **Kierkegaardian Ethics**).

The notion of authenticity leads in the direction of an extreme situation ethic*, not governed by rules or general principles but dependent on the unique circumstances and possibilities of each individual agent in each new situation. Would one have to say then that for some persons an authentic existence might take forms condemned by the commonly accepted moral standards of the human race, for instance, that authenticity might mean for some people becoming Nazis or racists? The more extreme exponents of this point of view would not hesitate to draw such conclusions. The error of such a position lies in its extreme individualism*. No human existence can be authentic without an affirmative relation to other human beings, and a true conception of authenticity would have to take account of this. Among Christian existentialists, it is recognized that there can be no authenticity without love and so there can be no purely self-regarding authenticity that would ignore the interests of the community.

See also **Autonomy; Self-Realization.**

S. Kierkegaard, *Fear and Trembling* (1844), ET 1954.

JOHN MACQUARRIE

Authoritarian State *see* **State; Totalitarian State**

Authority

Claims to authority made on the basis of revelation or religious faith have been very much under fire in modern times, and perhaps this is nowhere more the case than it is in the field of ethics. Standards of conduct can no longer be upheld by a simple appeal to the authority of the church or the Bible. In modern secular societies, Christian ethicists are agreed that it is unreasonable to try to legislate Christian standards for the whole body of citizens, for example, in such matters as marriage and divorce. Even members of the churches do not always follow the teaching of their churches on particular matters. If therefore we can still talk of an "authority" in Christian ethics, it can hardly be thought of as an authority that is imposed, for it rests on the voluntary acceptance of those who profess themselves Christians (*see* **Discipline**). But when we ask about this authority, we find wide divergences of opinion. Are there, for instance, authoritative rules of conduct that the Christian undertakes to obey in all circumstances? Perhaps some biblical Protestants would recognize the Ten Commandments as laws having divine authority, and thus to be obeyed without question. Catholics would recognize as authoritative many pronouncements of the church, even those regulating minute details of conduct. Perhaps most writers on Christian ethics nowadays insist on the primacy of charity, and avoid any rigid legalism. Whether any Christian community could get along without some minimum of rules is questionable, but even those who make a point of "persons before principles" recognize an authority, namely, the demand of love. The ultimate authority for all Christian ethics is Jesus Christ himself. But this statement is not in itself very helpful when it comes to deciding about some actual situation, for we have to find some means of relating this situation to Christ. It would seem that the most indisputably authoritative statements in Christian ethics are also the most general, not to say jejune, and that the more specific we become, the more careful we must be about laying claim to "authority." Amid the complexities of contemporary society, a certain degree of modesty is desirable, and moral pronouncements by the churches should have some flexibility and be open to revision. While those who believe that Jesus Christ is God's revelation to humankind will accept him as their ultimate and authoritative guide on matters of conduct, they will also admit that it is not always clear what his mind on some particular question would have been, and this is obvious from the fact that sincere and learned Christians are often sharply divided over the "Christian" thing to do in a given situation. In any case, there would always seem to be some "mediate" authority between Christ and the particular situation, and this mediate authority could not have the ultimacy belonging to Christ himself. Perhaps we could

visualize this mediate authority as a composite one, in which several factors have to be taken into account. First among these would be the teaching of the NT, especially any teaching of Christ directly relating to the matters about which guidance is being sought. But this biblical factor might not be decisive in itself—for instance, in such an important question as that of divorce, the evidence about Christ's teaching is ambiguous or even conflicting. The second factor would be the traditional teaching of the church on any given matter. Especially where the NT teaching is unclear, the consensus of the church's interpretation of it must be accorded a high degree of authority. The third factor would be one's own conscientious judgment in the concrete situation. To give a concrete illustration, it might be felt that the church's traditional teaching about the just war, though representing the consensus of Christian opinion in interpreting the NT teaching, was no longer applicable in the current situation. There is a sense in which conscience has always an ultimate moral authority, for no one ought to be ordered or compelled to act against conscience. But, on the other hand, conscience may be poorly educated, or it may be distorted in various ways. An appeal to conscience should not become an excuse for an irresponsible individualism. Thus, in admitting conscience into the composite authority, we are thinking of a Christian conscience that has been purged of individual idiosyncrasies and that has undergone Christian formation and illumination through prayer and study. Such a conscience, however, has its right to be heard after the NT and the church when there is a question of authority in Christian ethics.

See also **Conscience**.

JOHN MACQUARRIE

Automation

A general term to describe the control and operation of effective action, or work, by mechanical rather than human means (*see also* **Computers; Robots**). The roots of its modern evolution may be traced back to the division of labor in factories described most vividly by Adam Smith in *The Wealth of Nations*. By dividing the functions involved in manufacturing pins among a number of workers, the quantity produced could be vastly increased.

There are many advantages to such an increase in the volume of production. Companies can produce goods at a lower unit cost and more people can afford to buy their products. A more efficient production process means greater wealth for the community as a whole, more for the provision of services, education, health, and welfare, and more for the development of culture in the widest sense. The most recent advances in automation, using microprocessors and computer-controlled robots, can make possible less wasteful use of raw materials and a lower consumption of energy.

But automation also leads to structural changes in the labor market and in other aspects of human activity. Craftsmanship on the shop floor of industry is, for example, replaced by machines, and office work done by clerks and typists is taken over by computers and word processors. New skills are required and old skills become obsolete. Further developments in automation open up the possibility of increasing structural change. Mass production, with the standardization of parts, may well give way to a new "de-massification" as machinery is programmed to produce one-off products to suit the particular demands of individual customers. It may be no more difficult to cut a suit automatically to exact individual measurements when required than to cut a whole batch to standard sizes to keep in stock. More work may be done at home instead of in factories and offices, and the communal and socializing benefits of work done together with others may be lost. Fewer people traveling to work may change whole patterns of transportation and communications.

There are also other problems posed by the development of automation. As the pace of change increases, society may become both more sophisticated and more fragile. Pressure is put on human communities, forcing change on them and disrupting a sense of belonging and identity. The gap between rich and poor, developed world and developing world, may also become greater as some have access to new technology and others do not. Automation can change the perception that people have of their place and role in society. As skills that used to be passed on personally from one generation to another are transferred to machines, the worker loses part of himself or herself to something impersonal under the control of others. Automation, bringing greater production, encourages an increasingly materialistic society; and a steady reduction in the number of hours worked brings with it a greater role for leisure. In the process large numbers of people become unemployed, provision for substantial retraining and relocation needs to be made, and the transition is not achieved without hurt to individuals, their families, and the whole community.

Automation is also bringing a greater interdependence to the world. Television brings events into people's homes, as they happen, from every continent. The world is becoming a "global village." As communications become quicker the world also becomes more dangerous. Nuclear weapons can be delivered within minutes, and the time allowed for making the decisions about retaliation is frighteningly short. Advanced technological methods threaten environmental pollution or genetic, biological, or chemical change. Political relationships between countries are affected as they compete for resources, such as oil. Pollution deposited in the sea or pumped out into the air in one country may affect another many miles away. Exposure to radioactive waste may have genetic effects or induce cancers that do not show up for many years.

These developments, however, also offer opportunities for greater cooperation between nations in the pursuit of solutions to what are essentially common problems. Increasingly, science and technology know no national or ideological boundaries. Controlling the increased human potential made possible by automation and harnessing it to genuinely human ends is a technological and ethical task of growing importance.

See also **Risk; Science and Ethics; Technology; Work, Doctrine of; Unemployment.**

W. Faunce, *Problems of an Industrial Society,* ed. E. M. Munson, 1981; J. Forslin et al. (eds.), *Automation and Industrial Workers: A Fifteen Nation Study,* vol. 1, pts. 1, 2, 1979–81; G. Friedmann, *The Anatomy of Work: Labor, Leisure and the Implications of Automation,* ET 1962, repr. 1978; J. Shepard, *Automation and Alienation: A Study of Office and Factory Workers,* 1971.

PAUL BRETT

Autonomy

Etymologically, "autonomy" is compounded of *autos* (self) and *nomos* (law or rule). In Greek *autonomia* originally referred to the independence of city-states from outside control and their determination of their own laws. Autonomy, having been made central by Kant (*see* **Kantian Ethics**), is usually contrasted with heteronomy*, rule by other objects, persons, etc. The themes of independence, internal rule, and self-determination are all used to explicate the autonomy of morality, of institutions, and of persons and their actions. (This article focuses on autonomy in ethics in contrast to autonomy of ethics*.)

In Christian ethics there is debate about the autonomy of institutions*, such as the state and the economy, particularly in relation to the church and moral action. The process of secularization* has increased the autonomy of these institutions over against the church. More controversial is what this autonomy (German, *Eigengesetzlichkeit*) implies for moral action—for example, whether moral action, either religious or secular in nature, should or even must be tailored to the "inner laws" of these institutions. Emil Brunner (*The Divine Imperative,* ET 1937, especially ch. 25) noted that there are no "Christian bridges" and no "Christian states" and emphasized the role of reason in understanding autonomous forces of a technical and social nature. This view of social ethics* stresses that all moral actions must be in accordance with the inner laws or inner logic of the institutions themselves, including their technical requirements as well as the requirements of collective life. In view of the impossibility of fully realizing ethical norms in society, some Christians urge selective withdrawal, while others, such as Brunner, urge the indirect application of love—for example, through personal relationships or in the "cracks" and "crevices" of the institutions. Still others insist that institutions can be transformed, at least within limits.

Often autonomy refers to qualities of persons and their actions. An example of an autonomous person is one who, with the requisite mental capacity, reflects on and chooses his or her own moral framework. It might be thought that a person who follows the dictates of a church is merely heteronomous, but such a person may have exercised and may even continue to exercise (second-order) autonomy in reflectively choosing that church as the source of (first-order) judgments, e.g., that artificial contraception is wrong. Following Gerald Dworkin, it is possible to say

that such a person uses second-order autonomy to surrender first-order autonomy. In other situations, a first-order action, such as the use of drugs, may well be determined, for example, by addiction, but the agent may exercise second-order autonomy in seeking help to overcome the addiction (*see* **Behavior Control; Drug Addiction**).

Autonomy does not necessarily imply that an individual's life plan is created by that person *de novo,* but it does suggest that the individual has adopted, usually reflectively and critically, a life plan as his or her own, even if it was drawn from a community and a tradition. An autonomous person does some thinking on his or her own, at least in identifying with and appropriating a tradition*. Autonomy in this sense is close to authenticity* and has been praised as a moral and religious ideal, particularly in liberal Protestantism.

Even though autonomy necessarily involves some thinking for oneself, it does not imply thinking only of oneself. Just as the *source* of an autonomous person's life plan may be and probably is social, so the *object* of that life plan need not be egoistic. It may include various principles and values such as love* and altruism*. An adequate conception of autonomy would also recognize that not all obligations are self-created, but that many exist independently of an individual's will and actions. Sometimes, however, autonomy indicates a sphere of discretion, where individuals are not under obligations (*see* **Adiaphora**).

There is considerable debate about what qualities a person or an action must have in order to be autonomous. At the very least a person must have the capacity to deliberate rationally about his or her conduct, including the choice of ends and the means to those ends, and must adequately understand the situation in which he or she is acting. Another essential condition is that the agent's decisions and actions not be substantially controlled by others, for example, by manipulation or coercion*. Obviously, these qualities may vary by degrees, and some persons or actions may be substantially, but not fully, autonomous or substantially, but not fully, nonautonomous.

The principle of autonomy identifies a constraint or limit on our actions in relation to others. As such, it usually requires that we not override or control a person's autonomous actions unless they harm other persons or the society (*see* **Paternalism; Morality, Legal Enforcement of**). This principle of autonomy can be defended without invoking an ideal of autonomy that would praise autonomous persons and conduct. What is important in this principle can probably be better expressed in the principle of respect for persons*, including their autonomous, or substantially autonomous, wishes, choices, and actions. Respect for persons who are autonomous may differ from respect for persons who are not autonomous. When people and/or their actions are nonautonomous, our duties of beneficence* and nonmaleficence* may permit and even require some interventions that would otherwise be unjustified without violating the principle of respect for persons. Thus, Kant excluded children and the insane from his discussion of the principle of respect for persons, and John Stuart Mill applied his discussion of liberty only to persons in "the maturity of their faculties."

An adequate conception of personal autonomy within a Christian framework will necessarily emphasize that autonomy is severely limited because human beings are dependent creatures who are both finite and sinful, who are not merely or even primarily rational, who are determined as well as determining, who are essentially temporal and social, who have many obligations that are not self-imposed, whose tendencies to egoism* stand under criticism from the NT norm of love*, etc. The claim of autonomy as independence is often sinful self-assertion in denial of one's dependence. Yet creation in God's image and likeness (*see* **Image of God**) may undergird a limited conception of autonomy, and the principle of autonomy remains important for Christians, as well as for others, in constraining what may be done to others in order to protect or benefit them if they are substantially autonomous and not harming others. Furthermore, views about autonomy and heteronomy will certainly have a major impact on Christian moral education*.

To many it seems difficult, if not impossible, to combine autonomy with a divine command* morality, since such a morality appears to be heteronomous (*see* **Autonomy of Ethics**). Within a broad ontological framework, Paul Tillich contended that some principles, such as love, are binding on the self, not because they are self-created or imposed from the outside, but because the self is united with the ground and source of all being. Attempting to avoid both heteronomy and autonomy, Tillich called his approach theonomous ethics.

See also **Authenticity; Conscience; Freedom; Free Will and Determinism; Human Dignity; Individualism; Liberalism; Persons and Personality; Respect for Persons.**

T. L. Beauchamp and J. F. Childress, *Principles of Biomedical Ethics,* ²1983; S. I. Benn, "Freedom, Autonomy, and the Concept of a Person," *Proceedings of the Aristotelian Society* 76, 1976; R. S. Downie and E. Telfer, "Autonomy," *Philosophy* 46, 1971; G. Dworkin, "Autonomy and Behavior Control," *HCR* 6, Feb. 1976.

JAMES F. CHILDRESS

Autonomy of Ethics

Autonomy* means the power of self-determination and freedom from alien domination and constraint. Autonomy stands opposed to heteronomy or subjection to the determination of another. A distinction may be drawn between the autonomy *of* ethics and autonomy *in* ethics. With regard to the latter the focus is upon the individual self and its capacity for self-determination; autonomy in ethics means freedom and the power to bind the self by a law which the self promulgates. By the autonomy of ethics is meant the doctrine that the moral dimension of human life has a form and structure of its own that is independent of religion, of custom and convention, and indeed of any other sphere of life or form of authority. The autonomy of ethics has frequently meant the separation of ethics from religion, but there are other factors—mores and customs, psychological and cultural determinism—from which ethics is also to be free if it is to retain its autonomy.

The problem of the autonomy of ethics was focused for modern thought by the moral philosophy of Immanuel Kant, in which autonomy figured as the central principle (*see* **Kantian Ethics**). Kant was attempting to root morality in practical reason independent of external influences and constraints. The problem underlying Kant's attempt is much older than his treatment of the issues involved. Plato raised the question in a dramatic way in the dialogue *Euthyphro* where Socrates discussed the question, "Is the holy [good] act holy because the gods love it? or do the gods love the holy [good] act because it is holy?" The alternatives are clear: in the first instance, the holy is being defined by the judgment of the gods and the ethical is made subject to the religious, whereas in the second case the standard of the holy exists beyond the gods and must be recognized by them no less than by mortals. The second alternative marks the autonomy of ethics because the standard of the good is independent of all other factors in existence and requires only to be grasped by the knowing mind.

In recent decades the autonomy of ethics has been a central issue both in religious and in ethical thought. Those who are skeptical about the validity of religion in an age of science argue for the complete independence of ethics from religion in the belief that the good is not dependent on God, and that values can be preserved even if a religious interpretation of morality is no longer tenable. On the other side, the proponents of the religious view claim that ethics can never be entirely independent of religion because religion supplies the insights from which moral ideals are framed, and without the grace of God the moral self has insufficient power to perform its duty.

See **Morality and Religion, Relations of.**

H. D. Lewis, *Morals and the New Theology,* 1947; W. G. Maclagan, *The Theological Frontier of Ethics,* 1959; G. Outka and J. P. Reeder, Jr. (eds.), *Religion and Morality,* 1973; P. L. Quinn, *Divine Commands and Moral Requirements,* 1978; P. Tillich, *Love, Power and Justice,* 1960.

JOHN E. SMITH

Avarice

see **Covetousness; Mammon; Property; Wealth**

Axiology

Axiology denotes a value theory that typically indicates the nature, kinds, criteria, and status of values and value judgments and attempts to resolve such disputes as whether values are subjective or objective. Although moral value is important, axiology also includes other values such as religious and aesthetic ones. "Axiological ethics" determines right and wrong actions by reference to their values and disvalues, usually of their ends, consequences, or motives. Thus, it is very close to and often identical to teleological ethics*.

See **Agathology; Values and Value Judgment.**

J. M. Findlay, *Axiological Ethics,* 1970.

JAMES F. CHILDRESS

Axioms *see* **Middle Axioms; Norms**

Babylonian Ethics

The law codes (Ešnunna, Lipit-Ištar, and Hammurabi) might appear from their contents to deal with social contract rather than morality. (If people are to live in society, to marry, to inherit and bequeath, to practice agriculture and engage in trade, and generally to live a life that creates all kinds of relationships with others, rules have to be laid down and punishments prescribed in order to bring continuity and stability into this interaction.) But there is a genuine humanitarian element in these laws and this humanitarianism, which is already attested in the inscriptions of the Sumerian social reformer Urukagina of Lagaš, is probably the earliest expression of ethical concern in Babylonian society. Hammurabi's intention is "that the strong may not oppress the weak [and] so to give justice to the orphan [and] the widow" (Driver and Miles, vol. 2, p. 97). Moreover, in the prologue and epilogue Hammurabi relates his laws to a concept of moral order of which he is the executor, and the gods, particularly Marduk and Šamaš, the guarantors and upholders (Driver and Miles, vol. 2, pp. 13, 99, 103).

There are good reasons why the idea of theodicy* did not come easily to the Babylonians and why the alliance of religious belief and morality (notwithstanding Hammurabi's bold statement) was tentative and uncertain. The old myths contain no basis for this marriage of religion and ethics, for the gods do not themselves have the moral stability to guarantee a moral order. They tend to reproduce all the human foibles on a larger scale and they differ from human beings principally with respect to superior power and freedom from death. It required the spur of adversity in the Cassite period (1500–1200 B.C.) to urge the necessity of a more intrinsic connection between religion and ethics, and even then this new ethical sensitivity hinged on the belief that there is a direct relationship between sin and suffering.

What has been said above indicates that the element of self-interest was strong in Babylonian ethics. The belief in a moral order was not held rigorously and the function of the personal god on whom the individual Babylonian set such store was to secure for its patron preferential treatment with the great gods and to protect from evil demons—a reminder of the tenacious power of magic over the Babylonian mind. Nor was there any sense of moral obligation, of morality as a thing to be pursued for its own sake. It was understood that gods made certain moral demands and human beings had better keep them if they wished to avoid disease and misfortune and to enjoy a long and prosperous life. This outlook is reflected in those wisdom precepts (Lambert, pp. 96f.) which offer practical guidance on correct behavior. Some of these are pragmatic, others inculcate the observance of religious duties, but all of them subserve a frank eudaemonism* that is undiluted by any belief in life after death, for the message of the Gilgamesh epic is that immortality belongs to the gods and humans cannot grasp it.

Two compositions, "The Babylonian Theodicy" (Lambert, pp. 63f.) and "I Will Praise the Lord of Wisdom" (Lambert, pp. 21f.), throw doubt in different ways on the existence of a moral order and even the possibility of intuiting ethical values. The latter describes the perplexity of a pietist, a devotee of Marduk, who cannot reconcile his sense of blamelessness with his experience of suffering and whose belief in a theodicy is subjected to strain, for the "Šamaš Hymn" (Lambert, pp. 121f.) teaches that the righteous are rewarded and the wicked punished *now*. The interest of this work lies not in the pious conclusion that the sufferings of the righteous are temporary and that all will come right in the end (in a this-worldly sense), but in the suggestion which is thrown up that human beings may have no intuitive sense of sin and may have no access to those moral values that regulate the actions of the gods. "Good" and "bad," "right" and "wrong" may mean the opposite for gods and humans and so the behavior of the gods cannot be accounted for nor their theodicy challenged. The "Theodicy," which is in dialogue form, is a robust social protest directed toward the actual conditions of oppression and moral chaos in human society and their incompatibility with the postulates of a theodicy. Here too the orthodox friend counters the rebel by drawing on teaching about the inscrutability

of the gods, but the conclusion which they reach, and which apparently satisfies the apologist no less than the rebel, is that humans are born liars and oppressors and that this is how the gods made them. In other words, humans are incapable of morality.

———

G. R. Driver and J. C. Miles, *The Babylonian Laws,* 2 vols., 1952–55; W. G. Lambert, *Babylonian Wisdom Literature,* 1960.

WILLIAM McKANE

Baptism *see* **Anabaptist Ethics; Church; Ecclesiology and Ethics; Patristic Ethics**

Beatitude *see* **Blessedness; Happiness; Sermon on the Mount**

Behavior Control

Behavior control is getting people to do, believe, or feel something they otherwise would not, by means of some direct or indirect intervention. Several questions need to be answered to understand a case of behavior control. Whose behavior is controlled? What behavior is affected? Is the control of behavior in someone's interest—for instance, the controller's or the controllee's? Is the control intentional on the part of the controller? Does the controllee know about it or consent to it? What is the nature of the intervention? How well does it work, if at all? Can the effects of behavior control be measured clearly? Under what conditions is the intervention desirable, and under what conditions undesirable? Who decides whether the intervention is legitimate in a particular case or class of cases, and can this decision be appealed? What are the social costs and benefits of the existence or availability of a particular kind of intervention? What does the possible use of the intervention reveal about human life?

Interventions. Although some modes of behavior control (e.g., the use of violence and intimidation) have been understood since prehistoric times, others are interesting because of their novelty in the scientific age. Three classes of intervention deserve mention.

New technologies of direct intervention in individuals include neurosurgery to alter behavior (psychosurgery), psychoactive drugs, behavior modification techniques, and many forms of psychotherapy. There is currently an explosion of new theories and research findings in neuroscience, psychology, psychiatry, and cognitive science on the topic of how the human behavioral and mental organism works. For the most part, direct interventions are developed for medical or psychotherapeutic purposes.

Indirect intervention through the control of the total environment is not a new technological artifact but, rather, the result of a new understanding of the effects of the environment that enables control of individuals to be achieved by its shaping. Total institutions such as managed prisons, boarding schools, cults, and closed military situations are obvious examples. Increasingly, however, popular knowledge of how total institutions work makes it possible to achieve or seek to achieve "total" effects from less total institutions such as classrooms, families, and work environments.

Intervention in media of learning, expression, and action controllably affects the behavior of those who use the media. Censorship* of books, ratings of films, the very availability of television, video games, and other electronic media, with the obverse displacement of media such as conversational speaking and the literary, constitutes a new situation with regard to the control of behavior.

Examples of alterations in media illustrate the point that behavior control need not be intentional. The controllers need not know what they are doing, or that they are doing anything in the area of behavior control. Behavior control is frequently a side effect of interventions intended for other purposes. An essential task of the social critic is to establish just what does take place regarding the alteration of behavior, to ask whether it is worthwhile, and to determine who is responsible.

Models of analysis. There are at least two models of analysis for framing the more important questions about technological behavior control: the self-control model and the social-control model. (This assumes that there is no moral plausibility in the control of one person by another for the exclusive interest of the controller.)

The self-control model is found when individuals intervene in their own behavior, usually self-consciously and intending to serve their own alleged interests, e.g., drinking coffee to wake up or taking relaxants to go to sleep. Relevant questions are: Do the people in fact know what they are doing? Are there no adverse side effects to the intervention? Are the individuals' interests truly served? Is the intervention effective? If the answer to all these questions is yes, we generally approve the behavior control.

A variation on self-control is the case where, as in medicine, a person employs another person, an expert, to intervene. Informed consent* is supposed to guarantee that the expert behavior control agent acts according to the will of the patient. A further variation is the case where the patient's own understanding or will is incapacitated, as in severe mental illness, and a proxy must be established to maintain the moral propriety of the patient's self-control. Should the proxy will for the patient's good or according to what the patient would have willed if able?

The social-control model is found when some individuals intervene in other individuals' behavior for the alleged good of some larger context. This is a frankly political model, recognizing that many more people may be affected by a given behavior than the person alone; education and the law are deeply involved in controlling behavior on this model. And it might be wise to apply the model to cases of mental illness* where the good of others needs to be taken into account and where the continuity of self-control through informed consent and proxies is misleading or fictitious. Moral management on the social-control model includes the political process for setting goals and limits of control, licensing of controllers, and due process appeals from unwanted control.

Christian values. Initially, the value of freedom* is the one apparently most affected by new methods of behavior control. Except in cases of blatant dominance, however, the issue is always more complicated because many interventions, e.g., those that wake people up or cure their mental illness, enhance rather than threaten freedom. The value of stewardship* is more subtly involved with behavior control because it legitimates intervention. Dostoevsky's Grand Inquisitor directly pits stewardship against freedom, advocating the management of society as a total institution. At its best, stewardship reinforces charity*. But behavior control technologies provide powerful instruments for doing good to people whether they want it or not and whether or not the controllers are properly warranted. Also, the goals of stewardship are notoriously difficult to determine in some cases. The Christian value of being responsible is perhaps the one most amenable to service by many of the new behavior controls. The legitimacy and limits of self-control and social control in some cases can be articulated by a determination of whether the intervention leads to greater responsibility in the person being controlled and in relevant others. But greater responsibility is not the only justification for behavior control. Psalm 104:15 praises God for wine, which merely gladdens the heart.

See also **Autonomy; Free Will and Determinism; Morality, Legal Enforcement of; Paternalism; Persons and Personality; Responsibility.**

J. Feinberg and R. Neville, "Behavior Control," *EB* I, 1978; W. Gaylin et al., *Operating on the Mind,* 1975; E. Goffman, *Asylums,* 1961; G. Klerman et al., "Controlling Behavior Through Drugs," *Hastings Center Studies* 2, no. 1, Jan. 1974; P. London, *Behavior Control,* 1969; R. Macklin and W. Gaylin, *Mental Retardation and Sterilization: A Problem of Competency and Paternalism,* 1981.

ROBERT C. NEVILLE

Behaviorism

Behaviorism is the doctrine that utterances about psychological or mental states are ultimately reducible to, or should be replaced by, expressions about an organism's dispositions to behave in certain ways. The acknowledged father of this doctrine is the American psychologist J. B. Watson (1878–1958), its most famous recent defender being B. F. Skinner (b. 1904). The classic statement of philosophical behaviorism is Gilbert Ryle's *The Concept of Mind* (1949), which is directed against the Cartesian view that "inner states" are immediately known, essentially private, and capable of causing dispositions to behave without *being* dispositions themselves. Against this view, Ryle aimed to establish a conceptual connection between reports of inner states and behavioral dispositions, thereby vindicating the doctrine of behaviorism. Ryle's opposition to the Cartesian view of "inner states" has been widely influential. Philosophers have grown increasingly doubtful, however, that talk about "inner states" can be reduced to talk about dispositions—a claim that many now take to be an overreaction to Cartesianism. Some philosophers, influenced especially by the arguments of W. V. Quine (b. 1908), have tried to recast the case against Cartesianism without claiming to establish conceptual connections. Cartesianism and behaviorism are now often described as extreme positions that do not exhaust the alternatives.

G. Ryle, *The Concept of Mind,* 1949; J. B. Watson, *Behaviorism,* 1924.

JEFFREY STOUT

Beneficence

Beneficence is active well-doing. Christian ethics recognizes a duty to do good to the neighbor and even to the enemy, but almost all ethical theories, religious or secular, teach a duty of beneficence.

See **Altruism; Love.**

JOHN MACQUARRIE

Benevolence

Benevolence is an attitude of goodwill, and may be considered as the subjective disposition corresponding to the activity of beneficence*.

JOHN MACQUARRIE

Bible in Christian Ethics

An early Paulinist confidently declared that scripture is "profitable for teaching, for reproof, for correction, and for training in righteousness" (2 Tim. 3:16). Since that time the same declaration has echoed down the centuries and across the divisions of the Christian church—and with reference to the NT as well as the Hebrew scriptures. Christian churches have always considered it a part of their calling to teach, reprove, correct, and train in righteousness, and they have always considered the Bible "profitable" for that task. With virtually one voice the churches have declared that the Bible is an authority for moral discernment and judgment. And Christian ethicists—at least those who consider their work part of the common life of the Christian community—have shared this affirmation.

That single voice, however, becomes many voices when scripture is *used* as an authority*. To affirm the authority of scripture is to invoke the use of the Bible in moral discernment and judgment, but it is not to prescribe how the Bible is to be used. The use of scripture or the authorizations for moving in argument from the Bible to contemporary moral claims depend not just on scripture's authority, but on judgments (sometimes left implicit) about its nature and message, the questions appropriate to it, and the relevance of other sources of moral wisdom.

What are these writings? One important debate relevant to the use of scripture in Christian ethics concerns its nature. The Bible did not fall directly from heaven; all Christians acknowledge and affirm that the Bible is human words. But these human words have been heard in the churches and are acclaimed in the churches as the word of God. The Bible is both human words and the word of God.

The conjunction of the divine and the human—whether in Jesus of Nazareth or the sacraments or scripture—eludes precision. At the Council of Chalcedon (451) the church was content to make a series of limiting statements concerning the way divine and human were joined in Christ: The divine and the human must not be confused, transmuted the one into the other, divided into separate categories, or contrasted according to area or function.

This Chalcedonian perspective can also be applied to scripture and distinguished from the perspective of fundamentalism*, which identifies and confuses the human words of scripture with the divine word, transmuting the one into the other; and from the perspective of liberalism, which divides the two and contrasts the human words with the divine word.

Fundamentalism's identification of the human words of scripture with the word of God has justified an identification of biblical ethics with Christian ethics. A rule or command or any moral teaching found in scripture may be presumed to be normative for the church today. The presumption typically may be overridden if the rule or command was intended as a temporary obligation rather than a perpetual obligation. The tasks of Christian ethics are to harmonize, systematize, and apply the biblical ethic.

Liberalism's contrast of the human words of scripture with the divine word has sometimes justified the "liberation" of Christian ethics from the human words of scripture. When scripture is used, the authorization is that some of its moral teaching expresses the word of God as that has been independently identified. The tasks of Christian ethics are to

identify the word of God within scripture (e.g., the social idealism of Jesus or the law of love) and to articulate it in a contemporary way. The task of identifying the word of God, moreover, is undertaken by attending carefully to contemporary needs and problems, to the Spirit of God in the age, not particularly to the human words of scripture.

A Chalcedonian perspective will be appreciative of fundamentalism's concern to bind the church to the Bible, and will be appreciative of liberalism's concern to address contemporary issues and problems. But it will disown fundamentalism's identification of the human words of scripture with the divine word, and also liberalism's contrast of the human words with the Word of God. It will disown not only these judgments about scripture but also the authorizations for the use of scripture that rest on them. It will own the "important two-part consensus," identified by Birch and Rasmussen (pp. 45–46) that "Christian ethics is not synonymous with biblical ethics" and that "for Christian ethics the Bible is somehow normative." A Chalcedonian perspective does not entail any particular recommendation for the use of scripture, but it does rule out some uses, and it invites further reflection concerning the other methodologically significant questions.

What questions are appropriate to the Bible? The use of the Bible in Christian ethics depends in part on judgments about the questions appropriate to it. Two issues may be distinguished here: the *type* of question judged appropriate, and the *level* of moral inquiry at which scripture is thought to speak with authority.

With respect to the type of question judged appropriate, some enduring disputes in Christian ethics are reflected. Some see moral agency as responsibility to God, and scripture as addressing questions of God's character and work. On this model, theological questions rather than moral questions are judged appropriate; indeed, scripture's rules or moral principles may be judged to be quaint. Others, however, insist that explicitly moral questions are appropriate, that our responsibility to God is shaped and judged by scripture's moral teachings. The type of moral question judged appropriate to scripture still reflects judgments about moral agency: deontologists are likely to ask questions of duty or the right; teleologists are likely to ask questions of proper ends or the good; and virtue theorists are likely to ask questions of character (*see* **Deontology; Teleological Ethics; Virtue**).

Another enduring dispute in Christian ethics is reflected in whether questions concerning political or social ethics*, as well as questions of personal ethics*, are judged appropriate to scripture.

There is a growing consensus that it is inappropriate to expect scripture to address the sort of moral question that seems sometimes to monopolize ethical reflection in pluralistic societies, the question of an impartial and "autonomous" morality, a morality that obliges a person whatever (and in spite of, if need be) his or her moral commitments and communities. It is precisely the sort of questions from which an autonomous morality based on "impartial" reason prescinds that are particularly appropriate to scripture. The Bible claims our loyalty for God, gives us a community and a history, and requires integrity with that identity in our dispositions and intentions.

With respect to the level of moral discourse, all agree that the question "Why be moral?" is appropriate to scripture. Many insist that scripture also speaks with authority at the "ethical principle" level, where the question is, "What general principles are normative?" And some even claim that scripture speaks with authority at the "moral rule" level, where the question is the concrete one of conduct, "What ought I to do?" To ask this last question, however, comes perilously close to confusing the human words of scripture with the Word of God and to treating scripture as what it is not and did not intend to be, an eternal code. The scripture will and must continue to bear on the concrete decisions of Christians—not directly but, rather, in ways mediated by its response to inquiries concerning our moral identity, our fundamental loyalty and perspective, and the dispositions and intentions which inhere in that identity.

What is the message of the Bible? The question of what one understands when one understands scripture is not a new one, nor is the relevance of such judgments to the use of scripture in Christian ethics a recent discovery. Augustine candidly insisted that any movement from scripture to moral claims is licensed if and only if it is consistent with the double love commandment, which he identified as the message of scripture.

Many Christian ethicists have claimed that Jesus Christ is the center of the biblical message in its entirety and the key to scripture. Then, of course, Christological "judgments" become relevant to the use of the Bible in ethics. If Jesus is understood as one who comes announcing the kingdom of God* as an ideal social order, then the use of scripture in moral argument will be authorized if and only if it is consistent with the social ideals of the kingdom (e.g., Walter Rauschenbusch). If Jesus is seen as teaching and embodying "a social style characterized by the creation of a new community and the rejection of violence" (J. H. Yoder, *The Politics of Jesus*, p. 250), then the understanding and use of scripture must cohere with that vision. If Jesus is seen as the "transhistorical Christ" in whom Christians mysteriously participate, then even the use of Jesus' teachings will be limited and licensed by what can be apprehended of the mystery.

Some Christian ethicists prefer a more Trinitarian rendering of the message of scripture: What we understand when we understand scripture may be summarized in terms of creation, fall, redemption, and the future age. Both H. R. Niebuhr and Richard Mouw provide such a summary and use it to license and limit their use of scripture; they differ about the type and level of question appropriate to scripture, however, because they hold different views of scripture and of moral agency.

Currently a number of Christian ethicists, notably Third World theologians (e.g., Gustavo Gutiérrez, Rubem Alves), black theologians (e.g., James Cone), and feminist theologians (e.g., Elisabeth Schüssler Fiorenza), understand "liberation" or deliverance from oppression to be the message of scripture. What one understands when one understands scripture is a history of liberation, oriented toward the future, in which a contemporary praxis of liberation can and must participate. The use of scripture in contemporary morality is authorized if and only if the claims are consistent with the central theme of liberation. Critics of liberation theology (e.g., J. H. Yoder) have sometimes asked whether liberation does not need to be balanced or subordinated to other themes—whether, in effect, liberation really is the message of scripture, and whether the understanding of "liberation" is controlled by the Bible or other sources (*see* **Afro-American Religious Ethics; Feminist Ethics; Liberation Theology**).

Examples of judgments about the message of scripture and their relevance to its use in Christian ethics could easily be multiplied. In the midst of this diversity three general observations can be made. First, judgments about the wholeness of scripture are methodologically necessary; Christian ethics would be served by candor about these judgments. Second, these judgments rest not so much on an "impartial" exegetical demonstration as on the experience of the authority of scripture in the context of one's own moral struggles, on the one hand, and of the believing community and its moral tradition, on the other. Third, the judgments about the message may not be substituted for the writings themselves. They may only be fashioned and used in the context of reverently listening to the whole Bible in the context of the believing community. Then the diverse judgments need not be rued but may be appreciated, for they keep us attentive to the whole of scripture and to the whole believing community in our concern with and for the world.

What is the relevance of other sources? The use of scripture in Christian ethics finally also depends on judgments about the relevance of other sources of moral insight. Positions range from a theological veto on the contributions of other sources to the surrender of control over moral argument to other sources. Between these extremes there are many voices calling for some sort of dialogue between scripture and other sources.

The theological veto on the contributions of natural morality or philosophical ethics is sometimes represented as entailed by the Reformation slogan *Sola scriptura* and is usually based on the radical fallenness of human nature and all human projects, including the project of distinguishing good and evil (e.g., Jacques Ellul). Not only is there inconsistency in this position, but the dismissal of arguments based on reason alone is an *argumentum ad hominem* on the scale of an *argumentum ad humanum*.

The surrender of control over the formation of conscience* is a position that looks to the deliverances of an autonomous morality or of some ideology* (*see also* **Autonomy of Ethics**). Jack Sanders, for example, states

candidly that scripture "must not be allowed to stand in the way of what is humane and right" (*Ethics in the New Testament,* p. 130). Many liberation theologians charge that the understanding and use of scripture have been controlled by the ideological presuppositions of the powerful. They do not recommend as a remedy the model of impartial reason and value-free critical exegesis, which they take to be a deceptive pretense cloaking ideological control by the powerful. Rather, they recommend candid commitment to partiality for the poor and oppressed, to the interests of particular oppressed groups, and to a social analysis that stands in their service. And they would surrender control over the understanding and use of scripture to these other sources (thus Juan Luis Segundo, James Cone, Elisabeth Schüssler Fiorenza; whereas José Miranda's recommended remedy is objective critical exegesis). However, to surrender control over Christian ethics to sources other than those intimately related to the religious community's moral identity—whether to the autonomous morality of impartial reason or to the ideologies of either the rich or the oppressed—comes perilously close to surrendering Christian identity.

Instead of the theological veto or the surrender of control to other sources, many have recommended some form of dialogue. The dialogue is understood and undertaken in various ways, of course. Sometimes the Bible's part in the dialogue is to challenge and disrupt conventional moral certainties and securities. Sometimes its role is to confirm and collaborate moral decisions reached on the basis of other sources. Sometimes scripture is taken to supplement or transform natural moral wisdom. Sometimes other sources challenge and disrupt a conventional understanding and use of scripture and force a new examination of what it requires of the believing community. The consensus, however, seems to be that—at least with respect to questions of moral identity—scripture must have the last word in the dialogue and that the biblically based identity must limit, corroborate, and transform appeals to reason and to group interests.

Conclusion. There is no "Christian ethics" that would deny the authority of the Bible, for apart from scripture the Christian church has no enduring identity. It must be recognized, however, that even those claims made on the basis of scripture are quite human claims, arrived at by means of quite human authorization. The authority of scripture for Christian ethics does not license the religious pride of claiming the absolute view, the final word, God's truth about some hard case simply because we can appeal to scripture. Indeed, the authority of scripture (as well as the confession of human capacities for self-deception and rationalization) commits us to self-conscious and self-critical reflection about the authorizations we use in moving from scripture to moral claims. It calls us again and again to listen reverently to the whole canon in the midst of the whole believing community. In that way perhaps the God who bears toward us—in scripture and the community—the relation of sanctifier may cleanse and renew even our use of the Bible in Christian ethics.

See also **Christian Ethics.**

B. C. Birch and L. Rasmussen, *Bible and Ethics in the Christian Life,* 1976; C. E. Curran and R. A. McCormick, S.J. (eds.), *Readings in Moral Theology, No. 4: The Use of Scripture in Moral Theology,* 1984; T. W. Ogletree, *The Use of the Bible in Christian Ethics,* 1983; A. Verhey, *The Great Reversal: Ethics and the New Testament,* 1984.

ALLEN VERHEY

Biblical Ethics *see* **Jesus, Ethical Teaching of; Johannine Ethics; Mosaic Law; New Testament Ethics; Old Testament Ethics; Paul, Ethical Teaching of; Prophetic Ethics; Wisdom Literature, Ethics in;** *see also* **Bible in Christian Ethics**

Bigamy

Marriage* to a second wife or husband while a previous marriage is in force. Bigamy is a crime in Western countries, though in other parts of the world bigamy or polygamy* (the marriage of many wives) is commonly practiced.

HERBERT WADDAMS

Bioethics

The term "bioethics" is very recent, one of its earliest uses being by V. R. Potter in *Bioethics: Bridge to the Future* (1971). He defined bioethics as "the science for survival" and concentrated on the use of the biological sciences to improve the quality of life. A more common definition of bioethics is the application of ethics to the biological

sciences, medicine, health care, and related areas as well as the public policies directed toward them. The *Encyclopedia of Bioethics* (1978) adopts this approach. Since the term "bioethics" may suggest an independent discipline rather than the application of ethics to an arena of human activity, parallel to other applications such as political ethics and business ethics, and since the term *bios* (meaning "life") is much too broad for what is treated under the heading of "bioethics," the phrase "biomedical ethics" has been proposed, but "bioethics" is handier and more common. Widespread interest in problems of bioethics dates from the late 1960s and early 1970s, when such developments as heart transplantation and the allocation of scarce lifesaving resources (e.g., dialysis machines) raised serious questions about what ought to be done. Judaism and Roman Catholicism have had stronger traditions of reflection on medical ethics than Protestantism, but Joseph Fletcher's *Morals and Medicine* (1954) was a landmark book, followed by Paul Ramsey's *The Patient as Person* (1970), which appeared as interest in bioethics exploded. Many other religious thinkers have contributed significantly to the field of bioethics, being joined for the last decade by numerous philosophers who have returned to applied ethics*. Bioethics is necessarily interdisciplinary and interprofessional, involving scientists, physicians, nurses, and others, as well as theologians and philosophers. For an indication of the range of problems covered in bioethics, *see,* e.g., **Abortion; Death, Determination of; Euthanasia; Experimentation with Human Subjects; Genetics; Medical Ethics; Organ Transplantation; Reproductive Technologies; Science and Ethics.**

T. L. Beauchamp and J. F. Childress, *Principles of Biomedical Ethics,* ²1983; *Dictionary of Medical Ethics,* ed. A. S. Duncan, G. R. Dunstan, and R. B. Welbourn, new rev. ed., 1981; *Encyclopedia of Bioethics,* ed. W. T. Reich, 4 vols., 1978 (esp. D. Clouser, "Bioethics").

JAMES F. CHILDRESS

Biomedical Ethics *see* **Bioethics; Medical Ethics; Professional Ethics**

Birth Control *see* **Contraception; Population Policy; Procreation; Sexual Ethics**

Black Religious Ethics *see* Afro-American Religious Ethics

Black Theology *see* Afro-American Religious Ethics

Blasphemy

Blasphemy (from Greek, "miscalling") is an extreme lack of religious reverence* manifested primarily in the improper use of expressions referring to God or in the use of improper expressions about God. Israel had a particular horror of any hint of disrespect toward the name of God and so avoided all use of it. The taking of God's name "in vain" (Ex. 20:7) implied a manipulation of God for one's own purposes, whether in invoking it to curse an enemy (Lev. 24:11–16), or possibly in sorcery or perjury, or in profaning it by idolatrously breaking with the God of the Covenant (Ezek. 20:27, 39). The charge against Jesus was that he blasphemed in his claim to stand in a relationship of particular intimacy with God (Mark 14:61–64; John 10:33), and in his bid to exercise a share of divine forgiving power (Luke 5:21). But when his opponents ascribed to Satan the divine authority with which he cast out demons, it was they whom Jesus accused of unforgivable blasphemy against the Holy Spirit (Mark 3:22–30).

Theologically, blasphemy has been interpreted as impugning the goodness of God, e.g., by cursing him for misfortune or, more systematically, by considering him selective in his providence, as in the Roman condemnation of "blasphemous" Jansenist propositions. It has also been viewed fundamentally as a dishonoring of God by any questioning or mocking of his power or by denying the divinity of Christ or, in Roman Catholicism, belittling those particularly close to him, such as Mary and the other saints. In itself it is considered a serious sin, sometimes involving heresy, but admitting of degrees of moral culpability according to circumstances of thoughtlessness, anger, or habit, or insofar as certain originally blasphemous phrases have lost their force through popular usage.

Historically, various Christian countries have proscribed and legislated against blasphemy as an injustice to God, but such social protection of God's good name has in more recent times undergone modification in two ways. One has been a shift in focus from the rights of God to those of the individual citizen or religious minority, in a transition from protecting God from "injury" to the protection of religion as a social institution, to a protecting of individuals or groups professing religious beliefs from being attacked, ridiculed, or even deeply offended. The other has been to explore the dividing line between such offensive blasphemy and legitimate religious controversy and criticism, as a particular instance of the tension between censorship* and freedom* of expression in society.

See also **Cursing/Swearing; Morality, Legal Enforcement of.**

J. MAHONEY

Blessedness/Blessed

To be "blessed" or in a state of "blessedness" is to be happy. The Beatitudes (Matt. 5:3–12; compare Luke 6:17, 20–23) identify certain kinds of actions that happiness accompanies; Jesus pronounced "blessed" those who are "poor in spirit," who "mourn," who are "meek," who "hunger and thirst for righteousness," who are "merciful," etc. In each case the formula ends with a specification of the condition or cause of happiness; for example, the "poor in spirit" shall have the "kingdom of heaven" and the "meek" shall "inherit the earth." Even in the Matthean version of the Beatitudes there are both material and spiritual rewards, both this-worldly and otherworldly concerns. The Lucan version more clearly focuses on material benefits in this world—for example, "hunger" itself rather than Matthew's "hunger and thirst for righteousness"—and its several maledictions ("Woe to . . .") are similar. Thus, the NT itself reflects different conceptions of the nature, conditions, and location of human happiness, though these are not necessarily in opposition to each other. In Roman Catholic thought beatitude is the state of blessedness realized in the beatific vision, the vision of God, which represents the *summum bonum* (supreme good) for which humans were created. There are important debates about the legitimacy of seeking worldly happiness for oneself and the relation between human achievement and God's gift or grace in happiness, as well as about the nature and conditions of happiness.

See **Happiness; Kingdom of God.**

JAMES F. CHILDRESS

Body

The Christian understanding of the human body and its significance for ethics is centered in the belief that "the Word was made flesh." As the problem for ethics concerns how human beings ought to act *within the world* in relation to themselves and to one another, and thus within the conditions of material life, the central problematic of Christian ethics rests in a key way on how the human body (the "flesh") is understood. Historically, two main views have been evident, one stemming from classical Greek thinking, the other arising from Hebraic roots in the OT. Both implied, and gave rise to, specific anthropologies, which in turn prompted specific moralities antagonistic to one another.

The first view is essentially Hellenistic and assumes a sharp separation between the body and the soul. The soul is the pure, holy, and immortal part; the body is regarded as the source of evil, corruption, and mortality. The soul, belonging properly to a "higher," heavenly realm, is imprisoned in the tomb of the body, subject to and tempted by its appetites and inclinations, but has its true destiny elsewhere—a destiny it must pursue by becoming freed from its worldly, bodily prison.

Although resisted by several church fathers, this view was implied by some asceticism* and gradually became a core part of medieval and later Christian thinking. It is human reason or mind which was thought to be "in the image of God," and this was conceived as fundamentally separate from the body. That human being exists in a "fallen" condition is due to the body: the "sins of the flesh." To be redeemed, then, is to suppress the ways of the flesh, the world. Taking the body as the bondage, this view often led to an extreme asceticism or at least to a repressive and otherworldly ethics— one endorsing the "higher" virtues of the spiritual or inner person and condemning the pursuits of the carnal.

The other view in historical Christianity stems from the biblical sources of the OT. Here, human being is viewed, not as a composite of soul and body, but as unitary; matter is not the source of evil, but is, as created by God, essentially good. The Hebraic understanding of human being or "soul" (*nephesh*) evokes the person as an animated body, not as an incarnated soul (as in Greek thought). This is captured in Pauline theology, in which the main terms for "body" (*sōma* and *sarx*) evoke the whole person in his or her natural condition, and are often synonymous with the personal pronoun. That is, this view does not regard "body" and the "soul" as two parts of human being, the one good and the other evil; hence, it is deeply opposed to any dualism. This view endorses a belief in the inherent goodness of the created world and human being, a goodness signaled by God's so loving them that he sent his "only begotten Son," not to condemn the world but to save it. For alongside that belief is the conviction that the world and human being within it are "fallen," are in corruption and rebellion and thus in need of salvation. Human beings are called on, not to despise their bodies and depart to other more ethereal realms, but to remain within the world and therein work out their salvation and that of the world. In this view, then, "souls" do not exist for a time in a "tomb," yearning for and painfully making their way to a heavenly abode of disembodied, pure spirits. Just the opposite: as "the Word was made flesh," God comes down to earth, to human being, at once to remake and to redeem it from its "fallen" state.

For this view, "body" or "flesh" does not signify one part of human being; yet there is a sharp antithesis between "flesh" and "Spirit." These terms, however, do not stand for two separate and opposing parts of human being, but rather for two *different kinds* of person. "Flesh" stands for the kind of person in whom the whole person (spiritual and bodily) is misdirected because she or he expresses an attitude of denial of human dependence on God and thus reveals a bondage to the human worldly self, or self-centeredness. This is the fundamental meaning of sin* in Christian ethics: the deep-seated and pervasive corruption of the whole person, love of self or hubris, the denial of oneself as God's creature.

The two views, then, are deeply opposed on the meaning of "body," on the meaning of human being's "fallen" and "sinful" condition, and therefore on the central questions of ethics and the understanding of human life and human destiny. While the first view tended to predominate from medieval times to the early 20th century, the second, already evident in early Christianity, has reemerged in recent times.

See **Embodiment; Asceticism; Death, Determination of; Image of God; Life, Prolongation of; Life, Sacredness of; Organ Transplantation; Original Sin; Sin(s).**

J. A. T. Robinson, *The Body: A Study in Pauline Theology,* 1952; C. A. van Peursen, *Body, Soul, Spirit: A Survey of the Body-Mind Problem,* ET 1966; R. M. Zaner, *The Problem of Embodiment,* 1964.

RICHARD M. ZANER

Borderline Situations *see* Conflict of Duties; Dilemma; Dirty Hands; Norms; Situation Ethics

Boycott

The name is used for a collective refusal to have dealings with some individual or corporate group, and is derived from a certain Captain Boycott (1832–1897), a landlord's agent who was made the target for such collective action on the part of the landlord's tenants in Ireland. The boycott has been increasingly used in recent times as a method of bringing moral persuasion to bear on bodies that are allegedly guilty of malpractices and that have resisted verbal persuasion. The word "boycott" should be restricted to the actions of private groups. Similar action by governments is better called a "sanction" or an "embargo." Examples of boycotts in which Christians have joined include the boycotting of South African produce as a protest against apartheid*; the boycotting of schools in an attempt to obtain better education for underprivileged groups; the boycotting of commercial concerns in protest against their employment policies. In the complexity of modern society, it is extremely difficult to judge about the rightness or wrongness of particular boycotts. On the one hand, they do provide a way of bringing pressures to bear in a society that is controlled by large corporate groups —industrial concerns, government agencies, trade unions, and the like. On the other hand, the boycott is, like strikes* and nuclear armaments, a somewhat indiscriminate weapon and is bound to hurt a good many people other than those at whom it is aimed. The Christian must consider each case very carefully, and decide whether the harm that will be inflicted on innocent people will be outweighed by the eventual righting of wrongs through the pressure exerted. In practice, this will often amount to calculating whether the action can be swift and successful. In cases where there might be doubt, there would be the possibility of substituting for a full-scale boycott a token boycott, perhaps for a day or a week, simply as a demonstration for the purpose of bringing to the public notice the particular injustice against which the protest is being directed.

JOHN MACQUARRIE

Brainwashing

An extreme form of indoctrination*. It is the forcible manipulation of the human mind in such a way as to change its orientation, to establish new beliefs and attitudes, against the will of the person concerned. In ethical terms it is a violation of human personality in its most intimate aspects.

The word first came to prominence during the Korean War in the mid-1950s, when reports were received of prisoners who had been forced to make confessions by the application of psychological and physical techniques designed to break down mental resistance and open the way to ideological conversion. The reality has been known for much longer. Torture* is an elementary form of brainwashing. But the special quality of 20th-century brainwashing rests on the exploitation of Pavlovian theories of conditioning, modern insights into guilt and dependency, and the all-enveloping atmosphere of the totalitarian state*. Concentration camps in both East and West perfected some of the techniques, and Koestler's *Darkness at Noon* remains a classic description.

Since the 1950s the word has taken on wider connotations and can be used, not always helpfully, to describe all forms of conscious or unconscious mental coercion from propaganda to advertising. William Sargant, a neurologist, drew comparisons with certain types of religious ritual, and aroused particular controversy through his analysis in Pavlovian terms of the techniques employed in Wesleyan revivalism. This analysis has been vigorously repudiated. The charge of brainwashing has also been made against some of the newer religious groups that use stress, isolation from previous contacts, and containment within an all-enveloping community to build loyalty in their new adherents.

Invasive techniques, akin to brainwashing, have also been employed in psychiatry, but attempts to produce a therapeutically useful disorientation by extreme versions of electroconvulsive therapy or the administration of hallucinogenic drugs are now discredited.

See also **Behavior Control; Cults; Deprogramming; Persons and Personality; Respect for Persons; Human Dignity; Dehumanization.**

J. A. M. Meerloo, *Mental Seduction and Menticide,* 1957; I. Ramage, *Battle for the Free Mind,* 1967; W. Sargant, *Battle for the Mind,* 1957.

JOHN HABGOOD

Bribery

By bribery is understood the act or practice of receiving or giving a bribe. A bribe is an inducement improperly influencing the performance of a public function meant to be gratuitously exercised. What counts as "an inducement," what counts as "improperly influencing," what counts as "a public function," what functions are "meant to be gratuitously exercised" have changed as culture has changed. The core concept has been remarkably constant.

In nearly every primitive society it is usual to approach a powerful stranger with whom one desires peace and to bring a gift. The gift functions to allay hostility and create reciprocity. Even the gods must be approached with gifts in hand. It requires a powerful impulse to break this pattern and to stamp certain gifts as bribes. Religion supplied the impulse and the new paradigm.

Although the ideal of a figure who does not take certain gifts can be found in Egypt and in Mesopotamia, the decisive texts for Christian thought occur in the OT—Ex. 23:8, commanding witnesses not to take *shohadh;* the prophets (e.g., Isa. 1:23), denouncing rulers who take *shohadh;* Deut. 10:16–18, declaring that God does not take *shohadh;* and Deut. 16:18–20, requiring human judges not to take *shohadh.* Ancient Hebrew, like Greek and Latin, did not develop a single word meaning bribe. *Shohadh,* an ambiguous term meaning either a good or a bad gift, is best translated "offering." In the context of condemnation it meant "bribe."

The OT texts set out the paradigm of God as a Judge who does not take bribes and is to

be imitated by human judges. The NT added one more dimension: the interdiction in Acts 8:18–24 of Simon's attempt to buy the Spirit, an interdiction with two implications—first, that some things were beyond purchase and could never be reduced to commodities; second, that those who offered money for the unpurchasable were as bad as those who sold the unsellable.

Greek and Roman legal thought harmoniously joined biblical teaching to form the Christians' repudiation of bribery in the later Roman Empire. Impartiality in judgment was insisted upon by fathers such as Augustine. The corrupt judge was the object of Christian scorn; the upright judge, of Christian praise. Restitution of bribes was perceived as an obligation that went with repentance of the sin. In a special way the fathers attacked the sale of the Spirit within the church. Giving or taking money for holy orders was seen as contrary to the express command of the Lord: "You have taken freely. Give freely" (Matt. 10:8). The principle that ecclesiastical office was beyond purchase reinforced the perception that some public functions by their nature must be gratuitously exercised.

The 6th to 10th centuries saw waves of primitive peoples, used to the exchange of gifts with powerful strangers, being introduced to the biblical standard by the sporadic efforts of popes, bishops, and monks. In general, the ideal of nonreciprocity with a judge was transmitted. Practice to the contrary was common. Beginning in the 11th century and culminating in the 16th, waves of reformation swept through the church. Always one of the cries of the reformer was against corruption, meaning by corruption a monetary traffic either in ecclesiastical appointments or in judgments. At first the papacy spearheaded the reform; by the 12th century the papacy itself had become the target of reformers seeking to eliminate, high and low, the sin now described as simony, the sale of any spiritual good.

Condemnation of secular bribery also flourished in the Middle Ages as the biblical standard was inculcated. The high point was reached in Dante's *Inferno,* where cantos 21 and 22 are devoted to the bribe takers and their fate: immersion in a thick tar, a divine penalty inspired by the biblical verse, "He who touches pitch is stained by it" (Ecclus.

13:1). No more succinct definition of bribery exists than Dante's line on Lucca: "where No becomes Yes for money."

English culture had been deeply influenced by the antibribery ethic as is evidenced by the Dominican John Bromyard's *Summa Praedicantium,* the tracts of John Wycliffe, and the sharp satirical treatment of corrupt clerics in Chaucer's *The Canterbury Tales.* By the 16th century, English culture had produced a single unambiguous word for a corrupt gift: "bribe." The word appears in 16th-century translations of the Bible beginning with Coverdale's (1535). Reformers like Hugh Latimer thundered against bribery at the court of Edward VI. Shakespeare's plays, especially *Measure for Measure,* built on the strength of the Christian antibribery ethic and expressed it. In 1621, for the first time in English history, a high English judge was convicted of bribery and removed from the office: the fall of Lord Chancellor Francis Bacon began the full secular acceptance of the biblical idea.

God as incorrupt Judge was the basic paradigm. Only by degrees and slowly was the ideal of gratuitous official action extended to secular administrators, rulers, and legislators. The elimination of all reciprocity from the political process has sometimes been felt to be beyond attainment. Today a serious moral question in every democracy is the distinction between campaign contributions and bribes.

If a campaign contribution is given out of admiration for a candidate's position, there is no thought of binding his or her future actions, and if what is given is publicly given and acknowledged, the contribution has the characteristics of a gift. If the contribution is secretly made in expectation of the candidate's vote on an issue of importance to the contributor, the moral distinction between a gift and bribe is tenuous. Even under present American law, it has been vigorously argued, there are many contributions openly made by political action committees that are morally and legally bribes but go unprosecuted and unpunished.

Other difficult moral questions are the effect of custom in defining bribery, especially in Third World countries; the proper reach of national law in defining bribery abroad; and the proper limits on measures to discover bribery. Usually a secret crime, bribery is often only detectable by undercover measures. But are the means justified? Must we choose between evil means and impotence to reform? These and other ethical questions bearing on bribery require more discussion than modern Christian ethics, Catholic or Protestant, has accorded them.

J. Borkin, *The Corrupt Judge: An Inquiry Into Bribery and Other High Crimes and Misdemeanors in the Federal Court,* 1962; J. McCloy, *The Great Oil Spill,* 1976; J. T. Noonan, Jr., *Bribes,* 1984.

JOHN T. NOONAN, JR.

Buddhist Ethics

Buddhist morality in part reflects the special spiritual aims of the faith. The Buddha's teaching included both a diagnosis of the condition of human beings and a prescription on how that condition could be alleviated and finally cured. The regimen he prescribed is known as the "Noble Eightfold Path," which leads to nirvana, and moral perfection is considered to be part of the means for attaining that degree of peace and insight which will release a person from the round of rebirth. Thus the Path includes, as three of its eight aspects: right speech, right action, and right livelihood. The last indicates that a good Buddhist should not pursue an occupation that is necessarily in conflict with the moral precepts of Buddhism—in particular, one that involves the taking of life, such as being a butcher.

The moral requirements of Buddhism are more fully, though negatively, explicated in the Five Precepts (*pañcasīla*), binding both on lay people and on monks. These things one should refrain from: taking life, including nonhuman life; taking what is not given; sexual misconduct; wrong speech; and taking intoxicants. The ban on the deliberate taking of life partly flows from the sense of kinship with other living beings implicit in the doctrine of rebirth and partly from the nonviolent attitude (*ahiṃsā*) of Buddhism. The ban on intoxicants (both drugs and liquor) fits in with the strong emphasis on mindfulness (*sati*) or psychological self-awareness, which forms a vital ingredient in the training of oneself in serenity and perfection.

Further and more stringent rules are binding upon monks and nuns. These are designed to promote a moderate asceticism (the Buddha claimed to teach a "middle way" between extreme self-mortification and self-indulgence). Thus monks' personal possessions are drastically limited. Some offenses attract expulsion from the Order (*Sangha*), such as having sexual intercourse and falsely claiming to have attained nirvana. Since there is a strong stress on mental training, Buddhism teaches that one should restrain mental dispositions, such as lust and greed, which represent the psychological counterparts of prohibited actions. Various meditations are prescribed to uproot such dispositions. The stress on the mental side also means that a nonlegalistic interpretation of the rules is offered: it is intentional infringement which counts.

Laypeople have a central religious duty, that of giving food and alms to the members of the *Sangha* and in general of respecting and helping the community through pious works. Conversely, the monks have the duty of preaching and of instructing the laity in the doctrine (*Dhamma*). These duties are summed up as "giving" (*dāna*), as distinguished from the cultivation of personal virtue (*sīla*) as defined by the Precepts. But the need for giving extends beyond the bounds of the adherents of the faith: preaching must extend to the unconverted, while the provision of shelter and care for humans and animals is counted a meritorious act.

Behind the good behavior delineated above, there should lie a general attitude of compassion (*karunā*), which holds a place in Buddhism comparable to that of *agapē* in Christianity. Thus the scriptures record the legend of how the Buddha at the time of his enlightenment was tempted by the Evil One (Māra) to disappear into nirvana without teaching the saving truth. But out of compassion for living beings he rejected the temptation. This motif becomes prominent in the development of the Mahāyāna. The so-called Hīnayāna or "Lesser Vehicle" (a term that was originally abusive), now represented by Theravāda Buddhism in Ceylon, Burma, and parts of Southeast Asia, was criticized by adherents of the Greater Vehicle as holding up an essentially selfish ideal—that of achieving one's own salvation. By contrast the Mahāyāna pointed to the pattern of life found in the career of the Bodhisattva or Buddha-to-be, who sacrifices himself through countless lives for the welfare of living beings and who puts off his own nirvana to do this. Thus the true Buddhist treads the path of the Bodhisattva (*bodhisattvayāna*). With this there

went some reinterpretation of the doctrine of dharma. Instead of the view that one had to work off the results of prior deeds through one's own efforts, there was substituted the belief that a Bodhisattva or Buddha can transfer some of the immense store of merit accruing to him as a result of his vast series of heroic lives. It can be transferred to the otherwise unworthy faithful who call upon the Buddha; thereby they are assured of rebirth in a Paradise (the "Pure Land") where the conditions for the attainment of nirvana are especially propitious. The extreme outcome of this trend was Pure Land Buddhism, which, in its Japanese form, even went so far as to deny the efficacy of any works in bringing salvation: thus Nichiren (1222–1282) could argue that celibacy, itself a "work," was not required of monks.

The Bodhisattva ideal expressed the centrality of compassion, and became a new norm for religious conduct and self-sacrifice on behalf of others, which was built into the practice of a popular religion of worship (in the Theravāda, by contrast, the Buddha is not an object of worship).

But also, in the Theravāda, popular moral teaching of a not altogether dissimilar kind is catered for through the *Jātakas* or "Birth Stories": these are tales about previous lives of the Buddha, often incorporating, and giving a Buddhist form to, existing fables. Thus humility and self-sacrifice are commended in the story of the hare (the Buddha in a previous life) who immolates himself on the fire of a lonely and hungry holy man.

Because the Buddha rejected the claims of contemporary Brahminical religion, controlled by a priestly class, he was opposed to the religious inequality implicit in the social order later to develop into the fully articulated Hindu caste system. Thus anyone could join the *Sangha*, which transcended class and caste distinctions. The emphasis on nonviolence in Buddhism also had some social effects, for example, through the conversion of the emperor Aśoka (268–c. 233 B.C.) from a career of martial aggrandizement. These facets of the Buddhist tradition, together with the ideal of compassion, provide the basis for modern Buddhist programs of social justice. On the other hand, Buddhism has adapted itself in its long, widespread, and complex history to a variety of social orders; thus even military virtues, in medieval Japan, could come to be interpreted as a way toward liberation. This, however, was a rather exceptional application of the Buddhist way, which prides itself on the fact that it has not generated any religious wars.

S. Collins, *Selfless Persons,* 1982; H. Dayal, *The Bodhisattva Doctrine in Buddhist Sanskrit Literature,* 1932; F. E. Reynolds, "Buddhist Ethics: A Bibliographical Essay," *Religious Studies Review* 5, no. 1, 1979, pp. 40–48; H. Saddhatissa, *Buddhist Ethics: Essence of Buddhism,* 1970.

NINIAN SMART

Business Ethics

Business ethics is distinct from a more general economic ethics because of the unique roles and responsibilities of persons connected to the modern business corporation: stockholders, professional managers, entrepreneurs, and, in a different way, employees and labor. Business activities are as old as merchants and exchange but this special constellation of moral agents is relatively new, dating back to the advent of modern market society in the 18th century and developing in new directions in the 19th and 20th centuries with the growth of (1) stock ownership; (2) the separation of ownership and management in the large corporation; (3) the development of transnational corporations with their complex internal divisions of labor across national lines, their international financial structures, and their capacity to move capital quickly throughout the world, often rivaling governments in economic power and escaping various levels of government control; and (4) the emergence of a class of professional managers who, because of the power of the modern corporation, often act as "quasi-public officials" (Lindblom), and who move back and forth across the lines of private and public management. The critical role of management in the large institutions of modern society, private or public, capitalist or socialist, has blurred the line between a strictly business ethics and a more general management ethics.

Christian ethical teaching has been slow in coming to grips with these developments. Traditional teachings in the Middle Ages on the just price*, usury*, property*, and work* were part of a larger framework presupposing traditional forms of social and economic life and often hostile to business activities per se. After the development of modern market society Protestant social teaching has tended in two contrary directions: It has emphasized the individual's calling and personal integrity, often celebrating the businessperson's capacity for charity and usually ignoring the structural realities of modern capitalism*, thereby baptizing these realities; or, concerned about the competitive individualism of capitalism and the great social inequalities created by capitalism, it has proffered various communal and socialist forms of economic organization, sometimes influenced by Marxism but as often not. The great bulk of Protestant teaching has been too individualistic to mount a sustained critique of, and ethics for, the large corporate forms of modern economic life. In the USA, only during the 1930s did Protestantism find in the work of Reinhold Niebuhr and other "protestant realists" (*see* **Realism**) an articulation of the power realities of modern social life that countered prevailing individualistic assumptions. While this ethic of social power made signal contributions to legitimating labor movements and unions and, to a lesser extent, government regulation of business, it did not yet provide a framework for understanding large corporate institutions and moral agency within them.

Roman Catholic thought, never as intertwined with individualism, was much earlier and more thorough in offering teaching about modern industrial life. A series of important encyclicals, *Rerum Novarum* (1891), *Quadragesimo Anno* (1931), *Mater et Magistra* (1961), and *Populorum Progressio* (1967), recognized the exposed position of labor in modern society, arguing for the right to work, the importance of labor unions, and the obligation of government to protect the poor and weak; strove to find a middle way between "individualism"* and "collectivism"*; offered principles for the organization of social and economic life (including the principle of subsidiarity*) that would disperse power and responsibility and protect different levels of community; and called on the rich nations to help the poor nations in order to correct the defects of the world market (*see also* **Official Roman Catholic Social Teaching**). It should also be noted that the ecumenical movement* as represented by the World Council of Churches and various national church councils has done much to work for social justice and to draw attention to the plight of the hundreds of millions of peoples either outside the mainstream of modern industrial life or subservient to it. But all these efforts, as important as they are, have dealt chiefly with systemic economic problems and not with the ethical problems of modern corporate organization.

Three historical reasons lie behind this failure. First is the ironic relation between Protestant ethical life and capitalism*, documented by Weber and Tawney. The Weber thesis is that Protestant teaching, especially Calvin's, contained a tension between the moral command to pursue rigorously one's vocation* in this world as a response to and a sign of God's election, and the moral injunction against ostentation and spending, a tension that Weber called "this-worldly asceticism" and that yielded, unintentionally, a propensity to save (and thus to accumulate capital) as well as to prize rational calculation in business. Although much debated, Weber's thesis stands as a classic statement of the way in which a religious ethic can legitimate a social and economic form that was no part of its original intention. Most important, this ironic connection has made much capitalist business activity impervious to conscious ethical direction, a double irony in light of the fact that later Calvinists often forgot Calvin's teaching that abundance should be shared with the poor, and the fact that in modern capitalism an ethic of consumption has long replaced the ethic of asceticism.

Second, the classic statements of market capitalism have expressly disconnected normal conceptions of moral agency from economic action. In effect, Adam Smith and others suggested that in the economic realm the pure pursuit of self-interest would yield public benefits because of the disciplining coordination of competitive market exchange (called the "price system" in neoclassical economics). In this revolutionary transformation of the understanding of economics, ethics was reduced to privately held values and the face-to-face relations of family and small communities, while economic pursuits were released from ethical constraint. This viewpoint persists in much of the scholarly and the broader public alike, in spite of the fact that virtually no one subscribes to the 18th-century teleological world view that alone made Smith's hypotheses intelligible.

The third reason, peculiar to the USA, is that the American Constitution, following the concern of the Federalists that large private economic structures would threaten republican democracy, assigned the power of incorporation to the states on the fallacious assumption that the power of private corporations would thereby remain less than the power of the individual states. The contrary in fact happened. States competed with each other for business investment by writing liberal laws of incorporation, with the result that corporations far transcend state boundaries and purposes and, with the transnational corporation, national boundaries and purposes.

The upshot of this history is that modern business structures and activities have virtually no intended connection to their moral and political foundations and are often in direct conflict with those foundations. The fundamental task of Christian ethics in the modern world must be to formulate an ethic that takes seriously this situation and its history. Two developments in the last ten to fifteen years make important steps in this direction.

The first is the increased participation by churches and other eleemosynary institutions (especially universities and foundations) in a spectrum of shareholder activities designed to monitor, modify, and correct egregious social harm done by those corporations in which they hold stock. Not only have such efforts led to changed corporate behavior (notably in the areas of foreign investment in South Africa, environmental impact, Third World marketing practices, and community and employee relations), they also have contributed to legal decisions and literature clarifying the role of stockholders in the modern corporation.

The second development is the growth of ethics courses within business school curricula. Ethics courses had existed before, but these tended either to focus on problems of personal integrity in relation to specific cases or to be part of broader "business and society" programs that lacked genuine moral analysis. The more recent efforts have often involved teachers of ethics from the fields of philosophy, religion, and theology. The entrance of philosophers into this arena has occasioned a spate of writing on business ethics, especially on questions of moral agency in business institutions and on problems of competing claims and rights. On the whole, however, the philosophical approach to business ethics has suffered from the modern philosophical preoccupation with metaethics and epistemology. The standard approach of philosophical introductions to business ethics is to give a short outline of competing modern ethical theories (deontological, teleological, egoistic, etc.), not only rendering the issues unnecessarily abstract but also inadvertently lending credence to the moral relativism already rampant in the classroom.

In principle, theological approaches to business ethics, if they can overcome the initial alarm at (or familiarity with) things religious, have the potential to be more powerful and illuminating because of the prophetic-critical aspects of Christian moral inquiry. In this light, a complete ethics of business, focusing on management as the moral agent, would include the following themes and dimensions:

1. The development of those personal characteristics and capacities essential for all moral judgments: moral identity; character and virtue; moral perception and imagination; the capacity for ordering, judgment, and self-criticism; and critical reflection about vocation, work, and the human community.

2. A critical ethical analysis of institutions* in general, with special attention to institutional roles and moral agency; the parallel between individual virtues (and vices) and institutional patterns; the nature of power in institutions and the tendency of power to distort perception, communication, and moral agency.

3. A critical ethical analysis of the special features of the modern business corporation, including the history and ideology of the corporation and business; the various "constituencies" or "stakeholders" of the corporation (labor, owners, management, community, suppliers, customers, nation); and the inherent tension (but not necessarily opposition) between two corporate dimensions: (a) its pursuit of profits, the emphasis on instrumental reason and values, the focus on "external goods"; and (b) the corporation's moral subservience to—and reliance on—cooperation and the cooperative virtues, human ends, "internal goods."

4. A critical ethical analysis of market society and capitalism, including its history and ideology; the peculiar relation and roles of owners and workers and the special vulnerability of the latter; the strengths and weaknesses of the market as a system of social coordination; the impact of markets and business in the Third World; and especially a normative framework for understanding the appropriate spheres and limits of exchange relationships in human society.

5. An integrating of these elements of moral judgment with the perceptual and analytical tools of managerial judgment. This inevitably involves the use of cases and of cross-disciplinary work. If integrated, they may yield a fairly radical understanding of management responsibility together with possible institutional health. If not integrated, they will be perceived as external constraints to be observed when possible but the first to go as luxuries in difficult times.

Three concluding points about such a program. First, any one of these themes pushed far enough will reach its theological foundation and presuppositions about human vocation, the nature and meaning of community, of human work and creation, of freedom and history, of the ground and extent of evil and wrongdoing.

Second, and consequently, any such program of business ethics has necessarily subversive aspects insofar as the moral identity not only of the Christian but of any thoughtful person must transcend the roles, responsibilities, and purposes of the business institution. It is in such a light that programs of corporate responsibility within businesses must be evaluated. If they do not include a frank awareness that moral identity and loyalty *must* transcend the business world, they will turn out only to serve business interests.

Third, ultimately business ethics must find its chief place within the teaching of local churches, among business people and managers who find their basic moral identity there. Programs in businesses and in business schools can at best be allies.

The two classics on religion and business are M. Weber, *The Protestant Ethic and the Spirit of Capitalism,* ET 1930; and R. H. Tawney, *Religion and the Rise of Capitalism,* 1926. On the market system, democracy, and the business corporation, see C. E. Lindblom, *Politics and Markets,* 1977; G. McConnell, *Private Government and American Democracy,* 1967; J. Schumpeter, *Capitalism, Socialism, and Democracy,* ³1950. On stockholder responsibilities, see C. W. Powers, *Investments and Social Responsibility,* 1971; J. G. Simon, C. W. Powers, and J. P. Gunnemann, *The Ethical Investor,* 1972. At present writing the best selection of journal articles on business ethics, with an excellent bibliography, is T. Beauchamp and N. Bowie (eds.), *Ethical Theory and Business,* 1979.

JON P. GUNNEMANN

Calling *see* **Vocation;** *see also* **Calvinist Ethics; Lutheran Ethics; Work, Doctrine of**

Calvinist Ethics

For John Calvin (1509–1564), "the surest foundations of a well-regulated life" are in God's grace and our grateful response. "Ever since God exhibited himself to us as a Father, we must be convicted of extreme ingratitude if we do not in our turn exhibit ourselves as his sons" (*Institutes* 3.6.3). The Calvinist ethic is an ethic of grateful obedience* (*see* **Gratitude**).

Although "men cannot open their eyes without being compelled to see him" (1.5.1), and our consciences testify to his righteousness, yet our sinful corruption is such that a natural knowledge of God and of his law serves only to leave us without excuse. For although God's goodness is there before our eyes, we are so blinded by sin that we cannot see it. Therefore God gave the written law, which "removes the obscurity of the law of nature" (2.8.1).

In dealing with the law, Calvin, like Luther, draws much on Augustine (*see* **Law and Gospel**). The first use of the law is to lead us to Christ. It is a kind of mirror in which we see our iniquity (2.7.7). It leads us to implore the help of divine grace. "In the precepts of the Law, God is seen as the rewarder only of perfect righteousness . . . , but in Christ his countenance beams forth full of grace and gentleness towards poor unworthy sinners" (2.7.8). The second use of the law is to curb human violence and excess. "This forced and extorted righteousness is necessary for the good of society, its peace being procured by a provision but for which all things would be thrown into tumult and confusion" (2.7.10). This restraint is also a merciful provision for those who are not yet regenerate. In both these uses, the law is our schoolmaster. For Luther, these two, the spiritual and the civil, are the only uses of the law. For Calvin, the third use is the principal use, when believers "in whose hearts the Spirit of God already flourishes and reigns" find in the law a

teacher "to learn what that will of God is which they aspire to follow," and also a spur, a stimulus to encourage them (2.7.12).

Calvin denies that the law is totally abrogated. The curse of the law is certainly abrogated, for Christians are not under law, but under grace. The ceremonies of the Jewish religion are abrogated, as regards their use. But even the old ceremonial law still has a meaning, as pointing to Christ in whom it is fulfilled, and the moral law remains "a perfect rule of righteousness" (2.8.5), to show us that nothing is more acceptable to God than obedience. Calvin interprets the Ten Commandments in the light of the two great commandments, love to God and love to the neighbor, and regards the sayings of the Sermon on the Mount not as an addition to the commandments, but as their true interpretation.

Yet when he comes to speak of the Christian life, Calvin seems to set the law aside. "Although the law of God contains a perfect rule of conduct admirably arranged, it has seemed proper to our divine Master to train his people by a more accurate method, to the rule which is enjoined in the Law; and the leading principle in the method is, that it is the duty of believers to present their 'bodies a living sacrifice, holy and acceptable unto God, which is their reasonable service' (Rom. 12:1)" (3.7.1). This grateful self-offering to God, Calvin calls "self-denial."* "The Christian ought indeed to be so trained and disposed as to consider that during his whole life he has to do with God. . . . For he who has so learned to look to God in everything he does is at the same time diverted from all vain thoughts. This is . . . self-denial" (3.7.2). "We are not our own. . . . We are God's." These are the reiterated themes of self-denial.

Just as in his treatment of law Calvin holds together worship and ethics, love of God and love of the neighbor, as our grateful obedience, so self-denial has respect to God and to the neighbor. In regard to the neighbor it is that charity which seeks the neighbor's good, whoever he or she is, and is ready to share with that person our blessings. "Everyone should consider that however great he is, he owes himself to his neighbors, and that the only limit to his beneficence is the failure of his means" (3.7.7). But since human greed, self-seeking, and the dread of poverty spring from man's insecurity and fear, the principal part of self-denial has respect to God: that

Christians "must not long for, or hope for, or think of any kind of prosperity apart from the blessing of God; on it they must cast themselves and there safely and confidently recline" (3.7.8).

The belief that "all prosperous and desirable success depends entirely on the blessing of God" (3.7.9) restrains Christians from the unscrupulous quest for riches and honor, and enables them to endure hardship and to bear the cross with patience and resignation, as persons who have placed their lives entirely at God's disposal. There is a right use of earthly blessings (3.10.1), a moderation which avoids both excessive austerity and all license, while remembering that they are given "not only for our necessity, but also for our enjoyment and delight" (3.10.2). Calvin, it may seem, leans more on the side of austerity than on that of license, but he is concerned for that moderate enjoyment of God's good gifts which is never unmindful whence these blessings come, nor ever forgetful of the needs of the neighbor (*see* **Temperance**).

Christians will meditate on the future life, and this assists them to place their lives at God's disposal. "If heaven is our country, what can earth be but a place of exile?" (3. 9.4). Nevertheless, it is in this world that God's will is to be obeyed and his blessings enjoyed and shared. And, since we are to look to God in everything that we do, life is not divided into religious and secular spheres. All things are done to the glory of God and the good of the neighbor. Calvin, it has been said, "laicized piety."

The life of self-denial is clearly not ruled by legalism* but by personal devotion. Why then does Calvin lay such stress on the law, and in particular on the third use of the law, as the instructor and stimulus of Christian living? One reason for this may be that the law not only instructs us about what God requires, it shows us also what he does *not* require. Calvin considers the human heart to be a veritable manufactory of idols. "The human mind, in its wantonness, is ever and anon inventing different modes of worship as a means of gaining his favor. This irreligious affectation of religion being innate in the human mind, has betrayed itself in every age, and is still doing so, men always longing to devise some method of procuring righteousness without any sanction from the Word of God" (2.8.5). The law can be a means to prevent consciences from being enslaved to

human rules and requirements, and to liberate them from such enslavement, for "to go a-wandering after good works which are not prescribed by the Law of God is an intolerable violation of true and divine righteousness" (2.8.5).

The fact that scripture alone is the divinely given authority means also that the existing hierarchical authority of church or of state cannot claim ultimate authority. It has authority only by the sanction of scripture. Calvinists tended to apply this principle more immediately and fiercely to church polity and worship than to the political order. Calvin took the traditional view of authority as being "by God's decree." He was concerned to avoid both the anarchism* of some Christian idealists, rejecting civil government altogether, and the complacency of "the flatterers of princes," who did not see it as subject to the Word of God. Christians, he believed, should be content with the form of government they have, and the right of resistance* to tyrants belongs only to the lower magistrates, or to champions raised up by God. Nevertheless, Calvinism did produce resistance to tyrants, not least because Calvin maintained that the office of magistrate extended to both tables of the law, and that his first duty was to establish and support the true religion. It was where the magistrate sought to suppress the Reformed religion that resistance began. But the principle was capable of being extended to the reform of government, and Calvin's view that "the law is a dumb magistrate, the magistrate a living law" (4.20.14) would be developed in political thought by Samuel Rutherford and others. Calvinists generally seem to have moved toward a representative type of democracy*, perhaps because the church organization of Presbyterianism is congenial to that. However, the Calvinist ethic, like the ethic of natural law, can be developed either in a conservative or in a radical political direction.

Later Calvinism tended to interpret Calvin's ethics more in terms of law than in terms of self-denial, but the element of commitment to a personal divine will was never lost, and it can emerge in some modern writers in terms that are almost situationist— an ethic of the divine command rather than of the divine law (*see* **Modern Protestant Ethics**).

The controversy which arose over Max Weber's *The Protestant Ethic and the Spirit of*

Capitalism (1905; ET 1930) continues (*see* **Sociology of Ethics**). Calvin himself, who set severe limitations on usury* and saw divine blessings as a trust to benefit one's neighbor, scarcely represents the spirit of capitalism*. The revival of the OT concept of "divine blessings" and the sense that we look to God in everything that we do, did, however, give a dignity to worldly activity as the sphere of our grateful obedience (*see* **Vocation**). Whether this justifies the Weber thesis is another matter.

Today the authority of the Word, and the legalism in which that was often expressed, cannot be used in the simple way Calvinists thought possible in the past. Yet there are resources in Calvin's own thought which could be developed beyond the "work-ethic" toward a more human and caring community.

A. Biéler, *The Social Humanism of Calvin*, ET 1964; J. T. McNeill, *The History and Character of Calvinism*, 1954; G. Marshall, *In Search of the Spirit of Capitalism*, 1982; E. Troeltsch, *The Social Teaching of the Christian Churches* (1912), ET 1931, vol. 2; R. S. Wallace, *Calvin's Doctrine of the Christian Life*, 1959.

JAMES A. WHYTE

Canon Law

The body of rules which the Christian community makes for the government of its own internal affairs and the conduct of its members. The Greek word *kanōn*, meaning a rule, is used by Paul, and perhaps even the most enthusiastic champions of "situation ethics" would hardly deny that the church, like any other corporate body, needs some basic rules if it is to function or even survive. In Acts 15 it is stated that the apostolic college in Jerusalem laid down some minimal rules to be observed by Gentile Christians. As time went on, the number of rules multiplied, and in the Middle Ages they were codified in the Western church in the *Corpus Iuris Canonici*. When the Roman Catholic Church revised its canon law in 1918, there were no less than 2,414 canons. Following Vatican Council II, there was a further revision, effective in 1983. The Church of England adapted the medieval canons to its own needs. Its canon law dates from 1604, revised in 1969. The canon law of the Eastern church consists of conciliar decrees. The expression "canon law" is not used among Protestants, though of course they have their own regulations.

Much of canon law is concerned with ecclesiastical questions that have no particular ethical significance, e.g., rules about ordination and admission to the sacraments. But there are areas where canon law and ethics overlap, e.g., marriage* discipline. In earlier times, when church and state were intimately bound up with each other, the canon law relating to marriage and sexual conduct was similar to that of the state. But with the separation of church and state (*see* **Church and State**), either in law or in fact, canon law has likewise become separated from civil law. If, for instance, the Christian ideal of marriage as lifelong monogamous union is to be maintained, the church has to lay down certain rules for its own members, but even in strongly Roman Catholic countries it is now recognized that these rules cannot be imposed on society at large, and the civil laws are much less stringent (*see* **Morality, Legal Enforcement of**). In such matters therefore the authority of canon law depends on the free consent of the Christians who belong to the community in which this law holds.

R. C. Mortimer, *Western Canon Law*, 1953; E. W. Kemp, *An Introduction to Canon Law in the Church of England*, 1957.

JOHN MACQUARRIE

Capitalism

Capitalism as an economic system is difficult to define, partly because one's evaluation of it is often implicit in the definition, but also because of the variety of kinds of capitalism in the countries that profess to have such systems. However, a definition such as this can be proposed: capitalism is that economic system in which the price mechanism, working through supply and demand in workably competitive markets, provides the dominant mode of making economic decisions about what is produced, how it is produced, and in what way it is distributed. Capitalist systems are also characterized by nongovernmental ownership of the means of production; economic freedom to enter and exit the market as producer, consumer, investor, or laborer; a legal order that protects voluntary and peaceful exchange; and a motivational system that includes rational and systematic pursuit of profit as a primary spring.

Such a system for making economic

choices can be combined with a variety of political systems. Though capitalist economies and liberal democracies have been closely associated historically, it is possible to combine capitalism with authoritarian governments of various sorts. In fact, the strongest critics of capitalism claim that it can fit with totalitarian fascism*, although it is difficult to see how the economic freedom associated with open markets could be allowed in a totalitarian context (*see* **Totalitarian State**).

Parties in the economic debate generally grant that all human societies have markets of some kind due to the human propensity "to truck, barter and exchange one thing for another" (Smith, 1776). They also agree that this small-scale commercial capitalism developed into industrial capitalism in England during the 18th century (see **Industrial Revolution**). Most affirm Max Weber's thesis that a certain kind of Protestant piety (inner-worldly asceticism) provided important motivation and legitimation for that development. After Marx, however, it has been almost impossible to agree on the description of what indeed capitalism is, let alone an analysis and evaluation of its effects.

Marx, who first used the adjective "capitalist," argued that there never were such things as fair competitive markets. Owners of private property gained profits by extracting surplus from labor. Capitalism in his view was intrinsically exploitative. The Marxist tradition argues that we are in the period of "late" capitalism, in which the contradictions latent in monopoly capitalism will lead to inevitable crises, and ultimately to revolution* (*see* **Marxist Ethics**).

Another major negative, though non-Marxist, interpretation of capitalism emerged from the left wing of the Keynesian school. R. H. Chamberlain, J. V. Robinson, A. Hansen, and J. K. Galbraith argued that competitive markets in industrial capitalism were largely a fiction. Since noncompetitive markets could not be trusted to set prices efficiently and fairly, public interventions were called for. Such interventions would lead gradually to a more humane and just democratic socialism.

However, such views of capitalism have not been predominant in Western countries. Mainstream economics—in its classical and neoclassical forms—has argued that capitalist systems have been generally characterized by "workable" competition, and that competitive market systems have produced remarkable results in raising the living standards of the vast majority of persons in societies where such systems have operated. Mainstream economists have believed that governments must ensure the competitive nature of the economy by antimonopoly measures, and otherwise have affirmed an active role for the state in forging monetary and fiscal policy as well as providing minimum welfare for all.

A number of dissenting economists and philosophers of a libertarian bent—M. Friedman, L. von Mises, F. von Hayek, R. Nozick—challenge such an expanded role for the state. They argue that what distortions of the market exist are caused by unwise and ineffective government interventions. With great confidence in the self-regulating capacities of the market, they counsel a more limited state and more expansive use of market mechanisms, even in areas that are generally not viewed as "economic."

With such variety in viewpoint among economists, it is scarcely surprising that religious ethics is as divided as it is in its description, analysis, and evaluation of capitalism. While there are few proponents of libertarian economic philosophy (*see* **Libertarianism**) among theologians and ethicists, there are many supporters of laissez-faire* among the laity of the churches.

However, the dominant attitude among religious ethicists has been negative toward capitalism and positive toward some form of democratic socialism*. There are clear reasons for this attitude in the recent history of Christian ethics. Such English religious thinkers as C. Kingsley and F. D. Maurice offered a socialist analysis and critique of developing 19th-century capitalism. They in turn influenced American social gospel thinking. Further, the European tradition of religious ethics, carried out in the shadow of Marx, generated hostility toward capitalism and affinity for socialism, as evidenced in the ethical reflections of both Paul Tillich and Karl Barth. In America, the young Reinhold Niebuhr brought prophetic judgment to bear on American capitalism.

In general, American Christian ethics has carried on this critical orientation, reinforced in recent years by neo-Marxist analyses employed by Latin American, black, and feminist liberation theologies*.

While there is little unanimity among this majority about the shape of democratic socialism, they tend to agree on a basic critique of capitalism. It enshrines greed as the motivating force of economic life; its mode of decision-making is nondemocratic; its monopolistic character leads to concentrations of economic power that distort American politics; capitalism leads to intolerable inequalities of wealth and income; it is ecologically destructive; it generates cultural vulgarity and commercialism*; and it impoverishes the developing world.

Such a litany of abuses has been challenged by a growing number of religious ethicists who not only question the empirical validity of the charges but lift up a number of practical and moral values that are supported by capitalism. Writers such as P. Heyne, M. Novak, G. Gilder, and R. Benne argue for a more positive moral assessment of democratic capitalism, ranging from the celebrative to the ambiguously positive.

See **Ecumenical Movement; Collectivism; Communism; Equality; Freedom; Individualism; Laissez-faire; Liberalism; Official Roman Catholic Social Teaching; Property; Socialism; State; Welfare State.**

R. Benne, *The Ethic of Democratic Capitalism,* 1981; V. A. Demant, *Religion and the Decline of Capitalism,* 1952; R. H. Preston, *Religion and the Persistence of Capitalism,* 1979; J. Schumpeter, *Capitalism, Socialism, and Democracy,* ³1950; A. Shonfield, *Modern Capitalism,* 1969; Adam Smith, *An Inquiry Into the Nature and Causes of the Wealth of Nations,* 1776; R. H. Tawney, *Religion and the Rise of Capitalism,* 1925; C. West, *Prophesy Deliverance!* 1982; J. P. Wogaman, *The Great Economic Debate,* 1977.

ROBERT BENNE

Capital Punishment

The Christian faith came into a world in which capital punishment was an accepted feature of the legal system, as we can see from the words of the penitent thief on his cross (Luke 23:41) and of Paul before Festus (Acts 25:11). So it has been in almost all known states before Christ and since. Only in recent times has capital punishment been questioned; it has been retained by very few Western European countries or those of Anglo-Saxon origin in other parts of the world; in the USA the practice varies among different states. The Gospels do not directly bear on the matter, but when the church came seriously to consider the role of the state* and its duties it tended to take capital punishment for granted. Lactantius was one of the few early fathers to oppose it. In using the Bible as a textbook of detailed ethical injunctions, the fathers had recourse chiefly to Genesis, Romans, and 1 Peter. God said to Noah, "Whoever sheds the blood of man, by man shall his blood be shed; for God made man in his own image" (Gen. 9:6). This can be read as a statement of fact—God's providence will catch up with the slayer; or it can be read as a command to execute the death penalty for the reason stated—i.e., either because human beings made in God's image have the divine authority to do so, or because of the serious offense in killing someone made in God's image and thus assaulting God himself. The commandment translated "You shall not kill" clearly means "You shall not commit murder" (though without giving any guidance as to what kinds of killing are to be accounted as murder) and does not abrogate the Genesis text. Moreover, it is held that Jesus by implication did not abrogate it, although he did abrogate death as a penalty for adultery and substituted divorce (a precarious argument from silence). So we come to Rom. 13:1–7, and especially v. 4, which says that the ruler "does not bear the sword in vain; he is the servant of God to execute his wrath on the wrongdoer" (cf. 1 Peter 2:13–17). Those who depend on these passages maintain that there is a uniqueness about murder which demands a unique penalty; and that the reason advanced in Genesis, that humanity is made in God's image, is perennially relevant. They say that it is the duty of the state to administer capital punishment (to remove it from private vengeance) as part of its task, ordained by God, to maintain order and the possibility of the properly ordered human life that he wills for those made in his image. Note that these reasons preclude the death penalty for many crimes for which it has in fact had Christian approval in the past —though the list of crimes punishable by death might be stretched to include treason, on the grounds that treason undermines the state's task of maintaining order against aggression.

There are, however, many other considerations. The New Testament itself has other things to say about the same Roman state when it opposed Christians (e.g., Revelation). And what are we to say of basically brutal and unjust governments? Moreover, Jesus' gospel was primarily concerned with God's initiative in graciousness toward the most sinful, not primarily about his wish that an exact *quid pro quo* should be exacted from a murderer. This suggests at least that the death penalty should be enforced reluctantly, if at all. In considering the justification for the imposition of the death penalty (and other punishments) by the state, three theories have provided a possible common ground between Christians and others, and they all would modify the rigor of those whose position has so far been outlined.

1. Deterrence. If it could be shown that the death penalty had a significant deterrent effect on the number of murders, there would be a case for it. But exhaustive investigations in Europe and North America have shown that there is no such evidence, but rather that the number of murders varies little whether there is a death penalty or not. One is most likely to be murdered by a member of one's own family or a near relation as a result of some emotional crisis in which considerations of rational self-interest and the death penalty have negligible influence. In the case of cold-blooded murder it is the likelihood of being caught that is important. Capital punishment may on occasion be a regrettable necessity on this ground; but we need to ask ourselves what it is in so many people which leads them so firmly to advocate it as a deterrent and refuse to face the evidence of its ineffectiveness?

2. Reformation. Capital punishment can have little relevance on this ground, except on occasion to produce a deathbed repentance. But few would advocate such a drastic means of producing this possible effect; and it is disingenuous to argue that the more Christian one is, the less one is perturbed by the death penalty because of one's belief in life beyond death, for we are concerned with *state* policy.

3. Retribution. In July 1976 the US Supreme Court said that capital punishment was not "a cruel and unusual" punishment; the court agreed that it had no convincing deterrent effect but held that the question of retribution remained. Some Christians doubt whether this is a legitimate Christian basis for punishment, but most see that it does bear witness to the dignity of the human person in assuming that the individual is responsible for his or her actions, and that part of growth into maturity is facing the consequences of one's actions, in this case wrongdoing. But does the Christian faith *require,* in the case of murder, the taking of the murderer's life in retribution? Sometimes all these theories of punishment are denied on the grounds that crime is a sickness to be cured not punished, and that as such it requires therapy not judicial proceedings; this obviously rules out the death penalty. This position has some truth, hence our arguments about "diminished responsibility," but it is a dangerous one if taken too far, for it turns human beings into moral invalids (*see* **Responsibility**).

Capital punishment has many disadvantages. It is unpleasant for those who have to carry it out. It has a bad effect on the public, which alternates between fits of self-righteousness and morbid gloating over its victims. Miscarriages of justice cannot be corrected, and a number of such cases have come to light. If, however, capital punishment is thought by Christians to be necessary on occasion, they must will the means as well as the end. It must be a Christian vocation to be a judge, a prison officer, or an executioner and to carry it out for the common good; Christians cannot leave to others the doing of unpleasant tasks. In short, in the general Christian view of the state and of punishment, capital punishment is not excluded, but neither is it required; rather, what is required is a strong case in particular circumstances to justify it. A last attempt to do so is to say that a long prison sentence is worse than death. But (*a*) prisoners are not given the choice, nor is it proper that they should be; (*b*) a civilized community should find a constructive punishment that is not worse than death for a grave crime.

See also **Homicide; Image of God; Penology.**

H. A. Bedau (ed.), *The Death Penalty in America,* ³1982.

RONALD PRESTON

Capital Sins *see* Seven Deadly Sins

Cardinal Virtues

The tradition of the cardinal virtues stems from book 4 of Plato's *Republic*, in which the four cardinal or principal virtues are linked to the three parts of the soul (reason, spirit, desire) and to the three parts of the polity (philosopher-rulers, guardians, artisans). The four cardinal virtues recognized there are: prudence* or practical wisdom, justice*, temperance* or self-control, fortitude or courage*. They are treated in a more phenomenological fashion in the *Nicomachean Ethics* of Aristotle, who does not give them so clear a primacy as do most of the classical and medieval writers on ethics. Cicero organizes his treatment of moral obligations in the *De Officiis* (*On Duties*) under the heading of the cardinal virtues, among which justice occupies the first place. In the fourth century Ambrose takes the schema of the four cardinal virtues over into his Ciceronian treatise for the instruction of the clergy, *De Officiis Ministrorum*, and many subsequent patristic and medieval writers used the cardinal virtues in allegorical interpretations of scripture. The cardinal virtues also figure prominently in medieval iconography. Augustine makes two crucial contributions to the theological interpretation of the virtues. The first is to define the cardinal virtues of classical philosophy as forms of love with God as their primary object (*On the Morals of the Catholic Church* 15). The second is to maintain that virtues which make no reference to God and which are sought for themselves without true religion are not genuine virtues (*City of God* 19.25).

This contention was to be fundamental for the negative Reformation assessment of natural or secular or human virtues that are not rooted in God. Thomas Aquinas argues that there are exactly four cardinal virtues: (1) the good of reason present in the judgment is prudence; (2) the order of reason with regard to actions affecting others and present in the will as its subject is justice; (3) the order of reason with regard to the passions when these draw us to something irrational is temperance and is in the concupiscible appetite; and (4) the order of reason with regard to the passions when these draw us away from a reasonable course of action is fortitude and is in the irascible appetite (*ST* I-II.61.3c). These virtues then have distinct objects but are also interconnected as qualities of good actions. They are subordinate to the three theological virtues* of faith*, hope*, and charity*, which have God as their object and which are caused or infused directly by God. Virtues, for Aquinas as for Aristotle, are principles of action, "operative habits,"

which enable human beings to perform good actions easily and well. Aquinas teaches that in addition to the acquired moral virtues recognized by classical philosophy there are also infused moral virtues that enable us to perform actions of supernatural worth. This view was rejected by Duns Scotus, who held that this was a needless duplication of causes.

Precisely because virtues are necessary for good action and are constitutive of good character, controversy has raged among theologians and philosophers about the extent to which they can be possessed by persons who are not good or not in union with God. Disputes on this topic arise both from differing conceptions of nature and grace and from the fact that virtues are intermediate between the two standard starting points for our moral evaluations of persons, namely, their interior dispositions and intentions and their actions. The Aristotelian conception of virtue stresses the acquisition of virtue through action, whereas the Augustinian makes virtue dependent on the orientation to God.

Another area of uncertainty is whether cardinal virtues are to be thought of as forming a schema for the classification of good dispositions of character or as distinct causal powers that are effective in subordinate virtues.

See **Character; Virtue; Aristotelian Ethics; Augustinian Ethics; Platonic Ethics; Stoic Ethics; Thomistic Ethics.**

P. Geach, *The Virtues*, 1977; G. Gilleman, *The Primacy of Charity in Moral Theology*, 1959; G. Klubertanz, *Habits and Virtues*, 1965; O. Lottin, *Psychologie et morals, aux XIIe et XIIIe siècles*, 1942; J. Pieper, *The Four Cardinal Virtues*, ET 1965; J. Wallace, *Virtues and Vices*, 1978.

JOHN LANGAN, S.J.

Care

Often used interchangeably with agape, or love* of neighbor*, as in Jesus' parable of the good Samaritan (Luke 10:29–37), which explicates the love commandment through the language of care, compassion*, and mercy*. The good Samaritan "took care of" the injured man and instructed the innkeeper to "take care of him." It is important to distinguish "caring for," which involves attitudes and motives of compassion and mercy, from "taking care of," which involves effective actions often but not always out of the motive of care. For example, professionals who provide health care and medical care may have motives other than care (see **Mixed Motives**). Finally, there is the moral and legal requirement of "due care," which dictates at least minimally how caring for and taking care of others should be carried out (see **Negligence**).

See **Aged, Care of the; Charity; Handicapped, Care of the; Health Care, Right to; Love; Mutual Aid; Philanthropy; Sick, Care of the; Social Service of the Church.**

JAMES F. CHILDRESS

Caroline Moral Theology
see **Anglican Moral Theology**

Casti Connubii see **Contraception**

Casuistry

Casuistry carries, in English and European languages, a meaning almost exclusively pejorative. Derived from *casus,* "occasion" or "case," it refers to any form of argument, usually about moral or legal issues, that employs subtle distinctions and twisted logic in order to justify some act that would be generally considered disreputable. In this sense, casuistry is to moral argument what sophistry is to philosophical argument in general. However, casuistry also refers to an actual style of presenting and analyzing moral issues that developed in the late Middle Ages and flourished from about 1550 to 1650, particularly in the Catholic countries of Europe. In this sense, casuistry (or "cases of conscience" as the style was usually called) is the attempt to formulate expert opinion about the existence and stringency of moral obligation in typical situations where some general precept would seem to require interpretation due to circumstances. Although this literature occasionally lapsed into the sort of reasoning that earned the pejorative connotation, it was, on the whole, solid, discerning, and cautious in its treatment of moral issues.

The basic question for moral casuistry asks how some general, commonly acknowledged moral precept is to be understood in some typical set of circumstances. These circumstances might be such as to make observance of the precept very difficult or to lead to some burdensome and perhaps immoral result; they may be such that another contradictory precept would seem to have equal claim to

obedience. Sometimes, crucial terms of the precept are unclear or the situation is so new and unusual as to raise doubts whether the precept applies to it. These sorts of problems are common in all discussions of morality. They become particularly urgent when there is a strong sense of moral duty together with a definite set of moral precepts stated in universal terms. This is characteristic of the great ethical monotheistic religions, Judaism, Christianity, and Islam. In each, a sovereign God rules creation and humanity; the divine rule over humanity is accomplished by the revelation of imperatives and prohibitions regarding certain general forms of human behavior. The faithful must continually attempt to follow these commandments in their own cultural, historic, and personal situation. Thus, in these three faiths, it became common for religious teachers to formulate opinions instructing the faithful how they were to observe the law of God in their lives.

In Judaism, *halakhah,* the authoritative interpretation of the moral precepts of Torah and Talmud, became the constant study of rabbis. In Islam, *Sharī'a,* the holy law of Islam revealed in the Qur'ān, was interpreted by its students, the muftis, who issued opinions, *fatwā,* for the guidance of the faithful in civic affairs, economic matters, and daily life. Both of these religious activities were influenced by the rediscovery of Aristotelian philosophy in the Middle Ages, and forms of interpretation were shaped according to the canons of logic and rhetoric. This led, in both cases, to a body of moral interpretation that was extremely subtle and (in the eyes of its critics) sometimes quite perverse and evasive. In Judaism, the style of argument called *pilpul* ("sharp as pepper") was accused of excessive intricacy; in Islam, *ḥiyal* ("stratagems") stretched the law to take account of human frailty. In Catholicism, a similar pattern developed, as the subsequent section will show. Thus, the common problem of all morality, how to apply universal precepts to particular circumstances, has appeared with particular clarity in the ethical monotheistic religions. The history of their way of handling this problem is instructive: on the one hand, it reveals certain important features of moral reasoning, on the other, the temptation to slip into subtleties that subvert the meaning and intent of morality also is evident. In each of these religions there is a serious casuistry—the careful, devout effort to discover, by reflection and discussion, the right course of action in typical circumstances; and there is a sophistic casuistry—the clever exercise of ingenuity to evade the inconvenient. It is appropriate in this discussion to follow only the history of Christian casuistry.

The moral teaching of the Christian church, contained in the NT and the writings of the church fathers and the Councils, stressed the broad imperatives of love*, humility*, mercy*. The Gospels contain some "casuistry" when Jesus interprets rabbinic obligations (see the Gospel of Matthew). Paul becomes a casuist in explaining the relationships of Christians to Jews and Gentiles (see 1 Corinthians). The Stoic philosophers, particularly of the middle period (mid-2nd century B.C.), devised a casuistry of duties with which many church fathers were familiar (see **Patristic Ethics; Stoic Ethics**). Clement of Alexandria initiated this casuistry in the *Pedagogue* and *Who Is the Rich Man That Is Saved?;* Ambrose wrote *On the Duties of the Clergy,* modeled after Cicero's *On Duties,* which related many of the classical Stoic cases; and Augustine's *On Lying* is an extended, subtle casuistry. However, the first strong impetus to casuistry came in the Penitential Books, composed in the British Isles in the 7th to 10th centuries. These books listed sins and appropriate penances for the instruction of priests receiving the private confession of penitents—a novel practice that became common in the Western church only in the 13th century. After the Fourth Lateran Council (1215) mandated annual confession for all Christians, more elaborate books appeared that not only listed sins and penances but defined sorts of action, distinguished seriousness, presented mitigating circumstances, and stated, in brief fashion, reasons for these positions. These confessional books flourished for several centuries, but in the 15th century had become stereotyped.

In the mid-16th century it became obvious that a more creative approach was needed: many new problems arose in the wake of the Reformation, the discovery of new lands, the emergence of a mercantile economy, and the development of the nation-state (see **Counter-Reformation Moral Theology; Modern Roman Catholic Moral Theology**). The Society of Jesus was founded to come to grips with these problems (1540) and began to produce prodigious numbers of theoretical and practical books about moral issues. They be-

came the principal (but not the only) casuists. Rather than attempt global analysis of moral problems, they made "case by case" analyses, stressing the relevance of various circumstances to the stringency of principles in question. They attended not only to the major questions of politics, economics, and religion but also to the minor moral perplexities about lying, gossiping, cheating, etc. They were particularly concerned to state the degree of certainty which various opinions enjoyed (see **Equiprobabilism; Probabiliorism; Probabilism; Tutiorism**). In the mid-17th century the Jansenists, a devout but somewhat unorthodox party of French Catholics, entered into theological and political disputes with the Jesuits. One of the Jansenist sympathizers was the genius mathematician Blaise Pascal, who was persuaded to write a polemic against Jesuit theology. He chose to attack casuistry and did so with a witty sarcasm that made the *Provincial Letters* (1656–57) a classic. His accusation that casuistry fostered a laxity and skepticism incompatible with Christian morality, and his clever description of casuistry as a hash of logic-chopping and meaningless distinctions, tarnished the enterprise for the future.

Papal decrees condemned both laxist and rigorist casuistry (1679, 1690), but not casuistry itself. It continued to be an integral part of Roman Catholic moral theology. The greatest casuist was the mid-eighteenth-century bishop Alphonsus Liguori (d. 1787), who, drawing from the tradition, gave incisive original analyses of many moral problems. In the 20th century, some skillful and solid casuistry has illuminated issues such as the just wage, abortion, contraception, euthanasia, saturation bombing, and nuclear deterrence. However, contemporary Roman Catholic moralists are generally unenthusiastic, considering casuistry legalistic, minimalist, and individualistic rather than theologically informed, inspirational, and communal. Yet, as those whose tradition fostered casuistry neglect it, moral philosophers are coming to find its approach interesting as a mode of analysis of the many new moral problems in medicine, politics, business, etc. (see **Applied Ethics**).

Outside Roman Catholicism, casuistry has not flourished, with the exception of a vigorous "case divinity" in the Anglican and Puritan traditions during the 17th century (see **Anglican Moral Theology; Puritan Ethics**).

Taylor, Sanderson, Baxter, and Perkins stressed the importance of an informed conscience in the absence of an authoritative clergy and were more hortatory and inspirational than their Roman Catholic counterparts. This tradition survived in Anglican theologians like Kenneth Kirk, who wrote the only modern scholarly study of casuistry. Joseph Fletcher's "situation ethics"* is a faint image of this tradition.

In Protestant theology, casuistry was generally viewed with skepticism and regarded as a legalism* that fostered false conscience and salvation by works. Still, some Protestant theologians, such as Edward L. Long, have recognized the usefulness of the casuistic approach.

K. E. Kirk, *Conscience and Its Problems*, 1927.

ALBERT R. JONSEN

Categorical Imperative

Kant makes a distinction between hypothetical imperatives, which command an action merely as a means to a given end and therefore have no validity for us unless we wish to attain the end, and categorical imperatives, which command an act as good in itself and therefore as necessary if our will is to conform to reason. The latter only are held by him to be moral imperatives, so that the distinction leads to an ethical system which in opposition to all forms of utilitarianism* avoids basing our obligations on consequences. There is indeed one end which none of us can help desiring, happiness*, thus giving rise to what he calls an "assertoric imperative," but even the fact that the end is actually pursued by everybody does not make the imperative to pursue it "categorical."

See **Kantian Ethics.**

A. C. EWING

Catholic Moral Theology

see **Counter-Reformation Moral Theology; Modern Roman Catholic Moral Theology; Moral Theology; Thomistic Ethics**

Catholic Social Teaching

see **Official Roman Catholic Social Teaching**

Celibacy

Originally, simply the unmarried state—in Latin *coelebs* is "bachelor," as in the imperial laws intended to encourage marriage. But the term is commonly used for acceptance of the single state as a religious duty, whether by vow or under some general obligation. Perhaps in view of God's approaching judgment, the early church deprecated the marriage of adult converts (cf. 1 Cor. 7:20–27); some parts of the Syrian church in the 2nd and 3rd centuries seem to have insisted on either marriage or commitment to celibacy before baptism. In some heretical sects, and semi-Christian groups such as the Manicheans, only the celibate were considered full members, and others remained in a status similar to that of catechumens.

What was once expected of the laity continued to be demanded of the clergy, and marriage after ordination was rare if not unknown—a rule further strengthened by the reverence for ascetics which made it natural to select celibates for the higher positions in the church. In 451 the Council of Chalcedon (Canon 14) assumes that only the lesser clergy, such as readers and singers, are still marriageable. In 691 a Council at Constantinople (the so-called Quinisext) enforced the discipline that still prevails in the Eastern church: priests and deacons may be married before ordination, but bishops, if not celibate, must separate from their wives—they are in fact almost invariably chosen from the monastic order.

The Western church was already moving toward a general enforcement of clerical celibacy, although practice varied in the early Middle Ages. The rule of celibacy was a main point of the Gregorian reform in the 11th century—intended not only to encourage a semimonastic standard for the clergy, but also to prevent their absorption in the feudal system (at least technically).

The Reformers generally rejected compulsory celibacy as wrong in principle, and not merely because of the scandals that often accompanied it; and this has remained the general Protestant position. In England under Henry VIII the Act of Six Articles (1539) enforced clerical celibacy as required by divine law; but the marriage of the clergy was allowed by an Act of 1549 under Edward VI (repealed in 1553, reenacted in 1559), and defended in Article 32 of the Thirty-nine Articles, "Of the Marriage of Priests" (1553, revised 1563). There has always remained in Anglicanism, however, some recognition of a special call to the celibate state, some going as far as the 17th-century Bishop Ken:

A virgin priest the altar best attends,
A state the Lord commands not, but commends.

Modern Roman Catholic theology considers clerical celibacy, however desirable, a matter of ecclesiastical rather than divine law, and hence subject to exceptions such as the recognition of the Eastern practice among Eastern Catholics. In the Latin rite ordination to the subdiaconate is held to involve acceptance of the obligation of celibacy; but there have been occasional exceptions, e.g., in papal dispensations for the ordination of former Lutheran ministers. Some modification of the Roman discipline is possible in the future, as shown by the discussion at the Second Vatican Council of such possibilities as a married diaconate.

See also **Asceticism; Marriage; Sexual Ethics; Virginity.**

On the history, see H. R. Niebuhr and D. D. Williams, *The Ministry in Historical Perspectives,* 1956; on the theory of the celibate vocation, Lucien Legrand (Catholic), *The Biblical Doctrine of Virginity,* 1963; David P. O'Neill (Catholic), *Priestly Celibacy and Maturity,* 1966; Max Thurian (Reformed), *Marriage and Celibacy,* ET 1959.

E. R. HARDY

Censorship

Censorship is the scrutiny of material (literature, art, plays, films, etc.) before it is published, exhibited, or performed. It acts therefore as a sieve to prevent what is undesirable from ever reaching the public. The censor must have some official standing, though he or she may in some cases be employed by a semiofficial body, as, for example, the British Board of Film Censors. The prosecution of publishers and others after publication or performance is not, strictly speaking, censorship, but has the same ultimate effect of keeping the public from further access to the offending material, and may lead to more excessive timidity and caution in publishing, since successful prosecution involves serious financial loss.

Censorship is most commonly discussed today in terms of pornography, but it is possible that it has been more frequently used for political and religious than for moral ends.

The church itself has been the most ardent of censors, and the Bible the most censored book.

While the right of public authority to suppress material in certain circumstances (where it causes grave offense, or is a danger to the public good) can hardly be denied (even, e.g., the censorship of letters in time of war), it is open to grave danger of abuse (e.g., the suppression of news derogatory to one's own cause), and it is therefore axiomatic that severe censorship is a mark of tyranny, spiritual or political, and that freedom of speech and expression is a mark of a mature community. But even the noblest defenders of liberty of speech, such as John Milton and J. S. Mill, believe that it has limits.

Those who burn or suppress the writings of others believe in the power of these writings to influence or corrupt those who read them, and believe also that by suppressing or destroying the material they remove the danger caused by the opinions expressed. Both beliefs are probably much exaggerated. It is arguable that some forms of pornography act less as a stimulus to action than as an escape valve, allowing socially unacceptable interests to be expressed in fantasy rather than in action. Other forms may reinforce and exploit tendencies already present in society, or in the individuals—for example, the association of sex with violence, especially against women (*see* **Feminist Ethics; Women, Status of**). Strangely enough, the censors and would-be censors always believe themselves to be beyond corruption. But pornography and prudery share the same unhealthy attitude toward sex, as naughty or evil in itself. The prude dares not express an interest except through condemnation.

Censorship often operates through very arbitrary and rough-and-ready rules, and many anomalies could be cited. The effect of some recent legislation which insists that a work be considered as a whole, and allows account to be taken of literary merit, in any prosecution for obscenity, has been to encourage more intelligent discrimination. Unofficial censorship is often exercised by pressure groups, religious and other, working upon library committees and the police, and organized protests against television presentations, etc. For lack of any other pressure, such groups can sometimes dictate policy. Since they are frequently fanatical and undiscriminating, they do not merit the unthinking support that they often receive from the churches. There is need for an enlightened Christian judgment to distinguish the trivial, the shoddy, the debasing from the authentic, the genuine, the human—not only in the field of pornography, for the corrupting influences in our society are by no means confined to that particular human interest. A society with the maturity to discriminate would have less need to be protected by censorship.

See **Morality, Legal Enforcement of; Paternalism; Sexual Ethics.**

D. Copp and S. Wendell (eds.), *Pornography and Censorship,* 1983; D. H. Lawrence, *Pornography and Obscenity,* 1929; J. S. Mill, *On Liberty,* 1859; John Milton, *Areopagitica,* 1644; C. H. Rolph (ed.), *Does Pornography Matter?* 1961; D. Thompson (ed.), *Discrimination and Popular Culture,* 1965.

JAMES A. WHYTE

Censure

The word used for a reprimand or punishment awarded by the church for a breach of ecclesiastical discipline*.

JOHN MACQUARRIE

Character

Character refers to that combination of natural and acquired features which distinguish one individual from another. While each person's character is unique, human character itself exhibits important structural features. Analysis of these features enables the ethicist to identify factors contributing to the formation of character, and to ascertain the roles of moral and religious beliefs and their corresponding social practices in that formation. A theological ethics which emphasizes character draws on such analysis to make available to the believing community the vocabulary necessary for its members themselves to participate in the formation of their characters, and for corporate judgments as to whether and how the community should play a conscious role in this formation. This article will treat, first, various perspectives on character important to Christian ethics, and second, structural features or elements of the formation of character in community.

Perspectives on character.

Ordinary language. In ordinary language, character refers to something distinctive or unique, as a character in a play or novel, or a character in printing. It can also imply a collection of features which together distinguish one thing from another, as the character of a fine wine, or a character actor. The separate features in such a collection are called character traits. A person can be said to "have," "possess," or "be" a certain kind of character. Usually there are explicit or implied normative judgments in the list of traits or the kinds of character a given culture describes.

Modern psychology. Psychoanalytic thought locates character traits in relation to psychosexual development, and in particular to fixations arising from arrested or deviant development. In this perspective, character traits are generally held to be unchangeable. Developmental psychology differs in noting the essential malleability of character as a whole, whether forced through crises of stage transition or forged by an individual's conscious attempts at integration.

Classical ethics. Classical treatments of character include those of Aristotle and Thomas Aquinas (*see* **Aristotelian Ethics; Thomistic Ethics**). Character is seen as the account of an individual's relation to the world over time as he or she lives a life more or less determined by the good. Central issues include the formation and expression of character in the practice of virtues* (skills of the good life) or vices* (failures in the good life, or the pursuit of lesser or inappropriate goods); the importance of practical reason and desire in pursuing the good; and the particular normative vision of the good which gives sense to the notion "a human being of good character." Other classical traditions in ethics (especially those following the Enlightenment) tended to ignore character as a moral feature exactly insofar as it concerned the historical and affective, and hence was ill suited to moral theories emphasizing universal rationality. In the 19th and early 20th centuries, discussions of character were generally confined to whether a given trait was to be considered a virtue or a vice in relation to the prevailing moral and cultural conventions.

Contemporary philosophy. From around the middle of the present century Anglo-American philosophy focused increasingly on issues congenial to expression in the language of character. Matters of intentionality; the interaction of thought, action, disposition, and desire; the social location of moral practices; the perspective of the agent; the history of moral notions, including virtues and vices; and the connection between beliefs and behavior, all resurrected classical ethical claims on the importance of the complex formation of character over time.

Contemporary Christian ethics. Contemporary Christian ethics draws in part on the classical and contemporary philosophical perspectives just described. It also relies on the traditional Christian claim that faith in Christ along with God's grace have a transforming effect on human nature in general and on each Christian in particular, and that such transformation is at least potentially visible over time in individuals and communities. Finally, it employs a developing understanding of how religious narratives make accessible the virtues and affections of a life lived in conformity with the good, thereby enabling the attempt to live such a life.

The formation of character in community. The language of character in Christian ethics is a way of talking about the relation of the self to the world. As such, it begins phenomenologically by articulating the elements or structural features of that relation. The four elements mentioned here represent four basic features of human existence whose content and configuration in the life of an individual is what we call character.

The capacity for intentional action. This element of practical reason and choice* is essential for any account of character, for without it moral and social responsibility* for one's actions and way of being in the world would be difficult or impossible to ascertain. Infringement of this capacity, for whatever reason, seriously impairs the ability to participate in the formation of character (*see* **Intention**).

Feelings. Human emotions* in themselves are indicators of one's particular relation to the world, and stand in need of normative interpretation. Yet feelings are often the most characteristic feature of human relations, and theories of character which dismiss these experiences and the rich vocabulary that has developed over the years to interpret them do so only from a misguided rationalism. The relation between feelings and intentions must be explored for both its creative and destructive effects on character.

The accidents of history. This element refers to those things in life about which one has little or no choice, yet which set the limits and possibilities for the formation of a given person's character. Accidents of history include events that are beyond the control of any individual or group; given historical, biological, psychological, economic, and cultural circumstances, including, to some degree, the network of special relationships (friendship, marriage, family, professions) in which people live; and the past, insofar as one cannot change what has already occurred.

The heart. Intentions, feelings, and accidents find a configuration and direction in the heart, where memory, imagination, and the desire for union with the good come together with the human capacity for entering a narrative vision of the good life. Calling this element "the heart" draws on the ordinary language metaphor of the heart as the core of an individual's being, and on a theological tradition following Augustine that seeks a resting place for the heart in God.

The role of the community. The formation of character thus involves the response of the heart to stories of the good life and the virtues and convictions they contain. This response enables a reevaluation of an individual's subjection to the accidents of history, offers a way to discriminate affections and passions, and provides normative criteria for exercising the capacity for intentional action. The community in which this continual formation takes place is important in at least two ways. It provides the historical and cultural setting for the appropriation of stories and their moral vocabulary, which in our pluralistic society is part of the competition of many such stories for the allegiance of the heart; and insofar as the community self-consciously claims such tasks, it will charge certain members with the proclamation, teaching, and evocation of normative stories and with responsibilities in assisting its members with their attempts at character formation (*see also* **Ecclesiology and Ethics**).

Thus the community might almost be said to have a character itself. This raises many questions, among them the difficulties in defining "community" and "normative story"; establishing meaningful analogues with the elements of an individual's character; and allocating responsibility and authority for the formation of the character of a community. Nonetheless, questions of character on both the individual and the communal level will remain particularly important to a religion like Christianity, which calls not for the procreation but the new creation of a people by the response of their hearts.

See **Act, Action, Agent; Habit; Vice; Virtue.**

Aristotle, *Nicomachean Ethics;* S. Hauerwas, *Character and the Christian Life,* 1975; and *The Peaceable Kingdom,* rev. ed. 1985; A. MacIntyre, *After Virtue,* 1981.

RICHARD BONDI

Charity

Derived from Old French *charité* and Latin *caritas,* the term "charity" is used especially in Roman Catholic moral theology* to refer to the love of God and neighbor* mandated by Jesus in his summary of the law and evoked by God's love; charity is also one of the three infused theological virtues*. The Latin *caritas* is a translation of the NT Greek word *agapē,* other Latin terms having been considered too impure or worldly. However, the Protestant Anders Nygren (*Agape and Eros,* ET 1953) drew a sharp distinction between *agapē* and *caritas,* charging that *caritas* combines the desire and longing of *erōs* with the spontaneity and gratuity of *agapē* and thus distorts the distinctive Christian theme of *agapē.* (For further discussion, *see* **Love.**) Outside religious contexts, the term "charity" loosely refers to active benevolence*, beneficence*, philanthropy*, and mutual aid* in response to human needs even when there is no religious motivation.

See **Almsgiving; Social Service of the Church.**

Thomas Aquinas, *ST* II-II.23–27, 44; T. Gilby, "Charity," *New Catholic Encyclopedia,* 1967; G. Gilleman, *The Primacy of Charity in Moral Theology,* ET 1959.

JAMES F. CHILDRESS

Chastity

The preservation of sexual purity according to one's state of life—virginity* for the unmarried, continence* for the widowed, loyalty* to husband or wife for the married. Violation of chastity is fornication* for the unmarried, adultery* for the married (sometimes called double adultery if both parties are married). Perhaps in reaction against the laxity of the pagan world, the early church tended to hold that sexual intercourse was permissible only with the positive intention of procreation (cf. Athenagoras, *Embassy on Behalf of the Christians* 33). But the Middle Ages recognized that it was at least "a remedy against sin" for "such persons as have not the gift of continency" and an expression and encouragement of the "mutual society, help, and comfort" of the married couple. These three traditional purposes of matrimony, here quoted from the English *Book of Common Prayer* (Solemnization of Matrimony), are certainly in accordance with the teaching of the NT (cf. 1 Cor. 7:1–10 and Eph. 5:21–33). The reference in the latter passage to marriage as a "great *mystērion* (Latin *sacramentum*)" related to Christ and the church is probably responsible for the inclusion of marriage among the sacraments (Greek *mystēria*) in an age when the celibate life was highly esteemed. However, the church has always taught, against such heretics as the Manicheans, that salvation is open to the married as well as the continent (cf. Canon I of the Fourth Lateran Council, 1215) (*see* **Marriage**).

As a virtue, chastity is not merely, or even primarily, a matter of physical purity, but an aspect of the all-encompassing virtue of love. It is an expression of respect and honor for other human beings as children of God, and for one's own physical and psychical nature as the work of the Creator, redeemed in Christ (cf. 1 Cor. 6:9–20); and may be violated by other forms of indulgence besides the overtly sexual. (One may note that the *Rule* of Benedict, which assumes monastic chastity, has to guard against temptations to indulgence in food and drink and personal possessions.) Hence in the Sermon on the Mount the commandment against adultery is applied to unlawful desires as well as the physical act (Matt. 5:27–28). Monastic chastity has a similar double meaning. Externally it means the preservation of the virgin (or widowed) state by the monk or nun; spiritually it is the devotion of all powers of body and soul to the service of God. For this reason, perhaps, it does not appear as a special vow in the oldest monastic customs, but as a necessary aspect of the monastic state (*see* **Monastic Ethics**). Benedict, for instance, does not prescribe a separate promise of chastity but includes it in the general promise of monastic behavior (*conversatio,* or in later texts *conversio; Rule,* ch. 58).

E. R. HARDY

Child Abuse
see **Children; Incest; Pederasty**

Children
The significance of children.

Social. Traditional views of children have regarded them as the natural fruits of love to be cherished and nurtured with care; as accidents of passion whose value depends on the circumstances of their conception; as the survival of the race; and as an extension of the life, will, or status of the parents. These evaluations are all in question in an age of contraception, abortion, self-fulfillment, and an uncertainty about the future brought on by the threat of nuclear holocaust. Such developments make the raising of children seem optional or problematic in ways foreign to most earlier societies.

Theological. Theologically, children have been seen as gifts of God; as fruits of married love; as required by a duty to be fruitful and multiply; as born in sin and in need of discipline; as the continuation of the people of God; and as a metaphor for all human beings in their relation to God. In almost all Christian perspectives child-raising is an essentially moral act involving the formation of children in a character appropriate to Christian life, and representing a fundamental hope in God's care for God's people in the future. Differences in perspective concern the understanding of marriage* and family life (*see* **Family**); the practice of parenting (*see* **Parenthood**); and the place of children in the worship life of a given Christian community.

Care for children.

Needs of children. Contemporary thought sees children as developing individuals with distinct physical and psychological needs, including the need for physical care and protection, affectionate love, clear but not rigid limits, and a gradual shift from a dependent to an interdependent status as age and maturity increase. Difficulties in defining these needs include how to link development with age, the need to balance protection with the allowance of risk, and the conflict of loyalties that often occurs with increasing freedom from parental control. These issues are more

acute in adolescence, particularly as this nebulous time between childhood and adulthood becomes increasingly protracted by the ordering of work and education in contemporary society.

Responsibility for children. Responsibility for children involves a balancing act of the interests and duties of parents, providers of social services affecting children, communities within which the family lives, and the state. Each of the possibly responsible parties may have a different conception of the needs and interests of children, but with widely varying degrees of personal and emotional involvement. Other recent developments in parenting considerably expand the number of individuals with some authority and responsibility in the life of a given child (*see* **Parenthood**).

Intervention on behalf of children. The confusion depicted above has led to an increase in instances where an institution or person outside the immediate family feels compelled to intervene on behalf of the children. While sometimes a matter of the intervention of relatives, friends, or community members, it more often takes the form of an arm of the state intervening in the family, and thus ethical debate concerns the balancing of family liberty with the state's interest in protecting the weak. Such intervention usually concerns issues of preventing harm to children (child abuse; child labor laws; care for orphans, the disabled, and the medically incapacitated), or issues of promoting equal opportunity under the law (standards for and support of education, housing, job training, and aid to families with dependent children). Also involved is the setting of legal standards for maturity in matters such as driving, consumption of alcoholic beverages, the military draft, and medical consent. Less direct but still important are issues of the intervention of the state, mass media, and religious groups into family control of value-shaping.

Duties of children. The duties of children are generally held to include obedience and respect for parents and others exercising proper care for them, and participation (insofar as they are able at different ages and points of development) in family life and in their own formation (*see* **Decalogue**). As children mature and begin to form their own allegiances outside the family, it becomes less clear how these new priorities fit into the special relation of their own family life, or indeed whether parents and children can themselves become friends as adults. The most that can be said is that how these matters are resolved is in large part related to how parents have expressed their love for and authority over their children in the past. One of the challenges facing Christian ethical reflection on children is assisting parents and children alike with the nurture of long-term relationships within the family (*see also* **Aged, Care of the**).

See **Abandonment; Adoption; Exposition; Family; Infanticide; Orphans; Parenthood; Pederasty; Procreation.**

J. Blustein, *Parents and Children,* 1982; D. Curran, *Traits of a Healthy Family,* 1983.

RICHARD BONDI

Children's Rights *see* Children

Chivalry

The term originally meant a body of mounted warriors; then the qualities of the ideal warrior—valor and loyalty to both his lord and his own men; then the qualities of the ideal knight outside of battle—honor, disinterested justice tinctured with mercy, defense of the weak, and a great courtesy to women. The humanization of warriors was originally and largely the work of the church, which linked the Germanic form of knighthood, conferred by prince or father, with religion and a moral code. By the end of the 11th century it was becoming usual for the initiate to spend a whole night in solitary prayer in a church and on the next day to make his confession, receive Communion, be publicly sermonized on his duties, and be declared a knight in the name of the Trinity. The Crusades* provided a broad outlet for such Christian chivalry. There was also a striking literary expression of it. Indeed, vernacular poetry as a contrived art began with epics of the famous knights, for example, Charlemagne, Roland, Arthur. In the 12th century in southern France, which had more internal peace, a legacy of Greco-Roman culture, and a climate and leisure that encouraged refinement, the troubadours, singing in courts their own lyrics (of exquisite craftsmanship), virtually narrowed the notion of chivalry to the platonic love and devoted service of distinguished ladies. This celebration of "courtly love," idealizing womanhood, was neither adopted nor condemned by the church. It seems to have been influenced in some degree by the growing cult of the Mother of God, and by the preachers' theme of the beauty and purity of genuine love for God. Such poetry spread throughout France and into Italy, Germany, and Austria; it helped to form the versification of Dante and his glorification of Beatrice. Some of it was wholly aesthetic, metrical variations on the *idea* of woman and the *idea* of love.

T. E. JESSOP

Choice

Choice is crucial for any theory of ethics, since moral action is in some sense choosing aright. Right choice depends on three factors: (1) a due appreciation of values and obligations; (2) right belief as to the facts, including the consequences of one's action; and (3) willingness to do what the agent thinks right. It has been held, for example, by Socrates, that it is impossible knowingly to choose what is wrong and that all wrong action is due to mistaken or confused belief, but this is hard to square with the facts that theologians have discussed under the heading of "sin." It does seem as if many wrong choices have to be explained by the fact that the strength of a person's desires is not always proportionate to the value one supposes their object to have. Most (perhaps even all) people want to do right, other things being equal, but they sometimes want other things much more and then they are tempted to sin.

According to one school of thought, what we choose is always determined by the relative strength of our desires; but if more is meant by "the strongest desire" than the desire that prevails, which would make the statement a tautology, this seems to imply too mechanical a view of the self and its determination by desires, as though the latter were a kind of physical force, and it is hard to reconcile with the cases where people seem after a struggle to act against their strongest desires. Here, if anywhere, it is supposed, we have the occurrence of free will (or choice not completely determined by antecedent causes). The self is regarded as something over and above its successive mental states and can, so to speak, stand apart from its desires and choose between them. It is held that but for this undetermined intervention by the self we should always be governed by the desire felt most strongly at the time and there would be no such thing as moral action. It may be argued, however, that even on a determinist view we need not hold that we are always governed by the desire, or group of desires, felt most strongly, for we have no ground for saying that the causal efficacy of a desire needs always to be in proportion to its felt strength. Determinism is the thesis that all our actions are determined, but it need not imply that they are determined in any one particular way.

The whole idea of a mental action of volition has recently been questioned in some quarters, but while it is unreasonable to suppose that every voluntary act has to be preceded by a specific volition, one can hardly deny the occurrence of decisions and efforts as psychological events. And while we cannot limit voluntary action to action preceded by a choice, we can hardly regard an act as voluntary unless the agent could at least have done differently if he or she had chosen. Whether the act could be regarded as free unless the agent could also have chosen differently without previous circumstances having been in any way different is a point in dispute between determinists and indeterminists.

See **Act, Action, Agent; Decision; Deliberation; Free Will and Determinism; Responsibility.**

A. C. EWING

Christendom Group
see **Anglican Moral Theology**

Christian Ethics
Other entries deal with the ethics of various Christian traditions; this one attends to the patterns of Christian ethical writing, their elements and their relations to each other.

Themes. Writings that are systematic have organizing themes (metaphors, analogies, symbols, principles) around which other theological and ethical ideas and concepts cohere. The themes may be theological or ethical, or combinations of the two. Some examples follow: (*a*) The theme that backs H. R. Niebuhr's "ethics of responsibility" is anthropological; persons are responders or answerers more than "makers" or "citizens." The theological theme of "God acting in events" to which persons respond coheres with this, as do such procedures as the interpretation of events. (*b*) *Agapē* is the supreme moral principle of Christian ethics for Paul Ramsey. Its supremacy is backed by his in-

terpretation of biblical theology. Since it is a rule term for him, and since he believes that biblical ethics are deontological, his practical procedures for making choices cohere with his view of *agapē*. (*c*) Luther's theology distinguishes but does not separate the work of God as creator and as redeemer. His ethics of the civic use of the law and of an agent-oriented freedom and love cohere with these themes. They are related to each other; Christians act out of freedom and love in obedience to the law and in their offices in orders of creation. (*d*) Augustine interprets human action as motivated by desires and directed toward ends. His view of rightly or wrongly ordered persons and acts coheres with his theological principle that all things are to be ordered proportionately in relation to God, the supreme good.

Base points. Comprehensive Christian ethical writings have four distinguishable base points, or points of reference. They are coherent insofar as the base points are organized around themes, as stated above. The base points are: (1) theological interpretation in a restricted sense—that is, the understanding and interpretation of God, God's relations to the world and particularly to human beings, and God's purposes; (2) the interpretation of the meaning and significance of human experience and history, of events and circumstances in which human beings act, and of nature; (3) the interpretation of persons or communities as moral agents, and of their acts; and (4) the interpretation of how persons and communities ought to make moral choices and judge their actions, those of others, and the states of affairs in the world.

1. How the interpretation of God is developed is critical for ethics. Process theology has implications for ethics that differ from those based upon an eternal and immutable divine order. The use of personal or interpersonal concepts to understand God and God's relations to the world will yield different ethics than a view of God as impersonal being. Christological choices are critical. If Christ reveals God to be primarily a gracious God, and if interpersonal concepts are used to understand God's relations to persons, one has ethics like Karl Barth's. If Christ is the one in and through whom all things are created, there is a Christological foundation for ethics of natural law, as in the Roman Catholic tradition. If Christ is the one through whom the divinization of man takes place, as in

Eastern Orthodox theology, the ethical implications are different in yet another way.

2. The concepts or symbols used to interpret experience and events are critical. If God is acting for the liberation of human life, experience and events have a different religious and ethical significance than in an interpretation based upon an immutable moral order of creation. If events are interpreted on the basis of the great power of evil in the world, they have a different significance than in an interpretation that views the power of good to be more in control. Christological choices affect how experience and events are interpreted. If Christ is a new "seed" implanted in history that is "organically" spreading through life (e.g., Schleiermacher), events will have a different significance than in a view that sees the crucifixion as the primary way to understand them (e.g., H. R. Niebuhr on war). Judgments about eschatology affect the interpretation of events. If the coming of the kingdom of God is almost totally, or totally, a future event, eschatology will function differently in Christian ethics than in a view that sees the kingdom as the fulfillment of a historical end. If it is interpreted as a social ideal (e.g., Rauschenbusch) certain goals can be inferred from it to direct action; from other perspectives it stands basically as a critical principle relativizing and judging all human ends.

3. The interpretation of persons and their acts has ramifications for ethics. If human actions are strongly conditioned, or determined, by desires (e.g., Augustine and Jonathan Edwards), Christian ethics takes a different shape from views that accent more strongly the freedom of the will. The decision that theologians make on various grounds about a theory of human action qualifies decisively the ethics they develop. Christological judgments are important here as well. If human beings are basically sinners, though justified by the work of Christ, persons and actions will be interpreted differently than in a view that stresses the present efficacy of redemption and sanctification.

4. Both the procedures and the content of the prescriptive or normative ethics in Christian writings require specific development. How they are developed depends on different sorts of choices that a theologian makes. One choice is of the fundamental shape of ethics; theologians back their choices in different ways. Paul Ramsey, for example, argues that Christian ethics is deontic because biblical ethics is. For others (e.g., Paul Lehmann), biblical theology supports a view of acting in events in ways consonant with God's humanizing purposes. For both theological and philosophical reasons other writers develop Christian ethics in a teleological manner. Interpretations of Christ make a difference. If Christ reveals the norm or ideal of true humanity, his life and teachings become morally normative and the procedures of moral life are discipleship or imitation and the application of his teaching to current actions. If his significance is primarily related to the redemption of persons, the norm is more that of dispositions from which moral actions flow; one gets a more "agent-oriented" ethics.

If the writings are both comprehensive and coherent, the three base points will be integrally related to one another.

Sources. Comprehensive Christian ethical writings use four distinguishable sources: (1) the Bible and the Christian tradition, (2) philosophical principles and methods, (3) science and other sources of knowledge about the world, and (4) human experience broadly conceived. Writers make judgments about these sources and about the weight or authority each has. Four kinds of judgments are made, namely, about which sources are relevant and why; which sources are decisive when they conflict, and why; what specific content is to be used from these sources and what is to be ignored or rejected, and why; and how this content is to be interpreted and why it is to be so interpreted.

1. All four kinds of judgments are made in the use of biblical materials and sources from the Christian tradition. Even if, as some argue, Christian ethics begins with biblical exegesis, choices are made about what biblical themes and passages are central. A basic choice is whether the biblical material will be used primarily for theological purposes that ground or back the development of ethics, or whether the moral teachings of the Bible will be treated as a revealed source of ethics. For example, the ethics of liberal Protestantism tended to use the NT, and particularly the Gospels, as a "revealed" source of moral ideals, ends, examples, and teachings. With the turn toward "biblical theology," ethics were grounded in various theological themes from the Bible, such as God acting in history, human beings as sinners, or the kingdom of God as breaking into history. Different theological themes from the Bible ground differ-

ent emphases in ethics. How the moral teachings in the Bible are related to the biblical theologies varies—e.g., for Barth they are instruction and give direction; for others they are ideals, principles, or rules.

Discernible differences can be found in writings from various Christian traditions; great theologians or historical movements establish patterns that persist. Examples: the use of natural law in the Roman Catholic tradition; the distinction between law and gospel and between the heavenly and earthly realms in the Lutheran tradition; the emphasis on following Christ as he is portrayed in the Gospels and on rigorous obedience to his teachings in the Radical Reformation tradition; the marked mystical aspects of ethics in the Eastern Orthodox tradition. Received traditions undergo development and change; an example is the rethinking of natural law in contemporary Roman Catholic theology in the light of more historical consciousness and stress on the "personal" character of human life.

2. Judgments are made about philosophical principles and methods. Writers sometimes explicitly adapt patterns from philosophy (e.g., Platonism, Aristotelianism, Kantianism, existentialism) because they believe they are consonant with a theology, or they use them to explicate the ethical implications of a theology, or they determine on philosophical grounds what the science of ethics is to which theology must be related. Sometimes the judgments about philosophy are implicit, sometimes they are defended on theological or other grounds.

Persistent themes in Christian ethics are developed differently, depending on philosophical choices made by the author. For example, love functions differently in Christian ethical writings that are deontic in mode from those that are primarily agent-oriented; in the former it is basically a principle or rule term, and in the latter it indicates a disposition of persons. Appeals to the Bible are not decisive in this matter; there is no philosophical theory of ethics in the Bible, and terms like love are used to refer to different aspects of moral life.

3. Applications of Christian ethics, no matter what choices are made on any of the previous items, use sources of information and insight about the sphere of activity that is attended to. Differences occur in part as a result of the different data that are used, even

about the same general area of interest. For example, to understand persons as agents some writers turn to particular psychologists, others to particular philosophers. The choice of data requires defense on the basis of its adequacy. Concepts used to interpret information also vary; for example, Christians influenced by Marxist interpretations understand the relations between ethics and economics differently from those who judge modified free-market interpretations to be more accurate.

4. Broader understandings of human experience in general affect how Christian ethics are developed. Insight is drawn not only from academic disciplines, but also from literature and art, and from the residues of moral experience embedded in custom and habit. The choices affect some basic postures toward the world. For example, the weight of a writer's judgment on a continuum from determinism to radical freedom may be affected not only by philosophical and scientific scholarship but also by the author's own experiences or by reflections gained from observations about historical events, etc.

All four types of judgments mentioned above are made about all four sources of Christian ethical writings.

Whether and how ethical writings are Christian depends upon the significance that Christ or Christology has for them. Christological judgments are critical to how ethical writings are Christian. Writers who view the Gospel narratives and teachings exclusively as a source for a sublime moral code, or for an ideal moral and social life, think in terms of the application of the teachings or realization of the ideal. For them, the significance of Christ is restricted to morality. For others, Christ is the revelation of the nature of God and God's relation to the world; for example, in Christ God is known as a gracious God who is "for man." Sometimes the focus is on the redeeming work of Christ; this calls attention to the efficacy of that work for the qualities of life of persons. Further judgments about the doctrine of sanctification will affect the interpretation of the Christian moral life. If the significance of Christ's work is forensic, the freedom of the Christian is stressed; if it is also efficacious in the reordering of motives and desires, claims are made for moral progress in Christian life.

Combinations and qualifications of these tendencies occur in various writings. The view of Christ as teacher and example might be backed, not by the judgment that is strictly moral, but by the idea that the form of God's revelation (i.e., in and through Christ) provides the pattern of life appropriate to those who believe in Christ and receive his benefits. Or, if the principal significance is what is revealed about God's goodness, the life and teachings can be signs or indicators of the kinds of deeds that those who respond to God's goodness ought to be doing. In the NT there are grounds for various foci of Christological development, and thus for different explications of what and how ethics can be Christian.

See also **Anglican Moral Theology; Bible in Christian Ethics; Eastern Orthodox Christian Ethics; Modern Protestant Ethics; Modern Roman Catholic Moral Theology; Moral Theology.**

J. M. Gustafson, *Christ and the Moral Life,* 1968; *Protestant and Roman Catholic Ethics,* 1978; E. L. Long, Jr., *A Survey of Christian Ethics,* 1967; *A Survey of Recent Christian Ethics,* 1982; H. R. Niebuhr, *Christ and Culture,* 1951.

JAMES M. GUSTAFSON

Christian Social Movement
see **Anglican Moral Theology**

Church

This term is used in widely divergent ways. It is commonly applied to buildings for Christian worship, to a congregation gathered for worship, to the institution that owns the building and organizes the worship, to the regional or national collective membership of a denomination, to the membership of all denominations, or, in some branches of Christianity, to the official leadership of a denomination. More theologically, the term may be applied to the "mystical body of Christ," to the company of all believers of all times and places (church universal) or to those within and without the institutional church (including "anonymous Christians" who belong to other religions) who are known by (or "elected" by) God to be faithful (church invisible). The term has also been taken into Western jurisprudence in ways that mean, by extension, that Islamic mosques, Jewish synagogues, Hindu temples, etc., are given legal status as "churches" in

documents defining church-state relationships and religious liberties. Still further, some cross-cultural analysis has utilized the term "church" to apply to the typical kinds of "holy" or "sacred" social organization which every religion develops (although such organizations differ widely in character). Thus, the caste is held by some to be the "church" in some Hindu groups, the order of monks in some Buddhist groups, the "party" in Marxist-Leninist "secular religion," the clan in traditional "Chinese religion," or the tribe in primal religions, etc.

In Christian ethics since the historical-sociological work of Max Weber and Ernst Troeltsch, however, "church" has come to be understood as a technical term that refers to a type of Christian social organization, based on characteristic understandings of theological first principles as institutionalized in distinctive ways in society to form a social ethic. In the process of selecting, clarifying, organizing, and institutionalizing first principles in various cultural, political, and economic contexts, the "church" takes on a normative social form that is a compound of religious convictions, apologetic, pastoral, and cultic needs, functional organizational requirements in coordinating right teaching and practice, and compromise with secular institutional realities of the context in which it finds itself. The church, thus defined, attempts to be a socially inclusive institution both in the sense that it tries to draw the entire population into itself and in the sense that it attempts to cooperate with and normatively inform all other sectors of social life—familial, economic, political, intellectual, and social. The more absolutistic and perfectionistic demands of the gospel are, for the masses, modulated and adapted to the realities of natural and historical life, although the church may contain within itself specialized institutions (such as monastic orders) where these demands are taken as primary. The church usually attempts to establish a specialized and hierarchically organized priesthood with a relative monopoly on authoritative teaching, preaching, and sacramental care, and there is often close cooperation with political authority to maintain this pattern. On these bases, the church develops its ethic, an explicit "Christian social philosophy," intended to be a comprehensive guide to the common life. Troeltsch argues that only Roman Catholicism and Calvinism have been able to do this in ways significant for world history.

In this sense, "church" is contrasted with sectarian (see **Sect**) and with mystical types of religion. The latter are intensely personal and transcendental religious orientations that may exist in a church or a sect or among intellectual elites outside organized religion. They differ from churches in that they are characteristically unconcerned about normative patterns in doctrine, ecclesiology, or social order.

Since Weber and Troeltsch wrote on this topic, subsequent scholars have become aware of the emergence of "denominations," which are also often called churches. In Anglo-American lands and in many of the emerging countries where Western missionary activity has been influential, a church in the sense of "denomination" does not claim to have a monopoly on truth in doctrine, ethics, or sacrament as does a "church" or "sect" in the above senses. Instead, "church" is understood to be a species within a broadly acceptable genus with a distinctive understanding of creed, code, worship, and polity, organized on the basis of a voluntary association* of like-minded people who tolerate and often cooperate with other churches. A church in this sense usually is a further development of the "free church" tradition, but it may also derive from an exclusive established church that has entered a pluralistic environment shaped by the free church tradition, or from a sect that has developed a broader constituency and range of acceptable teaching in doctrine and morals and is thus willing to acknowledge other religious bodies as members of the same general family of faithfulness.

See **Church and State; Ecclesiology and Ethics; Institution/Institutionalization.**

MAX L. STACKHOUSE

Church and State

"Church" here means a Christian community and its ecclesiastical organization; "State" means a nation in its corporate capacity and organized for civil government. How ought these two institutions, and the claims they make upon the allegiance of humankind, to be related? Every normal human being has to be a citizen of some state: a "stateless" person is notoriously in an intol-

erable and pitiful condition. Although it is far from being the case that everyone has to belong to a church, yet, because churches exist in nearly every country in the world, relations between church and state are a worldwide problem. The problem is an ancient one too, and it has been solved, insofar as it ever has been solved, in a variety of ways.

There have been many different kinds both of church, such as papal, episcopalian, presbyterian, and independent (see **Church; Ecclesiology and Ethics; Sect**), and of state, such as monarchical, republican, democratic, and totalitarian. These differences have affected the character and extent of their interrelations. Then again, the problem has been posed differently according to whether the membership of a church was more or less coterminous with that of a state, or a church was a small minority within a state, or there were several churches or only one church in a state. Hence no simple description of, or prescription for, church-state relations is possible.

Christians have naturally searched the scriptures for guidance with regard to the circumstances in which they found themselves, but the scriptures are not as helpful as might be wished. Scriptural authority has been claimed for many divergent doctrines. It may be that Christians have tended to extract from, or read into, the Bible what they wanted to find there. The OT, though it testifies that both civil government and ecclesiastical organization are divinely ordained, is not otherwise directly relevant, since Israel was both church and state in one, not two distinct societies: there was no problem of the relation between them such as has arisen in the Christian era. After Pentecost the church of Christ soon became a distinct society, but in the NT period it was never more than a small minority within the Roman Empire. All it looked for, so far as civil government was concerned, was freedom and security for its missionary work. There was no question yet of formal relations between civil government and ecclesiastical organization. Moreover, since history was not expected to endure for long, the apostles had no occasion to theorize about future contingencies. They acknowledged that civil government was a necessary and beneficent institution and they prayed for the political authorities. It never occurred to them that

Christians might one day have the opportunity of shouldering responsibility for the political order, that is, an opportunity of administering the state as well as the church and a need to reconcile the two obligations. In spite of everything that commentators have said about a passage like Rom. 13:1–7, no one can say for certain what the apostles would have thought if they had lived three centuries later than they did.

The relations of church and state did not become as problematic, as in one way or another they have been ever since, until the emperor Constantine, early in the 4th century, inaugurated between the two institutions an alliance which may have been too readily welcomed by the church because of the relief it afforded from the threat of periodical persecutions. Before long, Christianity was made the official religion of the Empire.

From that time and right through the Middle Ages, the accepted idea was that church and state, while in principle distinct societies, were united in one commonwealth (the *corpus Christianum*): the distinction between them was to be seen chiefly in their separate hierarchies (pope and emperor, etc.) with their different functions and in the systems of law they administered. After the schism between East and West there were *two* commonwealths of this kind: otherwise the main idea was not affected, except that in Byzantium the emperor became the dominant partner. In the West there was ever-recurring tension or rivalry between the ecclesiastical and civil authorities, of which the Investiture Controversy is a famous example. All the same, there were in the Middle Ages undercurrents of misgiving about the accepted conjunction of church and state. There were groups of enthusiastic Christians who alleged that since the time of Constantine the church had succumbed, or been conformed, to the world and had compromised its witness, which should have been inspired by the Sermon on the Mount and the standards of the primitive church. There sprang up a number of nonconforming sects* which were deemed to be heretical and were subjected to persecution*, but they were evidence that the post-Constantinian developments could be called in question on evangelical grounds.

At the Reformation the unity of the Western church was broken up and there emerged a variety of national churches. Some continued to be in communion with the pope while claiming a considerable degree of national independence (e.g., Gallicanism in France); others—Lutheran, Reformed, and Anglican—had rejected the papal suzerainty. The Lutherans and Anglicans, it may be noted, were much more willing than the Reformed (Calvinists) to let the civil power (the "godly prince") manage the church. Still, the accepted idea was that in each country church and state were one commonwealth: in England, Richard Hooker was the classical exponent of this idea. Unity in religion was held to be necessary for the sake of the political coherence and stability of a nation.

On the other hand, the Reformation gave birth to new embodiments of the quite different idea that had found expression in the medieval sects, notably in the case of the Anabaptists (*see* **Anabaptist Ethics**). Their contention was that the true church, instead of veneering whole nations with a nominal Christianity, should consist of those who were called out of the world into separate communities—gathered churches instead of national churches. Churches therefore should not be established or depend on civil governments for support. Worldliness, compromise, even sacrilege, were inevitably entailed in establishment.

Nevertheless, until the French Revolution and the gradual disintegration of the *ancien régime* elsewhere, the union or alliance of church and state was generally maintained in Europe, with a more or less precarious toleration of dissenting minorities. In the USA after some uncertainty, the separation of church and state became an accepted principle. In European countries the civil and ecclesiastical authorities struggled for the upper hand. By the 18th century the former had the latter everywhere under control, as is strikingly illustrated by the fact that they induced the pope in 1773 to suppress the Society of Jesus.

The control of the church by the civil power is known as "Erastianism"* among Protestants, as "Josephism" or "Febronianism" by Roman Catholics, and as "Caesaropapism" in the Eastern church. When in the 19th century civil governments in Europe ceased to be professed upholders of the church or recognizably Christian, perceptive churchmen began to wonder whether establishment was any longer tolerable, witness the Oxford Movement in England and the

Disruption in Scotland. In fact, the idea of the union of church and state was now being eroded, giving way to the pluralist or liberal idea of the state. According to this, the function of the state is to preserve law and order and the freedom of citizens to profess and practice any religion or none: in other words, its function is that of a policeman and not of a father, still less of a father in God.

The logical outcome of this view would be the separation of church and state, as in the USA, or "the free church in the free state" and no interference by either in the affairs of the other. But churches in Europe, which retained the allegiance of a majority of citizens, preserved much of their involvement with the state with their traditional prestige and privileges, or at least some of the signs and ceremonies of the old order were kept on in states for which in all vital matters pluralism had really become axiomatic.

It looked as though the coming norm for church-state relations would be secular states, which would be religiously neutral, and churches, which would be voluntary societies (see **Voluntary Associations**) left to their own devices. However, pluralism* and liberalism*, and the freedom* of churches which they were supposed to secure, have been rudely shaken in the 20th century by the growth of collectivism* and the advent of totalitarianism*. Totalitarian states seek to impose a secular faith on all their citizens, and tolerate churches only if they are content not to challenge or criticize it. Churches are expected to confine themselves to "the salvation of souls" and preparation for the next world.

No self-respecting church can accept such limitations. "A free church in a free state" is an attractive formula, but it leaves many questions unanswered and may be so interpreted as to be incompatible with the Christian duty to bear witness to God's will for the whole life of humankind. How can non-Christian political leaders be persuaded that churches have an inherent authority directly derived from God, that is, rights which the state does not confer but is required to acknowledge? On what grounds can a church, whose freedom is being restricted by a state, convincingly and effectively base its resistance? Can the provinces of church and state be so easily demarcated as liberalism presupposed? As soon as education, in which both church and state have an essential interest, becomes universal and compulsory, either collaboration or conflict is inescapable. This is a particularly thorny subject even where church and state are formally separate as in the USA.

Questions such as these have been driving Christians to do some fresh thinking. The novel characteristics of the modern state, the breakdown of the old forms of establishment, and the inadequacies of the liberal solution mean that churches have to come to terms with an unprecedented situation and to articulate anew a doctrine of the church and of the state and of their interrelations. A critical reassessment of past attitudes and assumptions has been going on for some time both in the Roman Catholic Church and under the auspices of the World Council of Churches (see **Ecumenical Movement; Official Roman Catholic Social Teaching**). A particular urgency is given to this undertaking by the uncertain prospects of churches in the new states of Africa and the East with their strongly nationalistic dispositions.

The claims of churches to unrestricted liberty will always be viewed with suspicion by leaders of the state who remember the attempts of churches in the past to monopolize power and influence, and also the intolerant and persecuting spirit with which their history has been compounded. Churches are unlikely to have accorded to them the freedom which they seek and which is necessary for their mission until political leaders are satisfied that churches have irrevocably accepted the desirability of pluralist societies, wherever they may be had, and so can be depended on to defend the religious freedom of all citizens and not only their own. The Roman Catholic Church appeared to do this at the Second Vatican Council.

See also **State; Persecution and Toleration; Pluralism; Theocracy; Nonconformist Conscience.**

Lord Acton, *Essays on Church and State,* 1952; K. Barth, *Church and State,* ET 1939; J. C. Bennett, *Christians and the State,* 1958; D. A. Binchy, *Church and State in Fascist Italy,* 1941; W. Adams Brown, *Church and State in Contemporary America,* 1936; S. Parkes Cadman, *Christianity and the State,* 1924; A. J. Carlyle, *The Christian Church and Liberty,* 1924; *Church and State,* Report of the Archbishop's Commission, 2 vols., 1935; M. Cruikshank, *Church and State in*

English Education, 1963; O. Cullmann, *The State in the New Testament*, ET 1957; C. Dawson, *Religion and the Modern State*, 1935; F. Dvornik, *National Churches and the Church Universal*, 1944; S. Z. Ehler and J. B. Morrall, *Church and State Through the Centuries*, 1954; N. Ehrenström, *Christian Faith and the Modern State*, ET 1937; T. S. Eliot, *The Idea of a Christian Society*, 1939; J. N. Figgis, *Churches in the Modern State*, 1913; P. T. Forsyth, *Theology in Church and State*, 1915; C. F. Garbett, *Church and State in England*, 1950; F. Gavin, *Seven Centuries of the Problem of Church and State*, 1938; E. B. Greene, *Religion and the State: The Making of an American Tradition*, 1941; A. Keller, *Church and State on the European Continent*, 1936; J. Lecker, S.J., *Toleration and the Reformation*, ET 1960; C. C. Marshall, *The Roman Catholic Church in the Modern State*, 1928; D. L. Munby, *The Idea of a Secular Society*, 1963; A. V. Murray, *The State and the Church in a Free Society*, 1958; J. C. Murray, S.J. (ed.), *Religious Liberty: An End of a Beginning*, 1966; D. Nicholls, *The Pluralist State*, 1975; T. M. Parker, *Christianity and the State in the Light of History*, 1955; H. M. Relton, *Religion and the State*, 1937; P. C. Simpson, *The Church and the State*, 1929; L. Sturzo, *Church and State*, ET 1939; W. Temple, *Christianity and the State*, 1928; E. Troeltsch, *The Social Teaching of the Christian Churches* (1912), ET 1931; A. R. Vidler, *The Orb and the Cross*, 1945; M. A. C. Warren, *The Functions of a National Church*, 1964.

A. R. VIDLER

Circumcision

The cutting off of the foreskin of the male or the excision of the clitoris and/or the labia minora and/or the inner fleshy portions of the labia majora in the case of females. The more radical form of female circumcision has been traditionally termed pharaonic circumcision, due to a tradition that has ascribed its origin to the time of the pharaohs. The practice of male circumcision is recorded in Gen. 17 and Ex. 4:25, as well as elsewhere in the Old Testament. Herodotus advanced the account that the practice originated in Egypt, though it has been found independently among other groups such as Australian aborigines and some American Indians. Male circumcision remains integral to both Jewish and Islamic religious practices, while female circumcision continues to be practiced among Muslim and some Christian groups in North Africa. Female circumcision constitutes a major health risk due to blood loss at the time of circumcision and when the vagina is opened at first intercourse. Major medical difficulties may be encountered when a woman who has experienced pharaonic circumcision gives birth. In addition to the role of male circumcision in religious rituals and puberty rites, it has been widely advocated as a preventive of masturbation*, as well as for various health benefits. The value of routine male circumcision is widely challenged.

H. TRISTRAM ENGELHARDT, JR.

Circumstances
see **Norms; Situation Ethics**

Civil Commitment
see **Involuntary Hospitalization**

Civil Disobedience
Civil disobedience is one form of dissent* from and resistance* to the state, but, as with other forms of dissent and resistance, there is considerable debate about what it is and when it is justified. The phrase "civil disobedience" is often attributed to Henry David Thoreau and is associated with his influential essay "Civil Disobedience" (1849), which he had earlier entitled "Resistance to Civil Government." Civil disobedience is sometimes defined as a public, nonviolent, and submissive violation of law in protest of some actual or proposed law, policy, or practice (Childress). Yet each element in this definition is controversial. The controversy about the definition is in part a controversy about the moral and political status of civil disobedience, especially whether it involves disloyalty, rebellion, or revolutionary activity. It is often argued that resisters whose actions have these features remain within the political-legal system—even though only on its boundaries—particularly because they are nonviolent and submit to legal sanctions. However civil disobedience is defined, illegal actions with these features raise special moral and political issues—for example, Henry David Thoreau's refusal to pay his poll tax, Mahatma Gandhi's campaign against the British in India, Martin Luther King, Jr.'s struggle for civil rights for blacks in the USA, protests against US military actions in Vietnam, and protests against nuclear weapons

and deterrence in the USA, the UK, and elsewhere.

Civil disobedience is sometimes distinguished from illegal conscientious objection* or conscientious refusal by two criteria. First, there are the *grounds* of the disobedience. Some distinguish personal moral grounds, especially religious ones, from moral-political grounds. For example, John Rawls restricts "civil disobedience" to acts that are political in the sense that they are justified by "moral principles which define a conception of civil society and the public good" and by "common principles of justice" rather than personal or religious aspirations. Second, there is the *intention** of the disobedient. In civil disobedience, many argue, the agent is trying to effect or prevent social and political change, but in conscientious objection or refusal, the agent is bearing witness to his or her principles and perhaps seeking exemption from participation in evil, without being concerned to persuade or coerce others to bring about or retard change.

The moral justification of civil disobedience involves standards that are similar to those used to justify war, violent resistance, and other violations of prima facie obligations. A fundamental consideration is the basis and limits of the moral obligation to obey the law. Several theologians, including Augustine, Thomas Aquinas, and Martin Luther King, Jr., have held that "an unjust law is no law at all" and thus cannot obligate citizens to obedience; others have argued that there may be a prima facie obligation to obey the law, even unjust laws, in relatively just democratic states because of the duty to support and maintain just institutions, the duties of fair play* and gratitude*, and the need for order* in a fallen world (*see* **Democracy; State**). In any case, the moral obligation to obey the law is not absolute. In order to rebut the presumption in favor of obedience, it is often held to be necessary to show that the end of the illegal action is just; that other channels have been tried without success; that the disobedience would probably be effective, at least as a symbolic witness; and that its probable negative consequences, such as the threat to order, would not outweigh its probable positive consequences. The forms or means of disobedience are also important; for example, it is easier to defend nonviolent disobedience than violent disobedience and submissive than evasive disobedience. (Vio-

lent and evasive resistance and revolution may be justified, but they must pass stiffer tests.) Other distinctions are also significant, for example, between *direct* disobedience—violation of a law that is considered unjust—and *indirect* disobedience—violation of an admittedly just law in order to protest some other law or policy. Finally, in some circumstances civil disobedience may be morally obligatory as well as morally justified; as King insisted, there may be a "moral responsibility to disobey unjust laws."

See **Conscientious Objection; Law; Resistance; Revolution.**

H. Bedau, *Civil Disobedience: Theory and Practice,* 1969; J. F. Childress, *Civil Disobedience and Political Obligation: A Study in Christian Social Ethics,* 1971; D. Daube, *Civil Disobedience in Antiquity,* 1972; M. K. Gandhi, *Non-violent Resistance,* ed. B. Kumarappa, 1961; M. L. King, Jr., "Letter from Birmingham Jail," in *Why We Can't Wait,* 1964 (also in Bedau, *Civil Disobedience*); J. Rawls, *A Theory of Justice,* 1971; D. Stevick, *Civil Disobedience and the Christian,* 1969.

JAMES F. CHILDRESS

Civil Liberties *see* **Civil Rights**

Civil Religion *see* **Secularization**

Civil Rights

Civil rights are rights* that belong to people by virtue of their citizenship in a state* and are legally protected and enforced. They are thus distinguished from human rights* or natural rights* that belong to human beings as human beings. However, arguments for civil rights may proceed from convictions about human rights or natural rights. Although "civil rights" often encompass "civil liberties," the two terms are sometimes distinguished: Civil liberties often include freedom of conscience, of religion, of association, etc., while civil rights often include the right to work, the right to a decent minimum of health care, etc. (*see* **Welfare State**). In the USA the civil rights movement in the 1960s was an effort to eliminate various kinds of discrimination* against blacks (*see* **Afro-American Religious Ethics; Race Relations; Racism; Rights**). For a distinction between civil rights and political rights, *see* **Rights**.

JAMES F. CHILDRESS

Civilization

"Civilization" and "culture"* are frequently treated as synonyms, but it is heuristically advantageous to regard the former as a broader concept that includes the latter. In this reading, civilization refers to all of humankind's efforts to bring about order, security, efficiency, and elegance in its existence outside Eden, whereas culture is (to draw on Hannah Arendt's interpretation of classical categories) the special province of action—the arena of philosophical values, aesthetic expression, and educational or political endeavor which transcends the *labor* necessary for biological survival and the *work* of *homo faber* which provides convenience and comfort. This analytical distinction goes against the tendency of anthropologists to treat culture as inclusive of all artifacts and processes present in a given society, but it is faithful to their inclination to treat culture as a value-neutral term; moreover, it is an accurate reflection of the fact that civilization has typically been a normative concept. An *Encyclopaedia Britannica* definition that comes very close to equating "civilization" and "culture" nevertheless retains an evaluative dimension in its reference to "the aggregate characteristics displayed in the collective life of an *advanced* people or historic period" (italics added). When used as an antonym for "barbarism," it declares that humankind's efforts to build a collective life characterized by material sufficiency, security, justice, and the free pursuit of happiness is far more desirable than a putative "state of nature" where all are at war with all and life is "solitary, poor, nasty, brutish, and short." Indeed, the concept of civilization has tended since the Enlightenment to partake of evolutionary notions of progress* in which Renaissance fondness for *maniera* (i.e., the virtuosity of artifice, which outdoes Nature instead of merely imitating it) glorifies artificiality as the expression of the highest powers of *Homo sapiens*.

It would be difficult to quarrel seriously with the normative connotations of the term. Those who benefit from the achievements of modern technology have even greater reason than Sophocles' chorus in *Antigone* to exult in humankind's ability to harness nature to its purposes; those who have suffered the horrors of war or oppression have even more reason to appreciate the blessings of "law not changing with the strong man's pleasure" and of "language, and thought like the wind and the feelings that make the town." Yet we can acknowledge the advantages of civilization without being blind to its ambiguities. Apostles of romanticism have never ceased to remind us of the wisdom of staying close to Nature and of the "wise passivity" which makes us open to receive its gifts. Freud and his followers have helped us to understand the painful (and to some extent inevitable) conflict between the impulses of human nature and the requirements of civilization. Writers such as Jacques Ellul, Ivan Illich, and Theodore Roszak have attacked the dehumanizing effects of high technology and the mind-set it engenders, and Ernest Becker, Albert Camus, and also a host of Christian theologians have warned against the ironic dangers inherent in Promethean aspirations. The counterculture's protest against the inauthenticity of roles and rules of etiquette may be interpreted as a valid protest against unnecessary or counterproductive rigidities in contemporary civilization.

But surely it is possible to find a golden mean in which civilization is conceived of as a *sensible* ordering of humankind's energies that avoids the perils of modernity without relinquishing its benefits. A morally circumspect definition of civilization, in fact, would insist that its instruments be used to promote human welfare and fulfillment in a way that does not separate us from Nature or our own natures. Some restraints upon healthy human vitalities can be recognized as surplus repressions and relaxed. Appropriate technologies that do not deplete natural resources or smother us in pollution can be devised. And cultural, legal, and administrative checks and balances can protect us against the demonic excesses of the drive to shape our collective destiny.

K. Clark, *Civilisation*, 1970; F. S. C. Northrop, *The Meeting of East and West*, 1952; R. Redfield, *The Character of Civilizations*, 1956; A. Toynbee, *A Study of History*, 12 vols., 1934–61.

HENRY CLARK

Class *see* **Social Class**

Clinical Ethics *see* **Bioethics; Medical Ethics**

Cloning *see* **Reproductive Technologies**

Codes of Ethics

The earliest codes of ethics expressed the basic ethics and law of a culture. Ancient codes, such as the Code of Hammurabi, did not make sharp distinction between the legal and the ethical. They presented in concise fashion the behavioral norms for entire societies or for particular professions or occupations within them.

One of the primary identifying marks of a profession is its commitment to write its own code and enforce it upon its members (*see* **Professional Ethics**). Thus marginal professional groups have often tried to gain legitimacy by writing their own codes and claiming a right to apply them to their members. Now literally hundreds of groups, from the Comic Magazine Association of America to the American Watchmakers Institute, have written their own codes. They generally commit the professional to the welfare of the client, pledge confidentiality*, and commit members of the group to preserve and increase knowledge in the professional field. Often they spell out norms of behavior among members of the profession and in relation to other closely associated professions. Recently, codes have been revised to include commitment to the client's rights as well as welfare (thus combating the paternalism* inherent in many professional codes). They have also begun exploring the limits of the duty to the client, especially when the interests of society conflict.

The oldest and most well established professional codes have been in the medical profession (*see* **Medical Ethics**). Sometimes they appear in the form of an oath or a prayer, but in any case their function is to provide summaries of the ethical norms of the profession. In Western culture the earliest important manifestation was the Hippocratic Oath*, probably dating from the 4th century B.C. Most of the major religious traditions of the world also have codes that spell out physicians' ethical duties.

A number of important questions have surfaced in the recent study of codes of ethics. One is the relationship of code ethics to the basic religious and philosophical ethical systems of the culture. It is apparent, for example, that the Hippocratic Oath is incompatible with the Judeo-Christian tradition. It appeals to Greek gods and goddesses and endorses conceptual and moral perspectives unacceptable to Judeo-Christianity. A Chris-

tianized version of the Oath was prepared in the Middle Ages, but never gained great support.

A second question is whether the members of the profession or others (such as those responsible for teaching and transmitting a tradition) should be responsible for writing the codes. Rabbis have articulated a Jewish view of the ethics of professionals such as physicians that is not always consistent with the views of the professional groups. The most famous Jewish document is a prayer attributed to Moses Maimonides, but actually written in the 18th century. Various Christian traditions offer their own codifications. Thus the U.S. Catholic Conference has prepared a code entitled *Ethical and Religious Directives for Catholic Health Facilities* Protestantism, with its emphasis on lay access to ethical norms, might be expected to have codes written with extensive lay involvement. To the extent that a religious tradition offers a unique ethic, members of that tradition would plausibly want to adhere to a code based on that ethic.

The secular public is also questioning the legitimacy of professionally articulated codes. Several important recent legal opinions in the USA have rejected the idea that professionals can set their own ethical norms of conduct simply because they are professionals. No one seems to deny that many people—parents, patients, and public servants as well as professionals—have special ethical duties that attach to specific roles. What is being challenged is the idea that those in a particular role can define and codify the ethical requirements of that role—especially when their behavior has a direct effect on others such as clients or patients.

The literature in religious ethics has contrasted the ethic of codes with the ethic of contract* or covenant*. In a covenant or contract, emphasis is placed on reciprocal responsibility rather than on a unilateral specification by one group. All parties, drawing on a commonly held ethical perspective such as a religious tradition, jointly articulate the norms, which apply to everyone bound together in a moral community, rather than having the ethic bestowed philanthropically by the professional group. The result would be that each religious or philosophical tradition would generate its own ethical summaries for the various familial, professional, and other social roles. Whether they are in the form of a code or a covenant, oath, or prayer may not be critical.

J. Clapp, *Professional Ethics and Insignia,* 1974; G. R. Dunstan, *The Artifice of Ethics,* 1974; L. Edelstein, "The Hippocratic Oath: Text, Translation and Interpretation," in *Ancient Medicine: Selected Papers of Ludwig Edelstein,* ed. O. Temkin and C. L. Temkin, ET 1967, pp. 3–64; M. B. Etziony, *The Physician's Creed: An Anthology of Medical Prayers, Oaths and Codes of Ethics Written and Recited by Medical Practitioners Through the Ages,* 1973; W. F. May, "Code, Covenant, Contract, or Philanthropy?" *HCR* 5, Dec. 1975, pp. 29–38; U.S. Catholic Conference, Department of Health Affairs, *Ethical and Religious Directives for Catholic Health Facilities,* 1971; R. M. Veatch, *A Theory of Medical Ethics,* 1981.

ROBERT M. VEATCH

Coercion

Coercion is the threat or use of force to constrain another agent's freedom* of action. Coercion and deception are two major ways to control the actions of others without their fully voluntary cooperation. A coerced action is intentional (*see* **Intention**), but it is not totally voluntary (*see* **Responsibility**). Ethical issues in coercion obviously arise in the use of power* by the state* and through the law*, involving both authority* and force, including various sanctions*. They also arise in other actions such as economic boycotts* and strikes*. The justification of coercion is often a major part of the justification of both violent and nonviolent resistance* (*see* **Civil Disobedience**).

See **Behavior Control; Freedom; Paternalism; Penology; Respect for Persons.**

Roger Scruton, *A Dictionary of Political Thought,* 1982.

JAMES F. CHILDRESS

Cognitivism *see* **Metaethics;** *see also* **Descriptivism; Ethics; Intuition; Naturalistic Ethics**

Collective Bargaining

Most of the conditions and terms of work in industrial societies are settled by collective bargaining, if only because the discrepancy of power between a single worker and the management or employer is otherwise extreme. The bargaining is carried out by trade unions or professional associations. It includes conditions of work, pensions, etc., but attention is mainly fixed on wages and salaries. The bargaining can be done locally (plant bargaining), or on a regional or national basis; and there are adumbrations of bargaining beyond national frontiers now that transnational corporations have become powerful. Where worker power is weak, or in government-sensitive occupations, employers may still try to ban union representation, or may insist on a "company union," which is in a weaker position. In the making of wage and salary claims a sharp eye is kept on differentials, on comparability with other jobs that the bargainers consider closest to their own. Also the claims are usually put in terms of justice as fairness. In fact, there are considerable conventional elements in these differentials, mixed up with basic longer-term trends in the demand for, and supply of, workers in various jobs. Particular collective demands are argued for in the forum of public debate and are expressions of a legitimate vested interest. Other vested interests, e.g., those of the consumers of the product or the producers of other products, also need presentation. How successful the bargaining is depends a good deal on the power of the group making it to exercise pressure, with the strike as the ultimate weapon. Medical people are very powerful (because everyone in the community is concerned about health); so are some weekly wage earners in key industries, such as electric power workers; miners used to be, but have become less so with the development of alternative sources of energy. Some workers are in a weak position, either because they are not easy to organize (scattered workers) or because the nature of their jobs makes them unwilling to strike (e.g., nurses). The government and the electorate need to be specially sensitive to those without much negotiating "muscle"; and those with more of it need to be careful not to use it overbearingly against the common good*.

See **Industrial Relations; Labor Movements; Strikes; Trade Unions; Wages and Salaries.**

RONALD PRESTON

Collective Responsibility

Collective responsibility means that all members of an identifiable grouping are answerable, liable, and/or praiseworthy or blameworthy for events, persons, or conditions connected with the group as an entity, and to which some members of the group—but not necessarily all—are immediately or causally related. The principal ethical problem of the concept is whether individual persons justifiably can be held responsible simply by reason of their identification with the group and without reference to their own intention, agency, and awareness. Attempts to bridge the gap between individual and group responsibility usually take the forms of theories of (1) corporate oneness (common identity, mind, consciousness, will); (2) necessary interdependence between group structures and individual members; (3) representation (including tacit consent); and (4) common benefit.

Solidaristic notions of responsibility and guilt* are prominent in the OT, but are called in question in Jer. 31:29–30 and Ezek. 18. Philosophical liberalism, following Locke's individualism, generally has rejected collective responsibility, except as an extension of individual responsibility. Philosophical idealism, with Hegelian inspiration, often has supported it with metaphysical concepts of group reality. Collectivistic philosophies and movements (Marxism, fascism, Nazism) regard individual responsibility as an expression of collective responsibility. Noncollectivistic interpretations of human nature and selfhood as social and relational acknowledge both individual and collective responsibility, and also the tensions between them.

Movements for social justice recognize rightly that structural injustice cannot be explained and corrected solely with reference to individual responsibility, but they tend to forget the religious and humanistic warnings that concepts of collective responsibility and guilt can themselves be instruments of injustice and dehumanization.

See also **Responsibility.**

J. Feinberg, *Doing and Deserving: Essays in the Theory of Responsibility,* 1970; P. A. French (ed.), *Individual and Collective Responsibility,* 1972; K. Jaspers, *The Question of German Guilt,* ET 1947.

THEODORE R. WEBER

Collective Security

A concept or entity for joint action to prevent or resist military aggression. It was intended at the San Francisco Conference (1945) that the United Nations should organize collec-

tive security, but agreement among the great powers to provide the necessary military forces under Chapter VII of the UN Charter has not been forthcoming. In the absence of an effective UN system, states have entered into regional or local agreements that an armed attack against one of them would endanger them all, requiring the parties to meet the common danger by collective action, an arrangement that is consistent with Article 51 of the UN Charter, "until the Security Council has taken measures necessary to maintain international peace and security." Some collective security arrangements include a unified military organization and institutions for political consultation.

See also **Security.**

House of Representatives Committee on Foreign Affairs, *Collective Defense Treaties . . . ,* 1967 (U.S. Government Publication 73-233); A. Martin, *Collective Security: A Progress Report,* 1952.

SYDNEY D. BAILEY

Collectivism

In its more precise meaning collectivism is the theory of the collective ownership of property*, particularly land and the means of production, by the community or society as a whole and for the benefit of the people at large. As such, the theory is basic to the classical formulations of socialism*.

By extension collectivism is used to refer to any society that practices a high degree of governmental control over individual life. Thus Plato's hypothetical Republic and modern totalitarianisms are examples of collectivisms. Ideologically, collectivism is the polar opposite of individualism*, and no actual society is a pure type of either, although societies usually tilt in one direction or the other.

In Christian belief all property ultimately is God's: "The earth is the LORD's" (Ps. 24:1). Thomas Aquinas taught that the pure natural law, prior to the Fall, allowed for no human property rights; people simply shared the goods of creation. Property rights are a necessity for order and personal protection in a fallen world. But those property rights are not absolute; they remain subject to the public good and the needs of other people. Frequently in Christian history various groups (monastic orders and utopian communities) have sought to abolish private property within the community, and some groups (e.g., the 17th-century English Diggers, led by Gerrard Winstanley) sought to abolish private property and all "buying and selling" in society at large. Two centuries later, Karl Marx made the drive for collectivism a major force in the modern world.

In the theory of Marx and Engels private property, particularly private ownership of the means of production, was an illegitimate expropriation by some of what originally belonged to all. They advocated the "expropriation of the expropriators" and the return of property to a collective cooperative ownership. The state, which they expected ultimately to die out, was the temporary instrument of ownership and control. Actually those societies adopting Marxist theory have seen a heightening of the power of the state. So the issue has become the relation of private property and power to the power of the state, which may or may not serve the best interests of the people. The struggle for personal rights against the state becomes a critical issue in collectivist societies, comparable to the struggle for personal rights against corporate economic power in traditional capitalist societies.

Christian ethics often distinguishes between two uses of property. Thus Reinhold Niebuhr identifies the "defensive and offensive" uses of property. In its defensive use, property is a means of protection of individuals and families against the encroachment of others and is an expression of selfhood and creativity. In its offensive meaning, it is an instrument of oppression* against others. Similarly Vatican Council II described private property as "a wholly necessary area of independence," an "extension of human freedom," and "a kind of prerequisite for civil liberties." But it went on to say that "private property has a social quality deriving from the law of the communal purpose of earthly goods."

If there is a Christian consensus, it is that collectivism like individualism has a limited validity within an ethic of concern for the common good*. Continued debate can be expected on the relation between the two.

See **Capitalism; Communism, Ethics of; Individualism; Property; Socialism; Totalitarian State.**

R. Niebuhr, *The Children of Light and the Children of Darkness,* 1944, chs. 2–3; Na-

tional Conference of Catholic Bishops, *Pastoral Letter on Catholic Social Teaching and the U.S. Economy,* 1985; Vatican Council II, *Gaudium et Spes* (Pastoral Constitution on the Church in the Modern World), 1965, pt. II, chs. 3–4.

ROGER L. SHINN

Colonialism

Colonialism commonly refers to the direct and indirect rule of Europeans over the other peoples of the world from 1482, when the Portuguese established Castle Fort at El Mina in West Africa, to a period following World War II, the end being symbolized by the Bandung Conference of 1955. The colonial conquest took the Portuguese, Spanish, French, and English hegemony to India, North and South America, Australia, the Pacific, and other areas of the known world. This hegemony, which was made possible by discoveries in navigation, was motivated by the desire for trade and profit and a concern for national security. It resulted in the destruction of existing civilizations, such as that of the Amerindians; the African slave trade and its legacy; the dispersion of Indians and Chinese as coerced cheap laborers in Africa and the Caribbean; the exploitation of world resources for the betterment of the people of Europe, Russia, and North America; and the establishment of the doctrine of white supremacy.

The European primacy was sustained by technological and military supremacy; revolution in industry, transportation, and commerce; preeminence in science and research; and skill in government and finance. Some scholars, such as Max Weber, have argued that much of this achievement was due in part to a peculiar value constellation that included the Protestant ethic, the capitalist spirit, and individualism, but it was not limited to Protestant countries. The power and pride resulting from these achievements did much to establish the belief that white persons and races were metaphysically and physically superior and possessed the right to dominate all other persons and races and to control their land and resources. Even with the recent formal demise of colonialism, aspects of the system continue to exist.

Colonialism was a vehicle for the transfer across cultural boundaries of moral and religious beliefs, behaviors, and institutions, as well as wealth and power. Western religious and philosophical ethics helped justify every aspect of colonialism. But some Western ethical ideas also established for the first time among non-Western people or stimulated within them their own moral and religious aspirations to dignity and autonomy, including the rights of self-determination and control of their own nation-state. A major present and future task of ethics is to address moral issues resulting from the legacies of colonialism. Of particular importance is the establishment of an inclusive universal moral community with norms that apply equally to all individuals and groups. Failure to accomplish this will produce neocolonialism, that is, Western imperialism in a more subtle and less visible form, or the attempt by the previously ruled to fashion a partial ethic to assert claims that go beyond what might be required by just reparations for past injustices. Where colonialism endures and is recalcitrant, violent revolution may be justified; elsewhere nonviolent means ought to be employed to correct continuing injustices.

See **Exploitation; Imperialism; Race Relations; Racism; Resistance; Revolution.**

PRESTON N. WILLIAMS

Commandments see **Decalogue; Divine Command Morality; Law; Jesus, Ethical Teaching of; Love; Mosaic Law; New Testament Ethics; Old Testament Ethics**

Commercialism

Commercial exchange is an element in economic life in most economic systems, whether or not they are based upon free market assumptions. But the term "commercialism" suggests that individuals or societies have become dominated by acquisitiveness. Whenever commercial activity is taken to be an end in itself, exchange values dominate consciousness and all things are valued in terms of their price on the open market. When Western bourgeois civilization is subjected to cultural criticism, it is often through the charge that it fosters an inordinate spirit of commercialism. Thus, Marxism has asserted that capitalism* transforms all human relationships into a "cash nexus," substituting the "fetish" of money for authentic life process and relationship (see **Marxist Ethics**). Such criticism of commercialism was, of course, long anticipated by the 8th-century Hebrew prophets, by the scathing rebuke of deference to wealth in the NT letter of James,

and, indeed, by Jesus' own warnings about the spiritual consequences of laying up treasures on earth, where moth and rust consume.

Twentieth-century advocates of laissez-faire* capitalism, while not defending materialistic idolatries as such, consider it important for economic life to be driven as directly as possible by acquisitive motives. Disciplined by free market institutions, it is held, human selfishness can be enlisted in mutual service since the only way one can make a profit is by meeting the needs of others. A commercialist spirit is the one dependable motivation for production which accounts for the extraordinary improvements in material well-being in recent centuries. Capitalist writers emphasize that freedom* and justice* are best served when goods and services are accurately priced through the market mechanism: we should pay for what we get and get what we pay for, and we should be free to make our own decisions about all economic exchange. Such writers also emphasize that it is possible to engage in commercial activity without personal selfishness or idolatry.

Criticisms of commercialism that are based on the assumption that economic life can be conducted entirely on unselfish lines may neglect too much the truth of the Christian doctrine of original sin*. The early claims of some socialist countries to have created a "new socialist humanity" based upon selfless devotion to the common good have not stood the test of time (see **Socialism**). The human reality appears universally to manifest a mixture of self-centeredness and generosity of spirit, illustrating Reinhold Niebuhr's belief in human "capacity for justice" and "inclination to injustice." The problem confronting social policy is how to evoke generosity and creativity while ensuring that selfishness does not frustrate justice and corrode the shared values of a culture. Some use of market institutions may be consistent with this, but reliance upon the free market for all economic decisions surely is not. Where the price of all things must be calculated, the concession to commercialism is too great and the inversion of instrumental and intrinsic values too probable.

From a deeper theological perspective, all human institutions* should where possible embody the reality of grace*. When everything has to be paid for or sold, the gracious reality of giving and receiving freely is obscured and human society does not well provide visible manifestation of the theological reality. Some things should simply be available, so far as possible, to be used freely in accordance with human need; and people should be encouraged to contribute freely to the public good.

See **Advertising.**

R. Benne, *The Ethic of Democratic Capitalism,* 1981; E. Fromm (ed.), *Marx's Concept of Man,* 1961; B. Goudzwaard, *Capitalism and Progress: A Diagnosis of Western Society,* ET 1979; K. Polanyi, *The Great Transformation,* 1944.

J. PHILIP WOGAMAN

Common Good

While this teleological term is widely used to point to shared or public values and interests, as, for instance, Augustine's notion of "the advantageousness, the common participation in which makes a people" (*City of God* 19. 21), it is given particular prominence in the social teaching of Roman Catholicism. There it expresses the Catholic distrust of individualism* and concern for institutional order*. The doctrine of the common good is the antithesis of Bentham's claim that the interest of the community is simply "the sum of the interests of the several members who compose it" (*Principles of Morals and Legislation,* ch. 1). It insists on the conditions and institutions which are necessary for human cooperation and the achievement of shared objectives as decisive normative elements in the social situation, elements which individualism is both unable to account for in theory and likely to neglect in practice.

The notion has roots in classical political thought, for instance, in Plato's observation that the goal of his ideal state was not the special advantage of any one class, but "the greatest possible happiness of the city as a whole" (*Republic* 4.240B). Orientation to the common good is laid down by Aquinas as one of the defining features of law (*ST* I-II.90.2). In defending capital punishment, Aquinas proposes a teleological subordination of the individual to the community, and says that in the case of the dangerous criminal "the treatment to be commended is his execution in order to preserve the common good" (*ST* II-II.64.2c). The radical subordination of individual to community was challenged in this century by Jacques Maritain, who argued that the "human common good" had to in-

clude "within its essence the service of the human person," who was endowed with natural rights* (*The Person and the Common Good,* p. 19). Pope John XXIII taught that the common good provides "the whole reason for the existence of civil authorities" (*Pacem in Terris,* par. 54) and requires guarantees for personal rights* and duties. He also maintained that there is an international common good which requires a restructuring of the present order of states (ibid., par. 135). More recent Catholic social teaching has also stressed the contribution of economic development to the common good and the necessity of adapting the notion of the common good to different societies and historical conditions.

See **Official Roman Catholic Social Teaching.**

JOHN LANGAN, S.J.

Communication *see* **Advertising; Confidentiality; Honesty; Lying; Media, Ethical Issues in; Propaganda; Truthfulness**

Communism, Ethics of

As Marxist theory and practice define it, the word "communism" has two related but distinct meanings. On the one hand, it denotes the ultimate stage of human history in which, after the proletarian conquest of power, all human exploitation will end, all self- or group-centered enterprise will be transcended, and each person will contribute freely and rationally to the social product, receiving from it what he or she needs and finding personal fulfillment in the progress of universal humanity. In the *Economic and Philosophical Manuscripts* of 1844, Marx expressed it thus: "Communism as the positive transcendence of private property, or human self-estrangement, and therefore as the real appropriation of the human essence by and for the human being; communism therefore as the complete return of the human being to self as a social (i.e., human) being—a return become conscious and accomplished within the entire wealth of previous development."

This communism—which, he goes on to say, is the true resolution of conflict between human beings, between humanity and nature, between freedom and necessity, and between individual and species, in short the solution of the riddle of history—differs in three respects from other visions of property-sharing community. First, it is foreseen as a community of production—not only, as in the early Christian church (Acts 2:44; 4:32), of property and earnings gained elsewhere. Second, it anticipates a society embracing the whole human species. Radical sectarian communities, both Christian and utopian socialist, are appreciated in Marxist theory, but faulted for their withdrawal from the total class struggle. Third, it is understood not as an ideal but as the essential condition of human society, present naively at the beginning of history in primitive communism, working through the negative form of total deprivation among the proletariat of the capitalist system, ready to establish itself provisionally by state power after the revolution, then to mature into an ultimate solidarity of self-realizing humanity on the highest technological level, which will require no further coercion.

In Marx's words: "After the enslaving subordination of the individual to the division of labor, and therewith also the antithesis between mental and physical labor, has vanished; after labor has become not only a means of life but life's prime want; after the productive forces have also increased with the all-round development of the individual, and all the springs of cooperative wealth flow more abundantly—only then can the narrow horizon of bourgeois right be crossed in its entirety and society inscribe on its banner: From each according to his ability, to each according to his need" (*Critique of the Gotha Program*).

Lenin, in *State and Revolution,* turned the last two stages into a theory of (*a*) socialism, where a dictatorship of the proletariat is still needed to suppress the enemies of the revolution and to structure production so that selfish profit motives will be both used and curbed, and (*b*) communism, where finally "observing the simple, fundamental rules of human intercourse will become a habit" and the state will wither away. In so doing, however, he gave to the word "communism" its other meaning: a movement of workers and peasants, led, disciplined, and educated by Communist parties united in the Third International under the leadership of the Soviet Union, through such violent and coercive steps as are scientifically required by a dialectical materialist understanding of the laws of history, to the ultimate spontaneous solidarity of the communist society. There are passages in Marx and Engels, to be sure, notably

in *The Communist Manifesto* and in *The Civil War in France,* that foreshadow this meaning. But its definition, to the exclusion of all other interpretations of Marx (*see* **Marxist Ethics**), and the organization of a nation and a world movement around it, are the work of Lenin.

Ethics or morality in Communist ideology* so defined has a subordinate role to play in the promotion of social revolution and the construction of a socialist society. Ethical standards, Lenin followed Marx in saying, emerge from and serve the requirements of the particular economic conditions and powers that produce them. All morality therefore expresses the interests and struggles of a particular class. The idea of an eternal moral order whether based on human reason or on the commandments of God is a deception practiced by the possessing classes in defense of their privileged position.

Communist ethics then is subordinate to the revolutionary struggle. It repudiates and condemns the capitalist and feudal social orders as based on exploitation and justifies all steps necessary to bring about their destruction and replacement by a socialist society. Morality is discipline and inner commitment in this struggle. Good and right actions are those that promote this end (*see also* **Ends and Means**).

Communist ethics depend for their content, therefore, on the stage of the working classes' progress in socialism*. In a capitalist society they are the strategy and tactics of revolutionary activity aiming at the capture of power by the "exploited classes" under the leadership of the Communist Party. In colonial or underdeveloped countries an ethic of collaboration with nationalist forces and a positive attitude toward liberal democratic ideals or toward indigenous culture or religion may be called for. After the Communist seizure of power, however, the primary moral obligation becomes constructive and defensive. This means first the conversion of the whole society to "a spirit of collectivism, industry and humanism" (*Program of the XXII Congress of the Communist Party of the Soviet Union*). Negatively, this involves continual ideological struggle to eliminate "individualist" or "unscientific" attitudes and "religious superstition." Positively it calls for the creation of "a new man who will harmoniously combine spiritual and moral purity with a perfect physique" (*XXII Con-*

gress), for whose development the political and economic conditions are already present. This new man, as described by recent literature, will be imbued with an ethos of unstinting labor, a primary concern for public life and welfare, a comradely solidarity with fellow workers and with working people everywhere, a love of country and the entire community of socialist lands, a devotion to the building of communism in the whole world, and "an uncompromising attitude to the enemies of Communism, peace, and the freedom of nations" (*XXII Congress*). The content of this ethic is in many ways similar to the democratic idealism of many Western lands. Honesty, modesty, family loyalty, and responsibility are all given their due place among the virtues named above. The purpose and direction of the whole ethic, however, is the building of a communist society. All else is subordinate to this objective.

Thus the Soviet Communist self-portrait. There is much room in it for moral reflection, as the textbooks point out. "What will the human being be like in the communist future? What will be his moral principles and norms? Which of our present principles and norms will lose their meaning in communism and which will gain greater meaning?" (A. F. Schischkin, *Foundations of Marxist Ethics*). All of this will be reflection on the practice by which communism is in fact built: "The new man forms himself by active participation in the building of communism, by developing communist principles in economic and social life under the influence of the whole system of education through the Party, the state and social organizations in which the press, radio, film and television play a large role." The real issues are found, however, not in this idyll, but in the friction between it and the human reality to which it claims to give shape, both in the present and in the future.

In the present the basic issue is the authority of the Communist Party in defining both the laws of history that lead toward communism and the strategy and tactics by which it is realized. Marx and Engels had already set forth in *The Communist Manifesto* the doctrine of the Party as nothing more than "the most advanced and resolute section of the working class parties of every country" that understands the actual forces and direction of their movement in general terms and moves them toward their goal. The extreme

form of party discipline from which the Communist movement has suffered, however, is due primarily to Lenin, although it has been recently attacked as Stalinism. Lenin limited democracy* in the party to the provisional discussion of tactical matters. He openly argued in his first major work (*What Is to Be Done?* 1902; ET 1933) that the proletariat would never develop more than a trade-union consciousness if left to its own devices. The Party alone, governed by the theories of Marx, was capable of bringing the working classes to a proper understanding of their condition and their revolutionary destiny and the steps necessary to achieve it. Dogmatic unity in the interpretation of Marx was therefore essential in Lenin's scheme. Free debate was in order about immediate steps in Party action but once the Party had decided, rigorous unity was in order. Recalcitrant opponents in the organization were for Lenin dangers to the success of the cause.

Under Stalin and the Chinese Communists this Party discipline was further refined. The Chinese theoretician Liu Shao-chi raised "intra-party struggle" to a basic principle of operation, although he tried to protect it from being directed against personalities. This struggle, for Liu, is the continuing effort of the Party to define the central line of its policy against errors to the left and right, to help comrades purge themselves of such errors, and to expose enemies within the Party. Liu combines this with a concept of the personal self-discipline of a Communist Party member. The initial decision, he points out, does not make one a good Communist. It is only in ceaseless struggle against counterrevolutionaries that one learns to know one's enemy, oneself, and the laws of social development and revolution. In the process one develops into a more effective humble servant and leader of the masses. The same method was developed in more general terms by Mao Tse-tung in his theory of the role of contradictions in history, especially the distinction between antagonistic contradictions, which require total struggle, and nonantagonistic ones, which can be worked out among groups in a society building socialism.

All of this has been expressed in the Communist parties of China, the Soviet Union, and elsewhere by the process of criticism, self-criticism, and confession. This takes place usually in small groups where the members examine each other's attitudes, actions, and thoughts and are encouraged to confess any faults of which they may have been guilty. It is here that the most intimate ethos* of the Communist Party is formed and deviation most thoroughly rooted out. Confessions may be written and rewritten many times until they satisfy the group and its leader. Innermost attitudes are expected to be bared and corrected. The most vivid examples of this collective discipline of the spirit are from the early period of Chinese Communist rule, but a variant form of it is described in Arthur Koestler's story of the Moscow purge trials, *Darkness at Noon* (ET 1946).

Since the death of Stalin, and more recently of Mao, this whole concept of Party discipline has been seriously undermined. Khrushchev's denunciation of Stalin's crimes only three years after his death dealt the ideological authority of the Soviet Communist Party a blow from which it has never fully recovered. The excesses to which Mao's principles were taken by the Cultural Revolution and the radical leadership of the Gang of Four have discredited past discipline there. Resisters in both the Soviet Union and China have been rehabilitated and a few have become heroes. Meanwhile the unity of the Third International under Soviet leadership has been at least defaced by major parties calling themselves Communist—notably the Yugoslavian, the Chinese, and recently the Italian and the Spanish—going in their own directions. By invading Czechoslovakia in 1968 the Soviet Union was able to crush a creative ferment of socialist humanism in Eastern Europe, and to reestablish ideological control by force over the areas it controls. But it has lost ideological leadership and vitality. The union between moral conviction and a sense of the inexorable judgments of history that underlay Communist power a generation ago is gone.

This is reflected also in fading Marxist-Leninist confidence in the communist future. In 1939 Joseph Stalin could report to the XVIII Congress of the Communist Party of the Soviet Union that "the exploiting classes have already been abolished in our country; socialism has been built in the main; we are advancing toward communism." Only capitalist encirclement, the threat from outside, still required the repressive coercion of the state. Since that time official Soviet ideology

has remained stationary in a posture of perpetual advance. The expectation of communism still dominates, as we have seen above. It comes to function more and more however as a sanctification of present power and present policies inside states under Marxist-Leninist domination, and as a utopian ideal raising questions to this power and these policies among Marxists elsewhere (*see* **Marxist Ethics**). In the former case it fills a place remarkably like that which Marx accused religion of filling in a capitalist society. In the latter case it invites Marxism to return to a whole range of questions about judgment, redemption, and hope in human history which it had ruled out by claiming scientific validity for its analysis, strategy, and tactics.

See **Collectivism.**

T. B. Bottomore (ed.), *A Dictionary of Marxist Thought,* 1983; Anne Fremantle (ed.), *Mao Tse-tung: An Anthology of His Writings,* 1962; V. I. Lenin, *What Is to Be Done?* (1902), ET 1933; *The State and Revolution* (1917), ET 1919; Liu Shao-chi, *On Inner Party Struggle,* ET 1951; *How to Be a Good Communist,* ET 1951; *The Program of the XXII Congress of the Communist Party of the Soviet Union,* 1962; A. F. Schischkin, *Grundlagen der marxistischen Ethik* (Foundations of Marxist Ethics), German tr., 1965; R. C. Tucker (ed.), *The Marx-Engels Reader,* ²1978.

CHARLES C. WEST

Community

Two common meanings of community are of secondary interest, but must nonetheless be noted. It is frequently a spatial concept that refers to a geographical or demographic area that functions more or less self-sufficiently in an economic, political, or cultural sense. It is also an item in Ferdinand Tönnies's *Gemeinschaft-Gesellschaft* typology, where it refers to a traditional mode of human interaction characterized by face-to-face contacts with neighbors who are known as persons, clear role-definitions, and group norms which provide a great deal of order and security at the expense of freedom and variety.

But the most interesting and significant use of the concept in recent sociological and theological literature is one that focuses on the spiritual and emotional tone of a group of persons who are bonded by strong commitment to shared values. Christian theologians worthy of the name have always lifted up a vision of religious *koinōnia* that serves as a standard by means of which to measure the depth and worth of sentimental or shallow notions of "togetherness" or "belonging-ness," but in recent years this noble under-standing of community has been refined and enriched by important developments in secu-lar life and thought. The hypocritical and ideological dimensions of certain well-estab-lished conceptions of community have been unmasked and rebuked by movements for ra-cial justice, Third World independence, and equality of women. Humanistic psychology has called attention to the counterproductive effects of inauthenticity and the "antagonistic cooperation" so often found in "polite soci-ety." Sensitivity training has enabled many ostensibly benevolent and goal-oriented func-tionaries to gain greater awareness of their own will to power and the manipulativeness or cruelty it sometimes leads to, and asser-tiveness training has enabled many erstwhile victims to protest effectively against unjust domination or mistreatment. Many people no doubt have a far better comprehension of the kind of authenticity and power balance that are essential to genuine community.

Yet this new insistence on recognition of the legitimate claims of what Paul Tillich called the "power of being" of each individ-ual causes numerous complications that are not easy to discern and difficulties that are not easy to resolve. When the "nicely cal-culated less and more" of justice begins to preoccupy one's mind, the warmth and joy one hopes to experience in community may be to some extent and in certain ways dimin-ished; furthermore, as Reinhold Niebuhr ob-served, unless calculations of entitlement on all sides are reliably open to softening by a spirit of generous self-giving "above and be-yond the call of duty," even the stability of justice will degenerate into a disorderly mix of resentment and attacks. Perhaps Hans Schmalenbach's addition of *Bund* (commu-nion) to the *Gemeinschaft-Gesellschaft* typol-ogy offers a way of understanding what is taking place as people in our time strive to find an experience of community that is rooted in justice. According to Schmalen-bach, the "charisma" that fires intense feel-ings of devotion in a *Bund* must be rou-tinized into the stable commitments and loyalties of a *Gemeinschaft*. Thus community

is a mean between communion and society* just as justice is a mean between love and order.

E. Durkheim, *The Elementary Forms of Reli-gious Life*, ET 1947; G. H. Mead, *Mind, Self and Society*, 1934; F. Tönnies, *Community and Society* (1887), ET 1957; B. Zablocki, *The Joyful Community*, 1971.

HENRY CLARK

Comparative Religious Ethics

The comparative study of religious ethics as well as the practice of religious ethics in a comparative spirit is no doubt as old as the earliest forms of sustained cultural and reli-gious contact and interaction. When advo-cates of one set of religious beliefs and prac-tices begin to realize, reflect upon, and respond to alternate and perhaps conflicting sets of religious belief and practice, the condi-tions are created for "doing" comparative re-ligious ethics.

Still, as a disciplined, academic investiga-tion, the subject is the product of particular 19th- and 20th-century concerns and meth-ods of inquiry. The concerns were both apol-ogetic and scientific. With the dramatic ex-pansion of Christian missions to the non-Western world and with the extensive immigration into the USA of diverse Chris-tian and Jewish groups, contact and interac-tion among different religious people stimu-lated the various confessions to defend themselves explicitly against one another.

At the same time, the "scientific" or "criti-cal" approach to the study of religion, which deeply affected the investigation of the thought, history, and literature of Christian-ity and Judaism, also influenced the compar-ative examination of the world's religions. Here the objective was not so much to defend one confession against another as to describe, analyze, and compare accurately the variety of religious beliefs and practices, and thereby to "understand" them better.

However, there was no hard and fast line between investigators with an apologetic in-terest and those with a scientific one. Some religious apologists made important contri-butions to the anthropological and sociologi-cal study of religious belief and practice, as, for example, Father Bernard Haile's work on the Navaho (1950), and Ernst Troeltsch's contributions in *The Social Teaching of the Christian Churches* (1912, ET 1931). Some apologists also drew upon the results of the scientific study of religion to bolster their defense, as, again, Troeltsch did in *The Absoluteness of Religion* (1912, ET 1971).

Similarly, philosophers like L. T. Hobhouse (1916) and Edward Westermarck (1906–1908) employed sociological and anthropological approaches to support particular secular ethical positions as over against traditional religious views. And a social scientist like Durkheim believed he could construct a "science of morals" out of his cross-cultural studies that would not only exhibit the origins and functions of religious and ethical belief and practice but also provide constructive moral guidance.

In addition, several "grand theories" of social behavior produced in the 19th and early 20th centuries by thinkers like Marx and Engels, and by Freud (1913), purported to make scientific the study of religious and ethical life, and to draw comparative conclusions therefrom. At the same time, these theories were supposed to supply moral direction. From a different perspective, Nietzsche (1887) advanced a theory about the "genealogy of morals" (and religion), which led him to compare and evaluate the religious and ethical beliefs of Christianity, Judaism, and Buddhism.

Two central theoretical issues emerged from all this activity—some of which was impressionistic and offhanded, and some of which was serious and sustained. First, is it possible to develop a general theory for organizing and undertaking a comparative approach to religious ethics? Second, is it possible to find a way to resolve the problem of ethical relativism*? or, in Nietzsche's case, the problem of ethical nihilism*?

The interest in comparative religious ethics has increased, and presently much effort is being expended on the subject. Basically, the same mix of concerns has accompanied this growing endeavor. Some practitioners continue to lean toward the apologetic side, either with a theological interest, such as Hendrik Kraemer (1956), or with a secular point of view, such as P. H. Nowell-Smith (1966). Kraemer defends the superiority of a neo-Reformation version of Christian ethics against "all [other] ethics of the world." By contrast, Nowell-Smith argues that the religious-ethical beliefs, at least of Judaism and Christianity, are authoritarian or "heteronomous," rather than "autonomous." As such,

they represent immature ethical positions, which can be overcome only by adopting a sufficiently secular position. Both thinkers propose ways of organizing and investigating comparative ethical materials, and both, in their different ways, appear to be antirelativists.

Ronald Green in *Religious Reason* (1978) defends a semi-Kantian interpretation of religious ethics. Green believes that this position not only captures the underlying structure of practical reasoning in the world's major religions but also, properly understood, gives uniform moral guidance to members of different traditions.

The works of Christoph von Fürer-Haimendorf (1967), Alexander MacBeath (1952), Richard Brandt (1954), John Ladd (1957), and David Little and Sumner Twiss (1978) all incline toward the scientific side, with a special emphasis upon descriptive, rather than advocative or normative, comparative ethics. Especially Ladd, in his study of the "structure of ethical discourse" among the Navaho, and Little and Twiss try to develop a cross-cultural theory of practical discourse (the way the minds of various peoples work religiously and ethically as they think about and defend pursuing a given course of conduct). This approach stresses the need for careful definitions of terms like "religion" and "ethics," together with the elaboration of types or patterns of reasoning which purport to characterize some of the ways religious and ethical reasons work in different cultural settings.

Ladd, as well as Little and Twiss, conceive of their work in the terms of the traditional Western study of ethics. The basic terms and categories for comparative analysis are adapted from conventional moral philosophy. The approach also rests upon the belief, borrowed from Max Weber and others, that up to some point it is possible to distinguish between advocating a religious-ethical position and describing it, as well as between investigating the "meaning system" or the beliefs of a group and giving a sociological, psychological, economic, or other strictly social-scientific account of a group's way of life.

In keeping with philosophical conventions, this approach differentiates between "first-order" morality or positive ethics (the complex of judgments, standards, principles, and rules of conduct—actual and ideal—of a given group) and "second-order" ethics, in the sense of moral philosophy or moral theology—namely, the critical reflection on and perhaps the reasoned defense of a given morality. Thus, the comparative study of ethics will involve describing and comparing the first-order beliefs and practices of two or more groups and plotting and analyzing second-order reasons offered in justification of the first-order beliefs and practices.

Second-order reflection is itself subdivided. One aspect concerns various types of *normative justification:* Whether, for example, an end or a set of ends (however defined) is taken to justify specified means, or whether certain actions are regarded as simply right in themselves. The other aspect concerns a set of *metaethical considerations* (*see* **Metaethics**). The interest is in the sorts of reasons offered in defense of the normative system adopted by a given group or culture, including the basis for whatever religious and other cosmological and anthropological beliefs underlie that system.

For example, Little and Twiss, having laid out their definitions and analytical apparatus, examine the "patterns of practical justification" in the thought and practice of the Navaho, the Gospel of Matthew, and selected Theravāda Buddhist texts. The argument is that while first-order as well as normative and metaethical notions do vary among these different bodies of thought, the patterns are determinate (and comparable), and are developed in response to certain common basic human concerns.

This approach, in particular, is under critical review from several quarters, and there are emerging proposals for undertaking the comparative study of religious ethics in other ways and with other objectives.

Jeffrey Stout (1981) reflects the doubts of others about the utility of applying conventional Western philosophical techniques to non-Western settings. The attempt to export definitions of "religion" and "ethics" and to trace and compare types of practical justification assumes unwarrantedly, it is charged, that all the terms and categories that are perhaps appropriate in one context are accordingly appropriate in radically different cultures. Furthermore, Stout questions whether some of the basic assumptions of Ladd's and Little and Twiss's approach are in fact valid at all—assumptions, for example, about the disjunction between advocating and describing and between analyzing and explaining.

Stout's objections recall current philosophical disputes that obviously touch on the subject of the comparative study of religious ethics, but go beyond it and involve the larger questions of the possibility of believing in an idea of "cross-cultural rationality." If there can be no such thing, then comparative work, including comparative ethics and religion, must look very different, if they are possible at all.

The objections also raise again the abiding problem of ethical relativism and nihilism. If, as Stout contends, it makes no sense to posit objective structures of reason, which might be appealed to in face of ethical and religious (not to mention scientific) conflict, then it is hard to see how anyone might be held accountable by other than purely ethnocentric standards.

Stout's skepticism about the possibility of "global" theories of comparative religious ethics is echoed elsewhere. From another perspective, some students of religion propose a more "holistic" method of study, whereby, presumably, religious and ethical beliefs and practices are examined as part of a self-contained web of belief. Moreover, less attention should be given, it is argued, to investigating practical rules and principles, and more attention paid to the place of stories, myths, parables, and other more informal ways of guiding action.

See **Anthropology and Ethics; Sociology of Ethics;** and articles on different religious traditions (*see* **Religious Ethics**).

R. Brandt, *Hopi Ethics,* 1954; S. Freud, *Totem and Taboo* (1913), ET 1962; C. von Fürer-Haimendorf, *Morals and Merit,* 1967; R. Green, *Religious Reason,* 1978; B. Haile, *Legend of the Ghostway Ritual,* 1950; L. T. Hobhouse, *Morals in Evolution,* 1916; H. Kraemer, *The Christian Message in a Non-Christian World,* 1938; J. Ladd, *Structure of a Moral Code,* 1957; D. Little and S. B. Twiss, *Comparative Religious Ethics,* 1978; A. MacBeath, *Experiments in Living,* 1952; F. Nietzsche, *The Birth of Tragedy* and *The Genealogy of Morals* (1872; 1887), ET 1956; P. H. Nowell-Smith, "Morality: Religious and Secular," in I. Ramsey (ed.), *Christian Ethics and Contemporary Philosophy,* 1966; J. Stout, *Flight from Authority,* 1981; P. Taylor, *Normative Discourse,* 1961; E. Troeltsch,

The Social Teaching of the Christian Churches (1912), ET 1931; and The Absoluteness of Christianity (²1912), ET 1971; R. Tucker, The Marx-Engels Reader, 1978; E. Westermarck, The Origin and Development of the Moral Ideas, 2 vols., 1906–1908.

DAVID LITTLE

Compassion

In the parable of the good Samaritan (Luke 10:29–37), Jesus noted that when the Samaritan saw the victim of the robbers who had been left "half dead," he "had compassion, and went to him and bound up his wounds, pouring on oil and wine." When Jesus (Matt. 9:36) "saw the crowds, he had compassion for them, because they were harassed and helpless, like sheep without a shepherd." Compassion is one of the emotions, or attitudes with an emotional component, that are altruistic or other-regarding. Compassion presupposes sympathy*, is close to both pity and mercy*, and leads to acts of beneficence* —the Samaritan "showed mercy on "the victim and "took care of him." Compassion is often an expression of love*, or agapē. As L. Blum notes, "compassion is not a simple feeling-state but a complex emotional attitude toward another, characteristically involving imaginative dwelling on the condition of the other person, an active regard for his good, a view of him as a fellow human being, and emotional responses of a certain degree of intensity" and duration. Acts of beneficence that flow from compassion need to be rational and effective, as the good Samaritan's actions were. However, compassion is also appropriate where no action is possible or would be effective. An ethical perspective emphasizing compassion (see, e.g., A. Schopenhauer, The Basis of Morality, 1841, ET 1965) can provide a valuable corrective to ethical theories that downplay emotion in the name of duty and rationality (see Kantian Ethics).

L. Blum, "Compassion," in Explaining Emotions, ed. A. O. Rorty, 1980.

JAMES F. CHILDRESS

Compensationism

A moral system that resembles tutiorism* in favoring the safer course where there is doubt about the obligatoriness of an act. The name indicates that the doubt whether the law applies must be weighed against the person's imperfect understanding of the law, and suitable compensation made for the latter.

JOHN MACQUARRIE

Complicity see Cooperation with Evil

Compromise

The problem with which compromise is concerned arises when it is realized how radical is much of the ethical teaching of the kingdom of God in the NT. Christians seek to realize the kingdom in action, but it transcends any partial realization, and points to an eschatological realization beyond history. At the same time, its eschatological challenge in the present inspires efforts to improve on the status quo. This applies to the personal life of Christians, to the corporate life of the church, and to both Christians and the church as they live amid the educational, economic, industrial, and political structures of life in society, where they are placed by God cheek by jowl with persons of all faiths and none and have to find some way of living and acting with them. To some extent the dilemmas are softened by an appeal to "natural law" or "common grace" or "civic righteousness," all of which express in their own way the continuous creating and sustaining activity of God in society. The most radical elements of the ethic of the new creation in Christ are to operate in society as a leaven in the lump, but not to control it directly. But the dilemmas are not removed, because (1) all the structures and all the individual lives are corrupted by an entail of sin from the past, which means that they do not start in the present unblemished as ideally we would like them to; and (2) collective action means that one rarely secures a decision that is exactly what one would wish, and has to be content with only a proportion of it. Sometimes, indeed, the collective decision goes against what one would wish, and then one has to decide whether to stand aside as a conscientious objector or go along with the majority. Even in more intimate personal situations there often arises a tension between what seems feasible and what one would wish. In the last resort, both decisions in the more personal and those in the more collective aspects of life are decisions of the individual conscience* (see also Conscientious Objection).

How far are accommodations to the circumstances to be regarded as compromises? They can be looked at in two ways. If after all the factors have been weighed a decision is arrived at as to what action is best *in the circumstances,* and if no better is available, it is misleading to call it a compromise. That might imply that there was a Christian duty which was being evaded. On the other hand, it can be looked at in a more radical dimension as an inevitable falling away from the demands of the gospel because of the entail of personal and social sin of which one is inescapably a part; the only thing to do (as Luther said) is to "sin boldly," knowing that one is justified before God by faith, not works. Seen in the first way, it is still possible that the Christian's judgment may be distorted by sin. We may err in judgments about the facts of the case because of inevitable (invincible) or culpable (vincible) ignorance*, and we may fail in practice by weakness* to carry out what we have decided we ought to do. Christians are neither infallible nor sinless. However we look at it, we must try to find out what is the right thing to do in particular circumstances and do it, unless and until the evidence changes. This discussion presupposes an "ethic of responsibility" (*see also* **Ends and Means; Responsibility**). Some Christians have held to an "ethic of inspiration," which proceeds either from a biblical text or from a sense of direct guidance to a detailed conclusion about conduct. These persons do not have the sense of a tension between the radical gospel and the immediate possibilities. Many of them have formed separatist Christian "communes."

See also **Ecclesiology and Ethics; Sect; Conflict of Duties.**

RONALD PRESTON

Computers

Computers are fundamentally machines that count. Simple devices of this sort, such as the abacus, are of great antiquity. More recently, mechanical calculating machines, such as Comptometers and cash registers, have given way to much more sophisticated electronic computers able to perform many thousands of calculations in fractions of a second.

Earlier computers were powered by transistors invented in 1948 by William Shockley and colleagues at the Bell Telephone Laboratories. By the 1950s transistors were being made out of silicon, one of the earth's most abundant materials. Before the end of the 1980s it may be possible to build more than a million such transistors into small chips of silicon the size of a human fingernail. It has been estimated that silicon integrated circuits able to simulate the functions of the human brain could soon be put together into a space smaller even than the brain itself. The impetus for both the speeding up of the calculating process and the miniaturization of the machinery involved has come chiefly from the demands of space exploration as well as from government defense contracts.

Computers can be used either to control machines or to provide information. Electronic checkouts at supermarkets can be automatically linked to stock control records, electronically controlled tractors can plow fields without a farm worker in the cab, vehicles can be assembled in factories by machinery controlled by computers, computer-aided design (CAD) can speed up work in industrial drawing offices, funds can be transferred from one bank to another and credit card accounts kept under almost instant control by computers. Libraries can record information about millions of volumes in a computer, legal and educational information can be stored and made more widely available, medical information can be quickly handled, documents can be reproduced and transmitted without the need for any postal system.

The rapid growth of computer usage has posed a number of human problems. New skills, for example, are needed to develop, program, and use computers, and these skills need constant updating. Those whose jobs become obsolete as a result of technological advance may not easily be able to learn the new skills required. Miners or shipyard workers in one part of the country cannot easily become microprocessor assemblers in another. Information fed into computers may sometimes become available to unauthorized users, and there is concern about the protection of such data. Computers may be used for increased social control, speeding up surveillance by police and other authorities. Computer fraud, chiefly involving the misdirection of funds, is a large and growing area of criminal activity.

Access to information is also related to the exercise of power. Greater availability of information, through home computers and information systems linked to telephones and television networks, can make possible a more general participation in the decision-making process in the community as a whole. On the other hand, those with access to the large sums of money needed to use such advanced technology may gain a disproportionate degree of power over others if unchecked by democratic processes. Control by computers holds out both a threat and a promise to democracy* itself.

See also **Automation; Privacy; Robots; Technology.**

D. Burnham, *The Rise of the Computer State,* 1984; D. G. Johnson, *Computer Ethics,* 1985; E. J. Laurie, *Computers, Automation, and Society,* 1971; G. Simons, *Silicon Shock: The Menace of the Computer Invasion,* 1985.

PAUL BRETT

Concubinage

The habitual practice of sexual intercourse between a man and a woman who are not married to one another. Cohabitation may or may not be associated with it. Concubinage of the clergy was a problem for many centuries after clerical celibacy* had been made compulsory in the church of the West.

HERBERT WADDAMS

Concupiscence

Concupiscence refers to immoderate desires, especially sexual. Its kindred concept, lust*, has traditionally been condemned as one of the "seven deadly sins." The problems involved are psychological as well as spiritual. Substance abuse—overeating, alcoholism, drug-taking—are examples of inordinate desires stemming from psychological pain. More generally, contemporary thought recognizes that repression of desire can be as problematic as its inappropriate expression. Desire* as such is not to be condemned, and it can only be unbalanced to tackle the disorders of desire without at the same time maintaining a positive affirmation of the value of the human personality.

J. B. Nelson, *Embodiment,* 1979.

ELIZABETH R. MOBERLY

Conduct *see* Act, Action, Agent

Confession

The acknowledgment of one's guilt* to other persons or to God. Confession was described by Bonhoeffer as the "renewal of the joy of baptism," and it is intended not as an un-

healthy brooding over past sins but as a turning to new life, which can be done honestly if there is acknowledgment and renunciation of past wrongs. The NT enjoins the practice: "Confess your sins to one another, and pray for one another, that you may be healed" (James 5:16). In this passage there is a typical linking of confession with healing. Modern psychiatry has rediscovered the healing effects of confession. To make confession and to hear words of forgiveness* can be a release from guilt feelings and from the moral paralysis and impotence that sometimes go with them. On the other hand, an overconcern about confessing one's sins can be a mark of scrupulosity* or a morbid parading of one's intimate feelings, and there can even be a perverted boasting of one's sins.

The church provides for confession in various ways. (1) Most acts of public worship include a general confession, which is designed to promote self-examination*, repentance*, and the assurance of forgiveness. (2) A Christian may make confession of sin to any fellow Christian, and it is important that this should be done to anyone who has been injured, as part of the process of reconciliation. Christians to whom such a confession has been made should offer such advice as they can, and assure the penitent of forgiveness. (3) The sacrament of penance* (also called the sacrament of reconciliation*) provides for private confession to a priest, who is authorized to give to the penitent absolution*, counsel, and penance (an act designed to express sorrow for the sins committed—nowadays, often the reading of an appropriate psalm). (4) Sometimes strict ecclesiastical discipline has demanded a public confession followed by a public penance, but this would be very rare in modern times.

D. Bonhoeffer, *Life Together,* ET 1954; B. Häring, *Shalom: Peace—The Sacrament of Reconciliation,* ET 1968.

JOHN MACQUARRIE

Confidentiality

The two major contexts in which the confidentiality of verbal communication is thought to be especially important are the marital relationship and the relationship between clients and several of the helping professions—especially law, medicine, nursing, social work, and the ministry. Elaborate moral and legal rules have been developed in many societies to assure that communications in these special contexts will be protected from public view.

The most detailed ethical analyses of the duty to preserve the confidentiality of communications occur in Roman Catholic textbooks of moral theology (see especially Regan). Perhaps because of the importance of confidentiality in the relationship of priest and penitent, one finds in the classic textbooks detailed examination of such issues as the nature of a secret, mental reservation, and the circumstances under which secrets may or may not be revealed by professionals.

The major moral justifications for confidentiality fall into two broad categories: consequentialist and nonconsequentialist (*see* **Consequentialism; Deontology**). Consequentialists generally justify the social practice of preserving confidentiality in certain contexts by arguing that the efficient functioning of the physician-patient or lawyer-client relationship would be impeded without it. Nonconsequentialists (or deontologists) usually justify confidentiality by relating it either to the duty of promise-keeping, if an implied or explicit promise* has been made, or to the duty to respect the autonomy* of persons, who in this case would otherwise lose control over important information about themselves.

In both law and ethics the duty to preserve confidentiality is generally considered to be only a prima facie duty—one that can be overridden by other, more compelling duties in certain circumstances (*see* **Conflict of Duties**). The three general grounds most often adduced for breaching confidentiality are: (1) protection of the client from harm; (2) protection of an identifiable second party, e.g., an intended victim; and (3) protection of nonidentifiable individuals or the society at large, e.g., the airline passengers who may go down with a pilot whose failing eyesight is not reported by a sympathetic physician. These grounds for breaching confidentiality are more compelling when they are forward-looking—i.e., aim to prevent a possible future occurrence—than when they are backward-looking. They are also more compelling as the probability and magnitude of the hypothetical harm increase.

See **Secrecy**.

S. Bok, *Secrets: On the Ethics of Concealment and Revelation,* 1983; H. A. Davidson, "Professional Secrecy," in E. F. Torrey (ed.), *Ethical Issues in Medicine,* 1968, ch. 9; C. DeWitt, *Privileged Communications Between Physicians and Patients,* 1958; C. Fried, *An Anatomy of Values,* 1970, ch. 9; R. E. Regan, *Professional Secrecy in the Light of Moral Principles,* 1943; L. Walters, "Ethical Aspects of Medical Confidentiality," in T. L. Beauchamp and L. Walters (eds.), *Contemporary Issues in Bioethics,* [2]1982, pp. 198–203.

LEROY WALTERS

Conflict of Duties

Strictly speaking, this phrase is a misnomer because if something really is our duty, it cannot conflict with any other duty*, but the phrase is used to signify cases where there are moral reasons in favor of each of two or more incompatible actions. I think this is best discussed in terms of a phrase coined by Sir David Ross, "prima facie* duties." A prima facie duty is a possible action for which there would be a compelling moral reason in the absence of any moral reason against it, so that it is always obligatory to fulfill a prima facie duty if it does not conflict with any other. Thus it is a prima facie duty not to lie, but this may conflict with a prima facie duty to save a person from being murdered. The prima facie duties are sometimes regarded as ultimate, sometimes as dependent on the good they produce; also we think of ourselves as having prima facie duties that put us under special obligations to further the good of, e.g., relatives rather than the equal good of a stranger. It is arguable that they can all ultimately be explained on utilitarian grounds, but even if this is true—and it would be much disputed—the above account comes much nearer the way in which we usually think in practical life than does pure utilitarianism* (even if the good is conceived as wider than pleasure). No philosopher has succeeded in producing adequate general rules for dealing with conflicts of duties, probably because this is intrinsically impossible. Sometimes we can see quite clearly that one obligation is more weighty than another, but in many cases it is a matter of difficult individual judgment where one could not venture to condemn anybody who disagreed with one. The sharpest and most obvious cases of conflict of duties occur in war, but they are present in a lesser degree throughout life if only because time and resources devoted to furthering one end have to be taken from the time and resources devoted to furthering another.

A. C. EWING

Confucian Ethics

The core of Confucian ethics lies in the moral teachings of Confucius (551–479 B.C.) and the brilliant but divergent contributions of Mencius (371–c. 298 B.C.) and Hsün Tzu (fl. 298–238 B.C.). Significant developments, particularly along a quasi-metaphysical route, are to be found in the works of Chang Tsai (1020–1077), Ch'eng Hao (1032–1085), Ch'eng I (1033–1107), Chu Hsi (1130–1200), Lu Hsiang-shan (1139–1193), and Wang Yang-ming (1472–1529). Li Kou (1009–1059), Wang Fu-chih (1619–1692), and Tai Chen (1723–1777) have also made noteworthy contributions to the critical development of Confucian ethics. In the 20th century, the revitalization and transformation of Confucian ethics has taken a new turn in response to Western philosophical traditions. Important advances have been made by Fung Yu-lan, T'ang-Chün-i, Thomé Fang, and Mou Tsung-san. Most of the recent works in critical reconstruction are marked by a self-conscious concern with analytic methodology and, to a lesser extent, with phenomenology and existentialism. Still lacking, perhaps in the making, is a comprehensive and systematic Confucian ethics informed by both the history and the problems of Western moral philosophy.

While major Confucian thinkers differ in their conceptions of the foundation of morality, most of them accept Confucius's ideal of a well-ordered society based on good government that is responsive to the basic needs of the people and to the issues of wise management of natural resources and of just distribution of burdens and benefits. In this vision of social order, special emphasis is put on harmonious human relations in accord with virtues or standards of excellence*. In this respect, Confucian ethics is an ethics of virtue*, concerned primarily with the cultivation of moral character* rather than with the inculcation of moral principles or rules. Drawing freely from the contributions of major Confucianists and contemporary philosophical scholarship, this article presents the basic concepts in classical Confucian ethics and a sketch of its response to two distinct, though related, problems in ethical theory: rules and exceptions, and justification.

Basic concepts. The *Lun Yü,* commonly known as the *Analects,* are the main source of the teachings of Confucius, and provide a complex ethical vocabulary. This vocabulary contains a large number of aretaic terms, or terms referring to virtues. A careful study of the *Analects* discloses five basic concepts: *tao, te, jen, li,* and *yi.* The most incisive and comprehensive study of these basic aretaic notions, along with more than twenty others, has been made by Chen Ta-ch'i. While most aretaic notions can be rendered into English (e.g., those that refer to filiality, fraternal piety, courage, wisdom, respectfulness), the five basic concepts do pose a problem for conceptual explication. In the first place, terms such as *tao* have been appropriated by different Chinese schools of thought, and *jen* has undergone a complex conceptual evolution in the history of Confucian philosophy. In the second place, the basic Confucian notions have no exact equivalents in English; they can be rendered in a variety of ways. These translations do inevitably embody the writer's interpretations. Moreover, even in Chinese these terms can be used in different ways. *Tao,* for example, can be used as a verb, meaning "to speak" or "to guide"; and as a concrete noun, meaning literally a "road." In the latter sense, it can be rendered as "way." But in distinct Confucian ethical usage, it is *tao* as an abstract noun that is meant, and more specially in the evaluative rather than descriptive sense. Without raising the difficult and still unresolved problem of textual scholarship, perhaps the best approach to understanding the basic Confucian notions is to regard them as "focal notions," i.e., terms that function like focal lenses for conveying distinct, though not unrelated, centers of ethical concern. As generic terms, focal notions are amenable to specification in particular contexts of discourse, thus acquiring specific or narrower senses. This distinction owes to Hsün Tzu. But it must be noted that, in general, a term may be used as a specific term in one context, and yet in another context as a generic term subject to further specification. In other words, the use of a term in the generic or specific sense is entirely relative to the speaker's purpose on a particular occasion, rather than to any theory concerning the intrinsic characters of terms or the essential attributes of things. The following gives a brief explication of the basic Confucian concepts as generic notions amenable to detailed specifications.

As noted in the preceding, *tao* is an evaluative term. The focal center of ethical interest lies in the Confucian vision of the good life on the whole or an ideal of human excellence. *Tao,* commonly rendered as "the Way," is functionally equivalent to the notion of the ideal way of life. Unlike the other basic terms, *tao* is most distinctive as an abstract term in the highest generic sense that is subject to specification by way of *jen, li,* and *yi.* Before attending to these aretaic notions, something must be said about *te. Te* has a homophone which means "to get." In Chu Hsi, *te* is explained as that which an individual obtains (in following the *tao*). Thus when a person succeeds in realizing the ideal, *tao,* he or she has attained moral excellence. The specification of *te,* apart from *jen, li,* and *yi,* can take a variety of forms, e.g., courage, trustworthiness. In this sense, *te* is an abstract noun, like *tao,* but depends on *tao* for its distinctive ethical character. *Te* is thus functionally equivalent to "ethical virtue." Thus Confucian ethics, with its emphasis on *te,* is properly characterized as an ethics of virtue, but more informatively as an ethics of *jen, li,* and *yi,* since *te* requires these terms for specification. *Jen, li,* and *yi,* relative to other aretaic notions, are generic focal notions, though specific relative to *tao* as a generic term. *Jen* focuses on the love and care for one's fellows, i.e., an affectionate concern for the well-being of others. *Jen* is functionally equivalent to *agapē.* In Confucian ethics, the method of pursuing *jen* lies in *chung* and *shu. Chung* may be rendered as "doing one's best," and *shu* as "consideration of others." Much like the Christian Golden Rule, *chung* and *shu* focus on doing one's best in accord with one's desire to acquire *jen, li,* and *yi,* with due consideration to other people's desires. In this light, Confucian ethics displays a concern for both self-regarding and other-regarding virtues. However, the acquisition of these virtues presupposes a locus in which these virtues are exercised. Here Confucian ethics stresses the primacy of filiality and fraternal piety as a basis for the extension of *jen,* which focuses on love and care for one's fellows. The family is thus viewed as the basis for extending affection. In this way, the method of *jen,* i.e., *chung* and *shu,* presupposes its practice in the family. In Sung and Ming Confucianism (e.g., Chu Hsi and Wang Yang-ming), *tao* is sometimes used interchangeably with *jen.* In this manner, *jen* has attained the status of a supreme ethical ideal of extensive affection. Confucius's vision of a well-ordered society is now seen as a vision of *jen,* i.e., a good human community characterized by extensive mutual care and affection.

The notion of *li* focuses on the ritual code. For this reason, it is commonly rendered as "rites" or "ritual propriety." The ritual code is essentially a set of formal prescriptions or procedures for proper behavior, a set of ritual rules that pertains to the manner or style of performance. Since the ritual code represents a tradition or customary practice, the Confucians, particularly Hsün Tzu and the writers of some chapters of the *Li Chi* (The Book of Propriety), were concerned with providing a rational justification for complying with these traditional rules of proper conduct. The notion of *yi,* in part, is an attempt to provide a rationale for the acceptance of *li. Yi* focuses principally on what is right and reasonable. It has a near homophone which means "appropriate." The equation of *yi* and "appropriate" is explicit in *The Doctrine of the Mean,* and generally accepted by major Confucianists (e.g., Hsün Tzu, Li Kou, and Chu Hsi). However, since what is right and reasonable depends primarily on judgment, *yi* may be understood as reasoned judgment concerning the right thing to do, more especially in particular circumstances. In relation to *li,* it has a dual significance: (1) that the *li* are the right sort of rules to regulate conduct, and (2) that the *li* require reasoned judgment for their application to particular cases. Since the *li* embody a tradition, their acceptability depends on the exercise of *yi.* Where the *li* conform to *yi,* they may be accepted as reasonable rules of conduct. And since *yi* focuses on right and reasoned judgment, it may be said to be opposed to an exclusive concern with self-interests. In sum, as basic notions, *jen, li,* and *yi* express three distinct centers of ethical concern. As aretaic notions, *jen* expresses the virtue of extensive affection; *li,* the virtue of rule-compliance; and *yi,* the virtue of sound judgment. In Aristotelian language, *jen* and *li* are moral virtues, and *yi* an intellectual virtue, functionally equivalent to Aristotle's *phronēsis* or practical wisdom (*see* **Aristotelian Ethics; Prudence**).

Problems of rules and exceptions and justification. The problem of rules and exceptions, construed in terms of building exceptions to the rules, is not a genuine problem in Confucian ethics. For the notion *yi* can be employed in dealing with perplexities concerning what one ought to do in a particular situation. For classical Confucians like Mencius and Hsün Tzu, perplexities arise largely from changing circumstances of human life. As Hsün Tzu succinctly reminds his readers: "One must use *yi* to respond to changing circumstances." Difficult cases for deliberation are those that can be resolved by an appeal, not to an established rule, but to one's reasoned judgment of the right or fitting thing to do. Mencius is particularly emphatic on the exercise of discretion (*ch'uan*) in coping with exigent situations. When queried as to what a person ought to do when his sister-in-law is drowning, in light of the *li* requirement that male and female are not to touch one another in giving or receiving anything, Mencius appeals to discretion rather than to rule compliance. This appeal has nothing to do with making an exception to a rule of proper conduct, but refers to one's sense of rightness in exigent situations. In light of *yi*, a rule may be judged to be irrelevant to ethical perplexity, not because it has no authoritative status, but rather because the *li* as a set of ritual rules are not intended to cover all circumstances of human life. It is *yi* that responds to ethical perplexities. More explicitly, Li Kou considers *yi* as "decisive judgment that is appropriate (to the situation at issue)." In this writer's opinion, the characterization of Confucian ethics as an ethics of flexibility is quite accurate in light of *yi*. Moreover, there are grounds in the *Analects* for this flexible attitude toward changing circumstances. It is recorded that Confucius once said of himself: "I have no preconceptions about the permissible and the impermissible."

Quite naturally, one may raise the question of rational justification for such judgments in exigent circumstances. In normal situations, the *li* are quite sufficient when an action is informed by a concern for *jen*. The problem of rational justification has not received attention from most major Confucian thinkers, except Hsün Tzu. Even in the works of Hsün Tzu, we do not receive any explicit answer to this problem. However, his works do provide materials for constructing a response to this problem. In the first place, Hsün Tzu is quite explicit that any discussion is valuable because there exist certain standards for assessment, and these standards pertain principally to conceptual clarity, respect for linguistic practices and evidence, and to the requirement of consistency and coherence in discourse. A philosophical reconstruction along the line of ethical argumentation presents an interesting Confucian view of justification in terms of rational and empirical standards of competence, along with certain desirable qualities of participants in ethical discourse. In this reconstruction of Hsün Tzu's works, ethical justification is a phase of discourse that is preceded by explanatory efforts in the clarification of normative claims, which in turn presupposes that queries concerning the proper uses of terms are understood by the participants in ethical argumentation. It must be noted that Confucians in general are fond of appeal to historical paradigmatic individuals. This ethical use of historical knowledge or beliefs is a pervasive feature of early Confucianism. This feature of Confucian ethics deserves further inquiry.

In closing, it may be noted that Confucian ethics, like any normative system in the West, presents conceptual problems of interpretation and reconstruction. In addition to the problems discussed in this article, there are also important problems on the unity of virtues, the connection between morality and human nature, the relation between moral knowledge and action, and the metaphysical grounding of morality. A serious student of Confucian ethics must consider these problems with reference both to the tension and divisive efforts in coping with these problems within the history of Confucian philosophy, and to the significance of these efforts in light of systematic Western ethical theories.

Wing-tsit Chan (tr.), *A Source Book in Chinese Philosophy,* 1963; Wing-tsit Chan and Charles Fu, *Guide to Chinese Philosophy,* 1978; Chen Ta-ch'i, *Kung Tzu hsüeh-shuo,* 1977; A. S. Cua, *Dimensions of Moral Creativity: Paradigms, Principles, and Ideals,* 1978; *The Unity of Knowledge and Action: A Study in Wang Yang-ming's Moral Psychology,* 1982; and *Ethical Argumentation: A*

Study in Hsün Tzu's Moral Epistemology, 1985; H. Fingarette, *Confucius: The Secular as Sacred,* 1972; D. C. Lau (tr.), *Confucius: The Analects,* 1979; *Mencius,* 1970; B. Watson (tr.), *Hsün Tzu: Basic Writings,* 1963.

A. S. CUA

Conscience

The term is fairly often used in general speech, in such phrases as "in all conscience" or "I have it on my conscience," but its meaning varies and is often vague. For instance, the second phrase might mean "I must do something" or "I'm uneasy about what I've done." However, it is a sufficiently well known term to be embodied in Article 18 of the Universal Declaration of Human Rights, which refers to "the right to freedom of thought, conscience and religion." In popular Christian speech its meaning also varies. If a Christian says "My conscience tells me," it might mean "This is what I have thought out" or "God has told me this and I must obey." The latter is often called the "telegram from heaven" view. There has been much theological, philosophical, and psychological attention given to the term, but there is a mainstream Christian tradition that needs consideration before a brief reference is made to other views.

The classical definition is that of Thomas Aquinas: conscience is "the mind of man making moral judgments." More precisely, Aquinas held that human persons have an awareness of basic moral principles (which he called synderesis*), and that conscience is the judgment of the practical reason as it brings these to bear on particular questions of right and wrong. Just as the reason works on questions of true and false, so it works on questions of right and wrong. We can see that such a concentration on the mind without considering the emotions is too restrictive, but it does bring out the fundamental point that practical moral decisions need reasons to justify them. Feelings are not enough. I may, for instance, be full of "righteous indignation" at the behavior of the British to Ireland in the past and in the present, but that does not of itself justify any action of protest I may choose to take, such as planting a bomb in a disco or assassinating a judge. The emotions come in when we are committed to doing what our moral judgment (conscience) has decided is right, and to shunning what we have decided is wrong. So we might say that

conscience is the whole person passing moral judgments on issues of right and wrong, or that, as the poet T. S. Eliot said, "it is the power to feel our thoughts and think our feelings" in moral questions. In the same way, when conscience passes judgment on what *has been* done we feel either "pangs of conscience" or feelings of approval. Because humans are "fallen" creatures, the pains of conscience are familiar and, paradoxically, the more sensitive our conscience becomes, the less likely we are to enjoy a "good" conscience. It is the clear testimony of those we consider the most saintly that they have a sense of the gulf between what *is* and what they know *ought to be* in their own lives.

The traditional Christian teaching is that one must always obey one's conscience (*Conscientia semper sequenda*). This is not meant to bolster prejudices or to assert that conscience is infallible. Far from it. Conscience can err because our judgments can be corrupted by personal, social, and economic interests; it can err because it makes errors of factual judgment, and because of ignorance; it can err by not being sensitive enough to the personal and social factors involved in the issues at stake; and it can err by wrongly estimating the possible consequences of possible actions in deciding what to do (and there can rarely be practical certainty in advance about these). Yet the traditional teaching is that an erring conscience (objectively considered) must be followed. We must take responsibility as adults before God for our decisions; no one can live my life for me. Even if we take, e.g., a vow of obedience, the decision to do so must be a conscientious one, and even then if we are ordered to do something against our conscientious judgment we should disobey, whatever anguish or possible danger this causes. The Allies also took this view of German military personnel in the Nuremberg trials after World War II; it was held that on certain points they should have disobeyed their military oath to Hitler. It is a solemn and hard doctrine, which applies all around.

All this means that reasonable care must be taken to consider relevant factors in arriving at a moral judgment. We have therefore a duty to educate our conscience. As Christians we are to allow the mind of Christ to be formed in us (1 Cor. 2:16) so that we grow in sensitivity, in the art of moral discernment*. The right environment for the education of conscience is life in the fellowship of the church. Here we shall draw on the resources of prayer, sacramental participation in Christ, and Bible study. Here we shall learn from the practical wisdom the church has acquired over nearly two thousand years, as well as from its mistakes, and be prepared to face the unknowns of the future unafraid. Here we may receive corporate and personal counsel from our fellow Christians in general, and from clergy and ministers in particular. But these Christian aids do not exhaust the sources for the education of conscience. We cannot afford to ignore the whole sweep of human knowledge wherever it is relevant, and our sources for this are not peculiarly Christian ones but such as are available to the public at large. We need much more discussion of moral problems among Christians in diverse groups, if only to correct and check our judgments, for some of the worst deeds have been done with a "good" conscience and often in the name of religion. It has been said that humans never work such havoc as when invoking God—or an ideology. Technical moral theology* distinguishes between a "material" sin (where conscience is "objectively" in error) and a "formal" sin (where one goes against one's own conscientious judgment). The distinction is important, though the terminology is confusing. It also discusses certain, probable, indifferent, scrupulous, and doubtful consciences, and how they can be helped pastorally. And it differentiates between invincible ignorance (which is not our fault) from vincible ignorance (which is our fault, because we could have taken more trouble to be informed). (See also **Ignorance.**) Even more important, however, is the conviction that the Christian life is a joyful following upon our acceptance in Christ, and not an anxious effort to secure acceptance by a high record of conscientious moral achievement. It is because of the knowledge of what Christ has done *already* for them that Christians can face unafraid the inevitable uncertainties of moral decision.

Bringing to bear basic moral insights upon particular moral problems is known as casuistry*. There is much in its history that was dubious and gave it a bad name, but basically every Christian has to do this, to seek to act from the right motive and find the right content of action in particular circumstances. Most of our lives we have standard ways of behaving that are the result of the whole process of our upbringing and adult decisions, but there are constantly new aspects of old issues, as well as (in a rapidly changing world) new issues that need facing.

It follows from this teaching that conscience belongs to human persons as such, not just to Christians. Possessing the capacity to recognize basic moral distinctions between good and evil and applying it in particular cases is part of what we mean by a person. The actual deliverances of conscience are indeed profoundly influenced by time and circumstance, and must be if they are to be relevant. Of course, they can be *conditioned* in illegitimate ways, which need guarding against, but they are not *determined* by past and current factors. Christians may well believe they have potential advantages in the formation of conscience because of a deeper knowledge of human life and destiny and a deeper vision of goodness through Jesus Christ. Their responsibility is the greater. But all persons, in the Christian view, should act according to their conscience and educate it according to their circumstances.

This teaching is not spelled out systematically in the Bible but is presupposed by it and is a development of it. The word "conscience" is not found in the OT, but the reality is presupposed in the whole prophetic movement, in the light of which our present OT text has received its form. It underlies the Genesis sagas, the historical books, the prophetic books, and the Wisdom literature (Nathan's confrontation of David in 2 Sam. 12 is a good example). The word is not found in the Gospels either, but is presupposed in Jesus' parabolic and gnomic teaching (cf. Luke 12:57). The word conscience (*syneidēsis*) does occur twice in Acts and 27 times in the NT letters, chiefly in those of Paul. It was used in popular Greek ethical vocabulary mostly in the sense of an adverse judgment by the self on acts already committed, leading to remorse. Paul uses the word in that sense and also in a wider one. Conscience can also approve of past actions (cf. Rom. 2:14f.), and it can cover decisions, made before action, on what should be done. An erring conscience should be obeyed (cf. 1 Cor. 8 and 10). For a good conspectus of the uses of the word in the NT, see the five occurrences in Hebrews (Heb. 9:9, 14; 10:2, 22; 13:18). On the other hand, it has been alleged that Paul uses it only as the previous Greek writers had done, in a negative and retrospective sense, but this involves a strained interpretation of some texts (cf. 2 Cor. 1:12). Conscience clearly has a good sense in the pastoral epistles (cf. 1 Tim. 1:19), as it began to have in Greek literature by this time. We can say that in Paul the word is the ripe fruit of Israelite moral teaching, an interior norm free from legalism*, and an important enrichment of the idea of a person. There has, however, been a tendency in 20th-century Continental Protestant theology to interpret conscience only in a negative sense. Emil Brunner, for instance, in *The Divine Imperative* (ET 1937) treats it only as the experience of the wrath of God. Similar interpretations can be found in Thielicke and Bonhoeffer, among others. This is exegetically dubious and practically unfortunate in teaching the art of moral judgment, and may be a passing phase.

The traditional Christian teaching on conscience is akin to that taken up by most moral philosophy, whether the term is used or not. Confusion is caused by a quite different use of the term in Freudian psychoanalytic theory. Freud finds the seat of the conscience in the (necessarily) repressive superego*. What Christians mean by conscience he calls "the reality principle," and this is what he wants people to live by. Whether or not Freud's theories are sound, they do not contradict Christian teaching on this point, and they may throw light on the well-known phenomenon of the "scrupulous" conscience. He has confused the terminology by being unaware of the usual Christian understanding of conscience (*see* **Psychoanalysis; Scrupulosity**).

See also **Conscientious Objection.**

J. Donnelly and L. Lyons (eds.), *Conscience,* 1973; C. E. Nelson (ed.), *Conscience: Theological and Psychological Perspectives,* 1973.
RONALD PRESTON

Conscientious Objection

Conscientious objection or conscientious refusal is one form of dissent* from an institution's rules, policies, or practices. Although such dissent appears in various settings, including religious institutions, the phrase "conscientious objection," without further specification, often refers to refusal to participate in military service on moral or religious grounds (*see* **Pacifism**). In conscientious objection, the agent claims that the refused act, if undertaken, would violate his or her conscience and would result in a loss of integrity

and wholeness in the self, along with heavy guilt* and shame* (*see* **Conscience**). In a political context, conscientious objection is close to but sometimes distinguished from civil disobedience* mainly because it involves the agent's refusal to perform what the state demands (or insistence on performing what the state forbids) and the agent's claim for exemption from the legal duty in question without necessarily seeking to alter that institution's rules, policies, or practices in other ways. It is often dissociation from or noncooperation in what one takes to be evil (*see* **Cooperation in Evil;** for a fuller definition, *see* **Civil Disobedience**).

Early Christians were conscientiously opposed to military service for several reasons, including aversion to bloodshed, and pacifism* also emerged in several Christian groups after the church accepted Christian participation in war. In addition to conscientious objection based on pacifism, there was selective conscientious objection based on just war* criteria: the Christian might have to refuse to fight in an unjust war or to commit wrongful acts within the war. It was assumed that in clear cases the Christian should say "no," but that in doubtful cases the presumption should be in favor of obedience, with superior orders* protecting the soldier from guilt in those doubtful cases (but not in cases of clear injustice).

In both the UK and the USA, exemption of some conscientious objectors to military service has become an important part of the conscription* policies for pragmatic, political, and moral reasons. Conscientious objectors would not contribute to and would probably disrupt military service, and it would be difficult to deny exemption to such vigorous objectors as members of the "historic peace churches"—the Mennonites, the Brethren, and the Quakers. Furthermore, the principle of respect for persons*, including their consciences*, argues against forcing the conscientious objector to choose between military service and jail, if it is possible to avoid that conflict without imposing unfair burdens on others. It is at least prima facie wrong to force a person to act against his or her conscience, even though it may sometimes be necessary and justifiable to do so. Such a claim can be defended without answering the ultimate question of the relation between the individual conscience and the state.

There are important questions about the

scope, limits, and conditions of exemption from military service, particularly in the USA where the exemption is construed as a matter of privilege or "legislative grace" and where the war in Vietnam led to many crises of conscience. Two major questions of scope are whether the exemption should include (1) both religious and secular objectors, and (2) both universal objectors (pacifists) and selective objectors (applicants of just war criteria who claim that a particular war is unjust). In both the First and the Second World War the UK had a more liberal policy toward conscientious objectors than the USA, recognizing nonreligious as well as religious objectors and selective as well as universal objectors. The USA has gradually moved from recognizing only members of established peace churches, to accepting any religiously based pacifism, and finally to using a broad definition of religion that encompasses most moral objections. Britain exempted selective objectors even while under siege during the Second World War, but the USA has refused to recognize selective objectors, grouping them in official policies with political or economic rather than moral objectors, even though the selective objector can appeal to the just war* tradition, just as the universal objector can appeal to the pacifist tradition.

Another question is whether exemption of conscientious objectors from military service should be conditional or unconditional. The fairness* argument for conditional exemption is that conscientious objectors should render either noncombatant (e.g., medical service within the military) or alternative service (e.g., work of national importance) in exchange for exemption from direct military service as a way to assume a fair share of the social burdens. In general, but not always, the USA and the UK have required either noncombatant or alternative service. Neither the UK nor the USA has been lenient with noncooperators, who refuse to cooperate at all with the system of registration, testing of conscience, etc. The Jehovah's Witnesses, who deny the authority of earthly governments but who are willing to fight in the Battle of Armageddon, have also posed major problems. The US government has been willing to view them as pacifists, for all practical purposes, but has frequently prosecuted them for refusing to cooperate, for example, in the assignment to alternative service.

Societies usually try to distinguish sincere from insincere claims of conscience for purposes of exemption from mandatory social activities. Yet, as C. D. Broad noted, it is difficult, if not impossible, to determine the motives* of action for oneself or for others. The requirement of alternative service, perhaps even for a longer period of time, is sometimes considered one way to test the conscientious objector's sincerity.

Conscientious objection is not limited to military service. Some Christians and others are conscientiously opposed to taking an oath or to paying taxes for nuclear weapons, for preparation for war, or for state-funded abortion procedures. Before overriding the claims of conscience, the state* should show that it cannot secure its legitimate interests by alternative means. When the conscientious objector refuses to perform some *positive legal duty,* the state can sometimes tolerate the objection without serious difficulties (e.g., objection to jury duty), accept alternative service (e.g., in the case of military service), or perform the act in question for the objector (e.g., attach the tax objector's salary or bank account). Obviously, the nature of the service demanded, the number of objectors involved, and the risks to others (e.g., from a refusal to accept a vaccination) may affect the state's response. There are also *negative legal duties,* which prohibit conduct that the agent considers essential to his or her religious or moral convictions. Examples include proselytizing, polygamy, and rituals involving prohibited substances, such as peyote. It is commonly argued that the state should yield to conscience in matters that do not involve harm to persons outside a consenting community (or minors within the community). When the conflict is only between the state and the individual conscience, many would argue that the state's interest in paternalism* should yield to conscience (*see also* **Conscience; Autonomy; Freedom; Law; Morality, Legal Enforcement of; Respect for Persons**). During and after social conflicts, there is often a debate about whether pardon or amnesty* should be granted to conscientious objectors and other resisters.

R. Barker, *Conscience, Government and War: Conscientious Objection in Great Britain,* 1939–45, 1982; C. D. Broad, "Conscience and Conscientious Actions," in *Moral Con-*

cepts, ed. J. Feinberg, 1970; P. Brock, *Twentieth-Century Pacifism,* 1970; J. F. Childress, *Moral Responsibility in Conflicts,* 1982, chs. 5 and 6; C. C. Field, *Pacifism and Conscientious Objection,* 1948; J. Finn (ed.), *The Case for Selective Conscientious Objection,* 1968; D. Hays, *Challenge of Conscience: The Story of the Conscientious Objectors of 1939–1949,* 1949; R. J. Regan, S.J., *Private Conscience and Public Law: The American Experience,* 1972; J. Rohr, *Prophets Without Honor; Public Policy and the Selective Conscientious Objector,* 1971; L. Schlissel (ed.), *Conscience in America: A Documentary History of Conscientious Objection in America, 1757–1967,* 1968.

JAMES F. CHILDRESS

Conscientization

The theory and practice of consciousness-raising, first developed by Paulo Freire, began as a new approach to popular education and soon matured into a revolutionary philosophy of liberation. Alongside its campaign for basic literacy, the philosophy of conscientization involves: (1) recognizing the distinction between nature in its inevitability and culture in its changeability; (2) unmasking the myths that allow oppressors to dominate society by blurring this distinction; and (3) exploring the alternatives available under the fundamental "generative theme" of our epoch, namely, liberation. Implicit in all three stages is a teleological view of human nature that emphasizes the role of consciousness in overcoming "limit-situations" through revolutionary "limit-acts."

The significance of conscientization for Christian ethics is twofold. On the one hand, as a substantive philosophy of history it is the vehicle for creating and sustaining an authentically utopian ethos that provides critical leverage against elitist power politics of both the right and the left. On the other hand, as a critical methodology it provides the vehicle for challenging most of the inherited traditions of Christian ethics for their collusion in cultures of oppression*. While Gustavo Gutiérrez calls for a "conscientizing evangelization" synthesizing both these strategies, it remains to be seen whether conscientization can make a contribution to Christian ethics beyond its critiques of oppressive ethos. Crucial here will be further reflection on Freire's distinctively teleological view of human nature.

See **Liberation Theology.**

————

P. Berger, *Pyramids of Sacrifice: Political Ethics and Social Change,* 1976; M. Daly, *Beyond God the Father: Toward a Philosophy of Women's Liberation,* 1973; P. Freire, *Pedagogy of the Oppressed,* ET 1970; *Education for Critical Consciousness,* ET 1973; G. Gutiérrez, *A Theology of Liberation,* ET 1973; E. L. Long, Jr., *A Survey of Recent Christian Ethics,* 1982.

DENNIS P. McCANN

Conscription

Military service is one of the few positive actions of service, in contrast to obedience, expected in many modern states, which choose among several policies: compulsory citizens' militia (usually involving long-term reserve duty); compulsory universal service in either military or other social institutions; compulsory universal military service; compulsory but selective military service, often called a "draft" in the USA; voluntary military service, the current policy in the UK and the USA. Standards of justice* or fairness*, respect for persons*, and utility (*see* **Utilitarianism**), particularly in relation to national defense, are all important in assessing policies toward military service. For policies of compulsory military service, the question of exemption for conscientious objectors is often difficult. Karl Barth (*CD* III/4) has argued that the pacifist demand for the abolition of conscription is "shortsighted" because conscription makes military service personal as well as political (*see* **Pacifism**). When military service is selective rather than universal ("universal" in most contexts is limited to males), serious questions of justice arise. For example, should citizens engaged in nonmilitary work of social importance be exempted, deferred, or conscripted? Should a lottery be used to ensure equality of opportunity? There is also debate about the relative merits of conventional armed forces and nuclear forces, some contending that strong conventional forces are necessary in order to reduce reliance on nuclear weapons.

See **Conscientious Objection; Deterrence; Peace; War.**

————

M. Anderson and B. Honegger (eds.), *The Military Draft: Selected Readings on Conscription,* 1982; J. O'Sullivan and A. M.

Meckler (eds.), *The Draft and Its Enemies: A Documentary History,* 1974.

JAMES F. CHILDRESS

Consent

Consent is an act of agreement or acquiescence that deliberately changes the structure of rights* and obligations*. It creates rights in or transfers rights to another agent who did not previously have those rights; it authorizes that agent to act in certain ways. The other side of consent is refusal. Consent is a necessary condition (morally and legally) for sexual intercourse and for marriage. Where consent is absent or seriously compromised, sexual intercourse is unjustified and may be subject to the charge of rape, and a marriage is invalid. (Consent may be a necessary condition without being a sufficient condition to justify actions.) John Locke also held that a civil government requires the consent of the governed. He did not limit valid consent to express or explicit consent; for him so-called tacit consent, which emerges in "any possession or enjoyment of any part of the dominions of any government," is also valid consent (*see* **Social Contract; State**).

Wherever consent creates or transfers rights and thus authorizes others to act in certain ways, a critical question is what conditions have to be met before consent is valid, morally or legally. Consent is more than an attitude of approval. It is an intentional and voluntary act. As an intentional act, it requires awareness, knowledge, and understanding; a person cannot consent accidentally. Furthermore, consent is not valid if it is not voluntary, for example, if it is rendered under duress (*see* **Intention; Responsibility**).

The paradigm case of consent that creates or transfers rights is *express* consent, usually by written or oral statement or gestures; for example, a patient who expressly consents to medical treatment authorizes the physician to proceed without risk of battery. *Tacit* consent, which probably cannot be extended as far as Locke suggested, is expressed silently or passively by omissions or by failures to indicate or signify dissent. In tort law, according to William Prosser, "silence and inaction may manifest consent where a reasonable person would speak if he objected." If a woman does not protest verbally or in other ways when a man proposes to kiss her, he has her tacit consent. Whereas tacit consent is expressed through failures to dissent,

implied or implicit consent is not expressed at all; it is rather inferred from actions. For example, a patient's visit to the doctor's office or consent to one procedure may imply consent to certain other procedures. Closely related to, and often confused with, implied or implicit consent is *presumed* consent. Agents presume what a person would consent to if he or she could consent or were asked to consent. If consent is presumed on the basis of a person's actions, it is close to implied consent; if it is presumed on the basis of what we know about that person's values, it is farther removed from implied consent; and if it is presumed on the basis of a theory of human goods or a rational will, rather than on the basis of the person's actions or values, it is very different from implied consent. In their own distinctive ways, express consent, tacit consent, and implied consent refer to an individual's own actions and inactions, but presumed consent may not refer to them at all. For example, a physician may presume a patient's consent to a medical procedure in an emergency.

Not only does consent (or refusal, the other side of consent) take different forms; it also occurs at different times. For example, a patient may consent to a medical procedure one day, but refuse it the next day. Thus, present consent must be distinguished from past consent and from probable future consent. Not only may persons have several different and perhaps even contradictory wishes at one time, but their wishes may vary over time. Several questions arise about respecting people over time when they change their consents and refusals. One very difficult question is whether a person's present wishes (expressed in either consent or refusal) may be overridden in order to honor that person's past wishes or probable future wishes. The story of Odysseus and the Sirens dramatically depicts an agent's consent to a course of action that he expected to repudiate under certain pressures.

In the last fifty years "informed consent" has emerged as an important moral and legal requirement in medical care and research involving human subjects (*see* **Experimentation with Human Subjects; Bioethics; Hippocratic Oath**). The doctrine of informed consent holds that a person's consent to undergo a medical procedure or to participate in research is not morally or, in many settings, legally valid unless the person has adequate information about the nature of the procedures, their risks and probable benefits, alternative procedures, etc. And it imposes on health professionals and investigators a duty to disclose that information and, ideally, to ensure that the patient or subject has comprehended that information. This doctrine of informed consent, based on a principle of respect for persons* and their autonomy* is simply a fuller development and application of the conditions of valid consent to a particular arena of human interaction. Even though it emphasizes disclosure of information, it also presupposes voluntariness. Unfortunately, the doctrine of informed consent has sometimes been expressed in a ritualistic procedure which emphasizes the signed consent form, rather than in a process of interaction and communication that extends over time. Valid consent may not involve written or even oral statements, but these are frequently important, especially as documentation of consent. Most significantly, the doctrine of informed consent recognizes the patient's or the potential subject's right to accept or to refuse medical procedures or participation in research. He or she has the moral veto. (For some limitations, see **Paternalism**.)

J. F. Childress, *Who Should Decide? Paternalism in Health Care,* 1982; A. J. Simmons, *Moral Principles and Political Obligations,* 1979.

                                        JAMES F. CHILDRESS

Consequentialism

A term that received wide currency as a result of an article by Elizabeth Anscombe in 1958, "consequentialism" is closely related to and sometimes viewed as a subset of teleological ethics*, in contrast to deontological ethics (*see* **Deontology**). Consequentialism is the moral theory that actions are right or wrong according to the consequences they produce, rather than any intrinsic features they may have, such as truthfulness or fidelity. All plausible moral theories recognize that the consequences of actions are morally relevant, but a fundamental question is whether the consequences are the only or the dominant moral considerations. In Max Weber's classic distinction, an ethic of responsibility* (*Verantwortungsethik*) is consequentialist (sometimes called *Erfolgsethik*) whereas an ethic of

intention* or ultimate values (*Gesinnungsethik*) is deontological in character. Dietrich Bonhoeffer and Reinhold Niebuhr, among Protestant theologians, have emphasized consequences within an ethic of responsibility, while many Catholic theologians, such as Richard McCormick, use the language of proportionality* to emphasize the importance of balancing consequences. Although Paul Ramsey has worried about the "wasteland of consequentialism," few theologians view the consequences of actions as the only moral consideration. Joseph Fletcher's "situation ethics"* is probably an exception. However, utilitarianism*, the main contemporary version of consequentialism, is more common in philosophical ethics.

See also **Ends and Means.**

G. E. M. Anscombe, "Modern Moral Philosophy," *Philosophy* 33, Jan. 1958; J. Fletcher, *Situation Ethics,* 1966; I. Sheffler, *The Rejection of Consequentialism,* 1983; M. Weber, "Politics as a Vocation," in *From Max Weber: Essays in Sociology,* tr. and ed. by H. H. Gerth and C. W. Mills, 1958.

                                        JAMES F. CHILDRESS

Conservatism

Conservatism is the somewhat vaguely defined political stance of parties and individuals who, on the whole, desire to maintain existing social and economic structures and who therefore oppose sudden or radical change. In some countries, the term "conservative" still refers to those who seek to maintain the privileges of wealth and social status and oppose democratization. It is important to distinguish this conservatism of the extreme right, shading into fascism, from the much more moderate conservative parties of Britain and other Western democracies. This moderate conservatism has much in common with liberalism*, for instance, in defending individual freedoms against the encroachments of state control. Those who adhere to it may inaugurate social policies that would once have been considered "progressive," and they would not seek to turn back social change. While in economic affairs they prefer the free working of market forces to rigid state control, they are likely in practice to settle for a "mixed economy" rather than unrestricted laissez-faire. They would also accept such democratic principles as equality of opportunity and nondiscrimination. They commend the old-fashioned virtues of thrift and industry, and have usually claimed to be allies of the churches. Some European conservative parties have had close links with religion and called themselves "Christian Democrats," but these links have nowadays become weaker. There is no rigid conservative ideology, but the political thought of the Anglo-Irish statesman Edmund Burke (1729–1797) is often considered to be a basic (though unsystematic) statement of conservative principles. His teaching was called forth by specific events and situations, so there is an element of pragmatism and flexibility in it. At the time of the French Revolution, he deplored violent change and taught a doctrine of continuity, with respect for the past and tradition, yet with an openness to the future. In constitutional matters, he upheld the parliamentarian and party system, while also claiming that a member of parliament is a representative, not a delegate bound by the wishes of constituents. The more liberal face of conservatism was evident in his desire for reconciliation with the American colonists. Underlying these views is a strong natural law mentality and an organic conception of social life.

In the past, the churches have frequently supported conservative policies, perhaps because ecclesiastical privileges have sometimes been at stake in the course of social change. Nowadays political attitudes among members of the churches are much more mixed. Many, for instance, would think that an extreme right-wing conservatism is just as hostile to Christian ideals as is the extreme left. On the other hand, many Christians may be sympathetic to a moderate conservatism. It may be a question of balancing the legitimate rights and opportunities of the individual with the equally legitimate rights of the community. If the Christian considers it a duty to support those policies which lead to the enhancement of human life, he or she will have to ponder the words of the Irish statesman Garret FitzGerald: "The insensitivity of some liberals to economic injustice is more than matched by the insensitivity of some socialists to individual freedom."

E. Burke, *Works and Correspondence,* 1852; M. Friedman, *Capitalism and Freedom,* 1962; R. Kirk, *The Conservative Mind, from* *Burke to Santayana,* 1953; H. A. Kissinger, *A World Restored,* 1957; E. Powell, *Freedom and Reality,* 1969.

JOHN MACQUARRIE

Consumerism *see* Capitalism; Commercialism

Contemplation

In the sense of the intellectual vision of the highest good or the highest reality, contemplation is undisturbed by feeling or striving, and represented for Plato and for classical philosophy in general the summit of human possibility. This view passed over into Christianity, and such outstanding Christian thinkers as Augustine and Aquinas have maintained the superiority of the so-called "intellectual" virtues. In modern times there has been a reaction against the place formerly given to contemplation. Critics of the contemplative ideal see it as reflecting the notion that the soul must escape from the encumbrance of the body, and therefore as otherworldly and quietist. The modern temper calls for an ethic that is activist and thisworldly. Some of the criticisms are doubtless justified, but one should not underestimate the place of contemplation or brush it aside. The ancient Christian writers did not advocate contemplation in isolation, but saw it within the context of the whole Christian life. But more important, there can be no sustained and intelligent Christian action, properly so called, unless it is guided by Christian understanding; and this in turn arises from the immersion of the Christian mind in the contemplation of the vision of God, granted in Jesus Christ.

See Ascetical Theology.

JOHN MACQUARRIE

Contextual Ethics *see* Situation Ethics

Continence

Thomas Aquinas (*ST* II-II.155) says: "The word *continence* is taken by various people in two ways. For some understand continence to denote abstention from all venereal pleasure. In this sense perfect continence is virginity in the first place and widowhood in the second. Others, however, understand continence as signifying that whereby a man resists evil desires, which in him are vehement." (Continence for Aquinas, as a virtue of the will, is distinct from temperance*, which moderates the desires themselves.)

The distinction between perfect continence (*continentia virginalis, vidualis*) and marital continence (*continentia coniugalis*) is not formally maintained in Reformed thought, but "continence" is used in the same sense. Calvin (*Institutes* 2.8) interprets the Seventh Commandment as meaning "that every part of our lives ought to be regulated by chastity and continence." "Virginity, I acknowledge, is a virtue not to be despised. But as this is denied to some and to others is granted only for a season, let those who are troubled with incontinence and cannot succeed in resisting it avail themselves of the help of marriage, that they may preserve their chastity according to the degree of their calling."

Great stress was laid on continence in some early Christian writings. *Second Clement* is not untypical in regarding perfect continence as an important part of the perfect way. "Keep the flesh pure and the seal unstained to the end that we may receive life." (*2 Clement* 8; cf. 12–15). The virgins (*parthenoi*) of Rev. 14:4 may show the same emphasis within the NT itself. Augustine (*Confessions* 7) seems to have regarded his "conversion" largely as an embracing of continence. The church, however, consistently defended marriage* against philosophical and Gnostic sects that repudiated it altogether.

Christian writers adopted the current philosophical viewpoint that the agitation, physical and emotional, associated with sexual activity was peculiarly contrary to the calm self-control of the life ruled by reason. Pleasure* was suspect, even within marriage. "The marriage act that is done out of sensuous pleasure is a lesser sin than fornication" (Aquinas, *ST* II-II.154). Augustine's view that the violence of the passions in sexual activity is consequent on the Fall came to be widely held (see Calvin, loc. cit.) and colored Christian thinking about chastity* and continence within marriage (*see* **Original Sin**).

If Christian writers today can find within their faith and its biblical source grounds for a more positive evaluation of sex, it is largely because the secular attitude has radically changed. In a post-Freudian age it may be necessary to distinguish in a new way two kinds of continence: that which springs from a neurotic fear or hatred of sex and the sex impulses, and that self-control, responsibility of action, which is compatible with freedom and self-understanding.

Traditional Christian thinking was male-centered. Continence meant resisting desires, and for those without the gift, marriage afforded a remedy. Such a view is open to the objection that it makes marriage legalized prostitution; an argument reinforced by the doctrine of the *debitum coniugale,* the marriage duty. It was the Puritans who first understood the marriage relationship in terms of companionship and personal love. A modern reinterpretation of the virtue of continence must be in *relational* terms, in which continence is a part of Christian love, acting responsibly and in genuine concern for the other.

See **Asceticism; Chastity; Marriage; Sexual Ethics; Virginity.**

JAMES A. WHYTE

Contraception

By contraception is commonly understood the use of physical or chemical means to prevent sexual intercourse from resulting in the conception of a child. The term itself is a 20th-century coinage. The original Christian attitude toward the practice was shaped by the positive Christian value set on human life, human dignity, marital love, and human procreation and by the convergence of five contrary trends in the Mediterranean world in which Christianity took shape: (1) The difficulty of distinguishing between abortifacients (drugs that kill a living human being in the womb) and contraceptives (drugs that block conception). Ancient medicine, while familiar with drugs of both kinds, had inadequate resources to distinguish them. (2) The biology prevalent in the ancient Mediterranean world that taught that ensoulment of the embryo did not occur at conception but months later in pregnancy—a biology that led to the question of protection of the early embryo being treated as a question of contraception. (3) The association of contraceptives with their use by prostitutes, professionally averse to procreation, and their use in extramarital and adulterous affairs to prevent unwanted pregnancy. (4) The high value put on marital procreation by husbands desiring to perpetuate their family and by wives conscious that childbearing in lawful marriage gave them a status not possessed by slave concubines. (5) The ideological aversion to childbearing expressed among Gnostics within, or on the borders of, the Christian community. For many Christians the chief Greek reason for procreation—to achieve quasi-immortality in one's descendants—was no longer persuasive; and the chief Jewish reason—to perpetuate the race until the coming of the Messiah—had become obsolete. Questioning why procreation was desirable, some Christians on the right advocated the celibacy of Jesus for all his followers, while some Christians on the left argued that just as the Sabbath was made for man not man for the Sabbath, so all the Mosaic laws, including the sexual ones, were now subordinate to the freedom of the Christian. A middle position was found by what became mainline Christianity in adoption of the Stoic rationale for procreation—that it was in accordance with nature. "As the eye is to see, so the generative organs are to generate with" ran the basic maxim. Neither Christ's example nor the freedom enjoyed by Christians had repealed this basic norm provided by nature. It perfectly excluded all contraception.

Ideological challenge to procreation was again raised in the 4th century by the rival religion of Manicheism, whose basic myth taught that to procreate was to imitate man's devilish ancestor. Augustine, who was a Manichean in his twenties, on his conversion to Christianity wrote *The Morals of the Manicheans* and *The Morals of the Catholic Church.* He stressed that the cardinal moral point separating the two was the Manicheans' abhorrence of procreation and their taking steps to prevent it, while the Catholics believed that only procreative marital intercourse was moral. Augustine, the most influential writer on Western sexual ethics, thus repeated and put in succinct formulae the Christian rejection of contraception (*see also* **Manichean Ethics; Augustinian Ethics**).

In the Middle Ages, the Cathars appeared to be the Manicheans returned. The old Augustinian texts were inserted into the fundamental canon law, Gratian's *Harmony of Unharmonious Canons.* The theological position as set out by the great summists, such as Thomas Aquinas, firmly classified contraceptive acts with other sins against nature. Luther, Calvin, and the other Reformers did nothing to change the traditional teaching. The philosophers of the Enlightenment, skeptical of so many other Christian doctrines, did not assail it.

Only in the 19th century did advocates of "birth control," i.e., contraception, appear. They did not claim a Christian warrant for their position. They were greeted with hostility by most of the medical profession, academics, legislators, and the churches. In the first quarter of the 20th century a shift in medical, demographic, and popular opinion occurred. In 1930, at a Lambeth Conference, the Church of England by a vote of 193 to 67 went on record as permitting "other methods" besides self-control where there is "a clearly-felt moral obligation to limit or avoid parenthood and where there is a morally sound reason for avoiding complete abstinence." Partly in response to this departure from the old position, Pope Pius XI in December 1930 issued the encyclical *Casti Connubii* condemning as violative of "the law of God and nature" any use whatever of marriage "in the exercise of which the act, by human effort, is deprived of its natural power of procreating life."

During the next thirty-five years a large number of Protestant churches (e.g., Congregationalist, Methodist, Lutheran, Reformed) took a stand accepting the use of contraception in marriage as conformable to Christian morals, and a substantial number of leading Protestant theologians—among them Karl Barth, Emil Brunner, Reinhold Niebuhr—defended the practice. The 1958 Lambeth Conference emphasized the duty of "responsible parenthood," saying nothing as to the means of achieving it. The World Council of Churches issued a committee report in 1959 stating that there was "no moral difference between use of the infertile period, artificial barriers to the meeting of the sperm and ovum, and drugs regulating ovulation."

The Greek Orthodox Church, however, continued to condemn contraception; and the Catholic Church permitted only the choice of intercourse at times believed to be infertile. In the ferment of the Second Vatican Council the question of continuing the ancient prohibition was raised. Much had changed since the law had been formulated as a way of defending nascent life, strengthening marital love and wifely dignity, and repudiating ideological attacks on the goodness of procreation. A clear line was now drawn biologically between sperm and human embryo. Slave concubinage had disappeared, and procreation in modern industrial societies was not the only way of achieving status as a woman. Gnostics, Manicheans, Cathars were forgotten heretics. Above all, the old Stoic-Augustinian line of thought about the purpose of marital intercourse had gradually given way to a new view that saw conjugal acts as properly expressing conjugal love. At the Second Vatican Council this view was expressed in the pastoral constitution *Gaudium et Spes,* sec. 49, which declared that conjugal love was "uniquely expressed and perfected by the marital act itself."

The Council left to a papal commission established by John XXIII and continued by Paul VI the question of contraception itself. Factors favoring change were the social and theological shifts just enumerated. Against change was not only the force of the tradition so recently enunciated in *Casti Connubii* but the realization that the old evils against which the rule was aimed had not disappeared: it was still easy to confuse abortifacients and contraceptives and still easy to cross the line from contraception to abortion; in the sexual hedonism encouraged by modern industrial societies, contraception did facilitate sex outside of marriage; even the old Manichean haters of procreation were present as modern pessimists, alienated from God's creation and seeing procreation as a purposeless continuance of a purposeless universe. Nonetheless, the theology of Christian marriage had changed, and that was decisive for the papal commission: it recommended change.

In 1968, Paul VI issued the encyclical *Humanae Vitae.* At first reading it was taken to be a reiteration of the absolute ban proclaimed by *Casti Connubii.* Language in it can be cited to support this conclusion, which was reached by a number of national Catholic hierarchies including that of the USA. However, other national bishops' conferences (e.g., the Dutch, French, and German) read the encyclical with nuances and in the light of the marital theology of Vatican II. Seen in that light, it has been argued that the encyclical puts the natural law objection to contraception on a new footing. The union of the expression of conjugal love with the natural rhythm of fertility is taken as indissolubly established by divine providence. Nothing is seen as preventing human intelligence from exercising itself to determine the infertile periods and, further, to secure infertility in these periods according to the natural biological rhythm. Practically speaking, this reading means that contraception is prohib-

ited by the encyclical for the four days of normal fertility of a woman's twenty-eight-day cycle. Relying on such theological interpretations or on their own judgment, the majority of Catholics did not treat *Humanae Vitae* as requiring them in conscience to abandon all contraception. The matter is not closed for Catholics. Mild interpretations and common practice could be papally proscribed. At the present time the practical difference between Catholic and Protestant views is small.

See also **Marriage; Population Policy; Procreation; Sexual Ethics; Sterilization; Magisterium; Modern Roman Catholic Moral Theology.**

R. M. Fagley, *The Population Explosion and Christian Responsibility,* 1960; J. T. Noonan, Jr., *Contraception: A History of Its Treatment by the Catholic Theologians and Canonists,* 1965; "Natural Law, the Teaching of the Church and the Rhythms of Human Fecundity," *American Journal of Jurisprudence* 23, 1980, pp. 16–37.

JOHN T. NOONAN, JR.

Contracts

Contracts—voluntary agreements between parties that create or alter legal obligations—play a large role in human interactions and are usually enforced by legal sanctions. Even though contracts or quasi contracts appear in various societies, it has been argued that a major historical shift occurred as contractual relations supplanted status relations in the modern era. Contracts are particularly prominent in liberal individualist societies, where the marketplace is central, and the contract metaphor has often been used to interpret social and political life (*see* **Capitalism; Laissez-faire; Social Contract**). There is considerable debate in jurisprudence about the foundation of contract law. Some theorists contend that the promise* principle is its moral basis, but others interpret contract law in terms of reliance (if X is injured because he relied on Y, the question is whether Y was so responsible for that injury that he should be compelled to compensate X) or benefit (if X has benefited Y, the question is whether fairness requires that Y compensate X for the benefit). In contrast to these two latter approaches, an interpretation of contract as based on promise focuses on the will of the parties and their self-imposed, voluntary obligations. Also, in contrast to Aristotle's discussion of contracts as commutative justice, some theorists view contracts as a matter of distributive justice, emphasizing the society's role in distributing benefits and burdens rather than the will of the contracting parties. Whatever theory is held, individuals have moral obligations* to act in good faith in making and carrying out contracts, and the society has moral obligations not to enforce contracts that are based on fraud or duress or are unfair or unconscionable. There are obvious dangers in an overuse of contract, either as a metaphor for social and political life or as a way to interpret and direct various relationships, such as marriage*. Even if from a legal standpoint the term "contract" may be appropriate for marriage, for example, Christians may find the idea of covenant to be richer in part because it is less individualistic, voluntaristic, and minimalistic.

See also **Consent; Covenant; Justice; Promise.**

P. Atiyah, *The Rise and Fall of Freedom of Contract,* 1979; and *Promises, Morals, and Law,* 1981; C. Fried, *Contract as Promise,* 1981.

JAMES F. CHILDRESS

Contrition

Perfect sorrow for sin, arising from inner conviction and from the love of God. It is distinguished from attrition*.

JOHN MACQUARRIE

Conventional Morality

In any stable society there will be (almost by definition of "stable") a substantial measure of agreement on matters of moral principle—on what makes conduct right or wrong, a man good or bad, etc. This will mean that the "descriptive meaning" of the moral terms (*see* **Ethics**) will be constant as between one speaker and another; and some degree of constancy of this sort is necessary, if such terms are to have the use which they typically do have. We expect, when a man calls another a good man, to receive some idea of what qualities the man has; if he is being called good for very eccentric reasons, we may be seriously misled. Thus all stable societies have a "conventional morality"; and within the confines of this, moral words can be used to give information, in just the same way as descriptive words like "red." It is this fact

which lends plausibility to naturalist and descriptivist ethical theories (*see* **Naturalistic Ethics**). As a result of exclusive attention to the conventional aspect of morality, a use of moral words can grow up in which their "action-guiding" force is lost; in calling a man a good man we are no longer holding him up for imitation, but merely attributing to him certain properties.

In such a situation, moral reformers of various kinds can attack the dead morality of convention (cf. Christ's attack on the Pharisees, and the Communists' on "bourgeois morality") and attempt to restore the action-guiding function of the moral words while altering their descriptive content. For example, a 5th-century Athenian could have said, "Nicias is a bad man because he is a ruthless slave owner," although according to the conventional morality of the time Nicias was a typically good man, and slave-owning was held no bar to being called "good." The logical possibility of doing this is the strongest argument against descriptivism; if the descriptivism were true—that is, if the moral words had their meaning determined by the properties in virtue of which they are applied, the supporter of conventional morality could always say to the moral reformer: "In saying that a man is bad whose character is well known and whom everybody except you calls good, you are just misusing the language; for we *mean* by 'good man' a man like him." The very fact that they understand what the moral reformer is saying to them shows that this is not what they mean by "good man."

R. M. HARE

Conventions

The literal meaning of "convention" is a coming together. People come together to agree on something in their common interest, and while there is goodwill enough to do so, to lessen the harm they might do to one another when goodwill is gone. Their agreement is then also called a convention. In international relations it resembles, in some respects, a treaty. Among such are the conventions of The Hague, Geneva, the Red Cross, and the United Nations: attempts to set limits to the waging of war, and minimum standards for the protection of the wounded, prisoners, and refugees. Of present relevance are the Geneva Convention on Chemical Warfare (1925), now in need of renegotiation, and the UN Biological (Bacteriological)

Weapons Convention (1971). They bind signatory states only, and notice of withdrawal may be given; but states usually adjudge it to be in their own interest to adhere. Diplomatic conventions, covering embassies and their staffs, are designed to keep communications open even in times of mutual hostility or displeasure. Such are the sinews of a frail international morality.

Within sovereign states the final protector of social order is the law*. But law is a blunt and explosive instrument, setting minimum standards only, and relying for its effect on either acceptance in conscience by a majority of the community or on enforcement by police or military methods so drastic and far-reaching as to invade cherished liberties. A mature society does not so exalt the function of law. It relies more on social institutions*, intermediate between the state and the individual, each with its specific norms or patterns of conduct. Professional ethics* are thus in some respects conventional. The practice of, e.g., medicine, the law, accountancy, the stock exchange, is governed partly by rules of etiquette regulating internal relations and protecting the social and economic status of the body corporate, and partly by conventions deemed essential to maintain the confidence and trust of the lay public. Some medical conventions, like those of the World Medical Association, have international status. The final sanction of professional conduct is the relevant law; but within the law the conventions of professional ethics go a long way to maximize both the responsible freedom of the practitioner, within the corporate discipline of the profession, and the relationship of trust with the public in which the interest of patients or clients is best served. When trust fails, litigation paralyzes practice. As other bodies (e.g., social workers, or practitioners in advertising or marketing) aspire to professional status, the criteria by which the aspiration may be judged include the integrity of their conventions or corporate ethics and the degree of control they exercise over the education, practice, and discipline of their members. Published codes of practice now feature in commercial and industrial relations: e.g., the guidelines issued by the Association of the British Pharmaceutical Industry (ABPI) for the conduct of drug trials. The British Code of Advertising Practice is an instrument of self-regulation, administered by the Advertising Standards Authority on the basis of consent (*see also* **Codes of Ethics**).

Social life requires institutions* to provide security within which spontaneous relationships may flourish. Conventions contribute to this security. Beyond the associations of family and work, people gather voluntarily in a multitude of ways: for recreation, sport, pursuit of common interests and concerns. Many such associations have aims and rules, written and unwritten, that both govern their internal life and call for, or assume, degrees of moral commitment by their members. Even in social, family, and personal relations, conventions offer security as a condition of freedom: people are at ease when they know "where they stand" or "what is expected of them." To be unsure of oneself in social relations is unsettling, inhibiting. Conventions in sexual relationships—like those in bridge—because they offer signals for play as well as rules for restraint, enable men and women to enjoy their complementarity to the full, and to enrich the wider society by their doing so.

Conventions in ethics invite further study. They stand between the individualism that has possessed a generation of moralists and the older corporate, institutional, or totalitarian systems from which they reacted. Man is not an isolate. He is by nature a member of society, bound to it by sinews the stronger for being unseen. He has these by convention.

See also **Conventional Morality.**

S. D. Bailey, *Prohibitions and Restraints in War,* 1972; G. Best, *Humanity in War,* 1980; R. S. Downie, *Roles and Values,* 1971; A. S. Duncan, G. R. Dunstan, and R. B. Welbourn (eds.), *Dictionary of Medical Ethics,* ²1981, art. "Declarations"; G. R. Dunstan, *The Artifice of Ethics* (1974), 1978; D. L. Emmet, *Rules, Roles and Relations,* 1966.

G. R. DUNSTAN

Conviction of Sin

In an earlier age conviction of sin* was commonly seen as the normative state of mind preceding a crisis experience of conversion. The Westminster Shorter Catechism affirmed it as the work of the Holy Spirit and a first step toward salvation. Characteristic feelings (which might last for days, months, or even years) included a sense of general wretchedness and unworthiness, self-blame and contempt, often compounded by fear of eternal punishment. After the conversion crisis these feelings of despair, which could be extremely intense, normally gave place to a sense of release, peace, and joy. Revivalist preaching, as in the early Methodist movement and the Great Awakening, tried deliberately to secure conviction of sin in the belief that the person so affected would better appreciate, and more willingly accept, the proffered mercy of God.

Early students of the psychology of religious conversion in adolescence noted that there was frequently no direct relation between the intensity of the conviction of sin and the extent of any actual transgression. They concluded that fear and suggestibility were major factors in producing a conviction of sin. More recently it has been recognized that striving to produce feelings of worthlessness may actually render some people less capable of hearing the gospel message by confirming their neurotic tendencies (e.g., to self-punishment).

Ethical issues involved in conviction of sin include issues of responsibility for one's own past and issues of the propriety of attempting to secure a particular result by what amounts to the manipulation of feelings.

E. S. Ames, *The Psychology of Religious Experience,* 1910, pp. 258–264; Jonathan Edwards, *A Treatise Concerning Religious Affections,* 1746.

GRAEME M. GRIFFIN

Cooperation with Evil

Prior to Vatican Council II, Roman Catholic moral theology developed a detailed set of guidelines to deal with the problem of cooperation with the immoral acts of others. Though the applications of this doctrine in the past show the weaknesses of a now-dated theology, there is a value in the teaching that has enduring relevance.

Cooperation was seen as concurrence with another in some immoral action. Distinctions were made between formal and material, immediate and mediate, and proximate and remote cooperation. Formal cooperation involved consenting to and active participation in the evil action of another. Material cooperation did not imply consent*. It involved concurrence in an action that, though innocent in itself, was a preparation for an evil action. A non-burglar helping a burglar pack the loot was called immediate material cooperation. Mediate material cooperation involved an action that was secondary and subservient to the main and evil act. Selling burglars their tools would be an example of this. Proximate material cooperation is intimately linked to the evil act, as when one holds the ladder or a light for the burglar. Remote material cooperation is not closely connected with the evil act.

Formal cooperation was seen as a sin against charity* and against the virtue offended by the action. Material cooperation could be justified only if the action was in itself not sinful (since we need not intend all of the effects of our actions) and if there was a sufficient and proportionate reason for cooperating. The more closely one cooperates, the more serious must be the justifying reason.

Using this doctrine, the older moral theology justified cooperation by an assistant with a surgeon performing an "evil operation" even to the extent of sterilizing instruments, preparing the patient, and administering the anesthesia. The doctrine was also applied to participation in "heretical worship," to the sale of obscene or forbidden objects, to cooperation with evil employers, and to the problems of judges and juries in dealing with unjust laws.

The teaching had notable weaknesses: it was individualistically concerned with single deeds; it was preoccupied with an antiseptic or egoistic sense of guilt*; it inspired quibbling and simplism. It did, however, face the fact that in a complex world of sinful persons, total detachment from evil is impossible.

The problems we address today are different, but the question of cooperation endures, often addressed in discussions of proportionalism and consequentialism* (*see* **Proportionality**). Questions of cooperation today concern such issues as working for producers of nuclear weapons, paying taxes when the national budget is overly militarized, entering military service, buying from corporations engaged in immoral enterprises, joining a clergy that excludes women, and serving drinks to prospective drivers.

H. Davis, *Moral and Pastoral Theology,* vol. 1, 1949.

DANIEL C. MAGUIRE

Corporal Punishment

Experience shows that corporal punishment may be effective insofar as it is administered by someone in a sustained, predictable, and loving relationship with the person punished, but the more distant and impersonal the relationship and the less stable the character punished, the less effective it will be. That is why some (usually men) claim that a thrashing from their father when they were young did them a lot of good. It may have done so. A question remains, however, as to whether it was *necessary*. If the parents who apply it are unpredictable and capricious or threaten to cease loving, corporal punishment is unlikely to be effective and can be counterproductive. Much the same considerations apply to schools and indicate that corporal punishment is rarely likely to be effective. It is usually applied to disruptive, bored teenage boys where it is used at all, but more and more schools in the English-speaking world have abandoned it.

Judicially, corporal punishment usually takes the form of flogging as a penalty for crimes such as robbery with violence or sexual assault. The same reasons are used to justify it as are advanced for capital punishment*, and with the same doubtful cogency. Does it *deter?* There is a widespread tendency to exaggerate its deterrent effect, and much evidence shows that changes in the law on flogging bear no relation to the volume of crimes for which it may be the penalty. Does it *reform?* Only in the cases where corporal punishment is least needed. Is it a suitable *retribution?* Only if one deems it proper to behave in a physically harsh way to those who have themselves behaved to others in that way; and it is hard to maintain this view on *Christian* grounds (*see also* **Penology**).

The chances of harm in a judicial flogging are great. Elements of eroticism easily enter. Those who have suffered from violent behavior from others need patient counseling. Those whose violent conduct represents a conscious or unconscious reaction to violent treatment by asserting themselves need self-understanding, not flogging. Those who are so excitable that their conduct is not a rational choice but a relief of tension need a sheltered environment. Those who are mentally ill need hospital treatment. For those who are coolly brutal it is the certainty of detection rather than the fear of corporal punishment that is more important. The latter is hardly ever a remedy for serious disorders. A root question to ask is: What is it in human nature

that leads so many to be firmly in favor of corporal punishment?

RONALD PRESTON

Corporations *see* **Business Ethics; Capitalism**

Cost-Benefit Analysis

Cost-benefit analysis (CBA) is a formal "analytic technique designed to help a decision-maker consider systematically all the consequences of a possible course of action, arrayed as costs and benefits" (Fuchs). It involves identifying and assessing all the costs and benefits of alternative courses of action in order to determine which has the most favorable benefit-cost ratio. Developed in business, this approach has also been extended to public policy*, for example, in decisions about building airports, protecting the environment, and setting safety standards in the workplace. A subset of CBA is risk-benefit analysis, risk* being one kind of cost. CBA is essentially a form of ethical consequentialism* or, more specifically, utilitarianism*, and is subject to the criticisms that have been directed against such perspectives. Since maximization of welfare (utility) is considered morally important—though not necessarily sufficient—from practically all ethical perspectives, CBA may be accepted by nonconsequentialists and nonutilitarians within limits, particularly within the limits set by distributive justice*. Practitioners of CBA tend to sum up or to aggregate the costs and benefits of various policies without adequately considering how they are distributed, that is, who will bear the costs and who will gain the benefits. For example, according to one study, the most cost-effective approach to control hypertension in the USA is to concentrate resources on known hypertensives, but considerations of justice might dictate a different allocation because many poor people would not be aware of their hypertension since they have limited access to the health care system. (Cost-effectiveness analysis simply considers the costs of different ways to achieve some goal, such as saving lives, without converting the goal and the costs into a common measure, such as money.)

Narrow and broad versions of CBA differ according to the range of values they include and the extent of their efforts to reduce all costs and benefits to a common denominator, usually money, for purposes of determining trade-offs. Obviously, it is impossible to identify, weight, and balance costs and benefits or even to determine the alternatives to be compared without some values*. Since proponents of CBA tend to favor hard over soft variables, the question of *which* values becomes very important for assessing consequences, and often it becomes the question of *whose* values. Efforts to find a common scale or denominator of values, usually monetary value, become arbitrary when applied to goods not traded in the marketplace, such as life and friendship, which they then seriously distort. One major question is whether CBA, when open to a wide range of soft variables that may be incommensurable and when attentive to distributive justice, can be useful in decision-making, particularly to make explicit judgments that might have been only implicit. The process, perhaps even more than the results, of CBA may be useful as part of a democratic government's accountability despite the counterargument that sometimes the bases of decision-making should not be made public (*see* **Democracy; Secrecy**).

CBA is widespread, and alternatives may not be immediately available. Nevertheless, one of its own potential costs should be noted: the prevalence of the language and technique of calculation and quantification, which may come to dominate its users, subtly but significantly changing their perspectives. For example, in the USA the economic language already evident in medicine—"the health care industry," "providers," and "consumers"—may threaten the traditional conception of the physician-patient relationship, including its moral norms. John Stuart Mill noted that Jeremy Bentham's utilitarian philosophy could "teach the means of organizing and regulating the merely *business* part of social arrangements," but not family and friendship. The instrumental rationality of CBA is appropriate in some areas of life, but even in public policy, expressive values, such as care and compassion, are often important, for example, in allocating resources to rescue individuals despite the demands of instrumental rationality and efficiency.

See **Ends and Means.**

V. R. Fuchs, "What Is Cost-Benefit Analysis?" *New England Journal of Medicine* 303, Oct. 16, 1980, pp. 937–938; S. Kelman, "Cost-Benefit Analysis: An Ethical Critique," *Regulation,* Jan.-Feb. 1981; A. MacIntyre, "Utilitarianism and Cost/Benefit Analysis," in *Values in the Electric Power Industry,* ed. K. Sayre, 1977; E. J. Mishan, *Cost-Benefit Analysis,* 1976; R. Sugden and A. Williams, *The Principles of Practical Cost-Benefit Analysis,* 1978; J. N. Wolfe (ed.), *Cost Benefit and Cost Effectiveness,* 1973.

JAMES F. CHILDRESS

Counseling, Ethical Problems in

For the last forty years, ethical problems in both secular and religious counseling have been similar to one another. This is because both spheres of counseling have been informed by similar philosophical views about ethics, values, and the nature of human problems.

The influence of secular psychotherapy on religious counseling. These philosophical views largely have come from the commitments of secular psychotherapy. Freud believed that psychotherapy was an ethically neutral process that needed guidance only by a limited professional ethic covering the contract for therapy. Heinz Hartmann in his *Psychoanalysis and Moral Values* (1960) took a similar view and saw psychoanalysis as a technology for changing personality without commitment to particular sets of moral values. This view continued to prevail and received a widely popular articulation in the client-centered counseling of Carl Rogers. Rogers's emphasis was slightly different, however, from Freud and Hartmann. He recognized the value-laden nature of therapy but saw the values involved as coming from the client's inner motivations toward growth, maturity, and self-actualization.

The Rogerian view influenced pastoral counseling in both Protestant and Catholic circles through the writings of Seward Hiltner, especially his *Pastoral Counseling* (1949). Hiltner saw pastoral counseling as communicating acceptance of the person being helped. It also entailed clarification of the broken person's problems. Acceptance and clarification would help the broken person to regain his or her own initiatives and address life's problems within the individual's own value resources. Although Hiltner recognized the usefulness to counseling of the minister's role as representative of the church's religious and moral tradition, he believed it was inappropriate to impose this tradition upon the broken person within the intimacies of the counseling situation. To accomplish this, Hiltner, following Rogers, believed that a counseling relationship should be built around a warm process of communication through a nondirective and empathic "reflection" of the feelings and attitudes of the person being helped.

Value dimensions of counseling. Recent philosophical analysis of counseling relationships, whether secular or religious, has uncovered new ways to think about their value dimensions. Rather than ethically neutral, it is more accurate to see them as a kind of praxis with special moral and value commitments appropriate to their major task of reorienting personality toward the goal of greater autonomy, initiative, and freedom. Counseling may appear to be ethically neutral because it may bracket or temporarily set aside concern with certain more specific moral rules that conventionally govern typical everyday behaviors. But sometimes more abstract ethical principles such as respect for persons, fairness, or mutuality are still very much in evidence in many types of counseling and especially counseling that addresses marital or family problems involving more than one person.

In addition, the images of health associated with many forms of secular therapy can frequently be seen as covert concepts of character or human fulfillment with quite discernible ethical commitments. Joseph Margolis in his *Psychotherapy and Morality* has argued that contemporary psychotherapy is not ethically neutral. Rather, it has a specific type of ethics, generally teleological with an emphasis on virtue* in contrast to more deontological and principled approaches to ethics. Some moral philosophers have pointed out the ethical egoism* implicit in the concept of self-actualization which serves as the image of health and maturity in humanistic psychologies such as those of Abraham Maslow and Carl Rogers (*see* **Self-Realization**). Philip Rieff and Gilbert Harmon have found a kind of ethical egoism of a more hedonistic kind in Freud's image of health. Ernest Wallwork, on the other hand, has found in Freud a more Kantian and implicitly Jewish principle of respect for persons. These controversies at least have established the difficulty that any psychotherapeutic psychology has in drawing a firm line between its concepts of health and some more properly normative and ethical image of human fulfillment (*see* **Health and Disease, Values in Defining; Mental Health**).

Beyond ethical neutrality. In recent years, William Glasser, Perry London, Hobart Mowrer, and Thomas Szasz have all made statements recognizing that psychotherapy is an ethical process. They all admit that it uses scientific psychological concepts, but primarily at the level of diagnosis and analysis of the causal determinants shaping a particular life. But the scientific concepts function within a larger ethical praxis that becomes especially evident in the determination of the goals of counseling.

But few of these statements recognize the full consequences of their arguments pointing to the ethical character of counseling. They seem either to take some kind of arbitrary ethical stand or to believe that the problems of imposition of heteronomous ethics on unsuspecting clients can be solved if the therapist simply acknowledges his or her own ethics.

Ethics in pastoral counseling. In recent years, three distinct positions on the relation of religious counseling to ethics has emerged. Hobart Mowrer has influenced several pastoral counselors to believe that underdeveloped, in contrast to overdeveloped, superego* strength is a major cause of neurosis. Mowrer's counseling reinforces superego functions and also works to reconcile individuals with parental authorities. This position has the difficulty, however, of simply assuming the basic correctness of conventional ethical positions and sees no need for a more critically grounded ethic as a background to therapy. John Hoffman in his *Ethical Confrontation in Counseling* has argued for the therapeutic efficacy of ethical judgments in counseling, especially for a variety of problems where the client has sufficient freedom and ego strength to hear and appropriate ethical advice. Don Browning in *The Moral Context of Pastoral Care* and *Religious Ethics and Pastoral Care* has argued for the importance in all forms of counseling, religious or secular, of a stable, critically grounded, and publicly recognizable ethic as a contextual background to the healing process. In more distinctively psychological forms of counseling, this ethic is often temporarily set aside within the confines of therapy itself while more specifically psychodynamic problems that inhibit the client's freedom are addressed. But he argues that this ethic should be present in the background of all counseling so that individuals and the public know what kind of ethical world the subtle socializing forces of all therapies are opening up for clients.

D. Browning, *The Moral Context of Pastoral Care,* 1976; and *Religious Ethics and Pastoral Care,* 1983; H. Hartmann, *Psychoanalysis and Moral Values,* 1960; J. Hoffman, *Ethical Confrontation in Counseling,* 1979; J. Margolis, *Psychotherapy and Morality,* 1966.

DON S. BROWNING

Counsels

In moral theology, counsels are exhortations that are helpful toward the attaining of the good life, but are not binding, as precepts are. The "counsels of perfection," also called the "evangelical counsels," are the exhortations to poverty*, chastity*, and obedience*. This way of talking seems to suggest that the "religious" life is "higher" or "more perfect" than the life of involvement in the world, and this would be challenged by Protestant moralists. But it is a mistake to talk of "higher" and "lower," and it is a misunderstanding of the expression "counsels of perfection." The Christian social ethic demands that many persons should involve themselves in the life of the world, but especially in an age of affluence and of the overprizing of comfort and wealth, this same ethic equally demands that some should hear the evangelical counsels and witness to the realities of prayer, aspiration, and true holiness. This is far from being "escape" or "withdrawal," but it demands nonattachment and self-renunciation.

JOHN MACQUARRIE

Counter-Reformation Moral Theology

The Roman Catholic moral theology of the Counter-Reformation period can best be understood in the light of the previous history of moral theology and of the historical circumstances of the time. Catholic moral theology as a separate discipline distinct from all other theology came into existence at the end of the 16th and the beginning of the 17th centuries. In the *Summa Theologiae* of Thomas Aquinas (d. 1274) there was no separate discipline of moral theology, but reflec-

tion on moral life was connected in a systematic and integral way with one theology. After Aquinas, the influence of nominalism with its emphasis on the individual and the uniqueness of every moral choice negatively affected all systematic theology (*see* **Medieval Ethics; Thomistic Ethics**).

At the time of the Reformation there were two significant strands in what would be called today moral theology*. A Thomistic revival in the 15th-century university world made the *Summa* the primary text. Commentaries on Part II of the *Summa,* which deals with the moral life of the Christian and its virtues, were the primary form of publication. Thomas de Vio (later Cardinal Cajetan; d. 1534), Franciscus de Victoria (d. 1546), who contributed so much to international law, and the somewhat later Dominican school of Salamanca illustrate such an approach in the 16th century. The Jesuits Gabriel Vasquez (d. 1604) and Francis Suarez (d. 1617) were also well-known commentators of the *Summa.* At the same time there also existed *Summae Confessoriorum,* which had begun to appear in the 13th century. These were very practical books often arranged in alphabetical order with little or no abstract reasoning that dealt in a very positivistic way with the considerations of the moral life.

One of the first theological responses to the Reformation took the form of an apologetic in defense of the Catholic faith. Robert Bellarmine's (d. 1621) *Disputationes de Controversiis* well illustrates such a genre. Bellarmine considered all theological issues, including those which might be thought of as pertaining to moral theology—free will, sin, vows, sacraments, merit, etc. His whole approach was apologetic rather than systematic, and obviously polemical.

In the beginning of the Counter-Reformation period there came into existence an important new genre—the *Institutiones Theologiae Moralis,* which became the manuals or textbooks for moral theology until Vatican Council II. As part of the attempt to reform Catholic life and institutions, the Council of Trent stressed the importance of the sacrament of penance* and decreed that all Catholics in the state of grave sin were obliged to confess no less than once a year to the priest according to the number and species of their sins. To accomplish this reform it was necessary to train priests as confessors for the sacrament of penance, with special attention given to the role of the confessor as a judge of the existence and the gravity of sinful acts. In this connection, the *Ratio Studiorum* of the Society of Jesus proposed a special two-year course to train future priests which would begin with a brief treatment of the principles of fundamental moral theology (the end of human existence, human acts, the moral law, sin), then discuss the moral life of the Christian on the basis of the Ten Commandments, and finally treat the sacraments especially in the light of how they were to be administered and celebrated. John Azor (d. 1603), a Jesuit theologian teaching in Rome, followed this approach and published his class notes under the title of *Institutiones Theologiae Moralis*. The world of Catholic theology after Trent shifted from a primary university base to a seminary situation in which the professional training of future priests became the primary purpose. In this context the genre of the *Institutiones Theologiae Moralis* quickly spread. The method and tone of these manuals became generally accepted as the approach to moral theology existing within the Roman Catholic tradition until very recently.

Moral theology in this context became cut off from sacred scripture, dogmatic theology, and spiritual theology and became closely allied with canon law*. This discipline was not primarily interested in speculative or systematic concerns but only in the practical concern of judging if a particular action were sinful or not and the degree of sinfulness. Vital concerns in moral theology such as character and the virtues of the acting person were skipped over. The tone of these manuals was legalistic, extrinsic, and minimalistic as they dealt with their primary concern of whether or not particular actions were right or wrong on the basis of their conformity to the law of God primarily seen in terms of the Ten Commandments and the laws of the church.

In the 17th and 18th centuries a sharp controversy arose in moral theology between laxists and rigorists which centered on what was later called the moral systems. There can be no doubt that some of the manualists in the 17th century fell into laxism; e.g., Antonine of Diana, Anthony Escobar, Thomas Tamburini, and John Caramuel, a Cistercian monk who was later called "the prince of laxists." Extreme reaction against the laxists came primarily from the Jansenists in France and took the form of rigorism in the writings of Anthony Arnauld, Peter Nicole, and Blaise Pascal. Often the Jesuits as a whole were accused of laxism, but such a charge is not true. These controversies were quite heated and evoked strong reactions on the part of many. In 1679 the Holy Office under Pope Innocent XI condemned sixty-five propositions associated with laxism. Among laxist positions condemned as at least scandalous and dangerous in practice were the following: it is sufficient to make an act of faith only once in a lifetime; we are able to satisfy the precepts of loving our neighbor by only external acts. In 1690 Pope Alexander VIII condemned some extreme rigorist positions; e.g., those who do not have the most pure love of God, uncontaminated in any way, are to be excluded from the eucharist.

Much of the debate centered on the question, How does one move from theoretical doubt about the existence of a law or obligation to the practical certitude necessary to act? The one extreme of absolute tutiorism* maintained that when in doubt one had to follow the safer course; i.e., assume the existence of a duty, law, or obligation. The opposite extreme of laxism held that one could follow an opinion in favor of freedom from the law even if the arguments in its favor were only tenuously probable (the Latin word really means provable) or even much less probable than the arguments in favor of the obligation. Both of these extremes were condemned by the above-mentioned papal interventions, but the debate continued. After 1656 the Dominicans generally proposed probabiliorism*, according to which one could follow the opinion for freedom from the law only if it were more probable than the opinion in favor of the law or obligation. The Jesuits were generally supporters of probabilism*, according to which one could follow the opinion for freedom from the law provided it was probable, or as often phrased, truly or solidly probable. Unfortunately, the discussions often degenerated into polemics.

After the suppression of the Jesuits, Alphonsus Liguori (d. 1787) became the leading defender of a moderate probabilism that was attacked by the Dominicans Concina and Patuzzi. Alphonsus, who was the founder of the Redemptorist order, called his approach equiprobabilism*—one could follow the opinion in favor of freedom from the law if it were equally as probable as the opinion for the law. Perhaps the greatest reason for the ultimate success of Alphonsus was the prudential way in which he approached all moral problems and offered his solutions. Later popes declared him a saint, a doctor of the church, and the patron of moral theologians and confessors. Although Alphonsus wrote much on spiritual and ascetical theology, his manual of moral theology followed the general method and outline of the *Institutiones* which remained the primary Catholic approach to moral theology until Vatican Council II.

See also **Casuistry.**

T. Deman, "Probabilisme," *Dictionnaire de théologie catholique,* vol. 13, 1936; B. Häring, *The Law of Christ,* vol. 1, ET 1961, pp. 3–33; L. Vereecke, "Préface à l'histoire de la théologie morale moderne," *Studia Moralis* 1, 1963, pp. 87–120.

                                   CHARLES F. CURRAN

Courage

The place of courage in the moral life has always been acknowledged even if variously understood and debated. Christian ethical reflection on the subject owes much to ancient Greek and Roman thought, especially Aristotle and the Stoics. As one of the cardinal virtues* along with wisdom (*see* **Prudence**), justice*, and temperance*, courage was seen as necessary to all truly moral conduct, a mean* struck between rashness and cowardice, a capability of human character* to resist pain, danger, or adversity by enduring what cannot be changed and by changing what cannot be endured.

Christian conceptions of courage were greatly influenced by the experience of martyrdom in the early centuries. This left an indelible impression upon theology and ethics as well as in church art and liturgy. It had much to do with stressing the passive elements in courage, thus balancing the soldierly fearlessness so prized by Plato and Aristotle in their treatments of the theme. Nevertheless, the Latin *fortitudo* became the defining term for courage in the Christian mode, spelled out in manuals and treatises with a distinctly monastic flavor, and illus-trated in the lives of the saints told and retold all through the Middle Ages.

As is well known, Thomas Aquinas brought together the cardinal virtues with the three "theological virtues"* of faith*, hope*, and love*, thus constructing an ethical scheme that has intrigued and baffled Christian thinkers ever since. Is courage, for example, "only human" as compared with faith, divinely infused in the soul? Later Catholic thought went on to schematize fortitude as both a cardinal virtue and one of the seven gifts of the Holy Spirit*. This obviously tended to leave courage in a kind of ethical limbo, in which it might be regarded as "the emotion involved in the exercise of fortitude," to quote one recent Catholic statement, or as the very meaning of that virtue itself, in the view of another. It would seem that oversharp definitions which distinguish "Christian" from merely "human" courage raise more questions than they answer. Did Aquinas, by combining pagan insights with Christian truth, thereby diminish or instead transfigure them? Is an ethic of virtue really compatible with one of grace-through-faith?

These are of course as much Protestant as Catholic questions; it is not surprising therefore that the field of Christian ethics should increasingly engage both traditions in common inquiry and dialogue. Is "human" always a synonym for weakness contrasted with God's almightiness? Can an ethic of humility and obedience ever supplant one based upon healthy self-respect and the kind of self-assertion that belongs to courage as such? Is the one more "Christian" than the other? And if so, what actual moral difference should it make?

Part of the difficulty in locating courage, much less defining it, lies in the fact that it is psychosomatic in character, shared with the animals as well as the angels, and as versatile as the variety of perils and fears requires. Furthermore, courage cannot be thought of without an aesthetic as well as a simply moral reference; it occasions admiration whenever "danger is despised from a noble motive," as Aristotle says. The one word "courage" must cover such a great range of situations and responses—running all the way from coping to daring, resignation to resistance—that, like the character trait it represents, the word must have both flexible and firm possibilities of meaning. Perhaps therefore the best definition of courage would be one couched in the language of explicit metaphor and parable, evoking what it describes, but always in terms of that resilient steadfastness out of which human courage is made.

Aristotle, *Nicomachean Ethics,* bk. 3; R. Hazelton, *Graceful Courage,* 1985; J. Pieper, *The Four Cardinal Virtues,* ET 1965; P. Tillich, *The Courage to Be,* 1952.

ROGER HAZELTON

Covenant

Biblical covenants. The word "covenant" translates the Hebrew *berith,* which may be related to Akkadian terms meaning "to bind" and "bond." It also translates the Greek *diathēkē,* a term that can mean "last will and testament" but that in the NT is used primarily in the sense of an agreement between unequals. The concept has central importance in both Old and New Testaments, as reflected in the names that, in the 2nd century A.D., came to be given to these two parts of the Bible, which would more accurately be rendered Old Covenant and New Covenant.

Covenants in the OT between God and the people are initiated by God, not negotiated, and are expressions of God's power and grace. In some covenants, God's action is self-binding: e.g., those with Noah, Abraham, and David, in each of which God makes a promise to the people but does not lay corresponding obligations upon them. In other cases, God's covenant includes explicit obligations laid upon the people, as in the giving of the law at Sinai and in the covenant at Shechem (Josh. 24). The contrast between these two types of covenant should not be overdrawn; the latter type, and not only the former, strongly expresses God's grace, in that the God who covenants is the God who has brought the people out of bondage in Egypt, and in that the law which is given in the Sinai covenant is received by the Israelite people with immense gratitude, as a gift that gives shape and meaning to the people through the revelation of God's will (*see also* **Old Testament Ethics**).

One way NT writers interpret the significance of God's action in Jesus Christ is by reference to God's covenant with the people Israel. The writers frequently portray Jesus Christ as the fulfillment of God's promises to Israel. Elsewhere they contrast the new covenant in Jesus Christ with the old one written on tablets of stone and speak of the church as a community brought into being through the new covenant in Jesus Christ (*see also* **New Testament Ethics**).

Covenant and social relationships. The term "covenant" may refer either to a certain kind of social relationship or to the transaction that brings it about. In the former and more basic sense, a covenant among persons is a binding, enduring relationship of mutual loyalty*. Although a covenant is characteristically thought of as coming about through explicit mutual promises, as in a marriage, the term is also appropriate for relationships in which the members' entrusting themselves to one another and accepting one another's entrustment is implicit, though nonetheless binding and obligating, as in the case of life in civil society.

A covenant relationship, while it often includes contractual features, is to be contrasted with a contract* in most usual senses of the term. Covenants imply strong affirmation of each member in the relationship, a focus on the relationship between the members rather than mainly on the stipulated obligations, and emphasis upon mutual belongingness and enduring responsibility, even when the members are unfaithful. Although the obligations of a covenant vary somewhat with the type of relationship, they characteristically stress mutual faithfulness of a kind appropriate to the type of relationship (*see also* **Fidelity**).

Christian theologians have sometimes used the concept of covenant as the central vehicle for their theological and moral reflection (*see* **Puritan Ethics**). The "federal theology" of the 17th century developed an elaborate covenantal scheme, contrasting a "covenant of works" between God and Adam with a "covenant of grace" through Jesus Christ, and interpreting the church and the wider society in covenantal terms. Although a pervasive covenantal interpretation of life is in principle promising, serious exegetical and theological questions have been raised about how these theologians carried it out. Partly under their influence, a major element in the tradition of the Afrikaners of the Republic of South Africa is the belief that at a time of great crisis God entered into a covenant with the Boer people and gave them victory over their enemies. In this imagery God elected the Afrikaner people to special favor and wills the separation of that people from other races—a doctrine used to support theories of apartheid* and "separate development." The contrast could hardly be sharper between this view of covenant and the New Testament proclamation of God's love in Jesus Christ for all people. Christian covenantal interpretations, however, are not inherently exclusivistic, but more readily express the universality of God's love and the inclusive as well as the special moral obligations that follow from it.

J. L. Allen, *Love and Conflict: A Covenantal Model of Christian Ethics,* 1984; K. Barth, *Church Dogmatics* IV/1, ET 1956, pp. 22–78; D. J. McCarthy, *Old Testament Covenant: A Survey of Current Opinions,* 1972; G. E. Mendenhall, "Covenant," *IDB* I, 1962.

JOSEPH L. ALLEN

Covetousness

The last of the Ten Commandments* prohibits covetousness: "You shall not covet your neighbor's house; you shall not covet your neighbor's wife, or his manservant, or his maidservant, or his ox, or his ass, or anything that is your neighbor's" (Ex. 20:17). This is the only commandment that applies directly to thoughts rather than external actions. Jesus also warned of covetousness: "Take heed, and beware of all covetousness; for a man's life does not consist in the abundance of his possessions" (Luke 12:15). Covetousness appears prominently in lists of vices and sins in the NT (e.g., Rom. 1:29f.; Col. 3:5) and has traditionally been counted among the seven capital, or deadly, sins* because it leads to other sinful actions, such as theft. John Calvin observed that the point of the Tenth Commandment is to "banish from our hearts all desire contrary to love," since covetousness could lead to actions that harm the neighbor, and that its positive interpretation in accord with Christ, the interpreter of the law, is that "whatever we conceive, deliberate, will, or attempt is to be linked to our neighbor's good and advantage" (*Institutes* 2.7.49).

Covetousness is perhaps best defined as ardent, excessive, or immoderate desire not only for possessions but for the possessions of others (*see also* **Envy**). Covetousness is close to but often distinguished from greed, which is an excessive desire for goods, especially wealth, and from avarice, which is an inordinate desire to acquire and hoard goods, usually money. Following Aristotle, Thomas Aquinas (*ST* II-II.118) treated generosity or liberality as the virtuous mean between the vices of covetousness or avarice and prodigality or extravagance. There is considerable latitude in defining this mean. One important debate about the relationship between socioeconomic systems and motives is whether capitalism* depends on such motives as greed, avarice, and covetousness.

JAMES F. CHILDRESS

Creation *see* **Christian Ethics; Image of God; Law and Gospel; Natural Law; Orders**

Creation, Orders of *see* **Orders**

Crime

Crime is a pervasive but—as far as its definition is concerned—somewhat elusive characteristic of societies. The economic costs of crime in industrial societies are considerable: in Great Britain it is estimated that crime costs more than £4 million each day; the psychological costs to victims are often equally serious. Recorded rates of crime that are published publicly are gross underestimates of the extent of criminal activity in society. Large-scale surveys asking people if they have been the victim of a crime during a preceding period of time currently indicate that about 50 percent of all burglaries, 75 percent of woundings, and about 90 percent of acts of vandalism are not reported to or recorded by the police. White-collar crime rarely comes to light. Many people therefore cope with crime as a routine aspect of their lives without involving the civil authorities. Many persons commit offenses that are never detected.

Fear of being a victim of crime, especially among the elderly, has often been found to be based on poor evidence. Although crime is a pervasive and serious problem, it is widely dispersed in both time and space and is usually of a petty character. And in many offenses involving physical harm, the victim shares similar social characteristics with the assailant. Changes in the recorded rates of crime may be as much related to changes in reporting habits among the public, or recording practices by the police, as to actual increases or decreases in criminal activity. The published aggregate statistics of crime obscure such nuances of interpretation, possibly increasing anxiety and fear, compounding the problem of crime itself.

Although contestable at every point, an initial conception of crime indicates that it is behavior intended by a person who could have acted differently; activity harmful to the public welfare; prohibited by the criminal law, and usually prosecuted by representatives of the state. Some anthropologists have pointed to examples of societies where crime is identified without the existence of a centralized state, which may therefore be the least important feature. However, criminologists and sociologists do not dispute greatly over a definition of crime. Indeed, they have tended to expand their subject matter well beyond the concern of criminal law to include the making and breaking of social rules of conduct. Thus, the professional interest of the sociologist of deviance may range from robbery to nudity, from fraud to religious fundamentalism.

Dispute does focus on the causes of crime or, less ambitiously, on the social conditions that foster it. Legal positivists regard crime as human behavior that intentionally breaks the criminal law. Judicial decision-making concerns the relationship between a person's actions and the meaning of a statute, as well as an offender's mental state. Crime resides in the action of a willing person.

Early attempts to explain the causes of crime were directed to individual human characteristics, whether genetic, physical, or psychological. For example, on the basis of detailed anthropometric measurement, Lombroso (1836–1909) attempted to identify the born criminal. Human will plays a diminished role in this perspective, with little hope of reform offered to an offender. Scant attention is given to the fact that crime is defined socially and therefore brings different sections of the population within its scope as change occurs.

Another range of theories links crime to the malfunctioning of a social system. Robert Merton (b. 1910) argues that when particular groups cannot achieve generally shared societal goals by the accepted institutional means, they may resort to deviance and lawbreaking. A variety of "strain theories" have followed, including the proposition that crime can become a feature of a subculture that functions to sustain the material welfare of disadvantaged people.

Working from rather different assumptions about the nature of societal objectives, Marxist criminologists have tinged criminal acts with political significance. Crime is caused by the residual inequalities of capitalist society. With more or less certainty, it is argued that in a socialist society the amounts of crime will be small.

Sin is not a notion generally employed by criminologists. Evil intent or the hurt caused to victims is not a matter for frequent comment. It has been left to moralists to debate the relationship between crime and sin. In Britain, this has provided a complex literature that has echoes of the difficulty of holding to a notion of natural law and the tension of a more contextual ethic. The debate between Patrick Devlin, who, though not equating crime with sin, does identify an area of public morality to which the law should refer, and H. L. A. Hart, who urges a more critical appraisal of popular morality, has continued, but largely free from the intervention of criminologists (see **Morality, Legal Enforcement of**).

Finally, crime has been defined as a process of decision-making by the various personnel of the criminal justice system. A person perceives himself or herself as a victim, the police are called and decide on the validity of the claim. Through a complex series of relationships an event is molded into a final category of criminal activity. This perspective has led to the gathering of a fruitful body of knowledge about the assumptions that police officers, lawyers, and other people working within the criminal justice system make about their work and their differing definitions of crime. The tension between legal positivism and "law in action" has been highlighted. Such a perspective can present a highly relativistic concept of crime, neglecting a description and analysis of those actions which, across a range of contexts within and between different societies, may frustrate what Paul Lehmann (*Ethics in a Christian Context,* 1963) has described as "making and keeping human life really human."

See **Penology; Juvenile Delinquency.**

H. S. Becker, *Outsiders: Studies in the Sociology of Deviance,* 1964; P. Devlin, *The Enforcement of Morals,* 1959; D. Downes and P. Rock, *Understanding Deviance,* 1982; P. H. Ennis, *Criminal Victimization in the United States: A Report of a National Survey.* U.S. President's Commission on Law Enforcement and Administration of Justice, Field Surveys 11, 1967; H. L. A. Hart, *Law, Liberty and Morality,* 1963; Home Office, *The British Crime Survey,* 1983; R. K. Merton, *Social Theory and Social Structure,* 1957.

SIMON HOLDAWAY

Criteria *see* Norms; Situation Ethics

Cruelty

The willful infliction of unnecessary pain and suffering, i.e., pain and suffering that are not necessary to achieve morally important ends and thus cannot be justified by those ends (*see* **Ends and Means**). Cruelty is the infliction of pain and suffering for their own sake on any sentient creature that can experience pain and undergo suffering. Cruelty to animals as well as to humans is a moral offense and usually a legal offense too. Although cruelty is often physical, it may also be mental as in the case of humiliation. There are no moral defenses of cruelty; cruelty appears to be absolutely wrong, seriously harming both the perpetrator and the victim. But even if the moral rule against cruelty is absolute, there will still be disputes about its meaning, particularly about which acts that inflict pain and suffering are cruel and which can be justified by their ends (e.g., deterrence of crime or retaliation to force the enemy to respect the laws of war). For example, the Eighth Amendment to the US Constitution rules out "cruel and unusual punishment," but there is dispute about whether capital punishment* is cruel. Similarly, the laws of war rule out cruelty, but there is dispute about whether torture* is always cruel or whether it can be justified by some ends. Certain weapons are prohibited because they are designed to cause unnecessary suffering; for example, dumdum bullets and explosive or inflammable projectiles weighing less than four hundred grams are prohibited because they can incapacitate only one person and cause more suffering than is necessary to incapacitate that person. Other major disputes about cruelty include the use of animals* in research. Psychologically, there are some pathological conditions: the sadist enjoys inflicting pain and the masochist enjoys experiencing pain. Sociologically, some regimes and opponents of regimes create terror in part by the infliction of pain and suffering, but they usually deny that their acts are cruel by contending that they are necessary for their morally significant ends.

See **Humanitarianism; Necessity; Terrorism.**

P. P. Hallie, *The Paradox of Cruelty,* 1969; J. Shklar, *Ordinary Vices,* 1984.

JAMES F. CHILDRESS

Crusade

The idea of the crusade, or "holy war," is described by Roland Bainton as one of three Christian attitudes toward war, alongside pacifism and the just war idea. Bainton identifies the crusade by four characteristics: holy cause, belief in divine guidance and aid, godly crusaders and ungodly enemies, and unsparing prosecution. Other writers (e.g., Thomas Fuller) have stressed the close connection between the just war and crusade ideas. For the Decretists of the 12th and early 13th centuries, a crusade was simply a just war authorized by the pope. For the Puritan apologists of the 16th and 17th centuries, God's authorization and participation are similarly a sign of the most just kind of war. The idea of war ordained by God originates in the OT story of the conquest of Canaan; this paradigm was incorporated by Augustine in his nascent theory of the just war. In the OT such wars are to be fought unsparingly; yet Augustine undercut this theme by insisting on restraint in the use of force against evildoers. A similar mixed picture emerges later. The efforts of the medieval church to limit warfare among Christians (the Truce of God, the Peace of God, and the banning of certain weapons) were not extended to warfare with infidels, and the medieval crusades were not fought according to such restraints. Some apologists in the Puritan revolution argued that their soldiers' godliness implied scrupulously merciful treatment of the enemy; yet extreme cruelty and devastation sometimes appeared in this war and were generally characteristic of the Continental religious wars. The evidence is not that all crusades are necessarily unsparing, but that a transcendent cause tends to justify extreme measures in its service. Modern ideological wars share the characteristics of the crusade and present the same dangers.

See **Just War.**

R. H. Bainton, *Christian Attitudes Toward War and Peace,* 1960; T. Fuller, *The Historie of the Holy Warre,* 1639; J. T. Johnson, *Ideology, Reason, and the Limitation of War,* 1975; L. B. Walters, Jr., "The Just War and the Crusade: Antitheses or Analogies," *The Monist* 57, 1973.

JAMES TURNER JOHNSON

Cults

Derived from the Latin *cultus* (worship), the term "cult" generally either denotes the act or form of religious practice, or classifies a religious group as unorthodox or spurious. In the first sense, cult may refer to specific rites and beliefs, or their adherents, devoted to a particular deity, spirit, or saint, such as the cult of Apollo or the Virgin Mary. In the second sense, "cult" is often used interchangeably with "sect"* as a term in contrast to church* or denomination.

In popular American usage since the 1960s cults are "totalistic" religious groups which demand their members' complete commitment to absolutist beliefs and authoritarian leaders, regimented organizations, and deviant ways of life. To this end groups like the Peoples Temple of Jim Jones subject their recruits to "brainwashing,"* disrupt their families, and exploit their labor and assets. Defenders of many alternative religious movements labeled cults, as, for example, the Unification Church, point to their lack of overtly coercive measures as well as their ideological and communal integrity in responding to the problems their converts face in the larger society and culture (*see* **Deprogramming**).

Sociologists of religion have fixed no unified definition of the term or list of cases to which it applies. In the context of modern Christianity the seminal formulation is that of Ernst Troeltsch (1912), who views the cult as a form of radical mystical individualism. This entirely inward spiritual religion is indifferent to moral discipline, public worship, and social concerns. As opposed to the creedal and sacramental authority of the church and the ethical rigor of the sect, the antinomian and subjective cult "creates no community, since it possesses neither the sense of solidarity nor the faith in authority which this requires, nor the no less necessary fanaticism and desire for uniformity."

More recent church-sect classification schemes have stressed the organizational and institutional traits of cults, and their alien instead of schismatic stance toward the society's religious traditions. Thus Milton Yinger (1957) defines the cult as loosely structured, "small, short-lived, often local, frequently built around a dominant leader," and unlikely to develop into an established sect or denomination. Drawing on the work of Bryan Wilson (1959, 1973) and David Martin (1965), Roy Wallis (1977) distinguishes between cult and sect by observing that while both deviate from the respectable church and denomination, the sect, like the church, is seen by its members to be "uniquely legitimate as a means of access to truth or salvation." The cult, like the denomination, is seen to be "pluralistically legitimate, one of a variety of paths" to the truth. This absence of authoritative grounds for discerning heresy from orthodoxy stems from the cult's epistemological individualism. This central trait is what precludes stable doctrine, organization, and membership in the case of the cult. If cult leaders can claim some new revelation to consolidate doctrinal and moral authority, then a coherent sectarian group can develop from the diffuse, individualistic origins of a cult.

See **Sect.**

D. A. Martin, *Pacifism,* 1965; E. Troeltsch, *The Social Teaching of the Christian Churches* (1912), ET 1931, vol. 2, p. 796; R. Wallis, *The Road to Total Freedom,* 1977, pp. 13–18; B. R. Wilson, "An Analysis of Sect Development," *American Sociological Review* 24, 1959, pp. 3–15; also *Magic and the Millennium,* 1973, ch. 1; J. M. Yinger, *Religion, Society, and the Individual,* 1957, pp. 154–155.

STEVEN M. TIPTON

Culture

In common parlance, culture is a word that applies to the art and literature of a society or a period, and historians contrast the authenticity and spiritual value of *folk, high,* and even *popular* culture (e.g., vaudeville, which had a good deal of personal creativity and audience participation) with the superficiality and spectator character of *mass* culture (e.g., commercial entertainment). Despite its partiality, this emphasis on intellectual and artistic expression has the virtue of pointing to what scholars identify as the most important (or most distinctive) element of culture, namely, its codification of the "symboling" activities of people in a particular society. The focus on art, religion, philosophy, ethics, and communication through words and images in general also captures a crucial aspect of terms like "horticulture" and of the use of "culture" in connection with bacilli grown in a laboratory, for it suggests the earliest meaning of the word as applied to humankind's efforts to build civilization by cultivating or nurturing the highest capacities of the species. Applying the word to both flowers and germs also reminds us that social scientists now use the term in a value-neutral sense: just as Enlightenment *philosophes* such as Voltaire began to use culture to mean "the spirit of a people," anthropologists use it to refer to the "social heritage" or "way" characteristic of a particular group without blessing or damning its substance.

A purely descriptive understanding of culture would embrace at least the following four attributes:

1. Culture is not the result of biological or other natural factors; it is the work of human hands and minds. It may be heavily influenced by environmental or biological determinants, but it is a human *response* to these conditions, not an inevitable consequence of them.

2. It is not just a collocation of unrelated customs or attitudes; it is a patterned whole in which various cultural traits are interlocked with and functionally related to one another. Early functionalists (especially those whose conclusions were based on study of primitive societies) may have erred in assuming that *all* cultural traits were *necessarily* interrelated, but they were right in principle.

3. The concept implies both continuity in time and comprehensiveness in scope, and every society takes elaborate pains to transmit its culture to succeeding generations through appropriate rituals and socialization processes.

4. What Berger and Luckmann call "objectivations" and "cosmizations"—i.e., the metaphysical doctrines, the aesthetic images, and the utilitarian explanations which legitimate the way a society views and does things —are of special importance. Thus analysts lay particular stress on the symbol systems (the "superordinate meaning structure") of a culture.

Certainly one of the most remarkable achievements of any culture is its ability to induce the individuals who live and move and have their being within it to internalize its

version of socially constructed reality. The internal police of the cultural superego* can enforce respectable conformity much more adequately than the externally imposed threat of punishment by law enforcement officials. In addition, there is doubtless a lot to be said in favor of the psychospiritual cohesion promoted by the received wisdom.

Yet it may well be that ethicists have overemphasized the importance of religious and philosophical objectivations and of the methodological apparatus that usually accompanies conceptual sophistication and attempts to teach it. Programs in applied ethics may often be misguided insofar as they operate on the premise that an intellectual understanding of the moral dimensions of business or the professions will lead reliably to better institutional policy and/or better individual decision-making. Just as moralists had to learn to challenge racial *discrimination** directly through laws and administrative regulations which forced behavioral change instead of trying to attack indirectly through education and exhortation designed to show the irrationality or iniquity of *prejudice**, applied ethicists may need to give less attention to the communication of concepts and more to working directly for changes in law, organizational practice, and other forms of "recipe knowledge" or behavioral cues that determine in such large measure what people actually *do* in ordinary life situations (*see* **Applied Ethics**).

Or, to put the matter in terms that will doubtless be somewhat more palatable to religionists, perhaps what is needed is a stress on "spiritual exercises" which to some extent bypass the mind in its role as repository of cognitive mastery and simply shape behavior through repetition or collective effervescence. A virtue*, after all, is a *habit**, and particular virtues are habitual inclinations to act in specific ways deemed appropriate by one who has cultivated them. Thus ethics in the form of specific behaviors of benefit to other persons might be generated more effectively by traditional or modern types of behavior modification than they are likely to be by the attempt to promote the internalization of objectivations (*see* **Behavior Control**).

See also **Civilization.**

P. Berger and T. Luckmann, *The Social Construction of Reality,* 1966; E. Cassirer, *The Philosophy of Symbolic Forms,* 1953; A. L.

Kroeber and C. Kluckhohn, *Culture: A Critical Review of Concepts and Definitions,* 1953; R. A. Nisbet, *The Sociological Tradition,* 1966; T. Parsons, *The Social System,* 1951.

HENRY CLARK

Cursing/Swearing

The taking of the Lord's name "in vain" is forbidden in the Ten Commandments, and Jesus says, "Do not swear at all" in the Sermon on the Mount. These commands protect the sacredness of human testimony about God against the unholy or profane uses to which sacred language is often put.

In many cultures it is believed that by invoking "godly" symbols humans can manipulate the divine powers, willfully punish an enemy, or arbitrarily render ultimate judgment (as in "God damn them to hell"). Such practices are idolatrous and magical when it is presumed that such formulas have power over God's providence. Biblical cursing, however, invokes God's righteousness in a prophetic protest against desperate conditions legitimated by unrighteous cultural conventions.

Some wider implications of these restrictions are that the capacity for human communication needs to be seen as a gift of God and protected from corruption. Otherwise, humans cannot speak clearly about the most important things or engage in the profound sharing of information or perspective. Language shapes consciousness, belief, culture, and society. The meaning and power of the Word is obscured by the routine distortion of words.

Common meanings of "cursing" and "swearing" include restrictions on sexual and scatological language. These restraints prevent the depersonalization of intimate relationships and private bodily functions, but, legalistically enforced, can induce repressive guilt or shame.

The casual, aggressive, or facetious use of theological, sexual, and scatological language discredits the serious uses of human discourse and impoverishes a culture's linguistic system.

See also **Blasphemy; Oaths.**

MAX L. STACKHOUSE

Custom

Custom refers to the habitual behavior of a society. It represents the normal, typical response of any social group to the normal conditions of life, interpersonal relationships, and environment. It is the daily, immediate working out of the effects of tradition, ethics, religion, values, and world view. The American who turns a piece of pie so that the point is toward him or her when eating it, or who looks automatically to the left for oncoming traffic when crossing the street (whereas the Britisher looks to the right), or who becomes excited over World Series games, or who feels repulsed by the thought of eating fried caterpillars, or who feels that a distance of 12–20 inches between people engaged in conversation is "intimate" (whereas for a Latin American anything greater is cold and withdrawn), is following the customs of his or her group.

The customs of any group are not a collection of oddities, or of odds and ends of unrelated behavior, however. A people's customs, no matter how diverse and unrelated they may seem to the observer, are to varying degrees interwoven into a network of behavior, personality, emotion, and value system, which is unique for every society and constitutes its culture. Customs are the individual habitual traits of behavior by which people act out their culture, but a culture is far more than a listing of customs. It is a dynamic force rooted in a people's psychology, values, and history. Customs are part of its manifestation.

Most customs, or *folkways,* exist only on the level of the unconscious, unsophisticated ways of daily life. People act as they do because of their cultural preconditioning without ever giving it a thought or dreaming of being critical of what seems so "natural." Some customs, particularly those which are threatened by change or by the example of some other intruding culture may shift to the level of *mores,* of prescriptive behavior, but prescriptive behavior simply accepted as right, not formulated into law*. Laws and taboos* may then eventually derive from such customary behavior when even greater sanction* is required to keep it from being changed.

Once a custom is called to the attention of the people who practice it by being threatened in some way, it may be quickly rationalized, given a pseudohistorical explanation, or a mythological reason for existence. Anthropologists, on the other hand, have set themselves to find the historical, functional, and psychological factors within the culture which provide the basis for significant individual custom (*see* **Anthropology and Ethics**).

People's tendency to accept the greatest bulk of their own customs as right, natural, and comfortable leads to ethnocentricity when they look at the customs of other people. These seem odd, difficult, cumbersome, embarrassing, primitive, stupid, dangerous, or (on the other hand) glamorous, powerful, or exotic. In either case foreign customs may be copied and assimilated into the receiving cultural system, thus modifying the culture, but on the other hand, massive influence from another culture may be seen as a threat to be opposed bitterly.

Custom, therefore, can be understood in any nonsuperficial way only relative to other custom, and to the culture as a whole. It can also best be understood cross-culturally, that is, relative to other people's ways of meeting the same kinds of problems with other customs which are the manifestations of other cultural configuration.

B. M. Leiser, *Custom, Law, and Morality,* 1969.

WILLIAM A. SMALLEY

Cynics, Ethics of the

The Cynic preacher was a familiar wanderer in the ancient world, shaggy and unkempt, always uncompromising and sometimes heroic to the point of martyrdom.

Epictetus (*Discourses* 3.22.1–10) paints the picture of the Cynic saint. He cannot start without God. He has no desire but the desire for goodness. His self-respect is his only protection and his only guardian. He is the ambassador of God and the preacher of righteousness. He may be naked and penniless but he knows true freedom and true happiness. He will be flogged and he will love the man who flogs him. His governing principle, waking and sleeping, will be purer than the sun.

For the Cynic, virtue is all that matters. Ethics is the one and only science. And ethics is not theory; it is action (Diogenes Laertius 6.11). Virtue is something that can be taught and it can be achieved only in one way, by putting your mind to it.

Happiness to be real must be inalienable. The one thing one can never lose is one's mind. Therefore virtue consists in a certain attitude to life. What is that attitude? It is

complete self-sufficiency, complete independence of all material things and all external happenings.

Wealth must be abandoned, for wealth and virtue cannot exist together. "The love of money is the metropolis of all evils," Diogenes said (Diogenes Laertius 6.50). Pleasure must be abandoned. Antisthenes, the founder of the school, said that he would rather be mad than pleased (ibid., 6.3). "May the sons of your enemies live in luxury," he said (6.8). Pleasure is the supreme enemy of life and *ponos,* toil, is the supreme good. Love must be abandoned, for it makes one the slave of one's passions. "If I could lay my hands on Aphrodite," said Antisthenes, "I would shoot her" (E. Gomperz, *The Greek Thinkers,* ET 1901–1905, vol. 2, p. 143). But the Cynics were no ascetics, and took their pleasure where they found it.

Zeller sees cynicism as a series of renunciations (*Socrates and the Socratic Schools,* ET 1885, pp. 316ff.). It was a renunciation of civilization and a return to simplicity. Diogenes even tried eating his food raw (Diogenes Laertius 6.34, 76). It was a renunciation of social and political life. Diogenes called himself a citizen of the world. He may have coined the word *kosmopolitēs* (ibid., 6.63). The Cynics were the first thinkers to declare slavery unnatural, and to insist that the only difference between human beings is the difference in virtue and vice. It was for the Cynic the renunciation of modesty and shame. The Cynics notoriously did the most private things in the most public places, believing that, if it was right to do a thing, it was right to do it anywhere (Diogenes Laertius 6.69). It was a renunciation of the gods. Dill holds that the Cynics were "probably the purest monotheists that classical antiquity produced" (*Roman Society from Nero to Marcus Aurelius,* 1905, p. 363). They believed that the only true sacrifice was a life of goodness and virtue (Julian, *Orations* 6.199, 200; Xenophon, *Memorabilia* 1.6.9–15). Virtue was for them the only worship.

The Cynics believed that goodness was everything, worth any renunciation, and open to any person who would pay the price in toil.

WILLIAM BARCLAY

Cyrenaics, Ethics of the

Of all the Hellenistic schools of philosophy that of the Cyrenaics was the simplest and the most uncomplicated. Its founder Aristippus held that pleasure is the supreme good and the highest aim in life (Diogenes Laertius 2.85, 87; Cicero, *Academics* 2.13.131). And the pleasure in question is the pleasure of the body, for bodily pleasures are the most vivid and intense (Diogenes Laertius 2.87, 90). Still further, the pleasure in question is the pleasure of the moment, for the past is gone and the future is quite uncertain (Diogenes Laertius 2.66; Athenaeus, *Deipnosophistae* 544). The aim of the Cyrenaics was not *eudaimonia,* happiness, but *hēdonē,* pleasure, so that they were sometimes called the hedonists.

The Cyrenaic theory of perception adds still something else to the picture. The Cyrenaics held that the only thing we can know is sensation. We may have the sensation that something is sweet; the sensation we do know, but of the thing itself we know nothing. It follows that there is no possible knowledge of anyone else's sensations; all that we can know is our own. There are therefore no absolute criteria; the only possible guides are convention and tradition (Diogenes Laertius 2.93).

If there are no absolute criteria and if individual sensation is the criterion, then it is difficult to see how ethics enters into the Cyrenaic scheme at all. But the Cyrenaics did study moral philosophy under five parts—what to avoid and what to seek, passions, actions, causes, proofs (Sextus Empiricus, *Against the Logicians* 1.11).

The Cyrenaics admitted that in common sense the consequences of any pleasure must be taken into account. Simply to get the greatest pleasure out of pleasure the Cyrenaics respected prudence and wisdom, and simply to avoid unpleasantness they abstained from what law and convention regard as evil (Diogenes Laertius 2.87, 90, 93). No one denied that a man could leave the school of Aristippus a profligate (Cicero, *On the Nature of the Gods* 3.31.77), but if he did so it simply meant that he was not having pleasure at its most pleasant.

One thing remains to be added. The Cyrenaics insisted that people must be masters of pleasure and not pleasure master of them. In regard to his relationships with Lais, the famous courtesan, Aristippus spoke his most famous epigram, *Echō, ouk echomai,* "I possess, but I am not possessed."

For the Cyrenaics ethics existed simply to make pleasure more pleasant, and the odd

consequence was that Aristippus and many of his followers were far better than their creed. It was Plato who paid Aristippus the greatest compliment: "You alone are endowed with the gift to flaunt in robes or walk in rags" (Diogenes Laertius 2.67).

WILLIAM BARCLAY

Death, Determination of

Traditionally, at least in the modern West, there was little controversy over the determination of death. Medical science could not maintain people in ambiguous states, for example, where one's heart beats but brain function is destroyed. Beginning in the 1960s, however, as medical science began to be able to maintain such patients, the precise meaning of death and the techniques that should be used for measuring it have become important matters at both the practical and the theoretical level.

Contemporary developments. The evolution of the controversy is closely related to, though logically separate from, the development of organ transplantation*, since one reason to define death precisely is to retain the possibility of obtaining organs from the newly dead at a time when they would still be viable for transplant. In 1968, soon after the first heart transplant, a committee at Harvard Medical School proposed four medical criteria for measuring what they took to be irreversible coma, claiming that a person in such a state was dead.

Since then, there has been widespread agreement that two separate issues are really at stake in the debate over the determination of death. The first question is essentially philosophical, conceptual, and ethical: Under what circumstances do we consider a person dead? The question is asked in several ways. What are the necessary and sufficient conditions for a person to be alive? What is the essential characteristic of persons such that its loss can be said to constitute death? (*See* **Persons and Personality.**) The moral corollary of these questions is the question: Under what circumstances should we treat a person as dead? Certain social behaviors are normally associated with calling a person dead: certain treatments may be stopped that would not otherwise be stopped; a will may be read, plans for a funeral may begin; if the dead person was a public office holder, the process of succession will begin.

The traditional understanding of the

meaning of death was either the departure of the soul from the body or, in more recent secular thought, the irreversible stoppage of the flowing of the bodily fluids associated with heart and lung function. Now, however, individuals may have totally destroyed brains with the irreversible loss of the ability to integrate bodily functions, while their respiration is supported mechanically and their hearts continue to beat. This development has led many to argue that the irreversible loss of capacity for bodily integration is the necessary and sufficient condition for being dead. Many countries and many (but not all) states within the USA have opted through statutes and case law for a concept of death that relates death to loss of brain function. In Great Britain some professional groups have accepted determination of death based on brain-related criteria and some courts have made use of such a determination, but no definitive parliamentary or court policy has been established. This concept has been supported by public commissions as well as professional organizations.

Emphasis on loss of all functions of the entire brain, including the brain stem, differentiates this from a newer formulation of the concept of death, often referred to as the "higher-brain" position.

We now realize that irreversible coma is not identical with the death of the entire brain. It is possible for a person to be in a coma (or, more accurately, what is now called a permanent vegetative state) and still retain much brain activity, especially lower-brain activity that controls breathing and certain reflexes. Recent scholarly debate has centered on the question of whether persons should be considered dead if they are permanently unconscious but still retain the capacity to integrate bodily functions such as breathing and reflexes. If one adopts the philosophical or theological position that consciousness, capacity to communicate, or capacity to relate socially to others is necessary for being alive, then being irreversibly in a noncommunicative, vegetative state would be considered being dead (even though the body continues to breathe on its own). A number of philosophers and theologians have adopted this view, but as yet no national or state government or religious body has endorsed it.

Once a concept of death has been chosen, one can turn to a second, more scientific

question: How, empirically, does one measure the irreversible loss of whatever functions have been determined to be essential for life? Holders of the traditional heart-lung position would turn to cardiologists to tell them when the capacity to pump blood has been lost irreversibly. Holders of the whole-brain position would ask neurologists how to measure irreversible loss of all brain functions. Some holders of the higher-brain-function position now claim that a flat electroencephalogram alone is the measure that predicts loss of cerebral (i.e., higher) brain function.

Religious positions. Theologians and ethicists within various religious traditions have provided substantial leadership in this debate. Within the Roman Catholic Church, Pope Pius XII early in the discussion said, "The task of determining the exact instant of death is that of the physician." His statement has been interpreted as signaling the acceptability of new formulations articulated by medical experts. The statement, however, can now be seen as ambiguous. If it meant that the church will leave to the medical experts the scientific question of which medical criteria and tests should be used to measure the destruction of heart or brain function, it is not controversial. If, however, it meant that the choice of a concept of death should be left to medical experts, that position would be widely challenged both within the Roman Catholic Church and outside it.

Some Catholic thinkers, such as Bernard Häring, and some Protestant thinkers, such as Paul Ramsey and Joseph Fletcher, have generally endorsed the use of brain criteria for death pronouncement, although several have warned of the ethical danger of rushing too quickly to pronounce death (based on either heart or brain criteria) when the postmortem use of body parts is also on the agenda. There appears to be a division among both Catholics and Protestants over the theological question of whether an irreversibly unconscious person with lower-brain function including intact respiration should be considered dead. Some who answer yes argue that in Christianity the human being represents an essential unity of body and soul (mental function being a modern analogue for the soul). They hold that when consciousness is irreversibly lost, what remains is only the mortal remains of the person. More conservative critics argue that an individual should be considered alive as long as capacities remain for bodily integration even if consciousness is no longer possible.

Harvard Medical School, "A Definition of Irreversible Coma: Report of the Ad Hoc Committee of the Harvard Medical School to Examine the Definition of Brain Death," *Journal of the American Medical Association* 205, 1968, pp. 337–340; U.S. President's Commission for the Study of Ethical Problems in Medicine and Biomedical and Behavioral Research, *Defining Death: Medical, Legal and Ethical Issues in the Definition of Death,* 1981.

ROBERT M. VEATCH

Decalogue

Origin. The Decalogue, or Ten Commandments, is a collection of ten short, primarily negative guidelines for human conduct, presented in the Hebrew Bible as God's revelation to Moses on Mt. Sinai. The collection appears twice in the Bible, in Exodus (20: 1–17) and in Deuteronomy (5:6–21), with only minor differences in the wording. It is not possible to say with confidence just how much of the contents and the present form of the Decalogue goes back to Moses. Some of the prohibitions almost surely come from Moses, and the collection itself may also owe much to him. It was probably repeated regularly in connection with acts of worship in early Israel, and would also have been taught in the home and in the individual communities of early Israel. Such short, unqualified demands may have some relationship to ancient curse rituals such as the one found in Deut. 27:15–26, but the Decalogue contains no threat against those who disobey; it only states God's demands.

Form and Content. The demands of the Decalogue are similar in form to other categorical statements in the Bible and in other ancient Near Eastern literatures—especially to curses, laws carrying the death penalty (see, e.g., Ex. 21:12, 15–17), and provisions of ancient Near Eastern treaties. It is probable, but by no means certain, that originally the Decalogue consisted of ten negative sentences, each opening with the Hebrew particle *lo',* "not," continuing with a verb, and concluding with the object of the verb. The ten prohibitions would have been remembered by reference to the ten fingers. They would have been taught to children as well as repeated in communal gatherings for wor-

ship and confession of faith, and in these ways would have provided the fundamental religious and ethical orientation for the community of Israel.

While the content of the particular demands of the Decalogue can to a large extent be found also in the religious and ethical literature of Israel's neighbors, no *collection* of this sort is known outside the Bible, and none focuses so directly the exclusive claims of God upon a particular people. The prologue ("I am the LORD your God, who brought you out of the land of Egypt, out of the house of bondage," Ex. 20:2) ties the demands of the Decalogue to God's act of redemption of the Israelite slaves. The commandments to worship God alone, to make no sculptured images of the deity, and not to use the divine name to do violence or mischief against one's neighbors also underscore this exclusive claim of God. The commandment against idolatry is particularly striking and is of very great importance for biblical ethics. It underscores the difference between God and every part of God's creation. Nothing in the whole of creation can represent God, for nothing that God has made participates in the divine being and character. The human self comes nearest; in the language of the priestly community responsible for the creation story with which the book of Genesis opens, humankind, male and female, are created in the image and likeness of God (Gen. 1:26–27). The prohibition of images of God seems to have arisen from this understanding of the fundamental difference between Creator and creature, with the human being charged in a special way to affirm and preserve that distinction, while seeking the companionship and doing the will of the One in whose image human beings are made.

The prohibition against the misuse of the divine name is also of special importance for biblical ethics. It seems particularly designed to prevent the misuse of the power of religion, the numinous power of the holy, to further one's own ends at the expense of the life or welfare of others. Like the commandment against idolatry, it provides a check against authoritarian priestcraft, and especially against the use of fear to compel allegiance to religious demands.

The ethical import of the other commandments is even clearer. The observance of one day of rest in seven is identified in Deuteronomy as a provision that human beings and draft animals have rest and refreshment (Deut. 5:14–15). Human beings are made for work and also are made to rest from work. Life's meaning is not summed up in work or in usefulness to others. Human beings are not instruments but selves. God rested on the seventh day and rejoiced in the creation; human beings are to do the same (Gen. 2:2–3; Ex. 20:11).

The honoring of father and mother is akin to the Sabbath command in one way: it too insists that labor and the products of one's labor are not everything. When persons grow old and are no longer able to carry their load, their place within the community has not come to an end. Aged parents are to be shown honor and respect by their (adult) children. This commandment is not primarily intended to encourage small children to be obedient to their parents; it seeks to regulate the very difficult problem of how the *generations* are to relate to one another.

The remaining requirements of the Decalogue lay down flat prohibitions, not threateningly or with any indication at all of the consequences of a violation of the demands. This is not *law* in the modern sense of the term; it is the foundation for law. Human life is sacred and is not to be taken. There are wars, and there are human acts that, according to Israelite law, demand the death penalty. But the commandment against killing flatly asserts that one is not to take human life. Life, it clearly implies, is God's gift; life belongs to God. The community, in the light of such a demand, must then work out what it is to do about warfare, about capital punishment, and about the maiming and destroying of human life in other ways, always with an eye to the affirmation that life belongs to God and is not to be taken by human beings.

Adultery, the theft of persons and property, false testimony, and hankering for the life and goods of others are ruled out in the same way. Such acts are acts of violence against other persons and against the property that is closely identified with them. The command against coveting seems to have in view the lusting after others and their goods that damages and can destroy one's very life.

Influence. The Decalogue is at the foundation of the religion and ethics of Israel's prophets, even though it is only occasionally quoted or alluded to (e.g., Hos. 4:1–3; Micah 2:1–3; *see* **Prophetic Ethics**). Its demands are only intensified in the Sermon on the Mount*

(Matt. 5–7) and in other NT teachings. The summary of the Mosaic law*, the love of God and neighbor (Mark 12:28–31 and parallels), also rests upon the Decalogue and sums up its fundamental contents. The continuing Christian use of the Decalogue in catechetical instruction and otherwise has kept this treasure before the Christian community, despite some disagreements about its proper division and interpretation. For example, there are disputes about whether the prohibition of other gods and of images should be construed as one commandment (Roman Catholics and Lutherans) or as two commandments (Anglicans and Calvinists), and whether the prohibition of coveting the neighbor's goods should be construed as one commandment (Anglicans and Calvinists) or as two commandments (Roman Catholics and Lutherans), with an obvious impact on the numbering of the commandments. Nevertheless, the Decalogue, precisely in its largely negative form, is a positive guideline for religious and ethical existence. It uncompromisingly indicates what is *not* to happen, what simply cannot be done. When a commandment is violated, as commandments will be, the community must act. The community must know, however (as its individual members must know), what is demanded of it, what is contrary to its very character, its very life.

The Decalogue is like the Bill of Rights attached to the US Constitution. It defines and refines the character and ethos of Israel's life with God, and it does so in ways that liberate and also confine the life of the community. The confinement demands liberty, and the liberty confinement.

See also **Old Testament Ethics.**

A. Alt, *Essays on Old Testament History and Religion,* ET 1967; B. F. Childs, *Exodus, A Commentary,* 1974; W. Harrelson, *The Ten Commandments and Human Rights,* 1980; E. Nielsen, *The Ten Commandments in New Perspective,* 1967.

WALTER HARRELSON

Deception *see* **Honesty; Truthfulness**

Decision

In the most general sense, to decide is to give an answer (not necessarily in words) to any question; for example, logicians speak of "decision procedures" for deciding whether propositions are true or false. Most commonly, however, the word is used of answering, for oneself or another, the question "Shall I do this (or that)?" in the sense in which asking that question is deliberation*. It is commonly supposed that every voluntary action is preceded by a decision; but this is not so. To decide, or answer the question "Shall I do this?" I have first to *ask* this question (deliberate); if I act without having asked the question, I have made no decision. We sometimes act without having decided, because we have not had time to ask the question. For although it cannot be said that the actual deciding always takes time (it may be the mere boundary between being undecided and being decided), nevertheless there has to be time for asking the question before we can answer it. Additional time may be, but need not be, spent on considering this question; when we say that a man took a long time to decide, our meaning could otherwise be expressed by saying that he took a long time before deciding. But lack of time is not the only possible reason for acting without deciding; a man may (voluntarily) enter holy orders, to whom it has never occurred to do anything else (the youngest son, say, of an aristocratic family in which it is taken for granted that the youngest son becomes a clergyman). We might say: He never *decided* to enter the ministry; he had always intended to.

Therefore decision is not a necessary constituent of voluntary action, nor of the forming of an intention*. Nevertheless, a being who in principle could not make decisions (that is, ask, and answer, the question "Shall I do this?") could hardly be said to act voluntarily or to be a free agent in the fullest sense.

R. M. HARE

Defense *see* **Aggression; Deterrence; International Order; Just War; War;** *see also* **Defense Mechanisms**

Defense Mechanisms

The term "defense mechanism" is used generally of any adjustment adopted automatically to avoid having to come to grips directly with painful facts or situations, but having positive and adaptive intent. It is employed technically in psychoanalysis to describe measures by which the ego* resists unwanted impulses from the id* and unwanted feelings, both positive and negative. These measures are carried out below the level of conscious awareness, and hence the person concerned is normally unaware of their operation. Defense mechanisms are in part accompaniments of neurosis and in part substitutes for it. Individuals tend to be relatively consistent in the sort of defenses they employ.

The most significant of the defense mechanisms is *repression**. Other common mechanisms include *regression,* in which the person reverts to an earlier level of thinking, feeling, or behaving to escape the threat inherent in increasing responsibility and complexity; *reaction formation,* in which an impulse or conflict is rejected and a new personality characteristic (frequently embodying the exact opposite) is developed in its place as, for example, when an intolerable hatred is disguised in an excess of love. In such instances the new characteristic frequently subtly achieves the aims of the original impulse as, for example, where the excessive love smothers, cripples, and destroys the hated person; *projection,* in which one's own feelings, attitudes, or desires are attributed to other persons; *introjection,* or identification, in which the attributes or attitudes of others are taken over as one's own; *sublimation,* in which the instinctual aims that cannot be directly gratified are redirected into other and more acceptable channels. This last has been much disputed, particularly in relation to interpretations of creativity as sublimated sexuality.

The popular tendency is to treat all defense mechanisms as uniformly bad. They do have in common a distortion of reality, but there are occasions when the ego needs defenses in order to survive. Regression, for example, is common in adolescence but is only neurotic if it becomes a characteristic way of responding to threat. It can be so severe and debilitating as to be psychotic. It is positive both in intent and in fact when it gives the person concerned an opportunity to regroup his or her resources to deal more adequately with a presenting threat.

It is possible for strong defensive measures to become independent of the original conflict and to result either in bodily changes (e.g., rigidity or stiffness) or personality characteristics (e.g., an arrogant attitude masking insecurity or a "fixed" smile covering up deep hostility). Psychotherapy can help reverse the changes.

A. Freud, *The Ego and the Mechanisms of Defence,* 1937; H. P. Laughlin, *The Ego and Its Defences,* 1970.

GRAEME M. GRIFFIN

Dehumanization

Dehumanization may be defined as the process whereby human beings, either individually or socially, are oppressed and unable to exercise or develop their potential as human beings or societies of human beings. This process may be the result of a conscious decision by one individual, group, or nation to exercise power over other people, or it may be the result of other factors, for example, scientific or technological advances, that have the effect of denying human dignity. In coming to a sense of self-significance, human beings need to be able to affirm themselves. This self-affirmation is achieved through the exercise of power by the subject in the context of the self-affirmation of others. Dehumanization occurs when power is exercised by a person or group in such a way that it has the effect that others are unable to affirm their humanity. Erich Fromm termed this "destructive power" as against the "creative power" necessary for self-affirmation. Human affirmation with its potential for growth and development is also stunted by types of employment made necessary by modern technology that require an automaton role for men and women.

While the description of dehumanization owes much to the insights of the behavioral sciences, the awareness of it belongs to all ages and cultures. The refusal to allow people or groups to act as subjects has been a constant concern of philosophers and theologians, even though the word "dehumanization" itself belongs to the modern era. From the matrix of this experience and process of dehumanization has arisen the concept of "human rights,"* which attempts to protect those who are unable to affirm their humanity, and to secure the conditions whereby individuals and groups may be empowered to affirm themselves. The language of "protection" and "promotion" underlies the provisions of International Conventions and Bills of Rights in the attempt to alleviate dehumanization and encourage the affirmation of human dignity.

See **Human Dignity; Persons and Personality; Respect for Persons.**

R. May, *Power and Innocence,* 1976; E. Kamenka and A. Erh-Soon Tay (eds.), *Human Rights,* 1978; P. Tillich, *The Courage to Be,* 1952.

ALAN D. FALCONER

Deliberation

Deliberation is the name given to the process of asking and considering the question "Shall I do this?"; to answer this question is to make a decision*. The minimal form of deliberation is the mere asking of the question; but since normally we decide for reasons, deliberation is usually concerned with the consideration of reasons for or against some action. The two types of reason most commonly discussed by philosophers are: (1) that the action is of a certain kind; (2) that the action is a means to a certain end. Since (2) is a subcase of (1), an account of deliberation in terms of (1) is likely to be more complete than one which is confined to (2). Another reason for rejecting accounts of deliberation solely in terms of means and ends is the following: it is usually said that means precede their ends in time, and are causes or conditions of attaining them. But often we decide to do *a, although* it has the consequence c_1, *because* it has the consequence c_2. If c_1 precedes c_2 in time, and is the cause or condition of it, c_1 can in most cases be called the means and c_2 the end. But suppose that c_1 succeeds c_2 in time, as when we order oysters because they will give us pleasure (c_2), although they will give us indigestion (c_1); nobody in that case would call getting indigestion tomorrow a means to getting pleasure today; yet there is a close analogy between this sort of case and the preceding, which the means-end terminology obscures. In morals it is most important to realize that the relative position in time of the various things that we bring about by an action is normally irrelevant to the morality of the action. It is as bad to bring about a small good today at the cost of a greater evil tomorrow (both being equally certain) as to bring about a small good tomorrow at the cost of a greater evil today.

The following schema of deliberation is adequate to cover most cases. Faced with the necessity of doing one of several alternative actions, we consider in detail what we should be doing if we did each of them (including the consequences we should be bringing about). It will be found that certain of these details bring the actions under various moral or other principles (the word "principle" is here to be understood in its Aristotelian sense, to include, e.g., desires): if I did a_1, I should be transgressing principle p_1; to do a_2 is required in order to observe principle p_2; if I do a_3 I shall (or shall not) fulfill my desire for x, etc.

In the simplest case it will turn out that only one of the alternative actions is consistent with our principles; if so, then unless we have in the process been led to reconsider the principles themselves, we shall do that action. In other cases there is a conflict of principle and we cannot, as things are, observe or obey all our principles; this forces us to reconsider them and to qualify one of them so as to admit an exception in this type of case, if the principles are moral ones. If, however, a moral principle is in conflict with a nonmoral one, the latter may be merely overridden, not qualified. A moral principle, in one sense of the word, is one which cannot be overridden in this way. Therefore, if two moral principles are in conflict, one of them has to be qualified, unless we are content to say that whatever we do in certain situations is bound to be wrong—a conclusion which offends against the principle that it is always possible to avoid doing wrong, or that "ought" implies "can."

It is the finding of principles which will resolve such moral conflicts that constitutes the substance and the difficulty of moral thought, and is the source of most moral progress.

R. M. HARE

Democracy

The term comes from the Greek *dēmos,* "people," and *kratein,* "to rule." In its most general sense it might be understood as "rule by the people." Yet this definition leaves difficult questions unanswered: Who are the people? What can or should it mean for them to rule? Descriptive and normative issues are closely interwoven throughout the subject. The term is used both descriptively and to portray an ideal.

All democracies understand "the people" so as to exclude some from the vote, whether slaves, felons, women, persons failing to meet some property or poll tax qualification, or in any event those below a certain age. Some of these exclusions are generally held to be unjust today; yet some exclusion, and in particular an age requirement, is unavoidable.

A more difficult question is what it can or should mean for the people to rule. Some have interpreted it to imply direct democracy, where all the people enter directly into decisions about public policy. Only in relatively small communities, however, is this method feasible (cf. the assembly of a small Greek city-state or the New England town meeting). Otherwise the only practicable implication is representative democracy, where decisions about policies are made by a few persons designated to speak on behalf of the people.

How representatives are understood to speak for the people is decisive for distinguishing democracy from its counterfeits. A dictator might claim to speak for the people by acting (supposedly) in their behalf. Yet even if masses approve (and dictators can manipulate them to elicit approval), that would not constitute democracy. Neither the content of government decisions nor the people's approval is an adequate test for the extent to which democracy is present.

Appropriate tests for the presence of democracy are primarily procedural. The most important is whether representatives attain office through competition among candidates for the people's votes. Where competition for the vote is discouraged, election is no sign of democracy; thus the claims of countries to be democracies where only one party is legal are fatuous. For competition among candidates to be significant, however, other procedures must also be present, such as nonintimidation of voters, freedom of candidates and the media publicly to discuss issues, ascribing the same weight to all persons' votes, tallying the votes honestly, and permitting the winners to take office. Equally important with competition for office is the voters' ability to turn representatives out of office; hence, frequent elections.

Democracies ordinarily follow the principle of majority rule, both in elections and in votes within the body of representatives. Often, however, decisions about changing the constitution or about other crucial issues require more than a majority. On the other hand, sometimes a plurality rather than a majority suffices to elect. For still another reason it is not accurate to characterize democracy simply as "majority rule": the procedures listed above imply that respect for the political rights of minorities is essential if we are to distinguish democracies from nondemocracies.

Within this procedural framework opinions differ about the most desirable form of democracy. Should it be parliamentary, presidential, or some mixture? Should restraints on the majority to protect minority interests be primarily constitutional, social, or internal to individuals? To what extent should answers to such questions depend upon the circumstances of each society?

Today nearly everyone asserts that democracy is desirable, whether in one sense of the word or another. Why it is desirable, though, is a major theological-ethical issue. Because the people's will is God's will? Because rulers tend to be oppressive and must have their power limited? Because attaining greater justice requires balancing power among social groups? Because the indeterminacy of human nature calls for democracy rather than some more closed form of government? Or a combination of these and other reasons? Some theologians, most especially Reinhold Niebuhr, have given special attention to the bearing of a Christian view of human nature upon this issue.

Another theological-ethical issue has to do with the appropriate goals of government. Should we desire democracy so as to enable everyone to pursue individual self-interest, to assist persons to fulfill their potentialities, to preserve individual rights, to increase justice, to seek the common good, or some combination of these?

The widespread praise of democracy tends to cloak some of its recurring problems: that it can lead to sustained rule in behalf of some to the neglect of others; that many take advantage of it through graft, nepotism, and special favors; and that it easily falls prey to *coups d'état* by groups that dislike the outcome of its procedures.

Such problems raise the question whether democracy is a good in itself or primarily a means to a more just and desirable community. The two can conflict, as when a majority favors an injustice. If so, should democratic procedures continue to take priority? There is danger in either answer: in subordinating justice to democratic forms, or in absolutizing a narrow conception of justice at the expense of procedures that ordinarily restrain injustice.

See also **Aristocracy; Politics; State.**

R. A. Dahl, *A Preface to Democratic Theory*, 1956; C. B. Macpherson, *The Life and Times of Liberal Democracy*, 1977; R. Niebuhr, *The Children of Light and the Children of Darkness*, 1944; J. A. Schumpeter, *Capitalism, Socialism, and Democracy*, ³1950, pp. 233–302.

JOSEPH L. ALLEN

Denomination *see* **Church; Ecclesiology and Ethics; Sect**

Deontological Ethics *see* Deontology

Deontology

Deontology means literally the "science of duty." The word is used in several distinct senses: (1) the expression "deontology" seems to have been first used by Jeremy Bentham to designate his own utilitarian ethics, but it would not commonly be understood in this way nowadays; (2) among Roman Catholic moral theologians, "deontology" is sometimes used for the special ethics associated with a particular profession or vocation (*see* **Professional Ethics**); and (3) perhaps most commonly, "deontology" denotes a view of morality which takes as its fundamental categories the notions of "obligation" or "duty"* and the "rightness" of acts. This deontological view of morality may be contrasted with the views which stress the end of action (the "good"), sometimes called "agathology"* or more often "teleology" (*see* **Teleological Ethics**), or the consequences of action, often called "consequentialism."* At a minimum, a deontologist in the third sense must hold that some acts are obligatory, right, or wrong, independent of their ends and their consequences. Immanuel Kant, W. D. Ross, and John Rawls are all deontologists, as are many theologians.

JOHN MACQUARRIE

Depravity, Total *see* **Total Depravity;** *see also* **Original Sin; Sin(s)**

Deprogramming

The term refers to systematic attempts to deconvert adherents of controversial new religious movements (cults*). These attempts generally take place in a context of forcible confinement of the devotee, often subsequent to an abduction. The term "deprogramming" was developed by supporters of the procedure, who intended to imply that the convert has been "programmed" by intensive sectarian indoctrination to such a degree that free will* has been extinguished and forcible therapeutic intervention is necessary to restore personal autonomy* to the deprogrammee. Opponents of deprogramming tend to prefer the term "faith-breaking."

The most sophisticated defense of deprogramming has been formulated by Richard

Delgado, a legal scholar, who maintains that a religious indoctrinee's refusal of treatment may be legitimately overridden "if it appears that the indoctrinee is incapable of fully understanding the conditions to which he has been subjected that account for his recent change of outlook." Critics of this line of thought perceive a "rationalistic fallacy" whereby a faith is not viewed as authentic or worthy of legal protection from forcible intervention unless the believer can articulate the rational grounds of his or her faith. Some religionists discern an "antireligious" orientation underlying the apparent convictions of some supporters of deprogramming that acceptable modern faiths must be rational, not emotionally intense, and respectful of the essentially secular context of modern life.

Most legal and philosophical discourse relating to deprogramming has focused on the role of the state in religious deprogramming by means of temporary conservatorship and guardianship orders awarded to parents of adult converts by courts. Delgado has argued that the manipulative and "coercive" context in which commitments to cults are developed renders these involvements essentially involuntary from the standpoint of criteria of informed consent. Coercive intervention may be justified if "non consensuality" is accompanied by some degree of psychological harm to the devotee.

In a counterformulation, Robert Shapiro maintains that, notwithstanding the imagery of "programming," most allegations that someone has been "brainwashed" in a religious cult generally amount to a simple assertion that someone has *become a different person* under the impact of coercive and deceptive processes of influence. In such a situation, an imposition of therapy over the protest of the devotee is unwarranted, as the "new person" is still a *person,* whose beliefs are absolutely protected from state interference under the First Amendment to the Constitution in the USA. The argument for interference is stronger, according to Shapiro, if it can be established that the manipulated devotee *is no longer a person,* i.e., has regressed to a subhuman level (*see* **Dehumanization; Respect for Persons**).

Presently most deprogramming is extralegal, i.e., does not involve court custody orders. Although some mental health* professionals have engaged in deprogramming or worked with deprogrammers, increasingly even those psychiatrists and psychologists who discern both pathological phenomena in cults and a therapeutic imperative, tend to discourage participation in extralegal coercive intervention. Some professionals have declared that involvement in involuntary therapeutic relationships with religious devotees is unethical, as psychotherapy requires a voluntary client commitment.

See **Behavior Control; Brainwashing; Consent; Cults; Freedom; Indoctrination; Paternalism; Persecution and Toleration.**

D. G. Bromley and J. T. Richardson (eds.), *The Brainwashing-Deprogramming Controversy: Sociological, Psychological, Legal and Historical Perspectives,* 1984; R. Delgado, "Religious Totalism: Gentle and Ungentle Persuasion Under the First Amendment," *Southern California Law Review* 51, 1977; R. Shapiro, "Of Robots, Persons and the Protection of Religious Beliefs," *Southern California Law Review* 56, 1983.

THOMAS ROBBINS/DICK ANTHONY

Descriptivism

Descriptivism is a name sometimes given to the view that the meaning of moral terms is exhausted by their descriptive functions: for example, that "He is a good man" serves solely to describe a man as having a certain property or properties—so that to know the meaning of "good" is simply to know what property or properties objects have to have in order to be called "good." Often contrasted with prescriptivism*, naturalism is currently the most popular variety of descriptivism (*see* **Naturalistic Ethics**); others are intuitionism* and (in some senses) subjectivism*.

See also **Ethics; Conventional Morality.**

R. M. HARE

Desire

The English word "desire" indicates a set of ideas that can be weak or strong, from a mild wish to a yearning or a frantic lust. "I have no desire to go there," "You shall have your heart's desire," or "He was consumed by desire" are within its range. What is more to the present purpose, desire can be evil or excellent. In the NT strong desire (Greek noun *epithymia,* or verb *epithymeō*) can be base or innocent; e.g., Gal. 5:16, "Do not gratify the desires of the flesh"; Phil. 1:23, "My desire is to depart and be with Christ"; or Luke 22:15, "I have earnestly desired to eat this passover with you."

Religious people frequently treat desire itself as inherently sinful, and especially sexual desire, so uncontrollable and often irrational. Theologians of a more positive bent have blamed Augustine's horror of "concupiscence," mankind's fallen, distorted will, for much that is negative in Christian ethics (e.g., *City of God* 14.15ff.). Yet Augustine himself also supplied the corrective as, characteristically, he emphasized our longing for our true home and the delight God has in store for his people. "If you do not want to cease praying," he said, "do not cease longing" (*Discourse* on Ps. 38). He has the NT understanding that we have a *treasure* to find and enjoy.

The refreshed understanding that desire and delight matter, that the mainspring of the human personality for good or ill is the will and not the intellect alone, and that Christianity is a religion of promise and not only demand, is not new but has deep roots in Christian tradition (see, e.g., C. F. Evans, *The Lord's Prayer,* 1963, pp. 55–56).

See **Concupiscence; Lust; Repression.**

Augustine, *Confessions; City of God* 22.30; A. Nygren, *Agape and Eros,* ET 1953, pp. 437ff., part II, ch. II, sec. III; H. Oppenheimer, *The Hope of Happiness,* 1983, chs. 12 and 13; T. Traherne, *Centuries of Meditations* (e.g., 41–43).

                                        HELEN OPPENHEIMER

Despotism *see* **Fascism; Resistance; Totalitarian State; Tyrannicide**

Destiny

We confine ourselves to the ethical significance of this idea. Many nations or communities have believed themselves to have a "destiny," in the sense that a certain goal had been set before them. The use of the word "destiny" usually implies that this goal has been set by some transhuman agency, perhaps God; but the notion need not be fatalistic, since the community may have to strive to fulfill its destiny. The word "destiny" is not biblical, though one does find related terms, such as "determinate" and "predestinate." However, something like the idea of destiny is contained in the biblical doctrine of God's providence and his sovereign disposal of history. From an early time, the people of Israel were conscious of having a destiny, and it was this consciousness which held them together and gave them their identity. In the NT the church appears as the eschatological community, and such a community may be said to be conscious of a destiny. In modern times, the word has often had more sinister associations. German philosophy in the 19th and 20th centuries has made a good deal of the destiny (*Geschick*) of the German people, and there can be no doubt that this notion contributed to German nationalism. The notion of having a destiny is found also in the USA. There it takes the relatively harmless form of supposing that God has specially favored America and conferred on it the mission of leading the rest of the world to freedom and affluence. The pervasiveness of such ideas is evident from the habit of American politicians of decorating their speeches with pious references. A much more baneful conception of destiny is found among the white population of South Africa. From these few illustrations, it becomes apparent that the conception of destiny has very ambiguous implications for ethics. A sense of destiny can bring cohesion to a community, can invest its life with meaning and dignity, can inspire noble aspirations and ideals, and give courage to endure hardships in the pursuit of them. But it can also induce feelings of superiority and it has in fact contributed to aggressiveness, racism*, nationalism* and fanaticism.

See also **Fate and Fatalism.**

                                        JOHN MACQUARRIE

Determinism *see* **Free Will and Determinism; Libertarianism**

Deterrence

Deterrence is the act or process of discouraging or preventing other persons, groups, or nations from undertaking some actions, mainly by provoking their fear of the consequences of those actions. Questions about the morality and effectiveness of deterrence are prominent in debates about criminal punishment and nuclear weapons. This article focuses on nuclear deterrence; for deterrence in the context of criminal punishment, *see* **Capital Punishment; Corporal Punishment; Penology.**

Deterrence in the nuclear age implies the strategic deployment of nuclear weapons against targets of value belonging to a potential enemy to deter an attack; more specifically, it refers to the mutual policy of such targeting by the USA and the USSR. The roots of strategic deterrence are in the policies for nuclear use determined in the late 1940s and early 1950s. These policies were shaped by Cold War rivalry and mutual hostility between the USA and the USSR; they took form around the idea that Soviet aggression could best be deterred by a massive threat directed against Soviet cities and impossible to defend against. In the context of marked US superiority in nuclear forces, this doctrine found expression in such ideas as "massive retaliation," according to which even aggression by conventional forces would be deterred by the threat of nuclear response. With the development of substantial parity between the opposing nuclear forces this concept gave way to the deterrence strategies of "assured destruction" and "mutual assured destruction." This last idea, dating from the late 1960s, continues to provide the framework of American deterrence strategy.

The specific content of American deterrence has varied not only in response to the nature of Soviet power but also according to technological developments and changing fashions in strategic thought. Early deterrence concepts focused on targeting nuclear weapons against "soft" targets such as cities; this required relatively few weapons, and in fact few were available. The development of a Soviet intercontinental ballistic missile force, however, necessitated a shift to targeting of such "hard" targets, and not only were these more numerous but each required more than one nuclear weapon to "kill" it. By this time the introduction of fusion devices had made possible a large expansion in the number of warheads that could be manufactured from a given amount of fissionable material and also vastly increased the yield of each weapon. The introduction of "counterforce" targeting concepts alongside the concept of "assured destruction" produced a deterrence strategy that no longer relied only on counterpopulation threats but now also was conceived as deterring aggression by threatening destruction of Soviet military power by nuclear strikes. Current US nuclear strategy relies on such a mixture of deterrent threats.

Christian thought has been sharply divided over the question of nuclear deterrence. For some persons nuclear weapons themselves, because of their enormous destructive power, represent a threat to human life on earth and perhaps to the divine plan for creation. On this view it is immoral even to possess nuclear weapons for deterrence; the only moral course is nuclear disarmament*. This is nuclear pacifism* in the starkest form. Other persons apply traditional just war reasoning to nuclear deterrence, arguing that the deterrent threat is immoral if it relies on intended harm to an enemy's noncombatant population, but that deterrence may be just if only combatant targets are directly and intentionally targeted. A third view, falling somewhere between the other two, accepts deterrence, perhaps even if it involves strategic nuclear targeting of population areas, so long as the deterrent forces are never in fact used in war. Its proponents draw a moral distinction between threatening to do an immoral act without intending to do it and the threat coupled with the intent (see **Intention**). On this view the *intent* behind nuclear deterrence is to prevent nuclear war, a moral aim, though the *threat* on which it depends, unleashing a strategic nuclear strike, would be immoral if carried out. This position is sometimes termed deterrence by "bluff." A strong recent statement of this position appears in the 1983 pastoral of the American Catholic bishops, *The Challenge of Peace,* which sharply distinguishes "deterrence to prevent the use of nuclear weapons" from "war-fighting" plans, and says " 'no' to the idea of nuclear war."

Each of these positions presents peculiar problems for the proponents of the other two. Critics of the first position charge that if the disarmament it seeks is unilateral, it would amount to a selling-out of Western values and it might, through destroying nuclear parity, actually make nuclear war more likely. If multilateral disarmament is the goal, then the critics charge that this is unrealistic utopianism. Critics of the just war position generally deny its premise that nuclear war can be held in check and often point out that even a counterforce strategic strike would in practice be massively destructive of life and values. Criticism of the "bluff" position has been of two main sorts. One line rejects the moral distinction between threat and intention, arguing that for the threat to be realistic, the intention must be present, and pointing out further that the intention *is* present, since the strategic deterrent forces are not merely "possessed," as if in warehouses, but actually deployed with targets already chosen. Another line of criticism stresses that should such deterrence fail to prevent nuclear war, the war would inevitably be total, since it would be fought with massively destructive strategic weapons in the absence of preparation for limited, lower-level nuclear warfare.

See **Disarmament; International Order; Just War; Nuclear Warfare; War.**

A. Carnesdale et al. (Harvard Nuclear Study Group), *Living with Nuclear Weapons,* 1963; D. Davidson, *Nuclear Weapons and the American Churches,* 1983; L. Freedman, *The Evolution of Nuclear Strategy,* 1983; A. Geyer, *The Idea of Disarmament,* 1982, pp. 17–88; J. T. Johnson, *Can Modern War Be Just?* 1984; P. Ramsey, *War and the Christian Conscience,* 1961; and *The Just War,* 1968; (US) National Conference of Catholic Bishops, *The Challenge of Peace,* 1983.

JAMES TURNER JOHNSON

Development, Economic
see **Economic Development**

Development, Moral
see **Moral Development**

Dialectic

Stemming from the Greek word for "discussion," the term "dialectic" came to mean first the method of getting at the truth by the thrust and counterthrust of argument, and only later the unfolding process of world history itself, whose contradictions and resolutions are discerned through dialectic (in the first sense).

Plato (*see* **Platonic Ethics**) defined dialectic as a journey in which "the summit of the intelligible world is reached in philosophical discussion by one who aspires, through the discourse of reason unaided by any of the senses, to make his way in every case to the essential reality and perseveres until he has grasped by pure intelligence the very nature of Goodness itself." This is dialectic in the first sense. It is the highest *method* of philosophical and ethical inquiry. Goodness itself, the object of that inquiry, is eternal and unchanging.

Kant took a very negative view of dialectic.

The contradictions or antinomies of dialectical reason showed that it was overreaching itself and that supersensible reality is inaccessible to the knowing mind. Ethics, for Kant, is not dialectical. Its categorical imperative* is quite clear and precise and free from contradiction or change.

Hegel and Marx saw the structure of reality itself as dialectical. According to Hegel, "wherever there is movement, wherever there is life . . . there dialectic is at work." History itself, understood by Hegel as the history of the self-movement of Spirit, has the dialectical form of affirmation, negation, and "sublation" (*Aufhebung*). According to Marx, however, the dialectic of history has a material rather than a spiritual base; but materialism must, nevertheless, be dialectical precisely to account for the development, through contradiction and struggle, of higher forms of life, culminating in the classless society. For both Hegel and Marx ethics is socially conceived. It concerns the perfected state to be realized at the culmination of the dialectical process (*see* **Hegelian Ethics; Marxist Ethics**).

Kierkegaard's Christian dialectic carries the individual beyond the aesthetic and the ethical into the sphere of the religious (*see* **Kierkegaardian Ethics**). The absolute paradox of God made man is apprehended only by a leap of faith beyond all human forms of thought and existence. Similarly, 20th-century "dialectical theology," associated especially with the early Barth, insists on the use of statement and counterstatement to express the truth of God (*see* **Modern Protestant Ethics**). Christian dialectic, however, remains "Platonic" in that it constitutes no more than a method of access to and expression of the transcendent. In most theology and ethics the nature and will of God themselves are not conceived as dialectical.

R. Heiss, *Hegel, Kierkegaard, Marx* (1963), ET 1975; H. Zahrnt, *The Question of God* (1966), ET 1969.

BRIAN HEBBLETHWAITE

Dictatorship

Dictators were initially officials of the Roman Republic vested with emergency powers for specified periods. Dictatorship now signifies the legally unrestrained rule of individuals or groups governing for indefinite periods and in the absence of agreed procedures for transferring power to opponents. It typically arises in sharply divided societies confronting major economic crises or international pressures. In practice it involves substantial reliance on coercion.

Modern dictatorships are classifiable as follows: (1) Rule by "strongmen" typical of such backward and politically unorganized societies as Haiti. (2) Traditional counter-revolutionary regimes as in Franco's Spain. (3) Single-party "modernizing" regimes typical of such postcolonial societies as Tanzania. (4) Single-party revolutionary regimes such as Castro's Cuba. (5) Military regimes, as in Brazil or Nigeria. (6) Totalitarian regimes of the Nazi or Soviet varieties that in principle seek, through a single party, to control all aspects of social life.

See **State; Totalitarian State; Tyrannicide.**

C. J. Friedrich and Z. K. Brzezinski, *Totalitarian Dictatorship and Autocracy,* 1965; L. Schapiro, *Totalitarianism,* 1972.

KENNETH N. MEDHURST

Dignity, Human *see* **Human Dignity**

Dilemma

In moral discourse the term "dilemma" may refer to several distinct situations of moral conflict and perplexity when an agent is deliberating (*see* **Deliberation**) about what to do: (1) There is some evidence that an act is morally right or obligatory and some evidence that it is morally wrong. (2) There is conclusive evidence that an act is both morally right or obligatory and morally wrong. (3) The moral reasons for (or against) an act are in conflict with nonmoral reasons—such as prudential or political reasons—against (or for) an act.

Some philosophers and theologians deny that the third situation is a moral dilemma because the moral reasons are all on one side, but there are disputes about the distinction between moral and nonmoral reasons. Some also deny that the first situation is genuinely dilemmatic because the perplexity may dissolve upon closer examination; it is epistemological rather than ontological. There is general agreement that the second type of situation is a genuine dilemma, but there is disagreement about whether there are any moral dilemmas in this strict sense, i.e., situations in which the moral conflict is not in

principle resolvable if limitations of knowledge could be overcome. In particular, there is debate about the interpretation of the moral experience of perplexity in relation to theological doctrines. For example, Edmund Santurri has argued that some Christian beliefs in the coherence of the moral universe, whether in divine command* morality (*see* **Voluntarism**) or in natural law*, appear to exclude moral dilemmas in a strict sense (*see also* **Morality and Religion, Relations of**). However, such theologians as Helmut Thielicke identify "borderline situations" as "the crucial test of ethics" (*Theological Ethics,* vol. 1: *Foundations,* ET 1966, p. 609) in a fallen world. According to Thielicke, the theological doctrines of sin* and justification by faith* establish that guilt* is inevitable and forgiveness* necessary in some extreme conflict situations such as abortion where any action or inaction will incur moral guilt. Nevertheless, in these conflicts there may be a better course of action, which might be described as the lesser of two evils. From this perspective, forgiveness liberates the Christian to face moral dilemmas (*see* **Law and Gospel**).

In philosophical ethics, utilitarianism* eliminates moral dilemmas in the final analysis by its appeal to the single principle of utility; there can (only) be uncertainties about which action in the situation would maximize welfare. In deontological ethics (*see* **Deontology**) there is debate about whether there are moral dilemmas in the third sense. For example, W. D. Ross distinguished prima facie duties from actual duties in order to resolve conflicts of duties (*see* **Conflict of Duties**). One difficult question is whether an overridden prima facie duty leaves what Robert Nozick calls "moral traces" and engenders moral guilt*, duties of reparation, etc. (*see* **Dirty Hands**). Some interpretations of dilemmas focus on conflicts of values and ideals, as well as of duties and obligations.

Much of the recent work in applied ethics*, including business ethics* and bioethics*, has concentrated on moral dilemmas, quandaries, and conflicts; critics have charged that this concentration distorts the moral life, particularly the centrality of virtue* and character*.

See **Absolutes, Ethical; Casuistry; Compromise; Conflict of Duties; Dirty Hands;**

Double Effect; Ends and Means; Necessity; Norms; Right and Wrong; Situation Ethics.

John Lemmon, "Moral Dilemmas," *Philosophical Review* 71, 1962; E. N. Santurri, "Perplexity in the Moral Life: Philosophical and Theological Considerations," Ph.D. diss., Yale University, 1984.

JAMES F. CHILDRESS

Dirty Hands

In moral discourse, dilemmas* are sometimes interpreted as problems of "dirty hands." For example, in Jean-Paul Sartre's play *Dirty Hands* (1948, ET 1949), the Communist leader Hoederer says, "I have dirty hands right up to the elbows. I've plunged them in filth and blood. Do you think you can govern innocently?" Sometimes this moral phenomenon appears in the context of ritual purity as, e.g., in the comment by Basil the Great in the 4th century: "Killing in war was differentiated by our fathers from murder. . . . Nevertheless, perhaps it would be well that those whose hands are unclean abstain from communion for three years." Often, but not only, viewed as a conflict between responsibility* for the consequences of actions and inactions and responsibility for adhering to norms (*see* **Consequentialism; Deontology**), the problem of "dirty hands" often emerges in politics, where it is sometimes held to be necessary to lie or to use coercion* in order to realize good ends, or in war, where it is sometimes held to be necessary to kill innocent persons in order to avert defeat. The problem concerns both what is right and wrong in conflict situations and what weight should be assigned to the agent's integrity and purity. Part of the debate hinges on the interpretation of moral experience in the light of philosophical and theological convictions; for more on this debate, *see* **Dilemma**. For related issues, *see* **Absolutes, Ethical; Compromise; Conflict of Duties; Ends and Means; Guilt; Necessity; Responsibility; Right and Wrong.**

M. Walzer, "Political Action: The Problem of Dirty Hands," *Philosophy and Public Affairs* 2, no. 2, Winter 1973, pp. 160–180.

JAMES F. CHILDRESS

Disarmament

The elimination, reduction, or control of the means of making war*, whether imposed by a military victor; undertaken as a unilateral initiative for moral reasons or to set an example; or agreed to as a result of intergovernmental negotiations on a bilateral or multilateral basis. There are several motives for seeking disarmament: to reduce the risk of war by limiting military potentials, to save money, to comply with international humanitarian norms, to limit casualties and damage if war should occur, to facilitate war termination. Negotiations about disarmament provide opportunities for strategic dialogue between potential adversaries.

Negotiations. Conferences or meetings to negotiate agreements not to manufacture, stockpile, transfer, or use particular weapons were held at The Hague (1899, 1907), Washington (1921–22), Geneva (1925), London (1930, 1936), under the auspices of the League of Nations (1932–37), and at the United Nations almost continuously since 1946. Progress has been slow because of general political tensions among the negotiating parties, the difficulty of establishing balanced equivalences between different kinds and numbers of weapons and fighting personnel, and disagreements about national or international means of verification at each stage and means of enforcement should a violation be alleged.

Nuclear weapons. The advent of nuclear weapons in 1945 added a new dimension to the disarmament problem, for nuclear weapons have some indiscriminate effects and would almost certainly cause damage beyond that required by strict military necessity. In addition to treaties and negotiations for the limitation or reduction of stockpiles of long- and medium-range nuclear weapons and antimissile systems, conducted under various acronymic labels (SALT, START, LRTNF, INF), there have been treaties to limit or prohibit the testing of nuclear weapons, measures to inhibit their dissemination (the safeguards system of the International Atomic Energy Agency, the Non-Proliferation Treaty, and the guidelines of the Nuclear Suppliers' Group), and consideration of zones to be kept free of nuclear weapons. The Western nuclear-weapon states have resisted proposals to ban unconditionally all uses of nuclear weapons, believing that the possession of nuclear weapons and a conditional intention to use them is necessary to deter aggression. France and China have kept aloof from some negotiations and treaties about nuclear weapons (*see* **Deterrence; Nuclear Warfare**).

Chemical and biological (bacteriological) weapons. The manufacture, deployment, or use of biological (bacteriological) weapons are banned by international treaties. There has been little progress in stopping the manufacture or stockpiling of chemical weapons, but the actual use of chemical weapons in war is prohibited by the Geneva Protocol (1925) though some parties have reserved the right to retaliate against a violator or an ally of a violator. States are free to maintain stocks of chemical agents for riot control in nonwar situations.

Demilitarization. There are agreements not to militarize Antarctica and not to deploy nuclear weapons in outer space or on the seabed. The Treaty of Tlatelolco (1967) is designed to keep Latin America free of nuclear weapons, and a similar zone was established in the South Pacific in 1985. Small demilitarized zones have been established in the Middle East, Kashmir, and Korea for the negotiation or supervision of agreements to terminate armed conflict.

The arms trade. There has been little success in controlling the trade in conventional weapons, partly because of opposition from actual or potential recipients.

International humanitarian law. Efforts to control or reduce arms have been paralleled by agreements to ensure the immunity of noncombatants from direct attack, the outlawing of weapons that cause unnecessary suffering, measures for the protection of injured or shipwrecked combatants, care of prisoners of war, the protection of civilians in occupied territories, and the protection of cultural property (*see also* **Conventions**).

Collateral measures. It is generally agreed that progress in disarmament should be accompanied by strengthened institutions for preventing or resolving international disputes, for deterring or suppressing aggression, and for maintaining peace*.

S. Bailey, *Christian Perspectives on Nuclear Weapons,* rev. ed. 1984; A. Geyer, *The Idea of Disarmament! Rethinking the Unthinkable,* 1982; P. J. Noel-Baker, *The Arms Race,* 1958; N. Sims, *Approaches to Disarmament,* rev. ed. 1979; Working Party appointed by the Board for Social Responsibility of the Church of England, *The Church and the Bomb,* 1982; M. Wright, *Disarm and Verify,* 1964.

SYDNEY D. BAILEY

Discernment

The capacity to perceive and interpret the religious and moral significance of experience in order to make an appropriate response to God; an evaluative judgment of a particular situation, more specific than the application of general moral principles. In the Christian tradition it has three interrelated meanings:

1. Discernment of spirits. Weighing interior experiences to determine if their ultimate origins are divine. NT use denotes either a Pauline charism (1 Cor. 12:10), insight into God's will that stems from conversion (Rom. 12:1–2), or a capacity to determine doctrinal authenticity (1 John 4:1–6). Monasticism and Roman Catholic spirituality test ideas and dispositions by examining their origins and destinations through self-knowledge and affections of peace, joy, love, etc., that lead to God. (Origen, Cassian.) This leads to:

2. Discernment of divine calling. Interpretation of God's call to specific persons, moving to an important life decision, and also the *process* for subsequent decisions that correspond with the fundamental personal vocation*. Both presume ordinary moral boundaries. (Ignatius of Loyola, Jonathan Edwards, Karl Barth, Karl Rahner.)

3. Synthetic practical wisdom. Disclosure of meaning by locating particular events in larger frameworks of biblical narratives, symbols, and personal history. It interprets divine intentions in a more mediated way than (2), above; and it seeks the "fitting" response to God's action in all events. Like the virtue of prudence*, (3) synthesizes moral principles, situational factors, consequences, and insight from the religious tradition into a concrete moral judgment, employing such resources illuminatively rather than prescriptively. (John Henry Newman, H. Richard Niebuhr, James M. Gustafson.)

See also **Norms; Situation Ethics.**

J. M. Gustafson, "Moral Discernment in the Christian Life," *Theology and Christian Ethics,* 1974; E. Malatesta (ed.), *Discernment of Spirits,* 1970.

WILLIAM C. SPOHN, S.J.

Discipleship *see* **Imitation of Christ; Jesus, Ethical Teaching of; New Testament Ethics; Sermon on the Mount**

Discipline

The term has two related meanings. It may mean the maintenance of certain standards of conduct through the enforcement of them by appropriate penalties; or it may mean the training of persons so that they will conduct themselves according to given standards. When one talks of "ecclesiastical discipline," unfortunately one thinks too readily of only the first of these two meanings. It is true that from the beginning the church had to enforce some minimal standards for its members, otherwise it would have lost its distinctiveness and been rendered ineffectual for its mission. At some times in its history, the church has been very rigorous in its discipline and has even invoked the civil authorities for the enforcement of its standards. Nowadays the strict discipline that was once enforced is neither practicable nor desirable. It may well be, however, that the decay of discipline is due as much as anything to indifference. In any case, the discipline of the church should never be harsh. The church must find room within itself for "weaker" members, as Paul called them, and its aim must be to sustain these and eventually strengthen them. This is not to say that its standards are to be weakened, but that whatever is done must aim eventually at reconciliation and at the rehabilitation of those who have injured the community. This is where discipline, as the maintenance of standards, passes into the more important kind of discipline which has to do with the forming of disciples and their training in the Christian life.

See **Ascetical Theology.**

JOHN MACQUARRIE

Discretion *see* **Discernment; Discrimination**

Discrimination

The term "discrimination" refers to the drawing of distinctions and marking of differences, and it covers several different positive and negative actions from the standpoint of Christian ethics. First, it often indicates the power or act of making a judgment, particularly in distinguishing right and wrong actions. In this sense, it is often used interchangeably with "discernment."* Second, in the context of the use of force, particularly military force, discrimination refers to the distinction between combatants and noncombatants, and the principle of discrimination prohibits direct attacks on noncombatants (*see* **Just War; Resistance**). Third, discrimination against individuals and groups involves actions and policies that treat them differently and unjustly because of such characteristics as race, sex, or age. (*See* **Race Relations; Racism; Sex Discrimination; Women, Status of.**)

JAMES F. CHILDRESS

Dispensation

Permission by an ecclesiastical authority to perform an act that would normally be against some rule of the church, or the waiving of the penalty due for having done such an act. A dispensation would be granted because of some special circumstances obtaining in a particular situation. While this conception of dispensation undoubtedly lends itself to abuses, it has a legitimate function as mitigating the rigor of rules and introducing a situational element.

JOHN MACQUARRIE

Dissent

Disagreement with and refusal to consent to a belief, institution, practice, policy, or action (*see* **Consent**). It may be based on moral, religious, or other reasons, and it may involve withdrawal from, noncompliance with, or protest against what is objectionable. For dissent in social and political settings, *see* **Civil Disobedience; Conscience; Conscientious Objection; Cooperation with Evil; Freedom; Law; Resistance; Revolution; State; Totalitarian State; Whistle-blowing.** For dissent in religious settings, *see, inter alia,* **Church and State; Conscience; Cults; Discipline; Ecclesiology and Ethics; Magisterium; Modern Roman Catholic Moral Theology; Nonconformist Conscience; Persecution and Toleration.**

JAMES F. CHILDRESS

Dissociation from Evil *see* **Conscientious Objection; Cooperation with Evil**

Divine Command Morality

The name applied to any moral system or theory in which central moral elements are related directly to the commands of the deity.

The morality of the OT, with its focus on the Ten Commandments and other injunctions of God, can be developed as a prime example of a system of divine command morality. For example, the commandment "Thou shalt not kill" creates a moral obligation to refrain from killing. Variations in theories concern (1) what moral elements are tied to divine command, and (2) how they are connected. Most plausible is the view that moral duties, rights, wrongs, and other aspects of moral obligation are in some way logically derived from God's commands (cf. Adams, Graber). Value judgments (i.e., judgments as to what is good, desirable, worthwhile, etc.) are more appropriately tied to divine *approval* rather than command.

A divine command approach has been widely presupposed as the natural moral expression of piety. Explicit divine command theories of ethics have been proposed by numerous classical Christian thinkers, including notably Duns Scotus, William of Ockham, René Descartes, John Locke (in some writings), and William Paley (in some contexts)—as well as by contemporary theologians and philosophers (Patterson Brown, Robert M. Adams, Philip L. Quinn). (See Idziak for selections and references.)

Criticism of this ethical approach also has a long history. Plato posed a classic dilemma in his dialogue *Euthyphro.* One version of it can be stated thus: Either (*a*) God commands a certain act *because it is right,* or (*b*) it is right *because God commands it.* If (*a*) is true, then it appears that the fundamental standard of morality is logically independent of God's will or his commands (although God's authority might still form the basis of our *knowing* our duty, or of our *accepting* it, or of our *being motivated to do* it). If (*b*) is true, then there appears to be no independent reason to accept or do what God commands. (This is alleged to make morality "arbitrary" or "capricious.") Further, in (*b*) there appears to be no basis for praising God's *moral* qualities, since there is no moral standard independent of his will. Modern critics (e.g., Kai Nielsen, Antony Flew, Patrick Nowell-Smith, and R. M. Hare) raise extensions of these objections, as well as criticisms based on issues in metaethics.

See **Morality and Religion, Relations of; Voluntarism.**

R. Adams, "Divine Command Metaethics Modified Again," *JRE* 7, no. 1, pp. 66–79; G. Graber, "In Defense of a Divine Command Theory of Ethics," *Journal of the American Academy of Religion* 43, no. 1, pp. 62–69; J. Idziak, *Divine Command Morality: Historical and Contemporary Readings,* 1979.
GLENN C. GRABER

Divine Right of Kings

A theory that the king rules by divine right, a right granted to him (and not only to his office) directly by God (and not only indirectly through the people or through God's providential ordering of the world). Its most prominent spokesmen were James I and Sir Robert Filmer in the 17th century. While Rom. 13 holds that God ordains government as such and particular governments, the theory of the divine right of kings focuses solely on kingship, holding that royal absolutism receives its authority directly from God's special decree and that it is hereditary. This theory denied citizens the right to disobey or to resist the king.

J. N. Figgis, *The Divine Right of Kings,* 1896.
JAMES F. CHILDRESS

Divorce

If lifelong marriage is a norm, it is certainly a norm with exceptions. The problem of divorce, i.e., of marriage that breaks (as distinct from nullity, attempted marriage that never was real), has always beset human society.

There have been many procedures for divorce, from unilateral repudiation to mutual consent, from return of bride-price to bills of divorcement or judgments by family courts. There have been attempts to forbid divorce with remarriage altogether, though separation "from bed and board" has to be allowed. In some societies, in some situations, divorce has even been obligatory (cf. Matt. 1:19). There are many possible grounds for divorce, from falling out of love to cruelty. The most universal ground has been adultery*, especially a wife's adultery, which is felt by nearly all societies to cut at the root of marriage and family life.

God's people have been taught that the Lord hates "putting away" (Mal. 2:16), but they have still needed provision for it. The law laid down that a man might divorce his wife in proper form "if she finds no favor in his eyes because he has found some indecency in her" (Deut. 24:1). Much dispute ensued about interpreting this "indecency," this "unseemly thing." In Matthew, Jesus gives his teaching on divorce in answer to a question about this point: "Is it lawful to divorce one's wife for any cause?" (Matt. 19:3). The answer is no, "except for unchastity" (19:9). Christians have disputed ever since about the status and meaning of this exception. It is commonly held now that the "hard saying" in its more absolute Marcan form (Mark 10:2–12) is both more basic and more characteristic.

It seems clear that Jesus taught that divorce and remarriage are against God's will. The question has been whether this is a new Christian law, and if not, how it can be more than an unattainable ideal. The theological complexities are well illustrated by the interplay of church and state in England on the matter.

The belief that the Lord gave a new law and that the "Matthaean exception" was part of it formed the basis of the English divorce law of "matrimonial offence." Before 1857 divorces could be granted only by expensive private Act of Parliament. There were more than three hundred such cases, and those concerned were remarried in church as a matter of course. From 1857 divorce was made increasingly available to all. The grounds were gradually widened, for the sake of justice, to include other offenses than adultery, especially cruelty and desertion.

Meantime critical opinion was coming to believe that the "Matthaean exception" was just as much a product of the early church seeking to interpret the mind of the Lord as the so-called "Pauline privilege" (1 Cor. 7:15). If Jesus legislated, his law was rigorist. The most natural conclusion seemed to be either that he was legislating only for Christians or that he was not giving a law but establishing an ideal. Each of these positions had its intractable difficulties, both for scholarly accuracy and for Christian love. But neither of them required the church to try to enforce Christ's teaching upon the world (see **Morality, Legal Enforcement of**). So when the "matrimonial offence" increasingly showed itself an unsatisfactory basis for the

law, church people of different theological persuasions were able to encourage and even assist the state to substitute the principle of "irretrievable breakdown." (It needs to be noted that neither legally nor theologically is "breakdown" supposed to be itself divorce. A marriage remains in being unless expressly put asunder.)

Granted that the church can tolerate a secular divorce law, its real problem is what to say to its own members whose marriages falter. Can Christians ever encourage other Christians to divorce and remarry? Can the church offer such encouragement? Can it bless those remarrying? Can it bless the new vows? If a remarriage has any validity, does it not need all the grace it can have? Here, as elsewhere, both strictness and gentleness are trying to witness to real values but come into collision. Rigorism binds "heavy burdens, grievous to be borne" and lays them upon other people's shoulders (Matt. 23:4; Luke 11:46). Liberalism forgets hard sayings and never expects to take up a cross.

In looking for an answer the following points may be noted:

1. The Lord's teaching is more positive than negative. It is recounted that he was questioned about divorce and answered about marriage. If the church makes a ban on divorce the main concern of its teaching on marriage, no wonder it does not look very "Christian." But if the "one flesh" union is the main point, then divorce can be understood as an agonizing exception, an unnatural amputation rather than an attractive temptation. Instead of arguing about the indissolubility or dissolubility of faltering marriages, it is better to look for indissolubility where it really belongs, in the characteristic unity of a good marriage. Fidelity* is to a husband or a wife, not to an impersonal duty.

2. If anything is clear about the teaching of Christ, it is that whether rigorist or liberal it was not legalistic (see **Legalism**). If questions about whether people are "living in sin" depend upon dates of baptisms, upon technicalities and regulations, upon metaphysical bonds that seem to tie up God's mercy, surely something is wrong. The remarriage discipline of the Orthodox churches may look strange and inconsistent to Westerners; but their strength is their grasp of "the freedom and transcendence of God" and their conviction, strong not weak, that the purpose of

marriage is love (A. M. Allchin, Root Report, Appendix 3, pp. 114, 123).

3. The seemingly impossible commands of Jesus are meant to be obeyed: but they cannot be kept piecemeal. They belong in the whole context of a new covenant: "The Gospel preceded the demand" (J. Jeremias, *The Sermon on the Mount,* ET 1961, p. 29). They are illustrations of a way of living. To argue about whether they are "optional" or "compulsory," "ideals" or "laws," misses the point, just as it misses the point to say that they are binding only upon those who belong. They are kept as a response to something seen, human or divine, that overcomes hard-heartedness. When hard-heartedness remains, it is too much to expect them to be kept. We may have to admit even in the church that the harvest of the Spirit (Gal. 5:22–23) is not ready for reaping.

See **Marriage.**

D. Atkinson, *To Have and to Hold,* and bibliography, 1979; *Christian Marriage in Africa* (A. Hastings for Anglican Church), 1973; K. Kelly, *Divorce and Second Marriage,* 1982; *Marriage, Divorce and the Church,* including appendixes (Report of Root Commission), 1971; *Marriage and the Church's Task* (Report of the Lichfield Commission), 1978; H. Oppenheimer, *The Marriage Bond,* 1976; *Putting Asunder: A Divorce Law for Contemporary Society* (Report of the Archbishops' Group), 1966; P. Turner, *Divorce: A Christian Perspective,* 1983; A. R. Winnett, *Divorce and Remarriage in Anglicanism,* 1958; *The Church and Divorce,* 1968.

HELEN OPPENHEIMER

Domination *see* **Equality; Exploitation; Liberation Theology; Oppression; Power**

Donation, Organ *see* **Organ Transplantation**

Double Effect, Principle of

The principle of the double effect is a rule of practice that both allows for certain exceptions and attempts to limit them. It would be more accurate to refer to the actions involved as actions with a double dimension or aspect. Some effects of human activity were considered so radically wrong (intrinsically evil) that they could be tolerated only when they were *praeter intentionem,* or not directly sought (*see* **Intention**).

It is disputed whether what is now known as the principle of double effect is to be found in Thomas Aquinas's treatment of self-defense. Whatever the case, it can be said that the inspiration for the notion may be located in Thomas's notion of *praeter intentionem.* In the 19th century, actions involving certain evils were said to be justifiable under a fourfold condition: (1) The action from which evil results is good or indifferent in itself; it is not morally evil. (2) The intention of the agent is upright—i.e., the evil effect is sincerely not intended. (3) The evil effect must be equally immediate causally with the good effect, for otherwise it would be a means to the good effect and would be intended. (4) There must be a proportionately grave reason for allowing the evil to occur. These conditions have been variously stated over the years, but when they (or qualified versions of them) are fulfilled, the resultant evil was referred to as an "unintended by-product" of the action, only indirectly voluntary and justified by the presence of a proportionately grave reason.

A classic example is the situation of a woman with a nonviable pregnancy who is diagnosed as having cancer of the uterus. If nothing is done, the cancer (at least in many cases and in the case here envisaged) will spread and bring death to both mother and child. If, however, the cancerous uterus is removed, the woman would be saved but the fetus would obviously perish. Uterine excision was judged permissible under the conditions detailed above. Specifically, the action was seen as good or indifferent (removal of the uterus); the intention is upright (removing the uterus to save the mother's life); the good effect is equally immediate causally with the evil effect (thus, e.g., the uterus would be removed whether it was pregnant or not, an indication that the death of the fetus is not exactly a means in the strict sense to the attainment of the good); there is a proportionate reason.

This distinction has been used by theologians over the years, especially in three areas of concern: actions involving the sin of another (scandal), actions involving killing, and actions involving the use of the sexual faculties. Because of the importance of these areas and the almost limitless variety of human situations in which they can occur, a huge casuistry* concerning the double effect built up over the centuries.

Furthermore, the so-called double effect principle has been taken over and used extensively in official documents of the Roman Catholic magisterium*, especially in recent decades. For example, in discussing abortion*, Pius XI asked, "What could ever be a sufficient reason for excusing in any way the direct murder of the innocent (*directam innocentis necem*)?" Pius XII repeatedly condemned the "deliberate and *direct* disposing of an innocent human life" and argued that "neither the life of the mother nor that of the child can be subjected to an act of *direct* suppression." He also applied the direct-indirect distinction to sterilizing drugs. The most recent and authoritative use of this distinction is found in *Humanae Vitae*. Paul VI stated, "We must once again declare that the *direct* interruption of the generative process already begun, and above all, *directly* willed and procured abortion, even if for therapeutic reasons, are to be absolutely excluded as licit means of regulating birth." He immediately added, "Equally to be excluded, as the teaching authority of the Church has frequently declared, is *direct* sterilization, whether perpetual or temporary, whether of the man or the woman" (*see* **Sterilization**).

The use of this distinction has had two general effects. First, it has reduced the intolerable consequences of adhering to a simple rule against taking any human life (or, respectively, the fertility of the sexual act). An unqualified rule against taking any human life offers little difficulty most of the time. But unrestricted adherence to it means that we are, for example, helpless in the face of aggressors who do not respect it. Thus over the centuries Catholic tradition restricted the rule to apply to *innocent* life. However, there are still other instances (especially obstetrical) where adherence even to the modified rule would cause greater loss of life. So another refinement was called for. That refinement is the distinction between direct and indirect killing. Thus in certain life-threatening situations it is possible to save the mother even though the fetus is "indirectly killed." The second result of this distinction is that by such a process of restrictive interpretation of the rule against killing, it has been possible not only to save life in some conflict situations, but also to preserve a strong deontologically interpreted rule against killing. The upshot, then, of such restrictive interpretation of the rule against killing has been the combi-

nation of a commonsense need to save life when possible with a strongly felt need to maintain a strict rule against killing. In summary, the present "hard" (deontologically understood) rule against killing ("no *direct* killing of an *innocent* human being") is just as plausible as it has been teleologically modifiable to its present wording (*see* **Deontology; Teleological Ethics**).

Since around 1965 (largely through the writings of Peter Knauer, S.J., Bruno Schüller, S.J., and Louis Janssens) the determinative character of the double effect principle has been challenged. Though such analysts reveal important individual differences, they concur in their move toward a teleological understanding of the actions formerly justified by the double effect principle. Traditional analysts felt it necessary to use "direct" and "indirect" with regard to certain actions because they regarded them as "evil in se." They regarded them as such because of certain features independent of consequences. Once one judges that sterilization, for example, is not "contrary to nature," there is no reason for the direct-indirect appeal. The assessment is made teleologically and the truly decisive consideration is the presence or absence of a proportionate reason (*see* **Proportionality**).

See also **Modern Roman Catholic Moral Theology; Thomistic Ethics.**

R. A. McCormick, S.J., "The Principle of Double Effect," *How Brave a New World?* 1981; P. Ramsey and R. A. McCormick, S.J. (eds.), *Doing Evil to Achieve Good: Morality in Conflict Situations*, 1978.

RICHARD A. MCCORMICK, S.J.

Draft *see* **Conscription;** *see also* **Conscientious Objection; Pacifism**

Drives *see* **Instincts or Drives**

Drug Addiction

Cast against an ethic of independence and self-control, the term "drug addiction" communicates a negative value-judgment. Drug addiction has been seen as symptomatic of a personality disorder and has been classified as a variety of sociopathic personality disturbance. However, one must note that addiction is used loosely to include not only physical dependence but the habituated use of a drug without evidence of such dependence.

The second phenomenon, psychological dependence, is often referred to as habituation in order to contrast it with physical dependence. Generally, physical addiction can develop more easily with the use of substances such as opium and alcohol, but not usually with substances such as cannabis and cocaine. However, habituation can create a significant dependence. Drug addiction in the broader sense of habituation is rampant in most Western societies, as evidenced by the psychological dependence of many on nicotine in cigarettes or caffeine in coffee.

The social significance of addiction or habituation will depend in part on whether the drug involved is widely accepted and on the circumstance of its acquisition. Thus, a psychological dependence on the use of cannabis is likely to have more adverse social consequences than even more severe dependence on benzodiazepines and other minor tranquilizers, insofar as the latter are provided by prescription. Even a physical addiction to alcohol may appear more socially acceptable. This is in great measure due to a distinction informally drawn between proper use and abuse, in terms of whether the drug has been procured through legal channels. In addition, a line may implicitly be drawn between proper and improper use of drugs in terms of the extent to which the benefits of the drug's use are likely to outweigh the harms associated with it, according to generally accepted third-person standards. Thus, the use of a minor tranquilizer in the case of an individual suffering from a situational anxiety due to the hospitalization of a close family member is likely to be seen as a proper use of the drug, even if some slight potential of psychological dependence exists. Also, the use of highly addictive narcotics for the terminal pain of a cancer patient is usually justified. Concerns about the risks of addiction and the significance of addiction must be put in a context. Given the fact that the use of drugs ranges from the recreational to the purely therapeutic through many zones of gray, it is often difficult, where there is significant controversy about the prudence or propriety of using a drug with addictive potential, to judge concerning what should count as proper usage (see **Risk; Suffering**).

In fact, any characterization of the problems associated with drug addiction depends on particular social structures and particular systems of values. The criminalization of drug addiction presupposes that the profit made by organized crime and the death and injury of innocent individuals due to drug-related crime are outweighed by the benefits due to legal proscription. It may presuppose as well a set of paternalistic and nonlibertarian commitments on the part of the law to protect individuals from the consequences of their own actions. So, too, to see drug addiction as a disease carries with it its own assumptions regarding the proper role of medicine and the avoidance of pain and the provision of pleasure*, as well as the extent to which the outcomes of drug use should be understood within the confines of the sick role. The more that pain and anxiety* are seen as medical problems in their own right, the more plausible it becomes to risk addiction in ameliorating them. The more that euphoria and pleasure are seen as major human goals, the more plausible it becomes that recreational drugs may play a wholesome role in human societies. On the other hand, insofar as one sees medicine as able to blunt the adverse outcomes of drug usage, the more tempting it will become to construe such problems as medical problems. One thus finds a major section in the *Diagnostic and Statistical Manual of Mental Disorders* (³1980) of the American Psychiatric Association devoted to substance use disorders. The characterization of drug addiction is dependent on how the phenomenon is understood within the framework of legal, medical, and religious institutions, which may characterize such a state of affairs nonexclusively as circumstances of criminal behavior, disease, or sinfulness.

See also **Abstinence; Alcoholism; Autonomy; Counseling; Harm; Health and Disease, Values in Defining; Involuntary Hospitalization; Mental Health; Mental Illness; Morality, Legal Enforcement of; Paternalism; Responsibility; Sick, Care of the; Temperance; Tobacco, Use of.**

H. TRISTRAM ENGELHARDT, JR.

Drugs *see* **Drug Addiction;** *see also* **Abstinence; Alcoholism; Temperance**

Drunkenness *see* **Alcoholism; Temperance**

Duty

Duty, especially in modern moral philosophy, means primarily a motive or principle of conduct that serves as an indication of the individual person's moral quality. The meaning of duty is inseparable from that of obligation, the acknowledgment of what ought to be done, of what we are bound to do, of what we are "under orders" to perform. Immanuel Kant made the apprehension of duty the fundamental principle of his ethics and he took our human capacity for respecting and subjecting ourselves to a moral law to be the mark of our dignity as moral persons. In Kant's analysis, duty as a motive implies the existence in the moral self of counterfactors or temptations that stand opposed to, or in some way obstruct, the performance of duty. Kant spoke of inclinations or self-regarding springs of action that must be opposed, redirected, or outwitted if the moral law is to be obeyed and our duty performed. The moral law of conduct confronts us in the form of duty just because we are imperfect beings and not fully able to determine ourselves through the dictates of practical reason. God, by contrast, embodies the moral law in his holy will so that the idea of action out of duty in relation to a holy will becomes irrelevant.

Duty as a motive for action is generally regarded as "unconditional" and not subject to external qualifications. Here the term "unconditional" does not mean that we are allowed to ignore the actual situation and the conditions of action in determining what we are to do, but rather that once our duty becomes clear we must perform regardless of our personal inclinations and without calculating the advantages or disadvantages to ourselves based on the anticipated consequences of the act. If we fail to acknowledge our obligation and to act in accordance with it, we are morally without excuse.

Appeal to duty as a basic moral principle defines a morality of motives and locates the moral quality of the person in the character of his or her willing. Opposed to such a view is the utilitarian position in ethics (see **Utilitarianism**), according to which all human conduct is to be judged and evaluated not by its motive but by the extent to which the consequences of one's actions contribute to or prevent the realization of happiness or well-being. According to the morality of duty, on the other hand, the good person is the one whose will is good solely in virtue of the motive it expresses, and who is judged by the ability to do not only *as* duty requires but *because* duty requires.

While the religious person may regard the performance of duty as conduct based on a duty to God and thus be motivated by the love of God, the main aim of duty or obligation theories in ethics has been to ground duty in reason alone and thus to establish it as a self-sufficient spring of action. Human freedom and the autonomy of morality (*see* **Autonomy of Ethics**) are said to reside in the fact that nothing beyond the acknowledgment of obligation or duty is required for moral motivation. This point can be seen most clearly if we consider the questions that have frequently been raised in connection with the idea of obligation: Why should I perform my duty? or, Why should I be obligated? From the standpoint of the morality of duty, these questions themselves are fundamentally immoral because they presuppose some further end beyond obligation or some good that entices me to obey. The acknowledgment of obligation is the essence of morality; duty can have no ground or further reason beyond itself if its moral import is to be preserved. In Kant's thought, for example, respect for the law that obligates us is the fundamental moral spring of action; there is no thought of being motivated by the anticipated consequences of an action or the attainment of some good as an end.

It is important to notice the close connection that exists between the concept of duty and a community of moral persons as expressed, for instance, in Kant's idea of a kingdom of ends*. Acknowledgment of duty is at the same time acknowledgment of a universal law that is binding on all other beings capable of understanding their nature as moral persons. In one formulation of duty prescribed by the moral law, Kant held that I must so act as to treat all other rational beings as ends in themselves and never merely as means. The universal import of the duty principle can best be seen by attending to the fact that the principle is intended to exclude any conduct based on a maxim that is peculiar to myself; the morality of duty is set against my making an exception in my own case and it marks off as immoral any deed based exclusively on my own self-interest or on an "ulterior" motive that means a form of personal gain. Thus Kant would say that the good person is one who, for example, is honest not because it is the best "policy," for that means calculation of consequences and advantages, but the one who acknowledges an obligation to speak the truth without regard to "policy." Only if entirely self-regarding moral principles are excluded is it possible to have a community of moral persons.

In addition to duty understood as a motive or ground of action, we also speak of particular duties, by which we mean specific actions we ought to perform. It has sometimes been debated whether a duty and a right action are always the same (*see* **Right and Wrong**); the reason why such a question would arise is not difficult to find. Insofar as saying that some particular action is our duty also means that we have inclinations or predispositions against performing it, identifying right action with duty is questionable, for it would leave out of account right actions that we perform either habitually or without any clear sense of their being against our inclination. While it seems that duty can never be other than an obligation to perform the act that is right, there are right actions—for example, eating the proper food and resting adequately in order to maintain our health—that would not generally be regarded as duties in the sense that they confront us as obligatory over against natural inclination. And yet even in these cases we can see that should neglect of proper food and rest lead to illness jeopardizing both our own lives and the lives of others, it would be legitimate to say that it is our *duty* to obtain proper food and rest.

The ethics of duty has often been the subject of criticism on the ground that it is abstract and formal, leaving no place for action motivated by love. Thus the poet Schiller chided Kant by saying that whereas he wanted and liked to help his friends in distress, such action would be without moral worth in Kant's view because only what is done from a sense of duty is in accord with the moral law. There are, to be sure, profound and difficult problems connected with the relation between law and love, disposition and command, but these cannot be treated in brief compass. It is, nevertheless, important to notice that while Kant's morality of duty has often been cast in the legalistic form of "duty for duty's sake" it was actually intended to be a transcendence of law and not a form of legalism at all. Kant found the essence of morality in the person for whom morality means *respect* for a law that expresses the dignity of the moral person, the willingness to be bound by a universal principle. The good person is the one who has this respect and who needs no determining ground beyond it as a spring of action. By denying the moral standing of all self-regarding motives and reasons, Kant was excluding the possibility that, as he expressed it, the "dear self" could become a valid determining ground for the good act.

See **Categorical Imperative; Deontology; Kantian Ethics; Universalizability.**

F. H. Bradley, *Ethical Studies,* [2]1927; J. M. Gustafson and J. T. Laney (eds.), *On Being Responsible,* 1968; H. R. Niebuhr, *The Responsible Self,* 1963; G. Outka, *Agape: An Ethical Analysis,* 1972; D. Z. Phillips (ed.), *Religion and Understanding,* 1967; S. Toulmin, *The Place of Reason in Ethics,* 1950.

JOHN E. SMITH

Eastern Orthodox Christian Ethics

Ethics in Eastern Orthodoxy. As a separate discipline and area of theological study, ethics is a late development in Christian history, and in Eastern Orthodoxy in particular. It arose with the attempt to study the Christian faith and its teaching in an ordered and systematic fashion. The birth of the theological discipline of Christian ethics can be dated with some specificity to the 18th century. However, the subject matter of Christian ethics is found in the original sources of Christian life and faith.

Theological context. For Eastern Orthodox Christianity, the roots of its ethical teaching are identical with those of its faith and life. Eastern Orthodoxy understands itself as one in life, ethos, doctrine, ecclesial organization, history, spirituality, sacramental life and worship, canon law, and ethical teaching with the one united church of Jesus Christ of the first eight centuries. The church's chief authoritative source for its life and practice is divine revelation, as historically understood in the living tradition of faith, and reposing in the consciousness of the church. Concretely, this means that the authentic teaching and life of the church is both embodied and formed by the OT and the NT, the writings of the universally acknowledged fathers of the church whose interpretation of scripture helped form the doctrinal formulations of the seven ecumenical councils, the monastic tradition of Eastern Christian spirituality, canon law, sacramental and worship life, and in general, the theology, moral teaching, and ethos of Eastern Orthodoxy. Together, these form an ecclesiological whole, a spiritual ethos*. The ethical and moral teaching is only one of several major dimensions of this totality. It is both informed and guided by the whole teaching and, in turn, informs and guides the whole as well.

However, certain fundamental theological teachings provide several of the central determinative concepts for Orthodox ethics. Among the most significant are the doctrines of the Holy Trinity, creation and the doctrine of human nature, the incarnation and redemption, and the church.

The doctrine of the Holy Trinity significantly begins, in the Eastern Christian tradition, with the experience and knowledge of the persons of the Father, Son, and Holy Spirit, which then leads to the affirmation of the unity of God. Thus, foremost in Eastern Christian thought is the perception of God as a community of persons in organic relationship, rather than as an abstract impersonal essence. God is one, because the Son is born of the Father and because the Holy Spirit proceeds from the Father. The identity of the divine essence in conjunction with the plurality of the persons in the Trinity provides an important and fundamental model of community in unity for the ethics of Eastern Orthodoxy.

It is only as God communicates this divine reality that he is known. In his very essence and being God is unknowable and incomprehensible to us. Creation brings into being all that exists other than himself. Creation is other than God in its being. It has come into being by the will of God *ex nihilo*. Even though God is transcendent over the totality of creation, he communes with it, relates with it, and sustains it through his divine energies. This is grace—not a substance or thing imparted to creation, but rather the very presence of God. While we cannot know or experience or perceive the essence of God, we know God and experience his power and reality through his very presence in his energies.

Thus, nothing is divorced from his active and real power and presence, and nothing that is created achieves its fulfillment separated from the divine energies of the triune God.

In particular, this is true of human beings. As creatures of God, they are in a unique fashion in God's image. Human beings share in many of the divine attributes: intelligence, self-determination, moral perceptivity, creativity, the capacity for interpersonal relations and for personal identity in the *koinōnia* of personhood. They also have been granted these things with a potential for fulfillment and full realization. Creation is a gift as well as a potential dependent on human cooperation with God in the realization of full humanity, as persons and as a body. This provides a view of human nature that is dynamic and developmental, with a strong respect for self-determining choosing and acting.

Sin in life is primarily perceived as the breaking of the appropriate and fitting relation of the creature with the Creator. Its consequences are disastrous for human existence. Rebellion by the creature against God, with its primary motivation being pride, not only deprives human beings of the possibility of growth toward God-likeness, but concretely and essentially distorts the divine image in all of creation, most especially in human beings. From this perspective, all human beings are defective and less than truly human.

The saving work of Jesus Christ does not take place in the abstract. Through the incarnation, the second person of the Holy Trinity enters history and the created reality, and assumes human nature without its sin. Through his teaching, his dominion over nature, his submission to the demonic forces of death on the cross, and his victory over them through his resurrection, Christ saves humanity as a whole, providing forgiveness and the restoration of the potential for full humanity, both in personal and in corporate life. His work of salvation is an embodiment of the divine life of love in the Trinity.

In the church this life finds its fullest expression, for the task of the church and its life is to particularize, in persons and peoples, the image and likeness of God, that is, to realize the God-likeness that is the fulfillment of human existence. Part of this new life is moral and spiritual in character. Determining the motives, intents, behavior, and actions that are fitting and appropriate to this new life is the task of the discipline of Christian ethics. It is seen, however, as dealing with a life that is constantly growing and developing toward God-likeness and therefore cannot ever assume a stance of rigidness and legalism. Nor can it find its completion in this worldly existence. Though the kingdom of God begins in this life, it transcends it as well. So the ethical dimension will always have a provisional character to it, even while it seeks to provide direction and guidance for living the new life in Christ by persons and communities growing toward the fulfillment of the image and likeness of God.

Approaches. Various traditions of doing ethics in the Eastern Orthodox Church have come into being during this century. Most writings prior to 1930 were popular handbooks and did not have scholarly character. In the last fifty years three major approaches to Orthodox Christian ethics have emerged. One of these has sought close grounding in a broad, creation-based perception of the ethical experience. This view has emphasized the continuities, for instance, between philosophical understandings of the ethical experience and foundational Christian views. Its virtue has been the maintenance of a strong catholic concern with the world as a whole, and with the church. Another view has focused on the redemptive work of Jesus Christ as an analytical tool for doing ethics. It organizes itself around the redemptive work of Jesus Christ, with major foci on unredeemed human existence on the one hand and redeemed human existence on the other. Scripture and the Greek fathers of the 4th and 5th centuries are its main source. The third perspective from which ethics is approached seeks to incorporate the unique insights of the later Eastern Christian mystical and ascetic traditions in its formulations. The *Philokalia* tradition and Palamism are its most significant sources. More recently, attempts have been made to synthesize these three approaches into a single coherent approach to the understanding of Orthodox Christian ethics.

The theōria of Orthodox Christian ethics. The doctrinal teachings of Eastern Orthodox Christianity, as sketched out in part above, provide a framework for Orthodox Christian ethics. In the most broad context, the relationships of God with human life as created and redeemed and as growing in the image and likeness of God toward Theosis provided for an "ought" not based on the "facts" of a fallen creation and a distorted humanity, but rather on the *telos,* or goal, toward which human beings are directed by their calling to be fully human. Within this context, a theory of ethics is formed that deals with the "ought" dimensions of the Eastern Orthodox Christian faith and life (*see* **Teleological Ethics**).

The good. Eastern Orthodox Christian theology identifies the good with God. The triune God, as a community of divine persons —Father, Son, and Holy Spirit—is understood to be as well the very essence of the good for the created world. Eastern Christian teaching rejects a view of the good which is abstract, that is, which is an objective, impersonal principle, concept, or idea. Ultimate reality is God, who is a Trinity of persons. The Holy Trinity as the good is the ground from which the good in the created world (with major focus on humanity) is communicated. Inasmuch as created reality communicates with the source of all goodness— the triune God—it shares in and manifests goodness. Inasmuch as created reality, especially human life, severs communion with God, it equally fails to share in goodness, with the consequence that it is distorted, incomplete, and fails to fulfill its true and full potential for which it exists. However, because the Christian faith is catholic in scope, its ethical teaching cannot be limited and sectarian. Thus, nearly all of the major emphases of the various schools of philosophical ethics, as well as those of other religious traditions, find a place in the structure of the *theōria* of Orthodox Christian ethics. Though the triune God is understood as the source of human good, the good as inborn, as law, as pleasure, as evolution, as perfection, as value, as existential, and as love are included in a complete perception of the good. Each nonrevelatory approach to ethics shares in a portion of the truth of that which Maximos the Confessor has called "the good by nature," i.e., the triune God.

The essence of God is unknown to the created world. Just as there is no possibility of defining the nature (*ousia*) of God, so there is no possibility of defining the good in abstract terms in the created world. However, inasmuch as God relates to the created world, the Trinitarian existence forms the goodness of this world. This contact, relationship, and communication is variously referred to as the divine energies, divine grace, or divine presence. The terms are synonymous. It is the divine energies that make the good which is God as a community of persons present in human life.

Evil and sin. The ethics of Eastern Orthodox Christianity understands evil in an ultimate sense as "meonic" ($m\bar{e}\ \bar{o}n$ = nonbeing). Evil has no metaphysical reality of its own, since it is "the absence of the good." Of course, evil is experienced in many different forms. It is an empirical reality as sin, it is the willed rejection by self-determining intelligent beings of the fitting and appropriate relationships between themselves and God. Evil is also structural, in that the forms of the created world have been distorted and darkened by the condition of original sin. In Eastern Orthodox ethics, evil is considered to be a consequence of the choice of self-determination, which at heart is a rejection of the proper and appropriate relationship between human beings and the triune God. This means that in human beings, the very violation of that appropriate relationship creates a condition of incompleteness and distorted humanity. Both personal and social, it impacts upon all aspects of life, including the physical nonhuman created world. However, this does not mean that the image of God in humankind is totally lost. Rather, much of the image remains, even though it be in darkened and incomplete form. This is the Eastern Orthodox understanding of "original sin."* Human beings are still able to share in some measure in the good, and consequently still do a measure of good. As a result, Eastern Christian ethics is neither overly optimistic nor overly pessimistic regarding the moral capacities of unredeemed humanity.

Human moral capacities. Part of the image of God in human beings that remains, in spite of sin, is the universal existence of human moral capacities. Human existence is inextricably bound to the sense of the imperative of the moral. This imperative consists of the universal human tendency to see events and situations in ethical categories, and to make moral judgments upon them. Sometimes called the "moral drive" and the "ethical sense" by Orthodox ethicists, this imperative is understood as being part of the essential meaning of human existence, an irreducible aspect of the image of God. Flowing from this is the human capacity for self-determination (*autexousion*). The Greek fathers usually restrict the idea of freedom (*eleutheria*) for the condition reached at the highest levels of development in which there is no conflict or struggle in behaving inwardly and outwardly in a divine-like, and therefore, fully human manner.

The conscience. The conscience is the outgrowth of the inborn moral capacities, not a faculty. The sense of moral obligation is the distinguishing characteristic of the conscience. This imperative character is subject to development, and also capable of being deformed, by becoming over- or underformed. It must be cultivated, educated, trained, and formed. The conscience is the place where the "objective" moral good is made personal and "subjective." It is the locus of the moral life in the individual. As such it is a process or ability to discern, to distinguish, and to evaluate moral realities. This is distinguished from moral values and criteria. The conscience is the human capacity to function ethically.

The natural moral law (*see* **Natural Law**). For the Greek fathers, the first, elementary, and low-level moral content of the conscience, i.e., its basic norm, has as its purpose the maintenance of the basic patterns of human society. These essential norms are universally identified in all cultures, societies, and groups. They are frequently referred to as the natural moral law. Eastern Orthodoxy holds that such a normative reality is to be found "naturally" even in the fallen condition of the world. It remains functional even in the distorted reality of the fallen condition. One of the most adequate expressions of the natural moral law is the Decalogue*, though its major principles are to be found embodied in the scriptures of all major religious traditions and the laws of all societies. Thus, for example, "You shall do no murder" indicates an elementary respect for life, prohibiting the unjust taking of life. Its basic and first-level character is supported by the understanding that its widespread violation would destroy any society, tribe, or social group. The natural moral law is applicable to any social whole, assuring survival. As such, it cannot be considered as the only moral criterion in more complex situations.

The evangelical ethic. The evangelical ethic is to be understood within the Christian *Heilsgeschichte,* or salvation history, which in Eastern Christianity is dominated by the purpose of humanity to achieve Theosis, or God-likeness, and divine communion. This means that human beings become truly so when their lives reflect, both within and without, the life of the Holy Trinity. Thus, the specifically Christian ethic is more than an ethic just for Christians. It is a human norm. The context of the evangelical ethic, on the one hand, focuses on Christ's teaching which requires a coherence of inner dispositions, intents, and motives with overt behavior. On the other hand, the content of the evangelical ethic focuses primarily (though not exclusively) on *agapē* love*. On its first level, Christian *agapē* means selfless concern for the welfare and good of the other. This permits acts of love for the stranger, and even for the enemy. But the Trinitarian pattern for the Christian life growing toward Theosis also indicates a more full and complete aspect or level of love. Here, mutuality is transcended by communion and union, as the persons of the Holy Trinity are united with one another. The Greek fathers did not hesitate to call this love *theios erōs,* or divine love. Such love is to characterize all the relationships of those who grow toward Theosis—including relationships with God, neighbor, and self. It will involve numerous specific modes of behavior which can be specified and enjoined in normative language.

Moral being, deciding, and doing. Because the growth toward Theosis demands the transformation of life so that more and more it becomes reflective of the Trinitarian life in whose image and likeness human beings are created to become, it requires the formation of stable yet developing modes of existence and the avoidance of those modes of existence which do not conform to the life in conformance with Theosis. When these modes of behavior are considered as specifics, they are referred to as "virtues" and "vices." When they are seen as a whole, they are referred to as "character."* Ethically speaking, growth toward Theosis is a process of forming the God-like or Christ-like being, both in the individual person in community and in the total life of the community. This emphasis on being does not exclude the possibility or the requirement that the gospel may demand radical behavior. Yet these radical demands (e.g., "Greater love has no man than this, to give his life for his neighbor") cannot take place other than in a framework of a stable and developing ethos of a holistic God-like style of life.

The growth toward Theosis also is embodied in decision-making, a function of the conscience which takes place before, during, and after an act. The decision-making is properly determined by the act's participation or nonparticipation in the divine-like life. For this, discernment is needed, which can only come from the formation of character and virtues in the being of the decision maker. Nevertheless, decision-making will require attention to rules, consequences, intents, motives, means, values, the situation, and the consciousness of the church as well.

The good is accomplished and evil avoided through a cooperation of the energies of God and human self-determination. The Greek fathers refer to this as *synergeia,* or "synergy." On the human side, evil is overcome and the good done through a set of practices collectively known as *askēsis,* which are seen as the means by which the struggle for growth (*agōna*) in the God-like life is practiced. These include all the traditional religious practices, such as prayer and fasting, as well as other forms of spiritual and moral discipline. The doing of the good and the avoiding of evil are always understood as taking place within the corporate, ecclesial whole.

The praxis of Orthodox Christian ethics. In numerous and varied ways, the ethical tradition of Eastern Orthodoxy has provided guidance for the practical living of the faith for believers throughout the centuries. The scriptures all include concrete directives for the living of the Christian life. The writings of the fathers of the church are replete with practical enjoinders that were both sought and offered with the full sense of the appropriateness of such an exercise. Both canon law and the spiritual disciplines surrounding the sacrament of Holy Confession include such reference to the praxis of the Christian life. Yet, this guidance is not understood as legalism*. Moral rules and laws are rather understood as shorthand ways of saying that such and such behavior or such and such attitudes either fit and are appropriate to the ethos of growth in the image and likeness of God toward Theosis (prescriptions) or they do not (proscriptions). Yet the commandments are always treated seriously and with great respect, as the means by which the tradition of faith has chiefly embodied its ethical teaching. But they are not treated as absolutes and as rigid legalisms. A case in point is the Eastern Christian doctrine of *economia* (*oikonomia*). "Economy" is practiced when a rule is consciously not applied in a given circumstance when it is judged that the results of such application would, in fact, not embody or realize the growth in the image and likeness of God toward Theosis. However, the exercise of Economy in a given situation is not perceived as creating a precedent for future application. In the next similar circumstance, the rule will again be applied with its full force and without reference to the previous exercise of Economy. Needless to say, only proper authority may exercise Economy (in most cases a bishop, a synod, or a spiritual father).

There is no accepted and universal pattern for the formulation of the norms of Eastern Orthodox ethical praxis. Often, they are articulated after the fashion of the NT in reference to occasional situations, or as broad generalities. Sometimes they are the fruits of deep meditation (e.g., the *Philokalia*). Frequently, these moral directives are given as the result of questions asked by the faithful, such as the so-called longer and shorter *Rules of Basil.* An ancient tradition that embodies the rules of behavior for the guidance of *pneumatichoi,* i.e., spiritual father confessors, in the *exomologetaria* (confessors' handbooks) also serves this purpose.

In the modern tradition of Eastern Orthodox ethics, it is frequent that the praxis of the church's ethical teaching is included in a second or "practical" part. The most common, though by no means exclusive, approach is to delineate the praxis of Eastern Orthodox ethics in reference to the "other" with whom we are in communion, i.e., God, neighbor, and self.

Concern for the neighbor is not limited to interpersonal relations. It also includes concern for nature and for the basic institutions of life, such as family, state, and church. As these reach farther and farther into the society and world which is "not church," the church looks for a model for society which is coherent with its basic Trinitarian orientation. It finds this model in the concept of the kingdom of God. The spheres of Orthodox Christian ethics, therefore, encompass the personal, the ecclesial, and the broadly social.

S. S. Harakas, *Contemporary Moral Issues Facing the Orthodox Christian,* 1982; and *Toward Transfigured Life: The "Theoria" of Orthodox Christian Ethics,* 1983.

STANLEY SAMUEL HARAKAS

Ecclesiology and Ethics

The term "ecclesiology" first appeared in the 19th century in studies of the architectural forms and decor appropriate in the structure of church buildings. However, that question was quickly recognized as dependent on both theological and practical questions as to what the nature, purpose, patterns of authority and participation, boundaries and central values of the Christian community, the *ecclesia,* the company of believers, ought to be. Thus, the term "ecclesiology" was applied to the study of doctrines of the church, particularly as those doctrines take practical shape in institutional life. Wherever these studies turn to normative implications for establishing patterns of "right and good" behavior or structure for human community, ecclesiology is directly linked to ethics.

Nearly all theological studies of the organized Christian community acknowledge that the foundation of the church's existence is a mystery, a gift of grace. While familial, economic, political, cultural, and a number of other social institutions can be understood to be grounded, at least in part, on the needs or desires of humanity and society (*see* **Institution**), the community of faith cannot be so explained. Theological expositions of the foundations of the ecclesia thus focus on the interpretation of key images and symbols which attempt to identify the character of that grace-full mystery: body of Christ, covenant, communion of saints, people of God, temple of the Holy Spirit, etc. To be sure, an ecclesia is also an earthly institution, and even the most abstruse spiritual reflection on these symbols must sooner or later identify the "marks" of where these are truly present in the world. For early church leaders, and for many today, these marks are apostolicity, catholicity, unity, sacramentality, and obedience to the proper clergy in decisive matters of faith and morals. For the Reformation churches, the marks most often accented are "the gospel rightly preached and the sacraments rightly administered." Sectarian groups often focus on the marks of personal regeneration and righteous living. And throughout the long history of disputes on these matters, the water is widely muddied by ecclesiasticism—the attempt to prove that "our" church polity derives directly from the intentions of Jesus while everyone else's is tainted by nefarious pretenses of humanity's greed for power and authority.

The rich meanings implicit in these symbols and their marks have been spelled out by a range of modern scholars. Paul Minear, for example, systematically explicates the dominant ecclesial images that can be found in scripture; F. W. Dillistone lays out the metaphysical, anthropological, and organizational assumptions of the "organic" as compared and contrasted with the "societal" symbols of the Anglo-Catholic and Reformed traditions; and A. Dulles has recently analyzed the eight competing models of the church that overlap in Catholic and some Protestant ecumenical understandings. These and other theologians have been clear that each of the understandings of the church has direct implications for the ways in which normative authority is to be understood and structured in the community of faith and how that community is to relate to the society in which it finds itself.

However important these treatments are for Christian ethics, the mainstream of ethical reflection on ecclesiology has been shaped by two other developments: One derives from pioneering work in the sociology of religion and ethics in the traditions of Max Weber and, especially, Ernst Troeltsch as carried on in America (especially) by students of Troeltsch: H. R. Niebuhr, J. L. Adams, J. Bennett, and W. G. Muelder, and their students. The other is the development of ecumenical structures in federations and councils of churches around the world.

Troeltsch and Weber argued that in the history of Christianity, two essential types of ecclesial organization had developed: the church* type and the sect* type. These are analytically derived constructs which serve as genus categories for the two predominant ways in which primary religious concerns can be organized and institutionalized in social and ethical life. In Christian history, each has many species, and there are numerous mixtures as well as inevitable influence from both the natural requirements of worldly life and the specific historical conditions in which the ecclesia finds itself. Each is marked by a coherent body of social attitudes and teachings about the organization of authority in the community of faith, and about the Christian's obligations in society. Indeed, each develops a distinctive way of legitimating or ignoring, reforming or passively accepting the ethical authority of civilization's structures and institutions. For this distinction, Troeltsch and Weber are justly famous.

But another level of their work is of equal import and less often noted: The main forms of the Christian ecclesia in the past (the Catholic and the Calvinist) provided a core "religious social philosophy" by which Western civilizations found integrity and direction, and they did so by integrating the "highest" religious principles with the "base" demands of social existence into a guiding normative polity. Ecclesiology as polity is the center point at which theology and sociology join, and it is only at this juncture that profound and durable social teachings can give guidance to independent groups or to whole civilizations. (The "sects" are most concerned about the former, the "churches" about the latter.) Both Troeltsch and Weber express skepticism as to whether a fresh and compelling new synthesis can be developed, since old Catholicism and Calvinism have faded in influence. The reasons have to do with a simultaneous crisis of faith since the Enlightenment and the complexity of modern society since industrialization and massive urbanization, of which the fragmentation of the church is partly cause, partly effect, and partly symptom. Nevertheless, their work demonstrates that no ecclesial theory and hence no "Christian social philosophy" can be constructed simply on the basis of theological and religious elements alone; it is always an amalgam of religious, theological, and ethical first principles *in conjunction with* the intellectual, social, political, economic, and cultural resources present in the historical environment. Indeed, just as the building of cathedrals and chapels depends on the governing designs and ideals of the architects and engineers, it also depends on the kinds and qualities of building materials available and on the skills of ordinary craftsmen. Ecclesiology as normative social theory, i.e., as the attempt to incarnate in the real, historical world the kinds and qualities of worship (piety), human relations (polity), and programmatic actions (policies) which God wants of believers and for humanity, inevitably demands ever-new synthesis. Ecclesiology thus becomes the study of the dynamic and constantly transforming points of selective affinity, normatively ordered, between changing perceptions of the first principles of theology and religious ethics, on the one hand, and changing material conditions in civilization on the other. In the Troeltschian tradition, particularly, we find a historical-sociological-theological-ethical argument that the ecclesia is the incarnate moral soul of civilization and that its proper science, ecclesiology, is the fundamental clue to the social ethics of civilization.

As an example of those who have built their work on this tradition, one could cite the early works of H. R. Niebuhr. He showed, in one important study, the social influences on the formation of "denominations" derived from either "churches" or "sects" under specific social-economic pressures (1929). In another, he discusses the ways in which the symbol "Kingdom of God" has been variously interpreted in America to produce distinctive attitudes toward social and cultural materials to produce changing ecclesial and social-ethical structures (1937). And in a third, he traced the predominant logics by which the theological-ethical principles (summarized by the word "Christ") could be related to sociopolitical and intellectual ones ("culture") (1951). James Luther Adams, to mention another example, took the concerns of Troeltsch, as modified by Paul Tillich's theology of culture and "liberal" theories of democracy, in directions entailing the formation of modern pluralistic societies wherein "secular ecclesia," called "voluntary associations"* and "professional organizations," have been decisive for modern pluralistic societies (see **Pluralism**). And John Bennett took Reinhold Niebuhr's "Christian realism*" into ecumenical ecclesial forums with special focus on political and economic ideology, while W. G. Muelder and his students have attempted to connect philosophical studies of natural law to theological ethics, and the results with historical and contemporary social analysis, to find a new synthesis of "Christian personalism*" and "democratic socialism*."

The work of these Troeltschians is paralleled by that of a number of other significant ethicists who struggle with the formation of communities of commitment on the basis of theological rootage and sociopolitical involvement, in order to find means of constructing what Troeltsch and Weber feared could not be easily constructed—a new ecclesially based Christian social philosophy faithful to biblical Christianity and directly pertinent to the guidance and reform of civilization*. Their efforts are paralleled by Catholic figures from John Courtney Murray and Jacques Maritain to find an ecclesially sound "public philosophy." The history of the "social encyclicals" from the 1890s to the present gave wider impetus to other Catholic efforts (see **Official Roman Catholic Social Teaching**). Indeed, the main core of Christian social ethics as a discipline taught in Christian seminaries is rooted more in these quests than in any other single factor, and the most important professional society of working ethicists in North America, the Society of Christian Ethics, has had this concern at the center of its formation.

At the present time, at least one major debate rages in regard to ecclesiology and ethics in this tradition. If the center point of ecclesiology is "right order" or "polity," formed on the basis of theology and sociology, and if polity is inevitably influenced by both the demands of "pure" piety and the realistic cognizance of social dynamics, as it appears in "policy," which of the two influences should predominate in the formation of ecclesial polity—piety or policy? Is it the "being" of the church as a worshiping community that should shape polity? Is the priestly or "spiritual" impulse of the religious and ethical life of prime importance so that all patterns of organizational polity (and the policies entailed) established on earth by the people of God should follow from that which can sustain that core? Or is it the case that God has called the faithful together to accomplish godly purposes in the world? That is, should the ecclesia be conceived essentially as a people with a mission, a task, a direction of prophetic action, in short, a policy, so that the patterns of polity (and the forms of piety required to sustain motivation and solidarity for the task) should be so arranged to contribute to the fulfillment of these possibilities? The question can be put in other terms: is the normative order for church (and hence as a model for society) to be ontologically or functionally defined? Ought the church to be governed by deontological principles of righteousness derived from true piety or by teleological principles of purposes, ends, and objectives derived by the discernment of God's "policies"? Paul Ramsey has argued for the former (1967); Paul Lehmann for the latter (1963). Contemporary neo-evangelicals and liberationists have extended and further polarized the problems (see **Evangelical Ethics; Liberation Theology**).

And, of course, this question has wideranging implications for the understanding of the relationships of the Christian churches to other religions and movements. Can Christians in Hindu, Buddhist, Islamic, or tribal contexts utilize the authentic patterns of piety and ethics of those traditions to form entirely new polities for the ecclesia? And can Christians engaged in a social mission which they hold to be godly form solidarity structures with secular and even antireligious movements which are working for the same historical ends? In either case, is the result a true ecclesia? In posing the questions in these terms, we recognize some of the complexities of dealing with ecclesiology and ethics in our time. Every dimension of theological-ethical discourse and of sociocultural analysis must be identified, analyzed, and evaluated in a world where each level is vastly pluralized and complicated.

All of the above questions have been taken up in the 20th century by the second most important development in ecclesiology and ethics—the ecumenical movement*. After several centuries of fragmentation of the church by the rise of increased numbers of sects, denominations, nation-based "churches," and indigenous churches in decolonialized lands, the 20th century has seen a dramatic rise in the formation of ecumenical bodies. In nearly every land, federations or councils of churches exist. And everywhere one finds efforts to overcome previous divisions between religious groups— "united" and "uniting" churches, mergers, consultations on church union, and "family" reunions (World Alliance of Reformed Churches [Presbyterian and Congregational], Lutheran World Federation, etc.). Not only those communions rooted in the Reformation are joined in the councils of churches, but Roman Catholicism has both established new connections with previously separated bodies and, since Vatican Council II, engaged in an enormous range of interfaith and interreligious consultations. Further, denominations deriving from evangelical sects have formed national and international associations which raise comparable issues.

What is at stake for ecclesiology and ethics in these dramatic developments is that a trajectory of "conciliary denominationalism"— the federated linkage of religious bodies meeting as equals—is understood to be the normative pattern for ecclesial polity and is set for the future. The ancient tradition of the church councils which established key theological doctrines is being retrieved and reestablished on a new ground of participatory, pluralistic, representative, democratically ordered catholicity. These councils attempt to clarify matters of piety as they bear on polity (e.g., the ecumenical "Lima agreements" on baptism, eucharist, and ministry), and on prophetic policies as they demand modification of polity (e.g., the Commission on Racism or the Commission on Women and Men in the Church). None of these developments is without difficulty, severe criticism, and resistance, but the suggestions of a new Christian social philosophy can be discerned in the agendas and documents of these new ecclesial efforts.

Not clear in many of these developments, however, are the two things that are ultimately required for a profound and durable new synthesis: compelling clarifications of the guiding theological-ethical principles, properly informed, as they must be to remain authentically Christian, by clear warrants from scripture, tradition, reason, and experience; and clarity in regard to the analysis of the modern world with all its intricate relationships, structures, institutions, tensions, confrontations, and competing philosophical modes of thought between and within the plethora of civilizations now having to live in a shrinking world. The task of addressing these issues, partly begun in ecumenical debates about human rights, faith and science, and peace priorities, remains a primary part of the agenda of religious social ethics for the future. In this effort, ethicists will have to be in constant dialogue with, on the one hand, those theologians who continue to focus on the core symbols and marks of the ecclesia, and, on the other, with social analyists and theorists of complex civilizations, constantly attempting to find those points of "compromise," in the sense of "co-promise," for normative ordering of life in, for, and with the whole people of God.

See **Church and State.**

J. L. Adams, *On Being Human Religiously,* 1976; J. A. Bassett, *The New England Way and Vatican II,* 1981; P. Bock, *In Search of a Responsible World Society,* 1974; F. W. Dillistone, *The Structure of the Divine Society,* 1951; A. Dulles, *Models of the Church,* 1981; P. M. Harrison, *Authority and Power in the Free Church Tradition,* 1959; D. Hollenbach, *Claims in Conflict,* 1979; P. Minear, *Images*

of the Church in the New Testament, 1960; R.
J. Mouw, *Called to Holy Worldliness,* 1980;
National Council of Churches, *The Ecclesiological Significance of Councils of Churches,*
1963; H. R. Niebuhr, *The Social Sources of
Denominationalism,* 1929; *The Kingdom of
God in America,* 1937; and *Christ and Culture,* 1951; M. L. Stackhouse, *Creeds, Culture and Human Rights,* 1984; and *Ethics
and the Urban Ethos,* 1973; E. Troeltsch, *The
Social Teaching of the Christian Churches*
(1912), 2 vols., ET 1931; E. L. Underkoefler
and A. Harsanyi, *The Unity We Seek,* 1977;
M. Weber, *Economy and Society* (1922,
²1925), ET 1968, vol. 2.

MAX L. STACKHOUSE

Ecology *see* **Energy; Environmental Ethics; Future Generations, Obligations to;
Technology**

Economic Development

The theory and practice of the major Protestant churches with respect to economic development can be divided into three periods:
the missionary period up to the early 1960s;
the period between the World Council of
Churches Assemblies at Uppsala and Nairobi
(i.e., 1968–1975); and the period since the
Nairobi Assembly. These three periods could
conveniently be given the labels of naive
pragmatism, developmentalism, and structuralism.

In the period of naive pragmatism, the
churches sought to raise the standard of living of actual or potential members by providing education, health care, agricultural improvement schemes, and access to credit. At
its worst, the church acted as no more than
the agent of the state, but more frequently the
relations between church and state were ambiguous and conflictual. Although church
schools, for example, played a major role in
providing the colonial power (*see* **Colonialism**) with appropriately trained workers,
they also provided nascent nationalism* with
its leadership. The churches played a significant role in introducing new cash crops—
e.g., cotton to Uganda, cocoa to Ghana—but
they were also early critics of labor conditions in the mines of central Africa, and of
land apportionment in the settler colonies.
These critical voices tended to be in a minority, however, and the dominant theme was a
paternalistic concern to raise the living standards of the indigenous population in ways

and at a pace that were consistent with the
interests of the colonial powers.

In the postcolonial period the churches,
largely led by the Continental Roman Catholics, came to see economic development as an
important part of the incarnation of the gospel. This enthusiasm came from a number of
sources: postcolonial guilt, rising awareness
of international income disparities, the supposed need to demonstrate the "relevance" of
the gospel to an increasingly secular society,
and the need to redefine a role for the metropolitan church in the former colonies.

The theological understanding of enthusiasm for economic development lagged far behind the elaboration of instruments designed
to secure development. Common theological
themes were Pauline body imagery, love, and
thanksgiving. These were never successfully
integrated into a coherent framework that
transcended a biblicist sympathy with the lot
of global neighbors.

By contrast, institutional development was
rapid and widespread. The 1960s saw most
churches developing overseas service agencies, on either a denominational or an ecumenical basis. Some, particularly in the USA,
Germany, and Sweden, became significant
channels for the disbursement of government
development assistance, and/or food aid.
While this permitted the rapid growth of
these institutions, and their acquisition of a
high level of professional expertise, it stored
up largely unresolved problems for a later
period.

By 1970 developmentalism was under severe attack in both secular and ecclesiastical
circles. The failure of the UN Development
Decade, declining political commitment in
the industrialized countries, a strong suspicion (not amenable to empirical testing because of lack of data) that the numbers of
persons in absolute poverty were increasing
rather than diminishing, and a rediscovery of
the centrality of justice, mercy, and righteousness in biblical ethics all combined to
change the character of the development debate.

It is significant that the major intellectual
impetus for this change came from the developing world itself—from the Philippines,
from the small Christian communities of
South Asia, and supremely from Latin
America. The nodal expression of this new
thinking came from the conference of the
Roman Catholic bishops of Latin America at

Medellín in 1968. It was reflected in different vocabularies but the same substance in the WCC Assembly in Nairobi in 1975. The key to this style of thinking was the notion of liberation from oppressive and exploitative forces, of which the story of Exodus was seen as *the* biblical paradigm. Power* thus became a central issue, and its obverse, the powerlessness of the poor, was subjected to intensive theological reflection. "Participation" was seen as the programmatic embodiment of this concern, though it is arguable that this has not yet progressed beyond the status of a populist slogan.

The centrality of liberation made inevitable a reassessment of Marxist critiques of capitalism*. Although exploitation continued to be a theme of critics of developmentalism, theologians were not equipped to subject Marxian theories of value, on which notions of exploitation logically depend, to serious critique. While it would be an exaggeration to say that Christians were discovering classical Marxism at a time when Marxists were decreasingly confident of its logical foundation, it is nonetheless true that much Christian thinking in the late 1970s and early 1980s used the language of Marxian analysis, somewhat incautiously (*see* **Marxist Ethics**).

In this way structuralism gave a new urgency to development education, conceived as the process of raising the critical consciousness of the community, and particularly the Christian community, to issues of justice and impoverishment.

Insofar as this process has been taken seriously by the churches and conscientiously implemented—and it would be misleading to exaggerate the extent to which this has happened—it has tended to be accompanied both by a more overtly theological appreciation of the structural position of the poor in present-day society and in the development of biblical ethics, and by a deepening awareness of the need to reintegrate practice, reflection, and spirituality.

See **Colonialism; Ecumenical Movement; Hunger, World; Imperialism; International Order; Liberation Theology; Oppression; Poverty; Race Relations.**

CHARLES ELLIOTT

Ecumenical Movement, Ethics in the

The ecumenical movement, expressed in the 20th century by a growing web of contacts among Christians which have produced the World Council of Churches, regional councils in Asia, Europe, and Africa, structures of cooperation between Protestant, Orthodox, and Roman Catholic churches, and countless less formal forms of fellowship, is difficult to separate into its biblical, theological, and ethical components. Its activities have been on the action-research model, constantly seeking the form of the church's unity, mission, and social responsibility by reflection on, and renewal of, its life and practice. There are, however, two distinguishable strands of ecumenical work with special significance for the student of ethics. They arise separately out of the life and mission of the churches, and are today being woven together into what might be called a common ecumenical missionary ethical sense of church and world in the context of God's grace, judgment, and calling.

A. *Mission.* The first ecumenical strand of ethical significance is the effort of the churches to understand their missionary task through the great World Mission Conferences in Edinburgh (1910), Jerusalem (1928), Madras (1938), Whitby (1947), Willingen (1952), Ghana (1958), Mexico (1962), Bangkok (1972), and Melbourne (1980), the International Missionary Council and its successor the Commission on World Mission and Evangelism of the WCC, and the whole spiritual-intellectual ferment to which the foreign missionary enterprise of the past two centuries has given rise. The central ethical issue in all of these has been the faithfulness of a missionary church in the form of its life to the gospel it seeks to make known in a non-Christian society, be that society permeated by another religion or a form of secularized Christendom. Self-critical repentance and the urgency of proclamation stand in inevitable tension here. The experience of the churches in ecumenical mission during the 20th century has been an ever-deeper discovery of each of these poles and the dynamics of their interaction.

Awareness of this interaction was present in some form from the beginning. John R. Mott, setting forth for the Student Volunteer Movement his call for *The Evangelization of the World in This Generation* (1900), found the greatest hindrances to this goal in the "secularized, self-centered" conformity of the home church itself to its own society. The point was underlined in the Edinburgh Conference of 1910, where the success of the urgent missionary task was linked continually with the renewal of the sending churches and the reform of unchristian aspects of European and American society, not least its political imperialism and rapacious trade relations with non-Christian lands. The Jerusalem Conference in 1928 acknowledged explicitly that Christianity was not wholly accepted in the Western world, and proclaimed the missionary task as a worldwide one, in which every nation's "pride of national heritage or religious tradition" would be humbled before Christ. The burden of its deliberations concerned the proper appreciation of non-Christian systems of life and thought, both religious and secularist, in order to bring the gospel to them as fulfillment, not destruction, of their proper values.

In the years since, two ethical issues have dominated ecumenical missions, sometimes distinct, sometimes in close and confused mixture.

1. Relation to non-Christian religions and cultures. What is the relation of the Christian message in the wholeness of its claim and promise over human life to the religion and culture of non-Christian peoples? William Ernest Hocking, under whose direction *Rethinking Missions: A Laymen's Inquiry After 100 Years* was produced in 1932, suggested that the exclusive claim of Christ over the life of the world is itself an expression of Christian pride and domination. His alternative was nonevangelistic forms of service and the pursuit of ultimate truth with and through all religions. It was a broadly popular point of view among Hindu and some Christian scholars at the time. In contrast, Hendrik Kraemer argued, in *The Christian Message in a Non-Christian World* (1937), that human religion itself is a double phenomenon, partly human recognition of and reaching for God and partly the effort to make human interests, dreams, and cultural ideals divine in defiance of God. The Christian message is about historical events in which God reveals his judgment on all religions, including the religious habits and hopes of Christians, and subjects living people to the saving claim of Christ in the whole of their lives and cultures. Kraemer's point of view was the central issue, which remained unresolved, of the World Mission Conference at Tambaram near Madras in 1938.

2. Relation to political and social revolution. The question that dominated missions after World War II was still more radical. Political and social revolution*, driven by rising nationalism*, strongly influenced by Marxist ideology (*see* **Marxist Ethics**) though often nourished by the biblical vision of the new humanity in Christ, the righteousness of God, and the hope of his kingdom which Christian missions had brought, faced the church in every part of the world with the question of its own integrity as a witness to the power of God alone, not to the influence of Western culture or the technological-economic power of European-American society. In one country after another indigenous leadership took over from missionaries in the church, often at the cost of an internal struggle or a political upheaval. But this was only the first step, for an aggressive non-Christian nation then challenged the church to repent of its past association with imperialism* and to justify its continuing reason for existence, in the midst of the struggle for independence and nation-building. The early meetings of the East Asia Christian Conference and later of the All Africa Conference of Churches, the first regional ecumenical church associations, were primarily concerned to discover the form of the mission of Christ to this world of revolutionary change, wrestling with its problems and sharing while transforming its hopes and dreams. The most substantial literature in this field was produced in India by the Christian Institute for the Study of Religion and Society, by its directors M. M. Thomas and P. D. Devanandan, and by J. Lesslie Newbigin.

The issue, however, has its counterpart in the world that once was Christendom, where churches have become identified with some social classes or structures and have alienated others. Pre–World War II pioneers in this discovery were a Scottish Presbyterian, George MacLeod, from whose work in the slums of Glasgow the Iona Community arose, and a French Roman Catholic, Henri Godin, the first of the worker-priests of Paris. After the war such urban and industrial missions multiplied as thousands of evangelists made identification with some estranged and needy social group and/or the formation of experimental Christian communities the starting point for rediscovering the Christian message and for challenging and renewing the church. This ferment was focused and cultivated by the WCC's Department on Studies in Evangelism under the successive leadership of J. C. Hoekendijk, D. T. Niles, H. J. Margull, and W. Hollenweger and by the Department on the Laity under H.-R. Weber. Their writings, and the publications of these departments, are the best guide to the study of it.

Meanwhile in Eastern Europe the same question was posed in a third milieu. Whole nations of traditionally Christian culture fell, after the war, under Communist domination. Churches, used to centuries of power and prestige, were forced to rediscover their mission when faced with the moral attack of Marxist ideology on their association with the injustices of past regimes, and when subjected to the repression of Communist power, which made it costly and sometimes dangerous to be an active Christian in society. Temptations were of two kinds: to idealize and live from the past while withdrawing in hate from responsibility for the present; or to conform completely to Communist policy, reserving only the privilege of an "ideological difference" on religion. Between these alternatives, both widely adopted among Eastern European Christians, church leaders both Protestant and Catholic have tried to work out a theology and practice of evangelical community over against the mass organizations of the Party and the state, of critical solidarity with the aims of a socialist society, and of free witness in a distinctively Christian ethic to the justice of God over against the ideologies of East and West. Most of this work has been done in the languages of the countries involved, often privately reproduced and circulated, though some of it has appeared in English in the writings of J. L. Hromadka of Czechoslovakia and Johannes Hamel of East Germany, in the Hungarian Church Press, and in publications of the WCC and the Lutheran World Federation.

In the period since 1961 the two issues described above have increasingly intertwined in the mission of the church. A Dutch missiologist, Arend van Leeuwen, set the stage with a sweeping study (*Christianity in World History*, 1964), showing how the history and the message of the Bible have worked to historicize, secularize, and revolutionize human society and to challenge all "ontocratic" systems including the cosmic mythology of ancient Babylon, the rational philosophy of the Greeks, and the modern forms of religious culture whether Hindu, Buddhist, Muslim, or Christian. Christianity, van Leeuwen maintained, is in a constant struggle with its own temptation to become another sacred system of thought, worship, and organization, but continually it is revolutionized by the living word of God within it. The church and Christian society are always being reformed and secularized by this word, and set on the path of history with a gospel of transforming hope. This is the real dynamic behind the missionary movement in our time. It is also, in a distorted form, the dynamic behind Western technological, economic, and political expansion bringing both a promise and a new form of oppression to the rest of the world. Therefore the missionary encounter, he says, must redeem the worldwide technological society from its demonic distortions of right and left with the biblical gospel of sober hope. All human religions and cultures are being caught up in, and relativized by, this history.

Whatever the truth of van Leeuwen's basic thesis, he was mistaken in one prediction. Non-Christian religions, often energized and goaded by the historical dynamic he described, have again become major actors in the historical drama. Absorbing from Christianity while fighting it, they have often developed enough sense of history and ethics to become vehicles of personal faith for many modern people, and of national hope and self-assertion for many countries in a technologically developing world. As a result, Christian encounter with these religions has taken new forms: the discernment of Christ, acknowledged or hidden, in the dynamics of other religions; the discovery of biblical themes also in the history of non-Christian peoples; and dialogue with non-Christian faiths not so much about God and cosmology as about man and woman, about social and personal ethics, and about hope in history. A few examples among many of this new encounter are M. M. Thomas, *The Acknowledged Christ of the Indian Renaissance* (1970); *Man in the Universe of Faiths* (1975); C.-S. Song, *Third-Eye Theology* (1979); and the reports edited by S. J. Samartha of interreligious dialogues sponsored by the WCC.

Nevertheless van Leeuwen's theme has also persisted. The Communist transformation of China, the technological modernization of Japan, and the waning of traditional religious culture in Korea and many parts of Africa are secularizing facts too great to be ignored. For M. M. Thomas and many other

Christians in India, secularism* is a saving grace and secular ideologies an important factor in an overheated religious environment (*The Secular Ideologies of India and the Secular Meaning of Christ,* 1976). Liberation theology*, developed in largely Christian Latin America, has influenced also the ethics of mission in Asia and Africa, with its emphasis primarily on imperialism, class conflict, and solidarity with the poor as the arena of Christian engagement. The "base communities" of Latin American Christians have their ecumenical extension in the projects of Urban Rural Mission, an agency of the WCC concerned with the support of groups everywhere in the world that are struggling against oppressive powers in their own localities for control of their own lives (Leon Howell, *People Are the Subject,* 1980).

The diversity of this search for the form of witness and service in the church's mission increases every year as new participants from new cultures and social conditions join it. Nevertheless a few common features of it can be named.

(*a*) It is Christocentric. The original missionary motive to make Christ known takes the modern form of seeking the form of Christ in every culture and society as the true reality of that society. The old debate about the relation of Jesus to founders of other religions has been largely forgotten. Proclamation of Christ the Savior of the world is the goal of the search in almost all its expressions.

(*b*) It takes its sense of history from the biblical story and seeks to understand the suffering and hope of today's world from that source. No longer is it seriously argued that the religious history of some other culture be substituted for the OT; rather the effort now is to understand that history in the light of the story of the covenant people of God.

(*c*) Its central communal concept is "people." The term is understood in various ways: sometimes as a particular culture, sharing a language, a history, and a politico-social organization; sometimes as a class thrown together and formed by poverty and exploitation; sometimes in a broad sense as all who are seeking liberation and true humanity together. The relation of this concept to the people of God in the church is often unclear, perhaps because the experience of church is so fundamental that it is taken for granted, perhaps because church has meant for some

an alien institution. In any case the ecclesiology of mission, the social form of the body of Christ bringing judgment and redemption to every people, remains to be worked out.

(*d*) Liberation, or attaining full humanity, is its dominant expression of the content and goal of Christian life. Divine salvation is continuous with the human struggle for freedom and justice. This is one part of the gospel, but it underplays the other part: divine judgment on human pride and power, the forgiveness of sins, and the sanctification of the sinner by grace alone. Once again the experience of this grace is in the church on the mission frontier, in the humility and the openness of its life and community. An ethic of the full Christian life needs to be built upon it.

B *Social thought and action.* The second ecumenical strand of ethical significance is that represented by the Universal Christian Conference on Life and Work through its conferences at Stockholm in 1925 and Oxford in 1937, and since the formation of the WCC, in its Department on Church and Society, and the studies and statements that World Council Assemblies and other conferences have produced. In this ecumenical study and action nearly all the significant lines of Christian social thought and action in recent generations have come together. The Stockholm Conference was conceived, following five years of preparatory study, in the spirit of the social gospel, but already in its opening session this antitheological optimism was challenged. The Oxford Conference, with its seven preparatory volumes and forty-seven contributors, brought into conversation leading representatives of social thought in every branch of Christendom. Its report remains to this day the most comprehensive ecumenical statement on problems of church and society ever produced, covering the responsibility of the church in relation to (1) other human communities of nation and race; (2) the function, authority, and limits of the state; (3) the economic order and its reform; (4) public and private education; (5) war, peace, and the international order; and (6) the general problem of social order.

Between Oxford and the First Assembly of the WCC at Amsterdam in 1948 intervened the shattering experience of the Second World War. Ecumenical social thought turned naturally therefore to diagnosis of the dynamics of a world that had proved uncontrollable by the best of Christian principles and to the task of the church's witness and obedience in that world. The problem, as Amsterdam understood it, was to find ways of creative living for "little men in big societies" (J. H. Oldham), to plan for personal responsibility and community life in a world increasingly dominated by large aggregations of power having a momentum of their own. This was the context of the concept of the "responsible society," i.e., "one where freedom is the freedom of men who acknowledge responsibility to justice and public order, and where those who hold political authority or economic power are responsible for its exercise to God and to the people whose welfare is affected by it" (Amsterdam Report, Section III, p. 200).

On the basis of this understanding, Amsterdam condemned both communism* and laissez-faire* capitalism* and initiated a period of search for those forms of balance between freedom and planning in the economic order, efficient production and equitable distribution of goods, effective centralization of political power, and constitutional limits in the interest of free personal relations and local responsibility, which lasted through and after the WCC's Second Assembly at Evanston in 1954. Section III of the Evanston Report is an effort to explore this balance pragmatically in the midst of the powers and pressures of (1) Western technologically developed society, (2) Communist-dominated areas, and (3) the social revolution in Asia, Africa, and Latin America.

It has proved impossible since, however (as it was at Evanston), to hold these three areas together with one analysis and social program. In 1956, therefore, the WCC initiated a study of Christian responsibility in countries undergoing rapid social change. The term was understood to apply not to the rapid changes in relatively stable societies such as Europe or North America, but to those nations where the whole structure of political, social, and economic order is in upheaval. This study was diverse and detailed. Its primary purpose was to stimulate the churches on the spot to examine their own ministry to their changing world. Most of its results were published locally or in occasional papers by the Department on Church and Society in Geneva. Some common findings were drawn together, however, in P. Abrecht's *The Churches in Rapid Social Change* and in an international conference in Thessalonika, Greece, in 1959. Among the emphases of these reports were: (1) a more positive, hopeful attitude toward centrally planned technology and industrialization than in the West, despite the human costs involved; (2) an affirmation of nationalism as a creative force, despite the moral dangers of political idolatry, and of nation-building as a basic Christian responsibility; and (3) an urgently future-oriented ethic, prepared in principle to take chances with the unknown consequences of radical change rather than rest with known but unpromising securities.

Since the WCC's Third Assembly at New Delhi in 1961, worldwide problems have again come into focus. The third World Conference on Church and Society at Geneva, 1966, was in every way broader than the second at Oxford nearly thirty years before. Its four preparatory volumes, with eighty-four contributors from every part of the world and, for the first time, full Roman Catholic and Orthodox as well as Protestant and secular participation, give a good picture of its scope. *Christian Social Ethics in a Changing World* (ed. J. C. Bennett, 1966) raises the basic issues of theology in revolution, biblical bases of ethics, responsible society, and natural law vs. contextual ethics which underlay the whole conference. *Economic Growth in World Perspective* (ed. Denys Munby, 1966) provided the material for a special section on the ethics of technological change in developed societies, special problems of developing countries, and world economic relations. *Responsible Government in a Revolutionary Age* (ed. Z. K. Matthews, 1966) underlay two section reports on the nature and function of the state and the structures of international cooperation. *Man in Community* (ed. E. de Vries, 1966) dealt with the basic problems of ideology*, secularization*, cultural and ethnic tension, and the basis of human community. Its insights permeated the report as a whole.

Geneva 1966 was a watershed in ecumenical ethics in three respects. First, it led to a period of direct cooperation between the WCC and the Vatican in a program on Society, Development, and Peace (SODEPAX). Parallel strong statements were made by Pope Paul VI in 1967 (*Populorum Progressio*) and by the Fourth Assembly of the WCC in 1968 (Uppsala Report, Section III) about the urgency of world economic development, the evil of poverty, the danger of violence, and the moral demand on wealthier nations to put their resources at the service of human life for the poor. For nearly a decade these were implemented by SODEPAX in a series of exploratory conferences, in the coordination of policy by Catholic and WCC world service and development agencies, and in regional cooperative groups throughout the world. Second, Geneva 1966 brought together, for the first time in history on a world scale, a predominance of ethically concerned Christian laity, trained in their own professions or academic disciplines, to place the expertise of these spheres of life and thought at the service of the responsible social witness of the church. Theology was no longer the unifying universe of discourse; its place was taken by intense dialogue between the insights and problems of various human sciences, and of various fields of work in the common life. This dialogue has grown throughout recent years to include natural scientists, industrial technicians, and an ever-wider circle of concerned citizens in the WCC program on faith, science, and the human future. Third, Geneva 1966 confronted this whole dialogue among ethically concerned professionals with the revolutionary demands and politics of those who saw themselves as excluded from the process and victimized by it. To some extent this was a confrontation between the First World and the Third World, between developed industrial societies and underdeveloped nations, though not entirely, because some of the most articulate revolutionary spokesmen were Americans or Europeans, and leaders from the Third World took part fully in the moral-professional discussion. To some extent it was an ideological debate between Christians tempted by opposing forms of humanism: technological rationalist on one side and revolutionary idealist on the other.

In any case this confrontation led, in ensuing years, to a profound bifurcation of ethical method in the ecumenical movement, which continues to the present day. The traditional method, dating from the earliest years of modern ecumenicity, has been dialogical, sometimes confrontational, in the context of a common commitment to Christ and the church. Persons are brought into this dialogue from radically different, sometimes opposing, positions and convictions, churches and social backgrounds; issues are defined, and new truth is sought in the encounter. This truth is then offered as guidance for the churches, but questioned and tested anew in

the lives and actions of Christians and churches themselves. The process is continuous. It is a story of changing and being changed as one's strongest convictions encounter the faith and witness of others in Christ. In recent years it has broadened to include the contributions of morally concerned scientists, politicians, economists, revolutionaries, professionals, and others whose faith is not actively Christian but who respect and want to help the church. It seeks not so much consensus as the best insight available in each time and place about the form of Christian obedience. In extreme cases a church body has suffered ecumenical condemnation—as in the case of the pro-Nazi "German Christians," or, more recently, the pro-apartheid position of the white Dutch Reformed churches in South Africa—and dialogue has been broken off. But this is rare. More usually, critical reflection, even to a demand for repentance, takes place within the forum and under the judgment of a common allegiance.

A new approach to ecumenical action. In the late 1960s this method of ecumenical work came under sharp criticism. Paul Ramsey (*Who Speaks for the Church?* 1967) found it to be pretentious and haphazard, informed by too little research and expertise, and therefore of little guidance to acting professionals in the world's affairs. More vigorous, however, was the attack from the left, which criticized it as an abstract exercise without actual engagement in the social struggle. The ecumenical movement, these critics urged, must move beyond discussion to forms of action. Their plea was heard. In 1970 the WCC organized two new agencies, the Commission on the Churches' Participation in Development (CCPD) and the Program to Combat Racism (PCR) to implement a quite different method. A good overall description of these agencies and of ecumenical ethics from their perspective is Richard D. N. Dickinson, *Poor, Yet Making Many Rich* (1983). They have broken new ground in ecumenical action in several respects. They are designed and equipped to act on behalf of the churches, with church and some secular financial support, in social and political conflicts, sometimes working through local church bodies but often dealing directly with outside forces. In this way they differ from the previous work of the Division of Interchurch Aid, and from other ecumenical agencies primarily concerned with forming the conscience of the churches through theological and ethical reflection in dialogue with the actions of Christians. They are mandated to work for social justice as distinct from service to human need in itself. In this they are distinguished from the relief and aid work traditionally done by churches, and committed to a concept of justice through participation in political and social conflict. They, especially the CCPD, undergird this action with certain social convictions which are their working principles:

(a) Justice is achieved, not by appeals to reason and conscience within a given economic and political system, but by the conflict with the system to bring about structural change. Christian witness requires taking sides therefore with the forces that are working, even violently at times, to bring about this change.

(b) World development requires, not economic growth in itself, but political power changes. Under the direction of wealthy nations and transnational corporations it creates dependency and impoverishment in the Third World, with the connivance of a small Third World elite. Christian witness, therefore, requires the support of movements in the poorer nations for economic self-reliance with goals set by people's participation.

(c) God is at work and Christ is present among the poor of the world, in their struggle against oppressive powers to achieve full humanity. Solidarity with the poor in this struggle is a basic form of Christian existence. Some would say that there is where the church is found. Christian action should therefore take its form from movements of the poor themselves and serve those movements.

(d) The goal of Christian life is liberation of the oppressed, in order that they may become "subjects of their own history," co-creators with God of their own future, and participants in the shaping of their human life. This, rather than forgiving and justifying grace, is the way of divine action in the world (Julio de Santa Ana, *Towards a Church of the Poor*, 1979).

In the method at work here, biblical interpretation, theological understanding, and social analysis all arise out of a particular social experience or position in the social struggle. Those who are outside this experience are invited to identify with it and look at themselves, God, and the world from there.

Criticisms. Popular as it is, however, this method has raised serious problems in the ecumenical movement as a whole. To name a few of them:

(a) How far may a Christian support violence as a means of social change? The first grants of the Program to Combat Racism to southern African liberation movements threw this question into the Central Committee of the WCC. The result was a study on *Violence, Nonviolence and the Struggle for Justice* (1973) conducted by the Office on Church and Society, which involved the range of conviction and practice in Christendom from Mennonite pacifists to African freedom fighters. Though brief, it was a definitive guide, recognizing the pervasiveness of violence—governmental, oppositional, and civil; exploring the legitimacy and the abuse of government power for the common good, and the justice and limits of resistance to unjust power; wrestling with disagreements about the exemplary authority of Jesus for the Christian's responsibility toward human power; probing the positive possibilities of nonviolent action for justice and the limits of violence on which all could agree; and finally, asking probing questions to pacifists and nonpacifists, to supporters of the status quo and of revolution (*see* **Resistance; Revolution**).

(b) Is the model of system change by confrontation and conflict, including the engagement of church agencies on one side of a power struggle, always just, effective, and faithful to the gospel? In practice the CCPD and the PCR have not been as extreme as their theory. CCPD project grants have usually been to national church-sponsored development commissions that in turn have supported self-help projects to improve living conditions in poor local communities. PCR grants, even to African movements engaged in liberation warfare, have been for medical, educational, and relief purposes. Meanwhile, PCR has supported Zimbabwean and Namibian delegates' attendance at international negotiations on the future of these countries, has made studies of racial minorities and grants to church groups working for minority rights in places as diverse as Canada, India, the Philippines, the USA, Sri Lanka, New Zealand, and Japan. Only toward the Republic of South Africa has confrontation sharpened, and in this there is strong support from world public opinion.

(c) Is the community of promise the struggling poor, or is it the people of God who know themselves judged, redeemed, and made new in Christ? Some of the language of this perspective assumes the former, but the poor are seen, not in their own right, but as conscientized by a definition of their condition and their struggle which those who identify with them bring to and elicit from them (see **Conscientization**). Is the self-assertion of the poor, thus made aware, the earthly agent not only of immediate justice but also of true humanity and the salvation of God? Once again the practice of these agencies is more church-centered than the theory. Still the question of the prophetic witness of the church toward all sinful humanity, poor and rich, revolutionary and conservative alike remains.

Studies on the future of humanity. Questions like those listed above cannot be faced in the context of the method that raised them. They bring the activists, when seriously challenged by the church, back into dialogue about their assumptions. This has led to an uneasy but real interaction between them and the other main line of ecumenical ethics in the 1970s and 1980s: the study of "The Future of Humanity in an Age of Science-based Technology" sponsored by the Office on Church and Society. This problem was first posed by ethically concerned scientists themselves in a radical shift from the technological optimism of the previous years. Its range over the following years has included:

(a) A reconsideration of the relation between faith and science in the light of the form and the technological uses of scientific knowledge and Christian ethical concern about the role of science in society (see **Science and Ethics; Technology**).

(b) A new study of the role of nonhuman creation or nature in biblical and theological understanding as a control and guide to technological domination over and manipulation of nature for human purposes. Questions of the ecological integrity of nature in the covenant purpose of God, of the rights of nonhuman creation compared with human rights, of justice to future generations* compared with justice in the present, of preserving the environment versus meeting present human need, and of the harmony of nature and humanity in the promise of God, have been involved here (Thomas Derr, *Ecology and Human Liberation,* 1973). (*See also* **Environmental Ethics.**)

(c) Probing the dynamics of modern technology and its responsibility for directing limited world resources toward justice for all the world's people. The goals, determining powers, and dilemmas of technological planning, the vast imbalance of technological development in the world, appropriate technologies for differing societies and social goals, the waste and pollution of technological processes, resource-conserving technologies, and transfer of technology from the rich to the poor, are among the problems in this sphere.

(d) A new look at the economics of a "just, participatory and sustainable society." This has meant rethinking the goals of life in affluent societies toward less consumption of material goods, curbing the power of the highly developed world to coerce the economies of poorer nations through governmental policies, transnational corporations, international finance, and other means, projecting self-reliant economies in developing countries in accordance with their cultures and social goals, and shepherding the resources of the earth for a sustainable future.

(e) A special concern for the technology of energy production, consumption, and conservation. The largest item on this agenda is, of course, nuclear energy (J. Francis and P. Abrecht, eds., *Facing Up to Nuclear Power,* 1976). Second to it is the effect of various forms of energy use on the environment: air pollution, thermal changes in air and water, the generation of renewable fuel resources, the hope for solar energy, and the like. A third question is conservation of energy in light of the dangers that all mass energy sources pose (see also **Energy**).

(f) Facing the question of the biological manipulation of life, especially human life. The ethics of genetic research and of genetic engineering heads the list in this area (Charles Birch, ed., *Genetics and the Quality of Life,* 1974), but the influence of recombinant DNA technology on plant and animal life, the control of the human mind and behavior by pharmaceutical means, and distributive justice in the use of scarce medical resources are also its themes (see also **Genetics**).

(g) A continuing confrontation with the massive commitment of science and technology to military purposes (see **Deterrence;**

Nuclear Warfare). The unchecked development of nuclear weaponry is the most critical concern here. Its most recent expression was in an international hearing sponsored by the WCC (P. Abrecht and N. Koshy, eds., *Before It's Too Late,* 1983). The issue of chemical and biological weaponry has also come up, however, as well as the effect on the Third World of overmilitarization.

The ongoing discussion of this wide range of interlocking problems has been reflected primarily in the publication of the Office on Church and Society, *Anticipation,* from 1970 to 1983. Here the reports of several international conferences and an ecumenical variety of essays are brought. More accessible to most readers, however, are the published volumes of preparatory papers and the two-volume report of the World Conference on Faith, Science and the Future in Cambridge, Massachusetts, in 1979 (*Faith, Science and the Future,* 1978); *Faith and Science in an Unjust World,* vol. 1: *Plenary Presentations;* vol. 2: *Reports and Recommendations*).

The future of ethics in the ecumenical movement beyond its high point in the Cambridge conference is unclear. The tension between the two methods continues. It was expressed at Cambridge by statements from youth delegates and some from the Third World. It came to expression again at the Sixth Assembly of the WCC at Vancouver in 1983. The danger of separation into action dominated by a limited theology and social analysis versus sophisticated reflection without a clear influence on social behavior is real. Hope lies, however, in the fact that Christians continue to be thrown together across all lines of conflict by the urgency of the gospel and the urgency of the world situation. These urgencies in the past have helped greatly to dispel ideologies and compel engagement with human problems in their complex reality.

See **Ecclesiology and Ethics.**

In addition to items mentioned in the text: P. Bock, *In Search of a Responsible World Society,* 1974; H. Godin, *France Pagan?* 1949; W. A. Visser 't Hooft and J. H. Oldham, *The Church and Its Function in Society,* 1937; *The Church and the Disorder of Society,* Amsterdam Assembly Series, III, 1948; *Dilemmas and Opportunities:* Report of International Study Conference, 1959; M. Lindqvist, *Economic Growth and the Quality of Life,* 1975; G. MacLeod, *We Shall Rebuild: The Work of the Iona Community on Mainland and on Island,* 1945; D. T. Niles, *Upon the Earth,* 1962; R. H. Preston (ed.), *Technology and Social Justice,* 1971; *World Conference on Church and Society:* Official Report, 1967.

CHARLES C. WEST

Education, Christian Moral

Christian faith and morality are not synonymous terms; neither are Christian education and moral education. Nevertheless, for Christians, moral education is not something separate from or added to Christian education. Christian education is education for the Christian life. Since this life is inherently a moral life, Christian moral education means the way this particular form of moral life is taught.

Education may be understood both broadly and more narrowly. Education, broadly understood, involves all the influences of a person's social context which shape his or her values, beliefs, skills, and patterns of behavior, etc. In this sense, education is socialization, and is in part unplanned, unintentional, and unsystematic. More strictly defined, education is limited to the intentional, conscious, and willed actions of persons and institutions in relation to others in order to influence them in particular ways. There is wide agreement that morality is powerfully shaped by broad, socializing forces. Most moral and religious educators believe that moral education in the narrower sense is also possible—that planned educational strategies can be developed that will have significant impact on important dimensions of a person's morality. Many argue that effective moral education involves responsibility both for the shaping of broad social contexts and for direct teaching.

The various contemporary approaches to moral education are often directly related to theories of moral development (*see* **Moral Development**). Different approaches emphasize different strategies and goals. Many are often useful to Christian moral education. Christian moral education has historically involved several constant elements, however. The church has always found it important for the formation of moral life that people be intimately involved in the life of Christian community. Here children and adults learn and assimilate the values, convictions, and patterns of perception, interpretation, and action of the faith community through participation in myriad events of worship, fellowship, service, and creative expression. The Christian family has often been seen as the church in miniature and, because of its intimacy, a particularly significant institution of moral education. In addition to such socialization within Christian community, the church has also usually provided forums for moral discourse. Here explicit opportunities are set up both to learn and to inquire into the moral convictions, principles, and values of the Christian faith as these are carried by its stories, symbols, rituals, and theology, and to engage in debate and discussion about moral conflicts and decision-making that arise in the lives of people. Finally, the church has, in various forms, developed structures for moral action and vocation that provide communal support and guidance for its people's moral endeavors.

See **Ecclesiology and Ethics.**

H. Bushnell, *Christian Nurture,* 1861, repr. 1979; E. B. Castle, *Moral Education in Christian Times,* 1958; C. Dykstra, *Vision and Character,* 1981; C. E. Nelson, *Where Faith Begins,* 1967; T. Sizer and N. F. Sizer (eds.), *Moral Education: Five Lectures,* 1970.

CRAIG DYKSTRA

Egalitarianism *see* Equality; Justice

Ego

In Sigmund Freud's later understanding of the human mind the ego is the institution or structure responsible for perception, thinking, memory, and judgment. It develops out of the id* and endeavors to modify the id impulses to conform to the demands of reality. It is partly conscious and partly unconscious and in general performs the controlling and integrating function in the human personality. The conscious ego tends to act rationally and logically and is prepared to postpone immediate pleasure for the sake of anticipated future pleasures. Psychoanalytic theory (*see* **Psychoanalysis**) regards the conflicts between id, ego, and superego* as basic in the development of personality. Ego structure may also be influenced by external factors, and an ego is said to be strong when it is capable of dealing realistically with a wide variety of pressures from within and without.

More recently an "ego psychology" has developed which claims that the ego is somewhat autonomous of the id and has both its own sources of energy and its own aims and purposes. This position is particularly associated with Heinz Hartmann and David Rapaport and has found widespread acceptance among psychoanalysts. There are also modified forms of ego psychology such as that advocated by Gordon Allport.

There is no general agreement in psychology on the relation of the term "ego" to the term "self." Some theorists use the words interchangeably; others insist that there is a difference between them, but some of these use both terms in a manner directly opposite to their use by others. It is abundantly clear, however, that there is no warrant in the best contemporary psychology for the common misapprehension (from which theologians in particular are not exempt) that any considerations of ego or of self constitute a pandering to human pride*, egoism, or self-centeredness. The simple fact is that we could not survive as human beings without an adequate ego, that is, without some central integrating structure and function in the personality. The traditional issues in ethics about egoism* versus altruism* focus around a different concern.

See **Persons and Personality; Psychology and Ethics.**

G. Allport, *Pattern and Growth in Personality,* 1961; A. Freud, *The Ego and the Mechanisms of Defence,* ET 1937; S. Freud, *The Ego and the Id* (1923), ET 1927; C. S. Hall and G. Lindzey, *Theories of Personality,* ²1970, esp. pp. 515–523; H. Hartmann, *Essays in Ego-Psychology,* 1964.

GRAEME M. GRIFFIN

Egoism

The word means self-centeredness. Of course, a person could not be human or a moral agent unless he or she was a centered self or ego*. However, the word "egoism" is used in a pejorative sense to mean excessive self-regard. It may be the case that true self-regard does not conflict with regard for others, for genuine selfhood is attainable only in a community of selves. In many particular situations, whatever may be true in general about the ultimate coincidence of self-regarding and other-regarding conduct, the moral decision presents itself as one between one's own interests and the interests of other persons. The Christian ethic stresses the claim of the other and teaches that true selfhood can be gained only through willingness to lose oneself. More subtle than the egoism of the individual is what may be called "group egoism," the unrelenting pursuit of its own interests by, let us say, a family, a social class, a nation, without regard to the damage or injustice inflicted on others. Reinhold Niebuhr's contrast between "moral man" and "immoral society" points to the curbing of egoism in the individual and its relatively unrestrained exercise by the group; and it also makes clear that the Christian ethic cannot be thought of merely in terms of individual integrity but must seek to permeate the larger social structures as well.

See **Altruism; Persons and Personality.**

JOHN MACQUARRIE

Egyptian Ethics, Ancient

Maat ("order," "justice") is both a cosmological and an ethical concept and presupposes the integration of the order of nature with the order of Egyptian society. This harmony is achieved in the person of the pharaoh, who is a god, and kingship dates from the time of creation and belongs to the basic order of existence. Nature does not confront Egyptian society as threatening or unpredictable, but is a complex harmony alive with the gods who all have their allotted place, and such changes as are seen are predetermined rhythms that declare the utter stability of the created order. The Egyptian therefore lives in a world that was perfect from the day of creation, and this static view extends to Egyptian society so that history is no more than the inevitable working-out of the original constitution of that society. The Egyptian state is the pharaoh, who is the source of *Maat* and who preserves through the derivative powers of his officials that immutable order of society which derives from his person.

Akhenaton, the heretic king of the 18th dynasty, claimed that he lived on *Maat* (as his food), but his successor, Tutankhamen, declared that "His Majesty drove out disorder (or falsehood) from the Two Lands so that order (or truth) was again established in its place; he made disorder (falsehood) an abomination of the land as at 'the first time' (creation)" (*AER*, p. 54). From this point of view Akhenaton threatened to destroy the harmony of the created order and to reinstate chaos. Akhenaton's use of *Maat* is somewhat specialized; in art it meant something like

truth to life, while in other spheres (literature, social manners) it indicated a revolt against traditionalism and a zest for experiment. The god of the monotheistic cult that he established at his new capital, Tell-el-Amarna, was the sun disk, Aton, and this reform certainly involved the suppression of the Amon cult and the other Egyptian gods, although it should not be forgotten that Akhenaton himself was a god and that it is on the unique relationship of Aton to his person that the reform hinges. Its most important religious document is the *Hymn to the Sun* (*LAE*, p. 288), which has aesthetic and intellectual merit and which adores Aton for his creative, ordering, and sustaining work in nature, but in which there is little evidence of ethical emphasis. The so-called universalism of the Aton cult was not an entirely new departure (cf. *The Hymn to Amon, LAE*, p. 282) and its significance should not be exaggerated, for although parochialism was transcended the favored relationship of Egypt with the god was still asserted (see *LAE*, p. 292 n. 3).

"Order" or "justice" was not so much a concern of the private Egyptian as of the pharaoh and his officials, as is evident from the "Instructions" genre. These "Instructions" (*LAE*, pp. 54f., 234f.; *ANET*, pp. 412–425) are manuals on the art of statesmanship compiled for the benefit of those who were to serve the pharaoh in the upholding of *Maat*. They contain a vocational ethic and were used in the schools where apprentice statesmen were trained. Their authors are sometimes seasoned statesmen who at the end of a successful life conserve their stores of wisdom for those who are to succeed them in office. The "Instruction" for the most part inculcates a hardheaded wisdom and warns against intellectual rather than ethical flaws. One who is to succeed in affairs of state should bridle his tongue, cultivate silence, stifle impetuosity, and speak only when he has something weighty to say. He ought to avoid quarrels and make as few enemies as possible, and it is essential that he should know his limitations and not imagine himself to be more important than he is. Pride in a statesman leads to disaster. There is, however, a great variety of maxims in these instructions; they deal with matters of etiquette and they rise to genuine ethical injunctions. Probity and incorruptibility are demanded of the official, and he must take great pains to see that justice is done (this is perhaps the point of *The Complaints of the Peasant, LAE,* p. 116; *AER,* pp. 46, 146f.) and be ready to help the less fortunate members of the community. Frankfort and others have objected to the description of these maxims as "pragmatic" and have held that they are over-arched by religious belief and that *Maat* is everywhere presupposed. Nevertheless Frankfort agrees that they are empirical wisdom and that they do not have the moral fervor that accompanies the concepts of law and sin in biblical thinking (*AER,* pp. 73f.). The Egyptian gods do not "reveal" a social ethic to humans nor do they give extraordinary "guidance" on matters of state. Religion thus makes room for statecraft based on a bank of experience accumulated over many generations, and the native intelligence coupled with a rigorous educational process is part of the *Maat* which guarantees harmony to the created order. Empiricism is attuned to the divine order.

A. Erman, *The Literature of the Ancient Egyptians* (*LAE*), tr. A. M. Blackman, 1927; H. Frankfort, *Ancient Egyptian Religion* (*AER*), 1948, chs. 2 and 3; J. B. Pritchard, *Ancient Near Eastern Texts Relating to the Old Testament* (*ANET*), [2]1955; J. A. Wilson, *Before Philosophy,* 1949, ch. 4; *The Burden of Egypt,* 1951, ch. 6, on Akhenaton.

WILLIAM McKANE

Eleemosynary Activities *see* **Almsgiving; Charity; Philanthropy; Social Service of the Church**

Emancipation *see* **Afro-American Religious Ethics; Liberation Theology; Oppression; Race Relations; Slavery**

Embodiment

To be a human being is to be a whole of a special kind: at once self-conscious, purposive, corporeal, social, historical, and spiritual. But saying this already makes prominent a certain unease: human being is not "just" a string of such adjectives but is somehow "more." Not even the addition of other adjectives—rational, deceitful, imaginational, sinful—quells the unease. For what every such list leaves obscure is the sense of "whole" itself, which is the human being.

The phenomenon of embodiment, although suggestively educed in Pauline theology by its Hebraic sources (*see* **Body**), has only in more recent times been clearly appreciated as forming the core of that "whole." One way to make this phenomenon stand out is to contrast it with the entrenched idea that human being is a composite of "mind" and "body." Essentially a *metaphysical* postulate, this mind/body dualism is simply unresponsive to a plain fact: that persons experience their own bodies in specific ways that can be studied as such whether such dualism is true or false.

Another way of eliciting embodiment would be to note a remarkable feature of the work of René Descartes (1569–1650). In his metaphysics Descartes argued that mind (*res cogitans*) and matter (*res extensa*) are "substances": mutually exclusive, self-subsistent, and ontologically distinct entities, neither of which requires the other *to be* or *to be known.* This bifurcation stood dramatically opposed to Descartes's clearly stated conviction that, even though *metaphysically* dichotomous, human life is in its *everyday* modalities a unity. Mind and body somehow interact, even though that interaction could not be specified or understood within the metaphysics. The mind is not contingently or accidentally "in" the body as a boatman is in a boat. But the sense of that "intimate union" is the fundamental issue. If everything must be either mind or body and nothing can be both, how can the one be said to be united or to interact with the other? To this Descartes could not respond that in daily life there simply *is* no issue.

The insight is genuine, however much Descartes and others confused it: that one does in truth experience one's own body as profoundly "intimate." Blaise Pascal (1623–1662) noted with marked irony that if one, like Descartes's metaphysician, composed all things of mind and body, surely that mixture would itself be intelligible. Yet, not only do we not understand the body, and even less the mind, least of all do we know how a body could possibly be united to a mind. This, however, Pascal pointedly stated, *is our very being:* to be both and thus to be opaque to ourselves.

Benedict de Spinoza (1632–1677), too, saw that such a metaphysical bifurcation created real difficulties. While he focused his main argument in metaphysical terms (neither mind nor body could possibly be genuine substances, but rather only "attributes" of the one unitary substance that is reality itself), Spinoza nevertheless saw the importance of accounting for what Descartes had merely named a "union." Both mind and body are essential to one another; the body is mirrored in the mind as its "idea." Although his theory is far more complex, the point of major emphasis here is that by rejecting the dualism, Spinoza was able to achieve a clearer understanding of the sense of that "intimate union."

It was not until more recently, however, in the early writings of Henri Bergson (1859–1941), that the sense of embodiment became a specifically focal issue (even though Bergson did not fully explore it). The body is that whereby a person has a locus or placement in the world; this is a unique phenomenon. Unlike any other worldly object, this body is "intimate," that is, is experienced by the person as "mine": it is the "mineness" of the human body which makes it *sui generis.* As such, it is the center for the person's experience: the field of objects and events is spatially organized around "my body" as its center of reference. More than that, it is that by means of which the person engages in activities of any sort. Thus, spatial location and the familiar sensory perceptions of things are always experienced within specific contexts of *action.* "My body" is an actional center. Worldly things are not merely data, only later to be taken up into various bodily actions. Perception is not a matter of "data perception" (input) followed by "internal neural translation" and then by "externalization" (output). For the experiencing perceiver, things are at the outset menacing, helpful, handy, or obstacles,—in short, are experientially organized as "poles of action" appearing only in and through specific activities directed toward them. "My body" is a center, that *by means of which* the person is in the world, in the midst of things, people, language, culture, and it is that by means of which the surrounding milieu is presented for thought and action.

After Bergson, Max Scheler (1874–1928), and even more Edmund Husserl (1859–1938), carried out detailed studies of this "intimacy." The primary phenomenon, Husserl insisted, is the experiential relation of consciousness to its own embodying organism. It is this organism (*Leibkörper*), not merely the "body" (*Körper*), which is the locus of "intimacy" or "mineness," and it is solely due to

its being experienced as such that anything else in the world is able to be experienced.

Gabriel Marcel (1888–1973) advanced the issue substantially, pointing especially to the fundamental opacity at the heart of personal life which embodiment entails. Maurice Merleau-Ponty (1907–1961), too, located an essential ambiguity intrinsic to embodiment. So "intimate" is the "union" between the person and the embodying organism, indeed, that one is tempted to say, "I *am* my body," even while there is that opacity or ambiguity at the heart of this: I both "am" and "have" this body, as Marcel emphasized. My body is not only mind but is that by virtue of which anything else can be said to "belong" to me. So profound is that "mineness," indeed, that when it becomes compromised—as in certain cases of mental or physical disturbance—this can entail a compromise to the sense in which other things are experienced as "belonging" to the person.

By virtue of what is this singular embodying organism "mine"? This is an intricately complex issue. It seems generally agreed that this organism embodies the person solely to the extent that (1) it is the locus for the person's various fields of sensation; (2) it is the only "object" in which the person "rules and governs" immediately (through and by means of its various organs and the whole organism); (3) it enacts most immediately the person's "I can" (see, touch, talk, move, grasp, etc.); (4) it is the means by which the person perceives and otherwise experiences the surrounding world, and is thus the immediate access to the world and the focus of the world's and other persons' actions on oneself; and (5) it is itself experienced while other things are by its means also experienced (the organism is reflexively related to itself).

Embodiment is fundamentally actualized within various levels and modalities of bodily attitudes, stances, movements, personal striving or willing, and perceptual awareness of things. Wishes, desires, movements, etc., are actualized through various corporeal feelings and fields (kinesthetic, proprioceptive, coenesthetic, sensory), which embody these strivings (reaching, squinting, locomoting, etc.).

It needs to be emphasized that the opacity of embodiment has other facets. I *am* my body; but in another sense I am *not* my body —or not just that. The relationship of person to embodying organism is more complex: not only "mineness" but also radical *otherness* is inherent to it. This otherness is equally profound: I am my body, but this body is also "mine," and this belonging shows that "I" am in a way distanced from it. Yet, the union is so close that the experience of otherness can be shattering (whether it be my body's happy obedience, which I notice for the first time, or its hateful refusal to do what I want done). At times, I as a person feel genuinely "at home" with my organism. Yet, so other is it that I feel distanced from it (e.g., when I obsessively stuff it with food, or otherwise mistreat it; or when it seems to "have a life of its own," with aches, activities, and processes of its own; or in times of grievous illness).

Human being is embodied by an animate organism whose connections to that person *are themselves the very issue* of that life, and form an experiential impasse—an aporia in Plato's sense. Nothing so much as me-myself is at once so utterly familiar and usual (who else could I be?), yet so completely foreign and alien (who, indeed, am I?). This body, which is so utterly familiar, is yet so strange: I am "one" with it, yet "other" than it. This unique complex is not merely an inability to make up my mind; it is rather the disclosure of the core phenomenon of embodiment: this dialectic of "mineness" and "otherness" which is itself the heart of my experience, as a person, of my own body.

To speak of embodiment is thus to speak of something the person *is;* I am *my embodiment,* and it is not just that "I am my body." And this embodiment is itself a primal issue for any human life, as Pascal had already seen with remarkable insight: this "not-knowing" myself is precisely what it is for a human being to be, and is focalized within the opacity that is embodiment. Thus, embodiment is an *enactment* ongoing at every moment of every human life.

From this it is possible to appreciate that embodiment is also an essentially *expressive* phenomenon. It is by means of a person's embodiment that wishes, feelings, desires, strivings, and the like are in the first instance expressed, made known to others and to oneself (in grimaces, grins, bodily stances and postures, and the rich array of physiognomic and bodily gestures). This expressiveness is fundamentally a *value phenomenon.* Just because this specific organism uniquely embodies this person—me—and none other, and is

thus most intimately "mine" ("me-yet-not-me"), what can happen to it happens also to me. Although I as a person "govern" my body, I am also subject to it and its specific conditions: if an arm is broken, "I" am injured. Hence, it is fundamental to the experience of embodiment that it matters what can and does happen to my body.

Its value character can also be made clear if one considers, quite apart from specific moral positions, what one thinks of someone who is "loose" with his or her body. Indeed, embodiment, as "intimate union" between "mineness" and "otherness," is clearly at the heart of the prominent sense of inviolability of a person, and thereby of privacy* and integrity. Thus it is more understandable that there are constraints felt as regards interventions and intrusions into the lived-body (whether in medical encounters, on the street, or in one's private affairs).

These considerations also help clarify why certain current moral problems are so highly charged: abortion*, psychosurgery (*see* **Behavior Control**), euthanasia*, organ transplantation*, etc. On the one hand, these (and others) involve interventions into that most intimate and integral of spheres—the embodied person. On the other hand, every person is embodied, enacts the self through that specific animate organism which is his or her "own" and is thus expressive of that very person. Thus, bodily schemata, attitudes, movements, actions, as well as perceptual abilities, are all value modalities by which the person articulates and expresses his or her character, personality, habits, goals, beliefs—in short, life as a whole.

From the perspective of embodiment, then, human interactions (of whatever sort) are essentially "skin trades": interchanges, interventions, discourses, which invoke and have their place within contexts of specific bodily life. In all such exchanges, concretely embodied persons engage with one another in specific forms of valorized actions. Just because every social exchange is a complex of embodied gestures—i.e., is expressive and valorized—each of them is necessarily within the moral order. Embodiment is a moral phenomenon (and not only for Christian ethics), for at every moment of human life the person is "at stake" or "at issue" (Marcel). The "mattering" bodily organism which embodies the whole person is itself what "matters" for ethics. And for Christian ethics, what "matters" is the "special whole" which is human being, i.e., how the "flesh" (*sarx*) of embodiment, human being-in-the-world, is actually lived—whether a person lives "for" the world (centered on oneself: titanic pride, or sin), or whether a person lives "in" the world "for" God (as a creature).

See **Body; Human Dignity; Image of God; Life, Sacredness of; Persons and Personality; Respect for Persons.**

G. Marcel, *The Mystery of Being,* 2 vols., ET 1950; M. Merleau-Ponty, *Phenomenology of Perception,* ET 1962; R. M. Zaner, *The Context of Self,* 1962.

RICHARD M. ZANER

Embryo Transfer
see **Reproductive Technologies**

Emotion
The general term for the whole range of feeling states (affects) and the physiological changes accompanying them. Aquinas in the 13th century, following Aristotle, designated eleven basic emotions: love, desire, joy, hate, aversion, sorrow, hope, despair, courage, fear, and anger. There have been many such lists but little agreement as to how many emotions there are (hundreds have been recognized) and how many of these are basic in the sense of not being derived from others.

Much traditional philosophy has denigrated the role of the emotions (passions, feelings) in human life, but David Hume and many others since acknowledged them as important for morality. Psychologists of many different schools have emphasized their significance in shaping behavior. The dynamic or depth psychologists have demonstrated the damage that can result to the personality from either neglect of the emotional dimensions of life or overemphasis upon them.

Emotion is involved in almost all practices and attitudes of healthy religion. One of the functions of religious ritual seems to be a patterning of emotional experience so that one is neither overwhelmed by it nor deprived of it. Its use in religion is not always healthy, however. Some sects and other groups have been accused of manipulating emotional responses to achieve their own ends by appealing inappropriately to fear, frustration, alienation, etc. (*see also* **Conviction of Sin; Enthusiasm**). The power of emotion to influence attitudes and action make its

responsible use imperative in worship and in Christian living. There is no general agreement as to whether there are any specifically religious emotions or sentiments.

Contemporary research on the nature of emotions in many ways continues to follow the leads of outstanding pioneers of the late 19th and early 20th centuries: William James on the relationship between feeling and physiological response; Walter Cannon on the role of the brain in emotional expression; Sigmund Freud on the unconscious distortions of the emotional life (*see* **Repression; Guilt**); and Charles Darwin on the relation of emotional responses to survival needs.

Emotional responses are commonly characterized as positive or negative according to the dominant feeling tone (pleasant or unpleasant). Even the so-called negative emotions like fear or anger, however, may give pleasure in limited and controlled quantities, and the positive emotions become unpleasant in excess. Recent experimental work suggests that positive and negative emotional responses may involve different hemispheres of the brain. An important normative function of emotion is to motivate appropriate reactions to a wide variety of circumstances. Too high an emotional level may paralyze one for action; too low a level may leave one indifferent and fail to stimulate the needed response.

See **Anxiety.**

C. E. Izard, *Human Emotions,* 1977; C. E. Izard, J. Kagan, R. Zajonc (eds.), *Emotion, Cognition and Behaviour,* 1983; C. G. Jung, *Psychological Types,* ET 1923; J.-P. Sartre, *The Emotions: Outline of a Theory,* ET 1948.

GRAEME M. GRIFFIN

Emotivism
Emotivism is the view that the primary element in the meaning of moral judgments consists in their function of expressing the emotions or attitudes of the speaker, or arousing similar emotions or attitudes in his audience. It is to be distinguished from prescriptivism*, subjectivism*, relativism*.

R. M. HARE

Empathy
The human capacity to apprehend directly the state of mind and feeling of another person. Empathy involves, in effect, putting oneself in the place of the other, understanding and sharing the other's emotional experience,

and seeing the world as he or she sees it. The line between empathy and sympathy* cannot be drawn rigidly, but in general terms empathy involves a sharing in quality rather than in quantity, in kind rather than in degree. It is this which makes it possible to enter into the emotional situation even of persons incapacitated by the strength of their feelings without oneself being overwhelmed by those feelings.

Empathy is a desirable characteristic in all human relationships, and all of the various systems of psychotherapy acknowledge its importance for therapists. It is a valuable tool for gaining insight into the other person and thus for assessing his or her capacity to deal with a given situation. Empathy—particularly when coupled with a nonjudgmental approach to the other person—comes to be perceived by the other as genuine understanding. The sense of being heard and being understood can itself be very liberating and provides a stimulus for growth in a relationship. The capacity to empathize can be developed to a high degree, and its absence usually indicates that the person concerned is caught up in personal conflicts and difficulties.

See **Counseling.**

R. L. Katz, *Empathy: Its Nature and Uses,* 1963; C. Rogers, *Client-Centered Therapy,* 1951.

GRAEME M. GRIFFIN

Encyclicals *see* **Modern Roman Catholic Moral Theology; Official Roman Catholic Social Teaching**

Endogamy
The custom of marrying within the tribe.
See **Exogamy.**

JOHN MACQUARRIE

Ends and Means
"As a rule," writes Emil Brunner, "the notorious proposition 'the end justifies the means' conceals great confusion of thought, whether it is defended or rejected on principle."

It seems impossible to defend or reject the principle without qualification. Those who favor a teleological ethic, an ethic of consequence, may wish to defend it and to ask, "What but the end can justify the means?" but this can only mean that certain ends can justify certain means, not that any end can justify any means. Those who favor a deonto-

logical ethic, an ethic of principle, may wish to reject the proposition out of hand. "Shall we do evil that good may come?" Yet it is arguable that *Fiat iustitia, ruat coelum* (Let justice be done, though the heavens fall) is a more immoral proposition in its refusal to take seriously the disastrous consequences of a moral act. Shall we do good that evil may come?

Unhappy as most Christian writers are with the proposition that the end justifies the means, there are few who would say with Kant that a lie is never justified (e.g., to save innocent life or to mislead an enemy), just as there are few who would maintain that the violence used to push someone out of the way of an oncoming bus is as objectionable as the same violence used with the end merely of doing injury. On the other hand, those who defend the proposition (like Joseph Fletcher, with his claim that "love justifies its means") do not claim that the purpose of love justifies any means. The means must be "fitting."

Christians must act in an imperfect and sinful world in which, not infrequently, the possibilities of action or inaction all seem, in different ways, morally questionable. Harmless inactivity may not be harmless. In Arthur Koestler's *The Yogi and the Commissar,* it was said of the yogi that "he never hurt a fly" and "the flies he did not hurt destroyed a province." It is in such moral dilemmas that the principle that "the end justifies the means" may seem helpful. Brunner has this in mind when he says that "the necessary end hallows the necessary means." Traditionally, the doctrine of the just war* was an attempt to do this and to say in what extreme and limited circumstances war might be justified as a means to a just end. A doctrine of a just revolution* may be needed to do the same for rebellion.

The common understanding of the proposition that "the higher and more noble an end is, the more it justifies any means used in achieving it" seems to be the reverse of the truth. This is the deadly error behind the crusade*, or holy war (which is always the most bloody and barbaric of conflicts), and behind the modern idea of "the Revolution," which is thought by some to justify any bloodshed, crime, or treachery.

A contrary view might put forward the following considerations:

1. In moral matters, the means affects the end; i.e., the means are not morally indiffer-

ent, and a sharp distinction between means and ends is never possible. "The different routes most often lead to different places" (Flew). Those who believe that they can leave blood and treachery behind, once they have entered into their kingdom, find that they are mistaken. The evil means has permeated the end, and they and the kingdom are corrupted. All who take the sword will perish by the sword.

2. The more noble an end, the more restricted are the means appropriate to it. Public order requires a limited amount of coercion; the gospel of the kingdom can be served by love and by truth and by no other means.

3. The proposition may be more useful when the end is a negative one, combating a specific and limited evil, rather than advancing a positive and unlimited good. The just war is a defensive war, and severely limited at that, and the principle may be the same in matters of social and political action.

4. The less immediate and specific the end, the weaker is the causal connection between ends and means. It is one thing to have to shoot people as the only way to stop them from blowing the town sky-high. It is quite another thing to blow up the town in the belief that this will somehow bring closer the Communist revolution.

5. It is always possible, as Brunner insists, that "the means which may be used for a definite good may be of such bad quality that in this instance we feel it to be our duty to renounce the undertaking altogether."

6. Bishop Butler observed that our disapproval of falsehood, unprovoked violence, or injustice is irrespective of the happiness or unhappiness that may be supposed in any particular case to result from them. If morality were simply a matter of consequences, or of Fletcher's "agapeic calculus," the means would not be such a problem. The problem arises when we must balance the desirability of the end against our moral disapproval of the means: and these are not always commensurable. Thus to abandon a large prize for a small scruple may be a reasonable price of integrity.

7. To describe behavior in terms of means and ends is of only limited usefulness. Some Christian action is of value not as achieving specific objectives but as demonstrating the generosity of love, setting up in this world the signs of the kingdom.

See also **Compromise; Consequentialism;** **Deontology; Necessity; Responsibility; Situation Ethics; Teleological Ethics.**

E. Brunner, *The Divine Imperative,* ET 1937, pp. 243ff.; J. Butler, "Of the Nature of Virtue," dissertation annexed to *The Analogy of Religion,* 1736; J. Fletcher, *Situation Ethics,* 1966; A. Flew, "Ends and Means," *EP* II, 1967.

JAMES A. WHYTE

Enemy *see* **Conventions; Hatred; Jesus, Ethical Teaching of; Just War; Love; Malice; Neighbor; Pacifism; Resistance; Sermon on the Mount**

Energy

Since the advent of the Industrial Revolution, both human-manufactured needs for natural energy sources and the subsequent development and exploitation of those sources have increased exponentially. These increases have raised serious moral concerns in recent decades about the rate of our natural resource consumption and about its environmental effects. Many of these concerns are addressed in other entries in this volume (*see* **Environmental Ethics; Future Generations, Obligations to; Risk; Technology**). The present entry will focus selectively upon applications to energy policy of two basic moral principles, justice* and nonmaleficence, and upon anthropological assumptions implicit in energy consumerism.

Justice. The primary policy mode of assessing energy technologies, at least since the 1960s, has been cost-benefit* (or risk-benefit) analysis, a basically utilitarian method of weighing net expected benefits (e.g., cheaper electricity or transportation) of a given power source relative to its predictable costs (including harms or risks of harm) for the aggregate of persons involved (*see* **Risk**). In order to do this, the cost-benefit analyst must somehow convert all prospective factors under consideration into some common denomination, usually monetary. Critics of such analysis point out that many human values—especially life, health, and chosen life-styles—cannot and should not be fiscally weighed. More important, however, cost-benefit analysis is morally hollow without further attention to the claims of *distributive justice,* which demands at least equal concern for the interests of all involved parties and thus considers *who* will be positively or negatively affected and to what relative extent. Critics of nuclear fission as an energy source, for example, point out that electricity consumers near a nuclear power station gain no economic benefit relative to their more distant counterparts, yet must bear an estimated fifty-fold relative increase in carcinogenic and mutagenic risks. Further uncompensated health risks are associated with the mining, refining, enriching, and transporting of uranium and with the storage of nuclear wastes. Other modern environmental hazards such as acid rain, atmospheric "greenhouse effect" and smog raise similar distributive justice questions about coal-power and petroleum technologies. Even nonpolluting energy technologies involve issues of just cost-benefit distribution, as when primitive peoples are flooded out of their ancestral homelands by hydroelectric dam construction in developing countries.

Related to distributive justice considerations are those of *compensatory justice*. Justice-as-compensation seeks redress for the relative harms suffered by some in the process of benefiting others. One frequent energy application of this is in the argument that energy-consuming societies should bear the costs of providing extensive safety measures to prevent (and medical care to ameliorate) the peculiar health problems associated with coal mining and uranium processing. As a further example, in the USA (particularly since the nuclear near-disaster at Three Mile Island in 1979), compensatory justice arguments have been leveled against the Price-Anderson Act (1957), which was designed to protect utilities from bankruptcy by arbitrarily limiting compensation claims of homeowners to a small percentage of their actual property losses in the event of nuclear plant accident.

While both distributive and compensatory justice involve notions of "balancing" benefits and harms (or risks of harm) of energy technology among those affected, modern energy production also creates delayed "costs" for future persons who cannot share in the present benefits of cheap, available energy. Morally, these costs must be examined on independent, though related, grounds.

Nonmaleficence. The prima facie moral duty of nonmaleficence, or "Do no harm," also entails avoidance of causing risks of harm. And most of us recognize at least some obligation not to heap misfortune on those who follow us (though the nature and extent of that obligation is not easily specified; *see* **Future Generations, Obligations to**). Many philosophers and theologians are particularly concerned by two effects of current energy technology which may be considered objective harms to future persons. The first is environmental pollution—of which several examples have already been cited—and its associated health hazards. Nuclear waste pollution is perhaps the most feared. We have as yet no known proven safe way of packaging nuclear plant wastes: many thousands of gallons of radioactive liquid waste have already leaked from steel tanks in government storage areas. Moreover, plutonium, a radioactive by-product of reactor operation, requires 24,000 years to decay by half and 500,000 years to become innocuous. (It is also weapons-grade nuclear material.)

The second potentially harmful effect of present energy consumption is simply that we may be leaving our progeny a plundered planet. The natural resources necessary for our "hard" energy technologies (e.g., coal, petroleum, uranium) are, after all, nonrenewable. There is, so far at least, no clear and compelling moral formula for determining what coal and oil reserves we "owe" to our great-grandchildren. But advocates of more renewable "soft" energy paths (e.g., solar, wind, hydro) argue that unless we either increase our proportional dependence on these decentralized and less convenient paths, or reduce our overall energy demands, or both, we may be guaranteeing that our successors will have few energy options *except* those we now consider too costly or inconvenient for ourselves.

Nature and Anthropology. One other question that arises for many observers of the technological age is, What is the proper relation between humanity and the rest of nature, and is our growing energy-consumerism consistent with that relation? This is but a variation on a traditional concern of theological anthropology: our role in the created order. Particular anthropological themes or symbols do not function in our moral deliberations in the same way as principles or values do; instead, they function to form our perspectives or attitudes about who and what we are responsible for. For example, humankind's biblical "dominion" over the earth (Gen. 1:26) might suggest that humanity and nonhuman nature are radically discontinuous and that the latter exists for our use, to whatever extent makes human life more comfortable. Something like this view seems implicit in energy policies which emphasize greater current acquisition and use of fossil fuels to facilitate broad economic expansion (*see* **Commercialism**). Of course, a more moderating concern for the energy needs of future persons would also be consistent with this perspective.

On the other hand, the traditional Christian notion of our "stewardship" of creation might imply not just rational control over what God has created but also human continuity with, and protection of, what God sustains. If we accept this perspective as normative, then our responsibility extends beyond the needs and wants of persons (present and future) to encompass preservation of the non-human world for its own sake.

In summary, energy policymaking is invariably a moral enterprise—fundamental moral values and principles are at stake in decisions about energy production and consumption. And one of theology's key contributions to that enterprise is in offering perspectives for understanding the meaning of human existence in its relatedness to the world.

N. Evans and C. Hope, *Nuclear Power: Futures, Costs and Benefits,* 1984; M. Kaku and J. Trainer (eds.), *Nuclear Power: Both Sides,* 1982; A. B. Lovins, *Soft Energy Paths,* 1977; N. Myers, *The Sinking Ark,* 1979; R. and V. Routley, "Nuclear Power—Some Ethical and Social Dimensions," in T. Regan and D. VanDeVeer (eds.), *And Justice for All,* 1982; K. S. Shrader-Frechette, *Nuclear Power and Public Policy,* ²1983; and "Ethics and Energy," in T. Regan (ed.), *Earthbound: New Introductory Essays in Environmental Ethics,* 1984.

JAMES B. TUBBS, JR.

Enlightenment

Immanuel Kant (1724–1804), in the opening sentences of his essay *What Is Enlightenment?* (1784), gives this definition:

> Enlightenment (*Aufklärung*) is the movement of man out of his minority state, which was brought about by his own fault. The minority state means the incapacity to make use of one's understanding without the guidance of another. This

minority state is brought about by a man's own fault if it is caused by a deficiency not of understanding, but of the resolution and the courage to make use of it without the guidance of another. *Sapere aude!*— Have the courage to make use of your own understanding—is thus the motto of Enlightenment.

This definition implies the autonomy* of the rational self-consciousness. Human reason possesses the power to find the truth about the human race, the world, and God, and to live in accordance with this truth. The authoritarian claim of positive religion to possess special supernatural powers and evidences for the understanding and realization of the truth is denied. Sometimes it is tacitly excluded, sometimes (as with Lessing) it is modified to mean that while "revelation does not give man anything which human reason left to itself would not also discover," nevertheless revelation "gave and is giving man the most important of these things sooner" (*Education of the Human Race,* sec. 4). But in general it may be said that the Enlightenment works with an intramundane conception of morality in which the concept of grace has no place. Morality is therefore secularized. Religion is esteemed (if at all) simply as a buttress of morality.

The term "Enlightenment" is generally applied to the period from the mid-17th through the 18th century. Leibniz (1646–1716) is the great figure of the Enlightenment. In him may be seen the distinct connections with earlier movements (especially with Descartes and the 16th-century Renaissance), and the manifold powers and problems of the Enlightenment itself, which to this day have not been exhausted or resolved. Thus the principle of individuation leads to the conception of the human being as a microcosm, and to the cardinal importance of the individual conscience. Again, the doctrine of preestablished harmony between humans and the outer world establishes a cosmos that is basically the product of human thought. But it is insufficient to describe his ethical position as "Stoicism" (Karl Barth, *From Rousseau to Ritschl,* 1959, p. 57). For in Leibniz's view true piety consisted in the recognition of the divine providence behind the preestablished harmony.

But the Enlightenment took many different forms; in Britain empiricism (Hume), in

France positivism (Voltaire), in Germany both literary and critical metaphysical forms (Lessing, Kant), leading to idealism. In general, so far as ethics are concerned, the view of the Enlightenment may be summarized as intramundane, with the stress on the autonomy of the human reason, humanitarian, tolerant, and optimistic. Humans could discover for themselves what the good was, and they could achieve it. Thus the stress lay upon the continuity of cultural goods, and the means for maintaining and developing this continuity lay in education.

The effects of these views upon the traditional Christian teachings were immense and have not yet been completely worked out. The Enlightenment may be regarded as the first deliberate effort of the human spirit to think through the consequences of the breakup of the medieval synthesis. The doctrines of sin and atonement were reinterpreted in moral terms. The religion of Christ is preferred to the Christian religion. The teaching of Jesus replaces the dogmas concerning Christ. God is even regarded as a principle immanent in the human race.

From the standpoint of Christian ethics the emphasis was laid upon Jesus as a teacher of eternal truths, upon the fatherly love of God, upon human brotherhood, and upon immortality and freedom. "The goal and measure of history is to be seen in the self-produced progress of the truth" (W. Anz, *RGG*³ I, 716). While it is easy to dismiss much Enlightenment teaching as shallow and pretentious, especially in the notion of the progress and perfectibility of society, the autonomy of the human reason (as propounded by Leibniz) and the sense of the significance of history (as expressed by Lessing) are contributions of central importance for a creative assessment of ethics. The views of the Enlightenment, in general, represent a release from the heteronomies of authoritarian dogma.

R. GREGOR SMITH

Entertainment *see* Amusements

Enthusiasm

Enthusiasm is employed religiously in a number of different but imprecisely defined ways. It was used originally by late Greek writers, such as Plutarch and Plato, to denote the effect of divine indwelling in poets, mystics, seers, and philosophers. Later the term was applied to any claim to direct divine inspiration or to personal direction by the Spirit of God. Early Christian prophecy (e.g., the Revelation of John and the *Shepherd of Hermas*) was regarded as the product of enthusiasm. More commonly, however, the term is used pejoratively and implies a doubt on the part of the user as to the authenticity of the source of the claimed inspiration or direction. In this negative sense the accusation of enthusiasm has been leveled against many individuals over the centuries and against aspects of such disparate movements as Montanism, Donatism, Fraticelli, the Anabaptists, Jansenism, Quietism, the Society of Friends, the Moravians, early Methodism, the Great Awakening, the Shakers, Revivalism, the Irvingites, Seventh-Day Adventism, Christian Science, Pentecostalism, the charismatic movement, and many others of lesser consequence. Enthusiasm is found in all periods of history but seems to have been particularly luxuriant in the 17th and 18th centuries.

Early writers on the psychology of religion spoke of enthusiasm as the extravagant manifestation of religious devotion or practice, and a great deal of attention has been focused on the emotional and psychological accompaniments, which have included such phenomena as glossolalia (speaking in strange tongues), trance states, visual and auditory hallucinations, involuntary jerking movements of the head, body, or limbs, involuntary cries and ejaculations, barking. These have been interpreted by adherents as gifts of the Holy Spirit and evidences of divine favor. They are typically interpreted by critics as evidences of unhealthy emotionalism. Some dynamic psychologists have suggested that the ecstatic phenomena are group-approved ways of working out substantial inner conflicts within the individual members. They can thus serve as a positive alternative to personal psychic disintegration. Enthusiasts have usually attacked the ecclesiastical and sociopolitical status quo of their times. Their theology is often highly individualistic and frequently includes expectation of the imminent end of the age with the return of Christ and the separation of the "elect" from others.

R. A. Knox, *Enthusiasm,* 1950; U. Lee, *The Historical Background of Early Methodist*

Enthusiasm, 1931; H. N. Wright, *Christian Use of Emotional Power,* 1974.

GRAEME M. GRIFFIN

Environment and Heredity

Environment and heredity, taken together, exhaust the factors which determine and/or influence development and behavior. Strictly speaking, heredity is limited to factors transmitted through the genes. All other prenatal events are regarded as environmental factors, though all factors present at birth, whether actual or potential, are commonly regarded as a part of the individual's constitution, whether due to genetic determinants or prenatal conditions.

The controversy concerning whether hereditary or environmental factors are most important in shaping the individual is a very old one. In aristocratic societies in the past heredity has been emphasized, and in more recent democratic and socialist societies (exclusive of Communist societies influenced by Soviet genetics) environmental factors have been stressed.

The following factors are now known to be determined or influenced by heredity, with the degree of susceptibility to environmental influences increasing in rough parallel to the progression of the list: (1) blood groups, including type and other factors; (2) physiological defects, such as color blindness; (3) quantitative differences, such as stature and degree of skin pigmentation; (4) resistance and susceptibility to some disease; and (5) mental and emotional characteristics.

The fifth-mentioned factors are generally regarded as much less determined by heredity than the four preceding factors—and emotional factors less than mental factors. Studies of identical twins, the primary source of data concerning the relative importance of heredity and environment, show wide variations in mental and emotional traits in twins reared in separate environments. There are apparent hereditary limits to mental variability, however, as studies show no more than 25 percent difference between identical twins. See H. H. Newman, F. N. Freeman, and K. Holzinger, *Twins: A Study of Heredity and Environment* (1954).

Anthropological and educational studies have shown that race, as a genetic factor, is not determinative of mental ability and temperament in all cases. Difficulties presented by separating hereditary from cultural and social factors have so far made it impossible to determine whether and to what extent race may directly or indirectly influence these factors in some individuals, but the bulk of scientific opinion is against such influence.

There is little evidence that a program of eugenics* can be justified on the basis of the inheritability of "higher" functions alone, even aside from ethical considerations of individual rights. Examples of phenotypes of wide degrees of genetic determination are known for men. Yet the potential for behavior provided by heredity sets limits on humans' malleability and control by their fellow humans.

See **Behavior Control; Free Will and Determinism; Genetics.**

JAMES N. LAPSLEY

Environmental Ethics

Environmental ethics focuses the enterprise of ethics on what we should do and be disposed to do regarding nature or the material universe. The relation of humans to nature and their behavior regarding it are ancient concerns. However, new knowledge about ecosystems along with increased power of humans through technology* to impact the environment irreversibly, at a rate and scale that threaten severe damage to all life and destruction of the entire biosphere, have recently brought a qualitatively new dimension and an urgent note.

Pollution of air, water, and land; world human population levels and the rate of reproduction; increased demands for food and shrinking supplies of arable land, energy, and nonrenewable resources; the disappearance of whole species of animal and plant life; economic development and appropriate lifestyles on a finite globe; and the threat of nuclear holocaust are some of the issues engaged by environmental ethics over the last two decades. The biological sciences and ecology, with its study of the complex interplay of natural organisms and systems, have been added to the customary list of dialogue partners for ethics.

In addition to the familiar subjects of ethics, the following items are characteristic matters under discussion in environmental ethics:

1. Views regarding nature. There is widespread criticism of the still-prevalent view that objectifies nature, likens it to a machine, and places humans apart from it as observers and manipulators. Associated with classical science and technology, this approach concentrates on how things function rather than on what things are, and fragments knowledge of nature into specialized parts. It has brought enormous benefits and revolutionized the conditions of human existence. But many regard such a view as now scientifically outdated and an important if not the major factor in creating our ecological crises.

Some are convinced that this "despotic view" is endemic to the traditional metaphysics of Judaism and Christianity (L. White, J. Passmore, A. Toynbee). They look to Eastern philosophies and religions or to pantheism and animism to provide new foundations.

Others believe that the Christian tradition of trusteeship and stewardship (*see* **Image of God**) of nature provides grounds for a sound view of nature (R. Attfield, T. Derr, I. Barbour, L. Wilkinson). Indeed, for a century this subject has been neglected in Christian thought apart from the ongoing Eastern Orthodox tradition (P. Gregorius), process theology (J. Cobb), and a few others (J. Sittler, G. Hendry). But in recent reexamination interpreters agree that neither scripture in general nor the dominion passage in Genesis in particular indicates any kind of predatory role for humans in relation to the rest of creation (J. Barr, G. Liedke, O. H. Steck). All living things as well as human beings are part of God's creation, capable of reflecting God's glory and grace, and are the object of God's redemptive purpose (Rom. 8:19–23). The recognition that nonhuman creatures have intrinsic value is present in the Christian tradition (Basil the Great, Chrysostom, Augustine, Francis). Anthropocentric views are also to be found (Origen, Lombard, Aquinas, and Calvin) and border on the despotic in Bacon and Descartes. But even in this stream there is present a sense that humans are to be trustees of nature—protecting and developing the natural world in accord with God's purpose and after the model of Christ's dominion (Phil. 2:5–11).

2. The extent of the moral community. Who or what are to be acknowledged as having moral standing, deserving moral consideration in their own right? Differences regarding the definition of moral standing, criteria for determining who or what qualifies, and hence where the parameters of the moral community are drawn, tend to vary according to diverse ethical theories: having

an interest; or possessing an intrinsic good; or holding certain basic rights (the grounding, nature, and content of which in turn are matters of dispute); or being members of God's covenant community, and the like.

There is extensive agreement that future generations* of human beings have moral standing. But should the moral community be limited to human life or perhaps even to human persons (however defined)? Those who so argue develop a *conservation* ethic of care for the material universe in terms of its instrumental value for human rights and well-being (W. T. Blackstone, J. Passmore, N. Rescher).

Those who would extend moral standing beyond human life tend to develop an ethic with emphasis on *preservation* of nature. But they differ as to whether the moral community properly includes all sentient beings (J. Feinberg, P. Singer, T. Regan), or all living things (J. Cobb, A. Schweitzer, C. Birch, P. Taylor). There are also proponents, sometimes called holists, who argue that entire species or ecological systems or even the entire earth viewed as a single organism should be given independent moral standing alongside individual units of such wholes (A. Leopold, J. Rodman, C. Stone).

3. Ascertaining the likely impacts of human actions upon nature. This becomes more difficult as technology becomes increasingly sophisticated. How are risks* of danger to be measured and assessed? While quantitative effects can be measured most accurately, especially when there is enough previous experience to provide good data for statistical analysis, there are important kinds of impacts that cannot be quantified, and there are ever-new technological innovations for which there are few if any precedents. The extent and kind of influence that values, interests, and commitments have on estimates and measurement of likely impacts is another matter under discussion (R. Veatch).

4. Developing moral principles for establishing duties and virtues with regard to nonhuman nature and future generations. In addition, attempts are made to attach relative weight to various members of the moral community and priority to different moral obligations when they conflict—for example, when the interests or rights of animals or of a species clash with the need of human beings for expanded economic production. The importance of this task became apparent in the

1960s when the environmental movement was criticized (R. Neuhaus) for impeding by its zealousness for the environment the struggles of human groups to escape poverty and oppression. New theories of justice* are required not only to take account of more complex distributive questions but also common interests and nondistributable goods like those of the environment.

5. Political processes for public policy decisions that affect the environment. A cluster of related concerns include: What processes would ensure that relevant parties participate in such decisions and that matters of the common good receive appropriate attention? Who should these parties be, especially when it is frequently difficult to determine the boundary of the relevant public whose interests are affected? What groups in the polis can be relied upon to carry the interests and guard the rights of future generations and nonhuman creatures? Which of these rights, if any, should be given legal status? These, of course, lead into the wider issue of determining what political and economic institutions and systems are most appropriate not only to human justice but to good stewardship of the earth.

6. Social analysis to define environmental problems and ascertain their causes. The following are some of the theories advanced to account for our various ecological problems: capitalism; excessive regulation of the free market; the increase of human population (A. and P. Ehrlich, G. Hardin); the growth of affluence and increased rate of consumption (P. Rivers); new technologies and methods of production (B. Commoner); exponential growth (M. Mesarovic, E. Pestel, T. Derr); certain religious and metaphysical traditions (L. White, J. Passmore, A. Leopold, A. Toynbee). Such social analysis is both shaped by and itself influences the principles adopted, the theory of justice, and the view of nature held.

See **Animals; Energy; Future Generations, Obligations to; Hunger, World; Image of God; Population Policy; Risk; Technology.**

P. Abrecht (ed.), *Faith and Science in an Unjust World,* vol. 2, 1980; R. Attfield, *The Ethics of Environmental Concern,* 1983; C. Birch and J. B. Cobb, Jr., *The Liberation of Life,* 1981; R. L. Shinn (ed.), *Faith and Science in an Unjust World,* vol. 1, 1980.

TERENCE R. ANDERSON

Envy

Sadness, sorrow, or grief about another's goods insofar as they surpass, or are thought to surpass, one's own. According to Thomas Aquinas (*ST* II-II.36), this "sorrow for another's good" is distinguished from fear that another's good may be the cause of harm (e.g., an enemy's power), from zeal*, which is sorrow over another's good not because he or she has it but because we lack it (e.g., zeal for virtue), and from grief over another's good because we believe he or she is unworthy of it (e.g., worldly success). Though certain initial movements of envy may be venial, envy itself is a mortal sin, Aquinas contends, because it is contrary to charity*: "Now the object both of charity and of envy is our neighbor's good, but by contrary movement, since charity rejoices in our neighbor's good, while envy grieves over it." It is also directly contrary to pity, which grieves over another's evils, while envy grieves over the neighbor's goods. It is a capital sin, not because it is the worst of all sins or because it does not flow from other sins, but because it issues in other sins, such as hatred (*see* **Seven Deadly Sins**). The Anglican litany lists envy, hatred, and malice in that order, suggesting that envy issues in hatred* and that both issue in malice*. The Gospels (Matt. 27:18 and Mark 15:10) report that Pilate "perceived that it was out of envy that the chief priests had delivered him [Jesus] up," their envy probably being directed at his authority and power over the people. Envy may sometimes lead to right actions or good outcomes; for example, Paul (Phil. 1:15) notes that "some indeed preach Christ from envy and rivalry, but others from good will." Nevertheless, Paul condemns envy, linking it with various other vices (see Rom. 1:29; Gal. 5:19ff.).

In many Christian contexts, for example in the Anglican litany, envy is deemed to be an outgrowth of pride*. But according to John Rawls in *A Theory of Justice* (1971), "the main psychological root of the liability to envy is a lack of self-confidence in our own worth combined with a sense of impotence." Friedrich Nietzsche attempted to unmask Christian morality, finding back of it envy and resentment. Some contemporary writers, especially conservatives, attempt to discredit the struggle for equality by claiming that it expresses envy. But the norms of love* and equality* may be defended on theological grounds and applied for reasons other than envy.

JAMES F. CHILDRESS

Epicureanism, Ethics of

It might at first sight look as if Epicureanism had no ethics at all. Or, if Epicureanism had an ethic, it might seem bound to be the "ethic of the pigsty." This is so for a variety of reasons.

Epicureanism reduced humans—and everything else—to a fortuitous conglomeration of atoms," which came together by chance to form a human being, and which at death simply disintegrated. Epicureanism banished religion, which it held to be the chief curse of the human race (Lucretius 1.62–79), and removed the gods to a lonely isolation in which they had not the slightest interest in humankind. The word "epicureanism" has become a synonym for the worship of pleasure, and for Epicurus pleasure was the supreme good (Lucian, *Hermotimus* 36). Pleasure is "the alpha and omega of the blessed life, . . . the first and native good" (Diogenes Laertius 10.128, 129). Epicureanism is therefore admittedly the pursuit of pleasure.

Sometimes the Epicureans did speak as if they meant bodily and sensual pleasure, but the fact was that in the ancient world the Epicureans were notorious, not for their indulgence in physical pleasure, but for the austerity of their lives. Clement of Alexandria quotes a saying from a play of Philemon: "This fellow (Epicurus) is bringing in a new philosophy; he preaches hunger and his disciples follow him. They get but a single roll, a dried fig to relish it, and water to wash it down" (Clement of Alexandria, *Stromateis* 2.493; cf. Seneca, *On the Happy Life* 13.1; Aelian, *Historical Miscellanies* 4.13; Athenaeus, *Deipnosophistae* 4.163; Diogenes Laertius 10.11). How does this come about? It comes about because for the Epicurean the supreme pleasure is *ataraxia*, the calm serenity when the soul is at peace. The Epicurean definition is: "By pleasure we mean the absence of pain in the body and trouble in the mind" (Diogenes Laertius 10.131). This meant that it was always the long view of pleasure that had to be taken, and therefore the sensual pleasures which brought pain to follow were the very things the Epicurean avoided.

So for the happy life contentment is necessary. "If you want to make Pythocles happy, add not to his possessions but take away from his desires" (Epicurus, *Fragment* 28). The real necessities are all the simplest things (*Fragments* 67, 71). Physical love is to be avoided. The wise will not fall in love because it disturbs their peace (Diogenes Laertius 10.118, 119). Envy must be banished as injurious (*Fragment* 53). Ambition must have no place in life. Epicureans strenuously avoided politics and public affairs. Their motto was: "Live unseen" (*Fragment* 68).

The Epicurean believed in the necessity of virtue, but only from the purely selfish point of view that without virtue happiness is not possible. Epicurus advocated justice, for instance, not because justice is absolutely good, but because, if we do wrong, we may be found out, and, even if we are not found out, we cannot be at peace, because we will always be afraid that we may be (*Fragments* 2, 7; Seneca, *Letters* 97.13).

Epicureanism had a high ethic but its motive was prudent selfishness and enlightened self-interest.

WILLIAM BARCLAY

Epikeia

Aristotle gave the common Greek word *epikeia* ("fitting, suitable, reasonable") a technical meaning: "correction of legal justice when it is defective due to the universality of law" (*Nicomachean Ethics* 5.10). This correction consists of interpreting the intent of the legislator as it would be realized in a situation not expressly covered by the law.

Aquinas, following Aristotle as well as the canonists, defines *epikeia* as a "virtue that inclines to benign interpretation of the law in accord with what is good and just" (*ST* II-II.120). *Epikeia*, still used in this sense in Roman Catholic moral theology, is usually translated "equity."

———

B. Häring, *The Law of Christ*, vol. 1, ET 1964, ch. 5; E. Hamel, "La vertu d'epikie," *Loi naturelle et loi du Christ*, 1964.

ALBERT R. JONSEN

Equality

Human beings are empirically unequal in intelligence, skills, moral qualities, physique, and beauty. Yet there is a strong sense in many religious and humanist philosophies that in some ultimate "ontological" sense they are equal, and that this equality is more important than their empirical differences. In the Christian faith this is expressed by the belief that in creation all are "made in God's image"; that all have sinned and fallen short of what they ought to be (the "Fall"); that Christ died for all to reconcile them to God (the atonement) and bring them into a new creation (the church) in which basic human differences are transcended; and that God's intention is that all should find their fullness in enjoying him and one another in him (the "last things"), though it is possible some will refuse this. A vigorous humanist expression of this attitude was given by Walter Lippmann in *Men of Destiny* (1927): "There you are, sir, and there is your neighbor. You are better born than he, you are richer, or you are stronger, you are handsomer, nay you are better, kinder, wiser, more likeable; you have given more to your fellow men and taken less than he . . . and yet—absurd as it sounds—these differences do not matter, for the best part of him is untouchable and incomparable and unique and universal. Either you feel this or you do not: when you do not feel it, the superiorities that the world acknowledges seem like mountainous waves at sea; when you do feel it, they are slight and impermanent ripples upon a vast ocean."

The question is, to what extent is this insight to be expressed in public life? Equality before the law has been achieved in theory in "Western" societies, though there is not always in practice equal access to the law, for in this as in many other respects, wealth brings advantages. In the Western type of political democracies the position of "one adult, one vote" has mostly been achieved, though only after a great struggle by women to obtain the vote, and by a struggle against property carrying extra votes. Equality of opportunity is the next aim for many. This raises the question of the principle or principles of distribution of economic goods in society. There are three basic ones: right, merit, and need. Legal right tends to perpetuate inherited hierarchies from the past in wealth and prestige. Merit would in theory sweep these away—but for the empirically more unequal human persons, equal opportunity would allow no protection from the sense of failure; and a meritocracy could be an unpleasant society. Need does justice to certain necessities that every person has, and without which individuals cannot play their full part in the community. It seems unlikely that any

society can avoid giving some weight to all three principles, but there is a case for saying that need should have priority. After that, excellence has to be recognized, and inevitably hierarchies will establish some rights. The classic treatment of this is R. H. Tawney's *Equality*. Equality is closely related to justice* and to freedom* and, again, these have to be balanced against one another.

Equality, therefore, cannot be the sole, comprehensive social ideal. It starts from the affirmation that all persons are equal in inherent worth, and it ends by saying that all social and economic inequalities which are not necessary or justifiable in terms of the common good* should be eliminated. Equalities do not need special justification, whereas inequalities do. This position is not the same as egalitarianism, which is usually taken to mean that all social inequalities are unnecessary and ought to be eliminated, and that all persons ought to be treated alike—a position held by few. But there is wide scope for discussion on which inequalities are necessary or justifiable.

R. H. Tawney, *Equality,* 1931; J. Rees, *Equality,* 1971.

RONALD PRESTON

Equiprobabilism

This method of resolving practical doubts, taught by Alphonsus Liguori (1696–1787), seeks a middle course between probabilism* and probabiliorism*. It appeals to the legal maxim that in a case of doubt the one in possession has the better claim (*Melior est conditio possidentis*). Thus, if the doubt concerns the *existence* of a particular obligation, and if the argument in favor of liberty is at least equally probable, it is held that this suffices to confirm our liberty, which is already "in possession." But if the doubt concerns the *cessation* of a recognized obligation, and if the argument in favor of liberty is no more than equally probable, we must conclude that the law, which is already "in possession," continues to oblige.

See also **Casuistry; Counter-Reformation Moral Theology; Moral Theology; Tutiorism.**

THOMAS WOOD

Equity *see* **Epikeia; Fairness**

Equivocation
see **Honesty; Lying; Truthfulness**

Erastianism

The type of relationship between church and state whereby the former is subjected to the latter.

See **Church and State.**

JOHN MACQUARRIE

Eros see Love

Error see Ignorance; Sin(s)

Eschatological Ethics

As the result of the work of a large number of NT scholars beginning with Johannes Weiss and Albert Schweitzer, it is generally recognized that Jesus' conception of the kingdom of God* presupposes an eschatological and apocalyptic world view. In the teaching of Jesus the kingdom of God was essentially an eschatological event and its coming was conceived to be imminent. Its advent would be marked by a radical transformation of the present world order and the inauguration of a new aeon in which evil would be completely overthrown and the righteous rule of God would be fully manifest. (Apocalypse is a type of eschatology—a doctrine of the "last things"—that anticipates God's destruction of the forces of evil in a cosmic cataclysm and conflict.)

Recognition of the eschatological and apocalyptic presuppositions which underlay Jesus' understanding of the kingdom of God called for a reexamination of the nature and purpose of his ethic. In *The Quest of the Historical Jesus* (1906, ET 1910), Schweitzer argued that the purpose of Jesus' ethical teachings was to show people what they must do in preparation for entrance into the kingdom, the coming of which he believed to be imminent. Since it was intended only for a relatively brief interval between the proclamation of the kingdom and the actual advent of the kingdom, Jesus' ethic was in reality an "interim ethic."* Its content was so conditioned by the expectation of an imminent end to the present historical order, Schweitzer believed, that it is inapplicable to life in a radically different cultural situation in which a much longer chronological future is anticipated.

Subsequent biblical scholarship has modified Schweitzer's thoroughgoing eschatology at a number of important points. It is now generally recognized, for example, that Jesus' conception of the kingdom had a present as well as a future dimension. Moreover, it is also generally acknowledged, as we shall see, that Jesus' ethic cannot be adequately understood simply as an "interim ethic," even though it is also agreed that his ethic cannot be properly understood apart from its eschatological setting. But the basic question raised by Weiss and Schweitzer was not whether there was such an eschatological element in Jesus' teaching; rather, it had to do with the fundamental *meaning* of the latter. Insofar as Christian ethics is concerned, the basic question in this regard is: To what extent did eschatology condition Jesus' ethic? To what extent did the former determine both the sanction and the content of the latter? Does Jesus' ethic lose its entire validity once the expectation of the immediacy of the *eschaton* is no longer held?

As previously noted, Schweitzer argued that Jesus' entire ethic was an interim ethic, the purpose of which was to summon humanity to repentance in preparation for the advent of the kingdom of God. In this respect, Schweitzer went even farther than Weiss, who had acknowledged that some of Jesus' teachings—especially the commandments to love God and one's neighbor—do not seem to have been directly affected by his expectation of the imminent advent of the new age. Since Schweitzer some NT scholars have sought to distinguish in various ways between one set of Jesus' ethical teachings which appear to be eschatologically conditioned, on the one hand, and the remainder of his ethical teachings which seem to presuppose a relatively long continuation of the present historical order. Thus Hans Windisch, in *The Meaning of the Sermon on the Mount,* distinguishes between the following two main streams in the ethical thought of the Sermon on the Mount*: (1) radicalized wisdom teachings which had their origin in the nondualistic wisdom tradition of Judaism and hence were not originally affected by eschatological beliefs, and (2) prophetic-eschatological announcements of salvation and judgment, the content of which was directly related to the eschatological expectations. The content of the wisdom teachings—for example, the counsel to love one's enemy, the warning against anxiety, and the admonition that one about to go to court should make friends with one's accuser—was not determined by the nearness of the judgment; nevertheless, these sayings are given a radical eschatological interpretation as they appear in Matthew in contrast to Luke.

While it is possible to discern at least two types of ethical counsel in the teachings of Jesus—one reflecting the wisdom, or law, tradition; the other reflecting a more prophetic, eschatologically conditioned demand—and while the former may be more directly applicable to a nonapocalyptic setting than the latter, it is difficult to make a sharp, clear-cut distinction between the two. Moreover, the most distinctive ethical counsel of Jesus is couched in the form of certain stringent demands that he places upon his followers in view of the impending apocalyptic crisis. At the deepest level, therefore, the fundamental question concerning the relationship of eschatology to Christian ethics must be raised in connection with the prophetic, radically eschatological demands of the gospel. And, finally, the question arises as to whether there is any unifying element underlying the whole of Jesus' ethical teaching that may provide a basis for placing the questions of eschatology and an interim ethic in a larger perspective. In an attempt to indicate some of the most important interpretations of the significance of eschatology for Jesus' ethic that have been set forth in opposition to Schweitzer's concept of an interim ethic, we shall briefly consider the following: Rudolf Bultmann's existentialized eschatology, C. H. Dodd's "realized eschatology," Martin Dibelius's concept of an "eschatological stimulus," and Amos Wilder's distinction between the secondary and primary sanctions of Jesus' ethic. Finally, attention will be given to a number of recent attempts to build a distinctively Christian social ethic upon eschatology.

In *Jesus and the Word,* Bultmann argues that despite the apocalyptic character of Jesus' teaching concerning the kingdom of God, the validity of his ethic is not affected in the least by the failure of this expectation. Bultmann characterizes Jesus' ethic as one of "radical obedience," involving the claim of God upon the whole person to do the divine will in each present moment of decision. The basic significance of the eschatological element in Jesus' teaching is to be found in the fact that the proclamation of the coming of the kingdom points humanity to *"the present moment as the final hour* in the sense of the hour of decision" and that this "now" is always the last hour in that in it each person is

confronted with the necessity of making an existential decision for or against total obedience to the divine claim. Hence, it is a matter of indifference whether the specific content of Jesus' ethical teaching was derived from his eschatological expectations; for that which is permanently valid about his ethic is the demand that it makes for radical obedience to the demand of God, the precise content of which must be existentially heard in each new moment of decision. Jesus' ethic cannot, therefore, be dismissed as an interim ethic; moreover, his proclamation of the coming of the kingdom and his ethical teaching about the will of God have an indissoluble unity in the "word" of God—i.e., in that event in which humanity is confronted with the message of God's forgiveness and with the necessity of making a decision either for or against obedience to God.

While Bultmann maintains that for Jesus the coming of the kingdom of God lay wholly in the future, C. H. Dodd argues that Jesus viewed the kingdom as having arrived both as judgment and as grace in his ministry. In *The Parables of the Kingdom,* Dodd acknowledged that certain sayings of Jesus apparently imply a future coming of the kingdom, but he holds that such sayings refer, not to a future coming of the kingdom in this world, but to a "transcendent order beyond time and space"—an order in which "many who are not yet 'in the kingdom of God,' in its earthly manifestation, will enjoy its ultimate fulfilment in a world beyond this." The eschatological hope for the coming of the kingdom was thus being "realized" in Jesus' own lifetime, and he did not look for it to come again or in any fuller sense in this earthly order. Hence, Jesus' ethic cannot have been intended as an interim ethic. Rather, Dodd believes, it was intended as "a moral ideal" for persons who are even now living in the new age. Or, as Dodd puts the matter in *Gospel and Law,* it is intended "as the new law which supersedes the law of the Old Testament"; it is intended, in short, as "the law of the kingdom of God." As such the ethical precepts of the Gospels have two purposes: on the one hand, they serve as an aid to repentance, and, on the other hand, they serve as a guide for positive moral action for those who have received the kingdom and seek to live their lives in the presence of God's judgment and grace.

According to Martin Dibelius in *The Sermon on the Mount,* Jesus looked for the end of the present age to come soon, but his ethic was not for this reason intended as an interim ethic. On the contrary, the commandments of Jesus represent the eternal will of God, and as such they "were given for eternity." Indeed, all of the commandments in the Gospels, and not just those with an explicit reference to the coming of the new age, are eschatological in that their starting point is the absolute will of God, not human ability and the conditions of earthly life in the present age. Jesus' ethical teachings as well as his deeds are therefore "signs of God's kingdom." They were not intended as law but rather as "radical examples of what God demands" of those who want to be children of the kingdom even now in this present age. It is impossible for modern persons who do not share Jesus' apocalyptic expectations to be fully obedient to the will of God, since they cannot escape responsibility for the social problems of today; nevertheless, the ethic of the Gospels is just as relevant to life in the modern world as it was to Jesus' hearers. The primary purpose of this ethic then and its essential function today is to make men and women "well acquainted with the pure will of God" to the end that, although they are "not able to *perform* it in its full scope," they may be "transformed by it." Jesus taught neither an ethical ideal that people might seek to attain as the goal of their social life, nor a law for moral conduct either before or after the arrival of the new age; rather, his ethic serves as an "eschatological stimulus," which, because it is completely focused upon the reality of the kingdom of God and because it is intended as a sign of the kingdom's presence, confronts humanity with the pure and eternal will of God in a way in which it is impossible for either a set of laws or any other system of ethics to do.

In *Eschatology and Ethics in the Teaching of Jesus,* Amos N. Wilder recognizes that eschatology provided the "dominant sanction" for Jesus' ethic, but he argues that this appeal to rewards and punishments was only a formal and secondary sanction based upon a religious-prophetic apprehension of the divine will (*see* **Rewards and Punishments; Sanctions**). Hence, the essential and fundamental motivation for righteousness in Jesus' teaching is found in the appeals which he

made to a discernment of the nature of God, humanity, and the world; to intuition; to gratitude; to obedience; and to the desire to be children of the heavenly Father. The eschatological appeal to rewards and punishments is thus basically a symbolic albeit pedagogically necessary formulation of the consequences of human conduct in a world in which the primary human relationship is the personal one which each bears to the righteous and sovereign Lord of history.

Eschatology has three main functions in relation to Jesus' ethical teachings, according to Wilder. In the first place, insofar as the coming of the kingdom is conceived of in futuristic terms, the appeal to eschatology provides "the motive for repentance and for urgency in doing righteousness, and the particular demands are looked on as conditions of entrance to the future kingdom." In the second place, insofar as Jesus teaches that the kingdom is already present, he recognizes that a new ethical situation has been created by its presence; his ethical teaching points, therefore, to the new possibilities of life based upon the presence of the kingdom, and his ethic may be described as "an ethic of the present kingdom of God or a new-covenant ethic." Finally, eschatology is related to Jesus' ethical teachings in a third way, for the crisis associated with the coming of the kingdom, which Jesus identified with his own work, placed special claims upon his followers during this period. Particularly stringent acts of loyalty, witness, and sacrifice were required of his disciples during this time of conflict. This "discipleship ethic" was thus conditioned in a special way by the eschatological expectations of Jesus, but even here as elsewhere the fundamental sanction is Jesus' apprehension of the divine will.

Like Bultmann and Dodd, Wilder tends not only to de-emphasize the apocalyptic elements in Jesus' message but also to interpret the eschatological features of the latter symbolically. As a consequence the cosmic-universal and the sociopolitical aspects of Jesus' teaching are eliminated from his message and indirectly from that of the NT as a whole. When these elements are lost to view, Christian morality easily becomes spiritualistic and individualistic. Recent scholarship has shown, however, that the apocalyptic language of the NT cannot be separated from its eschatological content without betraying the

NT vision of the fulfillment of history and the entire cosmos as well as individuals. The language of NT eschatology is apocalyptic; "as such it is cosmological, universal, political, and mythological" (E. Schüssler Fiorenza). As noted above, there is also general agreement among scholars that the eschatological events described in the NT are in some sense both present and future.

For the most part (the major exceptions being the Fourth Gospel, Colossians, and Ephesians), the "already" and the "not yet" of the promised salvation exist in dialectical tension. The continuing problem for Christian ethics is how this dialectical relationship can be recovered and sustained in the present day.

The following authors and movements are representative of the attempt to recover the significance of eschatology for Christian ethics by relating the promise of the coming kingdom dialectically to historical forms of human life in the secular world in the period since World War I: Dietrich Bonhoeffer, Helmut Thielicke, Reinhold Niebuhr, Jürgen Moltmann, Gustavo Gutiérrez, and Thomas Ogletree. In his *Ethics* Bonhoeffer moved from the more radical eschatological concentration upon the "ultimate" in *The Cost of Discipleship* to an ethic that included both the "ultimate" and the "penultimate." Recognition of the penultimate provided the basis for the Christological affirmation of the secular on the basis of its relationship to the ultimate, i.e., "the last things." Understood in this perspective, Christian ethics is an ethic of formation, obedience, and responsibility *within* the mandates or orders*. For Thielicke, theological ethics is best typified by the "borderline situation" wherein the conflict between good and evil is irresoluble without guilt (*see* **Dilemmas**). The very possibility of Christian ethics rests, therefore, upon "justification by grace" whereby the believer is freed to participate responsibly in culture as a "worldly Christian." In Thielicke's view, the relationship between Christian faith and the world is wholly dialectical. For Reinhold Niebuhr, Jesus' teaching about the kingdom as both present and future means that history after Christ is an "interim between the disclosure of its true meaning and the fulfillment of that meaning" at the end of history. During this interim between the first and second coming of Christ, faith regarding the meaning and final consummation of history provides the basis not only for a critique of all human achievements within history but also for "the struggle for social justice."

According to Moltmann, biblical theology is fundamentally eschatological, and eschatology is interpreted primarily in terms of promise grounded in the resurrection of Jesus Christ. In relation to ethics, eschatology provides the basis for critiquing the negativities of the existing social order; it also provides the basis for openness to change and for hope and courage in the face of injustice. Due to his conception of eschatology in terms of the resurrection of Jesus, together with his conception of the contingency of creation, however, Moltmann is unable to provide moral guidance for concrete human action, especially in the area of social ethics. Writing from the perspective of Latin American liberation theology*, Gutiérrez also makes eschatology the key to an understanding of Christian faith. For him the central meaning of eschatology lies in the tension which it creates between the present social order and the coming kingdom. In liberation theology generally the eschatological promise is understood in historical, temporal, and social terms; the ethical norms of the Gospels—liberation, justice, peace, and love—are similarly understood as societal norms. Eschatology provides the theological basis for the transformation of society. Finally, attention should be called to Ogletree's study *The Use of the Bible in Christian Ethics*. According to Ogletree, the substantive meaning of eschatology for ethics is found in the fact that it "directs attention to new possibilities for human existence taking form in the midst of the old age." The "eschatological horizon" of Christian faith issues in an ethic of discipleship—an ethic that is basically perfectionist rather than deontological—and in the formation of new eschatological forms of community characterized by mercy, mutual forbearance, and forgiveness. A social ethic based upon the NT must be built first of all upon the eschatological promise of the coming kingdom rather than on creation or preservation. The relationship of the coming kingdom to creation is dialectical and to a certain extent transformationist. Thus understood, eschatology does not refer fundamentally to the expectation of an imminent end of the world; it refers, rather, to the presence of a new age in the midst of the old.

See **Hope; Jesus, Ethical Teaching of;**

Kingdom of God; New Testament Ethics; Sermon on the Mount.

D. Bonhoeffer, *Ethics*, ET 1955; R. Bultmann, *Jesus and the Word* (1926), ET 1934; and *The Presence of Eternity: History and Eschatology*, 1957; M. Dibelius, *The Sermon on the Mount*, ET 1940; C. H. Dodd, *The Parables of the Kingdom*, 1936; E. Schüssler Fiorenza, "Eschatology of the N.T.," *IDB* Suppl., 1976; G. Gutiérrez, *A Theology of Liberation*, 1973; W. G. Kümmel, *Promise and Fulfilment*, ET 1957; J. Moltmann, *Theology of Hope*, ET 1967; R. Niebuhr, *The Nature and Destiny of Man*, 2 vols., 1941–43; T. W. Ogletree, *The Use of the Bible in Christian Ethics*, 1983; N. Perrin, *The Kingdom of God in the Teaching of Jesus*, 1963; H. Thielicke, *Theological Ethics*, vol. 1: *Foundations*, ET 1966; A. N. Wilder, *Eschatology and Ethics in the Teaching of Jesus*, rev. ed. 1950; H. Windisch, *The Meaning of the Sermon on the Mount*, ET 1951.

E. CLINTON GARDNER

Essenes

Our information about the Essenes, a Jewish sect between the 2nd century B.C. and the end of the 1st century A.D., comes from four main historical sources: Josephus, *Antiquities* 15. 10.4–5; 18.1.5; *Jewish War* 2.8.2–13; Philo, *Every Good Man Is Free* 13–14; Pliny, *Natural History* 5.17.4; and Eusebius, *Preparation for the Gospel* 8.11. There is also evidence that the Qumran community of the Dead Sea Scrolls belonged to or was closely connected with this sect.

The Essenes were deeply devoted to the Jewish law. To them Moses came second only to God, and to blaspheme the name of Moses was a crime punishable by death. Their ethic was therefore basically the ethic of devout Jews. But in more than one direction they carried their ethic beyond the ethics of Judaism. E. Schürer (*History of the Jewish People*, vol. 2, ET, rev. ed. 1979) calls them "connoisseurs in morality."

1. Their ethic was a community ethic. They held everything in common. Food, clothes, money, even their tools were the property of the community. There was therefore among them no such thing as poverty, and they were famous for their treatment of the sick and the aged, who in the Essene community received such care that they had nothing to fear.

2. They worked for the community, but they had certain views regarding work. They would only work in villages and in the country, for they would not share in the immoralities of towns and cities. They were forbidden to make a weapon of any sort, or to manufacture anything that would hurt or harm any other human being.

3. They were abstemious and even ascetic. They ate only enough to keep them alive, and were content with one dish and with no variety in their food. They wore the simplest clothes, and wore them until they were completely worn out. Unlike normal Jewish practice, they forbade marriage and practiced celibacy, although some seem to have married, perhaps for the sake of the continuance of the community.

4. In certain things they were in advance of their time, and different from normal Judaism. They refused all oaths—except the oath upon entering the community—on the grounds that a statement which required an oath was already condemned. They rejected animal sacrifice, although they sent incense to the temple. They had no slaves and believed slavery as an institution to be wrong.

It may fairly be said that they practiced the ethics of Judaism, but intensified them in a monastic community which was based on a covenant theology and an apocalyptic eschatology.

A. Dupont-Sommer, *The Essene Writings from Qumran*, ET 1961; G. Vermès, *The Dead Sea Scrolls: Qumran in Perspective*, 1978.

WILLIAM BARCLAY

Ethicist, Ethician

An ethicist is a person who "does" ethics, in the sense of reflecting on morality, its nature, its presuppositions, and its applications. The term has sometimes been used, especially earlier, to refer to someone who supports ethics rather than religion (see OED). Now probably more common in religious than in philosophical or secular contexts, the term "ethicist" is interchangeable with "moral theologian" or "moral philosopher," as in the expressions "Christian ethicist," "religious ethicist," and "philosophical ethicist." It is apparently more at home in Protestant contexts, where the phrase "Christian ethics"* is more common than "moral theology."* Another equivalent term is "ethician," which is probably more popular in Roman Catholic moral theology.

JAMES F. CHILDRESS

Ethics

The word "ethics" is used in a variety of ways, and confusions between these uses are common. At least three main types of question are called "ethical" in different senses: (1) questions as to what is right, good, etc., or of how we ought to behave (normative ethics, morals); (2) questions as to the answers given by particular societies and people to questions of type (1) (descriptive ethics or comparative ethics, a branch of moral sociology or anthropology); and (3) questions as to the meanings or uses of the words used in answering questions of type (1), or the nature or logical character of the moral concepts, or, in older language, of what goodness, etc., are (theoretical ethics, philosophical ethics, moral philosophy). It is perhaps best, in philosophical writing, to reserve the word "ethics" (unqualified) for inquiries of type (3). The motive for undertaking them has, however, often been the hope that their results might bear on questions of type (1); whether and in what ways this is possible is the question that above all others vexes students of philosophical ethics, and divides the supporters of naturalism*, intuitionism*, emotivism*, descriptivism*, prescriptivism*, etc.

The simplest answer is given by naturalism and related theories, which hold that to understand the meanings of moral terms is already to be assured of the truth of certain general moral principles, from which, in conjunction with statements of fact, particular moral judgments can be derived. Against this it has been objected by the followers of G. E. Moore that moral principles are matters of substance, or synthetic, and therefore cannot be established by appeal to the meanings of words. More recent writers (prescriptivists) have added to this objection another, that, since moral judgments are prescriptive or action-guiding, they cannot be derived by logical deduction (with or without the use of definitions of terms) from merely factual premises. The substance of this objection goes back to Hume and Kant. Both these objections rely on the general logical principle (itself not undisputed) that the conclusion of an inference can contain nothing that is not there, at any rate implicitly, in the premises.

In a religious context, this controversy is most aptly illustrated by considering the suggestion that "wrong" *means* "contrary to God's will." If this were so, then we should at once be assured of the general moral principle that what is contrary to God's will is wrong (it would, indeed, be a veiled tautology); and from this, in conjunction with factual premises about what, in particular, God wills, we could deduce particular moral judgments about what is wrong. If objections about the difficulty of ascertaining God's will are ignored, there remain the objections: (1) that it must be matter of substance, not a mere tautology, that what is contrary to God's will is wrong; and (2) that no mere definition of terms could enable us to deduce the prescriptive judgment that something is wrong from the factual statement that it is contrary to God's will. It is further objected that it must be possible for a sufficiently perverse man to maintain without self-contradiction that an act is contrary to God's will but not wrong, or vice versa. Moreover, the word "wrong" is used, and apparently understood, by atheists, and it is not obvious that they are using it in a different sense from theists. For these reasons most philosophers would now reject the view that "wrong" *means* "contrary to God's will"; but this does not imply a refutation of the view that what (and only what) is contrary to God's will is wrong. The latter view (an answer to a question of type (1) rather than of type (3) above) is held by most Christians. It does not follow that Christians will agree with one another about all moral questions; for issues which among non-Christians would be treated as disputes about what is wrong, simply, will often be treated among Christians as "factual" disputes about what God's will is, it being assumed that, whatever it is, what is contrary to it is wrong. Often, there being no independent way of ascertaining God's will, it gets accommodated to the moral views of particular disputants. It is perhaps only when a speaker is prepared in this way freely to "tailor" what he calls "God's will" to his own moral opinions, that the expressions "contrary to God's will" and "wrong" can be said to be equivalents.

If we ask more positively what *are* the meanings, functions, natures, uses, etc., of moral words or concepts, we are, naturally, on controversial ground; but there are some points on which, perhaps, a majority of moral philosophers would agree, their differences lying in matters of emphasis and interpretation. (1) It is a widely accepted view that moral judgments containing such words are in some strong and special sense action-guiding (for example, that there is a more than merely contingent connection between thinking an act the best in the circumstances and being disposed to choose it). This is the feature of moral words which is most emphasized by prescriptivists. (2) Most thinkers would agree that when words like "right," "wrong," "good," and "bad" are used, they are applied to acts, etc., in virtue of some feature or features of them (apart from their mere rightness, etc.) which is the *reason* for using these words of them. It is held by many to follow from this that to call one act, for example, wrong, is to commit oneself to call any other act wrong which resembles it in all, or in the relevant, particulars. This thesis has been called "the universalizability of moral judgments."*

These two theses are not inconsistent, though they can be made to appear so by mistaken interpretation, thus giving rise to needless disputes. This in turn has led to the rejection of one of the theses as incompatible with the other. For example, some naturalists have rejected (1), holding that moral judgments are action-guiding only in the sense in which any factual judgment whatever may be; the information that an act is the best in the circumstances will lead me to do that act, *if* I want to do what is best, just as the information that a stone is the flattest available will lead me to choose it, *if* I want the flattest stone; the effect of this is to turn moral judgments into something like Kant's "hypothetical imperatives." They have done this because they thought that, if thesis (2) is correct, the only thing that we can be doing in calling an act the best act is to inform our hearers that it possesses those features which entitle it to this name. If this were so, then the information would guide action only given a prior disposition (which might be absent) to do acts which have those features.

Against this, adherents of Thomism on the one hand, and many modern prescriptivists on the other, have insisted, in different ways, on thesis (1). This doctrine is summed up in the maxim, which goes back in substance to Socrates, *Quicquid appetitur, appetitur sub specie boni* (Whatever is desired, is desired under the appearance of its being good).

Thesis (2) is incompatible with thesis (1) only if we take (2) as implying that when we call an act, for example, the best, and do so in virtue of something about it, we are doing the same sort of thing as when we call, for example, a surface red in virtue of something about it (its visual appearance under normal conditions). In the latter case to know the meaning of "red" is to know that we are entitled to call a surface red if, and only if, it appears *thus* under normal conditions. If "best" functioned like "red," then, once its meaning was known, there would be no choice left as to what sorts of acts we could call best. And this would lead to a dilemma. Either we should have to reject thesis (1); or else we should have to maintain that to think some act the best is, indeed, to be disposed to do it, but that, once we know the meaning of "best," what sorts of thing we are disposed to do become unalterably fixed; and this runs counter both to our common understanding of the meaning of "best," and to our feeling that to know the meaning of a word can never restrict our freedom of choice in this way.

Faced with this dilemma, some have felt that, sooner than reject thesis (1), it is best to reject thesis (2), and deny that acts are necessarily called "the best" in virtue of *anything* about them. But we can avoid this implausible conclusion by interpreting thesis (2) more carefully; it can be taken as implying, not that the meaning of words like "best" ties them to *particular* features of, for example, acts (the same for all users of the word) but rather that whenever anybody uses the word, he must have in mind, as his reason for using it, *some* features of the act in question (which, if repeated in any other acts in relevantly similar situations, would oblige him to call them, too, the best in their respective situations, or else to withdraw his judgment about this present situation); but these features might differ from speaker to speaker, depending on their various moral opinions, without thereby the *meaning* (in one sense) of the word "best," as used by them, altering. In other words, the user of the word 'best' thereby commits himself to *some* rule for its application, but there is no single rule to which all users of the word are committed by its meaning. The rule followed by any speaker will depend on his own moral principles as to what is best in this type of situation. For certain necessary qualifications to this statement, *see* **Conventional Morality.**

This issue has sometimes been stated in terms of the distinction between the descriptive and the prescriptive (or evaluative) meaning of moral words. The descriptive meaning is the features in virtue of which an act, for example, is called the best; the prescriptive meaning is the conceptual link whereby a judgment that such and such an act is the best is logically tied to a disposition to choose it. Most current controversies in ethics are essentially about the relations between these two sorts of "meaning," and the extent to which one or the other of them is properly called "meaning." It may safely be said that any ethical theory which ignores either of them is bound to be incomplete; if the prescriptive meaning is ignored, the action-guiding character of moral judgments, which alone gives them their importance and even their use, is lost; if, on the other hand, thesis (2) is denied, then the basis of the rationality of moral judgments, viz., that they are made for reasons, that is, because of *something about* their objects, is destroyed.

The issue just discussed has a bearing on the question of the so-called "objectivity" of moral principles, which has been the "philosopher's stone" of ethics. It is possible to interpret "objectivity" in such a strong sense that it can be established only by some form of naturalism—that is, by saying that the *meaning* of the moral words is such that, once it is known, there is no option left as to what we call, for example, right. Those who reject naturalism cannot in consistency seek to establish this sort of objectivity. However, it is likely that what most "objectivists" are really after is not so direct a link between the meanings of the moral words and the features of things in virtue of which the words are applied to them, but rather some way or other of establishing the rationality of moral thinking. Much recent controversy in ethics has been between those who think that it cannot be established without adopting some sort of descriptivism (that is, by denying thesis (1) above, in practice usually by espousing some kind of naturalism), and those who think, on the contrary, that thesis (1) is not incompatible with the rationality of moral thought, and may even be essential to it. The word "objectivism" and its opposites subjectivism* and relativism* have been used in so many different senses (often without the realization that they are different) that clarity

would be furthered by abandoning the terms altogether and characterizing the disputants in the current controversy by new terms such as "descriptivists" and "non-descriptivists." But, if this is done, it is important to realize that a non-descriptivist does not necessarily deny that moral terms have descriptive meaning; he merely affirms that this is not the only element in their meaning.

See also **Metaethics.**

For amplification of the argument of this article, see the author's articles "Ethics," in *Encyclopedia of Western Philosophy and Philosophers,* ed. J. O. Urmson, 1960; and "Descriptivism," in *Proceedings of the British Academy,* 1963; and see his books *The Language of Morals,* 1952; *Freedom and Reason,* 1963; and *Moral Thinking,* 1981. For a general survey of the field of ethics from a different standpoint, with further references, see R. B. Brandt, *Ethical Theory,* 1959.

R. M. HARE

Ethos

A transliteration of the Greek word for "custom" or "character," this term refers to the characteristic values, beliefs, and practices of a social group or a culture. It corresponds to the Latin *mores,* "customs," which refers to generally held moral beliefs and practices. While ethics* involves reflection on choices and decisions about action, an ethos is constituted by pervasive beliefs and values that are seldom questioned within the ethos. Thus, free speech is an element of the democratic ethos, while personal humility is part of the ethos of most Christian communities. Ethics aims at a consistent and unified moral system, but an ethos may contain elements that conflict with one another. Also, different ethoses may impinge on the same person, giving rise to contradictory expectations. In modern pluralistic societies, conflicts within and between ethoses become important occasions for ethical reflection. Political loyalties may conflict with a person's religious identity, for example, or ethnic family patterns may differ from the ideals promoted by the media and mass culture.

The study of an ethos is initially a descriptive rather than a normative task. Sociology* and anthropology* provide methods for an accurate account of cultural beliefs and expectations, which can then be subjected to normative scrutiny and systematization. At the same time, this critical study of society indicates that systematic moral philosophy and theology always depend in important ways on the ethos in which these reflections take place. Contemporary Christian ethics seeks to identify the economic ideologies, national cultures, and social class biases that may intrude upon its normative conclusions, and it attempts to articulate more fully the ethos of the Christian community that determines which problems will seem important and which solutions are likely to appeal to ethicists who are themselves shaped by that community.

See also **Custom.**

ROBIN W. LOVIN

Eudaemonism

The theory that holds happiness* to be the highest good.

JOHN MACQUARRIE

Eugenics

At least since the time of Plato, philosophers have exhorted healthy, productive, intelligent people to reproduce. Just as regularly, individuals whose natural endowments seemed to equip them less well for success in society, e.g., the chronically ill or the mentally disabled, have been discouraged both by custom and by law from bearing children. While the impetus for both a positive eugenics (rewarding childbearing among the most fit) and a negative eugenics (impeding parenthood among the "inferior") has ancient precedents, it was not until the late 19th century that a program of selective breeding based on systematic, ostensibly scientific principles was proposed (*see* **Genetics**).

In 1883 British physician Sir Francis Galton coined the term "eugenics" (from the Greek, meaning "wellborn") to describe a new branch of study that would focus upon improving the human race by judicious matching of parents possessing "superior" traits. Galton's study emphasized the hereditary transmission of intelligence. His disciples expanded upon the notion that certain behavioral patterns or characteristics of personality could be identified in individuals and passed on through a program of selective mating. They proposed that many negative traits could be traced to a hereditary legacy, i.e., that criminals, paupers, alcoholics, prostitutes, and others with undesirable propensi-

ties had reached their state in life simply as a result of their genetic inheritance.

In the 20th century, application of eugenical theory as a solution to social problems in America led to such ethically problematic practices as the wide-scale sexual sterilization of epileptics, the mentally ill, and the retarded, restrictions on the immigration of some ethnic groups, and prohibition of marriages between people of differing racial backgrounds. To support each of those practices, purportedly "scientific" criteria derived from eugenical studies were used to argue that hereditarily ill or handicapped parents always produced defective children; that the people of some nations and ethnic groups were genetically inferior to people of other nations; and that mixing the genes of superior and inferior races would dilute the total gene pool, to the detriment of all humanity.

Little attention was paid by the most doctrinaire eugenicists to the differential effects of environment on human achievement. The difficulty of analyzing a single character trait, e.g., intelligence, that might be the result of multiple factors such as education, family practices, and heredity was also often ignored. By the mid-1940s increased sophistication in the study of genetics put to rest many of the fallacies of eugenical theory that had arisen in the first third of the century. The demise of Nazi Germany, the nation that most aggressively enacted the tenets of eugenical theory into law, led to further discrediting of the conclusions of the eugenicists.

Today, while the most distasteful arguments of classical eugenics are held in general disrepute (e.g., that the handicapped should be strictly prohibited from marrying or that some races or ethnic groups are genetically inferior to others) and the term "eugenics" itself is rarely heard, the idea that society should have some say in regulating reproduction remains current. As in the early years of the century, there are those who would invoke the good of society to restrict the number of children born to poor parents. Such potential restrictions highlight the conflict between the burdens communities should be asked to bear (in taxes to support the indigent) and the rights to reproduction, personal autonomy*, and choice of family size that are arguably vested in all persons without regard to social rank or economic condition.

The development of medical technology to assess mental and physical abnormalities *in* *utero* or, even before conception, to diagnose individuals or groups more at risk to produce less than "normal" children throws the social good versus individual rights debate into even higher relief. Does a parent who conceives and delivers a severely malformed or handicapped child, even though the risks are known and the conception and birth are preventable, have a right to expect that scarce medical resources will be allocated to the child's care? What place do religiously controversial practices such as surgical sterilization* (or other means of birth control such as contraception*) and selective abortion* have as tools of public policy in encouraging "wellborn" children? Should the state fund such practices, or, from the opposite point of view, should they be forbidden by law? A perspective beyond that of state or parents could be attributed to the unborn child. For such potential persons we might ask: What rights are possessed by the medically abnormal fetus? Does its developing identity as a human being give it a full claim not only to life itself but also to whatever public resources may be necessary to sustain and nurture it? And finally, is there such a thing as wrongful life? That is, can we impute a eugenical value system even to the unborn, who, if they could know the suffering that a life of deformity or handicap might hold in store for them, might opt not to be born at all?

Such questions remain as part of the popular debate over population policy*, reproductive choice, and the appropriate exercise of both governmental and personal power over the kind of individuals who will people the future human community. These questions are not directly attributable to the intellectual heritage of the eugenicists, but force us to renew an analysis of the issues they posed originally: Who should be encouraged, who forbidden to bear children; and, What principles should be applied to evaluate the role of governmental coercion or parental choice in family planning?

See **Genetics; Handicapped, Care of the; Procreation; Race Relations; Racism; Reproductive Technologies.**

C. P. Blacker, *Eugenics: Galton and After,* 1952; F. Galton, *Natural Inheritance,* 1889; M. Haller, *Eugenics: Hereditarian Attitudes in American Thought,* 1963.

PAUL A. LOMBARDO

Euthanasia

The literal meaning of euthanasia (from the Greek *eu* and *thanatos*) is easy or gentle death. But its etymology is of little help in resolving the moral problem which it poses, for none of us would wish anyone to die in pain or distress.

In pre-Christian times what might be termed euthanasia was practiced in some countries, usually in the form of exposure of the very young and abandonment of the aged (*see* **Abandonment; Exposition**). Modern interest in the question dates from the 19th century. Few would now defend it in terms of a crudely utilitarian ethics as a means of forcibly disposing of those members of the community who, because of disease, mental deficiency, or physical uselessness, are felt to be burdensome. Such a policy was given a logical extension in Nazi Germany during the Second World War when it embraced those who were regarded as politically and racially an embarrassment to the state. Today euthanasia is usually referred to in a narrower context and, by its advocates and opponents alike, is generally understood to mean that when a person is acknowledged to have an incurable and/or distressing illness, his or her life should be terminated by some painless method approved by science to shorten the suffering. This might take a compulsory or voluntary form.

Compulsory euthanasia means the painless putting to death of the sick person, without his or her consent, by someone acting in a private or public capacity. This has been defended as "mercy killing" with special reference to grossly deformed or mentally defective children (*see* **Infanticide**) or adults who are in terminal, painful, or "humiliating" illness. It is said that to give them a speedy and gentle release would be an act of merciful kindness to them and to members of their family. This clinical homicide conflicts with Christian teaching. The right to life is God-given, and it is not within our moral competence deliberately and directly to take the life of any innocent human being either with or without his or her consent. To do this in the circumstances envisaged would be an act of injustice toward the sick person and an act of impiety toward God who gave the person life. True compassion* there should be, but it is incompatible with injustice and impiety. We have a general duty to relieve suffering, but not at any price. It is sometimes said that doctors commonly practice a benign euthanasia under a well-understood conspiracy of silence, but the evidence does not support such a claim. There is an important distinction between the *analgesic* and the *lethal* dose: it is one thing to deaden or reduce pain by an injection which may also have the unintended effect of shortening life, and quite another to give an injection with the direct object of terminating a patient's life (*see* **Double Effect**). To take with deliberate intent the life of any innocent person, whether incurably sick or in good health, with or without the aid of medical science, is to commit the grave sin of murder (*see* **Homicide**).

Voluntary euthanasia is that gentle clinical termination for which a person of sound mind asks, in the event of his or her becoming the victim of grievous illness or ravaging disease. It is the contention of the voluntary euthanasia legalization societies that, with various safeguards, the law should permit a person in these circumstances to be supplied with the means to terminate his or her own life or to authorize a doctor, by a signed and witnessed declaration, to do it. Some Christians support this view, arguing that a good person may conclude that he or she has already reached a stage when one can no longer do anything more to serve God or one's fellow humans by remaining alive. But this conflicts with the overwhelming weight of Christian opinion in the present as in the past. A human being is not the absolute owner of his or her life, whose creator and redeemer is God. One has the right to protect it but not the right willfully to destroy it. Is it not a denial of God's loving providence to assert at any given time that one's life can no longer serve any good purpose? It is true that suffering* can sometimes seem meaningless to us; it is never to be sought or endured simply for its own sake, and as far as possible it should be eased. It can be very terrible, but it is not the worst evil. Sometimes it is the occasion of spiritual growth. The manner in which it is endured can have moral effects of great value upon those who are privileged to be in attendance. Deliberately to take (or request another to take) one's life for any self-regarding motive, even that of escaping from the burden of what is at present an incurable disease (and, in this case, also denying one's family or society's public representatives the opportunity

to fulfill their duty of trying to provide the care one needs), is to commit the grave sin of suicide*. (There is, however, increasing debate about the adequacy of some of the traditional arguments against suicide.)

Often condemned by ecclesiastical authorities, voluntary euthanasia was also declared unethical by the World Medical Association in 1950 and subsequently by many regional associations in part for consequentialist reasons (*see* **Consequentialism; Wedge Argument**): Would not the practice gradually undermine the attitude of complete trust* hitherto assumed in the doctor-patient relationship, and introduce suspicion and insecurity into many domestic situations? Some who would otherwise be its supporters have acknowledged that the practical problems involved in drawing up a legally acceptable declaration might be insuperable, not least because of the need to be certain of the patient's valid consent* not simply at some earlier date but at the very moment of euthanasia.

Confusion is sometimes caused by using expressions like *"passive euthanasia"* to denote the *withholding* of *any* treatment that is capable of keeping alive the gravely ill, however briefly. It has been claimed that, until death occurs, it is always one's duty to continue using to the full every available life-sustaining procedure. But, when one considers all the highly sophisticated systems and techniques of modern medicine, it is frightening to envisage the possible consequences of a strict adherence to such a rule. It would be one thing (and exceedingly culpable) to allow a person to die by deliberately withholding or withdrawing treatments which, if applied or persisted in, would be remedial or curative. It is quite another thing, during the final stages of terminal illness, to refrain from extraordinary procedures which might intensify the suffering and, at best, only prolong the process of dying, providing simply the sedation and skilled nursing that will allow the patient to die a "natural" death, peacefully and with dignity (*see* **Life, Prolongation of**). This is no more an instance of euthanasia, rightly understood, than is the switching off of a life-support machine when brain death has already been diagnosed (*see* **Death, Determination of**).

Opposition to euthanasia might be held to imply the duty of striving to make ever more widely operative those standards of terminal care more especially associated with the modern hospice* movement in Britain and America, in the light of which—it has been said—euthanasia is seen to be not only mistaken but irrelevant.

See also **Life, Sacredness of.**

Church Information Office, *On Dying Well: An Anglican Contribution to the Debate on Euthanasia,* 1975; P. Ramsey, *The Patient as Person,* 1970; S. Stoddard, *The Hospice Movement: A Better Way of Caring for the Dying,* 1979; H. Trowell, *The Unfinished Debate on Euthanasia,* 1973.

THOMAS WOOD

Evangelical Counsels *see* **Counsels; Norms; Vocation**

Evangelical Ethics

Evangelical ethics heralds the Creator-Redeemer's revealed demand for both personal righteousness and social justice, and it echoes the imperative of love for God with our whole being and of love for our neighbor as ourselves. It looks to the substitutionary Savior Jesus Christ for unblemished fulfillment. The biblical vision of earthly justice and peace, it stresses, is messianically grounded.

The regenerate church views itself as the distinctive new society over which the risen Christ rules, and it anticipates the Lord's return to fully establish the kingdom of God. The Great Commission mandates not only world evangelism but universal instruction in the teaching and commands of Christ. Intellectual historians have noted that almost all Western humanitarian impulses sprang from the theology of the cross.

John Wesley denounced slavery and urged prison reforms and education for the masses. William Wilberforce, English politician and philanthropist, after his conversion in 1785–86 helped found societies to challenge obscene publications and to abolish the slave trade. Once the House of Commons, in 1807, ended the slave trade in the British West Indies, he promoted immediate emancipation. One of the 19th century's most effective social and industrial reformers was Anthony Ashley Cooper, 7th Earl of Shaftesbury (Lord Ashley), leader of the evangelical movement in the Church of England, who promoted asylums for the insane and legisla-

tion to curb and regulate child labor and to protect workers from economic exploitation. The evangelical social agenda included orphanages for foundlings, hospitals for the sick, restriction and rehabilitation of prostitutes. The Salvation Army, the YMCA, the Red Cross, and many other humanitarian enterprises had evangelical rootage.

Social ideals promoted by evangelicals at home were carried abroad by missionary pioneers. For example, William Carey secured the prohibition of widow-burning and child sacrifice in India. Missionaries also fought the slave trade, discouraged polygamy, promoted literacy and education, built schools, medical clinics, and hospitals.

The modern "social gospel"* sought millennial transformation of the world through education, legislation, and social evolution; it abandoned miraculous revelation and supernatural redemption, supposedly in deference to the empirical methodology of science. Its early advocates were committed to the indispensability of personal evangelism and spiritual rebirth, but the alteration of social structures soon became the main mission of ecumenism. Some church leaders were convinced that the unity of the world church, frustrated by debate over theological pluralism, could be achieved instead through a shared agenda of social reform. Some social gospel spokespersons alienated evangelical church leaders by implying that capitalism* is intrinsically immoral and socialism*, biblical; evangelicals defended the biblical propriety of private property* and fair profit.

Before the mid-20th century, American evangelicals were beginning to reverse fundamentalism's reactionary withdrawal from the social arena (*see* **Fundamentalist Ethics**). The evangelical journal *Christianity Today,* begun in 1956, made social ethics* one of its emphases. Evangelical leaders became increasingly aware that Christianity's social aspects had been unjustifiably sidelined (see David Moberg, *The Great Reversal,* 1972).

On specific issues in social ethics evangelicals diverge considerably, even as they do over church polity and eschatology. In evangelism they have forged a consensus for transdenominational cooperation despite theological differences on secondary matters. Whether they can articulate a moral consensus in the secular social milieu remains to be seen. Those who aggressively link biblical values with the political right include Francis

Schaeffer (d. 1984) and Jerry Falwell. The emerging left is represented by *Sojourners* magazine, edited by James Wallis, and by *The Other Side* and *Radix;* other spokespersons include Ronald Sider and Richard Lovelace. One of the major concerns of most evangelicals is abortion*, considered by many to be the most horrendous evil of our age.

Evangelicals consider God intrinsically good and the sovereign stipulator of the moral law. Evangelical ethics is basically a "divine command"* ethics (*see* **Voluntarism**); it attributes the current lack of objective moral authority to the modern grounding of morality in utility or observation rather than in transcendent revelation. Christ rules the church, it holds, through the Holy Spirit by the authoritative scriptures (*see* **Bible in Christian Ethics**). The good life, it contends, is not attained by realignment of one's natural abilities, but by crucifixion of the old nature and spiritual rebirth.

C. F. H. Henry, *Christian Personal Ethics,* 1957; and *A Plea for Evangelical Demonstration,* 1971; J. M. Idziak, *Divine Command Morality,* 1979.

CARL F. H. HENRY

Evil

Evil can be considered in terms of its nature, explanation, and remedy (or cure). Inevitably the Christian view of evil coincides at many points with the views adopted by non-Christian thinkers. But the gospel provides a wholly new answer to the problem of its cure.

The nature of evil. Most theologians distinguish between moral and nonmoral evil. Moral evil consists in transgression of the moral law or, when faith is present, disobedience to the will of God. Nonmoral evils comprise those ills which do not proceed directly from human sin.

Moral evil, or sin, will be analyzed elsewhere (*see* **Sin(s)**). Here it is enough to state that a human act can have evil effects without itself being evil in the moral sense. An act is morally evil only if it is a voluntary infringement of a moral law that is known to the agent. When the agent is invincibly ignorant of a law, or when he or she acts involuntarily, the act is not morally wrong, or sinful; so that any evil effects it may produce fall within the nonmoral category.

Nonmoral evils are various. One thinks chiefly of the human suffering produced by physical disorders—by earthquakes, famine, or disease. (Whether the wastage in the evolutionary process or the pain endured by subhuman animals is to be judged evil is a disputable question. But nature is unquestionably often evil in relation to its highest product—humankind.)

Yet what is the nature of evil in itself? What is its ontological character or status? Aquinas held that it is wholly negative—a "privation of good." His aim was to exclude a Manichean dualism that would be incompatible with the Christian doctrine of creation. Since everything is made by God, and since God is holy, evil cannot possess independent being. It is therefore a defect in a person or a thing. Just as blindness is lack of sight, so vice is lack of virtue. In both cases the human organism fails to actualize its nature and achieve its good.

Although the concept of *privatio boni* has often been criticized, four things can be said in its favor (in addition to its exclusion of cosmic dualism). First, even if it is not a complete definition of evil it can be regarded as a partial one. Secondly, it does not entail the view that evil is merely apparent or unreal. Thirdly, it does justice to the spiritual truth (stated by both Plato and Paul) that sin diminishes and corrupts the soul at the center of its being. Fourthly, it explains why we include both moral and nonmoral ills within the single category "evil," and why we view both with equal horror. We do so because they both distort reality. Both represent a declension from the creature's good and thereby from the perfect, loving will of the Creator.

The explanation of evil. Even if we accept the view that evil is negative, we still have to explain how it can occur in a world created by a holy God. Two general explanations must be rejected.

The first rests on the denial that God is omnipotent. He is limited, if not in wisdom, then in power. He is faced either by recalcitrant material or by other malign agencies that co-exist with him. Such a view (which was held by many Gnostics) is incompatible with Christian theism which asserts that God made the world *ex nihilo.* God is not omnipotent in the sense that he can do anything, for some things are contrary to reason or morality. But he is omnipotent in the sense that he controls all things by his creative word.

Some, again, have taken refuge in the contrast between God's "absolute" will and his "permissive" will. God does not will evil absolutely (by a direct expression of his nature), as he wills good. He merely permits it for a higher end. But this is an evasion, not a solution; for since God is simple he wills everything by a single, undivided act of power. If we say that he merely "permits" evil—and perhaps we are driven to say this in order to make his action intelligible—we must add that his will in permitting it is absolute. In any case we are left with the question why, if he is omnipotent, he permits it.

Having rejected these "solutions," we can to some extent explain evil in its two main forms along the following lines:

1. Sin*. According to the doctrine of the Fall, sin entered the human race through Adam's disobedience (*see* **Original Sin**). But even if the Genesis myth is taken literally, it only pushes the problem a stage farther back. How could Adam (or anyone in Adam's place) make a sinful choice if he was made in the image of a good Creator? It has been suggested that if we take the Adam story symbolically we can understand the origin of sin in evolutionary terms thus. If human beings were created as spiritually immature beings engrossed in the struggle for survival and endowed with dim, often distorted views of the divine, it was virtually inevitable that they should acquire sinful impulses. Many theists have attempted to justify the existence of sinful acts on the ground that their possibility is an inevitable consequence of free will*, and that the latter is a condition of a personal relationship with God. To this it has been replied that the harm done by such acts outweighs any value inherent in free will*, and that a personal relationship with God would be possible even if the agent always spontaneously performed good acts.

2. Human suffering*. This has always been regarded as a powerful obstacle to belief in the Christian God. Nothing can be said that is both new and true. Some suffering is caused by the prior sin of the sufferer. But (as Job's experience and Christ's explicit teaching show) some suffering is unmerited. Unmerited suffering is often justified on three grounds. First, it "purifies" the sufferer by affording an opportunity to strengthen his or her character. Secondly, suffering can produce virtues that would not otherwise be

shown. Thus it can produce courage in the sufferer and sympathy in those who care for the sufferer. Thirdly, examples of suffering endured with courage and faith can afford moral and spiritual inspiration to others. However, some suffering does not ennoble, but degrades. Some too does not evoke sympathy or inspire others. Some again is so prolonged and acute that it can scarcely be justified solely in temporal terms. Here theists have often made the following additional claims. (1) Insofar as suffering is caused by sinful acts, it is justified by the freedom that God has given us (see above). (2) Insofar as suffering is caused by nature, we must accept it on the ground that if God constantly intervened miraculously to prevent it, nature would become wholly unreliable. To the objection that God could have created the world in the first place without harmful elements, theists have replied that we do not have the knowledge enabling us to affirm this; that we cannot isolate ourselves and imagine that we would be the same persons in a different kind of world; and that in any case much suffering is caused by accidental collisions with natural forces. (3) We must see this life in the light of the next, when unmerited suffering will be both rectified and transformed by eternal joy.

However, it must be stressed that many, perhaps most, theists admit that evil is not now fully explicable when it is set against belief in an omnipotent God of love. Many too would add that the element of inexplicability is consonant with the facts that God and his providential ways surpass our understanding; that faith is always subject to trial or "probation"; and that faith's present knowledge always falls far short of the vision we shall possess hereafter (see **Theodicy**).

The cure of evil. Although Christians cannot fully explain the fact of evil, they possess the secret of its cure. God in Christ has saved them from the ravages of sin and suffering through his perfect sacrifice whereby he made of both a pathway to the heavenly world.

Hence, for the Christian, evil is characterized by a double paradox. On the one hand, its presence in a world created by a holy God cannot be fully explained. On the other hand, God himself, in his incarnate Son, has conquered evil and enabled us to share (by grace, not merit) in his victory. Again, evil is fully real—a terrible cancer at the heart of things. Yet we believe that, through the Spirit of the risen Christ, the greatest evil can become the occasion of the greatest good—if not of a good that is manifest here and now, then of a good that will be manifest hereafter.

Christians can and must face evil in its full reality and inexplicability. But their reaction to it is distinctive. They do not seek escape from it (as the Buddhist seeks escape in a passionless nirvana). They do not preach a Stoic "indifference" to it. Still less do they make it an excuse for a pessimistic *Weltanschauung*. They have two duties: (*a*) to combat it by every means and (*b*) to believe that God will vanquish it according to the perfect (but hidden) wisdom of his providence.

Thomas Aquinas, *Philosophical Texts*, sel. and tr. T. Gilby, 1956, pp. 163–180; J. Hick, *Evil and the God of Love*, 1966; H. P. Owen, *Christian Theism*, 1984, pp. 83–111.

H. P. OWEN

Evolutionary Ethics

The notion that ethical conduct should be seen as an extension of biological evolution was popularized by Herbert Spencer (see especially his *Data of Ethics*, 1879, ch. 2, "The Evolution of Conduct"). Evolutionary views of the development of cultures were prevalent among anthropologists of the late 19th century, assuming a pattern of stages of development from simple primitive forms to the complex rational forms of Western civilization. That social and ethical conduct should be looked on as a direct continuation of biological evolution, to be described in similar categories, was challenged by Thomas Huxley in his Romanes Lectures of 1893, "Evolution and Ethics," in which he maintained that ethical life, particularly insofar as it involved consideration for the weak, prescribed conduct directly opposed to the cosmic struggle for existence described by biological evolution. A version of the older view of ethical development as a further stage of evolution was given in 1943 in another Romanes Lecture, under the title "Evolutionary Ethics," by his grandson, Julian Huxley, the best-known recent exponent of this view. He sees ethical and cultural development as a new stage of evolution, where the human mind can deliberately shape the future course of evolution through purposive action. He shows the continuity with earlier stages by presenting the later stages as development of potentialities inherent in the earlier.

A difficulty about this way of looking at ethics is knowing just how the notion of evolution should be understood. Biological evolution is a theory of the differentiation of a number of species from a common ancestor, and the survival of some of these. The elimination of large numbers of species and the survival of others makes for a gradual change through the accumulative effect of small genetic variations. Whether or not the term "evolution" should be restricted to biological evolution in this sense, it can be broadly said to stand for processes of large-scale change over long periods through the accretions of small changes not attributable to the purpose or intention of individuals or to special creation. To use the term "evolution" as equally applicable to ethical and social development may obscure differences between purposive human actions and biological change. Nineteenth-century "social Darwinism" took success in competition for scarce resources as the condition for survival in nature and as a law of society. Yet such behavior is found disadvantageous to the individual and advantageous to its kin. "Sociobiology" is a neo-Darwinian view of "altruistic" behavior as making for the selection of those carrying the genetic inheritance. It is criticized as reading too much control into the genes.

The term "evolution" may also suggest a single line of human social development, and even an inevitable line of progress. The notion of potentialities can also be used to reinforce the metaphor contained in the word "evolution": the unwinding of something implicitly already contained in what is already there. In moral conduct, on the other hand, while a number of different courses of action may all be potential in the sense of possibilities, to decide which human potentialities—for instance, those making for aggression or those making for cooperation—should be encouraged and which inhibited is a matter for decision in the light of value judgments.

The strength of evolutionary theories of ethics lies in their attempt to show human beings as living in a natural environment, and also in bringing out the fact that, like all living things, they are dependent on adapting themselves to their environment. There can also be an incentive to moral effort in the idea that human life, as it emerges from nature, and as it has developed over long stretches of time, is still incomplete: that "the gates of the future are open," to use a phrase from Henri Bergson's *Creative Evolution* (1907; ET 1911). The weakness in this type of view consists in the slurring of the distinction between what is and what ought to be, between judgments of fact and judgments of value. If there are indeed natural tendencies in biological nature, for example, making for love and cooperation, and if human ethical behavior directed to furthering these qualities can draw on the energies such instinctive drives may supply, this is a matter for which those who value these qualities may be grateful. But if not, ought we to drop the conviction that these are qualities to be encouraged? If there are tendencies in nature strengthening ethical propensities, moral development will thereby be easier, but if not, we are not bound to take our moral cues from nature. Moreover, to hold that moral behavior must be deducible from natural facts is likely to lead to an unduly moral interpretation of phenomena of "mutual aid" in animal behavior. A sympathetic account of this is given by Mary Midgley in *Beast and Man: The Roots of Human Nature* (1978). She claims that our emotional nature is largely given by our animal inheritance, and much of it is shaped by social needs with which ethics is concerned.

The belief that ethical conduct is conduct in accordance with the direction of evolutionary change, and that "good" means "more evolved," rests on a valuationally loaded view of evolution by which it is seen as change in a line of direction, so that what follows is held to be more "advanced" and not only subsequent to what went before. There is some empirical support for this without making an assumption of universal progress, insofar as more complex stages make possible the achievement of a greater range of possible types of activity and of relationships, and these more complex stages have generally been preceded by simpler and less differentiated stages. But the ethical question can still be raised as to whether, in human activities, the achievement of all "possibilities" is desirable.

On the whole it is likely to make for greater clarity to speak of processes of social and cultural change in terms of development rather than evolution. This is of course a matter of recommendation; there is no authoritative legislation in matters of terminology and definition. But if the term "evolution" is used of social and ethical development, it is essential to be aware of the differences between this kind of change and biological evolution.

There is, however, a sense in which the term "evolutionary ethics" may be used, not as a view in which the standards and criteria of moral conduct are thought of as derivable from a process of change continuous with biological evolution, but as a theory that would be better described as "the evolution of ethics." This would be the view that ethical beliefs and principles have "evolved," in the sense that they have taken different forms at different times as ways in which human beings in societies have met their biological and social needs. So long as this view is not taken to imply some single pattern of successive stages through which all cultures must pass (a view that nowadays has little support among anthropologists), there is considerable empirical support for this. Its main limitation is that it fails to express the extent to which the institutions through which human beings seek to satisfy social needs may be matters of contrivance as well as of piecemeal and even unconscious adaptation. It also makes little allowance for aspirations after nonutilitarian ideals of moral excellence and for the purposive work of reformers.

A sustained attempt to present a view of evolutionary ethics in both these senses was L. T. Hobhouse's *Morals in Evolution* (1906). Hobhouse was concerned with "the advance of the ethical consciousness to the full understanding of its own origin and function, viz., that it has arisen out of the conditions under which mind evolves and that its purpose is to further and perfect that evolution." Hobhouse's view was a sophisticated one in that he did not assume automatic progress* and he saw that there was a need for criteria for evaluating social changes not simply in naturalistic terms. His own criteria were qualities making for the achievement of "rational good," such as the increasing control over the conditions of life and the harmonious development of human potentialities. (Some of the question-begging character of the term "potentiality" is corrected by introducing the qualification "harmonious.") Morris Ginsberg, in his *Evolution and Progress* (1961), has a sympathetic discussion of Hobhouse's work, along with a judicious estimate of the standing of this kind of thinking.

See **Science and Ethics; Naturalistic Ethics.**

A. L. Caplan (ed.), *The Sociobiology Debate,* 1978; M. Ginsberg, *Evolution and Progress,* 1961; L. T. Hobhouse, *Morals in Evolution,* 2 vols., 1906; J. Huxley, *Evolution and Ethics, 1893–1943,* 1947 (this is a publication of the Romanes Lectures of both the Huxleys, with an introduction by Julian Huxley); T. Huxley, *Evolution and Ethics,* 1893; M. Midgley, *Beast and Man: The Roots of Human Nature,* 1978; C. Sherrington, *Man on His Nature,* 1940; H. Spencer, *The Data of Ethics,* 1879; C. H. Waddington, *Science and Ethics,* 1942 (a discussion of some of the problems raised by "evolutionary ethics" from a number of points of view); E. O. Wilson, *Sociobiology: The New Synthesis,* 1975.

DOROTHY EMMET

Excellence

The person who excels is the person who is superior to others in ability and achievement. It is a simple fact of life that there must always be some persons who are above the average, and a very small group who are much above it. In the *Republic* of Plato, provision was made for this group to have special privileges and training, counterbalanced by special responsibilities laid upon them. Perhaps Nietzsche, with his doctrine of the superman (*Übermensch*), carried the ethic of excellence to its furthest extreme and also showed the dangers inherent in it—dangers that manifested themselves in the rise of fascist and racist movements, rooted in this whole tradition. But there is also the danger that in modern egalitarian societies, excellence may be stifled and all reduced to a monotonous mediocrity. The immense complexities of a technological society demand an increasing number of very highly qualified and able people. That such persons should have full opportunity to develop and exercise their superior talents is not only their due but is also necessary for the health of society. This may mean that there must be provided for them such advantages in education and such rewards and incentives as will ensure their optimal development and functioning. This sets up a tension between the claims of excellence and the claims of equality* which is not always easy to decide and which may become more acute as the technological revolution goes on.

JOHN MACQUARRIE

Exception *see* **Norms; Situation Ethics;** *see also* **Anglican Moral Theology; Modern Protestant Ethics; Modern Roman Catholic Moral Theology**

Excommunication

An ecclesiastical sanction for breaches of doctrine or morals that excludes the offender from full communion with the church. Excommunication regards ecclesiastical status, not necessarily a person's relation to God. The usual NT warrant for excommunication is Matt. 18:15–18; see also Matt. 16:19; John 20:23; 1 Cor. 5; 2 Thess. 3:11; 1 Tim. 1:19b–20; and 3 John 9–10. Excommunication first is mentioned in church documents in the 4th century; by the 15th it clearly had evolved into "greater" and "lesser" forms, which were complete social shunning of the excommunicates (called *vitandi*) and deprivation of the sacraments (for the *tolerati*). Some Reformation groups retained excommunication, e.g., the Anabaptist "ban" (see also on "disownment" in Quaker ethics*). Today, Roman Catholicism retains the two forms, but generally exercises only the lesser. It can occur automatically through one's action, even without public sentence. In Protestantism excommunication is infrequent.

See **Discipline.**

Codex Iuris Canonici, 1983, pp. 227–301; W. Doskocil, *Der Bann in der Urkirche,* 1958.

LISA SOWLE CAHILL

Existentialist Ethics

In his famous lecture on existentialism, Jean-Paul Sartre, the last existentialist to avow the title, tells of his refusal to advise a young man facing an ethical dilemma. In the subsequent discussion with the philosophers who heard the lecture, two criticized him. "You should have told him what to do," they said. One of these was a Christian, the other a Communist.

Existentialists make a virtue of not knowing what to do. They are not thereby as remote from Christian thought as some have judged. Basic concepts in Christian ethics are taken up into the viewpoint, especially in the attitude toward law and toward human freedom. Even the alleged acosmism, individualism, and atheism of existentialism have meanings which are closer to the Christian position than the casual observer generally concedes.

Living by laws, which is a way of knowing what to do, is regarded by existentialists as "bad faith" (Sartre and Simone de Beauvoir). Any abridgment of human freedom is "bad faith." A legalistic ethic abridges freedom by taking decisions out of the hands of responsible selves. Søren Kierkegaard's treatise *Fear and Trembling* anticipated this view. Abraham was a knight of faith because he remained open to God's word. His willingness to murder his son out of obedience to God is higher than ethics because it does not force the future to conform to revelations of God given for the past.

In existentialism what Kierkegaard called "the teleological suspension of the ethical" is itself ethics. Openness to the future has primacy over conformity to the past. Not that one annihilates the past. To use Sartre's term, one simply "nihilates," which is to say, "suspends" it, in order to let the demands of the future emerge. The past tells us what we ought to do. The future is a more reliable guide simply because it does not tell us what to do, but appeals to us to "invent" or "create" in the light of the emerging situation.

Christian ethics has accomplished the same movement away from legalism*. When the apostle Paul interpreted the preaching of Jesus as a reducing of the whole law to the one word, "love," he rooted Christian behavior in "the trans-moral conscience" (Paul Tillich), "an ethic without laws" (Paul Ramsey), an ethic of "creativity" (Nicolas Berdyaev) or "responsivity" (H. Richard Niebuhr). The transcendence of laws does not mean, however, the abrogation of norms*. For existential ethics, freedom*, by which one transcends laws in the direction of creative action, is itself the norm for freedom. Humanity is freedom. Freedom is the source of the human's possibility to act ethically, because freedom is nothing—a lack to be filled, a power of resoluteness which lets situations reveal their needs. And what is the norm by which to discern in any situation what is needful? One must so act as to let others be free while oneself remaining free (Sartre).

In fulfilling this ethical program, existentialists are known to be atheistic. What is less evident is that they are also acosmic. That is, they do not accept the world sponsored by cosmologists. If one could know why existentialism is acosmic, one would have important clues to why existential atheism is quite benign. The world of the cosmologist is an outthere world into which a human is invited to fit as a coin fits in a box. Existentialists, however, believe the world is not something one is *in*. Worlds are modes of *being-in*. There is the world of politics, of sports, of religion, of art. There is no "world" of ethics because ethics is the study of modes of being-in which results in revealing the possibilities for the worlds one creates through one's modes of being-in.

The model from art comes the closest to exemplifying how an existential ethic works. The artist does not record a world that exists, but rather creates through his or her aesthetic behavior, the possibility for a world one may not previously have known (Martin Heidegger and Maurice Merleau-Ponty). The Acropolis mobilized the earth, sea, and sky of Periclean Athens into a significant human world. Whether it still does so is questionable, so that artists continue to develop possibilities for today's world at the risk of reducing previous artworks to the status of museum pieces. Ethics, like art, nihilates the world as cosmos (earth, sea, and sky) in order to create the world as a mode of being-in (the Acropolis). Now it can be seen why it is a mistake to call existentialism an individualism*, implying that it has no social ethic. The primary term for existentialist ethics is neither "individual" nor "social" but "world," a reality in which the distinction between individual and social disappears, for "world" embraces *all* modes of being-in.

By analogy to acosmism, atheism does not mean the annihilation of God, but only his nihilation. God as a static reality is put in parentheses in order to let the world of humanity emerge as it is possible. Atheism has sometimes meant that humans have killed God. In existentialism it means that humans have used a static concept of God in order to endorse effete causes whose prolongation is murderous to humanity. Such a god is not simply dead; he is an executioner. Kierkegaard was a theist for the very same reason that existentialists today are atheists. Why is it that for Kierkegaard Abraham's willingness to slay Isaac was not a deficiency in his moral sense, so that he could be called a pioneer of faith? Because if there is a God, nothing else can be absolutized. All one's relations will be relative. Old worlds, like Isaac, must be allowed to die in order for new worlds to be born. In this case relativism* does not mean the absence of standards, but the freedom, that is, the responsibility, for creating in one's time the relevant mode of being-in.

See **Kierkegaardian Ethics; Phenomenology; Situation Ethics.**

S. de Beauvoir, *The Ethics of Ambiguity,* ET 1948; S. Kierkegaard, *Fear and Trembling* (1843), ET 1941; H. R. Niebuhr, *The Responsible Self,* 1963; F. Olafson, *Principles and Persons: An Ethical Interpretation of Existentialism,* 1967; J.-P. Sartre, *Critique of Dialectical Reason,* vol. 1 (1960), ET 1976.

CARL MICHALSON

Exogamy

The custom that prevents a man from taking a wife from within his own tribe. The opposite is endogamy*.

JOHN MACQUARRIE

Experimentation with Animals
see **Animals**

Experimentation with Fetuses
see **Fetal Research**

Experimentation with Human Subjects

Historical perspectives. The ethics of involving humans as subjects of biomedical experimentation has ancient roots. The physician Celsus (1st cent. A.D.) approved the vivisection of condemned criminals by his Egyptian predecessors, Herophilus and Erasistratus. His words became a classic defense of all experimentation: "It is not cruel to inflict on a few criminals sufferings which may benefit multitudes of innocent people throughout all centuries." In contrast, at the dawn of modern medicine, Claude Bernard (1813–1878) espoused a different view: "The principle of medical and surgical morality consists in never performing on man an experiment which might be harmful to him to any extent, even though the result might be highly advantageous to science, i.e., to the health of others." Between these two ethical positions stands Sir William Osler. Testifying before the Royal Commission on Vivisection (1908), he discussed Walter Reed's experiments in which human volunteers ran the risk of death in order to determine the cause of yellow fever.

Commission: I understand that in the case of yellow fever the recent experiments have been on man.

Osler: Yes, definitely with the specific consent of these individuals who went into this camp voluntarily. . . .

Commission: We were told by a witness yesterday that, in his opinion, to experiment upon man with possible ill result was immoral. Would that be your view?

Osler: It is always immoral, without a definite, specific statement from the individual himself, with a full knowledge of the circumstances. Under these circumstances, any man, I think, is at liberty to submit himself to experiments.

Commission: Given voluntary consent, you think that entirely changes the question of morality or otherwise?

Osler: Entirely.

When Osler spoke, "human experimentation" was a relatively rare event in medical science. He himself emphasized careful clinical observation rather than deliberate therapeutic manipulation. The pathology laboratory rather than the bedside was the locus of research. During the 1920s the model of "investigator-clinician" was shaped. In the early 1930s, Sir Bradford Hill and Sir Ronald Fisher provided essential statistical tools for the design and analysis of clinical experiments. By the late 1930s, the professional clinical investigator was established on the medical scene and research had become an integral part of hospital practice. Thus, with the experimental spirit abroad, the professors in position, the methods at hand, and the patients on the wards, human beings, and most often sick human beings, became the "animals of necessity" in theory and in fact.

These research developments aroused little indignation. Medicine was at the apogee of its scientific achievement. The conquest of many lethal infectious diseases by antiseptic practice, by immunization, and by antibiotics, as well as the conquest of pain by anesthesia, had come about through research and experiment. These triumphs not only impressed the public but brought undeniable benefit to the suffering and to society.

The revelation, in 1945, of the experiments carried out by German physicians on concentration camp prisoners shocked the world and forged an unhappy link between the words "experiment" and "crime." The influential article by Henry Beecher in the *New England Journal of Medicine* in 1966 began with the words, "Human experimentation since World War II has created some difficult problems." In the 1960s, several events in the USA then became public issues: the experiments at Jewish Chronic Disease Hospital, in which cancer cells were injected subcutaneously into senile patients without their knowledge; studies on viral hepatitis at Willowbrook State Hospital, in which retarded children were deliberately infected; the Tuskegee Syphilis Study, in which 300 rural black males were left untreated for diagnosed syphilis even after effective antibiotics became available. These events generated a negative view of medical experimentation.

These ethical problems soon became issues of law and public policy. In the USA, the federal government, sponsor of so much basic and clinical research in medicine and the behavioral sciences, produced guidelines and regulations of increasing explicitness and strictness. Then Congress established the National Commission for the Protection of Human Subjects of Biomedical and Behavioral Research (1974–78), which framed the federal regulations now in force (Code of Federal Regulations 45CFR46, 1983).

In Great Britain and in Canada, the debates over this issue have not been as vociferous as in the USA. However, the medical research councils in both nations have issued statements of principle similar to those incorporated in American regulations, although much less explicit about the particular problems surrounding use of children and incapacitated persons. On the international scene, the Council for International Organizations on Medical Sciences has issued international guidelines (1982) that go beyond the Helsinki Declaration of the World Medical Association (1964) in explicitness.

Principles of ethics of research. Research designates a class of activities directed toward the development of generalizable knowledge. Generalizable knowledge signifies theories, principles, or relationships based on data that can be corroborated by methods of observation, experiment, and inference. Research activities may seek new knowledge, reorganize existing bodies of information, verify extant theory, or apply existing knowledge to new situations. While the various scientific disciplines specify criteria for evaluating research performances within the scope of their respective domains, some components are common to all, including explicit objectives and formal procedures designed to attain these objectives. These components are commonly set forth in a research protocol.

The intended results of research are new or improved understanding of biological phenomena and the eventual development of diagnostic and therapeutic measures. These results benefit various parties: researchers in terms of knowledge, skills, and reputation; future patients whose illnesses are cured; society at large in the form of more effective health care. The benefits of research rarely come directly to the subjects of the research. It can be said that the basic ethical principle that justifies biomedical research is a utilitarian one: the prospect of improving the health of society. Yet, as the classical quotations from Celsus and Bernard show, there is a moral tension. The human subjects of research are themselves persons to whom moral obligations are owed. There is a need, then, not only of an ethic of research but an ethic of the protection of human subjects of research.

The Nuremberg Code (1949) states two elements of this ethic: voluntary consent* of the subject and the reduction of risk*. Although other codes and policies repeated these elements in various ways, the National Commission's "Belmont Report" in 1978 offered the first systematic statement of basic ethical principles emphasizing respect for persons*, beneficence*, and justice*.

The principle of respect for persons incorporates two fundamental ethical convictions: autonomous individuals should be allowed to make their own choices, and individuals with diminished autonomy should be protected. Respect for autonomy* consists in giving weight to persons' considered opinions and choices while refraining from obstructing their actions unless these are clearly detrimental to others. In accord with this principle, persons are invited to become research participants on the basis of an explanation of the nature of the research, its risks and probable benefits to themselves and to society. Participation should be entirely voluntary, and any coercive restrictions on free acceptance or refusal of participation should be eliminated. The practical requirement of informed consent arises from this basic principle (*see* **Consent**).

Since some persons who lack capacity for deliberation and consent might be suitable subjects for research, the principle of respect requires special protection in light of their limitations. The extent of protection depends on the risk of harm and the likelihood of benefit in relation to the importance of research. Protection may be of various sorts: some categories of persons might be totally excluded as research subjects, while others might be allowed to participate only in view of prospective benefits to themselves or to others suffering from the same or similar disorders. A strict standard might be imposed on guardians and special review might be required. (In one major debate in Christian ethics, Paul Ramsey argued that children who cannot consent should never be used in nontherapeutic research, i.e., research not intended to benefit them directly, while Richard McCormick, S.J., contended that with proxy consent, children could be used in nontherapeutic research of minimal or negligible risk.)

The National Commission used the term "beneficence" to designate the obligation to benefit individuals and, in the context of research, to reduce harms and to maximize benefits over possible harms. Beneficence thus required what might be called utility or proportionality: a practical "risk-benefit" assessment of each research project. Careful attention must be given to the identity of possible beneficiaries; the nature, probability, proximity, and importance of benefits; and the likelihood and seriousness of harms from the research (*see* **Risk; Proportionality; Utilitarianism**). Because of the divided loyalties of clinical investigators—to current patient-subjects and to future patients—it is important to make sure that current patient-subjects are not sacrificed to obtain future benefits (*see* **Hippocratic Oath**).

The principle of justice as applied to research requires that attention be given to the distribution of burdens and benefits of research. In the past, the sick, the poor, and the imprisoned were often recruited as research subjects, while the benefits of the research accrued to the more affluent members of the society. Justice requires that systematic discrimination in the selection of research sub-

jects be eliminated. Thus, research projects should be carefully examined to determine whether certain classes, such as welfare patients, racial or minority groups, or institutionalized persons, are selected simply because of their ready availability, their compromised positions, or their manipulability.

Obviously debates arise about the application of these basic principles of research. The National Commission endorsed the practice, started in the late 1960s by the U.S. Public Health Service, of Institutional Review Boards. Institutions conducting research under funds from the federal government must establish committees, composed of laypeople as well as researchers, to determine whether proposals to conduct research on human subjects satisfy these principles, particularly the risk-benefit ratio of the research, the appropriateness of the selection of subjects, and the adequacy of consent, but also other relevant principles and rules, such as the protection of privacy* and confidentiality*. The efficacy of this review process for protection of human subjects has been demonstrated (President's Commission for the Study of Ethical Problems in Medicine . . . , *Protecting Human Subjects: The Adequacy and Uniformity of Federal Rules and Their Implications,* 1981). In Great Britain and Canada, review committees are not required by law, but have become common in institutions performing research. They work with much less explicit guidance from regulatory agencies than the American committees.

C. Fried, *Medical Experimentation: Personal Integrity and Social Policy,* 1974; J. Katz (comp.), *Experimentation with Human Beings,* 1972; R. J. Levine, *Ethics and Regulation of Clinical Research,* 1981; and relevant articles in *DME* and *EB.*

ALBERT R. JONSEN

Exploitation

In moral discourse, "exploitation" denotes the process, condition, or result of X's taking unfair advantage of Y, usually through coercion*, deception, or undue influence, for X's own ends. Thus, it presupposes standards of justice*, fairness*, human dignity*, and respect for persons*. The term is widely used in Marxist thought (*see* **Marxist Ethics**) and in ethical positions influenced by Marxism, such as liberation theology*. In Marxist thought it has been defined as "withholding from another person, through the market or the production process, what is really his due" (P. J. D. Wiles, "Exploitation," *Marxism, Communism and Western Society: A Comparative Encyclopedia*, ed. C. D. Kernig, vol. 3, 1972). From this perspective any paid labor in capitalist economies is exploitative. This interpretation of exploitation has been rejected by all libertarian* and several more egalitarian theories of justice (*see* **Equality**). The concept of exploitation has also been applied to relations between nations (*see* **Imperialism; International Order**), to relations between the sexes (*see* **Feminist Ethics; Sex Discrimination; Women, Status of**), to relations between the races (*see* **Race Relations; Racism**), and to relations with nature (*see* **Environmental Ethics**).

See **Capitalism; Communism; Dehumanization; Economic Development; Human Rights; Justice; Oppression; Poverty; Socialism; Wealth.**

JAMES F. CHILDRESS

Exposition

Exposition of infants, that is to say, their exposure and abandonment, was a cruel form of population control, condemned by the early church.

See **Abandonment; Infanticide; Population Policy.**

JOHN MACQUARRIE

Extraordinary Means of Treatment *see* Life, Prolongation of

Fairness/Fair Play

The principle of fairness is widely invoked in ordinary moral discourse about the justice* of both the state's distribution of benefits and burdens and transactions among individuals (e.g., "that is not a fair contract" or "that is not a just wage"). It also undergirds a duty of "fair play," which appears in arguments to "play by the rules of the game," to "bear one's share of the burdens," not to be a "free rider," and, in short, not to take advantage of others' observance of the rules or contributions to a cooperative endeavor. The principle of fairness or fair play has received little explicit attention in Christian ethics, but it has been analyzed more carefully and imaginatively by philosophers, for example, by H. L. A. Hart (*Essays in Jurisprudence*

and Philosophy, 1983) and John Rawls (*A Theory of Justice,* 1971), in order to account for obligations that are distinct from fidelity* to promises* and contracts* and from debts of gratitude*. Both Hart and Rawls justify the obligation to obey the law in some settings by the principle of fairness, and this principle also appears in debates about punishment (*see* **Penology**). Rawls even labels his theory "justice as fairness' to reflect his use of a model of a hypothetical fair bargaining situation to generate principles of justice.

See also Epikeia; **Exploitation; Golden Rule; Just Price and Just Wage; Justice.**

JAMES F. CHILDRESS

Faith

Classical theology assigned two main functions to faith. (*a*) Faith is a necessary condition of authentic knowledge of God and of the human good. This is faith as belief and believing. The cognitional primacy of faith is expressed in the Augustinian theological principle *Credo ut intelligam* (I believe in order to understand). In the Augustinian tradition this means that one believes not only to attain an intellectual grasp of being and value but also to exist Christianly. (*b*) Faith is also construed as trust or loyalty. In this mode faith is held to be a religious virtue of the highest order, sharing that rank only with hope and love. Thus it could be said that faith as belief is the Martha of Christian existence, and that faith as trust is the Mary (Luke 10:38–42).

The dominant modern tendency is to widen the distinction between faith as belief and faith as trust. Thus the cognitive mode is sharply differentiated from the dispositional, and the status of faith as belief as a necessary condition of Christian existence becomes problematical. Accordingly, faith as trust, its ties with certifiable knowledge of God and of the human good loosened, is put under heavy pressure to posit in and for itself value absolutes—ideals and/or beings deemed worthy of unconditional loyalty. Thus, what was a polarity within faith itself deemed to be a unitary principle of life and spirit becomes a dichotomy in which the ascendency of either element—belief or loyalty—threatens the integrity if not the meaning of the other.

Barth's thought is a powerful critique of such tendencies. It manifests an Augustinian stress on the cognitive mode and function of faith. In Jesus Christ God makes himself known; in this transaction, and here alone, the divine moral imperatives for the faithful are ascertained.

Another distinction in the concept of faith has had a history something like that of belief/trust. This is the distinction between faith as gift and faith as achievement. In the classical traditions the content of belief (truths) as well as the ability to believe were held to be God's gifts; so also for faith as trust or loyalty. There were disagreements on the question of a created (natural) receptibility for the actual bestowal of supernatural truth and the endowment of heroic loyalty. Yet the objectivism of classical traditions could not have accommodated the notion of faith as an essentially human achievement. On this point Luther and his Tridentine opponents would make common cause against modernity.

The persistent subjectivism of modernity with respect to the realm of spirit construes the gift/achievement distinction as essentially intrahuman. Thus questions concerning the provenance and the authority of faith are adjudicated by appeal to anterior philosophical-anthropological principles. Liberalism transfers receptibility from human being to God's being: God responds affirmatively and creatively to human faith-ventures in behalf of ideal values. Thus faith as disposition enjoys primacy over faith as cognitive certainty.

Hence, modern conceptions of faith entail a direct and imperative engagement with an ethical realm deemed to be autonomous relative to religion. This can be seen in modern preoccupations with two questions.

1. What, if anything, is worthy of absolute loyalty? This question conjoins skepticism and certitude. It manifests skepticism about any and all absolutes. It betrays certitude concerning the provenance and authority of any legitimate ethical absolutes. In other words, absoluteness must be self-generated; it cannot be externally imposed or arbitrarily mandated. But absolutizing the power of the value of the private ego (the modern individual) is assuredly a sickness unto death. Not less formidable is the positing of a social structure or a cultural system as an object of unconditional loyalty. Moreover, the relentless pursuit of an abstract ideal has often proved to be a demonically destructive force. So perhaps nothing but the capacity for unconditional loyalty is to be trusted absolutely.

In terms of the practicalities, this amounts to believing that one cannot meaningfully aspire to a truly human existence without making enduring commitments, but none of these should be held as unrevisable.

2. How is faith to be related to other virtues and values? The answer to this question varies as attention shifts from the cognitional aspect of faith to the dispositional. The modern spirit is profoundly skeptical about beliefs that run counter to the (empirical) evidence; holding on to a faith that has lost real credibility is widely held to be a kind of immorality arguably more destructive of the fabric of self and society than violations of conventional morals. On the other hand, faith as loyalty to and unyielding confidence in the human enterprise is as widely and deeply held to be a transcendent moral value. In these modes, therefore, faith and love* are integral parts of a value continuum. This is also true for the relation of faith to courage*: Resolute devotion to ennobling ideals and beloved communities despite fearsome perils is held to be altogether, if not absolutely, good. What then of the relation of faith to wisdom? The modern inclination is to construe wisdom as practically efficacious knowledge (judgment) of the relation of available or conceivable means to duly accredited ends, with some confessed uncertainty about that accreditation. In classical philosophy and traditional theology, wisdom is granted a stronger cognitive status. For classical philosophers the ultimate ends of human thought and action are intuitively and rationally certain; in traditional theology they are accredited in or by revelation. Contemporary theologians continue to wrestle with the problem of historical and ethical relativity and dream of resolving the impasse between classical objectivism and modern subjectivism.

What is to be understood as "keeping the faith" offers yet another contrast between biblical and classical thought on the one hand and modernity on the other. New Testament Christianity strongly commends holding fast to the faith in the face of the most harrowing trials, for thus the authenticity and efficacy of the religious life are determined, and therein fitness for life with Christ in the eternal kingdom of God (the epistles of Peter; Revelation). In the modern context "keeping the faith" is much more likely to mean persistence in adhering to ideal values and their social embodiments. It is tempting to write this contrast off as a function of the difference between Christianity as a persecuted minority and Christianity as a triumphant cultural consensus. This explanation lacks plausibility in an age that daily registers new triumphs of secularization.

There is a significant linkage of modernity with tradition in the conviction that believing that Christianity—in some form or element—is true entails a commitment to act persistently for the good of other persons. So if one really believes that God is love, it will be evidenced in character and conduct. Unloving conduct and character devoid of benevolence do not falsify the belief that God is and commands love; they tend, rather, to discredit the presumptive believer. By the same token, even the most resolute adherence to the principle and policies of *agapē* does not prove that God exists and is absolute benevolence. It is not merely a modern presumption that these must be taken on faith. Even so, the problem expressed by the father of the epileptic boy seems strikingly modern: "I believe; help my unbelief!" (Mark 9:24).

See also **Fidelity; Justification by Faith; Loyalty; Trust; Cardinal Virtues; Theological Virtues.**

Paul, *Epistle to the Romans;* J. Calvin, *Institutes of the Christian Religion,* book 1; K. Barth, *Church Dogmatics* II, III.

JULIAN N. HARTT

Faithfulness *see* **Faith; Fidelity; Loyalty; Trust**

Fall *see* **Original Sin**

False Witness

False witness is forbidden in the Decalogue* and throughout the OT; this prohibition is echoed in the NT. The term particularly refers to false evidence in court cases. Its prohibition was of vital importance in days when there was no counsel to protect the accused. An individual's fate could be determined, and life perhaps jeopardized, by false witness. It remains a most serious offense against God and humanity, though there may be extreme borderline cases* where the general prohibition has to give way before an even more vital obligation.

See **Lying; Slander; Truthfulness.**

RONALD PRESTON

Family

The family is a feature of human society that precedes Christian ethical reflection upon it. It is both a social institution and a special relationship. As a social institution* the family regulates sexual intercourse, assigns responsibility for children, conserves lines of descent, and orders wealth and inheritance. It assigns roles for the division of labor for everyday living, supports the roles of its members in the external economy, participates with other institutions in the socialization of the coming generation, and plays a role in the physical and psychological welfare of family members. Christian theology and ethics reflect on how to exercise these functions in ways appropriate to Christian conviction and experience.

As a special relationship the family constitutes a moral arena unlike most others formed in the public sphere. The family both forms and expresses the identity and character of its members. Members of one family are not interchangeable with those of another, as each is a part of the formation of others within the family unit. Families also contain voluntary members (parents) and involuntary members (children), and can grow or decrease both naturally (birth and death) and socially (adoption, divorce, remarriage). The family is subject to inescapable tensions between its personal and institutional aspects, whether these are visible within the family or between the family and other institutions such as the state, church, or economy. Indeed, one important task in ethical reflection is distinguishing the special relations of "marriage," "family," and "parenthood" and their corresponding social settings today (*see* **Marriage; Parenthood**).

Sources of Christian thought. Of the many historical sources of Christian thought on the family only the most prominent may be briefly mentioned here.

The understanding of marriage and family in *Greco-Roman culture* left assumptions still visible in secular as well as religious perspectives: that marriage is a contract entered into by the consent of individuals and thus dissolvable by law; that the state can and should regulate marriage and divorce but should be reluctant to intervene in family life; that any religious dimension to marriage and family life is a private matter.

Christianity's roots in *Jewish tradition* contributed heavily to its understanding of the family. Three themes are of special note: that sex is a good of creation ordained by God for procreation and pleasure; that marriage and family are human institutions understandable on a convenantal model; and that women, men, and children have definite roles in daily family life.

Two kinds of sources appear in the NT: those which refer specifically to marriage and family (such as Eph. 5:22–33) and those broader NT themes and narratives which have been or might be employed to understand marriage and the family (such as Gal. 3:23–29). Important also is the setting of family life as a vocation alongside the legitimate choice of the single life in the service of the Lord. Since it is often difficult to separate explicit references from their sociocultural background, and the interpretation of broader texts depends on other theological convictions, the actual use of the NT in Christian ethical reflection on marriage and family varies widely.

The writings of *Augustine of Hippo* shaped the direction of Christian thought on these matters for centuries in a way that is still widely influential. Augustine taught that the natural procreative intent of sexual intercourse was the foundation for marriage and the justification for family, and that the fruits of marriage were children, companionship, and participation in the sign of the union of Christ and the church. Later Catholic thought stressed an increasingly biological and juridical interpretation of the natural state of marriage and family, and gradually incorporated the sign of which Augustine spoke into the sacramental system of the church. Both developments stressed the indissolubility of marriage and the integrity of the family as natural and spiritual goods.

The chief impact of the *Reformation* was to eliminate the sacramental (but not the symbolic) element of marriage and family. This effectively removed them from church jurisdiction and assigned them to a sphere that became increasingly private. Ethical reflection within this sphere came to depend either on secular models of authority and propriety or on basically OT themes of convenantal relations.

Types of ethical reflection. Sources of Christian thought thus reveal biological (natural law), social (free consent, companionship, and child-raising), and spiritual (sacramental, convenantal, and vocational) foundations for the family. Six types of ethical reflection can be noted following the differing metaphors employed to image marriage and the family and the ordering of their respective foundations in relation to Christian convictions.

The *happy-ever-after* and *contract* * metaphors take their context in part from stories of romantic love and from the free market. They provide social foundations for the family with a minimum of explicit normative reflection and a correspondingly high reliance on cultural expectations. They persist because romantic love is not so much a wrong foundation as an inadequate one; and as long as marriage and family are regulated by the state they will to some degree be contractual relations.

The metaphor of *natural union* provides a biological and social foundation for the family, which may be supported by a spiritual one as well. Reflection within such a metaphor is controlled by the prevailing scientific wisdom on human sexuality, as it seeks an order in nature which ought then to be visible in human society. Christian ethics tending in this direction characteristically has trouble with nonprocreative sexuality within marriage, with nonprocreative foundations for the family, and with distinguishing cultural from theological norms.

The *command-of-God* metaphor sees the primary normative issue in marriage and the family to be obedience to the will of God, whether found directly in scripture or mediated through the elders of a given community. Such reflection tends toward the first sort of NT source mentioned above, and often fills out descriptions of roles and relations by recourse to OT or traditional cultural models.

Metaphors of *covenant* * and *vocation* * seek primarily spiritual and social foundations for marriage and family life. Reflection within the covenant metaphor appeals to the long-standing analogy made between Yahweh and Israel or Christ and the church on the one hand, and husband and wife on the other. While it is a rich tradition, it is often at a loss whether to interpret the covenant analogy as one of obedience or of faithful love; it is subject to the temptation to assign gender-specific roles rather than understand both wife and husband as sharing at times qualities of both Christ and church; and it frequently falls back on the historic origins of a covenant as a treaty among unequals in a patriarchal society, thus underwriting a low status for women and children in the family. Reflection within the vocation metaphor emphasizes the voluntary entrance into marriage as a way of life, and the related assumption of parenthood as an intentional activity (or of assent to a state not entered by design), and sets roles and relations within family life in the context of the Christian call to faithful love. Such reflection often turns to broadly covenantal or sacramental themes to prevent its understanding of the family from becoming overly private.

Issues in contemporary discussion. Ethical reflection on concrete issues is affected by the metaphors and sources used in the reflection and thus varies widely. Nonetheless, several issues that challenge any Christian ethics of the family may be noted here (*see also* **Children; Parenthood**).

The Christian understanding of *human sexuality* includes issues of gender formation and identity; sex roles and their social transmission; the transformation of sexual desire into conjugal love; the place of sex before, within, and outside marriage; sexual dimensions of child abuse; and the implications of shifting from a chiefly biological foundation for the family, including questions of nonprocreative sexual relations, homosexual unions, and the distinction between procreation and child-raising (*see* **Sexual Ethics**).

To the degree that Christian ethics takes up a position critical of prevailing cultural assumptions, and emphasizes the covenantal or vocational nature of marriage and the family, it takes on a responsibility for assisting in *preparation for marriage and parenthood,* and for the ongoing *nurture and support of family life,* as moral tasks of the Christian churches. Such efforts find their focus in exploring the *formation of character* in daily family life (*see* **Character**), as well as in offering reflection on *moments of crisis* such as divorce*, death, disability, generational and interpersonal conflicts. As the increasingly competitive demands of marriage, parenthood, economic necessity, and professional expectations take their toll, church support for families experiencing a *conflict of vocations* is also a crucial issue, visible in church sponsorship of day-care centers or other assistance for families where both parents work.

Finally, Christian ethics faces a creative challenge to integrate its perspectives and contributions with those of *pastoral care and counseling*.* Ethics has too long been seen as a source of rules for proper living, and pastoral care cast in the role of picking up the pieces of those who could not conform. At best, theological ethics can offer a normative vision of Christian family life along with the reflective skills necessary for attempting to live it out, while pastoral care can offer insight on the psychosocial dimensions and interpersonal dynamics of making the attempt. Some understanding of the shared task of ethicists and counselors alike is necessary to further each Christian's ability better to embody his or her faith in family life.

Church of England, *The Family in Contemporary Society,* 1958; J. B. Elshtain, *The Family in Political Thought,* 1982; E. Fuchs, *Sexual Desire and Love,* ET 1983; C. Gallagher, G. Maloney, M. Rousseau, and P. Wilczak, *Embodied in Love,* 1983.

RICHARD BONDI

Family Planning *see* **Children; Contraception; Family; Parenthood; Population Policy; Procreation; Sexual Ethics**

Famine *see* **Hunger, World**

Fanaticism *see* **Enthusiasm; Zeal**

Fascism

The name given to a type of political movement of which the classic defining examples were the Italian Fascist Party (from the Italian *fascio,* a group) under Benito Mussolini (1883–1945), which ruled Italy from 1922 to 1943, and the German National Socialist Party under Adolf Hitler (1889–1945), which ruled Germany from 1933 to 1945. Their principal characteristic was extreme nationalism*. In National Socialism this took the form of a virulent racism* whose climax was the attempt at genocide* of the European Jews and persecution of so-called "inferior Slav races" (Poles, Russians, and others) as the German "master race" expanded eastward toward its goal of world domination. In Italy anti-Semitism* had no local roots, but Italian fascism was also expansionist and sought to conquer a new Roman Empire. Mussolini like Hitler prized the values of force and war as (in the language of social Darwinism) the inevitable conflict for the survival of the fittest.

In domestic politics. Fascist theory required an authoritarian state under a single leader. Fascist movements were correspondingly antidemocratic and anti-Left (whether Communist, socialist, or trade-union). Fascism was also, however, distinct from the traditional Right. It was anticapitalist and inclined to antimonarchism and anticlericalism. This mixture of ideologies reflected the outlook of its major electoral sources of support, the lower middle class and peasant proprietors. The radicalization of these classes is explained by experience of the First World War (defeat in Germany, humiliation in Italy); economic disruption in which inflation and depression had a severe effect on countryside and towns; and fear of deadlocked democracies leading to civil war and Bolshevik revolution. The threat to small entrepreneurs both from powerful trade unions and from big business made them responsive to an ideology* that condemned both and that offered an escape from the conflicts of industrial society in the irrational values of blood and soil, expounded by Alfred Rosenberg in *The Myth of the Twentieth Century* (1st ed., 1930).

In power. Fascism relied on coercion, crushing resistance with secret police and concentration camps. An attempt was made to integrate social and occupational groups into the state by specialist party organizations, in Italy by the concept of each industry forming a "corporation" of the state. In practice Fascist dictatorship* was not as total as in theory (see **Totalitarian State**). Compromises were made with the churches, which received institutional guarantees in return for their political inactivity (Lateran Agreements in Italy, 1929, and Concordat with Germany, 1933), but this did not prevent subsequent conflict, and Hitler looked forward to the replacement of Christianity by a new racist religion. The monolithic theory of Fascist administration was also undermined in practice by constant disputes between state and party agencies and between rival party leaders.

Elsewhere fascism found many imitators. Fascists were junior partners in General Franco's dictatorship in Spain (1936–1975) and in the Vichy government of France (1940–1944); collaborators (known as Quislings after the Norwegian Fascist leader) shared power in German-occupied Europe. Only in Romania and Hungary, however, did local Fascist movements enjoy significant support. The term fascism has also been applied loosely to nationalist regimes in Latin America and Japan and to any authoritarian or racist movement.

———

G. Allardyce (ed.), *The Place of Fascism in European History,* 1971; W. Laqueur (ed.), *Fascism, A Reader's Guide,* 1976; S. J. Woolf (ed.), *Fascism in Europe,* 1981.

                                                                J. R. C. WRIGHT

Fasting

Abstention from food as a religious exercise is found in many parts of the world, either as an expression of humiliation before deity or as producing a state suitable for religious impressions; as such it is often part of primitive initiation rites (cf. the Isiac initiation described in Apuleius, *The Golden Ass* 11.23). Both ideas appear in the OT, for example, in Ps. 35:13 and Deut. 9:9, 18. Penitential fasting became more common after the exile (cf. Zech. 7–8), but the one universal fast of Israel was (and is) the Day of Atonement, from sunset to sunset (referred to in Acts 27:9 as "the fast"). Pious souls might fast more often, even twice a week (Luke 18:12); the practice is assumed rather than directed in Matt. 6:16–18. By the 2nd century, Christians prepared for Easter by a fast of one or two days, which also prepared candidates for the Easter baptisms; not until the 4th century was the idea of a historical memory of the passion on Good Friday emphasized. A fast to the ninth hour (the common Roman dinner hour in midafternoon) or later was widely observed on the "Station Days," Wednesday and Friday, and at Rome also on Saturday. (Buddhist monks traditionally follow a converse practice, eating only before noon.) Roman and Anglican rites preserve a relic of stations in the Ember Days at the four seasons. From the 4th century the pre-Easter fast came to be extended over the Lenten season, necessarily less intensely; it often, however, was kept until broken by Communion at the time of vespers in the late afternoon—in the Middle Ages this was gradually relaxed by anticipating vespers in the morning, a custom still common in the Eastern

Orthodox Church, and assumed in the Roman rite until 1960. The medieval Latin church also fasted on Christmas Eve and the vigils of a number of other festivals. By the 13th century the observance of a fast day was defined as one main meal at noon or night, with one or two other slight refections permitted.

The Reformers generally objected to the legalism they saw in the traditional fasts—though in the Church of England they were kept up by custom, and since 1662 have been listed in the *Book of Common Prayer,* which also recommends fasting before adult baptism. But fasting out of private devotion or by special order of the church was common in Reformed circles and not unknown in Lutheran—cf. the austerity still expected in Finland on the quarterly national days of prayer. In New England the Puritan colonies developed the custom of an annual fast day in the spring—this still survives formally in New Hampshire and in Connecticut (where since 1797 traditions have been combined by proclaiming the civic fast day on Good Friday).

In our time prescribed fasting seems to be obsolescent, except for such symbolic gestures as the Friday abstinence. In 1949 Pope Pius XII simplified the Roman Catholic rules, which had been complicated by many special exemptions; but even his rules are often further reduced by local dispensations. In 1966 Pope Paul VI reduced the canonical requirement to abstinence on Fridays, and fasting on Good Friday and the first day of Lent (the American hierarchy has decreed that abstinence from meat is no longer legally required on Fridays, though it is encouraged on a voluntary basis, or "good works" may be done instead). Modern Anglicanism has followed a similar course—for example, the 1977 American *Book of Common Prayer* designates Ash Wednesday and Good Friday as fasts, and calls for special acts of discipline and self-denial (but not precisely defined) in Lent and on Fridays (except in the Christmas and Easter seasons). The fast before Communion was often observed in the Reformed churches—in Scotland for some time in the form of preparatory fast days—and was revived among Anglicans under the influence of the Oxford Movement. But it also seems to be obsolescent in view of the complex time schedule of modern life and the widespread desire for more frequent Communion. For

Roman Catholics Pius XII reduced the obligation in 1957 to three hours, and Paul VI in 1964 reduced it to one.

But the call for temperance and discipline which fasting expresses still remains. Early Christian preachers often stressed that the true fast must include abstinence from sin (cf. Isa. 58), and that what was saved by fasting should relieve the needs of the poor. A modern form of fast has been developed in Great Britain and America since the Second World War, by which a simple meal is served at a church gathering (or at home) and the price of a full meal given to refugee relief or other special causes. "Let us conduct ourselves becomingly as in the day, not in reveling and drunkenness . . . but put on the Lord Jesus Christ" (Rom. 13:13–14) as Paul bids us in his name.

See **Abstinence; Discipline; Hunger, World; Mortification; Self-Denial; Temperance.**

E. R. HARDY

Fate and Fatalism

The idea of fate, with variations in various cultures, is that of a force (sometimes half-personified) or law governing some or all of human affairs. The concept has sometimes been connected with an attitude to life known as fatalism—a kind of passivity in the face of the future. Fatalism has also appeared as a philosophical doctrine, as apparently entailed by determinism.

Paradoxically, fate can cover both what is thought of as necessitated by some inner law working in the universe and what is thought of as due to chance. Thus the relevant cluster of concepts in ancient Greek thought include both *anagkē* (necessity) and *tychē* (chance). The reason for this ambivalence is that fate is invoked to account for occurrences to human beings, in particular where these events (such as death) are regarded as striking and inscrutable. Thus a personal disaster may appear an accident (mere chance), and yet may be assigned a deep-seated cause. The most comprehensive pattern of such thinking is the Indian doctrine of *karma,* which in principle explains all events that happen to living beings in terms of a law (though theistic thought in medieval India saw this as an expression of God's will) and of an invisible force (*adṛṣṭa*). However, the necessity is normally thought of as conditional: there are ways in which one's future fate may be changed—through meditation, austerity, moral effort, faith in God, etc. Analogous to this is the way in which the Greek gods, and even humans, might interfere with otherwise foreordained destinies. Thus Zeus (*Iliad*, book 16) contemplates saving Sarpedon from his doom, long since fixed by fate. Similarly the determinism implicit in Qur'ānic teachings is held in conjunction with the doctrine of the capacity of the individual to perform the duties laid upon him or her by faith.

On the other hand, in Islam and elsewhere, there have been attempts to interpret destiny as unconditional and universal. Thus the Ājīvikas (a movement contemporary with the Buddha) held a doctrine of fate (*niyati*) as wholly determining the future. Hence the good works (such as austerity) associated with a liberated life are symptoms, not causes, of salvation. A similar conclusion, not based, however, on the concept of fate, but rather on that of the will of God, is found in Muslim and Christian predestinationism.

Fatalism as an attitude involves resignation to one's future lot, together with a sense of its unalterability. The first of these elements can appear, in theistic religions, as faith in providence. The second is a deduction sometimes made from determinism, whether the latter is conceived in terms of God's governance of events or in terms of empirical causation.

The standard reply to fatalism is that it depends on an invalid inference. Thus "Either I shall be alive in 2000 or I shall not; and suppose that I shall be alive: then I shall be no matter what I do. Consequently, I can smoke fifty cigarettes a day." This is invalid reasoning, because my actions enter into the causation of future events. Even if my actions are determined, this gives no ground for doing A rather than B, unless I know which way I am determined to act. But even here the very knowledge of the future gives me an opportunity to avoid disasters, etc.

See **Free Will and Determinism.**

A. J. Ayer, *The Concept of a Person,* 1964; S. G. F. Brandon, *Man and His Destiny in the Great Religions,* 1962; *History, Time and Deity,* 1965; D. Davidson, "Mental Events," in *Philosophy as It Is,* ed. T. Honderich and M. Burnyeat, 1979.

NINIAN SMART

Feminist Ethics

In its most general sense "feminist ethics" refers to any ethical theory that locates its roots in feminism, and especially in the contemporary feminist movement. Feminism, in its most fundamental meaning, is a conviction and a movement opposed to discrimination* on the basis of gender. It opposes, therefore, any ideology, belief, attitude, or behavior that establishes or reinforces such discrimination. In terms of social structure, feminism is opposed primarily to patriarchy. The ultimate aim of feminism is equality* among persons regardless of gender. Since discrimination on the basis of gender (sexism) is perceived by feminists as pervasively discrimination against women, feminism aims to correct this bias by a bias for women. This includes a focal concern for the well-being of women and a taking account of women's experience as a way to understand what well-being means for women and men.

Feminist theory appears in a variety of disciplines, including philosophy, the social and behavioral sciences, and theology. It is also expressed in principles of interpretation for literary and historical texts and for religious scriptures. Major tasks undertaken by feminist scholars include the critique of sources of sexism (for example, religious, social, political, economic); retrieval of women's history and pro-woman myths; reconstruction of theories of the human person and the human community. Feminist ethics, insofar as it is done systematically, draws on all of this work.

There is pluralism within feminism, and hence within feminist ethics. Differences are sometimes identified according to analyses of the causes of sexism and strategies to correct it. Thus, for example, a liberal feminist ethic advocates the extension of the liberal tradition of political rights to women and a corresponding reform of discriminatory policies of gender role differentiation. A socialist feminist ethic is primarily concerned with changing the forms of production in society in order to secure economic parity and autonomy for women. A radical feminist ethic believes that the only way to alleviate women's oppression is to achieve total autonomy for women (political, economic, sexual, and reproductive), and to do this through separatism or by seizing power from men. Much of feminist ethics incorporates varying combinations of these views.

Despite the pluralism in feminism and feminist ethics, there are generally shared issues and basic principles. Major questions in feminist theology and philosophy that have produced common ethical issues include: the meaning of human embodiment* (especially issues of human sexuality); the nature of the human self (including possibilities for the development of character); the value of the world of nature; patterns for human relationships (both personal and political). Significant methodological and substantive principles can be formulated that express strong currents of feminist ethical reflection on these issues.

There is a firm methodological commitment to maintaining a focus on the experience of women as the primary source for feminist ethics. Like feminism in general, feminist ethics traces its origins to women's growing awareness of the disparity between received traditional interpretations of their identity and function and their own experience of themselves and their lives. It also claims an important hermeneutical vantage point in a focus on women's experience precisely as disadvantaged. Methodologically, feminist ethics has been open to both deontological and teleological patterns of reasoning. On the one hand, it has taken seriously the possibility that human actions can be judged unethical insofar as they contradict values intrinsic to the concrete reality of persons. On the other hand, feminist ethics sustains a concern for consequences, for an ethical evaluation of means in relation to ends and of parts in relation to the whole; overall it is favorable to an ecological view of reality, and it allows the relativization of values in situations of conflict (as, for example, when dealing with issues of abortion*).

Feminist ethics as a systematic discipline is new enough that it is difficult to generalize its substantive principles. One way of identifying them could go something like this. The most fundamental substantive principle is the principle that women are fully human and are to be valued as such. The content of this principle differs significantly from similar but nonfeminist affirmations. It is not, for example, to be mistaken for the view that women are human, though derivatively and partially so. Rather, feminist belief about the humanness of women is specified by the inclusion of further principles of equality and autonomy*, and it is qualified by a principle of mutuality. Even radical feminism accepts these principles in some form, though both separatism and matriarchy present serious difficulties for a principle of equality, unless they are understood as necessary means to egalitarian contexts.

The insistence on the combination of principles of autonomy, equality, and mutuality differentiates feminist ethics from some other ethical theories. Feminist ethics wants to specify the formal principle of "equal treatment for equals," noting the necessity of discerning who are equals in terms of basic humanity. Moreover, feminist ethics rejects strong theories of complementarity that, in the name of "different but equal" identifications, disguise patterns of inequality (relationships in which the role of one partner is always inferior to, dependent on, or instrumental to the role of another). Feminist ethics insists, therefore, that the essential feature of personhood, which modern liberal philosophy identified for human persons as such (that is, the feature of individual autonomy, grounded in the capacity for free self-determination), be appropriated for women as well as for men. On this basis, the feminist principle of equality, of the equal right of all persons to respect as persons, is maintained (*see also* **Respect for Persons**).

Feminist ethics, however, extends the principle of equality to a principle of equitable sharing. That is, out of women's experience of disadvantage and their perception of the disadvantaged histories of other groups, feminists argue for a universalized right of all to an equitable share in the goods and services necessary to human life and basic happiness. Feminist ethics generally includes, therefore, a positive form of the principle of equality, one based not only on the self-protective right of each to freedom, but on the participation of all in human solidarity.

Closely aligned with this, feminist ethics could be described as rejecting a view of human persons that is self-isolating. Hence, it tends to combine some form of the principle of mutuality with the principle of equality. Its basis for doing this is a view of personhood that identifies relationality along with autonomy as an essential feature of human persons. Feminist ethics insists, then, on the need for a corrective to a liberal philosophy that fails to understand persons as embodied subjects, with an essential capacity and need for union with other persons. But feminist ethics generally sees itself also as a corrective to romantic theories of sociality, organic models of society, or theories of complementarity in which relation is all, without regard for free agency or for personal identity, power, and worth, which transcend roles.

Generating principles of equality and mutuality, feminist ethics includes a critique not only of sexism but also of racism and classism. Moreover, in opposing a general pattern of dominance and subjugation, it gives ethical priority to models of human relationships characterized by collaboration rather than competition or hierarchical gradation. In some of its forms it is also an advocate of nonviolence.

Methodological and substantive principles for feminist ethics have been identified. It must be added that some feminist ethicists prefer to avoid the language of "principles" altogether. This follows a recognition of past abuses where principles were used to oppose, rather than serve, the well-being of persons and relations, and where principles were maintained without any acknowledgment of the historical and social nature of human knowledge.

Some feminist ethical reflection can be more specifically described as Christian feminist ethics. This can include much of what has already been noted, but also a more direct concern with issues shaped by Christian belief and theology. Thus, for example, Christian feminist ethics takes a critical stance in relation to past theological justifications of the inferiority of women to men. It opposes the distinction of male and female as polar opposites (representing mind/body, reason/emotion, activity/passivity, dependency/autonomy). It challenges the association of women with religious symbols of evil, but it is also opposed to religious "pedestalism," or the expectation that women will be more virtuous than men. A Christian feminist ethics takes seriously the radical feminist critique of Christianity as a religion that can lead to the exaltation of dependence and suffering. As Christian and feminist, then, it takes as one of its tasks the formulation of a theory of moral and religious development and a feminist theory of virtue or character. Christian feminists have also identified problems with traditional concepts of *agapē*, and they seek

to balance principles of equality and mutuality with the notion of self-sacrifice. Finally, Christian feminists are concerned with the formulation of a theory of justice*, one that will illuminate more adequately every form of human and Christian relationship.

See **Love; Sex Discrimination; Women, Status of.**

M. Daly, *Gyn/Ecology: The Metaethics of Radical Feminism,* 1978; E. Fiorenza, *In Memory of Her: A Feminist Reconstruction of Christian Origins,* 1983; B. Harrison, *Our Right to Choose: Toward A New Ethic of Abortion,* 1983; R. Ruether, *Sexism and God-Talk: Toward a Feminist Theology,* 1983; L. Russell, *The Future of Partnership,* 1979.

MARGARET A. FARLEY

Fetal Research

Ethical issues in fetal research are associated with but are not reducible to those involved in abortion*. The ethical standards involved are similar to those involved in experimentation with human subjects*, but their application to fetal research is controversial because of debates about the moral status of the human fetus, defined as the human embryo from conception to delivery. Some distinctions are important: fetal research may be conducted on live or dead fetuses, on fetuses *in utero* or *ex utero,* on fetuses to be aborted or to be brought to term, and on pre-viable or viable fetuses. It is also important to distinguish research that may benefit the subject as well as others (sometimes called therapeutic research) and research that is designed only to benefit others (sometimes called nontherapeutic research) and to distinguish degrees of risk (e.g., minimal, moderate, and serious). Questions about the proper balance of risks or burdens and benefits arise in this area as in other research, but pointing to the benefits of research for fetuses as a group—and there have been major benefits—may not justify the risks or burdens imposed on particular fetuses in particular experiments.

As André Hellegers (1978) noted, the guidelines proposed by the Peel Commission in Great Britain in 1972 and by the National Commission for the Protection of Human Subjects in the USA in 1975 share several features: "They have in common that dead fetuses and their tissues are to be afforded the respect of other dead human bodies and tissues. Fetuses with a chance of survival are to be treated like children. Willful damage to the fetus *in utero* may not be caused, presumably lest a mother change her mind about abortion. Significant differences are that in the United States regulations, fathers can veto the research, while in the Peel Report there is no such specific provision. In Britain it is proposed that no nonbeneficial research . . . be done on the fetus *in utero* or the viable fetus. In the United States it may be done if there is minimal or no risk." Paul Ramsey (1975) has argued against any nontherapeutic research on fetuses as well as on children who cannot consent, and many have questioned whether a pregnant woman who has decided to have an abortion can give valid consent for the use of the fetus in research.

In recent years a controversial context of fetal research has been *in vitro* fertilization. In the UK in 1984 the Warnock Commission (discussed under **Reproductive Technologies**) recommended that some research be permitted on human embryos up to the end of the fourteenth day after *in vitro* fertilization, but that no embryo used in research be transferred to a woman. Some members of the commission opposed any research on "spare" embryos. The debate about fetal research can be expected to continue as society grapples with questions of moral responsibility to the fetus.

See **Abortion; Experimentation with Human Subjects; Reproductive Technologies.**

———

Great Britain, Department of Health and Social Security, *The Use of Fetuses and Fetal Material for Research* (Report of the Peel Commission), 1972; A. E. Hellegers, "Fetal Research," *EB,* 1978; National Commission for the Protection of Human Subjects of Biomedical and Behavioral Research, *Research on the Fetus: Report and Recommendations,* 1975; J. Peel, "Fetuses and Fetal Material, Use of for Research," *DME,* 1981; P. Ramsey, *The Ethics of Fetal Research,* 1975.

JAMES F. CHILDRESS

Fetus, Responsibility to *see* Abortion; Fetal Research; Genetics; Reproductive Technologies

Fidelity

The core meaning of fidelity is faithfulness, in the sense of loyalty*. However, the term also connotes truthfulness*, as in the sentence "The apostles' fidelity to the message of Jesus is debatable." Some of this complexity of connotation is best captured in the synonym "faithfulness." Fidelity also connotes marital faithfulness, in contrast to loyalty, which may seem more at home in a political context. In any case 20th-century writers like H. R. Niebuhr and Paul Ramsey tend to use the terms "loyalty" and "fidelity" interchangeably, although Josiah Royce, to whom both are indebted, distinguished them. Royce stressed loyalty, holding that fidelity—which he understood to mean habitual obedience to another—was possible for a dog. On a strictly etymological level fidelity has connotations of faith and truth, while loyalty relates to law. In fact, however, a clear distinction between them would have to be stipulated by a contemporary writer in English. Both terms imply a commitment or involvement of the self with another, which for Christians may be related to God's covenantal or incarnational involvement with humankind. Augustine's conceptions of love and the self are in the background of much of this literature on fidelity.

The major 20th-century writer whose thought develops the concept of fidelity is Gabriel Marcel. He studied Royce's work extensively and evidently found the French *fidélité* a more apt translation than "loyalty." For Marcel true fidelity must involve the emotions and the heart. Rote obedience to duty and formally correct behavior make a relationship stale. This pathology arises when selves focus on their own virtue rather than on the one to whom they should be faithful. True fidelity can only be measured by the one to whom it is pledged. Does this make fidelity impossible, given that affections obviously change? No, for in true fidelity I commit myself to forming my attitudes and directing myself in certain ways. True fidelity calls on the will to make the self and is in this sense creative.

Ultimately fidelity to another runs the risk of disappointment through confusion between the other and my idea of him or her. Consciousness centered on God and fidelity to God are rooted in humility* and make hope* possible. Hope in turn alters more limited fidelities.

It is clear that fidelity, like loyalty, is both a moral and a religious concept. It captures an important dimension of the moral life, suggests a searching for a relationship with something absolute, and may symbolize the saving acts of God.

G. Marcel, *Creative Fidelity,* ET 1964; and *Royce's Metaphysics,* ET 1956.

DAVID H. SMITH

Filial Piety *see* **Aged, Care of the; Children; Family; Parenthood;** *see also* **Confucian Ethics**

Finality

A general term that was used in Aristotelian philosophy to designate one of the causes of creaturely substances (the final cause or *telos*). It could refer to either an extrinsic *telos* (a substance for which it exists) or an intrinsic one (the full maturation of the being in question).

Scholastic philosophers adopted the notion and made a principle of action of it: "Every agent acts for an end" (Aquinas, *Summa Contra Gentiles* 3.2). Intelligent beings can comprehend this end, whereas nonintelligent beings depend on an extrinsic intelligence. Thomas Aquinas used the notion of finality by appealing to basic inclinations. The objects of these inclinations are the basic goods suitable for the agent because they complete and perfect it. It was on this substructure that Aquinas built his understanding of the natural law*. This law was completely transformed by its penetration by charity, which oriented the responsible, intelligent creature toward its ultimate supernatural end. In recent Christian (especially Catholic) writing, the *telos* that animates and underlies human ethical activity is seen to be Christ, God's self-manifestation and therefore the manifestation of the meaning and destiny of the world.

See also **Teleological Ethics; Thomistic Ethics.**

"Finality," *New Catholic Encyclopedia,* 1967.

RICHARD A. McCORMICK, S.J.

Flesh *see* **Asceticism; Body; Embodiment; Mortification**

Force *see* **Coercion; Power; Resistance; State**

Forgiveness

Strictly considered, forgiveness is a conception and an experience in which religious and ethical sensibilities, perspectives, and responsibilities are intimately related. They are so intimately related that it is scarcely possible to distinguish one from the other without neglecting one in favor of the other.

The religious reality of forgiveness identifies a certain relation between God and humanity. This relation is marked by the awesome holiness of God, by human offenses against this holiness, by human guilt, and by the ineradicable human need for assurance that sin against God has been pardoned and right relations between God and humanity have been restored.

From the earliest apprehensions of the numinous to the classical Christian doctrine of justification by faith*, the experience of forgiveness has been that of the setting aside, on God's initiative, of enmity between God and humanity and the restoration of right relations between them. In primitive religions, this transformation is an experience of ritual cleansing. In more highly developed religions, ritual undergoes the more conscious and symbolic refinement of liturgy, together with a theological clarification of the initiative of God in restoring humanity, despite sin, to free and uninhibited fellowship with God and one another. Understood in this way, forgiveness tends often to be loosely interchanged with justification and/or reconciliation.

More carefully considered, however, forgiveness may be distinguished from justification, as well as from reconciliation*. Such a distinction differentiates between an offense against God, set right by God's action (justification) and the consequent restored relation between humanity and God (reconciliation). As justification expresses the *fact* of a restored relation between God and humanity, so forgiveness expresses the divine assurance and human acceptance of this fact. As reconciliation expresses the *result* of this restored relation in *behavior,* namely, the overcoming of enmity between God and human beings and between human beings and each other, so forgiveness expresses the divine and human acknowledgment and practice of this result. Thus, forgiveness is not so much a middle term between justification and reconciliation as one that includes them both.

This inclusiveness is grounded upon the

perception and conviction of Christian faith that in the death and resurrection of Jesus Christ an atonement has happened. This "at-one-ment" between God and humanity has come about through the death of Christ, whose offering up of himself—one for all, and once for all—is a height, range, and depth expiation of human sin and guilt which—in the power of his resurrection—has at once nullified and fulfilled all need from the human side to "get right with God," and has surrounded and sustained human failure, frailty, and hope with the promise and the power to live humanly, as God has purposed his human creatures to live and to be. The atonement identifies the reality, possibility, and power of trust in God's assurance that things are *so right* with him that we are set free to trust and to risk trusting our neighbors *and* our enemies, as companions of the gift of being human which God has given.

The ethical reality of forgiveness, on the other hand, underlies the unique relation between forgiveness, justice*, and love* (*see also* **Mercy**). This relation is the distinguishing mark of a Christian account of ethics and the unique contribution of Christian thinking about ethics to ethical theory and practice. Indeed, the relation between forgiveness, justice, and love is the *summum bonum* of Christian ethics, in notable contrast to and correction of philosophical and other religious accounts of ethics. Whereas these ways of thinking about ethics are preoccupied with rational or mystical determinations of the highest good, and with descriptions of virtues and vices, rights and duties, obligations, rewards and punishments, Christian ethics centers upon the relations between forgiveness and love and between love and justice, as providing the context for human freedom and responsibility in renewal and fulfillment.

The source and resource of these religious and ethical sensibilities, perceptions, and responsibilities is the Bible. Consequently, the Bible is the authoritative guide to their meaning and practice. From Genesis to Revelation, and with a remarkable thematic unity in variety, and variety in unity, the Bible is preoccupied with the human living of human life in the world that belongs to God. In this world the gift, promise, and foretaste of God's covenantal faithfulness and grace, will and purpose, claim and responsiveness, deliverance and renewal, point to and point up what it takes to be and to stay human.

According to the OT, the way of God's being God to, with, and for the people whom he has chosen is marked by God's patience and providence, righteousness and justice, love and law, mercy and forgiveness. The focal watchword is that the people whom God has chosen—and because of them, all humanity—have been shown what is good. What is required is "to do justice, and to love mercy, and to walk humbly with . . . God" (Micah 6:8). The test cases are the poor and the stranger within the gate. The least and the unlikeliest are the immediate and the ultimate human occasions for the practice toward one's neighbors of the love, forgiveness, and justice that God has unfailingly shown in the bounty of the earth, the deliverance from slavery and exile, the gift of a land of promise and—despite all sin and rebellion, faltering and failure, mistrust and violence—the promise of a new covenant through "an anointed One" who

> shall not judge by what his eyes see,
> or decide by what his ears hear;
> but with righteousness he shall judge
> the poor,
> and decide with equity for the meek
> of the earth.
>
> (Isa. 11:3–4)

According to the NT, this way of God's being God to, with, and for the people whom he has chosen for covenant faithfulness and caring in the world includes—in foretaste and fulfillment—all the people in the world, both now and in the world to come. In Jesus of Nazareth, the "anointed One" has come, the new covenant has begun, the sacrifice to end all sacrifices, the atonement to end all atonements has been made. There is a straight thematic line—howsoever the accents and circumstances vary—between Micah (and all the company of the prophets with him) and the Magnificat, which celebrates who Jesus is, and what he is about, and what those called to a life of discipleship with him are to be about.

> For he who is mighty has done great
> things . . .
> and holy is his name.
> And his mercy is on those who fear
> him
> from generation to generation. . . .
> He has scattered the proud in the
> imagination of their hearts,

he has put down the mighty from their
thrones,
and exalted those of low degree;
he has filled the hungry with good
things,
and the rich he has sent empty away.
(Luke 1:49–53)

In the NT, as in the OT, the words "love,"
"forgiveness," and "justice" identify the key
tonalities of the thematic line. But this identification is made by way of descriptions of
varied contexts of relations between God and
humanity rather than by carefully analyzed
definitions of terms. The Gospels report the
central message of Jesus as that of the kingdom of God, implicitly identify him with the
OT prophets and their teachings, underline
the parabolic character of Jesus' teachings,
and give major attention to Jesus' crucifixion
and resurrection. The passion confirms not
only Jesus' messianic identity but also the
inauguration of the kingdom of God in the
midst of the world of time and space and
things and people. (See, e.g., Mark 8:27–30;
9:2–13; Matt., chs. 5–7; 17:1–22; 25:31–46;
Luke 4:16–37; 6:32–36; 11:42–44; 21:1–28;
John 1:1–18; 3:1–21; ch. 17.) The power,
prospect, and promise of this new world
under way is attested in the Acts of the Apostles (cf. Acts 1–4, passim) as a report on the
life of a new human community in the world.
This is the community which has discovered
in the life, death, and resurrection of Jesus a
surprising and renewing power of deliverance
from sin, death, and the devil and of a freedom *from* self-seeking security and self-jus-
tification and *for* the responsibilities of reciprocal caring for the needs and weaknesses,
sufferings and sorrows, hope and fears that
make the concrete difference between human
and inhuman, meaningful and meaningless
life. This new righteousness of freedom and
freedom for righteousness is the central
preoccupation of the Pauline epistles. These
epistles declare and explore the fact that
God's love, forgiveness, and justice have happened and do happen in the world through
the formidable and fulfilling power of grace
over sin, truth over falsehood, wisdom over
foolishness, the fruits of the Spirit over the
works of the flesh, steadfastness amid tribula-
tion, and trust over premature certainties. Indeed, the principalities and powers are being
brought to book by a radically new way of
displacing alienation, futility, and enmity by

the healing experience and practice of love
through forgiveness and justice. (See, e.g.,
Rom. 1; 7; 8; 13; 1 Cor. 1:18–31; ch. 13; Gal.
3:23–29; ch. 5; Phil. 3; Col. 1.)

If the correlation between love and forgiveness tends to overshadow the correlation of
love with justice in the Pauline letters, the
catholic epistles may be said to redress the
balance. These letters are preoccupied, to be
sure, with the reality of the new covenant in
Jesus Christ, especially in the face of false
prophets and teachers, with the persistent
temptation to take up attractive, because
easier, alternatives, and with the debilitating
anticipation of the imminence of Christ's
coming again. Nevertheless, the link between
love and forgiveness is eloquently and insist-
ently joined to the link between love and justice, i.e., with the claims and needs of the
least of Christ's brethren: the weak and the
poor, the stranger and the destitute. (See,
e.g., 1 Thess. 5:12–22; 1 Tim. 6:11–20; Heb.
4; 8; 11; 13:7–16; James; 1 Peter 2:1–10; ch.
3; 5:1–11; 1 John.)

Thus, the Bible ends as it began. Its thematic correlation of love with forgiveness
and justice leads from Micah and the Magnificat to the parable of the Last Judgment
(Matt. 25:31–46) and thence to the penultimate perception and assurance of what is already more than on its way: "A new heaven
and a new earth; for the first heaven and the
first earth had passed away, and the sea was
no more" (Rev. 21:1).

A Christian ethical account of forgiveness,
therefore, underlines the practice of love
through forgiveness and justice. *As actions of
God,* these relations exhibit God's free initiative toward humanity, and God's sustaining,
renewing, and fulfilling concern for and companionship with his human creatures. In
love, God faithfully favors humanity with his
presence and grace. In forgiveness, God
"sends away" or "pardons" or "covers"
human disavowals and violations of this divine initiative. In justice, God's presence in,
with, and under the human aspiration and
struggle to be human is discerned and experienced in the setting right of what is not
right in personal and social interaction. The
religious factor in these relations is the priority and freedom of the divine initiative toward the human condition. The ethical factor
in these relations is God's unfailing and liberating involvement in and with the human
struggle to be human in the world.

As human actions, the practice of love through forgiveness and justice expresses the response in behavior toward God and toward one's fellow human beings of what God characteristically and revealingly does toward and for the human meaning and fulfillment of life. The religious factor in these actions is the recognition and acceptance of the claim that in so doing, the will of God is being done on earth as it is in heaven; and that power is available to do what otherwise could not and would not be done. *Laborare est orare!* The ethical factor in these human actions of love, forgiveness, and justice is the recognition and acceptance of the coexistence and destiny, the aspirations, capacities, and needs of the neighbor as the bearer and giver of selfhood, and thus of the primacy and priority of the claims of the neighbor over the claims of the self. Love is the unexceptionable readiness in word and deed to "bear one another's burdens, and so fulfil the law of Christ" (Gal. 6:2). Forgiveness is the "sending away" or "pardoning" or "covering" what has come between persons who as neighbors have become enemies. Justice is the steadfast commitment to setting right what is not right in personal and social relations at those acute points in social interaction which expose structural denials in interpersonal relations of openness and trust through the intensification of enmity.

The critical instance of the religious and ethical meanings of forgiveness and love in human behavior is exhibited in the relation between justification by faith and justice. The juridical interpretation of these relations, owing to a juridical view of the sacrificial and atoning death of Christ, in the tradition of Christian theology and ethics, has greatly contributed to the failure of justification and justice creatively to intersect. The consequence has been an unhappy divorce between soteriology and ethics, between the religious and the ethical practice of love through forgiveness. When justice is understood as the setting right of what is not right in human interrelations, both private and public, the struggle for justice becomes the concrete expression, in behavior, of the human response to what God has done, and is doing, to set things right between humanity and himself. The faith by which we are justified becomes what Luther called "a busy, living, active thing" by which we learn, in the struggle for justice, what it means concretely to forgive

and to be forgiven, to love God and one another. In the struggle for justice, the religious and ethical meaning of forgiveness converges and emerges as the practice of reconciliation.

It is noteworthy that the discussion of forgiveness in the literature of Christian theology and ethics is conspicuously slight. The grounds for this are traceable to the dominance of a liturgical, sacrificial, juridical view of the atonement; and to the persuasion that the OT and the NT, canonically accepted and interpreted, warranted this reading of what God in Christ was primarily doing in the world. Nor must one underestimate the divorce between justification and justice in the practice of reconciliation perpetuated in (and despite the rereading of the Bible in) the churches of the Reformation. There are, of course, exegetical discussions, and those which find their way into theologies of the OT and the NT. As for systematic theology and ethics, Albrecht Ritschl's three-volume work on justification and reconciliation (1870–74), of which vols. 1 and 3 have been translated (the latter in 1900 by H. R. Mackintosh as *The Christian Doctrine of Justification and Reconciliation*), is still the most extensive and instructive. Ritschl's attention to forgiveness lies behind the moving, personal treatment by Wilhelm Herrmann in *The Communion of the Christian with God* (ET from the 4th German ed. of 1903 by R. S. Stewart, 1906; also tr. by J. S. Stanyon, 1971); and also behind the influential treatment of the subject by H. R. Mackintosh, *The Christian Experience of Forgiveness* (1927). A perceptive, substantive, and systematic discussion, which goes beyond Ritschl's and Mackintosh's, is at hand in the constructive, critical, and contemporary interpretation of Karl Barth in *Church Dogmatics* IV/1 (ET 1956; repr. 1974); and in an admirable chapter on forgiveness and love in Reinhold Niebuhr's *An Interpretation of Christian Ethics* (1935). Mention may also be made of P. Lehmann, *Forgiveness* (1940); A. Miller, *The Renewal of Man* (1956); N. Wolterstorff, *Until Justice and Peace Embrace* (1983).

PAUL LEHMANN

Formalism

Formalism is an excessive insistence on the outward observances of religion at the expense of a due regard to their inward spirit and meaning. It involves a preoccupation with the formal correctness of rites and ceremonies together with a neglect of their inward content. Similarly in the sphere of morality it is an undue insistence on the form or letter of a moral code and neglect of the spirit or purpose of the code (*see* **Legalism**). "Ethical formalism" also refers to a type of ethical theory that determines moral rightness and goodness by formal rather than material considerations. It focuses on the agent's disposition and intention and a formal test for determining concrete duties (e.g., the Golden Rule* or universalizability*), rather than on material ends and consequences of acts. It is one type of deontology, especially but not exclusively Kantian (*see* **Deontology; Kantian Ethics**).

R. C. MORTIMER/JAMES F. CHILDRESS

Fornication

Fornication is sexual intercourse between unmarried persons. In the case of casual and promiscuous relations, the relation lacks any dimension of commitment and is an act of mutual exploitation. In such a case, the sexual act is demeaned and depersonalized. Sometimes intercourse takes place between unmarried persons who are engaged to be married or who intend a stable relationship. The presence of a measure of commitment makes it undesirable to apply the word "fornication" indiscriminately in such cases, though there may be irresponsibility, lack of self-control, and a failure to appreciate the Christian understanding of marriage*.

In some English versions of the Bible, the word "fornication" is used in a very general sense for sexual immorality, and this is also seen as a type of Israel's unfaithfulness to Yahweh and its promiscuity with the idols.
See **Sexual Ethics.**

JOHN MACQUARRIE

Fortitude *see* **Cardinal Virtues; Courage**

Free Church *see* **Anabaptist Ethics; Church; Ecclesiology and Ethics; Nonconformist Conscience; Sect**

Free Will and Determinism

Together with the problems of God and immortality, the problem of the freedom of the will* is one of the three great metaphysical problems named by Kant as lying beyond the powers of the human intellect. Believers in free will hold that at least some human actions (and all on which moral judgment may be passed) are the result of free rational choice* on the part of agents. They are not compelled to act by forces outside of their moral consciousness. It is important to say this, because freedom of the will does not imply that moral actions are uncaused or originate out of nothing. In other words, they are not chance or random events, but flow from the values and character of the agent. This also means that freedom has nothing to do with unpredictability. The actions of mature moral agents may be highly predictable, because they will flow consistently from a stable moral character*. If such persons were to behave in unpredictable ways, this would not be evidence for freedom, but rather the reverse: the persons concerned are so unfree that they are easily blown off course by passing whims.

By its very nature, as something unobjectifiable and unobservable, free will would seem to be something that could be neither proved nor disproved. The observable overt happenings belonging to any human act may be seen as constituting a chain of causally linked physical events, while even the internal states of mind of the agent, if they are taken into account at all, might be explicated in terms of a determinist psychology. Yet the agent may have been aware of deliberating between different possible policies of action, and of having chosen one rather than another. Thus, although a great many arguments have been put forward in the history of philosophy, aimed either at establishing the reality of free choice or at showing it to be an illusion, none of these arguments has been decisive.

It is claimed by the supporters of determinism that all human behavior is due to the operation of causes of the same order as those which determine the course of events in the natural world. Some of these causes are physical and chemical and arise from the natural functioning of the body, including the nervous system, and its environment. Other causes are psychological, and it is claimed that individuals act as they do because of their past personal history, including heredity as well as environment. There is also sociological determinism, for most people simply conform to the standards and patterns of behavior prevailing in the societies to which they belong. There have also been a few upholders of theological determinism; for instance, Calvin's strong emphases on divine providence and predestination leave little scope for choice on the part of the individual. In Marxism we encounter economic determinism, the view that human behavior is shaped by economic factors. It need not be denied that much human action is determined in one or another of these various ways, yet most people believe that we are not wholly determined and that some areas in life remain open for freedom of choice.

The case for free will (like the case for the reality of the external world or the reality of other selves) does not finally rest on some subtle philosophical argument, but on the fact that it is an inevitable presupposition of our everyday thinking and acting. Thus, having shown the impossibility of a metaphysical proof of free will, Kant went on to claim that it is a postulate or presupposition of the moral life (see **Kantian Ethics**). We warn and we advise, we praise and we blame, we reward and we punish, we have a good conscience or a bad one, we set goals and strive after them, and all this makes sense only on the supposition that there is some freedom of choice and action. Such freedom is never unlimited (never a *libertas indifferentiae*), for it is always circumscribed by a great many "givens," such as environmental circumstances, the past acts of the agent or of others, personality traits, and the like. These limit freedom of the will at any given moment, and perhaps it is sometimes reduced to near the vanishing point. Yet it would be senseless to speak of ethics and moral responsibility at all unless some human action enjoyed at least some range of freedom (see **Responsibility**).

Parallel to the argument that free will is a postulate of the moral life is the argument of A. M. Farrer that it is a postulate of science and of intellectual activity in general. All such activity includes judgment, whereby we decide that one position is true, another false, or one argument valid and another fallacious. Our judgment must be a free act, based solely on rational grounds. If the determinist were correct, then our judgments too would be determined by personal history, the chemistry of the body, social pressures, and the like. Carried to its conclusions, this argument clearly leads into a self-destroying skepticism, for even the determinist's own argument is something determined by these fac-

tors and cannot claim to be based on rational judgments. Indeed, rational discussion has, like morality, been reduced to an illusion.

The question of freedom* in relation to a specifically Christian ethic becomes acute at two points in particular—where it impinges on the doctrines of original sin* and grace*. The awareness of this tension found its classic expression in the controversy between Augustinianism (see **Augustinian Ethics**) and Pelagianism. The first of these views held that the human will is so disabled by sin that it cannot choose good except through the supervention of divine grace; the second, that a genuine autonomous freedom remains. In practice, the church seems to have settled for a compromise between these extremes. Even if we allow that our fallen nature pulls us toward bad choices, we are not absolutely determined by this pull, and the very fact that there is a natural awareness of sin is itself a breach in the domination of sin. On the other hand, if we allow that the human will needs enabling grace, it cannot be supposed that such grace is irresistible or imposed in such a way that we become mere puppets. The dialectic of sin and grace is the theological counterpart of the ethical dialectic between freedom and determinism. In both cases, the dialectic must be maintained and explicated in fully personal terms.

See **Libertarianism**.

H. Bergson, *Time and Free Will* (1889), ET 1910; A. M. Farrer, *The Freedom of the Will,* 1958; I. Kant, *Critique of Practical Reason* (1788), ET 1883.

JOHN MACQUARRIE

Freedom

Freedom in the NT and most often in the context of Christian theology is a category not of social or political ethics but of the ultimate relationship between the Christian and Christ. Freedom is seen as freedom from sin and freedom for obedience to God. Paul emphasized freedom in these terms in Romans and Galatians especially, and always freedom as spontaneous loyalty* and obedience* to God in Christ is ultimate for Christian understanding. Deliverance from all hindrances to this loyalty and obedience is the negative dimension of freedom in this religious context. There has always been a problem in relating freedom understood in these terms to the specific social and political forms of freedom. For one thing it is possible to think of the freedom of the Christian as being independent of all external circumstances such as political tyranny or imprisonment. In this spirit Paul could say, "In any and all circumstances I have learned the secret of facing plenty and hunger, abundance and want" (Phil. 4:12). This may be true of persons who have attained considerable mature strength, but external deprivations in childhood, such as serious malnutrition and lack of early emotional supports, may keep persons from developing the stamina that makes possible inner freedom which is independent of external circumstance.

There is a relationship even between this exalted form of Christian freedom and freedom for the citizen when the Christian feels obliged by his or her obedience to God to take freedom to speak and act in the world. It sometimes becomes necessary to disobey the powers that seek to limit this freedom. "We must obey God rather than men" (Acts 5:29). Here we can see how Christian freedom in the most distinctive sense may become a source of political ferment. Those who take freedom to obey God in the world, as they understand this obedience, often break through the structures that limit their freedom to speak and act, and they have in Western history opened the door to political forms of freedom (see also **Civil Disobedience; Resistance**).

Until the 17th century in Christendom it was generally taken for granted that, either to protect souls from the spiritually deadly effects of heresy or to preserve social unity by permitting only one religious allegiance within a political community, it was right for Catholic or Protestant Christians to limit the freedom of those whom they believed to be in error. Gradually over a period of three centuries this assumption has been eroded, and today it is explicitly abandoned by nearly all Christians. At present there is a very broad ethical consensus in the church not only that it is bad public policy in pluralistic societies to use the power of the state to enforce religious uniformity but also that it is a sin against Christian love to "force consciences," to tempt persons to hypocrisy by intimidating them when they fail to conform in their religious life and witness (R. H. Bainton, *The Travail of Religious Liberty,* 1951). The Dec-

laration on Religious Freedom of the Second Vatican Council puts the Roman Catholic Church on record in favor of religious freedom for all on principle. Thus the Roman Catholic Church, which until Vatican II had no doctrinal basis for supporting religious freedom, especially for those in grave religious error, has become one of the strongest defenders of the freedom of all persons, Christians and non-Christians. This has had great effect especially in Latin America (see also **Persecution and Toleration**).

Freedom is not an absolute. Any society, even when committed to the kinds of freedom of expression and action guaranteed by the American Bill of Rights and other such affirmations, may be justified at times in setting limits to freedom for the sake of public order or national security or of some aspects of publicly supported morality. It is easy to recognize extreme cases of the abuse of religion as a front for racial discrimination or such an abhorrent practice as the coerced mass suicide or murder of the members of an ostensibly religious community—Jonestown in Guyana in 1978. The state may be justified in requiring various inoculations for the sake of public health even when they go against the religious scruples of some citizens. Nations threatened by serious disunity or subversion may at times be justified in abridging some usually sanctioned freedom of action. The healthier the society the heavier the burden of proof it should place on such abridgments of freedom. The provisions for conscientious objection* to the military draft (see **Conscription**) are widely supported by churches and are a fine example of the recognition by the state of the freedom of conscience of its citizens. Censorship* of what is regarded as pornography can be justified especially when it is on public display or made readily available to minors, but there are often disagreements as to what constitutes pornography, and the process of such censorship should be kept under criticism as it provides precedents for wider censorship of art or ideas (see also **Morality, Legal Enforcement of**).

The relation between the various forms of "civil liberty" and freedom of private initiative in economic life varies from country to country and there is no one Christian view of the matter. The issue is settled in favor of the dominance of public initiative and planning in Communist nations, and this is not in itself generally rejected in principle by churches in those countries. Elsewhere there is preference for a mixed economy which, while emphasizing the state's responsibility for welfare, allows considerable scope for private enterprise. Both the encyclicals of recent popes and the reports of the Assemblies of the World Council of Churches agree in presenting a flexible position in this context leaving much room for both private and public initiative. In the USA the extent of intervention by government in limiting free enterprise is more resisted than in other industrialized democracies because of a deeper strain of individualism* in American culture, but even in the USA there is acceptance of limited intervention by the state when public health is threatened by dangerous drugs or noxious waste and also to provide "welfare" and medical care for those recognized officially to be in need, but there are continuous political debates about the range of such need (*see* **Welfare State**).

Under Hitler and Stalin the uses of terror by the state to prevent expressions of public dissent and to intimidate whole populations have shown how far the state can go and sometimes does go in restricting the political and also the cultural and personal freedom of its citizens. Religious freedom is often limited to the sanctuary, and religious affiliation has been a cause of public discrimination. In recent decades there has been an increase of such abridgment of freedom on both the political left and the political right. Indeed, there are probably more rightist regimes than leftist regimes that severely restrict political and cultural freedom. Internationally the issues of freedom are most often discussed under the heading of "human rights."* There are several levels of such rights, beginning with the most basic rights to be free from arbitrary imprisonment or torture, moving up to such rights as freedom of speech and of the press, and moving beyond them to the right to engage in political organization and the right to vote. There are debates as to the extent to which all three levels of human rights are interdependent, but there may be priorities in emphasis in various countries. In recent decades there have been both diminution of human rights in many countries and also a much wider public awareness and concern about human rights and much more publicity about their denial wherever there is

freedom of speech and of the press. The issue of human rights, we may say, has been put on the global map.

Freedom in this article has been considered chiefly in terms of freedom *from* many forms of external hindrance to persons as they seek to make their own choices, to express their own convictions, to be true in the public sphere to their own consciences. (The same considerations apply to groups and institutions especially when they respect the freedom of conscience among their members.) But Christian thinking about freedom does return full circle to freedom in the positive sense, freedom to be bound by loyalty to God's will revealed in Christ. Those who do not share the commitment of Christian faith may have the same form of positive freedom which consists in a commitment that both limits the freedom of the person and expresses it. Freedom *from* external hindrance may be understood as opportunity for the person to speak and act as one bound by his or her deepest commitments.

See also **Authenticity; Autonomy; Conscience; Conscientious Objection; Libertarianism; Paternalism; Voluntary Associations.**

JOHN C. BENNETT

Friendship

In Western culture the love of friendship is more discussed in the literature of Greece and Rome than in writings from the Christian era. The most important classical treatises on friendship are books 8–9 of Aristotle's *Nicomachean Ethics* and Cicero's *Laelius de Amicitia.* Plato's *Lysis* and *Phaedrus* are also noteworthy. Friendship was highly prized among the Epicureans, but very little of Epicurus's writing is extant. Christian thinkers have written few detailed treatises on friendship. A notable exception is Jeremy Taylor's "Discourse on the Nature and Offices of Friendship." Friendship has also received attention in the literature of the Christian monastic tradition. In the modern period, friendship has been the subject of famous essays by writers as diverse as Montaigne and Emerson. It has also been a concern of thinkers seeking to recapture an emphasis on public virtue, civic solidarity, and "civic friendship."

Friendship may be defined in terms of its focus on the friend (as a reciprocal goodwill founded in sentiment or choice) or in terms of the friends' shared focus on some common interest, value, or cause. Both emphases are needed to characterize friendship adequately. The shared focus helps differentiate friendship from erotic love, but an emphasis on shared focus alone makes friendship more impersonal than our experience suggests it is.

Among issues often discussed in the literature on friendship are (1) how many friends it is possible or desirable to have; (2) loyalty to friends vs. loyalty to the political community; (3) the necessity of friendship for human flourishing; (4) the degree to which friendship requires reciprocity but can be contaminated when seen as a mere "exchange"; (5) change within friendships and the possibility that friendship may end; (6) the possibility of friendship between men and women.

Friendship stands in some tension with Christian love* (*agapē*) because agape is to be more universal in scope and open even to the enemy, whereas friendship is preferential and reciprocal. Three basic strategies have been followed in attempting to reconcile the loves: (1) build down from agape to friendship by seeing friendship as a narrower specification of agape, a narrowing made necessary by the constraints of finitude; (2) build up from friendship to agape by seeing the narrower preference of friendship as a "school of virtue" in which to learn what love for any human being may require; (3) build around friendship by using agape to set boundaries to the preference friendship may legitimately show.

L. Blum, *Friendship, Altruism, and Morality,* 1980; S. Kierkegaard, *Works of Love* (1847), ET 1962; C. S. Lewis, *The Four Loves,* 1960; G. Meilaender, *Friendship,* 1981; G. Outka, *Agape,* 1972.

GILBERT MEILAENDER

Fundamentalist Ethics

In the USA, fundamentalism distinguished itself theologically from Protestant modernism by the so-called "five points of fundamentalism," which were prepared at the Niagara Conference in 1895: the total inspiration and inerrancy of scripture, the deity of Jesus, the virgin birth, the substitutionary atonement, and the physical resurrection and premillennial second coming of Christ. In its early stages, fundamentalism was neither anti-intellectual nor hostile to social ethics. Scholars like James Orr joined in writing The

Fundamentals (a series of books beginning in 1909), and J. Gresham Machen, while preferring to be identified as Reformed, made common theological cause with the fundamentalists against theological liberalism and the social gospel.

But fundamentalism soon underwent noteworthy changes. Before mid-century it became increasingly polemical, largely through the rise of independent ecclesial agencies. It expounded ethical pietism mainly in terms of individual abstention from worldly vices (drinking, gambling, smoking, movie attendance). In *The Uneasy Conscience of Modern Fundamentalism* (1947) this writer warned that, in reaction to ecumenical sociopolitical preoccupation, fundamentalists had recoiled from a significant stance on sociocultural matters. The modernist social gospel sought a transformation of society without the spiritual rebirth of fallen humanity despite Walter Rauschenbusch's early insistence on personal regeneration. This prompted fundamentalists to link all social concern with evangelistic aims and to neglect issues of public justice. Reinforcing this stance was a dispensational premillennial conviction of the imminent end of this age, now apostate; before Christ's return salvific possibility remained for only a remnant.

Emergence in the late 1970s of the Moral Majority led by Jerry Falwell marked a partial and belated return by the fundamentalist movement to sociopolitical engagement. Falwell acknowledged that by social withdrawal fundamentalism had lapsed from its evangelical heritage. His vigorous entry into political matters aroused the ire of some fellow fundamentalists. Moral Majority presuppositions were at first somewhat obscure except for energetic support of the political right. Its call for biblical morality seemed to approve legislation of Christian positions upon secular society, but Falwell subsequently stressed that Moral Majority was not theologically based. The movement took positions on some issues (e.g., the Panama Canal treaty) that were matters merely of secular prudence*. It increasingly focused on anti-abortion and pro-Israel emphases, promoted prayer in public schools, and vigorously opposed pornography and homosexuality. Fundamentalists have established a network of Christian day schools, Bible institutes and colleges, and now venture increasingly into liberal arts learning from which they had long recoiled.

But the movement tends still to be more aphoristic than academic in its responses.

See **Bible in Christian Ethics; Evangelical Ethics.**

J. Falwell (ed.), *The Fundamentalist Phenomenon,* 1981; C. F. H. Henry, *The Uneasy Conscience of Modern Fundamentalism,* 1947; G. Marsden, *Fundamentalism and American Culture: The Shaping of Twentieth Century Evangelicalism, 1870–1925,* 1980; J. I. Packer, *Fundamentalism and the Word of God,* 1958.

CARL F. H. HENRY

Future Generations, Obligations to

Do we have moral obligations to members of future generations? If so, what is the nature of these obligations and how far into the future do they extend? These are novel questions. Until recently, human beings had little ability to inflict serious harm* on their distant descendants, but recent technological developments have changed this (*see* **Risk**). Some of the most urgent moral problems of our day—issues of environmental responsibility, energy alternatives, genetic engineering, and nuclear arms policy—all raise the question of how much we are obligated to protect those who follow us (*see also* **Deterrence; Energy; Environmental Ethics; Genetics; Nuclear Warfare; Population Policy; Technology**).

Many persons are convinced that we do have important obligations to the future. They believe that it would be wrong, for instance, to leave our descendants a world badly polluted by radioactive wastes, even if this made possible cheaper energy in the present. But recent efforts by philosophers and ethicists to account for these intuitive convictions have revealed how difficult the task is.

For example, efforts to ground this sense of obligation in the claim that future persons have "rights" face many problems. Rights* language ordinarily makes reference to identifiable living individuals who are the bearers or claimants of the strong entitlements rights involve. But can there be rights when, as in this case, the "rights holders" do not yet exist? And if so, to which nonexistent persons do rights extend? To all those who could possibly ever live? Or only to all those who, pending our reproductive decisions, actually do live? Major moral decisions in the areas of genetic and reproductive medicine and in population policy hinge on the answers to these questions. To complicate matters further, some philosophers have argued that the very contingency of future persons makes it difficult to harm them in an ordinary sense. This is because some efforts to avoid injuring future persons—say, through the adoption of more costly but less polluting energy policies—may actually alter which identifiable specific persons are born in the future. Do we really benefit people by improving the quality of a world into which, as a result, they are never born? Do we harm people by handing on to them a degraded world which, had it not been degraded, they might otherwise never have lived to see?

The peculiarities of these questions and of the effort to comprehend our responsibility to the future in terms of obligations to specific and identifiable persons has attracted some ethicists to an alternative, utilitarian way of understanding our responsibility to the future. Since utilitarianism* traces all moral obligation to a nonpersonalized duty to maximize the sum total of human well-being (the duty to promote "the greatest good for the greatest number"), it does not appear to matter when or for whom this well-being is produced. Hence we have as much of an obligation to promote and to protect the well-being of our distant descendants as we do that of our contemporaries.

Unfortunately it has been noted that utilitarianism, too, leads to a series of puzzling conclusions where future generations are concerned. If we are obligated to maximize the sum total of human well-being, for example, should we not also increase the *number* of future persons enjoying well-being? Indeed, so long as the per capita decline in welfare created by crowding and resource depletion does not jeopardize the total increase in well-being brought about by the existence of more persons, it would seem that utilitarianism requires policies of rapid and burgeoning population growth. Efforts have been made to avoid this conclusion, including those which interpret utilitarianism as requiring us to promote the highest *average* as opposed to highest *total* level of well-being. But not only is it uncertain whether these efforts can avoid all the populationist implications of the utilitarian position, they also appear to forfeit utilitarianism's great strength in this area: its grounding of obligation to the future in a nonpersonalized duty to maximize human welfare generally. What utilitarians must show is why we should further limit this obligation to protect only those individuals we allow (through our reproductive decisions) to come into being at some future time.

None of these perplexities should surprise us. As one writer has noted, we are in the "early days" of systematic thinking about our intergenerational moral responsibilities. That we have such responsibilities and that, discounting for the factor of uncertainty about the impact of present deeds on future persons, these responsibilities are roughly the same as those we have to our contemporaries is intuitively evident to many persons. What is currently lacking is a convincing philosophical account of these intuitions. Such an account might well return for clarity to an understanding of the basic conditions of moral justification. For example, if one adopted a Rawlsian "contractualist" understanding of moral justification some of our puzzles might dissolve (see **Social Contract**). This approach views morality as a peaceful means of adjudicating possible disputes among rational persons. Thus, it views moral rules as a form of abiding public legislation adopted by rational persons under conditions of impartiality and objectivity. The fact that in this framework moral legislators are necessarily thought of as living persons who can become parties to moral disputes means that moral principles are relevant only to those who will actually come into existence. This may underlie our intuitive perception that we need only be concerned about really existing persons in the future and that we are not responsible for proliferating possible future lives. Similarly, the requirement of impartiality in moral justification means that, where disputes between generations are involved, moral legislators must be asked to reason to principles without knowledge of the specific generation to which they belong: hence our intuitive sense that in our judgments and conduct we must be fair to those who live in the future. This account needs further development, but it is a promising way of understanding and advancing commonsense thinking in this area.

In view of the urgency of these basic questions and the attention given them in the philosophical literature, it is remarkable that to date they have received so little treatment at the hands of theological ethicists. None of the major Christian ethicists of the past generation addresses this issue. While the significance of human involvement in history occupies attention in the work of Barth, Brunner, Tillich, Niebuhr, or Thielicke, and while thinkers like Häring, Ramsey, or Gustafson sometimes address issues (such as eugenics or environmental responsibility) that bear on the welfare of future persons, none of these writers explicitly discusses the extent or limits of our obligations to future persons. Clearly resources for such a discussion exist within the biblical tradition, where God's relationship to humankind is typically viewed as one spanning generations. But these resources have yet to be systematically assessed or explored.

R. M. Green, *Population Growth and Justice,* 1975; G. S. Kavka, "The Paradox of Future Individuals," and D. Parfit, "Future Generations: Further Problems," *Philosophy and Public Affairs* 11, 1982, pp. 93–112 and 113–172; E. Partridge (ed.), *Responsibilities to Future Generations,* 1981; J. Rawls, *A Theory of Justice,* 1971; J. Schell, *The Fate of the Earth,* 1982; R. I. Sikora and B. Barry, *Obligations to Future Generations,* 1981; J. P. Sterba, *Morality in Practice,* 1984, pp. 65–113.
                                        RONALD M. GREEN

Gambling

The determination of the possession of money, or money value, by an appeal to an artifically created chance, where the gains of the winners are made at the expense of the losers and the gain is secured without rendering in service or in value an equivalent of the gains obtained. Thus the playing of a game of chance wholly for amusement is not gambling. Insurance, which is a statistical reduction of the risks of chance, is not gambling. The acceptance of a gift, though it is literally "money for nothing," is not gambling because there is no appeal to chance. Gambling may be *gaming,* that is, playing for money in a game of chance; *betting,* that is, staking money on an event of which the outcome is doubtful; *lotteries,* that is, the distribution of prizes by lot or chance; and *pools,* which combine the latter two.

The habit of gambling is deeply rooted in human history. The knucklebone, the original of the dice, was used for this purpose in the 16th century B.C. Many ivory, porcelain, or stone dice—some of them loaded—were found in the ruins of Pompeii. Twice the apostle Paul uses words that in their literal meaning refer to gambling (Eph. 4:14; Phil. 2:30). It is generally agreed that immoderate addiction to gambling is to be condemned. An individual or a community in whose life gambling plays too prominent a part betrays a false sense of values which cannot but impair the full development of the personality or the society. It should therefore be the concern of the state to control the indulgence within reasonable bounds.

Most Christian moralists who accept this general judgment assert that the danger lies in the excess. It is extremely difficult, they contend, to establish by abstract arguments that all gambling is inherently immoral without adopting views on the nature of good and evil that do not commend themselves to general acceptance. A small stake in a raffle for a worthy cause, for example, inflicts no conceivable hardship on the purchaser of the ticket and is motivated more by generous desire to help than by anticipatory greed. In much actual gambling, the element of amusement or harmless excitement is not dominated by cupidity. If a number of people join together in a competition in which, by completely voluntary agreement, some will win and others lose, those who win need not be ashamed. In short, when gamblers firmly control their indulgence and are not dominated by it, they may obtain from it legitimate enjoyment that adds color and modest excitement to their life. The essence of this argument is that gambling is not wrong in itself. It may reveal, but does not cause, defects of character in the participants.

The answer of the minority of moralists who take a stricter view is that "gambling in itself" is a meaningless phrase. Every gamble is a particular and concrete action. They contend that in no circumstances is any gamble morally justified. The essence of their argument is that the command to love one's neighbor rules out gain at the other's inevitable loss, even if he or she is a willing partner. The decisive consideration should not be the ability of the bettor to risk a loss, but the willingness to accept an undeserved gain. In the totality of transactions, large sums of money are transferred by the random operations of chance from one set of pockets to another set. To all the other tensions of economic life—the consequences of exploitation,

mismanagement, waste, and social injustice —is added an arbitrary, unpredictable, and unnecessary tension. It is further argued that the moralistic condoning of small-scale gambling weakens the case against commercial exploitation on a large scale, and so puts a stumbling block in others' way. Finally, it is contended that resort to gambling is a virtual denial of faith in God and an ordered universe, putting in its place an appeal to blind chance, prompted by neither love nor rectitude.

The two positions cannot be reconciled. They illustrate clearly two distinct ethical approaches. The "Catholic" approach deprecates what is regarded as an exaggerated scrupulosity concerning acts and notions that can be reasonably argued to be harmless in their effects on the individual and on the community. The "dominical" approach deprecates what is regarded as the condoning of acts that can reasonably be held to conflict with the law of love to one's neighbor. One is basically sociological, the other basically theological.

The undoubted fact, however, that the great majority of Christian moralists condemn excessive addiction, commercial exploitation, and government participation in the provision of facilities for gambling suggests that there may be a considerable measure of rationalization in the less rigorous approach.

W. D. Mackenzie, *The Ethics of Gambling,* 1895; R. C. Mortimer, *Gambling,* 1933; S. Longstreet, *Win or Lose: A Social History of Gambling in America,* 1977.

EDWARD ROGERS

Gaudium et Spes see **Official Roman Catholic Social Teaching**

Gene Therapy, Human see **Genetics**

Generosity see **Almsgiving; Charity; Love; Philanthropy**

Genetic Counseling see **Genetics**

Genetic Engineering see **Eugenics; Genetics**

Genetic Screening see **Genetics**

Genetics

Human genetics involves the study of human variability in terms of its causes and effects. Hardly any feature of human existence draws more conflict and disagreement than the origin and meaning of differences between human beings themselves, and between human beings and other animals. Therefore, human genetics and evolutionary thought have been more influential in the development of modern theology, ethics, and politics than many other branches of science.

Human genetics in historical perspective. The earliest societies to keep records (Babylonian, Assyrian, and Egyptian) attributed malformations to supernatural causes and viewed birth defects as signs of good or evil for the society itself. Such views spread to Greece, Rome, and Europe. Even though the supernaturalistic explanation was dominant, naturalistic explanations also emerged for malformations and for physical differences and similarities between members of the same family. Concepts of inherited differences appear in the Hippocratic texts and in the writings of Anaxagoras (500–428 B.C.).

Aristotle based a theory of inheritance on his philosophy of form. He held that the generation of males and females was due to differences between "principles" of movement and matter that were embodied in semen and female secretions. When the male principle was dominant, sons were conceived who were more like their fathers than their mothers, and vice versa. These ideas, incorrect in the biological sense, were the major source of prescientific guidance on such questions until the Enlightenment period.

In the religious context, an impression exists, probably false, that part of the Mosaic Code (Lev. 18:6–13) prohibiting incest* was *also* related to eugenic concern, due to insight into the frequency of birth defects from sexual union between close relatives. No biblical text specifically deals with prevention of birth defects through marital laws, but incest is clearly regarded as a grave moral offense. The Talmud, a collection of rabbinic writings dating from A.D. 400, rules that a man may not marry into a family afflicted with epilepsy, leprosy, or a similar disease. The rabbis noted that such diseases were transmitted more frequently in such families. D. M. Feldman commented that these texts are the first eugenic edict in any social or religious system. In a strict medical sense, he may be correct, although Plato's utopia was based on eugenic principles for selection of spouses for reproduction.

European physicians in the 17th and 18th centuries debated the "preformationist" theory in terms of whether the whole organism was preformed in the ovum or sperm. The debate foundered on the lack of empirical evidence until Gregor Mendel's experiments, reported in 1865. Mendel, an Austrian monk and botanist, experimented with crossing varieties of the pea in terms of color and shape of seed. He then counted all types and combinations in the offspring for several generations. From these experiments he deduced the statistical laws that shape the foundations of modern genetics and provided the correct biological theory for the similarities and differences between offspring, namely, that the germ cells (sperm and ova) are the constant forms in the dynamics of inheritance.

The fact that Darwin knew nothing of Mendel's work, despite their publications during the same period, is a comment on the cultural isolation of creative scientists of that time. Mendel's concept of the *gene* would have provided answers to many of Darwin's major intellectual insights and contradictions, especially as to the mode of inheritance of specific characteristics. Furthermore, Mendel's work remained unused by scientists and was eventually rediscovered only in 1900.

During this same period, Sir Francis Galton (1865) published papers asserting that qualities like talent and social achievement were strongly influenced by heredity. Later, he proceeded to develop the basis for biometric genetics, or the study of variations in whole populations by statistical methods. The eugenic theme was strong in early 20th-century genetic studies and led to unethical sterilization*, restrictive immigration, and discriminatory political measures in Europe and the USA (*see* **Eugenics**). Nazi racist-eugenic programs were the most ethically and legally objectionable expressions of eugenic motives in human genetics. Galton's lasting work continues in studies of population and behavioral genetics.

Mendel's discoveries gradually led to clear and less controversial applications in medical genetics, and to evidence that genes were composed of the content of DNA molecules, the building blocks of protein synthesis common to life in all of its forms. Techniques in molecular biology gradually laid a foundation for understanding the basic principles of gene action. Today, molecular biologists routinely recombine particles of DNA to produce new life forms in bacteria, plants, and chemicals. Some thinkers have likened the potential for good or evil to the world's people of this biological revolution to that of atomic energy.

Applied human genetics. Concurrent with the development of a powerful theory of Mendelian genetics, physicians and other scientists applied genetic knowledge to problems of inherited disorders. Today applied human genetics involves practices of genetic screening of newborns and carriers, genetic counseling, prenatal diagnosis of genetic disorders, and the treatment of harmful results produced by some genes. Applied human genetics was a major source of moral and ethical problems addressed by Christian ethicists, among others, in the 1970s and 1980s.

Genetic screening is done for three reasons: (1) to uncover a disorder that is latent or actual, so that treatment or support can follow; (2) to detect persons of reproductive age who are at higher risk to transmit a genetic disorder, so that information about reproduction can be given to people involved; and (3) to answer questions about the natural history of a disorder, how frequently it appears in the population, and how the gene(s) for the disorder is (are) distributed. Large-scale screening programs were organized to screen for carriers (those who carry the trait but do not manifest the disease) of Tay-Sachs disease, beta-thalassemia, and sickle cell disease. Because these disorders are found frequently (but not only) in those of European Jewish, Mediterranean, and African ancestry, respectively, screening creates occasions for racial and ethnic discrimination and misunderstanding. Questions also can be raised as to whether screening should be mandatory to prevent the recurrence of disease. Religious ethicists joined other professionals (Research Group, 1972) in providing social and ethical guidelines for screening programs. This early statement emphasized a goal of information for parents and voluntaristic methods, rather than screening of entire populations and mandatory sanctions. Dissent by some religious ethicists was apparent, however, due to the implications of genetic screening for abortion. The core principles of these guidelines were embodied in the influential recommendations of the President's Commission for the Study of Ethical Problems in Medicine and Biomedical and Behavioral Research (1982) as to practices in counseling and screening.

Genetic counseling, as practiced today, is an informational process between a qualified counselor and the individuals(s) or family at higher risk to have or transmit a genetic disorder. Goals of counseling are (1) to establish a diagnosis, (2) to evaluate the risk of recurrence, (3) to communicate these risks to those with a primary interest, and (4) to inform as to the severity and potential burdens of the disorder. Beyond these goals is one of informing the family as to the options that exist for reproduction. Each goal can be an occasion for moral problems, such as truth-telling and breaching confidentiality*. As a practice, however, genetic counseling has not aroused significant controversy in Christian literature.

Prenatal diagnosis of genetic disorders is carried out by a number of technically successful modes: (1) amniocentesis, extracting amniotic fluid by needle puncture between the sixteenth and eighteenth week of pregnancy, by which fetal cells can be obtained and cultured in the laboratory for diagnosis; (2) fetoscopy, the insertion of a small-gauge endoscope into the abdomen of the pregnant woman, to remove fetal blood or tissue; (3) ultrasound, the transmission of the fetal image onto a screen by high frequency, low intensity sound waves; and (4) an emergent technique of chorionic villus sampling in late first trimester by means of ultrasound-guided catheterization. The main purpose of prenatal diagnosis is to screen high-risk pregnancies for malformations, to provide parents with a diagnosis and information about the disorder. If presented with evidence of a serious disorder, parents face choices of waiting until birth to attempt treatment if one is available, or relinquishing parenthood before or after treatment followed by adoption, or elective abortion. Many parents who take the third course do so in the hope of trying again for a healthy child, but not without considerable moral suffering.

Ethical questions have been raised about the risks of prenatal diagnosis, controversial indications (e.g., maternal anxiety, sex choice unrelated to sex-linked disorders), and fairness of access to services. Abortion* was the most controversial problem debated by

Christian ethicists during the 1970s in relation to prenatal diagnosis. Critics of the practice such as Bernard Häring and Paul Ramsey were not opposed to the technology as such but to its link with abortion and implications for selective treatment of persons based on inheritable qualities. Two dominant themes appear in their arguments: (1) a basic purpose of medicine—to save life—is violated by the practice of abortion; and (2) while some abortions may be justified, the use of prenatal diagnosis tends to set apart certain fetuses as deserving of abortion and thus treats fetuses unequally and unjustly. The theological views from which such ethical views proceed tend to secure the sanctity of all human life in the protection of God, who confers an "alien dignity" on each new life that is not to be overridden by any other reason or source of human evaluation.

The main argument by religious ethicists for elective abortion following genetic diagnosis is based on the principle of reducing or preventing suffering for the family in the absence of any approach to treatment for the disorder. Some physicians and geneticists offer further reasons, namely, to prevent genetic disorders in future generations or to prevent a lifetime of suffering for the affected individual. The number of abortions of carriers needed to prevent genetic disorders raises a clear moral barrier to the possibility that prenatal diagnosis might be used to screen pregnancies for selection of fetuses at lowest risk to transmit or suffer genetic disorders. For these reasons, prenatal diagnosis in its present forms is unlikely to affect the future incidence of the most prevalent genetic disorders. In fact, many more persons who are carriers for genetic disorders live longer and reproduce more, creating the paradox that advances in applied human genetics cause more and not less reproduction among couples at risk.

Treatments for genetic disorders after birth span a gamut from transplantation of organs to alteration of diet. The common feature of contemporary treatment focuses on reducing harmful expressions of underlying genetic causes. However, many scientists and physicians believe that a *genetic* approach to the treatment of genetic disorders will soon be technically feasible. The possibility of human gene therapy creates moral and ethical concerns that Christian ethicists, among others, have discussed.

Assuming that successful animal experiments to correct inherited disorders lay a scientific foundation, prospects for human gene therapy involve three levels of potential intervention: somatic cell therapy, prevention of genetic disorders by gametic correction, and deliberate attempts to alter human traits like height, longevity, and intelligence by correction of either somatic or gametic cells.

Protestant, Catholic, and Jewish ethicists tend to agree that gene therapy at the simplest level would be ethically acceptable, as long as its experimental beginnings were conducted with proper review and consent. The first treatments may possibly be tried in patients with diseases caused by deletions or other problems at a single gene, thus permitting insertion of fragments of DNA directed toward the cells that operate incorrectly. Somatic gene therapy will affect only the treated patient, and thus the disorder will recur in later generations. Only those who fear that the other two levels of intervention are inevitable, given the introduction of gene therapy, oppose human gene therapy as a pretext for potential abuse of genetic engineering.

A strong presumption exists among supporters of gene therapy that sufficient ethical and social controls exist, due to recent efforts to shape stronger bodies of research ethics, to guide the early uses of somatic cell therapy. However, there is little evidence that sufficient ethical guidance exists for the uses of knowledge of how to alter gametic (sperm and ova) cells. Scientists have already conducted experiments in fruit flies and mice that demonstrate the capacity to alter inherited traits permanently by introducing DNA into the pronuclei of embryos. Some offspring inherit the humanly altered trait from the parent. Scientists will probably learn how to do similar experiments with human gametes before the ethics of human gametic correction have been thoroughly debated and policy guidelines formulated to prevent abusive consequences and encourage the most beneficial results.

Theological issues. On the question of the future of applied human genetics and its interaction with religious traditions, sharp divergences appear in the views of religious ethicists. Theological convictions and their bearing on the meaning of the future are a major source of these differences. One view is that even somatic gene therapy is a thin wedge of a much wider danger of future wholesale genetic engineering of human traits in the name of a perfectionism that threatens religious faith. This view stresses human tendencies toward self-interest, hubris, domination of other species, and the willful abuse of power. Underlying this view is a belief in an infinite qualitative difference between the Creator and the creation's creatures, of which humans are but one, albeit a gifted, dangerous, and complex creature. In this view, creation is essentially finished. The Genesis texts on creation are drawn upon strongly for support and guidance for the churches' positions on genetic issues (Granberg-Michaelson, 1984). A future is portrayed that is full of danger.

Others, such as James Gustafson and Roger Shinn, view the biological and social sciences as necessary to theological and ethical reflection about the proper meaning and direction of any genetic interventions. The real limits of genetic knowledge are a source of insight and help to lessen cause for concern about immediate dangers. Scripture tends to be used as an orientational source of ethical guidance on medical and biological research, rather than a source of direct guidance. The creative and ordering works of God are seen as unfinished and continuing. Human beings, as well as other species, participate in creation, but humans have the greatest present role and responsibility in such co-creativity. The future is viewed with less sense of danger and more expectancy of novelty and creativity breaking in upon history. These alternative views show less interest in judging specific experiments as right or wrong and more in attempting to guide the ultimate goals of biological and medical research.

Finally, the theory of genetics and evolution by natural selection raise even broader theological questions about how God acts in the world and whether human existence is rendered meaningless by the random genetic mutations that are supposed to have been the major objects of the process of natural selection. And insofar as most mutations are harmful to humans and other species, in what ways is God's goodness and power compromised or defeated by such events? The work of God as Creator, Redeemer, and Emancipator as explicated in contemporary theology must continue to come to terms with genetic and evolutionary theory as a proper background for Christian ethical thought about the many and potent ethical problems raised by applied human genetics. Human genetics will be a subject of ethical reflection throughout the century and beyond.

See **Abortion; Eugenics; Sterilization.**

D. M. Feldman, "Eugenics and Religious Law: Jewish Religious Law"; J. C. Fletcher, "Prenatal Diagnosis: Ethical Issues"; and R. L. Shinn, "Gene Therapy: Ethical Issues in," all in *EB*, 1978; J. C. Fletcher, *Coping with Genetic Disorders: A Guide for Clergy and Parents*, 1982; W. Granberg-Michaelson, *A Worldly Spirituality*, 1984; President's Commission for the Study of Ethical Problems in Medicine and Biomedical and Behavioral Research, *Genetic Screening and Counseling*, 1982; Research Group on Ethical, Social, and Legal Issues in Genetic Counseling and Genetic Engineering, "Ethical and Social Issues in Screening for Genetic Disease," *New England Journal of Medicine* 286, 1972, pp. 1129–1132; R. L. Shinn, *Forced Options*, 1982; F. Vogel and A. Motulsky, *Human Genetics: Problems and Approaches*, 1979; and the relevant articles in *DME*.

JOHN C. FLETCHER

Genocide

Genocide is a form of discrimination* that aims at the extermination of a religious, racial, or cultural group. Although genocide has occurred throughout human history, the term was coined specifically to identify the policies of the German National Socialist regime (1933–1945) which led to the Holocaust, in which some six million Jews were killed in Germany and the territories it occupied (*see* **Anti-Semitism**).

International law. In 1946, the United Nations General Assembly affirmed that genocide is a crime under international law. The UN Convention on the Prevention and Punishment of the Crime of Genocide (1948) specifies five policies which, when implemented with intent to destroy a group, are acts of genocide: "(*a*) killing members of the group; (*b*) causing serious bodily or mental harm to members of the group; (*c*) deliberately inflicting on the group conditions of life calculated to bring about its physical destruction in whole or in part; (*d*) imposing measures intended to prevent births within the group; (*e*) forcibly transferring children of the group to another group." The Convention makes it clear that genocide is not simply a crime during the conduct of war, but violates international law whenever it occurs. Policies of genocide are forbidden in all circumstances, and any contracting state can call upon the UN to take action against genocide wherever it occurs.

Genocide and racism. Although armed conflicts since 1945 have repeatedly led to massacres of civilian populations that seem genocidal in intent, no sustained policy of extermination comparable to the Nazi "final solution" has come to light. Charges of genocide made in international forums have centered on policies that put identifiable racial groups or aboriginal populations under severe disadvantages that tend to reduce the size of the group and limit the well-being of its members. The US declined to ratify the UN Convention on Genocide because ratification might have invited international action against the racial segregation then widely protected by US law. Other nations have responded to accusations of genocide by asserting sovereign rights to regulate their own internal affairs. Except in cases of overt extermination of a group, then, the international community has not widely accepted the Convention's principle that actions taken against racial or religious groups are not simply matters of internal policy. The prohibitions of genocide in international law have not been effective against policies of racial discrimination (*see* **Race Relations; Racism**).

Moral considerations. The meaning of genocide in moral and political discussions has come to include not only policies of overt extermination, but any intentional discrimination that exposes a group to material hardships or erodes the self-respect of its members. Warfare, too, may be denounced as genocidal when it is pursued with unusual vigor or extraordinary means against people who happen to belong to a different racial or ethnic group. The moral meaning of genocide thus expands considerably beyond the legal definition in the UN Convention to encompass virtually any harmful policy directed against persons solely because of their membership in an identifiable group. While it is important to reserve a strong moral condemnation and to preserve a legal basis for direct action against policies that directly result in the deaths of innocent persons, it is also true that any policy which adversely affects the welfare of a group or makes it difficult for its members to retain their identity tends, over time, toward the elimination of that group. To that extent the broadened meaning of genocide in contemporary moral and political discussions is probably justified, even though it tends to weaken the term's condemnatory force.

ROBIN W. LOVIN

Gluttony

Food and nonintoxicating drink are essential to life and health, and the desire* for a sufficient quantity and quality—and even for pleasure in their consumption—is not sinful, according to the Christian tradition. What is sinful is excessive or inordinate desire for them and the pleasure they bring. Nevertheless, gluttony does not figure prominently in the lists of sins and vices condemned in the NT. Jesus himself was accused of being "a glutton and a drunkard" because he came "eating and drinking" in contrast to the ascetic John the Baptist (Luke 7:33–34; Matt. 11:18–19). Jesus' parable of the rich man who "feasted sumptuously every day" and the poor man Lazarus who lay at his gate desiring "to be fed with what fell from the rich man's table" suggests that gluttony can dull compassion* and love* for the neighbor (Luke 16:19–31). In making gluttony one of the seven capital sins—the so-called "deadly" sins*—the Christian tradition has stressed that inordinate pursuit of the desirable end of food and drink can lead to other sins such as theft and injustice. Gluttony may even reflect or contribute to a lack of faith in and love of God, as in the case of those of whom Paul said "their god is their belly" (Phil. 3:19). According to Thomas Aquinas (*ST* II-II.148), gluttony is contrary to the general virtue of temperance* and the special virtue of abstinence*. Fasting* may be an appropriate form of mortification* and self-denial* in the exercise of self-control. In a world where people are suffering from malnutrition and dying from starvation, gluttony both symbolizes and contributes to policies that are unjust and uncaring (*see* **Hunger, World**).

JAMES F. CHILDRESS

Gnosticism, Ethics of

Until recently the little that was known about Gnostic ethics was gleaned from orthodox Christian opponents and the Neoplatonic philosopher Plotinus. On the basis of these reports the conclusion was drawn by scholars that Gnostics rejected all conventional moral norms because of their deep aversion to the material world and its Creator. This would express itself either in asceticism* or more typically in libertinism*. Reports about libertinism from late antiquity were generally assumed to refer to Gnostics. However, the large collection of ancient Gnostic writing discovered near Nag Hammadi in Egypt does not support this reconstruction of Gnostic ethics. Not only do these texts show no hint of libertinism but the obvious ascetic stance of the collection is not motivated by defiance over against an evil creator and lawgiver but rather by the ideal of an otherworldly perfection that can only be reached if the bodily passions are denied. In this Gnostic ethics does not stand over against contemporary Hellenistic culture but is a radical form of a common ascetic trend found within most religious movements of that time as well as in Middle Platonism and Neoplatonism*.

The discrepancy between the ethical stance of the Gnostic treatises and the reports of the anti-Gnostic polemicists needs an explanation. Upon closer examination it becomes clear that with few exceptions the claims of Gnostic libertinism are not based on firsthand observation but rather on hearsay and inference. In the heat of controversy opponents are usually put in the worst possible light. For the orthodox church fathers it was inconceivable that heretics could lead a godly life. They felt sure that false teaching would lead inevitably to immorality even if this did not become public. They dismissed the ascetic life of Gnostics as a false front to deceive the orthodox and win them over. The encratic marriage (one without sexual intercourse) which was practiced among the Valentinians was ridiculed and called a fraud even though this ideal was shared by orthodox circles in Syria.

The main mistake Plotinus and the church fathers made was the assumption that the Gnostics would draw the same consequences from theology for ethics that they drew themselves. They considered the affirmation of creation as an essential factor underlying the virtuous life. Since the Gnostics considered the creator a villain and the world an evil, alien place, the ethical consequence could only be libertinism. There was no need to observe immoral practices to be sure of this. However, it is clear from the Nag Hammadi texts that the Gnostics did not follow this line of reasoning. They connected the creator with the evil passions and saw asceticism as the ethical consequence.

Another questionable claim made by some of the church fathers was that Gnostics did not think it necessary to live a virtuous life because they were saved on the basis of the spiritual nature they possessed. The Gnostic writings known to us do not support this claim. They pose some form of asceticism as an essential prerequisite for salvation. The Gnostic is involved in a moral struggle in this world and will be judged accordingly.

There is no need to claim that all reports of Gnostic libertinism are false inferences or slander. The movement may indeed have produced some individuals or groups that rejected conventional moral standards or were involved in orgiastic rites. However, these would have been exceptional. Gnostics appear not to have produced ethical writings. This may be because they were well served by such non-Gnostic ascetic treatises as were found among the Nag Hammadi texts. Another reason may be that the Gnostic literature available to us does not appear to reflect the existence of organized Gnostic communities with distinct rituals and life-style.

K. Rudolph, *Gnosis: The Nature and History of Gnosticism,* ET 1982; F. Wisse, "Die Sextus-Sprüche und das Problem der gnostischen Ethik," in *Zum Hellenismus in den Schriften von Nag Hammadi,* 1975.

F. WISSE

Golden Rule

"Whatever you wish that men would do to you, do so to them" (Matt. 7:12; Luke 6:31) has been designated as the Golden Rule or Golden Law at least since the 17th century. Since it occurs both in Matthew's Sermon on the Mount and in Luke's Sermon on the Plain it may be presumed to have belonged to the early tradition of Jesus' sayings that the two Gospels had in common (Q). Probably Matthew added the phrase "for this is the law and the prophets." It has long been recognized that this principle, at least in its negative form, had been enunciated prior to and apart from the teaching of Jesus. In Judaism it appears in Tobit 4:15; *Testament of Naphtali* (Hebrew) 1.6; *B. Shabbath* 31a; *Letter of Aristeas* 207; Philo, *Hypothetica* 7.6; and *Ahikar* 2.88 (Armenian text). At least a similar formulation is found in other religious and ethical traditions, e.g., Confucius, *Analects* 15.23; *Li-Ki* 39.23; the Zoroastrian *Dâdistân-I Dinik* 94.5; Herodotus, *History* 3.142.3; Thales (reported in Diogenes Laertius, *Lives of Eminent Philosophers* 1.36); Isocrates, *Nicocles* 61; Seneca, *Epistles* 47.11; and, according to Lampridius in the *Life of Severus* 51.7f., the latter wrote this axiom on his palace wall.

Apart from the Gospel references, other traditions present a negative version of the Rule (but see *Letter of Aristeas* 207 and, in a sense, *M. Aboth* 2.10, 12). The merits of the two versions have been debated, some contending that the positive is superior because it makes greater demands on the altruism of the hearer; but others have praised the negative version on the grounds that it is more realistic and "goes deeper into the heart of the problem" (Abrahams). Chrysostom, *Concerning the Statues* 13.7, quotes both versions, commenting that the negative requires "a departure from evil," while the positive version demands "the exercise of virtue." Despite the positive form in the Gospels, the negative version circulated also in the Christian tradition. See the Western text of Acts 15:20, 29; *Didache* 1.2; Clement, *Stromateis* 2.23; Pope Fabian, *Epistles* 2.2; Cyprian, *To Quirinius* 3.119. The positive form, however, was the most frequently quoted by the church fathers.

As a principle of conduct the Golden Rule is another way of stating, "You shall love your neighbor as yourself," and the Jerusalem Targum on Lev. 19:18 adds the negative Golden Rule to the earlier precept. But neither statement represents a universally applicable norm, since our desires for ourselves are not necessarily commendable. It is no accident that some quotations of the Rule qualify it to read "Whatever *good* thing you wish . . . ," as Augustine testifies (*City of God* 14.8). However, the function of the Golden Rule or of "You shall love your neighbor as yourself" is not to provide a rule of thumb for all interpersonal relations. Rather, it is intended to shatter the radical self-centeredness that obscures our awareness of the rights and needs of others.

See also **Universalizability of Moral Judgments.**

I. Abrahams, *Studies in Pharisaism and the Gospels* 1st–2nd series, rev. ed. 1968; D. M. Beck, "The Golden Rule," *IDB* II, 1962; G. B. King, "The 'Negative' Golden Rule," *Journal of Religion* 8, 1928, pp. 268–279; M. Singer, "Golden Rule," *EP* III, 1967.

HARVEY K. MCARTHUR

Good, The *see* **Agathology; Axiology; Finality; Good Works; Goodness; Teleological Ethics**

Good Works

The phrase is used in controversy about justification and the place in it of faith and works. The debate runs into the question of the fruits of justification, as to whether it conveys righteousness or merely imputes it; whether it removes only guilt or also some unrighteousness. Further, whether good works before justification have any merit and even whether good works of the redeemed aid their salvation (*see* **Justification by Faith; Merit**).

Paul's writings contain some antinomies on the question. His emphasis on the primacy of faith as against works (Rom. 3:27; 4; 11:6; Gal. 2:16, 21) seems to have been a protest against the excessive legalism* of Judaism. He also recognized the value of good works (2 Cor. 8; Phil. 2:12; 2 Thess. 2:17). There is no ultimate opposition between his teaching and that of James who, in his letter, maintained that the evidence of faith is the doing of good works (2:14, 17, 18, 22).

The differences of Catholics and Protestants in the Reformation period were around the question whether reconciliation* was a matter of faith alone or whether the faithful signify their faith by their good works. None doubted that the grace* of God, accepted by faith*, was the efficient cause of justification. Aquinas, who is credited with maximum concession to the necessity of good works, nevertheless is more Pauline than Jamesian in ascribing the first movement of salvation to the believer's faith in God's justifying initiative (*ST* I-II.13.8–9). But he also said that faith without works is *fides informis* and faith that leads to loving works is *fides formata* (*ST* II-II.4.3–5). Augustine had taught that good works established merit, but that grace alone enabled humans to perform them (*En-*

chiridion 107; *Epistle* 194.19). Calvin combated the Catholics for holding that "a man once reconciled to God through faith in Christ is accounted righteous on account of his good works" but added that "there is no controversy between us and the schoolmen as to the beginning of justification" (*Institutes* 3.14.11). In some respects the Puritans brought in a more moralistic belief in good works than the earlier Reformers had, while liberal Christianity with its Pelagian bias almost made good works the beginning as well as the end of salvation, one sect even setting up a formula of belief: "salvation by character."

For fuller treatment of the differences between Catholics and Protestants, see A. Ritschl, *The Christian Doctrine of Justification and Reconciliation* (1870–74), ET 1900, from an ethical Lutheran point of view; and for a Catholic interpretation of the controversy, see J. A. Moehler, *Symbolism* (⁵1838), ET 1843, pt. I, ch. 5, section "Of Good Works." See also articles "Merit, Introductory," and "Merit, Christian," in *HERE*.

V. A. DEMANT

Goodness

In ethics goodness has two main senses.

1. Moral goodness. The aim of this article is to state the *Christian* view of goodness. But one must begin by affirming two principles that fall within the scope of secular philosophy.

(*a*) Moral goodness is irreducible, or unique. Many attempts have been made to equate it with a nonmoral factor. Thus hedonists have equated it with "pleasure."* A good action is one that produces pleasure (or happiness) either for the agent or for someone else. Others (e.g., Julian Huxley and C. H. Waddington) have equated it with the direction of the evolutionary process. A good action is one that satisfies the criteria which a morally neutral study of evolution can provide (*see* **Evolutionary Ethics**). All these attempts to reduce moral to nonmoral terms were brought under the heading of the Naturalistic Fallacy by G. E. Moore, whose refutation of them in his *Principia Ethica* (1903) is widely accepted by philosophers of every school (*see* **Naturalistic Ethics**).

This fallacy can take a religious form. Thus Ockham held that an act is good simply because God wills it. But it is obvious that "the good" cannot be equivalent to "divinely willed" unless God's will is good and unless we know that it is good (*see* **Divine Command Morality; Voluntarism**). It is obvious too that we could not know this unless we had a prior knowledge of the good as a purely moral, nonreligious category.

(*b*) Moral goodness is objective. It actually inheres in the object of which it is predicated. Whether it so inheres in things and circumstances may well be doubted. But most of us have no doubt that it inheres in those *persons* to whom we attribute it. It is (we think) a spiritual property of them. Yet modern empiricists (such as Ayer and Nowell-Smith) hold that goodness is entirely subjective. In calling a person "good" we are merely expressing our "approval" of that person.

The purely philosophical objections to subjectivism* are well stated by Brand Blanshard in his *Reason and Goodness* (1961). These are confirmed by Christian theism. It is absurd to say that when we call God good we are simply expressing our approval of him. He *is* goodness, for in him essence and existence are identical, so that creatures are good to the extent that they mirror him.

2. Teleological goodness. In this sense "the good" signifies an end or goal in which a person or thing fulfills his, her, or its nature or specific form. While this sense can include the first, it need not do so. It is logically possible to maintain that the good life for a human being is one devoted to the pursuit of (let us say) wealth or fame.

The Christian and the non-Christian can reach a large measure of agreement in their views on goodness. They can agree on many of the qualities that make a person good (for instance, the cardinal virtues). Also they can agree on many of the values that constitute the good life. This area of agreement is part of the *lex naturae* (*see* **Natural Law**).

The specifically Christian contribution consists in the following elements:

1. Moral goodness.

(*a*) The ideal of goodness is the character of God. Jesus sums up his moral teaching in the words: "You, therefore, must be perfect, as your heavenly Father is perfect" (Matt. 5:48). The context makes it clear that the element in divine perfection that disciples are to copy is self-giving love*. (The NT calls God "love," not "goodness." But since his goodness is by nature self-diffusing, it is identical with his love.)

The view that moral goodness consists in the imitation of God's attributes was not original. The Jewish law was summed up in the precept, "You must be holy, for I am holy." Plato and the Stoics also regarded God as the model for human excellence*. The originality of the gospel on this score consists in two facts: the incarnation and the gift of the Spirit.

The incarnation is primary. The apostolic writers urge converts to imitate the love, gentleness, patience, and humility of *Christ* who is the Word and Image of the Father. Furthermore, we participate in Christ through the Holy Spirit who is his "other self." Christian goodness is thus doubly *supernatural* (that is, beyond the scope of the natural intellect and will).

(*b*) Through Christ the *content* of moral goodness is transformed. It is dominated by three virtues: faith*, hope*, and charity*. Each of these exhibits the dependence of Christian ethics on Christian revelation. Human goodness consists in the imitation of God's love through faith and hope in Christ. The church did not reject the natural virtues described by pagan moralists. But two of its greatest thinkers—Augustine and Aquinas—insisted that in the Christian life these virtues must be governed and transformed by charity (*see* **Cardinal Virtues; Virtue**).

Love* (*agapē*) distinguished, and continues to distinguish, Christian from non-Christian forms of goodness. Although Greco-Roman moralists sometimes commended selfless generosity, they did not give it the prominence it had in Christianity. Thus Aristotle's ethics rested on the ideal of prudence* (as the prerequisite of contemplation*), while the Stoics preached self-sufficiency. Moreover, even the closest parallels to *agapē*—such as Buddhist "compassion"—lack the example and motive power of God Incarnate.

(*c*) Christian goodness is unmerited. We cannot achieve it by our works; it is a gift of grace. Even if we were wholly virtuous on the plane of nature, we could not claim supernatural perfection as our due. As it is, we fail even to enact the *lex naturae*. We all know the inner conflict that Paul described: "I do not do what I want, but I do the very thing I hate" (Rom. 7:15).

As D. M. Baillie noted, there is a paradox in acquiring goodness, just as there is in acquiring happiness. If we make happiness (in the sense of "pleasure") an end that we deliberately pursue, it will evade us. Similarly if we make goodness a goal that we try to reach by our unaided strength we shall both fail to achieve it fully (on account of our inherent sinfulness) and stand in danger of falling into the further sin of pride* by taking credit for the limited moral victories we may win. Hence growth in humility* is always a constituent in, and sign of, moral progress.

(*d*) Christian goodness is essentially corporate in two ways. First, each Christian is indebted to the guidance and encouragement afforded by both past and present fellow Christians. Secondly, it is God's purpose to establish, not merely good individuals, but a holy church—a community united by his triune love.

2. *Teleological goodness.* Augustine and Aquinas followed Plato and Aristotle in basing their ethics on the concept of the human being's "good" or "end." What can fulfill human nature and be the cause of permanent beatitude? Not riches, fame, or pleasure; not even human friendship or the natural activity of the human mind in seeking beauty, truth, and moral goodness. Our final end is the vision of God (*see* **Finality; Teleological Ethics**). Nothing less can satisfy our deepest longings.

This vision is related to moral goodness in two complementary ways. On the one hand, it is through this vision (received partially and indirectly now, but fully and "face to face" hereafter) that we grow in goodness. On the other hand, the holier we become the more clearly we see God. From the merely human standpoint goodness in the second sense is wider than goodness in the first, for God exceeds any moral goodness we are able to conceive. Yet in reality the senses coincide; for the God who is our "good" *is* goodness (or holiness*), so that in our perfect vision of him *per connaturalitatem* morality is, not abolished, but transformed.

Teleology is overlapped by eschatology. According to the NT, our end (*telos*) will not be reached immediately after death. It will be part of the "last stage" (*eschaton*) in God's purpose for his whole creation. We shall not be perfected—we shall not fully possess our moral good and reach our final end (the beatific vision)—until all things are summed up in the Word by whom they were created (*see* **Eschatological Ethics**).

The Christian attitude to the world is therefore "dialectical." On the one hand, we accept it as the sphere in which we can grow in goodness through submission to the will of God. On the other hand, we know that God's will cannot now be embodied fully either in himself or in society. But we hope for a fulfillment in the kingdom that is yet to come.

I. Murdoch, *The Sovereignty of Good,* 1970; A. E. Taylor, *The Faith of a Moralist,* vol. 1, 1930; G. F. Thomas, *Christian Ethics and Moral Philosophy,* 1955, pt. 4.

H. P. OWEN

Government *see* Politics; State; World Government; *see also* Anarchism; Anarchy

Grace

Grace, *charis,* in its Greek religious usage means "divine gift" or "favor." Thus a "grace" was a quality or power usually bestowed by the gods, a quality that could be exhibited by a mortal. The English word "graceful" reflects this meaning.

Here as in so many cases the Christians used the Greek word in such a way as to make it express a special meaning in the context of the biblical understanding of the relationship of God and humanity. The foundation of the NT meaning of grace is given in the Hebrew *hesed,* God's mercy and love through which he overcomes and redeems the sin of his covenanted people. The Septuagint usually renders *hesed* by *eleos,* pity. There is evidence, however, that there was an increasing tendency in the Hellenistic period to use *charis.* Thus the way is prepared for the NT use of *charis* to express the specific redemptive action of God in Jesus Christ. Grace thus means the divine forgiveness* of sin constituting the new creation, and it also means the power of God communicated to those who enter upon the new life of faith*, hope*, and love*. Thus Paul says, we "are justified by his grace as a gift, through the redemption which is in Christ Jesus" (Rom. 3:24), where grace is the quality and power of the divine action which redeems human beings from sin. Paul also speaks of grace as the continuing action of God which enables the Christian to live the new life. "God is able to provide you with every blessing (grace) in abundance" (2 Cor. 9:8). Thus also the writer of the letter to the Hebrews appeals to his hearers to have grace whereby we may serve God acceptably with reverence* and godly fear (Heb. 12:28).

Christian theologians have made distinctions with respect to the different functions or relationships in which grace is manifest. The central meaning remains always the mercy* and forgiveness* of God given freely to sinners along with the empowerment to meet the demands of the new life, and to resist temptation. The power of grace always remains God's power but it becomes operative in humans and thus fulfills, sustains, and renews human nature.

In the biblical view all God's action is ultimately gracious, for it expresses his love toward the world. Hence there is an inevitable extension of the use of the term "grace" to cover all the divine action from creation to last things. Catholic theology has been based upon the foundation of the distinction between prevenient grace and saving grace. The former is God's sovereign will establishing the world and electing his people to redemption. The latter is God's forgiveness mediated to those who are brought within the company of the saved, and mediated through the church and the sacraments.

The Protestant Reformers tend to confine the use of the term "grace" more strictly to the forgiveness given in Christ. For them grace does not so much complete a human nature which has lost its endowment of faith and hope and love, as it re-creates an almost totally fallen nature. At the same time Protestants developed a doctrine of common grace which pointed to the uncovenanted mercies of God manifest in his provision for humankind in the orders of creation and in the unexpected and creative events in life which sustain and renew the human spirit.

The doctrine of grace has always raised questions about the relation of the divine power and mercy to the human moral situation. The distinction between grace as forgiveness and grace as empowerment sets the terms of the problem, for grace is asserted to deal with the problem of sin*, which has a moral dimension, and it enables the person to love God and neighbor. Hence there has been a continual discussion in theology of the relation of grace to human freedom* and action, and there are perennial tensions in various theological standpoints.

Certain major areas of concern can be distinguished:

1. Grace is understood in the Christian tradition as the mercy of God which solves the ultimate moral problem of human beings,

that is, their inability to fulfill the requirements of perfect love* and obedience* to the divine will. Grace as forgiveness transcends all ethical categories, for it resolves the moral problem at another level than that of moral justification or fulfillment. The doctrine of justification by faith* must be understood as meaning justification, that is, being made righteous, by grace which is received and grasped by faith, not by moral effort. It is true that grace so understood deals with more than ethical failure, for sin is also a transmoral category. The sins of pride* and idolatry* cannot be classified simply as immoralities. Yet sin as violation of the divine law, and as specific acts of injury to self or neighbor, is moral wrongdoing, and the affirmation of the grace of God has always included its power to restore the morally right relationship between a human being and God, and between one human and another.

2. The assertion of grace as empowerment to live the moral life raises the question of human freedom and moral responsibility. Ethical systems which assert that only the free act can be understood as within the realm of moral behavior have rejected the conception of humankind as dependent on grace for the power to act rightly. Kant asserts that the structure of moral obligation implies the power of humans to fulfill the moral requirement else it is meaningless. A strong argument for this point of view is made by W. G. Maclagan in *The Theological Frontier of Ethics* (1961). He holds that moral action must be self-wrought to be moral action "even though there are environmental pressures and solicitations which render the will's action to an indefinite extent easier or more difficult" (p. 131). His position is that "It is a condition of the very being of a moral personality that a man's willing, in its goodness as in its badness, should be absolutely his own, into which in neither case does God's action enter constitutively" (p. 118). This would appear to mean that grace operates wholly in a transmoral dimension of life. But from another theological standpoint the situation is more complex, for it is asserted that human beings can recognize an obligation without being able of their own will to fulfill it, and that the actual moral experience is that of discovering a power beyond the self which enables one to make a right response. Grace is sometimes described as having a cooperating function once the

initial restoration to right relationship is achieved by God's action.

The issue here has divided Augustinians and Pelagians through the centuries. It appears not only in the theological debate but also between all those who find the moral situation of human beings that of being bound to powers they cannot control and those who assert humans' freedom to direct their action. The issue has appeared, for example, between schools of psychology in the modern period (*see* **Free Will and Determinism; Freedom**).

The Augustinian position and all its followers have tried to interpret the actual situation of the person who is not free to become what he or she ought to become, or wants to become. Empowerment must come from outside. The problem of the position is to make clear in what sense there is moral accountability for humans in this situation. The Pelagian theological tradition, as in Pelagius himself, never rejected the concept of grace. But it asserted that the human being as accountable must retain some freedom and power of action toward moral growth and that the function of grace, therefore, is educative and cooperative.

3. In the 20th century many Christian theologians have attempted to show by an analysis of the ethical problem how the search for meaning in the human moral experience leads to the need for grace, not only as forgiveness for individual guilt, but as the redemptive power of the divine working in history. This argument has been prompted by the increasing secularization* of human life and the resulting questioning of the need for or relevance of grace as conceived in the religious tradition. The autonomous person has no need of grace. Christian apologists, many under the direct influence of Kierkegaard, such as Gogarten, Tillich, Barth, Bonhoeffer, H. Richard Niebuhr, and Reinhold Niebuhr, have sought to show through an analysis of human moral existence and its ambiguities and failures that a meaningful human existence cannot be secured through ethical principle and action alone. Realization of the wholeness of life amid the tragedies of history is possible only through reliance upon the divine redemptive working which can best be designated by the word "grace." The mediation of the divine mercy is present in communities of acceptance and forgiveness, within the recognized church and beyond it,

in which grace is present as the spirit of forgiving love transcending the demand for moral rectitude as the sole justification for human action. Thus the concept of grace set alongside the ultimate ethical dilemmas leads to a reconsideration of the theology of history and of the doctrine of the church.

W. G. Maclagan, *The Theological Frontier of Ethics,* 1961; J. Moffatt, *Grace in the New Testament,* 1931; R. Niebuhr, *The Nature and Destiny of Man,* 2 vols., 1941–43, esp. vol. 2; J. Oman, *Grace and Personality,* 1917; W. T. Whitley (ed.), *The Doctrine of Grace,* 1932.

DANIEL D. WILLIAMS

Gratitude

Gratitude and gift. Gratitude is the virtually universally expected response to a gift as an unearned benefit from a well-intentioned giver. Gratitude becomes central to Christian life and ethics when Christians take seriously their confession that all they are and have comes undeserved from God, that they live by grace* alone. The Hebrew *barak* (bless, blessing) and the Greek *charis* (grace, gratitude) reveal the relatedness of "grace" and "gratitude," of gift and appropriate response to it.

Moral functions. Gratitude has several functions in the moral life. As motivation generating action reflecting one's thankfulness for past benefits, it is to be contrasted with the morally problematic motivation springing from future reward and punishment. Gratitude is also the appropriate attitude or sentiment for a beneficiary to exhibit toward a donor. This interpretation complicates gratitude's moral status, however, since attitudes are usually not thought to be under the agent's direct control as moral actions must be. Gratitude is sometimes treated as a virtue, often linked to justice, reflecting the agent's readiness to respond appropriately to the donor. Most likely to be overlooked—because in some tension with the widely presumed spontaneous, voluntary, even optional character of gratitude—is gratitude as grounding, or as itself being a form of obligation of recipient to donor. Here gift-giving and grateful response derive significance not only from the personal relation between donor and recipient but also from the larger cultural setting, which defines them as an obligation-grounding sociomoral practice.

Obligations. Gift-based obligations root largely in the gift's continuing identification with the donor and the donor's intentions in giving the gift (Mauss), a linkage that qualifies and limits the recipient's ownership of the gift. Duties of gratitude take two major forms: grateful conduct toward the donor, by which gratitude for the donor's beneficence is shown; and grateful use of the gift, by which respect is shown for the significance of the gift itself, the context and the relationship in which it was given, and the donor's intentions for it. Duties of gratitude are freer and more flexible than contractual or promissory ones. For example, the donor cannot demand recipient performance, and the recipient may choose among several ways to fulfill gift-based obligations.

As moral stance. Finally, gratitude can characterize the entire moral life of an agent or of a community when people see life as extensively enriched by the generosity of persons or powers outside themselves. (Cf. Paul's challenge to the Corinthian Christians: "What have you that you did not receive?" 1 Cor. 4:7.) The logic of such a grateful stance should lead to generosity toward others.

Problems. Unresolved problems concerning gift and gratitude as moral realities include: tension between the free, nonobligatory dynamics and the apparently obligatory ones; the similarities and dissimilarities between human and divine gift-giving and gratitude; the tension between the gift as an expression of generosity and benevolence eliciting gratitude, and the gift as an instrument of domination eliciting resentment.

P. M. Blau, *Exchange and Power in Social Life,* 1964; P. F. Camenisch, *"Gift and Gratitude in Ethics,"* JRE 9, Spring 1981, pp. 1–34; M. Mauss, *The Gift: Forms and Functions of Exchange in Archaic Societies* (1925), ET 1967; P. Tournier, *The Meaning of Gifts,* ET 1963.

PAUL F. CAMENISCH

Greed *see* **Covetousness; Mammon; Property; Wealth**

Greek Ethics, Ancient

see **Aristotelian Ethics; Cynics, Ethics of the; Cyrenaics, Ethics of the; Epicureanism, Ethics of; Platonic Ethics; Skeptics; Socratic Ethics; Sophists; Stoic Ethics**

Guidance *see* **Casuistry; Conscience; Moral Theology; Norms**

Guilt

It is important to distinguish at the outset between guilt as a moral or legal concept and guilt as a feeling. The former has a primary objective reference to the breaking of some law or commandment or some accepted code or standard of values. One does not have to acknowledge culpability to be adjudged guilty in this sense. Roman Catholic moral theology makes a further distinction between "formal" guilt (the willful commission of a transgression) and "material" guilt (which involves no act of will).

People who are guilty of some actual transgression may also experience guilt feelings, that is, feelings of distress such as self-reproach, self-blame, remorse*, anxiety*. Ideally these are unpleasant enough to stimulate remedial or expiatory action. A common sequence of such action is repentance*, confession*, seeking of forgiveness, reparation. Here the guilt feelings (the sense of guilt) are performing their normative function. If there were no capacity for guilt in human beings, there could be no sense of responsibility in personal relationships. One way of understanding guilt feelings is to see them as signaling that some act or omission on our part has broken or put at risk a relationship important to us. The feelings exist to impel appropriate effort to heal the breach.

As social and ethical norms change, so the behaviors about which it is seen as appropriate to feel guilty also change. In Western culture, guilt over masturbation, for example, is now widely seen as inappropriate, and in many subcultures the appropriateness of guilt with respect to other forms of sexual expression is ambiguous. Guilt feelings require an internalization of norms, and when the norms themselves are in question the guilt feelings (if any) can be quite unpredictable in effect and intensity.

Guilt feelings may also be experienced by people who are, in the objective sense, not guilty of any transgression. And guilt feelings may persist after all appropriate remedial measures have been taken. Guilt may remain a potent motivating factor in human behavior but not be felt as guilt at all. It is also common for guilt feelings to be displaced, that is, for the feelings to be aroused by something quite different from whatever it is the person says he or she is guilty of. This phenomenon has been demonstrated both in Roman Catholic studies of scrupulosity* and in dynamic psychology. Many guilt feelings amount to an obsessive preoccupation with one type of responsibility* as a defensive measure to avoid having to come to terms with other, deeper, and even more threatening problems. Since the guilt feelings are painful, the "inner avenging forces" of the personality are satisfied, but at the price of concealing the true conflict and hence of rendering ineffective the measures of atonement adopted. All of these variations on the normative relationship of guilt feelings to objective guilt can be characterized as neurotic guilt.

There are many conflicting theories about the origin of guilt both in the human race and in the individual person. There does appear to be an interrelationship between guilt, hostility, and anxiety. Guilt is often contrasted with shame*, which arises with the threat of being exposed in our inadequacies. The Christian understanding of the sinner's guilt before God begins at the point where that guilt is effectively dealt with, at the cross of Jesus Christ. In consequence, the Christian who continues to feel guilty about his or her sin is exhibiting something of the neurotic guilt noted above.

The new insights into guilt raise some acute questions for ethics and for theology generally. There are ways of proclaiming forgiveness*, for example, that play into the helplessness which underlies some of the hostility element in guilt feelings and which therefore compounds the problem. There are many areas of ethical debate in which the complex role of guilt has been inadequately explored, especially from a Christian perspective. These include bioethics, sexual ethics, euthanasia, politics and international relations, and the whole area of ethics and criminology. The issue of diminished responsibility raises questions for ethics, as does the difference between the criminal who is caught accidentally and the one who unconsciously arranges things so that he or she will be caught.

In recent years the notion of social or collective guilt has become important (*see* **Collective Responsibility**). Groups, and even nations, have been spoken of as being influenced in their present policies by an often undefined sense of responsibility for past actions (including actions of a past generation). Issues of ethical significance, such as land rights for aboriginal peoples in many countries, are often complicated by such a sense of guilt. Similarly, many issues of international relations are made more complex by the expectation that West Germany (for example) should continue to feel guilty about Nazi atrocities.

A. H. Becker, *Guilt: Curse or Blessing?* 1977; L. J. Sherrill, *Guilt and Redemption,* rev. ed. 1957.

GRAEME M. GRIFFIN

Habit

The word "habit" is used generally of well-defined patterns of behavior or modes of thought in which a person engages without having consciously to initiate the process on each occasion or to give assent to each step in the process. Explicit decisions, trial-and-error judgments, and conscious acts of will may well have been necessary to establish the pattern, but once it has become established, it assumes a certain autonomy. One need not even be aware that the habitual action takes place; in the common phrase, it is done "without thinking."

The formation of habits is important in everyday life. It makes learning possible and reduces the time and effort involved in repeated activities. Our habits reflect our individuality, since they include characteristic patterns of thinking and ways of speaking and responding to the world around us. The unreflective nature of habits can sometimes mean that we behave in stereotyped ways that are not appropriate for some particular occasions. Some habits (the addictions) are sustained by physiological needs created by the substances first used to satisfy psychological desires.

Ethical distinctions between "good" and "bad" habits are commonly based on cultural judgments about those acts or modes of thought acceptable or unacceptable to particular groups. The perceived goodness or badness reflects the values of the group. Another basis for differentiation is whether a particular habit frees or inhibits the person for the responsible discharge of his or her obligations.

Specific theories as to how habits are formed, broken, or modified are related closely to particular understandings of the learning process. William James pioneered the modern understandings of habit at the close of the 19th century. He and John B. Watson (1925) proposed that habits are formed as consequences of the establishment of definite pathways in the nervous system which are reinforced by repetition (conditioning) and which tend to fade if not repeated. Many experimental psychologists have adopted this basic position, and therapies (aversion therapies and behavior therapies) have been devised to break the old habits and form new ones by planned counterconditioning. Dynamic psychologists have put their stress on the development and maintenance of habits as stereotyped forms of reaction to internal stresses and conflicts. They have been concerned primarily with such "habit disorders" as nail-biting, bed-wetting (enuresis), and temper tantrums. Psychoanalysis has stressed the importance of the psychosexual developmental stages in personality in the formation of habits. Others have stressed the role of social forces and of imitation. The dynamic position, in its various forms, warns that even the best-intentioned will is ultimately powerless to break or modify a habit if the internal conditions that led to the formation of the habit are not dealt with effectively. Roman Catholic theology speaks of supernatural habits, i.e., the gifts of the Holy Spirit and "the infused theological and moral virtues" which have the effect of uplifting and shaping the "natural" habits.

See **Character; Virtue; Cardinal Virtues; Theological Virtues.**

J. B. Watson, *Behaviorism,* 1925.

GRAEME M. GRIFFIN

Handicapped, Care of the

An *impairment*—which results from a disease, disorder, accident, or defective gene—can be anatomical, physiological, or mental. If the impairment persists and interferes with an individual's ability to do something (e.g., breathe, walk, talk, see, hear, speak, take care of personal needs, perform manual tasks, learn, or work), we say that person has a *disability*. When a disability, in interaction with environmental conditions, causes an individual to have a permanently or temporarily limited adaptability in performing one or more major life activities, we say he or she is *handicapped.*

One ethical issue in the care of the handicapped is labeling. Labeling persons as handicapped is useful for procuring special services, but may so stigmatize the disabled that they receive a new handicap, for the social identity created by the label may invite others to prejudge the subjects' capacities, underestimate the importance of their views, and thus reduce their chances for habilitation.

Second, issues of the overall style and quality of the care of the handicapped are best addressed through virtues. Compassion* is the virtue* by which, on the basis of a deep feeling of sharing the suffering of others, we are inclined to stand by them (the handicapped), alleviate their suffering, and offer them assistance in the suffering that cannot be eliminated. Care*, which is related to friendship* and love*, is a virtue whereby one person is inclined to pay close and respectful attention and offer thoughtful service to the other (the handicapped) in a relationship that is characterized by a commitment to help the other grow, in part by helping the person care for himself or herself and something or someone else. Stanley Hauerwas mentions other virtues that support this virtue of care: patience (to wait even when the other fails); honesty* (to tell the truth even when it is unpleasant); trust* (to let the other take the risk of the unknown); and humor (that the other may know that no mistake is a decisive defeat).

A third issue is the survival of the handicapped, especially in a medical context (*see* **Euthanasia; Life, Prolongation of**). In this complex debate the general tendency in Christian ethics is to defend a principle prohibiting direct and deliberate killing of the handicapped, and a prima facie principle that human life should be sustained, particularly by those holding special responsibilities. There is considerable debate, however, on whether certain kinds of mental or physical disabilities should either place a qualification on the fundamental normative value of life—and hence on the prima facie duty to preserve life—or be included among those so-called "extraordinary" factors (hardship and suffering) that can limit such a duty. While some defend a more egalitarian principle of life sustenance (though placing limits when circumstances of suffering or hardship warrant it),

others hold categorically that individuals lacking self-consciousness and/or a potential for some meaningful level of human relationship lack the moral status required to ground a serious duty to preserve life. Different from these principle-based approaches are those which appeal to ethical models of behavior that present values for emulation: e.g., the values inherent in the parents' response of bonding with their retarded child.

A fourth issue pertains to welfare services for the handicapped (e.g., special education, medical care, and housing). Norms governing these services focus on charity, rights, and justice. In one model that joins love with political power, namely, in a liberation theology*, the aim of charity* would be to provide all the handicapped the means to as much freedom as possible from their plight, including the social power and specific remedies required for them to be personally and spiritually liberated. In another model, which disengages love from political power, the duty in charity is to see to it that the church teaches its members how to patiently love the tragically weak and disadvantaged (e.g., the handicapped) as neighbors, without measuring that love in terms of its effectiveness in changing worldly structures.

Human and legal rights of the handicapped to welfare services are strong claims recognized, for example, by the United Nations and by legislative and judicial authorities, and supported by moral arguments that are sometimes rooted in notions of the dignity of all humans (*see* **Human Dignity; Human Rights**). While remarkable benefits have been gained for handicapped persons through rights language, one objection among several is that of practicability: many specific rights claims are for maximum services or a very high level that cannot be met by many governments because of poor or shifting economies.

Justice*, regarded as a norm for treating people fairly, raises the issue of equal treatment of the handicapped, for equality* is an essential characteristic of fair distribution (*see also* **Fairness**). Robert Veatch points out that an egalitarian foundation for justice affecting the handicapped is emphasized by biblical and early Christian themes: the radical equality of all humans before God, the bond of mutual responsibility among all humans arising from their having the same divine Parent, and the concept of stewardship* that places restraints on ownership of property*. One reasonable concept of equality—equality of opportunity to function at a level commensurate with one's abilities—can account for highly controversial preferential policies, which require socioeconomic redistribution and the neglect of some claims of the nonhandicapped. For example, the mainstreaming of mentally and physically handicapped children in public schools requires costly adjustments: architectural changes, special education and rehabilitation programs, therapies, equipment, and extra personnel. A theory of justice can justify preferential policies by linking distributive justice with social justice—the justice that is concerned with a vision of the general welfare and the goods that a society should promote and share in meeting needs that are crucial to human flourishing.

A fifth issue pertains to the setting and goals of care. Institutionalization is sometimes justified, for example, when the mentally ill will cause physical harm to themselves or others, or when care of the profoundly and severely or hyperactive retarded would cause a major hardship to the family who cannot be adequately aided by community-based assistance. Deinstitutionalization and normalization of the care of the mildly to severely mentally impaired has been promoted on the basis of several principles: the humanization of care, better promoted in a family and community setting; the promotion of the freedom of the handicapped by the least restrictive reasonable care; the utility to be gained from the productivity of the handicapped; the enhancement of their sense of self-worth by moving from the dependency of an institution to an environment that promotes personal responsibility; and the reduction of public costs for institutionalization. Conflicts often occur among these principles: reduction of costs is sometimes achieved by housing the handicapped in community residences but in violation of the principles of humanization of care and enhancement of self-worth, due to the low standards of the housing, poor training opportunities, and de facto segregation. Frequently, all these principles are defeated by the unwillingness of others to share their neighborhoods with those who deviate from familiar standards of normalcy.

See **Genetics; Health and Disease, Values in Defining; Health Care, Right to; Sick, Care of the; Social Service of the Church; Welfare State.**

M. Cohen, T. Nagel, and T. Scanlon (eds.), *Equality and Preferential Treatment,* 1977; S. Hauerwas, with R. Bondi and D. Burrell, *Truthfulness and Tragedy,* 1977; R. F. Weir, *Selective Nontreatment of Handicapped Newborns: Moral Dilemmas in Neonatal Medicine,* 1984.

WARREN THOMAS REICH

Happiness
The distinction between happiness and pleasure* is frequently blurred. In ordinary language happiness is frequently used to indicate a more stable, less intense state than pleasure; for instance, one speaks of the happiness of a marriage, but of the pleasure of an orgasm. Yet one could hardly predicate happiness of a life that was altogether without pleasure. While those teleological moralists who have favored utilitarian conceptions of moral obligation have (apart from the late Professor G. E. Moore and his followers) usually adopted a hedonist conception of the end of moral action, those moralists who have combined teleological ideas with the rejection of utilitarianism* have inclined to speak of a happy life as the end of human beings, happiness being found in, and sometimes identified with, a life of fulfillment and harmony both within the individual and in that individual's relations with others (*see* **Teleological Ethics; Eudaemonism**).

In much contemporary thinking about ethics the notion of happiness is frequently invoked in criticism of moral conceptions which exalt such ideas as duty, obedience to superiors and established traditions, heroic engagement, and even commitment, and at least by implication depreciate the significance of the individual's concern for his or her own and others' welfare. Against such views (not without their representatives among avant-garde theologians) the importance of happiness as an unsophisticated, but comprehensive, human end receives justified and intelligible emphasis.

E. Telfer, *Happiness,* 1980.

D. M. MACKINNON

Harm
Harm is damage to a person's interests, for example, in physical integrity, psychological

integrity, or reputation. It can be distinguished from "hurt" (a person may be hurt without being harmed) or "offense" (a person may be offended without being harmed). (*See* **Scandal.**) In the important debate about whether interests can be reduced to wants and desires*, most Christian theologians affirm some objective interests that are not reducible to subjective preferences. A related term, "injury," often refers to specific bodily damage, such as a broken leg, but it also has meant a wrong, an injustice, or a violation of rights (*injuria* in Latin, meaning a wrong or injustice).

See **Homicide; Justice; Nonmaleficence; Rights; Risk.**

J. Feinberg, *Harm to Others,* 1984.

JAMES F. CHILDRESS

Hatred

Hatred, as ill will, hostility, and enmity, is the direct opposite of love*, and it may be directed against God, against the neighbor, or against oneself. Hence, it violates the love commandment (Matt. 22:37–40 and parallels), which includes two major parts, love of God and love of neighbor as oneself. According to Jesus, hatred is ruled out and love required of his disciples, even toward enemies (Matt. 5:43ff.), because of God's perfect righteousness* which humans should emulate. The attitude of hatred is condemned not only because of the evil actions that result from it but also because of its own intrinsic nature. Thomas Aquinas (*ST* II-II.34.4, Blackfriars' trans.) notes: "Sins against our neighbour are evil on two counts; the first is the disorder in the sinner, the second is the hurt done to the one sinned against. On the first count hatred is worse than actions hurting another, since it implies a disordered will, and the will, that most powerful force in man, is at the root of all sin. . . . But on the other count, the harm done to one's neighbour, the external sins are worse than the internal hatred." And yet hatred is not one of the capital, or deadly, sins because it does not lead to other vices, even though it obviously leads to sinful acts (*see* **Seven Deadly Sins**). Hatred often flows from two capital vices, anger* and envy*, but more directly from the latter. According to the dominant Christian tradition, it is possible to hate the sin without hating the sinner, even in such acts as warfare, capital punishment*, and self-defense

(*see* **Pacifism; Resistance; War**). According to John Calvin (*Institutes* 4.20.18), for example, lawsuits are not permissible if hatred is one of the motives, and right intentions, motives, and attitudes have been required by the just war* tradition. For some of the debate about whether certain actions necessarily express or reflect certain vices, attitudes, or motives, see **Malice.**

JAMES F. CHILDRESS

Health and Disease, Values in Defining

Certain concepts are central to the apportionment of tasks among major human endeavors and to the involvement of major constellations of values. Thus, salvation and sin belong to the province of priests, ministers, and rabbis, legal infractions belong to the province of lawyers, and matters of health and disease belong to the province of physicians and other health care professionals. For example, to see excessive drinking as a moral problem, a religious problem, a legal problem, or a medical problem is to predestine the way it will be described and the professions that will be recruited to deal with it. Determining that an individual is a sinner, or a criminal, or is diseased involves different value judgments. When one decides that a state of affairs is best interpreted in terms of the concepts of health and disease, one commits oneself at least in general terms to the languages of medical description, evaluation, explanation, and social control. The precise role of values in concepts of health and disease is a matter of keen philosophical dispute. Normativists have argued that the language of health and disease is intrinsically value-infected, because seeing a state of affairs as a condition of health or disease involves making a nonmoral value judgment based on usually implicit physiological and psychological ideals. To appreciate a phenomenon as a disease is to see it as a failure to achieve an ideal of functional ability, of freedom from pain, of human form and grace, or of life expectancy. In short, terming someone diseased is an adverse nonmoral value judgment, just as terming the person ugly is. Having a disease is, all else being equal, not good. Being healthy is a good to pursue, and different understandings of health are dependent in part on different values associated with anatomical, physiological, and psychological conditions. Normativists disagree as to the extent to which values in concepts of health and disease are culture dependent. Neutralists deny any role for values and hold that concepts of disease do not presuppose value judgments.

See **Alcoholism; Drug Addiction; Mental Health; Mental Illness; Values and Value Judgment.**

H. TRISTRAM ENGELHARDT, JR.

Health Care, Right to

It is important to distinguish rights *in* health care (e.g., the right to consent* to or refuse medical treatment) from rights *to* health care (*see* **Rights**). There was little interest in a right *to* health care until it became clear that modern medicine could save lives, improve their quality, and reduce insecurity. Earlier the charitable activities of religious institutions and individuals played a major role in health care (*see* **Sick, Care of the; Social Service of the Church**). Now many countries have established political-legal rights to health care. For example, as part of its welfare system, Britain instituted the National Health Service in 1948 and, despite some criticisms, there is general acceptance of the right to health care, in part because it reduces anxiety about the ability to pay. However, in the USA governmental Medicare and Medicaid, in combination with private insurance*, fall far short of a right to health care, and it is estimated that approximately twenty-five million American citizens do not have adequate insurance coverage.

Elizabeth Telfer has identified four major systems of health care according to the weight they assign to the principles of liberty* and equality*, which may be viewed as regulative principles of justice*. First is the *laissez-faire* approach, which rejects the welfare state* altogether and makes health care solely a matter of voluntary transactions between individuals, that is, contracts* and charity*. It repudiates equality for the sake of liberty. This approach prevailed in the USA until the 1960s, but it has few defenders now. However, modified versions appear in some efforts to contain the costs of health care through competitive strategies. Second, the *liberal humanitarian* approach provides a decent minimum of health care with minimum coercion through taxation. It establishes a "safety net" in order to protect people from catastrophic illnesses. The USA has taken this approach since the mid-1960s, but its safety net fails to protect many sick people, some of whom do not even seek medical care because of their limited funds. Third, the *liberal socialist* approach moves further toward equality, while allowing professionals and patients to make private contracts outside the public system (*see* **Socialism**). This approach, which provides equal access to medical care, prevails in Britain where there has also been some pressure to eliminate private medical care in favor of a single public system. However, Telfer has argued that individuals may have a moral duty (not only a right) to purchase private health care when they can in order to relieve the demands on the public system. The final approach is *pure socialist,* and it sacrifices liberty to equality by prohibiting private health care. China has taken this approach, but in the mid-1980s it permitted some private initiatives in health care.

In Western democracies, the major debate in recent years has been between the second and third positions, and it has centered on the value of equal access to health care versus the value of efficiency in a system that preserves incentives and yet provides a decent minimum of health care. There is also debate about how well either of these approaches does in practice. Apart from general egalitarian arguments that would support the equal distribution of all goods in a society, most arguments for a political-legal right to health care—whether equal access or a decent minimum—appeal to moral principles of justice*, equality*, equity*, or fairness*, on the one hand, and compassion* or charity*, on the other hand, in conjunction with claims about the special nature and importance of health needs, particularly as random results of the "natural lottery." For example, defending equal access, Gene Outka has argued that health needs are undeserved, randomly distributed, unpredictable, and overridingly important when they appear. Thus, it is unjust to distribute health care according to such criteria as merit, societal contribution, or ability to pay. In addition, Outka argues that Christian *agapē* (*see* **Love**) overlaps with and requires an egalitarian conception of justice as distribution according to need.

The content, scope, and limits of a right to health care must be specified, in part because health needs and desires (which are not always easy to distinguish) could consume an excessive amount of the society's budget, including its welfare budget. The three main variables are access, level and quality of care, and associated costs or burdens. Even in a system of equal access, as in Britain, some rationing (*see* **Triage**) is practiced; in addition to queues, access to such medical care as kidney dialysis and transplantation (*see* **Organ Transplantation**) has been rationed according to nonmedical criteria such as age. Controversies about the criteria of patient selection (who should receive a scarce medical resource?) may lead to a reconsideration of the society's policies of macroallocation, which determine how much of a scarce good will be made available. For example, because of the controversy about allocating kidney dialysis according to ability to pay and social worth, the US federal government decided in the early 1970s to provide practically universal coverage for treatment for end-stage renal disease, its main experiment in socialized medicine. In view of major developments in biomedical science and technology as well as the increasing costs of medical care, vigorous debates can be expected about the content, scope, and limits of the right to health care, as well as about other health policies, such as preventing ill health through reducing environmental hazards and controlling life-styles and behavioral patterns (*see* **Paternalism; Risk**).

See also **Bioethics; Professional Ethics; Science and Ethics; Sick, Care of the; Technology.**

H. S. Aaron and W. B. Schwartz, *The Painful Prescription: Rationing Hospital Care,* 1984; G. Outka, "Social Justice and Equal Access to Health Care," *JRE* 2, 1974; President's Commission for the Study of Ethical Problems in Medicine and Biomedical and Behavioral Research, *Securing Access to Health Care,* vol. 1, Report, 1983; E. Shelp (ed.), *Justice and Health Care,* 1981; E. Telfer, "Justice, Welfare, and Health Care," *JME* 2, Sept. 1976.

JAMES F. CHILDRESS

Health Promotion *see* Health Care, Right to; Paternalism; Welfare State

Heaven

The traditional picture of heaven portrays the universal human aspiration to reach a highest good in this world and to achieve its lasting consummation in a cosmic and hierarchical order. The modern world view, however, has not only abolished the literal equation heaven = sky, but also calls into question the famous Kantian dictum that the moral law within has its sanction in the eternal order. The denial of the Christian tradition of heaven derives from political and cultural hostility, especially the Marxist-Leninist attack upon the idea of eternal life. Religious teachers, too, dislike the mystical otherworldliness which they associate with an escape from "real" life. Modern ethical systems distrust a system of celestial incentives and the implicit self-interest which such a system encourages. Moreover, whereas heaven is a concept which presupposed that there is perfect truth and goodness as a transcendental fact related to God, moral empiricism denies its existence on the grounds of patent contradictions. The evidence taken from contemporary experience leads to the formulation of a moral relativism, in which all actions are seen and evaluated in the light of a complexity of motives. The skeptic uses this evidence as proof for the absence of the providential moral order.

Nevertheless a strong case can be made for the traditional belief on empirical lines, such as the survival of the naive belief in "the other world" among the less sophisticated, the revelations of "the above" in dreams, the data of parapsychology, the self-transcendent properties found among ecstatics. The relevance of aesthetic activity to celestialism lies in its "unearthly" quality and serves as evidence that human beings are not wholly self-enclosed. Most important for Christian moralists is heaven as the goal of ascetic practice, for it asserts that the discipline of desires in this world not only brings strength of character in this life but also sows the seeds of eternal life. Asceticism*, positive in purpose and balanced in accord with reason, denies the gratification of appetites in order to secure the gradual ascent to heaven. The peculiar Christian emphasis on all mortifications* lies in their connection with positive loving and a way of sacrifice which reflects Christ and the indwelling of the Holy Spirit. Heaven comes to stand thus for the glorious future and mystical union and eternal bliss, which God initiates among human beings to be made perfect, the "there and then" of virtuous conduct "here and now."

See **Rewards and Punishments; Sanctions; Hell.**

J. Baillie, *And the Life Everlasting,* 1950; F. H. Brabant, *The Everlasting Reward,* 1961; E. Brunner, *Eternal Hope,* ET 1954; U. Simon, *Heaven in the Christian Tradition,* 1958; *The Ascent to Heaven,* 1961.

ULRICH SIMON

Hebrew Ethics *see* **Jewish Ethics; Mosaic Law; Old Testament Ethics; Prophetic Ethics**

Hedonism
Hedonism is the doctrine that pleasure* is the chief good.
See **Utilitarianism.**

JOHN MACQUARRIE

Hegelian Ethics
While being the continuation of the idealist philosophy initiated by Kant, Hegel's philosophy is also perhaps the most thoroughgoing compatibilist program in the history of philosophy. G. W. F. Hegel (1770–1831) attempted to bring together into one system the seemingly opposed philosophies of Aristotle, Kant, and Spinoza, showing that each needed the complement of the others to attain a full truth. His method for doing so was what he called dialectic*. In its Hegelian sense, dialectic resolves apparent incompatibilities between two concepts or philosophies by locating them in a larger categorial framework. Ultimately, the various categories and their resolutions are seen as posits made by mind (*Geist,* often rendered "spirit") in order to explain itself and its world. Hegel extended this idea to a philosophy of history, seeing history as the gradual dialectical development of mind seeking to understand itself by overcoming the apparent incompatibilities in its posits.

Hegel's ethics is part of this system. It has three parts: a section on Abstract Right, a section on Morality, and a section on Ethical Life (the translation of the German *Sittlichkeit*). Hegel takes each section as if it were to be a complete explanation of the possibility of ethical life and shows that each fails in this pretense. Abstract Right is that area of ethics in which we try to explain the possibility of ethical life by very general and abstract principles of right and wrong. However, such a view cannot explain the difference between,

e.g., revenge and punishment. Hegel argues that punishment must be given as retribution meted out according to both the amount of wrong done and the extent of responsibility of the wrongdoing party for the wrong done. Abstract principles of right and wrong do not, however, give us any way of assessing the responsibility of the parties for the wrong done. Although the intent of the moral language of Abstract Right is to distinguish, e.g., between revenge and punishment, it finds that its resources are incompatible with such a distinction. The language of Abstract Right contradicts its intent; it must therefore be complemented by some conception of the role of the agent in choosing and being responsible for his or her actions.

This complement is given in Morality. Hegel offers a trenchant critique not only of Kant's views but of the role of morality in ethical life in general. Morality is that area of ethical life in which we try to assess the responsibility of an agent for his or her acts by determining whether the agent was freely under an obligation to act a certain way and was responsible for that action. The requirements of obligation and responsibility lead naturally to a Kantian ethics*, in which the right is determined according to some universalizable rule valid for any rational agent (e.g., Kant's Categorical Imperative*: "Act not unless you could will that act to be universal"). Such a rule will unfortunately always turn out to be empty; a rule that applies to any rational agent will not be able to generate any particular moral content for specific people. This emptiness is compounded by the requirement of responsibility. Since the agent must choose the act and the rule, the agent is responsible only for that which he chooses. Hegel argues that this radically shortchanges ethical life; it eliminates all that is specific to the person, including the elements of character*, since it must focus not on the particularities of a person in a specific social and cultural setting but only on the character of the person as a rational agent in general. In fact, even moral success will turn out not to be morally important, since success is in part a matter of empirical luck; instead, the agent is only obligated to try to achieve the morally proper conclusion. By employing only the abstract concepts of obligation* and responsibility*, Morality finds that, like Abstract Right, it contradicts its claim that it can completely explain the whole of ethical life. This is a criticism not only of Kant's attempt to explain all of ethical life in terms of morality but also of the whole social practice of making morality and its correlate, the concept of obligation, supreme in social practice. Morality requires the complement of Ethical Life.

Ethical life is life lived in accordance with the conceptions of human well-being (and concrete rights and duties) formed within certain basic kinds of social unities. These are for Hegel the family, civil society, and the state. In the family, there are specific rights and duties which arise from the nature of the social unity present: the relation between the man and the woman is in part a legal relation but one whose catalyst is love; the children do not choose to be born into this or that family, etc. The bonds that hold the family together are those of intimacy and affection. To try to construe the ethical life of a family in terms of universalizable rules would be a catastrophic error, according to Hegel. Civil society, on the other hand, is that social unity in which the requirements of morality find their home. The bond that holds civil society together is that of mutual self-interest; each believes that this quasi-contractual arrangement is in his or her interests. Hegel argues that civil society represents the form of social unity which would be chosen in the social contract; to stabilize itself, it sets up a state apparatus to protect property, promulgate and enforce laws, and regulate commerce so that the interests of the individual parties are maintained. Hegel calls this the "state based on need" (der Notstaat).

According to Hegel, however, the "state based on need" should not be confused with the state proper. Hegel rejects the social contract* model as inadequate to capture the political element of ethical life. The state based on need is primarily a result of individual choices; it is an economic unity. The state proper, however, is primarily a political unity, established in order to further common values and to provide for a common good*. People can choose to be members of a state based on need; they cannot choose to be members of the state proper. Hegel's point is that an important element of ethical and ethical-political life is that one does not choose the national community into which one is born, although the values of that community influence one's conception of self, of the good, and so on. Certain things may be valued simply because they are part of one's

identity as a citizen of this or that community. The state proper is the political expression of that. Hegel thus profoundly breaks with the voluntarist model of ethical life represented by Kant and others.

Hegel's ethics form the part of his system called Objective Mind, the area in which mind erects particularized institutional structures in the world as expressions of itself. His system culminates in Absolute Mind, expressions of mind which are indifferent to their particularizations. These are art, religion, and philosophy. Art is absolute because the great works of art remain available to all; Homer's poems and the architecture of the Greeks are as valid for us as they were for them. Religion also displays a truth outside of history; the Christian faith remains as true and valid for us as it was for the founders who lived in a much different time. Philosophy, however, is the sublation of religion. It presents in adequate conceptual form what religion can only present in symbols, namely, the full coming to self-consciousness of mind. It has always been unclear in Hegelian scholarship if Hegel thought of philosophy as a replacement of religion or just as its intellectual complement. In any event, he certainly thought of himself as having resolved the apparent incompatibility of faith and reason.

Hegel's influence on later thinkers was profound. Karl Marx transformed the Hegelian system into a materialist system; rather than being propelled by mind's overcoming of intellectual incompatibilities, history was to be seen to be driven by conflicts between the social relations of production (the oppositions between classes as to which class owned the means of production) and the forces of production, with revolutionary change bringing about new social forms in which the old oppositions were temporarily overcome. Like Hegel, he sought a resolution to oppositions; in Marx's case, he postulated a point in history in which all class oppositions would be overcome, viz., communism* (see **Marxist Ethics**). Kierkegaard rebelled both at Hegel's intellectualism and at his belief that all basic oppositions were in principle resolvable. Kierkegaard held that this radically misunderstood the nature of religion, which was one of finite people having to make choices about something of which they could have no knowledge, the infinite; Hegelianism made religion into an intellectual problem to be resolved in seminars in philosophy rather than the serious existential matter which it was. Nonetheless, Kierkegaard employed Hegelian concepts and themes to make his points (*see* **Kierkegaardian Ethics**). (For a discussion of Hegelian themes in 19th-century British thought, *see* **Idealist Ethics.**)

Hegel also inspired several competing schools of biblical interpretation, the most famous of which were those that attempted to discover the real historical truth underlying the symbolism of the Bible. His influence on contemporary theology remains profound; the Catholic theologian Hans Küng is one example of a contemporary theologian who can be described as "Hegelian." Many European Marxists in the 20th century, such as Georg Lukács, attempted to reintroduce Hegelian elements into Marxian thought, producing what has been called humanist Marxism (sometimes just called Hegelian Marxism); this remains a powerful trend today in European Marxist thought. Ernst Bloch used Hegel to reintroduce a quasi-religious element into Marxism, reinterpreting Marxism as an eschatological doctrine which attempts to answer the basic questions of hope addressed by the prophets and the NT. The French existentialists, particularly Sartre, adopted themes, techniques, and terminology from Hegel to spin out their sometimes existentialist, sometimes Marxist philosophies (*see* **Existentialist Ethics**). What generally appeals to all these neo-Hegelian thinkers is the sweep of Hegel's system, his focus on the role of basic oppositions in thought and his belief that abstract principles divorced from concrete life are a one-sided representation of the ethical life. Hegel is also remembered in many areas of contemporary Anglo-American philosophy as the best (or worst, as the case may be) example of philosophical charlatanism. His influence thus remains profound and controversial.

G. W. F. Hegel, *Phenomenology of Spirit,* ET 1977; and *Philosophy of Right,* ET 1942; J. N. Findlay, *Hegel: A Re-Examination,* 1958; M. J. Inwood, *Hegel,* 1983; C. Taylor, *Hegel,* 1975.

TERRY PINKARD

Hell

The conception of hell as a place under the earth where the damned receive everlasting punishment derives from mythology. The realm of the dead, Hades, beyond the Styx, the pit of destruction called Abaddon, the valley of Hinnom (Gehenna) where the people of Jerusalem burned their rubbish, the anonymity and oblivion of Sheol, became fused in the picture of the final destination of the unredeemed. With the rise of lurid portrayals of the end of the world and literal interpretations of apocalyptic teaching, hell assumed proportions similar to those of heaven. This symmetrical arrangement features popular belief and is best studied in the iconography and sculpture of the Middle Ages (e.g., Bourges). Hell is ruled by the enemy Satan or Antichrist and governed by a hierarchy of evil powers and demonic angels. Hell stands for the permanent enclosure of evil, an enclave in God's universe. The best authorities, among them Thomas Aquinas, refused to regard its fire and pains as metaphors and insisted on the reality of the tortures of the wicked which are endless. They make up in endlessness that which they lack in severity.

The modern liberal reaction against this dogma has been sharp and is largely based upon ethical refutations. Hell is felt to be an offense against the deepest human moral convictions inasmuch as it sets up an eternal state of evil. In assigning reality to evil, hell conflicts with the Christian apprehension of the character of God and his purpose for the world. Hell surrounds human responsibility with a web of mythological speculations. To argue that it sanctions goodness and grants emotional satisfaction to the victims of evil is to misread the experiences of martyrs and the sufferers of contemporary crimes. It is said that no one gassed at Auschwitz would have wished the perpetrators of the crime to continue to exist in an eternal concentration camp.

A way out of this very serious impasse may be found by a psychological understanding of hell. Humans are demonically bent upon destruction, and every virtue has its shadow, and a heaven-hell dialectic governs human conduct. C. G. Jung shows with the aid of his archetypes that such an evaluation of evil gets to the root of human deviations. The imagery of hell is part of our existence. C. S. Lewis, too, corrects the balance in the moralists' too easy dismissal of Satan and outside demonic forces. Spiritual conflict without the antagonist and the symbol of perdition becomes meaningless. This new understanding of hell as a present reality recovers the essential strands of ancient thought without committing us to its eternal torments.

See **Rewards and Punishments; Sanctions; Heaven.**

Dante, *The Divine Comedy;* K. Barth, *Church Dogmatics* III/3, ET 1961; A. Huxley, *Heaven and Hell,* 1956; C. S. Lewis, *The Screwtape Letters,* 1942; *The Great Divorce,* 1945; A. Winklhofer, *The Coming of His Kingdom,* ET 1963.

ULRICH SIMON

Heredity *see* Environment and Heredity

Hermeneutics *see* Interpretation

Heteronomy

Kant condemns as "heteronomous" (as opposed to "autonomous") any system that tries to derive ethics from anything but the nature of the rational will as such. He includes under heteronomous systems egoistic hedonism, the moral sense theory, the metaphysical theory which derives morality from the concept of perfection, and any theological theory of ethics. They are considered heteronomous because they all derive ethics from something else, thus destroying its unique character.

See **Autonomy; Autonomy of Ethics; Kantian Ethics.**

A. C. EWING

Hindu Ethics

Ethical attitudes within Hinduism possess a complex diversity. Hinduism or the "Everlasting Law" (*sanātana dharma*) is the result of the synthesis of a whole variety of religious and cultural elements in the Indian subcontinent. Since it contains within it a spectrum of theologies and customs, its unity is in certain respects rather formal. Thus on the theological side, Hindus look to the Veda or sacred revelation, but the interpretations placed thereon differ very widely; while the unity of customs is provided by the framework of the caste system, in which diversities are related through a complex of exclusive social categories. Certain motifs, however, in Hindu ethical thinking can be picked out; and it happens that in the modern period (from about the beginning of the 19th century) there is an increasing consensus on doctrinal and moral beliefs among educated Hindus.

In the principal Upaniṣads (8th to 5th centuries B.C.) there is to be found the beginnings of a theory, later to become commonly accepted in Indian philosophy, about the ends of human life. These ends are: wealth (*artha*), desire (*karma*), and duty (*dharma*)—all of which should in principle subserve the supreme end of liberation or salvation (*mokṣa*). Since much, though not all, of Hindu thought has conceived of the means of liberation as involving the practice of meditation (*yoga*) and of withdrawal from worldly concerns, this theory of ends has been made practically consistent by a theory about stages of life (*āśramas*), which assigns different pursuits to different phases of the individual's career (by extension, the doctrine of reincarnation performs a rather similar function). Thus wealth, desire, and duty are ends for the family man or householder; one graduates to this position after a period as a celibate student. Gradually the householder, as his children reach maturity, withdraws from these concerns; and the highest ideal is to reach the fourth *āśrama,* that of the wandering recluse or *sannyāsin,* bent solely upon spiritual knowledge and attainment. Since the realm of caste is defined by *dharma,* and since the recluse has left *dharma* behind, he is beyond caste and beyond social custom. This human arrangement is reflected in the doctrine sometimes stated in the Hindu tradition that likewise the Divine Being is "beyond good and evil."

The particular duties falling upon a person are defined by his social station. Certain rules (vegetarianism and abstention from liquor) apply to Brahmins, but not necessarily to other classes. The tensions created by such an ethical pluralism are expressed in the problem facing Arjuna in the *Bhagavad-Gītā,* before the battle to which he was committed and in which he would have to fight against, and perhaps kill, relatives and friends. Krishna, in the guise of Arjuna's charioteer, tells him that inactive detachment from the world is impossible. It remains Arjuna's duty to fight, for this duty belongs to his station in life. On the other hand he should practice a kind of active detachment—by renouncing the fruits of the deeds that he performs, and by performing them for the sake of the Lord. In this way liberation (*mokṣa*) will be granted by God. This teaching in the *Gītā* is in opposition to a widely held belief in ancient India—that any action (even a good one) is liable to bind one to the world and to the process of rebirth. It also expresses the relationship between faith in God and action which was to be worked out more fully in medieval Indian theism, with its stress on self-surrender to the Lord.

The *Gītā* encourages the warrior to fight on the ground that "there is more happiness in doing one's own duty badly than in doing another's well"; but paradoxically it was the favorite spiritual reading of Gandhi (1869–1948), who was deeply committed to *ahiṃsā* or nonviolence. He was giving a political dimension to another ancient motif in Indian ethics—the careful reverence for all forms of life, and by consequence the refraining from slaughter and cruelty to animals. On the other hand, the provisions of the ancient legal code could make applications of this sense of the sacredness of both human and nonhuman life which effectively cheapened the former. Thus the killing of a *śūdra* (a person belonging to the lowest of the four recognized classes) by a Brahmin attracted the same penalty as the killing of a dog or cat.

The last two centuries have seen a renaissance of Hinduism, partly under the stimulus of the challenge presented by Western culture and Christianity. Reformers, beginning with Ram Mohan Roy (1772–1833), advocated social changes, social service was seen as flowing from the principles of religion, as in the teaching and practical endeavors of the Ramakrishna Mission, expressed most articulately by Swami Vivekananda (1862–1902). Gandhi, on the basis of the Hindu tradition itself, attacked casteism, and in particular the exclusion of untouchables (whom he renamed Harijans, "children of God") from social and religious life. In addition, modern Hindus have seen as central to religious attitudes the virtue of tolerance, which reflects the all-embracing nature of Hinduism, together with the long, at least partial, emphasis on nonviolence in the tradition. It is thus a common criticism of Western Christianity that it often seems (to Indian eyes) to be exclusive and intolerant. These modern developments have given a new dynamic to the Upaniṣadic text that stresses the centrality of self-control (*dama*), giving (*dāna*) and mercy (*daya*).

The first of these is a reminder that the religious path in Hinduism has often been conceived as involving austerity and withdrawal, elements present in Gandhi's program, which has helped to reinforce the puritanism of contemporary Indian society. Yet in terms of the total fabric of Hindu life it would be misleading to regard its ethic as "world-negating."

S. C. Crawford, *The Evolution of Hindu Ethical Ideals,* 1974; I. C. Sharma, *Ethical Philosophies of India,* 1965; S. Thakur, *Christian and Hindu Ethics,* 1970; B. Walker, *Hindu World,* 2 vols., 1968; R. C. Zaehner, *Hinduism,* 1962.

NINIAN SMART

Hippocratic Oath

Hippocrates of Cos (c. 460–c. 377 B.C.) has long been thought to have formulated the oath that bears his name, but modern scholarship has discredited the tradition. As the "Father of Medicine" he remains an almost ghostly figure about whom much legend has gathered. Literary and historical criticism have also shown that the earliest extant version of the Oath is of the 9th century A.D. The Greek pioneer in experimental physiology, Galen, who about A.D. 200 edited the Hippocratic Collection of treatises on medical subjects (for which no "canon" is any longer possible), appears to have done something with the Oath. There is a considerable literature dealing with the critical problems involved, comparable to studies of parts of the biblical materials. Investigation by modern methods shows that the Oath and other parts of the "Hippocratic" corpus have gone through untraceable and myriad changes at the hands of scribes, booksellers or manuscript merchants, and expositors.

Its earliest versions appear to have been indenture agreements between master physicians and their apprentice-pupils, probably at the point of their becoming independent practitioners. Thus the opening promises were to be loyal to the master and to hand on medical knowledge to his descendants free of charge, if they want it. This part has been generally dropped from current versions, as schools of medicine have replaced apprentice training and as their graduation rituals have taken to administering the Oath as a corporate promise, *en bloc,* in the second personal plural. Physicians are nowadays asked in each case to swear their professional oath* "by whatever he holds most sacred," thus allowing for the religious and nonreligious pluralism* of modern culture. The very earliest versions may have had no vow* at all, not even to Aesculapius (son of Apollo and father of Panacea, medicine's god-sponsor, and Hygeia, health's). There are grounds for viewing the Oath as ethically archaic.

A logical reduction of the Oath yields four promises of ethical importance for medicine: (1) to make the patient's interests supreme (my work will be "for the benefit of my patients" and "not for their hurt or for any wrong"); (2) to refuse to give a "deadly drug to any, though it be asked of me"; (3) to refuse to terminate any pregnancies, that is, "aid a woman to procure abortion"; and (4) to preserve professional secrets and the patients' privilege of communication ("whatsoever things I see or hear" in medical attendance "which ought not to be noised abroad" will be kept as "sacred secrets"). (See text at **Professional Ethics.**)

The first promise is undisputed as an ideal, but nevertheless is constantly infringed by the increase of direct human medical experimentation with new drugs and procedures (see **Experimentation with Human Subjects**). Sometimes these experiments and tests are carried out without the patients' knowledge and could not practically be revealed or interpreted, their moral defense being rested on claims of the general welfare. Issues arise around a fair interpretation of "benefit" and "hurt" and "wrong."

The second promise has commonly been broadened to mean a repudiation of euthanasia*. But this vow is thought to have been originally aimed against physicians becoming accessories to poison murders and assassination, especially political and familial. Some scholars have reasoned that the Pythagoreans, with their mystical doctrine of escape from this life to another, were the targets aimed at, but disciples of Hippocrates actually engaged in direct medical euthanasia. (Indirect euthanasia, "letting the patient go" *in extremis,* is not in question.) (See **Life, Prolongation of.**) One scholar, Ludwig Edelstein, recently offered a new theory: that the Oath was in fact of Pythagorean design, not aimed against them.

The third promise, if taken to be against abortion* as such, runs into trouble with the modern acceptance of voluntary medical or "therapeutic" abortion, and with voluntary terminations for "nonmedical" causes (mental health and social welfare). But there is good ground for taking the promise to have

been against the unsafe and medically unsound use of *abortifacients* in ancient Greece.

The fourth promise, like the first, is an undisputed principle of medical respect for professional confidences, and has considerable (but not universal or constant) support in civil law; moral and legal exceptions are taken when the preservation of such secrets would victimize innocent third parties, as in the case of a seaside lifeguard suffering from serious cardiac failure and unwilling to let it be known (see **Confidentiality**).

See **Bioethics; Codes of Ethics; Medical Ethics; Professional Ethics.**

L. Edelstein, *Ancient Medicine,* ed. O. Temkin and C. L. Temkin, 1967.

JOSEPH FLETCHER

Holiness

For the Judeo-Christian ethical tradition holiness is first and foremost a divine attribute, indicating the radical otherness of God's inner world. The supreme majesty and purity of what Rudolf Otto termed the "numinous" inspires in humans awed reverence before "the divine ground of being" (Tillich). Yet it is this overwhelmingly thrice-holy God (cf. Isa. 6:3) who has chosen to be "the Holy One of Israel" (Isa. 41:14), and Israel is consequently to be differentiated from other nations as "a people holy to the LORD" (Deut. 14:2), called to "be holy, for I am holy" (Lev. 11:44). The "Holiness Code" at the heart of the book of Leviticus (chs. 17–26) spells out in terms of institutions and of ritual as well as moral cleanness the purity of worship and life incumbent upon God's holy people, and in the process designates certain places, times, objects, and priestly persons as set apart and sacrosanct, in some sense charged with God's own holy presence.

Within the new covenant this divine otherness is focused upon Jesus, who was conceived of the Holy Spirit to be called holy (Matt. 1:20; Luke 1:35), and who "sanctified" himself to his "holy Father" so that his followers might be made holy in the truth of his word and protected in the world (John 17:11, 15–19). The church of God thereafter is composed of those made holy in Christ Jesus (1 Cor. 1:2), who have been chosen out to be washed clean and made holy and spotless through Christ's own self-dedication (Eph. 1:4; 5:25–27). They are a chosen race, the "holy nation" foreshadowed in Israel and called by the Holy One to be themselves holy in all their conduct, as befits saints (1 Peter 1:15–16; 2:9; Eph. 5:3). Thus singled out rather than set apart, they will devote all their actions "to righteousness for sanctification" (Rom. 6:19), so manifesting that "holiness and righteousness" which was promised by God of old (Luke 1:75), personified in God's "Holy and Righteous One" (Acts 3:14), and now a consequence of God's renewal of creation in his own likeness "in true righteousness and holiness" (Eph. 4:23–24).

Holiness, then, for the individual Christian unites the characteristics of divine initiative (election), distinctiveness from all that is not of God, and dedication to God's holy purpose. It is an eschatological participation in God's own righteousness, in which, as Aquinas observed, "grace is nothing else than a beginning of glory in us" (*ST* II-II.24.3, ad 2). It is not a quality that by contrast brands the creaturely as profane and unclean, or that differentiates between sacred and secular, whether in times, places, or states of life. For the hour has come when the whole of creation is now God's holy place and sphere of action (cf. Ps. 24:3; John 4:21). Rather, it is a gift that betokens inner transformation to recognize "what is good and acceptable and perfect" (Rom. 12:1–2). It entails a horror of moral defilement (cf. 2 Cor. 7:1) and requires a complete break with one's former state of death, darkness, and sin (cf. 1 Cor. 6:9–11). In God, and therefore in his saints, holiness is a consecration of power in the service of love. It combines the mystery of holy election with that of God's will to save all people (1 Tim. 2:4); and God's moral requirements for his holy ones are no set of voluntarist injunctions, but a revelation of his own concern for universal justice.

It is God's intrinsic holiness that prevents him from imitating humans in being vengeful: "For I am God and not man, the Holy One in your midst, and I will not come to destroy" (Hos. 11:9). Similarly, it is only the righteousness of God's kingdom that will enable his sons and daughters to rise above themselves and love even their persecutors, so imitating their heavenly Father who is "perfect" in his undiscriminating love (Matt. 5:44–48). In fact, the Sermon on the Mount, which is a disquisition on the righteousness of the Christian disciple (Matt. 5:20), is also the deployment in human history of divine integrity and holiness. As such, it shares with all Christian ethics the "numinous" qualities of being both captivating and daunting in its moral purity. But as it was God who chose us from the beginning to "be saved through sanctification by the Spirit" (2 Thess. 2:13), so it is the Lord who will accept our offerings "sanctified by the Holy Spirit" (Rom. 15:16) and establish our hearts "unblamable in holiness" at the coming of our Lord Jesus "with all his saints" (1 Thess. 3:13).

See **Ascetical Theology; Perfectionism; Righteousness; Sanctification.**

R. Otto, *The Idea of the Holy,* ET 1923.

J. MAHONEY

Holocaust *see* **Anti-Semitism; Genocide**

Homicide

It is necessary to distinguish between types of homicide (the taking of human life) that can be said to be accidental, culpable, or justifiable.

Accidental. It is not difficult to think of situations in which a person has been killed as a result of actions that have been in no sense willed either by the dead person or by others. A mountaineer might slip and knock a colleague, who falls to his death as the rope snaps which links him with his companions. Let it be assumed that he and his friends were fit and qualified to make the climb, and that there had been no negligence* when they checked the serviceableness of the climbing gear. It is evident that in this and all comparable instances neither the victim nor his associates are morally blameworthy.

Culpable. A person's right to life is conferred upon him or her not by other persons but by God, the Lord and giver of all life. My life is my own to use and fulfill, but God remains its absolute owner, and I am answerable to God for my use and treatment of it. Since life does not belong to human beings absolutely, it is not within the moral competence of any individual deliberately to destroy it. Thus, it is never permissible to make any deliberate attack upon the life of oneself or of another person (even at the other's invitation), whether such an attack be the immediate effect or the inevitable, foreseen, and directly intended consequence of one's action (or inaction). When such an attack is made and death ensues, it is an instance of culpable homicide. This is the act of murder to which the Sixth Commandment refers. Examples of culpable homicide include compulsory and voluntary euthanasia*, infanticide*, and suicide* ("self-murder"), though there are now disputes about which acts fall under these descriptions and whether they are always culpable. In any particular case the degree of culpability will depend upon all the circumstances in which the act was committed, including the mental condition of the offender or offenders.

Justifiable. It is sometimes claimed that in no circumstances can an action be justified which involves the taking of human life. This, however, has not been the traditional Christian view. The right to life implies the right to protect and defend one's own life or the life of another person against an unjust attack. Since the defense can only be effective if it is in proportion to the violence of the unjust attack, it is possible that in the act of defending himself or another the victim may kill the assailant. In such a case, assuming that any appeal to public justice was at the time out of the question, it may be said that the defendant acted justifiably and was in no sense guilty of homicide. His purpose was *not* to kill his adversary but only to preserve his own or another person's life against an unjust attack (*see* **Double Effect**). It would be an act of culpable homicide only if the victim could have been adequately defended without causing the assailant's death. It is by this same principle of self-defense against unjust aggression* that capital punishment* and killing in war* can be justified. Under God the state* is responsible for the maintenance of law* and order* and the protection of its citizens as a whole. This implies the right to adopt the extreme measure of the capital punishment of particular offenders *when the state cannot otherwise fulfill its general duty of defense.* When, however, the state finds it no longer necessary to exercise this right, it cannot justly continue to do so and it should revise its criminal code accordingly. At any given period opinions may differ about the correct interpretation of the available relevant information; but many countries have already concluded that with them capital punishment* can safely be abolished. The state is also responsible under God for the protection of the lives and property of its citizens against unjust attack from without. The fulfillment of this duty may involve the extreme measure of resorting to war. Thus in a just war* (which is, by definition, essentially of a "defensive" kind), a soldier cannot rightly be accused of unjustifiable homicide when the taking of an enemy's life becomes an unavoidable consequence of the performance of his or her military duty to disarm the enemy. Whether in any particular instance a country may truly be said to be engaged in a just war is another question; and it is a matter of present debate whether the "defending" country could continue to claim that it was engaged in an otherwise just war the moment it resorted to the use of nuclear bombs and missiles, which are by their nature, and in varying degrees, weapons of indiscriminate destruction (*see* **Deterrence; Nuclear Warfare**).

See also **Crime; Life, Prolongation of; Life, Sacredness of; Pacifism; Resistance.**

K. Barth, *Church Dogmatics* III/4, ET 1961; P. E. Devine, *The Ethics of Homicide,* 1978.

THOMAS WOOD

Homosexuality

Homosexuality is the presence of a predominant and persistent psychosexual attraction toward members of the same sex. The homosexual *orientation* must be distinguished from same-gender sexual *acts,* which may be engaged in by persons who are predominantly heterosexual or which may be refrained from by celibate homosexual persons. Today many same-sex oriented persons in the USA and Britain prefer the terms "gay men" and "lesbians" to "homosexuals," believing that the latter term carries negative clinical associations and conveys a narrow genital focus in the definition of the person.

Presently, there exists no scientific consensus on the causes of homosexuality or, for that matter, of heterosexuality. However, because traditionally homosexuality has been viewed in most Western societies as a divergence from normal sexual development and orientation, a wide variety of theories regarding its causation have arisen. Such explanations currently can be grouped as biological, psychoanalytic, and social learning theories, or some combination thereof. The best that can be said is that little is understood conclusively about the genesis of either homosexual or heterosexual orientation. There appears to be general agreement, however, on several ethically relevant factors: (1) that basic sexual orientation becomes relatively fixed in early childhood, usually by ages five to seven, quite apart from the individual's conscious choice; (2) that efforts to reorient adult sexual preference may change certain sexual behaviors but do not usually have significant or lasting effect upon feelings, desires, and sexual fantasy; (3) that most persons are neither exclusively heterosexual nor exclusively homosexual but have predominant tendencies toward one of those orientations; and (4) that predominant homosexual orientation as such carries with it no clinical pathology, though some gay men and lesbians will experience psychological and/or behavioral problems stemming from social oppression, problems similar to those found in other socially oppressed groups.

While there is ample evidence of homosexuality in all known cultures from ancient times to the present, there has been no consistent pattern of societal or religious response. Homosexuality has been affirmed as representative of the deity, institutionalized, tolerated without approval, ignored, or penalized and persecuted, depending upon the given culture and period of history. But in the Judeo-Christian West homosexuality has been viewed with particular abhorrence, an attitude undoubtedly strongly linked with certain biblical teachings.

The relatively few biblical passages dealing with the subject do not treat homosexuality as a psychosexual orientation (a distinctly modern concept) but rather refer to certain types of homosexual acts. The major references *appear* to make completely negative judgments upon same-sex genital expression. The destruction of Sodom and Gomorrah frequently has been attributed to homosexual acts (Gen. 19). The Levitical Holiness Code prescribes the death penalty for male homosexual acts (Lev. 18:22; 20:13). The NT denounces both male and female homosexual relationships as expressions of idolatry (Rom. 1:26–27) and indicates that certain types of same-sex acts preclude entry into the kingdom and contravene the law of God (1 Cor. 6:9–10; 1 Tim. 1:9–10).

However, most biblical scholars now question the accuracy of understanding these references as blanket condemnations of all homosexual relationships. To the extent that the Sodom story focuses on homosexual acts, its judgment is upon the homosexual rape of divine messengers, and its larger judgment appears to be against social injustice and in-

hospitality to strangers (see Ezek. 16:49–50). The references in 1 Corinthians and 1 Timothy quite clearly take the sordid and dehumanizing dimensions of Greco-Roman pederasty as their image of homosexual relations. The uncompromising condemnation in Leviticus is clear, though it must be understood in the context of the concern for cultic purity in the face of defiling pagan incursions as well as beliefs about male dignity and the nonprocreative loss of the revered life-bearing semen in a patriarchal culture. Finally, Paul's unequivocal denunciation (Rom. 1:26–27) is directed at homosexual *lust** understood as the consequence of idolatry (his main concern), and it appears predicated on the assumption that such homosexual acts were performed by heterosexual persons who freely chose to act contrary to their own "natural" inclinations.

Thus, the serious hermeneutical question remains: Do the scriptures give clear guidance for evaluation of homosexuality as a predominant psychosexual orientation or for evaluation of homosexual acts between adults in loving relationships?

While the Christian church has often been accused of sustaining an unrelenting persecution of gay men and lesbians, the historical record is much more mixed. During its earliest centuries the church exhibited considerable toleration, though with the dissolution of the Roman state hostility arose. Yet, throughout most of the Middle Ages, Christian moral theology was either silent on the issue or at worst compared homosexuality to heterosexual sins. Indeed, a major gay subculture was tolerated by the church during the 11th and 12th centuries. After the 12th century, however, considerable intolerance arose, perhaps closely related to a general increase in the intolerance of minority groups in a changing European economic and social structure. That hostility was both reflected in and perpetuated by the church's theological and ethical writings of the later Middle Ages and continued to influence European society for centuries, frequently contributing to the persecution of homosexual persons by the state. During and following the Protestant Reformation the generalized hostility continued.

Four theological-ethical positions regarding homosexual orientation and its expression appear to represent the continuum of current Christian understanding. The first is a *rejecting-punitive* position. Homosexuality is unconditionally rejected as not Christianly legitimate, either as orientation or in its genital expressions. Further, there is a punitive attitude toward lesbians and gay men. Such arguments usually rest upon literal, noncontextual interpretations of certain biblical passages and are usually buttressed by various cultural stereotypes of gay and lesbian people.

The second position is *rejecting-nonpunitive*. Homosexual acts are condemned as unnatural, idolatrous, and in violation of God's creative intent. Nevertheless, a distinction is made between acts and orientation or person. The argument typically takes two forms, sometimes in combination. One is that the procreative possibility is essential to legitimate sexual intercourse. Thus, Thomas Aquinas argues that, since the sexual organs must not be used for acts that preclude generation, homosexual intercourse is a sin against nature and is next in gravity to bestiality. The other argument is the essential gender complementarity of male and female in the *imago Dei*. According to Karl Barth, since one comes to "fellow humanity" only in relation to a person of the opposite sex, to seek one's humanity in a same-sex relationship is self-worship, perversion, and idolatry. While this general position uncompromisingly rejects all homosexual *acts* as "intrinsically evil," two qualifications must be made. First, homosexual *orientation* itself is not always morally condemned even if it is understood as essentially flawed. Second, this position seeks to be nonpunitive toward the homosexual *person* who, in light of God's mercy, is to be treated compassionately as one in need of the church's ministry.

The third position is that of *qualified acceptance*. This stance agrees with the previous one in affirming God's heterosexual intent in creation. However, constitutional homosexuality is now understood as largely given, fixed early in childhood, and in adults frequently unsusceptible to reorientation. If homosexual persons can change their orientation, they are morally obligated to do so. But those who cannot should attempt to sublimate their genital desires and practice abstinence. If this is not possible, genital relations must be ordered in an ethically responsible manner, i.e., in adult, monogamous commit-

ments. Thus, homosexual orientation is still viewed as incomplete, not normative, or even as contrary to nature and God's design. Hence, even those homosexual acts within monogamous commitment are distortions of God's ideal, yet they are not to be absolutely condemned. Such acts, though "essentially imperfect," for some persons are the lesser of the evils and hence qualifiedly accepted.

The fourth position on the continuum is that of *full acceptance* of homosexual orientation, with homosexual acts themselves to be evaluated by the same standards used for heterosexual acts. While this position was scarcely articulated in Christian ethics until recent decades, it rests historically upon a development in certain Protestant understandings of human sexuality and heterosexual marriage that took place in the 17th century. That shift elevated "the unitive purpose" of marriage and sexuality to the primary position and dethroned the centrality or even coequality of "the procreative purpose." While contemporary adherents of full acceptance of homosexuality generally assume that sexual orientation is a given rather than a matter of meaningful choice, that is not their major argument. More fundamentally, they contend that same-sex relationships can fully express God's central purpose for sexuality, the unitive. Thus, affirming homosexual as well as heterosexual orientation, this position holds that all sexual acts ought to be evaluated by their relational qualities: What behaviors and relationships will serve and enhance rather than inhibit or damage human fulfillment, faithfulness, mutuality, and genuine intimacy and communion? While holding this single standard of ethical judgment as the appropriate ideal, some adherents of this position insist that sensitivity and fairness dictate that the realities of social oppression be taken into account when evaluating specific acts of homosexual expression.

The central questions that appear to distinguish the above positions are these: the meaning of human sexuality, the interpretation of scripture, the use of empirical data, and the criteria for evaluation of moral action. While the positions as described cannot do justice to the nuanced understandings of any particular individual or group, they do indicate the wide spectrum of current understanding. Of those churches which have taken public positions, the majority embrace the rejecting-nonpunitive stance, with a few expressing qualified acceptance, and a small minority committed to full acceptance.

In addition to the general theological-ethical question concerning homosexual orientation and expression, a number of more specific moral issues now face the churches. A major issue is the support of civil rights and social justice for lesbians and gay men, an issue on which most major church bodies now publicly agree. More divisive are those which directly affect internal church life. These include the acceptance of gays and lesbians into full church participation, the provision of enlightened and effective pastoral care, the ordination of publicly affirmed lesbians and gay men, the liturgical blessing of gay or lesbian unions, the support of legal rights for gay or lesbian unions analogous to the legal rights of heterosexual marriages, and interdenominational recognition of largely lesbian and gay Christian communions such as the Universal Fellowship of Metropolitan Community Churches. Perhaps the most difficult and far-reaching challenge of all, however, is that of dealing with the moral and spiritual dynamics of homophobia, the irrational and compulsive fear of homosexuality, as it is expressed both personally and socially.

See **Sexual Ethics; Lesbianism; Marriage; Morality, Legal Enforcement of.**

D. S. Bailey, *Homosexuality and the Western Christian Tradition,* 1955; E. Batchelor, Jr. (ed.), *Homosexuality and Ethics,* 1980; J. Boswell, *Christianity, Social Tolerance, and Homosexuality,* 1980; A. Kosnick et al., *Human Sexuality: New Directions in American Catholic Thought,* 1977; E. Moberly, *Homosexuality: A New Christian Ethic,* 1983; R. Scroggs, *The New Testament and Homosexuality,* 1983.

JAMES B. NELSON

Honesty

This and related words occur at several places in the NT (though not in the OT). In AV at Luke 8:15; Rom. 12:17; 2 Cor. 8:21; and 1 Peter 2:12, "honest" translates the Greek word *kalos,* meaning good or excellent. Similarly, at Phil. 4:8 it translates *semnos,* meaning honorable or proper. At 1 Tim. 2:2 "honesty" translates the abstract noun *semnotēs,* meaning gravity or dignity. At Rom. 13:13 and 1 Thess. 4:12 "honestly" renders an adverb meaning decently or with propriety. These words all refer to conduct that is appropriate to one who responds to the call of the kingdom of God. In part, this vocabulary reflects the social virtues of those who are to live at peace with their neighbors, most of whom are not of their faith, and it is without the eschatological emphasis of some of the NT language. Honesty involves thoughts, words, and deeds, exhibiting a harmony between one's fundamental beliefs and their manifestations. Honesty in thought means willingness to follow evidence wherever it leads, not concealing or falsifying it for intellectual security or material gain, and not rushing to conclusions on inadequate information. (For honesty in word, *see* **False Witness; Lying; Slander; Truthfulness.**) Salespersons, copywriters, publicity agents, journalists, and other writers and speakers have special temptations to dishonesty in the use of words. Continual concern for accuracy and appropriateness of speech (the search for *le mot juste*) is a safeguard against giving way to them. Honesty in deed involves accuracy in money transactions, openness in relationships, and a careful use of things.

RONALD PRESTON

Honor

Honor is the appreciation of the worth of, and the expression of esteem for, a person, an officeholder, etc. While the term "honor" refers primarily to a social response, it may also refer to the state of being worthy of such a response or to a person's own self-esteem. The Fifth Commandment in Ex. 20:12 requires: "Honor your father and your mother," adding the motivating reason, "that your days may be long in the land which the LORD your God gives you." This requirement to honor parents was extended to other superiors, especially rulers, and Paul (Rom. 13:7) insisted on "honor to whom honor is due" along with payment of taxes, revenue, and respect.

Both direct honor and indirect honor of God are significant motives and standards in Christian ethics. John Calvin emphasized the direct honoring of God (*Institutes* 3.26.3), observing that "God has in his own right the reverence of a father and of a Lord"—reverence* consisting of both fear and honor—and that the knowledge of God "carries with it the honoring of him" through adherence to the law.

The passage in 1 Peter (2:17) that beseeches Christians to "honor the emperor" also beseeches them to "honor all men." In Christian ethics both requirements are ultimately connected to honoring God because God has ordained rulers who are his "ministers" (Rom. 13:6), and because his image and likeness is in all people (Gen. 1:26ff.). (*See* **Image of God.**) Regarding the latter, Thomas Aquinas (*ST* II-II.41.4) noted that reverence "paid to a person as the image of God redounds somewhat to God." Regarding the former, Calvin (*Institutes* 2.7.35) held that the sum of the Fifth Commandment is "that we should look up to those whom God has placed over us, and should treat them with honor, obedience, and gratefulness," their preeminence being reflected in such titles as "lord" and "father," used alike of God and selected human beings, and the fact that God "lights [them] up with a spark of his splendor so that each may be distinguished according to his degree." This hierarchical view of society has been rejected by some Christians who seek to level the social order, emphasizing the equal honor and dignity of all who are created in the image and likeness of God. For example, the Quakers in 17th-century England refused to render "hat honor," to recognize titles, and to use various gestures of honor (e.g., they addressed superiors by "thee" and "thou" rather than "you"; *see* **Quaker Ethics**).

Peter Berger has observed that through the process of modernization, the concept of honor has become obsolescent and has been replaced by the concept of dignity: honor "implies that identity is essentially, or at least importantly, linked to institutional roles," while "the modern concept of dignity, by contrast, implies that identity is essentially independent of institutional roles" and can be achieved only by reversing the process of alienation*, bad faith, etc. (*see* **Human Dignity; Institutions; Persons and Personality; Respect for Persons**). Honor is often viewed as an aristocratic theme associated with hierarchical societies, but this association is not necessary although the concept of honor tends to survive and even to flourish in such settings (e.g., the military). (*See* **Chivalry.**)

However much particular conceptions of honor and even the concept of honor itself appear to have declined, honor and dishonor and their surrogates remain important "as a mediator between individual aspirations and the judgment of society" (Pitt-Rivers). Honor in the sense of external acknowledgment still influences moral conduct, even though few people may accept Thomas Aquinas's view that honor for virtue is the greatest external good at human disposal (*ST* II-II.129.1). On the one hand, it is one of society's ways to control conduct. Although, as Jesus noted, prophets are frequently without honor in their own country, seeking honor is one motivation for virtuous conduct. It may, however, lead to hypocrisy*. On the other hand, a person's own sense of honor may be a strong motive for conduct apart from a social response. Finally, there are also moral duties not to violate the honor of others through such acts as calumny and slander* and significant moral questions about the Christian's defense of his or her own honor. One of the criteria Karl Barth (*Church Dogmatics* III/4, ET 1961) offers for determining when Christians may and should defend their own honor is whether they can undertake such a defense "with a final and profound unconcern" because of a recognition that "only the existence of God as man's Creator and Lord, and man's existence as His creature and under His rule, constitutes the honor of man."

P. Berger, "On the Obsolescence of the Concept of Honor," in *Revisions*, ed. S. Hauerwas and A. MacIntyre, 1983; B. Häring, *The Law of Christ*, vol. 3, ET 1966; J. Pitt-Rivers, "Honor," *International Encyclopedia of the Social Sciences*, ed. D. Sells, 1968.

JAMES F. CHILDRESS

Hope

Hopes exhibit a common formal identity while being quite diverse in their psychological textures and human significance. To hope is to desire that which is believed possible of realization (*see* **Desire**). Yet desires can be strong or weak, so hopes can vary in their intensity. Possibilities can be awaited or pursued with assurance or anxiety, thus hopes can be confidently or tenuously held. Hopes are directed to objects, but those objects can be definite and discrete or global and encompassing. Thus the term "hope" alone opens us to a complex array of often dissimilar phenomena.

Classical philosophy paid little attention to this array. Classified as a passion, hope was regarded as an obstacle to rational living. Aristotle compares hopeful selves to callow youth, regarding them as somewhat unrealistic in their expectations of life. Biblical religion, however, identifies a certain kind of hope as an essential response of the believer who grasps his or her situation before God. Given God's love, mercy, and sovereign mastery of human possibilities, believers are to display an enduring and pervasive hope that is both grounded in and directed toward divinely instituted realities. The NT elaborates the hope of Israel in Christological and eschatological terms. Christ's work and the coming full disclosure of his triumph become the basis and object for a hope not circumscribed by the dimming possibilities of death and sinful darkness.

The Christian tradition has continued to feature hoping in and for God in its account of the Christian life, but the moral implications of such a hope have often been left undeveloped. This can even be said of such an important elucidation of Christian hope as that provided by Thomas Aquinas. Aquinas carefully integrates his analysis of the theological virtue of hope with the doctrine of grace, yet he does not explore the moral import of hopeful living founded on God's gracious help. Moreover, his philosophy of hoping, advanced in his accompanying philosophical anthropology, does not progress much beyond the perspective found in Aristotle (see **Thomistic Ethics**).

Recent theological developments have brought overdue attention to the question of the moral significance of Christian hope. The "theology of hope" movement, spearheaded by Jürgen Moltmann, has challenged the frequently voiced criticism that the otherworldly dimension of Christian hope purchases personal consolation at the cost of this-worldly social and political involvement. In Moltmann's view it is precisely the eschatological thrust of Christian hope that makes it such a dynamic for social and political change. Drawing on both biblical material and themes developed by the revisionist Marxist philosopher Ernst Bloch, Moltmann argues that God's new and coming future makes the claims of history and nature provisional. A hope targeted on that future would,

then, foster both an openness to and a readiness for social and political change.

Resurgent interest in the dispositions that undergird and define Christian moral selfhood is also bringing attention to the moral significance of Christian hope. Displaying such an interest, the work of James M. Gustafson has included hope among the dispositions that shape Christian moral agency. Drawing on the phenomenological reflections of Gabriel Marcel, Gustafson has sketched how Christian affirmations can ground a disposition of hopefulness which counteracts that despair which would cripple moral activity while fostering that courage* which effective moral agency presupposes.

The theological trends cited here locate the moral relevance of Christian hope within the sphere of moral psychology. Intensified dialogue with philosophers and reflective psychologists on the role of hope in moral psychology will enhance and sharpen the insights already advanced. A precondition for such dialogue is discrimination in regard to the different kinds of hopes and their effects. For their part, theologians will have to become as discriminating in their analysis of the array of hopes as they generally are in their analysis of the array of loves (see **Love**). When Christians can clearly distinguish between hopes that are and hopes that are not analogous to the hope fostered by the Christian faith, between hopes that are basic to human fulfillment and moral existence and hopes that are morally empty and demonic, they can expect such a dialogue with nontheological disciplines to further highlight the moral significance of their own hope in and for God.

See also **Eschatological Ethics; Evolutionary Ethics; Kingdom of God; Optimism; Progress, Belief in; Promise; Realism; Transcendence; Utopian Thought.**

Thomas Aquinas, *Summa Theologiae* II-II.17–22; D. Evans, *Struggle and Fulfillment*, 1980; J. M. Gustafson, *Can Ethics Be Christian?* 1975; G. Marcel, *Homo Viator*, ET 1962; J. Moltmann, *Theology of Hope*, ET 1967.

PHILIP A. MUNTZEL

Hospice

Hospice care, whether it be in a separate unit or ward or by a home-care or consulting hospital team, is concerned with the quality of life* remaining for patients whose illness has become terminal. The whole family is the unit of care both before and after bereavement and, where possible, part of the caring team.

Since the first hospices were founded at the turn of this century on both sides of the Atlantic, a main concentration has been upon patients dying with advanced malignant disease. Some hospices today include patients with other incurable diseases and the frail elderly.

Hospice care is concerned with enabling patients to live to the limit of their physical, mental, and spiritual capacity, with control and independence, as far as is possible in the place of their choice. Skilled medical relief of symptoms is essential and sometimes makes further active treatment possible. Team nursing is supported by members of other disciplines and trained volunteers. Some patients may require admission to a specialized hospice bed, but it has been shown that home care is the choice for many people and their families and reduces the time of a final admission.

The academic model of care, research, and teaching was introduced into this field with the opening of St. Christopher's Hospice in London in 1967, and since that date there has been a worldwide proliferation of hospice units and teams, each responding to local needs and possibilities to give a complementary, integrated service. The basic principles are also being introduced and interpreted throughout the general field of medical and nursing practice.

See **Life, Prolongation of; Sick, Care of the.**

CICELY SAUNDERS

Hospitality

The term means taking in strangers or travelers; the practice was common in ancient Israel and is referred to in several places in the Hebrew Bible, notably in Abraham's hospitality to the "three men" in Gen. 18:1–5. A responsibility to care for travelers was congruous for a people who remembered their history of wandering in the wilderness.

Hospitality was also to be shown to enemies or those of whom one was afraid. The Christian church placed great stress on an obligation of hospitality. Jesus' ministry depended on the practice, and he is portrayed as exemplifying it (as in the footwashing of John 13) and exhorting his disciples both to count on hospitality and to be hospitable (e.g., Matt. 10:11f.; Luke 10:5; 14:12–14).

The responsibility for hospitality fell particularly on bishops in the early church. As an institutionalized practice of hospitality the first hospitals or hospices are associated with Basil the Great (c. 375). Specialized hospitals for the sick, orphans, or the crippled were started by Chrysostom in Constantinople (c. 400). The Western practice goes back to Benedict; it is enjoined in chapter 53 of the Benedictine rule. Western hospices provided shelter for travelers and were often associated with monasteries; hospitals served the sick and quickly evolved so that they had specialized functions.

Neither the virtue nor the institutional practice of hospitality have been much stressed in recent Christian ethics, which has tended to stress more assertive traits of character and the welfare obligations of the civil state.

T. Gilby in *Encyclopedic Dictionary of Religion* II, pp. 1716f.; "Hospitality," in *HERE* VI, pp. 797–820; T. Ogletree, *Hospitality to the Stranger: Dimensions of Moral Understanding,* 1985.

DAVID H. SMITH

Hospitals *see* **Bioethics; Health Care, Right to; Hospice; Hospitality; Medical Ethics; Sick, Care of the; Social Service of the Church**

Household Codes

At least since Luther's time the term "Household Codes" (*Haustafeln*) has been applied to Col. 3:18–4:1 and Eph. 5:21–6:9, in which exhortations are given *ad seriatim* to the various members of a household. Characteristic of these passages is the direct, second-person address and the arrangement in pairs with the "subordinate" member mentioned first: e.g., "wives . . . , husbands . . . ." Elsewhere in the NT, 1 Peter 2:13–3:8 is similar to the Colossian and Ephesian passages but not so tightly structured, while passages such as 1 Tim. 2:8–3:13; 5:1–22; and Titus 2:1–10 are primarily Congregation Codes (in the third person). It has long been noted that Hellenistic writers, especially Stoics, arranged ethical instruction in terms of the relation of an individual to the other members of the family and the larger society. See, e.g., Diogenes Laertius, *Lives of Eminent Philosophers* 7.108f., 118–125; Seneca, *Epistles* 94.1f.; 95.45; Epictetus, *Discourses* 2.10.1–23; 14.8; 17.31; Plutarch, *On the Training of Children* 10; Marcus Aurelius, *Meditations* 5.31. Similar patterns appear also in Hellenistic Jewish writers and their usage is a more likely source for the early Christian writers. See, e.g., Ecclesiasticus 7:18–36; Tobit 4:3–19; Philo, *On the Decalogue* 165–167; *Hypothetica* 7.3; 4 Maccabees 2:10–13; Pseudo-Phocylides 175–228; Josephus, *Against Apion* 2.198–210. In Rabbinic literature, see, e.g., *M. Kiddushin* 1.7; *T. Kiddushin* 1.11; *M. Kethuboth* 5.6–7. Early Christian literature continued this form of parenesis without following strictly the NT format. See *Didache* 4.9–11; *Barnabas* 19.5–8; *1 Clement* 1.3; 21.6–9; Ignatius, *To Polycarp* 4.1–6.2; Polycarp, *To the Philippians* 4.1–6.3. It has been argued, but never completely demonstrated, that a common catechetical tradition stood behind the various Household Codes in this Christian literature.

Scholars have debated whether these NT Codes reflect specifically Christian insights or were taken over from earlier sources and lightly "Christianized." Clearly, the writers were anxious to bring the relationships of the home into obedience to Christ, but the particular injunctions do not appear to be novel or distinctively Christian. It is scarcely novel to suggest that wives, children, and slaves should be obedient to their husbands, fathers, and masters respectively. However, Ephesians has a distinctive digression on the husband-wife relation as a parallel to Christ and his church; Colossians has a disproportionately long exhortation to slaves, which may reflect special problems in the Christian community. Also the repeated references to the "Lord" indicate that for the believer Christ was to be master of every relationship and the motivating force for ethical behavior.

The eschatological expectations of the Christian community might have led to a rejection of all the social patterns by which ancient life was held together, but the Household Codes are one of the evidences that this possibility was resisted. While awaiting the coming of the kingdom, Christian leaders wanted all earthly relations to continue not only decently and in order but "in the Lord." This was the beginning of the long struggle through which the church strove to bring personal and community life into obedience

to the will of Christ. Certainly not everything was clear to Christian leaders from the beginning, and modern readers will note a significant tension between the "subordination" principle of the Codes and the "egalitarian" principle proclaimed elsewhere in the gospel for all who are in Christ.

In addition to commentaries on the relevant passages, see D. J. Balch, *Let Wives Be Submissive: The Domestic Code in I Peter,* 1981; J. E. Crouch, *The Origin and Intention of the Colossian Haustafel,* 1972; W. Lillie, "The Pauline House-Tables," *Expository Times* 86, 1974–75, pp. 179–183; O. J. F. Seitz, "Lists, Ethical," *IDB* III, 1962.

HARVEY K. MCARTHUR

Hubris *see* Hybris

Human Dignity

Human dignity is the inherent worth or value of a human person from which no one or nothing may detract. Through different philosophical or religious premises, the concept belongs to every age and culture, as Hersch demonstrates, and is the basis for the contemporary claims for human rights*.

The predominant explanation given for this dignity has been one which links humankind with God. Socrates posited a certain community of nature between God and humanity, thus stressing that to detract from a human person was to detract from being in harmony with the universe. This idea was later developed by the Stoics, who posited an ascending scale of dignity from inanimate objects to a final culmination in humanity. As in earlier and subsequent systems of philosophy, Stoicism considered human reason to be essentially a spark of the divine, thus making it the distinctive element associated with the dignity of being human. In systems of thought which are essentially nontheistic, human reason alone provides the basis for the understanding of human dignity. Such a rationale provided the philosophical foundation for the *Déclaration des droits de l'homme et du citoyen* (1798), upon which a number of subsequent bills of rights are modeled. The rationality of human beings is deemed to provide the individual with a dignity, anterior to the demands and requirements of the state.

In the Judeo-Christian tradition, the concept of human dignity belongs to the understanding that human beings are made in the image of God*. Human beings are declared to be created by God and in relationship with God, the "thou" in relation to God. Human beings then are not to be considered simply as selves, but as selves in relation to God. God is portrayed throughout this tradition as treating men and women with respect, never as "things." Because of this love of and relationship with God, every human being is a subject of reverence to other people. Human dignity arises from the self-giving of God, described in the creation and covenant narratives. Even although men and women have broken this relationship with God and each other through sin, the image of God* has not been eliminated from them (see also **Natural Law**). John Calvin, for example, maintained that while God's image had been vitiated by the Fall it had not been eliminated. Thus, because of the remnant of God's image in them, men and women possess no small dignity. Since Jesus Christ died for all, Calvin stressed that God has demonstrated a purpose for human beings. This remnant and this purpose, conferred by God, carry the implication that people are to be honored and treated as sacred. Other theologians also stress this gift of the image of God in humans, and the purpose of God for humankind demonstrated in Jesus Christ, as the foundation for human dignity. Such dignity permits no derogation.

An appeal to human dignity provides the basic premise for the contemporary understanding of human rights, be these conceived in civil and political or social and economic terms, as evidenced in the use of such words as "inalienable" in constitutions and international covenants. This concept has also justified opposition to injustice and dehumanization, irrespective of its source.

See **Dehumanization; Honor; Human Rights; Humanistic Ethics; Image of God; Natural Law; Persons and Personality; Respect for Persons.**

K. Barth, *Protestant Theology in the Nineteenth Century: Its Background and History,* ET 1972, pp. 33–79; D. Cairns, *The Image of God in Man,* 1973; J. Hersch, *Birthright of Man,* 1969.

ALAN D. FALCONER

Human Experimentation

see **Experimentation with Human Subjects**

Human Nature see **Free Will and Determinism; Freedom; Image of God; Natural Law; Original Sin**

Human Rights

As the notion "human rights" has come to be understood in contemporary international usage, it means a set of justifiable or legitimate claims with at least six features: (1) they impose duties of performance or forbearance upon all appropriately situated human beings, including governments; (2) they are possessed equally by all human beings regardless of laws, customs, or agreements; (3) they are of basic importance to human life; (4) they are properly sanctionable and enforceable upon default by legal means; (5) they have special presumptive weight in constraining human action, and (6) they include a certain number that are considered inalienable, indefeasible, and unforfeitable.

The language of various international human rights instruments that have been generated since World War II, including sections of the Charter of the United Nations, the Universal Declaration of Human Rights, and others, all clearly presuppose an asymmetrical relation between morality and law. The set of human rights enunciated in these documents, and others like them, is affirmed as justifiable and legitimate on grounds *independent of and prior to* the determinations of sovereign legal entities or states. The words of the Preamble to the Covenant on Political and Civil Rights are typical: "Considering that, in accordance with the principles proclaimed in the Charter of the United Nations, recognition of the inherent dignity and of the equal and inalienable rights of all members of the human family is the foundation of freedom, justice and peace in the world . . . Recognizing that these rights derive from the inherent dignity of the human person . . ." There is here what may be called the assumption of a prior and independent moral belief in some common and permanent human characteristics that enjoin certain universally specifiable ways of treating human beings and that prohibit others. The conviction is that whether particular states agree and adhere to the covenants or not, whether they decide to denounce them or not, states do not control, finally, the authority of the covenants, because that authority is regarded as being distinctively *prelegal* and *prepolitical*. This conviction underlies each of the above six features.

At the same time, as the Universal Declaration states, "if man is not to be compelled to have recourse, as a last resort, to rebellion against tyranny and oppression, . . . human rights should be protected by the rule of law." The assumption is both that human rights constitute a fundamental standard for determining the legitimacy of a given government or legal order, and that they provide the primary impulse for instituting governments in the first place. In short, law follows from and depends upon a prior moral belief in universal human rights.

This observation calls attention particularly to features (3) and (4). While in common usage not all rights are either human or legal, the general notion of a right does carry with it the implication that one who possesses it is entitled to sanction any default by an appropriate form of blame, criticism, or punishment, depending on the kind of right involved, and thereby, if possible, to compel compliance. Rights-language, even outside the context of human rights and legal rights, ascribes a special sort of control over those who are bound to observe the rights*. Human rights are believed to be of such critical importance to human life (feature 3) that they are thought to require especially strong and reliable guarantees and forms of enforcement (feature 4).

In fact, as a deposit of the natural rights tradition, which had such a formative influence upon modern human rights thinking (*see* **Natural Rights**), human rights are understood to comprise the basic standard for regulating the use of coercion. Coercion that violates human rights is, in general, illicit, and coercion that protects them is licit. Legal rights in various domestic legal systems are frequently combinations of internationally recognized human rights and other more culturally specific provisions. Although legal enforcement is clearly assumed in the notion of human rights, the arrangements for international enforcement are still matters of intense dispute.

While the international human rights instruments assume by their language a prelegal moral reference, they do not identify any particular moral theory as the ground for that reference. Debate over this subject is widespread. A few examples of the types of defense of the basis of human rights must suffice.

Noncognitivists (*see* **Metaethics**). M. Mac-Donald gave definitive expression to this view in her famous 1947 essay. For her, as for all noncognitivists, choices among values can never rest, as can scientific judgments, upon veridical knowledge. Statements about values, like registering approval of the Universal Declaration, are nothing more than announcements of preference, and as such have no rational foundation. In one way or another, the noncognitivist position has been adopted subsequently by philosophers like H. L. A. Hart (1955), J. Feinberg (1973), and A. I. Melden (1977).

Cognitivists (*see* **Metaethics**). While Locke (*see* **Natural Rights**) is anything but consistent on the subject, there is a strong strain in his writings to the effect that certain kinds of behavior, such as the deliberate infliction of pain or disablement, or the destruction of another human being "at one's pleasure," are knowably wrong and contrary to reason. This knowledge is "fixed and permanent" and applies universally, and thereby provides the basis for a moral commitment to natural or human rights.

In a very different way, A. Gewirth (1978) offers a more recent version of a cognitivist ground for human rights. Gewirth believes that human beings are indisputably and unavoidably "agents." By a kind of conceptual analysis of the generic features of agency —purposiveness and freedom—Gewirth believes he can show that each agent "must" claim a right to these features and, by extension, ascribe the same rights to all human agents. From this basis, Gewirth infers an elaborate scheme of human rights (1982).

There are of course many more kinds of religious and philosophical defenses of human rights (see Swidler, 1982).

In respect to feature (1), there is much debate in the literature over whether human rights are essentially "negative"—matters of forbearance or noninterference, or whether they are also "positive"—requiring the performance of acts of welfare assistance. The human rights instruments clearly include both. The Covenant on Political and Civil Rights enjoins restraints on governments, while the Covenant on Economic, Social and Cultural Rights enjoins quite positive forms of economic and other assistance. The conviction that an easy line of distinction can be drawn between rights of noninterference and rights of assistance has been tellingly challenged (see Okin, 1981).

Finally, features (5) and (6) raise the much-discussed questions of the absoluteness and the inalienability and indefeasibility of human rights. Many of the human rights instruments themselves contain "public emergency" provisions according to which states may permissibly derogate from certain specified human rights "to the extent strictly required by the exigencies of the situation." Consequently, not all rights are assumed to be absolute and inalienable for these and other reasons. Still, certain "nonderogable" rights, such as the prohibitions against slavery* and against subjection to "cruel, inhuman or degrading treatment or punishment," and requirements for a fair trial, appear to come closer to that understanding. It is widely accepted that no one ought under any circumstances to be allowed to transfer to another, have annulled, or forfeit the right not to be sold for profit, not to be brutally treated in or out of prison, or the right to an impartial trial. Whether any of these rights is also "absolute" in the sense of being unconditionally binding and completely exceptionless is a matter of much controversy.

See also **Civil Rights; Human Dignity; Natural Law; Natural Rights; Persons and Personality; Respect for Persons.**

P. G. Brown and D. MacLean, *Human Rights and United States Foreign Policy,* 1980; A. Falconer (ed.), *Understanding Human Rights,* 1980; J. Feinberg, *Social Philosophy,* 1973; A. Gewirth, *Reason and Morality,* 1978; *Human Rights,* 1982; H. L. A. Hart, "Are There Any Natural Rights?" *Philosophical Review,* 1955; *Human Rights Documents,* U.S. Congress, House Committee on Foreign Affairs, 1983; E. Kamenka and A. Erh-Soon Tay (eds.), *Human Rights,* 1978; M. MacDonald, "Natural Rights," *Proceedings of the Aristotelian Society,* 1947–48; A. I. Melden, *Rights and Persons,* 1977; S. M. Okin, "Liberty and Welfare: Some Issues in Human Rights Theory," *Human Rights,* 1981; A. S. Rosenbaum, *Philosophy of Human Rights,* 1980; A. Swidler, *Human Rights in Religious Traditions,* 1982; K. Thompson, *Moral Imperatives of Human Rights,* 1980.

DAVID LITTLE

Humanae Vitae *see* **Contraception; Modern Roman Catholic Moral Theology**

Humanism *see* **Humanistic Ethics**

Humanistic Ethics

The title of this article, while necessarily elastic, designates some recognizable principles and stresses within a broad spectrum of ethical reflection. Humanism, as we meet it in the contemporary world, is a recurring accent which may be best expressed by the ancient axiom that humans are "the measure of things." Current forms of humanism, like their Renaissance* and classical counterparts, commonly reject belief in God as either sanctioning or explaining moral conduct, and insist that human beings themselves have the sole responsibility for bettering and fulfilling their existence in this world.

During our century, to be sure, humanism has taken on added depth and density because of the untimely, tragic character of the many situations which are, to say the least, ethically questionable. As its former optimism* regarding human perfectibility has receded sharply, its function as anguished protest against dehumanizing forces and structures has been gathering strength. Humanism now assumes a darker, more defensive posture: a drastic sense of human precariousness and ambiguity, a heightened anxiety over the threats to cherished humane values coming from technology, social conflict, or nuclear warfare, and a greater willingness to deal with questions of human *being*—all these have profoundly marked humanistic ethics of the present.

Nevertheless some older strains persist as well: the dignitative use of the word "man" (or its inclusive-language substitutes) as against reductive or destructive tendencies judged to be at work in philosophy, the sciences, political and economic conditions; the conviction that "ethics without God" (Kai Nielsen) has by now become a culturally necessary option; and a standing protest, usually issue-oriented, against what Erich Fromm called our "humanoid" mode of present-day existence.

It has been customary to describe humanistic ethics as "nontheistic" or even "atheistic," which though true enough is much too narrow and negative to be very illuminating. Quite apart from any simple opposition over the question of God, Christian ethics is profoundly indebted to humanist thought for clarifying ideas of what being human can be said to mean. The judgment of Paul Tillich (in *Morality and Beyond*) that the conflict between reason-determined ethics and faith-determined ethics is now obsolete must be taken seriously. Moreover it seems to be borne out by much recent work in the field. Instead of reasserting a revelational or "deontological" position, Christian ethicists appear far more ready to assume a problem-centered, contextual orientation which affords much common ground and cause with humanists.

Whether the issue under discussion concerns political morality, genetic manipulation, the right to live or die, racist or sexist oppression, theological commitments are more often muted than made explicit. If the recent debate between "context" and "principles" is as "misplaced" as James Gustafson believes, it has at least made clear that what humanists reject is not what Christians generally affirm, i.e., "authoritarian" or "divine command"* legitimizing of the moral life. The ethical work of those who affirm the latter is more and more being done in an indicative-descriptive mode, because dealing with such problems as brain death or abortion makes precise reference necessary. Such problems are not settled by appeals to scripture or Christian moral tradition, but are only made more compelling and complex thereby (see **Situation Ethics**).

So when Paul Lehmann refers to the "human indicative" as "the primary ethical factor," we notice unexpected affinities with humanistic ethics at a significant point; and similar statements by other Christian ethicists like Robert Johann and David Little stress that what makes an act moral is not obedience to some external imperative but rather one's freely chosen decision to make and keep human life human (Lehmann), to "order life cooperatively" (Little) or to "build the human" (Johann). At any rate the older pejorative dismissals of humanistic ethics as "rationalistic" or "hedonistic" have undoubtedly lost much of their former virulence, as Christians and humanists think and

act together in an ethically unacceptable state of affairs in the world common to both.

Is it nevertheless the case that the primary opposition between Christian and humanistic ways of ethical reflection remains in force? Where questions of human freedom* and responsibility* are involved, especially, can these ways be reconciled in theory? Humanistic ethics sees in freedom to choose and act the signal instance of "man's" unique standing in the known universe. It seeks to preserve and protect such freedom by distinguishing it from natural conditioning, on the one hand, and from supernatural invasion of privacy, on the other. In Auguste Comte's words, "man" has his own highest being, his so-called "God," in himself; according to Sartre, human life just happens and remains "absurd." Here freedom as self-motivation can only mean nonaccountability to any higher or lower determining power. That human beings can and do know, seek, and realize their own real good without relying upon any standard or support beyond themselves—is this not still the hallmark of any humanistic ethics?

Christian ethics, far from denying or belittling the truth of human freedom or its power of effective choice*, has always intended to affirm it, since any moral obligation would of course be meaningless without it. Yet it regards such freedom as a gift rather than a right, a created good which humans have abused and which therefore needs to be renewed and redeemed. "We are not our own light," in the words of Flannery O'Connor. Our freedom is the ambiguous source in us of both our alienation from and our reconciliation to God, who wills to realign and reinvigorate our freedom. Whatever obligation persons may have to seek and serve the good of others—an obligation recognized by humanists—is owed to a more-than-human endowment, creative and redemptive with respect to all human good.

Is the growth of modern and contemporary humanism only the fruit of a "tragic misunderstanding," as Henri de Lubac held? That is, can it be shown that humanism, instead of being inimical to Christian faith, is actually its corollary and explication? After all, there has always been, however hampered theologically, a Christian humanism. Present-day "liberation theologies" insist upon giving humankind its due, quite apart from considerations of a supernaturalist or extraneous law, will, or sanctioning; so too do the so-called theologies of process, hope, and political involvement (*see* **Liberation Theology; Political Theology**). The best defense of what Walter Muelder terms "the ethical edge" of Christianity would then become, not a contradicting antihumanism but rather a reassessment of the human situation and enterprise in terms afforded by Christian understanding of human "misery and grandeur," in Pascal's words.

The Christian estimate of humanistic ethics cannot be either a simple rejection or a straightforward acclamation. One may rejoice in the fact that humane values and virtues are indeed great and claim a high degree of devotion without presuming that they are self-explaining or self-justifying. A Christian doctrine of the human is no mere transcription of despair; Christianity can no longer be supposed to have a monopoly on the tragic sense of life. Human wretchedness and greatness are but two sides of the same truth. This truth comes to Christian expression with singular clarity in Berdyaev's "God is the meaning of human existence." But this declaration from the side of faith can only be made good if Christians are willing to confess and rectify those perversions of their faith which have made humanist protest possible and its critique at many points cogent. In order to show that belief in humanhood and belief in God belong together, Christian ethical thinkers will need to advance sounder interpretations and elicit stronger motivations with respect to what being human means than humanism alone has thus far been able to provide.

See **Dehumanization; Human Dignity; Human Rights; Image of God; Morality and Religion, Relations of; Persons and Personality; Respect for Persons; Secularism; Worldliness.**

H. J. Blackman, *Humanism,* 1968; E. Fromm, *Man for Himself,* 1947; J. Gustafson, *Theology and Ethics,* 1981; and *Christian Ethics and the Community,* 1971; R. Johann, *Building the Human,* 1968; P. Lehmann, *Ethics in a Christian Context,* 1963; K. Nielsen, *Ethics Without God,* 1973; R. Shinn, *Man: The New Humanism,* 1968; P. Tillich, *Morality and Beyond,* 1963.

ROGER HAZELTON

Humanitarianism

Humanitarianism is the principle of commitment to improve the human condition, particularly with regard to the exploited or marginalized members of society or of world society.

Drawing from humanist insights (*see* **Humanistic Ethics**) and from the concern with humanity in religious traditions, humanitarianism emerges as the commitment to improve living conditions for human beings, so that the basic necessities for living are available to all, and so that the possibility for a life-enhancing existence is available to all. This commitment is often based on compassion* or a sense of fellow feeling in the face of deliberate cruelty*. The response to such situations has been to try to alleviate the suffering*, especially where no solution to the situation is immediately foreseeable. On an international scale, the first "humanitarian laws" were the Declaration of St. Petersburg (1868), the Hague Convention (1899, 1907), and the Geneva Protocol and Convention (1925, 1949) which sought to apply humaneness even in time of war (*see* **Conventions**). By drawing on the humanitarian impulses of diverse philosophical and religious traditions, a universal principle focusing on the welfare of human beings was established. This impulse has also motivated action to alleviate distress within societies (*see* **Welfare State**). Increasingly the term is also being used to cover the humane treatment of other animate beings (*see* **Animals**).

Humanitarianism, through its ability to phrase a common impulse in diverse religions and philosophies, has been a force for the positive improvement of human living, especially where the diversity of such traditions and ideologies would have tended to make cooperation on the human project unlikely or impossible.

See **Charity; Dehumanization; Human Dignity; Human Rights; Hunger, World; Image of God; Persons and Personality; Philanthropy; Social Service of the Church; Welfare State.**

ALAN D. FALCONER

Humanity *see* **Human Dignity; Human Rights; Humanistic Ethics; Humanitarianism; Image of God; Natural Law; Natural Rights; Persons and Personality; Respect for Persons**

Humility

Though pride is a sin, humility—its opposite —is not so much a virtue as a grace. According to K. E. Kirk, "Worship alone can make us humble" (*The Vision of God,* abr. ed., p. 186).

Yet there are paradoxes about humility to be teased out. Augustine found it surprising that "there is something in humility to exalt the mind, and something in exaltation to abase it" (*City of God* 14.13). Aquinas noted the possibility of being proud of one's humility (*ST* II-II.38.2). What is odd on the face of it is the Christian teaching that the *reward* for being humble is to be exalted (Matt. 23: 12). Is humility really a good thing in itself, or a means to an end that will not be humility at all?

In biblical usage, there is the state of lowliness, undesirable to the natural human being, and the promise that the mighty shall be put down from their seats in favor of the humble (Luke 1:52). One might suppose that "Blessed are the meek, for they shall inherit the earth" (Matt. 5:5) is parallel with "Blessed are those who mourn, for they shall be comforted" (Matt. 5:4), and that to humble oneself, even to find oneself humiliated, is just part of the way of the cross, a doorway into the kingdom, not the kingdom itself (1 Peter 5:6). Yet humility and meekness* in some sense are praised for their own sakes as truly Christian characteristics (Matt. 11:29; Eph. 4:1–2; Col. 3:12). Theologies of liberation encounter similar paradoxes over "Blessed are you poor" (Luke 6:20).

Must humility, like some other kinds of human well-being, tend to be ruined by its attainment? Is it meant to be a lasting good at all? Is creaturely humility required just because we are sinful; or more fundamentally, because we are finite?

More fundamentally still, is human humility always in stark contrast with the unique worshipfulness of God? Or is there also a divine humility, of which human humbleness is not the correlative but the imitation? (Cf. John 13:1–17.)

Five senses of humility may be distinguished. Let it be said that two of them are erroneous. (1) Humility ought to have nothing to do with a *false* low opinion of oneself. If it is a matter of grace, it must somehow also be a matter of truth. (2) Even when the low opinion is justified, humility does not require self-loathing. The servile self-abase-

ment that comes from either of these misconceptions is a misleading caricature.

Three good senses remain. (3) There is objective lowliness: the unimportance which, paradoxically, is important to God. (4) There is creaturely reverence acknowledging glory not one's own (cf.1 Cor. 4:7). (5) There is the humility that is not foreign to God himself, the humility that is an aspect of *agapē* (1 Cor. 13:4–7), which empties itself for other people's sake (Phil. 2:5–11), which is the opposite of pride in the sense of self-centeredness. The humble in this sense can be exalted without losing their characteristic grace. They can exalt one another and find themselves heirs of the kingdom (Rom. 8:15–17). It is not paradoxical to say that this kind of humility has self-confidence, the self-confidence that can afford to take delight in attending to other people.

See **Pride.**

W. Beach and H. R. Niebuhr (eds.), *Christian Ethics: Sources of the Living Tradition,* 1955, esp. pp. 54–55, 61–62, 155–157, 164–165; K. E. Kirk, *The Vision of God,* 1931, VIII, II (b); abr. ed. 1934; W. Law, *A Serious Call to a Devout and Holy Life,* 1728, chs. 16, 17; C. S. Lewis, "The Weight of Glory," *They Asked for a Paper,* 1962, pp. 204–206; H. Sidgwick, *The Methods of Ethics,* 1874, ch. 10, sec. 2.

HELEN OPPENHEIMER

Hunger, World

Prior to 1970, Christian ethicists and church leaders focused little attention on the question of *world* hunger. Ancient settled biblical principle called for the provision of food as an act of charity* to sustain the poor, but in traditional subsistent agricultural economies, large-scale remedies for famine were few; and global remedies were unimaginable. "Feed the hungry" seemed an adequate summary of Jewish and Christian tradition in the matter.

The late 1960s and early 1970s saw an upsurge of ethical and church interest in world hunger. The subject quickly lost its apparent simplicity under the impact of global economics and communications. Surplus and famine became world economic facts. National economies flourished or staggered in response to international markets. Ecologists entered the world debate on "development," calling attention to the limit of the global ecosystem to sustain unlimited economic growth among humans. Demographers warned national and world policymakers that population curves drastically influence economic curves. Caught in the cross fire of this relatively new set of considerations, both capitalist and socialist politicians found their systems subjected to a critical test—what was their promise for feeding half a billion people on earth who are currently starving or undernourished?

That way of initiating the discussion was congenial to many Third World leaders and representatives of churches. But the economic, political, ecological, demographic, and ideological complexity of the subject— all on a global scale—faced ethics and theology with new issues, new also to the human community as a whole. A chief catalyst of the ethical and political debate among intellectuals was the biologist Garrett Hardin, author of a pair of widely read articles, "The Tragedy of the Commons" (1968) and "Lifeboat Ethics: The Case Against Helping the Poor" (1974). Central to the discussion that swirled around the claims of such articles were issues such as the following:

1. *What price should world society pay for the survival of all its current member societies?* Jesus said that "man shall not live by bread alone," in reply to demonic temptation that he assuage his own hunger by turning stones into bread. The text has often suggested to Christian ethicists that physical survival can be an idol. Humans must live by "every word . . . of God" (Matt. 4:4). This start toward a normative theory of value pluralism echoes in the refusal of some Third World leaders to "modernize" their local economies at the price of abolishing their traditional culture, which may call, for example, for large families and the leisure of village society. Hunger is a great evil, they agree; but industrialization and the dependencies of the world agricultural market may bring greater evil yet. Who are "developed" people to tell us otherwise?

Hardin and company replied to these claims bluntly: Choose your own compromise with world economics, but don't count on world charity. Either solve your food problem through world commerce and population control or consent to mass starvation of your people. Third World reaction to this message turned against the social injustice that Hardin seemed so blithely to accept on a world scale: Who are scientists and politicians from rich countries to tell us in poor countries what we must do to pull ourselves up in the world? What holds us down so much as the power of rich countries to shape our economies to *their* wants rather than our needs? Are we not supplying luxurious wealth to them when we sell our bananas or our uranium ore at prices which they determine? And as for sacrifices, the rich countries, by sacrificing little, could benefit us much. They owe us the cost of at least our survival, since we are helping to pay the cost of their affluence.

The precipitate of this stage of the debate was twofold among Christian ethicists: acknowledgment, with the scientists, that human survival has its costs and conditions; and acknowledgment, with Third World leaders, that rich nations do have the capacity and the obligation to pay some of the costs of at least the survival of the threatened "Fourth World." But how many of the costs? At what level of sacrifice to their own peoples and cultures? The neighbor-ethic of the gospel, if not the natural law of nations, requires Christians to side with the world's poor in this matter. But what that may mean for national and international policymaking of both rich and poor governments remains a bundle of open questions. Rejected here by Christian ethicists were all forms of egoistic and evolutionary-competitive normative theories of social ethics, such as are detectable in Hardin. At the root of the debate yawned drastically different views of social justice.

2. *Is starvation, in the modern world, ever just?* Hardin's unambiguous "yes" to this question came clothed in his lifeboat metaphor for the world resource crisis: exceed the "load" which the world ecosystem can carry, and you capsize the whole thing. In the name of survival for some, you may have to deny survival to others. The policy guide has to be the familiar triage ethic of military medicine: let the slightly wounded get well on their own, treat those who can only get well with help, and ignore those who will die anyway (*see* **Triage**).

The metaphor and its exposition were full of ethically enticing assumptions: the world context of the hunger problem, scientific claims about the future fate of whole nations, and notions about the just deserts of people inside and outside the world lifeboat system.

A few American ethicists such as Joseph

Fletcher reluctantly but firmly sided with the Hardin analysis and the Hardin version of justice here. But a majority moved to challenge the theory on all its levels—its science, economics, and theory of justice. The ethical use of scientific prediction, said they, is not to foresee the future but to state what it may be *if we do not act to make it otherwise.* Hardin thus tends to turn present fact into future fact, but his greatest fallacy is his assumption that people whose opportunities or ancestry puts them in a social lifeboat are exemplars of justice. The losers of history lose again. What justice is there in that?

Quite a bit, answer all those philosophers from Thomas Huxley to Robert Nozick who believe that inherited advantage can be just (*see* **Libertarianism**). Hardly any, answer all those from Augustine to John Rawls who believe that a just society requires norms of equality* and perpetual focus on the goal of making the weakest members stronger (*see* **Justice**).

On the whole, theological ethicists in the 1970s sought to avoid the scientism of Hardin and the evolutionary conservatism of Nozick. They maintained that biblical ethics requires Christians to "feed the hungry" (and "feed your enemy") even in a complex global economy. The right to life cannot be rationed. Human systems of power and exchange must be influenceable to just ends, or they are demonic. *Especially* in the age of world economic systems, with their food surpluses and planned economies, it is never just that "the least of these" should starve. World hunger, in this view, remains "the world's largest solvable health problem."

3. Who then should produce more, who consume less? With great persistence Third World critics have sought to turn the assumptions of the "lifeboat ethic" against its originators. On Hardin's overgrazed world "commons," said one theologian from South India, "American 'sheep' are consuming annually some thirty times as much per capita as are African or Asian 'sheep.' . . . The only way to save the commons is to starve the 'fat sheep' and stop them from multiplying at all!" Right now they are "multiplying" through their ability to import far more food than the poor countries, often at the cost of distorting the economies of the poor who should be raising corn and cattle on land now producing coffee and bananas. But stubborn questions remain. Do such export-import

systems only perpetuate the historic injustices of world imperialism? Or are they hedges against yet further deterioration in a poor country's ability to feed itself?

The answers of any contemporary person to these questions will identify him or her with contrasting ideologies, political policies, and ethical theories. Jacques Loup of France spoke from the middle of the world development debate when he said in 1980, "In the coming years, the reconciliation of the imperative of justice with the necessity of growth may indeed constitute the greatest challenge of world poverty." Growth for whom? At whose expense? And by what yet-uninvented mechanisms of world power and exchange? Many of these questions lead away from ethical discourse toward the discourse of policymakers; but—as we have seen—a salient dynamic of the discourse among ethicists in the 1970s was its rapid escalation from simple concern for hungry people to a wrestle with the imponderables of economics, politics, and ideology on a world scale. Accordingly they found themselves entering into analysis and prescription concerning such questions as economic life-styles and foreign aid policy in their own nations. If Christians of affluent countries discipline their consumption of food, will they make more available to the world's poor; or will they merely lessen the effective demand for food production in a sector of the world market that will not, in any event, give or sell its surplus to poor countries? Must American and British Christians continue to consume their coffee and tea while working to reform the world trade system so that the price of these products rises enough to benefit their Third World producers? A new version of the old split between personal and social ethics heaves into view here: Do personal consumption habits influence international economics, or does a serious ethic of world hunger focus on the policies of governments and multinational corporations? What is the proper Christian leaven in the lump of rich-nation politics: exemplary modest life-styles, or the hard political work of getting an entire affluent society to show preferential treatment to the world's poor?

Debate on this range of questions in the 1970s concentrated among Christian ethicists and church leaders in the USA. At its beginning, European and Third World leaders cast a suspicious eye at the focus on hunger in the American churches: "There go the rich Americans again, thinking that they can feed the world with their charity and ignoring the systematic injustices of world commerce from which they benefit." But in the USA and elsewhere, the discussion headed straight toward those systematic concerns, opening a wide door upon an arena where clashing assumptions of ethics and giant organized interests contend for power to shape the global future. For many, to go through that door was to change their world view, to discover multiple obligations to world neighbors, and to repent of their intellectual provincialism.

See **Charity; Economic Development; Ecumenical Movement; Environmental Ethics; Equality; Future Generations, Obligations to; International Order; Justice; Liberation Theology; Life, Sacredness of; Love; Mutual Aid; Oppression; Philanthropy; Population Policy; Poverty; Property; Social Service of the Church; Triage; Wealth.**

L. R. Brown, *By Bread Alone,* 1974; P. G. Brown and H. Shue (eds.), *Food Policy: The Responsibility of the United States in the Life and Death Choices,* 1977; W. Byron (ed.), *The Causes of World Hunger,* 1982; G. R. Lucas, Jr., and T. W. Ogletree (eds.), *Lifeboat Ethics: The Moral Dilemmas of World Hunger,* 1976; J. A. Nelson, *Hunger for Justice: The Politics of Food and Faith,* 1980.

DONALD W. SHRIVER, JR.

Hunting *see* Animals

Hybris

Hybris (or hubris) is a Greek term taken over by Christians with its Greek meaning. It is used to denote the madness of human pride* arrogantly setting out to defy the gods. Christians would describe hybris as the sinful folly of human beings setting out to control what humans cannot control, even if they wish to do this for the glory of God, the furtherance of the gospel, and the welfare of all people.

R. E. C. BROWNE

Hypocrisy

"Hypocrisy," which in Greek denoted playing a part in a drama, is defined by the OED as "the assuming of a false appearance of virtue or goodness, with dissimulation of real character or inclination, especially in respect of religious life or belief." In the Sermon on

the Mount Jesus admonished his followers not to be like the hypocrites, who give alms ostentatiously "that they may be praised by men," or who "love to stand and pray in the synagogues and at the street corners, that they may be seen by men," or who "disfigure their faces that their fasting may be seen by men," noting that their public reputation is "their reward" (Matt. 6:1–5). Jesus also condemned as hypocrites those who criticize others, observing the speck in their neighbor's eye, while neglecting the log in their own eye (Matt. 7:3–5). Hypocrisy masks a person's true feelings and thoughts and is thus deceptive, insincere, and inauthentic. It is common for groups as well as for individuals; for example, as Reinhold Niebuhr noted, nations often mask their motives of self-interest by appeals to moral principles. Yet hypocrisy is not unambiguous, because, as La Rochefoucauld observed, it is "a tribute that vice pays to virtue." Right actions may be performed and good outcomes may be produced hypocritically. "The exposure of hypocrisy," Michael Walzer writes, "is certainly the most ordinary and it may also be the most important form of moral criticism." But unmasking hypocrisy has its own perils and may lead to cruel and vicious actions.

See **Authenticity; Honesty; Self-Deception; Truthfulness.**

R. Niebuhr, *Moral Man and Immoral Society,* 1932; J. Shklar, *Ordinary Vices,* 1984.

JAMES F. CHILDRESS

Id

The Latin form used in psychological literature in English to render Sigmund Freud's term *das Es* (literally "the it"). The id designates one of the three structures, levels, orders, or institutions into which psychoanalytic theory divides the human mind. Freud first introduced the id in 1923, but while the term came into popular usage along with ego* and superego* (the names he gave to the other two structures) the idea of an id has not found much support in nonpsychoanalytic approaches to psychology (*see* **Psychoanalysis**).

The id is said to be the most primitive level of psychic organization. It contains the basic instinctual drives concerned with such matters as hunger, sex, and self-preservation, and these are said to be invested with large quantities of psychic energy seeking discharge. The forces of the id are blind forces, fundamentally amoral, and not concerned with considerations of prudence, discretion, or the needs or rights of others. They simply seek to find expression. Within the id the so-called *primary process* prevails: the contents are chaotically organized so that opposites, for example, are not mutually exclusive, ideas lack synthesis, affects or feelings may be related to inappropriate objects, and the whole process is governed by the overriding principle of obtaining gratification or pleasure. The id does not learn more acceptable forms of behavior and has to be controlled by the ego, which develops from it to bring some reality factors into the picture. Id-ego conflict is, in Freud's view, a major source of neurosis.

Contrary to some popular misconceptions, Freudian theory does not advocate the uninhibited or unrestrained expression of id impulses. It clearly recognizes that this would be intolerable both for the individual and for society. It was Freud's own dictum that "where id was, there shall ego be," and one of the functions he saw for psychoanalysis was to help people develop positive and appropriate regulation of basic impulses.

S. Arieti (ed.), *American Handbook of Psychiatry,* 1959; S. Freud, *The Ego and the Id* (1923), ET 1927.

GRAEME M. GRIFFIN

Idealism *see* Idealist Ethics; Realism

Idealist Ethics

An idealist, in common parlance, is anyone committed first and foremost to pursuing ideals. The expressions "ethical idealism" and "idealistic ethics" are thus sometimes used to mark a contrast with the "realism"* of moralists who stress sober assessment of things as they really are. But the phrase "idealist ethics" typically conveys a different sense altogether, especially in philosophy, where idealism names a metaphysical or epistemological doctrine. An idealist, in this sense, holds that reality—or the only reality we can know—is ultimately mental or spiritual in nature. Idealist ethics, then, refers to the moral philosophy or social outlook associated with some form of this doctrine, and is often restricted further to the views of post-Kantian idealists in Germany, England, and America.

Philosophers began using the term "idealism" in the 18th century. Gottfried Leibniz (1646–1716), one of the first to use the term, contrasted idealism with materialism, and defended the antimaterialist view that the ultimate constituents of reality are *monads,* which he took to be perceiving and appetitive (though not necessarily conscious) entities. Matter, he argued, is composed of monads and hence cannot be ontologically basic. George Berkeley (1685–1753), who referred to his own position as immaterialism, was concerned to resolve a problem in Lockean psychology—that of figuring out how, if the mind perceives only its own ideas, one could ever tell which ideas resembled their objects. He argued that "nothing can be like an idea but an idea" and that we can therefore avoid skepticism about objects of perception only by dispensing with belief in a mind-independent world and with the theory of knowledge as accurate representation of such a world.

Immanuel Kant (1724–1804) did not dispense with belief in the world of things as they are in themselves, or *noumena,* but he did argue that only the "world of appearances," or *phenomena,* can be known. Space, time, and the categories of the understanding are, according to Kant, conditions of the possibility of experience, not features of noumenal reality. The phenomenal world is, therefore, a constructed world, dependent upon the activity of a "transcendental ego" and the structures of the knowing mind. Empirical science, by means of which theoretical reason attains knowledge of phenomena, is, however, only one important sphere of intellectual activity. Another is morality, the realm in which practical reason legislates for itself the basic law of right action, the categorical imperative, and procures its own coherence by postulating God, freedom, and immortality—the indispensable tenets of rational faith. By limiting the scope of theoretical reason to knowledge of the world of appearances, Kant meant to make room for such faith. If science neither supports nor undermines beliefs about noumenal reality, practical reason is free to entertain faith in God and immortality. If science's deterministic explanations cannot reach beyond the world of appearances, it cannot rule out the possibility of freedom. Kant's program, then, involved marking out the basic domains of human thought and culture, offering a separate account of each, and establishing limits beyond which each fundamental employment of reason should not transgress.

Kant's "transcendental idealism" is the great transitional moment in the history of idealism, and his successors took inspiration from his attempt to map the entirety of human thought and culture. They were also quick, however, to abandon his division of culture into essentially separate domains grounded in distinct compartments of mind, to dismiss his notion of unknowable noumena, and to extend his conception of freedom. Subsequent idealism was in many ways deeply indebted to Kant, but many of its major themes, not least of all in ethics, can only be defined as reactions against his thought.

Johann Gottlieb Fichte (1762–1814) transformed the free rational will of Kant's moral philosophy into an absolute will that generates both itself and the field in which it acts. This absolute is expressed in the individual's consciousness of duty and also in the institutions and laws of society. The individual's task is to find and fulfill his or her vocation as part of society, thereby achieving self-realization in free identification with universal will. Fichte intended this conception of self-realization to overcome Kant's sharp separation of duty from self-interest.

G. W. F. Hegel (1770–1831) thought Fichte's conception of the absolute as universal will was one-sided, and portrayed the absolute instead as spirit dialectically realizing itself in history. Hegel followed Kant in holding that all knowledge is mediated by concepts, but concepts, for Hegel, are subject to change as the history of spirit progressively unfolds. From Hegel's vantage point, Kant's philosophy was not a timeless critique of reason as such but rather the expression of spirit in one stage of its development, a stage in which spirit had become alienated from itself. This self-alienation is evident, according to Hegel, in Kant's skepticism about things-in-themselves, in the formal abstraction of his categorical imperative, and in his separation of duty from inclination. The form of consciousness expressed in Kant's philosophy is one of division and discord of a sort that can finally be overcome, on Hegel's view, only in his own conception of absolute spirit. Kant's moral philosophy lost sight of the origins of ethical consciousness in the immediacy of an unreflective ethos, and it could not yet foresee the realization of fully self-

conscious ethical spirit in the rational state. Now that Kant's age has been overcome, we are freed from the empty abstractions of the categorical imperative and free to identify ourselves with the concrete ethos of our community, assured that this ethos expresses the immanent rationality of spirit (see **Kantian Ethics; Hegelian Ethics**).

The leading English idealists, Thomas Hill Green (1836–1882), Bernard Bosanquet (1848–1923), and Francis H. Bradley (1846–1924), turned to German idealism for help in combating British empiricism. Their ethical writings were directed mainly against individualism* and utilitarianism*, but they borrowed from Kant and Hegel very selectively. Of the three, Bosanquet was the most dependent upon Hegel. Green, in particular, was highly suspicious of dialectical method. None made much of Hegel's historicism. All three, however, used Hegelian ideas to give moral duty a concrete locus in social life. Green did not preach the identity of finite minds in the infinite, though he did maintain that the manifestation of the infinite in the finite constitutes a sort of social bond such that the self can achieve its realization only in community. Green used idealism as a metaphysical backdrop for attacks on laissez-faire individualism and for a highly influential defense of the state's responsibility in matters of social welfare and education. Bradley, whose political vision was more conservative than Green's, relied heavily upon a Hegelian conception of "the concrete universal" as a way to overcome the individualism and abstractness he found in both Kant and the utilitarians. For Bradley, the goal of moral striving must be highly concrete without falling short of the universal—the duties of a particular station in an organic community that transcends merely individual interests.

The American philosopher Josiah Royce (1855–1916), who contributed significantly to idealist ethics in his own right, criticized Bradley for allowing individuality to dissolve too completely in the absolute. Still working within Hegel's influence, Royce sought to restore what he took to be a proper balance between the personal and the communal in the fully realized self. Moral obligation, for Royce, consists in loyalty* to the community of all individuals.

Idealism no longer survives as a philosophical movement, but many of its major ethical arguments and themes have proved remarkably resilient when separated from idealist metaphysics. Both Marxism and American pragmatism*, for example, have adopted and retained criticisms of individualism, utilitarianism, and Kantianism first articulated in the idealist tradition, while also echoing the historicism and holism of Hegel's approach to ethics.

A. C. Ewing (ed.), *The Idealist Tradition: From Berkeley to Blanshard,* 1957; A. J. M. Milne, *The Social Philosophy of English Idealism,* 1962.

JEFFREY STOUT

Ideals *see* **Aspiration; Excellence; Norms**

Ideology

The term "ideology" was introduced into political discourse by the French philosopher Destutt de Tracy in 1795 to denote the general science of ideas, and the term passed into general usage almost immediately and was used by Napoleon and subsequently by Marx. In the 20th century the term has come to acquire two rather different usages.

The first and more general usage refers to the range of theories, ideas, concepts, and values that characterize a particular sociopolitical doctrine or belief system. So today we frequently refer to Marxist ideology, Fascist ideology, liberal ideology, etc. Such ideologies have at their center a theory of human nature—our needs, interests, rights, etc.—and from this theory more specifically political doctrines are derived relating to the nature of the state and the fundamental types of obligations that human beings may be thought to have to one another.

A central feature of the tradition of Western political thought has been a concern about whether such general theories, which purport to be about universal characteristics of human nature and human life, can be rationally grounded. The pervasive conviction in the 20th century that they cannot be so grounded and that they rather reflect the value preferences of those who hold them perhaps explains why they have come to be called "ideologies."

The second usage is more technical and is internal to Marxist historical materialism. It is central to Marx's view that the basic explanatory tool in the explanation of human history is the production and reproduction of material life or economic activity. This activity has two aspects: (1) the means of production—labor, tools, raw materials; (2) relations of production, notably the class relation, which enable a particular set of the means of production to be exploited. Corresponding to this material base are forms of social consciousness or ideology concerning human nature, the state, the economy, art and human spirituality which change as the economic base changes. These modes of consciousness, or ideologies, are not to be seen as their protagonists see them, as all-embracing, true theories about such things, but rather they serve the interests of the dominant economic class. As such, ideologies embody false consciousness: they purport to teach general and universal truths about aspects of the human condition, whereas they serve the widest possible social and political function of making the existing class and power relations appear natural and legitimate to those who are most disadvantaged by them. Ideology therefore performs a mystifying and consoling function, misrepresenting social reality in various respects and inducing acceptance of the status quo. This view of ideology was clearly applied to Christianity by Marx. In his view this Christian ideology encouraged political quietism and transferred the hope for a better life to the world to come.

See **Marxist Ethics; Rationalization.**

D. McLellan (ed.), *Karl Marx: Selected Writings,* 1977; K. Mannheim, *Ideology and Utopia,* ET 1936; B. Parekh, *Marx's Theory of Ideology,* 1982; M. Seliger, *Ideology and Politics,* 1976.

RAYMOND PLANT

Idolatry *see* **Decalogue; Patristic Ethics**

Ignorance

I. General Theological, Philosophical, and Ethical Issues

In Christian ethics, discussions of ignorance are usually related to problems about the culpability of agents for their actions. When, and how, does ignorance exculpate someone who has performed a morally wrong action?

Much of the discussion in Western tradition, and especially in Roman Catholic moral theology, takes its origins from Aristotle's treatment of it in his *Nicomachean Ethics* 3.1. Aristotle distinguishes between ignorance of the universal, which, in his view, does not excuse, and ignorance of the particular, which does (or may). An example of this might be found in the story of Oedipus. He was ignorant of the fact that it was his mother he married, and this is an excuse. Had he, however, been ignorant of the wrongness of marrying one's mother, he would have had no excuse.

It may be that Aristotle's discussion should be read in a legal context. But the distinction he drew between the two kinds of ignorance was frequently taken over into moral contexts, and was thereby linked with a discussion whether it was possible for a responsible adult to be ignorant of moral principles. The general answer (to be found, for instance, in Aquinas, *ST* I-II.94.3) was that it was not possible for any (responsible) human being to be ignorant of the basic moral principles, though a person might well be ignorant of more detailed and specific principles (*see* **Synderesis**). Aquinas held that such ignorance could excuse, since he held that a person was morally obliged to do what he or she believed to be right, even if mistaken in this belief (*ST* I.19.5–6). And it was generally acknowledged that ignorance of facts could excuse. But neither in the case of ignorance of moral principle, nor in the case of ignorance of fact, was it held that ignorance excused if the ignorance was itself the result of blameworthy behavior on the part of the agent, such as an unwillingness to take reasonable pains to discover the true state of affairs, or deliberately putting oneself into a condition (e.g., drunkenness) in which one would not realize the true state of affairs. Noncognitivist theories of ethics (*see* **Metaethics**), denying as they do that there is any such thing as moral knowledge, must also deny that there is such a state as ignorance of moral principles. In such theories, it does not seem that disputes could even arise about whether such ignorance would or would not constitute an excuse. And many cognitivists (*see* **Metaethics**) also would dispute the view that ignorance of a moral principle was ever culpable, despite what Aristotle might have held. Such ignorance might perhaps be attributable to inadequate education, or to mental illness, rather than to moral defect.

Moreover, the sharp distinction between ignorance of moral principle and ignorance of facts is more difficult to sustain than appears at first sight.

It has been alleged that Rom. 1:18–21 provides biblical support for the view that there are at least some moral principles which no normal adult human being can honestly fail to know, though the precise exegesis of this passage is controversial.

What is not in dispute is that when ignorance does properly function as an excuse, it does so because it is regarded as appropriate to take the agent's description of the action as the proper basis on which to make assessments of blameworthiness.

See **Intention; Responsibility.**

GERARD J. HUGHES

II. Distinctions in Moral Theology

In the moral sphere, the word "ignorance" is used to denote a lack of knowledge which one ought to have. The word "error" is used by some moral theologians in the same sense, and no distinction from ignorance is intended.

From the point of view of that which is not known, there can be ignorance of a fact and ignorance of the law (see above).

From the point of view of the person who is ignorant, ignorance may be "*invincible*" or "*vincible.*" Invincible ignorance is that which persists after all reasonable efforts have been made to dispel it. Vincible ignorance is that which a reasonable effort could and should overcome. What is reasonable depends on the circumstances, for example, the importance of the subject matter, and the opportunities afforded for inquiry or reflection. Vincible ignorance, since it is in some degree a person's own fault, does not excuse from blame any action to which it may lead. Invincible ignorance, on the other hand, does excuse.

The textbooks subdivide vincible ignorance into "simple," "crass," and "affected" or "deliberate." "Simple" is where some effort has been made to overcome the ignorance, greater effort might have been made, but failure to do so is not very blameworthy. "Crass" is where virtually no attempt has been made to dispel it, and there is little or no excuse for the omission to do so. "Affected" ignorance is a deliberate act of will by which people determine to make no effort to find out the truth in order that they may feel free to do whatever it is they want to do.

From the point of view of the action which follows from the ignorance, the textbooks distinguish between "antecedent," "concomitant," and "consequent." Antecedent ignorance is an involuntary ignorance which is the cause of an action which, but for it, the agent would not have performed. For example, a motorist driving with all reasonable caution runs over a man whom she does not know to be in the road. Concomitant ignorance is also an involuntary ignorance, but is not the cause of the action which follows, in the sense that the agent would still have performed the action even if he or she had not been ignorant. For example, a murderer intent on killing his enemy "accidentally" runs the person over in his car. Such a man is morally guilty of murder, though technically and in law probably only of homicide or at worst manslaughter. Consequent ignorance is willful ignorance and therefore the same as affected ignorance, if directly willed, or crass ignorance if indirectly willed, that is, the result of gross negligence.

The relevance of ignorance to a judgment on the culpability of an action, and the importance of an accurate understanding of the different kinds of ignorance, are obvious. It is not surprising that moral theologians devote considerable space to the subject.

R. C. MORTIMER

Illegitimacy

An illegitimate child is one born out of marriage, not being the child of validly married parents. Legitimacy is an important element in most laws of inheritance. The Roman Catholic Church has clear definitions of legitimacy, and illegitimate children can be legitimated by the Holy See. English law has removed some of the disabilities of illegitimate children.

HERBERT WADDAMS

Image of God (*Imago Dei*)

"Then God said, 'Let us make man in our image, after our likeness; and let them have dominion. . . . ' So God created man in his own image, in the image of God he created him; male and female he created them" (Gen. 1:26f.; cf. 5:1 and 9:6; see also 1 Cor. 11:7 and James 3:9). The NT also views Christ as the image of the invisible God (2 Cor. 4:4; Col. 1:15), reflecting God's glory (Heb. 1:3), and

the Christian as renewed in God's image by God's regenerative power through the Holy Spirit (2 Cor. 3:18). In theological anthropology, so important to Christian moral theology and ethics, the image of God has been central in debates about what was present before, what was lost in, and what remains after the Fall. E. Brunner (*Man in Revolt: A Christian Anthropology,* ET 1947, p. 92) contends that "the whole Christian doctrine of man hangs upon the interpretation of this expression [in his image and after his likeness]. . . . The history of this idea is the history of the Western understanding of man."

Distinguishing *imago Dei* and *similitudo Dei,* rather than viewing them as Hebrew parallelism, Roman Catholic theology has held that *similitudo Dei,* which consisted of certain supernatural endowments (*donum superadditum*), was lost in the Fall, but that the *imago Dei* (including reason and free will) was not fundamentally affected. According to Reformation theology, original sin* affects the core of human nature, but there were also disputes among Reformation theologians. As Van Harvey writes, "In general, the Lutheran tradition emphasized the loss of the image of God while the Calvinist tradition regarded it as corrupted but not lost. Roman Catholic theologians considered the Protestant view antihumanistic and destructive of natural morality. Protestants, on the other hand, regarded the Roman Catholic view as implying that sin did not go to the root of human existence." Questions of natural law* and natural theology are obviously connected with doctrines of the image of God.

Although the image of God is often construed as reason and free will, it has also been interpreted as spiritual capacities, such as self-transcendence or the capacity for and the call to relationship with God, and as excellences, such as righteousness*. Some theologians have objected to the concentration on intellectual and spiritual aspects of humanity to the neglect of the external body. A few have argued that the image of God is the body, while others have argued that it is a combination of the spiritual and physical in psychophysical unity (*see* **Body; Embodiment**).

There are numerous ethical implications of different interpretations of the image of God, but a few examples will suffice. (1) The Genesis passage connects creation in the image of God with human "dominion" over the rest of creation. Humans are in but are distinguished from the rest of nature. Even if, as in the royal ideology of the ancient Near East, humans are God's representatives in parts of his kingdom, their rule should be like God's and should not be exploitative. (For a discussion of stewardship, *see* **Environmental Ethics.**) (2) Human dignity* is an alien dignity, not intrinsic dignity; it is bestowed on human beings through their creation in God's image and their redemption. (3) Genesis (9:6) connects the prohibition of taking human life with creation in God's image (*see* **Life, Sacredness of; Homicide**). (4) As the NT passages suggest, the doctrine of the *imago Dei* can support a call to conform to the "image" of Christ, who is "the image of the invisible God" (*see* **Imitation of Christ**).

J. M. Childs, Jr., *Christian Ethics and Anthropology,* 1978; V. A. Harvey, *A Handbook of Theological Terms,* 1964; N. W. Porteous, "Image of God," *IDB* II, 1962; G. von Rad et al., *"eikōn," TDNT* II, 1964; G. von Rad, *Genesis,* ET 1961, rev. ed. 1972.

JAMES F. CHILDRESS

Imitation of Christ

Human ethical ideals seem to require some particular focusing in a personal life to integrate values and provide motive power. The life of Christ for Christians is such a unifying and integrating factor, and the imitation of Christ as an ideal is of both psychological and theological importance.

Imitation in human development is not something that belongs only to childhood; mimesis continues to play an important role in the growth of human personality. There seems to be a universal tendency to regard one life history as a paradigm and to treat some historical personage as an archetype.

Theologically one of the presuppositions of belief in the incarnation in Christ is humanity's need of an exemplar. Moreover, the fact that the Christian sees Christ as a *redemptive* model shows that more is at stake in the imitation of Christ than the satisfaction of a psychological need. The imitation of God in Christian belief is not a means to salvation but the fruit of it, and it inevitably assumes the form of the imitation of Christ, which is a possibility through grace by the work of the Holy Spirit.

According to the NT the imitation of Christ consists of a being conformed to his humility, patience, hope, and love. This is the essence of the Christian ethic as modeled on the attitude of Christ.

It is a pity that the word "imitation" suggests uncreative copying. A reminder of the way that word is used in the history of art would prevent this misunderstanding. In the arts and in music imitation as commonly understood would be a hopelessly feeble word for the creative and original quality of variations based on previous themes. In the NT the imitation of Christ as an ethical ideal is not some endeavor to copy literally the historical Jesus, but is conceived to be the work of the Holy Spirit molding the life of the Christian into some likeness of Christ. Both John and Paul in their writing on the work of the Spirit think of it as a kind of doing a Christ over again in terms of the life and action of the Christian communities.

The history of the imitation of Christ in Christian ethical tradition does show a tendency toward literal *mimesis.* One thinks, for example, of the literal attempts of Francis of Assisi to copy Christ, and in the light of this Luther was right to prefer the term *conformitas* to *imitatio.* In a fully developed exposition of the place of this ideal in the Christian tradition, the terms *conformitas* and *imitatio* would need to be related. The imitative life of the Christian involves both God's activity by the Spirit in grace in conforming human beings to his image in Christ (*conformitas*), and that of human beings focusing their moral and spiritual attention on the exemplar Christ (*imitatio*).

Any modern presentation of the Christian ethical ideal of the imitation of Christ needs to come to terms with contemporary historical criticism. Certainly the NT Gospels are not historical biographies in the sense that they were written to satisfy curiosity about personal facts concerning Jesus. The NT Gospels are "lives of Christ" for potential disciples. The Gospels are about discipleship at the same time as they are about Christ, and in this sense one can speak of them as allegories of Christian discipleship, with the corollary that the life of the disciple can be to the discerning eyes of faith to a greater or lesser degree an allegory of Christ. The use made of the tradition about Jesus was determined by something very like the *imitatio Christi* ideal. This provided a main impetus to tell stories about Jesus, but it would be foolhardy to suppose that this was the only motive or that it was entirely free from historical controls. It is more likely that one of the assumptions behind the early transmission of the material about Jesus was the imitation of Christ, and this may have exercised a conserving influence before the idea was sufficiently formative to have strong inventive potency. This may have led to the retention rather than the loss of reliable fact. There are features of the character of Jesus, for example, which, clearly, were imperfectly assimilated during the time of his life but which yet find a place in the records. One could instance his attitude to children and animals. There is no evidence that these attitudes were appreciated in the early church. It is possible to argue that it was the faithfulness of the Evangelists to historical memory which led them to represent Jesus as dealing with children and speaking of animals in a way that they did not understand or really sympathize with but felt to be clearly characteristic of him.

Finally the imitation of Christ as an ethical ideal needs to be conceived in terms not of a constant looking back to a past model but of a living process that attains its goal in the future. Christians are in the process of being made like Christ, but full likeness is always for historical persons that which is yet to be. "It does not yet appear what we shall be, but we know that when he appears we shall be like him, for we shall see him as he is" (1 John 3:2). For the Christian the model lies in the future as much as in the past. Christ is, to use Gabriel Marcel's phrase, "a memory of the future."

See **Norms; Goodness; Jesus, Ethical Teaching of; New Testament Ethics; Eschatological Ethics.**

D. Bonhoeffer, *Ethics,* ET 1955; I. Gobry, *Le modèle en morale,* 1962; J. M. Gustafson, *Christ and the Moral Life,* 1968; E. Malatesta, S.J. (ed.), *Imitating Christ,* 1974; K. Ward, *Ethics and Christianity,* 1970.

E. J. TINSLEY

Immigration *see* **Race Relations; Racism; Refugees**

Immorality *see* **Norms; Right and Wrong; Righteousness; Sin(s)**

Imperative *see* **Categorical Imperative; Divine Command Morality; Norms**

Imperialism

Imperialism is not condemned in the NT. On the contrary, Jesus shows no sign of seeing the struggle against the Roman Empire as being any part of his mission, or of setting his face against the numerous imperialistic passages of the OT. One has therefore to bring modern imperialism under moral judgment with at best indirect guidance from scripture. In liberation theology* this is done in ways that attach central importance to selected scriptural material, but the following remarks are prudential rather than theological.

At the present time, we are living close to the end of a period of intense political change constituted by the collapse of the European empires in which the states of Western Europe explicitly and proudly subjected a large part of the world to colonial status (*see* **Colonialism**). Much of what is said about imperialism by religious commentators and in international forums needs to be understood in this historical context. For example, the UN General Assembly has, increasingly since the late 1950s, become an organization whose majority is committed to supporting and furthering the process of decolonization. One of its main reproaches to the so-called pariah states, Israel and South Africa, is that they are objectionable vestiges of the era of European imperialism. This charge continues to be reiterated even though they are in fact sovereign states with aims and interests which conflict at many points with those of the colonial power (the UK) which can in some sense be said to have created them.

Another major preoccupation of the successor states which have emerged with the "end of empire" is their abject dependence on the richer and stabler countries of "the north." Their resentment of this dependence is often articulated in terms of the "covert imperialism" to which they see themselves as being subjected.

The notion of imperialism is stretched still further in the widely believed argument that the two superpowers (USA, USSR) have subordinated almost all of the world to a "bloc system" in which nominally sovereign states are reduced to being mere pawns and proxies. "Soviet imperialism" is thus often used to refer to *both* the internal domination by Russia and Russians over the other republics and peoples of that vast country *and* the Soviet claim to have a right to intervene in its sphere of influence (recognized by the great powers at the Yalta Conference, asserted more vigorously in the Brezhnev Doctrine, and now perhaps interpreted to cover Afghanistan as well as Eastern Europe). The term "American imperialism" is used in a somewhat similar way (not always by the same people!) to refer to the long-established US practice of intervention in Latin America (first declared in the Monroe Doctrine) and the growing tendency since 1945 for US military intervention to occur in many parts of the world.

Has the word "imperialism" become so stretched by these and other analogies to the legally constituted empires of former times that it is no longer useful, an empty pejorative? Probably not: international order*, as we now know it, is grounded in the mutuality of sovereign states, and imperialism is a systematic, barefaced affront to the sovereignty of peoples, involving, as it does, the claim of one state to subject alien peoples to political rule. Even if there are no formal empires at present, many degrees of subjection to foreign domination continue to exist, and argument is bound to continue about where the line is to be drawn between legitimate control of the weaker by the stronger, and intervention so extreme as to amount to the fundamentally objectionable practice of imperialism. It seems clear that the idea of national self-determination, according meaningful statehood to any people desiring it, which was mooted by Woodrow Wilson after World War I, is doomed to remain a dream. So long as it does so and disparities of state power continue, moral and political dispute about which political inequalities amount to imperialism seems bound to continue.

See **International Order; National Sovereignty; State.**

G. W. Gong, *The Standard of 'Civilization' in International Society,* 1984.

BARRIE PASKINS

In Vitro Fertilization *see* Reproductive Technologies

Incest

Incest involves sexual contact between persons within prohibited degrees of kinship. Most frequently incest takes place between father and daughter, or stepfather and stepdaughter. Sibling incest is also found, and for some generations the Egyptian pharaohs and pre-Columbian Incas considered brother-sister marriage normative. Grandfather-granddaughter, uncle-niece, and (rarely) mother-son incest may occur; and the relationship may be homosexual as well as heterosexual. Typically, incest arises within a family unit that is already disturbed. Chronic disharmony in the marital relationship is often to be found. Where incest occurs, the consequences for a girl may include neurotic symptoms, depression, disturbed self-evaluation, and mistrust of men, the latter often having an adverse effect on subsequent marriage. Stability and good nonsexual relationships within the family are important for the development of the child's personality. In addition, incest is genetically risky. Children born of incest have an increased risk of recessive disorders and congenital malformations.

H. Maisch, *Incest,* 1973; J. Renvoize, *Incest,* 1982.

ELIZABETH R. MOBERLY

Indeterminism *see* **Free Will and Determinism; Libertarianism**

Indifferent Acts *see* **Adiaphora; Norms**

Individualism

The essential Christian belief in the person-in-community is easily polarized into two opposing abstractions, individualism and collectivism*. Each expresses a partial truth and a partial distortion of the Christian understanding.

Individualism magnifies the valid experience of the self and minimizes the social formation and involvement of the self. It starts with individual persons. Society*, then, is the aggregate of individuals, and social institutions* exist to serve individuals. The individualist esteems freedom* and autonomy*, and is skeptical of social solidarity and authority*.

Individuality is not, in historic fact, the primary datum in human experience. Primitive tribes and ancient empires have usually been more impressed with the social unit than with the individual. But individualism, like so many of the themes of Western society, has roots in the history of both the Greeks and the Hebrews.

In Hellenic society there were individualist impulses, variously related to social identification, in the Promethean myth, in the Periclean oration in Thucydides, in the tragic heroes of drama, in the satires on personality in comedy. The Sophists* of the 5th century B.C. included radical individualists, highly critical of society and tradition. Socrates (*see* **Socratic Ethics**) is remembered as the relentless questioner, whose martyrdom in 399 B.C. demonstrated the power of a conscience that refused to surrender to the popular will, even while affirming his loyalty to Athens. Although his disciple Plato (*see* **Platonic Ethics**) advocated an organic, hierarchical society, the Cynics* claimed to follow the Socratic logic to its consequences in a stubborn, eccentric individualism. Epicurus (*see* **Epicureanism, Ethics of**), with an atomistic doctrine of nature and of the self, minimized the importance of society.

The Bible took a different path in the discovery of the person. The early sources emphasize the "corporate personality" of the tribe or of Israel. But the call for fidelity* and personal decision* came to distinguish the individual from the society. The hope for the nation became the hope for a remnant. The punishment of the family or tribe for the sins of some of its members gave way to law that fixed guilt and responsibility upon individuals (e.g., Deut. 24:16). The prophets (*see* **Prophetic Ethics**), while feeling solidarity with their people, became lonely in their alienation from their kin. "I sat alone," wrote Jeremiah (Jer. 15:17); and his writings showed a quality of self-awareness never before expressed. Ezekiel emphasized personal responsibility to the extent of an unreal denial of social solidarity (Ezek. 18:1–4). The exilic and postexilic psalmists frequently showed a penetrating quality of introspection and recognition of the inner life of the person. Late Jewish eschatology transferred the locus of hope from the historical society, in which persons found gratification by anticipation, to a consummation in which each person would participate and be judged individually.

The NT developed this Hebrew consciousness of the person to the highest possible pitch. Jesus taught that God numbers the hairs on the heads of persons, that there is more joy in heaven over one sinner who repents than over 99 people who need no repentance, that an act done to "one of the least of these my brethren" is done to God. Jesus

himself went to his lonely death on the cross. Yet the NT interprets this solitary man as representative person, suffering and conquering sin for all. He teaches and exemplifies love. He calls persons, not into solitary devotion, but into a community of faith. His followers understand themselves as the household of God, as the body of Christ, as a holy nation.

In subsequent history Christians brought to society both an intense concern for persons and a commitment to community. Although Augustine in his *Confessions* (about A.D. 400) produced a genre of writing hitherto unknown in the probing of selfhood, he had an overwhelming sense of the solidarity both of humanity in sin and of the redeemed in the city of God. Medieval society accented the human social awareness in an organic, hierarchical society. Mystics and rebels kept alive the Christian awareness of personal experience; and ordinary persons knew that their sin, judgment, and redemption were highly personal. But inasmuch as salvation was sacramental, it was communal.

The modern world has seen the emergence of an individualism that has both Christian and heretical roots. What is commonly called "Protestant individualism" has little to do with Christian faith or the Reformation. Yet it remains true that, just as the Renaissance awakened an exultant appreciation of human powers, the Reformation put a heightened emphasis on personal responsibility. Luther (*see* **Lutheran Ethics**) taught that all persons must do their own believing just as they must do their own dying. Repentance and faith are personal, not institutional. Luther sought to recover the NT sense of the person-in-community when he said that all Christians are called to be priests, even Christs, to their neighbors. The Anabaptists (*see* **Anabaptist Ethics**) emphasized the personal nature of faith in their insistence upon believers' baptism. They tended to see the church as the community of those persons who have made decisions for Christ rather than as the organic community that nurtures persons in faith. The later English Independents and Quakers (*see* **Quaker Ethics**) emphasized in various ways the importance of personal decision and responsibility, the value of freedom, the significance of conscience, and the inadequacy of external authorities.

These Christian movements, however, kept an awareness of the work of faith and love in creating community*. Other streams of thought had to arise in order to bring about modern individualism, with its affirmation of the autonomy* of the self. Hobbes and Descartes in the 17th century separated the individual from the meaningful social nexus —Hobbes by reviving an ancient atomism and Descartes by defining the self as "a thing that thinks." (Hobbes shows how easy it is to start with individualism, yet end with an authoritarian society.) Defoe's *Robinson Crusoe* (1719) depicted the autonomous self fictionally. Locke, Hume, Adam Smith, Bentham, and Mill in the 18th and 19th centuries did the same thing, with many variations, philosophically.

Some of these names suggest the importance of the modern economy for individualism. An industrial economy, where persons and wealth are mobile and interchangeable, encourages individualism. Such an economy may also esteem individual initiative, free enterprise, and the doctrine of laissez-faire*.

Curiously this very individualism has seemed to many to destroy the significance of the individual person. Industrial society, often substituting a process or system of production for personal relations, can generate an abstract rather than personal individualism. It tends to deal with masses rather than persons, to value individuals for their functions rather than their selfhood, and therefore to make persons expendable (*see* **Industrial Revolution; Industrial Relations**).

One result has been the romantic and existentialist rebellion against Enlightenment rationalism in the name of an appreciation of authentic selfhood (*see* **Authenticity**). Emerson, Thoreau, and Whitman in America, like some of the Romantic poets of Europe, exalted the self. Later existentialism, whether Christian, agnostic, or atheistic, emphasized the individual person. Kierkegaard, with his emphasis upon self-exploration and decision, and Nietzsche, with his exultancy in the uniqueness of every person, were the early leaders of the movement. Heidegger and Sartre carried it farther.

It may be asked whether such writers, in their concern for individual freedom and decision, have lost the significance of community. But it is noteworthy to see them reassert the importance of the individual in the face of the very society that had so often stifled the person while flying the banners of individualism.

By this time individualism has come to mean many different things in the Western cultural tradition. (To make comparisons with Eastern traditions would require a longer essay than this.) Among the many varieties are these: (1) the insistence upon the autonomy of the self which rejects any external authority, yet may (in its Kantian form) have a high sense of social duty in its appeal to the self-legislating will and its insistence that every person is an end, not merely a means; (2) the romantic and existentialist forms that emphasize individual uniqueness; (3) the political individualism that resents intrusion of the state and asks minimal government; (4) the competitive economic individualism represented by Herbert Spencer's Social Darwinism and popularized in America by Andrew Carnegie and Herbert Hoover ("rugged individualism"); (5) the compassionate individualism that values every person, including the "least of these." It is possible to combine some of these meanings as in contemporary American libertarianism*, which unites radical versions of political and economic individualism. It is not possible to combine them all.

Individualism is the development of one aspect of the Christian understanding of the person-in-community. It needs continuous correction from those who understand that the self lives only in relation with others. But it is itself, in some of its forms, a correction of any doctrine of society or nation that submerges persons.

See **Autonomy; Collectivism; Community; Existentialist Ethics; Human Dignity; Liberalism; Libertarianism; Persons and Personality; Respect for Persons.**

Augustine, *Confessions;* M. Buber, *I and Thou,* ET ²1958; J. Dewey, *Individualism, Old and New,* 1930; S. Lukes, *Individualism,* 1973; J. S. Mill, *On Liberty,* 1859; R. Niebuhr, *The Self and the Dramas of History,* 1955; R. Nozick, *Anarchy, State, and Utopia,* 1974; J. Rawls, *A Theory of Justice,* 1971.
                                    ROGER L. SHINN

Individuality *see* **Individualism; Persons and Personality; Self-Realization**

Indoctrination

The word literally means instruction in doctrine, and is morally neutral. It has gained a pejorative sense from its overtones of authoritarianism, and from unfavorable contrasts drawn between unproven doctrines and established facts. In an ideal type of liberal education pupils learn, not by the exercise of coercive authority, nor by the suppression of alternative beliefs, but by the free use of their own reason on evidence presented to them without bias. In practice it is doubtful whether any educational system could or should operate according to this ideal model. Indeed, the model itself depends on presuppositions about the value of liberal educational methods, and the capacity of pupils to respond to them, which are imposed without argument despite being disputable. Some degree of indoctrination is inevitable in any educational system, if only because learning has to start somewhere, time is too short for everybody to discover everything for themselves, and reason is not sufficient to establish in each person *de novo* the complex matrix of beliefs, values, and attitudes that make civilized life possible.

This indoctrinational element in all education, however, does not justify the deliberate use of procedures designed to silence criticism and to inculcate disputable beliefs without any indication that they are disputable. There is a point at which legitimate guidance, and help given in establishing criteria, passes into lack of respect and ultimately into violation of personal integrity.

See **Brainwashing; Education, Christian Moral; Respect for Persons.**

B. G. Mitchell, "Indoctrination," Appendix B in *The Fourth R: The Durham Report on Religious Education,* 1970.

JOHN HABGOOD

Industrial Relations

Industrial relations involves the conduct of, and the theories analyzing, relationships among people working for large organizations in a modern industrial setting. Earlier the term was limited to the interactions between employers and workers or managers and employees, particularly in business corporations. Now it is also applied to the relations among all those who contribute to the activities of any large organization, private or public, profit or nonprofit, manufacturing or service.

The problems with which industrial relations is concerned are those encountered by people dealing with others in hierarchical, bureaucratic, collegial, or other systematic organizations. An issue of central importance is the kind of responsibilities superiors have in directing their subordinates and the nature of the obligations owed by subordinates to those above them in performance of their tasks. Another major issue is the amount of freedom an individual may assume within his or her work or occupational group and the extent to which individual and group goals can diverge from those of the larger organization. These issues arise in various forms, posed as problems of special conditions, circumstances, and time. What people are to be hired and by what standards are they to be judged? How will their tasks be assigned and by whom? Why should special communications devices be used and for what purpose? How will work standards be defined? Who will enforce the performance and carry out any disciplining? When will promotions, layoffs, or discharges be effected and for what reasons? Determination of the rates of pay, hours of work, and job conditions along with the introduction of technological change are among the most difficult problems.

Industrial relations as an area of systematic study did not develop until the 20th century. Before then scholars generally assumed and business people believed that the market automatically and appropriately governed the relations of employers and workers. Employers relied upon the market to regulate their dealings with workers; but they also looked to the tradition and law of the master-servant relationship to define the role of each party. Classical economists argued that individuals seeking work in a free market could not be injured since competition would force employers to pay the highest wages and provide the best conditions possible. While the argument possesses some validity, experience has not always confirmed it. Workers all too often enjoyed little choice of employment and thus gained none of the protection a competitive market was supposed to offer.

To their considerable market power employers added the traditional "rights" of a master's prerogatives and of an owner's property. They were socially superior, as proven by their position—the chosen of God or Nature—and their authority was reinforced by the law, which warded off all attacks upon their arbitrary directives and absolute rules because it guaranteed them the right to dispose of their property and to manage it as they saw fit. Though today managers seldom appeal to the old traditions to bolster their prerogative claims, many still insist that they do and ought to possess at least some unquestioned rights in directing or administering the organization.

In the mid-19th century, Karl Marx (*see* **Marxist Ethics**) powerfully criticized the capitalistic market system, which gave overwhelming power to employers. He argued that it allowed exploitation* which impoverished laborers and that it degraded men by alienating them from their works. Some employers, of which Robert Owen is an outstanding example, recognized the inadequacy of the market in providing healthful conditions of work and living standards conducive to an efficient, effective labor force. Interested as well in social reforms, Owen established a model industrial town, New Lanark, in 1800, encouraging education, productiveness, and moral behavior. Throughout the 19th century other employers experimented with programs similar to Owen's. They provided conditions for their workers superior to those which the market would have provided, but the improvements usually depended upon the paternalistic concern or "enlightened" self-interest of the employer, not upon the right of workers. Neither their voices nor their views were allowed free expression, initiative, or decisive role. The employers' values were almost always served first, and in time of depression or low profits the workers' interests were disregarded completely.

Employers were tempted to puff up their concern for their workers into the presumptiousness of the president of the Philadelphia and Reading Railroad Company in 1902 when he declared that "the rights and interests of the laboring man will be protected and cared for, not by labor agitators, but by the Christian men to whom God in his infinite wisdom has given the control of the property interests of the country." A more common temptation today is for managers to assume a new paternalism*, asserting that they can comprehend the needs of their employees and serve them equitably and justly.

Beginning around the turn of the century and reaching full flower after the First World War, the theories and movement of scientific management proposed a new kind of industrial relations. Specially trained, naturally talented managers were to determine the one best way of performing job tasks; workers were to be chosen rationally on the basis of tests that revealed their individual aptitudes and willingness to follow the minute rules and regulations imposed upon them. Advocates argued that all concerned would benefit, both workers and employers sharing the assured productivity increases.

While it contributed greatly to improving work efficiency, scientific management wrongly assumed that there was only one best way of performing a task and expected a rationality in organizations that probably does not exist. The diversity of abilities, talents, and temperaments among people allow different workers to achieve the same efficiency in their job in a variety of ways; and selection, direction, and administration continue to involve a great deal of art and subjective evaluation despite the use of tests, objective measurements, and rigorously defined standards. Moreover, groups of employees seldom remain passive instruments to be ordered about or manipulated to fulfill the needs and demands of even a scientific manager. They have continued to insist upon their own approach to their work, on occasion subverting the purpose of scientific management. Under piece rate (piecework) systems, for example, work groups not infrequently learn to use prescribed techniques to serve their purposes of maintaining or raising earnings without a corresponding change in production.

The recognition by social scientists that employees in factory, shop, or office formed social groups, imposing work norms upon their members, led to the development of a new approach to industrial workers—that of human relations, which was popular from the late 1930s through the late 1960s. Managers were urged to listen to their employees' problems and complaints, not simply to act upon their own diagnoses. They were told to make workers *feel* they were important and to convince them that their interests were carefully and seriously considered when solutions and remedies were proposed. The heart of human relations is an open unimpeded channel of communications between manager and employees through which managers learn the foibles, weaknesses, and needs of their employees. Managers can then help employees solve their problems, teach them the necessities of business, and encourage them to develop socially useful (that is, business-oriented) attitudes and habits.

At its best, human relations can give employees a sense of participating in the governing of their work lives. At its worst, human relations degenerates into attempts to manipulate employees as instruments solely to serve managerial purposes. It is seldom helpful in confronting conflicts of interests and values among employees or between employees and managers, however. Improved communications resolve conflicts only insofar as they arose from misunderstandings. Conflicts of interests and values may be left unresolved or even heightened. If employees possess no organization of their own or method of forcefully supporting their interests, the superior position and power of the managers will, of course, tend to resolve these conflicts in favor of management.

To ensure themselves the right to participate in managerial decisions and to help resolve conflicts of interest in their favor, some workers have striven for recognition of collective bargaining as a lawful, regular means of conducting industrial relations.

Collective bargaining* is seldom a process of unilateral imposition of demands; usually it involves mutual accommodation and adjustment on both sides. The very success of collective bargaining in the industries where it is prevalent has brought about the growth of large, bureaucratic unions and raised the same issues and problems for workers that the rise of the large factories did. The workers on the job now find that they may have exchanged one master for two—management and the union. To guarantee their rights as workers and protect their job interests they must also ensure their rights as union members (see **Trade Unions**).

While collective bargaining receives the most public attention because of its contentious procedure and the dramatic strikes* that sometimes accompany it, only a minority of those in the labor force use it to determine the rules under which they work. Not all workers desire to use collective bargaining. Some believe that the individual bargaining they enjoy is appropriate and adequate to their demands. Others, such as many professionals and white-collar workers, find that the labor market protects and rewards them satisfactorily. Workers democratically choose representatives to bargain for them. The collective strength of the union allows workers to deal with managers on the basis of some equality. If managers will not agree to conditions of work which workers feel they must have, they can impose sanctions, disrupting production, interfering with distribution, or cutting off sales of the product. Through such exercise of economic power unions can sometimes force managers to act in ways they might not otherwise have chosen. Collective bargaining thus allows workers to help establish and administer through representatives the rules and regulations that govern their work lives.

All the several varieties of industrial relations mentioned above can be found in any of the Western industrial nations. An organization may follow several of them at the same time depending upon the kinds of workers and occupations involved. No one of them excludes the other, nor should one expect it to do so. Each can be useful to both manager and worker, depending upon circumstances. And each can be injurious to the parties and problematical for society.

See **Capitalism; Industrial Revolution; Labor Movements.**

JAMES KUHN

Industrial Revolution

The term commonly used for the first phase of the industrialization of Great Britain, which is dated approximately 1760 to 1820 or 1830. The term seems to have originated in France early in the 19th century and in its original use there was an implied comparison with the French Revolution. The currency of the term in Britain can be traced to Arnold Toynbee (1852–1883), who in 1881–82 gave a course of lectures, published after his death, entitled *Lectures on the Industrial Revolution of the Eighteenth Century in England.* Toynbee and his successors stressed the social losses through industrialization rather than the technical advances and economic gains.

The term has come in for criticism and has been largely abandoned by economic historians owing to its lack of precision. Some writers have applied it to the process of industrialization that has taken place in country after country down to the present day, while others have used it loosely for any sudden and striking technological change in even a single industry. In this way many industrial revolutions may be detected by the historian, for example, economic changes in the woolen industry in England in the 13th century, and even by the prehistorian, who has found an industrial revolution in the late Bronze Age.

Moreover, the term suggests greater suddenness than the facts warrant. While Britain saw a rise in population, the industrial use of many important new inventions and a concentration of population near sources of power in the later 18th century, the way to these changes had been pointed by developments in the previous century. Further, no reason can be assigned for regarding the revolution as ended early in the 19th century. To all appearances it is still in progress.

Nevertheless the vagueness of the term should not blind us to the unique and decisive character of what happened in Britain's classic period of industrial revolution when a new relationship emerged between human beings, machines, and resources. It was then that the economic and social pattern of the contemporary world, with the ethical problems involved, began to command attention.

See Energy; Environmental Ethics; Industrial Relations; Revolution; Technology; Urbanization.

T. S. Ashton, *The Industrial Revolution,* 1948; G. N. Clark, *The Idea of the Industrial Revolution,* 1953.

STEWART MECHIE

Industrialization see **Industrial Relations; Industrial Revolution;** see also **Energy; Environmental Ethics; Technology; Urbanization**

Inequality see **Equality; Justice**

Infanticide

Infanticide is the killing of a newborn child either by the parents or with their consent. Many primitive and non-Christian peoples (including the Greeks and Romans) are known to have approved the practice (by direct killing or abandonment* or exposition*), as a form of religious sacrifice (rarely), as a means of population control, or as a matter of domestic convenience. In Christian teaching it has been consistently condemned.

In modern times three arguments have been used by way of defense or mitigation in the case of infants known to have some gross physical or mental handicap: (1) The interests not only of their own family but of society as a whole are best served by the painless killing of such infants, because they would otherwise become an increasing social and economic burden to the community. (2) They

should be put to death painlessly for their own good as an act of compassion*: they cannot expect to enjoy the pleasures and opportunities available to normal children and adults, and it is kinder to spare them the frustrations and hardships they must otherwise inevitably experience. (3) Though infanticide may not be morally permissible, it should be regarded as a less heinous offense than the murder of a grown child or adult, because an infant cannot experience fear or terror or even pain in a comparable degree, nor does its removal impose any significant hardship or loss on the family circle.

From a Christian standpoint all three arguments are unacceptable. (1) All human beings derive their essential value not from society (or from their parents) but from God who gave them their life and to whom they are infinitely precious; and society is judged by the extent to which it cares or fails to care for its weaker members. (2) The parents may feel profoundly sorry for their handicapped child (and not only sorry for themselves, as is sometimes the case), but the decision to kill the child even for what they deem to be his or her "own good" is one which they are not morally competent to make. The right to life is the infant's, and on what grounds other than their own subjective feelings can they claim to know that it would be "better for the child to die," or that he or she would not wish to live if given the opportunity? There are in fact many grievously handicapped children and adults who rejoice that they are alive, who know happiness despite their sufferings, and who give joy and sometimes practical service to others despite their limitations. (3) Legally the question can be one of some complexity (and varies from country to country), but factors like age and physical or mental handicap have no bearing on the right to life. It is never morally permissible deliberately and directly to kill any innocent person. Morally the distinction between infanticide and murder has no significance, though it may be a convenient one in some systems of criminal law. This is not to deny, however, that in any particular instance of infanticide there may be extenuating circumstances. The mother may be virtually inculpable because of her mental condition at the time (though the same is unlikely to be true of any of her accomplices); and she may be in urgent need of medical and spiritual care.

In an age when medical advances have

made possible the healthy survival of infants who would previously have died, it is a sad irony that there are occasions when doctors and parents are suspected of conniving at "clinical infanticide." It is one thing to refrain from subjecting to complex surgery and medication a newborn child whose life will be thereby, at best, only very briefly extended. It is quite another thing deliberately to withhold available lifesaving procedures from an infant capable of a very favorable response, and to treat only with a "negative care" which must end with a speedy death, simply on the grounds of "parental rejection" and/ or an otherwise predictably handicapped and "qualitatively poor" existence. As we have seen, factors like parental emotions and physical or mental handicaps have no bearing on an infant's right to life which is conferred by God alone.

See also **Abortion; Children; Handicapped, Care of the; Life, Quality of; Health Care, Right to; Life, Prolongation of; Life, Sacredness of; Parenthood; Population Policy; Sick, Care of the.**

R. Weir, *Selective Nontreatment of Handicapped Newborns,* 1984.

THOMAS WOOD

Informed Consent *see* Consent

Inhibition
The term is used generally of a restraint on behavior, movement, thought, or feeling that may come either from within or from beyond the person and may be occasional or habitual. In physiology inhibition refers to the blocking of one set of bodily processes by another.

Inhibition can be important in the psychological understanding of memory and of the learning process. In dynamically oriented psychology, inhibition usually refers to the operation of automatically functioning, unconscious mental mechanisms that curtail the free recognition or expression of thoughts, impulses, etc. Inhibition may be distinguished from self-control on the grounds that self-control is essentially a conscious restraint.

Some inhibitions are necessary in the process of socialization; hence psychotherapy does not seek to remove all inhibitions so much as to replace psychically destructive forms of control with other forms that are more flexible and more responsive to the complex demands of reality.

In another usage of the term, most conflict theories of personality regard the inhibition, or blocking, of natural growth tendencies as a root cause of later psychic distress.

GRAEME M. GRIFFIN

Injury
Injury may mean the infliction of harm* (*see* **Nonmaleficence**) or the violation of rights* (*see* **Justice**).

Innocence
Older theology tended to identify innocence and perfection, to see in Aristotle the ruins of an Adam. More recent study has tended to distinguish between the two. Thus F. R. Tennant pointed out that a child could be sinless but could not be morally perfect: "There are heights of considerateness and courtesy, for instance, which are inevitably beyond the compass of a child's nature, in that they involve knowledge of ourselves and of our fellows derived from experience such as cannot lie within the child's reach" (*The Concept of Sin,* 1912, p. 28).

On its positive side innocence has been analyzed most acutely by Kierkegaard in his *The Concept of Dread* (first published in 1844). Innocence, says Kierkegaard, is ignorance. Consequently when God said to Adam, "Of the tree of the knowledge of good and evil you shall not eat, for in the day that you eat of it you shall die" (Gen. 2:17), Adam understood neither the command nor the threat. But both command and threat open out possibilities to Adam, possibilities that may follow on his actions, possibilities which he does not understand and which for that reason make him anxious. This state of anxiety or dread is thus a product of that situation of freedom and finitude in which humanity finds itself. This state of dread is an unpleasant one and it is inevitable that innocent humans should try and escape from it, and it is in this escape that the leap into sin —ultimately inexplicable—takes place. Innocence therefore involves this state in which humans are overcome by dizziness at the thought of their own finite freedom. When they emerge from it, they find that their freedom is real enough, but that its reality has been shown forth in sinful action. In theory, the dread could have been resolved by faith —why it is not is the enigma of sin, which

Kierkegaard never professes to resolve. But in fact what happens is that the soul, caught up in this state of dread, attempts to escape from it by flying from either the finitude or the freedom, which are its two constituent elements. In the one case, humans treat themselves as gods. In the other, they surrender their freedom in exchange for servitude to their own lusts or the will of a dictator. In either event innocence has been lost.

IAN HENDERSON

Insemination, Artificial *see* **Reproductive Technologies**

Instincts or Drives

The basic notion denoted by the term "instinct" is that of an enduring tendency or disposition to act in an organized way without previous performance or foresight. The term "drive," though sometimes equated with instinct, usually refers to a motive with an intense "demand" character which must be met by the organism in some way. Drives are generally instinctual, but some writers speak of secondary or acquired drives which are partly learned.

The concept of instinct has long been a controversial one in psychology, and many psychologists prefer not to use it on grounds that it is too vague and inferential. For those who do use it, it has the following major connotations.

1. Instinct refers to innate hereditary potentials for behavior, as opposed to learned or acquired motives. Although some psychologists deny that it is possible to discriminate between innate and learned behavior, the work of the ethologists, such as Konrad Lorenz (see *On Aggression,* ET 1966), has shown that much animal behavior is not learned, in the sense of learned by trial and error or conditioning, but is activated by the *imprinting* of the response on the young of the species at an appropriate time by an adult of the species of a particular sex. Lorenz has demonstrated, for instance, that sexual responses are not completely innate in geese, but that young male geese will develop as homosexuals unless exposed to an adult male at the appropriate stage of development. Instinct is, then, an innate potential which must be developed.

2. Instincts in human beings refer generally to the irrational aspects of the personality, and as such may cause difficulty or distress, while in the lower animals instincts are generally adaptive in character, facilitating life and not hindering it. The adaptive nature of instincts formerly aroused controversy over their presumed teleological implications. They were regarded by many as evidence of purpose, and frequently instinct theories were accepted or rejected for that reason. Now instincts are not widely regarded as evidence of purpose, but as the result of mutation and natural selection.

The instinctual behavior of animals is more highly developed and pervasive than that of humans, which results in the relatively fixed character of their adaptive pattern, as, for example, in the ant. Humans are more flexible because of the less specific determinants of their instinctual life.

3. The number of instincts in human beings has been a subject of dispute. William McDougall, a prominent instinct theorist, tended to posit relatively large numbers, which fluctuated to some extent. In his *Outline of Psychology* (1923) he listed fourteen instincts: escape, combat, repulsion, parental, appearance, mating, curiosity, submission, assertion, social or gregariousness, food seeking, acquisition, construction, and laughter. These embrace all dimensions of the psychic life. Freud, taking a more genetic approach, emphasized the drive-like quality of the instincts and their small number. He first held to one basic drive or instinct, the sexual, but later changed his view to include a second drive—the aggressive. There is considerable ambiguity in translating Freud at this point, as he used the word *Trieb* to indicate both the drive quality and the instinct quality, at least in the phrases translated "life instinct" and "death instinct," by which he meant basic tendencies rather than immediately demanding motivations. See his *Beyond the Pleasure Principle* (1920), ET 1961 (*see also* **Id**).

While one may speak of strong or weak instincts, drives are strong by definition. They may, of course, diminish in intensity, as does the sex drive with the passing of years, but in such instances it is perhaps not appropriate to speak of a drive. Drives may be displaced, as in animals sexual frustration sometimes results in overeating. The principle of displacement was also used by Freud to account for the substitute character of much human gratification, and it formed the basis of his view that the person who could love and work was the optimal human being, having displaced his or her primitive sexual and aggressive drives. Drives may also be frustrated, turned back on the self, or inadequately expressed. In such cases mental illness develops.

Acquired drives develop according to the laws of learning through conditioning and reward, though partly through unconscious displacement. Alcoholism is an example of an acquired drive. Such drives can be "extinguished," though with difficulty.

The present climate in psychology favors minimizing the role of instincts and maximizing the role of learning in the development of motivational drives. An instinctual base is acknowledged, but it is regarded as relatively vague and inaccessible for study, while secondary drives can be more easily studied and controlled. However, specific drive centers for eating have been discovered in the brain of rats, giving promise of behavior control* through cortical stimulation. Other "pain-pleasure" centers are being searched out, so that sex and aggressive needs may also be met through the medium of electrodes placed in the brain.

Studies of drives and instincts, then, afford some comfort for those interested in the flexible capability of humans for higher functioning. They also suggest that human drives do not have to be thwarted to produce ethical behavior, but rather sometimes can be displaced through regulation by the ego. The drives serve the positive social function of limiting the malleability of humans at the hand of humans, though the cortical stimulation experiments mentioned above warn that even the drives may become subject to control by others.

See also **Aggression; Behavior Control; Evolutionary Ethics; Motives and Motivation.**

JAMES N. LAPSLEY

Institution/Institutionalization

An institution is an organized practice (such as an initiation rite or a marriage ritual) or a social body (such as a hospital or an army) established to meet a basic human need, social function, or felt desire. Institutions do not spontaneously spring from needs, functional requirements, or desires, however; they have to be constructed and maintained by intentional human actions. That is, the needs or social requirements or desires have

to be acknowledged as right or good by someone or some group and multiple resources of thought, personnel, financial support, time, and space have to be marshaled and organized in order to establish an institution. Institutions are thus artifacts, organized establishments, which both "incarnate" certain values and functionally meet perceived needs, social requirements, or desires.

"Institutionalization," therefore, can refer to the "routinization" of specific compounds of value and perceived needs into established embodiment in practices and organizations in social history; or it can refer to the placing of some person or group in an establishment for socialization, care, constraint, or rehabilitation—as in schools, nursing homes, prisons, or reformatories. The patterns of institutionalization in a civilization constitute the basic fabric of social authority predominant in it, and they are inevitably preferential to some groups. One of the tasks of social ethics* is to analyze and critically evaluate the perceptions of needs, requirements, or desires on the one hand, and the definitions of what is right or good on the other, to see whether that which is institutionalized is morally valid.

In all civilizations, at least four basic needs must be met for the human community to exist: sex (and support systems for the nurture of the progeny it produces); *technē* (i.e., means of extracting food, clothing, and shelter from the environment); order (especially defense against arbitrary violence from within or without); and symbol (i.e., means of communication and expression). Every civilization will define right and good ways to meet these needs and establish institutions to do so "properly." Thus, every viable human community will have some institutionalized form of family, economy, government, and culture and will institutionalize penalties or punishments for those who break the established patterns.

The basis of normative understandings of the right and good ways to structure these institutions, however, is not given in the needs or in the institutions themselves. Nor is the proper relationship of these institutions provided by the necessity of their existence. Should families control politics, economics, and culture, for example; or should politics control family life, economy, and culture? Some "transcendent" basis is inevitably invoked by peoples and civilizations to certify or legitimate the normative principles that are to guide institutionalization. In short, institutional life requires a governing "metaphysical-moral vision." Thus, to the initial four basic, or "natural," institutions of society must be added a fifth, supranatural one—"religion" (or its substitutes: authoritative tradition, philosophy, or ideology). Those forms of social ethics which focus on institutional analysis, therefore, must eventually reckon with "religious social ethics" and develop a normative polity for institutional existence or its reform.

In highly developed societies, not only basic needs but also increasingly differentiated systemic requirements and wider ranges of human desires also become the bases for institutions. Universities, libraries, and pornographic bookstores; stock exchanges and multinational corporations and crime syndicates; clubs, recreation industries, and brothels, to name but a few examples, are institutionalized as well. These too embody specific values, but their relationships to a governing metaphysical-moral vision are often attenuated. Religious values become more focused in specific voluntary associations* and distinct from the increasing influence of nonprimary establishments. The latter are regulated more by legal procedure, public opinion, the ethical codes of relatively autonomous professional groups, or the passionate concerns of interest groups than by the direct influence of religious ethics.

In every age where complex civilizations have developed, religious reformers, prophets, and seers have developed a hostility to "artificial" institutions (see also **Conventions**). Where this hostility does not lead to theocratic attempts to total control, it usually eventuates in an anti-institutionalism and the quest for a pure spirituality and a pure morality. However, if the metaphysical-moral visions of reformers are not institutionalized and connected to patterns that can meet basic needs, human desires, and complex civilization requirements, either the normative vision dissipates as a force in society or the civilization falls into chaos, without moral coherence in its institutions. Civilizational history can be written according to the changing definitions of the governing metaphysical-moral vision as they become more or less institutionalized and as they engender positive attitudes toward institutions as the preservers of civility against chaos or negative attitudes toward institutions as the artificial constrictors of spiritual and moral vitality.

The characteristic institution of Christianity is the church (see **Church; Sect; Ecclesiology and Ethics**). Internal to the church, patterns of sacrament, proclamation, and polity shape the character of this religious institution. Every church (or sect or denomination) also develops characteristic teachings about "the world's" institutions and ways of relating, positively or negatively, to the surrounding institutionalized patterns of civilization. Every church will have at least an implicit ethic of sex and the family, of politics and power, of economy and work, and of communication and the arts consistent with its core beliefs. In complex societies, any church that hopes to develop a relevant social ethic will also have both an explicit doctrine of differentiated institutions and ways of providing normative guidelines for believers who participate in them. The clarification of Christian principles of the right and the good as they bear on urban, military, international, scientific, technological, professional, and paraprofessional institutions is one of the most important tasks of Christian ethics as the church faces an increasingly complex network of local, societal, and global institutions.

J. R. Earle, D. D. Knudsen, and D. W. Shriver, *Spindles and Spires,* 1976; C. Geertz, *The Interpretation of Cultures,* 1973; R. M. MacIver and C. H. Page, *Society,* 1949; T. Parsons, *The Social System,* 1951; D. Reeck, *Ethics for the Professions,* 1981; M. L. Stackhouse, *Creeds, Society and Human Rights,* 1984.

MAX L. STACKHOUSE

Insurance

A device for securing a payment to offset loss occasioned by some foreseeable risk through a system of equitable payments from members of a group exposed to the risk. For centuries it has been possible to insure against fire, death, shipwreck, theft, and other hazards with commercial insurers. State insurance is relatively modern. It arose from the insecurities of industrial society and was designed to secure against sickness, industrial injury, old age, invalidity, and loss of a breadwinner. Social insurance, financed out of compulsory contributions of employers and employees, is distinguished from social assistance to the needy, financed from government resources, and from public assistance, given to all in a particular group from government revenues (*see also* **Mutual Aid; Welfare State**).

Insurance is an expression of human solidarity and offers several advantages. It lessens dislocations of business, reduces business insecurity, relieves anxiety, prevents poverty, and encourages saving. Compulsory insurance limits freedom but reaches more people than commercial.

Church documents have welcomed social security for the security it gives and because it redistributes wealth. They have stressed the obligation of governments to provide this service.

The ethical obligations of the insurer are to establish an equitable relation between the premium and the risk and to carry out the terms of the contract. The insured party must not make false declarations or indemnify for contingencies that he has caused, e.g., by arson. Both parties should abide by the civil law. Professionalism on the part of the insurer benefits both parties, and consumer ignorance can damage the public interest.

G. Clayton, *British Insurance,* 1971; B. Häring, *The Law of Christ,* vol. 3, ET 1967, pp. 469f.; Pope John XXIII, *Mater et Magistra,* 1961.

BRENDAN SOANE

Integration *see* **Apartheid; Race Relations; Segregation;** *see also* **Persons and Personality**

Integrity *see* **Conscience; Dirty Hands; Persons and Personality**

Intention

The concept of intention has been thought to be important for ethics mainly because whether a man is blamed for an act can sometimes depend on whether he did it intentionally. It belongs to the same group of "mental concepts," whose nature is still very obscure, as belief and desire; two people who had the same belief or desire or intention could in all cases be said to be "of like mind." It is characteristic of these states of mind that they have what are called "intentional objects"; that is to say, what is the object of my intention is determined, not by what actually takes

place, but by a certain description of it (true or false) which I "have in mind." Thus I may intend to dial ABBey 4520 (if asked what I was doing, I should say "Dialing ABBey 4520"), but in fact be dialing ABBey 4250. A man who intends to do what he does under one description may not intend to do it under another description; he may intend to wound a man, but not to kill him, though the act of wounding does kill him. Similarly, I may believe that I am wounding a man, but not that I am killing him, although by wounding him I am in fact killing him.

The fact that we can intend to do what we do not actually do shows that intention is not any sort of knowledge of the future or the present. Nor is it any sort of belief. It is more akin to the kind of thought that is expressed by commands and requests; indeed, when I tell somebody to shut the door, I might be said to express the intention that he should shut the door. It is therefore tempting to compare intentions with self-addressed commands—but this remains an obscure metaphor.

If the genus to which intention belongs is "being of a certain mind" the species is to be sought by asking what counts as "having the same intention" or "having a different intention." Suppose that at a certain time I intend to do *a* at time *t* in the future. If, when time *t* comes, and I know that it has come, and am not forgetful of my intention, and can do *a,* I shall be said to have changed my intention (changed my mind) if I do not do *a.* An attractive definition of "intention" (though not a complete one) is: "A man is said to have an intention to do *a* if and only if he is of such a mind that he will have changed his mind if he fails, other than through inability or mistake or forgetfulness, etc., to do *a.* If the "etc." could be satisfactorily filled out, this definition would at any rate differentiate intention from belief, though not without a perhaps unavoidable circularity, in that, by the reference to mistake, a prior definition of "belief" is presupposed.

The definition, however, requires at least the following qualifications: (1) We do many acts intentionally without having had, *previously,* an intention to do them; (2) it must not be thought that to have an intention (any more than to have a belief) is to have something going on currently in one's mind (a man whose mind is at the moment a complete blank, or who is thinking solely about the game of football he is watching, can still be truly said to intend, or even to be intending, to return to London tonight); and (3) at the same time, a definition of intention solely in terms of dispositions to action will have difficulty in distinguishing between intentional and unintentional actions.

It has recently been disputed whether all foreseen consequences of an action must be intended, even if not desired. That this is so is suggested by the legal maxim that a man must be presumed to intend the natural consequences of his actions; for this is arrived at by deduction from the two premises, "A man must be presumed to foresee the natural consequences of his actions" and "All foreseen consequences of actions are intended." The maxim would lose its basis if either of these premises were false. Some, however, reject the second, on the ground that there are always many foreseen consequences of my actions which I should not properly be said to intend: for example, when I dive into the pool, I know that I shall make a splash, but I do not dive in with the intention of making a splash. Nor is the making of a splash unintentional; but on this view "intentional" and "unintentional" are not contradictory terms but only contrary—a consequence of an action may be neither.

If this view be accepted, it alters the relation, with which we started, between intention and blame; for, if I foresaw a consequence of my action, I shall be blamed for it, whether or not I intended it in the narrow sense proposed. Thus absence of intention, in this narrow sense, does not excuse. This has a bearing on the so-called "Law of Double Effect" (see **Double Effect**). The Law is sometimes put in the following way: if an act, not sinful in itself, has two consequences; and if one of these consequences is something which it is normally sinful to bring about, and is a necessary condition of the other, which is good, it may not be sinful to do the original act, because only the good consequence is intended, the other not. It may be that this doctrine rests upon an equivocation between wider and narrower senses of "intend": in the sense in which absence of intention excuses, we intend all the foreseen consequences of our actions, bad as well as good; but in the sense in which undesired consequences are not intended, the absence of intention is no excuse, but only the absence of knowledge.

See also **Negligence; Responsibility.**

R. M. HARE

Interest *see* **Usury and Interest**

Interim Ethic

The expression was used by Albert Schweitzer for the ethic of Jesus. This teaching was given in the expectation that there would be an almost immediate end to the age. It is to be understood therefore in relation to the situation of the imminent end and not as applying universally to any and every situation.

See **Eschatological Ethics; Jesus, Ethical Teaching of.**

JOHN MACQUARRIE

International Order

A paradoxical and elusive, but necessary, concept. When one contemplates the cruel, chaotically opportunist way in which states conduct their rivalries with enemies and friends alike, one is tempted to ask, if this is order, what disorder would look like. But long term historical perspective suggests strongly that a measure of international order already exists, containing within itself fairly clear indicators of the direction in which further progress is to be sought.

In the wars of religion that preceded the Treaty of Westphalia (1648), the princes of Europe strove without success to impose by force a universal definition of the meaning of Christianity, and hence of religious truth. At and after Westphalia, they acknowledged failure in a potentially creative way. They recognized one another as possessing *sovereignty**, the legitimate authority to decide matters of great moment within agreed frontiers. In this new way of thinking, two rulers might come to opposed conclusions about the most vital matters and both have the right for their views to hold sway in their separate countries. Sovereignty, the basis of international order, is *the* alternative to absolute war between militant faiths. Iran since the Shah has shown some signs of posing a basic challenge to sovereignty in favor of the promotion of a particular conception of Islam without respect for boundaries but, for good or ill, most states show some respect, however grudging and imperfect, for sovereignty as the organizing principle of international relations.

The sovereign states of the world constitute one another sovereign by recognizing one another. Since the end of World War II, they have done so largely in terms of the United Nations, whose grand design is revealing about the conclusions of the most sophisticated thinking to date about how to organize a world of sovereign states. The UN is a two-tier organization. All recognized states are members of the General Assembly, a grand debating group with majority voting and very limited powers. Private individuals do not have direct access to the General Assembly, since states reserve to themselves the right to address one another as equals. (Contrast with this the arguably more progressive rules of the European Court of Human Rights, to which individuals can gain access.) The General Assembly has little real power, but is a potent symbol of the equality of states, for there even the mightiest must respond to the reproaches of the weakest, and must face the possibility of humiliating denunciation by a majority of its equals.

In counterpoint to the General Assembly is the Security Council, whose permanent members are few, and who operate a unanimity rule for voting on serious matters. At present, the permanent members happen to comprise all of the avowed possessors of nuclear weapons (USA, USSR, UK, France, China), but this is an accident of history. The main original idea was that the permanent members would be the great powers of the day, acting in concert to order international relations for the common good. With this grand aim in mind, they were endowed with draconian powers (e.g., of intervention). When the UN was created, tensions were already increasing between the USSR and the Western powers, so it is not surprising that a veto was built in, allowing Security Council powers to be exercised only when all the permanent members were in favor. This has been a grave limitation on the UN's effectiveness. So much of the disorder since 1945 has resulted directly from, or been exacerbated by, East-West tensions, and great power relations have been so poor and petty, that the Security Council has lacked the coordinating powers envisaged by the more idealistic of its creators. Many serious-minded people view the UN with deep skepticism as a result, but it is arguable that they should be criticizing the great powers rather than the

institutions whose smooth running is prevented by the deplorable state of great power relations.

One of the main instruments by which sovereignty and international organization operate is diplomacy. The members of the UN have inherited from the European states a highly developed system of diplomacy that permits mutual communication without endangering the lives of the communicators. The necessity and immunity of diplomats is almost universally recognized, but has been subject to two major challenges in recent years which bring into sharp focus central problems of international order.

1. The Iranian hostage crisis occurred in the latter part of the administration of US President Carter. For weeks and months, the President was seen on television as being powerless to act against desperadoes who, with the blessing of a minor power, held American diplomats hostage. Many commentators consider this episode to have been a crucial factor in Carter's subsequent election defeat, and in the swing of American public opinion toward a highly interventionist, militarily assertive foreign policy. The important point for thinking about international order is that the USSR did nothing to show solidarity with the US administration. Superpower relations were so poor that on an issue as noncontentious as the immunity of diplomats, letting the opponent be humiliated took precedence over considerations both of principle (including the vulnerability of Soviet diplomats to similar attacks) and of interest (the consequent electoral success of a President still less congenial to Moscow than Jimmy Carter). International order is bound to be feeble when the great powers are so ill-coordinated for minimal cooperation as they proved to be in this episode.

2. Diplomatic immunity is getting a bad name from the practice of smuggling arms, and even the attempted smuggling of a kidnapped individual, under cover of the diplomatic bag. If this practice grows, the feasibility of diplomatic immunity is bound to be subverted. But a very simple technical remedy is possible. X-raying of the diplomatic bag would reveal the presence of guns and kidnap victims without exposing documents to the scrutiny of enemy intelligence agencies. Revision of the law to provide for such x-raying would be simple, and it is hard to see

that any state could oppose it in good faith. But even if technical means are available to restore the credentials of the diplomatic bag, (1) above indicates that international organization can operate effectively only if states in their sovereign wisdom strive to make it do so, rather than indulging in acts or omissions of petty spite.

Mutual communication by diplomacy is a very minimal kind of international order, because underlying it may be the kind of unbridled egoism in which every state is essentially opposed to every other, and none is guiding its conduct by reference to a shared concept of the common good. Even in that sort of world, diplomatic contacts are necessary. But what do we need for a configuration of international relations more worthy of our ordinary understanding of what order means and requires?

Perhaps the most illuminating discussion of this is to be found in a difficult but rewarding essay by the great German philosopher Immanuel Kant (1724–1804). The meaning of his *Perpetual Peace* (1795) is much debated. One interpretation of it is roughly this. We are irretrievably committed to sovereignty, and can move beyond its more destructive implications only by the sustained will of states to exercise their sovereignty in pursuit of mutually compatible definitions of the common good* on an organized basis. In other words, the great powers and other states must strive, actively and constantly, to make some such organization as the UN a central part of their common pursuit of justice and peace (whose value is universally acknowledged, but whose meaning is the subject of profound ideological and pragmatic dispute).

In the present bad state of international relations, Kant's argument is a dismaying one, since it demands that human beings learn from their errors and make their way toward a better world by self-consciously willing to do so, without benefit of any hidden hand. We know too much history to find this a comforting argument. Ever since the French Revolution, the state has been dominated by popular passion, nationalism, and ideology. The simpler environment of the 18th century, in which foreign policy was the prerogative of narrow elites with limited and relatively easily reconciled interests at stake, is not available to us. We must will the inter-national common good in a way that can find broadly based popular support despite the grave ideological disputes that set so many nations at odds, and despite the new wave of nationalism that has been unleashed by the replacement of the European empires by a vast number of internally unstable successor states. Some find slight hope in the possibility that nuclear deterrence enforces a new sobriety in the mutual dealings of nuclear weapon states, but if this sobriety does exist, it has shown no sign of driving the great powers into constructive cooperation. Furthermore, by far the majority of states face one another with traditional military power untrammeled by fear of nuclear reprisal. The huge number of wars since 1945 shows little sign of abating, and there are many reasons for doubting that the spread of nuclear weapons is a desirable way of spreading such mutual restraint as the great powers do display toward one another.

Is there some alternative to Kant's idea of creating a more civilized order by self-consciously pursuing it? Some speak of the need for world government, but the establishment of such a thing would surely be as impossible now as it was before the Treaty of Westphalia signified its abandonment as an objective by the princes of 17th-century Europe. Some put their faith in functionalism, i.e., in the idea that underlying economic necessities are drawing states into closer accord against their will and without their knowledge, forcing them to cooperate on an ever-growing range of functions and creating a web of interdependence that will necessitate more prudent policies. There is certainly something to be said for this hidden hand argument: witness as one example the arguably constructive web of interdependence between the USSR and the countries of Western Europe. But functionalism is not necessarily a vehicle of justice and peace: witness the fears of many Europeans and many in the Third World that on the rare occasions when the superpowers are driven to cooperate, they do so for their mutual advantage at the expense of the rest of the world. Furthermore, so long as some states or peoples are intensely aggrieved about their place in international relations, their relation with their principal adversaries is bound to be a focus for rivalry and conflict among the stronger powers to whom they turn for help. Only an organizing consensus on the desirability of minimizing and isolating conflicts in order to overcome them through reconciliation can offer a realistic hope of an international order that is informed by substantial justice.

A much less ambitious definition of "order," but somewhat more substantial than the minimal order of diplomatic communication, is espoused by writers who contrast order* with justice*, and assert that order must take priority over justice. One influential expression of this view has been from writers on US foreign policy who have argued that Washington should support governments that lack a secure domestic base in the interest of strategic stability. This argument has the merit of taking legitimate Western interests very seriously, but has two serious drawbacks. First, it is very difficult to be confident that according priority to "order" over justice in fact facilitates the subsequent pursuit of justice. If one is supporting a narrow clique against an oppressed majority or substantial minority, then one's clients are unlikely to be able or willing later on to move toward justice. They are likely to be less capable of movement because more dependent on military dominion over their opponents, and are likely to be in a position to exploit their very vulnerability to deter their protector from putting them under serious pressure to reform. Giving priority to order over justice is thus likely to amount to signing a blank check of support for tyranny and oppression*. Second, in a time of great power rivalry (and the great powers have always tended to rivalry), support by one power of one faction in the furtherance of one definition of order is very likely to motivate support of another faction by another interventionist power seeking a different definition of order. In short, order before justice is a recipe for ever-growing great power animosity of the sort that is bound, in an age of ideology and nationalism, to confine international order to the bare minimum.

See **Internationalism; Nationalism; Peace; State; World Government.**

H. Bull, *The Anarchical Society,* 1977; H. Butterfield and M. Wight (eds.), *Diplomatic Investigations,* 1966; M. Frost, *Towards a Normative Theory of International Relations,* 1985.

BARRIE PASKINS

International Relations
see **International Order**

Internationalism
The conviction that all human beings share certain basic common characteristics and are of equal worth, and that the shared attributes are more significant than differences of national or ethnic origin, language, culture, religion, or ideology. The spirit of internationalism was behind the attempts to outlaw slavery, the colonial system, racial discrimination, and war, and to provide aid for the victims of natural or human-made disasters through the Red Cross movement, agencies of the UN, or voluntary humanitarian organizations. It has also been the driving force of attempts to bring together adherents of different Christian churches, members of national parliaments, and people of different professions and vocations such as doctors, scientists, writers, and athletes.

Nongovernmental organizations based on an aspect of internationalism began to flourish in the West in the second half of the 19th century with the convening of international peace congresses and with the foundation of such organizations as the International Committee of the Red Cross, the International Workingmen's Association, movements advocating Esperanto or some other world language, the Inter-Parliamentary Union, the Olympic Games, the Nobel prizes, and movements for arbitration or judicial settlement of international disputes. In the 20th century, the international spirit has found expression in movements for disarmament*, human rights*, and world government* and, at an intergovernmental level, in the League of Nations, the United Nations and its agencies, and regional organizations. The international idea has also been evident in literature, music, art, and other forms of aesthetic expression, because culture cannot be confined within borders. It is a basic element in the Christian message, the belief that all men and women are children of one God and in equal need of liberation (1 Cor. 12–13; Gal. 3:28; Eph. 4:4–6).

The intense strength of national or local feeling (*see* **Nationalism**) has in some parts of the world been a barrier to the growth of internationalism, especially in states based on exclusivist religious or ethnic sentiments (Israel, Pakistan, South Africa) or in areas with acute communal tensions (Cyprus, Northern Ireland).

See also **International Order; National Sovereignty.**

SYDNEY D. BAILEY

Interpretation

Interpretation has two references in Christian ethics: to the mediation of traditions of moral understanding, and to the assessment of contemporary situations calling for moral response. Though both references have roots in Christian origins, they have taken on new importance since the rise of historical consciousness in 19th-century Europe.

The reference to tradition* reflects the fact that Christian thought is governed by happenings in the past and by biblical witnesses to those happenings. A crucial component of Christian ethics is the interpretation of moral understandings contained in the biblical witnesses in a fashion that is pertinent to contemporary experience. Interpretation involves three processes: (1) exegesis, reading the biblical materials in their own social and cultural settings, aided by the tools of historical and literary criticism; (2) critical engagement, reading the biblical materials as speaking to questions which are also our questions, and, therefore, as possibly saying something true to us; (3) constructive appropriation, unfolding a coherent, contemporary account of the moral life which contains a reformulation of biblical notions. Attention to the full scope of Christian tradition figures in each of these processes (*see also* **Bible in Christian Ethics**).

The reference to situations reflects the fact that our perceptions and assessments of the realities we confront in our social world are governed by preconceptions and biases of which we are not necessarily aware. The first question to be asked in each situation, H. Richard Niebuhr argues, is, What is going on? This question is not simply an empirical one, an admonition to get our facts straight. It is itself an ethical question, a summons to cut through prejudices and taken-for-granted assumptions that distort or obscure our correct seeing. It involves self-consciousness about our social location and about the impact of the movement of history upon us. For Niebuhr it finally entails responding to all situations as elements in our response to God, understood in the tradition of radical monotheism. The interpretation of situations becomes important when there are deep underlying problems in social existence that tend to escape awareness. It is a critical undertaking, an attempt to open up avenues of thought and action that previously have not even come into consideration. A correct reading of a situation implies a social consensus reached through a process of unrestrained public discourse, an ideal that presupposes the transcendence of the underlying bases of social conflict. In practice, the moral import of complex social situations remains ambiguous (*see* **Situation Ethics**).

H.-G. Gadamer, *Truth and Method,* ET 1975, pp. 235–345; J. Habermas, *Communication and the Evolution of Society,* ET 1979; H. R. Niebuhr, *The Responsible Self,* 1963; T. Ogletree, "The Activity of Interpreting in Moral Judgment," *JRE,* Spring 1980, pp. 1–26; P. Ricoeur, *The Symbolism of Evil,* ET 1969, pp. 347–357.

THOMAS W. OGLETREE

Intuition

Intuition is the name given to supposed direct knowledge by rational insight of states of affairs; for example, in the ages when Euclid's axioms were thought to be absolute (in spite of the criticism of the "parallels postulate," which goes back at least as far as Proclus) and believed to obtain in respect of the space of the physical world, these axioms and the theorems deduced from them were thought to embody universal and necessary truths concerning the structure of configurations in actual space. The axioms were believed to be established by immediate inspection of their terms, or by construction of these terms in an ideal medium. Thus one only had to think what one meant by a straight line to see, by a kind of direct intellectual insight, that it was the shortest distance between two points. The development of non-Euclidean systems of geometry, beginning with the work of the Russian geometer Lobachewski (who numbered Lenin's father among his outstanding pupils) and Bolyai and culminating in the use of such systems for the effective correlation of measurements in actual space in Einsteinian physics, constituted an intellectual revolution of the greatest importance, in that the claim made on behalf of geometry, viz., that it was a non-inductive study, giving us incorrigible insight into necessary relations within the actual world, must be regarded as invalidated, although philosophers of mathematics are by no means agreed in their understanding of the nature of pure geometry, the logical character of its proofs, etc. This revolution is particularly significant where moral philosophy is concerned. Thus many philosophers (e.g., John Locke in the 17th century and H. A. Prichard in the 20th) had supposed an analogous insight where the first principles of conduct were concerned, to that supposedly enjoyed where the axioms of Euclidean space were at issue. It is not for nothing that several moralists, who like Prichard would be regarded as intuitionists, fought a sustained, if somewhat pathetic, rearguard action against the claims made for non-Euclidean geometry. But the sort of apologetic for moral absolutism that has relied on the supposed analogy of geometry must be judged finally invalidated. The moralist, therefore, who is convinced that the intuitionist tradition embodies genuine perceptions concerning the nature of moral experience is faced with the task of presenting alternative models of the direct insight into the moral universe he or she claims that we enjoy.

Other uses of the term which must be distinguished carefully from the foregoing and from one another and which should be noticed include the following: The term is sometimes used to refer to the synoptic vision of all forms in the light of the "Idea of the Good," which Plato distinguishes from the preceding grasp of individual forms. It occurs also in exposition of Bergson's contrast between two sorts of temporal experience, measured and immediate. In common parlance it is used to refer to allegedly feminine quick perception concerning, for example, human motives sometimes hardly defensible by inductive argument but often disquietingly correct.

Finally in Kant's theory of knowledge in the *Critique of Pure Reason* (1781) the term is used to refer to the passive sense-awareness by which the subject receives the temporarily successive, and spatially discrete, data which through the cooperation of imagination and discursive understanding yield us knowledge of the single world of space and time, the detail of whose causal order it is the task of the physical sciences to establish. In his third *Critique* Kant makes use for purposes of illustration of an important distinction between such an understanding as ours, which is inherently discursive and relies for the possibility of objective knowledge on resources (viz., a sensible intuition) extraneous to itself, and one which he calls intuitive such as the understanding enjoyed by God, if he exists, which posits its own objects, and to which therefore all things are transparent. Kant develops this distinction in order further to elaborate his fundamental awareness of the limitations of characteristically human knowledge; he is not in any sense arguing for the existence of God; but in his discussion of the notion of an intuitive understanding and the contrast he draws between its condition and that of a human being relying on perception, theory building (itself dependent on the elaboration of more powerful forms of mathematics), experiment (bound to the state of technical apparatus available as well as to the inventive genius of the experimenter), induction, observational invalidation, etc., he throws an enormous amount of light on the nature of that omniscience predicated of God in traditional metaphysical theology.

See **Ethics.**

H. A. Prichard, *Moral Obligation,* 1949.
D. M. MACKINNON

Intuitionism *see* **Intuition;** *see also* **Ethics; Metaethics**

Invincible Ignorance *see* **Ignorance**

Involuntary Hospitalization

The involuntary hospitalization (civil commitment) of the mentally ill is a particularly problematic issue for modern psychiatry, the courts, and moral philosophers. Coercive confinement, even for therapeutic reasons, violates deeply held values in a free society and scarcely provides an auspicious beginning for a collaborative physician-patient relationship. Moreover, commitment to an institution for treatment does not guarantee that effective therapy is available or, if it is, that it will be provided in individual cases. Yet the severity of some mental disorders with their profoundly destructive impact upon personal function and the social fabric have impelled civilized societies to enact legislation authorizing involuntary hospitalization under certain conditions.

In the USA these laws are the responsibility of the states; hence there is considerable variation across the country. Usually three criteria have been specified: (1) dangerousness to others, (2) dangerousness to self, and (3) mentally ill and in need of treatment. In most states (e.g., California), the third criterion is disallowed, while in others (e.g., New York), it is legally sanctioned. Notoriously difficult to define reliably and precisely, these criteria frequently must be applied in crisis situations with incomplete data.

Political and legal forces have brought about a number of changes in psychiatric practice regarding involuntary hospitalization and treatment in the past decade through the passage of legislation. These changes have been in the direction of tightening the criteria for involuntary hospitalization, mandating periodic review of patients' involuntary status, protecting the individual patient's right to treatment and right to refuse treatment, and requiring that the justification for involuntary treatment is fully documented, including the opinion of a qualified consultant.

Similar social and legal forces in Great Britain generated extensive parliamentary debate culminating in the Mental Health Act of 1983. This legislation greatly increased involuntarily detained patients' access to appeal of their detention through a Mental Health Review Tribunal and established a new body, the Mental Health Act Commission, to review the care and treatment of detained patients. Moreover, if a psychiatrist wishes to administer electroconvulsive therapy or prescribe psychopharmacologic agents for a period exceeding three months to a patient who is incapable of giving informed consent, a second psychiatric opinion is required.

Currently the psychiatric profession is assessing the impact of these regulatory changes. There is concern that some of this legislation, well-intentioned though it is, has resulted in failure to hospitalize, inadequate treatment of, and/or premature discharge of patients who later committed violent acts against themselves or others or who were relegated, without adequate financial, social, and medical support, to a life of street vagrancy (e.g., the "bag ladies" of New York City).

From a moral perspective, two major issues are at stake. First is the double agency problem—the psychiatrist utilizing involuntary confinement to achieve social ends, as in commitment on grounds of "dangerousness." Here it is the welfare of others and of society at large, not the welfare of the patient, that primarily justifies the commitment. Although in modern Marxist states the welfare of the state is accorded preemptive importance, physicians in the free West follow the Hippocratic tradition (*see* **Hippocratic Oath; Professional Ethics**) in ethically grounding treatment on the patient's best interest. Moreover, the Western criminal justice system is founded upon the presumption of a person's innocence until proven guilty. To involuntarily hospitalize patients, then, who have not yet harmed anyone, upon the pretext that they are "dangerous" is problematic legally, clinically, and morally. Combined with the lack of evidence establishing the predictability of violent behavior, these factors have diminished support for the "dangerousness" criterion.

Psychiatrists are far more comfortable resorting to involuntary hospitalization for patients refusing treatment who are suffering from severe mental illness that endangers their life and health. But this poses a second ethical dilemma by coercively instituting treatment without the patient's informed consent*. The doctrine of informed consent has become securely established as fundamental to ethical medical practice in the past twenty years. But in psychiatry its application has never been satisfactory. Because in cases of severe mental disorder it is the patient's ability to make prudential judgments which is itself malfunctioning, it is clear that such patients may repeatedly "choose" behaviors that are self-destructive and even suicidal. The determination of the level of self-harm at which coercive treatment is justified is highly contentious. A large literature has developed utilizing the concepts of rights*, including the right to suicide*, justified paternalism*, patient autonomy*, competence, and rationality. The consensus among ethicists appears to be that the morally decisive judgment is the determination of the rationality or competence of the patient. The decision of competent patients to refuse hospitalization is to be respected while involuntary hospitalization may be ethically recommended for incompetent patients.

Yet problems remain. The attempt to evaluate patients' competence without basing that judgment on their treatment choices is an effort to discern their capacity to make rational decisions without judging the decisions they make. But ultimately we must judge the process by the product. Sooner or later we must specify which patient decisions we ought ethically to respect and which, for the patient's good, we ought to override. Clinicians are particularly concerned that many psychiatric patients who are legally competent are, nonetheless, incapable of making adaptive choices. Profound disturbances in self-esteem, persistent emotional states of depression or rage, and severe defects in the ability to maintain interpersonal relationships scarcely qualify patients for the label of "incompetent." But compassionate concern for their suffering and ultimate well-being may indicate temporary involuntary treatment.

See **Mental Health; Mental Illness; Health and Disease, Values in Defining; Consent; Coercion; Paternalism; Autonomy; Human Dignity; Respect for Persons; Sick, Care of the.**

J. R. Hamilton, "Mental Health Act 1983," *British Medical Journal* 286 (May 28, 1983).
ROGER C. SIDER

Irresponsibility   *see*   Responsibility; Sin(s)

Islamic Ethics

Islamic ethics is based on religious sources: primarily the Qur'ān, the scripture of Islam, supported and expanded by the *ḥadīth* (traditions of Muḥammad), with other elements derived from pre-Islamic tribal morality, from custom, and from Persian and Greek sources.

Emphasis is on conformity to the law: an action is commanded or forbidden by God, rather than inherently right or wrong. All aspects of life are regulated by the *sharī'a,* the religious law, which covers belief, worship, social and individual morality, warfare, hostages, the family. The primary authority, the Qur'ān, has the status of the Word of God as revealed to the prophet Muḥammad (d. A.D. 632), and since its appearance in the early 7th century has been for Muslims the ultimate criterion of good and evil.

Earlier suras (chapters) of the Qur'ān stress monotheistic belief, worship, good works, and social justice. Individual and community alike are called to repentance: the rich and the idolaters are warned of disaster and punishment, while worshipers of the One God are promised Paradise. "Righteousness" is described in the Qur'ān (2:177) as: belief in Allah (God), the Last Day, the angels, the Book (scriptures) and the prophets; spending one's wealth for love of God on kindred, orphans, the needy, the wayfarer, the beggar, and ransom of captives; performing worship and paying the alms tax; keeping one's promises and covenants; patient endurance in adversity and in battle. The Qur'ān lists most of the religious requirements of the Muslim (17:23–40). Commanded are: worship of the One God; kindness to parents, kindred, the poor, and travelers; protection of the property of orphans; just dealings in trade; humility. Forbidden are: wastage of goods; the killing of unwanted children; adultery; killing except in a just cause.

Muḥammad himself is described in the Qur'ān as "a fine example" (33:22) and one who possesses "high moral excellence" (68:4). As such, he has been taken as a model of good conduct, and his practice (*sunna*) followed in minute detail. The *sunna* is preserved in the *ḥadīth*—narratives of his words, deeds, and silent approval on a vast range of subjects. These, whether or not historically accurate, reflect the thinking of the Muslim community, and have come to form the second source of law. Despite the stress on detail, a famous *ḥadīth* states that "actions are judged by the intention" (*niyya*).

Qur'ān and *ḥadīth* are supported by *ijmā',* the consensus of the community, and by *qiyās,* analogy, when no specific ruling can be found. In practice this means the teaching of the theologians and lawyers of the first centuries of Islam.

The religious duties of the Muslim are fivefold: profession of faith in the One God (the *shahāda*); worship (*ṣalāt*) five times a day; fasting (*ṣaum*) during the month of Ramaḍān; almsgiving (*zakāt*); pilgrimage (*ḥajj*) to Mecca at least once in a lifetime if possible. To these is added *jihād,* often explained as "holy war" but also interpreted as the struggle against evil inclinations of the soul, described as "constantly inciting to wrong" (Q. 12:53).

Within the *sharī'a,* there are two types of duties (*farḍ*): individual and collective. Actions themselves are recognized as falling within five categories: obligatory (*farḍ* or *wājib*), recommended but not obligatory (*mandūb, sunna*), neutral or permitted (*mubāh, jā'iz*), disapproved (*makrūh*), forbidden (*harām*).

Another source of ethics was the pre-Islamic legacy of tribal nomadic life. This strict code enjoined honor, loyalty to the chief and the clan, hospitality, courage, and endurance. To a large extent this was refined and Islamized, and tribal loyalty replaced by religious allegiance, for "all Muslims are brothers." Further, customary law ('*āda*) was in some regions absorbed into the Islamic system.

This might seem to leave little room for any ethical theory. However, the concept is indicated early in Islam by the term *adab* (good conduct, refined manners). Hence the titles of two books by the Persian Ibn al-Muqaffa' (d. 757). Later, Ibn Qutayba (d. 889) harmonized the pre-Islamic and Persian elements with the Islamic, in his *'Uyūn al-akhbār*. In time, ethics came to be denoted by the term *akhlāq* (pl. of *khuluq*, character, disposition). *Makarim al-akhlāq* (noble qualities of character), a phrase attributed to Muhammad, is also the title of some collections of *hadīth*.

Only within the comparatively restricted milieu of philosophy was ethics a study in its own right, *'ilm al-akhlāq*. Greek philosophy, especially works of Plato and Aristotle, were introduced to the Muslim world from the mid-8th century onward, translated into Arabic generally via Syriac. Many ideas, such as the Aristotelian mean and the need for moral education, were in harmony with already existing views, while others were condemned by religious circles. During the 8th and 9th centuries the Mu'tazila, a theological school relying chiefly on the use of reason to support revelation, tackled the question of free will and predestination. In an attempt to preserve the absolute justice of God, they taught that humans are the sole source of evil actions, for which therefore they are totally responsible. The orthodox, on the other hand, saw this as denying the absolute power of God. The two extremes were moderated by the formulations of al-Ash'ari (d. 935), with the principle of acquisition (*iktisāb* or *kasb*): humans are given the ability to "acquire" what God has decreed, and thus they acquire the merit or censure due to their actions, and deserve the reward or punishment promised by the Qur'ān.

The physician and philosopher al-Rāzī (d. c. 923) wrote on the virtues and vices to be imitated and avoided in the proper conduct of life, avoiding extremes (*al-Tibb al-rūhānī*, translated by A. J. Arberry as *The Spiritual Physick of Rhazes*, 1950). The Brethren of Purity (*Ikhwān al-Safā'*) in the 10th century taught in their Epistles that the soul could raise itself above the limitations of the body, through ascetic practices. Ibn Miskawayh (d. 1030) considered that the soul, the spiritual element in man, needed ethical formation. In his *Tahdhīb al-akhlāq* he spoke of the inner value of religious duties (C. K. Zurayk, *The Refinement of Character*, 1968).

This last point, and others from his work, were taken up by one of the greatest Islamic theologians, al-Ghazālī (d. 1111). He stressed the importance of conformity to the religious law, but even more the inner spiritual dimension: the intention (*niyya*) being necessary for all religious duties. Ghazālī considered that knowledge ('*ilm*) would produce the right attitude in the soul and thus lead to good action ('*amal*). He too put forward the example of Muhammad as the highest ideal of human virtue.

Ghazālī's teachings were founded on mysticism, on the ideals of the Sufis, who preached a way of life based on poverty, prayer, and rejection of the world. The movement was inspired by Qur'ān and *hadīth*, and arose in the early 8th century, partly as a reaction to the worldliness of the ruling classes and the dry legalism of the theologians. Some of the Sufi values are explained by Ghazālī in his great work *Ihyā' 'ulūm al-dīn* (Revivification of the Religious Sciences): *sabr* (patient endurance and resignation to God's decrees); *tawakkul* (absolute trust in God); *dhikr* (constant remembrance of God)—the foundation for the Sufi ritual of *dhikr*. Sufi brotherhoods are widespread throughout the Islamic world, and while they preach the search for perfection they also offer a way of practical ethics for the ordinary Muslim and have had a considerable influence on personal morality and devotion.

Comparatively little development in theology or ethics has occurred since Ghazālī. In more recent times Muslim thinkers have looked again to Qur'ān and *sunna* for guidance for their community, while seeking freedom from Western influence; such are exemplified by Jamāl al-Dīn al-Afghānī (d. 1897) and Muhammad 'Abduh (d. 1905). Some Islamic states today are seeking an idealized

Qur'ānic legislation, as in Saudi Arabia, Pakistan, and Iran. Others while officially Islamic have allowed considerable freedom of interpretation and are more open to external influences. While most are in sympathy with the United Nations Charter and Universal Declaration of Human Rights, they would claim that Islam has already made full provision. Such a view is seen in the Universal Declaration of Human Rights in Islam (1981), which, while addressing modern political and social questions, contains some hundred references to the Qur'ān and fifty to the *ḥadīth.* In general, Islam is able to absorb a great deal from external sources, but any ethical theory must be in full accord with Islamic principles.

D. M. Donaldson, *Studies in Muslim Ethics,* 1953; L. Gardet, *La cité musulmane,* 1954.

PENELOPE JOHNSTONE

I-Thou Relationship

Although the concept of "I-Thou" relationships has roots in the thought of Kierkegaard and Feuerbach and was also developed by others, such as F. Ebner, its most striking and influential formulation appears in the writings of Martin Buber, the 20th-century Jewish philosopher. According to Buber's renowned *I and Thou* (published in German in 1923), there are two basic attitudes, postures, or stances toward the world, represented by the two primary words of "I-Thou" and "I-It." The former is relation, dialogue, encounter; the latter experience; the former involves the whole self, the latter only a part of the self, such as reason. The distinction is between openness and engagement, on the one hand, and objectivity and detachment, on the other. Only through relationships or encounters does a human being become a person and live authentically. The world itself is not divided into "Thous" and "Its," and it is possible to have an I-Thou relation with a thing, such as a tree or a work of art, as well as with other persons. I-It is not evil and is necessary for human life. In fact, every "Thou" must become an "It" since it is impossible to live only in encounter. But to live only on the level or from the stance of I-It is evil. Some critics have suggested that "I-You" interactions, for example, in cooperative endeavors, are not reducible to either "I-Thou" or "I-It." In ethical terms, Buber's key themes were responsibility* and dia-

logue. His influence has been particularly strong in Protestant theology and ethics—e.g., in Emil Brunner, Friedrich Gogarten, H. Richard Niebuhr, and Reinhold Niebuhr. In Brunner's theological ethics, for example, themes similar to Buber's appear in his interpretation of human life in personalistic terms, particularly responsibility, his sharp distinction between personal and institutional realms, his affinities with the "no-church" movement in Japan, and his suspicion of modern technology. As Brunner's work suggests, one of the major questions for this sort of personalistic ethic is its assessment of and guidance for institutional life.

See also **Existentialist Ethics; Institutions; Personal Ethics; Personalism; Social Ethics.**

M. Buber, *I and Thou* (1923), ET 1937; new ET 1970; E. Brunner, *The Divine Imperative* (1932), ET 1937.

JAMES F. CHILDRESS

Jealousy

In the Decalogue* the reason for God's prohibition of graven images and idols is his jealousy for his people: "for I the LORD your God am a jealous God" (Ex. 20:5). Despite this positive assessment of divine jealousy, human jealousy is generally, though not always, criticized. For example, it appears in lists of condemned "works of the flesh" (Gal. 5:19–21), and of acts, emotions, and attitudes that are not appropriate for Christians (2 Cor. 12:20). Thomas Aquinas makes jealousy almost synonymous with envy, a capital sin, but envy* may be viewed as a strong desire for a good that someone else possesses, while jealousy is a desire* to possess a good exclusively for oneself.

JAMES F. CHILDRESS

Jesus, Ethical Teaching of

The ethical teaching of Jesus is virtually confined to the first three Gospels, though a small number of instructions given by Jesus are to be found in the letters of Paul, and one ethical saying appears in Acts 20:35. Important preliminary questions arise before the teaching can be understood and interpreted.

First, recent study of the Gospels makes plain that each of them is a more or less coherent theological whole, the work of a writer who was not merely assembling stories and sayings of Jesus but presenting a theological account of Jesus' significance. While opinion differs concerning the extent to which the Evangelists have adapted or even created material, it is evident that the presentation of Jesus' teaching in each case is indebted, in part at least, to the writer and the Christian outlook he represents. It is hard, therefore, to be sure of drawing accurate lines between the ethical teaching of Jesus and that of, e.g., Matthew, all the more so if each Evangelist can be shown to present a really distinctive and consistent account of Jesus' teaching.

Second, there is the question of what is meant, in the context of the early church, by the ethical teaching of *Jesus.* Some have held that his sayings were transmitted verbatim by his followers, as the teachings of a revered rabbi. But it is increasingly clear that the matter is not so simple. In the first place, an understanding of the conditions of oral transmission in constantly changing settings indicates the naïveté of such a view. In the second place, it is evident that factors in early church belief and life led to the creative growth of the tradition of Jesus' teaching, in particular to the existence of prophets who, seized by the Spirit, mediated the teaching of the present, living Lord to his church. Such activity is seen most vividly in 1 Cor. 14, and its fruits are probably found in some of the (admittedly few) moral teachings of the Lord given by Paul (e.g., 1 Cor. 14:37; 1 Thess. 4:2); in the letters to the churches in Rev. 2–3; and, less identifiably, in sayings in the Gospels. In 1 Cor. 7:10, Paul shows that this kind of access to Jesus' teaching was compatible with a concern for the historically mediated tradition coming down from his ministry. The very fact that the tradition of Jesus' teaching developed so freely (witness the evidence of both the canonical Gospels and a document like the *Gospel of Thomas*) shows how powerful and legitimate such prophetic activity, with ancillary literary processes, was in the view of many Christians.

Third, there is the question of how far it is proper to abstract Jesus' ethical teaching from the rest of his work. The best understanding of his ministry is that his prime concern was for the sovereignty (the kingdom) of God, seen as the reality of his power, soon to be triumphantly revealed in an act of cosmic scope. In that case, Jesus' message was a challenge to decision: for or against the cause of God. It was therefore ethical in the sense that it was a call to repentance, but scarcely

in the sense that it contained detailed guidance for ordinary daily living—for such living would soon be a thing of the past. On this view, the comparative (though by no means total) lack of ethical material in the Gospel of Mark, seen as the first of the four to be written, is understandable. Indeed, such ethical material as Mark gives is itself to be taken as part of the proclamation of God's new age rather than as standing in its own right as anything like moral law. The command to a prospective follower to sell his possessions (Mark 10:17–22) is a challenge to his whole direction of life in the light of God's call, not the enunciation of a timeless rule on the rightness or wrongness of possessions; and the forbidding of divorce (Mark 10:2–16) is a picturing of life in the kingdom, a renewed Eden, not law for the church. It is then necessary to hold that the subsequent Gospels of Matthew and Luke show some movement away from this overwhelmingly theological conditioning of ethics. Their much more abundant presentation of Jesus' ethical teaching may reflect neither the emphasis of his lifetime nor indeed a genuine legacy of it, but rather the need of somewhat less eschatologically minded congregations in the later 1st century for authoritative guidance on a host of everyday problems. Here our third question links with the first two: Both the activity of the Evangelists in developing the tradition and that of inspired Christian preachers representing the voice of the living Lord may have contributed to the meeting of this need. At all events, the ethical teaching of Jesus came to be, in the Gospels of Matthew and Luke, a much more substantial and, to a degree, independently identifiable entity than it had been before, so far as our evidence goes.

The third of the preliminary questions amounts to a caveat about the very status of this subject: It is not as isolable as it may seem, and to take it as an independent topic may be to falsify. The other two questions have a different role. They show how problematic is any attempt to discover the ethical teaching of Jesus. Granted that it should not be set apart from his message as a whole, its content can only be reached by making a judgment about the contributions of members of the early church, whether prophets or the Evangelists themselves, to the teaching that lies before us in the Gospels; and it is impossible for that judgment to be made with finality and certainty. In that case, the subject may dissolve altogether, and we may have to be content with "the ethical teaching of Mark," etc. Certainly, the problems are not such that they can simply be raised in a theoretical way and then put aside while we proceed to a straightforward account of the Gospel material, topic by topic.

Nevertheless, it is important to balance the account so far given. There are certain thrusts in the Gospels that are so dominant, and often so original, that they bear every mark of representing to us the authentic emphases of Jesus' teaching.

The most pervasive and far-reaching in its effects is Jesus' attitude to the Jewish law. Though, as it is presented in the Gospels, this is a prime example of overlay by later Christian developments, that attitude seems to have had both negative and positive aspects. In Judaism, the law was far more than a code of ethics. With its stories of primeval events and the foundations of Israel, as well as its detailed provisions for life and worship, the Mosaic law*, contained in the Bible's first five books, gave a comprehensive framework for the life of God's people. Essentially, it was the gracious gift of God to Israel, the chief expression of the bond between them. But the center of Jesus' message was the kingdom of God*: The new immediacy of God's relationship with his own could not but set the law in a wholly new light. In its fundamental role, as providing the structure of an ordered life, it was redundant. A new situation had arrived, and "ordered life" was not a way to describe its character and concern. So there is a major shift of interest. By comparison with the Judaism of his day, Jesus represents (even in the somewhat exceptional Gospel of Matthew; see below) an abandonment of interest in the major issues of the law as discussed in his day: matters of ritual cleanliness and table fellowship, which in practice dominated the current scene, and questions of calendrical and ritual observance, especially in relation to the Sabbath. The emphasis falls instead on direct response to God's urgent summons, forcibly expressed in obedience to the dual command to love God and love the neighbor.

All this is most clearly seen in the Gospel of Mark, where the Sabbath law is dismissed (2:23–3:6), ritual cleanliness set at nought (7:1–23), and the love command emphasized (12:28–34). There is of course a chance that we have here the doctrine of a Marcan church that had radicalized the teaching of Jesus. But it is easier to see this as the authentic note of a Jesus who thereby attracted the hostility of the more orthodox of his contemporaries and who was distinctive enough to launch, in effect if not necessarily by design, a movement that survived. This has a strong claim to be the truth, even though parts of the church proved unable to maintain Jesus' radical teaching on some of the matters before us. In particular, the Gospel of Matthew testifies to a reaction against the radicalism found in Mark. The crucial statement on the Sabbath in Mark 2:27 is omitted and the love command is specifically said to offer no mitigation of the rest of the law (Matt. 22:40), which plainly remains in force (Matt. 5:17–19; 23:3, 23), even though that command, brought to a position of primacy and in effect expounded in Matt. 5:20–48, sets the law in a quite new perspective. It enables an ethic of law to be received in the new and invigorating spirit of Jesus, the gentle, saving Messiah for whom love is central (11:28–30). In making such a fusion of elements, Matthew's Gospel is a major achievement in the development of Christian ethics. To be sure, it retains an attachment to the Jewish law as valid for Christians—though some important aspects of it, such as circumcision, make no appearance, and we cannot tell whether they have been dropped or are taken for granted. But this attachment to the law did not, it seems, long survive the circumstances of Matthew's church, and Matthew's Gospel was widely interpreted in less strenuous terms. It is true that while Matthew's dependence on Mark need not be taken to mean that, on this crucial issue, his different presentation moves away from an authenticity that Mark preserved, there is no adequate ground for believing that he was better informed historically than Mark, and the words of condemnation of Mark's radical Jesus are more credible than those of Matthew's less deeply disturbing figure.

In the Gospel of Luke, too, there is some "deradicalizing" of Mark (e.g., Mark 2:27 is once more omitted), but in the interests of a weaker endorsement of the law than Matthew's, apparently in line with Luke's sense of Judaism's vital preparatory role for the gospel. The two later Evangelists, in other words, have theological convictions that make it possible for us to see why they should amend Mark's picture. And while it cannot be demonstrated that Mark's picture is itself not similarly motivated (indeed, there is no reason to deny that Mark believed the teaching he presents), there is good ground for saying that it makes the best historical sense to take Mark's picture as broadly faithful to Jesus' own outlook.

This is all the more likely to be so because on other related matters the Evangelists are at one, and on at least one matter there is greater coherence with Mark's general picture than with Matthew's. This is the matter of Jesus' open acceptance of social (and legal) outcasts, especially into table fellowship. Mark's fundamental statement of this theme (2:13–17) is taken over by his successors without significant modification. It is apparent that Jesus issued a merciful and gracious call that brushed aside moral and ritual qualification as a prerequisite for acceptance into his circle. In Matthew, this aspect is bound to seem a piece of messianic largesse, an exception to a general policy of acceptance of law. We note that once more it is hard to distinguish ethics from doctrine: Is this a picture of the life of the kingdom, God's way with human beings, or an expression of the ethic of love? Or is it false to distinguish?

Nevertheless, ethical guidelines may be discerned. Even if the words to the rich man (Mark 10:17–22) are best seen as the expression of God's call, there is still a refusal to ratify the possession of wealth. The Gospel of Luke makes this one of its major themes, with its blessing of the poor (1:53; 4:18; 6:20) and its condemnation of the rich and the extortionate (16:19–31; 19:1–10), but the basis is there in Mark: This is not to be dismissed as a piece of Lucan creativity, even though it is certainly a Lucan emphasis.

Moreover, it is not a feature that is out of line with other aspects. The blessing is upon not only the poor but also those who mourn and are persecuted (Luke 6:21–22). Once more, these words may or may not be close to those of Jesus in his lifetime, but they typify an emphasis that is too strong and pervasive to be put aside. It is partly a matter of the reversal of worldly fortunes and worldly values, partly a matter of an outlook characterized by the coming kingdom: the assurance of the future determines attitudes in the present. Again, ethical matters do not stand alone.

But not only do they merge into belief, they are also close to what later times would call spirituality. It is a matter of the character of a whole response to God, of which moral action is one crucial expression. That character is one of simplicity and openness—the childlike attitude enjoined in Mark 10:13–16. There is an absence of hankering after worldly gain and prestige, and a readiness to serve rather than to rule (Mark 10:35–45; Luke 22:24–27), to forgive and be forgiven (Matt. 6:14–15). Though it is no doubt possible to see here the values of a small charismatic and missionary community—perhaps the Palestinian churches in the decades after Jesus' lifetime—there is every reason to suppose that there was no discontinuity in these matters between Jesus and his subsequent as well as his immediate followers. This is all the more likely when, clearly, it was precisely features of this kind which were hardest to maintain in the more settled urban congregations that soon came to predominate in the church of the eastern Mediterranean lands.

In giving an account of the ethical teaching of Jesus, it is hard to avoid securely and scrupulously all the pitfalls that the nature of historical investigation and the character of the Gospels place in our path. It is hard to avoid being at some points more confident than the evidence strictly allows or more cautious than probabilities indicate. It is misleading simply to abstract sayings from the Gospels and arrange them subject by subject. This would represent not the ethical teaching of Jesus but exactly what has been said: a topically arranged abstract of the ethical sayings in the Gospels. But it is also misleading to suppose that in the Gospels we have no access to anything below the surface. The Evangelists were inspired and nourished by a tradition that stemmed from the life and work of Jesus. What we do not know is where authentic tradition ends and later development takes over. And we must reckon that in considering spoken teaching we are dealing with something so fluid, shifting from occasion to occasion and audience to audience, that fixity and authenticity are false objectives. A grasp of major thrusts, such as those we have identified, is the best we can hope to achieve. There is a likelihood that, while both the theological message and the ethical teaching of Jesus were open to modification in the years following his ministry, the latter was particularly prone to such change, under the pressure of the needs of the churches. That is the fundamental reason why appeal to the teaching of Jesus for present-day guidance is so risky. The Evangelists themselves, even dealing with such general questions as the proper attitude to the law, differ very considerably in their presentation of Jesus' attitude. How false then to dogmatize for quite different circumstances on the basis of teaching found in only one of the Gospels or, worse, an uncritical and incoherent mixture of them all that corresponds to what no one actually taught. A discernment of the major thrusts gives no license for any such assembling of texts with a view to direct modern application.

What is called the Sermon on the Mount* (Matt. 5–7) is often the victim of such mishandling. On the surface it seems to be the quintessence of Jesus' moral teaching and fit to serve as a basic text for the ethics of those who wish to follow him. But quite apart from its numerous parallels in Jewish teaching, this is clearly a literary composition as it now stands, one of five major discourses introduced, largely, by Matthew into the narrative taken over from Mark, and made up—in uncertain proportions—of traditional elements and his own doctrine of the Christian life in the community to which Jesus' message and work had given rise and to which Jesus continued to give his presence (Matt. 28:20). As we have seen, its balance of endorsement of the old law and new stringency, but under the gracious tutelage of Jesus the Messiah, is a change from Mark's radicalism and is the specific achievement of Matthew's genius in the circumstances that faced him. That is where the Sermon belongs: it is not timeless.

This is not to say that such long-ago achievement has no relevance to other times and places, such as our own. But it is to say that it must come to us through the filter of the best understanding we can gain of its historical origins, with their complexity and uncertainty. Only in the light of such discrimination can we expect both to hear the voice and grasp the context of Jesus' teaching about the human response to God's call. We shall then hear a voice that met the coming end of all things, not with passive or fearful acceptance, but with joyful and life-giving activity. This voice replaced the casuistry of Judaism by a grasp of the total demand of God and of the essential features of the life he required; and it substituted, for a way of religion in which ethics threatened to legislate their way into the whole of life, one in which

ethics were swallowed up in the overwhelming claim of God to human allegiance.

See also **Eschatological Ethics; Neighbor; New Testament Ethics.**

R. Bultmann, *Jesus and the Word* (1926), ET 1934; J. L. Houlden, *Ethics and the New Testament,* 1973; W. H. Kelber, *The Oral and the Written Gospel,* 1983; R. Schnackenburg, *The Moral Teaching of the New Testament,* ET 1965.

J. L. HOULDEN

Jewish Ethics

Numerous issues divide scholars seeking to characterize the ethics of Judaism. Two general difficulties prevent easy delimitation of the field: lack of agreement as to what constitutes "ethics" and the philosophic contention that theocentric moralities, such as that of Judaism, may not properly be termed "ethics." More troublingly, the authoritative Jewish sacred texts, the Bible and the Talmud, do not use the term "ethics" or reflect so Hellenic an intellectual category. The holy, rather than the good, seems to be their most inclusive value. Efforts to describe the ethics of Torah, God's "instruction," began only in the 9th century C.E. when Jews encountered Greek philosophy via Muslim culture. These treatments struggled to discover generalizations that would be true to the multiple, discrete behests of the Written and Oral Torahs (one dynamic whole), God's instructions.

When the fifteen-century European segregation and persecution of Jews ended (beginning about the time of the French Revolution), Jewish thinkers responded to the grant of equality by creating new theories of the ethics of Judaism. The most notable of these, that of Hermann Cohen (1842–1918), radically identified the ethics of Judaism with neo-Kantian ethics. In some watered-down sense, that notion lies behind the use of the term "Jewish ethics" in most discussions. But despite the continuing efforts of a few to rehabilitate this position, most Jewish thinkers, for historical and philosophical reasons, have abandoned it. Consensus now exists only on the problems involved in working on the ethics of Judaism and on certain themes it encompasses. But how to respond to the former and structure the latter remain highly contentious. This article seeks to communicate a representative historical overview plus an account of divergent contemporary approaches to this field, all necessarily filtered through one perspective.

For the biblical authors, human responsibility derives from God's reality. One God and no other created the universe, set its rules, oversees its affairs, and participates in its activities in both ordinary and extraordinary ways. This sovereign yet involved God created humankind different from other creatures, making people uniquely capable of knowing and doing God's will. Remarkably, the undisputed Ruler of the universe gave human beings the freedom to do or not to do the divine commands. The ethics of Judaism begins at this juncture: a God who might but does not coerce persons and a person created for special intimacy with God who may freely will to obey or transgress God's stated will (see **Old Testament Ethics**).

The distinctive urgency connected with the Bible's injunctions to action stems not only from their being God's stated behests but from the knowledge that God "cares" supremely about human action. Diverse human metaphors are employed to make the divine priorities plain. God weeps, pants, suffers, roars, regrets, rages, threatens, punishes, and much else, in response to humankind's freely chosen sinfulness. God's concerns embrace much more than the Greeks considered ethics, e.g., the interdiction of idolatry. Nonetheless, moral considerations occupy a major place in the biblical legislation, are a constant theme in the historical books, run strongly through wisdom literature and dominate the prophetic condemnations of their people. Classic Judaism summons humankind and the Jewish people to action for God's sake. One can only hope to understand its character and the ethics it encompasses if one appreciates the manifold religious levels on which its teaching is communicated and experienced.

This centrality of ethics in the service of God applies to all human beings equally. Neither the Bible nor the Talmud contains serious denial that God is the God of all humankind and established and maintains a covenant with them all. The early chapters of Genesis specify God's ethical expectations of humankind. As the fate of Sodom and Gomorrah indicates, God cares about Gentile behavior even after there are Jews. More tellingly, God's acceptance of the repentance of the utterly sinful Ninevites, for all that Jonah found it a personal affront, indicates how firmly the relationship between God and the Gentiles remains in force.

In rabbinic Judaism, this universal doctrine was reflected in Jewish law. On the basis of the covenant God made with Noah and his children, the rabbis held Gentiles to be bound by seven fundamental commandments: not to blaspheme, or to practice idolatry, or to steal, or murder, or commit sexual offenses, or to cut limbs off living animals and, positively, to establish courts to administer justice. Obviously, authoritative Jewish teaching has an embracing sense of the (religious) ethical competence of all human beings, one which rabbinic tradition amplified in its customary extension of these basic laws.

The rabbis' teaching about human nature similarly applies equally to Gentiles and Jews. Two inner urges, the will-to-do-good and the will-to-do-evil, battle within each human soul. No one ever fully staves off the will-to-do-evil, but like Moses, God's most intimate servant, all eventually sin. With sin understood as a choice, its rectification also takes place by a free human act: repentance, the turning back to God. If, however, one has sinned against another human being, one must first make such restitution as one can before asking for God's forgiveness (which, the rabbis stress, is always forthcoming to the sincere soul). All this transpires without benefit of special rite, personnel, or occasion, as the case of the Ninevites demonstrates.

One other aspect of the ethical theory of human nature deserves attention. For the biblical authors and the rabbis, human nature remains critically social. One is indissoluble not only with one's family but with one's folk or nation. Thus the classic ethics of Judaism address the community or society as much as the individuals who constitute them. So seamlessly do these notions blend that often in the book of Psalms we cannot tell whether an individual or the nation speaks or is being addressed—and occasionally the poet moves between the two with no apparent unease. So too the traditional ethics of Judaism manifests an utter interpenetration of what might elsewhere be distinct domains of individual and social ethics*.

The biblical authors and the rabbis believe God brought the Jewish people into being and established a special covenant with it because the Gentile nations consistently sin. God's election involves the gift of God's Torah, the divine "instruction." The Torah proper, i.e., the first five books of the Bible, indicates the acts God's people ought to do, expressing this more in the form of law than of the stories and teaching which extend its application and give it its meaning. The rest of the Bible—the rabbis spoke of the whole as the Written Torah—includes considerable exhortation but little commandment. In the latter books of the Bible, Torah-instruction occurs as intimate poetry and practical apothegm, touching short story and detailed history, social criticism and bizarre vision of a distant future.

The ethical thrust of the covenant* with the Jews hardly comes as a surprise given the biblical view of God and humankind. It urges Jews to be just with others and yet more than just. A repetitive theme in the commandments demands special concern for the powerless: the widow, the stranger, the orphan. So, too, the community must take care of the poor; not to the point of perverting justice for them (one may also not pervert justice for the rich), but in acknowledging the right of the indigent to community support. Such laws, so to speak, command compassion*, seeking to make personal response as urgent a responsibility as obedience to specified duties. For God's justice* and mercy* can never be completely spelled out, and the fullest service of God must come through living up to one's personal likeness to God.

The Oral Torah, i.e., the dynamic, still continuing, rabbinic elaboration of the Written Torah and the received traditions, only amplifies these tendencies (for Jews read the Bible through the rabbinic tradition). Ethics remains a subcategory of holiness*, and the rabbis impart ethical instruction in many different ways.

Their vast literature has customarily been read in terms of two levels of authority. The one, *halakhah,* "the way," had the power of law and was enforceable in Jewish courts (though some of it remained more ideal than practical). The other, *agadah* (or *haggadah*), perhaps "the lore," included all that was not *halakhah;* while an integral part of God's Oral Torah, it allowed for greater individual freedom of response and action. Ethical prescriptions abound in the *halakhah* with its detailed concern, for example, about fair business practices. Since much of the agadic

literature is homiletic or exegetic, it contains many general comments on how one ought to live—but also a puzzling diversity of opinion. Students of ethics have found agadic teachings of particular interest because they appeal to one's self-determination. Thus, while the *halakhah* enjoins some obligations of parents to their children, the bulk of the famous Jewish family ethos is taught in the *agadah* and in the community traditions which are its complement.

While neither the teachers of the Bible nor those of the Talmud define duty* primarily in terms of virtue* (or vice), it may convey something of the flavor of Jewish ethics to indicate some characterological concerns of the rabbis. They abominate lying, stealing, sexual immorality, violence, and bloodshed. They decry gossip, slander, faithlessness, injustice, hard-heartedness, arrogance, and pride. They glorify the industrious, honest, compassionate, charitable, trustworthy, humble, forgiving, pious, God-fearing soul. Their sense of the social emerges in homey fashion in their continuing emphasis on "acquiring a good name" and such customs as requiring even the poor supported by community funds to contribute to the communal philanthropic funds.

The rabbinic understanding of duty focuses on this world and prizes life as an ultimate if not absolute good. The rabbis believe devoutly in the resurrection of the dead. (They made it central to postbiblical Judaism.) And they often invoke its promise of eternal life and its threat of judgment-punishment as motives for righteous living. But these themes, like the love and fear of God, which medieval thinkers were to write about, remain in the background of their thought. Being intensely conscious—overawed would not be too strong a word—at possessing God's own instruction/instructions, they devote themselves to studying, explicating, applying, and living them. They disparage speculation on what happened before creation, have some greater tolerance of theories of what will happen in the days of the Messiah, but remain resolutely agnostic about what will follow it in the future-to-come.

One result is a passion for life and whatever will make it possible (*see* **Life, Sacredness of**). Should someone's life be at stake, every law of the Torah which stands in the way of saving it *must,* as a divine command, be broken, save three: the prohibitions against idolatry, murder, and sexual sins. Thus, Jewish medical ethics has been relatively open to experimentation and advance whenever they could be shown to save threatened lives. This "bias toward life" cannot be reduced to an easy formula. Thus, rabbinic law on the dying patient is strongly weighted against hastening the end. But though the rabbis have great respect for a fetus as a potential person, if its mother's life is threatened by it, it must be aborted. In the latter case, note that the "is," as determined by competent medical personnel, becomes fundamental to the legal-ethical decision of the rabbi.

From the completion of the Talmud to the beginnings of Jewish modernity (roughly from 500 C.E. to the French Revolution), several intellectual movements affected the further development of Jewish ethics. Each based itself on the Bible and the Talmud and accepted the ongoing developments in Jewish law as the context of its teaching. They all learned from one another, making the distinctions between them somewhat artificial. Nonetheless, for clarity's sake scholars speak of the separate genres of *musar,* or pietistic literature, of philosophy, and of mysticism.

The nature of *musar* literature is epitomized in the title of its first major work, Bahya ibn Pakuda's *Hovot Halevavot,* the Duties of the Heart, a Spanish-Jewish book of the late 11th century. Bahya sought to clarify the inner responsibilities that devolve upon the Jew and complement the external obligations specified by the rabbis. Primarily, he urged individuals to cultivate an intimate sense of God's greatness. That would lead them to act so as to gain God's favor and avoid God's judgment. This inner sensitivity would also bring them to deep concern for others, seeking to do more than merely fulfill their obligations toward them. The cultivation of piety and with it compassionate living so characterizes this work and the literature which followed it that some scholars have characterized the *musar* books as primarily ethical.

The pietists introduced other themes of ethical import into medieval Jewish thought. They counseled heightening one's sense of the evil of sin and of the terror of God's punishment so as to strengthen one's will-to-do-good. They also thought of the body as the antagonist of the soul in the fight to remain pure in heart and deed. Though rabbinic Judaism recognizes some dichotomy between body and soul, the rabbis had a far more integrated and less dualistic notion of the self than that of the musarists. However, whatever temptation they had to move on to full-scale asceticism was reined by the law which commanded marriage, procreation, festive celebrations, and other worldly activities.

The *musar* literature was intended for the masses and became widely read. Its influence may be judged from the growth of the custom, in late medieval times, of writing an "ethical will" for one's family. Few significant pietistic works appeared after the 18th century, largely because they seemed out of place in the humanistic, self-confident 19th century. An attempt to recast the insights of the pietists was made by Israel Lipkin (1810–1883). He founded the Musar movement, which introduced pietistic-ethical devotion and practices into the traditional East European *yeshivot,* the academies devoted almost entirely to the study of *halakhah.*

Medieval Jewish pietism arose amid Muslim civilization, and scholars have sought to explicate its roots in Muslim piety, particularly in Sufi mysticism, as well as in the Neoplatonism* that figures so strongly in them. This Hellenic-Muslim mixture also formed the background of medieval Jewish philosophy and was responsible for the ethical treatises which form a minor part of it. In these, however, the Aristotelian heritage, with its emphasis upon intellect and its understanding of human nature, became dominant.

Medieval Jewish mysticism was, like Jewish philosophy, an essentially elitist enterprise until its last period, that of Hasidism (beginning in the 18th century). Through its long history it retained a strong ethical content. While teaching its adepts the proper way to intimate communion with God, it affirmed the immutability of God's Torah and hence of the content it commanded. Thus, Jewish mystic experience did not become antinomian. Rather, it reinforced and extended the content of classic Jewish teaching, particularly the *musar* stress on ethical sensitivity as a means to holiness.

After fifteen centuries of segregation and persecution, the grant of equality* which came fitfully to various European Jewries shattered the old patterns of Jewish life and thought. Modernity meant secularization*, certainly for Jews, whose only hope of social equality lay in the creation of civic domains where religion, i.e., Christianity, did not rule. It also changed the scope of Jewish responsibility. Where Jews had once been excluded from civic affairs they were now expected to be good citizens and think in terms of the general welfare. The classic Jewish sources had not considered such an eventuality. Much talmudic and later Jewish law assumes (with good reason) existence in a hostile social environment. It therefore divides Jewish duty into the spheres of those who share one's laws and values, other Jews, and those who do not, Gentiles. One's kin receive more generous treatment than do the oppressive outsiders, though God's covenant with Gentiles mandated significant ethical duties toward them. When, however, social equality came, it required a new Jewish social ethic. Elaborating it became a major intellectual task for 19th-century Jewish thinkers.

Producing a more explicitly universal Jewish ethics required facing another challenge: secularization made human experience the substitute for divine revelation, the foundation of classic Jewish thought and ethics. The successful resolution of this intellectual problem gave rise to what has become the accepted ideology of contemporary Jewry—and also to the criticisms which have brought into being three alternative theories of modern Jewish ethics.

In Immanuel Kant's ethics, 19th-century Jewish thinkers found a philosophical framework by which to specify what they now took to be the essence of Judaism (see **Kantian Ethics**). In the work of Hermann Cohen, the founder of Marburg neo-Kantianism, this effort achieved academic fulfillment. Cohen argued that the ethical dimension of human rationality must be said to undergird its other Kantian modes, scientific and aesthetic thought. To integrate these three activities of the mind, every rational world view requires a unique, transcendent idea, what religions call God. Philosophy therefore mandates religion of reason, ethical monotheism.

In actual history, Cohen argued, this idea first appeared in the prophets of Israel and it remains the rational unity integrating all the subsequent development of Judaism. Thus, Jewish law is at heart a training for ethics, and that ethics, for all its limitation to one community, ideally aims at universal inclusiveness. In the modern period, with Jews freed from the ghetto, this universal core could now freely express itself. Jews should give up anything in their tradition that contradicts ethics and preserve everything that either teaches or abets it. Contemporary Jewish duty must now be as directed toward humankind as to the Jewish people. Indeed, Cohen argued that Jews had a historic mission to teach this concept of ethical monotheism to all of humanity since their religion possessed it more purely than did any other.

Ideas such as these had an almost incalculable influence upon the lives of all modernized Jews, though they were for long particularly cherished in Reform Judaism. Even those Jews who have given up Jewish belief have often still maintained a commitment to ethics as the criterion of true humanity. The statistically disproportionate involvement of Jews in every activity for human betterment derives from this reinterpretation of Jewish responsibility. The same is true of the standard apologies for Jewish practice—that they are, essentially, training for ethics; and for Jewish continuity—that no other religion produces such devotion to ethical living.

Critics have challenged the Jewish and ethical adequacy of this theory. Its identification of Judaism with a universalistic ethics has been rejected as untrue to Jewish history and destructive of particular Jewish duty. Over the centuries, Jews have thought of themselves as rabbinic rather than "prophetic" Jews and rabbinic law may have some universal, ethical themes but cannot, without distortion, be equated with a humanistic morality. Rather, this theory says more about 19th-century German philosophy than it does about the Jewish tradition. If proof of this charge is required, it can be found in the "commandments" generated by this system. It commits Jews primarily to universal ethics, relegating Jewish ritual and communal responsibility to a secondary, optional role. That may create good people but might also lead to the disappearance of the unique Jewish service of God.

In reaction to Judaism-as-ethics, some thinkers advocated a historicist approach to Jewish duty, and though it has found institutional expression in Conservative Judaism it has not been given academic theoretical explication. These thinkers contended that history indicated that there could be no Judaism without its legal system, *halakhah.* Any modern Judaism, to be worthy of the name, must therefore operate within the classic legal framework. That, however, should now be understood in terms of the modern notion of historic development. As scholarly research indicates, Jewish law has changed over the centuries, not infrequently as the result of growing ethical sensitivity. Were a modern scholar class to respond dynamically out of Jewish law to questions of the day, contemporary Jews might hope to have a properly ethical and Jewish determination of their responsibility.

This view, too, has had its critics. Orthodox Jewish thinkers have charged that while it properly identifies Judaism with *halakhah,* it perverts the classic Jewish understanding of how the law develops. Changes in Jewish law in the past arose primarily out of concern for Jewish teaching and only secondarily to adapt to the Gentile world. The inauthenticity of the historicist treatment of the law has been made manifest by its validating changes in practice that traditionalist scholars and the bulk of the observant community have found contrary to *halakhah.* Considering the moral and spiritual emptiness of much of Western civilization—a civilization which could give rise to the Holocaust—its values should not become a guide to the Jewish service of God. Rather, the determination of Jewish law and ethics should be left to those who have come to merit the respect of the observant, learned Jewish community. Reverent continuity, not presumptuous change, should be the hallmark of Jewish obligation.

Feminists have radically challenged the ethical sufficiency of the historicist and Orthodox interpretations of Jewish duty. By universal standards, Jewish law is sexist and unethical. This is not to deny that the *halakhah* may have extended women's rights over the ages and given Jewish women a higher communal status than that of other women of their time. Nonetheless, it denies women equality with men, most troublingly by insisting that men make all the decisions about women's Jewish religious status. Despite these charges, the sages of Orthodoxy have ruled that *halakhah* prohibits any major changes in Jewish law and practice with regard to women. The historicists have split over this issue. The more traditional among them agree with the Orthodox that loyalty to the procedures and precedents of Jewish law makes it impossible to grant many of the changes feminists desire. Others argue

that Jewish law does not explicitly prohibit greater equality for women, such as their right to be ordained, but, dynamically read, can authorize changes in women's status.

A personalistic, Buberian approach to these issues has also been advocated. It accepts the liberal notion that a universal ethical sensitivity must be basic to a modern Judaism. But it denies the continuing adequacy of the Kantian understanding of the ethics, which derives from a conception of the self as fundamentally a construction of one's reason. Instead it proposes to integrate rationality into a more comprehensive, existentialist sense of the self, producing thereby an ethics of relationship rather than of rational rule. Likewise, it reinterprets Jewish authenticity in relational terms, suggesting that Jewish responsibility derives from personally sharing the Jewish people's covenant with God. The *halakhah* and *agadah* may then be the Jew's best guides to authentic obligation— but they must now be read in terms of a given individual's present response to God as one of God's dedicated ethnic community. The proponents of this view find its pluralism amid traditionalism appealing, but its critics charge that its individualism will destroy the community cohesiveness necessary for the Jewish people to continue to serve God in history.

Two centuries of growing freedom have so ingrained the expanded ethical commitment of Jews that it has become fundamental to their Jewish existence. But the community and its thinkers remain deeply divided as to just how to define the character and content of Jewish ethics.

J. D. Bleich, *Contemporary Halakhic Problems,* vols. 1 and 2, 1977–83; E. B. Borowitz, *Choosing a Sex Ethics,* 1969; H. Cohen, *Religion of Reason Out of the Sources of Judaism,* 1972; D. Feldman, *Birth Control in Jewish Law,* 1968; S. Spero, *Morality, Halakhah and the Jewish Tradition,* 1983.

EUGENE B. BOROWITZ

Johannine Ethics

A cursory reading of the Gospel of John in the interests of a quest for ethical material is bound to lead to disappointment. By contrast with the Gospels of Matthew and Luke in particular, there is here no teaching on such practical topics as marriage, divorce, possessions, tax-paying, or even on desirable moral qualities such as mercy, humility, or peaceableness. All that emerges—and then not until the Gospel is half over—is the "new commandment," to "love one another" (John 13:34; 15:12, 17), and three references to keeping the commandments of Jesus, which remain unspecified (14:15, 21; 15:10). The reference to "my commandment" (singular) in 15:12, following close on the reference to Jesus' commandments (plural) in 15:10, suggests that in fact in all these passages the writer had in mind only the single command, that Jesus' followers should love one another, and used the plural either loosely or to signify "what Jesus commanded," i.e., to love, in its many applications. The "new commandment" itself is excessively general, but there appears to be a clue to its content in the story of the foot washing in ch. 13, with which it is (if a little distantly, vs. 12–17, 34) associated. To love one another is to serve one another in deep humility and against worldly expectation.

Two points are to be noted. First, this emphasis on the reversal of worldly values and on the duty of mutual service (see **Mutual Aid**) in the community of Jesus is a link with other parts of the tradition, even though the story of the foot washing itself is confined to John: Mark 10:35–45; Luke 22:24–27. Thus it is a common and pervasive feature of Jesus' teaching. Second, the message of the foot washing story is not purely ethical, it is also, probably primarily, doctrinal. It sets forth the character of Jesus' condescension and self-abasement as God's Son to the lowliness of human existence, exemplified dramatically in his servile act. This fusion of ethics and theology is an important clue to the Johannine outlook. What is enjoined in ch. 13 is not so much a particular line of behavior ("love one another") as a total standpoint, or rather the recognition of the true position of each of us in relation to God and humankind, realized in the new life brought by Jesus.

This fusion goes some way to explain the single-minded concentration on the one commandment and the form in which it is put. To take the latter point first, it is notable in its divergence from the Synoptic Gospels (and Paul, Rom. 13:9), where the moral law is summarized by direct quotation of Lev. 19:18: "Thou shalt love thy neighbor as thyself." That command, originally taken to apply to one's fellow Jews, was greatly widened in the teaching of Jesus to include not only all in need, even where taboos meant an absence of obligation (the point of the story of the good Samaritan, Luke 10:25–37), but even enemies (Matt. 5:43–48). When we turn to the Gospel of John, that remarkable and attractive openness has been lost and, in one perspective, there is a return to the old narrowness of feeling loyalty and duty only to one's own: "Love one another."

We may account for this Johannine teaching both sociologically and theologically. It is likely that it reflects the peculiarly close-knit quality of the Johannine congregations. In modern terms, they were sectarian in assumptions and outlook, and, while able to survey the universe in their doctrine, lived in practice segregated from "the world," viewed largely as alien or hostile (see **Sect**). Theologically, this teaching reflects not so much a narrowing of horizons or a meanness of spirit as the writer's understanding of the nature and mission of Jesus. He is God's envoy to the world, who reproduces among the believers that relationship of intimacy which Father and Son have enjoyed from all eternity. "Love" signifies not simply a style of moral disposition but rather the loyalty and attachment that binds together first Father and Son, and then the believers to one another through their shared relationship with Christ (John 13:34; 15:9–10). There is an important sense then in which even this commandment is not appropriately classified as a purely ethical statement, for it betokens a mode of being more than a program for action. Yet it has an ethical aspect: set forth in Jesus' own self-giving for his own (15:13; 13:12–17)—though his laying down of his life is itself not only an act of love but also one of salvation (3:13; 12:32).

The Johannine epistles, probably coming from a later stage in the life of these congregations, testify to a sad and notable shift in the bearing of the command to love one another. Although it is expressed here in sublime language, it is apparent that its application is now limited still further as far as this writer is concerned: to those members of his churches who have not fallen into what he regards as false belief (especially in the unreality of Jesus' humanity and their own immunity to sin), and have not broken away in schism (1 John 3:18–24). Nevertheless, as in the Gospel of John, Christ's love, shown in his death, is the source and model for love of the brethren (3:16), and love certainly receives a practical application here that the Gospel lacks (3:17; 4:19–20). It also carries with it a clear future hope (2:28; 3:3). In the First Epistle, this insistence on love here and now, yet in the light of future destiny, yields a sense of the need for continued repentance (1:8, 10) combined, perhaps uneasily, with a conviction of Christian life as always essentially one of sinlessness, even though restoration after falls is clearly provided for (3:5–6; 2:1; 5:16–17), at least in cases that fall short of the ultimate sin of separation from the true community of believers. As in the Gospel, but now more institutionally, the framework of God-given existence is the context of the moral life.

See **Ecclesiology and Ethics; Jesus, Ethical Teaching of; Love; Mutual Aid; Neighbor; New Testament Ethics.**

R. E. Brown, *The Community of the Beloved Disciple,* 1979; J. L. Houlden, *Ethics and the New Testament,* 1973; J. T. Sanders, *Ethics in the New Testament,* 1975.

J. L. HOULDEN

Jurisprudence *see* Law

Jus ad bellum
The right to go to war or the justice of resorting to war. *See* **Just War.**

Jus in bello
Right or just conduct in war. *See* **Just War.**

Just Price and Just Wage
The doctrine of the just price, and that of the just wage which is a special case of it, arose out of the medieval attempt to apply a detailed system of Christian ethics to every aspect of life. In any transaction, it was held, justice* requires that the seller receives a value equivalent to that of the goods and services which he or she provides to the buyer. In practice, this price was taken to be that arrived at by common evaluation, as reflected in prevailing market prices. Hence it was recognized that it must reflect changes in the general conditions of demand and supply, though it was also strongly maintained that a buyer's exceptional necessity did not give the seller the right to exact a higher return. Taking advantage of temporary shortages to extort high prices was regularly condemned.

The just wage, similarly, was a price for labor fairly regarded as equal to the value of the service provided by the seller to the buyer. Hence it was held to imply equal pay for equal working capacity, and that in each type of occupation the pay should be adequate to enable the worker to maintain the status associated with his or her position in life.

The detailed application of these principles to actual prices and wage rates was obviously easier in a slowly changing society, where customary rates were known and accepted over long periods, than it could be amid the rapid technological and social changes of the present day. When new products are always appearing and when technical innovation is constantly changing costs of production, creating a demand for new skills and destroying the demand for others, it is very difficult to say in practice exactly what a just price or a just wage should be. Modern economic theory, being thoroughly positivistic, does not use such concepts, but seeks rather to analyze the forces which lead to actual market prices and wage rates.

Yet the idea of fairness* or justice inevitably underlies much of our thinking on these matters. Consumers are concerned about the high prices charged by monopolies, or the results of resale price maintenance, whereas producers feel that prices should not be cut below what they consider to be a fair level. Trade unions* defend the "rate for the job" and seek to maintain comparability of pay with other occupations. During the inflationary years of the 1960s and 1970s, many countries tried to develop price and income policies, which inevitably involved the establishing of fair norms for pay and price rises.

M. P. Fogarty, in *The Just Wage* (1961), made an interesting attempt at a critique of contemporary British wage and income policy in the light of the doctrine. More recently, the papal encyclical *Laborem Exercens* (1981) reaffirmed the moral basis of the just wage as being the means by which workers and their families can have access to a fair share of the goods and services produced for common use. Hence it is seen as a means of verifying the justice of the socioeconomic system.

See **Wages and Salaries; Work.**

M. P. Fogarty, *The Just Wage,* 1961, repr. 1975; Papal Encyclical, *Laborem Exercns,* 1981.

JOHN F. SLEEMAN

Just Wage *see* **Just Price and Just Wage; Wages and Salaries;** *see also* **Justice**

Just War

The term "just war tradition" properly applies both to the moral tradition on war, its justification, and its limitation that has developed historically within Western culture as a whole, and to the Christian component of this larger tradition. The nature of the Christian idea of just war can be understood both thematically and historically. Thematically, it is the result of thinking through the implications of what may be called the "original just war question": May a Christian ever justifiably take part in violence? A negative answer to this question implies nonviolent pacifism, a major strand alongside just war tradition in Christian attitudes toward war. A positive answer requires going a stage further to address a number of corollary questions defining the conditions under which use of violence is morally permissible for a Christian. Thematically, Christian just war tradition is the collective response, over history, of individual Christian thinkers and of the church as an institution to these corollary questions.

Historically Christian ideas of just war may be said formally to begin with the writings of Ambrose of Milan and especially Augustine of Hippo in the 4th and 5th centuries. Both these early writers drew upon the existing Roman idea of *justum bellum* as well as on the OT paradigm of war commanded by God; Augustine additionally identified the reluctant and limited use of force as one of the ways in which a Christian might be required in charity to serve the needs of an innocent neighbor under attack by an assailant. The historical context of this reasoning was provided by the perceived need for Christians to participate in defending the Roman Empire, by that time a Christian state, from invading Germanic peoples. Just war tradition in Christian thought thus historically came into being as a product of a close relation between church and secular society, and it has ever since developed in dia-

logue with the requirements of statecraft as manifested in different eras.

In the Middle Ages the problems posed by the historical context were quite different: how to restrain internecine warfare among petty nobles and the depradations of marauders. Beginning with the Council of Narbonne in 1054 the church sought to impose limits by the Truce of God, which defined certain days as illicit for fighting. Another effort at restraint was the Peace of God, a version of the idea of noncombatant immunity, which sought to spare persons on religious duty the ravages of war. Weapons limitation was attempted by the Second Lateran Council in 1139, which banned crossbows, bows and arrows, and siege machines. All these restrictions were somewhat piecemeal and applied only to wars among Christians, where the church had moral authority over both sides. The 12th-century compiler of canon law Gratian in his *Decretum* (first published in 1148) began the process of systematization. His definition of just war drew heavily upon Augustine. Gratian's emphasis, like Augustine's, was on the justification for use of force (that which later came to be termed the *jus ad bellum*), though the beginnings of a doctrine on restraint in prosecuting just war (*jus in bello*) can be found in his retention of the earlier conciliar statements.

Before Gratian there was no unified body of Christian teaching on just war, only isolated and occasional statements. In the 13th century, largely on the foundation of the *Decretum,* such a coherent doctrine began to coalesce. Two generations of canonist successors (known as the Decretists and the Decretalists) clarified who might justly authorize war and elaborated on the Peace of God to produce a recognizably modern idea of noncombatant immunity. (In both cases they drew copiously on existing *jus gentium* and chivalric mores.) Simultaneously, theologians (most notably Peter of Paris and Thomas Aquinas) focused also on defining just cause and right intention. Right authority, just cause, and right intention, listed by Aquinas as the conditions for a just war, all derive from Augustine and entered medieval consciousness through Gratian; they have remained the nucleus of the *jus ad bellum.*

By the end of the Middle Ages just war tradition had solidified into a general cultural consensus on the justification and proper limits of the use of force; this was reflected in the thought of the Renaissance-Reformation period, in which this body of doctrine was assumed. Not only the concepts of authority, cause, and intention existed here; the *jus ad bellum* that was passed on included as well the ideas that force should be a last resort, should be proportionate to the evil remedied (*see* **Proportionality**), should expect to succeed in its ends, and should contribute to a new state of peace*. The *jus in bello* was defined by a broad and concrete consensus on noncombatant immunity (*see* **Discrimination**) and a concern for proportionate means in war. Regulation of weapons and of the days for fighting had disappeared as ineffective.

Among the chief problems posed for just war thought by the historical context in this period were how to limit religious warfare and the use of excessive force. In the mid-16th century Franciscus de Victoria declared baldly, "Difference of religion is not a cause of just war." But a century of religious warfare remained necessary to bring the point home. Apart from this issue, both religious and secular just war thought in this period concentrated on restraining the prosecution of war, a tendency marked in subsequent Western moral thought on war up until the present.

Much religious concern regarding war in the 19th century focused on the existence of large standing armies among the European powers, along with the expense of new military technologies. These concerns have continued into the present, where they are found in opposition both to what is often described as "militarism"* and to nuclear weaponry (*see* **Deterrence**). While partly rooted in a resurgent Christian pacifism*, much of this properly should be understood as following from such just war concepts as opposition to force except as last resort, the need that violent means be proportionate to the values served, and the concern to protect the innocent. That force may nonetheless sometimes be employed by Christians has also been strongly argued in this period, as for example in Reinhold Niebuhr's break with Christian pacifism in the 1930s and his writing during World War II, Paul Ramsey's application of just war reasoning to nuclear deterrence and the Vietnam War, and a stream of Catholic doctrine including the 1983 pastoral letter of the American Catholic bishops.

The relevance of just war thinking to the age of nuclear weapons is often challenged in contemporary debate, and it may be that pacifism is again, as at other times in the past, moving into the forefront of Christian consciousness. But in any case the question should not be the relevance of the just war idea as such; unless the use of force for the protection of values is to be utterly repudiated, then it is necessary to have some such body of moral wisdom and cultural practice on when force is justified and what limits should circumscribe it. For Western culture and within Christian thought, that body of moral wisdom is just war tradition. The more important questions are, as always in the past, how to relate Christian moral concerns to the larger tradition of just war and to the exigencies of the time. In the present context this implies such diverse lines of inquiry as asking whether arms limits should not now, as first in the Middle Ages, be a means of choice to set limits on war; or whether limited conventional war may not be the upper limit of allowable force for Christians; or whether "wars of liberation" may not be just in spite of the unsavory means, including terrorism*, they often employ; or what should be the limits to conscientious objection* in a national draft law. All these are the sorts of questions that have shaped just war tradition in the past; to engage in present debate over them is to enter that tradition and to help to shape its further development.

See also **Conventions; Crusade; Deterrence; Disarmament; Humanitarianism; International Order; Militarism; Nuclear Warfare; Pacifism; Peace; Torture; War.**

G. Best, *Humanity in Warfare,* 1980; J. F. Childress, *Moral Responsibility in Conflicts,* 1982; J. T. Johnson, *Ideology, Reason, and the Limitation of War,* 1975; and *Just War Tradition and the Restraint of War,* 1981; W. V. O'Brien, *The Conduct of Just and Limited War,* 1981; F. H. Russell, *The Just War in the Middle Ages,* 1975; L. Walters, "Five Classic Just-War Theories," Ph.D. diss., Yale University, 1971.

JAMES TURNER JOHNSON

Justice

Christian interpretations of justice have drawn in part on Greek thought, particularly Aristotle's categories as mediated through Thomas Aquinas. Aristotle distinguished general or legal justice from particular jus-

tice, the former being close to righteousness*
in human relations, the latter being divided
into commutative and distributive justice.
Commutative justice, which focuses on relations of members of a society to each other,
rectifies both voluntary transactions, such as
contracts*, in which both parties consent*,
and involuntary transactions, such as theft or
robbery, in which only one party consents.
Its main setting is civil law rather than criminal law, but it often includes criminal penalties because of the state's interest in prohibiting, deterring, and punishing such actions as
theft (see **Penology**). Distributive justice,
which considers the whole in relation to its
parts, focuses on the community's distribution of benefits, such as honors and wealth,
and burdens, such as taxation, to individuals
and groups. Especially since Pius XI's encyclical *Quadragesimo Anno* (1931), the phrase
"social justice" has been widely used to focus
on the common good* of the community,
including the distribution of benefits and burdens and respect for rights* (see **Official
Roman Catholic Social Teaching**).

Four senses of justice often employed in
theological discussion will be considered
here: (1) a norm for human moral agency
that has its source in the being and agency of
God; (2) a virtue of the moral agent; (3) a
norm for the governing of human relationships that compares and contrasts with a
standard of love for neighbor (*agapē*); (4) the
normative ordering and distribution of social
benefits and burdens among citizens of a
commonwealth. These senses are distinguished from, but not exclusive of, one another; they may and do overlap in various
contexts, and each may be understood to give
content to a certain formal sense of justice:
the rendering to a person what is due him or
her (*reddere suum cuique*).

1. The biblical conception of God depicts
him as one who is just or righteous, and who
as such remains faithful to the demands of a
relationship with human beings that is divinely established and constitutive of human
well-being (see **Righteousness**). God's justice
may be expressed in deeds that liberate the
weak and vulnerable from bondage, as well as
in judgment on the unfaithfulness of the people; yet both expressions reflect God's role as
Lord of a covenant* relationship. Correspondingly, the justice of human activity is
measured by its faithfulness (see **Fidelity**) to
the covenanting God, who may be identified

in creation and history, in the Law and the
Prophets, and ultimately for Christians, in
the story of Jesus Christ. The exact character
of the link between human justice and its
source in correspondence to the being of God
may vary across different Christian traditions. For example, in much Protestant
thought correspondence is established primarily by the analogical correlation of
human action to the pattern of God's saving
righteousness for the world as depicted in
scripture. Another position, prominent in
Roman Catholic ethics, focuses on the way
human moral action corresponds to the mind
of God, who as creator orders all things to
their proper ends; hence one may speak with
Thomas Aquinas of the natural moral law as
participating in God's eternal law (see **Natural Law**). In the first case human justice
mainly consists in imaging God's saving justice, while in the second it involves discernment* of and response to God's ordering of
creation to natural and supernatural ends.

2. Considered traditionally as a cardinal
virtue*, justice stands with and in relation to
prudence*, temperance*, and fortitude*. As
virtue*, justice is a trait of character* em-
powering and disposing an agent to act in
ways constitutive of human flourishing. As a
cardinal virtue, justice is an operative habit
setting the will in the direction of impartially
rendering to each his or her due or desert; but
justice requires for its effective realization the
power to discern the right means to secure
the good toward which justice disposes (prudence), the ability to order the passions for
single-minded pursuit of the good (temperance), and steadfastness in the pursuit even in
face of threats to the self (fortitude). As a
virtue relevant to Christian ethics, justice and
the other cardinal virtues are shaped and directed by charity*, the love of God and
neighbor. Given the idea that charity is the
"form of the virtues" (Thomas Aquinas), one
can say that the claims to which the charita-
bly just person attends are those proper to
one's status as indebted to God the creator
and redeemer, and those proper to the "alien
dignity" of persons created by and beloved of
God. Persons may also derive claims from
their membership in a particular group (e.g.,
family, political community), and these
claims gain fuller theological justification by
reference to theological anthropology and accounts of how particular human relationships witness to the being and agency of God.

3. There is a tradition of thought in contemporary Christian ethics that compares and contrasts the norm of Christian love* with the norm of justice. Contrasts often take their point of departure from the different moral situations to which the norms apply. For example, love in the sense of sacrificial regard for another's well-being may apply in relations between the self and the neighbor; justice, the impartial and evenhanded consideration of competing claims to well-being, may be the more fitting Christian response to the claims of third parties. Sometimes this contrast is softened to permit justice claims to apply to the self in the former case and agape to operate beyond the requirements of justice in the latter. Alternatively, justice may refer to contexts deeply conditioned by finitude and sin, in which individuals and especially groups assert themselves over against one another from dominantly self-interested motives and perspectives. As the norm of adjudication of claims to achieve a tolerable peace and harmony, justice is distinguished from the law of utterly disinterested love, which presupposes for its realization the absence of conflict and inordinate self-assertion (Reinhold Niebuhr). More simply, a contrast is sometimes drawn between personal and impersonal bonds among persons. Finally, contrast shades into strict opposition when the situation appropriate to justice encompasses considerations of merit *simpliciter,* over against the radically unmerited, unconditional, and gracious character of neighbor-love, for which God's own love is paradigm.

Several positive relationships have also been proposed for love and justice. Principles of justice entailing equal consideration of (competing) interests and respect for individual freedom may be viewed as approximations of neighbor-love under the conditions of history. Criteria of justice for the distribution of goods according to need also approximate Christian love. One way to reflect on the positive relationship is to locate the relevant bases for moral regard for each norm. What is due a citizen or medical patient or buyer in the marketplace is determined through a relevant, and therefore nonarbitrary, assessment of the claims of these persons, given their status in political or medical or economic relationships. Specification of justice requires specification of criteria appropriate to the nature of the re-

lationships in question; for example, it can be argued that ill health and not ability to pay is the relevant reason for receipt of medical care, and that justice, therefore, requires prima facie that health care be distributed independently of such ability (*see* **Health Care, Right to; Triage**). But the basis for moral regard in the case of Christian love is one's status as "beloved child of God," or as "sister or brother for whom Christ died," or as "one made to be a companion in the sharing of beatitude." Apart from all particular statuses, and in virtue of this "alien dignity," the neighbor's well-being is to be sought simply as such. Thus a pattern of regard for the neighbor* may and must embrace regard for the citizen or patient or buyer insofar as human well-being or flourishing is in some way at stake with respect to those roles. So agape may and does require more, but never less, than the demands of justice. (For further discussion of the relations of agape and justice, *see* **Love**).

4. A renewed and sophisticated interest in the justice of the political community has emerged since the publication of John Rawls's *A Theory of Justice* (1971). Conceived as "the first virtue of social institutions," justice concerns the fitting assignment of rights and duties, and of the benefits of social cooperation, to persons who participate in political society as free, and equal, and in pursuit of plans of life according to particular conceptions of the good. It applies to social circumstances characterized by scarcity of resources and by disagreement among persons about what sort of life makes for human fulfillment. Principles of justice are warranted through arguments which depict a hypothetical agreement about the organization of major political and economic institutions among persons who abstract from their particular life plans, and who thus would agree together as free and equal. For Rawls, a deeply egalitarian conception of justice emerges from this procedure; rights to equality* of liberty and opportunity are to be guaranteed, and social and economic inequalities must work to the benefit of the least advantaged persons in society.

This vision contrasts with utilitarian conceptions that identify justice with the maximization of total or average "happiness" or desire-satisfaction in society, rather than with equal respect for persons' separate life plans (*see* **Utilitarianism**). In its effort to *combine* values of liberty and material equality into a uniform moral ideal, Rawls's view (and others like it) is to be distinguished from two other approaches: (1) *libertarianism* * (*see also* **Capitalism**), which gives priority of place to protection of arrangements freely consented to and therefore uncoerced; and (2) *socialism* *, which stresses above all an ideal of social and material equality* through the overcoming of private privilege. Libertarians criticize socialists for the way their proposals interfere with private freedom of choice, and socialists respond with the charge that libertarian recommendations effectively undermine genuine human freedom by their inattention to human needs, and to the domination of persons by the accumulation of political and economic power* in private hands. Modified versions of each of these criticisms may be directed at Rawls's egalitarianism as well.

Questions about social and political justice in Christian ethics are often posed along the lines of the different positions sketched above. May one commend the deprivation of individuals' life prospects for the purpose of maximizing happiness overall, as some utilitarians claim? Is the threat of governmental intrusion into private engagements so great as to warrant severe restrictions on state power in providing for basic material needs of its citizens? On the other hand, does the satisfaction of basic human needs for health care, food, shelter, and the like have a special priority, compatible with public intervention when private initiatives fail? What ought to be the proper balance between respect for human needs and respect for human preferences? Disagreements among Christian ethicists about the answers to these questions finally hinge on disagreements over various background beliefs, such as the propriety of claims to sacrifice for others, the character of political community in a created but fallen world, and the concrete meaning of that dignity* which attaches to human beings in virtue of their common origin and destiny in God.

Reflection on the notion of justice may address the issue of specifying each of these four senses; but it also needs to pursue questions posed, as it were, to one context of use from others. For example, how is the justice of political life compatible with the idea that justice is a virtue? How exactly does the jus-

tice of God differ, for the purposes of human behavioral requirement, from the love of God? How compatible are theological and particular nontheological conceptions of social justice? Thus the agenda for Christian ethics is as imposing as it is important.

See **Charity; Equality; Exploitation; Fairness; Freedom; Liberalism; Love; Respect for Persons; Rights; Social Service of the Church; State; Welfare State.**

J. C. Haughey (ed.), *The Faith That Does Justice,* 1977; J. R. Lucas, *On Justice,* 1980; G. Outka, *Agape: An Ethical Analysis,* 1972; J. Pieper, *The Four Cardinal Virtues,* 1966; P. Ramsey, *Basic Christian Ethics,* 1950; J. Rawls, *A Theory of Justice,* 1971; J. Sterba (ed.), *Justice: Alternative Political Perspectives,* 1980.

WILLIAM WERPEHOWSKI

Justification *see* **Justification by Faith; Justification, Moral**

Justification, Moral

Moral or ethical justification is usually demanded and provided only when there are reasons to think that an act is wrong or bad, and it involves offering moral or ethical reasons for the act in question and showing that they outweigh the reasons against it. This sort of justification is common in ordinary moral discourse, being demanded by our consciences* as well as by others. And there is an ongoing assessment of these reasons, often involving various principles, rules, and values, as well as critical reflection on these reasons by moral philosophers and theologians, among others. Nevertheless, some theologians are very suspicious of moral or ethical justification of such actions as abortion, resistance, and war—e.g., justified abortion— not because they believe that such actions are always wrong, but because they so fear legalism* and self-righteousness (e.g., Helmut Thielicke) or restricting the sovereign freedom of God's command (Karl Barth) that they repudiate ethical justification. Hence, some theologians replace ethical justification by an assurance of justification by faith* or by an inner certainty of the divine command*. According to Jacques Ellul (*Violence,* ET 1969), "it is not so much violence itself as justification of violence that is unacceptable to Christian faith." For other Christians moral justification, including appeals to moral principles, rules, and values, is important and even indispensable, but it does not eliminate the need for God's grace or limit God's freedom. Its place is modest but significant, as long as agents are aware of the dangers of self-deception*, rationalization*, bad faith, ideology* (in its negative sense), and hypocrisy*. For a discussion of the process of justification, which is social as well as individual, *see* **Deliberation**.

See also **Casuistry; Decision; Norms; Situation Ethics.**

JAMES F. CHILDRESS

Justification by Faith

Justification by faith or, more fully, justification by grace through faith has been called "the article by which the Church will stand or fall." The usual designation, "justification by faith," is subject to such misunderstanding that the fuller statement "justification by grace alone, for Christ's sake, through faith active in good works" is preferable. Faith then is to be regarded as "the comprehensive name for the Christian God-relationship" (Gustaf Aulén).

For Paul, the only righteousness that saves is the active righteousness of God which is imparted to human beings (especially Rom. 1:16–17; Eph. 2:8–10). The agent in justification is entirely the gracious God, who covers the human being's sin, thus justifying the ungodly (Rom. 5:6–11) and at the same time creating the "new being" in Christ, that is, sanctification (2 Cor. 5:17–21). This view is abundantly substantiated by the total biblical witness.

Luther understood "justification" comprehensively: "Where there is forgiveness of sins, there is life and salvation." In distinction from the Roman conception of justification as a gradual process of growth in sainthood via sacramental infusions of grace employed in good works, he affirmed the all-at-once, gracious act of justification, which is at one and the same time a forensic act and an act of renewal. Grace* is not a power infused by God himself in his gracious disposition toward human beings and his gracious self-impartation to them. It is the *sinner* who is *declared* righteous and at the same time *made* righteous. One does not become good by doing good, but a person must first *be* good before he or she can *do* good. Only a

good tree brings forth good fruit (Matt. 7:16–20). At the beginning of the life of the Christian stands the once and for all, complete act of justification, which makes the sinner fully the forgiven child of God and heir of all the blessings of salvation. Full assurance of salvation thus rests wholly upon God's word which accomplishes what it says, and not on our faith in our own faith or on our good works. The Christian remains always "simultaneously righteous and a sinner" and, therefore, in need of daily repentance and renewal.

This has profound implications for the Christian life, for it is only when our pride and egocentricity, in which we seek ourselves in all we do, are broken by the act of justification, that we are free not to use our neighbor as a means to personal salvation. Then we become, by God's grace, channels through which God's *agapē* flows through us out to the neighbor. The direction is altogether from God down to humanity and out to the world's needs. There is a genuine "life together" based on openness to the neighbor where each one knows himself equally sinful yet equally beloved and accepted. This rules out false "perfectionism."* In all respects and at all times, in thoughts, words, and deeds, a person is justified only by grace through faith, which is never a meritorious work on the person's part since it is the work of God in him or her (*see* **Good Works**).

Thus it is invalid to object to "by faith alone." Works are not added to faith as its consequence, because faith is present only as it is alive in works, just as the sun is present only in its shining. Therefore, also, there is no contradiction when James says that faith without works is dead (James 2:17) or when, in the final judgment, it is the deed of love which is decisive (Matt. 25:31–45).

Thus the quality of the Christian life can always be judged by whether or not there is the realization that a person lives only by forgiveness* and is thereby freed and empowered to do God's will of love in service to the neighbor in his or her particular standing place. But it does not follow that this must at all times be put in terms of "justification." The NT is rich in variety of expressions and different times demand different emphases, just so the substance of the gospel, which is the "justification of the sinner by grace alone," is preserved.

See also **Faith; Law and Gospel; Lutheran Ethics**.

G. O. Forde, *Justification by Faith: A Matter of Death and Life,* 1982; W. H. Lazareth, *Luther on the Christian Home: An Application of the Social Ethics of the Reformation,* 1960, esp. pp. 34–165; G. Quell and G. Schrenk, *Righteousness,* Bible Key Words, vol. 4, ET 1951 (also in *TDNT* II, pp. 174–225); G. Rupp, *The Righteousness of God,* 1953.

MARTIN J. HEINECKEN

Juvenile Delinquency

Be they infringements of the criminal law or of an unwritten rule of conduct, the misdemeanors of young people are often called acts of delinquency. The phrase "juvenile delinquency" tends to encompass not only crime, but also behavior like truanting from school, resistance to parental discipline, and attitudes of an intolerant nature. This definition is related to a particular legal, social, and moral understanding of youth.

In most industrial societies the law sets an age of criminal responsibility, which differs across jurisdictions and is subject to historical change. In Great Britain, children under ten years of age cannot be charged with a criminal offense. A special system of judicial administration and justice has been established in America and in Britain to deal with juveniles. There have been some attempts to make the juvenile court a place of last resort and a provider of welfare, but this remains a contentious proposition.

The roots of this understanding of young people are diverse. Of particular importance is the belief that the learning of appropriate rules of conduct and of morality during the early years has a significant impact throughout adulthood. It has been argued that juvenile delinquency, like a contagious disease, may lead to an established pattern of criminality. There is a small amount of evidence to support this view but most juveniles, convicted or not, seem to mature into law-abiding adults.

The perceived threat to societal disorder posed by young people—especially males—who display and sustain a highly visible, if fragile, membership of a youth subculture has stimulated academic curiosity. "Hippies," "Rockers," "Rastas," "Acidheads," and so on, are likely to invoke what one sociologist has called "moral panic," which in turn can provoke a firm controlling response from the police or other agencies. It has been suggested that attention like this may actually give the subculture an exaggerated status and credibility, strengthening and nourishing it.

The diverse range of behavior that may be called delinquent and a strong moral concern for youth have prompted important developments in the diagnosis and classification of symptoms of delinquency, as well as the establishment of programs of treatment. In particular, social workers have been given the responsibility for the "care and protection" of juvenile delinquents. A mandate like this affords professionals in the social services a wide measure of discretion and power. There is now a significant view which, while wanting to retain some special facilities for young offenders, asserts "children's rights." Young people, then, may require a measure of protection from those social influences which could precipitate adult criminality, and from the particular morals of the caring professions.

See also **Children; Crime; Penology**.

A. Morris et al., *Justice for Children,* 1980; M. Rutter and H. Giller, *Juvenile Delinquency,* 1983.

SIMON HOLDAWAY

Kantian Ethics

Immanuel Kant (1724–1804), a native of East Prussia, is generally regarded as the greatest modern philosopher. Brought up in the rationalist (Leibnizian) school, he nevertheless became convinced of the impossibility of justifying "metaphysics" (*a priori* theoretical knowledge of reality). In his major work, the *Critique of Pure Reason* (1781, [2]1787), he maintained that all judgments capable of giving new information about matters of fact must include both an empirical and an *a priori* element, the former providing matter or content and the latter form or organization. This enabled him to furnish a justification of causality and other *a priori* categories against philosophers like Hume, on the ground that they were necessary if we were to make any judgments at all, but also to refute theoretical metaphysics on the ground that it depended for its arguments on using the categories illegitimately beyond the realm of experience. But he took a quite different view of judgments as to moral principles, regarding these as essentially *a priori*. This enabled him to produce ethical arguments for the objective validity of the only metaphysical ideas that he considered of practical interest to man—namely, God, freedom, and immortality. For according to his view an ethical proposition could say something new (be "synthetic") without being dependent on empirical facts and therefore could yield conclusions that went beyond the realm of experience, thus escaping his objections to *a priori* arguments in theoretical metaphysics. The general principle behind his argument for God and immortality is that the moral law bids us pursue the supreme good as attainable. It cannot, however, be attained in this life or in any finite time, hence immortality, and since the possibility of realizing it depends not only on ourselves but on external circumstances we must think of the latter as ordered for the greatest good, which we can only do by envisaging everything as created and controlled by a being who is both perfectly good and omnipotent. (This is the essence of the argument, but its actual form would have been improved if Kant had not restricted his idea of the good to "good will" and happiness; see below.) The argument is held by him to give indeed not theoretical knowledge but sufficient evidence to justify a subjectively certain practical belief. It occurs in the *Critique of Practical Reason* (1788). He not only regards religious belief as justifiable solely by ethical arguments but takes the view that religion is of value only as a means to leading a good moral life, and in *Religion Within the Bounds of Reason Alone* (1793) he reinterprets the dogmas of Christianity in terms simply of ethics and of a belief in the moral government of the world.

Kant's view of freedom is very difficult, and he admits that the concept, though we must accept it, is unintelligible to us. As the result chiefly of various epistemological arguments and the antinomies about infinity he had come to the conclusion that everything in space and time is appearance and not reality. This he applied even to our view of ourselves in introspection. The appearance self, he thought, must be like everything in time completely subject to causation by previous events, but the real self was timeless and so could be free, not being determined by previous events. Its freedom consisted in the possibility of moral action, "ought" implying "can."

Kant's best-known work on ethics is his *Groundwork of the Metaphysic of Morals* (1785), though we must remember that it was intended as the introduction to a work in which he would develop ethics more in detail, as he did in the *Metaphysic of Morals* (1797). ("Metaphysic" is here used not in the sense in which Kant denied its possibility, that is, *a priori* theoretical knowledge of reality, but simply to mean a systematic investigation of the *a priori* elements in our moral thinking.) His ethics, as already suggested, is noted for its *a priori* character. He holds that only "hypothetical" and not "categorical" (genuinely moral) imperatives can be derived from considering the consequences of actions. If I am to attain a certain end, I am subject to a hypothetical imperative to adopt the means needed for this purpose, but the imperative is binding on me only insofar as I desire the end, and even so it is only a prudential and not a moral "ought." A categorical imperative, on the other hand, is concerned with the principle ("maxim") of an action and not with its consequences.

This is connected with Kant's view of what is good in itself. The *Groundwork* opens with a statement that the only thing unconditionally good is the *good will*, by which is meant the will to do our duty just because it is our duty. This is not the same as saying that the good will is the only thing good otherwise than as a means. Kant regards happiness also as good in itself but only if the happiness is deserved by the exercise of the good will, and so only conditionally on the other higher good being attained. He does, however, seem to deny the value of anything else besides good will and happiness, even of intelligence and knowledge, love, aesthetic and religious experiences, except as a means. He points out that the goodness of the good will does not depend on its being successful in its endeavors or on its actual consequences. He denies any merit to action that is not morally motivated, however well it conforms outwardly with the moral law, and this has aroused criticism on the ground that many acts are better done out of love than out of a sense of duty. It is, however, doubtful whether Kant meant to deny moral value to an action that was done both from love or some other (good) desire and from a sense of duty, provided the latter was strong enough to bring about the action of itself even if the other motive had not been present also. And he insists that, if we are really moral, we will do our duty gladly despite the prima facie opposition between duty and desire. His rather rigorous attitude is to be understood as a reaction against the view, very common in his day, that the reason for doing our duty was ultimately to be found in the agent's own happiness.

Since the good will is a feature of the action itself and its motives and not of its consequences, and since happiness, although an end that could serve as a ground for action, is regarded by him as of comparatively subordinate importance, his view of the good debarred him from setting up an ethic that derived our obligations mainly from an appeal to consequences. Instead he uses universalizability as his main criterion. He does not indeed hold that we ought to act according to every principle that could be universali˜ed, but he does hold that we ought not to act according to any principle that could not be universalized. What cheats want is not that everybody else should cheat them, but that an exception should be made in their own case. And Kant thinks there are certain principles such that it would be impossible for us to will their universalization. Thus we could not have a state of affairs in which all people always made any promise they chose without any intention of keeping it, because there would be then no point in making the promises since they would not be believed. Similarly he tries to base the obligation to help others in need on the argument that we could not will the universalization of the opposite principle since we ourselves might need help from others. This must be distinguished from the merely prudential argument that we ought to help others because we are then more likely to be helped ourselves. Kant is appealing not to the actual consequences of any kindness we may show but to the purely hypothetical situation that would arise if kindness were never shown. I think his contention is in essence that it would be unfair to break ourselves a general rule which we cannot help expecting others to obey in their dealings with us. Kant assumes that the moral principles he establishes hold universally, as one would indeed expect an *a priori* principle to do, but then the question arises what we are to do if two of them clash in a particular case. Kant expressly defended the view that one ought never to tell a lie even to save the life of a man pursued by a would-be murderer, but it is not clear why the principle

of truthfulness should be given priority over the principle of preserving life. But Kant has the merit of being the first moral philosopher to realize the immense importance of the concept of universality for ethics. It is an essential part of the moral attitude that any reason for or against an act must be capable of statement in general terms and must be such that it would apply to anybody without exception granted similar circumstances.

Kant's second formulation of the central moral imperative is the direction to "act so as to treat humanity never only as a means but always also as an end." We must note that he does not say that we should never treat people as means—which would be incompatible with our ever employing them to do work for our benefit—but that we shall never treat them only as a means, that is, we must never employ them under such conditions as involve a disregard of their well-being or human dignity. These words of Kant have had as much influence as perhaps any ever written by a philosopher; they serve indeed as a slogan for the whole liberal and democratic movement of recent times. But for their application we seem to need a fuller idea of the ends of humankind than Kant supplies, together with more empirical content.

In the most important version of his third formulation Kant introduces the concept of a kingdom of ends, all the members of which treated each other as ends as well as means. Kant insists that we ought to act as if we were members of such a kingdom, though we know that not all our fellow beings are such in their actions; for example, we ought not to cheat because others cheat us.

Kant emphasizes very strongly the "autonomy" of ethics*, by which he means that moral principles must be derived from the nature of the rational will which refrains from acting on any principle that it could not consistently will to be universalized, and not from any idea of private advantage, nor from some feeling, nor from metaphysics or theology. He is insisting on the unique status of ethics.

In the 1960s James Gustafson wrote that "surely Kant remains *the* philosopher of greatest impact on European Protestant ethics—Brunner and Barth particularly." Perhaps in part because Kant reflected Protestant thought to a certain extent, his influence in Protestant ethics has been strong (*see*, for example, **Ritschlian Ethics; Modern Prot-**

estant **Ethics**). Nevertheless, it has occurred in various ways, sometimes shaping only part of the perspective; for example, neighbor-love (agape) has been interpreted in the light of the Kantian principle of respect for persons* (G. Outka, *Agape,* 1972; A. Donagan, *The Theory of Morality,* 1977). In addition, Kantian themes have been prominent in recent moral philosophy, for example, in the work of Alan Donagan and that of John Rawls (*A Theory of Justice,* 1971). Kantian ethics has been subject to various criticisms, including charges of overemphasis on moral reason in contrast to the inclinations, on deontological ethics (*see* **Deontology**) in contrast to teleological ethics*, on principles and rules rather than virtues, on the moral self apart from time and community, etc. For further discussion of Kantian ethics, *see* **Respect for Persons**.

See **Categorical Imperative; Duty; Heteronomy; Kingdom of Ends; Practical Reason; Universalizability, Principle of**.

B. Aune, *Kant's Theory of Morals,* 1980; Immanuel Kant, *Groundwork of the Metaphysic of Morals* (1785), tr. H. J. Paton as *The Moral Law,* 1948; *Critique of Practical Reason* (1788), tr. L. W. Beck, 1949; O. Neill, *Acting on Principle: An Essay in Kantian Ethics,* 1975; H. J. Paton, *The Categorical Imperative,* 1947; W. D. Ross, *Kant's Ethical Theory,* 1954.

A. C. EWING/J. F. CHILDRESS

Kierkegaardian Ethics

Søren Kierkegaard (1813–1855) turned repeatedly to ethical questions in his books and journals. His views, or in many cases the views attributed to him, have proved highly influential in both Christian and secular circles in the 20th century. Matters are complicated because among his most relevant works some are pseudonymous (e.g., *Either/Or* and *Fear and Trembling*) and others are under his own name (e.g., *Purity of Heart Is to Will One Thing* and *Works of Love*). Claims about ethics in the pseudonymous works do not always represent his own constructive proposals, yet they figure prominently in subsequent discussion. Thus, to speak of "Kierkegaardian ethics" one must attend to various distinctive claims considered in his corpus and widely canvassed in later generations, not all of which are, or were intended to be, compatible.

Three stages on life's way. A beginning theme is that human life consists in stages of development. Each stage must be confronted as a preparation for the next, and each generates its own characteristic values. Kierkegaard distinguishes aesthetic, ethical, and religious stages. All of us begin at the aesthetic stage where the pursuit of pleasure and enjoyment holds sway. Whenever this starting point turns into a way of life, all of the varied expressions lack individual decisiveness. "Entirely finitized" expressions include sensuous eroticism and sheer conformity to social custom and etiquette. More reflective expressions play out an "imagination existence" intoxicated by infinite possibilities: boredom is the great enemy and the strategy for avoidance is endlessly to "rotate the crops." The "decisions" of reflective aesthetes are plagued by a both-and or neither-nor quality. Manipulation marks all of their social relations. Certain commentators see in Kierkegaard's depiction of the aesthetic stage a version of eudaemonism* or hedonism*. A. MacIntyre ties the portrayal of reflective aesthetes to emotivism (*After Virtue,* 1981, pp. 23–24). Kierkegaard himself reserves the term "ethical" for precisely the sort of individual decisiveness the aesthete lacks. Judge William, the quintessential ethical pseudonym, claims that the aesthetic stage has to do with what a person immediately *is,* the ethical with what a person *becomes.* "Becoming" involves an affirmative effort of the will, initiative-taking, and the assumption of responsibility*. The person at the ethical stage acquires narrative continuity and biographical depth. Such activity is fraught with religious significance, albeit of a dialectical kind. On the one hand, as another pseudonym, Vigilius Haufniensis, insists, "the good signifies continuity, for the first expression of salvation is continuity" (*The Concept of Anxiety,* p. 130). This first expression is the narrow gate that leads to the religious life. The ethical and religious accordingly form a "glorious alliance" over against the aesthetic. On the other hand, ethical personalities like Judge William underestimate the power of the forces that foster disorder and discontinuity; the limits of the ethical are revealed when such persons succumb to these forces despite stringent standards and earnest effort. Here Kierkegaard sometimes sounds a Pauline and Lutheran note: "What is said of the law is also true of ethics: it is a disciplinarian that demands, and by its demands only judges but does not bring forth life" (*The Concept of Anxiety*, p. 16). The life in question turns out to be unavailable apart from divine grace known as such only at the religious stage. Judge William's own views are nevertheless a key source for the idea developed by secular existentialist writers that moral autonomy* rather than moral truth is the fundamental concept in ethical theory (*see also* **Existentialist Ethics**). But for Kierkegaard, the doctrine of the stages contains a religious *telos* (which we certainly remain free to frustrate); it plots various steps in the individual's concern for eternal blessedness.

A teleological suspension of the ethical. Other widely discussed claims are advanced by the pseudonym Johannes *de silentio* in *Fear and Trembling*. Johannes examines the biblical story of Abraham's near sacrifice of Isaac in obedience to a direct divine command, calling Abraham's action "a teleological suspension of the ethical." As *Fear and Trembling* is often read to commend the action, it supports four claims: (1) we should not commit ourselves in principle to a necessary link between antecedently known moral prohibitions and God's will, but instead should remain dispositionally open to God's self-disclosures here and now; (2) the distinctive and irreducible importance of the individual's relation to God requires that it remain direct and unmediated; (3) such a relation is constituted only by a personal encounter with God; (4) given God's nature, this encounter takes the form of a divine command and a primal response of obedience (*see also* **Divine Command Morality**). While the "ethics" that is suspended differs from its more favorable depiction elsewhere in Kierkegaard's literature (e.g., *Concluding Unscientific Postscript*), the claims themselves are appropriated in part by a group of 20th-century theologians all of whom share a special wariness of legalism*. The group includes K. Barth and E. Brunner most clearly; and also, with qualifications, D. Bonhoeffer, H. R. Niebuhr, and P. Lehmann. They endeavor to retain some element of personal encounter in which God's command is immediate, concrete, and requisitely self-interpreting (*see also* **Modern Protestant Ethics**).

Commitment to the highest good. A case where the ethical is favorably depicted is *Purity of Heart,* a nonpseudonymous work with striking affinities to Kant. We meet with a doctrine of the highest good (*summum bonum*) which, as with Aquinas and Kant, is eternal. Ethical practice consists in actually "willing one thing," and this rules out not only purely personal ambitions but all goals that can be exhaustively specified in temporal terms. Various kinds of "double-mindedness" are exposed, including the "reward disease." What emerges is the claim that no temporal goal can be the one thing successfully willed; every such goal when pursued to excess turns into its opposite, and this because the goal cannot bear the single-minded commitment appropriate solely to the eternal. The anthropological consequence is that the will itself, and not what it does or achieves in the world, is the ethically good. This work displays two of Kierkegaard's own most notable points of influence: (1) The claim that the eternal is the only appropriate object of a single-minded commitment lends support to Kierkegaard's well-documented vindication of *the individual.* The person who strives to will one thing must realize that one cannot succeed unless he or she acquires independence from, even invulnerability to, the way the world goes (including the judgments of other people). One's commitment cannot be made hostage to the uncertain flux of limited temporal goals: this condition obtains for every person. (2) A particular type of writing serves to cultivate commitment. Kierkegaard calls his work an "edifying discourse." Here, unlike Kant, he writes to promote an actual transformation of the will and not only to offer an intellectual examination of the practical reason.

Ethics after dogmatics. Haufniensis distinguishes between a "first ethics" which is shipwrecked on the individual's sinfulness and a "second ethics" which presupposes dogmatics and "has the actuality of sin within its scope" (*The Concept of Anxiety*, p. 23). Several of Kierkegaard's most confessional writings treat ethical questions as governed by Christian concepts. In *Training in Christianity,* for example, the authority of Christ relativizes one's station in life and frees the established political order from deification; and in *Works of Love* the biblical commandment to love one's neighbor casts a shadow over the motives of all preferential loves (*see* **Love**). More generally, Kierkegaard brings Christian beliefs critically to bear on the received moral opinions of the age, a practice perpetuated in the 20th century by otherwise quite different thinkers. K. Barth, for instance, annexes philosophical ethics to theological ethics, and R. Niebuhr employs a doctrine of sin* (with an acknowledged debt to Kierkegaard) to illuminate the possibilities and limits of ethical and political life. The legacy of Kierkegaardian ethics includes a nonapologetic and radical attempt to tell the age something it cannot tell itself.

S. Kierkegaard, *Either/Or*, ET 1971; *Fear and Trembling*, ET 1983; *Purity of Heart Is to Will One Thing*, ET 1956; *Works of Love*, ET 1962; *Concluding Unscientific Postscript*, ET 1960; *The Concept of Anxiety*, ET 1980; *Training in Christianity*, ET 1972; A. Hannay, *Kierkegaard*, 1982; G. Malantschuk, *Kierkegaard's Thought*, ET 1974; M. C. Taylor, *Kierkegaard's Pseudonymous Authorship: A Study of Time and the Self*, 1975.

GENE OUTKA

Kingdom of Ends

This term was used by Kant for an ideal society in which the members treated each other never merely as means but always at the same time as ends. He insisted that we ought to act as if we were already members of such a society, even though others may not do likewise in their dealings with us.

See **Kantian Ethics.**

A. C. EWING

Kingdom of God

Writers on Christian ethics sometimes use this phrase as a shorthand for the ideal state of affairs to whose realization Christian effort is to be directed. The petition in the Lord's Prayer, "Thy kingdom come," is taken to be an obvious aspiration toward such an outcome. The kingdom is the world order that God desires. Characteristically it is seen as an order marked by social justice, freedom for the oppressed, fulfillment for the individual —the whole gamut of liberal values. Such a use of the term has had a wholly understandable revival (in more Marxist dress) in the crisis-evoked liberation theology* stemming from South America, and it has often been linked with the writings of that school with the exegesis of the Gospels.

Yet in truth, this direction of thought is almost wholly misleading if it is a question of attending to the meaning of the term in the NT where, after all, it found its origin in Christian writing, and, as far as its prominent use is concerned, in any writing at all. Its known use in Judaism in the period is so rare that it has the strongest possible chance of being the central theme of Jesus' preaching, just as the Synoptic Gospels show. But though the phrase is relatively rare in the Judaism of the time, the idea—that of God's sovereign rule over his people or over the world—has its roots deep in Jewish theology —in theology, not ethics. Although God certainly has a will and law for his people, the idea is essentially that God rules as king (Pss. 93; 97; 99). It expresses a conception of God's being and position, not a program for human living and social improvement.

The usage of the Gospels, in their account of the preaching of Jesus, is wholly in line with this. Jesus proclaims the nearness of the revealing of God's victory (Mark 1:14–15). His acts of power fill out the character of God's rule; and the parables evoke both its mysteriousness (Mark 4:26–29) and the urgency (Matt. 13:44–46; 25:1–13) of its challenge.

Yet it is easy to see how this essentially theological term, signifying God's initiative and the assurance of his power, has come to be treated as predominantly ethical. While the underlying Semitic phrase involved the idea of sovereignty, the Greek word *basileia* (kingdom) brought into prominence the concomitant image of the sphere within which sovereignty is exercised, and so the nature of the life within that sphere. Sayings in the Gospels (particularly Matthew) express this quasi-territorial idea of kingdom, which is itself only a step away from the later tendency to equate the kingdom of God with the church: Matt. 16:28; 19:28; 20:21; and note 13:41. Indeed, a strong impulse in this direction was already given by one of the most striking features of Jesus' preaching. In sayings like Matt. 12:28 and Luke 17:21, there is the idea that Jesus' presence and deeds are more than signs of the kingdom—they are the very proof of its realization already in the world. Around Jesus, among his followers therefore, in this language of realized eschatology (as C. H. Dodd named it), the expected end is brought forward and seen as planted in the midst of human life and affairs.

As for the character of life in the kingdom, prophetic passages, such as Isa. 35:5–6 and 61:1–3, colored the picture of the coming new age and illuminated Jesus' acts of healing and restoration. It is no wonder that in the long term, charitable work and Christian social effort came to be seen as the building or (with a greater retention of the eschatological origins of the idea) the hastening of the kingdom, with a prominence given to human effort that the writer of the Gospel of Mark would not have understood.

In this way, "the kingdom of God" has been the great bearer of the two major shifts in the perspective of Christian faith after its earliest days: the shift from the dominance of eschatology and the shift to the prominence of the church as the institutional embodiment of Christianity and provider for practical Christian living. The ethicizing of the idea of the kingdom is then the ultimate development of the process thus initiated (*see* **Kantian Ethics; Kingdom of Ends; Ritschlian Ethics; Social Gospel**).

Alternatively, the process may be described as a movement from the kingdom of God as a theological term (almost a periphrasis for God himself in his purposive and ultimately triumphant activity) to the kingdom as the community where this rule of God is already welcomed; thence to the church in a more formalized sense, and finally to the church in its work of extending the sphere of life in accordance with God's demands, whether seen in predominantly religious or social and political terms, to the world as a whole, a program of which Rev. 11:15 might be seen as the visionary statement.

See **Ecclesiology and Ethics; Eschatological Ethics; Hope; Jesus, Ethical Teaching of; New Testament Ethics.**

R. H. Hiers, *The Kingdom of God in the Synoptic Tradition,* 1970; N. Perrin, *The Kingdom of God in the Teaching of Jesus,* 1963; J. Weiss, *Jesus' Proclamation of the Kingdom of God* (1892), ET 1971.

J. L. HOULDEN

Kingdom of Heaven *see* Kingdom of God

Koinonia

A NT expression, *koinōnia* may be translated as "fellowship," "communion," "participation," or even "community." The basic idea is that of sharing. The Christian life is a shared life, shared with God through Christ, and with the other members of the body of Christ, the community of the Spirit. In eth-

ics, the term is used by those who hold that Christian action is determined by the living context of the community.

See also **Ecclesiology and Ethics.**

JOHN MACQUARRIE

Labor Movements

Modern industry and technology have produced a type of society new in the history of the world; in turn this has produced new types of political movements among its workers. Britain was the pioneer in the "Industrial Revolution,"* as it is commonly called, and the labor movements it provoked are a good example of them. After inchoate movements in the early years (including the Christian Socialist experiment sponsored by the theologian F. D. Maurice and his friends 1848–54), and a quiescent period after that, a three-pronged labor movement developed.

1. Trade unions. These began with craft unions in, e.g., engineering, and the general or "industrial" unions of relatively unskilled workers came later, from about 1880. In some European countries unions developed under Christian labels as counterparts to secularist ones, but not in the UK.

2. Cooperative societies. Consumers' Cooperation began in Rochdale, Lancashire, in 1844; the shops were owned and managed through elected representatives of the customers, who received a dividend on purchases, and from this the societies developed and owned manufacturing enterprises to supply their shops, through the Cooperative Wholesale Society. They grew rapidly and became a powerful social, educational, and cultural force in working-class communities, and today are used by a wider public, particularly in the grocery trade. Lately they have been meeting severe competition from supermarkets. There have also been Producers' Cooperatives, particularly in agriculture, which have had a less strong corporate sense, since farming is more an individualist family occupation than industrial work. However there have also been a number of manufacturing units owned and managed by the workers, but they have been fewer and on a smaller scale until the recent Mondragon Cooperative in northern Spain, which is attracting wide attention. Some co-partnership schemes in industry and commerce have been established but they have more of a "liberal" than a "labour" flavor.

3. Political parties. In the UK the Independent Labour Party, which later became the Labour Party, arrived in Parliament at the 1906 election (which swept the Liberals into power) when they won 29 seats. In the early 1920s they replaced the Liberals as the main opposition party. In Europe, Social Democratic parties were formed in opposition to Christian Democratic parties; these latter have been conservative, and so the Social Democratic parties have tended to be anticlerical and often anti-Christian; in the UK there were enough links between the churches and working-class institutions to avoid this. In the USA the open frontier and the large-scale immigration have meant a less defined situation.

In addition there have been various Marxist parties deriving from the First, Second, and Third Internationals. They have had a checkered history and proved very fissiparous. Some have been anarchist; others have arisen from the split between Stalin and Trotsky, with great hostility between them. The Communist Party is the most "official" and least radical of the Marxist parties. The influence of all of them in the UK has been small, and chiefly among middle-class intellectuals. In Marxist countries there is usually one party operating, on Lenin's theory of democratic centralism. In Third World countries the situation varies considerably between and within Asia, Africa, and Latin America.

Individual Christians have made striking contributions to labor movements, but churches have not yet come to terms with the phenomenon of the industrial worker.

See also **Industrial Relations.**

RONALD PRESTON

Laborem Exercens *see* **Official Roman Catholic Social Teaching**

Laicity

A term used (chiefly in France) to mean the control of civil affairs by laypersons, to the exclusion of clerical influence. The principle is similar to that known in the USA as "separation of church and state."

See **Church and State.**

JOHN MACQUARRIE

Laissez-faire

This phrase, literally meaning "let do," was first used by the French physiocratic writers of the 18th century. It has come to stand for the belief that it is best to leave the working of the economy to the free play of the self-interest of producers and consumers, relying on the "invisible hand" of competition in the market to bring about the best interests of the community.

Christian thought would emphasize the importance of individuals being free to exercise responsible judgment and choice, and the dangers of excessive state power, but extreme laissez-faire has usually been condemned. It has been held to be incompatible with Christian beliefs about the fallibility of human nature, which makes it impossible to rely solely on an invisible hand to restrain the effects of greed and exploitation. Christians who believe in the need for self-seeking to be transformed by the love of God into self-denial in the service of others could not accept as adequate a social philosophy of possessive individualism* based expressly on self-seeking. Christian responsibility for one's neighbors' welfare made it imperative to advocate collective action by the community to correct the inevitable abuses of self-interest.

Thus the Amsterdam Assembly of the World Council of Churches in 1948 condemned laissez-faire capitalism* as well as communism*. The papal social encyclicals from *Rerum Novarum* (1891) onward have also condemned it. R. H. Preston points out that a free market economy presupposes not only a legal structure of law and order and property rights but also a commitment by all concerned to basic moral virtues, such as honesty* and charity*. Ideally it involves also freely contracting individuals who have complete knowledge of the market, can move freely from place to place, and are completely rational in their attitudes to present wants as against future growth.

Given these limitations, the practical choice becomes one of how much freedom of the market should be advocated, and in what framework of corporate community action. Where the choice falls tends to reflect fundamental political, philosophical, and theological beliefs. Among Christians, those in what may be called the Social-Catholic tradition have tended to believe that the market can only work equitably and efficiently within a strong framework of community action, in the form of social services to meet the needs of the less fortunate and government overall planning of the economy. This tradition came to be the most influential from the

1930s on through the 1960s. Those in what we can call the Individualist-Evangelical tradition have always been more concerned with the dangers of state action and the importance of individual responsibility, and their strength has grown more recently as the rise of the new Radical Right has coincided with the economic recession of the late 1970s and early 1980s.

See also **Ecumenical Movement; Evangelical Ethics; Official Roman Catholic Social Teaching; Socialism; Welfare State.**

N. Bosanquet, *After the New Right,* 1983; G. Gilder, *Wealth and Poverty,* 1981; R. H. Preston, *Church and Society in the Late Twentieth Century: The Economic and Political Task,* 1983.

JOHN F. SLEEMAN

Law

In its primary sense law is a guide or directive of human actions. Specifically defined, law is a directive judgment of lawmakers regarding means necessary for the common welfare. This view of law, as essentially a directive, is part of the great tradition in human thinking. "Teach me, O LORD, the way of thy statutes; and I will keep it to the end. Give me understanding, that I may keep thy law and observe it with my whole heart. Lead me in the path of thy commandments, for I delight in it. . . . Thy word is a lamp to my feet and a light to my path. . . . Therefore I direct my steps by all thy precepts" (Ps. 119:33–35, 105, 128).

Sometimes law has been looked upon as an undesirable restriction on human freedom or as a necessary evil for remedying trouble situations. Such a myopic outlook is usually the result of a foreshortened prelegal education that precludes viewing law in its true perspective. Law seen in its total sweep is, rather, like the guide marks on a map that restrict people only that they may more certainly reach a definite goal, even when this is the seeking of remedies.

Law is also used in a secondary sense that refers to a uniform order of sequence observable in nature. Such a usage is not uncommon in the physical sciences to denote the order perceived in natural phenomena or events. This use of the word "law" was undoubtedly related originally to an interpretation of nature that saw in it the handiwork of a maker. When this maker was also seen in the formality of a lawmaker, the ordered sequences observable in nature were recognized as the expression of his directive judgments and the word "law" was attributed to them. But such a use of the word "law" is imprecise and equivocal, because law refers to the directive judgments of a lawmaker and not to the promulgation of these judgments. All the more is the use of the word "law" equivocal when it designates this uniform order in itself and unrelated to its intelligible rationale.

Similarly in the science of ethics, the word "law" is used in such phrases as "law of nature" or "natural law"* to denote either the basic drives that humans observe operative in themselves, or the value judgments naturally made according to the demands of these drives and even the conclusions deduced therefrom by a reasoning process. Here likewise the use of the word "law" is lax and equivocal. Human drives at best, when seen related to a higher cause, are not law but the expression of a law. Nor are the basic value judgments that humans make "law," because they are not the directive judgments of a lawmaker who has the authority to direct all people to their common welfare.

In the perspective of God and humans, there are two basic kinds of law: God-made, eternal law and human-made, temporal law. God-made law is known either through positive means such as the Decalogue or through natural means such as the elementary drives of human nature. The positive promulgation of God-made law has been called by some "divine law" and its natural promulgation has been termed "natural law." But, as already indicated, the use of the word "law" to designate the publication of a law is incorrect and equivocal.

Human-made law is made for the most part by legislators. Judges, however, sometimes also make law. This is done interstitially when, in applying statutes, they have to fill up gaps left by the statute, or when they decide cases of "first impression," or when as members of a highest court they render decisions by way of judicial review. Executives also may in certain circumstances make law by proclamation. Finally the people themselves, the political source of all lawmaking authority, make law by means of the customs they have established. Customs are ways of acting that are necessary for the common welfare, have been in use by the people over a long period of time, and are recognized as such by legislators and judges. The lawmaking judgments of lawmakers out of office or long dead continue as law inasmuch as it is a matter of recorded fact that they did so directively judge, and succeeding lawmakers are assumed to have made the judgments of their predecessors their own unless they give evidence of the opposite by attempting amendment or appeal.

The promulgation of human-made law to the people is, of course, a condition prerequisite for its effectiveness in directing the people to their common welfare. But the making known of a law does not constitute it as law. A law is fully fashioned before it is made known, somewhat as a road map is complete and finished before it is distributed as a guide. Custom law has its own particular kind of promulgation. It is made known by the publicly repeated actions of the people which manifest their directive judgments regarding some practice as necessary for the common welfare.

The end of law, the common welfare, is a unique kind of good—the common good*. This is not a total of goods proper to all individuals such as the sum of all producer and consumer goods. Nor is it a collective good such as the family fortune which diminishes as it is communicated to each member. The common good is, rather, the kind of good that is communicable to all and is not lessened by being so communicated. The peace, security, and protection of law itself are prime examples. They are not lessened by the number of participants nor does this number cause each to have less. The effectuation of the common good is in proportion to the amount of cooperation put forward by the members of the society.

The content of law includes whatever is necessary for the common welfare—either absolutely necessary such as police protection or relatively necessary such as directional turning indicators on automobiles. Statutes that would purport to dictate, for instance, what people should believe or how they should worship would invade areas that pertain directly to the private welfare of individuals and not to the common welfare of the community. Such laws would be the embodiment of tyranny and dictatorship*. On the basis of content, laws are either substantive or procedural, depending on whether they are concerned with claims themselves or with methods of enforcing these claims. Laws are also private or public inasmuch as some laws regard the private claims of one citizen as against another and other laws are concerned with the public claims of all the citizens against one or many. Private law embraces torts, property, contracts, domestic relations, equity, and the like. Public law is concerned with the constitution, administration, crimes, and procedure.

The obligation of law derives from the necessity of the content of a law for the common welfare. For obligation is the moral necessity of choosing a means that is necessary for a desired end. If I desire the safety of myself and others, I must choose to restrict my speed according to the limit set by the speed law. If I choose to exceed this limit, the safety of myself and others is in jeopardy.

In the long history of law, this objective, means-end foundation of obligation has at times been lost sight of. Some have said that obligation had a subjective basis in the will of the lawmakers. A statute obliged me only if the lawmakers so desired. Otherwise, the law was merely indicative of what the lawmakers wanted done but it was not obligatory. This type of philosophico-legal thinking gave rise to the theory of "merely penal law." This phrase was used to designate a law that supposedly did not oblige me to the execution of what was commanded (because the lawmakers did not so desire to oblige me) but merely to the payment of a penalty if I was apprehended violating the law (because this was what the lawmakers wished). Others, also considering human will or practical reason to be autonomous and incapable of being put under any determination by an objective, means-end relationship, said that obligation derived from the interior reverence that I should have for law itself. The nobility of law itself, and not what it specifically stipulates, commands my respect. In this theory, obligation is for obligation's sake.

Still others, rejecting all models explaining obligation philosophically or morally, said that obligation was the same as sanction, that the obligation of a law was the same as its enforceability by power. Some who held this position did so not because they denied the validity of morals but because they wished to keep morals and legal obligation separate (*see also* **Morality, Legal Enforcement of**). Others who held this position did so because they believed that morals rested on an emotional basis and were consequently noncognitivist and nonscientific. Morals therefore, according to them, had no place in scientific thinking.

But time, the great practical tester of theories, has shown that once obligation is cut adrift from its means-end anchor, it loses all meaning. It becomes a will-o'-the-wisp of either the lawmaker's will or of my own; or else it becomes synonymous with force and power, and this connotes might is right. Obligation is anchored in my desire for an end. There is one end which I cannot help desiring and this is my own complete self-actualization or happiness. It is the objective relation of a particular fact-situation to this end which gives substance to my obligation.

The sanction* of law is of a different nature than obligation. Sanction refers to the rewards that are consequent upon the keeping of a law and to the punishments that follow the breaking of a law. Sanctions are either extrinsic to the law itself insofar as they are affixed to it, or they are instrinsic to the law insofar as they follow from the very content of the law. Examples of extrinsic sanction would be rewards offered by law for the apprehension of criminals, or punishments that consist in the deprivation of property by fine, of freedom by imprisonment, of physical well-being by flogging, or of life itself by execution. Examples of intrinsic sanction would be the reward of safe driving conditions that result from observing traffic laws, or the punishment of dangerous driving conditions that ensue from violating the laws. Inasmuch as intrinsic sanction has to do with the accomplishment or nonaccomplishment of the end of law and this same end is the anchor of my obligation to observe the law as explained, there is this relation between intrinsic sanction and obligation. The extrinsic sanction of force and physical punishment is undoubtedly needed to ensure the enforcement of law —the perverseness of humans being what it is. But it is not of the essence of law itself and there can be valid laws without a stipulated, affixed punishment. The constitutions of many nations are examples of this.

Law, then, is a directive for humans regarding those things that are necessary for their common welfare, and obligation to observe law is based on this means-end relationship. This concept of law and obligation finds verification not only in the written laws of literate peoples but also in the unwritten cus-tom laws of preliterate peoples. Recent and reliable research in anthropology and ethnology has shown that in many situations found among preliterate groups, regulations are observed and order preserved without the threatened sanction of physical force. Many times the threat of public ridicule, a much-needed sanction in so-called civilized societies that so frenetically shun adverse publicity, is sufficient. Further, preliterates' idea of why they are obliged to follow their regulations appears explainable only on the grounds of their implicit recognition that what is required by these regulations is in most instances something necessary for their own common welfare.

See also **Civil Disobedience; Law and Gospel; State.**

T. Davitt, *The Elements of Law,* 1959; L. Fuller, *The Morality of Law,* 1964; and *Anatomy of the Law,* 1969; H. L. A. Hart, *The Concept of Law,* 1961.

THOMAS E. DAVITT, S.J.

Law and Gospel

The whole content of the word of God may be summarized in terms of "law and gospel." Martin Luther maintained that the ability to make the distinction and preserve the right relation was the most difficult of all theological tasks, at which no one really succeeded.

Accordingly, law* is what God demands. It means a lawgiver who coerces, rewards, and punishes. Nothing less than unconditional and complete obedience can fulfill the demands of the law. The law, therefore, by definition, excludes mercy*, grace*, forgiveness*. Under the law there can be no escape from its demands. Under the law a person gets what he or she deserves. The law is inviolable; it allows of no exceptions, or else it is not law. That is why an elaborate system of casuistry* is necessary in order to apply the law in all fairness to specific cases.

The gospel, on the other hand, is what God gives. It runs counter to the law as the good news of God's grace and forgiveness, which does not deal with persons in accordance with their deserts, but accepts them as they are, in their unworthiness. It is love of the unworthy, of the enemy, it is "justification by grace alone without the works of the law" (Rom. 1:16–17; Eph. 2:8–10) (*see* **Justification by Faith**).

Defined in this way, the law and the gospel stand in direct opposition and are mutually exclusive. The gospel goes counter to the law, which always accuses. The very meaning of the reconciling act of God in Christ is that it breaks through the order of justice. The fact that God is gracious can be defined in no other way. Otherwise the law loses all its meaning and power. If the law can be broken with impunity, all ordered living becomes impossible. Law has to be dependable or it is not law. Any game must be played strictly according to the rules, with no forgiveness permissible; so it is then, *a fortiori,* with God's law and the game of life.

This alone makes meaningful the good news that God does not deal with us according to our iniquities. Forgiveness is not forgiveness if it is based on conditions that must first be met and if the law must somehow first be kept, unless it breaks through the order of justice and goes counter to the law. Love* is not *agapē* except as love of the unworthy; it is most clearly manifest as love of the enemy and in vicarious suffering, which is never just, but loving.

On this definition the law necessarily precedes the gospel. It presupposes the human being's fall. The fact that God must make demands is the sign of the human being's sinfulness, for if the relationship were right there would be only the indicative (1 John 4:19). Thus the law serves to reveal the human being's sin and lead him or her to Christ (Rom. 3:20; 7:7; Gal. 3:24). This is the so-called proper, theological, pedagogical, or elenctical (judging) use of the law. The law is never itself salvatory, but it reveals humanity's bondage under God's wrath. It is, therefore, an essential part of Christian proclamation to awaken the terrors of conscience before the gospel can do its gracious work. True contrition of heart is worked by the preaching of both law and gospel, while trust and confidence are worked by the gospel alone.

In addition to leading to a sense of sin, the law, however, also serves a second function, the so-called political use which prompts and coerces human beings to do God's will, even when they are not willing to do it freely. Since all human beings are sinful, and the believers, too, continue to be sinful (simultaneously righteous and sinful), all human beings are at all times subject to this "big stick" use of the law. This is God's rule with his "left hand," made necessary because of sin. It is God's "strange work" of coercion as opposed to his "proper work" with the "right hand" of grace. It applies not only to the laws of the state, but applies wherever human beings live, work, and play together and cannot get along without rules to impose order upon them. Among sinful human beings it is unrealistic to dispense with law and to rely upon spontaneous obedience. As Luther said, the sheep would keep the peace, but they would not live long. Law and justice must be enforced, as is so evident in the whole struggle for human rights and racial equality. The law must continue to function justly and with proper rigor in the home, the school, the state, and even in the church as an institution. This is the meaning of the God-given power of the sword (Rom. 13).

Although some have advocated a third use of the law, the so-called didactic use, to serve as a guide to the Christian, this Lutheran orientation would not allow such a third use. The law always functions *either* in its pedagogical use to convict sinful human beings of their sin *or* in its political use to keep sinful human beings in line. Insofar as a person is reborn as the new human being he or she is free from the law and does the will of God spontaneously. Love is both the fulfillment and the end of the law (Matt. 22:37–40; Rom. 13:10; Gal. 5:14; 1 John 2:7–10). Love in obedience to law is not love. The one who acts in love is free to meet the needs of the neighbor creatively in the moment without being bound by principles or a code morality, even though, because still a sinner, he or she will submit also to the political use of the law out of love for the neighbor. The Christian is free to frame such laws as will meet the neighbor's needs (a contextual ethic).

This orientation does not deny the primacy of God's love, which is manifest in creation before it is manifest in redemption. God *is* love *and manifests that love in many different ways.* Creation is a work of love by the same God who in Christ redeemed the fallen creation; it is creation through the Word and in the power of the Spirit; it is a work of the entire Trinity. God's love is manifest, therefore, also in the structures of creation (*see* **Orders**), the lawful order of the world, which makes the world a fit theater for the realization of God's purpose.

Human beings are set down into the midst of interdependency; they are persons-in-community, whose *human* life depends upon their observing the created order. The law of creation is love. Here, however, law does not mean the law which is connected with God's wrath and always accuses, but it means the dependable order which furthers human well-being. On it are based and from it flow all human beings' potentials for conquering the earth and also for the development of a "civil righteousness," that is, a righteousness before humanity, which, however, has no merit in the place of justification before God. All this (the family, the economic order, the state, education, entertainment, etc.) is "under the law," in the realm of creation and not of redemption, not to be derived from the gospel in the sense of the redemptive work accomplished in Christ. (This is Christocentricity as opposed to Christomonism.) The "new age" inaugurated in Christ does not change these given, created structures which remain under the law. It does, however, affect, the men and women who enter into these given structures as new creatures, and through them the creative possibilities of those structures are opened up, without the law ever becoming redemptive in the sense in which only the gospel is redemptive. Though the whole creation is to share in the eventual fulfillment (Rom. 8; Eph. 1) in the *eschaton* when this age and history are over, it remains under the law as long as this present age endures. Only this positive emphasis upon the law enables one to claim the realm of culture for God. God claims all humans in virtue of their creation and the fact that they have nothing which they have not received. There is "good" in the world which is not derived from the reconciling act of Calvary but from the fact of creation. There is no profane realm, but the whole creation is God's. The so-called "secular," too, is holy in a "sacred secularity" and persons may take real delight in the law of God (Ps. 119).

If now the order is reversed, this may be only to show that love is primary, that the choice of Israel (the covenant) antedated the giving of the law to Moses (Gal. 3:17), and that therefore the appeal for keeping the law is based on the prior fact of love's gracious act of deliverance. On that basis the law and the keeping of it within the covenant relation are not a burden but a delight. It is not the condemning voice of the accuser but the loving will of the gracious heavenly Father.

This, however, does not alter the fact that the law must first do its *judging* and *condemning* work before the gospel of the redemption in Christ can do its *gracious* work. Nor does it alter the fact that insofar as the Christian is still under the law he or she is so as a sinner who is in need of coercion. When, therefore, the law is called "the necessary form of the gospel" (Karl Barth), the terms are confused. Law is, to be sure, a manifestation of God's love in the sense defined above. In its political use it is the form which love takes under the circumstances of human sinfulness. To refuse to enforce the law would not be loving. Also, in its pedagogical use it is a manifestation of love by leading persons to repentance. But the law, which accuses and condemns, can never be a form that the gospel, which accepts and forgives, takes on.

Moreover, if the law follows after the redemption, then the Christian life will again become a life under the law. With the best will in the world it cannot be prevented that the gospel becomes a new law and that legalism, code morality, and work righteousness take over, as the history of Christian ethics clearly shows. The danger of antinomianism*, where the sequence is law and gospel, is not as great as the danger of legalism* and the loss of Christian freedom*, where the sequence is gospel and law (John 8:36).

The situation may be clarified if the NT distinction between the will of God (*thelēma theou*) and the law of God (*nomos theou*) is observed (Paul Althaus). The will of God for human beings is always a will of love and the doing of it will be the delight of the redeemed. But the law of God is the tyrannous, coercive element which has no place in the new life in Christ. As a way of salvation in which humans put their trust it must be altogether rooted out.

The alternatives can thus be set in bold relief. On the one hand, the law precedes the gospel and always accuses, while only the gospel redeems. Moreover, the law continues to coerce the unwilling and thus preserves order. There is a "sacred secularity" of the created world. And finally, the new life under the gospel is one of creative freedom meeting the needs of the neighbor in love. On the other hand, when the gospel precedes the law, the law loses its power and the gospel becomes a new law. The created order loses its goodness under God and is turned over to the devil.

See **Lutheran Ethics; Orders; Two Realms.**

P. Althaus, *Divine Command: A New Perspective on Law and Gospel,* ET 1966; W. Anderson, *Law and Gospel,* 1961; G. Aulén, *Church, Law and Society,* 1948; K. Barth, *God, Grace and Gospel,* ET 1959; C. H. Dodd, *Gospel and Law: The Relation of Faith and Ethics in Early Christianity,* 1951; C. F. W. Walther, *The Proper Distinction Between Law and Gospel* (1893), ET 1929; G. Wingren, *Creation and Law,* ET 1961.

MARTIN J. HEINECKEN

Law, Uses of *see* Calvinist Ethics; Law and Gospel; Lutheran Ethics

Legalism

Legalism is the type of ethic that seeks to prescribe rules for every conceivable occasion of moral choice; or for the type of mentality that follows what is supposed to be the rule in every situation. Some systems of ethics have in fact worked out extremely detailed rules of conduct, so that merely to remember them, let alone fulfill them, would be extremely burdensome. In practice, however, such systems have always allowed some flexibility, according to the demands of the situation. A legalistic mind is probably much more dangerous than a legalistic code of ethics.

See **Law; Law and Gospel; Formalism; Moralism; Norms; Situation Ethics.**

JOHN MACQUARRIE

Legitimacy *see* Illegitimacy

Leisure

see **Amusements; Work, Doctrine of**

Lesbianism

Female homosexuality of any kind. The word came from Lesbos, the home of the Greek poet Sappho, who was said to have practiced it.

See **Homosexuality.**

SHERWIN BAILEY

Letting Die *see* Euthanasia; Life, Prolongation of; Life, Sacredness of; Omission, Sin of

Liberalism

"Trust of the people, qualified by prudence" was how that great British Liberal William Gladstone once described the approach of the party he led into government on four occasions. An appeal to people—rather than classes, racial or religious groups, or property interests—lies at the heart of liberalism.

In turn, that is itself a reflection of the cornerstone of liberalism—the belief in the supreme value of the individual, and the individual's freedom* and rights*; and a conviction that the only value of the State* is to remove obstacles in the path of liberty, and to create the positive conditions of freedom whereby human beings might realize their human potential to the full.

The earliest struggles of liberals the world over have been in affirming the necessity for *limited* government—for confronting arbitrary power and asserting that the individual possesses rights and liberties which no sovereign power has the authority to take to itself. Such principles are recognizable in Magna Carta, imposed on an unwilling King John by his barons in 1215. The continuing struggles between King and Parliament in England, culminating in the Civil War and the English Republic, were part of the same tradition. But the flowering of liberal thought, and its decisive struggle with absolutism, was in the 17th and 18th centuries, in the American War of Independence from British rule; in the French Revolution; and in the philosophy of such figures as Spinoza, Locke, Paine, Montesquieu, Bentham, and J. S. Mill.

Liberal thinkers have argued that the individual has natural rights*, which are universal, springing from a human condition that transcends time and place. The goal of humans everywhere is to realize their freedom —and if they accept the emergence of the State, it is as a necessary evil, a guarantor of their liberty, justifiable only to the extent that it maximizes freedom and protects the individual from those who would deprive the person of his or her liberty. The individual's obligation to the state is balanced by the state's recognition and fulfillment of its own duties. State power rests upon the consent* of the people. That much is common to all liberal theories of government, with Rousseau's doctrine of the social contract* perhaps being the prime example.

Hand in hand with such principles goes a belief in democratic freedoms; in the rule of law and the right to national self-determination, in freedom of speech and association, in tolerance of the religious and political convictions of others, and—flowing naturally from a view of human beings possessing a common dignity*—in the rights of the minority against what J. S. Mill called "the tyranny of the majority." It was this element seized upon by José Ortega y Gasset when he said: "Liberalism . . . is the supreme form of generosity; it is the right which the majority concedes to minorities and hence it is the noblest cry that has ever resounded in this planet."

Nor is liberalism unchanging. Liberals in Britain have all drawn upon liberal thinkers and writers of the past hundred years—from J. S. Mill, L. T. Hobhouse, and T. H. Green through to Jo Grimond and many more recent figures. But their texts are not sacred, nor are their assumptions beyond question. Liberalism is a dynamic philosophy, moving with the demands of the new age.

It was this conviction that led liberals in 19th-century Britain to recognize that laissez-faire* liberalism was not enough. True, it proved essential in unlocking the new economic forces of the Industrial Revolution* and in loosening the grip of privilege and the landed interests. But it offered few solutions to the social misery which was the outcome for many of that economic upheaval. Political rights alone were not enough. Freedom from oppression* needed to be matched by freedom from want—by the State promoting the positive conditions for the liberty of all its people.

Thus it was that the foundations of the welfare state*—of old-age pensions, unemployment benefits, public education, and health insurance—were laid and developed by liberals like Asquith and Lloyd George and by the later pioneering work of William Beveridge. And under the influence of Keynes and others, liberals accepted the need for state intervention, providing a framework within which a genuinely free enterprise system could operate and safeguarding a society from which the scourge of mass unemployment* could be lifted. In the USA New Deal liberalism resulted in reforms that were similar but less extensive.

Finally, the belief in the universal dignity and worth of humanity makes liberalism unassailably internationalist in outlook (*see* Human Rights). Once again, it was Gladstone who captured this essential dimension of liberalism:

"Remember that the sanctity of life in the hill villages of Afghanistan, among the winter snows, is as inviolable in the eye of Almighty God as can be your own. Remember that He who has united you as human beings in the same flesh and blood, has bound you by the law of mutual love; that that mutual love is not limited by the shores of this island, is not limited by the boundaries of Christian civilisation; that it passes over the whole surface of the earth, and embraces the meanest along with the greatest in its unmeasured scope."

DAVID STEEL

Liberalism has not lacked critics, in part because its commitments to freedom* and to equality* are sometimes in tension. Some liberal thinkers have argued that both are grounded in a principle of respect for persons*, human dignity*, or "equal concern and respect" (R. Dworkin), but difficult questions remain about how to balance claims to freedom, privacy*, autonomy*, property*, etc., on the one hand, and claims to equal access to a decent minimum of welfare. (For examples of this debate, *see* **Capitalism; Health Care, Right to; Justice; Socialism; Welfare State;** for other issues, *see* **Autonomy; Morality, Legal Enforcement of; Paternalism; Pluralism.**) Libertarianism* defends the priority of freedom; communism* the priority of equality. Liberals criticize the former for its excessive individualism* and the latter for its collectivism*. Liberalism itself has been criticized for its concentration on rights* and for its failure to attend sufficiently to the common good* (*see* **Official Roman Catholic Social Teaching**) as well as for its inadequate appreciation of community*, tradition*, ritual, etc. (*see* **Conservatism**). Some critics have proposed retaining the spirit of liberalism along with its institutional achievements while modifying some of its principles. Major disputes also emerge on the international level, where liberal conceptions of human rights* are controversial, particularly when they are invoked to justify intervention in other countries.

See **Capitalism; Conservatism; Democracy; Equality; Freedom; Human Dignity;**

Individualism; Liberation Theology; Persecution and Toleration; Pluralism; Politics; Poverty; Property; Socialism; State; Voluntary Associations; Welfare State.

R. Dworkin, *Taking Rights Seriously,* 1977; H. K. Girvetz, *The Evolution of Liberalism,* 1963; L. Hartz, *The Liberal Tradition in America,* 1955; D. MacLean and Claudia Mills (eds.), *Liberalism Reconsidered,* 1983; J. Rawls, *A Theory of Justice,* 1971; M. J. Sandel, *Liberalism and the Limits of Justice,* 1982.

JAMES F. CHILDRESS

Liberation *see* **Afro-American Religious Ethics; Conscientization; Ecumenical Movement, Ethics in the; Feminist Ethics; Justice; Liberation Theology; Political Theology**

Liberation Theology

First popularized in the English-speaking world by Gustavo Gutiérrez's *A Theology of Liberation,* this term refers to a range of practical theologies having the following characteristics: (1) All claim to represent the concrete experience of groups seeking to understand their Christian faith in the midst of organized struggle against various forms of oppression*. (2) All conceive the theological task within certain philosophical assumptions regarding the unity of theory and practice. The methodological focus shifts from perceiving the truth to doing the truth. (3) Since the practice of these groups is confrontational, their theoretical reflections take the form of criticism of the reigning ideologies of oppression and construction of alternative ideologies of liberation. While the latter inevitably project utopian images of the future, they remain functionally ideological to the extent that they are oriented to the present struggle against oppression. (4) Such ideological reflection qualifies as theology, precisely because liberation theologians affirm an intimate connection between their struggle and the authentic meaning of Christian faith. Typically, they seek to understand this connection in terms of a vast *communicatio idiomatum,* transferring the episodes and images of biblical narrative to the concrete struggles experienced by these groups, and vice versa. (5) This "new way of doing theology" ensures each of these groups

an uncompromisingly "prophetic" perspective against both the mainstream churches and the dominant patterns of society. Both are confronted in their oppressive characteristics by the divine judgment of Christ the Liberator.

Within this generic description, it should be possible to analyze the structures common to the entire spectrum of liberation theologies. This is not to say that there are no differences, say, among various Latin American liberation theologians on the uses of Marxist perspectives in their work, or that all North American feminists agree in their analyses of the degree to which sexism has distorted the Christian ethos, or again, that black liberation theologians in the USA resonate to the same Christian traditions that empower Latinos and other oppressed minorities in the USA (*see* **Afro-American Religious Ethics; Feminist Ethics**). Nevertheless, while each group with its distinctive history of oppression and appropriate style of theological reflection deserves serious study for its own sake, generic analysis of liberation theology makes a limited contribution in illuminating the basic structures that need to be understood if an adequate diagnosis of the strengths and weaknesses of these theologies is to be made.

What are these strengths and weaknesses? Liberation theology has been most successful in challenging the dominant styles of "academic theology" to do some consciousness-raising about their own ideological dynamics, tacit or otherwise. Orthodoxy—and most forms of neo-orthodoxy, for that matter— cannot be sustained in the light of demands by liberationists for critical reflection on the concrete historical experiences of the Christian churches and groups. Their insight into the unity of theory and practice, once appropriately qualified for specifically theological reflection, may turn out to be an epoch-making achievement in the history of Christian theology. Moreover, during the past decade or so liberation theologians have probably done as much as any group in the English-speaking world to keep the plight of the oppressed before the conscience of public opinion. Theirs is the thankless task of effective "prophetic" witness.

Equally impressive, however, are their weaknesses, both substantive and methodological. Not surprisingly, the two are interconnected. At the methodological level, the unity of theory and practice advocated in this genre of theology places a certain form of "political analysis" or critical social theory in a theologically constitutive position. The problem is not so much that the analysis is often inspired by Marxism (see **Marxist Ethics**), but that any social theory placed in this position tends to predetermine the theologian's approach to biblical interpretation. While all biblical interpretation is inevitably theory laden, placing a particular theory in this constitutive role makes it extremely difficult for theologians to hear the Word of God as a possible judgment against their own convictions and commitments. At a substantive level, the question arises: What if, in fact, the preferred form of political analysis turns out to be inadequate? What if the critical social theorists revise their theories? At that point wouldn't the very unity of theory and practice that dictated the theological construction in the first place now call for its dismantling? This is not a hypothetical problem: Latin American liberation theology, for example, bases its focus on "liberation" on the assumption that "dependency theory" adequately accounts for the experience of oppression in Latin America. Yet after a decade or more of debate, dependency theory has all but met the death by a thousand qualifications that eventually awaits all forms of political analysis. At the very least, those advocating this "new way of doing theology" may have to resign themselves to making a routine of shaking their own foundations.

None of this would be of much direct concern to Christian ethics were it not that liberation theologians typically exercise their prophetic mission by confronting the ideological residue of oppression embedded in Christian moral teaching. This confrontation, so far, has had salutary effects. It has reawakened most fair-minded ethicists to what John C. Bennett refers to as Christianity's "radical imperative" for social justice and peace. Liberation theologians have also strengthened the hand of those ethicists who have independently concluded that ethical analysis cannot proceed responsibly without careful attention to a variety of "contextual" dimensions. But liberation theologians have not been very helpful in breaking new ground for ethical reflection. Apart from notable exceptions, like José Miguez-Bonino, they have been content to reduce the ethical task to ideologi-

cal criticism of a variety of oppressive ethoses. Unlike Miguez-Bonino, they have felt no need to recognize that their very own struggles present all the moral ambiguities that heretofore have given rise to ethical reflection. When those ambiguities have been discussed, too often they have been couched in terms of the single problem of revolutionary violence, a uniquely perplexing place to begin (see **Revolution; Resistance**). It is not surprising that such discussions have tended to yield little more than a superficial endorsement of situation ethics*.

It is too early to tell what, finally, will be liberation theology's ultimate contribution to Christian ethics. The weaknesses identified here may be overcome in genuine dialogue if both liberation theologians and their critics keep uppermost in mind the overriding obligation placed upon all true Christians, wherever they may find themselves among the structures and ideologies of the particular historical moment, to seek justice and peace for the sake of the kingdom of God.

See **Conscientization**.

J. C. Bennett, *The Radical Imperative: From Theology to Social Ethics*, 1975; J. Cone, *A Black Theology of Liberation*, 1970; M. Daly, *Beyond God the Father: Toward a Philosophy of Women's Liberation*, 1973; J. M. Gustafson, *Can Ethics Be Christian?* 1975; G. Gutiérrez, *A Theology of Liberation*, ET 1973; B. Mahan and L. D. Richesin (eds.), *The Challenge of Liberation Theology: A First World Response*, 1981; J. Miguez-Bonino, *Toward a Christian Political Ethics*, ET 1983; M. Novak et al. (eds.), *Liberation South, Liberation North*, 1981; R. Ruether, *New Woman/ New Earth: Sexist Ideologies and Human Liberation*, 1975; J. L. Segundo, *The Liberation of Theology*, ET 1976; C. West, *Prophesy Deliverance! An Afro-American Revolutionary Christianity*, 1982.

DENNIS P. McCANN

Libertarianism

There are two distinct though allied meanings to libertarianism. The older sense of the term refers to a metaphysical or ethical doctrine that the human will* is free, rather than determined (see **Free Will and Determinism; Freedom**). In this sense, libertarian views contrast with necessitarian or deterministic viewpoints. Distinctions have been drawn with regard to the degree of freedom or determination, in that libertarian viewpoints range from those holding that individuals are absolutely free and undetermined (the *liberum arbitrium indifferentiae*) to those holding that, though there are influencing or predisposing factors, persons* are able to choose despite such influences. Libertarians in this sense include philosophers such as F. H. Bradley, Alfred North Whitehead, and Charles Hartshorne, who have argued that the outcomes of decisions by persons are not fully predictable because of the role played by self-determination. Others, such as Immanuel Kant, have distinguished between the ways in which individuals are regarded as persons, and the ways in which individuals are regarded as objects of science. In the first case, they must be considered to be self-determining as a condition of the very possibility of morality (*see* **Autonomy**). Libertarian viewpoints have been criticized, insofar as they rely on metaphysical assumptions or construe human choice* as unpredictable, therefore making human actions* chance occurrences.

The more popular sense of libertarianism refers to a political doctrine stressing the rights* of individuals vis-à-vis the state and other societal organizations, including corporations and large associations (e.g., unions). Libertarian understandings of political theory see governments as fashioned through the consent of individuals, as having no rights not possessed by individuals, as limited in their moral authority*, and as properly existing on as local and decentralized a basis as is feasible (*see* **Individualism; State**). A major source for libertarian viewpoints is to be found in traditional Western thinkers such as John Locke in his *Letter Concerning Toleration* and *Second Treatise of Government,* as well as in the writings of Richard Overton, Edmund Burke, and Alexis de Tocqueville.

Libertarianism has been drawn as well from the debate between anarchist and Communist thinkers over the last century (*see* **Anarchism; Communism**). Ideal Communist views with regard to the withering of the state and the decentralization of authority bring such views close to individualistic anarchists and their concern that society be in the hands of individual persons, in particular, individual workers. Contemporary libertarian views have in great proportion abandoned such explicit anarchist and syndicalist commitments in favor of a general defense of a limited state, which would function primar-

ily to provide protection against external and internal aggressors. For example, Robert Nozick's *Anarchy, State, and Utopia* (1974) argues that the state does not possess more authority than is needed for minimal police functions. Since 1971, there has been a Libertarian Party in the USA, which supports this last sense of libertarianism as a doctrine of a limited state and of paramount individual rights. Its presidential candidate received over 930,000 votes in the 1980 election, but less than a quarter of a million in 1984.

H. TRISTRAM ENGELHARDT, JR.

Libertinism *see* **Gnosticism, Ethics of**

Liberty *see* **Free Will and Determinism; Freedom; Libertarianism; Persecution and Toleration**

Liberty of Religion *see* **Church and State; Conscientious Objection; Freedom; Persecution and Toleration**

Life, Prolongation of

Prolongation of life is an imprecise term of medical ethics that refers to decisions whether to initiate/withhold or continue/withdraw life-sustaining efforts. This long-standing moral problem is frequently symbolized by the question of whether to use "life-support systems" (e.g., respirators, artificial hearts) for critically ill patients, but potentially embraces questions of the use of both simple and sophisticated means of both diagnosing and treating impairments of vital functions (by aiding, supporting, or supplanting them), and of health more generally (e.g., through medication and surgery not directly and immediately related to vital function).

In Christian perspective, the life of humans is the most fundamental of goods, underlying all other values; but concrete bodily existence is not the highest of values. A framework for guiding decisions about the prolongation of life is offered by the principles of "ordinary" and "extraordinary" (hereafter abbreviated o/e) means of treatment, which have a long history in Christian thought and are employed in professional directives, in court decisions, and in the language of clinicians and ethicists. The o/e principles in their classic form state that there is an obligation to use ordinary means to preserve life, but no strict obligation to use extraordinary means. Extraordinary means are all medicines, treatments, and operations that (1) do not offer a reasonable hope of success or (2) cannot be obtained or used without excessive hardship—i.e., excessive pain, cost, or other inconvenience. Because of ambiguities ("ordinary" does not mean customary in medical practice but morally obligatory), vagueness (e.g., does "hope of success" refer to restoration to full health, to a prior condition of health, to a satisfactory quality of life?), and misleading categorizations (due to rapid medical advances the means themselves cannot be o/e; circumstances may render them nonobligatory), it is now commonly urged that the terms "ordinary" and "extraordinary" be replaced by more precise terms: "obligatory" vs. "optional" measures, determined by what is judged "proportionate" or "disproportionate" when one weighs "benefits" and "burdens" in the use of available treatments (*see* **Proportionality**).

Relevant to any discussion about whether the o/e principles themselves should be abandoned is their significance, for they are not a mere distinction; they are code terms for a cluster of values, obligations, and limits to obligations. They also presuppose and embody important moral distinctions: between duties of beneficence* (doing good) and nonmaleficence* (not inflicting harm), killing and letting die, and direct and indirect effects (*see* **Double Effect**). While these principles have served for centuries to remind us chiefly that there are *limits* to the duty to preserve life, their principal service to the current era may be to convey a *presumption of a duty* to preserve life.

The two standards of "hope of success" (or the prospect of proportionate benefit) and disproportionate hardship necessarily involve judgments about various qualities of life; but there is considerable debate about single, overriding quality-of-life norms. Thus, while some hold there is no obligation to sustain a human life when, in the absence of mental activity, there is "only biological life," others argue that the "only biological" assessment manifests an inadequate concept of embodiment* associated with personhood (*see* **Persons and Personality**). Similarly, some hold that it is "extraordinary" (nonobligatory) to prolong the lives of newborn infants with serious impairments that will cause an incapacitating disability in the area of meaningful social relationships; others

hold that such standards offend the principle of fundamental equal worth of human lives and create a "slippery slope"* on which there is no logical or practical way of halting the slide toward excluding other categories of humans from sustenance.

Additional key issues in applying o/e principles are: development of "do not resuscitate" orders; whether and according to which principles of socioeconomic allocation a second party may deny life support to a patient on grounds of "excessive cost"; and whether use of food and water can ever be disproportionate. Elements in the latter dispute include whether hydration and alimentation viewed as *medical* therapies may become disproportionately intrusive means of artificial life support, or whether giving food and water is always an obligatory, minimal support because of the symbolism of this basic human gesture.

Regarding the question *who* should decide about life prolongation, principles of autonomy* and conscience* favor primacy of the patient; principles of beneficence* and social justice* ground a secondary role for physicians/hospitals and the state, respectively. Following this principled ranking, proxy decisions for the incompetent but formerly competent—made by a designee of the patient or by family where possible—should employ a "substituted judgment" standard, making the decision the patient would have made, based, if possible, on the patient's previously expressed (orally or in writing) wishes; while proxy decisions for those who have never been competent should be made—by family, physicians, committees, or court (in that order)—based on objective standards of the best interests of the patient.

See **Euthanasia; Life, Quality of; Life, Sacredness of; Paternalism.**

Anglican Working Party, *On Dying Well: An Anglican Contribution to the Debate on Euthanasia,* 1975; T. L. Beauchamp and J. F. Childress, *Principles of Biomedical Ethics,* [2]1983, pp. 106–147; U.S. President's Commission for the Study of Ethical Problems in Medicine and Biomedical and Behavioral Research, *Deciding to Forego Life-Sustaining Treatment: A Report on the Ethical, Medical, and Legal Issues in Treatment Decisions,* 1983; relevant articles in *EB* and *DME*.

WARREN THOMAS REICH

Life, Quality of

Quality of life is often distinguished from quantity of life (which might include the length of an individual's life or the number of lives affected), equality of life, and sanctity of life, particularly in debates about actions and policies to prolong or to save lives, such as abortion* and euthanasia*. One issue is whether biological life should always be prolonged regardless of its quality, "quality" sometimes indicating the value of the life to society, but often indicating the value of the life to the human being himself or herself. Theologians generally find the former unacceptable and the latter sometimes acceptable, within carefully defined limits, but there is vigorous debate about the ethical relevance of either interpretation of the quality of life.

See **Embodiment; Life, Prolongation of; Life, Sacredness of.**

R. McCormick, "The Quality of Life, the Sanctity of Life," *HCR* 8, Feb. 1978; P. Ramsey, *Ethics at the Edges of Life,* 1978.

JAMES F. CHILDRESS

Life, Right to

see **Life, Prolongation of; Life, Sacredness of**

Life, Sacredness of

Christian belief in the sanctity of human life is derived from the doctrine of God as Creator. Humankind was made in God's image with power to reason and the capacity to choose (see **Image of God**). Each individual is infinitely precious to God and made for an eternal destiny. Thus the Christian attitude to human life can only be one of reverence* —enjoined by the whole of the Decalogue (not only by the Sixth Commandment) and confirmed by the incarnation—which is to be extended to every individual from the moment of conception to extreme old age and death. Our right to life, grounded in our divine origin, is the basis of all other human rights, natural and legal, and the foundation of civilized society.

Our worth to God implies the duty of cherishing, protecting, and preserving human life, and the taking of all moral means for the relief of suffering and the eradication of disease. It implies a proper regard for the human body itself and a refusal willingly to accept or deliberately to inflict any physical mutilation that is not necessary for the health of the whole organism (see **Sterilization; Totality, Principle of**). Respect for both life and physical integrity sets limits to the mode and extent of therapeutic and nontherapeutic medical experimentation with fetuses and fetal material as well as with children and adults (see **Experimentation with Human Subjects**). Because all human beings derive the right to life from God, our value as persons is constant, whether we be rich or poor, strong or weak, handicapped or normal, socially "useful" or "useless"; therefore neither our life nor our well-being can rightly be sacrificed to the economic or political welfare or convenience of society: indeed, society itself is to be judged by its protection of and the solicitude it shows for its weaker members. Since all persons have been given life that they might fulfill themselves in the service of God and their fellow humans, we may properly take actions that endanger our life, and even be ready to sacrifice it, in a weighty and righteous cause. In certain exceptional circumstances, we may also be held to be lawfully deprived of it. But, since God remains the absolute owner of all our lives, the Christian tradition has held that it is a sin deliberately and directly to kill an *innocent* person, not simply for revenge but for any reason whatever (see **Homicide**). It is in the light of this conception of the sanctity of human life that the Christian must consider questions relating to procreation*, and practices like abortion*, infanticide*, suicide*, euthanasia*, organ transplantation*, capital punishment*, and war*.

Because God is the Lord and giver of all life, humans have a duty to respect and act responsibly toward forms of subhuman life. God has given to humankind authority to exercise dominion over all other living things: we may kill them for food and harness them to our use, but we must not exploit them for our greed or inflict unnecessary pain upon them (see **Animals**). Even more is it a matter of Christian concern that this sacred gift of God which is human life shall itself become truly *sanctified:* that all humans, by the grace of God, as members of the body of Christ, shall grow in the way of holiness (see **Holiness; Sanctification**).

See also **Body; Double Effect; Embodiment; Handicapped, Care of the; Human Dignity; Human Rights; Image of God; Natural Rights; Pacifism; Persons and Personal-**

ity; **Resistance; Respect for Persons; Reverence.**

THOMAS WOOD

Lifeboat Ethics see Hunger, World; Population Policy; Procreation; Triage

Living Will
A somewhat misleading term used in the USA to denote a person's advance directives regarding treatment in case of terminal illness and incompetence to make his or her own decisions. *See* **Consent; Life, Prolongation of.**

Lottery *see* Gambling

Love

I. Historical Perspectives
Few words so indispensable to discourse upon Christian ethics as well as Christian theology are so imprecise in their denotation as the word "love." In common English usage love means a sentiment of strong attachment entertained toward a particular object or class of objects. A person may be said to love anything in which he or she takes special delight—the sea, flowers, birds, music, poetry. When the object of love is personal, it is usually individual rather than generic: we do not naturally speak of loving musicians or poets. In the Hebrew of the OT, the commonest word for love—'*ahebh*—generally has a personal object, though it can be used, for example, of savory meat (Gen. 27:4) or cursing (Ps. 109:17). In Hebrew as in English, the word gets its most characteristic overtones from the fact that the strongest and most enduring form of personal love is that between man and woman. Neither language has a separate word for erotic love. The Septuagint translation of the OT generally renders '*ahebh* and its derivatives by the Greek *agapan* and its noun *agapē,* even when as in the Song of Songs the natural word for the love described would be *erōs.* In prebiblical Greek *erōs* is a passion, an ecstasy, a madness; while the verb *agapan* and the noun *agapēsis* (the form *agapē* seems not to occur earlier than its use in the Septuagint) denote the cooler and calmer love of rational preference, which chooses its object and holds to it freely. This is in accord with the most important feature of biblical usage, which is that the love of husband and wife includes the

obligation of fidelity; and it is this element of loyalty in a covenanted relationship that is reflected when love, which as a spontaneous sentiment cannot be forced, is required in the Deuteronomic law (Deut. 6:5) as Israel's liege duty to the God who had entered into covenant with this people. The love of God is indeed often coupled with the keeping of his commandments (Deut. 11:1, etc.); but there is no need to evade an apparent paradox by arguing that the command to love God really means the requirement of obedience to God's law in all the actions of life. The command assumes that love in the natural meaning of the word is the natural response to the love so wonderfully bestowed by God himself upon the people whom he has chosen. To fail in this response would be to have forgotten the unique relationship in which Israel stands to Jehovah. Before the Deuteronomist, the prophet Hosea had already found in the figure of an adulterous wife the most telling image for Israel's apostasy: Israel *ought* to be true in love to its divine husband. So Joshua demands that Israel shall "cleave" to the Lord (Josh. 23:8), as the law of nature requires a man to "cleave" to his wife (Gen. 2:24). In the same way, the command in the Holiness Code of Lev. 19:18—"You shall love your neighbor as yourself"—is to be understood as a real command, based upon the natural bond of common membership in the elect nation.

It is possible that the combination of Deut. 6:5 with Lev. 19:18 had already been made in rabbinic teaching before Jesus; for it appears in the *Testaments of the Twelve Patriarchs* (e.g., Issachar 5:2; 7:5). In any case, the scribe in Mark 12:28ff. welcomes as "truly said" Christ's summary of the law as love to God and love to neighbor; and both Jesus and his questioner must be taken to have understood the operative word in each of the two commandments so associated as having the same meaning: the second is really (as in Matt. 22:39) "like" the first. There has been much discussion about the meaning of "as yourself," and the nature of the "self-love" which the saying appears to sanction. But the phrase will not bear the weight of any such far-reaching inferences; it simply describes a love as intense and compulsive as that of Jonathan who loved David as "his own soul" (1 Sam. 20:17)—so that the fortunes of the beloved are as important to the lover as his own. But it should be clear that to love one's neighbor as thus commanded does not *mean* to succour him in distress, any more than to love God *means* to keep his commandments. It is a separate question, in what kind of behavior must the love of God or neighbor be exhibited and its genuineness verified?

In the teaching of Jesus, the pattern love is God's, which is displayed (1) in his indiscriminate goodness to all his creation, (2) in his free forgiveness for the repentant sinner, and (3) in his redeeming activity, going out "to seek and to save." So we are bidden to imitate the divine love (1) by doing good to all without distinction, (2) by forgiving as we have been forgiven, and (3) by ready response to every call of need. The love-ethic of the NT epistles is true to that of the Gospels in the second and third of these characters; but the universalism implicit in Christ's extension of love to enemies is replaced by an emphasis on "love of the brethren" which is hardly less marked in the Pauline than in the Johannine writings. For Paul, love is the greatest of the Spirit's gifts because it serves for the "building up" of the Christian community. Love is the solvent of all divisive forces, all individualism which threatens the life of the one Body; it is the "bond of wholeness [*shalom*]" (Eph. 4:3; Col. 3:14). For John, the new commandment is that we love one another: this mutual love of Christians is to be the proof for all people that we are Christ's disciples, and by the love which unites us, as it unites Father and Son in the Godhead, the world will know that the Father has sent him (John 13:34f.; 17:22f.). Here certainly OT influence is at work. The church is the true Israel, whose members are bound in the new covenant, sealed in Christ's blood, to be true in love to God and their brethren. It is the nature of love to be the supreme *unifying* power.

Apart from the summary of the law, there is not more than a single reference (Luke 11:42) in the Synoptic account of Jesus' teaching to human love for God. In the rest of the NT the "love of God" nearly but not quite always means God's love for humanity. In 1 John 5:3 love for God is expressly identified with the keeping of his commandments (cf. John 14:15, 21); and Paul in Gal. 5:14 and Rom. 13:10 calls love of neighbor the *fulfillment* of the law. But these texts are insufficient justification for assuming an intentional reduction of the first great commandment to the second. Paul does speak of love for God without qualification, for example, in 1 Cor. 8:3; and we may be sure that it was not a love of neighbor but an answering love to the God whose own forgiving love he had known in Christ that took him to his death in Rome. For him as for Rabbi Akiba and many another persecuted Jew, martyrdom "for the Name" was the ultimate fulfillment of the great commandment.

What is harder to find in the NT is any expression of love toward God which recalls the "thirst" of the psalmists (Pss. 42 and 63). And this is the sense of unsatisfied longing which dominated the minds and hearts of later Christians educated in the philosophic atmosphere of Platonism (*see* **Platonic Ethics; Neoplatonism**). The *eros* which in Plato was the desire for vision of the ideal beauty became for the Neoplatonist the desire for union with God; and union with God was not to be distinguished from the eternal life which was the promise of the Christian gospel. The famous words of Augustine in the *Confessions* (1.1), that our hearts are restless till they find their rest in God, would have been echoed by nearly every one of his great predecessors, at least in the Greek-speaking church, as voicing the essence of religion. And Augustine is the mainspring of the great tradition of Catholic mysticism which flourished throughout the Middle Ages. The tradition received its intellectual formulation from Thomas Aquinas. In the *Summa Theologiae* all natural love is treated as a passion, stirred by some good to which the love is adapted; but the "love of concupiscence*," which is the desire of possession, is distinguished from the "love of friendship*," which seeks only the good of the friend. Charity* as the supernatural gift of grace is a love of friendship, based on God's self-communication to humanity, in which God is loved "for himself" and not for anything to be obtained from him.

The scholastic distinction, however, did not impress Anders Nygren, who in his influential study of the doctrine of love in Christian theology maintained that the "*eros*-motif" predominant in Catholicism is irreconcilable with the "*agapē*-motif" of the NT because *eros* is always egocentric as the pursuit of a good to be acquired for the self. The acquisitive nature of the desire is not affected by its transference from a "lower" to a "higher" good, from things earthly to things heavenly. *Agapē* on the contrary is entirely unselfish, seeking only the good of others, and is therefore theocentric because it is the reproduction of God's own outgoing love, a love "uncaused" by any existing goodness in its object. In Nygren's view, Augustine attempted to achieve a synthesis of *erōs* and *agapē,* in which the restless longing for God in the human heart—a longing implanted by God himself—is met by the descent of the divine love in the incarnation, so that the union with God which is the object of desire is participation in the selfless love which is the very nature of God. But (so Nygren holds) the synthesis must be pronounced a failure, because it involves (contrary to Augustine's own principles) "using" God for the satisfaction of a human need. The synthesis was shattered by Luther's "Copernican revolution," in which the *erōs*-inspired Catholic doctrine of love was seen to be the expression of "works-religion," seeking fellowship with God on God's own "level" by an ascent Godward on the wings of spiritual desire; whereas the doctrine of justification by faith means that fellowship with God is only to be had "on the level of sin," where God's love meets the sinner in Christ. *Erōs* is always the attempt of human beings to "establish their own righteousness," to make themselves fit for the vision of God; and it must therefore be ruthlessly extirpated to make room for the entry of *agapē.* The logical conclusion, accepted by Nygren, is that since humans may not love God in the sense of *erōs,* and cannot love him in the sense of *agapē*—the creature cannot "seek the good" of the Creator—the love enjoined in the first great commandment is really indistinguishable from the faith which is the only proper human attitude to God; while the Christian love of neighbor is nothing less than God's own *agapē* flowing through human hearts (*see* **Augustinian Ethics; Lutheran Ethics**).

Nygren's confrontation of *erōs* and *agapē* may be compared with the position of Søren Kierkegaard in his *Works of Love* (1847). Kierkegaard contrasted Christian love not with the mystic's desire for union with God but with the love between man and woman or friend and friend, which is selective, concentrated upon a particular person or persons preferred to all others. Such love, depending as it does upon the presence of certain qualities in its object found lovable, is for Kierkegaard (as *erōs* is for Nygren) only a disguised

form of the love of self; and it is necessarily exposed to alteration and failure. Christian love, which does not choose its object but goes out to the neighbor who is everyone, is secure from change just because it is accepted as a duty, as obedience to a "you shall" (*see* **Kierkegaardian Ethics**).

Karl Barth in his *Church Dogmatics* (IV/2, p. 68) agrees with Nygren that *erōs* and *agapē* are contraries; for *agapē* conforms to the true nature of human beings as created for relationship to God and to their fellow humans, while *erōs* opposes it. So, though in most if not all of us, both loves are present and active in varying degrees, they must always be in rivalry: the love which seeks self-fulfillment must be at issue with the love which is *Hingabe,* total surrender of the self. But Barth is too good a biblical theologian to approve the "Puritanism" of Nygren's refusal to allow that humans can have love toward God. Christ accepted the loving extravagance of Mary's offering, and rebuked the moralistic protests of his disciples. Without love to Jesus there can be no following of Jesus: without love to God there can be no obedience to God. Love is the *presupposition* of all else in the Christian life; and it is precisely the freedom to love both God and neighbor that is the gift of grace, the creation of God's own redeeming love in Christ. So Barth can see only an intolerable legalism in Kierkegaard's insistence that love must be made "secure" by the obligation of obedience to a command. He holds equally firmly against Nygren (or Luther!) that the love of neighbor which springs from and is "like" human beings' love for God must be a genuinely human activity; Christians are not mere "channels" for God's love. But he maintains that because God's own love is not a disposition or a sentiment but an *act,* the same must be true of the love humans have for their fellow humans. The act in which it consists is essentially an act of witness to the gospel, to the accomplished fact of redemption; and accordingly Barth follows the Pauline and Johannine example in treating Christian love as in principle an act that is not indiscriminate in its reference, but has the "brother" as its object—though it must always be ready to find a "brother" in one who was not such before.

Differences in the understanding of Christian love arise to a large extent from the incurable ambivalence of a religious ethic. For secular morality there is an obvious distinction between the love which links persons to one another because of something peculiar to them as individuals or members of a class, and the love of humanity as such which expresses itself in the service of others not because of their characters but because of their situation. Kantian rigorism will allow moral quality only to the second of these loves. The "problem of love" in Christian ethics is posed by its theological basis: What is the consequence for Christian behavior of the belief that God is love? The image of divine fatherhood which was central to the teaching of Jesus does not suggest a love that is exhibited in pure altruism, regardless of any personal relationship to its recipients. The love of God of which the gospel speaks is more than a love of beneficence, it is a reconciling, in the strict meaning of the word an atoning love. We cannot suppose that the heavenly Father does not care whether his children love him or not. The labor of his love is to overcome the pride and covetousness that estrange people alike from God and from one another, and to bring them to that state of mutual attachment and mutual dependence which is proper to a family. Christian love, therefore, cannot be perfected without the warmth of personal affection which is the cement of unity between parent and children, brothers and sisters. The grace of our Lord Jesus Christ is what gives that warmth to people's service of one another and to their loyal obedience to the law of God.

E. Brunner, *The Divine Imperative,* ET 1937; J. Burnaby, *Amor Dei,* 1938; M. J. D'Arcy, *The Mind and Heart of Love,* 1945; J. Guitton, *Essay on Human Love,* 1951; S. Kierkegaard, *Works of Love,* ET 1962; J. Moffatt, *Love in the New Testament,* 1929; R. Niebuhr, *An Interpretation of Christian Ethics,* 1936; A. Nygren, *Agape and Eros,* ET 1953; G. Quell and E. Stauffer, *Love,* Bible Key Words, vol. 1, 1949 (also see *TWNT* I, pp. 21–55).

JOHN BURNABY

II. Contemporary Discussion

Love in Christian ethics remains a pervasive subject in recent writing. Studies of relevant biblical materials continue to be published; the legacies of Augustine, Aquinas, Luther, Kierkegaard, Nygren, and Barth described in the previous article persist. What distinguishes contemporary discussion above all perhaps is the amount of attention certain normative questions receive. These questions center on the meaning of neighbor-love itself and its implications for modern problems in both personal and social life. Sketches of four questions follow.

1. Universal human dignity and the question of its recognition and enhancement. Many writers begin by affirming that God's love in the teaching of Jesus serves as pattern and prototype for love between human beings. This affirmation (formally, divine exemplar theory) means at a minimum that we should imitate on our own level and with our own capacities God's bestowal of value or dignity on every person. Love conforms to grace when it is unconditional: nothing a person does in particular qualifies or disqualifies him or her from respect and active help. The question discussed extensively is what this affirmation implies for our spatiotemporal existence. Does it, for example, call for certain patterns of personal, social, and legal recognition and enhancement, patterns that may disrupt and transform as well as ratify any particular set of status quo arrangements? Some refuse to ascribe "final" significance (for our religious prospects at any rate) to *our* drawing of patterns. For them, if God's bestowal of dignity is constitutive of our human condition, so that we do not establish it by any act of ours and cannot undo it, then we betray a false temporal seriousness when we suppose we must work to guarantee that dignity is recognized and enhanced. Does our work not disclose an absence of confidence that our dignity is "real" after all? Do we not attest to our dignity most fittingly by rising above or transcending all of our spatiotemporal determinations? Most, however, do engage in the work of recognition and enhancement. Not to do so risks abstraction and fails to confront the realities of a sinful, conflict-ridden world. Our efforts may be flawed and transient, but they represent the strictly human imitation of which we are capable.

The story of these contemporary efforts occurs especially in three areas. (*a*) To recognize dignity requires us to attend to the generic characteristics all persons share, such as the requirements for physical survival and development of talents ("welfare") and the conditions of agency ("freedom"). One influential effort lies in the growth of a human rights* tradition in 20th-century Roman Catholic social ethics, where moral claims are specified in terms of a right to noninterference and a right to an equal share of goods and services which meet basic human needs (*see* **Official Roman Catholic Social Teaching**). (*b*) To recognize dignity requires us to confront situations of conflict. Different kinds of conflict must be distinguished: (i) the case of a single other person: protection from harm and honoring free choice; (ii) between myself and another person: here regions of responsibility differ; (iii) between two other persons: where the same characteristic is at stake, e.g., the common need for a scarce kidney dialysis machine, and where different characteristics are at stake, e.g., the freedom of the woman and the physical survival of the fetus (at least as a potential person); (iv) between several or many other persons: distribution of the community's resources, rulers and ruled, employers and employees, wrongdoers and wronged and the possibility of justified coercion. (*c*) To recognize dignity requires us to determine which particularizing differences among persons make a moral difference. Some differences are acceptably relevant: differential treatments for different needs, a "preferential option for the poor" as a rectifying bias, (more contestably) certain claims of merit based on the differential exercise of an equal liberty. Other differences are seen as irrelevant, or rendered permanently suspect, or renounced altogether. For example, age, physical attractiveness, gender, and race are irrelevant; hierarchies carry always the burden of proof; chauvinism of every kind is rejected. The hardest cases involve the urgencies of special relations. We live within special bonds of varying kinds, e.g., between friends, lovers, spouses, parents and children, coreligionists, members of a given class, party, tribe, or society, and so on. Can any view which stresses the sameness of human dignity accommodate these bonds? Can it even stabilize and strengthen as well as relativize and limit some of them, and challenge others? To try to ignore them is to abandon moral particularity. Yet the force and tangible effects of a commitment to human dignity must be retained in their midst (*see* **Human Dignity; Persons and Personality; Respect for Persons**).

2. *Self-sacrifice queried and cohumanity reaffirmed.* To extol a love that "seeketh not its own" is foundational to a Christian ethic. Yet special pains have been taken recently to distinguish justifiable self-sacrifice from faithless self-abnegation; and to insist that the justified forms apply to men and women alike. Self-sacrifice is justified, one argument runs, if and only if it confers actual benefits on others, and not merely because it displays an internal disposition of the self. To this a philosophical argument is sometimes appended: self-sacrifice proves to be self-frustrating if everyone acts on it. No self ever benefits if all are engaged in endlessly giving themselves away. The case for commending self-acceptance and self-affirmation is religious or theological. It rests finally on the same grounds that obtain in the case of all other persons: our common status as creatures of God. If human dignity depends on God's unmerited bestowal, then effectively to exclude oneself from this judgment of worth is faithless and arbitrary. This case also reflects a heightened sensitivity to the sins of sloth* as well as pride*. The Protestant tradition perhaps especially has attended to the latter "Promethean" sort, against which self-sacrifice stands most intelligibly opposed. Now it is seen that the absence of self-direction corrupts, and not only selfishness, acquisitiveness, possessiveness.

Moreover, women writers contend that the ideal of self-sacrifice has been applied one-sidedly in the Christian tradition. Women far more than men have devalued their humanity by giving up too much of their own identities and quests for the sake of husbands and children. Any standard which combines self-affirmation and fidelity and devotion to others should govern impartially (*see* **Feminist Ethics**).

Yet a combination is the crux. The questions about self-sacrifice never imply praise of isolated self-sufficiency. Indeed, one claim that recurs is that some degree of achieved self-affirmation coincides with and conduces to *effective* help of others. Another background claim reinforces this: human persons are essentially interpersonal and social, beings-in-encounter; our humanity is actually cohumanity. This claim too receives pronounced emphasis in 20th-century theology.

3. *Love and justice reexamined.* Accounts of love and justice* offered earlier in this century sometimes assume that love contains no principle of justice within its meaning, and

that any principle proposed could conflict with, as well as supplement or be required by, love. Contemporary accounts usually assume justice is contained in the meaning of love, or at least that they are inseparable, if still distinguishable. This turn derives in part from interpretations of love as a standard of social and not only personal relations; and is exemplified in the stress already mentioned on rights as a recognition of dignity. One question posed about both earlier and later accounts is whether they too often succumb to simplifying formulae. It proves ambiguous in many instances to announce "*the* relation" between love and justice because there may be different relations to different conceptions, on either or both sides. In the case of justice, for instance, standard conceptions include: to each according to need, desert or merit, societal contribution, ability, rank, legal entitlement, covenants made, similar treatment for similar cases, etc. Love that centers on human dignity will obviously overlap with some of these conceptions (e.g., need) more than others (e.g., rank) and influence any priorities proposed.

4. Love and the authority of moral rules. During the past four decades several major debates have occurred in both Roman Catholic and Protestant circles concerning the bindingness of moral rules, and whether any are exceptionless, irrespective of consequences. The rules predominantly at issue include the parts of the second table of the Decalogue* which forbid killing, stealing, adultery, and lying. These rules share two features. First, they are comparatively specific: they locate action-kinds which are delimited, spatially and temporally. Second, they are basic: they refer to certain actions perceived as undeniably significant by virtue of the depth of their impingement on fundamental human interests. In one of these debates, proponents of the position called "situation ethics"* hold that love itself is exceptionless, but moral rules never are. The authority ascribed to the latter is at most prima facie: they may never be disregarded, because they carry with them in any situation to which they apply a presumption in their favor. But they may be overridden if in so doing the best consequences, all things considered, are realized. Critics of this view defend certain rules as exceptionless, though on differing grounds. Some construe the content

of love itself as a compendium of specific biblical commandments which are themselves exceptionless. Others maintain that certain action-kinds are forbidden by nature. Still others argue that human well-being is best served by holding certain actions closed to future possible exceptions. In such debates the tradition is reaffirmed, criticized, and selectively appropriated, in combinations that display some of its present internal conflicts, and that sustain and extend it.

J. L. Allen, *Love and Conflict,* 1984; J. Fletcher, *Situation Ethics,* 1966; J. Gremillion (ed.), *The Gospel of Peace and Justice: Catholic Social Teaching Since Pope John,* 1980; D. Hollenbach, *Claims in Conflict,* 1979; G. Outka, *Agape: An Ethical Analysis,* 1972; P. Ramsey, *Basic Christian Ethics,* 1950.

GENE OUTKA

Loyalty

Josiah Royce defines loyalty as the "willing and practical and thoroughgoing devotion of a person to a cause." As an attribute of a fundamental relationship it has been a central concept in the theological ethics of Royce and other 20th-century writers, including H. R. Niebuhr, Gabriel Marcel (*see* **Fidelity**), and Paul Ramsey.

"Loyalty" is related to the French *loi* (law). Loyalty within an organically conceived society was a fundamental social conception in medieval Europe. In contrast, utilitarian or egoistic ethical theories do not treat loyalty as an intrinsic good. Thus an ethic based on loyalty will have closer affinities with deontological moral theories of the Kantian and pre-Kantian types. Yet it is differentiated from these by its twin concerns for the fulfillment of the moral self and the object of loyalty.

An important criticism of an ethics of loyalty concerns a tendency to justify fanaticism. Blind loyalty to perverse causes—religious or secular—has done great damage in the 20th century, and an ethic that might give credibility to fanaticism is rightly discredited. Therefore thinkers using the concept of loyalty must give particular attention to the choice of an object of loyalty. Royce's idea was that loyalty must be separated from its political and militaristic connotations. Causes are evil if they live by overthrowing the loyalties of others; good causes manifest "loyalty to loyalty." For Niebuhr the proper object is a monotheistic god whose transcendence makes possible the integration of selves who see his power in all things. Ramsey insists that "covenant loyalty" be directed solely to needy individuals, primarily for their protection.

Royce argues that loyalty is morally decisive because it unifies the public world and the private world. The moral life needs definiteness; persons are fulfilled when they "limit their personal range" and then grow according to their interests and choices. One can go wrong by blindly conforming, ignoring one's own interests, or latching on to a false cause. Individualistic seeking for liberty or autonomy* is anathema: "The only way to be practically autonomous is to be freely loyal." Niebuhr sees sin as misdirected or conflicting loyalties associated with distrust. Even a unified world may appear as the destroyer, and only grace makes possible trust in the One. In Ramsey an experience of God's loyalty is primary; selves show their loyalty in giving to others. The deepest human pathology is anxious self-centeredness. It is striking that the obvious metaphor of betrayal is very little utilized, but these writers are agreed that a moral (loyal) life delivers something incomparable to the self.

Obviously loyalty is a social term. Royce and Niebuhr stressed the extent to which selves are formed by their environments; Ramsey's theory is less concerned with this. Several general questions remain, e.g., Is loyalty thought to be a sufficient moral principle? Royce thought not, but his development of derivative principles of justice and benevolence is at best embryonic. For Niebuhr there is at least a supplementary principle of equality. Ramsey, despite some appreciation for natural law, comes very close to developing an entire ethic from the one conceptual root. More specificity about derivative or supplementary principles would be helpful throughout.

Other issues remain as well: the relation between loyalty and affection, trust, and duty; conflicts between loyalties to persons and institutions; loyalty to the choices or the needs of another; the relative importance of loyalties to family, church, economic institutions, and civil government—to say nothing of the basis of the concept in scripture, tradition, and reason. It remains to be seen whether the general conception of loyalty will be as fruitful at the end of the century as it was at the beginning and middle.

———

J. Ladd, "Loyalty," *EP* V, 1967; H. R. Niebuhr, *Radical Monotheism and Western Culture,* 1960; P. Ramsey, *The Patient as Person,* 1970; J. Royce, *The Philosophy of Loyalty,* in J. J. McDermott (ed.), *The Basic Writings of Josiah Royce,* vol. 2, 1969.

DAVID H. SMITH

Lust

"Lust" is defined as a strong desire especially, though not exclusively, for sexual pleasure. Many expressions of lust, such as fornication* and adultery*, are condemned in the scriptures (see Rom. 1:24–28, which denounces the "shameful lusts" of the pagans, and Gal. 5:19–20, which condemns "works of the flesh"), and lust itself has been viewed as one of the seven deadly, or capital, sins* because it leads to so many other vices and sins. It is opposed to the specific virtue of chastity* and the general virtue of temperance*. According to Augustine, the sexual organs and sexual intercourse were originally subject to human reason and will; after the Fall, however, the sexual act involves concupiscence*—ardent sexual desire. Despite the inevitable presence of concupiscence, sexual intercourse has traditionally been viewed as not sinful if it takes place within marriage* and is directed toward or at least open to procreation* as well as mutual love. However, moral theologians have also held that if sexual intercourse in marriage involves lust that is indifferent about its object, e.g., whether one's spouse or someone else, then it is sinful. In general, because of their beliefs about the Fall and original sin*, Catholics have viewed concupiscence as a tendency to sin, not as a sin, while Protestants have viewed it as sinful. Most moral theologians and ethicists recognize that efforts to control lust and concupiscence should not lead to suspicion of all desires* or to repression*.

See **Contraception; Sexual Ethics.**

JAMES F. CHILDRESS

Lutheran Ethics

For Martin Luther (1483–1546), the biblical message of salvation is a tension-filled unity which can be viewed from the perspective of any one of its constitutive elements. He can speak of "grace alone," "Christ alone,"

"Scripture alone," or "faith alone" and mean thereby the same saving event in terms of either its eternal source, historical expression, apostolic witness, or personal appropriation.

In fidelity to this Christ-centered faith, Luther roundly condemned the moral and rational work-righteousness inherent in the philosophical theology of Rome. Before God, reason must submit to scripture and works must bow to faith. In an evangelical "theory of the cross," human beings humbly confess that the righteous shall live by faith (Rom. 1:17).

With their salvation thus assured in the unmerited forgiveness of Christ, grateful and obedient Christians are free to redirect their reason and good works toward serving their neighbors' welfare. Luther grounds his ethic in the paradoxical nature of Christian freedom, which accepts liberation from satanic bondage as the divine invitation for human service. All people act as "their brother's keeper": willingly in faith, begrudgingly in rebellion. Since Christians are at once righteous and sinful, their enforced service aids their self-discipline while their voluntary service meets their neighbors' needs. Against the presumption of Roman clericalism, Luther insists that all baptized Christians be permitted the beneficial exercise of their royal priesthood in loving service to their God-given neighbors.

In opposition to all unevangelical ethics of principles, "blue laws," ideals, or rules and regulations, Luther portrays the biblical pattern of a life of "faith working through love" (Gal. 5:6). A Christian ethic based on the "divine indicative" of God's grace (rather than the "divine imperative" of God's law) preserves the freedom of the believer under the guidance of the Holy Spirit through the Bible, the church, and prayer, to discover anew in each concrete situation what the will of God permits or requires of him or her then and there.

For the biblical foundation of his Christian social ethic, Luther rooted his doctrine of the "two realms" of creation and redemption in the Pauline eschatology of the "two ages" (aeons) in Adam and Christ (Rom. 5). In the kingdom of God, the Redeemer rules all regenerate believers through Christ and the gospel in personal faith and love. In the human kingdom, the Creator rules all sinful creatures through Caesar and the law in civil justice and obedience. As both Redeemer and Creator, God is at once the Lord of both kingdoms; as both righteous and sinful, the Christian is at once a subject of both kingdoms. Hence for an evangelical theology of society, the two kingdoms must always be properly distinguished, but never separated in secularism or equated in clericalism.

In this doctrine of the "two realms" of creation and redemption, Luther reaffirmed the "sacred secularity" of the ordinary tasks of the common life as those which best serve our neighbors' needs to God's glory. Whether empowered by Christ in faith-activated love (Christian righteousness) or compelled by Caesar in law-abiding reason (civil righteousness), the Christian saint-citizen lives not for self but for the benefit of others.

Christian social action was a major concern in Luther's own life and thought. The profound effects of the Reformation in the area of religion are common knowledge to all. What is not so well known—or, at least, not so commonly acknowledged—is the impressive social reformation which Luther's theology envisaged and even partially brought about in the broad and inclusive expanse of the common life. Here again, Luther's contribution to a better world is incalculable.

This emancipation of the common life was not so popular a crusade as it might at first appear. Luther's understanding of the Christian ethical life compelled him to combat both extremes of clericalism and secularism as unevangelical. Against Anabaptists, he had to fight for the preservation of music, art, and sculpture in the worship life of the church (Against the Heavenly Prophets). Against Roman Catholics, he had to struggle for the opening of the monasteries and the freedom of all Christians to marry and to engage in secular pursuits without endangering their salvation (On Monastic Vows; On Married Life).

Against recalcitrant parents and lax public officials, he also fought for educational reforms and the establishment of community chests to replace the illiteracy and begging so prevalent in his day (On Keeping Children in School; Preface to an Ordinance of a Common Chest). Against irresponsible merchants, he attacked economic injustice and proposed government controls to halt unfair commercial and labor practices (On Trading and

Usury). Against both the reckless mobs which confused their Christian freedom* with their civil rights, and the arbitrary rulers who disregarded their responsibility under God for their subjects' economic and social welfare, Luther appealed constantly for both civil obedience and—less strangely!—for political justice in a community of law* and order* (*Admonition to Peace; Exposition of the Eighty-second Psalm*).

It is true, however, that Luther does not normally conceive of the Christian's social responsibility as transforming the existing structures of society. While persons can be transformed by the gospel in the kingdom of God, institutions* can only be reformed by the law in the human kingdom. We are to accept the social structures for what they are (the Creator's dikes against sin), and to try to act as responsible Christians within them (as the Redeemer's channels of serving love). When our secular occupations among human beings are faithfully acknowledged to be part of our religious vocation under God, then love provides law with its ethical content and law provides love with its social form.

For example, against those who would spiritualize marriage into a Christian sacrament, Luther protests that marriage* belongs essentially to the realm of creation and not redemption. It is therefore ruled by God's law and not his gospel, and, as such, is one of God's temporal remedies against sin and not a sanctifying means of grace.

On the other hand, against those who would interpret this liberating message as justification for carnal lust and license, Luther is equally insistent that marriage is rooted firmly in the creative will of God as one of his own divine ordinances. Although it is not a sacrament of the church, there is nevertheless no higher social calling in which Christians can exercise their faith in deeds of serving love for family and neighbors. Hence, the ex-monk Luther himself eventually married as a public testimony of faith in witness to his restoration of the evangelical view of marriage and home life under God.

For Luther's social ethic, all offices and stations of life—ecclesiastical, domestic, economic, political, etc.—embodied in institutional form a particular command of God's law. They are all integrated within the earthly kingdom of humankind as the Creator's divinely ordained bulwarks in his ongoing struggles against Satan. There is no

particularly "Christian" form of these "orders."* Though corrupted by sin themselves, the "orders" are the means by which the Creator preserves his fallen world from even greater chaos, injustice, and suffering.

This is why the church can "christianize" politicians and economists but not politics and economics. These "orders" are ordained by God to remain secular, enjoying a relative autonomy* of their own under the sovereign law of the Creator. Hence not faith and love but reason and justice are normative for the temporal realm of life. At the same time, however, faith can illumine reason and love can temper justice whenever Christian citizens meet their civil responsibilities as part of their religious discipleship.

It is obvious that the authority of Luther's theology cannot legitimately be used to endorse many of the unhealthy social and political developments which have since appeared in the church bearing his name. To cite only the most notorious recent example, Luther could never have sanctioned a totalitarian regime (*see* **Totalitarian State**) ruling over a class-bound society in which a spiritually emasculated clergy could desist from prophetic criticism of the state in return for political and social favors. The vicious attempts to discredit Luther as "Hitler's spiritual ancestor," for instance, must be denounced as theological and political fantasy—despite some deceptive wartime propaganda to the contrary.

Four articles may be cited from the Augsburg Confession to show that Luther's restatement of the central thrust of Paul's ethic is afforded normative authority by the Lutheran Church.

On the personal level, Article 4 rejects all moral work-righteousness by grounding human salvation solely in one's being justified by God's grace for Christ's sake through faith alone. Then Article 6 militates against any ethical quietism by affirming that this Christian faith—"a living, busy, active thing"—is bound to bring forth good fruits, and that it is also necessary for Christians to do those good works which are commanded by God for the neighbors' benefit.

On the social level, Article 16 guards against any secularism by insisting that Christians are not to espouse any rigorous dualism between the two kingdoms of creation and redemption but are rather to permeate all of society with personal love* and social justice* in the exercise of their Christian ethical responsibility*. Finally, Article 28 complements this stress with a like rejection of all clericalism by sharply distinguishing the valid functions of the church and the state in the two kingdoms. On the one side, the church should not impose its will on the civil community by usurping the power of enforcement that rightly falls within the domain of government. On the other side, the state ought not interfere with the church's prophetic role in holding public life accountable to the sovereign law of God.

Hence, in fidelity to the twofold rule of their Creator and Redeemer through his law and gospel, Lutheran Christians are to remain reverent to God's Word and relevant to God's world by exercising both their priestly "yes" through faith active in love and their prophetic "no" through love seeking social justice.

See **Faith; Justification by Faith; Law and Gospel; Love; Orders; Two Realms.**

———

G. Forell, *Faith Active in Love,* 1954; W. H. Lazareth, *Luther on the Christian Home,* 1960; H. R. Niebuhr, *Christ and Culture,* 1951.

WILLIAM H. LAZARETH

Lying

In John 8:44 Jesus is portrayed as saying that the devil is the father of lies. There is no doubt of the general evil of lying: it destroys the basis of human association and is in the end stultifying. Christian thought, however, has been much concerned down the centuries as to whether it is ever right to tell a lie. For instance, the church fathers debated whether one was entitled to tell a lie to a pirate, and were much exercised about lies in scripture (e.g., the answer of the Hebrew midwives of Ex. 1). Partly in a controversy with Jerome, Augustine wrote two treatises against lying in any circumstances (*On Lying* and *Against Lying*). Centuries later he was to be followed by the philosopher Kant, who wrote against the supposed right of telling lies from benevolent motives. Theologians subsequent to Augustine did not like to contradict him, but his conclusions did not seem sound. A way around was found by not characterizing certain concealments of truth as lies. An immense literature grew up on ambiguity, mental reservation, economy of truth, "white lies," lies of etiquette, etc., which it is easy to

caricature, but which point to a genuine problem. Problems of war (e.g., in occupied countries) and espionage provide many more examples, and modern books on Christian ethics, moral theology, and moral philosophy abound in examples. It seems clear that there are occasions when it is right to tell a lie, but most of the time people tell lies when they should not. The temptation comes suddenly, perhaps to get out of an awkward situation or to practice some petty fraud or deception, and they succumb. In order to have the discernment to know when a lie is called for, one needs to be habitually truthful.

See **False Witness; Honesty; Slander; Truthfulness.**

———

S. Bok, *Lying: Moral Choice in Public and Private Life,* 1978.

RONALD PRESTON

Magisterium

The magisterium of the Roman Catholic Church is its teaching office. While many in the church exercise a true teaching function (e.g., catechists, religious educators, preachers, theologians), this prerogative resides in a special way with the pope, and with the bishops in union with the pope. The object of this teaching is "faith and morals," the latter referring to the behavioral implications of our "being in Christ." It is sometimes called the "moral magisterium." Thus in practice the church issues teaching statements in such practical areas as war and peace, economic and social justice, sexuality, contemporary medicine (*see also* **Official Roman Catholic Social Teaching**).

The binding force of such teaching is a matter of widespread misunderstanding, both outside and inside the Catholic community. The probable reason for this is that the Catholic Church understands its teaching authority to extend even to absolutely definitive and irreversible proclamations (infallible teachings demanding the unconditional assent of faith). Such proclamations are very rare. Most church teaching takes the form of authoritative but noninfallible teaching that does not exclude error in principle (the so-called "ordinary magisterium"). This is especially true of the moral sphere. There have been no irreversible definitions or decisions pertaining to concrete moral questions. Yet because the church maintains its prerogative of infallibility, many people unduly expand ordinary, day-to-day teaching into practically definitive statements.

When practical moral guidance is issued to Catholics, they are expected to put aside any residual obstinacy and to make sincere and arduous efforts to accept such authentic teaching, to assent to it. However, since ordinary teaching does not carry an absolute guarantee of its accuracy, but only the presumption of truth, the claims of such teaching are not absolute. Inability to assent (dissent) remains possible in principle. Indeed it is through such occasional dissent* that the church may be led to a more apt self-expression with regard to its substantive moral concerns. History reveals examples of this; for instance, the church's teaching on religious liberty (compare Gregory XVI and Pius IX with Vatican Council II).

See also **Authority; Modern Roman Catholic Moral Theology.**

C. Curran and R. A. McCormick, S.J. (eds.), *Readings in Moral Theology, No. 3: The Magisterium and Morality,* 1982; F. Sullivan, S.J., *Magisterium: Teaching Authority in the Catholic Church,* 1983.

RICHARD A. McCORMICK, S.J.

Magnanimity

Aristotle (*Nicomachean Ethics* 4.3) described the virtue of *megalopsychia* ("greatness of soul or mind"), which was translated into Latin as *magnanimitas,* from which "magnanimity" is derived. According to Thomas Aquinas (*ST* II-II.129), magnanimity, "the stretching forth of the mind to great things," is a moral virtue that inclines people to excellence*, especially but not only in the virtues, and it moderates the pleasure that a person derives from external honors: "Magnanimity is about honors in the sense that a man strives to do what is deserving of honor, yet not so as to think much of the honor accorded by man." It is part of the virtue of fortitude or courage*, because it is directed toward firmness or steadfastness in the face of what is difficult. Its opposite vices by way of excess are presumption (striving for excellence beyond one's ability), ambition (inordinate desire for honors), and vainglory (inordinate desire for glory); its opposite vice by way of defect is pusillanimity ("small-mindedness"), which keeps a person from attempting what is commensurate with his or her ability. There are obvious problems in adapting mag-

nanimity to Christian ethics, especially its temptation to pride* and loss of humility*. One possible corrective is to attribute abilities, excellences, and successes to God; for example, Thomas Aquinas noted that "magnanimity makes a man deem himself worthy of great things because of the gifts he holds from God."

See **Honor; Pride.**

JAMES F. CHILDRESS

Malice

The desire to hurt, injure, or harm someone. Malice is active ill will, malevolence, or hatred* and contravenes the norm of love* of neighbor. Sometimes translated as "wickedness" but most often as "malice," the Greek term *kakia* appears in several lists of vices condemned in the NT (e.g., Eph. 4:31; Col. 3:8; James 1:21; 1 Peter 2:1; see also Rom. 1:29). In Christian ethics there has been vigorous debate about whether certain actions, such as killing in war, necessarily involve malice. Augustine stated the dominant position when he argued that beneficence* rules out malice (*malitia*), not military service (*militia*), and that it is possible to kill in war* without malice (*see* **Just War; Pacifism**). In the Anglo-American legal tradition, "malice aforethought" in cases of murder has acquired a technical meaning of intent to do wrong, and it does not necessarily imply active ill will toward the victim.

JAMES F. CHILDRESS

Mammon

An Aramaic word meaning wealth, gain, or possessions. It could be used in Rabbinic literature without any pejorative meaning, e.g., in *M. Aboth* 2.12, "Let the property (*mammon*) of thy fellow be dear to thee as thine own"; but it was also used with negative connotations sometimes strengthened by associated terms, e.g., "unrighteous mammon" (*Targum Jonathan* 1 Sam. 8:3; 12:3; etc.). The word appears four times in the Greek NT: "unrighteous mammon" in Luke 16:9, 11; and "You cannot serve God and mammon" in Matt. 6:24 and Luke 16:13. In this last and best-known passage, wealth is personified as an idol standing over against God in the struggle for human allegiance. Through its NT usage the term became part of the general Christian tradition. See Tertullian, *Against Marcion* 4.33; Augustine, *Sermon on the Mount* 2.14.47; Chrysostom,

Homilies on Matthew 21.2 ("Tell me not of them that are rich, but of them that serve riches"); Thomas Aquinas, *ST* II-II.32.7, obj. 1.

In the medieval period its personification led to the mistaken impression that "mammon" was the name of a god or demon. See Nicholas of Lyra or the commentary attributed to Thomas Aquinas on Matt. 6:24. This view was further popularized by Milton's *Paradise Lost* 1.678, etc. The term continues to be used for wealth or earthly possessions. It connotes the capacity of material possessions to fascinate persons so as to lead first to their devotion and then to their enslavement.

See **Covetousness; Property; Wealth.**

———

D. M. Beck, "Mammon," *IDB* III, 1962; F. Hauck, *"mamōnas,"* *TDNT* IV, 1967; H. P. Rueger, "Mamōnas," *Zeitschrift für die neutestamentliche Wissenschaft* 64, 1973, pp. 127–131.

HARVEY K. MCARTHUR

Mandates *see* **Orders**

Manichean Ethics

Manicheism was a syncretistic religion that originated in the 3rd century A.D. and survived well into the Middle Ages. Its founder was an Iranian prophet, Mani (216–c. 276). He grew up under the influences of a sect that had Jewish, Christian, and Gnostic characteristics, and in his mid-twenties began to proclaim a new religion of his own, meant to be truly universal and to sum up all previous revelations. Mani, called the "Apostle of Light," was believed to be fully indwelt by the Holy Spirit, and to be the successor of Adam, Zoroaster, Buddha, and Jesus. In fact, elements from many religions are found in the system of belief that he propagated. His mission met with considerable success, but in the end he came into conflict with the Iranian authorities and the prevailing Zoroastrianism and was eventually put to death after a long trial and severe mistreatment.

The new religion continued to flourish and spread through the Middle East and North Africa. It reached its zenith in the 4th century, at which time it also made its most famous convert, Augustine, later to be a great Christian theologian and bishop of Hippo. Although Manicheism had later successes in central Asia and even as far away as China,

it gradually declined and became extinct around the 15th century. Some medieval Christian heretics, including the Bogomils in the East and the Cathari or Albigenses in the West, taught doctrines similar to those of the Manicheans, though the precise relationship between them is unclear. Manicheism was strongly dualistic and falls within the type of religious movements known generally as Gnosticism. According to the Manichean mythology, there were originally two separate realms: a realm of spirit, goodness, and light, and another realm of matter, evil, and darkness. The mythology tells how at a time in the past there took place a "fateful mixture" of these two realms, some of the particles of divine light becoming entrapped in matter. The human being is part of this unhappy mixture, the soul being imprisoned in the body. Salvation consists in the liberation of the spiritual particles from the matter into which they have been absorbed. The world itself is a kind of refining mechanism, in which the light is being disengaged from the darkness, and the eschatological goal of the process will be attained when once more there will be two separate unmixed realms, the one of pure light, the other of sheer darkness.

Against this background of belief, the Manichean ethic is naturally characterized by puritanism and otherworldliness. When one's heavenly origin has been understood, then the quest of salvation takes the form of turning away from everything material and of escaping from its influences. For the fully committed Manicheans (known as the "elect") this meant renouncing possessions, abstaining from sexual intercourse, and living on a meager vegetarian diet. For those who could not go so far (the "hearers") the rule was less strict but still included ascetic practices. The elect, it was believed, would after death pass immediately to the realm of light, while the hearers would require to undergo further reincarnations before they could reach that point.

The word "Manichean" is sometimes used nowadays to describe anyone who takes up an ascetic stance and, in particular, regards material and bodily enjoyments as inherently evil. It may be noted too that although Augustine abandoned Manicheism and wrote polemical works against it, he never quite shook off its influence, and this is seen in his doctrine of original sin, his teaching about the two cities, and his belief in double predestination.

See also **Asceticism; Augustinian Ethics.**

Augustine, *On the Manichean Heresy;* F. C. Burkitt, *The Religion of the Manichees,* 1925; H. Jonas, *The Gnostic Religion,* ²1963, ch. 9.

JOHN MACQUARRIE

Market, Free *see* Business Ethics; Capitalism; Laissez-faire; Socialism

Marriage

Marriage is a joining of two lives. It is defined in law as the voluntary union for life of a man and a woman. Christianity has no exclusive rights in it. Aristotle said, "Between husband and wife friendship seems to exist by nature; for man is naturally disposed to pairing" (*Nicomachean Ethics* 8.12). There are "pairbonds" among some animals and birds; but the institution of marriage, recognizable in many different forms, is undoubtedly characteristic of humankind. It has even been suggested that the earliest beginnings of the genus *Homo* were associated with pair-bonding, and that our ancestors were, so to speak, "personal relationship animals" more fundamentally than "toolmaking animals."

From the point of view of the evolution of the race, the role of marriage is to make possible the important long childhood of nurture and learning that a human being needs to grow to maturity. In this sense it is true that procreation* is the first "end" of marriage. Relationship is required for the sake of offspring. But from the individual point of view it is all the other way round. The characteristic fertility of marriage is a by-product of a union between man and woman which is valuable for its own sake. To give relationship priority in importance is not 20th-century perversity. It picks out a strand in our tradition that has always been there (cf. 1 Sam. 1:8); though no doubt reliable contraception* makes that strand easier to find.

The Christian church has sometimes seemed obsessed with the biological aspect of marriage and its function of peopling the earth. This is lopsided both humanly and theologically. Important as the command to "be fruitful and multiply" (Gen. 1:28) has been in the history of the people of God, it is not the aspect of the OT understanding of marriage which has been most emphatically taken up into Christianity. The creation stories affirm that humankind is made male and female "in the image of God" (Gen. 1:27) and that the fit companion for man is woman (Gen. 2:23). Man and woman are to be "one flesh" (Gen. 2:24) and this is what Jesus quotes (Mark 10:6–8).

It is not a far cry from this to the idea that human marriage is a good image for the union between Christ and his church (Eph. 5:25–32), from which much sacramental theory about marriage has developed. However ascetic and even antisex Christian thinkers might subsequently become, affirmation of the fundamental goodness of the marriage union could not be entirely lost.

In practice, this positive understanding has been used negatively. The lofty comparison of human and divine has been much called upon to emphasize the irreverence of divorce. It has seemed to be overlooked that the comparison in Ephesians "was meant to help" (J. Gosling, *Marriage and the Love of God,* 1965, p. 117), that to call marriage sacramental or even a "sacrament" ought to mean that it is in its own right a means of grace. At least there should be a corrective here to the persistent notion that marriage is a hindrance to holy life, a barely permissible way of avoiding actual lust, justifiable only by the need for offspring.

However high a doctrine of marriage is being propounded, it is still a thoroughly human institution* which is its subject. Divine comparisons cannot get started unless something earthly is their basis: as in the eucharist nourishment already has human significance beyond mere eating. The divine meaning has human meaning to work upon.

Among human relationships marriage is a particularly good image of divine reality because of, not in spite of, the fact that natural marriage is both spiritual and *physical.* The God of the Christian creeds is responsible for and entered into a material universe. To call this universe sacramental is to insist that the spiritual and the physical belong together. "It is a characteristic of human beings that they are persons for whom the deepest personal relationships are expressed by physical means" (Root Report, 30). To "make love" is an accurate expression. In physical lovemaking a man and a woman both create and express their unity: or rather, their unity-in-plurality. Their separate individuality is not destroyed but enhanced. The "one flesh" union of marriage is not an odd thing to find in this universe if Christianity is the truth.

It does not denigrate marriage to say that it belongs to creation rather than to redemption. It is made, not by prayer, but by the consent of the spouses. When they marry, they themselves effect the union. They are its ministers and anyone else, however priestly, is there as a witness. Even Christ does not found "Christian marriage." He recalls his hearers to its origins at the beginning of humanity. When he is present at a wedding and the wine flows at his word (John 2:1–11), he is not instituting a new sacrament but enhancing something that is there already. (This "holy estate" he "adorned and beautified," in the words of the *Book of Common Prayer.*)

Nor does it denigrate divine grace to find a "human grace" which is capable of illuminating its meaning. In the very ordinariness of the immense claims they make upon each other—the give-and-take of everyday life—married people have a humanly valid mystery which is able to be a model of the grace of God (cf. H. Oppenheimer, *The Marriage Bond,* 1976, ch. 3). In an almost routine way they say to each other something like what Augustine said to his God, "Give what thou commandest and command what thou wilt" (*Confessions* 10.29). Austin Farrer in a wedding sermon (in *A Celebration of Faith,* 1970) spoke of "the union of duty with delight," which he called, in the same breath, "the new miracle of Christ's religion." Nor is it surprising, still less blasphemous, that the language of worship and adoration has been used for love between human beings. Human love and human grace can be an image, not a parody, of divine love and divine grace.

For all this to be true, there is needed an essential fact about humanity. The embodied spiritual beings that are human creatures must characteristically be capable of *fidelity**, not as a rare heroic virtue but as part of everyday life. The idea of the pair-bond demands, not necessarily a metaphysically unbreakable *vinculum,* but a capacity in men and women to pledge themselves to one another with a reliability strong enough to be considered normal not extraordinary. The "ought" of marital duty must come from an "is" of natural tendency. The permanence and exclusiveness of monogamous marriage must not be notions brought in by theologians or moralists, still less by lawyers, but must in some way be integral to the concern

of the spouses themselves. The use of *covenant** language expresses this character of marriage more fully than "contract."* A vow is something people want to make, into which they put their hearts. To make it "for better, for worse" is to envisage "mutual help, society and comfort" through happiness or misery, not to envisage infidelity and abjure it.

The legal and institutional aspects are supports for what marriage is in its nature: they do not constitute marriage. The importance of the bond between two people for society at large, for their children, and for their families is so great that formal frameworks are necessary: laws making clear when a marriage exists, rituals of celebration and blessing, customs designed for support and encouragement. All of this can become tyrannical in various ways, can stiffen or weaken or collapse, so as to become hindrance rather than help. The basic fact, agreed by church and state, that in marriage a man and a woman join their lives by mutual consent* is easily obscured. In theory two people marooned on a desert island could validly marry each other. Yet it comes to be supposed that a particular ceremony or particular permission, that consummation or progeny, or even baptism, is what authenticates a marriage. So cohabitation is stigmatized as "fornication," not for lack of true intent but for lack of a ceremony.

Religious people have been notoriously prone to negative attitudes: antinomianism* and permissiveness have followed in reaction. Marriage has been deemed to be totally inferior to celibacy, sexual pleasure to be evil concupiscence, women to be she-devils or nitwits. Some of these notions might seem more forgivable if the real perils of unregulated sexuality without reliable contraception were recollected. Fear of our physical nature, however false to Christian theology at its best, once seemed only too well founded. The indifferent record of the Christian church in recognizing women as full human beings is partly based on protectiveness for mothers as well as on male brute strength.

Less excusable manifestations of fear are legalism and complacency. "It is the curse of 'Christian morality,' " said Brunner, "that it always regards the most legalistic view as the 'most serious' " (*The Divine Imperative,* ET 1937, p. 355). Complacency counts the known good as the only good. In the name of happy families, virtuous people make life hard for the unconventional, the childless, the deviant, even the lonely. In this context the NT "hard sayings" come into their own, traditions in which the Lord encourages celibacy* as well as marriage (Matt. 19:10–12), and warns against the possessiveness and self-assurance that beset family life (e.g., Mark 3:31–35). One is at least reminded (e.g., Mark 12:25) that "no human institution can be translated straight into heaven. Resurrection needs death and rebirth" ("Marriage," *New Dictionary of Christian Theology*, 1983).

See **Divorce; Family; Parenthood; Sexual Ethics.**

D. S. Bailey, *The Man-Woman Relation in Christian Thought*, 1959; J. Dominian, *Cycles of Affirmation*, 1975 (among others); G. R. Dunstan, "The Marriage Covenant," *Theology*, May 1975; R. Fletcher, *The Family and Marriage in Britain*, ³1973; B. Friedan, *The Feminine Mystique*, 1963; *Marriage, Divorce and the Church* (Root Report), 1971, Appendix IV; H. Oppenheimer, *Fidelity*, Mary Sumner Lecture, 1978; E. Schillebeeckx, *Marriage: Secular Reality and Saving Mystery*, vols. 1 and 2, ET 1965.

HELEN OPPENHEIMER

Martyrdom *see* **Patristic Ethics; Suicide**

Marxist Ethics

To speak of Marxist ethics is to confront a paradox. On the one hand, Karl Marx (1818–1883) was a vigorous foe of any normative philosophy of human behavior, whether the teleology of Aristotle, the deontology of Kant, the pleasure-pain calculus of Bentham, or the commandments of God in the Bible. On the other hand, the whole of his life and thought was driven by a profound moral passion—for the free activity of the universal human subject against the forces that he believed fettered human beings and turned the fruits of their labor against their own humanity. The roots of this paradox are proximately in the philosophy of Hegel, ultimately in a humanist inversion of Hebrew and Christian prophecy.

Marx and Hegel shared the belief that human freedom* is not individual but the activity of a self-realizing whole; that truth and goodness can be known only from within the struggle to realize group-limited concepts of them; and that out of the historical struggles of these groups will emerge the universally human free society (*see* **Hegelian Ethics**). Marx was, however, both more pessimistic and more radical. He found history to be at a moment not of relative fulfillment, but of intense alienation*. The concepts of *Recht* (legal and moral right), of God, and of the Spirit which Hegel discerned at work, were for Marx ideological mystifications of the power and interest of the ruling classes. The real forces in history were for him "material," i.e., the forces of production behind which is human labor captured and turned into a commodity serving the system itself, which dehumanizes both exploiter and exploited. The operations of this system, he believed, can be analyzed with scientific accuracy and their laws determined, for they work independently of human wills or decisions. These are the laws of history. They express the inner contradiction of the capitalist system: its devotion to money in place of the real values of human life, its ever-intensifying exploitation and alienation of ever-larger masses of workers, and its inevitable catastrophic end in the workers' revolution.

The conscious ethic of Marxism, then, is simply the strategy and tactics of the proletarian class in its struggle for, and consolidation of, power according to these historical laws. Marx and Engels fought throughout their lives against every effort to subsume this struggle under more general moral sanctions or goals shared by liberal reformers and utopian socialists, such as human equality, freedom of expression, the fight for civilization, or universal justice. Such principles they regarded as abstract substitutes for action at best, deceptive tools of bourgeois dominance at worst. Engels wrote: "All moral theories have been hitherto the product, in the last analysis, of the economic conditions of society obtaining at the time, and as society has hitherto moved in class antagonisms, morality has always been class morality" (*Anti-Dühring*). Marx, in defense of inequalities during the early stages of postrevolutionary society, wrote: "Right can never be higher than the economic structure of society and its cultural development conditioned thereby" (*Critique of the Gotha Program*). Lenin and Soviet communism have built their ethics systematically on this foundation (*see* **Communism, Ethics of**).

This, however, is only the outer half of the

story. Marx could reject ethics, whether philosophical or religious, because he believed so completely in the free, universal activity of the human being as such. Humanity was his ultimate; in this he was a true child of the Enlightenment*. But the uniquely human was not for him reason (Diderot et al.), the moral passions (Hume), the categorical imperative (Kant), the Spirit realizing itself in history (Hegel), or the elaboration of species being in relations of love between I and Thou (Feuerbach), but free, conscious productive activity whereby the human being universalizes self as "species being." "The practical production of an objective world, the working up of inorganic nature is what proves man [the German inclusive term *Mensch*] as a conscious species-being.—This production is his working species-life. Through it nature appears as his work and his reality. The object of labor is therefore the objectification of human species-life: in which man duplicates himself not only intellectually as in consciousness, but actively, really, and views himself therefore in a world that he has created" (*Economic and Philosophical Manuscripts*). There is clearly no room here for any ultimate limit on the active productive life of the human species. It is the universal with which every individual identifies himself or herself and seeks to embody in the self. This is the heart of Marx's atheism and of the atheism of the more rigorous forms of Marxism since. In the preface to his doctoral dissertation Marx wrote: "The confession of Prometheus, 'In one round sentence, I hate all the gods,' is philosophy's own confession against all the gods in heaven and on earth that do not acknowledge the human self-consciousness as the highest deity. No other may stand beside it." The later Marx substituted "free, conscious activity" of species humanity for consciousness, but this only intensifies the point. God is not only the finest essence of humanity projected on the heavens (Feuerbach); God is an intolerable limit on free, universal, active species humanity.

Against this background the moral character of Marx's controlled sarcastic rage at the conditions of early industrial capitalism* in his time becomes clear (*see* **Industrial Revolution**). It was a dialectical passion. On the one hand, the growing concentration of the means of production in the hands of a few leads to new heights of technological development, intensifies productivity, promotes the mastery of nature for human ends, and sweeps away the barriers to a worldwide human society. On the other hand, the primal evil of the division of labor has led human history from an idyllic primitive communism through successive stages of increasing dehumanization*. The human person *is* productive labor. When this labor is hired by another and only a part of its fruits returned, the laborer loses a portion of what makes him or her human. This then becomes "surplus value," objective congealed labor power, and takes on a life of its own, enslaving both exploiter and exploited to itself. Private property* becomes the goal of life, and because it cannot truly satisfy human need the thirst for it is insatiable. In earlier society this was somewhat curbed and humanity somewhat respected by a network of social relations, but today, in the words of the *Communist Manifesto*, "The bourgeoisie, wherever it has got the upper hand, has put an end to all feudal, patriarchal, idyllic relations. It has pitilessly torn asunder the motley feudal ties that bound man to his 'natural superior,' and has left remaining no other nexus between man and man than callous 'cash payment.' . . . It has resolved personal worth into exchange value, and in place of the numberless indefeasible chartered freedoms, has set up that single, unconscionable freedom—Free Trade. In one word, for exploitation, veiled by religious and political institutions, it has substituted naked, shameless, direct, brutal exploitation."

Upon this intensifying "capitalist accumulation" of ever more in ever fewer hands and the impoverishment of ever larger masses, the judgment of history is forming, Marx believed. He saw it already in a proletarian class deprived of every shred of private existence, whether property, nation, or even family, and forced into the solidarity of total negation and revolutionary will. In this solidarity, he thought, a new human reality was taking shape. Immediately it was dedicated to the total overthrow of existing production relations and the whole superstructure of government, law, culture, morals, and religion that was built upon them. Ultimately it would express a classless communist society in which all would contribute to the common product and draw from the common wealth, in which there would be no private property and no class distinctions, and where each individual would both identify with, and embody in himself or herself, the universal humanity which the work of the whole society expresses.

The true ethic of Karl Marx then is, like biblical ethics, a calling to participate in the judgments and the redeeming powers at work in history. To the proletariat it is an appeal to unite in revolutionary awareness and action, confident that this already is the true consciousness of the dispossessed and the inevitable direction of history. To the others it is a warning of things to come and an implicit (never directly expressed) demand that they identify themselves with the workers' revolution, for it is only by death to their bourgeois selves that they too can be liberated.

This paradox of morally passionate economic determinism Marx bequeathed to the movement that bears his name. It left major questions—about power and authority, about means and ends, about human agency, human nature, and human hope, about ethics in short—for his successors to solve. They did so in various ways. Although Leninist communism has been the most disciplined and powerful Marxist movement of the 20th century, there have been many others, ranging from the moderate social democracy of the Second International which forms governments in Western Europe and elsewhere today to the leftist extremes of China's cultural revolution or Italy's underground Red Brigade. To chart these variations would exceed the scope of this article. Some questions, however, will bring them into focus.

First, Marxism asserts an intimate interaction of theory and practice. Out of the growing oppression of the capitalist system emerges the revolutionary will, strategy, and tactic of the proletariat, to which Marxist theory gives direction. Who, then, has authority to interpret this theory aright and decide policy correctly? All Marxists agree that this authority resides in some organization for political and social action informed by reflection on Marxist principles; but here the agreement ends. The answer of the Social Democrats has been a democratic political party and labor movement with strong intellectual leadership, devoted to winning a majority of the popular vote as a base for building an experimental socialism with an open conception of the forms of public control over the means of production, respecting human rights and liberties. The Leninist response has been to concentrate power to define both theory and practice in the Party and its leadership, the scientists and engineers of revolution, and the construction of socialist society. Mao Tse-tung used the formula "democratic centralism" to describe a policy of mass education and political participation closely controlled, in both ideology and program, by the Communist Party. For a brief period in the 1960s Czechoslovakia, and to a lesser extent Poland and Hungary, began to develop a policy of pluralism in theory and openness in practice within a hitherto closed socialist society under the motto "socialism with a human face." But the question where authority and power lie in a Marxist understanding of the workers' movement and the socialist society remains fundamentally in contention.

Second, what, in Marxist understanding, is the relation between the end (transformation of the world into a socialist and eventually communist society) and the means used to achieve that end? In one sense Marx repudiated the question, for the means of struggle in his view were determined by the material conditions of the system of production. In another sense he clearly foresaw a violent revolution and justified it, as his comments on the Paris Commune of 1871 demonstrate (*The Civil War in France*). Despite this, however, he continually entertained the question whether the revolution could be achieved by nonviolent reform. He lived long enough to see with satisfaction the electoral achievements of German Social Democrats. He explicitly opened the possibility of socialism "by peaceful means," especially in Britain and America. Social Democracy has developed this theme into a principled advocacy of peaceful transformation, by electoral politics and by building the new within the bounds of the old—in the comradeship of labor unions, the Party, and associated groups that embody the solidarity of shared wealth and labor. This approach brings means and ends together. The new humanity to come determines the style of action to achieve it.

The intense experience of alienation among the victims of the present system, however, often demands a stronger response. To this experience Leninist communism claims to speak. Here the dichotomy between means and ends is acknowledged and complete (*see* **Ends and Means**). Change must be revolutionary and will be violent. The dictatorship of the proletariat is a necessary stage, using state power to destroy the remnants of the old system and establish socialism. Only at the end of this struggle will the new humanity spontaneously arise. But this approach has been no more successful. The means of struggle have created their own ends in a bureaucratic, repressive police state. Marxist movements and societies still wrestle with the relation between the humanity that is to come and humanity amid the battle to realize it in a world of conflict and oppression.

Third, Marx was quite clear that the basic forces at work in history are found in "material" conditions, i.e., productive relations that constitute social existence. From these conditions arise forms of human consciousness—political, cultural, moral, or religious—through which people become aware of economic conflicts and fight them out. Yet, his whole lifework was a passionate moral appeal to the human species to join in revolutionary action for a classless society. What then is the function of what later Marxists called ideological struggle in bringing about economic change? What effect can the religious, moral, or political superstructure have on the material basis of society? No question in Marxist thought has brought forth more confusion than this. The Mensheviks in Russia, Kautsky in Germany, and Mao's early opponent Li Li-san in China took Marx's historical stages as a science of social change and believed that capitalism has first to be developed to the full before the conditions for revolution would be ripe. Lenin, and later Mao, in furious opposition, located the power for revolutionary change in the Party's consciousness of the laws of history as the agent of an industrial working class that might not develop its full role until after the revolution. Revisionist Social Democrats, notably Eduard Bernstein in Germany, and the father of French socialism, Jean Jaurès, rejected the very idea of economic determinism. It is not necessary, wrote Jaurès, "to oppose the materialist and the idealist conceptions of history to one another. They interweave in a single and indissoluble line of development because, if you cannot abstract man from economic relations, neither can you abstract economic relations from man and history" (*Idealism in History*, 1895). Through this channel moral ideals of justice*, equality*, democracy*, and human rights*, which Marx had rigorously condemned as bour-

geois ideology*, found their way again into socialist language. The only exception to this was religious beliefs, which were regarded by all sides as, at best, outdated vehicles of human protests and aspirations; at worst, escape into another world from the oppression and revolutionary struggles of this one.

Today the picture has changed. The humanist philosophy of the early Marx, in large part published in the 1930s and seriously studied after World War II, has convinced even Leninists that Marxism is a form of humanism (*see* **Humanistic Ethics**). A few scholars, such as Louis Althusser in France, have disputed this by denying the continuity of the older "scientific" Marx with his younger ideas, but they have not prevailed (*For Marx*, 1970). The chairman of Social Democrats of America, Michael Harrington, describes Marx as a "spiritual materialist" on the basis of the early writings and goes on to propose a "Marxist paradigm" of self-critical, value-laden engagement of men and women as "both creatures and creators of their society" using Marxist social analysis as a guide to fundamental relations and conflicts, but not as a dogmatic system (*The Twilight of Capitalism*, 1976). This approach is typical of Social Democrats in other countries as well. Meanwhile Marxist-Leninist societies appeal increasingly to universal values such as "people's democracy," justice, equality, liberation, and peace, at least in their propaganda. Whether Marx would have approved is a disputed question.

Fourth, the relation of Marxist humanism to other views of what is human has therefore become a major question. Here Marxists and Christians have had their deepest encounters. Marx has bequeathed to his movement the vision of a universal species humanity reaching out collectively through the domination of nature toward unlimited goals. The Soviet Union today is filled with symbols of this Promethean faith. In practice, however, this absolute collective humanism has produced brutal inhumanity toward nonconformists, toward more intimate communities, and toward individuals, valued only as parts of the whole. Recognizing this has driven Marxists to searching anthropological reflection. In recent Christian-Marxist dialogues this reflection has focused on three points: (1) What might be a Marxist counterpart for the judging and redeeming transcendence of God? Clearly the collective wisdom of the people expressed in the Party will no longer do. From what source, then, can Marxist theory and practice be effectively criticized and reformed? (2) How can the claims of other persons in the give-and-take of human relations be given their true value in Marxist understanding, in some analogy to the biblical covenant and the communion of believers with Christ in the church? The solidarity of a class and a movement is not adequate here. Nor is the functional cooperation of the workplace even when it no longer is the instrument of exploitation. Humanity is not only productive labor. Community involves respect for genuine individual difference wherein persons limit and fulfill each other. How can Marxist humanism become interpersonal? (3) What Marxist expression can be found for the saving sacrifice of Christ in human relations? Heroes of labor will not do; there is no saving grace in them. The brooding spirit of Lenin guiding the affairs of the Soviet government no longer seems real. Leaders rehabilitated after unjust imprisonment and torture come closer. But the underlying question concerns the place of sacrificial love*, of forgiveness* and renunciation of power, in a Marxist understanding of the human.

Finally, for what may a Marxist now hope? The official Soviet answer has not changed for forty years: communism, the natural harmony of producers contributing creatively to the development of society without the coercion of the state, is just about to be realized. This is hardly believable anymore. In some socialist countries the vision has glimmered of a more flexible humanized socialism which will give place to the free exchange of ideas and free personal initiative in a pluralist atmosphere. But these visions either have been quashed (Czechoslovakia) or have moved away from Marxist roots toward a pragmatism of uncertain goals (China). The nonconformist philosopher Ernst Bloch made "the principle of hope*" the very center of his Marxist world view. Humanity realizes itself by moving forward in rebellion against every constraining order toward a utopian vision (*see* **Utopian Thought**) not yet fully understood but to be realized in the struggle. His influence, however, may have been greater in Christian than in Marxist circles because of his use and atheist reinterpretation of biblical and later Christian faith and eschatology. Here again Christians and Marxists question one another about a common human theme that underlies all ethics.

See **Communism, Ethics of; Dialectic; Liberation Theology; Oppression; Revolution; Socialism.**

L. Althusser, *For Marx,* ET 1970; E. Bloch, *Das Prinzip Hoffnung,* 3 vols., 1954–59; *Man on His Own,* ET 1970; T. Bottomore (ed.), *A Dictionary of Marxist Thought,* 1983; A. Fremantle (ed.), *Mao Tse-tung: An Anthology of His Writings,* 1962; A. Fried and R. Sanders (eds.), *Socialist Thought: A Documentary History,* 1964; M. Harrington, *The Twilight of Capitalism,* 1976; L. Kolakowski, *Main Currents of Marxism,* 3 vols., ET 1978; J. Plamenatz, *Karl Marx's Philosophy of Man,* 1975; R. C. Tucker, *Philosophy and Myth in Karl Marx,* [2]1972; R. C. Tucker (ed.), *The Marx-Engels Reader,* [2]1978.

CHARLES C. WEST

Masturbation

Although there is debate about whether Scripture clearly prohibits masturbation— the stimulation of one's own sexual organs for pleasure with or without reaching orgasm—the Christian tradition has generally considered it to be a grave moral evil and even a mortal sin, if it is deliberate and with consent*. Indeed, male masturbation was viewed as comparable to abortion* and contraception* because the male seed was thought to contain the whole human offspring, the woman's role in procreation being viewed as purely passive. Whether practiced by males or females, masturbation is still condemned in official Roman Catholic teaching as a moral evil: "Whatever the motive for acting in this way, the deliberate use of the sexual faculty outside normal conjugal relations essentially contradicts the finality* of the faculty" (Declaration on Sexual Ethics, 1975). It is rejected because it is not directed toward procreation* and mutual love, and it is variously described as self-abuse, self-pollution, and onanism. Even if masturbation is mutually performed by spouses or is for purposes of obtaining sperm for artificial insemination or for medical tests, it is still rejected by official teaching; many moral theologians dissent from this position, sometimes on the grounds that masturbation is not always a moral evil even if it is an ontic evil. The pastoral response has often been more lenient than the official position.

Masturbation has also been viewed as a disease and the cause of various illnesses, including insanity (*see* **Health and Disease, Values in Defining**). But there is no evidence that it causes physical or psychological problems, and there is evidence that masturbatory activity is natural rather than pathological, beginning with young children and culminating after puberty and before marriage.

Outside Roman Catholicism, masturbation is generally ignored in moral discussions and is usually neither encouraged nor condemned. Most Christian ethicists view it as morally neutral, its meaning, significance, and morality depending on the circumstances of the agent and the act.

See **Contraception; Procreation; Reproductive Technologies; Sexual Ethics.**

JAMES F. CHILDRESS

Mater et Magistra see **Business Ethics; Official Roman Catholic Social Teaching; Subsidiarity, Principle of**

Mean, Doctrine of the

The doctrine of the mean is part of Aristotle's definition of the moral virtues. Having shown that virtue is not an occasional or fitful quality but an established or habitual disposition, and not the mere having of certain feelings or desires but a choice or decision, he proceeds to specify as the mean the kind of object to be chosen. The idea of moderation* involved in this was already traditional among the Greeks: Aristotle sharpens it by using the mathematical term "mean" with its sense of what lies between two extremes. As a biologist, he notes that both too much food or exercise and too little spoil health, and as a writer on aesthetics, that a perfect work of art is one to which nothing can be added and from which nothing can be taken away. The point for ethics is that each virtue is opposed to *two* vices, one of excess and one of deficiency; for example, courage is the mean between foolhardy rashness and cowardice (he illustrates also from thirteen other virtues). He explicitly denies, however, that the precise mathematical sense of *equal* distance from two extremes is applicable to moral choice. He speaks of "the mean relative to us," that is, to our individual status, our given particular situation, and our strong

points and weak ones, on the last making the observation that if we have a proneness to one of the extremes we should lean toward the opposite extreme. With respect to emotions, pleasures, and pains the mean is the feeling that is not only of the right quantity but "at the right time, toward the right objects, toward the right people, for the right reason, and in the right manner." In short, the mean is what the experienced and sagacious person would detect to be such in each case. Almost at the beginning of his *Nicomachean Ethics* Aristotle had said emphatically that in moral matters general prescriptions are true only "on the whole," because we are here thinking of what is contingent and individual. Thomas Aquinas took over from him the notion of the mean, but did not make it the guiding one of his system of the natural moral virtues, returning instead to the pre-Aristotelian conception of four cardinal virtues.

See **Aristotelian Ethics; Thomistic Ethics.**

T. E. JESSOP

Meaning/Meaninglessness

Christian ethics is concerned subjectively with a person's sense that life is meaningful, and objectively with *the* meaning of life.

A sense of meaninglessness is one of the most pervasive forms of human alienation* and is particularly characteristic of modern Western society, with its loss of a shared communal conviction that life has a meaning. While it is quite possible to give one's life a meaning or meanings in terms of relationships, interests, and commitments, the lack of an overall given framework of meaning can lead to disorientation or despair.

What Tillich calls "the courage to be" is found, according to Christian ethics, in the discovery or belief that life finds fulfillment in relation to "an infinite, unthreatened ground of meaning." Thus God's purpose and love give human lives and the created world itself their ultimate point.*

K. Britton, *Philosophy and the Meaning of Life,* 1969; P. Tillich, *The Courage to Be,* 1952; and *Systematic Theology,* 3 vols., 1951–63.

BRIAN HEBBLETHWAITE

Media, Ethical Issues in

Advances in technology* have made possible communication with mass audiences through newspapers, magazines, radio and television, video recorders, etc., on an increasingly extensive scale and one great debate is the extent of the influence of the means of communication on the formation of beliefs, values, and standards. The major question of social ethics* posed by these developments is therefore whether the media are to be regarded as public services accountable to the people or whether they are to be operated by private enterprise. The problem is how to achieve a method of public accountability without state control or a form of private enterprise which is not so dependent, for example, on revenue from advertising* as to be wholly concerned with what will attract and keep the largest possible audiences and readership. In this case the newspapers, for example, run the risk of becoming more and more part of the entertainment industry. Large-circulation newspapers controlled by a shrinking number of owners already illustrate this tendency. The result is a restriction on the amount and range of material considered suitable for the mass audience. Minority features and programs are squeezed out. Furthermore, if the chief aim is to hold mass audiences, there would be little serious and sustained attempt to challenge or change public opinion* on major contentious issues, although occasionally some "pseudo-event" will be created and treated contentiously for sensational purposes. There is therefore an inevitable tendency for the media to develop propagandist habits unless adequate safeguards are maintained (see **Propaganda**).

The major Christian point of reference in the consideration of the media in relation to ethics will be the doctrine of humanity made in the image of God "fallen" and re-created in Christ (see **Image of God**). A Christian anthropology firmly based on belief in an authentic historical incarnation and in its realistic implications should provide resources for detecting the debilitating kind of fantasy that poses as the real, what Richard Hoggart has called the "candy-floss world." The media by their very nature are likely to exhibit the distortion of human life and experience which William Lynch has called "the grandiose imagination: that kind of work in literature and art which leaps too quickly to the splendid, the spectacular, the dream, the magnificent, skipping in the process all those intermediate realities of man and nature which might give some support to our leaping."

Thoroughly analyzed, this attitude to human beings with its easy acceptance of the glib and shallow generalization, its appeal to easily aroused emotions, and its avoidance of thorny, controversial issues implies a "gnostic" inability or unwillingness to live genuinely near the full range of realities of human life and experience.

A significant feature of the development of the media, because of its influence in the long run on the formation of values*, is persuasive advertising where powerful and ingenious attempts are made based on extensive and expensive market research in "motivation" to "sell" more than the article itself. This kind of advertising with its commendation of ambition, constant appeal to snobberies and desire for status, and the insistent suggestion there is a magical shortcut to the satisfaction of basic human needs for security, love, and significance presents a popular alternative to the NT concept of the good life and elevates to the level of virtues the deadly sins of, for example, avarice* and envy* in traditional systems of Christian moral theology (see **Seven Deadly Sins**).

The difficulty is how to devise some form of public control of the media that is compatible with basic human rights* and freedom*. Such control would run the risk of a charge of "paternalism,"* but it is hard to see how the serious and courageous exercise of responsibility in this field could avoid that. The long-term need is for the development of high standards of literary and visual appreciation, especially ability to detect attempts made to blur judgment by the use of emotive language or sentimentality. A Christian humanism informed by the corollaries of belief in the incarnation and the atonement, with a fully articulated theology of the relation between the creation of God and the creativity of human beings as "procreators," is one of the safeguards necessary to sustain the humanizing of modern culture.

R. Hoggart, *The Uses of Literacy,* 1957; F. Lynch, *The Image Industries,* 1959.

E. J. TINSLEY

Medical Ethics

Physicians, philosophers, and theologians have long reflected on moral ideals, virtues, and duties in medicine, which have been expressed in numerous medical oaths, declarations, and codes (see **Codes of Ethics; Hippo-**

cratic Oath; Professional Ethics). Medical ethics has also included matters of etiquette, courtesy, etc. Often the phrase "medical ethics" has been construed narrowly to include only ethics for physicians, but sometimes it has been interpreted broadly to include the ethics of various health care professionals such as nurses and social workers as well as physicians. Now topics of medical ethics are frequently discussed under the broader rubric of biomedical ethics or bioethics*. See also the articles on various topics in medical ethics and bioethics, such as Abortion; Euthanasia; Genetics; Life, Prolongation of; and Reproductive Technologies.

G. R. Dunstan, "Medical Ethics," DME, 1981; and the relevant articles in ED, 1978.

JAMES F. CHILDRESS

Medieval Ethics

In the Middle Ages ethics is found chiefly in Greek and Latin writings by Christians. Some Jewish and Islamic ethical literature influenced Christian moral works from the 12th century onward (Avicenna, Averroës, and Moses Maimonides). Practically all ethicists in the period from A.D. 600 to 1450 were theists. Up to the 13th century the Platonic philosophy of the *Republic* and *Laws* was used to structure a moral science that combined the ethical views of OT and NT with Greco-Latin classical notions of happiness, the good life on earth, and the development of character through practice of the virtues of prudence, temperance, fortitude, and justice. Stoic teachings on passions and virtue somewhat influenced early Christian ethics (H. Chadwick, *The Sentences of Sixtus,* 1959). Greek fathers such as Gregory of Nyssa and John Damascene provided a moral psychology in which the human will became the decisive power in ordering life. Greek writings attributed to Dionysius the Pseudo-Areopagite (6th cent.) stressed the otherworldly theme of a return of man to union with God and they became influential in Latin from the 9th century onward. Parts of Aristotle's *Nicomachean Ethics* came into Latin in the 12th century, and the entire work was translated under the direction of Robert Grosseteste around 1245. Greek Christians (Michael of Ephesus and Eustratius) wrote commentaries on the *Nicomachean Ethics* that were put into Latin and partly incorporated in Grosseteste's *Notes* on the Latin version. From the mid-13th century the philosophic influence on Christian ethics shifted from Platonism to Aristotelianism. With the growth of the universities in that century Christian ethics became an academic discipline, as found in the moral sections of the many theological summas and in the questions and commentaries on Aristotle's ethics.

Medieval ethics is nearly always teleological. The basic question is: What is the ultimate good, or end, toward which the free actions of human beings should be directed so that they may live well? This final end is identified objectively with the perfect good (God). Diversity is found, however, on the manner of attaining to God, or on the subjective character of man's ultimate happiness (*beatitudo, felicitas*). Arguments to show that God is the only highest good (*summum bonum*) are found in Augustine (*City of God* 19), Boethius (*Consolation of Philosophy* 3), Aquinas (*Summa Contra Gentiles* 3), and many other treatises. Some thinkers situated the final beatitude of humankind in will activity and others placed it in the intellect.

Another broad characteristic of medieval ethics is the use of natural law* as an approach. Humans are able to know, by intuition and by reasoning from life experiences, certain general precepts or rules of good behavior. The primary principle is: Good is to be sought after and done; evil is to be avoided. This is grasped through the intuitive habit of intellect or will called synderesis*. Other natural law precepts are: do no harm to other persons; avoid extremes and be moderate in desires; stand firm in facing difficulties; treat others as you would be treated. Such rules are regarded as participations in the eternal law which only God knows fully. Their applications to the judgment and choice of one's individual actions are made by *conscientia* (T. C. Potts, *Conscience in Medieval Philosophy,* 1980).

In his *Division of Nature* (9th cent.) John Scotus Erigena merged Augustinian ethics with Neoplatonic views on the return (*reditus*) of human beings to God by a sloughing off of matter and its concerns. (See the critical edition and translation by I. P. Sheldon-Williams, 1981ff.) Two centuries later, we find Augustinianism in the simple ethics of Anselm of Canterbury. Moral righteousness (*rectitudo*) is a disposition of the human will (*affectio voluntatis*). After the fall of Adam the human will retained a disposition toward what is good in the sense of being useful on earth (*affectio commodi*), but divine grace is required to restore the higher disposition to righteousness (*affectio justitiae*) which is a gift of God. In his dialogue *On Truth,* Anselm concludes that justice is rightness of will preserved for its own sake (*rectitudo voluntatis propter se servata;* see R. McKeon, tr., *Selections from Medieval Philosophers,* 1929, vol. 1, pp. 173–179).

Peter Abelard (1079–1142) further emphasized the interior character of the moral act. He was one of the first to use the name *ethica* (ethics) for moral philosophy. (See the critical edition of his *Ethica* by D. E. Luscombe, 1971.) Abelard felt that the external bodily action derived its moral quality from what went on within human consciousness. Intention is the key factor. The goodness or evil of what a person is doing lies not so much in the objective nature of the complete action as in what he thinks he is doing. Yet Abelard's ethics is far from being wholly subjective, for good intentions must conform to the law of God (*Abailard's Ethics,* tr. J. R. McCallum, 1935, pp. 19–33).

Christian ethics before the 13th century is generally a theistic approbative teaching in which God's wisdom, or will, or law, is the highest and ultimate norm of morality. Human actions are good and right when they conform to this norm; bad and wrong when in discord with the *lex aeterna.* God's law is known in two ways: (1) through faith in divine revelation—for instance, the Decalogue and the NT precepts of love of God and neighbor; (2) through reasoning from natural experience to what is fitting to the nature and ultimate end of human beings. Efforts to develop the second mode of ethical knowledge led to the growth of natural law teachings (Y. Simon, *The Tradition of Natural Law,* 1966).

After the mid-13th century the English Franciscan Roger Bacon wrote three different versions of his plan for a reorganization of Christian learning: in it he placed ethics at the peak of the learned disciplines (J. H. Bridges, ed., *The Opus Majus of Roger Bacon,* 3 vols., 1900; ET by R. B. Burke, 2 vols., 1928). Others in the Franciscan school at Paris (John of La Rochelle, Bonaventure) produced a very thorough moral psychology, using elements of Aristotelian faculty theory and Christian views on the functions of the human soul. The focus of this Franciscan psychology was on the will and the preeminence of love (*caritas*) in morality. Agapistic ethics today may owe something to this emphasis.

In the Order of Preachers (Dominicans), Albert the Great and his pupil Thomas Aquinas (*see* **Thomistic Ethics**) were the leading 13th-century ethicists. Both produced influential commentaries on Aristotle's ethics and also devoted large sections of their theological works to moral questions. The patristic tradition lived on in university classes through the collection of the "judgments" (*sententiae*) of the church fathers (chiefly Augustine) made by Peter Lombard in the 12th century. Albert's ethical writings have not yet been fully studied. His original course on the *Nicomachean Ethics* is quite possibly the outstanding commentary on this work in the 13th century. Right reason (*recta ratio*) is a central feature of Albert's ethics (as also in Aquinas) and this rightness in moral thinking depends on a thoughtful reflection on ordinary life experiences as well as on divine revelation. Aquinas's ethics enlarges on this theme and has become better known in later centuries, partly because his writings are more readily available. Aquinas is usually considered the greatest ethical writer of the Middle Ages. His influence is found in many schools of modern ethics. (See V. Bourke, "Thomas Aquinas and Early British Ethics," *Rivista di Filosofia Neo-scolastica* 46, 1974, pp. 817–840.) Where Aquinas viewed the final beatitude of the good person as an intellectual act, Bonaventure and other Franciscans took ultimate felicity to be a volitional act of love (*see* **Thomistic Ethics**).

By the 14th century Duns Scotus and William of Ockham were continuing the Franciscan teachings and developing Scholastic ethics into more complex forms. Scotus endeavored to balance the roles of volition and intellection in the moral life, but Ockham became more evidently a voluntarist. Late medieval ethics thus tends to identify moral law with a fiat of an omnipotent divine will, to locate human awareness of moral duty in a will experience of righteousness, and to focus on obligation as the central feature of ethics. Thus Ockham writes, "By the very fact that the divine will so wills, right reason dictates that it must be willed." (*In Libros Sententiarum* I, d. 41, q. 1, k; see also Ockham, *Philosophical Writings,* tr. P.

Boehner, 1957, pp. 158–163.) Early Renaissance Scholasticism continued to stress this legalistic and voluntaristic approach to ethics (F. Suarez, *On the Laws,* selections tr. G. L. Williams et al., 1944).

See also **Divine Command Morality; Voluntarism.**

V. Bourke, *History of Ethics,* pt. 2: *Patristic and Medieval,* 1968; F. Copleston, *A History of Philosophy,* vol. 2, pts. 1 and 2, 1950; G. W. Forell, *History of Christian Ethics,* vol. 2: *Middle Ages and Reformation,* 1986; O. Lottin, *Psychologie et morale aux XIIe et XIIIe siècles,* 6 vols., 1942–60.

VERNON J. BOURKE

Meekness

In the Beatitudes, Jesus praised the meek: "Blessed are the meek, for they shall inherit the earth" (Matt. 5:5). And Paul entreated the Corinthians "by the meekness and gentleness of Christ" (2 Cor. 10:1). Elsewhere in the NT meekness is commended along with such qualities as gentleness, patience, kindness, humility, lowliness, and love (see, e.g., Gal. 5:22–23; Eph. 4:2; Col. 3:12). The image of Jesus as meek, gentle, and mild has been prominent in much Christian thought and piety, but the term "meek" in current English usage may suggest more passivity than the full portrait of Jesus' life and teaching warrants. The crux of the matter is the legitimacy of anger*, since meekness mitigates anger. Jesus said that "every one who is angry with his brother shall be liable to judgment" (Matt. 5:22; some ancient texts insert "without cause"). Yet Jesus is reported as being "indignant" (Mark 10:14), and his various denunciations ("Woe unto . . .") suggest anger and outrage. With many in the Christian tradition, Thomas Aquinas (*ST* II-II.157–158) distinguished between the passion of anger and the sin of anger, the latter occurring when anger is directed against the wrong objects or in the wrong manner. The sin of anger is one of the seven capital, or deadly, sins*. For Aquinas, meekness is part of the virtue of temperance*, controlling the irascible appetite: "Clemency moderates external punishment [thus avoiding cruelty], while meekness properly mitigates the passion of anger." Aristotle (*Nicomachean Ethics* 4.5) viewed meekness or gentleness as the "mean in feelings of anger." But he also noted that it inclines toward the defect, in part because we tend to view the excess as more opposed to meekness or gentleness than the defect and because people who are excessively angry are more difficult to live with than people who are deficient in anger.

See **Anger; Pacifism; Resistance.**

JAMES F. CHILDRESS

Meliorism

Usually credited to William James, meliorism stands midway between optimism* and pessimism* on the grounds that they misread the facts about humanity, history, and ultimate reality. Holding that existence is neither predominantly evil nor incontrovertibly good, meliorism says that humans are able to make it *better.* It is one form of the American challenge to responsible action. Human beings, William James held, are able, by the use of their creative intelligence and through education, to improve their physical, mental, social, and moral condition.

Meliorism regards history as a record of humanity's tortuous emancipation from magic and superstitious beliefs and its employment of the scientific method for understanding and controlling itself and its environment.

Finally, with reference to ultimate reality, meliorism holds that even God's very being may be said to draw sustenance from the human effort to improve life—a metaphysical and ethical line of thought appearing in Whitehead and others.

See **Progress, Belief in.**

CHARLES W. KEGLEY

Mennonite Ethics

The Mennonites—their name comes from Menno Simons, a 16th-century leader of the Anabaptists in Holland—represent a group of Christian communities all of whom are the descendants of 16th-century Anabaptism (*see* **Anabaptist Ethics**). They are therefore the heirs of a dissenting ethical tradition of which some of the spirit and various particulars are still intact.

For most Mennonites ethics are as important as theology. The old Anabaptist view that works are necessary to salvation is alive and well, and with it the tendency to perfectionism*. Mennonites believe that the Bible clearly spells out how a Christian ought to behave, and that it is incumbent on every believer to obey Christ in terms of specific ways of acting. Mennonites therefore often suffer from guilt at not being able to perform at the expected level or at living in a situation in which their affluence produces injustice for others.

In Europe and North America, Mennonites have become extensively acculturated. The old Anabaptist separation between church and world has become seriously blurred. Hence they have become much less distinct in their separatism than formerly. Very few Mennonites can still be detected to be such by their clothing or demeanor. This is particularly noticeable in their relation to the civic and national communities in which they live. Very few today refuse to vote. Participation in government at all levels has become relatively common, especially in the Netherlands and Canada. European Mennonites have long since abandoned the refusal of military service, although there is a revival of opposition to military service on a small scale. In North America, too, many Mennonites do not consider war a serious ethical issue.

Precisely because Mennonites too have come to feel at home in the earthly city, they are having to face an ethical landscape full of ambiguity. Simple biblical nonresistance, while still an important element, appears to many Mennonites today to be too small and simplistic a vessel to contain issues of international affairs such as disarmament and the control of nuclear weapons (see Resistance). There is thus increasing merger with a broader Christian and humanist pacifism*, although for Mennonites it remains biblically oriented. The concern for the dignity of human and other life which goes beyond simple obedience to Gospel imperatives has brought issues such as biomedical ethics, abortion, and euthanasia into the orbit of what Mennonites traditionally called nonresistance. The same is true of environmental concerns and the issues of population and poverty. Simple dogmatic solutions to problems posed in all these areas are increasingly being rejected.

In addition to all that, children born out of wedlock, adultery and divorce, abortion, homosexuality, and the place and role of women have in the last several decades emerged into the light of day among Mennonites. The concerted attempts to address the problems of sexuality and related issues reveal the tension in the Mennonite soul accustomed to living in a simpler world and always committed to perfection. No unique solutions to these problems can be anticipated. However, the commitment to mutual aid* at all levels of life continues strong in the Mennonite community and may help to reduce and heal the ravages so often wrought by these problems. Commitment of personnel and funds to aiding the victims of war, poverty, and natural disasters continues strong along with the conviction that it is done "in the name of Christ."

Such Mennonite thinkers as John Howard Yoder and Gordon Kaufman have significantly influenced ethical reflection in other traditions in the late 20th century.

See **Ecclesiology and Ethics.**

The best access to Mennonite discussions on ethical issues is provided by the files of three church papers: *The Gospel Herald* (Elkhart, Ind.), *The Mennonite* (Newton, Kans., and Winnipeg, Man.), and *The Mennonite Brethren Herald* (Winnipeg, Man.). See also *The Mennonite Encyclopedia,* 4 vols., 1955–59; J. H. Yoder, *The Priestly Kingdom: Social Ethics as Gospel,* 1985.

WALTER KLAASSEN

Mental Deficiency, Handicap, Retardation, Subnormality, etc.
see **Handicapped, Care of the**

Mental Health
Mental health is a term with complex clinical, social, and ethical dimensions. To the clinician, it denotes the desirable state of the integrated human organism's well-being toward which treatment is aimed. To the sociologist, it is a society's collective ideal regarding individual psychological and behavioral function. To the moral philosopher, mental health is one good among others, whose relative value is established within the framework of each philosophical school or system. Moreover, since the terms "mental health" and "mental illness" are mutually implicative, they cannot be conceptually separated. In practice, theorists focus on one of the pair, regarding the other as a derivative category.

The apprehension of mental function in terms of the health-illness paradigm first achieved prominence in the 19th century and was an outgrowth of the empirical, scientific study of the human being initiated during the

Renaissance. By the turn of the century, the basic biological understanding of the human organism in terms of adaptive, homeostatic well-function provided a conceptual framework within which to interpret mental and behavioral phenomena. Initially concerned with delineating syndromes of mental illness, attention was shifted to positive conceptions of mental health by the Mental Hygiene movement. Karl Menninger's influential definition, written in 1930, is illustrative: "Let us define mental health as the adjustment of human beings to the world and to each other with a maximum of effectiveness and happiness. Not just efficiency, or just contentment —or the grace of obeying the rules of the game cheerfully. It is all of these together. It is the ability to maintain an even temper, an alert intelligence, socially considerate behavior, and a happy disposition. This, I think, is a healthy mind." Similar expansive sentiments were expressed in the World Health Organization definition of health adopted in 1963. In such schemes, mental health becomes virtually synonymous with human happiness*, and is viewed as an inclusive, highly desirable human good, meriting priority in the lives of individual citizens as well as in the framing of government policies. This idealistic concept of mental health remains influential among adherents to holistic, humanistic, and some religiously oriented schools of thought.

The preponderance of opinion has shifted, however, during the past two decades as these expansive definitions have attracted severe criticism. Clinicians have realized that the pursuit of mental health, construed as a human ideal, is often an unachievable clinical goal, if not an indefinable mirage, and have reasserted their proper function as that of alleviating the suffering* caused by mental illness. In this way, they have returned to the earlier views of Sigmund Freud, who distinguished between the normal and pathological miseries of human life, the former lying beyond the reach of therapy.

Social scientists have emphasized the use of the mental health-illness paradigm as a social label with attendant role implications. Seen in this light a state of mental health or illness is an attributed characteristic relative to a society's criteria and categories for deviance. This social relativity of the concept raises the distressing possibility that a citizen who is well adapted to an evil social system

(e.g., Nazism) may be seen as a paragon of mental health from within that context.

Moral philosophers have been concerned by the illicit uses to which a concept of mental health may be put. In politically repressive regimes (e.g., the USSR), citizens may be coercively restrained for political views which, it is claimed, demonstrate that they are not mentally well. In free societies, experts in mental health may be accorded influence and power that extends beyond legitimate limits. But the most problematic contemporary issue for moral philosophers regarding mental health is the determination of its status as a human good. Specifically, to what degree is the specification of personal mental health appropriately self-defined by each competent individual, and to what degree can it be construed as a prescriptive good based upon norms of mental function that are socially or clinically based? Around this core question swirls much of the debate currently framed in terms of personal autonomy*, professional paternalism*, and social control.

Much of the disputation concerning the specifications of mental health norms is avoidable if the term is used conservatively to denote certain basic, adaptive, psychological, and behavioral competencies that human beings require in order to function with reasonable effectiveness. Among these are three primary functions—cognition, affectivity, and social bonding. Basic aspects of cognitive function include perception, memory, attention, concentration, and the capacity for coherent, logical thought. Important affective capacities include the ability to experience and modulate a range of human emotions and to maintain a homeostatic emotional state of stable, positive self-regard, free of profound depression, uncontrollable rage, or chronic apathy. Social bonding involves the ability to establish and maintain reasonably stable, mutually satisfying interpersonal relationships as well as the potential for human intimacy. Viewed in this way, the achievement of mental health requires adequate levels of neurologic and general biologic function as well as the provision of a minimally adequate relational environment during the critical developmental years. Moreover, there is broad cross-cultural consensus for these minimal criteria for mental health. Yet, such a conservative definitional strategy is not entirely satisfactory, for it omits any reference to the transcendent dimension of life.

For the modern Christian, mental health as a personal and social value poses several questions. First, to what degree can mental health be evaluated without reference to certain minimal commitments to fundamentally religious questions? The perennial existential triad of guilt, suffering, and death are ubiquitous in human experience. Can the mental health of persons be meaningfully assessed apart from their attitudes toward these realities? Yet, if responses to these issues are included within the domain of mental health, then the concept loses its unitary character and becomes relative to one's ultimate metaphysical and religious commitments. Then, we must formulate different definitions of mental health for Hindus, Muslims, Christians, etc.

Second, what importance ought to be accorded to mental health in terms of personal priorities? On one side are those who regard mental health as constitutive of God's purpose for persons, thereby meriting high priority. Moreover, a minimal level of mental health is a prerequisite to achieving other worthy goals. Others argue, however, that the pursuit of mental health is prone to corruption and that psychotherapy itself can become a narcissistic, even hedonistic, pursuit in which concern for others or for more worthwhile personal goals is eclipsed. Interestingly, this problem has recently received attention in the professional psychoanalytic literature.

Third, to what degree are the mental health needs of others a legitimate concern of compassionate Christians, both in their personal relationships and in their responsibility as citizens? Contributing to a relational environment in which others can realize their mental health would appear to be a moral requirement issuing from the Christian love ethic for all those toward whom we have clear personal responsibility (immediate family, close friends). At the social level, the mental health of its citizens can be viewed as a moral objective of a just state. Accordingly, Christian citizens will be active in fostering this value in government policy, particularly as it relates to those who may be disenfranchised because of poverty or prejudice.

Finally, despite the individualism* of the times, we should acknowledge that mental health is not a solitary achievement. Rather, it is gained or lost in relationship. Therefore, the church, as the Christian community, constitutes a powerful mediating resource in the realization of this worthy goal.

See **Mental Illness; Involuntary Hospitalization; Health and Disease, Values in Defining; Counseling, Ethical Problems in; Psychoanalysis.**

S. Bloch and P. Chodoff (eds.), *Psychiatric Ethics,* 1981; R. B. Edwards (ed.), *Psychiatry and Ethics,* 1982; M. Jahoda, *Current Concepts of Positive Mental Health,* 1958.

ROGER C. SIDER

Mental Illness

Mental illness is the term given to those dysfunctional psychological and behavioral patterns attributable to a demonstrable or imputed pathological disturbance in the healthy functioning of the individual which merits the concerned attention of a qualified mental health professional. Accordingly, it is a complex, poorly delineated concept whose boundaries with normality (the sane), eccentricity (the odd), and moral culpability (the bad) are disputed. Since classical times, Western thought has entertained three major explanations for such behavioral disturbance: demonic possession, moral depravity, and illness. These diverse theories reflect, no doubt, the intense ambivalence with which these persons were viewed as well as the genuine perplexity evoked by their behavior. Only since the latter half of the 19th century, with the ascendency of scientific medicine and psychiatry, has the illness paradigm achieved prominence.

Anti-psychiatry critics like Thomas Szasz categorically deny the existence of mental illness unless an organic etiology can be identified. But there is general consensus that mental illnesses are real, not in a reified, Platonic sense, but rather as recurring patterns of dysfunctional disturbance. A recent trend has developed, particularly in ethics and the law, to define mental illness narrowly in terms of competence or rationality. For legal and moral purposes, then, to be mentally ill is to be found incompetent. Clinicians have resisted this move, arguing that normative mental function extends beyond rationality and that many persons who are quite competent are nonetheless persistently self-destructive, suffering, maladapted, and in need of treatment. Accordingly, mental health professionals utilize broad, functional criteria in identifying mental illness, looking for regularly recurring patterns to which diagnostic labels can be applied, while leaving unsettled the question of a single all-encompassing definition for the domain of mental illness.

From the ethical perspective, two extremely important issues recur in cases of mental disorder. The first is that of personal responsibility* for actions taken while mentally ill. Fundamental to human moral agency is the capacity to voluntarily control one's behavior. It is acknowledged that floridly psychotic persons who commit crimes ought not to be held fully responsible for their actions. But how far ought this excusing function to extend? Clearly, the more broadly one defines mental illness, the more likely it is that personal responsibility will be diminished. The result of several recent celebrated legal cases in the USA (e.g., that of John Hinckley, who attempted to assassinate President Reagan) has been a reversal of earlier trends toward excusing personal responsibility on broad psychiatric grounds. But a discriminating balance is needed here. Too easily we could revert to a punitive social posture in which the profound conditioning influence of mental illness upon human behavior is ignored.

The second ethical issue regarding the mentally ill relates to establishing moral grounds for their involuntary treatment. This is discussed in the article on involuntary hospitalization.

See **Mental Health; Involuntary Hospitalization; Health and Disease, Values in Defining; Sick, Care of the; Health Care, Right to.**

R. E. Kendell, *The Role of Diagnosis in Psychiatry,* 1975.

ROGER C. SIDER

Mental Illness, Certification of
see **Involuntary Hospitalization; Mental Health; Mental Illness**

Mercy
In the NT God's mercy, expressed especially as forgiveness*, serves as both a motive and a standard for human actions: "Be merciful, even as your Father is merciful" (Luke 6:36) and "Blessed are the merciful, for they shall obtain mercy" (Matt. 5:7). Augustine (*City of God* 9.5) defines "mercy" as "heartfelt sympathy for another's distress, impelling us to succor him if we can," and Thomas Aquinas

(*ST* II-II.30) notes that "mercy takes its name *misericordia* from denoting a man's compassionate heart (*miserum cor*) for another's unhappiness." Mercy is distinguished from justice* and rights*. Mercy may be expressed when one assists a neighbor in need even though that neighbor had no right or claim of justice to that assistance (e.g., almsgiving) or when one refuses to stand on or exercise one's own claim of right or justice (e.g., forgives a debt or refuses to sue for damages). This distinction between mercy and justice is frequently important. For example, it makes considerable difference in the laws of war whether a policy of not killing enemy soldiers who are wounded or who have surrendered is based on justice or on mercy.

See **Compassion; Justice; Love; Sympathy.**

JAMES F. CHILDRESS

Merit
Merit is the worth or esteem that someone acquires as a result of good actions or special abilities; or again, it is the deservingness of recognition or reward on the part of such a person. The use of the concept of merit in Christian moral theology has been the subject of fierce controversy. The Protestant Reformers were vehement in their denunciations of the medieval penitential system, and stressed the utter worthlessness of all human achievements in the sight of God. We may well agree that no one could be meritorious before God, and that salvation must be by divine grace. In this regard, the Reformers' insistence on justification by faith through grace alone (*see* **Justification by Faith**) was correct. But we must not allow this valid insight to be exaggerated into a doctrine of total depravity* that levels all human action down to the undifferentiated worthlessness where "everything proceeding from the corrupt nature of man is damnable" (Calvin). This rules out all the relativities of conduct, whereby one course of action may be reckoned more meritorious than another, even if no human life is free from sin or can claim merit before God. The Christian acknowledges that in the last resort, true merit belongs to Christ alone. Christians have no merit of their own, but in the life of the body of Christ, and especially its sacramental life, they participate in the merit of Christ.

JOHN MACQUARRIE

Metaethics

A philosophical discipline that reflects on the cognitive status of our moral judgments. Metaethics can be regarded either as the epistemology of ethics or as the analysis of ethical language. It has been an especially important topic in Anglo-American moral philosophy of this century. The basic division is between cognitivists, who regard basic ethical statements as expressing propositions that can be true or false, and noncognitivists, who regard ethical statements as expressing emotions, attitudes, preferences, resolutions, or commands. Nearly all noncognitivists now recognize a significant place for moral reasoning in arguments from basic moral judgments. Cognitivists are divided into those who define basic ethical terms in such a way that there is no logical gap between facts and values and those who treat moral judgments as stating a distinct class of facts usually known by intuition*. G. E. Moore's presentation of the naturalistic fallacy was widely regarded as the definitive criticism of definist and naturalistic forms of cognitivism. Since the late 1960s many philosophers have begun to espouse some form of naturalism, accepting relations of entailment between some nonmoral facts and basic value judgments. Earlier moral theories usually contain elements of both positions. Thus expositions of divine command* theory often take reports of God's commands as statements of fact and regard the contents of the command as the object of a nonrational divine preference. Many contemporary theologians would reject the positivistic conception of knowledge and the distinction between facts and values which are commonly presupposed in classifying metaethical positions.

See **Ethics; Descriptivism; Emotivism; Naturalistic Ethics; Prescriptivism.**

W. Frankena, *Ethics,* ²1973, pp. 95–116; W. Hudson, *Modern Moral Philosophy,* 1970; G. E. Moore, *Principia Ethica,* 1903, pp. 1–36.

JOHN LANGAN, S.J.

Methodist Ethics *see* Wesleyan Ethics

Middle Axioms

A misleading term used to cover a middle ground in questions of social ethics between (*a*) general statements of goals or principles and (*b*) the details of policy that it may be appropriate for a church or churches to oc-cupy (if they can be agreed upon). General statements, e.g., in favor of peace or justice, are not much help, whereas detailed policies (which of course in the end have to be chosen and implemented) are subject to so many empirical uncertainties that it is usually unwise for churches as such to advocate them, though individual Christians as citizens have to decide upon them. A middle axiom seeks to find agreement on the general direction social policies should take and thus to guide opinion. If they are arrived at, it can only be by bringing theological considerations alongside empirical evidence from experts and "lay" persons who have relevant experience of the question at issue. If opinions differ too sharply, it will not be possible to do more than explore the options (perhaps advising against some as not meeting Christian criteria). If there is enough agreement to formulate them, they are inevitably provisional and subject to reexamination as circumstances change, but they do help to direct Christian attention in forming judgments amid the welter of information and opinion that constantly confronts it in public discussion. The word "axiom" suggests something that is arrived at by a logical deduction from a fixed premise, but it will be evident that this is misleading. The term "middle axioms" was coined by J. H. Oldham in the course of the preparatory work for the ecumenical Conference on Church, Community and State held at Oxford in 1937 and has influenced a good many of the studies in social ethics in the ecumenical movement, though it is by no means generally understood or accepted.

J. C. Bennett, *Christian Ethics and Social Policy,* 1946; J. H. Oldham, "The Function of the Church in Society," in *The Church and Its Function in Society,* by W. A. Visser 't Hooft and J. H. Oldham, 1937; R. Preston, *Church and Society in the Late Twentieth Century,* 1983.

RONALD PRESTON

Militarism

"Militarism," according to Radway, denotes "a doctrine or system that values war and accords primacy in state and society to the armed forces. It exalts a function—the application of violence—and an institutional structure—the military establishment. It implies both a *policy* orientation and a *power* relationship." Ordinarily the term is used in a derogatory sense because it suggests excess. Even though many Christians have been militarists, militarism is not consistent with the dominant interpretations of Christian doctrine. It glorifies military force, but non-pacifist Christianity tends to view military force as a necessary evil in a fallen world, both as a sign of sin and as a partial remedy for sin.

See **Just War; Pacifism; Peace; Power; War.**

L. I. Radway, "Militarism," *International Encyclopedia of the Social Sciences,* ed. D. Sills, 1968; A. Vagts, *A History of Militarism: Civilian and Military,* rev. ed. 1960.

JAMES F. CHILDRESS

Military Service *see* **Conscientious Objection; Conscription; Just War; Militarism; Pacifism; War**

Mixed Motives

Motives are said to be mixed when an action is performed from a principal motive while a subsidiary motive is also at work. A wealthy person may endow a charitable trust from the motive of benevolence, but may also be somewhat swayed by the prospect of receiving a public honor; the motive of vanity is mixed with that of benevolence. Morally indifferent acts also can have mixed motives, for example, taking exercise to keep fit and to please a companion.

The question of mixed motives in morals is almost exclusively the result of that "interiorization" of morality which Christianity brought about, distinguishing the good or the bad of an outward action from the movements "of the heart" which prompt it. Augustine emphasized the force and value of these inner motives in his exposition of the Psalms. Aquinas held that the outward act (the object) and the motive (which he designated "the end") each has its own moral quality (*ST* I-II.18, 19). (*See* **Thomistic Ethics.**)

Later moralists differ on the relation between the two objects of moral judgment, the act and the motive; and this variation affects the treatment of mixed motives. Bishop Butler held that acts of benevolence* are not morally invalidated by mixture with self-love* (*Fifteen Sermons,* 1726; 1897 ed., Preface and sermon 11). Others have appealed to the Beatitudes of Christ for biblical confirma-

tion that the desire for rewards is not necessarily incompatible with hungering and thirsting after righteousness, in other words that fulfillment of some desires can go along with a sense of duty or love to God (*see* **Blessedness; Rewards and Punishments**).

The view that a perfectly pure motive is absolutely necessary for a morally good action would condemn nearly all human behavior, though this appears to be the view of Kant (*Groundwork of the Metaphysic of Morals,* 1785, ET 1948, pp. 8–13). (*See* **Kantian Ethics; Duty.**) To this Rashdall replies: "It does not follow that the desire to do one's duty must always be the sole and exclusive motive of right conduct, or that conduct not consciously inspired by respect for the moral law as such must possess no moral value at all" (*The Theory of Good and Evil,* vol. 1, [2]1924, p. 119). Many moralists hold that a right act is often done, perhaps always so far as we can tell, from mixed motives; further, that if we are constantly concerned with the purity of our motives only, we shall be neglecting the most obvious duties. J. S. Mill maintained that motive has nothing to do with the morality of actions, but much with the worth of the agent. "He who saves a fellow creature from drowning does what is morally right, whether his motive be duty or the hope of being paid for his trouble" (*Utilitarianism,* 1861, repr. 1954, p. 17).

See **Motives and Motivation.**

V. A. DEMANT

Moderation *see* **Mean, Doctrine of the; Temperance**

Modern Protestant Ethics

This article covers trends and movements in Protestant thinking about ethics in Europe and America from the early 1920s to the early 1980s. The beginning of this period was marked in Europe by the dominance of autonomous reasoning in ethics built upon Kantian practical reason and in America by the influence of the social gospel*, which did much to turn Christian ethics toward the search for a more humane and just social order on premises drawn from the Enlightenment*. As Protestants on both continents, often independently and sometimes symbiotically, reacted against both of these perspectives, ways of thinking that were reminiscent of major options in the long history of Christian thinking about the relationship of faith to morality sprang forth, and even some interpretations that had no precedents. The last fifty years have seen Christian ethics* shaped and reshaped in so many ways that the process is probably better thought of as a kneading than as a remolding—and the end is not yet.

The pivotal figure in breaking the grip of liberal Protestant thinking in Europe was Karl Barth. His emphatic *Nein* to the grip of liberal ideas such as the Fatherhood of God and the brotherhood of man as advocated in Christian terms by Adolf Harnack, accompanied by belief in human progress* and confidence in European cultural achievements, was first uttered just about the time of the First World War. The pivotal figure in challenging the optimism* associated with the social gospel tradition in America was Reinhold Niebuhr, whose influence reached a peak about the time of the Second World War. Neither of these figures can be understood, however, apart from the thought of many others whose thinking played in either resonance or dissonance with that of the pivotal figures.

Barth's challenge to the culture-embracing Protestantism of his compatriots stressed God's action as independent of every existing human order. The priority of the divine will, embodied in a free grace that espouses the cause of the poor and needy, and puts the gospel before law (in contrast to the reverse ordering in conservative Lutheranism), rules out all norms that claim an independent validity. The divine will cannot be encapsulated in any set of rules, in any rationalistic moral ideals, or even in any traditional moral theology. Barth, in time instrumental in drawing up the Barmen Declaration that set the Confessing Church against the Nazi regime, declared that the command of God knows no prior restraint by any rational necessity, ecclesiastical tradition, political power, or cultural value system, yet allows moral concern about the world to utilize those factors for penultimate purposes.

Barth was indebted to those, like Christoph Blumhardt, who had a social vision of Christianity. Barth always deplored purely personalistic privatism in religion, but he did not want the social dimension to sanctify any existing social status quo. He was impressed by the cogency of, but never wholly embraced, the Marxist criticism of economic injustice and the church's complicity with exploitation. Barth's method for relating the Word of the Bible (through which the divine will is mediated) to social and political life was an *analogy of relation* in which Christ, church, and kingdom were utilized for the insights they yield about contemporary social circumstances and responsibilities. Barth's judgments about particular matters stemming from this method produced social stands of great intensity, such as his opposition to Nazism, as well as stands that perplexed many of his friends, such as his openness to the Communist presence in Eastern Europe.

Like Barth, Rudolf Bultmann wrote ethics only as an integral aspect of writing theology. His main contribution was to explicate the relevance of existential philosophy for understanding the Christian faith. Bultmann saw this as portraying the moral life to be one of a relationship to the Word of God in particular situations, not to any general or essential set of human values. The "radical obedience" entailed was faithful without reliance upon rules, prescriptions, ideals, or principles. While Bultmann reinforced Barth's view of ethics as relational in its foundation, he had considerably less guidance to offer for dealing with political or social realities.

Emil Brunner was almost unique among the European theologians in giving his ethical views separate and systematic articulation. *Das Gebot und die Ordnungen. Entwurf einer protestantisch-theologischen Ethik* (1932), published in English as *The Divine Imperative* (1937) was one of the most extensive of the limited number of systematic works in ethics published in Europe during the 1930s. It set forth a divine command* ethic which eschewed laws and principles, but it also embraced secular orders* for living out the Christian duty. Brunner emerged with a dualism not dissimilar to that of Luther, in which the Christian's responsibility as carried out in the family, the economic process, the state, the community of culture, and the church was governed by the laws of such orders—often demanding harsh official behavior more than an idealism of love or a spontaneous response to the divine will.

The last of the European figures whose thought was initially influential in the creation of a new orthodoxy, and whose thinking was influential in America through the 1940s was Dietrich Bonhoeffer. He grew up in a theological world dominated by the liberalism of Harnack, was touched by the thinking of Bultmann, and was inspired by Barth to take a heroic stand against the policies of Hitler. He had come to America planning to study under Reinhold Niebuhr, only to return and join the resistance. His premature death in a Nazi prison prevented him from bringing his ethical thinking to systematic completion, but enough of his writings have been published to have sparked much response. Like each of the other figures, Bonhoeffer was a relationalist who argued that God's command is utterly free of prior rational and legal necessity. He set forth a view of Christian responsibility that at first seems similar to that of Brunner, but he used the term "mandates" instead of "orders," and made four realms—labor, marriage, government, and the church—subject more to Christological sanctioning than to a created necessity. The relationship between the two realms was thus seen as dialectical rather than dichotomous. Bonhoeffer rejected what he called the "pseudo-Lutheranism" of the two-realms theory as it had come to be interpreted in conservative church circles.

The revolt against theological liberalism in America as spearheaded by Reinhold Niebuhr was both similar and dissimilar to the repudiation of Kantian autonomy and culture-bound Christianity on the Continent. Niebuhr took his academic training under professors committed to Protestant liberal thinking, but his career began as a pastor in a church in one of America's most brutalized industrial communities. There, the harsh realities of economic life began to erode his confidence in human goodwill to resolve disputes by persuasion alone. Like Barth, he saw the complicity of the churches in cultural realities contradictory to the gospel, but his point of attack was more on the anthropological side of the problem than on the theological side. After several works that probed the place of religion in the world, the inadequacies of individualistic views of the socioeconomic sphere, and the place of power in political life, Niebuhr published *The Nature and Destiny of Man* in the early 1940s. This work refurbished biblical, Augustinian, classical Reformation, and Kierkegaardian views of the human situation. Each of these had been especially articulate about the human situation as one dominated by sin. The optimism that had come to be associated with Christian liberalism—not least because it often engendered a pacifism that was unwilling to make the necessary responses to the military defeat of totalitarianism—was repudiated with massive strokes and rhetorical brilliance.

Niebuhr's strictures were aimed at a number of prevailing interpretations of Christian faith that had been espoused in America for some time, and which continued to attract adherents despite Niebuhr's onslaught against them. However, it is too simplistic to interpret Niebuhr merely as attacking the social gospel. He attacked the idealistic/rationalistic liberalism that had often become identified with the social gospel. He shared the impulse of the social gospel to look upon Christian faith as calling for social responsibility and economic justice, but he found the idealistic theology that had become associated with this impulse unrealistic. Among the exponents of such a basic theological rationalism, whom Niebuhr did not necessarily attack by name, Newman Smyth was an early example, and Douglas C. Macintosh and Albert C. Knudson later instances. Their understanding of the gospel was marked by belief in God's immanence, by a reliance upon human experience as the decisive measure of religious truth, and by a collapsing of the kingdom of God into a human achievement associated with spiritual progress in patterning life on the ideals and example of Jesus. In many cases this religious liberalism also eschewed coercion as an ineffective way to deal with social evil, and Niebuhr parried this with a scheme in which love was seen to be an impossibility for corporate life and justice the operative test in social process. Niebuhr's attack upon the anthropology and love ethic of liberalism was of controlling importance. It also cast the dialogue into terms that were somewhat more easily handled by the American intellectual frame of mind than the theological frameworks used in the European discussions could have been.

The situation created by Reinhold Niebuhr in American Protestant ethics can be described only in complex terms. Few thinkers were unaffected by his chastening of theological liberalism, but equally few were willing to formulate their own approach in the same way as Niebuhr did. For instance, Martin Luther King, Jr., acknowledged his indebtedness to Niebuhr's understanding that power* plays a crucial role in human affairs, but he advanced a very different view of the ways through which that power should be exercised (*see* **Afro-American Religious Ethics; Resistance**). His insistence that nonviolence is the only legitimate means of social change was as much a product of the idealistic personalism* against which Niebuhr wrote as his concern for power* was a product of Niebuhr's Christian realism*.

Paul Tillich, Niebuhr's colleague at Union Theological Seminary in New York, gave love, power, and justice ontological foundations which avoided the contrast between them central to Niebuhr's approach. Others, among them Ernest Lefever, utilized Niebuhr's thinking as the foundation for embracing realism in a tough-minded political way, but they have tended to end up as public policymakers and as members of the political/intellectual community more than as church-related theologians. Evangelical conservatives, like Carl F. H. Henry, never adopted Niebuhr's formulations of the Christian ethic even though they fully shared his opposition to Christian liberalism. Niebuhr's closest colleague, John C. Bennett, especially in his early and later writings, used the term "realism" in ways that held out more hope for the possible reordering of society through political and social action than Niebuhr encouraged. While almost every Protestant ethicist was greatly indebted to Reinhold Niebuhr for sharpening issues and setting certain trends, few, if any, were his mere protégés.

Modern Protestant ethics has also been influenced by developments that have occurred in England during the last hundred years—developments reflecting the legacy of the Anglicans Charles Kingsley and Frederick Denison Maurice (*see* **Anglican Moral Theology/Ethics**). The trends in Britain provide an instructive counterpoint to the European and American story, because the search for a Christian social order, enriched by the theological heritage of the established church and seeking to obtain justice through democratic socialist principles has been followed more consistently in Britain than elsewhere. The reactive repudiation of the Enlightenment in the name of radical faith has been much less pronounced. William Temple, one of the great leaders of the Christian social movement in England, had a penchant for synthesis rather than dialectic or polemic. He believed in an objective status for the moral good, in the necessity of the personal dimension, and in the need to give material and historical expressions to love and justice. Kenneth Kirk, who was more attentive to the role of conscience in decision-making, sought after a casuistry that would be consistent with a vision of God informed by inspiration and able to give specific guidance without being marred by legalism (*see* **Casuistry**). John Macquarrie of Oxford and N. G. H. Robinson of St. Andrews have both developed Christian ethical systems favorable to the place of natural morality.

In America the liberal tradition came to be re-expressed in a variety of chastened ways. Walter G. Muelder restated the importance of human reasoning in moral decision-making, and the significance and importance of autonomy in ethics, and argued for coherence as an important test for the laws of moral action. He also placed much importance on the social control of power in the responsible society instead of urging reliance upon the conflict of interests in a balancing of vitalities. James Luther Adams, in several scattered articles of considerable importance, restated the liberal Protestant tradition with special appreciation for the left-wing heritage of the Reformation. He discussed the importance of power, but described it as involving the capacity for enablement as well as the exercise of clout—being influenced in this regard by Paul Tillich's ontologically rooted thought. Adams also advanced with special cogency the concept of the voluntary association*, which introduces a quite different leaven into the civic order than do the traditional double realm and double kingdom theories appropriated from the heritage of Augustine and Luther.

Just as Brunner developed the most conservative extension of the Barthian impulse in Europe, Paul Ramsey may be thought of as having developed the most conservative (yet not fundamentalist) modification of the Niebuhrian impulse in America. Both Ramsey and Brunner were deeply indebted to the pivotal figure, yet both emphasized order to a greater extent than that figure. The emphasis upon order became evident in Ramsey during the 1960s and 1970s, as his stands on issues such as the sit-ins for civil rights, war, and medical ethics crystallized in increasingly conservative patterns. Ramsey employed the idea of covenant as well as the idea of creation for explicating his positions. He also increasingly articulated the value of rules and norms for guiding the Christian life.

Relationalism, which was central in the European repudiation of the liberal Protestant tradition, has been espoused in American variations by thinkers like H. Richard Niebuhr, Paul L. Lehmann, and Joseph Sittler. In H. Richard Niebuhr's thought, the best clue to which is *The Responsible Self,* ethics is a response to a Person, not obedience to principles or rules. Niebuhr built less upon exegetical or theological approaches than upon analyses of the social self borrowed from sociologists like Charles Horton Cooley and philosophers such as George H. Mead. Proposing relational ethics as a third option (in contrast to the ideals of the teleological and the rules of deontological approaches), Niebuhr portrayed ethics as the response which persons make to the redemptive activity of the Center of Value. Paul Lehmann's version of the relational approach, more polemical toward moral philosophy and moral theology than Niebuhr's, is heavily Christocentric. It relies upon the community of faith (designated by Lehmann with the term *koinōnia** rather than the term "church") as the source of decision-making and response to what God is doing to make life more fully human. Joseph Sittler's exposition of the engendering deed provides a biblically centered version of the relational approach. Situation ethics* (or "the new morality," as it was sometimes designated) was an easily popularized approach that stressed the priority of circumstances over norms* in determining appropriate action, but which usually lacked the divine-command elements in other relationalism. Its most popular American proponent was Joseph Fletcher and its English advocate, John A. T. Robinson.

The repudiations of optimistic liberalism were so strongly made that they were felt by many at the time to be decisively significant. However, the movements that began to appear in the late 1970s and early 1980s challenged the patterns that were so prevalent during the previous half century. In Europe, Jürgen Moltmann developed a theology of hope which emphasized ethical and social achievement instead of the need to resist evil. J. B. Metz, a Roman Catholic, and Dorothee Soelle called for a new attention to the secular order of politics in which the pursuit of freedom and justice is made central. Their political theology* laid foundations that were congenial to the rise of liberation theology* as it developed among oppressed groups in America and in a theological vitality arising in the Third World. James Cone, Letty Russell, and José Miguez-Bonino are representative of many who from different perspectives are forcing ethical reflection to take serious account of overcoming oppression* and to devise ways for thinking about and transforming social experience. The debate between this emphasis on justice* and freedom* and traditional concern about order* has affected the whole ecumenical church (*see* **Ecumenical Movement**). In England, for instance, it shows up in the contrast between the approach of John Vincent and that of Edward Norman.

Meanwhile, a number of American thinkers turned their attention to the moral agent as the locus of the ethical enterprise. James Gustafson did much to prompt this trend, but when his own systematic work was published it placed the emphasis upon the rediscovery of the need for theocentrism in ethics. Attention has been paid to the nature and function of the conscience*, to the development of an ethic of virtue* and character* (rather than an ethic of norms and strategy), and increasingly to describing the nature of moral development* and moral choice*. The work of Stanley Hauerwas is especially important in the development of an ethic of virtue and character, and that of Gibson Winter, Howard Harrod, and Thomas Ogletree in outlining the phenomenology* of moral choice.

The word "freedom"* has figured very prominently in current writing, being important in liberation theology, in Paul Lehmann's description of a transfigured politics in which freedom and justice are prior to order, and in Jacques Ellul's cultural iconoclasm. The left-wing reading of the New Testament imperative has been given a vigorous restatement by John Howard Yoder in *The Politics of Jesus* (1972), a book that challenges the Augustinianism that has been so dominant in most of the thought of this century. William Stringfellow also decried the post-Constantinian quality of contemporary Christendom.

In the last several years many of the Protestants trained in theological ethics have concentrated on applied ethics*, such as bioethics*, business ethics*, and political ethics, including issues of war and peace. Roger Shinn may be the most exemplary ethicist who works mainly in this way. Others, like Frederick Carney, have emphasized philosophical ethics, often in conversation with William Frankena. A few have become concerned with comparative religious ethics*.

At present no overriding set of concerns or identifiable consensus marks the Protestant ethical enterprise. It is impossible to foresee where trends are likely to turn in the next two or three decades. Much will depend upon whether a more practical concern about the establishment of justice and the making of peace produces a world in which there can be hope for the human enterprise or whether a cataclysmic conflict churns everything all over again.

See **Afro-American Religious Ethics; Ecumenical Movement; Evangelical Ethics; Feminist Ethics; Fundamentalist Ethics; Justice; Liberation Theology; Love; Political Theology.**

W. Beach and J. C. Bennett, "Christian Ethics," in A. S. Nash (ed.), *Protestant Thought in the Twentieth Century,* 1951, pp. 123–144; W. Beach and H. R. Niebuhr, *Christian Ethics: Sources of the Living Tradition,* 1973, pp. 475–508, 531–545; H. Cox, *The Situation Ethics Debate,* 1968; I. C. M. Fairweather and J. I. H. McDonald, *The Quest for Christian Ethics,* 1984, esp. pt. 3; J. M. Gustafson, "Christian Ethics," in P. Ramsey (ed.), *Religion,* 1965, pp. 285–354; E. L. Long, Jr., *A Survey of Christian Ethics,* 1967; and *A Survey of Recent Christian Ethics,* 1983; and J. B. Mow, "Trends in Christian Ethics," *Wesleyan Studies 1967–68,* pp. xx–xxx.

EDWARD LEROY LONG, JR.

Modern Roman Catholic Moral Theology

Until the time of Vatican Council II (1962–1965) modern Roman Catholic moral theology was practically identified with the manuals of moral theology*. These textbooks employed a natural law* methodology and had the primary purpose of preparing priests for the role of confessors in the sacrament of penance*. Their orientation was pragmatic and casuistic with the ultimate goal of determining what was sinful and what was the gravity of the sin (*see* **Casuistry**). The most renowned moral theologian was Alphonsus Liguori (d. 1787), who had successfully defended the middle course of a moderate probabilism* between the extremes of rigorism and laxism. Subsequent papal proclamations making Alphonsus a canonized saint, a doctor of the church, and the patron of moral theologians and of confessors confirmed the manualistic approach to moral theology. The manuals often consisted of three volumes. The first volume of fundamental moral theology discussed the ultimate end of human beings, human acts, law as the objective norm of morality, conscience as the subjective norm of morality, sin, and virtue. The second volume treated the morality of specific actions, with the Jesuit and the Redemptorist manuals following the format of the Ten Commandments whereas the Dominican manuals were organized around the virtues. The third volume considered the moral obligations arising from the celebration and reception of the sacraments and was heavily based on the requirements of canon law*.

Some changes began to appear in Germany even in the 19th century. The Tübingen school started with the pioneering work of John Michael Sailer (d. 1832), who attempted a systematic presentation of the ideal of the Christian way which all are called to follow. John Baptist Hirscher (d. 1865) based his moral theology on the biblical concept of the kingdom of God. The approach of the Tübingen school continued to have some effect especially in Germany and was represented in the 20th century in the work of Fritz Tillman (d. 1953).

In the mid-20th century especially in France (e.g., T. Deman) the neo-Thomist movement stressed an intrinsic, intellectualistic, and realistic understanding of natural law as the basis for moral theology as distinguished from the extrinsic, voluntaristic, and nominalistic approach of the manuals, which often gave the impression that something is good because it is commanded. This Thomistic renewal insisted that the good is the primary ethical category, held that something is commanded because it is good, emphasized the centrality of the virtues, and rejected the legal model of most manuals.

These various reforming trends in Catholic moral theology continued to grow somewhat before and after the Second World War, but the manuals of moral theology remained entrenched as the primary way of understanding and teaching moral theology. The most significant work in the revival of moral theology in the 20th century was Bernard Häring's *The Law of Christ,* published originally in Germany in 1954 as a 1146-page volume, which later went through many different editions and has been translated into more than fifteen modern languages (ET 1961–63). Häring followed in the footsteps of the Tübingen school but also did not neglect many of the concerns of the manuals of moral theology. The German Redemptorist emphasized the scriptures and saw all the moral life in terms of the believer's response to the gracious gift of God in Christ. *The Law of Christ* did not overlook the morality of particular acts, but it stressed the person and the growth of the person through continual conversion. Häring attempted to relate moral theology to the broader concerns of scripture, systematic theology, and liturgy. At the same time his philosophical understanding rested heavily on the phenomenology* of Max Scheler. In addition to Häring, Josef Fuchs and Gerard Gilleman contributed to the renewal of Catholic moral theology in the pre–Vatican II period.

There can be no doubt that great changes have occurred in Catholic moral theology since Vatican II. The rest of this article will summarize these developments, but two cautions are in order. First, although Vatican II represents a significant turning point, the Council must be seen in its proper historical context. New developments in scripture, theology, liturgy, and catechetics had begun to appear before Vatican II, and the Council gave authoritative and official approval to these developments.

Second, while change has taken place in the last few decades in Catholic moral theology, there has also been great continuity as well. The most distinctive characteristic of Catholic moral theology has been its insistence on mediation by the connecting "and": scripture and tradition; faith and reason; grace and nature; Jesus and the church; faith and works. At times distortions have arisen in the past by giving too independent a role to the second element in the couplet. Contemporary Catholic theology in continuity with its own tradition has held on to the second elements but now sees them in closer relationship with and even dependent upon the first elements. Traditional Catholic natural law theory well illustrates this emphasis on mediation. To determine what is to be done, one does not go immediately to God and God's will, but rather, to the plan of God, as discovered by human reason reflecting on human nature. Contemporary Catholic moral theology continues to insist on the role of reason and the human, but now tries to understand it in a more integral way in the light of a total faith perspective. Mediation continues to characterize Catholic moral theology.

Major developments in Catholic moral theology have occurred in the following areas: the role of the scriptures; its relationship to all theology; its philosophical underpinnings; its life-centered emphasis; and its emphasis on dialogue.

Role of the scriptures. The papal encyclical *Divino Afflante Spiritu* in 1943 cautiously opened the door for Catholic exegetes to employ a critical method in understanding the scriptures. Vatican II continued this approach and affirmed the primary role of the scriptures in all theology. The Decree on Priestly Formation of Vatican II specified that the scientific exposition of moral theology should be more thoroughly nourished by scriptural teaching.

The recognition of the scriptures as the "soul of all theology" had significant repercussions on moral theology. Above all, morality is seen as a religious morality—as response to the gift and call of God. This theme from the scriptures also argues against the Pelagianism and danger of works righteousness that was a perennial temptation in Catholic thought. A scripture-oriented approach changes the whole scope of moral theology which could no longer be primarily oriented to train confessors as judges in the sacrament of penance. A life-centered moral theology shows the need for the Christian to respond ever more fully to the gracious gift of God in Christ Jesus. The work of Bernard Häring best illustrates such a biblically based approach to moral theology.

However, moral theologians are also conscious of the limitations in the use of the scriptures, especially in terms of the hermeneutical question of going from the time and circumstances in which the scriptures were written to the different historical and cultural realities of our age. There is widespread agreement that the scriptures play a more significant role in the more general aspects of moral theology such as the dispositions of the person and the important values present in social life but a lesser role on particular questions more influenced by changing historical and cultural circumstances. The scriptures cannot be used as a proof text for a very specific moral conclusion that is often arrived at on other grounds. The proper role of scripture in moral theology requires continued study, particularly in relation to the place of tradition and reason, both of which remain important (*see* **Bible in Christian Ethics; Interpretation; Tradition in Ethics**).

Relationship to all theology. Moral theology has become more integrated into the whole of theology. Perhaps the most significant change occurred in understanding the relationship between the natural and the supernatural. Previously the Catholic tradition often understood the supernatural as a realm above the natural. Life in the world was under the guidance of the natural law, whereas those who wished to follow the gospel left the world and entered religious life. Vatican II recognized that both faith and the scriptures had to be related ever more intimately to daily life in the world. Theologians, especially Karl Rahner, have overcome the supernatural-natural duality on the grounds that nature is at best a remainder concept in Catholic theology. Pure nature as such has never existed. The remainder concept is an abstract reality to prove that God's gift of sharing in the fullness of God's grace is sheer gift and not due to us as human beings. All human beings have been created to share in the fullness of God's love. The older duality and extrinsic relationship between the realm of the supernatural and the realm of the natural can no longer be accepted. Overcoming the dualism between the natural and the supernatural has occasionally resulted in downplaying the traditional view of mediation and natural law, but for the most part mediation and natural law have been integrated into a more holistic approach. At times efforts to overcome the dualism have led to an overly optimistic theology which neglects the realities of finitude, sin, and the fullness of the eschaton as future, but most moral theologians affirm an eschatology that recognizes the tension between the now and the not yet (*see* **Eschatological Ethics**).

In addition to anthropology and eschatology, contemporary moral theology recognizes the importance of Christology,

particularly a Christology from below that emphasizes the importance of Jesus and his life. Political and liberation theologies stress the struggle of Jesus against the forces of oppression and the call for a salvation that embraces the whole person as well as the social and political structure of human existence (*see* **Liberation Theology; Political Theology**). With an emphasis on praxis contemporary Catholic moral theology also explores much more the relationship between moral theology and liturgy.

Philosophical underpinnings. In pre–Vatican II moral theology the human and human reason were understood in terms of manualistic Scholasticism's approach to natural law. Three significant criticisms of the older philosophical understanding have been made by revisionist Catholic moral theologians. First, the shift from classicism to historical consciousness has given greater importance to the particular, the individual, and the changing rather than to the universal, the essential, and the unchanging, as in the older Scholastic understanding. Historical consciousness calls for a more inductive methodology in addition to deductive and syllogistic logic. Second, there has been a turn to the person and the subject and away from nature and the object as illustrated by the new emphasis on freedom. Some want to ground all moral theology in the self-transcending subject. Even many (e.g., Ashley and O'Rourke; Wojtyla) who come to the same conclusions as the older Catholic approach still emphasize the personalistic aspect of their understanding. A third criticism accuses the older approach of physicalism in identifying the human moral act with the physical structure of the act and thus condemning contraception or direct killing as understood in terms of the physical causality of the act. On this matter sharp debate continues.

A pluralism of philosophical approaches now exists in Catholic moral theology. Perhaps the most common philosophical approach is a form of transcendental Thomism associated with Karl Rahner and Bernard Lonergan. Phenomenological, linguistic, and pragmatic philosophies also undergird different approaches in contemporary Catholic moral theology. Some political and liberation theologies have emphasized the importance of praxis and of orthopraxis. Although the insistence on the human and human reason underscores the continuity with the tradition, the human and human reason are now understood differently.

Life-centered moral theology. In general, almost all contemporary moral theologians recognize the need for a life-centered moral theology whose primary function is not merely to prepare confessors as judges in the sacrament of penance. In some ways this new emphasis can claim continuity with the broader theological tradition in the past and with a Thomistic emphasis on the role of grace and the virtues in moral theology.

The person is both agent and subject. Especially in the light of the biblical renewal, conversion has been stressed as the fundamental response of the Christian to the call of God. Conversion or change of heart makes one a disciple of Jesus who will then walk in the way of discipleship. From a more philosophical perspective, conversion has been seen in the light of Lonergan's understanding of the self-transcending subject. A very significant development is the concept of fundamental option which is most often construed in the light of transcendental Thomism. In Thomistic moral theology the basic human choice is that of the ultimate end and this choice then directs and governs the other particular choices that one makes. One either loves God above things and directs all other actions to that end or one chooses a creature, ultimately oneself, as the last end and directs all other actions to that end. Transcendental Thomism sees the basic option on the level of the subject and of transcendental freedom as distinguished from the level of the object and of categorical freedom. In every categorical act (e.g., walking, praying, lying) there is also present the I who performs the act. The fundamental option or the relationship with God is on the level of transcendental freedom. The subject is related to God not as object but as the absolute horizon of human reality. The concept of fundamental option as the basic orientation of the person can then serve as the philosophical starting point for a more positive and dynamic moral theology.

Most often the concept of fundamental option has been used to interpret mortal sin as a change of the fundamental option away from union with God—a change that usually occurs as the result of a process and obviously cannot be judged merely on the basis of the categorical act alone. A categorical act

may be called right or wrong, but it alone cannot be an adequate criterion for judging if there has been a change in the fundamental option. In an older approach mortal sin as a serious act against the law of God was considered to be a somewhat common occurrence. Mortal sin understood as a fundamental option occurs much less frequently in Christian existence.

The emphasis on the person in moral theology has focused attention on growth and development in the moral life. Such growth is often understood in terms of continual conversion which has both scriptural and philosophical roots. Moral theology has also been in critical dialogue with psychological theories of growth as espoused by Piaget, Erikson, Kohlberg, Gilligan, and others.

With a greater emphasis on the person, character* and virtue* have again become important topics in moral theology. Contemporary approaches to virtue usually abandon the Thomistic concept of the cardinal virtues* and the faculty psychology on which they were based. There have been no systematic approaches to the whole question of virtues and to the development of a moral theology on the basis of the virtues, but individual virtues such as hope* and truthfulness* as well as justice* and peace* have been stressed. The importance of the person as agent and subject has linked moral theology with spiritual theology, liturgy, and sacramental theology. The interest in narrative in contemporary theology finds its most appropriate application in the attitudes, character, and dispositions of the person.

Some, however, have pointed out the danger that emphasis on the subject might obscure the social, political, and cosmic dimensions of the Christian life. But Catholic ecclesiology and the Catholic theological tradition in general have consistently recognized the communal and social dimensions of human existence, and the eschatology described above also underscores the political and social dimensions of Christian life in this world.

The dialogical nature of contemporary moral theology. Perhaps the most significant characteristic of the entire work of Vatican II was its emphasis on dialogue, which also marks contemporary Catholic moral theology. Above all there is ecumenical dialogue with other Christians. Such a dialogue has brought about significant convergences in Protestant and Roman Catholic moral theology. There is also a dialogue with contemporary philosophical approaches so that Scholastic philosophy no longer serves as the monolithic philosophical basis of contemporary Catholic moral theology. A dialogue with the sciences has been encouraged by a more inductive methodology with its emphasis on the signs of the times. Official church documents now recognize the need for dialogue with all people of goodwill.

Other developments. There can be no doubt that very significant changes have occurred in Catholic moral theology since Vatican II. Since these changes are recent, few systematic approaches to moral theology have yet been developed in the light of new tendencies. Methodological shifts logically involve significant changes on specific substantive issues as is evident in the controversy over artificial contraception. In the 1960s some Catholic theologians gingerly suggested the possibility of change in the official Catholic condemnation of artificial contraception* for married couples. The pope announced a commission to study the question. More theologians began to argue for a change, but Pope Paul VI on July 25, 1968, issued the encyclical *Humanae Vitae,* which reiterated the condemnation of artificial contraception. Continued discussion of this particular issue merged with newer developments in methodology, and the revisionist approach to Catholic moral theology spread. Many revisionists also questioned other accepted teachings of the Catholic Church in the areas of personal, sexual, and medical morality. However, in all these areas the official teaching has remained the same.

Methodological and some substantive changes have also occurred in social and political ethics, e.g., liberation theologies involving women, the poor, and blacks, the acceptance of religious liberty, a greater stress on the communal nature of the goods of creation that exist to serve the needs of all, the possibility of dialogue between Catholics and Marxists, the acceptance of pacifism* as a legitimate option for the individual. Many of these changes have been accepted by official church teaching (*see* **Official Roman Catholic Social Teaching**). However, there has also been opposition to these methodological and substantive changes.

It is impossible to chronicle all the areas of debate in contemporary Catholic moral theology, but three significant disputes stand out: the existence of a unique Christian morality, the question of universal moral norms, and the possibility of dissent from official church teaching.

On the methodological level the question of the relationship between Christian ethics and human ethics has been raised. Many moral theologians maintain there is no unique material content to Christian morality in terms of norms and proximate goals, attitudes, and dispositions. History and experience indicate that non-Christians in theory and in practice often recognize attitudes and actions that sometimes have been thought to be uniquely Christian, such as self-sacrificing love or reconciliation. A theological acceptance of the fact that all people are offered the gift of salvation also tends to downplay differences between Christians and others which would be based on the presence or absence of saving grace. Proponents of this position cite Thomas Aquinas in their favor and maintain that Catholic moral theology has viewed the Christian as bringing the human to its fullest perfection. In this view the specifically or uniquely Christian affects the levels of intentionality, motivation, and the thematic understanding of the transcendental aspects of the Christian life. The other position maintains that faith, grace, and Jesus Christ should have some unique effect on Christians and how they act. Even those who deny that Christian morality has unique content recognize that a Christian moral theology must reflect on moral experience in the light of specifically and distinctively Christian understandings and symbols. At the same time, those who hold to a unique Christian content to morality also recognize that there is much in common with all human beings.

Perhaps the most divisive debate in contemporary Catholic moral theory concerns the existence and grounding of universally binding norms. The Scholastic moral theology of the manuals held that certain acts were intrinsically evil on the basis of the object of the act itself independent of intention, circumstances, and consequences. Revisionists maintain that the evil in acts such as contraception or even direct killing is not moral evil but physical ontic or premoral evil which can be justified for a proportionate reason. In subsequent discussion proportionalists have attempted to refute the charge that their position leads to sheer consequential-ism* and utilitarianism* (*see* **Proportional-ity**).

Another significant debate centers on the teaching function of the hierarchical magis-terium* and the legitimacy of dissent* from authoritative but noninfallible church teach-ing on specific moral issues. Catholics accept the hierarchical teaching office committed to the pope and bishops, but there are different ways of understanding this teaching office and how it functions. Technically speaking, the question of dissent in the areas of moral theology deals with the authoritative, nonin-fallible church teaching on specific questions such as contraception, sterilization, and di-rect killing. Only a small minority holds that these questions involve the infallible church teaching office. Many argue for the possibil-ity of dissent both by theologians and by the faithful on a number of grounds. Ecclesiolog-ically, the total teaching function of the church is not exhausted by the hierarchical teaching office and function. Theologically, these specific moral questions are not central to the faith, so that disagreeing with them does not entail denial of faith. Epistemologi-cally, on such complex specific questions one can never achieve a certitude that excludes the possibility of error. The argument against dissent stresses the presence of the Spirit in the official teachers of the church so that the faithful can have confidence in following their teaching in different matters. However, the revisionist position recognizes the possi-bility of pluralism with regard to some spe-cific moral questions even where the hierar-chical magisterium has already spoken.

See **Counter-Reformation Moral Theol-ogy; Double Effect; Magisterium; Natural Law; Official Roman Catholic Social Teach-ing; Thomistic Ethics.**

B. M. Ashley and K. D. O'Rourke, *Health Care Ethics: A Theological Analysis,* ²1982; C. E. Curran and R. A. McCormick (eds.), *Readings in Moral Theology,* Nos. 1–4, 1979–84; J. Finnis, *Natural Law and Natural Rights,* 1980; J. M. Gustafson, *Protestant and Roman Catholic Ethics: Prospects for Rap-prochement,* 1978; B. Häring, *Free and Faith-ful in Christ,* 3 vols., ET 1978–81; R. A. McCormick, *Notes on Moral Theology 1965 Through 1980,* 1981; K. Wojtyla, *The Acting Person* (1969), ET 1979.

CHARLES E. CURRAN

Modernization *see* **Industrial Revolu-tion; Secularization; Technology; Urbani-zation**

Monastic Ethics

Monk, *monachus* (fem. *monacha,* nun; from the Greek *monos,* alone) was origi-nally the general term for a Christian as-cetic who separated himself or herself from the common life of the world (*see* **Asceti-cism**). The word is commonly used, however, for one who lives with others in a monastic community—the cenobite (*koinobitēs*) as distinct from the individual anchorite (from *anachōreō,* to withdraw) or hermit (from *er-ēmos,* dweller in the desert). Beginning in the late 3rd century, traditionally with some who fled to the desert from the persecution of Decius (250–51), monasticism became the outstanding form of intense Christian piety in the 4th. Egypt was the classic cen-ter of the monastic movement, but Syria was not far behind, and it soon spread to Asia Minor and the Latin West. The nu-merous hermits of northern Egypt inevita-bly came together in informal communities, such as the crowds of disciples who gath-ered around Anthony (c. 260–343); in upper Egypt the organized common life was devel-oped under the leadership of Pachomius (d. 356). Monastic communities became wide-spread, though the East has continued to admire the apparently more heroic life of the hermit. However, Basil of Caesarea (d. 379), the great legislator of Greek monasti-cism (*Longer* and *Shorter Rules*), definitely preferred the common life as the normal sphere for the exercise of Christian virtues. Eastern monasticism has not gone through the varied developments of Western, but is not without history. In the early Byzantine period monks were numerous near the great centers of church life, and so were often in-volved in ecclesiastical and even secular pol-itics; since the 10th century Mt. Athos, the "holy mountain," has been the outstanding center of Greek monasticism. The stricter Greek monasteries are cenobitic; in others, called idiorhythmic, the monks lead more separate lives, assembling only for certain meals and services. Eastern monasteries have not developed the active ministries of Western monasticism, but have been impor-tant as centers of devotion and art, and as places of pilgrimage. Their ancient tradition of spiritual guidance flourished again in the monastic elders (*startsi*) of 19th-century Russia.

The early history of Western monasticism is reflected in the writings of such fathers as Augustine and Jerome, and later in a series of rules drawn up by various leaders for monks or nuns. A remarkable development was the monasticism of the Celtic church, which combined the austerity of monastic Egypt with the enthusiasm of the Celtic spirit. In the absence of cities, monasteries were the chief centers of church life—and Celtic monks became missionaries and explorers, more it seems out of a zealous desire to be strangers and pilgrims on earth than for the sake of the results achieved. The germs of this tradition can be seen in Patrick of Ireland. Its greatest figures are Columba (d. 596), whose monastery of Iona was for two centuries the center of the Scottish church, and his younger contemporary Columban. Meanwhile in Italy the experience of two centuries of monasticism was brilliantly codified in the *Rule* of Benedict (c. 540), which combines ascetic piety with the classic spirit of moderation and the Roman feeling for law and order. By the time of Charlemagne (d. 814) the Benedictine Rule had replaced all others in the Western church, except for some lingering Celtic survivals. But in the feudal age Benedict's pattern of work, study, and worship was distorted by the abandonment of physical labor. For those not occupied in business or intellectual pursuits this left a gap that was only partially filled by the increase of devotional exercises. The result was to give medieval Benedictinism a certain ponderosity that even its great reforms did not escape, such as those associated with the great center of Cluny (founded 910), or the revival of the monastic life in England inspired by Dunstan (after 940).

New forms of the monastic life developed as medieval life became more complex and sophisticated. The *Rule* of Augustine (derived from two of his letters) was revived after the 10th century. Having the advantage of simplicity and flexibility, it was found useful by those who wished to combine the monastic life with active work for the church—missionary, educational, pastoral, even military. On the other hand, longings for a return to ancient austerity led to the appearance of settlements of hermits. Out of these grew several orders that combined the common and the solitary life. The most significant of these

are the Carthusians (founded by Bruno, but organized by their third prior, Guigo, after 1110). Among Benedictines the Cistercians (after 1098) aimed at a return to the primitive life of the *Rule,* while avoiding the dangers of isolation by a federal organization of their numerous monasteries. A new inspiration entered the ascetic tradition with the vocation of Francis of Assisi to follow "the naked Christ" in poverty and joy. In 1209 Pope Innocent III recognized Francis's followers as the Order of Lesser Brothers (Friars Minor), and meanwhile Dominic had organized the Order of Preachers, to fight the spiritual battle of the church by preaching and teaching. The two groups influenced each other and were imitated by others, so the active and centralized order became the typical form of the monastic movement (for which the term "friar," as distinct from monk, should be used).

In the later Middle Ages there was more official regulation of the monastic life than before. In 1215 the Fourth Lateran Council ordered Benedictines and Augustinians to federate, and forbade any new monastic Rules; in 1274 the Second Council of Lyons recognized four orders of Friars (Franciscans, Dominicans, Carmelites, and Augustinians). There were few new developments in the following centuries. Catholic reformers combated in various ways the trend to secularism which was aggravated by the decline in numbers after the Black Death of the mid-14th century. The more mystical and personal piety of the age found its home in several new groups, such as the Order of the Savior founded by Bridget of Sweden (d. 1373) and the Brothers of the Common Life, who derived from the work of Gerard de Groot in Holland. The latter was an informal association, but had a monastic wing, the Augustinian Congregation of Windesheim, from which comes the best-known classic of monastic spirituality, the *Imitation of Christ* of Thomas à Kempis.

In the 16th century most of the Reformers attacked the idea of a special ascetic vocation*, and monasticism was weakened even in Catholic countries. But the Counter-Reformation led to revival and reform in many of the older orders (through such movements as the Capuchins in the Franciscans, and the Carmelite reform, after 1562, famous for its missionaries and mystics) and produced a new type, the "Regular Clerks," whose emphasis is less on renunciation of the world than on work for the church. The Society of Jesus (recognized 1540) is one of the first, and the most conspicuous, of these. Active sisterhoods devoted to education followed, and in the 17th century Vincent de Paul (d. 1660) succeeded in the radical step of bringing his Sisters of Charity out from the cloister into active work in the world. In modern Catholicism all forms of monasticism, from the strictly contemplative to the primarily active, play an important role. Though challenged by the 18th-century Enlightenment, and in many countries suppressed after 1789, the monastic life revived with the 19th-century Catholic revival, and has grown steadily since 1830. In recent years efforts have been made to integrate the ascetic vocation with the common life of humanity—as in the Little Brothers and Sisters of Jesus, inspired by the example of Charles de Foucauld, the soldier-hermit of the Sahara—and a new type of society recognized in canon law since 1947 as the Secular Institute.

Most remarkable has been the revival of monasticism in areas where it had been either condemned in principle or abandoned in practice. There has always been some aspiration in the Church of England toward the monastic life, suppressed under Henry VIII. Under the influence of the Oxford Movement the first modern sisterhood was founded in 1845, followed by active orders for men and women, and later by the more traditional forms of the monastic life as well. In definitely Protestant circles 18th-century Pietism* included several attempts at monasticism, and the Lutheran deaconess societies (since about 1830) have many aspects of active sisterhoods. Much as ancient monasticism flourished amid the crises of the late Roman world, Protestant monasticism has become conspicuous since the Second World War. Its best-known center is the Community at Taizé in Burgundy; and mention should also be made of such disciplined though not strictly monastic societies as the Iona Community in Scotland (comparable to which is the Zoë Brotherhood in the Greek Orthodox Church, which works in the world in a way that the traditional Eastern monk does not).

History seems to show that the special monastic response to the call to leave all and take up the cross is, in one form or another, a permanent feature of the Christian life (*see* **Asceticism**). In the words of a modern Benedictine scholar: "The true monk, in whatever century he is found, looks not to the changing ways around him or to his own mean condition, but to the unchanging everlasting God, and his trust is in the everlasting arms that hold him" (David Knowles, *The Religious Orders in England*, vol. 3, 1959, p. 468).

D. Baker, *A Short History of Monasticism*, 1982; F. Biot, *The Rise of Protestant Monasticism*, ET 1963; L. Bouyer, *The Meaning of the Monastic Life*, ET 1955; W. Capps, *The Monastic Impulse*, 1982; D. Knowles, *Christian Monasticism*, 1969; T. Merton, *Contemplation in a World of Action*, 1971; and *The Silent Life*, 1975; R. Panikkar et al., *Blessed Simplicity: The Monk as Universal Archetype*, 1982; H. Workman, *The Evolution of the Monastic Ideal*, 1913.

E. R. HARDY

Monergism *see* **Synergism**

Monogamy

Monogamy is the condition of having a single marriage partner at any one time. The qualification "at any one time" implies that if one of the partners dies, the survivor may remarry and this will not be counted a breach of the monogamous rule. While monogamy is virtually universal in Western countries, there are many other parts of the world where polygamy is accepted as part of the culture. The Christian ideal of marriage* visualizes a lifelong monogamous union of husband and wife. The institution of such monogamous marriage can be defended on the general moral grounds that it best provides for and protects the fullest development of conjugal love, and that it best safeguards the human dignity of the marriage partners.

See **Polygamy**.

JOHN MACQUARRIE

Moral Argument

One of the arguments for the truth of theism proceeds from the facts of the moral life to the alleged need for their completion or supplementation in the life of religion.

See **Morality and Religion, Relations of.**

JOHN MACQUARRIE

Moral Autonomy *see* **Authority; Autonomy; Autonomy of Ethics; Morality**

Moral Development

The concept of moral development points to the fact that human beings are not born morally mature and suggests that people grow morally through a sequence of more or less gradual changes. This basic thesis is not widely questioned. But beyond this, there is wide disagreement among theorists working in the field. The key questions are: What is morality? What does it mean to be morally mature? What develops in moral development? What is the sequence of changes that take place? How can these changes be accounted for? As this list makes clear, the study of moral development requires answers to questions that are philosophical and theological as well as psychological, sociological, and anthropological. Differences in theories of moral development arise from different answers to any and/or all of these questions.

The concern for growth in the moral life is ancient. Its long history is centered mostly around varying conceptions of "conscience."* The idea of moral *development* is modern, however. Four major alternative approaches can be identified.

1. The psychoanalytic approach. The first full theory of moral development is the psychoanalytic theory of Sigmund Freud (*see* **Psychoanalysis**). In Freud, conscience* for the first time comes to have a natural history the roots of which are exhausted in human biological development and social interaction. For Freud, the development of morality is coincident with the formation within the child's personality of a structure called the superego*. Through a process of identification, parental restrictions and ideals become internalized by the child and act as an internal moral judge. Rather than appearing all at once, the superego develops through a series of crises revolving around changes in infantile sexuality.

2. Social-learning theory. Freud's theory is ultimately a socialization approach to moral development. Moral norms are socially constructed and moral development involves their internalization. A similar view of morality, but a vastly different account of moral development, is found among social-learning theorists. Here morality is understood to involve learned cognitive and behavioral patterns. There is, such theorists claim, no need

for positing the development of a mediating internal psychic structure. Morality is learned directly through rewards and punishments which condition cognitions and behavior, as well as through imitation of models which provide indirect cues as to what behavior does or does not have positive consequences. Development takes place through training. As a person matures, there is increasing self-regulation, though this too is at least an indirect result of reinforcement and modeling cues. Social-learning theorists recognize that moral thought and behavior depend upon the cognitive, verbal, and social competences available to a person. As these not exclusively moral competencies develop, they interact in varying ways with socializing forces. This accounts for at least a general scheme of moral development.

3. Cognitive-structural theory. A major problem for both of the above theories is philosophical: the problem of relativism.* The cognitive-structural theory, most fully formulated by Lawrence Kohlberg, deals with this problem by appealing to a revision of an essentially Kantian formulation of a universal moral order. This order, though it may have metaphysical dimensions, is seen by Kohlberg to be embedded in universal structures of social interaction, the most basic of which is the structure of justice. As people develop in their cognitive capacities and engage with others in social interaction, role-taking, and social conflict, internal cognitive patterns develop in individuals which enable them to comprehend and operate in relation to these structures at increasingly more complex, integrated, and comprehensive levels. Kohlberg differentiates and places in hierarchical order six such cognitive patterns, and argues that moral development involves invariant sequential movement through them (though development may stop at any one of them). Each of these six patterns (or stages) gives rise to particular forms of moral judgment and reasoning which, according to Kohlberg, are the major determinants of moral behavior and affect.

In his most recent statement of his theory, Kohlberg (1984, Appendix A), lists the following stages: (1) heteronomous morality; (2) individualistic, instrumental morality; (3) interpersonally normative morality; (4) social system morality; (5) human rights and social welfare morality; (6) morality of universalizable, reversible, and prescriptive general ethical principles. The definition of each stage delineates a qualitatively distinctive way people at that stage think in making moral judgments, the *kind* of reasoning they use (rather than the conclusions they come to) in deciding how to resolve conflicts fairly in situations where there are competing claims. Kohlberg describes the stages in terms of the "sociomoral perspectives on norms in general and upon the justice operations of equality, equity, reciprocity, prescriptive role-taking, and universalizability" specific to each stage (1984, p. 624). The broad movement through the stages of these "sociomoral perspectives" is out of embeddedness in egocentric and concretely individualistic perspectives toward perspectives deriving from participation in and identification with interpersonal relationships and social systems; and then out from the latter toward perspectives based in rights, values, and principles which transcend particular relations, societies, and cultures.

Kohlberg has also suggested the possibility of a hypothetical Stage 7 which deals not with the question of *what* is just or fair or moral—as the others do—but with the question, Why be moral at all? This stage is of quite a different kind than the others, since it does not identify a kind of reasoning process so much as suggest the need to come, at the end, to discover some deeper, more metaphysical—even, perhaps, religious—ground and justification for the whole enterprise of morality; something which the reasoning patterns of moral judgment cannot alone provide.

One significant critique of Kohlberg's work has come from a feminist point of view (*see* **Feminist Ethics**). Carol Gilligan (1982) argues that Kohlberg's stages and understanding of morality, with their emphasis on increasing autonomy* and differentiation and on conflicting rights*, contain an inherent masculine bias. Women, she argues, move toward moral maturity seen and understood as increasingly more complex and appropriate forms of mutual care and connectedness with others—dimensions that autonomy and differentiation obscure if not discount entirely. Women usually score low on Kohlberg's scale, not because they are actually less mature than men but because Kohlberg's scales are skewed toward one-sidedly male concepts of self and morality.

4. Character formation. Kohlberg has come under criticism for other reasons as well. The intense focus by Kohlberg on moral judgment and reasoning is criticized by some who argue that moral character* and agency are more adequate and inclusive categories for discussing moral development (see S. Hauerwas, D. E. Miller, C. Dykstra). The concern for character is the concern for the unity of direction of a person's moral life involving not only judgment and behavior but also intention*, perception, outlooks, language, dispositions, habits*, hopes, values*, and visions (*see* **Virtue**). The concern for agency is the concern for the development of personal responsibility* in relation to one's character and with how this intentionality is related to moral intentionalities that transcend individual and social life. Although no fully developed theory of character formation in this sense has yet been accomplished, a psychological theory which helpfully describes the development of agency is that of Erik Erikson, who relates the development of ego strength to basic human virtues. Ego strength and the virtues develop, according to Erikson, through an eight-stage epigenetic cycle that covers the life span.

No unified theory of moral development now exists. Whether one ever can exist, given the variety of understandings of morality that are likely to remain, is questionable. But any comprehensive understanding of how people grow toward moral maturity will have to make sense of insights arising from all of the approaches discussed.

See **Education, Moral; Psychology and Ethics.**

A. Bandura and R. H. Walters, *Social Learning and Personality Development,* 1963; C. Dykstra, *Vision and Character,* 1981; E. Erikson, *Insight and Responsibility,* 1964, chs. 4–6; S. Freud, *New Introductory Lectures on Psychoanalysis* (1932), tr. James Strachey, 1965; C. Gilligan, *In a Different Voice,* 1982; S. Hauerwas, *Character and the Christian Life,* 1975; L. Kohlberg, *The Philosophy of Moral Development,* 1981; and *The Psychology of Moral Development,* 1984 (Essays on Moral Development, vols. 1, 2); D. E. Miller, *The Wing-footed Wanderer,* 1977; C. E. Nelson (ed.), *Conscience,* 1973.

                                    CRAIG DYKSTRA

Moral Philosophy

Used interchangeably with "ethics"* to denote philosophical reflection on morality.

Moral Systems, The

see **Casuistry; Compensationism; Equiprobabilism; Probabiliorism; Probabilism; Tutiorism;** see also **Anglican Moral Theology; Counter-Reformation Moral Theology; Modern Roman Catholic Moral Theology; Moral Theology**

Moral Theology

Moral theology is the discussion of the principles which govern, or should govern, the behavior of a Christian, and of their application to particular circumstances or classes of cases. Its sources are scripture, reason inspired by faith, the teaching of the church and in particular of certain preeminent church fathers and doctors—for example, Augustine and Thomas Aquinas.

Moral theology judges and advises on the morality of actions and of agents in the light of man's true end, the vision of God. It judges everything by one simple standard and principle: Does it conduce to the attainment of man's last end; does it conform to what is known of the will of the Creator; does it obey the laws which the Creator has laid down for attaining man's last end, as those laws are revealed in scripture or perceived by enlightened reason or apprehended in the teaching and tradition of the church, where faith illumines and guides reason?

Textbooks of moral theory, accordingly, all start with a section on humanity's last end. But because moral theology is the study of human behavior, they continue with sections which analyze the nature of a human act, the necessity for it to be the result of a free act of will accompanied by adequate knowledge and intention of the end or purpose of the act. Having established the essential ingredients of a human act*, moral theology goes on to consider the morality of actions, the grounds on which an action is to be judged as right or wrong; the considerations which are to be taken into account; the interaction of the immediate and inevitable consequences of an act and the intention of the agent and the circumstances in which the act was performed. Of obvious importance in this connection is a judgment whether the act does or does not conform with law. And so there follows a section on the different kinds of law* under which human beings live—the eternal law, natural law, positive divine law, and human law both civil and ecclesiastical —and the obligations which they impose and

how and when those obligations cease or are altered.

Next the distinction must be drawn between the objective morality of the act and the subjective morality of the agent. For the act may be wrong but the agent have thought it right. And so there follows the important section on conscience*, with the distinctions between a true and an erroneous conscience, lax and scrupulous, clear, doubtful and perplexed. In this discussion is included a description of the so-called systems of moral theology, which are different ways of enabling a person whose conscience is in doubt to arrive at a state of certainty as to what he or she ought to do. The systems are: tutiorism, probabiliorism, equiprobabilism, and compensationism (see the articles on these systems).

All this may be regarded as prolegomena to moral theology. The main business of moral theology is the consideration of the general norms or principles with which Christian behavior should conform and their application. The usual scheme adopted for this purpose is to treat them either under the heading of the Decalogue* or of the seven virtues. Each of the commandments in order is analyzed into the actions which it commands, explicitly or implicitly, and the actions which it prohibits. Or the virtues are examined and the kind of conduct to which each prompts is discussed and the vice or vices opposed to the virtue are similarly dealt with. For example, in the case of prudence, first comes a definition, then an analysis of its different parts, then the opposed vices of imprudence and anxiety.

Though the moral theologian is primarily concerned with describing and analyzing that conduct which is in closest agreement with the will of God for humanity, and in expounding and commending those virtues which all people should seek to acquire and those types of action through which the virtues find expression, yet there is no way to avoid dealing with difficult cases when two or more virtues seem to conflict and to impose irreconcilably opposite duties. Then the moral theologian has to try to determine which is the least of the evils and to advise its choice. Nor can the moral theologian altogether avoid answering questions which are couched in the form "May I do this or that?" "Is such and such permissible?" For the moral theologian has the duty of advising and helping the pastor in his task of leading the errant and sometimes unwilling sheep gently up "the steep ascent to heaven." Sometimes to recommend the heroic or the highest course of action does more harm than good, and it is important, if not more important, to know what is the lowest course of action to fall below which would be gravely sinful. It is, no doubt, from this part of the moral theologian's work that casuistry has acquired its sinister reputation. Yet casuistry*, in the best sense, is expert moral and spiritual guidance in solving difficult problems of conscience, in resolving an agony of doubt and indecision. The method is to introduce a number of parallel and analogous situations and by comparing them to bring to light the essentially relevant considerations and pinpoint the precise area of difficulty or obscurity.

But there is, also, the other side of casuistry, the delineation of minimum standards of conduct. Here the moral theologian overlaps the canonist. Every Christian community has to lay down some minimum standard of external conduct below which it cannot allow its members to fall. This is demanded by the duty of the community to bear faithful witness to the ethical teaching of the Christian religion. It is also demanded by the duty of the community to protect Christ's little ones. Some standard must be publicly maintained so that "the little ones" are not made to stumble by an apparent condonation or even approval of conduct which is obviously and scandalously contrary to the demands of the Christian life. In consequence every Christian community must lay down certain minima in the form of laws. It then becomes the business of the moral theologian and the canonist to interpret these laws and to determine precisely what they do and do not require—in other words, to answer the question "Is this or that permissible?" (see Canon Law).

It is usual to devote the second half of a textbook of moral theology to a treatment of the sacraments. Books on moral theology have tended to be written more as guides and helps for the clergy than aimed directly at the laity. A great deal of the work and thought of the clergy is taken up with the administration of the sacraments and with instructing and preparing the laity to receive them. This, perhaps, is one reason why the sacraments occupy such a large place in the moral theol-

ogy textbooks. Then again, advance in holiness* and the living of the good life depends so much on a reverent use of the sacraments, since holiness cannot be attained without grace, that it is perhaps natural to follow the exposition of the good life by a treatise on the sacraments which are so important a means for attaining it. And thirdly, canon law prescribes the conditions necessary for the valid administration of the sacraments, and the dispositions required for their lawful and worthy reception. The clergy need expert help in the interpretation of these canons, especially in the case of the sacraments of marriage* and penance*. A great mass of law attaches to these two sacraments and it requires expert handling to explain its application and its purpose.

In the Roman Catholic Church moral theology has been the subject of continuous study (see **Thomistic Ethics; Counter-Reformation Moral Theology; Modern Roman Catholic Moral Theology**). In the Church of England the 17th century produced a number of eminent moral theologians, notably Jeremy Taylor, R. Sanderson, and J. Hall. From the 18th century to the 20th the subject was little studied. An attempt to revive interest was made by K. E. Kirk between the wars, but it has met with limited success (see **Anglican Moral Theology**). The Protestant churches have always mistrusted moral theology because of its alleged tendency to fall into legalism* and formalism*. Protestant writers have tended, therefore, to concentrate on "Christian ethics,"* that is, a treatment of general principles and ideals, rather than get involved in the details and qualifications which the moral theologians can scarcely avoid.

For a selection from the extensive Roman Catholic literature, see **Counter-Reformation Moral Theology; Modern Roman Catholic Moral Theology.** For Anglican writings, see **Anglican Moral Theology.**

R. C. MORTIMER

Moral Weakness see **Weakness, Moral; Original Sin; Sin(s); Will**

Moralism

Historically, the term "moralism" has denoted thinking about life and actions or living and acting in light of morality. Although the term "moralist" is still somewhat neutral (e.g., "Samuel Johnson was a great moralist"), the connotations of "moralism" and "moralistic" are now mainly negative. Moralism, as Bernard Williams notes, is a "deformation of morality." "Moralism" and "moralistic" suggest excessive, rigid, and inappropriate applications of morality, particularly to areas, such as art or politics, that should allegedly be governed by other standards. In Christian ethics, when realists reject moralism and idealism in politics, especially in foreign policy, they do not deny the relevance of morality to politics.

See also **Legalism; Realism.**

JAMES F. CHILDRESS

Morality and Religion, Relations of

For many religious people, morality and religion are the same or inseparable; for them either morality is part of religion or their religion is their morality. For others, especially for nonreligious people, morality and religion are distinct and separable; religion may be immoral or nonmoral, and morality may or should be nonreligious. Even for some religious people the two are different and separable; they may hold that religion should be moral and morality should be religious, but they agree that they may not be. In thinking philosophically about such matters we must ask two sorts of questions: first, questions about the definitions of morality and religion, and, second, further questions about their relations.

Before addressing such questions, however, it is necessary to notice two points. The first point is that a religion typically involves three things: (1) a world view, e.g., a belief that there are one or more gods, that they are important in the affairs of the world, that they command or desire a certain conduct on our part, and that we are immortal—let us call this a religious world view (RWV); (2) an associated way of behaving and feeling that is regarded as right or good for us, i.e., what is called its "ethics"—let us refer to this as a religious value system (RVS) or religious action guide; and (3) an associated institution or church.

The other point is that morality is different from religion. A morality is not as such linked with an organized institution like a church; it may involve only a set of social or individual rules accompanied by sanctions of praise or blame, and feelings of conscience. It does, of course, involve an ethics or value system (VS) and a way of life; in fact, a morality *is* precisely a code or view about how we should or should not conduct ourselves; in morality this is primary, whereas in religion it may be secondary to a world view. A morality does presuppose some beliefs about the world and life, of course, but these need not be of a religious sort; they may be only beliefs about people and what they do or do not do to each other, that they are more or less rational, or that they are in some sense free to choose what they do. In fact, it is not hard to imagine a society of people that has no religion but has a morality, as well as a legal system, just because it sees that people cannot live together without rules against killing, etc., and that it is not desirable for these all to be legally enforced. There have also certainly been individuals who have had a morality but no religious beliefs. Moreover, it will not do to reply that such societies and individuals necessarily have a religion just because they have a value system or a world view, for it boots nothing to say that what one lives by is one's religion if it is atheistic or secular. Such maneuvers cannot win even a Pyrrhic victory. What one lives by may in fact be neither moral nor religious, e.g., if one lives by an aesthetic code or by the principle of egoism*.

If these points are correct, then a moral value system and a religious value system must be distinct kinds of value systems or action guides, even if or when they require or prohibit the same conduct or character trait. Besides, they do not ordinarily call for quite the same conduct; prayer, sacrifice, worship, and sacraments are normally parts of a religious value system but not of a moral one. That we should rest and worship on the seventh day is not as such a moral requirement; as such all days are morally the same. Thus, even theologians have often distinguished between moral and ceremonial or cultic laws within a religious value system, and between the Sabbath day commandment and those of the second table of the OT law. In fact, morality and religion might not call for the same conduct at all or might call for conflicting kinds of conduct. It might be, for instance, that the god or gods of a certain religion have no concern for human welfare or for how we treat each other, as long as we worship and serve them in the ways they desire. Even the OT and NT writers found it necessary to emphasize that their God was not interested only or even primarily in burnt offerings and sacrifices. Aristotle's God was not even aware of our existence, let alone being concerned about us.

Coming to the question of defining morality and religion, then, we must conclude that they are to be defined differently and have no definitional connections with each other. Conceptually and in principle, morality and a religious value system are two distinct kinds of value systems or action guides. Some of the criteria for an action guide's being a morality and some of those for its being a RVS must be the same, of course, since a morality and a RVS are both value systems or action guides, but at least one of the most important criteria, formal or material, must be different in such a way that, though a morality and a RVS may overlap, it is not analytically or logically necessary that they do. The same is true of etiquette and morality, or law and morality. Incidentally, one must remember that the questions here are about defining, not morality as opposed to immorality or "moral" as opposed to "immoral," but morality and the moral as opposed to the nonmoral. They are about defining, not religion as opposed to irreligion or "religious" as opposed to "sacrilegious," but religion and the religious as opposed to the nonreligious.

This seems to mean that the moral and the religious points of view are importantly different, and that different kinds of considerations are ultimate for judging from them about what we should do or be, e.g., from the religious point of view facts about what God or the gods command, desire, or are like, and from the moral point of view facts about what is beneficial or harmful to human beings and other sentient creatures. There is not space here to discuss further the problems of defining morality and religion, but, granting that they are definitionally distinct, we must ask how they are or may be related. Then there are a number of things to be said.

Even if morality and religion are conceptually distinct in the way indicated, it still may be that morality is dependent on religion. Religious believers need not think that morality is dependent on religion in any way; they may, for instance, hold that morality is a valid kind of value system that is wholly independent and self-sufficient as far as it goes, but regard a religious value system as em-

bodying a better, higher, or ultimately more satisfactory way of life. For example, a Christian may hold that morality is a matter of "natural law"* that can be grasped, perhaps inadequately but perhaps even adequately, by an unbeliever, and that one's own religious value system is a matter of revelation and simply more sufficient as a guide to life. But religious people usually do believe that morality is dependent on religion, or rather on a religious world view. This claim is, however, ambiguous and vague; there are several different senses in which morality has been held to depend on a RWV: (a) that it is genetically or historically dependent on religion in the sense that its emergence in the world was tied up with that of a RWV; (b) that it is psychologically or motivationally dependent on religion, since without a RWV, people are not adequately motivated to be moral; (c) that a RWV is necessary to show it to be rational to be moral or do what is morally right; and (d) that a RWV is needed to show that something is morally right or virtuous in the first place.

Morality may be dependent on religion in any one of these ways without being dependent on it in the others. None of these claims are easy to establish, and it may in fact be doubted that any of them are true, but they can hardly be adequately discussed here. It must suffice to make a few remarks—for example, showing that the question raised by (b) has no simple answer. Some individuals have been adequately motivated to be moral without having religious beliefs; many have not, even though they had religious beliefs. No complex actual society, religious or not, has solved the motivation problem satisfactorily, but one may suppose that it might be solved in the nonreligious society imagined earlier. As for (d), the logic of justifying basic moral principles by appeal to a RWV is infested with problems, and in any case it is not clear, given the difficulties of justifying a RWV, that one is ahead if one seeks to justify moral principles in this way. In connection with (a) it must at least be pointed out that, as morality has been influenced by religion in our history, so religion has also been influenced by morality, e.g., in Plato's criticisms of classical Greek theology and later in Christian ones.

Still, even if it is true both that morality and religion are distinct and that morality is not dependent on religion, they may be related in a number of significant ways. (1) Morality and religion (or rather a RVS) may overlap, as morality and law do, i.e., they may call for or prohibit some of the same things. Most people think this is the case. But then, as was indicated, morality and religion would or might ultimately, if not proximately, give different kinds of reasons for requiring or forbidding the same things. (2) It may be that a certain RVS would include all of what morality includes; this would be so, e.g., if God takes the moral point of view in making his commands (other than ceremonial ones), as is thought by those who hold that God commands those things because they are right, rather than the other way around, and as seems to be implied in the fact that the story of God's calling on Abraham to sacrifice Isaac had a "happy ending" except for the ram. (3) Of course, a person can have both a morality and a RVS, thinking, e.g., that for some areas of conduct there are two distinct grounds for regarding actions as right or wrong, good or bad; and then he or she might see the two either as overlapping or as merely supplementing each other. (4) Or she or he might think that they can on occasion make conflicting demands and that then one takes precedence over the other. It would usually be thought that morality takes precedence over ceremonial rules in cases of conflict, but, in the case of the story of Abraham and Isaac, Kierkegaard (and perhaps Abraham too) regarded the ethical and the religious requirements (the latter a ceremonial one) as being in conflict and the religious one as having priority. (5) However, being religious and recognizing the difference between a moral and a religious value system, a person might choose to live wholly in the religious way (whether seeing it as possibly conflicting with the moral way or not), thinking it to be not only sufficient for all of life but also in some sense better or higher, in effect letting the "merely" moral way drop out of the picture, except perhaps as something valid for unbelievers to live by—as Sir Thomas Browne did. In medieval language, such a person might hold that the RVS contains all of morality, but eminently rather than formally, much as a quarter contains all of the value of a dime and more. (6) Even if morality is not dependent on or logically derivable from a religious world view, it may still be that believing in a certain RWV makes it reasonable to believe in a certain

morality, though, of course, this can be so only if believing in that RWV is itself reasonable on independent grounds.

We may conclude by supposing that a person, A, has both a moral value system and a religious value system and is serious about them both (without seeing them as possibly conflicting), and then asking what difference adding religion to morality makes. For such a person, being morally good would not be just a "splendid vice," as Augustine thought, but a genuine virtue, though not a religious one and not the whole of virtue. Our question is usually answered by saying that religion adds a new dimension to A's moral life, but there are several respects in which this may be so. A's religion may just add ceremonial duties of prayer and religious observance to A's moral ones. Indeed, if God is conceived of as a being who can be benefited or harmed, helped or hindered (and not merely pleased or displeased) by what we do or do not do, then belief in God would add genuine *moral* duties to God to A's list of duties to self and others, human or subhuman, as well as ceremonial ones. However, religions have not always conceived of God or the gods in this way. In any case, A's religious world view may provide A with new factual premises to use in deriving secondary moral principles and particular moral judgments from basic moral principles. For example, from the moral premise that one ought to do good and not harm to others plus the religious belief in a hereafter, A can deduce new conclusions about what one morally ought or ought not to do, such as that one ought to work to save souls. That is, A's RWV gives A new insight into ways of doing good and harm. Perhaps most important, A's RWV may put A's moral life in a new perspective, adding a religious consciousness to A's earlier merely moral one. A will then see the moral life in a new light, as service to a being that is uniquely authoritative, powerful, perfect, holy, or sacred, and who expects, not only sacrifices, burnt offerings, and other observances, but also whatever morality requires of A. This general point can be and has been expressed by saying that A's motivation is changed and increased, that A now has an additional obligation to do what one is also morally obligated to do, or that A now has a further rationale for doing what there was only a moral reason for. It has also been put, e.g., by N. Culverwel in 1652, by saying that while what is morally right or good for A to do or be is right or good in itself and is commanded by God because it is morally right or good, it becomes law and obligatory for A only if and because God commands it. *See also* **Divine Command Morality; Voluntarism.**

B. Mitchell, *Morality: Religious and Secular,* 1980; G. Outka and J. P. Reeder (eds.), *Religion and Morality,* 1973; I. Ramsey (ed.), *Christian Ethics and Contemporary Philosophy,* 1966.

WILLIAM K. FRANKENA

Morality, Legal Enforcement of

The question at issue in the continuing debate about the legal enforcement of morals is whether the fact that certain behavior is, or is commonly held to be, morally wrong is a sufficient reason, or any reason at all, for it to be prohibited by law. The *Book of Common Prayer* gives expression to one view in the prayer that those in authority "may truly and indifferently minister justice, to the punishment of wickedness and vice, and to the maintenance of thy true religion and virtue." The opposing view was classically expressed in John Stuart Mill's essay *On Liberty:* "The only purpose for which power can rightly be exercised over any member of a civilized community against his will is to prevent harm to others. His own good either physical or moral is not a sufficient warrant. He cannot rightly be compelled to do or forbear because it will be better for him to do so, because it will make him happier, because in the opinion of others to do so would be wise or even right."

In modern liberal societies the "harm condition" has been generally accepted as the starting point for discussion, though in a slightly broader form than Mill gave it: no conduct should be suppressed by law unless it can be shown to harm someone. But there are considerable differences of interpretation among those who accept it, in particular as to what is to count as harm and as to whose harm is to count (*see* **Harm; Risk**).

What is to count as harm. A very broad interpretation of "harm" allows for a great deal of what is generally regarded as "morals legislation," e.g., about homosexuality*, prostitution*, pornography*, euthanasia*, abortion*. It is argued, notably by Lord Devlin in *The Enforcement of Morals,* that a

recognized morality is as necessary to a society as a recognized government. A society may, therefore, take steps to protect its morality in order to protect itself. If a society's very existence is threatened, its members are thereby exposed to harm, and so the morals legislation satisfies the harm condition. The case for a narrower interpretation has been argued by, among others, H. L. A. Hart. Hart accuses Devlin of failing to observe a crucial distinction between two sorts of morality. One is a morality of "universal values" whose recognition and observance is a necessary condition of the survival of any society whatever. The other is a morality of variable tastes and conventions, of which sexual morality is a conspicuous instance. What counts as harm, in a liberal society, should be determined by the morality of universal values.

The attempt to distinguish in this way is open to the objection, made by Devlin, that every society* possesses institutions*, such as those of marriage and property, which may differ in form from one society to another, but which in each society are, as they stand, essential to its existence. If they break down, the society itself is harmed and so are the individuals who compose it. These institutions are associated with, and require the support of, a recognized morality. Hence there may be justification, in terms of the harm condition itself, for morals legislation in support of these institutions.

Hence, within a broad area of agreement about the harm condition, there remains a division between those who would ban a certain kind of appeal to morality and those who would allow such an appeal; that is to say, between those who want the law to be morally neutral and those who do not.

One way in which some have sought to make the harm condition more precise and to narrow its scope is by distinguishing between *tangible* and *intangible* harm. In terms of this distinction it is possible to accept Devlin's insistence upon the centrality of institutions and the need to give them legal protection while allowing no moral defense of institutions and no moral assessment of people's interests in them except in terms of what can be measured by tangible benefits and tangible harms. On this view it is proper for the law to be used to protect, e.g., the institution of monogamy*, and for the maintenance of marriage* and the family* to be accepted in the interpretation and application of the law as objects of public policy, but only insofar as the particular form of marriage recognized by the law can be defended by these basically utilitarian criteria. Thus marriage as securing regular cohabitation and providing a stable home for the upbringing of children is worthy of public support; but that marriage should be for life and entail mutual fidelity are, arguably, requirements that derive from a moral and religious tradition and are justifiable only in terms of it. Doubtless marriage, so understood, enables the partners to enjoy a deeper and more trusting relationship, but these are intangible benefits, whose value it is for individuals to assess.

Thus homosexual relationships should, from this standpoint, be treated in the same way as informal heterosexual ones, and any law concerned with the protection of minors should be based only on the need to protect them from the physical or psychological harm they might suffer from premature exposure to adult sexual behavior. The criteria employed emerge clearly in the Williams Report, in its treatment of the involvement of children in pornography: "We were not able to conclude that participation in these activities was a cause of harm. Allegations to this effect were sometimes made to us, but these were usually in the context of evidence that assumed pornography to be evil and any association with it to be contaminating. We received very little evidence of a more objective kind" (6.70, 71).

Critics of this position would argue that it is difficult or impossible to arrive at a value-neutral definition of psychological harm and that, in any case, society has a legitimate interest in enabling children to develop as normal adults (where some value-laden concept of normality is presupposed). They would in addition be inclined to argue *ad hominem* that opponents of morals legislation in the area of sexuality are often in favor of it in other areas, such as those of racial and sexual discrimination.

Harm to others and harm to self. Mill was firmly opposed to paternalism* but, since his day, there has been so much legislation designed, with common consent, to protect individuals from self-inflicted harm that those who stand in his liberal tradition have sought to discriminate more precisely between legitimate and illegitimate paternalism. One criterion has already been mentioned, that it is only with respect to tangible harm that an individual may properly be protected from himself or herself. Another has been suggested by Neil MacCormick and relies on the concept of autonomy* or self-respect: "Hence there is a particular inappropriateness in enforcing upon others performance of any duties which we conceive as duties of self-respect. For example, if obscene publications tend to deprave or corrupt a person, and if it is a duty of self-respect to avoid temptation to self-depraving experiences, there is nevertheless good reason not to use coercions or coercive punishments against one who breaches that duty."

MacCormick's principle does indeed help us to understand why, other things being equal, the law should not be invoked to prevent individuals doing to themselves what self-respect requires them not to do, but it does not seem to be an absolute principle. It is no doubt desirable for the law to treat people, so far as possible, as if they were fully autonomous, but account has, arguably, to be taken of the extent to which people in practice fall short of this ideal.

At this point a further consideration enters in. In practice it is difficult, if not impossible, to draw a sharp line between conduct that affects oneself only and conduct that affects others. The behavior of most people is affected as much by the ethos of the society in which they live as by their own deliberately chosen moral principles. Hence, although it is desirable that individuals should refrain from, e.g., drugs or excessive use of alcohol out of self-respect alone, their failure to do so may tempt others similarly to fail and so to suffer harm. Legislation against drinking while driving may, therefore, have as one of its objects not simply the deterrence of those who will not respond to any other influence, but also the encouragement of a reasonable standard of habitual good behavior in the population at large. This sort of aim in legislation is, perhaps, most plainly discernible in laws against various sorts of racial and sexual discrimination*, in which, of course, duties to others are directly involved; but a concern to prevent the spread of self-harming activities may also, in a similar way, motivate some legislation.

The debate about the legal enforcement of morals tends to reflect certain underlying conceptions of morality. Utilitarians have generally, with Mill, wished to circumscribe the role of law in relation to morality, especially if they base morality upon human preferences rather than upon some objective concept of human nature. Since most of the existing morals legislation in Western societies derives from a Christian tradition, the attempt to dissociate law from morality has been seen largely as a struggle against religious control. But the debate is not a simple instance of the opposition between religious and secular. Mill's strong emphasis on liberty is not easily defended on purely utilitarian grounds and has its roots in traditions of religious independence which have also attached importance to the individual's responsibility for his or her own actions. Meanwhile in the Roman Catholic Church traditional emphasis upon the common good* as the proper end of legislation has been complemented since Vatican Council II by a greater stress upon the rights* of the individual conscience* as against the state.

See **Autonomy; Freedom; Law; Liberalism; Pluralism; Respect for Persons; Secularization; Sexual Ethics; State.**

P. Devlin, *The Enforcement of Morals,* 1965; H. L. A. Hart, *Law, Liberty and Morality,* 1963; D. N. MacCormick, *Legal Right and Social Democracy,* 1982; J. S. Mill, *On Liberty,* 1859; D. A. O. Williams (ed.), *Report of the Committee on Obscenity and Film Censorship,* 1979.

BASIL MITCHELL

Mortal Sin *see* **Counter-Reformation Moral Theology; Modern Roman Catholic Moral Theology; Sin(s)**

Mortification

Mortification as a term in ascetic theology* derives from the Pauline injunction to "put to death" (Latin *mortificate*) selfish desires (Col. 3:5). It expresses strikingly the character of the life of the Christian as one who is crucified with Christ (Gal. 2:20; 5:24), and who can say with Ignatius of Antioch "My desire (*eros*) is crucified" (*To the Romans* 7.2), or with John Wesley "Nail my affections to the cross" ("O thou to whose all-searching sight," 1738, based on a hymn by N. von Zinzendorf). The term is commonly used in a lesser sense for acts of self-denial* going beyond the common rules of prayer and fasting* (*see* **Asceticism**). For instance, ancient ascetics would deprive themselves of comfortable sleep and normal food or cloth-

ing (cf. the practice of Origen in his youth, Eusebius, *Church History* 6.3, 9–12)—recite the Psalter daily, perhaps standing in cold water (a practice of Celtic hermits), or renounce baths, considered in ancient times as a luxury. Benedict suggests more mildly that his monks could give up during Lent some of the allowance of food, drink, sleep, or conversation usually permitted (*Rule,* ch. 49). In the Middle Ages painful mortifications were often undertaken as a challenge to worldliness, in the cloister or outside it—the hair shirt of Thomas Becket is a famous example. For the Reformers discipline and self-denial should characterize the whole Christian life rather than being a special part of it (see *Augsburg Confession* II.5). In modern Catholicism the more spectacular mortifications are unusual, though not unknown. But the etiquette of pious houses and convents still offers opportunities for refusing slight indulgences otherwise permitted—and many Episcopalians preserve the custom of "giving up" this or that for Lent. Serious discussion of the subject often takes the line that "voluntary mortifications" are less useful than involuntary, that is, the acceptance of the stresses and frustrations which life itself and our particular vocation* impose upon us. And as writers as different as Thomas à Kempis and Martin Luther have emphasized, we must still come to the kingdom by the bearing of the cross (*The Imitation of Christ* II.12; *Ninety-five Theses,* no. 95).

For a classic treatment of the subject, see Augustine Baker, *Holy Wisdom,* 1657 (repr. 1874 and 1972), Second Treatise. For some medieval and later examples, see L. Gougaud, *Devotional and Ascetic Practices in the Middle Ages,* 1927; A. O'Rahilly, *Father William Doyle, S.J.,* 1920.

E. R. HARDY

Mosaic Law

The term has a number of meanings. Most narrowly defined, the law of Moses is the Decalogue, or Ten Commandments, the pithy, brief, primarily negative demands laid upon the people of Israel by their God and mediated through Moses, according to biblical tradition. They are found in two places in the Hebrew Bible, Exodus (20:1–17) and Deuteronomy (5:6–21), and are alluded to or quoted in part in several other places in the Jewish and Christian scriptures (Ps. 81:10

[11 Heb.]; Hos. 4:2; Micah 2:2; Mark 10: 17–31 and parallels). The Ten Commandments (the Decalogue*) give the Mosaic law in its best-known, summary statement.

More broadly defined, the Mosaic law comprises the classical legal heritage of the Hebrew people, including the collection of *cases* used by judges to guide them in the administration of justice, and also including the many legal prescriptions and principles found especially in Exodus, Leviticus, Numbers, and Deuteronomy. Even more broadly defined, the Mosaic law refers to the entire Mosaic heritage, found both in the Pentateuch (the first five books of the Bible) and in the authoritative interpretations of this heritage preserved in postbiblical Jewish literature, especially in Mishnah, Gemara, and Tosephta. The term "Torah" is often applied to this whole tradition, a word better translated "teaching" or "guidance" rather than "law."

Origins. The Mosaic heritage stems from many times, persons, and settings. Just how much of the Mosaic law comes from Moses himself it is not possible to say with certainty. Jewish tradition presents Moses as the deliverer of Israel from bondage in Egypt and as the giver of the law received on the holy mountain. Moses also appears in the tradition as a person passionately concerned with the weak, the oppressed, and the defenseless, and the Mosaic law underscores the protection of such regular victims of injustice as these. From the earliest stories of Moses to the account of his death (from Ex. 2 through Deut. 34) he appears as such a champion of public justice and of the rights of the poor and the oppressed. It seems probable that the Levitical tradition responsible for much of the present form of the book of Deuteronomy is to be credited with making Moses the lawgiver of Israel *par excellence.*

Contents. The legal heritage assigned to Moses is found in four chief collections of materials: the Decalogue (Ex. 20 and Deut. 5); the collection known as the Covenant Code (Ex. 20:23–23:33); the book of Deuteronomy (chs. 12–26 in particular); and the Holiness Code in the book of Leviticus (chs. 17–26). The first two of these are the oldest; the laws of Deuteronomy and the Holiness Code come from the 7th century B.C. in their present form, or perhaps from the 6th century.

In this collection, certain elements may belong to Moses quite specifically: the demand for exclusive loyalty to the God of Israel; the prohibition of the making of sculptured images; the insistence on rest every seventh day; and the laws protecting the natural victims of violence from the exercise of such violence by the powerful.

Among other noteworthy laws belonging to these collections we should mention the laws on slavery (Ex. 21:1–11 and parallels in the later laws). Slavery* was permitted in Israel, but it was regulated and checked, not so much to protect the "property" rights of slave owners, as in much of the ancient Near East, but to check the mistreatment of slaves by their owners. The sabbatical year provided for an end to slavery after 6 years; the jubilee year, after 49 or 50 years (see Lev. 25), meant release from indebtedness as well. The laws on slavery clearly treat slaves as human beings, not merely as property, and check the exercise of the authority of slave owners in many ways. One of the most interesting laws appears in Ex. 21:7–11. A slave woman is presumed to be a wife along with any other wives that the slave owner may have. She is guaranteed her food, clothing, and marital rights (Hebrew *'onah,* a special time—the time for sexual relations, in all probability). Should the woman be deprived of any one of these fundamental rights, freedom from slavery was supposed to be granted immediately.

The protection of aged parents from neglect or abuse by their (adult) children was also provided by the Decalogue, an element in the Mosaic heritage that may well stem from Moses himself. The prohibition of adultery and of murder, and the other laws prohibiting the exercise of violence against one's neighbor or the members of one's family, also probably rightly reflect this same concern on the part of Moses for those within a society who easily become victims of violence and oppression.

Developments. The commandment to love God (Deut. 6:4–5) and neighbor (Lev. 19:18), put together in the NT (Mark 12:28–34 and parallels), make an excellent summary of the Mosaic law (*see* **Love**). When the law of Moses is understood in this way, one can see that the contrast drawn between law and gospel* has often been overstated, both within the NT and in subsequent Christian history. Actually, law and gospel, rightly understood, go together and reinforce one another, just as they depend upon one another. Love of God and neighbor is not only a free act, born of God's own love and grace, but also an obligation, a service, resting on God's demand. The Mosaic law was recognized to follow upon God's gracious redemption of the slaves from Egypt (see the prologue to the Decalogue, Ex. 20:2 and Deut. 5:6). It was recognized to be a special gift of God's love, a delight of heart and soul (see Pss. 19:7–14 [8–15 Heb.] and 119), an unmistakable mark of God's love and grace to Israel. The Mosaic law could of course become a burden, as Christian obligation frequently became in the course of Christian history. But the demands of God could also be stressed too little, when Christian freedom and divine love were underscored without the accompanying demands of both law and gospel.

It is remarkable that, in the course of time, Moses should have become virtually the one and only lawgiver in the history of Israel. The Hebrew Bible credits no king with having instituted laws; all law comes to Israel prior to the kingship, prior to the time of the judges, out of the wilderness. We know that the legislation actually developed over the centuries, long after the death of Moses. But the tradition insists that Israel's kings did not make laws; God gave the law through his servant Moses. Law is *revealed*, and it is revealed in a setting of worship and adoration and openness to receive the law's demands on the part of slaves delivered from bondage and protected and guided in the wilderness. To follow God's law means to share the revelation of God at Mt. Sinai, where Moses went to hear God's disclosures, speak with the deity, and even seek to see the very face of God (Ex. 33:12–23).

See also **Old Testament Ethics.**

A. Alt, *Essays on Israelite History and Religion,* ET 1967; B. F. Childs, *The Book of Exodus, A Critical, Theological Commentary,* 1974; E. Nielsen, *Law, History and Tradition,* 1983; M. Noth, *The Laws in the Pentateuch, and Other Studies,* ET 1967.

WALTER HARRELSON

Motives and Motivation

Motives and motivation are involved in explanations of human actions. Derived from Latin (*motus*, from *movere,* move), they des-ignate the internal factors that move people to act. We are interested in motives as part of our interpretation and assessment of both agents and their acts.

In ordinary discourse, motives include aims, purposes, desires, wants, needs, and the like. In general, we use these other terms, rarely using the language of motives. Indeed, as R. S. Peters suggests, we seek or ascribe motives only "when a breach with an established expectation has occurred and there is need to justify some action." According to Eric D'Arcy, there are several types of motive-statements, all of which are explanations of the agent's objective in action. These motive-statements are offered and ascribed when there is some reason to think that an act is good and its motive bad, or that an act is bad and its motive good. The first type of motive-statement is forward-looking and explains an act in terms of its function as a means to an end (*see* **Ends and Means**). For example, "I accepted this job in order to please my parents (or my spouse)." The second type of motive-statement shows how a course of action that is not intrinsically attractive is worthy of pursuit because of some extrinsic circumstance. This may be a past circumstance (leading, for instance, to acts of revenge, gratitude*, or reparation) or a present circumstance (e.g., love* or a sense of duty*). For example, "I am sending him most of my money out of a sense of gratitude." The third type of motive-statement is not properly a motive-statement at all since it functions mainly to deny that ulterior motives, that is, motives other than the natural outcome of the act, are at work. For example, "I am taking care of my elderly father simply and solely out of love." Such a statement is designed to dispel suspicion about the motive for the action.

It is important to distinguish justifying reasons from motivating reasons for action (*see* **Justification, Moral**). Justifying reasons are the ones that the agent invokes to indicate why the act is right, all things considered; these justifying reasons (e.g., the action is required by love* or the natural law*) may also function as motivating reasons. But the action may be motivated by other moral or nonmoral reasons. For example, if an action is justified because of God's command (*see* **Divine Command Morality**), it may be motivated in part because of the sanctions* attached to that command (*see* **Rewards and Punishments; Heaven; Hell**). Similarly the desire for honor* may motivate actions that are justified by principles of justice*. T. S. Eliot remarked that "the greatest treason is to do the right deed for the wrong reason." Even though that statement is too strong, particularly as an assessment of acts in contrast to agents, it does suggest the importance of motives, especially in the overall assessment of agents (*see* **Character; Virtue**). For example, a Christian who does X, Y, and Z out of gratitude* for God's love more closely approximates the ideal of the Christian life than one who performs the same acts out of fear of eternal damnation. Some ethicists, such as Joseph Fletcher (*see* **Situation Ethics**), have argued that what is distinctive about Christian ethics is only its motives, such as love* or gratitude, not its material content. In modern Roman Catholic moral theology* recent debates have also focused on whether motivation or some other feature marks the distinctiveness and uniqueness of Christian morality. For a discussion of the role of motives in several ethical theories, particularly Kantian and Utilitarian ones, *see* **Mixed Motives.**

It is difficult, if not impossible, for the agent or others to determine either the existence or the strength of various motives. There are complex motivations for most actions; for example, in requesting exemption from military service, a person may want both to avoid the risk of injury and death and to avoid cooperation in evil* in an unjust war. Should this person's action be counted as conscientious objection* because of the presence of the motive of conscience*? As C. D. Broad has suggested, an objector's conscience may be (1) necessary and sufficient, (2) necessary but not sufficient, (3) sufficient but not necessary, or (4) neither necessary nor sufficient for his or her opposition to participation in war. The second and third are probably the most common and also the most difficult to assess. If conscience is necessary but not sufficient, both conscience and fear are the agent's motives, but neither is strong enough by itself to move the agent to action, while both together are strong enough. While it is debatable whether this should be viewed as conscientious objection, most interpreters would hold that where conscience is sufficient but not necessary, the action is conscientious objection. Similar points could be made about various other motives; this mixture of motives complicates the interpretation and evaluation of both acts and agents (*see* **Mixed Motives**; *see also* **Hypocrisy; Rationalization; Self-Deception**).

Some theories of motivation have held that this apparent diversity of motives can actually be reduced to some dominant or overarching motive such as pleasure*, as in psychological hedonism*, or happiness*, as in eudaemonism*. But such monistic theories have been widely criticized for oversimplifying human experience and action. In any event, there are controversies about what sorts of wants and desires people actually have.

In psychology, motive has been defined as any factor that "arouses, sustains and directs activity" (P. T. Young, *Motivation and Emotion,* 1961). Such a broad definition obscures some important distinctions, and many psychologists have adopted narrower definitions, often focusing on the model of motivation as "in-order-to" (Alston). As James Lapsley noted in the first edition of this dictionary, psychologists are divided in their approach to motivation: "Most agree that the paramount questions are what needs are being met in behavior—that is, what deficiencies are felt, and what goals are being sought to meet these needs. Goals are either intrinsic or extrinsic (learned)." Beyond this psychologists are divided on four significant issues: Which methods, such as direct or indirect, can identify and measure motivation; "whether motivation should be understood as a molecular or a molar phenomenon; whether it can completely be comprehended in terms of tension reduction; and whether it is primarily conscious or unconscious*." Lapsley classified motivation theories according to their emphasis on one of three aspects of mental functioning—drives*, emotions* or affects, and cognition. (1) Theories that emphasize such innate or instinctual drives as hunger, sex, and aggression. Freud offered one such theory in his psychoanalysis*. (2) Theories of emotions or affects as amplifying and modulating the underlying motivational drives. (3) Theories that stress the controlling and regulating functions of cognition, such as cognitive dissonance (L. Festinger) or adaptive cognition (e.g., G. Allport). (4) Theories of stimulus-response offered by behaviorists (*see* **Behaviorism**). The latter are somewhat similar to (1) even though they dispense with the concept of drive. The theories take various approaches to the four main issues identified earlier. For example, positions 1, 2, and 4 all view motivation primarily in terms of tension reduction, whereas position 3 recognizes the possibility of tension-increasing motives. There are debates about the merits of all of these theories, but together they suggest the complexity of human motivation and the impossibility of simplistic approaches to motives of action, whether in ethics or elsewhere. Of particular importance and continuing controversy is the relation between social structures, such as capitalism*, and motivation (see **Sociology of Ethics**) and between biology and motivation (see **Aggression; Evolutionary Ethics**).

See **Deliberation; Desire; Free Will and Determinism; Id; Ideology; Instincts or Drives; Intention; Original Sin; Psychoanalysis; Psychology and Ethics; Unconscious; Will.**

W. P. Alston, "Motives and Motivation," *EP*, 1968; C. D. Broad, "Conscience and Conscientious Action," in *Moral Concepts*, ed. J. Feinberg, 1970; E. D'Arcy, *Human Acts: An Essay in Their Moral Evaluation*, 1963; R. S. Peters, "Motives and Motivation," *Philosophy* 31, April 1956; and *The Concept of Motivation*, 1958.

JAMES F. CHILDRESS

Murder see **Homicide**

Muslim Ethics see **Islamic Ethics**

Mutilation see **Circumcision; Organ Transplantation; Sterilization; Totality, Principle of**

Mutual Aid

Often "mutual aid" refers to voluntary participation in an association or community of mutual assistance in cases of need—for example, communal sharing in the early church and in some groups of the Radical Reformation (see **Anabaptist Ethics; Mennonite Ethics; Quaker Ethics**). Henry Bullinger criticized the Swiss Brethren for holding that "every Christian is under duty before God to use from motives of love all his possessions to supply the necessities of life to any of his brethren." Such communities of mutual aid built on Acts 4:32, "They had everything in common," usually interpreting this passage to permit private goods coupled with sharing

to meet needs. Persecution made mutual aid even more important. These groups were sometimes criticized for limiting their aid to fellow believers, but such limits were usually practical rather than principled.

Mutual aid has also been embodied in insurance* programs, some of which have become obligatory (see **Welfare State**). And the term has referred to the sorts of associations advocated by Proudhon and Kropotkin (see **Socialism**). Most often, then, "mutual aid" is rendered by agents who can expect assistance when they need it because of their participation in an association of reciprocal aid. But in some ethical theories the principle of mutual aid is independent of institutions, voluntary commitments, and reciprocity. For example, David A. J. Richards (*A Theory of Reasons for Action*, 1971) views the principle of mutual aid as "requiring that, when a person is in a position where he can do a great good to another person, at little cost to himself, he is to do that good." It requires that individuals save others from grave pain, injury, or death, in contrast to works of supererogation* that actively promote their interests. John Rawls (*A Theory of Justice*, 1971) defends a natural duty of mutual aid because of its "pervasive effect on the quality of everyday life" through the knowledge and confidence that others will help if we are ever in need. In these philosophical accounts, mutual aid is close to "good Samaritanism," based on Jesus' parable of the good Samaritan; there are vigorous debates about whether the nature and extent of such a duty of mutual aid—sometimes called beneficence*—and whether it should be enforced in law (see **Morality, Legal Enforcement of**).

See **Charity; Fairness/Fair Play; Love; Social Service of the Church.**

D. F. Durnbaugh (ed.), *Every Need Supplied: Mutual Aid and Christian Community in the Free Churches, 1525–1675*, 1974; "Mutual Aid," *The Mennonite Encyclopedia* III, 1957.

JAMES F. CHILDRESS

Mysticism and Ethics

Discussion of the relation between mysticism and ethics has often rested on the assumption that mysticism is homogeneous, going back in one way or another to the kind of neo-Platonism made influential in Christian history by the work of pseudo-

Dionysius (5th century). The essence of this kind of mysticism is that that is most spiritual which is most removed from the material and the bodily. Hence there is a tendency to "angelism" in its anthropology and to an asceticism based on metaphysical dualism. Matter as such is thought to be unredeemable; history and time are unrealities from which the spiritual person will seek to be detached. "Sin" is a combination of ignorance and imperfection, redemption from which is a process of enlightenment. By spiritual exercises a mystic can achieve the proper destiny of humanity, which is absorption into deity.

If this is how mysticism is understood, then it is easy to see why certain charges are brought against it in the field of ethics. (1) There is the suspicion that ethical rights and duties are being rooted not in a divine act of redemption and seen as the fruit of the tree but are being radically reinterpreted so as to be identical with a new experience of heightened awareness which mystics seek to cultivate and retain by their system of discipline. The "ethics" of mysticism are derived from this particular experience and hence have no necessary relation to the historical incarnation and atonement of Christian belief. (2) Mysticism is held to involve an attitude toward asceticism that is incompatible with Christianity. In Christianity, asceticism* is eschatologically and not metaphysically conditioned. That is to say, it is based on the inevitable tension of a life lived in two ages simultaneously and not on the notion that matter itself is inherently evil (*see* **Body; Embodiment**). Hence it is assumed that mysticism is bound to lead to a self-centered asceticism where the practitioner is absorbed in his or her own self-culture. Mysticism is understood as unreservedly but unconditionally world-renouncing in a way that is incompatible with the Christian doctrines of creation and redemption. (3) Closely associated with this stricture is the criticism that mysticism is noticeably feeble in its social ethic. A tendency to treat evil as unreal means an absence of indignation or protest and an emphasis on contemplation and ecstatic experience that dulls social awareness. The "ethics" of mysticism are believed to be inevitably aristocratic in temper and content. It has "no message for the toilers" (John Oman) and is "unavailable for the burden bearers of the world" (Reinhold Niebuhr). Fundamentally mysticism is a self-centered cult of a particular experience. A fundamental theological objection to mysticism is that it is accordingly thought to be inevitably a form of salvation by works. And so the Protestant emphasis on divine grace* and justification by faith* strikes "a fatal blow at mysticism" (E. Brunner).

These are some of the strictures brought against what Teilhard de Chardin has called the "mysticism of the East." With it he contrasts the mysticism of the West, which is closely attached to the Christian doctrines of creation, incarnation, re-creation in Christ, and a sacramental view of the universe. In Western mystics like Julian of Norwich, Meister Eckhart, Teresa of Avila, or John of the Cross there is an emphasis on the necessary context of grace and the need for an active ethic ("It is better to feed the hungry than to see even such visions as St. Paul saw"—Meister Eckhart) which turns the criticism that mysticism is inevitably Pelagian in its attitude toward ethics and concentrates on the higher flights of religious experience for their own sake.

Recent studies have suggested that there is in the Christian tradition a type of mysticism to which the usual strictures against the neo-Platonic variety do not apply (*see* **Neoplatonism**). This is the Christian patristic concept of "mysticism as mystery." The early fathers used the word "mystical" either of scripture as containing more than meets the literalist's eye and pointing typologically or allegorically to Christ, or of the sacraments as again signifying more than meets physical sight. Mysticism in this sense is a compelling awareness mediated through the "mystery," which is some revelatory object situation, what Tillich calls the "sign event." This is a type of mysticism that is extroverted and maintains the closest contact with the "mystery," the concrete historical sign. Hence the incarnation is here not peripheral but central, and sacraments are seen as the normal and essential means of mystical apprehension. Against mysticism of this kind the conventional strictures against the ethical insensitivities of mysticism are not justified.

F. von Hügel, *The Mystical Element of Religion,* 2 vols., 1908; U. King, *Towards a New Mysticism,* 1980; A. Pié et al., *Mystery and Mysticism,* 1937; K. Ward, *Ethics and Christianity,* 1970.

E. J. TINSLEY

National Sovereignty

The dominant principle of legal authority in the nation-state system since the 16th century has been the doctrine of national sovereignty. Ethically, sovereignty has a double-edged character: its appeal is at once to *authority** and to *freedom**: authority within domestic society and freedom within the society of nation-states. Political philosophers commonly define sovereignty as "supreme legal authority over all persons and objects within a territory, and freedom from external control."

While there were biblical, Greek, Roman, and medieval-papal antecedents to modern ideas of sovereignty, it was the breakdown of medieval unity and the emergence of nation-states after 1500 that provided the historical context for the comprehensive development of such ideas. John Calvin (1509–1564) sought to resist the secular tides of modern nationalism by appealing to a stern political theology that preached an OT vision of the sovereignty of God and promised a theocratic society. But it was a more secular French lawyer and political philosopher, Jean Bodin (1530–1596), who is generally acknowledged to be the prime formulator of the doctrine of national sovereignty. In 1576 Bodin was appointed royal attorney to King Henry III, whose realm was beset by fractious religious and political strife. In that same year Bodin published his *Six livres de la République,* which sought to provide a secular rationale for national unity in which the authority to govern would derive from human need, not from the invocation of God's will. The philosophy he propounded was no mere appeal to force: his concept of a "well-ordered state" proclaimed that the realization of virtue, morality, and intellectual excellence was the highest purpose of the state. Bodin defined sovereignty as "supreme power over citizens and subjects, unrestrained by law." He held that a strong centralized monarchy offered the best polity for the effective exercise of sovereignty.

Thomas Hobbes (1588–1679) developed the naturalistic foundations of sovereignty into an authoritarian social contract*: an Absolute Sovereign Will which denies the authority of God, subordinates church to state, and accords coercive power a priority before any ethical principles. With John Locke (1632–1704), the social contract was liberalized in favor of natural rights*: sovereignty was made responsive to constitutional government and the separation of powers. Modern parliamentary and republican governments are heirs of Lockean liberalism*.

National sovereignty is invoked today as a positive principle of self-determination by virtually all national governments. Its typical corollaries are the right of self-defense and nonintervention in the affairs of other states.

Sovereignty is subject to ethical criticism by some who see it as contrary to universal human rights*, or anachronistic in an interdependent world (a view held especially by world federalists), or an idolatrous rival to the transcendent loyalties that belong to a world community—or to God.

See **Autonomy; International Order; Internationalism; Nationalism; State; World Government.**

J. C. Bennett and H. Seifert, *Foreign Policy and Christian Ethics,* 1977; F. Bonkovsky, *International Norms and National Policy,* 1980; G. and P. Mische, *Toward a Human World Order,* 1977; R. Niebuhr, *The Structure of Nations and Empires,* 1959.

ALAN GEYER

Nationalism

The sentiments of identification with a particular nation are rightly called nationalism, particularly when such sentiments assume an ideological character. In its more extreme forms, nationalism-as-ideology is sacralized into the highest good and the ultimate loyalty. More than a century ago, in his *Abhandlungen und Versuch,* German historian Leopold von Ranke described this fusion of political and religious sentiments in the phenomena of nationalism: "In most periods of world history nations were held together by religious ties alone." Salo Baron's 1947 study of *Modern Nationalism and Religion* provided a somewhat more dialectical interpretation: "Positively or negatively, religions served as the most powerful vehicle of nationalization and denationalization, while receiving in turn enormous stimuli from the patriotic, ethnic and cultural loyalties of their adherents."

Catholic-Protestant conflicts polarized emergent nationalisms in the 16th and 17th centuries. In the 20th century, Hindu-Muslim conflicts led to the partition of India, Jewish nationalism created Zionist Israel, and Islamic revival is a prime force in Arab and Iranian nationalism. For four decades, the Soviet mythology of Holy Mother Russia (more powerful and more enduring than Bolshevik ideology) has been in global conflict with an American Puritan ethos of a Chosen People.

Christian ethicists have frequently noted that these religious or quasi-religious aspects of nationalism-as-ideology intensify its moral ambiguity. Nationalism can evoke the most courageous, sacrificial behavior—or it can provoke the most brutal, self-aggrandizing acts.

In its early development, nationalism has typically inspired its apostles to a humanitarian struggle for justice* and freedom*. But the very success of a nationalist movement, particularly if it involves victory in a violent revolution* or warfare, is likely to be memorialized in a cult of militaristic virtues that, in turn, become the sanction for new acts of imperialism, oppression, and violence.

Nationalism assumes various forms and functions according to its political locus. There is a nationalism of colonial status: the cause of a people struggling for their political independence. There is a nationalism born of economic oppression*: an ideology* of liberation from structures of poverty and exploitation. The bitter Latin American experience in the Great Depression of the 1930s generated modern nationalism as a social force a century after most Latin states had achieved sovereign independence—a force that has more recently given expression to liberation theology*. There is a nationalism of political satellites: the passions of a people having the trappings of sovereignty but under the heavy political weight of a greater power. The vigor of Polish Catholic nationalism endures and is stimulated by the impositions of Soviet hegemony. There is a nationalism of ethnic separatism: the demand of a people for self-determination and sovereign identity based on a tribal, linguistic, or religious community with unsatisfied grievances against the larger political entity to which it is subjected. Biafra, Bangladesh, and Quebec are modern examples.

These "bottoms-up" forms of nationalism —nationalism as demands for social justice and liberation—contrast with the civil religions of established nation-states. The invocation of nationalist sentiment by rulers and leading citizens can be a force for unifying the people, preserving a cultural heritage, promoting artistic creativity, conserving the natural environment, inspiring acts of courage and sacrifice. But nationalism is often invoked to solidify the status quo, suppress dissent, rationalize economic interests, obstruct international cooperation, launch aggressive conquests, or wage total war.

If the darker side of nationalism suggests to some ethicists that its abolition is an imperative for a peaceful world community, others continue to view nationalism as an irrepressible cultural force, if not the most powerful force, in the world today.

See **International Order; Internationalism; National Sovereignty; State; World Government.**

S. Baron, *Modern Nationalism and Religion,* 1947; J. C. Bennett, *Foreign Policy in Christian Perspective,* 1966; H. Butterfield, *International Conflict in the Twentieth Century: A Christian View,* 1960; E. Tuveson, *Redeemer Nation: The Idea of America's Millennial Role,* 1968.

ALAN GEYER

Natural Law

The origins of the notion of natural law can be traced back at least as far as the 5th century B.C. In the *Antigone* of Sophocles a contrast is drawn between the written laws of the state and the unwritten laws, which have a higher moral claim on us just because of our common humanity. This contrast is related to the dispute about the status of moral duties generally. Are moral obligations derived from human nature (*physis*) or convention (*nomos*)? The most fully articulated early theory of natural law is to be found in Stoic ethics*, and in the principle that the good life consists in *physikōs zēn,* living in accordance with nature, where "nature" includes not merely our human nature but the entire natural scheme of things in which human beings have their place.

Subsequent uses of the term "natural law" have been various. We shall here be concerned with theories of natural law within moral philosophy. It can in general be said of all such theories (and there are several distinct ones) that they start from a view of human nature arrived at by scientific and/or philosophical reflection; and they assert that this view of human nature will provide the basis for an account of moral values and obligations. The classical moral philosophers in the Western tradition have almost all adopted some form of natural law theory. However, it must also be said that while they share the crucial tenet of a natural law theory, i.e., that moral duties can be ascertained by reflection on human nature, they differ widely in their views about what human nature is and, as a result, about the moral theory that can be derived from it. Thus, for example, Hobbes believed that human beings are motivated entirely by their desire for pleasure and aversion to pain, and that this entails that moral theory should be egoistic in character. Butler and Hume take a different view of human desires and hence reject a Hobbesian egoism. For Kant, human beings as moral agents are essentially rational, and the binding force of morality is not connected with human desires at all. On a Sartrean view, there is no human essence that could serve as the basis for morality; it is characteristic of authentic human nature to create its essence in the exercise of freedom. Again, for philosophers like Plato or Augustine, who adopt a dualist view of the mind-body relationship in human beings, the moral theory which results differs markedly from that derived by Aristotle or Aquinas, who do not adopt such a dualism, especially in regard to the moral value to be placed on the body and its drives, and on the emotions.

In the Christian tradition, the theory of natural law was developed in some detail by Aquinas, along fundamentally Aristotelian lines. It was Aquinas's view that by using our reason to reflect on our human nature, we could discover both the specific ends toward which we naturally tend (such as to live, to reproduce, to acquire knowledge, to have a role in an ordered society, to worship God) and the general end for which God created us, a blessed immortality. When we have discovered these ends, it is then possible for us to determine the means required to achieve them. This understanding of God's plan for us, built into our nature by his act of creation, Aquinas called natural law.

This general approach was taken much further by later Roman Catholic moralists, whose detailed applications of the method illustrate both the approach and its difficulties. They take as their starting point the Aristotelian notion of a natural teleology, the view that the human person as a whole has a function, and that the various human organs and capacities have their functions which subserve the good functioning of the whole. An examination of the proper functioning of each human capability leads to the derivation of moral duties. Thus, one functions best, as a matter of natural necessity, if one has good health, is given an education, is allowed to make free choices, and so on. It is therefore immoral so to act as to damage anyone's health; it is likewise immoral to deprive people of an education, or of their freedom. So far, the approach would be reasonably uncontroversial. However, the same method was used to derive much more specific conclusions. The function of the human reproductive system is to produce children: it is therefore immoral to act in any way that will impede this natural function. Or again, the natural function of sexual organs is reproductive: therefore any use of them for other functions (such as to express homosexual love) is likewise immoral.

Evidently, such uses of the term "natural" are more controversial. It is one thing to say that the natural function of the eye is to see. But even bodily organs can and do serve several functions. And if one asks of the body as a whole what its function is, the answer is much less clear. Even less clear is the answer to questions such as "What is the function of a human life?" or "What is the function of sexuality in a human life?" The way one might try to answer these questions seems quite unlike the way one might try to answer questions about the function(s) of the endocrine glands or the heart in the human body. The notion of "function" at this point becomes much more a matter of moral assessment than of scientific inquiry. It might yet be possible to find some morally neutral way of examining such notions as human fulfillment in the scientific manner that is required by natural law theories in general. But no such approach has as yet been satisfactorily elaborated, and natural law theories can be regarded as adequate only to the extent that such elaboration is forthcoming.

The very possibility of a natural law theory of ethics has been attacked on other grounds as well. G. E. Moore argued that the very attempt to base ethics on any nonmoral account of what human beings are like is radically flawed by the naturalistic fallacy, since it argues from what human beings are like to what they morally ought to be like (*see* **Naturalistic Ethics**). This criticism is perhaps less conclusive than it was earlier thought to be, but it does point to the major difficulty confronting any natural law theory, that its view of human nature is likely to be at least as controversial as the moral conclusions at which it arrives. Those who disagree with the conclusions are likely to question the picture of human beings on which those conclusions are based. Unless that picture can be firmly established in sufficient detail to warrant the moral inferences drawn from it, the theory as a whole will lack credibility. In particular, it will often be argued against natural law theories that the picture of human nature on which they rely will itself be the product of a moral outlook, rather than an independently established basis by which a moral outlook can be supported.

The entire approach has also been attacked on theological grounds. It has been argued that to assert that our human reason of itself, reflecting on our human nature, can arrive at a proper understanding of God's will for us is to undercut the need for grace, and also to ignore the fact that fallen humanity stands in need of the revelation given in Christ if human beings are to know what is good in God's eyes. The attempt to use our merely human estimate of right and wrong as a basis for Christian conduct is, on this view, regarded as a blasphemous willingness to exalt human reason, and fallen human reason at that, at the expense of God's revelation given to us in Christ. Controversy has arisen about the precise understanding of the term "nature" as it is used in Paul, especially in Rom. 1:18–21. Theologians of the different Christian traditions have understood this passage variously to refer to fallen nature, or to nature as originally created by God.

Whereas those theologians who hold a natural law theory of ethics will tend to play down or deny entirely the specificity of Christian ethics, those who reject a natural law approach will be much more ready to claim that Christian belief brings with it a radically new moral demand.

See **Christian Ethics; Law; Medieval Ethics; Thomistic Ethics; Modern Roman Catholic Moral Theology.**

J. M. Finnis, *Natural Law and Natural Rights,* 1980.

GERARD J. HUGHES

Natural Rights

The belief that all human beings are equally entitled or justified, prior to all laws, cus-

toms, or agreements, in claiming against appropriate others certain kinds of performance or forbearance, which are sanctionable or enforceable upon default. This belief emerged as a relatively self-contained doctrine at the end of the 16th century in northern Europe and England, and was highly influential in that form through the 18th century. It is taken to be knowable by "natural" faculties, which means that it is available to all adult, sane human beings without special religious or other privileged inspiration. The ascriptions "inalienable" and "indefeasible" or "imprescriptable" are often attached to conceptions of natural rights. This belief in its classical form has been modified and revised in numerous ways in the 20th century (*see* **Human Rights**).

The sources of this belief are deeply embedded in the Greco-Roman and Western Christian outlooks, particularly in the conviction found in the Stoics, Paul, the Christian fathers, and much medieval Catholic thought, that all human beings are born with an equal potential for individual self-direction with respect to fundamental matters of conscience, namely, basic questions of faith and morals. The idea that individual conscience* is in some important sense naturally sovereign over, and thus prior to, all earthly authorities has underlain numerous Christian reform movements, and most prominently the Protestant Reformation. References to a "natural right" to hold religious belief and to consent or not to political authorities are sprinkled throughout the writings of 16th-century Calvinist revolutionaries like Christopher Goodman and Robert Browne, and 17th-century English Puritan radicals like the Levellers, ideas that were in part inspired by Calvin's own utterances.

However, the systematic and self-conscious formulation of this doctrine occurred first in the thought of Hugo Grotius, the Dutch Protestant theologian and international lawyer (b. 1583). The crucial step was to state unequivocally, as Grotius did, that certain moral requirements might "naturally" be known without benefit of belief in God (though Grotius was a believer himself). Grotius held that human beings were born free and equal agents with a deep aspiration for peaceful, cooperative existence, and that the only way to achieve that end was to create laws and institutions that honored and protected the natural condition of equal freedom. The concept of natural rights in Grotius's hands thus constituted a fundamental standard of legitimacy for all laws and governments. According to his teaching, individuals were invested at birth with the authority (claimable upon reaching maturity) to exercise control by their consent over property and over the use of force. Governments are simply the contrivance of human beings (though also authorized by God) to regularize the distribution of property and the correction of offenses.

There is an ambivalence in Grotius's teaching which played itself out in the two opposing interpretations of natural rights that were definitively and influentially articulated in 17th-century England by Thomas Hobbes (b. 1588) and John Locke (b. 1632). The conflicting assumptions underlying these two constructions still fuel much of the contemporary philosophical discussion of natural rights doctrine.

Hobbes grounded his theory in what he believed was every individual's dominating preoccupation with self-promotion and self-preservation. From that assumption, Hobbes proceeded to define "natural right" in a rather peculiar way: All human beings are born with a right "to all things," even to the bodies and possessions of others. Strictly understood, that means that every person is entitled or justified, prior to all agreements, laws, or customs, to claim "everything" from all others and to demand that they forbear from interfering with the due exercise of this right! Since this is the right of everyone, the end result is social (if not conceptual) chaos. If chaos is to be avoided, the only rational solution, on Hobbes's view, is for everyone to agree to a system of laws and an agency of enforcement.

However, since "by inalienable and indefeasible right" everyone continues to be at war with everyone else, all will need to agree, in their own interest, to an absolutist political system. Only then will every person's "right" to self-preservation be guaranteed, for there is no other basis for unity and cooperation.

Locke's view is radically different. He explicitly denied that the natural rights of human beings rest in each person's self-interest. Rather, by a process of rational self-reflection and cogitation, human beings come to discover certain "fixed and permanent" moral truths, according to which they know that the gratuitous infliction of suffering,

maiming, and destruction of other human beings is wrong and ought to be avoided, and that assisting others in dire need at minor inconvenience is right and ought to be performed. These beliefs form the basis for Locke's doctrine of natural rights. They constitute the standards for the distribution of property and the organization and use of force. Governments are created to regularize these functions, that is, to promote and enforce the inalienable and indefeasible right to protection against arbitrary force and exploitation.

Hobbes's and Locke's theories of natural rights have been of the greatest influence upon later 18th-century liberal revolutionary thought. Particularly Locke's version resonated among some of the intellectual leaders of the American Revolution, like Thomas Jefferson and George Mason, and it lay behind the formulation of many of the documents of the international human rights movement.

See also **Human Rights; Natural Law; Rights.**

J. Finnis, *Natural Law and Natural Rights,* 1980; H. Grotius, *The Rights of War and Peace* (1625), ET 1901, repr. 1979; T. Hobbes, *Leviathan* (1651), 1958, chs. 13–15; J. Locke, *Two Treatises on Government* (1690), 1965; *Essays on the Law of Nature* (c. 1660–64), ET 1954; M. MacDonald, "Natural Rights," *Proceedings of the Aristotelian Society,* 1947–48; R. Tuck, *Natural Rights Theories,* 1979.

DAVID LITTLE

Naturalistic Ethics

This may be defined as covering any theory which seeks to reduce all ethical concepts to concepts of a natural science, usually psychology, but sometimes biology or sociology. If "good" be taken as the fundamental concept of ethics and be defined as meaning, for example, "desired" or "satisfying," or "right" be taken as the fundamental concept and defined as, for example, "generally approved," ethics becomes on principle a branch of psychology; if either is defined as "in accordance with the line of evolutionary development" or as "conducive to social stability," it becomes respectively a branch of biology or sociology (*see* **Evolutionary Ethics**). The term "naturalism" in this sense is derived from G. E. Moore, who in *Principia*

Ethica (1903) maintained that any naturalist definition of good was on principle impossible. By "definition" is here meant "analysis in terms of something other than itself," and not the naming of a property which merely accompanies the property defined. It might be possible to mention properties which are always present when anything is good and vice versa without analyzing goodness; to take an analogous example, the scientist can give a definition of yellow in terms of the accompanying wavelengths, but the color yellow as seen still cannot be analyzed in terms of something else in such a way that someone who had not experienced it could know what it was like. To say that ethical concepts cannot be reduced to nonethical is by no means an implausible statement, and if it is true it must be impossible to give a naturalist definition of them all. It would be a mistake to suppose that what was indefinable could not be known, because it might be known by direct apprehension of what it was like, that is, yellow. It must further be borne in mind that Moore's theory was applied only to one of the senses of "good," that one in which it signified good in itself. A person who held Moore's view on this might well accept a naturalistic definition of some other sense of "good," for example, instrumentally good.

Moore held that we could see directly (by "intuition") that what had certain empirical qualities must also have the quality of goodness (or badness), but he called the quality itself "non-natural" so as sharply to differentiate it from qualities which were themselves empirical. "Ought" might similarly be regarded as signifying a non-natural relation. Opposed to this is any view which regards ethical terms as standing for a quality observable in introspection or a causal property. Moore called the confusion of good with any such property the "naturalistic fallacy." No doubt there have been many writers in whom it was a fallacy, since they implicitly assumed or committed themselves to such a definition of good without being clear what they were doing, but since Moore's work the doctrine of naturalism has been deliberately reasserted by people who were well aware of Moore's position, and this conscious assertion of naturalism, even if held mistaken, should not be described as just a confusion or fallacy.

The advantages of a naturalist theory are that it provides an empirical basis for ethics and assimilates it to the natural science which represents the modern ideal of knowledge and that it avoids the need of appealing to intuition* in ethics. It has also been widely felt that it is extremely doubtful whether we can detect in ourselves any awareness of the alleged indefinable quality of goodness, but it would be easier to claim that we had such an awareness of the distinctive notion signified by "ought" and a theory which took ought as fundamental could be non-naturalistic as well as a theory which thus took good.

The main general objections to naturalism in ethics are as follows: (1) If naturalism be true, ethics should be an empirical science and its conclusions should then be capable of establishment by simple observation or empirical generalization, but this is not at all the method one follows in order to arrive at ethical conclusions. (2) In regard to any particular naturalist definition offered of right or good, it seems plain that it would not be self-contradictory to assert that something was right or good and yet deny that it conformed to the definition, so the definition cannot give what is meant by "right" or "good." (3) "Ought" is essentially different from "is" (though perhaps inferable from what is), but naturalism would reduce all ought-propositions to propositions about what is, that is, propositions about the actual attitudes of people or about the kinds of empirical things which are good. The only alternative to naturalism is not Moore's; many thinkers would say that both sides have a false assumption in common, namely, that the function of what we call moral judgments is not to give us information about the properties (natural or non-natural) of the real but to do something quite different, namely, express a practical attitude (emotive theory). The chief difficulty about such a theory is to reconcile it with the degree of objectivity we have to admit in ethics and the fact that we do not merely express an attitude in moral judgments but claim to have good reason for it, but very many philosophers are seeking a middle ground between these rival theories.

See **Descriptivism; Ethics; Metaethics.**

R. B. Perry, *General Theory of Value,* 1926, and the earlier philosopher David Hume, *An Enquiry Concerning the Principles of Morals,* 1751, are among the best examples of a naturalistic ethics. For criticisms of naturalism, see A. C. Ewing, *Definition of Good,* 1947, ch. 2; R. M. Hare, *The Language of Morals,*

1952, ch. 5; G. E. Moore, *Principia Ethica,* 1903, ch. 1, B. For a criticism of Moore's attack on naturalism, see G. C. Field, *Moral Theory,* 1921, ch. 5.

A. C. EWING

Nature *see* **Natural Law; Natural Rights; Orders**

Necessity
Several views of necessity are relevant to ethics. Logical necessity and metaphysical or ontological necessity are obviously important. For example, Reinhold Niebuhr contended that the doctrine of original sin* should be interpreted as meaning that sin is inevitable but not necessary, on the grounds that necessity would undermine moral freedom and thus moral responsibility (*see* **Sin(s); Free Will and Determinism**). Appeals to necessity are also important in morality and law, where they are invoked to explain, excuse, or justify conduct that would otherwise be wrong. Although necessity is sometimes conflated with self-defense, they are not identical since necessity may be invoked even though no identifiable agent is guilty of threatening one's life or goods. One paradigmatic situation is the lifeboat on the high seas when jettisoning or eating some passengers is claimed to be necessary. In one famous case of cannibalism (*Regina* v. *Dudley and Stevens,* 1884, 14 Q.B. 273), the judge held that "it is not correct . . . to say that there is any absolute or unqualified necessity to preserve one's life." This sort of necessity has long been rejected by most Christians, for example, when they discussed the well-known Stoic case of the board of Carneades—what should a person do when the only available plank after a shipwreck cannot support both his neighbor and him? In contrast to the Stoics, Ambrose (*On the Duties of the Clergy*), among others, held that the Christian should sacrifice himself for his neighbor. But when the survival of several neighbors or even the society is threatened, matters may not be so clear, and some Christians, e.g., Reinhold Niebuhr (*see* **Realism**), have argued that violence in various forms may be the "lesser of two evils" and even "necessary evil." It may be necessary for agents to accept "dirty hands"* and even incur guilt*. The language of necessity implies that agents have "no choice" and that some action, such as war or indiscriminate bombing, is thus justified or at least excused.

But the language of necessity obscures the specific value choices that are in fact being made. A society can and perhaps in some contexts should choose to surrender its political autonomy or yield some of its territory without war; the term "necessity" appears to give weight and finality to a judgment that, after all, is based on a calculation that certain means are necessary to achieve certain ends. Even if those ends cannot be achieved without means that are ordinarily considered immoral, there is still room for debate about whether both those ends and those means are necessary (*see* **Ends and Means**). Hence caution is in order in making and accepting appeals to necessity; even when a society has its back against the wall and has no other means to preserve itself from imminent destruction, the language of necessity may obscure more than it illuminates.

A. Donagan, *The Theory of Morality,* 1977; K. E. Kirk, *Conscience and Its Problems,* 1927; A. W. B. Simpson, *Cannibalism and the Common Law,* 1984; M. Walzer, *Just and Unjust Wars,* 1977.

JAMES F. CHILDRESS

Negligence
There are various ways in which people may act without thinking what they are doing; they may be tactless, inconsiderate, or absentminded. One such lack of thought is carelessness. "Negligence," which is more commonly used in legal than in ordinary language, is usually defined by lawyers as legally culpable carelessness. Carelessness, or negligence, is a failure to give thought or to pay attention to the risks inherent in one's actions and to take the appropriate precautions against these risks. This failure of attention may appear either in the manner in which one does something, as when someone shows carelessness, or negligence, in driving, or in the very commission or omission of the deed itself, as when through carelessness someone drives too near the middle of the road or omits to sound the horn on a corner. But an instance of carelessness, e.g., failing to sound the horn, is not an effect of carelessness, e.g., killing a pedestrian. One's carelessness might, fortunately, have no effects; but it could not be without an instance.

Each kind of task has its peculiar mistakes, blobs, muffs, errors, accidents, dangers, and pitfalls. Because attention to these risks in what one does may be necessary to ensure the successful doing of it, carelessness, or negligence, is something one ought not to show; it is something necessarily blameworthy. Yet because lack of care is not intentional, neither common sense nor the law blames the careless, or negligent, offender as harshly as the intentional offender.

What is done from carelessness need not be done from ignorance either of what one is doing or of its nature; I know that I did not sound my horn on rounding the bend and I know that not to sound my horn in such circumstances is dangerous. But I am negligent insofar as my failure to sound my horn was a failure to give my attention to the risks involved in my driving and to take the proper precautions against them.

As well as the lack of care that may be displayed in the commission of particular illegalities, modern law takes account of what is known as an independent tort of negligence. In such a tort it is immaterial whether what is done was due to lack of thought or to ignorance, incompetence, mistake, or even deliberate intent. What matters is that the offender has neglected a definite duty of care, for example, to use lights when driving at night or to fence in dangerous machinery.

See **Intention; Responsibility.**

A. R. White, *Errands of Liability,* 1985, ch. 7.

ALAN R. WHITE

Neighbor

Because of its use by Jesus when, highlighting Lev. 19:18, he stated the two great commands (Mark 12:28–34 and parallels), the term "neighbor" has become customary in discussion of Christian duty to other people. Its characteristic appearance in the singular ("thy neighbor," not "others") focuses attention on the specific case. Love is to be for *this* person in his or her individuality rather than for the human race in general. The Lucan version of the command, with the appended parable of the good Samaritan (Luke 10:25–37), made this even more striking: the neighbor is the one who acts for good precisely where there is no normal obligation. With original reference to the fellow Jew, the definition of the neighbor was a subject of intense controversy in the time of Jesus. His teaching opens the gate as wide as possible.

From this beginning, the word has become the common Christian term for speaking, in ethical contexts, of the status of other people in relation to oneself, and so of the claims that they exercise.

See **Jesus, Ethical Teaching of; Love.**

Art. *"plēsios,"* *TDNT* VI, 1968; V. P. Furnish, *The Love Command in the New Testament,* 1972.

J. L. HOULDEN

Neo-orthodox Ethics *see* Modern Protestant Ethics

Neoplatonism

A philosophical movement of late antiquity which originated in the teaching of Plotinus (205–c. 269). It represents the culmination of the 1st- and 2nd-century revival of Platonism which, in the thought of such writers as Albinus, Atticus, and Plutarch, had created an eclectic philosophy that grafted varying elements of Stoic and Aristotelian thought onto the Platonic stem. Plotinus, working on the problems engendered within this broad tradition, produced a new philosophical synthesis which was at once an integrated picture of the cosmos and an analysis of human experience informed by a strong mystical vision.

Plotinus's career as a teacher began in his fortieth year, when he gathered a circle of disciples at Rome. Only after the age of fifty did he begin to produce the series of essays— intended simply for circulation among his pupils—which Porphyry (c. 233–c. 305) collected and arranged topically in six sets of nine: the *Enneads.* In these closely written, unrevised pieces Plotinus sets out his interpretation of the teaching of Plato.

The ultimate ground and source of all being—itself "beyond being" and hence beyond description or comprehension—is the "One" of the first hypothesis of Plato's *Parmenides,* which Plotinus identifies with the "Good" of the *Republic.* From this transcendent first principle, by a kind of automatic overflow, there derive three "hypostases" in which its unity and goodness are successively, and ever more dimly, imaged. Each of these hypostases represents a level at once of being, of value, and of knowledge, and each is continuous with its neighbors. The first—*nous,* i.e., "Intellect"—embodies both Aristotle's Prime Mover and Plato's realm of Forms or Ideas. It is that intuitive contemplation which, in knowing itself, knows all things in one: a realm of light and life in which the subject and object of knowledge can be distinguished only notionally. From Intellect there derives the second hypostasis, Soul, which, because it subsists at a lower level of being, cannot grasp all things in one. At the level of Soul, therefore, the subject of knowing sees its world one thing at a time, in succession and separately. Hence with its appearance time and space, as well as individuation, come into being. The lowest level of being and knowing is that of Nature (*physis*), Soul's offspring; and its power of contemplation is so reduced that it grasps the truth of itself only by giving rise to an external image of itself which dances on the face of formless matter the corporeal world. The outflow of being from the One, then, is a movement from unity to multiplicity, from perfect self-possession to the point where being knows itself only as outside itself. At the same time, each of these levels is a level of being, and hence of goodness. Even the corporeal world is a derivative reflection of the One, and to be honored as such.

In this scheme, the human person has its normal conscious existence at the level of Soul. Nevertheless its being and action touch and include the levels above and beneath it. In one direction it functions at the level of Nature even while—in another, higher dimension of its selfhood—it shares the life of Intellect. This picture of human nature provides the foundation of the Neoplatonic ethic, whose basic imperative calls for the particular soul's realization of its highest nature as contemplative intelligence. Obedience to this imperative entails an inward conversion of the soul from Nature's obsession with the external, corporeal image of itself, and an ascent by way of intellectual training and exercise (*askēsis*) to the intuitive life of Intellect. The virtuous soul, therefore, purifies itself of attachment to worldly affairs and fleshly pleasures in order to move inwardly to the highest level of life of which it is capable: that of the impassive contemplation of intelligible reality in its integrated wholeness. And from time to time, in moments of ecstasy, the soul may experience its ultimate identity with the transcendent One.

Plotinus's successors systematized and elaborated his picture of reality. Beginning with the Syrian Iamblichus (d. c. 330) and culminating in the work of Proclus (c. 410–485) at Athens, they also contrived a revision of the religious sense of his teaching. Where Plotinus had emphasized intellectual discipline and contemplation (*theōria*) as the soul's way to self-realization, these thinkers stressed ritual and magical techniques (*theourgia*) for bringing the soul into the presence of the Divine. In part this shift of emphasis was occasioned by a desire to make of Neoplatonism the systematic theology of paganism, which was now fighting for its life within the Christian empire. It is also attributable, however, to a loss of Plotinus's essential optimism—his sense of a given, natural continuity between soul and the divine sphere of Intellect.

At its best and at its worst, Neoplatonism was a pagan philosophy. Many of its prominent exponents (and notably Plotinus's immediate disciple, Porphyry) were openly hostile to Christianity. It was in Neoplatonist circles that the emperor Julian nourished his hope for a revival of traditional religion. Nevertheless this philosophy was an intellectual resource for Christians as well as for pagans. In the East, its influence can be discerned in the writings of Gregory of Nyssa—and above all in the thought of the 6th-century theologian and mystic who wrote under the pseudonym of Dionysius the Areopagite. In the West, Neoplatonism touched Christian thinking through the converted philosopher and rhetorician C. Marius Victorinus Afer (fl. 355), whose writings against Arianism influenced Augustine of Hippo, and through Augustine himself, for whom Neoplatonism was the intellectual means of his conversion to Christianity. It became in the end the principal intellectual vehicle of the Christian mystical tradition.

See **Augustinian Ethics; Mysticism and Ethics; Platonic Ethics.**

A. H. Armstrong, *An Introduction to Ancient Philosophy,* 1947; E. Bréhier, *The Philosophy of Plotinus,* 1958; J. Dillon, *The Middle Platonists,* 1977; Plotinus, *The Enneads,* tr. S. MacKenna, 3rd ed., rev. B. S. Page, 1962; Proclus, *The Elements of Theology,* ed. and tr. E. R. Dodds, ²1963; R. T. Wallis, *Neoplatonism,* 1972.

R. A. NORRIS, JR.

New England Transcendentalism

A liberal religious, philosophical, ethical, and literary movement that arose in reaction to the limitations of orthodox and Unitarian Christianity in the 1830s. Ralph Waldo Emerson (1803–1882) was the central figure in the movement, but with him were associated a number of other young Unitarian ministers, including George Ripley, Frederic Henry Hedge, James Freeman Clarke, and William Henry Channing. Theodore Parker was also related to Transcendentalism, though his position blended certain Enlightenment and transcendentalist views. All of these men had studied at Harvard College and Divinity School. Orestes A. Brownson, who lacked the advantage of much formal education, belonged to the movement while in the Unitarian phase of his spiritual pilgrimage, which later led him to Roman Catholicism. A number of others who were to make their mark in the world of literature—chiefly Margaret Fuller, Bronson Alcott, and Henry David Thoreau —were members of the Transcendental Club, which customarily met in Emerson's study in Concord.

Unitarian thought was strongly rooted in the Enlightenment tradition and in Lockean philosophy. To Emerson and the others, that position was too cold, too narrowly rational, too negative. Influenced by various streams of idealism—Platonic, Neoplatonic, and German classical or essentialist philosophy as mediated by Carlyle and Coleridge—the transcendentalists rejected authoritarian patterns in thought and religion to stress the intuitive approach to truth. Their name came from the fact that they believed in an order of truths that transcends the sphere of the external senses. Some of the ministers resigned their posts, as Emerson had done in 1832, but others, including Clarke, Hedge, and Parker, remained in the ministry. Emerson, after travels abroad in which he met Carlyle and other leaders of thought, became a lecturer and an author, reaching a wide public through his tours and writings. In *Nature* (1836), the main outlines of his transcendental philosophy are set forth; some of his best-known essays, such as "Self-Reliance" and "The Oversoul," popularized the transcendentalist gospel.

A central belief of the transcendentalists was in the immanence of God, i.e., the nearness of the divine. This view underlay their strong differences with Unitarianism at several points, for they denied a sharp antithesis between nature and the supernatural, between natural and revealed religion, between Christianity and non-Christian religions. The transcendentalists also presented a more optimistic doctrine of human nature than was then current, for they stressed the native capacity of humans to apprehend spiritual truth by intuition. The more extreme among them, especially Emerson and Parker, denied that Jesus had any final authority: he was to be seen as a remarkable man but not divine in any other sense than all could be. When Emerson stated his views in the famous "Divinity School Address" of 1838, he was accused of infidelity by many Unitarian leaders. Some of the more conservative transcendentalists, like Clarke and Hedge, did have a more positive assessment of historic Christianity, yet rejected classical Christological views and traditional doctrines of the atonement.

The social ethics of the transcendentalists were predicated on the belief that everyone had the divine reason within. They affirmed the existence of a rational order that all can know directly and intuitively. Resolutely devoted to democracy and freedom, the transcendentalists were radical reformers in the church and society of their day, active in many such social crusades as those against war, alcohol, economic injustice, and slavery. Brownson was especially forthright in his social views; in his *Boston Quarterly Review* (1838–1841) he expressed the radical reformist side of the movement. More moderate was Brook Farm, a communitarian experiment under transcendentalist auspices that was expected to provide an example of a social utopia. Ripley resigned his parish in 1841 to guide the experiment, but by 1845 it became a Fourierist Phalanx before dissolving.

Transcendentalist influence spread into Unitarianism despite resistance to it, contributing to the theologically leftward drift of that denomination. Emersonian ideas were also appropriated by the harmonial "new thought" and "divine science" movements in the later 19th and early 20th centuries.

W. R. Hutchison, *The Transcendentalist Ministers: Church Reform in the New England Renaissance,* 1959; P. Miller (ed.), *The Transcendentalists: An Anthology,* 1950; S. Paul, *Emerson's Angle of Vision: Man and Nature in American Experience,* 1952.

ROBERT T. HANDY

New Testament Ethics

Just as the ethical teachings of Judaism presuppose the faith of the OT, so the ethical teachings of the NT are incomprehensible apart from the faith which underlies the latter. Taken as a whole, biblical morality is so closely related to the worship of one sovereign and righteous God that the biblical writers seldom distinguish clearly between ethics and faith or between ethics and religion. Throughout the scriptures morality is rooted in religious faith, and the latter is always understood as including a moral demand because God is apprehended as righteous will.

The characteristic features of NT ethics, then, can be adequately understood only in the context of the basic convictions of Christian faith as the latter finds expression in the various writings of the NT. The attempt has frequently been made to extract certain of the ethical maxims of the Gospels from their religious setting and to assume that they have a universal applicability; it is evident, however, that the ethical teachings are themselves altered in the process, for it is the underlying religious faith which both determines the distinctive content which these teachings have in the Gospels and provides the distinctively religious motivation for fulfilling them. New Testament ethics does have points of contact with nonreligious ethics, but the former cannot be reduced to the latter. Jesus was not primarily a teacher of morality, but the prophetic perception of moral possibilities and moral claims was inseparable from his apprehension of God's nature and will. That which is distinctive in the ethic of Jesus is determined by the particular quality of his faith in God and his conviction about God's relationship to humanity and the world. Moreover, the ethic of Jesus cannot be adequately understood either as an ethic of duty or as an ethic of aspiration after certain goods or values, although it contains elements both of duty and of aspiration. Rather, the ethic of Jesus and the ethics of the NT as a whole are best understood as an ethic of human *response* to the divine action in the establishment of the promised kingdom and in the person and work of Jesus.

The teaching of Jesus in the Synoptic Gospels. In view of the diversity—despite the underlying unity—of ways in which faith and morality are understood in the NT, one cannot properly speak of *the* ethic of the NT; one must speak instead of the variety in NT ethics represented by different strands in the NT, including the teachings of Jesus in the Synoptic Gospels and the ethics of the early church. The central theme of Jesus' message was the announcement that "the kingdom of God is at hand" (Mark 1:14), and this proclamation of the nearness of the kingdom was accompanied by the summons to repentance and obedience to the divine will (discipleship). In his teachings concerning the will of God, Jesus drew upon the ethical teachings of the OT, including both the law and the prophets, but he went beyond these in that he intensified, radicalized, and universalized the ethical demands of Judaism. He extended the Mosaic prohibitions against killing and adultery to include the attitudes of anger and lust (Matt. 5:21–22, 27–28). He radicalized the traditional demand for forgiveness by making it unlimited (18:21–22) and replaced the principle of retaliation—"an eye for an eye and a tooth for a tooth"—with the injunction to turn the other cheek (5:38–39). Similarly, he universalized the commandment of neighbor-love by extending it to include one's enemies (vs. 43–48). Jesus' ethic differed from that of the OT and of Judaism, moreover, both in the close relationship which he saw between love for God and love for one's neighbor and in the absolute priority which he gave to love* in relationship to all other virtues.

Jesus' ethic may be characterized as an "ethic of the kingdom of God"* in the sense that it describes the rule of God which will prevail when his kingdom is fully established (*see* **Eschatological Ethics**). But this ethic is not intended only for life in the future age when evil has been completely overthrown and presumably there will be no more occasion to turn the other cheek or go a second mile after one has been forced to go the first mile. Neither is it merely an "interim ethic"* (Schweitzer) intended only for a short interval between the proclamation and the imminent advent of the kingdom. The content of the ethic of Jesus is not fundamentally conditioned by the expectation of the nearness of the end. On the contrary, it represents the perfect will of God who is even now acting to establish his kingdom and who, through Jesus' own ministry, summons humanity to repentance, to trust in God, and to obedience to God in the present age. The ethic of Jesus is an ethic of grace*, and the moral demands which he makes are both demands and possibilities which arise out of his understanding of God's grace, which is manifest in the giving of the kingdom. The radical nature of the divine grace and love impose upon those who would enter the kingdom the demand for wholehearted trust in God, unlimited forgiveness, and unselfish concern for the neighbor in need.

While the ethical teachings of Jesus are frequently cast in the form of law, it is evident from the Gospels that Jesus did not prescribe answers to moral problems in the fixed, rigid way in which the Pharisees did. Indeed, he rejected the legalism* of the Pharisees because of its inevitable tendency to issue in spiritual pride and also because it placed greater importance upon the letter of the law than upon human need. Jesus fulfilled the law, but he did so by being faithful to the intent of the latter rather than to its precise wording. On the whole, instead of speaking in terms of generalized ethical maxims and laws, he characteristically illustrated the kind of action which was required in terms of parables and specific demands which were laid upon particular individuals and especially upon his disciples in view of the crisis created by the coming of the kingdom and his own peculiar relationship to it.

While Jesus' ethic represented the fulfillment of the law in the sense noted above, it was neither legalistic nor purely contextual. To reduce Jesus' ethic to the demand for "radical obedience" (Bultmann) to God is to make his moral teaching excessively individualistic and existential; it is to empty his ethic of its richness which it has in the Gospels—his teaching about grace and forgiveness, the importance of attitudes and other virtues in addition to obedience (e.g., trust, humility, love, gratitude), and the setting of his ethic in a new community of his followers. The God whom Jesus summoned his followers to obey was the God of Abraham, Isaac, and Jacob; he was the God who had made himself known in a concrete way in the history of Israel through the law and the prophets. It was this God who even now was acting to establish his kingdom and whose will is to be done "on earth as it is in heaven." The specific content of the divine will must be continually discerned anew in relationship to the needs of the neighbor; but the ethical teachings of Jesus, as well as the law and the prophets, are indispensable guides and directives for the Christian, pointing the latter to the will of God which transcends any formulation of that will in terms of an unexceptional law other than the love commandment.

The ethic of Jesus also differed from many other types of ethics in the sanctions* to which he appealed. While it is true that he sometimes appealed to eschatological sanctions of rewards and punishments*, this was not the fundamental sanction for his ethic. As Wilder points out, the eschatological sanction was a formal and secondary appeal; moreover, it was basically a mythological representation of the consequences of accepting or rejecting his call for repentance* and discipleship*. The essential sanction for Jesus' ethic was the religious-prophetic appeal to gratitude*, to obedience*, to the desire to be children of the heavenly Father. His ethic is an ethic of trustful, joyful acceptance of the divine grace and love and a humble, grateful, and wholehearted commitment to the will of the "Lord of heaven and earth" who has taught people to call upon him as their Father. Participation in the divine grace is its own reward. The acceptance of forgiveness*, the overcoming of human estrangement and alienation from God, and the joy of perfect fellowship with the Father in the kingdom—these are the true rewards of faith* and obedience.

The ethics of the early church. When we turn from a consideration of the ethic of Jesus as this is portrayed in the Synoptic Gospels to an analysis of the ethics of the early church as this is reflected in the remainder of the NT, we find here also a variety of motifs and emphases. In general, however, the ethics of the early church was shaped not only by the teaching and life of Jesus but also by his crucifixion and resurrection and by the gift of the Holy Spirit to the church. Taken together, the cross and the resurrection were the climactic events in the disclosure of God's redemptive grace; they symbolized the forgiveness of sin and the "new creation" which was already coming into being in the community of believers (the koinōnia*, the New Israel). The revelation of God's love in the death and the resurrection of Christ called forth the response of faith and love for the neighbor for whom Christ died: "Beloved, if God so loved us, we also ought to love one another" (1 John 4:11). "God shows his love for us in that while we were yet sinners Christ died for us" (Rom. 5:8). The love of God sustains the believers; they in turn are admonished to "abound" in mutual love (1 Thess. 4:10, ASV) and to continue the ministry of reconciliation which Christ has entrusted to the church (2 Cor. 5:14–21). So close was the relationship between a living faith in God and love for the neighbor that the former spontaneously expressed itself in the latter (1 Cor. 13; Gal. 5:6; cf. 1 John 4:20).

As the early Christians sought to be obedient to Christ, they were faced with the necessity of interpreting his teachings and applying them to a variety of new situations. Some attempted to turn his teachings into a new legalism; others tended to reject all forms of discipline and moral rules in the name of their newfound freedom. In opposition to such tendencies the writers of the NT on the whole recognize the authority of Jesus' ethical teachings without turning them into a system of casuistry*. This was true, as we have seen, of the authors of the Synoptic Gospels. Apart from Jesus in his confrontation with the Pharisees, Paul is the outstanding advocate of Christian liberty in the NT; but he also clearly warns against the subversion of liberty into license. Those who believe in Christ have been freed from sin, but to be free from sin means to be slaves of righteousness, i.e., slaves of God (Rom. 6:18–22). Christ has called his followers to freedom, but to be free from the law means to be bound to Christ and to one another in mutual love and service (Gal. 5:13). Those who live by the Spirit ought also to walk by the Spirit (Gal. 5:25). While believers are no longer bound by the law, the law remains good and serves as a guide to the will of God in daily life. For Paul, the entire law is summarized in the commandment of neighbor-love (Rom. 13:8; Gal. 5:14). For the Fourth Evangelist, also, Jesus' ethical teaching is summarily included in the commandment to "love one another" (John 13:34–35). The writer of this Gospel calls this "a new commandment," and Jesus' love for his followers is made the norm for their own mutual love (v. 34).

While the other writings in the NT do not purport to preserve Jesus' ethical sayings themselves to the same extent as the Synoptics, the words of Jesus are frequently reflected in their moral exhortations. This is particularly evident, for example, in the letters of Paul and in Acts. It is apparent, moreover, that the early church continued to recognize the validity and the authority of Jesus' ethical teachings after the hope of an immediate end of the present age had waned. Not only did the writers of the NT appeal to Jesus' ethical sayings, however, in their own moral exhortations, but they also appealed to his personal example. Christians were summoned to be imitators of the life, death, and resurrection of Christ (see **Imitation of Christ**). Thus, they were encouraged to be faithful even to martyrdom. Since they were now already made new creatures through God's reconciling action in Christ (symbolized, for example, by baptism), they were exhorted to live as the new persons which they in actuality already were—forgiven, reconciled, set free, made new. Moreover, the appeal to believers to be imitators of Christ was not limited to the exhortation to imitate in their own lives the redemptive action of God in Christ; more particularly, it included also a call to imitate the virtues of Jesus in the daily round of living (1 Cor. 11:1; 1 Thess. 1:6; 1 Peter 2:21–23). Paul's letters, for example, are filled with exhortations to imitate Jesus' love, meekness, gentleness, humility, patience, forbearance, generosity, and mercy as well as the generally self-giving quality of his life.

While both the words and the pattern of Jesus' own life remained normative for the early Christians, it became increasingly difficult to rely exclusively on these for ethical guidance in the NT church. Indeed, they could not be made a blueprint for Christian conduct without violating the very spirit of Jesus' teaching and his openness to the divine will and the neighbor's need. Following a long struggle within the church between the Judaizers, on the one hand, and such defenders of liberty from the law as Stephen, Paul, and even to a certain extent Peter, the NT church recognized that obedience to Christ was dependent upon the gift and guidance of the Holy Spirit. The Spirit was given, not to isolated individuals, but to the community of believers (John 14:16–20, 26; Acts 2:1–4; 1 Cor. 12:4–13). Moreover, the Spirit is represented in the NT— especially in the farewell discourses of the Fourth Gospel (John 13–17) and in Paul—as having a strongly ethical quality and not primarily as an ecstatic power. Thus Paul gives a catalog of virtues which he calls "the fruit of the Spirit" (Gal. 5:22–23) and makes love the criterion of the Spirit's presence and activity (1 Cor. 13). In a word, the ethic of the NT church may be described as a *koinōnia** ethic, i.e., as the ethic of a community which had been called into being by the action of God in Christ and which looked finally to the Spirit rather than to law or tradition for moral guidance.

In the early church the dominant attitude toward civil rulers was that of obedience to the rulers as deriving their authority from God (Rom. 13:1–2; 1 Peter 2:13–14). In cases of conflicts between the commands of the state and the commands of God, however, Christians were admonished to obey God rather than temporal rulers (Acts 5:29; cf. Mark 12:7) and to endure persecution with patience and faith (Rev. 13:10). According to Paul, the barriers between slaves and free persons and also between men and women have been broken down in the Christian fellowship, for all have been made one in Christ (Gal. 3:28). Celibacy* and marriage* are both understood as gifts. Paul's reservations about the latter are based upon his eschatological expectations rather than any ascetic depreciation of sexuality (1 Cor. 7:25–31) (*see* **Social Ethics**).

The body of each marriage partner should be at the disposal of the other except perhaps by mutual agreement for a limited season for prayer (1 Cor. 7:3–5). In contrast to the writings of Paul, the other letters in the NT generally reflect a more conventional attitude toward relationships within marriage, admonishing wives to be subject to their husbands. In the early church, as in the teachings of Jesus, there were also strong warnings against the dangers of wealth and injunctions to share with those in need.

Finally, it remains to be pointed out that neither in the ethic of Jesus as this appears in the Gospels nor in the ethics of the NT is there any explicit concern with the role of Christians in the transformation of society at large. In part, this is due to the expectation that God would soon intervene in history to overthrow evil and establish his kingdom; hence, there was little time remaining for the reformation of society by human action, and indeed the latter seemed unnecessary. In part, the absence of concern with social reform generally was also due to the cultural situation in which the early Christians found themselves: they constituted an extremely small portion of the population, and they lived in an authoritarian society in which they had no effective political or economic power.

Yet, despite the fact that the NT is not directly concerned with social ethics* in the sense of participating in the struggle for social justice, a strong basis for such a concern is implicit in the NT understanding of God's sovereignty, his righteous will, his grace, and the commandment of neighbor-love. As Christians have come to exercise a greater responsibility* in society and as their understanding of the extent to which human capacities and needs are socially determined has increased, these elements of their faith have caused them to join in the struggle for social justice out of love for the neighbor and as an act of obedience to God who is the Creator and the Judge even while he is the Redeemer of humankind.

See **Bible in Christian Ethics; Eschatological Ethics; Household Codes; Imitation of Christ; Interim Ethic; Jesus, Ethical Teaching of; Johannine Ethics; Kingdom of God; Love; Old Testament Ethics; Neighbor; Parenesis; Paul, Ethical Teaching of; Sermon on the Mount.**

C. H. Dodd, "The Ethics of the New Testament" in *Moral Principles of Action,* ed. R. N. Anshen, 1952, pp. 543–558; V. P. Furnish, *The Love Command in the New Testament,* 1972; and *Theology and Ethics in Paul,* 1968; J. L. Houlden, *Ethics and the New Testament,* 1973; T. W. Manson, *Ethics and the Gospel,* 1960; G. H. Marshall, *The Challenge of New Testament Ethics,* 1947; R. Schnackenburg, *The Moral Teaching of the New Testament,* ET 1965; H. Windisch, *The Meaning of the Sermon on the Mount,* ET 1951.

E. CLINTON GARDNER

Nihilism

What this term suggests philosophically fits only the dictum attributed to Gorgias, an Athenian teacher of rhetoric of the 5th century B.C.: Nothing exists, and if it did it could not be known. In fact the term is used (very little in English) as a condemnatory label for a theory supposed by the critic to imply the undermining of certainty or truth (e.g., skepticism), the impossibility of metaphysics (e.g., phenomenalism), or the denial of either objective moral standards or generally accepted moral convictions. The only writer who used it of his own theory seems to have been Nietzsche, to indicate his need to destroy traditional moral notions in order to set up radically new ones. In the latter part of the 19th century it was a name for the political reformism of a mixed lot of Russian radicals, and popularly for the violent ideas and practices of a minority of these.

T. E. JESSOP

Noncognitivism see Metaethics

Nonconformist Conscience

The term originated in the last years of the 19th century and first appeared in print in the correspondence columns of *The Times* in connection with Captain O'Shea's divorce of his wife (November 17, 1890) on the ground of her adultery with the Irish political leader Charles Stewart Parnell. On the Sunday following the court finding, Hugh Price Hughes, Methodist preacher and Christian philanthropist, speaking in the name of English Nonconformists publicly denounced Parnell's immorality and called for his resignation. The result was that the Irish politician was deposed by his party and disappeared from political life.

The force, of which Hughes was the mouthpiece, had been at work many years before this public scandal. Nonconformists are English Protestants who refuse to conform to the patterns of belief and action of the established church of England. The Nonconformist conscience was rooted in Puritanism and revealed itself in the positive aims of nonconformity which were heard in the repeated calls for liberty of conscience, the right to worship without state interference, and equal opportunities for all.

In the Industrial Revolution the Nonconformist conscience was the moving spirit behind the constant pleas for integrity, justice, and compassion. Proof of this is seen in the number of journals that commenced publication at this period—*The Nonconformist, The Christian Weekly*. The Unitarian editor of the *Manchester Guardian* was also an advocate of the same opinions. In the social life of England the best practical example of the Nonconformist conscience was the founding of the Salvation Army, and the same influence was also at work in the beginnings of the British Labour Party in 1893.

The present century, however, has seen a waning of its power except for the champions of Sunday observance*, total abstinence (*see also* **Temperance**), and anti-gambling (*see* **Gambling**) campaigns. Its last advocate was probably the Baptist preacher John Clifford, who led the movement for "passive resistance" to the Education Act of 1902 because of its supposed injustice to Nonconformists. It was largely due to his influence that the unionists lost the 1906 election. However, the continuing British preference for democracy, liberty of speech, and equal rights for all are in no small measure the outcome of the once-vigorous Nonconformist conscience.

C. Binfield, *So Down to Prayers: Studies in English Nonconformity, 1780–1920,* 1977; H. L. Cocks, *The Nonconformist Conscience,* 1943.

S. J. KNOX

Noncooperation see Civil Disobedience; Conscientious Objection; Cooperation with Evil; Resistance

Nonmaleficence

The word "nonmaleficence" means not harming or injuring others, and the principle of nonmaleficence establishes the duty not to harm* or injure others, or impose the risks* of harm on them, at least not without compelling justifications for doing so. This duty is part of the bedrock of social morality, and in many ethical theories (e.g., W. D. Ross and John Rawls) it is considered to be stronger, *ceteris paribus,* than the duty to assist or rescue others. It is expressed in the maxim from the Hippocratic tradition (*see* **Hippocratic Oath**) of medicine, *Primum non nocere*—"First of all [or at least], do no harm." And it is one component of love*.

See also **Beneficence; Homicide; Resistance.**

JAMES F. CHILDRESS

Nonresistance see Resistance

Nonviolence see Civil Disobedience; Conscientious Objection; Pacifism; Resistance; State

Norms

Norms are guides to being and doing, particularly guides to types of action that are right or wrong, obligatory or permitted (*see* **Adiaphora; Duty; Obligation; Right and Wrong**).

Norms that refer to character* and traits of character, such as virtues* and vices*, are discussed more fully elsewhere, and this article will focus on norms for actions (see **Act, Action, Agent**). The language of norms is general and encompasses such other language as ideals, laws, standards, principles, and rules. But the choice of language is not itself theologically or morally neutral; for example, the language of law* presupposes a different conception of morality than the language of ideals or even the language of norms (see **Law and Gospel**). The distinctions among these concepts are only rough; for example, although "principles" and "rules" are often used interchangeably, they are sometimes distinguished on the grounds that principles are more general and foundational (Solomon) and rules are more specific and derived.

One model of ethical deliberation* and justification* recognizes tiers or levels: (1) particular judgments in situations; (2) rules; (3) principles (see Beauchamp and Childress; Solomon). Often an agent appeals to rules and to principles to justify particular judgments in situations. However, the relation between the tiers or levels is more dialectical, and rules and principles may be modified because of convictions about particular judgments that do not appear to be adequately accounted for or justified by the principles and rules. In approaches to ethics that emphasize principles and rules (contrast **Situation Ethics**), there is more agreement about the importance and the identity of some principles and rules than there is about their foundations—e.g., whether divine command*, natural law*, or social contract*—and than there is about their implications for particular judgments (see **Applied Ethics; Casuistry**). Thus, there would be widespread agreement about many of the principles and rules discussed in this volume, such as love, respect for persons, beneficence, nonmaleficence, fairness, justice, truthfulness, and fidelity. However, there are disputes about why these norms are important and what they imply for practical judgments, particularly when they appear to come into conflict with each other. The application of principles and rules, especially in conflict situations, requires attention to both their meaning (see **Interpretation**) and their strength or weight.

What is the strength or weight of a rule? Is it absolute, prima facie, or relative? If a rule is absolute, it cannot be overridden under any circumstances and it has priority over all other rules with which it might come into conflict (see **Absolutes, Ethical**). But if several rules are defended as absolute, it is necessary to work out the boundaries of those rules in order to avoid conflict. If, however, a rule is prima facie binding (see **Conflict of Duties** for a discussion of prima facie), there is always a strong moral reason for acting in accord with that rule, but this reason may not always be decisive. Even though the rule is always morally relevant, it may sometimes yield to stronger rules. Finally, if a moral rule is construed as relative, it is a mere maxim or rule of thumb that illuminates but does not prescribe what ought to be done. Even a situationist such as Joseph Fletcher admits that moral rules drawn from tradition* can function in this third way to offer advice about decisions; but they cannot bind conduct because they only summarize what others have found to be expressive of love or productive of utility.

The connection between the weight and the meaning of rules can be illustrated by two examples. First, if the commandment in the Decalogue* reads "You shall not kill," it is more plausibly viewed as prima facie rather than absolute, for the Hebrews admitted killing in self-defense, punishment, and war. If, however, it reads, "You shall not commit murder," it can be taken as absolute, but the difficult task of moral interpretation* would focus on which killings are to count as murder (see **Homicide; Life, Sacredness of**). Second, if a lie is defined as intentionally telling a person what one believes to be untrue in order to deceive him or her, it is implausible to hold that it is absolutely wrong to lie. If, however, a lie is defined as intentionally deceiving a person who has a right to the truth, it could be viewed as absolutely wrong, but all the important "exceptions" could be brought under the determination of who has a *right* to the truth (see **Truthfulness**). A would-be assassin would not have a right to information about a potential victim's location. These approaches are also connected with theological convictions and interpretations of moral experience (see **Dilemma; Dirty Hands;** see also **Casuistry**).

The charge of legalism* does not apply to every appeal to norms in morality, and it may not even apply to conceptions of morality that recognize some absolute norms, particularly since those absolute norms may have "exceptions" built into them. Furthermore, some moral principles, such as love and respect for persons, and some moral rules, such as the prohibition of murder, cruelty, and rape, may be absolute, while others may be prima facie, and still others may be only rules of thumb. One difficult and controversial question is what strength or weight should be assigned to different principles and rules. Some of the major disputes in Christian ethics focus on whether and when priority is to be given to deontological norms (*see* **Deontology**) and to consequentialist and teleological norms (*see* **Consequentialism; Teleological Ethics**), since the most defensible ethical theories, whether religious or secular, include the intrinsic quality of actions as well as their ends and consequences (*see* **Ends and Means**). Finally, the practical application of principles and rules is not mechanical since it presupposes discernment* and prudence*.

Norms offer other "oughts" than those of obligation* or duty* (or, correlatively, rights*). For example, some norms identify ideals of moral life and action to which we ought to aspire (*see* **Aspiration; Excellence; Imitation of Christ**). The life of self-sacrifice might be viewed as an ideal from the standpoint of natural law*; hence, it might be viewed as praiseworthy rather than obligatory. This aspect or level of Christian morality has been expressed in Roman Catholic thought by the distinction between counsels* of perfection and precepts, a distinction rejected by the Reformers, who also rejected the idea of works of supererogation*. But even within a Reformation perspective, it is possible to distinguish morally praiseworthy from obligatory acts without viewing them as good works* that somehow increase one's merit* before God. Some Christian ideals obviously include traits of character*, such as virtues* to be developed and vices* to be avoided.

Another fundamental dispute about norms concerns whether they are natural or revealed and how human beings can apprehend them (*see* **Divine Command Morality; Discernment; Intuitionism; Morality and Religion, Relations of; Natural Law; Bible in Christian Ethics; Tradition in Ethics**; *see also* **Evangelical Ethics; Fundamentalist Ethics; Modern Protestant Ethics; Modern Roman Catholic Moral Theology**). In addition, there are questions about how human beings can

live up to norms, particularly in view of original sin* (*see* **Grace; Holiness; Righteousness**).

See also **Casuistry; Christian Ethics; Love; Situation Ethics.**

T. L. Beauchamp and J. F. Childress, *Principles of Biomedical Ethics,* ²1983; C. E. Curran and R. McCormick (eds.), *Readings in Moral Theology, No. 1: Moral Norms and Catholic Tradition,* 1979; P. Ramsey, *Deeds and Rules in Christian Ethics,* 1968; W. D. Solomon, "Rules and Principles," *EB,* 1978.
                                    JAMES F. CHILDRESS

Nuclear Power *see* Energy; Environmental Ethics; Future Generations, Obligations to; Technology

Nuclear Warfare

The term refers to the use, or plans for use, in warfare of either of two types of weapons, fission and fusion, according to any of a variety of tactical and strategic conceptions.

The earliest nuclear weapons were fission devices with yields (explosive power) measured in kilotons of TNT. These were treated in accord with assumptions and practices already developed for aerial bombing with conventional high explosives. World War II saw the development of two rival concepts of air power: one, called "tactical," had as its mission the support of ground troops in contact with the enemy; the other, called "strategic," had the mission of attacking support for the war among enemy civilians. In practice, strategic air power meant the bombing of targets that might or might not have had a genuinely military support function. The Japanese cities Hiroshima and Nagasaki, against which atomic bombs were used in 1945, were described at the time as "mixed" (civilian and military) targets; yet strategic bombing concepts allowed the direct targeting of civilians alone for purposes of destruction of the enemy's will to fight.

The postwar development of nuclear strategy followed as a direct development of the concept of strategic air power. Some commentators (cf. Brodie) stressed the discontinuities between nuclear and conventional weapons, while those involved in strategic planning stressed continuity: nuclear weapons, considered principally in terms of their blast effect, were regarded simply as larger and more efficient means toward an end already determined in an age of dependence on conventional high explosives. The development of fusion devices, with yields measured in megatons, not kilotons, of TNT did not alter this direction of policy. Supporting factors were the small number of nuclear weapons available in the early years of the nuclear age, which implied reserving them for "high-value" targets; and the large radius of destruction of each weapon; both these factors, together with the assumptions of strategic air power, led to a nuclear strategy based on countercity targeting. This meant that nuclear weapons would likely never be used except in an all-out war, but it also meant that any war in which nuclear weapons were employed would thereby become an all-out war.

A step in a different direction was taken when battlefield nuclear weapons began to be developed and deployed in the 1950s. Their deployment by American forces in NATO was matched by decreases in personnel and in conventional strength, implying that any Soviet attack in Europe would be met with a nuclear defense. Now nuclear war might be "limited" war, contained within the theater of land combat.

The concept of limited nuclear war was further developed by influential authors in the late 1950s and early 1960s. By this time the USSR also had substantial countercity strategic nuclear capability, enhancing the idea of a strategic "stalemate." An all-out nuclear attack would imply all-out response and total mutual destruction. To avoid this, three related concepts were put forward: limited war (the most general); graduated deterrence, implying a sliding scale of nuclear use in war; and counterforce targeting, a move away from the prevalent counterpopulation strategy. All three reflected a return to more traditional military principles such as economy of force and engagement with the enemy's military power; they also held the promise of fighting nuclear war by just war principles (cf. Ramsey, 1961, 1968).

With these developments the essential dimensions of subsequent discussion were established. Nuclear war continues to be discussed in terms of the counterpopulation-counterforce dichotomy, and the idea of limited nuclear war continues as a challenge to strategic dependence on what has come to be called "mutual assured destruction." Within the idea of limited nuclear war is a further distinction between limited "strate-gic" war (one-at-a-time strategic strikes) and limited "tactical" war involving the use of tactical/theater nuclear weapons within a discrete geographical area.

Christian thought has divided sharply on the question of nuclear war. A minority of Christian ethicists, including Ramsey and some Catholic authors, have argued that ideas such as limited war and counterforce targeting, together with technological improvements (reductions in the yield and collateral radiation effects of nuclear weapons, and enhanced accuracy of delivery systems) have opened the possibility that nuclear war may be fought according to the moral standards of just war tradition. A more widely held opinion, however, regards the idea of limited nuclear war as illusory and "war-fighting" plans involving nuclear weapons as dangerous. On this view, the only possible moral use for nuclear weapons is deterrence, and even this is suspect.

See **Just War; Deterrence.**

J. C. Bennett, *Nuclear Weapons and the Conflict of Conscience;* 1962; B. Brodie, *The Absolute Weapon,* 1946; L. Freedman, *The Evolution of Nuclear Strategy,* 1981, 1983; R. E. Osgood, *Limited War,* 1957; P. Ramsey, *War and the Christian Conscience,* 1961; *The Just War,* 1968; U.S. Catholic Conference, "The Challenge of Peace," 1983.

JAMES TURNER JOHNSON

Nuclear Weapons *see* Deterrence; Disarmament; Just War; Nuclear Warfare; Pacifism; Peace; War

Nullity

A declaration of nullity in regard to a marriage* establishes that there has never been a true marriage, whatever may have appeared to be the case, and however long the parties may have lived together. Various reasons, such as defective consent* or other impediments, may make a supposed marriage null. Nullity must be clearly distinguished from the Roman Catholic act of annulment, in which the pope dissolves the marriage bond in certain cases.

HERBERT WADDAMS

Oaths

Many Christian bodies have interpreted Matt. 5:33–37 as a total prohibition of all oaths and have forbidden their members ever to take an oath in any circumstances. The Roman Catholic and more general interpretation of the passage is that it forbids unnecessary, promiscuous, and frivolous swearing (*see* **Cursing/Swearing**). The Church of England in Article 39 interprets it this way and expressly authorizes the taking of an oath before a magistrate.

An oath may be either a solemn affirmation of the truth or a solemn declaration of an intention to do this or that. To say under oath what one knows to be untrue is to commit the grave sin of perjury. It is a grave sin to swear to do something without the intention of doing it or without in fact doing it. The binding nature of an oath is roughly the same as that of a vow* and is terminated in the same ways and for the same reasons.

See **Affirmation.**

R. C. MORTIMER

Obedience

Christian tradition glorifies obedience. In the OT God's people, often disobedient, are required to hear and obey. In the NT *obedient* love is emphasized more, not less. The Son obeys the Father even to death (e.g., Heb. 5:7–10). Full trinitarian doctrine builds obedience into the being of God.

This is filial, not political obedience; responsive, not external; yet contrary to today's ideals. It has tended to foster hierarchical notions of human relations (though it could encourage equality before God). Moralists today, with totalitarianism in mind, oppose obedience to ethical *autonomy**, not to rebellion. When the obedient spirit is deplored, characteristic Christian ethics seem repudiated. But if Christian obedience is allegiance and not subservience, then (since the worst is the corruption of the best) pseudo-religious oppression and capitulation can truly be understood as aberrations.

See also **Authority; Dissent; Freedom.**

P. Baelz, *Christian Obedience in a Permissive Context,* John Coffin Memorial Lecture, 1973; R. Harries, *The Authority of Divine Love,* 1983; H. Oppenheimer, *The Character of Christian Morality,* ²1974.

HELEN OPPENHEIMER

Objectivism

For objectivism, *see* **Ethics.** For opposition to objectivism, *see* **Emotivism; Relativism in Ethics; Subjectivism, Ethical.**

Objectivity *see* **Ethics; Metaethics**

Obligation

Often used interchangeably with "duty"* in moral and legal discourse. However, it is sometimes distinguished from duty on the grounds that obligations involve special relations and presuppose voluntary actions, such as making promises* or contracts*, receiving benefits (*see* **Fairness/Fair Play; Gratitude**), and harming or wronging others (*see* **Restitution**), whereas duties rest on status, stations, and roles in institutions. Both obligations and duties impose "oughts" that oppose contrary desires and inclinations (*see* **Duty**).

R. B. Brandt, "The Concepts of Obligation and Duty," *Mind* 73, no. 291, July 1965, pp. 374–393.

JAMES F. CHILDRESS

Octogesima Adveniens *see* Official Roman Catholic Social Teaching

Official Roman Catholic Social Teaching

Since the pontificate of Pope Leo XIII (d. 1903) there has existed in Roman Catholicism a body of official teaching on social issues. Papal encyclical letters addressed to the whole church have often been the vehicle for such teaching, but the official teaching includes less authoritative papal statements, as well as documents from Vatican Council II and the International Synod of Bishops. The most significant of these statements, especially from the earlier period, deal primarily with economic ethics. Leo XIII first addressed these questions in 1891 in his encyclical *Rerum Novarum,* which dealt primarily with the rights of the worker. Subsequent documents were often issued on the occasion of the anniversary of this ground-breaking encyclical. The number of official documents dealing with the issues is great, but the more significant ones include: Pope Pius XI, *Quadragesimo Anno* (1931); Pope John XXIII, *Mater et Magistra* (1961); *Pacem in Terris* (1963); Vatican Council II, Pastoral Constitution on the Church in the Modern World, *Gaudium et Spes* (1965); Pope Paul VI, *Populorum Progressio* (1967); *Octogesima Adveniens* (1971); International Synod of Bishops, *Justice in the World* (1971); Pope John Paul II, *Laborem Exercens* (1981).

These documents thus constitute a totality.

The very nature of authoritative church teaching often commemorating an earlier document emphasizes the continuity in the approach. However, the interpreter must also be alert to recognize the development and changes that have occurred in the course of this teaching. The three most significant aspects of this teaching are the ethical methodology, the content, and the binding force of the authoritative teaching.

Ethical methodology. Pope Leo XIII, who declared Thomas Aquinas to be the patron of Catholic theology and philosophy, employed Thomistic methodology with its emphasis on natural law in his encyclicals (*see* **Thomistic Ethics**). Natural law* is the plan of God as mediated in human nature and human reason created by God. In ethical discussion, two different aspects of natural law should be distinguished—the theological and the philosophical. From the theological perspective, the natural law maintains that the Christian finds ethical wisdom and knowledge not only in scripture and in Jesus Christ but also in human nature as understood by human reason. The early papal encyclicals on labor and social justice appealed almost exclusively to natural law and did not employ distinctively Christian sources of ethical wisdom. The nature of human beings and the nature of the state are the basis for the teaching on the rights of workers and the various roles of labor, capital, and the state in society. *Pacem in Terris* (1963) well illustrates a natural law methodology. The laws governing the relationships involving individual human beings and the state are to be sought in the nature of human beings, where the Father of all things wrote them. John XXIII makes no sustained appeal to Jesus, to revelation, or to Christian love, but only to the order which the Creator has put into the world and which human beings are able to discern in their consciences.

A significant change occurred at Vatican Council II. The Council called for a renewal of all theology, with sacred scripture being the heart of the theological endeavor (*see also* **Bible in Christian Ethics**). The Pastoral Constitution on the Church in the Modern World, *Gaudium et Spes* (1965), laments the gap existing between faith and daily life. The gospel, faith, grace, and Jesus Christ must be more directly related to life in the world. *Gaudium et Spes* understands Christian existence and activity in the world in the light of the mysteries of creation, sin, Jesus Christ, and the future of the kingdom. Subsequent church documents tend to adopt a similar methodology which does not deny the role of human reason and natural law, but tries to integrate them into a broader Christian perspective.

Such a methodological shift also provides a more intrinsic connection between faith and the gospel on the one hand and the struggle for social justice on the other. Before Vatican Council II, the church justified its involvement in the area of social justice because of its obligation to point out the law of God in all areas of life and to help people attain their eternal salvation. In the light of the newer methodological approach, *Justice in the World* (1971) maintains: "Action on behalf of justice and participation in the transformation of the world fully appear to us as a constitutive dimension of the preaching of the Gospel, or, in other words, of the Church's mission for the redemption of the human race and its liberation from every oppressive situation."

The philosophical level or aspect of natural law concerns the understanding of human nature and of human reason. Here too a shift has occurred in these documents which can best be described as moving from classicism to historical consciousness. Classicism tends to see reality in terms of immutable essences and uses a deductive reasoning process, whereas historical consciousness emphasizes historicity, growth, and change and uses inductive reasoning. The classicist approach associated with the earlier documents emphasized the essence of human beings and of the state and deduced universal moral norms from these essences. Perhaps the best illustration is the plan for the reconstruction of the social order proposed by Pius XI in *Quadragesimo Anno* (1931). The pope recognized that society is an organism and called for cooperative functional groups involving all elements in a particular industry—capital, labor, and consumers. These functional organizations, perhaps best described in English as the industry council plan, were to include all individuals in a particular industry and would be quasi-public organizations with quasi-legal rights, thereby setting the necessary policies for a particular industry. Cooperation rather than conflict should be the basic attitude among all those involved in the same industry. These organizations would then be related to other similar organizations on a national level in a hierarchical manner. Not only do later documents abandon such a plan, which was originally proposed for the whole world, but in the last few decades official church teaching has moved somewhat away from the classicism and deductive reasoning behind such proposals. *Pacem in Terris* finishes each of its four chapters with a section on the signs of the times. *Gaudium et Spes* begins its consideration of particular topics not with an abstract definition or essence but with a reading of the signs of the times. Pope Paul VI in *Octogesima Adveniens* (1971) insists much more on historical consciousness: "In the face of such widely varying situations it is difficult for us to utter a unified message and to put forward a solution which has universal validity. Such is not our ambition, nor is it our mission. It is up to the Christian communities to analyze with objectivity the situation which is proper to their own country and to shed on it the light of the Gospel's unalterable words and to draw principles of reflection, norms of judgment, and directives for action from the social teaching of the Church."

Content. The cornerstone of official Catholic social teaching is the dignity and social reality of the individual human being, which later documents refer to as the human person (*see* **Human Dignity; Persons and Personality; Respect for Persons**). The basic value, dignity, and inalienable rights of the individual form the foundation for official Catholic teaching from Leo XIII's defense of the rights of the worker to John Paul II's insistence on the priority of labor over capital. However, one cannot forget that the human being is also social. The social aspect of human beings grounds the recognition that the state is a natural society. Human beings are by nature called to form political society so that in and through the society they can do what individuals alone cannot do, and thus achieve their end and fulfillment. The end of the state is the common good*. There have been some differences of interpretation of the common good in the Catholic tradition, but *Mater et Magistra* (1961) understands it as embracing "the sum total of those conditions of social living, whereby human beings are enabled more fully and more readily to achieve their own perfection." The official Catholic teaching does not see the state primarily as coercive or with purely negative

functions but with the positive goal of striving for the common good, which ultimately redounds to the good of the individual. Obviously there is an important role for authority in the state, but authority is not understood primarily and only as coercive.

Such an understanding gives a positive but limited role to the state*. Within society, the state must respect, uphold, and promote the rights of the individual and of the family, which is the basic unit within society. In addition, there are many other intermediate associations that must function in a properly organized society, such as educational, fraternal, and religious organizations.

Leo XIII's approach to the rights of the worker well illustrates how such a view of the individual and of the state functions. The worker as a human being has a right not to be treated as a mere commodity in the production process. Among the rights of workers is the right to a living wage, because in the present industrial situation a wage is the only way in which workers can provide for themselves and their families. To secure their rights, workers have the further right to join labor unions (*see also* **Labor Movements**). The state itself has the right and the obligation to interfere to bring about justice and to make legislation in this regard. "Whenever the general interest or any particular class suffers or is threatened with harm, which can in no other way be met or prevented, the public authority must step in to deal with it." *Rerum Novarum* (1891) admits, however, there are limits on state intervention: "Law must not undertake more, nor proceed further, than is required for the remedy of the evil or the removal of the mischief."

Quadragesimo Anno explains the principle of subsidiarity*, which should govern the role of the state in society. The state should offer help (*subsidium*) to individuals and to intermediate associations. It should not take over what individuals and smaller groups can do, but rather should provide those functions which it alone can do—directing, watching, urging, and restraining. This principle thus tries to recognize and encourage the legitimate freedom and responsibility of all who make up political society. John XXIII in *Mater et Magistra* upset some conservative Catholics by insisting on the fact of socialization, or an increase in the complexity of social relationships, which calls for a greater intervention of the state even in some areas that are of intimate concern to the individual.

The primary virtues guiding life in political and economic society are social charity* and especially justice*. The Catholic theological tradition recognizes three types of justice: commutative justice, based on an arithmetic equality, governs one-on-one relationships; distributive justice, based on proportionality, need, and abilities, governs the distribution of goods and of burdens to the individual members of society; legal justice governs the individual's relationship and obligations to the society. *Quadragesimo Anno* introduced the term "social justice," but commentators cannot agree on the exact meaning of the term. Many understand social justice as a new species of justice which directs the individual to seek the common good with emphasis on organized action as the way to achieve that goal.

These general approaches were applied to the different problems that arose in the course of time. As mentioned, *Rerum Novarum* and *Quadragesimo Anno* dealt primarily with the rights of workers and the proper relationships involving labor, capital, and the state. John XXIII in *Mater et Magistra* emphasized the need for justice for those in agricultural work. *Pacem in Terris* and *Populorum Progressio* (1967) emphasized that the social problem has now become worldwide and cannot be considered only within the confines of one country.

In the course of the last century there have been significant developments in official Roman Catholic social teaching on a number of issues. Contemporary Catholic teaching stresses human rights* and the freedom*, equality*, and participation of all in determining life in society. However, such approaches were foreign to Leo XIII. In *Rerum Novarum,* Leo did stress the rights of workers and their need to participate in unions, but in many encyclicals on the political order his primary target was individualistic liberalism with its overemphasis on human freedom. Liberalism* taught the individual's independence from God and God's law, and failed to recognize the social nature of the human being. In addition, in Leo's time the vast majority of people were illiterate and needed to be governed by the rulers. As the 20th century developed, the Catholic Church saw its primary opponent no longer as liberalism but as totalitarianism (*see* **Totalitarian State**). Against fascism* and Nazism on the

right, but even more against socialism and communism on the left, the popes began to stress not only the duties and obligations of individuals, but also their freedom and their rights. Earlier popes were, in general, indifferent about the concrete form of government, but Pius XII definitely favored democracy*. *Pacem in Terris* contained the first in-depth elucidation of human rights within the Catholic tradition. The tensions involved in the developing tradition toward a greater emphasis on freedom and human rights came to a successful settlement when Vatican Council II affirmed the principle of religious liberty as a human right of all—a position that had not been acceptable to Roman Catholicism before that time (*see also* **Persecution and Toleration**). *Octogesima Adveniens* recognized that in the new context in which human beings are better informed and better educated, two aspirations persistently make themselves felt—the aspiration to equality and the aspiration to participation, two forms of human dignity and human freedom.

The understanding of the individual and of the state serves as the basis for the Catholic dissatisfaction with both the individualism* of liberalistic capitalism* and the collectivism* of socialism* and communism*. The condemnation of socialism was somewhat stronger than that of capitalism. *Quadragesimo Anno,* for example, recognized the existence of a moderate socialism which mitigated the emphasis on class struggle, violence, and the condemnation of all private property, but Pope Pius XI concluded that socialism which remained truly socialism cannot be reconciled with the teachings of the Catholic Church. Catholic Church teaching and Vatican diplomacy strongly emphasized anticommunism in the Cold War period following the Second World War. However, intellectual discussion, a willingness to work somewhat with Communist regimes, and contact on a practical level between some Christians struggling for social justice and some Marxists changed the picture. In *Pacem in Terris,* John XXIII signaled an opening to the left by distinguishing between false philosophical teaching and historical movements that have originated from such teaching. Meetings and discussions with such movements might even be opportune and productive at the present time. Later, *Octogesima Adveniens* recognized a certain splintering within Marxism and also pointed out different levels of expression of Marxism. Christians can never accept atheism or materialism, but some Christians do appreciate the Marxist concern for social justice and see in it an apt sociological tool for analyzing social and political realities (*see also* **Liberation Theology**).

Leo XIII strongly defended private property* as a right of the individual human being and saw ownership of some private property as the solution for the oppressed worker. Some would judge, however, that he did not adequately address the abuses of private property by the rich. Subsequently the tradition, without denying the individual aspect of private property, gave greater importance to the social aspect, rooted especially in the God-given destination of the goods of creation to serve the needs of all. *Populorum Progressio* cited the teaching of *Gaudium et Spes* on the universal destiny of the goods of creation to serve the needs of all and maintained, "All other rights whatsoever, including those of property and of free commerce, are to be subordinated to this principle." *Laborem Exercens* (1981) taught that the ownership of the means of production, whether in the form of private or public ownership, must serve labor and thereby make possible the first principle of the economic order, namely, the universal destiny of goods and the right to common use of them.

Pacem in Terris and especially *Gaudium et Spes* dealt with peace*, war*, and disarmament*. The teaching recognizes the need of all to work for peace and the importance of international structures to bring about peace. Operating within the context of the just war* theory, *Gaudium et Spes* recognizes as a last resort the right to go to war but only in self-defense. The way in which such a defensive war is waged is morally limited by the principle of discrimination*, which forbids acts of war aimed indiscriminately at the destruction of civilian populations, and by the principle of proportionality*, which requires that the good to be achieved is not outweighed by the evils involved in the war. The arms race is condemned as a treacherous trap which affects the poor to an intolerable degree and is not a safe way to preserve peace. Multilateral disarmament is a moral obligation for all. The Council document for the first time conditionally recognizes the pacifist approach within the church and also calls upon the state to recognize conscientious objection* (*see also* **Pacifism**).

Binding force. In these documents the Roman Catholic Church's official teachers claim the right and the duty to state authoritatively the principles of the natural law, but also realize they do not have competency in economics or politics as such. In the technical theological terminology, these documents belong to the authoritative or authentic, non-infallible hierarchical church teaching (*see* **Magisterium**). Commentators often speak of the principles that Catholics are bound to accept, which remain at a somewhat general level, and the concrete applications and judgments that are left to the consciences of the individuals. Some contemporary Catholic theologians now recognize the possibility of dissent* from such authoritative church teaching in general and would logically have to apply the same principles in the area of social teaching. In practice, the principles contained in these documents tend to be somewhat general and allow some diversity of interpretation and judgment within the Catholic Church on specific questions. Some commentators stress the more evolutionary aspects of the social teaching, whereas others emphasize long-term radical solutions. The official teaching calls for a change of structures and a change of heart, but the exact importance of both is debated among Catholics. The principle of subsidiarity can be interpreted differently either to enhance or to limit the role of the state. The principles of the just war also allow different possible interpretations.

J. Y. Calvez and J. Perrin, *The Church and Social Justice: The Social Teaching of the Popes from Leo XIII to Pius XII, 1878–1958,* 1961; R. L. Camp, *The Papal Ideology of Social Reform: A Study in Historical Development, 1878–1967,* 1969; J. Gremillion (ed.), *The Gospel of Peace and Justice: Catholic Social Teaching Since Pope John,* 1976; D. J. O'Brien and T. A. Shannon (eds.), *Renewing the Face of the Earth: Catholic Documents on Peace, Justice and Liberation,* 1977.

CHARLES E. CURRAN

Old Age see **Aged, Care of the**

Old Testament Ethics

Within the society of ancient Israel there was considerable diversity. Historically, one of the main components of that society was the pastoralists who entered the land, either as peaceful infiltrators (e.g., the patriarchs) or as armed invaders (e.g., those who came in under Joshua). Some of these retained their pastoralist life-style; some settled and became peasant landholders. They eventually incorporated into their national community the agrarian and urban population which they found already in the land.

Thus we have a society composed of pastoralists, peasants, and city dwellers, each group with its own life-style and not all having the same historical roots or traditions. Each of these groups makes a contribution to the ethics of the OT, and that ethics is to an extent created by the tension between the groups, their different traditions and their different needs. Developments that might readily have taken place in a more thoroughly urbanized society were resisted by pastoralists and peasants whose position gave them different perspectives and sometimes gave them an interest in preserving more traditional values.

We do not, therefore, expect OT ethics to be totally homogeneous and consistent, especially when we consider that the OT contains material from a period covering at least a thousand years. We find, for instance, that some very "primitive" notions of sin and guilt occasionally find expression. Some of these apparently primitive features have evidently been reinterpreted, whereas others persist without such reinterpretation.

The OT literature draws no sharp distinction between ethics and religion. In concerning itself with right conduct it does not distinguish between right *moral* conduct and right *religious* conduct. The law indiscriminately mixes commands on moral matters with commands on religious matters (as, e.g., the Decalogue* does), and in the prophetic writings likewise religious offenses such as idolatry are frequently condemned virtually in the same breath as social injustices (Ezekiel provides some especially striking examples, e.g., Ezek. 22). Hence, in speaking of OT ethics at all we are imposing a distinction of which no ancient Israelite would have been conscious.

Demands for right conduct are, not surprisingly, regularly grounded in religion. Yet, not all OT writers make their appeal to religious authority or religious motives in the same way. In the Pentateuch the basis of Israel's relationship with God is the covenant*. The conditions of the covenant are enshrined in the law, and Israel is committed to obe-dience to the law in order to maintain its side of the covenant relationship (*see* **Mosaic Law**). The same understanding may be presented in rather different perspective by saying that obedience is Israel's fitting response to what God has done for it, in making Israel his people and in delivering it through his mighty acts of salvation; notably through the exodus. Israel's obedience is thus an expression of the people's love for God, responding to the love he has shown to them. This view of the matter is most prominent in Deuteronomy (see, e.g., Deut. 6).

The prophets (*see* **Prophetic Ethics**) ground their appeals for right conduct in God's demand for righteousness, and they assert his determination to punish *un*righteousness. The prophets show themselves to be very familiar with the traditions of God's saving acts, and they take it for granted that theirs is a special relationship between Israel and Yahweh. But very rarely indeed do prophets earlier than Jeremiah refer to this relationship as a covenant, and only relatively rarely do they appeal explicitly to law.

The wisdom literature*, which is very largely concerned with questions of right conduct, is not very explicit about the basis of its morality. It does say frequently that "the fear of the Lord is the beginning of wisdom," implying that it is the relationship to God which is primary, and that wisdom, which manifests itself in right conduct, proceeds from this. Wisdom, as the wisdom writers appear to understand it, is a matter of acting in harmony with a cosmic order which is "given," and of which God is apparently assumed to be the guarantor. But the sanctions that the wisdom writers threaten are usually pragmatic ones, and the motives to which they appeal are generally those of enlightened self-interest. They do not usually urge God's demand for righteousness, as the prophets do, or appeal to law or covenant. Neither have they much to say about any special relationship between Yahweh and Israel attested by its peculiar history. The wisdom writings' only substantial references to the saving acts of God are in chapters 10–19 of the book of Wisdom and Ben Sira's praise of famous men (Ecclus. 44–50).

Clearly, the covenant and its associated law were not seen by Israelites as the *only* basis for morality. As additional evidence of this we may observe that the patriarchs, and others who lived before the introduction of the law, are assumed to know what God's requirements are and to have an obligation to meet them. Moreover, the OT everywhere takes it for granted that Gentiles, who are outside the covenant, who have not received the Mosaic law and have not experienced the historic saving acts, nevertheless recognize, or ought to recognize, universal standards of behavior. This is implied most strikingly in Amos 1:3–2:3.

These facts, together with the observation that neither the wisdom writers nor the prophets, in appealing to a popular audience, make much explicit reference to law or covenant, suggest that these themes were less decisive for the thinking of the average Israelite than for those who put the OT into its present shape.

What of the *substance* of OT ethics? What were the values by which the ancient Israelite actually lived? In practice, the chief concern in life was the maintenance of the *family** and its integrity. It is true that, if there is a conflict, loyalty to God is expected to come before family (Deut. 13:6–11), but normally this does not arise. Not only as a child but throughout life it is the Israelite's duty to honor father and mother (Ex. 20:12; Deut. 5:16; cf. Ex. 21:15, 17; Lev. 20:9, Deut. 21:18–21; 27:16; Prov. 15:20; 19:26; 20:20; 23:22). To "honor" one's parents meant for the Israelite not only obeying them but supporting them in their old age.

It is worth noting that the mother stands alongside the father as an authority figure (Prov. 1:8; 6:20; 30:17), even though from some points of view the Israelite family and Israelite society appear to be male-dominated. The continuity of the family is normally expressed in the male line, descent being traced through males and property inherited through males. The head of the household is a male, if a senior male is available, though widows and other unattached women may have their own households. It is not common for women to play much part in public affairs, though there is no absolute barrier to their doing so (see, e.g., Judg. 5:4ff.; 2 Sam. 20:14–22; 1 Kings 21:5ff.; 2 Kings 11:1–3; 22:14–20). Woman's sphere is thus primarily a domestic one, but in that sphere her authority is great (Prov. 31:10–31). That women are to be respected, and treated equally before the law, is everywhere assumed in the OT. The statement occasionally made that women were regarded as chattels

is totally without foundation. It rests on a misinterpretation of the custom of making bridewealth payments on marriage. There is no suggestion anywhere in the OT that marriage was seen as involving a purchase of the bride.

One apparent inequality is that men have the right to divorce wives whereas women have no corresponding right to divorce husbands. Our knowledge of OT divorce law rests on a single text (Deut. 24:1–4), and the grounds on which divorce was allowed are ill understood. It is possible that other ways were open to a woman of putting an end to an unsatisfactory marriage.

The *continuity* of the family is all-important, and the right to produce children is accorded a high priority. There is a positive duty to marry, reflected in the divine command of Gen. 1:28. Polygyny is allowed, though in practice it was probably made use of only by the rich and by men whose first wife proved infertile. The levirate law (Deut. 25:5–10) seems designed to protect not only the deceased, by giving him a kind of posthumous right to have children credited to him, but also the widow, by giving her the right to produce children within her late husband's family.

The safeguarding of the family *property** is also given high priority. In theory, land was regarded as inalienable. It was understood that at the conquest the land was divided among the tribes and that the tribes had divided it among their component families. Thereafter the land was supposed to remain in the family in perpetuity. It is clear, especially from the prophets, that this principle was not always honored (e.g., Isa. 5:8; Micah 2:1–2). Various laws and customs were designed to ensure that land sold because of hardship eventually reverted to its proper owners (see, e.g., Lev. 25:8–55, which is concerned both with the institution of the jubilee and with rights of redemption). Here we have an ethical principle that does seem to be rooted firmly in an understanding of Israel's particular history.

Loss of land meant, for the peasant, loss of livelihood, and this could lead to loss of liberty for the family's members through debt-slavery. A high value is placed on liberty. This is natural enough, but the feeling for liberty was probably heightened by the folk memory of Egyptian bondage, and by the exodus tradition which proclaimed it to be the will of God that all his people should be free. The OT law acknowledges that debt-slavery was sometimes inevitable, but the laws are designed to limit its duration and ameliorate its conditions (Ex. 21:2–11; Lev. 25:39–46; Deut. 15:12–18).

Important in maintaining the family were the functions of the go'el (traditionally translated as "redeemer" but perhaps better described simply as "kinsman.") If anyone fell on hard times his go'el was meant to come to his rescue; to avenge him if he was murdered (Deut. 19:4–12; Josh. 20); to redeem his property for the family if he was forced to sell it (Lev. 25:25ff.; cf. Ruth 4:1–4; Jer. 32:6–15), and to redeem his person if he was sold into debt-slavery (Lev. 25:47ff.). The go'el should also stand by a man if he was threatened, especially if he was accused at law. In theory, at least, if a man died childless, the go'el might be expected to marry the widow and raise children by her (Deut. 25:5–10; cf. Ruth 3:9–13; 4:1–13).

After the maintenance of the family the next priority was the maintenance of the community*. It is the duty of everyone, but especially of the wealthy, to support the community's poorer and more disadvantaged members, i.e., both to support them economically and to protect them from injustice (Job 29 is a description of how the ideal rich man functions in his community). The community to whom this duty is owed not only consists of Israelites but includes resident aliens (who were often, in origin, refugees). The duty to support the poorer members of the community in this way is by no means peculiarly Israelite. Other ancient Near Eastern cultures recognized similar obligations.

The leader of society par excellence is the king, and he above all is to be the protector of the rights of the poor and underprivileged. There were strong pressures in Israel at some periods favoring the development of a hierarchical, feudal structure of society, with very autocratic powers being exercised by the king, but there were also strong pressures from some quarters in resistance to such developments. Kings were not immune to criticism (see, e.g., 1 Sam. 15; 2 Sam. 12:1–14; 2 Kings 20:1–7); they did not make laws, only applied the laws, and they had no rights over land, to redistribute it (1 Kings 21). Deuteronomy lays down firm rules governing kingship (Deut. 17:16ff.).

The resistance to the development of a rigid class structure was at least partly successful. That at some periods there were gross disparities of wealth is not in question, but all free persons, including foreigners, were equal before the law (Lev. 24:22; Num. 15:15f., 29), and slaves, too, had their rights safeguarded (Ex. 21:2–11; Lev. 25:39–46; Deut. 15:12–18; cf. Ex. 21:20f., 26f.; Lev. 19:33f.). This is in contrast to some other ancient Near Eastern legal systems under which different social classes did not have the same rights before the law and were often subject to different penalties for the same offense.

A marked feature of OT ethics is what has been called its "worldliness." The good life, as the Israelite sees it, consists in having numerous offspring, in living to a ripe old age, in enjoying the respect of one's fellows, and in acquiring enough wealth to be comfortable and secure. These are very materialistic values and could easily be represented as selfish ones. What sets them all in perspective is the proviso that all these blessings must be justly acquired and justly used. Wealth is not to be gained by squeezing every last drop of profit. The righteous man does not reap his field to its very edges, or gather the windfall fruit of his orchard, or return for the forgotten sheaf (Lev. 19:9–10; 23:22; Deut. 24:19–21). The wealth he acquires is to be used for the support of others, and his influence in society is to be employed in the defense of the weak.

Property is less important than persons. Offenses against the person are consistently treated more seriously than offenses against property. The death penalty, for instance, is never invoked for offenses against property. This again contrasts with some other ancient Near Eastern systems.

Above all, if the pursuit of any of the good things of life, however legitimate, ever conflicts with loyalty to God, the Israelite is expected to put loyalty to God first, whatever the cost. This is the clear message of the book of Daniel, for instance.

The ethical demands of the OT can be summed up under the overarching demand for righteousness*. Righteousness is obedience to God. Righteousness is an expression of love for God, for love inevitably (as an Israelite would see it) expresses itself in obedience. Righteousness is at the same time an imitation of God. Leviticus 19:2 sums up God's demands as, "You shall be holy; for I . . . am holy." God not only demands righteousness in those who serve him but is himself righteous. His righteousness expresses itself not alone in rectitude and fairness but in mercy and grace. It is an expression of God's righteousness that he saves the oppressed, delivers those who are threatened, feeds the hungry and the poor. Those who serve him are expected to act similarly. To love him, to obey him, and to be like him are all synonymous.

It is not, however, true to say that for the OT writers righteousness is *defined* by what God does; i.e., an act is not made righteous by the fact that God does it. There are at least hints in the OT that righteousness is somehow self-authenticating and that in principle God himself might be judged by it. This is the whole basis of the complaint of Job, and is implied in Abraham's argument in Gen. 18, summed up in his rhetorical question: "Shall not the Judge of all the earth do right?"

J. Barton, *Amos's Oracles Against the Nations,* 1980; E. W. Davies, *Prophecy and Ethics,* 1981; W. Eichrodt, *Man in the Old Testament,* ET 1951; J. Hempel, "Ethics in the Old Testament," *IDB* II, 1962; W. C. Kaiser, *Toward Old Testament Ethics,* 1983; H. W. Wolff, *Anthropology of the Old Testament,* ET 1974; C. J. H. Wright, *Living as the People of God,* 1984.

HENRY McKEATING

Omission, Sin of

The sin of omission is the failure to do that which one has a duty* to do. To choose not to act may be a choice of considerable moral import. Omission is not the same as inaction or passivity since it may be psychologically active and intense. Omission connotes deliberateness and decision*; inaction and passivity do not.

The sin of omission receives prominent attention in the biblical theology of sin. In the Bible, it is omission, not commission, that best shows where the heart is. The scribes and Pharisees were excoriated by Jesus not so much for what they did as for what they did not do. "Woe to you, scribes and Pharisees, hypocrites! for you tithe mint and dill and cummin, and have neglected the weightier matters of the law, justice and mercy and faith" (Matt. 23:23). In Matthew's judgment scene, it is the omitters who are condemned, those who did not bring food, drink, and clothing to the needy, and who did not visit the sick and the prisoners (Matt. 25:31–45). This is consistent with the vision of Isaiah: "If you pour yourself out for the hungry and satisfy the desire of the afflicted, then shall your light rise in the darkness and your gloom be as the noonday" (Isa. 58:10).

The sin of omission is prominent in the Bible because the theory of duty and responsibility* is so sweeping. Biblical morality is biased in favor of the poor. Because "the poverty of the poor is their ruin" (Prov. 10:15), we are enjoined to eliminate poverty*: "There shall be no poor among you" (Deut. 15:4). No one will be without "his own vine" and "his own fig tree" (Micah 4:4; cf. Zech. 3:10). We are to make our own the cause of those whom we do not even know, becoming eyes for the blind and feet for the lame (Job 29:14–17). Such a massive commission to activism and social responsibility opens the door to the Bible's salient stress on sins of omission (*see also* **Sloth**).

The distinction between omission and commission is widely discussed in contemporary bioethics*, particularly regarding the difference between hastening death and letting die. Some few authors argue that since it is at times permissible to let persons die, it is *inferentially* moral also to actively induce death. This conflating of omission and commission is ill considered because omission and commission represent different moral and psychological realities (*see* **Double Effect; Euthanasia; Life, Prolongation of**).

Omission and commission differ in the following ways: (1) They differ in their effects. Though omission is not always more benign in its potential psychological effects, the impact on the bereaved is foreseeably different if death is passively allowed or actively induced. Omission and commission in this context would also have differing effects on the medical profession and on social attitudes toward illness and dying. (2) Omission and commission may differ also in their deliberateness, or voluntariness. Both omission and commission involve myriad and distinguishable modes of consent.* The decision not to operate and the decision to give a fatal injection are not volitionally identical choices, no matter how they are evaluated ethically. (3) The notions of agency* and responsibility differ for omission and commission. Agency is diffuse in omission. It is easier to say who did something than to say who did not do but should have done something. Since the sin of omission is a failure to respond to duty, the determination of whose duty and responsibility it is or was has its own special complexity.

The differences between omission and commission show up in the practice of law, which often applies ethical categories. The efforts of various systems of law to cope with problems of omission, seen, for example, in "Good Samaritan" laws, show the infeasibility of collapsing omission and commission into the same moral and human reality. *See* **Sin(s)**.

D. C. Maguire, *Death by Choice,* [2]1984; S. C. Mott, *Biblical Ethics and Social Change,* 1982.

DANIEL C. MAGUIRE

Oppression

The use of power* or coercion*, whether violent or nonviolent (*see* **Resistance**), to constrain another's freedom*, to violate another's rights*, to exploit another (*see* **Exploitation**), or to deny another's just claims (*see* **Justice**).This theme has become a crucial category in politico-ethical and religious interpretation since World War II. Oppression is probably as old as the human species; for example, biblical narrative is replete with stories of exploitation*, including the suffering of Israel under Pharaoh and the later judgments pronounced by the prophets against oppressive practices within Israel (*see* **Prophetic Ethics**). The decolonization that followed the Second World War brought into full view several centuries of oppression by the Western powers (*see* **Colonialism**). The churches had conspired in this exploitation for the most part, but began to break with the established powers by the mid-1960s. The Magna Carta of this new ecclesiastical movement was forged at Medellín in 1968 (*see* **Liberation Theology**). Other movements for liberation have emerged simultaneously in Africa and Asia. In the same period, the women's movement revitalized what has been called the "oldest revolution," forging new lines of attack on sexist exploitation (*see* **Feminist Ethics**).

Perhaps the most significant politico-ethical insights emerging from these movements for liberation are the retrieval of the fully political character of the biblical faith and the awareness that structures of oppression such as patriarchy and anti-Semitism* are interwoven with the moral and spiritual disclosures of the biblical heritage. This consciousness has opened the way for a thoroughgoing integration of sociopolitical analysis with theological and hermeneutical work. Thus the compartmentalization of theological studies is now coming seriously into question, though the established faculties continue to pursue rather fragmented inquiries.

See **Afro-American Religious Ethics; Colonialism; Ecumenical Movement; Exploitation; Feminist Ethics; Genocide; Human Rights; Liberation Theology; Marxist Ethics; Political Theology; Race Relations; Racism; Repression; Resistance; Revolution; Sex Discrimination; Totalitarian State; Tyrannicide; Women, Status of.**

Kim Yong Bok (ed.), *Minjung Theology: People as the Subject of History,* 1981, rev. ed. 1983; E. D. Gray, *Green Paradise Lost,* 1979; G. Gutiérrez, *A Theology of Liberation,* ET 1973.

GIBSON WINTER

Optimism

Optimism is a way of thinking and living that on the one hand affirms the capacity of individuals to improve themselves and the whole human condition, and on the other hand claims that ultimate reality, being under the control of good rather than evil, supports, if not guarantees, this improvement. There are various degrees of optimism, various grounds on which it is affirmed, and several different philosophical and theological frameworks of which it is an integral part.

An extreme version of optimism is expressed in Browning's phrase, "God's in his heaven, all's right with the world." A second extreme version is exemplified in Leibniz's philosophy that because God is all good, all wise, and all powerful he has created this "the best of possible worlds." Both of these fit with the derivation of the word (from *optimus,* superlative of *bonus,* good)—that is, belief that the best is in control. More moderate versions of optimistic philosophy, directly related to belief in progress, are illustrated in the Spencerian evolutionary naturalist and Hegelian Marxist beliefs in the inevitability of progress, and in the Deweyan affirmation that human beings can, by the use of intelligence, i.e., applied scientific knowledge, achieve the enrichment of all human life.

The *grounds* for optimism may be said to

center chiefly on judgments about the nature of humanity, history, and ultimate reality. As a philosophy of life it involves sometimes a belief in the basic goodness of human beings, at other times a more cautious affirmation that they are capable of improvement and of increasingly achieving well-being and happiness. In both the Roman Catholic and evangelical Protestant theologies there have been surprisingly optimistic estimates concerning the human achievement of goodness, always, it must be noted, as a result of God's guidance and grace*. In the former, people's capacity both to perform good works by their own effort and to achieve saintliness with God's help is affirmed; among the latter, one encounters John Wesley's counsel to Christian perfectionism*, and the social gospel* movement, which was certainly optimistic in talking about building the kingdom of God in the future.

Historical grounds for optimism usually involve teleological assumptions—that is, not merely that history has discernible meaning and purpose, but that it is actually moving toward a particular end. The Hegelian and Marxist view is of a patterned historical process moving toward a rational and good end. The Marxist view is Promethean: it sees human beings as capable, like Prometheus, of defying the gods and stealing their fire to provide themselves with the warmth of physical comfort and the light of understanding (see Hegelian Ethics; Marxist Ethics).

In contrast with dialectical materialism, one Christian version holds that God acts and guides within history in such a way that it is moving toward the kingdom of God* and/or toward an eschatological end (see Eschatological Ethics).

Optimism has related the above beliefs about humankind and history to metaphysical assertions. Central among these is the claim, expressed by William James as the essence of all religion, that "the eternal is good." Still more contemporary instances are modern theologians such as Paul Tillich, who, in agreement with classical theology, emphasizes that the ontological ground of being is good. Optimism has appeared within such differing and even conflicting frameworks as that of Herbert Spencer's biologically grounded belief in the inevitability of progress, the writings of the transcendentalist poets, and the Christian theologies indicated above (see also Progress, Belief in).

All varieties of optimism have been criticized and its extreme versions ridiculed on the following grounds: (1) on general grounds of personal experience, namely, that events in the lives of individuals are at best a frightening mixture of good and of very real evil, issuing into despair as well as hope; (2) on the religious grounds that original sin*, though it may be forgiven, leaves the human being always a sinner, capable of incredible cruelty and destructiveness; (3) on historical grounds, citing not only the disasters of two world wars but, much more frightening and urgent, humankind's present capacity and preparation for total destruction. These and similar considerations appear to render the outlook of optimism unwarranted at best, absurd at worst.

Is a Christian necessarily optimistic? Those who say "yes" usually emphasize Paul's statement: "In everything God works for good with those who love him" (Rom. 8:28). Jowett coined the phrase "apostolic optimism," a view that is temporarily pessimistic, i.e., about the actual condition of humankind, but ultimately optimistic, holding that God is the Lord of history. Finally, Jesus' statement, "Be of good cheer, I *have overcome* the world" (John 16:33), is often used as a basis for the qualified affirmation that Christ has already won the victory of good over evil* and so furnished the ground for Christian hope* and joy.

See also Enlightenment; Meliorism; Pessimism.

CHARLES W. KEGLEY

Order

Order, viewed as a structured state of affairs rather than as a command, has been a perennial concern of social ethics* in both philosophical and theological contexts as well as of politics*. According to Thomas Hobbes, anarchy* prevails in the state of nature, where life is "solitary, nasty, brutish, and short." Christian social ethics has traditionally emphasized the need for order—and the threat of disorder—because of its convictions about the universality of sin (see Original Sin; Sin(s); Total Depravity) and God's will to preserve the world from chaos. Thus, order is viewed as a requirement of love*. For example, Paul Ramsey (*Deeds and Rules in Christian Ethics*, 1967) argues that "there will be an inner pressure within acts that seek to be concretely loving also toward order (and not only order so far as it is just) as among the fundamental needs of men." There has been debate about whether order is a good in itself or a conditional good, but it has often received priority in Christian social ethics. When order has been viewed as the primary end of the state*, justice* has received correspondingly less attention.

Emil Brunner (*The Divine Imperative*, 1932, ET 1937) contended that the Christian's first response should always be one of accepting and preserving the existing order, even though the second response may be one of resisting and reforming that order. But even when Christians have recognized the legitimacy of the second response of resistance* or revolution*, they have emphasized the threat of disorder and the importance of establishing another order after the revolution. Order is not only a matter of rational calculation, for it is dependent on forces beyond human control and is construed as a matter of divine providence. This emphasis on order, particularly in Protestant doctrines of the orders* of preservation, has not gone unchallenged in the last twenty-five years. Theologically, G. Wingren has argued that we should attend to God's *ordering* of the world rather than to established orders, and H. R. Niebuhr has held that in all of God's actions upon us, God is creating, ordering (ruling or governing), and redeeming human life; thus, Christians should respond to all of the dimensions of God's actions, rather than to a single dimension such as ordering. Reinhold Niebuhr tried to escape conservatism* through a dialectical relation between justice and order: justice cannot be realized without order, but order cannot survive without justice, which for Reinhold Niebuhr includes both liberty (*see* **Freedom**) and equality*. Liberation theology* and theologies of revolution* hold that the traditional focus on order ideologically obscures the need for social change and limits the options for the realization of justice, liberation from oppression*, etc. Whether they in turn have paid sufficient attention to the need for order and to the structure of particular orders after the revolution is a matter of controversy. For related issues, *see* **Anarchism; Democracy; Institution; Law; Resistance; Revolution; State; Ecumenical Movement; Modern Protestant Ethics; Realism;** for the dangers of assigning priority to order over justice in international relations, *see* **International Order; Peace.**

Order is also important in Christian communities, and the balance between freedom and order requires constant attention and readjustment; *see* **Discipline; Dissent; Ecclesiology and Ethics; Excommunication; Magisterium; Scandal.**

P. C. Kuntz (ed.), *The Concept of Order*, 1968.

JAMES F. CHILDRESS

Orders

In his doctrine of the "two realms" of creation* and redemption, Luther reaffirmed the "sacred secularity" of the ordinary tasks of the common life as those which best meet our neighbors' needs in the service of Christ. He further refined this doctrine with his view of the three "orders" or "estates" of society which provide human beings with divinely ordained bulwarks against sin in the fallen realm of creation. He wrote (*WA* 26, pp. 504f.):

> The holy ordinances and foundations instituted by God are these three: the ministry, marriage, and civil authority. . . . Service in them constitutes true holiness and pious living before God. This is because these three ordinances are grounded in God's Word and command (Gen. 1:28), and are thereby sanctified as holy things by God's own holy Word.
>
> Above and beyond these three foundations and ordinances is the general order of Christian love which constrains us even beyond the boundaries of the three ordinances to serve the needs of our neighbors by feeding the hungry, giving drink to the thirsty, forgiving our enemies, praying for all men on earth, suffering all kinds of evil on their behalf, etc. These are good, holy works.

This means for Luther's social ethic that the earthly kingdom in the "old age" of Adam must be ruled primarily by God's law through human reason. Since most of God's creatures are not numbered among his saints, and because sin persists even in the life of the redeemed, the "fruits of the Spirit" can play only an auxiliary role in governing the world of temporal affairs.

"Faith working through love" (Gal. 5:6)

can nourish a sinful and unjust world only indirectly through the social action of Christians. The church can never directly "christianize" the secular "orders" of politics, economics, education, etc., even though it is essential for loving Christian politicians, economists, and educators to hold society and the state accountable to God's sovereign law by making justice as humane as possible.

Luther's dialectical teaching on the relative autonomy* of the "orders" (free from church-rule yet bound to God-rule) belies those ethical dualists, like the Nazified *Deutsche Christen* ("German Christians"), who have tried to give a "Lutheran" sanction to the "orders of creation" (*Schöpfungsordnungen*) which would permit the "orders" (especially the state) to become absolutely autonomous unto themselves (*Eigengesetzlichkeit*).

To stress both sides of these theonomous but historical "orders"—that they are divinely ordained but also subject to God's law, dikes against sin* but also corrupted by sin themselves—many Protestant theologians now prefer to speak of the Creator's "orders of preservation" (*Erhaltungsordnungen*) or "emergency orders" (*Notordnungen*) or even "mandates of God" (*Mandaten Gottes*).

See also **Lutheran Ethics; Justification by Faith; Order; State; Two Realms.**

WILLIAM H. LAZARETH

Orders of Creation *see* Orders

Ordinary and Extraordinary Means of Treatment
see Life, Prolongation of

Organ Transplantation

The first transplantation of an organ from one human being to another occurred in 1954, when a kidney was removed from one identical twin and transplanted in his brother. Since that time there have been over 40,000 kidney transplants in the USA. Other organs (heart, liver, pancreas, lung, and heart-lung) have been transplanted with varying degrees of success, and tissue transplantation (e.g., cornea, bone, bone marrow, and skin) is also widespread. In addition, blood is commonly transfused, and hormone extracted from pituitary glands can enable dwarfs to grow. Thus, several transplanted organs and tissues can increase a recipient's chances of survival or improve a recipient's quality of life. Rapid progress is being made in the 1980s, particularly with the development of improved immunosuppressive drugs that reduce the rejection phenomenon. Yet the supply of organs and tissues is inadequate to meet the need and demand for transplantation. Enough cadaveric organs exist, but society has not yet found an effective, efficient, and morally acceptable way to obtain them. For example, enough deaths occur in the USA each year under conditions that would permit salvaging so that more transplantable organs would be available than are needed (estimate: 20,000 of approximately two million deaths). And yet in 1982 only 3,681 postmortem kidneys were transplanted in the USA.

There are few religious objections to organ transplantation. Orthodox Jews are opposed to autopsies and to the removal of organs from cadavers, but most Jewish and Christian groups do not oppose the use of living donors of renewable tissue or of nonvital or paired organs (such as a kidney), or the use of cadaveric organs where there has been appropriate consent*. Indeed, it may be an act of love* to donate one's organs before or after death, or a deceased relative's organs, in order to meet a neighbor's needs, whether the neighbor is identified or unknown, and some Christian groups have urged postmortem organ donation. While even a risky premortem donation could be justified by love, it would probably be condemned as suicide* if it would certainly or with high probability result in the donor's death (*see* **Risk**). Within the Catholic context, mutilating surgery (e.g., amputation) was justified by the principle of totality*—sacrificing a part of the body for the welfare of the whole body. This principle was extended to justify a donor's use of part of his or her body in order to benefit another person and also benefit the donor as a whole moral-spiritual person. However, as many theologians have noted, this expanded principle of totality would be dangerous if it reduced the potential donor to a mere part of a larger social whole. The principle of respect for persons* or autonomy* and derivative rules such as privacy* dictate a policy of not removing tissues or organs from a person's body, whether dead or alive, against that person's will even to save someone else's life (though, of course, compulsory autopsies are performed after certain deaths). It is difficult to imagine a sufficiently compelling state interest to warrant a policy of conscription* of organ donors. Relevant religious perspectives also include convictions about the body*, embodiment*, and stewardship*.

Several ethical issues appear in debates about public policies to increase the supply of organs.

First, there is the issue of *cadaver organs.* In both the UK (Human Tissues Act of 1961) and the USA (The Uniform Anatomical Gift Act adopted by all fifty states in the late 1960s and early 1970s) the law allows individuals to determine what will be done with their organs after their deaths and allows the next of kin to donate a dead person's organs unless the decedent previously objected. Furthermore, in both countries brain death legislation was passed to facilitate organ donation (it has not yet been passed in all states in the USA). (*See* **Death, Determination of.**) Yet in both countries there is a shortage of cadaver organs for transplantation, despite the reports of opinion polls that large numbers of people are willing to donate their organs or their relatives' organs after their deaths. Within this policy of express consent, it is possible that vigorous efforts to educate the public and health care professionals about the need and procedures, etc., and to strengthen organizations for organ procurement, would reduce the scarcity. Since it is difficult for health care professionals to raise the subject of organ donation with a grieving family, one proposal is to provide incentives or even require hospitals to set up organ procurement teams and to request organ donations. Other proposals would modify the express consent policy to require individuals to make a decision for or against organ donation or even to presume consent where individuals have not explicitly dissented or objected. Such presumed consent legislation has been enacted in several countries, including Denmark, France, Israel, Italy, Norway, Spain, Sweden, and Switzerland, but no English-speaking country had adopted it by 1984. Yet the ethical objections to a policy of "contracting out" or "opting out" rather than "contracting in" or "opting in" may not be insurmountable, as long as individuals and perhaps their families have a clear right to object and understand that they have this right. Indeed, such a policy could be understood as one of "tacit consent" and might be considered ethically acceptable (see **Con-**

sent). However, a policy of express consent is ethically preferable, because it promotes active generosity and community.

A second ethical issue is that of *living donors* of renewable tissues, such as skin and bone marrow, or nonvital or paired organs, such as kidneys. Living related donors now provide a smaller proportion of the kidneys for transplantation than earlier, and there are now very few cases of living unrelated kidney donors, who provided 14.5 percent of the transplanted kidneys in the USA prior to 1967. The use of cadaver organs should be favored if possible because it avoids risks of morbidity and manipulation and coercion of living donors—e.g., a family may put pressure on a reluctant donor to provide a kidney to another family member. But not using kidneys at all from living unrelated donors may represent unwarranted paternalism* since such a donor's decision may be adequately informed, voluntary, and based on a strong moral or religious sense of love* or compassion*. There is, however, widespread suspicion about the motivation of living unrelated donors who claim to be acting altruistically toward their neighbors in donating organs. Furthermore, the medical profession is reluctant to impose medical risks on one person for the medical benefit of another person since it violates the principle *primum non nocere* (first of all do no harm) and may create the risk of a malpractice suit.

Judgments about the adequacy of a living *related* donor's understanding and voluntariness can only be made in the situation, and professionals should be sensitive to subtle signs of coercion* from other members of a family. Physicians sometimes justifiably provide a "medical excuse" for potential donors under severe pressure to donate. Two classes of living related donors are particularly controversial because their autonomy* is severely limited and even nonexistent in some cases: children (especially preadolescent children) and mentally retarded persons. Because of the limitations on their capacity to give valid consent, it may be unjust to impose the burdens and risks of organ removal (especially kidneys) on them in order to benefit some other member of the family. The counterargument is that children and mentally retarded persons frequently derive significant nonmedical benefits from "organ donation," for example, from the survival of a family member who contributes greatly to the "donor's" well-being and happiness. Some have proposed independent review of such cases to determine whether the heavy presumption against using organs from a nonconsenting person can be rebutted because of significant nonmedical benefits to him or her in the absence of alternative means to save the recipient's life.

A third issue is a more radical proposal to tolerate or encourage a *market* in organs and tissues (*a*) to alleviate the shortage of organs and tissues for transplantation, and (*b*) to respect the freedom* of individuals to do what they want to with their lives as long as they do not harm others. The main rejoinder to the first argument is that there are other effective, safer, and ethically preferable ways to increase the supply of organs. The main rejoinder to the second argument is that individuals are not acting freely but are being exploited when they dispose of their bodily parts in a commercial transaction (*see* **Exploitation**). Opponents also contend that a commercial system would be costly, would drive out altruism*, would be similar to prostitution*, and would reflect, symbolize, or express societal values that are not defensible. In the USA, an earlier market in blood was replaced by a voluntary system, which already existed in the UK, in part because of arguments by Richard Titmuss, among others, that the commercial system, when compared to the voluntary system, was ineffective, wasteful, and dangerous and that it expressed and encouraged nonaltruistic conduct. Despite the opposition to a market in organs, some have proposed incentives for individuals to donate (e.g., tax deductions). It may be instructive to consider where the line should be drawn: coverage of a donor's medical expenses, compensation of a living donor's lost wages, payment for the burial expenses of a deceased donor, etc.

A fourth issue is that of organs from *animals**. Despite futuristic visions of animal farms for organs, at the present transplanting animal organs into humans is considered only as a last resort and a stopgap or bridge to gain time while a human cadaveric organ is sought. Controversy erupted in the USA in 1984 when a baboon heart was transplanted into a young baby. The taboo on interspecies transplantation is difficult to take seriously, apart from immunological considerations, especially when a human life is at stake; after all, animal parts are already being used—for example, pig valves in heart surgery. The moral objection to the sacrifice of animals should be taken more seriously, but for most moral theories, religious or secular, it is outweighed when there is a significant chance of extending human life or reducing pain and suffering.

Finally, organ transplantation appears in the context of decisions about macroallocation (how much of a good should be made available?) and microallocation (who should receive that good when its supply is limited?) in health care. In part, the question is whether there is a right to a decent minimum of health care (as in the USA) or to equal access to health care (as in the UK), and whether this right includes funds for organ transplantation or for artificial organs, such as the dialysis machine and the artificial heart (the former being routine, the latter currently experimental).

See **Bioethics; Health Care, Right to; Life, Prolongation of; Medical Ethics; Sick, Care of the.**

R. Fox and J. Swazey, *The Courage to Fail,* ²1979; P. Ramsey, *The Patient as Person,* 1970; R. Scott, *The Body as Property,* 1980; R. Titmuss, *The Gift Relationship,* 1971. Also see articles on "Organ Donation" and "Organ Transplantation" in *EB* and *DME,* as well as various articles in *JME* and *HCR.*

JAMES F. CHILDRESS

Original Sin

Biblical authority for this doctrine has been found in Ps. 51:5 and Rom. 5:12ff. The latter passage states a causal connection between Adam's sin and our sin, and this connection was defined more closely and linked with the sexual act by Augustine. His argument goes as follows: The church is baptizing infants. Baptism cleanses from sin. Infants have not sinned themselves (Rom. 9:11). Therefore they must have inherited sin. They do this because conceived in the act of sexual intercourse. "That alone was not sinful flesh which was not born of such concubinage" (*On Marriage and Concupiscence* 1.13). What Augustine professes to find wrong in sexual intercourse is that in it the sexual organs are not under the direct control of the will (the same is true of the secretion of the gastric juices when eating). Augustine finds this a consequence of the Fall. Because Adam rebelled against God, his body rebelled against him. That is at any rate true of human sexual organs. It is because they are not like, for example, the arm, in direct control of the will, that human beings find shame in connection with them. This rebellion is transmitted through the act of sexual intercourse and as a result unbaptized infants are excluded from heaven (presumably a test-tube baby would not be). Calvin refused to accept Augustine's exclusion of unbaptized infants from heaven. But the latter's influence on the doctrine of original sin remains as one main, and by no means academic, problem for the church. The church today is to distinguish between the good and the not so good in Augustine's teaching. Over against his clear view of the universality of sin and the need for divine grace must be set his unbalanced view of sex. It must at least be considered whether any sound Christian view of marriage can be framed today without some break with Augustine.

It would, however, be unfortunate if the idiosyncrasies of Augustine's view of sex or the lack of historicity of Gen. 3 were to blind people to the importance and necessity of the Christian doctrine of original sin. It is an attempt to provide a solution to the problem that sin* though universal is not necessary.

All theories of original sin, artificial though some of them are, are attempts to solve this real difficulty. That is why Adam plays in them a central role that he does not play in the biblical teaching about sin. (Jesus and the prophets who speak profoundly about sin do not mention Adam once.) But in theological treatment of original sin Adam inevitably plays a leading part. For he, their common ancestor, is one thing all humans have in common. If in some sense it can be shown they have a share in and—though this is more difficult—a responsibility for his sin, then the problem seems well on the way to solution. In Adam's act all humans sinned and yet since Adam's act was voluntary, there is no necessity about the matter.

The later theology of original sin can be seen as a series of attempts to provide a solution to the causal connection asserted by Paul: Is it that we were all present in Adam's loins and so had a share in his sin? Possibly, but if so, it is not an easy conception, for most of us do not feel responsible for the sins of our more remote ancestors. Is it that Adam acted as the representative of humankind and that we are responsible for his actions as some

(though by no means all) Germans felt themselves responsible for the actions of Hitler? That again is a possible meaning of Paul, who sometimes indulged in this type of group thinking. But again it is a difficult conception, for while it might be argued that the Germans could have done something about Hitler—though plenty will point out that they could not—it is hard to see what we could have done about Adam. Or does it mean that we have inherited Adam's sinfulness? Maybe, but if so, are we responsible for our inheritance as distinct from the use we make of it (cf. the example of people who inherit a tendency to alcoholism)? Or does it just mean that since Adam sinned, everybody has been born into an evil environment and in the end environment gets us all down? Again maybe, and yet all human sin cannot be attributed to environment. One of the earliest and most creditable motives for monasticism was the desire to get away from an evil environment. Yet even in the desert and the cloister men met with temptation.

All these interpretations of the causal connection between Adam's sin and our sin have their obvious difficulties. But they are attempts to find a solution to the real problem arising out of the fact that sin while universal is not necessary. Even more important, they express the conviction that evil is something which cannot be eradicated from human life by social and political measures, valuable though these may be. The evil in life is something like the dent in a burst ball, something which can be got rid of in one place only to reappear in another.

Of modern writers on sin, among the most significant are T. R. Malthus, whose *Essay on the Principles of Population* (1798) while not directly concerned with the subject makes the salutary point that evil is something that cannot be eradicated by social and political revolution. Then there is F. R. Tennant, whose *The Sources of the Doctrine of the Fall and Original Sin* (1903), *The Origin and Propagation of Sin* (1902), and *The Concept of Sin* (1912) were written at a time when sin was an unfashionable topic. Tennant made a sustained effort to correlate the traditional teaching with the fact that human beings have evolved and that moral standards change so that what is sinful action to one generation is not so to a later one. Written earlier but influential later is Kierkegaard's *The Concept of Dread* (1844), one of whose insights has been the recognition that the sins of the flesh and the sins of the spirit are basically the same flight from the *Angst* which is a feature even of the state of innocence. In *Moral Man and Immoral Society* (1932) the young Reinhold Niebuhr faced courageously up to the fact that religion by absolutizing the relativities of the human struggle for power, has sometimes, though not always, served to intensify rather than to ameliorate sin. Niebuhr's *The Nature and Destiny of Man* (2 vols., 1941–43) offers a major influential reinterpretation of original sin. Other important works include G. C. Berkouwer, *Sin* (ET 1971), and Paul Ricoeur, *The Symbolism of Evil* (ET 1967). Emphasis on the social context and dimension of sin appears in liberation theology* and political theology*.

See **Image of God; Innocence; Temptation; Sin(s).**

IAN HENDERSON

Orphans

Children who have lost or have been deserted by *both* parents. The Bible mentions full orphans only once, the fatherless a great deal, and the motherless not at all. From this one can assume that the Hebrews were able to absorb orphans and motherless children into the extended family system, but that the lot of the fatherless child was tied up with that of the widow*.

The numbers of true orphans have always been small and within extended families provision for them was comparatively easily made. The medieval church took a considerable responsibility for the care of orphans and as early as the 6th century the diocese of Trèves accepted all children placed in the church porch. The Second Council of Nicaea (A.D. 787) extended the practice and the first true foundling home was started in Milan in the same year. Most countries have since then set up a variety of hostels of different kinds for the care of parentless children. In England the Foundling Hospital started by Captain Thomas Coram in 1739 was the first of the large institutions. It must be remembered of course that the development of systems of public assistance in most countries gave such authorities responsibility for orphans, and in England the Elizabethan act setting up the Poor Law made specific mention of orphans and charged those responsible for the Poor Law with their special care. Though this responsibility was not always

exercised as humanely as one would have liked, it is arguable that since 1601 more orphan children in England have been cared for by public authorities than by private charity. In 1867 Dr. Thomas Barnardo, who was distressed by the large number of homeless children in London, started a Home of Refuge, financing it from voluntary funds. This started a great national movement for the provision of homes for children; the Nonconformist "National Children's Homes" in 1869 and the Church of England "Waifs and Strays Society" (now the Church of England Children's Society) in 1881. In the USA the Infants Hospital was started in New York in 1868, the Sisters of Charity Foundling Asylum in 1869, and the Infant Asylum in 1871. In spite of the fact that under the Children Act of 1948 the basic responsibility for the provision of children's homes in England (unlike the USA) is now a local authority function, a very large number of children are now being cared for by voluntary societies. In the past, large numbers of children in the care of the big English children's societies were sent to Canada, Australia, and New Zealand as emigrants when they grew up.

The ideal solution to the sad problem of the orphan is, of course, adoption*. This was made possible in England by an act of 1926. Adoption is not, however, suitable for all children and must be rigorously controlled if exploitation is to be avoided. Public provision for orphans now include children's homes, preferably very small homes which are like ordinary houses in ordinary districts, and the boarding out of children with recognized foster parents.

See **Children; Social Service of the Church.**

M. P. Hall, *The Social Services of Modern England*, 1952; J. S. Heywood, *Children in Care*, 1959; M. Hopkirk, *Nobody Wanted Sam*, 1949; D. Owen, *English Philanthropy, 1660–1960*, 1965.

BRIAN RODGERS

Orthodox Ethics, Eastern *see* **Eastern Orthodox Christian Ethics**

Otherworldliness

While the Christian life contains an element of world renunciation, this is a dialectical element that must be held along with world affirmation. Nowadays the expression "otherworldliness" is generally used in a somewhat pejorative sense for an undialectical withdrawal from the world and an excessive preoccupation with the world to come. *See* **Eschatological Ethics; Secularism; Worldliness.**

JOHN MACQUARRIE

Pacem in Terris *see* **Official Roman Catholic Social Teaching**

Pacificism *see* **Pacifism**

Pacifism

Pacifism, which means "making peace," encompasses many different activities because "peace"* itself can be narrow or broad, because "making" involves various positive and negative actions, and because it can be applied to personal, group, or national policies. Peter Brock holds that contemporary pacifism combines "advocacy of personal nonparticipation in war of any kind or in violent revolution with an endeavor to find nonviolent means of resolving conflict." A minimal, negative definition covers a wide range of historical positions: opposition to war* and/or to direct participation in war through military service. Both violent resistance* and revolution* raise somewhat different problems about the Christian's relation to the state and have often been rejected even by Christians who have accepted war and participation in war. They have frequently drawn a sharp distinction between using violence *for* the state and using violence *against* it.

Despite the emphasis on "peace" in several senses in the NT, there is considerable debate about whether the NT is a pacifist document, in part because of ambiguities in Jesus' attitudes toward violent resistance (*see* **Resistance**). Although Jesus' response to the centurion (Luke 7:9) suggested that it was not necessary to reject military service in order to enter the Kingdom of God, many nonpacifists concede that the dominant tendency of Jesus' life and message is pacifist. However, it is clear that Paul and others justified the government's use of the sword, both internally and externally (see Rom. 13:1–7; 1 Peter 2:14). Until A.D. 170–180, there is no direct evidence that Christians participated in military service or that they abstained from such service. For various reasons, including their position in society and their re-

lation to the Roman Empire, it is probable that few Christians were soldiers. In the 2nd century, Celsus criticized Christians for not participating in military service, but there is evidence from A.D. 170–180 that some Christians were in the army. Their numbers increased in subsequent decades, and it appears that soldiers who converted to Christianity were not expected to leave the army. Dramatic changes occurred in the early 4th century with the conversion of Constantine, and by A.D. 416 only Christians could serve in the army. Nevertheless, Roland Bainton's comment is apt: "The age of persecution down to the time [of] Constantine was the *age of pacifism* to the degree that during this period no Christian author to our knowledge approved of Christian participation in battle." (*See also* **Patristic Ethics.**)

These Christian writers had many different grounds for their opposition to participation in war: Rome's persecution of Christians, anticipation of the imminent end of earthly society, suspicion of the world, fear of idolatry and divided loyalties in military service, immorality among soldiers, and aversion to bloodshed. All but the last reason were only contingently connected with military service, and many of them became irrelevant with the conversion of Constantine and the increased role of Christians in the military. Contemporary nonpacifists tend to emphasize all of these reasons but aversion to bloodshed, while pacifists tend to emphasize aversion to bloodshed based on neighbor-love. (There is also debate about whether the early church drew a sharp distinction between the police functions and the military functions of soldiers.)

Even early Christian pacifists offered a "relative justification of war" (Cadoux) as part of their interpretation of the role of government in a fallen world. And in their apologetics, they argued that Christians assumed their fair share of the burdens of social life, including indirect participation in war through their prayers for the emperor. They were part of the *militia Christi* and constituted what Origen called a "special army of piety" and the "salt of the earth" that held the empire together. Even though they avoided direct participation in military service, they rendered a more efficacious alternative service. As threats to the Pax Romana increased, it became harder to justify Christian participation only through prayer rather than through military service, especially under a Christian emperor.

When military service became acceptable for Christians, pacifism was channeled into a higher way of life based on the counsels* of perfection. Earlier there had been a division between the church and the world, now there was a division within the church and among Christians. According to Eusebius of Caesarea, Constantine's bishop and adviser, there were two levels of Christian vocation: lay people could participate in just wars, marry, etc., while the clergy could not participate (by bearing arms) even in just wars, could not marry, etc. The monastic* movement also reflected pacifist tendencies. In addition to distinctions between higher and lower ways of life and between counsels and precepts, other dualistic strategies evolved to accommodate the "hard sayings" of the NT to participation in war: (1) The distinction between actions for oneself and actions for others (e.g., Ambrose, Augustine, and Thomas Aquinas). Even when the church accepted participation in war it continued for a long time to prohibit killing in self-defense. (2) The distinction between attitudes and bodily actions (e.g., Augustine and Luther). According to Augustine, Jesus ruled out *malitia* (hatred), not *militia* (military service). (3) The distinction between private and public actions (e.g., Augustine and Luther). As Augustine developed this distinction, war is just only when it is fought under divine or governmental authorization, and rebellion has no place.

These distinctions did not satisfy all Christians, and during the Middle Ages such groups as the Waldenses and the Czech Brethren were pacifists. During the Reformation, the Swiss Brethren and some other Anabaptists (but not all) were pacifists; for example, the Schleitheim Confession of Faith (1527) rejected the sword as "outside the perfection of Christ." Erasmus, among others, defended humanistic pacifism. Pacifism has been common, but not universal, among the members of the "historic peace churches"—Quakers, Mennonites, and Brethren—and it has attracted such adherents as Leo Tolstoy.

Although any typology will oversimplify the many different versions of religious and secular pacifism, it is possible to identify several major types: (1) *Deontological pacifism* (see **Deontology**) holds that war and/or Christian participation in war is wrong because it violates the commandment against killing (better translated as "murder"), the norm of neighbor-love, the *imitatio Christi*, the requirements of discipleship, the demands of the suffering community in the world, etc. One of the most important contemporary proponents of Christian pacifism is John Howard Yoder, who draws on the broad Christian tradition, as well as the Mennonite tradition, to argue that Christians do not have a duty to make history come out right since it is in God's hands. Stanley Hauerwas also defends pacifism in the framework of Christian narrative, story, and character. This first type of pacifism emphasizes the Christian's witness rather than the consequences of that witness. (2) *Pragmatic pacifism* (see **Consequentialism; Pragmatism; Teleological Ethics; Utilitarianism**) holds that pacifism will work for individuals, groups, and nations and that it will produce a net balance of good over bad effects in the world. It affirms pacifism as a policy and usually presupposes an optimistic view of human nature. (3) *Redemptive witness*, a combination of (1) and (2), holds that pacifism is both right and effective, perhaps through the transformation brought about by unmerited suffering. This position has been defended by some Quakers (see **Quaker Ethics; Resistance**), and it has been vigorously rejected by realists (see **Realism**), such as Reinhold Niebuhr, who sometimes find (1) tolerable and even meritorious because of its representation of Christian love, but who repudiate both (2) and (3) because their claims about effectiveness overlook the reality of sin and evil in the world. (4) *Technological pacifism* —usually *nuclear pacifism*—is very different because it only opposes *modern* wars and not necessarily all of them. It usually appeals to just war* criteria to hold that such wars, particularly nuclear wars, would be unjust because disproportionate, indiscriminate, or both (see **Deterrence; Nuclear War**).

Some religious pacifists have displayed sectarian tendencies to withdraw from the world, while others have thought that the world itself could renounce the use of armed force. Pacifism has been more common in various Protestant groups, but in the last few decades it has become increasingly familiar in Roman Catholicism (e.g., Gordon Zahn, Dorothy Day, and the Catholic Worker Movement). Pacifists and nonpacifists share more than is often recognized because both begin with a presumption against the use of armed force but disagree about whether that presumption can be rebutted. Both also have a stake in securing national compliance with the standards of the just war tradition in order to limit the resort to and the conduct of war. Nevertheless, there are fundamental divergences, not only in the interpretation and application of moral norms, such as love and justice, but also in conceptions of human nature, society, and the church.

See **Conscientious Objection; Conscription; Just War; Militarism; Peace; Power; Resistance; Revolution; State; War.**

R. Bainton, *Christian Attitudes Toward War and Peace,* 1960; P. Brock, *Pacifism in Europe to 1914,* 1972; and *Twentieth-Century Pacifism,* 1970; C. J. Cadoux, *The Early Christian Attitude to War,* 1919, repr. 1982; J. F. Childress, "Moral Discourse About War in the Early Church," *JRE* 12, no. 1, Spring 1984; A. Harnack, *Militia Christi* (1905), ET 1981; S. Hauerwas, *The Peaceable Kingdom,* 1983; J.-M. Hornus, *It Is Not Lawful for Me to Fight,* ET 1980; G. Nuttall, *Christian Pacifism in History,* 1958; J. H. Yoder, *Nevertheless: The Varieties of Religious Pacifism,* 1971; *The Politics of Jesus,* 1972; and *The Priestly Kingdom,* 1984.

JAMES F. CHILDRESS

Paederasty *see* **Pederasty**

Pain *see* **Evil; Suffering**

Papal Social Teachings *see* **Official Roman Catholic Social Teaching**

Pardon *see* **Absolution; Amnesty; Forgiveness; Mercy; Penology**

Parenesis

A word from Greek meaning advice, admonition, or exhortation (also spelled paraenesis). It identifies a form of ethical discourse or writing commonly employed in the literary analysis of biblical writings, e.g., Matt. 7; Rom. 12. The hortatory mode of ethical statement is characteristic of religious ethics. It presupposes a strong basis for duty and the need for improvement, and often a doctrinal framework in which the mere outlining of moral reasoning is inadequate.

J. L. HOULDEN

Parenthood

In most cultures "marriage"* refers to the public bonding of a woman and a man for the purpose of sharing a common life. Since this common life involves sexual relations, marriage has usually been the foundation of family life, though not all marriages produce families. "Family"* refers to an intergenerational unit formed through procreation* or adoption* and involved with the raising of children. In traditional Western culture, marriages have been monogamous, though families headed by single parents, usually women, have often resulted from separation, divorce, death, or unfavorable socioeconomic conditions. Today more and more families exist beyond the marriages that initiated them, or become combined with families from two or more marriages. Together with the increased use of contraception* within marriage, and changing attitudes toward child-raising itself (*see* **Children**), these developments have cast parenthood more clearly as a state related to but separable from marriage. Two-parent, single-parent, and multi-parent (formed through remarriage with more than one set of parents having a role in child-raising) families, and same- or mixed-gender households (child-raising pairs or groups not formed by traditional marriage), immensely complicate the social, psychological, ethical, and theological understanding of parenthood.

Traditional views in Christian ethics on parenthood have been closely tied up with views on marriage and family, with parenthood usually seen as a gift or duty received or assumed in marriage. Yet it is also possible to see marriage and parenthood as vocations* (*see* **Family**). Such a view must still contend with the many instances of parenthood not entered intentionally, though these may in time come to be regarded as a vocation.

Virtues and vices of parenthood. Whether entered by procreation, adoption, or marriage into an existing family, and whether seen as gift, duty, or vocation, parenthood exhibits virtues and vices related to the practice of child-raising.

Combination of love and authority. Providing care and nurture for each child along with discipline and the setting of limits contributes to the psychosocial and spiritual development of children. It fosters a sense of self-worth in a setting of interpersonal responsibility, and in Christian terms reflects the mercy and justice, grace and law of God. Related vices include the rigid separation of love and authority along gender lines, disciplining by physical or psychological abuse, and setting no limits or vague limits in the name of love.

Modeling and training. Parents inevitably provide role models and training in social skills, as well as exercising primary responsibility for the assignment of certain specialized child-raising tasks to others (educators, day-care center operators, etc.). Evaluation of how they perform these tasks is related to what vision of the good of children one holds (*see* **Children**). Related vices clearly include trying to live through the lives of the children and demanding an unrealistic perfectionism.

Balance of loyalty and interdependence. Both within the family and between the family and the rest of the world parents can do much to foster personal allegiance and social responsibility, including affirmation of support and love at times of failure, assignment to children of important tasks in family life, and explicit recognition of the family's inter dependence with other families and communities. Related vices include neglect of responsibilities, abuse of loyalty by fostering isolationism, and refusal to admit errors or failures of parents or children.

Problematic issues of ethical reflection include the following:

Impact of marital relations and status. Sexual, power, role, and other related issues in the parent's marriage, and also whether the parent is single, married, remarried with a stepparent and a biological parent now involved in child-raising—all offer problems and possibilities for a given family.

The social network in which families exist. Schools, governments, media, the economy, class and ethnic status can both support and threaten individual families.

Disruptions of parenthood. Illness, disability, death, unemployment, generational conflicts, alcohol and drug abuse, pre- and extramarital affairs, and divorce all present special problems in the families in which they occur.

Conflicting visions of a good family life. Ethical reflection on parenthood is complicated by the diversity of convictions as to what constitutes good family life. This problem is exacerbated when family life is seen as a private and thus arbitrary matter. Conflicting sources of normative visions include the theories of experts in education, psychology, and sociology; diverse religious traditions; popular culture; each parent's own upbringing; and the peer groups of parents and children. Christian ethical reflection tries to sort out these issues in ways appropriate to Christian belief and experience.

J. Blustein, *Parents and Children,* 1982; S. Hauerwas, *A Community of Character,* 1981, pp. 155–229.

RICHARD BONDI

Passion *see* **Emotion**

Pastoral Constitution on the Church in the Modern World
   see **Official Roman Catholic Social Teaching**

Paternalism
The term "paternalism" first appeared in the 1880s, but the idea is much older. Paternalism is "the principle and practice of paternal administration, government as by a father; the claim or attempt to supply the needs or to regulate the life of a nation or community in the same way as a father does those of his children" (OED). Although the term "paternalism" is widely used, especially in a pejorative sense, other terms such as "parentalism" have been proposed because paternalism is sex-linked and because it reflects the image of the 19th-century father. Even though family structures have changed greatly in the 20th century so that fathers do not generally act "paternalistically" (i.e., the way the metaphor "father" appears to presuppose), the metaphor may still be useful because of what it suggests and evokes. Furthermore, women in various roles, such as mothers and physicians, may also act paternalistically.

What is evoked by the metaphor of father in paternalism? First, the father's motivations and intentions are assumed to be benevolent, caring, and loving, and the father is assumed to seek the child's best interests. Second, the father makes some of the decisions regarding the child's interests, even if the child opposes those decisions. A paternalist, such as the government or a professional, refuses to acquiesce in another person's wishes, choices, or actions for that person's own benefit, often by using force or controlling information (e.g., by deception or nondisclosure of information). The debate about paternalism frequently appears in the context of such matters as suicide* and suicide intervention, refusal of lifesaving medical treatment (*see* **Life, Prolongation of**), involuntary hospitalization*, and health promotion (e.g., laws discouraging the use of tobacco*, alcohol, and drugs). (*See also* **Alcoholism; Drug Addiction; Morality, Legal Enforcement of; Risk.**)

Paternalism clearly expresses some important moral principles in Western religious, humanistic, and professional traditions. For example, the Hippocratic tradition in medicine holds that the physician's primary duty is to benefit the patient, and traditionally codes of medical ethics have emphasized patients' needs rather than their rights (e.g., the right to information). (*See* **Hippocratic Oath; Medical Ethics; Consent.**) The principle of love* of neighbor* also supports paternalism: the agapistic agent should seek the neighbor's welfare and best interests. For the most part, the Christian tradition has assumed an objective interpretation of the neighbor's needs and interests and has paid little attention to the conflicts that are generated when the neighbor has a different interpretation of those needs and interests. After all, the good Samaritan did not encounter a resistant stranger who refused assistance and asked to be allowed to die.

There are various reasons for suspicion of paternalism in a pluralistic society where there are different interpretations of human interests: concerns about increasing the power of the state or professionals by allowing them to use force or control information in order to benefit people; concerns about whether the paternalist's own interests distort his or her interpretation of the neighbor's interests; concerns about the subjective values that enter definitions of needs (e.g., such categories as health, disease, and illness). (*See* **Pluralism; Health and Disease, Values in Defining.**) One of the main reasons for opposition to paternalism appears in John Stuart Mill's classic essay *On Liberty* (1859): Paternalism tends to violate the principle of respect for persons*, or autonomy*, at least in settings where no one else is harmed. Paternalism is generally wrong because it tends to violate a person's dignity and to insult or display disrespect to that person to treat him or her as a child in need of paternal control (*see* **Human Dignity**). Friedrich Nietzsche suggested that all assistance is a form of insult, but according to the line of argument just identified, all assistance against a competent person's wishes is an insult.

Even vigorous opponents of paternalism usually recognize some exceptional circumstances under which paternalistic actions can be justified. Mill limited his antipaternalistic principle to people in "the maturity of their faculties," and he justified the use of force to stop someone from crossing a dangerous bridge, at least temporarily, in order to make sure that the person is competent, informed, and acting voluntarily. Using similar examples, philosophers and theologians have distinguished strong and weak paternalism or extreme and limited paternalism. For strong or extreme paternalism, it makes no difference whether the person whose wishes, choices, and actions are overridden is competent, informed, and acting voluntarily; the only question is whether paternalistic actions would provide a net benefit to that person. By contrast, for weak or limited paternalism, it is necessary to show not only that the paternalist's actions would probably provide a net benefit to the neighbor, but also that the neighbor suffers from some encumbrance, defect, or limitation in deciding, willing, or acting. In weak or limited paternalism, benevolence* or love* provides the motivation, but the action is also constrained by the principle of respect for persons*. Only if the neighbor is not able to determine or pursue his or her own interests will that person's wishes, choices, and actions be overridden. It is not insulting or disrespectful to treat an incompetent person so as to benefit that person, even if he or she desires something else (*see* **Autonomy**). According to some interpretations, weak or limited paternalism is not controversial and should not even be considered a form of paternalism.

Several major conditions have been proposed for justified (weak or limited) paternalistic actions toward a neighbor: (1) the neighbor's defect, encumbrance, or limitation in deciding, willing, or acting; (2) the neighbor's high probability of serious harm apart from a paternalistic intervention; (3) the probability that a paternalistic intervention will produce a net balance of benefit over harm to the neighbor—this is the condition of proportionality*; (4) selection of the least restrictive, least insulting, least humiliating means of intervention (Childress). In a pluralistic society where there is disagreement about substantive ends and goods, this sort of weak or limited paternalism recognizes the neighbor's right to make his or her own decisions where able to do so and where this does not harm anyone else or the society. It is a procedural solution to conflict about the good life: it allows each competent person to decide for himself or herself (*see* **Pluralism**). The Christian doctrine of sin* implies that people's preferences may not be identical with their true interests, and this doctrine, along with others, lends support to paternalistic actions. But since Christianity recognizes the universality of sin, it may also support procedures to prevent one sinful person from overriding the wishes, choices, and actions of another sinful person when no one else is threatened. Opposition to paternalistic actions rules out the use of force and the control of information, but it does not rule out efforts to persuade others of the value of certain ways of life.

The tendency of a love-ethic to become paternalistic has often been neglected, with unfortunate theoretical and practical consequences. Determination of the neighbor's welfare has been assumed rather than analyzed, and little attention has been paid to which of the neighbor's interests has priority if not all of them can be realized, or if the agapist has a different ranking than the recipient. The principle of neighbor-love frequently becomes paternalistic when conjoined with certain values and beliefs about human nature, the soul, the body, life after death, and so forth. For example, if an agapist believes that an act of suicide not only ends the suicide's earthly life but deprives the suicide of eternal salvation, he or she may be likely to intervene to prevent suicide.

As the discussion of weak and limited paternalism suggests, it is important to view *agapē* as limited, constrained and restricted by the principle of respect for persons, or, alternatively, as including concern for the neighbor's wishes as well as his or her needs. The neighbor's freedom, including choices, decisions, and preferences, may count as one of the neighbor's interests, along with others. Still there is a problem of ranking interests. Thus, it may be important to balance agape and respect or, within agape, to balance the neighbor's interest in freedom and other interests. The temptation of paternalism, motivated by agape or benevolence, is pride*, arrogance, and self-righteousness; but the temptation of respect for persons or autonomy, uncoupled from agape or benevolence, is sloth* and indifference to the needs of others.

It may be useful to distinguish active paternalism from passive paternalism. In *active* paternalism, the paternalist attempts to thwart the preferences of the neighbor (e.g., having the neighbor involuntarily committed for medical treatment), while in *passive* paternalism, the paternalist refuses to carry out the neighbor's wishes (e.g., a physician refuses to sterilize a young woman at her request because of a belief that elective sterilization would not be in her best interests). It is easier, *ceteris paribus,* to justify passive paternalism than active paternalism. Passive paternalism is, after all, an expression of the paternalist's conscience and refusal to be a mere instrument or means in the service of the neighbor's wishes. Love does not issue the neighbor a "blank check" (Outka).

Most criticisms of paternalism presuppose Mill's distinctions between self-regarding and other-regarding actions (the former primarily affecting the self and the latter primarily affecting others), and between voluntary and nonvoluntary actions (the former involving competence, information, and voluntariness and the latter lacking one or more of those characteristics). Several arguments for increased control by the state, professionals, or others hold that the boundaries between self and other or between voluntary and nonvoluntary actions have become increasingly tenuous, and that the actions Mill exempted from external control—voluntary, self-regarding actions—are almost nonexistent. It is true that in an interdependent society "no man is an island" (John Donne) and many actions may adversely affect others; but these adverse effects are not always sufficient to justify restrictions on actions. Furthermore, it is not clear that all of our actions are so conditioned or determined, for example, by social forces, that we have no autonomy and that weak paternalism is commonly justified. Smoking is a good example of some of these debates about paternalism (*see* **Tobacco, Use of**).

See **Behavior Control; Individualism; Liberalism; Libertarianism; Morality, Legal Enforcement of.**

J. F. Childress, *Who Should Decide? Paternalism in Health Care,* 1982; G. Dworkin,

"Paternalism," in *Morality and the Law,* ed.
R. A. Wasserstrom, 1971; W. Gaylin et al.,
Doing Good, 1980; J. Kleinig, *Paternalism,*
1983; G. Outka, *Agape,* 1972; R. Sartorius
(ed.), *Paternalism,* 1983.

JAMES F. CHILDRESS

Patriotism

Pride in one's nation, a zealous devotion to
its welfare, and a fervent loyalty* to its government are the common marks of patriotism. Typically there is a mingling of the secular and the sacred in the sentiments of
patriotism. It is the sacred exaltation of national loyalties above all other loyalties
which makes some forms of patriotism a religious issue and an ethical burden. In Hegel's
Philosophy of Right, patriotism is pictured as
the sentiment which is fully conscious of obligation to the state itself as the fulfillment of
the Divine Idea in history.

Historically, patriotism has typically been
a function of international conflict: antipathy
to enemies may be the prime source of patriotic emotions. Modern warfare has not only
demanded heroism and sacrifice and the utmost of national unity: its propaganda* has
whipped up inhuman images of enemies, the
conduct of war has tended to collapse moral
constraints, and the legacy of war has been an
unreconciled and chauvinistic portion of the
public, if not the whole public. Thus war and
international rivalry tend to make patriotism
a love-and-hate phenomenon.

It is the manipulation and exploitation of
these nonrational elements which makes the
pretense of patriotism a constant temptation
to demagoguery. Patriotism may begin, then,
as a noble virtue but it may end as a vulgar
vice. When reason retreats and fairness flees,
and the only thing that matters is to discredit
political opponents, flag-waving is a common
weapon. Patriotic rhetoric has sought to
sanctify racism, sexism, antiunionism, excess
profits, witch hunts, religious bigotry, and
environmental plunder. In 1775 Samuel
Johnson declared to James Boswell that "patriotism is the last refuge of a scoundrel."
Arnold Toynbee's *Study of History* described
patriotism as "the last infirmity of noble
minds."

Among modern ethicists, Reinhold Niebuhr provided perhaps the most ambiguous,
if not cynical, estimates as to what the dynamics of patriotism really amount to. In
keeping with the central thesis of *Moral Man*
and Immoral Society (1932), which held that
group morality is inferior to personal morality, Niebuhr portrayed the "altruism" of patriotism as "simply another form of selfishness." Nation-states have become the
embodiments of a collective egoism which
asserts a will to power typically unrestrained
by any rational social force.

A more positive valuation of both patriotism and world community is suggested by
several modern prophets. Dietrich Bonhoeffer felt driven to return to Germany from
America to share in his compatriots' struggles against Hitler in order to earn the right
to participate in a postwar peace. Dag Ham-
marskjöld insisted that separation from nationhood can lead not to life but to spiritual
death; his own Swedish pride mixed marvel-
ously with a profound appreciation of other
cultures which was crucial to his style of
peacemaking. Martin Luther King, Jr., was
second to none in his power to evoke images
of the American dream which were consonant with prophetic theology.

The tendency of liberals to forfeit the
struggle over the symbols of nationhood to
regressive groups, such as the New Right,
has deprived both the churches and the public debate of some of their most potent ethical
resources.

See **International Order; International-**
ism; Loyalty; National Sovereignty; State.

M. Janowitz, *The Reconstruction of Patriot-*
ism: Education for Civic Consciousness, 1983;
J. Morray, *Pride of State: A Study in Patrio-*
tism and American National Morality, 1959;
R. Niebuhr, *Moral Man and Immoral Soci-*
ety, 1932; J. Yoder, *The Politics of Jesus,*
1972.

ALAN GEYER

Patristic Ethics

The phrase "patristic ethics" refers in the
first instance to the prescribed and accepted
life-style of Christian communities in the 2nd
and following centuries, and then to the theoretical and practical teaching of certain
prominent Christian thinkers and leaders
about Christian morality and its foundations.
In all cases, the Christian morality of the first
four or five centuries was understood to have
its basis in the gifts of repentance and of new
life which were conferred in baptism. It had,
therefore, a negative and a positive moment.
On the one hand, it was a turning from the

world and its ways—from a life in the service
of the demonic powers, which were the pagan
gods, and from the acquisitive, luxurious,
and licentious habits that prevailed under
their sway. On the other hand, it was a turning to the way of Christ—a way of triumphant suffering and of sharing in love, which
was not only a fulfillment of the precepts of
the gospel but at the same time an anticipation of the immortal life of the future age. It
was, therefore, the ethic of a community that
sought not to reform the world, but to demonstrate God's alternative to the world's
ways. In substance, this ethic owed much, in
its original shape, to the moral traditions of
Judaism. At the same time, it soon recognized analogies to its own values in those
commended by the philosophical schools—
Stoic and Platonist alike—and was able not
merely to employ the ethical terminology of
the philosophers but also to assimilate its picture of the Christian life to the philosophical
ideal of a practice of virtue that led to fellowship with, and likeness to, the Divine (see
**Neoplatonism; Platonic Ethics; Stoic Eth-
ics**).

The earliest sources (apart from the letters
of Paul and the Gospels themselves) that set
out an ethic for the Christian communities are
concrete descriptions of a way of life and
reflect for the most part the ethical catechesis
which accompanied Christian initiation (see
Matt. 28:20). The general shape, if not the
invariable content, of such instruction can be
gathered from a traditional catechesis which,
in different forms, is incorporated both in the
Didache (1–6) and in the *Epistle of Barnabas*
(18–21). Drawing both on the Hebrew scriptures and on sayings of Jesus, it sets out "the
Two Ways," of life and death, darkness and
light. It enjoins love and gentleness, sincerity
and truthfulness. It insists on sexual purity,
and on the avoidance of anger, idolatry, and
money-loving. It calls for evenhandedness
and for sharing of goods with the needy. Similar ideas and standards are reflected in the
letters of Ignatius of Antioch (d. c. 113), for
whom the Christian life is a way of discipleship and an imitation of God and Christ that
begins in faith and culminates in love. Con-
temptuous of worldly goods and values and
on guard against "the Prince of this world,"
the Christian lived, according to Ignatius, in
view of God's kingdom and the resurrection,
prepared to share Christ's suffering in martyrdom for the sake of a new and immortal life.

The seriousness with which these standards and ideals were taken is evident from
the problem that was created for 2nd-century
communities by the phenomenon of serious
postbaptismal lapse into sin. Baptism and the
repentance which it presupposed were understood as the beginnings of a new life—a life
in full accord with the spirit and the precept
of Christ. Some (see Heb. 10:26) had held
that there could be no forgiveness of postbaptismal sin; and this seems to have been the
assumption on which the Christian prophet
Hermas operated when, in his work *The
Shepherd,* he announced a single, extraordinary, and final opportunity of repentance for
the Roman congregation. Others, like the
writer of the Johannine letters, held that
there was forgiveness for sins which were not
"mortal"; and in time a discipline of repentance ("penance") grew up for the benefit of
believers who had sinned gravely, but without committing the irremissible sins of murder, apostasy, or adultery. It was not until the
3rd century—and then only in the face of
great controversy—that this "rigorist" position was relaxed and the possibility of a "second repentance" for any and all sins was admitted. Even so, it continued to be the
common understanding that baptism entailed a complete reformation of life—including, if necessary, the surrender of professions
or occupations that were tied in with the service of the pagan gods (see **Penance; Reconciliation**).

Three problems about the character of the
Christian life were foci of discussion or controversy in the early period. The first and
most obvious of these was the question of the
relative merits of marriage* and the life of
continence* (*egkrateia*). Paul had expressed
a preference for the latter (1 Cor. 7:25ff.),
though he saw nothing to condemn in the
married state. Within a generation or two,
however, it had become necessary, at least in
certain communities, to insist, sometimes in
the face of teachers who forbade marriage (1
Tim. 4:3), that that state "be held in honor
among all" (Heb. 13:4). Marcion (fl. c. 140)
forbade marriage to full initiates, and the
Montanist movement, toward the end of the
century, discouraged it. Clement of Alexandria (c. 150–c. 215), who in this regard
represents the view that came to prevail
among the churches, mounted a systematic
attack on Gnostics who denied the propriety
of marriage (*Stromateis* 2, 3), insisting that

marriage was a natural provision for the pro-creation of children and "the perfection of the world" (*Stromateis* 2.23.141), and that continence consists not so much in absten-tion from marriage as in freedom from domi-nation by desire of all sorts. Thus, honor can be given both to those who marry and to those who practice sexual continence as long as, in both cases, their state stems from ratio-nal choice and not from the compulsions of desire.

Clement applies the same principles to the question of wealth*—a second problem that had preoccupied Christian moralists. The strictures of Jesus against the rich were well known and caused embarrassment to Chris-tian communities which found persons of some wealth and property among their num-ber. The letter of James had reiterated the primitive polemic against the rich (5:1–6), and the pastoral epistles had asserted baldly that "the love of money is the root of all evils" (1 Tim. 6:10). Like the author of 1 Timothy, however, Clement of Alexandria saw the evil not so much in the possession of wealth as in the desire for it and the conse-quent misuse of it. Even the rich man, he thought, could be saved if he used his money generously to succor others.

A third, and perhaps even more difficult, subject of debate was provided by the issues surrounding martyrdom. In early Christian communities, martyrdom was more than just a conscientious witness to religious or moral principle. It epitomized the shape and sense of Christian existence insofar as the martyr imitated—and was indeed united to—Christ in his conflict with the powers of evil and in his triumphant suffering. Hence, martyrdom was the perfect baptism—a completed re-pentance that went hand in hand with initia-tion into the life of the coming kingdom; and the martyr was remembered and honored as one of Christ's living companions. Yet there was debate about whether it was right ac-tively to seek martyrdom. Gnostic Christians —no doubt because their *gnōsis* was in itself the assurance of ultimate salvation—tended to hold that martyrdom was unnecessary and were frequently charged with "denying" Christ (*see* **Gnostic Ethics**). By contrast, the Montanist movement, with its strong apoca-lypticism and its equally strong repudiation of all secular powers as tools of Satan, en-couraged believers to seek the opportunity of public witness and death. Tertullian (d. c.

225), himself a Montanist in his later years, wrote that Christians not only "have no dread" of the sufferings visited on martyrs, "but on the contrary, even invite them" (*To Scapula* 5); and Origen of Alexandria (c. 185–c. 254), in his own way as much a rig-orist as Tertullian, wrote an *Exhortation to Martyrdom,* which portrays the martyr as the "athlete of piety" who fulfills his baptis-mal vow to renounce Satan and practices the self-denial enjoined by Jesus.

A more reserved view of martyrdom was taken by Clement of Alexandria, who while regarding it as "the perfect work of love" to which the mature Christian gladly goes when called, nevertheless emphasizes that what is of ultimate importance is confession of Christ "before men" by "conduct and in . . . life." The most perfect martyrdom is that of per-sons who, for love of Christ, have loved their fellows. Further, Clement regards the Chris-tian who deliberately offers himself or herself for martyrdom, or seeks it, as cooperating in the evil deed of the persecutor (*Stromateis* 4.9–10). In his eyes, then, the attitude of folk like the Montanists is contrary to the true meaning of martyrdom, which consists in a life lived according to Christ, in self-control and love.

In the late 2nd and early 3rd centuries—with Clement, Origen, and Tertullian—the morality of the early Christian communities became a subject of more systematic reflec-tion. These writers had much in common. For all three, the Christian life was essen-tially a "way"—an engagement with God through Christ which took the form of a practice. All, moreover, saw the heart of this practice to lie in obedience and responsive-ness to the commandments and teachings of God, conveyed in the first instance through the moral instruction of the Mosaic law, but supremely in the perfect law of Christ's gos-pel. At the same time, all three, though in different ways, drew on the tradition of Hel-lenistic philosophical ethics for their han-dling of particular themes and, to one degree or another, for their understanding of the basis and aims of Christian praxis. In spite of these agreements, however, there was a sig-nificant difference of spirit between the two Alexandrians, Clement and Origen, and the North African Tertullian.

For Clement, the life of the Christian after baptism was conceived as an educative pro-cess whose goal was likeness to God. Under the tutelage of the divine Logos himself, who acted first as "trainer" (*paidagōgos*) and then as "teacher" (*didaskalos*), believers learned through practice of self-control to actualize the freedom and knowledge given in baptism, and so were purified of the "passions" that marked their subjection to and domination by external influences. Thus liberated, they could rise to the level of the "true gnostic," whose autonomy and understanding of things human and divine expressed itself in love for God and neighbor and in assimilation to the divine Logos who is the image of God and hence the archetype after which humanity was originally created. For Clement, then, the Christian way was an *askēsis,* a process of training, whose goal was the appropriation, through knowledge and rational freedom, of humanity's transcendent identity in God's Word.

Tertullian, by contrast, envisaged Christian existence not so much as a process of training and growth but as a matter of keeping the declared will of God as revealed supremely in Jesus Christ—an obedience that would be rewarded in the immortal and joyous life of the age to come. Believers lived in a world whose values and accepted patterns of behavior were determined above all by its idolatry—its service of demons who proclaimed themselves as gods. Christians, therefore, must live apart from this world and its illusions, exhibiting in their behavior their commitment to reality—that is, to the God who would in the end vindicate their commitment, and the suffering it entailed, by acknowledging them as his own people. They were to practice the mutual love that Jesus had enjoined, to cultivate continence, purity, and simplicity, and to avoid all actions or occupations which might be interpreted as countenancing the world's idolatry, from attendance at public shows and entertainments, to service in the military. They were, in short, to keep that *disciplina,* that way of belief and life, which Christ had handed on to the churches through the apostles, and by such strenuous obedience prepare themselves for the impending judgment in which God would claim those who had claimed him.

Origen, though more the rigorist than Clement, followed in the path that his predecessor had laid down. For him, the only proper goal of human aspiration is knowledge of God in God's Wisdom or Word, and the likeness to God which such knowledge brings. Sin as he saw it arose when the free rational spirits whom God originally created lost their hold on God and found their love, and themselves, uncentered, dissipated among the distractions of a material world. This situation is rectified by two means: through the incarnate presence of Wisdom herself in Jesus, whose human life is a "shadow" of the divine reality that is humanity's model and original; and through the inspired scriptures, which similarly, by their literal sense, intimate the mysteries summed up in God's Logos. Grasped by these realities through the faith and knowledge which the Spirit enables, believers enter upon the way of purification from passion, detachment from material concerns, and the practice of virtue. By this means they are once again centered and brought to themselves in the knowledge of God. Origen's is thus essentially a Platonist interpretation of the Christian way, in which the moral life is an *askēsis* through which the human person is led, under the tutelage of Word and Spirit, to fulfillment in fellowship with the Divine.

In none of these writers—despite the criticism of the world's ways and values that was embodied in early Christian practice—was much note taken of social or political issues. Like most inhabitants of the Roman Empire, the early Christians saw much to admire in the peace and order that Rome had brought to the Mediterranean world. Further, they tended to take for granted the social order on which it was based. The gravamen of their complaint against Rome was, in any case, religious: the trouble with the Empire itself and the peoples within it was that they were in the service of false gods—demons. This subtle combination of admiration and disapproval was continued when, after Constantine, Christianity was tolerated and then gradually became the official religion of the Empire. On the one hand, it became natural for Christians to admit their loyalty to the imperial system, since it had relinquished its commitment to idolatry. On the other hand, this new situation meant that Christian standards and values now applied to the society at large, which could be expected to reflect and embody them. This fact—not to mention the issues that arose about the relations of church and Roman society—introduced new themes, and a new critical note, into Christian moral discourse.

This does not mean, however, that the central thrust of patristic moral teaching was altered. The morality of the primitive communities as that was interpreted in the ascetic tradition remained the core of the Christian ideal. Indeed, this traditional, and strenuous, morality found, in the late 3rd and 4th centuries, a new institutional embodiment in the monastic movement, with which all of the great moralists of the Christian empire were associated in one way or another.

Beginning among the peasantry of Egypt and Syria, monasticism represented both a rejection of the burdens and complexities of society and culture in late antiquity, and a search for simplicity and single-mindedness in the service of God and in the pursuit of salvation for soul and body. It embodied the martyr spirit of struggle against the powers of evil; it espoused continence in matters of food, drink, and sex; and it enjoined the renunciation of material possessions—customs that echoed in a new and self-conscious form the spirit of the early Christian communities. Furthermore, in thinkers like Athanasius of Alexandria (d. 373), Basil of Caesarea (d. 379), and Basil's younger brother Gregory of Nyssa (d. c. 395), the monastic movement found guides and interpreters who set its practices within the frame of a theology of the ascetic life that drew, though not without severe modification, on the tradition of Clement and Origen. In this way, monasticism became the embodiment for this era of the heritage of Christian ethical and spiritual practice, and thus the matrix of Christian thinking about social and political problems (*see* **Asceticism; Monastic Ethics**).

In Eastern Christianity, the fruit of the monastic ethic is probably best studied in the sermons of John Chrysostom (c. 354–407), who was ordained to the priesthood in 384 after a failure in health forced him to give up the life of an anchorite. As presbyter in Antioch and as bishop of Constantinople, he preached with the aim of turning his flock from conventional Christianity to a faith that expressed itself in inward and outward dedication of life. He emphasized an active and loving obedience to God, which would express itself, on the one hand, in abstention from worldly pleasures and preoccupations and, on the other, in the positive practice of love and justice in personal and social life. He attacks what seems to him a scandalous neglect of the poor and underprivileged and calls for sacrificial almsgiving* on the part of

Christians. He sees the economic contrast between poor and rich, resting on the institution of private property, as the product of envy and avarice; and he denounces the double standard for men and women in sexual behavior.

Similar views appear in the West in the writings of Ambrose of Milan (c. 340–397), who on the one hand developed the Western ideal of the state as ally and protector of the church catholic, and on the other hand insisted on the moral (and doctrinal) autonomy of the church in relation to secular authority. A firm advocate of the ascetic ideal, who saw the practice of the moral virtues as a preparation of the soul for the enjoyment of God in a blessed immortality, Ambrose emphasized renunciation of worldly goods, whose possession he regarded as an affliction for which the only remedy was sacrificial almsgiving. A broadly similar position was taken up by Augustine of Hippo (354–430), whose conversion to Christianity under the influence of Ambrose was at the same time a conversion to the ascetic life of continence and personal poverty*. Like Ambrose (and others before him), Augustine accepted the classical Stoic-Platonist scheme of four virtues (prudence*, justice*, temperance*, and courage*, but insisted that it was only as these were actuated by love for God, the ultimate good, that they became true excellences of the human being (*see* **Cardinal Virtues**). Such love for God— the product, as he insisted against Pelagius and Coelestius, of the Holy Spirit's gracious working within the soul—involved love of neighbor as well as of self, and so dictated a life devoted to seeking the good of others. By contrast, Augustine thought, human loving that did not have God as its object (and source), but was directed to the goods of the temporal and material orders for their own sake, arose from self-centeredness and engendered competitiveness and violence. It was such sinful loving that had given rise to patterns of domination (e.g., slavery) and to the contrasts of wealth and poverty which were institutionalized in the system of private property.

It was these two contrasted ways of loving to which Augustine appealed when, in the *City of God*, he addressed himself to the problem of the relation between the secular order and the church. The church, as Augustine understood it, aimed at the transcendent peace and justice of God's kingdom. It represented, even though its life did not fully actualize, love for God—for the ultimate good which belongs to all persons in common. By contrast, the state aimed at an earthly peace and justice: its life was formed by a love that sought fulfillment in created goods and therefore presupposed self-seeking and violence. There could, then, be no question of identifying any secular order with the City of God, or of ascribing (as some Christians had done in the wake of Constantine's conversion) a sacred character to the Roman, or any other, political system. Not even the church embodies the City of God, which for Augustine remains an eschatological reality. But love for God is real in the church and so in the world; and such love will cooperate in the search for earthly peace and justice, even though these will always be temporary, relative, and flawed. Augustine's perspective on social and political issues is thus informed—as were Chrysostom's and Ambrose's—by his conviction that the true human good is to be found only in the vision or knowledge of God, in an order of things which transcends that of the present age (see **Augustinian Ethics**).

C. J. Cadoux, *The Early Church and the World*, 1925; H. Chadwick, *The Sentences of Sextus*, 1959; and *Early Christian Thought and the Classical Tradition*, 1966; J. Daniélou, *Platonisme et théologie mystique*, 1944; G. W. Forell, *History of Christian Ethics*, vol. 1, 1979; A. von Harnack, *The Mission and Expansion of Christianity in the First Three Centuries*, 2 vols. (1902), ET 1904–1905; K. E. Kirk, *The Vision of God*, 1931; E. Osborn, *Ethical Patterns in Early Christian Thought*, 1976; W. Telfer, *The Forgiveness of Sins*, 1960; E. Troeltsch, *The Social Teaching of the Christian Churches* (1912), ET 1931, vol. 1.

R. A. NORRIS, JR.

Paul, Ethical Teaching of

Three major matters are discussed here: sources and motivation, content and development, and the status of ethics in Paul's work as a whole.

1. Sources and motivation. Paul's moral teachings derive from no single source, and not all aspects are equally deeply integrated with his Christian beliefs. Some of his teachings come from the conventional wisdom of the culture in which he lived (e.g., lists of vices and virtues, 1 Cor. 6:9–10), and while he is inclined to add Christianizing phrases even to lists of duties to which all would subscribe (e.g., Col. 3:18–4:2; 1 Thess. 4: 1–12), on occasion he is hard put to find convincing reasons to support what his view of commonsense morality ("nature") dictates (1 Cor. 11:13–16). So at the level of everyday ethical assumptions Paul owes much to his Jewish background (e.g., in his deep abhorrence of sexual misbehavior) and to the conventions and ordinary moral intuitions of the Hellenistic world (e.g., 1 Cor. 5:1).

But for a few items he draws upon the teaching of Jesus in what we, if not Paul, would distinguish as two different ways. There is explicit appeal to the tradition of Jesus' sayings: in 1 Cor. 7:10, on divorce; in 1 Cor. 9:14, on the support due to Christian missionaries. There is also appeal to what the Lord here and now enjoins, probably through the inspired utterance of Christian prophets, including Paul himself: in 1 Cor. 14:34, on the conduct of women in church meetings; probably in 1 Thess. 4:2, on sexual purity. He can, however, also give directives on his own authority, apparently lacking such inspiration, in 1 Cor. 7:12, 25, on aspects of marriage and celibacy. The guidance of which he is aware can be ascribed to the Spirit (1 Cor. 7:40) as easily as to the Lord. It is noteworthy and problematic that at numerous points where Paul's teaching has parallels in the teaching of Jesus in the Gospels, no ascription to Jesus is made, most startlingly with regard to the love command (Rom. 13:9).

Jesus is the source of ethical judgments in another, deeper sense. Though Paul may have in mind specific instructions such as we have just referred to, it is probable that when he writes of imitating Christ (1 Cor. 11:1; 1 Thess. 1:6) he means a comprehensive following of the moral implications of Christ's saving work as a whole. This is brought out most clearly in two passages: In Phil. 2:1–11 Paul urges humility on the basis of Christ's self-abasement, his taking the form of a slave and dying by crucifixion. In 2 Cor. 8:9 Paul urges financial generosity on the grounds of Christ's act of self-impoverishment, whether in his manner of life or in his forsaking heavenly glory to live in the world (see also Rom. 15:3). This Christological basis for ethics is one of the two most striking and distinctive features of Paul's teaching. It is innovative too in that it means bringing to a position of prominence, not paralleled in Jewish or Greek ethics, qualities like humility and profound self-sacrifice.

The other distinctive feature is the influence of Paul's eschatological convictions on his ethical outlook. This comes out most dramatically in 1 Cor. 7, where his judgment on a series of cases arising in the area of marital relations is largely determined by this perspective. Responsibility for what now appears as a predominantly negative attitude is to be laid at this door. Marriage ties are to be eschewed if at all possible, in view of the nearness of the coming end of all things, an eventuality demanding of the believer austere vigilance and singleness of mind and purpose. It affects other matters too: though in the new Christian community ("in Christ") social and other differences are erased (1 Cor. 12:13; Gal. 3:28), nevertheless Paul does not recommend action to give practical expression to this judgment. In the interim before the end, people are to remain content with their lot (1 Cor. 7:17–24), though certainly a wholly new spirit of acceptance and fellowship is to pervade the Christian community, notably in its gatherings for worship. Paul is at pains to see how the interests of the simpler and poorer members can be safeguarded in face of the richer and socially more powerful (1 Cor. 8; 11; Rom. 14).

Undoubtedly, the church's situation as the community of the redeemed, but as awaiting the final consummation, led to tensions and inconsistencies in a number of respects. True, "in Christ there is neither male nor female" (Gal. 3:28), but the subordination of women to men remains part of Paul's practical scheme of things, even in most aspects of church life (1 Cor. 11:3, but note v. 5; 14:33–38), though it is plain that women could occupy an important place in the life of Paul's congregations (Rom. 16:1; 1 Cor. 1:11; and names in Rom. 16). It is true that the approaching end gives a prospect of Christians being in a position of superiority over all, so that recourse now to earthly judicial authorities is out of place (1 Cor. 6:1–8; in fact, other groups like pagan "clubs" felt similarly about the regulation of their internal disputes); nevertheless, this prospect gives no license to idleness (1 Thess. 4:11–12) or even for a dismissive attitude to the imperial authorities (Rom. 13:1–7). Admittedly, those authorities were at a remove from the

city governments more immediate to life in Paul's churches, but (as for Jews at the time and as indeed in Paul's own life) they were also a safeguard against local oppression. So perhaps it is not surprising that Paul sees divine backing for their power.

However, he gives a reason: they are a force for "the good." In Rom. 12–13 Paul, coming closer to a philosophical basis for ethics than elsewhere, makes much appeal to "the good" as the objective of moral action. Even so, there is no doubt that in Paul (as in the teaching of Jesus) the overriding moral imperative is the command to love*. It pervades the many injunctions of Rom. 12 and is stated explicitly in Rom. 13:9 (as in Gal. 5:14). It overrides even his belief in Christian freedom, in the matter of the treatment of tender consciences (1 Cor. 8). And Paul lays out its character in 1 Cor. 13, a passage that is fairly closely tied to the difficulties (social divisions and overregard for spectacular spiritual gifts) facing him in Corinth, but that also may well be inspired by his beliefs about Jesus. The emphasis on self-giving in Rom. 12 is wholly in line with what Paul sees as the essential mark of Christ's continued life in his people through the Spirit (Rom. 8:11; Gal. 5:22). So, though Paul does not tell us whether his highlighting of the love command derives from knowledge of Jesus' teaching, it is closely related to his adherence to Christ and his faith concerning Christ's significance.

2. Content and development. Much that might properly be said under this heading has appeared above, but we should now draw Paul's teaching together and look at it as a whole. This immediately raises the questions of development and of consistency. Paul's letters were written ad hoc. Even Romans, his most considered and judicious work, was probably directed to the known needs and circumstances of the Christians in Rome. Much of his ethical teaching is better classified as pastoral counsel aimed to alleviate specific difficulties and draw the misguided to a fuller appreciation of their Christian commitment. We should therefore not be overzealous to force Paul's teaching into too tight a straitjacket of rational system.

Nor should we resist the rather different possibility that his outlook as a whole altered as his experience grew. Thus there are signs of balanced statement in a later letter like Romans on matters where earlier teaching was, by comparison, a response to immediate need (see the broad treatment of the issue of food regulations in Rom. 14 alongside 1 Cor. 8 and 10). And it has been plausibly suggested that behind 1 Corinthians lies a process of discussion between Paul and the congregation in the course of which he shifted his position considerably on a number of issues. For example, 1 Cor. 7, which on the face of it seems negative in its attitude toward marriage, may well represent an attempt by Paul to move to a much more pro-marriage position than he had adopted before—in the light of a realization that his earlier asceticism, motivated by the expectation of Christ's imminent return, had led to serious difficulties in the area of sexual relations.

The fairest way to sum up the content of Paul's ethics may then be to have regard to the picture given in each letter, that is, at each stage in his ministry or in relation to each situation that faced him. Each made its own demands and drew from him its own kind of response. For example, it is clear that the multitude of difficulties in the Corinthian church compelled him to a degree and range of rule-making that was at odds with his convictions about Christian freedom, which are to the fore in Galatians. Yet this must not be taken too far. In the early 1 Thessalonians there is a notable quantity of firm moral teaching that, from a libertine or enthusiastic viewpoint, would appear to be of a restrictive or law-centered kind. There is in all of Paul's many letters an ethic that, dominated by Christ-inspired love though it is, combines freedom in Christ with quite specific moral teaching on matters of behavior, as well as with more general commendation of virtues and condemnation of vices. But still, the balance is not always the same: 1 Corinthians is full of advice on particular matters; Romans contains much more reflection on ethics in general (Rom. 12–14) than any of the other letters; and Galatians trusts much more to Christ's indwelling of the believer, showing a tendency toward a kind of intuitive ethic. This immediately raises the connected issue of the status of ethics in relation to Paul's outlook as a whole.

3. *Ethics in Paul's work.* A superficial account of Paul's theology might give the impression that he was not much interested in ethics. In the first place, the end was near. In the second place, his attitude to law, and the Jewish law in particular, was so negative that

freedom in Christ seemed to be the primary characteristic of the new Christian dispensation, with love displacing rules and regulations as the summation of what God required. It takes only a reading of one of Paul's major letters to show that this is a caricature of his teaching.

The key to the matter lies in an understanding of what law meant to him. To us the term "law" belongs almost wholly in the realm of ethics, or at any rate in the realm of the ordering of social behavior. For Paul it was not so: Greek *nomos* (law) represented the Hebrew *torah,* which signified the first five books of the scriptures, regarded as normative in Judaism and containing not only moral and cultic regulations but also the story of God's activity in the world from creation to the eve of his people's entry into the land of Israel (*see* **Mosaic Law**). It was, as a totality, God's gift to his people, the outstanding instrument of his gracious covenant. And it was in this function that Paul saw the law as superseded by Christ, so that its role had shifted: it was chiefly prophetic and preparatory. These writings foreshadowed Christ's work (Rom. 4) and provided for Israel before his appearance (Rom. 7:12; Gal. 3:19, 23). But as in any way conveying salvation, they were now of no account. They did, however, retain a place as a repository of moral guidance. Paul is nowhere explicit on the matter of the principle by which he distinguished between obsolete and still valid commands in the law. Clearly (at any rate for Gentile Christians), circumcision and food laws are at an end (Rom. 4:14; 1 Cor. 8), as are the traditional observances of the calendar (Gal. 4:10); and for all Christians the rules forbidding table fellowship between Jews and Gentiles are abrogated (Gal. 2:11–13). Equally clearly, the basic moral provisions of the Decalogue* and the command to love the neighbor remain in force for all (Rom. 13:8–10). So it is by no means the case that law, in the sense of rules for moral conduct, is done away with. While love "fulfills" the law (Rom. 13: 10; Gal. 6:2), there are other commands too that fill out its meaning. And while Paul sometimes offers suggestions about conduct in the manner of a pastor (1 Cor. 7:35; 2 Cor. 1:24), he is also capable of a much more authoritarian note (2 Cor. 6:14) and rigorous apostolic judgment (1 Cor. 16:22). And final judgment remains (2 Cor. 5:10).

But as we have seen, the morality Paul

puts forward is, as the emphasis on love vividly illustrates, chiefly determined by the gospel which he has received and of which he is the apostle; by the person and work of Christ, sent by God to acquit the guilty and receive them as sons and daughters, as free persons, reconciled to himself. In fact, so Christ-centered is Paul's thought that sometimes the autonomy of the individual as a moral agent may appear to be almost obliterated (1 Cor. 2:16; 2 Cor. 5:14; Gal. 2:20). Yet precisely the control of Christ or the Spirit is, in Paul's eyes, the condition of true freedom (2 Cor. 3:17), a condition he can even express (with a degree of paradox?) as being under Christ's law (1 Cor. 9:21; Gal. 6:2).

The word that most succinctly summarizes the relationship in Paul's thought between theology and ethics, the gospel and the moral life, is *righteousness**. The moral strength of God is no passive quality, but it is his dynamic determination, expressed in the sending of Christ, to restore alienated humankind to his company, that is, to a sphere of life where each human being can also live in righteousness (Rom. 1:16–17; 5: 1–5; 6:13–14). Such is the primacy of God's gracious act, which alone makes moral life— as Paul envisages it in the light of Christ— both possible and attractive, as the new age dawns and moves toward its glorious consummation.

See also **New Testament Ethics.**

J. Drane, *Paul: Libertine or Legalist?* 1975; V. P. Furnish, *Theology and Ethics in Paul,* 1968; J. L. Houlden, *Ethics and the New Testament,* 1973; E. P. Sanders, *Paul and Palestinian Judaism,* 1977; J. A. Ziesler, *The Meaning of Righteousness in Paul,* 1972.

J. L. HOULDEN

Peace

In ordinary usage, "peace" denotes the absence of conflict, the state that obtains between wars. It is also the term used to describe the end of a war. Similarly, an individual is "at peace" when not disturbed by internal conflicts. In Christian thought, however, the idea of peace carries more than this negative implication; it also refers to a positive state of individual and communal life in the presence of the power of God.

This broader concept first appears in the OT, where peace is depicted both in terms of the covenant of Israel with God and as a description for the eschatological time of the coming of the Messiah. Jeremiah (6:13– 14) connects the lack of peace in Israel with false dealing by everyone from prophet to priest; a similar message is found in Ezek. 13, where this lack of peace is tied to widespread idolatry. Isaiah 48 depicts the absence of peace as God's anger at Israel's failure to follow his commandments; had the people attended to them, he asserts, Israel would have had peace "like a river," "righteousness like the waves of the sea," innumerable offspring, and immortality. The eschatological theme surfaces also in these prophets. Ezekiel 37:26 looks to the establishment by God of an everlasting "covenant of peace" with his people; Isa. 32:16–18 describes the messianic time as one in which justice and righteousness will prevail, with the effect being "peace," "quietness and trust for ever," and "a peaceful habitation, in secure dwellings." Other examples include Ps. 85:10–11, linking righteousness and peace, and Isa. 42:2–3, joining the themes of justice and peace. Even without the explicit use of the word "peace," the same idea is found in many other places, as for example in Micah 4, where the vision of the messianic age is one in which nations shall no longer "learn war" and every man shall sit "under his vine and under his fig tree," at peace with himself and with his neighbors.

Carried forward into the NT, these concepts are linked there with the person and work of Jesus. Jesus opened his ministry of preaching with the message, "The kingdom of God is at hand" (Mark 1:15); many of his followers saw in him the actual presence of that messianic kingdom. As the ethic for this new age he proclaimed meekness, righteousness, mercy, and peacemaking (Matt. 5:3– 10). Going beyond the mere doing of justice, Jesus asked his followers to love not only one another but also their enemies (Matt. 5:43– 47; Luke 6:32–36) and to meet injustice and even violence with forgiveness, prayer, and blessings for the enemy and attempts at reconciliation (Matt. 5:38–42; Luke 6:27–30). All this is in clear continuity with the concept of peace found in the OT prophets, where the achievement of a just, righteous, and tranquil life in community was depicted as the goal of the covenant between God and Israel and expected to characterize the age of the Messiah. If Jesus was the Messiah, then peace—justice, righteousness, and tranquillity in life within human community—was at hand. Another theme from the OT, that the lack of peace is the result of God's anger, is not pursued in the Gospel accounts of Jesus' life, but it does surface in Paul's writings, where "peace with God through our Lord Jesus Christ" (Rom. 5:1) is the fruit of justification by faith. Here the focus is on the individual in community with God, not on the peace of the human community in the messianic age. A similar concept is found in John, who reports Jesus as leaving to his disciples a gift of peace linked to the presence of the Spirit (John 14:15–29). This same connection is made in John's telling of Jesus' meeting with the disciples after the resurrection (John 20: 19–22): Jesus greets them with the words, "Peace be with you," then breathes on them and says, "Receive the Holy Spirit." In these passages, as in the case of Paul noted above, peace is the presence of God, implying inner transformation.

The early church sought to embody the ideal of peaceful life together in its communitarian practices (cf. Acts 4:32–5:11), its addition of Gentiles to what had originated as a Jewish sect, and its efforts to distance itself from the state in such ways as avoidance of lawsuits and of military service. But, as we see clearly in Paul (cf. Col. 1:18–23), this was explicitly tied to the reconciliation with God and the presence of "the fulness of God" given to Christians through the risen Christ. A continuing problem was the tension of living this sort of life "in but not of the world," a world that obstinately refused to accept reconciliation, renounce war, and correct injustice. In the early Christian centuries the desire to escape this tension led some to embrace the life of the hermit; somewhat later the same desire fueled cenobitic monasticism; later still it became an impetus for separation from "the world" by entire communities of men, women, and children. Alone, the hermit could experience peace with God but not with other people. The monastery made the extension of the peaceful experience to other persons possible within a community still markedly artificial by the measure of society outside the cloister walls. Lay movements such as the Waldensians of the Middle Ages and the Anabaptist separa-

tists of the Reformation period sought to find the peace that presumably characterized the early Christian community in enclaves that included family groups. The tension remains and may be put in the form of a question: Is the peace of God to be realized by the Christian through efforts to achieve social justice through the transformation of society, or is this peace only to be experienced inwardly through the transformation of an individual's heart by the presence of God?

A special problem in Christian thought is the relation of nonviolence to peace. The early church was nonviolent, both out of necessity and out of conviction; such separatism as that mentioned above also has often (though not always) been accompanied by a profession of nonviolence. But just as the Christian notion of peace is not simply the absence of war, the achievement of peace in Christian thought is sometimes linked with war: God's anger, in the OT prophets, was often manifested in a war that chastised and purified Israel; the eschatological time, as in the books of Daniel and Revelation, is to be a time of war; in the just war tradition, war itself may not be fought except for the "end of peace." Just as there exists a continuing tension in Christian thought between the communal and personal aspects of peace, so there is also a similar tension over whether the achievement of that peace requires nonviolence as a precondition, or whether it may be secured by violent means.

See **Deterrence; Just War; Pacifism; Resistance; War.**

JAMES TURNER JOHNSON

Pederasty

Pederasty, or pedophilia, is the sexual love of children. Such love may be homosexual, but it is important to note that the majority of homosexuals are not pedophiles, and much pedophilia involves heterosexual contact with young girls. Although Freud highlighted the significance of the psychosexual strivings of the young child, this does not imply that overt sexual contact is appropriate or beneficial for normal maturation. In any case, the child is not able to give meaningful consent to such contact. Moreover, the adult who prefers pedophilia to adult sexual contact is typically insecure in his sexual identity. On a psychodynamic perspective, many pedophiles are still involved in an infantile relationship with their parents. As a result, they are unable to relate to adults as equals, and only feel at ease with children.

M. Cook and K. Howells (eds.), *Adult Sexual Interest in Children,* 1981; W. Kraemer (ed.), *The Forbidden Love,* 1976.

ELIZABETH R. MOBERLY

Penance

Penance is a sacrament of the church, though nowadays it is often called the sacrament of reconciliation*, to emphasize its affirmative character. This sacrament, like baptism and the eucharist, may claim NT evidence for its dominical institution (John 20:23). In the early church it was developed to take care of sins committed after baptism. The penitent makes a full and sincere confession of sins, declares genuine sorrow for them, and promises to amend his or her life and to make restitution to those whom he or she has wronged. The priest, on his part, gives counsel, sets a penance in the limited sense of some act (such as reading a psalm) which the penitent must perform as an earnest of repentance, and pronounces absolution.

See **Absolution; Confession; Restitution; Sin(s).**

B. Häring, *Shalom: Peace—The Sacrament of Reconciliation,* 1968.

JOHN MACQUARRIE

Penitence *see* Repentance

Penology

The philosophy of punishment is generally conceived of in terms of two main approaches, the retributive and the utilitarian. The retributive understanding of punishment may be said to date back throughout history, and in recent centuries it has been supported by philosophers such as Kant and Hegel and the Christian writer C. S. Lewis (*see also* **Retribution**). Retributivists insist on the centrality of the concept of desert. Other considerations are not precluded, but must be regarded as derivative from this. Thus, Hegelians such as Bradley and Bosanquet combined retributivism with a considerable emphasis on annulment or reformation. Subsequent to the Hegelians, the retributive approach met with increasing disfavor, and by the second half of the 20th century retribu-

tivists were placed on the defensive. The 1950s saw the attempt to establish the retributive understanding of punishment by making it a matter of definition: logical rather than moral considerations were placed to the fore. However, postwar criminology in general has been dominated by the reformative ideal.

Deterrence, reformation, and rehabilitation are expressions of the utilitarian understanding of punishment. The classical deterrent approach was shaped in reaction to the capriciousness and employment of savage penalties common in the 18th century. Prominent among the reformers were Beccaria and Bentham, who considered that no more pain should be inflicted than was necessary to deter. The application of utilitarian philosophy was of great benefit in the sphere of criminology, and led to substantial improvements in penal systems.

Unfortunately, the right and necessary opposition to practical abuses was on the theoretical level equated with the rejection of retributive principles. Thus for two centuries the utilitarian and retributive approaches have often been defined in contrast to each other, rather than as truly complementary. The chief effect of defining utilitarianism* in opposition to retributivism has been the rejection of the concept of desert. The original motivation behind this may have been humane, but its implications are alarming. By what right may one deprive a person of liberty, and subject him or her to reformative treatment, if this is not *deserved?* By undermining the concept of desert, the utilitarians have in effect exposed themselves to the criticism of advocating *un*deserved suffering. Either the given individual has been found to be delinquent, in which case intervention *is* retributive, in that it is based on this fact. Or an individual has not been found to be delinquent, in which case there is no need, or justification, for such intervention. In any case, it is not sufficiently realized that deterrent theory logically includes retributive considerations. Why should punishment deter anyone *from* crime, unless it is in fact imposed *for* crime? Deterrence clearly implies a prediction of retribution, and is meaningless without such retributive considerations.

It has sometimes been suggested that the pursuit of deterrence or reformation may justify indefinite or even lifelong deprivation of liberty. In this way, an originally benevolent concern for the offender may prove to sanction manifest injustice. Utilitarian theory is also held to allow of the possibility of high penalties generally, or proportionately higher penalties for smaller crimes, in order to maximize their deterrent value. Ironically, the study of history makes it clear that it was precisely this that the original utilitarian reformers were protesting against! The harsh penalties of their time were realized to be both unjust and ineffective. Originally, deterrence implied no more punishment than was necessary to deter, and it contrasted with the harsh penalties of retributivism. More recently, these positions have been reversed. Deterrence can be interpreted as justifying maximal rather than minimal penalties, and it has become the contribution of the retributive school to insist on a due sense of proportionality in punishment.

Certain major points emerge from this discussion, above all the tendency to draw an unsatisfactory dichotomy between the retributive and utilitarian approaches to punishment. The history of penology in recent centuries, above all in recent decades, has been the history of an oscillation between these two viewpoints. Moving from one extreme to another has proved a poor substitute for an adequate integration of the two viewpoints as being essentially complementary. The reformative ideal of recent decades has proved inadequate, and contemporary criminology is often considered to be confused or even in a state of crisis. Certain trends may be discerned. One is the resurgence of certain forms of retributive model, most notably the "justice model" on the one hand, and the call for measures of increased severity on the other hand. Unfortunately, neither of these proposals retains the insights of the reformative approach, and for this reason they are likely to prove unsatisfactory. Another significant trend is the call for reparation, which may at a theoretical level be linked with the reformative ideal. In practice, it stresses compensation to the victim, rather than restraint of the offender, and it is significant as being one of the few theories of penology that gives any serious attention to the victims of crime —an important oversight in many theories of punishment. A third trend is to speak of containment or incapacitation as the justification for imprisonment (which is of course only one form of punishment—many others are noncustodial, such as fines, probation, and community service orders). To regard punishment merely in terms of containment would seem to be a counsel of despair, stemming from the current inability to see an adequate rationale for dealing with an offender.

Another possible response to contemporary difficulties in penology is to seek reintegration of the retributive and reformative viewpoints. The Hegelians achieved this at the beginning of this century, and more recently their general approach has been renewed and developed by Sir Walter Moberly and Dr. Elizabeth Moberly. An integrated theory—of moral realism or personal realism—is proposed.

The Moberlys affirm that wrongdoing brings its own retribution, of moral deterioration. This is the truest and most congruous retribution of wrongdoing. Strictly speaking, punishment is not itself a consequence of wrongdoing, but rather, an instrument for dealing with the inherent entail of wrongdoing in the personality. By punishment it is hoped to check this inherent process of retribution, and to promote reformation. Traditional retributive statements are not usually capable of drawing the vital distinction between punishment and the intrinsic retribution of wrongdoing. Blameworthiness implies that there is a situation to be remedied. The essential insight of the retributive approach is not that punishment is retributive in itself, but that there is such a thing as retribution and that punishment is to be applied in an attempt to deal with this. Moreover, it is needless to contrast reformation with punishment, since punishment is itself the instrument for checking moral deterioration and for promoting reformation. The desire to eliminate vindictiveness from the practice of punishment must not be equated with the rejection of the concept of desert, since this renders punishment meaningless, and in practice has led to serious difficulties. Reformative thought is to be reintegrated with retributive presuppositions, and the Moberlys insist on the essential complementarity of the two approaches.

Penology must be concerned not only with punishment as such and the various forms it may take, but also with a number of wider concerns. The reintegration of ex-offenders into society needs careful attention, especially at times of economic recession when employment may be particularly difficult to obtain. Concern for the victims of crime is essential, and yet has often been relatively neglected. However, it is a questionable sense of priorities to focus largely on the offender, and not to make adequate provision for giving help and ongoing support to victims. Insurance schemes and self-help victim-support groups are of great value, but these do not cover the full range of help that is needed for all concerned. They are in any case largely dependent on private initiative, whereas the question of dealing with offenders is undertaken by community initiative. The overall question of crime prevention is important, and this depends not only on adequate policing but on such factors as street lighting, alarm systems, and the willingness of householders to install and use suitable locks, thereby reducing the actual opportunities for some forms of crime. Are the training and working conditions of police, prison officers, and other personnel satisfactory? Do the media engage in selective and sensational reporting of crime, or do they provide a responsible and unexaggerated commentary? What effect do political and economic trends have on society's response to crime and the criminal?

Finally, it should be noted here that the quest for justice will be undergirded by varying religious and ideological assumptions. Much contemporary criminology is set within the framework of the Christian-influenced perspective of secularized Western society. However, recent years have seen the resurgence of Islamic fundamentalism, with its application of Qur'ānic penalties for crime, such as physical mutilation. Most Western criminologists assume a certain general ethical consensus as to the limits of what is acceptable in penal policy. However, it will be important to bear in mind that many of its values are inspired by Christianity and are not to be taken for granted on a worldwide perspective. The Christian affirmation of the value of the person will remain of fundamental importance for criminology. Crime requires action, but it does not give the community unlimited rights over the offender. Ethical seriousness and redemptive possibilities must be continually interlinked in the concerns of penology.

See also **Capital Punishment; Corporal Punishment; Crime; Rewards and Punishments.**

A. E. Bottoms and R. H. Preston (eds.), *The Coming Penal Crisis,* 1980; G. Ezorsky (ed.), *Philosophical Perspectives on Punishment,* 1972; E. R. Moberly, *Suffering, Innocent and Guilty,* 1978.

ELIZABETH R. MOBERLY

Perfectionism

In Christian ethics perfectionism may mean (1) taking the "evangelical counsels of perfection" (*see* **Counsels**) as binding duties; or (2) John Wesley's doctrine of "perfect love" (also called "scriptural holiness"), in his sense, a state of regeneration in which attitude and motive are sinless, even though conduct may be objectively faulty because of creaturely limitations of knowledge, etc. (*see* **Wesleyan Ethics**). The term is sometimes applied to an ecclesiastical view that church membership should be restricted rigidly to those who are wholly committed and show the moral fruits of such religious sincerity. In philosophical ethics the original Latin sense of *perfectio,* completeness, persists: it indicates the full development of one's distinctively human capacities, cognitive, aesthetic, moral, religious. In this wide sense the notion comes from the Greeks, who included health or bodily perfection. It rose to a philosophical doctrine in Plato and Aristotle. In the 19th century a new metaphysical turn was given to it in Hegel's doctrine of completeness as wholeness: the individual mind is an organ of the world-spirit, which latter presses on from potentiality to actualization and from individuality or separateness to union with the whole. Hegel held that in its moral aspect the process is achievable not in the individual but only in the social whole. T. H. Green, though largely Hegelian in metaphysics, conceived perfection as self-realization*, and spelled this out into the Greek and Christian virtues, insisting on its social reference but preserving individuality (*see* **Hegelian Ethics; Idealist Ethics**).

See also **Holiness; Saintliness; Sanctification.**

R. N. Flew, *The Idea of Perfection,* 1934.

T. E. JESSOP

Persecution and Toleration

Persecution carries the connotation of unjust injury or harassment, usually because the victim espouses values or beliefs contrary to those dominant in a society or because he or she belongs to a group that does so. Toleration, in this context, refers to the degree to which nonconformist belief or behavior is accepted within a society. Pressure toward social conformity exists in all communities, particularly at points where the existence of the community is perceived to be at stake, and some level of nonconformity is tolerated in every society. But the degree of toleration varies widely among human societies.

Christian ethics has a long history of dealing with persecution and toleration, not only because the Christian church began its existence as a persecuted minority espousing deviant beliefs and values but also because Christians have found it difficult at times to accept the existence of dissident groups themselves. The history of the transition of Christianity from the status of persecuted minority in the Roman Empire to that of a dominant and sometimes intolerant social force is well known. But persecution and intolerance are not confined to previous history. In our own time Christians are frequently persecuted in Marxist countries and Marxists are frequently persecuted in Christian countries. Shiite Islam exhibits great intolerance of dissent wherever it enjoys social power, some Oriental countries prohibit Christian missionary activity, Christian socialists are harassed in some Latin American countries, sectarian and cult groups are sometimes treated intolerantly in North America, and some of these same groups practice the most rigid control of their own adherents. On the evidence, the subject of persecution and toleration is perennial, however much the particulars may vary from age to age.

The intuitive view of much contemporary Christian thought is that tolerance is a virtue and persecution an evil. That has not always been the dominant Christian attitude. To be sure, Christian thinkers from Paul to the present have claimed freedom to worship and to proclaim the faith without hindrance. But many notable thinkers, including Augustine, Thomas Aquinas, and John Calvin, have considered it the duty of the state to act against religious nonconformity. Thus, Aquinas prescribes in the case of a persistent heretic "that the Church gives up hope of his conversion and takes thought for the safety of others, by separating him from the Church by sentence of excommunication; and, further, leaves him to the secular court, to be exterminated from the world by death" (*ST* II-II.11.3). While remaining concerned about the soul of the heretic, Aquinas was even more concerned about the spiritual well-being of those whose faith, and therefore whose souls, might be destroyed by the public teaching of false doctrine. Later, by endorsing the execution of Michael Servetus, John Calvin took the same view. Actual execution of heretics subsided by the 19th century, but religious persecution under Christian sponsorship has continued here and there to the present.

Catholicism before the Second Vatican Council often justified a double standard on the subject of religious liberty by means of the "thesis-hypothesis" formulation. According to this, under optimal conditions (in "thesis") when Catholicism is in power, error should be suppressed. Only when Catholicism is not dominant should error be tolerated as a lesser evil (in "hypothesis"). The church, as possessor of the truth, should claim full freedom for its own mission under any historical circumstances; but it should tolerate error only when forced to do so by the historical situation. This is a double standard only from the standpoint of the norm of religious toleration; but the church's more basic norm was understood to be the truth of Christian faith and whatever might be required to express it freely and convincingly in the world. Since error can cause real damage to those who believe it, the church must suppress it wherever there is sufficient social power to do so. While this approach to religious liberty was roundly criticized by many Protestant thinkers as a peculiarly Roman Catholic hypocrisy, it was never exclusively Catholic. Many religious groups and ideological movements have claimed a freedom while in minority status which they have not been willing to accord others after arriving at social power. This is not necessarily inconsistent if one believes oneself to be in possession of the truth. It is easy enough to believe that the truth should be given every advantage when its advocates are in power and that it should claim at least the right to freedom of expression when the advocates of error are in power.

In the 20th century, Christian ethics has increasingly departed from this kind of double standard by condemning persecution and treating toleration as a norm in itself. John Courtney Murray, S.J., was particularly influential in reversing the longstanding Roman Catholic position prior to and during the Second Vatican Council. He gave particular emphasis to the pragmatic principle that policies conducive to social conflict ought to be avoided. The practical effect of the thesis-hypothesis approach has always been the exacerbation of social conflict in a pluralistic society. Murray argued that it was this consideration more than any other that prompted the founders of the United States to adopt the peculiarly American approach to religious freedom and separation of church and state. Freedom and separation were understood to be "articles of peace," that is, social agreements among competing groups necessary to preserve the peace*. Centuries of bitter warfare among competing religious groups in Europe threatened to erupt anew in the pluralistic New World if rules of competition guaranteeing equal rights to all religions could not be observed. Of course, such a pragmatic basis for toleration presupposes high regard for social peace as a necessary condition for the achievement of all other objectives, including the advancement of true religion. It might not be effective where one considers peace secondary to the truth (which one believes one possesses) or where a dominant group has sufficient power to quash dissent with little disruption of social peace.

Other Catholic and Protestant thinkers wished to go beyond Murray's more pragmatic and juridical argumentation to ground a doctrine of tolerance in the duty of Christian love* and the inherent inviolability of the conscience*. Christian love, the central norm of Christian ethics, was understood to provide deeper grounding for tolerance than the juridical norm and to be more faithful to the meaning of Christian faith than older distinctions between abstract truth and error. Indeed, many thinkers came to understand that religious persecution cannot even be effective on its own terms because faith cannot be coerced into being. Only those who freely assent to the truth really believe it; a coerced conscience is no conscience at all; so it appears to be a contradiction in terms to try to force the acceptance of beliefs or values —just as it is against love to do so. This line of argument was embodied in the Second Vatican Council's own declaration that "religious freedom has its foundation in the very dignity of the human person as this dignity is known through the revealed word of God and by reason itself" (see **Human Dignity**). The point, accepted now by many (perhaps most) Christian ethicists, provides substantial support for tolerance even in countries where Christians might have sufficient political power to persecute dissidents and adversaries.

It should be remembered, however, that this line of argument does not supply unambiguous support for toleration. Persecution has sometimes been undertaken, no doubt, in order to create converts or to express vindictiveness toward the "enemies of God." But the classical rationale for intolerance has not been to punish the persecuted or influence their beliefs so much as to stop them from infecting others with their heresies. Love sometimes is understood to require negative actions. Aquinas did not advocate that Christians should cease loving heretics; but he believed that deviance should still be punished in order to protect others. If error threatens the well-being of the soul, then it seems to be an act of love to protect people from its corrosive influences. The medieval mind sometimes even understood the burning of heretics to be the loving thing to do for the unfortunate victims: purified by a few moments of earthly fire, they might avoid the fires of eternal damnation! It is still possible to rationalize policies based upon intolerance as being best for everybody concerned if it is believed that truth and error can easily be identified and that the expression of error is fundamentally harmful.

Theological views based upon the positive contributions of the expression of dissent avoid such rationalization of intolerance. Toleration then can be perceived not as a reluctant acceptance of the right of people to believe and do harmful things, but rather as a positive openness to criticism and new truth. The theological basis for such an attitude can include the respect for human dignity and love cited above; but it also finds grounds in the transcendence* of God. God is understood to be greater than all human manifestations of truth and goodness, and humanity itself is limited and sinful. Accordingly, no human expression of truth and goodness can be taken as complete, final, and all-inclusive. God's truth and goodness may break forth in unanticipated ways at unexpected times. When one prevents a sister or a brother from bearing witness to truth and goodness as she or he sees it, therefore, one runs the risk of opposing an authentic, though unrecognized, word of God.

While such argumentation may appear to be based upon skepticism or indifferentism, that is not necessarily so. Christian love of truth and goodness commits one to bear witness to the faith, as one sees it, and to live out its implications in the life of love. It commits one to criticize what one considers to be evil or in error. But it also opens one up to take seriously what other people believe, to enter into dialogue, to protect the right of all to express their views freely, and to respect actions motivated by conviction.

Is such a view really an expression of Christian faith? It is interesting to note that some authorities on the history of persecution attribute religious intolerance to the monotheism of the Hebrew-Christian faith tradition. For instance, the Italian jurist Francesco Ruffini held that intolerance is a logical corollary of that tradition. From "the idea of a single and universal God," he argued, there followed "not only an inextinguishable spirit of proselytism, but also the principle that he only could be saved who worshipped the true God; that is to say, the principle of absolute intolerance." One cannot deny that that implication has been drawn by many adherents of Hebrew or Christian faith from the beginning, or that it is logical. If there is but one God, it appears to follow that those who worship other gods or support other religions are simply wrong. But there is another logically possible application of the monotheistic principle: If there is but one God, who is center and source of all being, then no finite human being can claim to know all that is worth knowing about God. God is thus understood to transcend every human manifestation. This humbler view also has a long history; and alongside the arrogance of those who have justified persecution on the grounds of their superior knowledge of and devotion to God, there has been a persistent tradition of tolerant openness that also appears to be grounded in the faith. The chauvinism of Ezra-Nehemiah is countered by the broader universalism of the OT books of Ruth and Jonah, the intolerance of crusade and inquisition by the generous spirit of Francis of Assisi, the arrogance of many Puritans by the tolerant spirit of many Baptists and Quakers.

How, then, are Christians to understand the open expression of what they consider to be error? They may well reflect that even what one considers to be error may make important contributions, such as (1) the example of deeply honest, though misguided, commitment to what a nonconforming believer regards as true—thereby at least bearing witness to the importance of honesty and conviction; (2) an emphasis upon some aspects of the truth which the community needs to hear, even though combined with much that is untrue; (3) a stimulation to the clarification of truth; (4) the continued opportunity for nonconformists to make other important contributions which may be unrelated to their errors; (5) the expression of social interests, issues of justice, which have been neglected—since heresy or social deviancy often has a social basis in the alienation of oppressed people; (6) the prevention of premature consensus, it being remembered that in one sense every consensus is premature in a world peopled by finite, sinful human beings; and (7) the expression of what we now consider to be wrong but what we ourselves may later come to regard as true.

In light of such values, should society tolerate all forms of deviancy? Clearly not. Such values justify a very high degree of tolerance, but the continued existence of human society places some limits upon deviancy. Certain distinctions may be useful in determining the justifiable limits to tolerance. First, Christian ethics may well subscribe to John Stuart Mill's principle that nobody should enjoy the freedom to infringe upon the equal rights of others. Antisocial behavior injurious to others may fairly be constrained by law. This leads to a second distinction between the expression of deviant ideas, as ideas, and behavior based upon such ideas. The expression of ideas can enjoy greater toleration in light of the foregoing theological considerations. But not all behavior can be tolerated just because it claims to have theologically principled motivation. Even the most heinous crimes have sometimes been committed by people claiming to be motivated by religion, including the awful mass suicide of Jonestown and the ritual murders of some offbeat cult groups. Even the normal presumptions of parental responsibility sometimes have to be set aside when parents, prompted by sincere religious faith, have withheld medical care or neglected the education of their children. Since almost any kind of behavior can be motivated by some form of religion, behavior itself cannot claim absolute tolerance within the community. Nevertheless, the general theological rationale for toleration might establish a presumption in favor of freedom of action, with this right of freedom overridden only when it seems clear that particular behaviors are injurious to individuals or to the community.

A more difficult distinction involves forms of communication which incite antisocial behavior or defame persons or debase the public culture. Those who oppose the general norm of tolerance argue that heresy has precisely such effects, so the distinction between communication of serious beliefs and values and the degradation of public society with inciting or corrupting beliefs and values may be a difficult one to maintain in practice. Absolutizing freedom of expression could allow any kind of public display imaginable and permit open incitement to riot or the verbal injury of other persons. On the other hand, these dangers should not be taken to justify intolerance and prohibition of unpopular ideas in general. The burden of proof should be borne by all those proposing to limit freedom of expression to show that objective harm to the community or to individuals is threatened.

A somewhat more absolute principle can be stated concerning the requirement that members of society express values or beliefs they do not hold. Early Christians and Jews were sometimes persecuted for refusing to worship the Roman emperors, and in our own time members of some sectarian groups (such as Jehovah's Witnesses) have suffered legal disabilities for refusal to pay formal homage to the state. But it is difficult to imagine any circumstances that would warrant a social policy requiring people to affirm as true or good that which they do not believe to be true or good. The absolute right to silence ought to be preserved even in those circumstances where overt behavior has to be regulated for the public good. A more difficult problem is posed by the question whether people should ever be compelled to act on the basis of the religious scruples of others. Should women in a Muslim country, for example, be compelled to wear a veil in public on the basis of the teaching of the Qur'ān? The fact that any law can reflect in some degree the religious motivations of lawmakers suggests the difficulty of a simple negative answer to the question. But where no rationale other than a religious one exists in support of a law, it would appear intolerant

to compel persons not sharing the religious scruple to obey the law.

There is a sense in which the foregoing remarks can be held to support the concept of a secular state or one in which formal neutrality among religious viewpoints is preserved. But there may be a difference between negative and positive forms of secularism*. A negative secularism avoids all religious values and beliefs because it considers them to be superstitious or divisive. A positive secularism is formally neutral because of the possibility that any and all religious viewpoints may have important contributions to make to the well-being of the community. This article has suggested that the weight of Christian ethics should be felt on that side in light of the recognition of God's transcendence and human finitude.

See **Church and State; Conscience; Conscientious Objection; Cults; Deprogramming; Dissent; Freedom; Liberalism; Morality, Legal Enforcement of; Nonconformist Conscience; Official Roman Catholic Social Teaching; Order; Peace; Pluralism; Secularization; Totalitarian State.**

M. S. Bates, *Religious Liberty: An Inquiry,* 1945; A. F. Carrillo de Albornoz, *The Basis of Religious Liberty,* 1963; Declaration on Religious Freedom, in *The Documents of Vatican II,* ed. W. M. Abbott, S.J., 1966; J. C. Murray, S.J., *The Problem of Religious Freedom,* 1965; and *We Hold These Truths: Catholic Reflections on the American Proposition,* 1960; F. Ruffini, *Religious Liberty* (1901), ET 1912; T. G. Sanders, *Protestant Concepts of Church and State,* 1964; A. P. Stokes and L. Pfeffer, *Church and State in the United States,* ²1964; J. P. Wogaman, *Protestant Faith and Religious Liberty,* 1967.

J. PHILIP WOGAMAN

Personal Ethics

The term does not have a generally accepted or technical meaning in the field of Christian ethics. Adding "personal" to "ethics," the disciplined, critical inquiry into moral selfhood and moral action, suggests several ideas.

First, personal ethics might be contrasted with nonpersonal interpretations of human behavior. In Christian ethics this usage emphasizes that human beings are centered selves, moral agents, accountable for their moral behavior, always existing in relationship to God (also understood in a significant sense as personal) and to one another, and under the necessity of deciding who they are and what they will do. They are thus not mere materials to be manipulated, not simply results of the conditioning of their heredity and environment, not interacting machines. This usage likewise stresses the personal qualities that are often hidden in the impersonality of much of life in urbanized industrialized society. However valid these ideas are, the term "personal" may be superfluous in this sense of the phrase, in that Christian ethics as a discipline appears to presuppose such assumptions.

Second, personal ethics might be contrasted with social ethics. In this sense the former might represent a focus upon those aspects of the moral life which involve direct interpersonal relationships, in contrast with the focus of social ethics upon the larger and more complex aspects of human life in society (*see* **Social Ethics**). This is a useful distinction so long as it is not assumed that personal ethics are in any way separable from wider social structures and processes, or that moral judgments and behavior or important ethical questions are private or merely individual matters.

Third, the term might refer to ethical inquiry that gives special attention to the moral agent, i.e., what it means for a person to be morally responsible, which moral traits are virtues and therefore commendable and desirable, and which are vices. Although the term is not ordinarily used in this sense, the usage would be understandable.

Finally, one might speak loosely of personal ethics when one means what would more precisely be called personal morality, referring to persons' actual moral dispositions, convictions, and behavior, rather than to the discipline that inquires into them.

See also **Social Ethics.**

B. Häring, *Free and Faithful in Christ,* 1978; S. Hauerwas, *Character and the Christian Life: A Study in Theological Ethics,* 1975; C. F. H. Henry, *Christian Personal Ethics,* 1957.

JOSEPH L. ALLEN

Personalism

Modern personalism has its roots in the idealist tradition since Plato, with major German representatives in W. Wundt and H. Lotze, French thinkers like C. Renouvier and E. Mounier, and recent British philosophers like J. Macmurray (*see* **Idealist Ethics**). In America, personalism was formulated by Borden Parker Bowne (*Personalism,* 1908) and developed by E. S. Brightman (*Moral Laws,* 1933; *A Philosophy of Religion,* 1940), A. C. Knudson, R. T. Flewelling, L. Harold DeWolf, Peter Bertocci, and others. In these thinkers theism and natural theology are closely related, and have theological affinities with Christian evangelical liberalism, being critical of fundamentalism and of irrationalism in neo-orthodoxy (K. Barth, E. Brunner, R. Niebuhr). Personalists affirm self-conscious experience to be the nonreducible synoptic key to reality and define value as of, by, and for persons-in-community. Person is the ontological ultimate, and personality is the fundamental explanatory principle. Personalism, broadly conceived, has several types. Personal realism interprets ultimate reality as spiritual and supernatural, but recognizes a natural order of nonmental being created by God and not intrinsically spiritual or personal. In the scholastic tradition such realism includes J. Maritain, E. Gilson, and E. Mounier (*A Personalist Manifesto,* 1936). Nonscholastic-oriented realists include J. B. Pratt (*Personal Realism,* 1937), G. Harkness, and A. C. Garnett. They view the categories of scientific thought—space-time, motion, cause, substance—as incredible in the mentalistic idea of nature. Idealistic personalism of the absolutist type holds that finite persons literally participate in one Absolute Mind (J. Royce, M. W. Calkins, B. Blanshard). Panpsychistic idealism has been presented in America by A. N. Whitehead and C. Hartshorne, who have developed an organic process philosophy. Personal idealists (Boston tradition) typically view all reality as personal and pluralistic. Reality is a society of persons grounded in the Supreme Person who is the creator of finite persons. As "world ground," God's self-directing intelligent agency shows itself in the order and continuity of the phenomenal world. In Brightman the epistemological and metaphysical argument distinguishes the "shining present" as experienced and the "illuminating absent" as a hypothesis of objective order, including nature and others' minds. Personalism stresses the unity of subjective and objective orders of being on a broader and more synoptic empirical basis than is postulated in science. Its view of being is activist, including values, and hence emphasizes both ethics and religion. The problem of "good and evil" tends to divide personalists between those who hold traditional views of God's power and finitists like Brightman, Bertocci, and S. P. Schilling (*God and Human Anguish,* 1977).

The impact of personal idealism on theological ethics includes: the interdisciplinary character of Christian social ethics; stressing metaphysical issues in the ideas of creation, nature, and personality; emphasizing the interpenetration of faith and reason; developing a critical value theory; rejecting irrationalism and heteronomy; offering a system of regulative moral laws (Brightman, *Moral Laws*) in contrast to deontological cultural prescriptions; emphasizing the purposive and relational aspects of personality, particularly of rational love; and insisting on the dialectical unity of theory and practice. These ideas form an ethic of personal development and social structural transformation. Brightman applies the metaphysical characteristics of personality directly to ethics since personality is an empirical complex whole, both active and interactive, a unitary agent, free to choose among given possibilities. In Britain, John Macmurray (*The Self as Agent,* 1957; and *Persons in Relation,* 1961) has argued that all meaningful knowledge is for the sake of action and all meaningful action for the sake of friendship. Moreover, he insists on the social nature of person and that the political is derivative from the moral.

In the field of social action M. L. King, Jr. (*Stride Toward Freedom,* 1958), based his nonviolent philosophy of social change on the metaphysics of Brightman and the Christian doctrine of love. Theologically, his mentor was DeWolf. For King, nonviolence was not simply a method or tactic but a coherent way of life.

See **Human Dignity; Idealist Ethics; Love; Persons and Personality; Respect for Persons; Self-Realization; Values and Value Judgment.**

WALTER G. MUELDER

Personality *see* Persons and Personality

Persons and Personality

Such ambiguity surrounds these terms, especially in modern usage, that no simple defini-

tion can be offered. Several interrelated meanings can be noted, clustering round the notion of the individual human being as the possessor of unique or at least distinguishing characteristics. The contexts of use are important, the term "person" being employed mainly in ethical and theological discussion, while "personality" features more prominently in psychological literature, particularly in theories derived from psychotherapy and counseling.

Philosophy and theology. The classical source for ethical and theological accounts of the nature of person is the definition of Boethius in his *Against Eutyches and Nestorius:* "the individual substance of a rational nature" (*naturae rationabilis individua substantia;* 3.5). The hallmarks of this approach are individuality and rationality. Designed originally to establish a case in the controversy concerning the nature of Christ, this definition has wider significance, since it captures a tendency (evident in Western thought especially) to isolate the individual from the community and to emphasize rationality at the expense of other aspects of human nature. In theology the stress on individuality has found many articulations, perhaps nowhere more passionately and eloquently than in the writings of Kierkegaard, the precursor of the existentialist theologies of the 20th century: "Had I to carve an inscription on my grave, I would ask for none other than 'the individual' " (1847; *The Journals of Kierkegaard,* sel. and tr. A. Dru, 1959). Such a view represents a reaction against essentialist philosophy and theology in which human nature and God's nature have been described in the language of substance and attributes, an outmoded terminology, ill suited to living beings whose uniqueness consists as much in action as in static characteristics (*see* **Existentialist Ethics; Kierkegaardian Ethics**). Thus both in Christological theory and in theological anthropology the notion of the person as an agent rather than simply as a rational individual is gaining prominence. In this context the writings of John Macmurray (*The Self as Agent,* 1957; *Persons in Relation,* 1961) are an important source of an action-oriented, personalist philosophy (*see* **Personalism**).

Ethics. In ethical theory "person" has been used to denote a *status* accorded to human individuals, which describes them both as the possessors of rights and as the bearers of the responsibility to respect the rights of others.

This view derives from Immanuel Kant's account of a moral law enjoining duty by virtue of its universal applicability to rational beings. Kant's formulations of the categorical imperatives* of morality included the imperative to treat all rational beings, including oneself, as ends in themselves and never as mere means (*see* **Kantian Ethics**). This formulation finds a modern equivalence in the norm of *respect for persons**. Kant's theory, however, depended upon a radical disjunction between reason and emotion, since he believed that the obligations of morality could never depend upon the vagaries of emotion. Modern accounts have tended to reinstate nonrational elements, while still seeking to avoid the emphasis on feeling and desire of egoistic or utilitarian theories. What is worthy of respect, it is argued, is the awareness, sensitivity, and consistency that make it possible for humans to seek moral ends in community with others. This version of Kantianism seems to accord well with the Christian value of love* of neighbor as oneself (*agapē*), and writers as diverse as Paul Tillich, Paul Ramsey, Reinhold Niebuhr, Paul Lehmann, and Joseph Fletcher have all offered interpretations of *agapē* that relate it to the requirement to respect others as persons. This approach has also proved influential in a number of contemporary moral debates, notably in the establishment of a list of basic human rights* (Universal Declaration of Human Rights, 1948) and in the search for norms to guide the judgments of modern scientists and physicians (see Paul Ramsey, *The Patient as Person,* 1970). Nevertheless, theories based on personalist values tend to lack precision and to miss some aspects of moral obligation. The communal and nonrational elements of morality remain on the periphery, and the function of moral principles which transcend individual choice remains a matter of controversy. This is especially evident in the continuing debate within Christian ethics about whether *agapē* is productive only of an attitude toward others or whether it is the source of exceptionless, or nearly exceptionless, rules that have social as well as individual applicability.

Psychology. Within psychological theory the concept of person and the related concept of personality have had a different but no less controversial history. They have found favor with those schools of psychology which have attempted to develop a comprehensive account of human nature rather than concentrate on research which isolates those aspects of human behavior amenable to study in laboratory or quasi-laboratory conditions. The need for such an account has been especially felt by theoreticians interested in the practical applications of psychology to counseling*, therapy, or education. In the writings of the psychotherapist Carl Rogers the phrase "becoming a person" is extensively used to denote a transition achieved by therapy from an inauthentic, socially conditioned self to "that self one truly is." An implication of this approach is that most individuals are *not* persons, most of the time. Rogers's view derives from the more thorough exposition by C. G. Jung of the contrast between the *persona* (the actor's mask, the Latin term from which the word "person" originally derives) and the "self." The *persona* is the social presentation of the self, but the "whole person" or "self" is much richer, containing elements concealed from consciousness, but nonetheless part of the individual's unique identity. According to Jung the archetypal self reveals the wholeness of the individual. This self is open to discovery through psychotherapy or through the symbolic communication of dreams, art, and religion.

Theories of the type espoused by Rogers and Jung are regarded by other schools of psychology as insufficiently supported by empirical evidence. Most psychologists would accept some distinction between the social self and that blend of personal consciousness and public behavior which constitutes the particular character of individuals. It is evident that the term "personality" can be used to describe either. We speak of someone having a strong personality or an attractive personality. Here we are referring to self-presentation in social situations, and this lends itself relatively easily to study through the experimental methods of social psychology. A large body of psychological literature is now devoted to personality theory based on the study of traits that can be ascertained through the use of personality inventories and other questionnaire methods. Parallel to this is the study of personality *development,* where changes in attitudes and behavior typical of different "life crises" are identified from observation of samples drawn from different age groups and different cultures. More elusive, however, is that supposed "personality," or self, which underlies the self-reporting and the social presentation. Behaviorists regard the search for such a subjective entity as misguided, indeed as mere metaphysical speculation. But many theories of personality in this second sense have been formulated. Apart from those stemming from the psychodynamic schools of Freud and Jung, there have been theories based on factor analysis, organismic organization, field theory, and the mathematical models of cybernetics. No single personality theory has gained widespread acceptance, but the requirement to explain how the separate aspects of individual experience and behavior gain a central organization seems inescapable for psychology. Despite the methodological difficulties a human psychology must take account of the uniquely personal (*see* **Psychoanalysis; Psychology and Ethics**).

Conclusions. Debate about the nature of person and personality raises a number of interesting issues for Christian ethics. First, the notion of "becoming a person," with its related ideas of wholeness, maturity, and self-actualization, may provide a contemporary interpretation of the Christian hope for human flourishing through love (*see* **Self-Realization**). But the quest for "authentic personhood" can also be regarded as both elitist and egocentric. It is unclear how a gospel of self-actualization can incorporate the prophetic elements of Christianity, in which justice for the oppressed is more important than self-development, and love may entail sacrifice and self-denial. Secondly, issues of freedom and determinism are raised by all sociological or psychological theories seeking a total explanation of human character and behavior (*see* **Free Will and Determinism**). The more comprehensive the theory, the less room there may appear to be for individual choice and responsibility. Some personality theories attempt to include notions of self-determination and self-transcendence within their compass (see A. H. Maslow, *The Farther Reaches of Human Nature,* 1976). Nevertheless, the tension between freedom and responsibility and "bondage of the will" characteristic of most Christian ethical theory is not easily captured in purely psychological categories. The need for Christian ethics to take account of God's purposes for humankind and of God's specific vocation to each individual within his or her life span appears to leave behind the ethical category

of rational agent and the psychological category of an organized, self-directing system of individual consciousness and behavior. Eventually Christian ethics has to return to some form of Christological formulation in order to express fully the dignity and uniqueness of the individual person as the recipient of God's gracious call. It must do this, however, in a manner that avoids the inadequacies of past formulations. The language of theology must always be sought from contemporary sources. It is probable that in the debates of contemporary moral philosophy and social psychology at least some of the appropriate terminology will be found.

Finally, it may be observed that the controversial and ambiguous character of the terms "person" and "personality" need not be a matter of regret. These terms attempt to describe that which must inevitably elude precise definition—the particularity and open-endedness of individual human existence. So long as debate flourishes among the moral philosophers and the social scientists there is some prospect that the richness of personal being will be better understood and respected. The person fully explained could easily be the person lost. (For a discussion of some of the issues about when personhood begins and ends, *see* **Abortion; Death, Determination of.**)

See **Human Dignity; Humanistic Ethics; Respect for Persons; Responsibility.**

H.-M. Barth, *Fulfilment,* ET 1980; R. S. Downie and E. Telfer, *Respect for Persons,* 1962; C. S. Hall and G. Lindzey, *Theories of Personality,* ³1978; J. Macmurray, *Persons in Relation,* 1961; R. Ruddock, *Six Approaches to the Person,* 1972.

ALASTAIR V. CAMPBELL

Persuasion

Usually refers to the act, process, or result of convincing a person to accept a belief through arguments, in contrast to such other acts, processes, or results as brainwashing*, indoctrination*, coercion*, and physical force. *See also* **Behavior Control; Deprogramming; Science and Ethics.**

Pessimism

Pessimism may be understood as a reflective attitude, asserting as a philosophy that reality is evil, either predominantly or essentially and totally. The pessimist puts the least favorable construction on actions and events, and views life as basically futile. Both as a set of beliefs and as an outlook on life it says that human nature is weak and evil, and an individual's capacity for improvement small or nonexistent. For example, those Christian estimates of human beings which emphasize not only their original sin but also their continuous state as sinners even when forgiven, are matched by other, less theologically informed interpretations which hold that humankind is basically stupid and indolent. And on a deeper level, the latter dwells upon psychological and sociological research which now seems to show that humans are controlled by nonrational and irrational forces to a far greater degree than had hitherto been imagined.

Pessimism also involves historical evaluations. Thus, it characteristically judges history to be, if not meaningless, then at least without any discernible meaning. Its attitude is basically one of gloom and despair. Russell, while not a pessimistic philosopher, sums up this view when he cites the comparison of life to a bird which flies from the darkness and cold through the momentary light and warmth of a castle and thence out again into the endless night. Hindu and Buddhist philosophies of life are often described as pessimistic, but theirs is a pessimism only with respect to this world. The Buddha's teaching that "all is suffering" refers only to experiences short of nirvana, while the Hindu's involvement in samsara—the struggles and disappointments of worldly life in one incarnation after another—will in time give way to the bliss of final release. In a somewhat similar vein, Christian thought, especially that of NT times and of the period of monasticism, is pessimistic about the present world but looks with anticipation toward the world to come.

In addition, pessimism embodies central metaphysical assertions, some of them directly related to one's philosophy of history. Thus, one school of thought claims not only that the total amount of evil exceeds that of the good, but that things are going from bad to worse. Another point of view has its best-known embodiment in Schopenhauer's *The World as Will and Idea* (1819, ²1844; ET 1883, 1958), in which he claims that life expresses blind will. Life is intrinsically self-defeating, because in seeking to fulfill its desires humankind is doomed to alternate between the pain of want and the boredom of satiety.

Finally, pessimism, whether on grounds of its doctrine of humanity, history, metaphysics, or all three, has usually led to the following attitudes: (1) belligerent resentment by human beings of their nature and condition—e.g., the "angry young man"; (2) resignation—e.g., the conservatives (religious and secular) who reject progress and yearn for a past age; (3) despair and anxiety, as analyzed by depth psychologists and by theologians (Tillich); and (4) people oriented to the next world.

Is the Christian pessimistic? A distinction must be made between the object and grounds of the estimate; that is, human beings are said to be sinners in a sinful world, nonetheless they are capable of response to and rapport with God's love, and history may be seen as the drama under his guidance. Concerning the ultimate ontological status of good and evil, Christianity has consistently rejected Manichean dualism, that is, the belief that good and evil are equally ultimate forces in reality.

See **Buddhist Ethics; Hindu Ethics; Manichean Ethics; Meliorism; Optimism; Progress, Belief in.**

CHARLES W. KEGLEY

Phenomenology

Phenomenological method in philosophy originated principally with the work of Edmund Husserl (1859–1938). He sought to clarify the truth of intentional acts of consciousness by a method of description and imaginative variation that would yield access to the "things themselves." In his view, such a grasp of the essences of things would yield apodictic truth or rational knowledge in a world plunging into irrationality. According to this method, questions of existence or nonexistence of the objects of consciousness would be bracketed, and the inquirer would ask only how the objects give themselves in lived experience. This openness to lived experience commended the method to scholars in history of religions, ethics, theology, and the arts, for a reductionistic positivism* had relegated their inquiries to a realm of nonrational subjectivity.

Alfred Schutz developed this method in

the human sciences, Mircea Eliade in history of religions, Paul Tillich in systematic theology, and more recently Edward Farley in theology, and Howard Harrod in moral philosophy. Significant differences in the work of these authors are indicative of the wide variations in appropriation of the phenomenological method.

Martin Heidegger, an early collaborator with Edmund Husserl, pursued this method in his first inquiries but shifted away from the concern with apodictic truth to the question of *being*. This break with Husserl's project opened the way to a hermeneutical phenomenology that is now unfolding in linguistic studies and political ethics.

H. G. Gadamer, *Truth and Method,* 1975; H. Spiegelberg, *The Phenomenological Movement,* 2 vols., 1960; G. Winter, *Elements for a Social Ethic: Scientific and Ethical Perspectives on Social Process,* 1966.

GIBSON WINTER

Philanthropy

The ideal of philanthropy commends a love* of humankind that issues in concrete deeds of service to others. These gifts of service can take the form of goods, time, or money. They help either to meet the basic needs of others (food, clothing, shelter, and medical care) or to foster their excellence (support for art, culture, research, parks, museums, public buildings, and education). Ancient religious traditions of charity* largely directed gifts to relieve or console those in misery (the hungry, the thirsty, the sick, the imprisoned). Modern managers of philanthropic foundations have largely concentrated their resources on the fostering of excellence, believing that support for research and education will help prevent and eliminate the structural causes of human misery rather than merely treat its outer manifestations.

Historically, aid to others has articulated itself through a variety of institutions. In traditional societies, the family, the kinship group, caste, or extended clan largely organized aid. In classical Western society, the church, which at one time possessed over one third of the usable land in Europe, supplemented familial support systems. (The sacred writings of Jews, Muslims, Hindus, Buddhists, Confucians, and other religious traditions also provide warrants for giving.) In the modern world, the welfare state, which had

its proximate origins in Bismarck's Germany and its remote precedent in ancient Rome, has increasingly assumed philanthropic functions. But the term "philanthropic" more narrowly refers today to giving by private donors, voluntary communities, or incorporated foundations rather than to giving within the reciprocities of family life or citizenship.

In the UK, philanthropic giving (donations by private individuals, companies, trusts, and government grants to private agencies) has increased from £2,400 million in 1976 to £10,000 million in 1984, in part as the result of new fund-raising efforts. In the USA, voluntary communities, aided and abetted by the principle of the separation of church and state, have played a significant role in the meeting of communal needs. Foreign observers from de Tocqueville forward have singled out the strength of voluntary communities as the distinctive feature of American social life. By 1982, philanthropic giving reached a total of 60 billion dollars. Recent advocates of the minimal state have sought to divest the government of its welfare functions and return them altogether to voluntary communities.

The proposal to meet human needs and foster excellence through individual initiative and voluntary giving faces a variety of difficulties. First, very practically, voluntary communities depend for their continuing vitality on the contributions of treasure and time from their members. Prolonged inflation, however, has eroded the financial base of churches, synagogues, and service organizations; and the women's movement (combined with the pressures of inflation) has propelled women into the work force, thereby reducing the number of people available to contribute their services. Voluntary communities have not had enough money or time at their disposal to take up the slack created by the abrupt withdrawal of the government from welfare responsibilities. Further, modern communities have so organized themselves as to provide the rich and the poor little contact with one another.

The ideal of philanthropy at its best divides the human race into two groups: relatively self-sufficient benefactors and needy beneficiaries. It presupposes a unilateral or one-way transfer from giver to receiver, overlooking the fact that the benefactor receives as well as gives. A two-way street of giving and receiving marks human community, and not merely in the setting in the family.

A society that relies too heavily on the voluntarist/philanthropic approach falls into a series of moral traps that derive from the pretense of the self-sufficient giver. Donors can be too overbearing, too demeaning, too given to covert control, too insensitive to long-range side effects of their interventions, too given to monumentalism, too oriented to their own glory, and sometimes too inflexible or narrow.

While agreeing with some of these criticisms of the ideal of philanthropy, the Christian moral tradition hardly justifies withdrawal from personal and organized giving. Rather, it puts the imperative to give on a different basis. Specifically, it breaks with the philanthropic division of the world into benefactors and beneficiaries from which many of the philanthropist's moral pretensions and difficulties flow.

Scripture provides powerful warrants for giving but always within the setting of a primordial receiving. The Jewish farmer leaves some of his crop for sojourners but as one who long ago received while himself a sojourner in Egypt. The Christian's love, from beginning to end, can only respond to primordial gift. "Herein is love, not that we loved God, but that he loved us. . . . [So] we also ought to love one another." The trivial gifts that men and women give, from the widow's mite to the Rockefellers' fortune, take place within a transcendent receiving.

The Christian tradition also supplies powerful warrants for the expenditures of time and treasure in the institutional setting of voluntary communities. A society should not, for all the reasons already cited, try to solve its welfare needs exclusively through voluntary communities, but these "little platoons" of organized charity supplement the capacities of a community to serve the needs and excellences of its members beyond the limited resources of the family or the impersonal distributions of the state alone.

See **Charity; Social Service of the Church; Voluntary Associations; Welfare State.**

Council on Foundations, Inc., *The Philanthropy of Organized Religion,* 1985; W. Gaylin et al., *Doing Good,* 1978; D. Owen, *English Philanthropy,* 1964.

                                    WILLIAM F. MAY

Philia *see* **Love**

Philosophical Ethics
Contrasted with theological or religious ethics. *See* **Christian Ethics; Ethics; Moral Theology.**

Physicalism *see* **Double Effect; Modern Roman Catholic Moral Theology**

Pietism, Ethics of
Pietism in Germany originated toward the end of the 17th century as a reaction, on the one hand, to Protestant orthodoxism with its one-sided emphasis upon intellectual assent to correct doctrine, which, however, represented a departure from the Reformation emphasis upon the right proclamation of the gospel as alone leading to faith and renewal of life in Christ. On the other hand, it was also a reaction to the legalistic attempts that were being made to bring order and discipline into the disrupted church life, particularly after the ravages of the Thirty Years' War. Instead, the Pietists advocated a deepening of the inner "spiritual" life.

Its chief proponents in Germany were Philipp Jakob Spener (1635–1705) and August Hermann Francke (1663–1727), who gave a great impetus to the work of social as well as foreign missions. Count Nicholas Zinzendorf (1700–1760) developed a community of Brethren who cultivated a religion of the heart and an intimate personal relation to the Savior. Pietism is particularly in evidence today in Württemberg. Through Schleiermacher it has influenced modern theology with its attention focused on inner religious experience. It has again and again manifested itself whenever the church has become formal and institutionalized and too much "conformed to this world" (as in England, e.g., at the time of the Wesleyan revival).

In general it may be said that Pietism insists upon a conscious conversion experience and a living faith relation to Jesus as personal Savior from sin, resulting in a changed life and in outward evidence of this change. Right *belief* is set over against *right* belief, with the former receiving the major emphasis. Reliance upon sacramental ministrations is regarded as a mechanical *ex opere operato* not requiring personal response. The objectivity of the means of grace is thus set in opposition to the subjective reception of God's grace, distorting the unity of the divine-human encounter in which revelation and faith are always corollary, with God as the author of both. Hence faith in one's own faith tends to replace reliance upon God's promise.

Likewise, with insistence upon outward evidence of inner conversion, the emphasis falls upon externalities of conduct under an individual's control. The Sermon on the Mount is taken as a set of principles rather than as paradigms of the new life of love. It is forgotten that it is the *hidden* life of love which is known by its fruits.

Moreover, the continued presence of the old sinful self along with the "new man" is obscured, leading to false "perfectionism."* The complexity of the human situation is underestimated along with the ambiguity of moral choices. It is forgotten that the will of God is always particular, at a time and place, affecting a unique individual within given structures. The gospel tends to become a new law, while the law loses its coercive power.

Nevertheless, Pietism has been and continues to be a valid protest against sterile orthodoxism and false sacramentalism and constitutes a proper plea for a genuine break with the old sinful self and an unregenerate "world." In its best manifestations it has resulted in active concern for the needs of human beings. In the genuineness of their piety the Pietists led simple, quiet, peaceful, joyous lives. They sent missionaries into many parts of the world in their zeal to save souls and to relieve human misery, poverty, and injustice. The danger lies in a self-righteous separation from the world instead of a free and joyous living "in and for the world" in the servant-form. It destroys the "hiddenness" of the one, holy, Christian, apostolic Church.

R. N. Flew, *The Idea of Perfection in Christian Theology: An Historical Study,* 1934; E. W. Gritsch, *Born Againism: Perspectives on a Movement,* 1983; A. W. Nagler, *Pietism and Methodism,* 1918; K. S. Pinson, *Pietism as a Factor in the Rise of German Nationalism,* 1934.

MARTIN J. HEINECKEN

Platonic Ethics

Plato (428/7–348/7 B.C.) was closely associated with Socrates in Athens in the years leading up to the latter's trial and execution for "impiety" and "irreligion" in 399, when Plato was twenty-nine or thirty (*see* **Socratic Ethics**). He was also the co-founder of an Athenian school known as the Academy, one of whose students was the young Aristotle (see **Aristotelian Ethics**).

The generally accepted corpus of Plato's writings includes (in addition to a few letters) some twenty-four philosophical works written in the form of dialogues. Most of these dialogues include Socrates as protagonist or at least a minor character; Plato himself is mentioned by name in only one (the *Apology*). In most of the early dialogues Socrates is portrayed as searching for definitions of virtue*, or excellence* of character* (*aretē*) by means of his method of "dialectic,"* in which one disputant attempts to defend a position while his questioner attempts to lead him into statements refuting that position by asking questions requiring a Yes or No answer. In the early dialogues, Socrates demolishes arguments for definitions of particular virtues and for answers to such questions as "Can virtue be taught?" While these dialogues identify the deficiencies of various conventional notions, they rarely construct particular definitions themselves. Glimpses of ethical doctrines do, however, emerge; and one to which Plato seems clearly drawn is Socrates' equation of virtue (*aretē*) with knowledge (*epistēmē*), although Plato has Socrates offer caveats to that equation in the *Protagoras* and *Meno.*

This idea of virtue-as-knowledge provides a good starting point for examining Plato's complex and evolving moral theory in the great ethical and political dialogues of his middle period (such as the *Republic*) and his late period (such as the *Politicus* and the *Laws*). For it presages the development of several Platonic doctrines that inform his ethics, including his theory of knowledge, particularly the Doctrine of Forms, and his divisions of the soul (*psychē*).

Knowledge. Rejecting the idea that truth is relative or a matter of convention (*see* **Sophists**), Socrates distinguished between mere sense-perception, on the one hand, and knowledge of eternal values (*epistēmē*), on the other. True knowledge must be of universals. Plato's doctrine of Forms (or Ideas) is both an epistemological and an ontological theory. There is an immutable, objective reality corresponding to each true universal concept. Though Plato's language sometimes suggests an utterly transcendent world of

pure Forms, these essences are also immanent in the phenomenal and particular. The
Forms give being to that which partakes in
them. The Idea of courage, for example, is
the source of courage in all who are truly
courageous. The Forms are also in an ontological hierarchy; their being is grounded in
the Absolute, which is transcendent to and
yet immanent in them. This Absolute is identified in the *Republic* as the Idea of the Good.

Ideas of virtue (courage, temperance, wisdom, justice) are subordinate to, and yet partake in, the absolute Good. We apprehend
these timeless essences and the absolute
Good discursively, that is, by means of dialectic. (Here Plato's interpretation differs
from that of latter Neoplatonists like Plotinus, who conceived of an "ecstatic" rather
than intellectual approach to the Ultimate
One; *see* **Neoplatonism**).

Plato held that man's attraction to his perceived good is through the motivation of
Eros (desire for the good). The "level" of
perceived good to which he is drawn by Eros
is a function of the rational development of
his soul in apprehending true essences. One
cannot be virtuous by nursing fleeting, muta-
ble sensations of goodness, but only through
proper orientation toward their real essences.
Virtue is, then, a quality of the well-ordered
soul.

The Soul. Plato believed the soul to be separate from (and superior to) the body. It is
the human being's greatest possession, and its
orientation his or her greatest concern.
Plato's famous tripartite division of the soul
is sketched in the *Republic* (and recurs in the
Phaedrus and *Timaeus*). The soul is said to
consist of a rational part, a "spirited" part,
and an appetitive part. The dominant theme
of the *Republic* is the nature of justice, and
Plato's Socrates defines the "just" person as
one in whose soul each part performs only its
proper function: bodily appetites and physical spiritedness should be under the direction
of reason. For the rational part is akin to the
divine in its approach to true Forms and is
immortal, while the other two parts operate
in the phenomenal realm and are thus bound
by mortality. In addition to defining the virtue of *justice** as the harmonic operation of
the soul, Plato also assigns other virtues to
the soul's parts and their relations: *wisdom**
is the virtue of the rational part; *courage** the
virtue of the spirited part; and *temperance**
the virtue of the union of spiritual and appeti-

tive parts under reason's rule (*see* **Cardinal
Virtues**). The proper rule of reason in the
virtuous soul clearly requires true knowledge, in the sense of discovering the absolute
and unchanging nature of goodness; this is
but another way of stating the doctrine that
virtue is knowledge. And with such virtue
comes true happiness.

Happiness and virtue. Plato's moral theory
is not primarily an ethics of judging particular actions. Indeed, one of the points of book
1 of the *Republic* is that moral virtue cannot
be defined simply in terms of "right" action
even when done in the "right" spirit. For
while there is a close connection between *aretē*
and right action, all actions must occur in the
world of sense and change, a world in which
virtue must be expressed under varying phenomenal conditions. Platonic ethics is eudaemonistic in the sense that it is centered
around the attainment of man's highest good,
his true happiness, which involves the right
cultivation of his soul and the harmonious
well-being of his life (*see* **Eudaemonism;
Happiness**).

For all his emphasis on true knowledge
and rational direction of the soul, Plato does
not characterize the good life as pure ascetic
contemplation*. The spirited and appetitive
parts must "justly" be given some rein as
well; so the good life is a "mixed" one of
intellectual pleasures and moderate satisfaction of desire. Happiness must be attained
through the pursuit of virtue—by becoming
"like the divine so far as we can." And while
Plato distinguishes particular virtues according to their objects or the parts of the soul of
which they are the habits, he also holds that
they form a "unity" as expressions of the
same knowledge of good and evil. "Prudence"* is his term for this unified virtue—
the knowledge of man's good and of the
means of attaining it. Ultimately the virtues
are inseparable.

In addition to his general equation of
knowledge and virtue, Plato also seems to
have held fast to the idea that no one ever
does evil willingly and knowingly. The urge
of Eros is always toward the good as we perceive it. We may perceive an (objective) evil
to be our good through ignorance* of our
"real" good; or our knowledge of the real
good may be obscured temporarily by passion (an imbalance of the functional parts of
the soul). In either case, however, we would
not be deliberately choosing evil but rather

misperceiving the good. Doing the good follows naturally and logically from knowing the good.

Political theory. In the *Republic,* Plato draws an analogy between the just person and the just state and constructs a model of the just state with three social classes representative of parts of the soul: workers and artisans, auxiliaries (soldiers), and guardians. The guardian class is composed of people, male and female, who have shown excellence in every phase of their education and who have been chosen to undergo rigorous physical and intellectual training. The most capable guardians will become philosophers and will be given complete political rule, since every good ruler is one who governs in virtue of knowledge of the truth.

Plato's insistence upon the ideal of philosopher-kings is a political manifestation of his doctrine of Forms coupled with his moral psychology. For the state exists to guarantee the good life for its citizens and should thus be ruled by those with a developed capacity for approaching the essence of good life (just as the reason must rule the soul because it is the part of the soul which has this capacity). Plato's famous story of the "Cave" in book 7 of the *Republic* is an allegorical presentation of this.

Having thus proposed and defended an ideal philosophical aristocracy*, Plato proceeds in books 8 and 9 of the *Republic* to describe its inevitable degeneration through plutocracy into democracy* and tyranny*. This foreshadows the more pessimistic, or "realistic," approach of Plato's later political works, particularly the *Politicus* ("The Statesman") and the *Laws.* For example, in the *Laws,* Plato's vision of the ideal ruler with knowledge of moral values is replaced by a polity of law.* Although Plato's anthropology is darker here than in earlier works, human beings are still viewed as capable of achieving virtue by observance and fulfillment of law. And Plato still affirms the responsibility of the *polis* to promote the good life for its citizens through education in virtue. In this century there has been vigorous debate about whether Plato's political thought was authoritarian, totalitarian, and racist (*see* **Totalitarian State; Racism**), as Karl Popper charged in *The Open Society and Its Enemies,* 1945. (For this debate, see T. L. Thorson, ed., *Plato: Totalitarian or Democrat?* 1963.)

The Platonic tradition. A. N. Whitehead noted that the history of philosophy is a "series of footnotes to Plato," and yet only some of those footnotes are actually in the Platonic tradition of ethics. This tradition closely connects metaphysics and ethics and holds that it is possible for humans to apprehend transcendent realities. According to D. A. Rees, "Platonism holds that a valid system of moral conceptions will reflect the nature of the universe, and morality is thus seen as more than merely human. Correlatively, Platonic ethics stresses the importance for conduct of knowledge and enlightenment and tends to place the highest good for man in the contemplation* of truth (the theoretical life); moreover, Platonic ethics lays less stress on duty* and responsibility* than on virtue* and the realization of good. . . . There is also a disposition sometimes manifested to assimilate the moral and the aesthetic (as through the notion of the fitting or the appropriate)." In this tradition, then, ethics is teleological rather than deontological (*see* **Teleological Ethics; Deontology**), and there is no sharp distinction between the self and others in the realization of good. Self-realization* involves happiness* rather than pleasure* in a narrow sense; it is thus eudaemonistic rather than hedonistic (*see* **Eudaemonism; Hedonism**).

As Rees further suggests, when Platonism was combined with Christianity, several themes often—but not always—emerged: denial of a sharp dichotomy between reason and revelation; emphasis on the divine spark in humans and their drive toward the good rather than on the effects of original sin; emphasis on the incarnation rather than on the atonement; high evaluation of contemplation; appreciation of the "spirit" rather than the "letter"; and suspicion of rules and institutions. In early Christian ethics, both Clement of Alexandria (c. 150–c. 211) and Origen (c. 185–c. 254) combined Christianity with the Platonism that was common in Alexandria (*see* **Patristic Ethics**). The Neoplatonic school (*see* **Neoplatonism**) embodied several of the above themes and significantly influenced Augustine (*see* **Augustinian Ethics**), who combined Christianity with a Neoplatonic structure while muting several of the above themes. In many syntheses of Christian and Neoplatonic perspectives—for example, the Pseudo-Dionysian writings, which were wrongly attributed to Dionysius the Areopagite—the mix was Christian mysticism, which valued contemplation as the highest way of life (see **Mysticism and Ethics**). By the 13th century the rediscovered Aristotelianism eclipsed Platonism in Christian thought, and the Thomistic synthesis of Aristotelianism and Christianity became dominant. However, Platonic perspectives were prominent in the Renaissance* and then in the latter half of the 17th century among the Cambridge Platonists, such as Ralph Cudworth. In the 19th century, the Platonic tradition influenced such Anglican thinkers as F. D. Maurice (see **Anglican Moral Theology**) and such philosophers as Hegel and the English Idealists (see **Hegelian Ethics; Idealist Ethics**); for example, the English idealists drew on Plato's organic interpretation of state and society to oppose individualism*. Although Plato has been the subject of numerous philosophical studies in the 20th century, Platonic thought has been only partially reflected in moral philosophy. For example, as Rees notes, G. E. Moore (*Principia Ethica,* 1903) reflected the Platonic tradition in making the good rather than the right central to his ethics and, in contrast to many of his fellow utilitarians (see **Utilitarianism**), in emphasizing several goods, rather than pleasure, that could be known by intuition*, even though he departed from the Platonic tradition in rejecting any naturalistic ethics* on the grounds that it is not possible to derive an "ought" from an "is," or ethical propositions from metaphysical propositions.

D. J. Allan and H. E. Dale (gen. eds.), *The Dialogues of Plato,* tr. B. Jowett, 4th ed., rev., 4 vols., 1953; F. C. Copleston, *A History of Philosophy,* vol. 1, 1946; I. M. Crombie, *An Examination of Plato's Doctrines,* 2 vols., 1962; J. C. B. Gosling, *Plato,* 1973; J. Gould, *The Development of Plato's Ethics,* 1955; E. Hamilton and H. Cairns (eds.), *The Collected Dialogues of Plato,* 1961; P. Huby, *Plato and Modern Morality,* 1972; T. Irwin, *Plato's Moral Theory: The Early and Middle Dialogues,* 1977; D. A. Rees, "Platonism and the Platonic Tradition"; and G. Ryle, "Plato," *EP,* 1967.

JAMES B. TUBBS, JR./JAMES F. CHILDRESS

Pleasure

The study of this topic is best approached initially along the lines of Aristotle, for whom it sometimes represented the unimpeded exercise of an activity (whether eating, swimming, doing mathematics or philosophy) and sometimes the crown, which, as it were, perfected the manner of a person's presence to the successive phases of his or her life, supervening on those phases as its bloom upon the spring of the year. For Aristotle pleasure is not something abstractible from the states of affairs to which it belongs. We cannot separate the pleasure of swimming from swimming nor that of doing mathematics from mathematical work. Yet we know that sometimes we enjoy ourselves in these activities and sometimes we do not. On this view pleasure is identified with enjoyment and enjoyment is intimately bound up with the activity or the state enjoyed. In consequence when we ask what various pleasures have in common, or on what principle they are grouped together as pleasures, we have to recognize that they cannot be regarded as possessing a generic or specific identity; rather, they must be judged properly grouped together as pleasures by analogy, viz., in the same way in which Aristotle grouped together in the last chapter of his *Categories* various forms of having, whereby a man may be said to have a wife, an overdraft, a Siamese cat, a copy of the Archbishop of Canterbury's sermons, a hole in his trouser pocket, etc. It is Aristotle's view (often denied on abstract, dogmatic grounds by earnest Christian apostles of self-sacrifice, and by their modern existentialist successors, but very often true, for all that) that people do best what they most enjoy doing and that therefore in certain cases their relish for a given form of activity is evidence that they are morally wise in adopting it (see **Aristotelian Ethics**).

For the thoroughgoing hedonistic utilitarian, for whom pleasures are ultimately homogeneous and measurable, pleasure is identified with satisfaction and assumes in the end the status of a technical term in that system. The utilitarian denies the viability of any critique of satisfactions, and urges moral tolerance as well, of course, as religious, within a framework capable of either providing for persons an increasing overall product of satisfaction or else guaranteeing their private and individual pursuit of happiness against interference by those who, from selfish motives or from dogmatic conviction, menace the kind of life which most fulfills their needs (see **Utilitarianism**).

In the history of the theory of pleasure we

must distinguish Aristotle's logical analysis of the concept of enjoyment from the utilitarian so-called "psychological hedonism" which is less an empirical generalization (if it is so, it is certainly false) than a program for abandoning any attempt at a critique of satisfactions in the name of an empirically based tolerance where questions of value are concerned, coupled with a determination to gear moral principles, customs, laws, etc., to the fulfillment of actual human needs.

See also **Hedonism; Happiness.**

D. M. MACKINNON

Pluralism

There are three different types of pluralism relevant to the discussion of Christian social and political ethics, all of which are allied to a liberal political perspective.

The first form concentrates upon the political consequences of moral and religious diversity in modern societies. Given as a matter of fact, groups of individuals in modern society differ over their conception of the good, the purposes and the ends of life; how should social and political institutions accommodate themselves to this diversity? The answer given by liberal pluralists such as Ronald Dworkin in *Taking Rights Seriously* and John Rawls in *A Theory of Justice* is to argue that the state cannot treat its citizens equally if it prefers one conception of the good to another. Consequently the state should as far as possible be neutral over questions of morality and should be concerned to secure that framework of law and institutions within which individuals and groups would be able to pursue their own good in their own way. On this view, interference with the rights of others to pursue their own good could only be justified when their pursuit causes harm to others. Of course, this qualification gives rise to difficulties if the concept of harm is itself value dependent in a morally pluralistic context. The central thesis of this form of pluralism is that a liberal society does not need substantive moral agreement over and above basic agreement on the importance of the mutual toleration of diversity. This thesis contrasts with views from both the left and the right which hold that a stable political society requires a common culture on what Hegelians call an ethical life—an agreement on a common good* which is not just an aggregate of individual goods as a focus for communal identity.

The second conception of pluralism is allied to the first but is more philosophical in inspiration. Whereas the first takes it as a fact that there is moral diversity, the view now under consideration takes this to be an ineradicable feature of the nature of moral concepts. Moral concepts are embedded in more general metaphysical theories about the self, its relation to other selves, and a person's place in the world. Given that these different metaphysical and religious theories are incommensurable and that disagreements between them are intractable, value diversity is inevitable. As such, this form of moral pluralism is a philosophical theory about the intractability of moral dispute as opposed to monism, which turns on the assumption that all of our values form a coherent and consistent structure which can be objectively grounded, with the result that moral disagreement is a ubiquitous consequence of the limitations on our rational capacities (*see* **Natural Law**). This vision of pluralism is closely allied with the first in the sense that if there is no single, true, objective way of combining values into a rationally grounded, coherent whole, then it could well be argued that it would be wrong for the state to seek to impose a particular structure of values upon society—it is, rather, a matter of individual citizens pursuing a conception of the good in their own way.

The third conception of pluralism constitutes a particular theory about the nature of politics in Western societies. In contrast to Marxist theories which see power in capitalist societies as class based, and in opposition to elite theories which hold that democratic politics is always a sham, with power being concentrated into the hands of a ruling elite, pluralists argue that in modern Western societies power, the capacity to make decisions and to get them implemented, is widely dispersed among diverse groups in society. It is also central to the theory that these groups are such that they countervail one another so that no group has absolute effective power in society. This theory is based upon a recognition of the growing complexity and specialization within society which has led to the formation of more and more interest groups. Government, both national and local, became the focal point for interest group pressure, and political leaders have to make policies which require a high common factor in interest group demands. Political leaders exercise power only when they are able to rely on coalition between interest groups, and these coalitions are always in a state of flux. Groups are therefore diffuse but at the same time powerful bodies in society. This does not mean that some groups will not have more power than others, but nevertheless power is more widely diffused than Marxist or elite theorists can explain. This type of theory was particularly characteristic of a good deal of American political success in the 1960s and 1970s and drew much of its impetus from the writings of Robert Dahl.

Pluralism in this conception not only is an empirical explanation about how power in Western societies is in fact distributed, but also came to have normative overtones—that in a complex and diffuse society the competition for power between a plurality of groups, none of which can exercise a monopoly of it over the rest, is what democracy relevant to an advanced society should mean. The diffusion of power between competing interest groups, rather than individual participation in decision-making, on this view articulates a more realistic and feasible conception of democracy.

See **Democracy; Liberalism; Morality, Legal Enforcement of; Paternalism.**

I. Berlin, *Four Essays on Liberty,* 1969; R. Dahl, *Who Governs?* 1961; R. Dworkin, *Taking Rights Seriously,* 1977; D. Nicholls, *The Pluralist State,* 1975; J. Rawls, *A Theory of Justice,* 1971.

RAYMOND PLANT

Political Parties

Political parties are characteristically modern devices for facilitating popular political participation. Acting alone or in coalitions they seek decision-making power at national and/or local levels and consequently maintain national or local organizations aimed at mobilizing mass support. Some (e.g., the British Conservative Party) were created by traditional rulers seeking support from newly enfranchised voters and others (e.g., Britain's Labour Party) were created to acquire power for previously unrepresented groups. Their organizations are of four main kinds: loosely structured groups of prominent politicians lacking permanent local machines (characteristic of developing countries); parties dependent on a mass local membership (as with Social Democratic parties); mass parties

based on cells at workplaces (notably Communist parties); and parties with military discipline (e.g., the Nazi Party). Their routine functions include facilitating communication between rulers and ruled; articulating popular political demands, defining policy objectives, recruiting future leaders, and nurturing the intellectual or emotional loyalties of adherents.

Party competition may exist in the context of two-party systems (as in the USA) or multiparty systems (as in most of Western Europe). Alternatively, as in contemporary India, one party may de facto be dominant despite the existence of legalized opponents. Typical of many Third World and Communist states is the legal monopoly of a single party.

Party systems tend to reflect major conflicts experienced during the relevant nation's development. Typical conflicts are owners or employers vs. workers; centralizing vs. regional forces; church vs. state; and urban vs. rural interests. Recently some Western democracies have witnessed a resurgence of local nationalist parties and the emergence of parties dedicated to, e.g., environmental issues. Economic crisis could mean polarization along more traditional lines.

See also **Democracy; Politics.**

M. Duverger, *Political Parties,* ET 1964; L. Epstein, *Political Parties in Western Democracies,* 1979; G. Sartori, *Parties and Party Systems,* vol. 1: *A Framework for Analysis,* 1976.

KENNETH N. MEDHURST

Political Theology

Political theology, in its contemporary meaning, originated in the 1960s as a movement among Roman Catholic and Protestant scholars to develop a new hermeneutics in Christian thought responsive to the temper and problems of modernity. Stressing the social context and historical character of reflection, political theology is critical of other forms of theological method: traditional Thomism, with its doctrine of nature and natural law, is ahistorical; transcendental Thomism (Karl Rahner), with its turn toward the subject, is apolitical; Lutheranism, with its two-kingdom theory and orders of creation, is dualistic and static; modern Protestantism (Rudolf Bultmann), with its existentialist commitment, is individualistic. The movement, strongly influenced by revisionist Marxism (Ernst Bloch, Theodor W. Adorno, Max Horkheimer, Jürgen Habermas), conjoins a Marxian concept of praxis with a Christian doctrine of eschatology as a ground for constructing its understandings of relations between the world and God, sin and salvation, church and society. The primary proponents of political theology are from Germany (Johannes Baptist Metz, Jürgen Moltmann, Dorothee Soelle, Helmut Peukert), but the movement has been influential in other Western nations as well (in Spain, Alfredo Fierro; in Canada, Charles Davis; in the United States, Matthew Lamb, John Cobb). Despite its praxis orientation, political theology has yet to develop a systematic approach to ethics. However, several distinctive themes of ethical significance are evident throughout its work.

1. The moral agent is a political subject. The world, according to political theology, is not a cosmos, a finished whole, in which each entity occupies a predetermined place and is intended to fulfill a fixed function. Rather, it is a social-historical process whose direction and form remain always to be decided anew. To be human, therefore, is not to be part of a natural order, but to be a subject, one who in interaction with others is engaged in the creative formation of the future. On this basis, political theology is critical of the implied determinism of a strictly scientific-technological approach to social problems and of the explicit determinism of historical materialism. Moreover, it is critical of all social structures that deny political participation to any class of persons as dehumanizing, and it encourages participation in historical struggles for emancipation.

2. The ground of moral judgment is the promise of God. From the perspective of political theology, the character of God's presence in the world is represented in Christ's crucifixion and resurrection, dialectically related as present and future. As crucified, God is understood as present in the suffering of all creation. The human counterpart of this side of God's presence is, in the strictest sense of the term, sympathy*. As resurrected, God is understood as future, as the effective promise of a new kingdom of peace and justice. The resurrection is an eschatological symbol in contradiction to which the actual conditions of the present world can be discerned and judged for what they are. The promise of God thus functions in a twofold way: as the ground for the formation of moral judgment and as the basis for hope that the structures of the world can be transformed.

3. The moral problem of history is suffering. In political theology, the concept of suffering* is central in depicting human experience throughout history. Suffering, in its moral aspect, is induced and sustained by social sin, by traditions and institutions through which, while some persons benefit, many are oppressed and dehumanized. Moltmann characterizes five "vicious circles of death" typifying suffering in contemporary society: in economic life, poverty; in politics, the domination of one class or nation over others; in cultural relations, structures of alienation among races, sexes, and ethnic groups; in the ecosphere, industrial pollution; and overall, a sense of meaninglessness and loss of purpose. To Metz, these circles taken together are signs of a "looming social apocalypse." To Lamb, they constitute an "anguished world" calling for "solidarity with victims."

4. The ultimate purpose of moral action is solidarity. Since the moral problem is the result of social sin, moral action must be directed toward social transformation. Moral action begins in solidarity with those who suffer, with the poor and exploited, but its ultimate motivation is "the indivisible salvation of the whole world" (Soelle, Cobb). While moral action, by itself, is insufficient to effectuate redemption in its full mystical sense (indeed, it is pretentious and dangerous to think that it might), it does intend, according to political theology, a new global society: a society beyond class struggle and domination, a society of friendship (Moltmann) and of open and free communication (Peukert). Solidarity thus signifies a kind of social identity that is more inclusive and public than the I-Thou relation, yet more intimate and devoid of narrow self-interest than relations of exchange (Metz).

5. The moral critique of society is a fundamental mission of the Christian church. The church, according to political theology, is a messianic association within society, bearing witness to the two-sided history of suffering and liberation. Through its "dangerous memory" (Metz) of Christ's crucifixion and resurrection, it is a call to identify with forgotten and victimized peoples and to engage in emancipatory praxis. The church is always political in some sense, but to be true to its mission under modern conditions it must undergo a radical reformation. Internally, it must overthrow its patriarchal tradition and become a church of and for the people. Externally, it must become an effective force representing the meaning of the kingdom of God in history through a critique of prevailing economic, social, and cultural idolatries and through a specification of justice and love, the mandates of discipleship.

6. *A predominant principle of social morality is democratic socialism.* Correlative to the five "vicious circles of death," Moltmann specifies a set of "ways toward liberation": in economics, socialism; in politics, democracy; in cultural relations, respect for others; in the ecosphere, peace with nature, and, overall, the courage to be. All these ways are marks of the promised kingdom of God, the consummation of righteousness. Political theology generally is supportive of democratic socialism* and human rights*, but Cobb, joining political theology to process thought, would deepen and extend its principle of justice to embrace the ecological sphere. On the use of violence in social change, political theology tends to adopt principles of last resort and limited use. However, Moltmann suggests that pacifism is the only realistic response to the threat of a nuclear holocaust.

Thus, while political theology is lacking in a rigorously developed ethical theory, these six themes—on the world and God, sin and salvation, church and society—represent a remarkably coherent ethical orientation to the modern world derived from its hermeneutical principles.

See also **Liberation Theology.**

J. B. Cobb, Jr., *Process Theology as Political Theology,* 1982; A. Fierro, *The Militant Gospel,* ET 1977; J. B. Metz, *Faith in History and Society,* ET 1980; J. Moltmann, *On Human Dignity: Political Theology and Ethics,* ET 1984.

DOUGLAS STURM

Politics

It is impossible to give a set of necessary and sufficient conditions for the use of the term "politics" which would then yield an unambiguous and uncontroversial definition. This is so for two interconnected reasons. The first is that the term is complex, there are a wide range of criteria which go to make up this complexity, and not all of these criteria have to be satisfied in order to justify the identification of a particular action or event as political. Secondly, the judgment about which criteria are relevant and the relative importance of particular criteria and their ordering in relation to one another is not independent of political and ideological preferences. To emphasize one criterion as against another will yield a different conception of politics, its scope and place in human life. That is to say, the selection and ordering of the criteria which then define a particular sphere as political is itself a politically salient action in that the criteria are selected and ordered in relation to the more general social, metaphysical, religious, and political beliefs of the actors (see **Ideology,** the first meaning identified).

Consider the following range of criteria, which are not exhaustive, and the ways in which emphasis upon one as opposed to another will yield a different view as to the scope and nature of politics.

1. The view associated historically with Aristotle and defended again by B. Crick in *In Defence of Politics* that politics has to do with the regulating, conciliation, and reconciling of the diverse range of interests which occur within a state. The difficulty with this definition is partly that it turns upon an undefined concept of interests over which there are equally many disputes, and the fact that it confines politics to complex, differentiated societies in which a wide divergence of interests is allowed to be expressed. This would have the effect of denying political activity in homogeneous societies in which there was no sense of diverse interests and in totalitarian societies in which conflicts of interest are not allowed to surface. In this sense, politics would be typically confined to Western-style societies.

2. Politics has to do with actions which relate to the basic welfare of the community. However, without a further definition of the basic concept of welfare this criterion does not take us very far, and clearly the use of this criterion would mean that politics could occur without the idea central to (1) of conciliating diverse interests.

3. It is possible to contrast politics with the organization of an authoritarian regime in that, for politics to exist, some form of consent is necessary. On this view, politics exists not only where laws and rules are enacted and implemented but where an attempt is

made to secure consent and the agreement of the relevant population to these rules. Politics requires relations between citizens not subjects; autocratic regimes on this view do not have politics.

4. Politics can exist only where there is a demonstrable relation to the legally binding authority of the state in government. Certainly this is a widely held view, both at the level of common sense, that politics has to do with the actions of government organs and agencies, and at the level of political philosophy, in which the problem of political obligation—why should individuals obey the state?—is a central question. However, it cannot without controversy be regarded as a necessary condition because it would rule out the idea that unions, corporations, committees, universities, and football clubs, for example, have a political dimension or engage in politics. Equally it cannot be a sufficient condition because many of the regulative functions of the state, for example, in securing adherence to standards of weights and measures, would hardly be called political.

5. Politics is about the exercise of power and the conflicts which arise from this. However, depending upon one's view of power, this can yield a very narrow or almost ubiquitously wide view of politics. If power is defined in terms of the ability to make decisions and implement them against the articulated interests of others, then it gives a very narrow definition of politics. Politics occurs only where there is a clear decision-making center and a clear conflict of interests. However, radicals such as H. Marcuse have wanted to argue that the way we come to conceive of our interests may be the result of an exercise of power, operating through culture and ideology, without this being the result of anyone's particular decision and without overt conflict. On this view of power, culture and ideology are both intrinsically political because they relate to how power is exercised over the definition of interests.

In addition, power is exercised in a wide range of contexts—in corporations, unions, universities, and family life, for example— and these would then become political, on this view, in opposition to criterion (4).

6. Politics requires formal organization with clear structures of authority and decision-making. On this view politics can exist outside formal government agencies as

against (4) but would be restricted to areas where there is a clear rule-governed structure —for example, in unions and universities. However, this criterion is too restrictive for some who believe that politics can exist in informal groups and encounters—for example, in football crowds and on campsites. This makes politics a ubiquitous human activity.

7. Another criterion which would make politics an endemic feature of human life is that politics is fundamentally about conflict and cooperation over the use of resources. However, unless some restriction is placed on the range of resources in question, politics would be a feature of a very wide range of transactions.

8. A further view is that politics is closely connected to the extensiveness of the effect of a discussion or policy. It seems plausible to suggest that a decision which affects all the population on a significant point is political, but it is difficult to pin this down. It would mean that politics could not occur in small groups, whereas many commentators have wanted to argue that politics does occur in groups such as families, groups of kin, and tribes as well as in interest groups.

9. One suggested criterion has been that the extent to which the outcome of an action is intended by the actors concerned is crucial to its identification as political. This of course could only be a necessary condition because not all intentional actions are political. However, even its status as a necessary condition has been disputed by radicals who want to argue that while certain outcomes—for example, of free market transactions—are not intended by anyone, nevertheless the distributive consequences of these outcomes are of central political concern.

These are only some of the range of criteria which have been brought to bear when trying to identify the sphere of politics, and several points need to be noticed. The first is that some of these criteria make use of terms which are themselves complex and contestable—for example: interests, consent*, the state*, authority*, and power*. A conception of politics goes hand in hand with these other concepts and cannot be abstracted from them, and the interrelations between these terms will constitute a part of a belief system or ideology. These belief systems are themselves pointedly engaged and presuppose political preferences. Thus, we cannot attain a "real" definition of politics which can be used independently of the ideological preferences of political agents.

Aristotle, *Politics;* B. Crick, *In Defence of Politics,* 1962; A. Leftwich, *Redefining Politics,* 1984; H. Marcuse, *One Dimensional Man,* 1964.

RAYMOND PLANT

Pollution *see* **Energy; Environmental Ethics; Future Generations, Obligations to; Technology**

Polygamy
The condition of having more than one spouse at a time. Usually the term "polygamy" is taken to mean what is more strictly called "polygyny," the possession by one man of several wives at one time. Very rare indeed is "polyandry," in which a wife has more than one husband at one time. Polygamy is an accepted institution in many cultures throughout the world and is sanctioned by many religions. It has sometimes been defended on economic grounds; for instance, some claim that the early Mormon experiment with polygamy served a colonizing purpose in a sparsely populated territory. On moral grounds, however, polygamy may be criticized as tending to produce family tensions and jealousies, and as being harmful to the dignity of women (*see also* **Women, Status of**).

While Christianity has always espoused the monogamist ideal, it is recognized today that it is unwise to seek to impose this too rigidly in cultures where it is novel. The older Christian missionaries sometimes insisted that converts should get rid of all their wives but one, and this caused much undeserved suffering among the women concerned. Today Christian moralists recommend a more humane approach to the problem. While still believing in the ideal of monogamy, they recognize that in cultures where polygamy has long been the rule, it cannot be instantly abolished, even where families or tribes have been converted to Christianity. It should be remembered too that although Western societies have turned away from open polygamy, the prevalence of prostitution*, sexual promiscuity, and easy divorce* means that something very like polygamy re-

mains a phenomenon beneath the surface in these societies.

See **Monogamy.**

E. Hillman, *Polygamy Reconsidered,* 1975.

JOHN MACQUARRIE

Pontifical Social Encyclicals
see **Official Roman Catholic Social Teaching**

Poor, Care of the *see* **Almsgiving; Justice; Poverty; Social Service of the Church; Wealth; Welfare State**

Population Policy
The explicit concern with population policy as a response to population growth is recent. Catholic responses to falling birth rates in the late Roman Empire, in the medieval period, and in the 19th century consisted of criticisms of the idea of restraining population growth. Protestants in the 19th century were also concerned with falling birth rates. By the First World War, Protestants began to take up birth control as a way of relieving human suffering, and to explore the relations between population size and resources. Yet in the 1930s some Protestant bodies urged Christians not to limit the size of their families, except out of necessity, because of falling birth rates.

For Catholicism, a systematic treatment of the morality of population policy as a distinct issue began during the time of Pius XII. In 1951 ("Address to the Italian Catholic Union of Midwives") Pius XII discussed population in relation to resources, and the move by governments to formulate policies to influence demographic trends. In 1958, Richard M. Fagley, a Protestant, published "The Population Problem and Family Planning," which argued for voluntary family planning, reviewed Catholic opposition to contraceptives, and urged an ecumenical conception of responsible parenthood*. The broad consensus on responsible parenthood for which he hoped has been realized, except for official Roman Catholic opposition to artificial contraception*.

Christians generally agree on the moral acceptability of limiting family size and doing so with some attention to the population situation. Churches have granted that governments may have a legitimate role in policies that affect population size. That does not mean that governments should be coercive. The consensus for voluntary family planning, and for procreation* as a right, is strong. Equally strong is the ecumenical agreement that special assistance be given to the poor and hungry (see **Hunger, World; Poverty**) and that justice* be served by governmental facilitation of socioeconomic development in all less developed areas of the world (see **Economic Development**). Equitable distribution of resources is a key concern of the churches and of Christian literature in ethics.

Christian groups and individuals are not of one mind with regard to whether it is appropriate to speak of "overpopulation" in the world, and whether present population growth rates constitute some kind of immediate, or fairly imminent, crisis. A number of Protestant bodies, though by no means all, do view population growth with alarm and urge government action to help solve what are considered very serious population problems. For example, the United Methodists (1970) made a number of suggestions: (1) creating major governmental agencies to work on "the population crisis"; (2) creating special committees on population in the US Congress; (3) international cooperation and assistance in implementing family planning and population policies; (4) approval by the states of abortion on request; and (5) no restrictions on voluntary sterilization*. Indeed, the various churches opposed to any legal restrictions of abortions do refer to excessive population growth as one of the reasons for their stand.

Official Catholicism, and some other Christian theologians and ethicists, have not seen population growth as the major source of problems such as malnutrition, poverty, and environmental degradation. That is not to say that such growth is not, or never will be, a problem. The priorities for governments lie in programs of social and economic justice. In *Populorum Progressio* (1967) Pope Paul VI explicitly recognized the obligation of governments to help people curb population growth (voluntarily) when population begins to outstrip development. In commending socioeconomic development that benefits those in need as the first step toward solving problems many associate with population growth, he was not very far apart from a number of the policy suggestions adopted by the United Presbyterian Church (U.S.A.) in 1972. Equal Rights for women, however,

is not understood in the same way by these two groups, and that is part of a larger split that divides Christians. Abortion* as a woman's legal right to decide for herself is a key part of the difference, already discussed above, insofar as population policy is concerned. Equality of opportunity and compensation in the work force is not disputed, and the positive role of sexual equality* in keeping family size small is widely perceived (see **Sex Discrimination; Women, Status of**).

The United Presbyterians in 1972 raised the possibility that government tax incentives or disincentives be used to discourage births. However, they did not accept any of the current tax schemes; they were persuaded of their unfairness (see **Fairness**), sharing the view of Christian ethicists who have analyzed such schemes. Moreover, the most recent literature on procreative matters of the United Presbyterians, and of a number of other churches, has emphasized procreative freedom. However, this literature has generally not addressed policies in China and elsewhere to reduce population growth. Whether this stress on freedom is intended to rule out all coercive measures remains to be seen.

The Christian consensus that the hungry should be fed has come under attack in the past decade. Proponents of "lifeboat ethics" have charged that it is not actually charitable and not morally justifiable to aid starving people in nations whose governments do not pursue effective population policies. The argument is that saving some lives now will cost more lives in the future because of overpopulation, accelerated by the lives saved through food aid. Christian ethicists have largely held firm against this. Some will not relinquish their commitment to save lives as the need arises even if it should mean disaster for the world: some values are seen as more important than survival. Others argue that it is not survival as such that is the issue, but rather the survival of a way of life. The only reason to "write off" certain poor nations now is to maintain the status quo for the wealthy nations, and that is unacceptable from a Christian perspective. Still others attack the relationship drawn between saving lives and fostering overpopulation. There are reasons to believe that food aid is itself a way of helping to reduce birth rates: people will only plan for their families and risk small families when they have some assurance that their children will live (*see* **Hunger, World**).

Love* and justice*, some Christian ethicists contend, are at the heart of what population policies are all about. From this perspective, population policy should emphasize governmental or private facilitation of self-help in communities where life is still too precarious for planning small families, and government involvement in family planning should concentrate on the provision of information and health services. There are growing hints of such an approach in some church literature as development is increasingly seen as something that happens insofar as people make it happen.

See **Abortion; Contraception; Coercion; Economic Aid; Environmental Ethics; Fairness; Family; Freedom; Hunger, World; Oppression; Parenthood; Poverty; Procreation; Sexual Ethics; Sex Discrimination; Sterilization; Women, Status of.**

R. M. Fagley, "The Population Problem and Family Planning," *Social Action* 25, no. 4, 1958, pp. 3–17; S. S. Harakas, "Population Ethics: Eastern Orthodox Christian Perspectives," *EB*, 1978; J. B. Hehir, "Population Ethics: Roman Catholic Perspectives," *EB*, 1978; G. R. Lucas, Jr., and T. W. Ogletree (eds.), *Lifeboat Ethics: The Moral Dilemmas of World Hunger*, 1976; W. Yates, "Population Ethics: Protestant Christian Perspectives," *EB*, 1978.

ARTHUR J. DYCK

Populorum Progressio *see* **Business Ethics; Official Roman Catholic Social Teaching**

Pornography *see* **Censorship; Morality, Legal Enforcement of; Sexual Ethics**

Positivism

Positivism, in its original sense, refers to the doctrines of Henri, comte de Saint-Simon (1760–1825) and Auguste Comte (1798–1857), who held that science has displaced theology and metaphysics as the sole legitimate means for seeking truth, informing action, and governing society. In contemporary usage, positivism more often denotes the "logical positivism" of the Vienna circle that gathered around Moritz Schlick (1882–1936) in the 1920s. Logical positivists maintained that all cognitively meaningful utterances are either true by definition or testable in principle by scientific method narrowly conceived. This view achieved wide influence in Britain and America through Alfred J. Ayer's *Language, Truth and Logic* (1936), which argued that theological and ethical utterances fail the test of cognitive meaningfulness. The movement waned in the years after 1950 as its assumptions about knowledge and meaning came under increasing criticism. Critics found the positivist conception of science too narrow to account for revolutionary moments in the history of science and too rigid to justify ordinary inductive reasoning. They also found positivist distinctions between truth by definition and factual truth, between theory and observation, and between fact and value too sharp to explain actual linguistic practice.

A. J. Ayer, *Language, Truth and Logic*, 1936; A. J. Ayer (ed.), *Logical Positivism*, 1959; W. M. Simon, *European Positivism in the Nineteenth Century*, 1963.

JEFFREY STOUT

Poverty

There are two articles on this subject. The first considers poverty as a voluntary condition accepted by Christians who have a vocation to the religious life; the second considers poverty as a social problem.

I. Poverty as a Voluntary Condition

Poverty is in the OT an object of sympathy (cf. Ps. 41:1), especially when suffered by the righteous, but not considered in itself desirable. The praise of poverty as bringing freedom from the burdens and temptations of wealth can be found in Hinduism—where traditionally the householder, having discharged family obligations, should end his life as a wandering ascetic—and among some Greek philosophers, of whom Diogenes in his tub is the most famous example. In the NT poverty is commended by the example and precept of Jesus (cf. Luke 9:58; 6:20) and by the call, addressed at least to some disciples, to abandon property in order to follow him more closely (cf. Luke 5:11; 12:33; 18:22; etc.). (*See* **Counsels.**) Paul gave a further example of "apostolic poverty" in laboring for his support and refusing to live by the gospel (Acts 18:3; 1 Cor. 9:18; 2 Thess. 3:8). And the voluntary generosity of the Christians of Jerusalem (Acts 2:44–45) provided a precedent for later monastic communities. But about 190 Clement of Alexandria (*Who Is the Rich Man That Is Saved?*) suggested the milder interpretation that the essence of true poverty is freedom from the desire* of wealth*, which may be consistent with its actual possession (*see* **Covetousness**).

However, the early church generally admired and often practiced the "philosophic life" of poverty and simplicity (Eusebius used the term of Origen's asceticism: *Church History* 6.3.13). The more ascetic hermits carried this to the greatest possible extreme, yet even they had to possess some means of subsistence. A different interpretation was developed in cenobitic monasticism, and finally codified by Benedict. He wished his monks to have no personal property whatever, but to find their needs provided for by the community adequately though not luxuriously. But in a well-administered and perhaps hardworking community individual poverty may be combined with corporate wealth; this experience was repeated more than once in monastic movements which began with a return to apostolic simplicity—for instance, the Cistercians often became prosperous agriculturists and graziers. Francis of Assisi attacked this danger by committing his followers to corporate as well as personal poverty, living by work or alms (as long as not received in money); his ideal was adopted, though less rigorously, by the Dominicans and other active orders. But the effort to turn the Franciscan challenge into a law led to difficulties—the Conventual Franciscans accepted adjustments which became evasions, while the "Spirituals" fell into a rigoristic legalism. Nevertheless a return to the freedom of poverty was the mark of later Franciscan revivals, such as the Observants in the 15th century and the Capuchins in the 16th. The Franciscan call, with its basis in the Gospels (cf. Matt. 10:9–10) remains as a challenge to easy acceptance of any property* system, whether feudal, capitalist, or socialist.

Protestantism has generally thought in terms of stewardship* of wealth, with an awareness of its dangers (cf. Luke 12:21), rather than of renunciation, except in the case of a special missionary or evangelistic vocation, for example, the quasi-Franciscan discipline imposed on its officers by the Salvation Army. As with medieval monks, movements dedicated to simplicity and work have sometimes found themselves facing the

problems of prosperity—for instance, the English Quakers in the 18th century, and somewhat later the Methodists. In a world aware of the problems of poverty we need witnesses to the balancing truth that property also can be a spiritual danger. Modern religious communities, Catholic and Protestant, and others who voluntarily adopt the life of the poor bring the challenge of Francis or the milder witness of Benedict to our time. In the words of the *Rule of Taizé* (1961, p. 57), which may be considered as presenting an existential interpretation of holy poverty, "the spirit of poverty is to live in the gladness of today."

See **Asceticism; Mammon; Monastic Ethics; Vocation; Vows.**

C. Butler, *Benedictine Monachism*, ²1924, ch. 10; J. F. Fletcher (ed.), *Christianity and Property*, 1947; D. Knowles, *The Religious Orders in England*, vol. 1, 1948; M. D. Lambert, *Franciscan Poverty*, 1961; *Poverty*, Religious Life, vol. 4, ET 1954.

E. R. HARDY

II. Poverty as a Social Problem

Great concern about poverty can be found in the biblical tradition. From the 8th century B.C. onward there is sharp criticism of unjust oppression of the poor (cf. Amos 2:6f.; 4:1; Isa. 3:15; Jer. 2:34; etc.). Failure to uphold the rights of the defenseless is also criticized (Isa. 1:23), as is the withholding of wages (Jer. 22:13). In the Psalms we hear the voice of those who call themselves poor and who appeal to God for justice. These represent either a group within the nation or, at least in some cases, more likely the nation as a whole. The parallelism of the psalms (with synonyms and antonyms) makes it clear that real need is in question as well as piety. The poor are contrasted with those who oppress them (e.g., Ps. 72:4) and see themselves as having a righteous claim on God (e.g., Ps. 86:1–2; cf. v. 14). In the laws there is also concern to protect the poor by legislative enactment. Gleanings are for the poor (Lev. 19:9f.), and limits are set to harsh contracts (Ex. 22:25–26) involving loans and pledges. Equality before the law is demanded (Lev. 19:15). Land sold can be redeemed (Lev. 25:25–28).

In the NT there is very positive treatment of the theme of poverty. Disciples are urged to renounce property and follow Jesus (Mark 1:18; Luke 9:58ff.; 14:33) as itinerants announcing God's kingdom. But that message is also good news for the poor (Luke 4:18; 6:20; 7:22), just as it brings healing to the sick. God's kingdom will transform the existing order, and already brings hope and healing through the activity of Jesus and his disciples. Jesus did not teach political revolution, but neither did he teach passive acquiescence. A sharper note is found in pre-Lucan passages which envisage reversal of fortune in the new age (Luke 1:53; 6:21–25; 16:25). If later than Jesus and earlier than Luke, these passages may reflect the famine when the rich feasted while the poor starved. Such gross inequalities and injustices are sharply condemned. Luke himself likes to show Jesus and Paul on good terms with the wealthy and influential, while retaining warnings of the dangers of riches. The account of so-called communism of Acts 4:32 contains literary allusions to Plato and Greek utopianism. The historical reality seems to have been epitomized in the story of Barnabas selling property to aid the needy. Paul emphasized the importance of work when faced with apocalyptic disorders in Thessalonica. He himself renounced the right to aid from his converts and worked to support free proclamation of the gospel. But he also proclaims an ideal of equality* (2 Cor. 8:14) which was not so much egalitarianism as the duty of communities with resources to assist poorer communities (Gal. 2:10; Rom. 15:26), especially those in Jerusalem impoverished after the famine. First John 3:17 condemns the failure to aid those in need. James 2:1–5 declares the poor heirs of the kingdom and condemns disrespect to them and in 5:4 the withholding of wages.

In the early Christian centuries asceticism*, voluntary poverty, and the obligation to charity* form a constant refrain. Hermits, and new monastic foundations, and later the Franciscans, returned again and again to this ideal. The problem was that orders tended to become rich. The alleviation of poverty was to some extent attempted by means of almsgiving*, condemnation of usury*, and maxims such as that of the just wage*.

Luther sympathized with the just grievances of peasants but bitterly criticized the Peasants' Revolt. Calvin taught equality before God but inequality in society, though his scheme to provide work for the poor in Geneva deserves mention. Systems of poor relief were set up in Europe; in England they were based on civil parishes. It was some radical Reformers who proposed more drastic remedies and encountered fierce resistance. The Quakers stand out for their emphasis on simplicity and social concern. In the 19th century, poor relief was made harsher as a result of a concept of "less eligibility." But alongside much approval of economic inequality should be set the campaigns of Christian and other social reformers, and the contribution of Methodists and others to the struggle of trade unions for a just wage.

In more recent decades analysis of the causes of poverty was followed eventually by legislation to provide pensions, social insurance*, unemployment* relief, and health care*, more so in Europe than in the USA. Christians and others have recognized that it is important to address poverty as relative deprivation in addition to eliminating poverty as absolute deprivation. Awareness of absolute poverty and gross inequality on a world scale has produced voluntary associations*, directly or indirectly promoted by Christians, and proposals for fairer regulation of basic commodity prices. In Latin America liberation theologians have again, though sometimes in a more political manner, voiced the sharp criticism of oppressive inequality to be found in the Bible, and the theme of hope for the poor to be found in the Gospels.

See **Almsgiving; Capitalism; Charity; Equality; Hunger, World; Health Care, Right to; Justice; Liberation Theology; Love; Mammon; Mutual Aid; Oppression; Philanthropy; Property; Revolution; Social Service of the Church; Socialism; Unemployment; Usury and Interest; Wealth; Work; Welfare State.**

J. F. Fletcher (ed.), *Christianity and Property,* 1947; D. L. Mealand, *Poverty and Expectation in the Gospels,* 1980; J. F. Sleeman, *Economic Crisis: A Christian Perspective,* 1976.

DAVID L. MEALAND

Power

Power is the capacity to effect intended results. According to the Bible all power belongs to God, who is himself Power (Matt. 6:13; 26:64). God shares his power with humanity and with the created order. He gives us the freedom to choose how we will exercise that power, in the service of our neighbor and the care of the earth, or for prideful self-deification. Our choice to exercise power irresponsibly results in our becoming the slave of the forces we were created to command. God's purpose for us is to restore us to a responsible and loving exercise of power. God discloses this purpose in history, centrally in Jesus Christ, in whom the power of love is lived out to the death and by whom dehumanizing and destructive forms of power are dethroned and harnessed, not annihilated. Thus the gospel calls humanity to share in and exercise power (*dominium terrae*), and our abdication of our responsibility as God's stewards is the sin of sloth* (acedia).

Christian theological ethics has often made the mistake of assuming that any exercise of power was sinful, but sin has more to do with how power is exercised. Although Lord Acton claimed that power corrupts, it is also true that the unwillingness or inability to exercise power also corrupts. By using power humans order their common life, specify the goals of society and distribute its goods. Not to share in power means not to share in the life of the community. Since sharing in the community is an indispensable ingredient of human life, misusing or being deprived of power reduces human beings to something less than humanness.

The problem of civil power has long been a central issue for theological ethics. State* sovereignty is the way civil power is organized and legitimated (*see* **Sovereignty, National**). There is no single biblical view of state power. Luke-Acts accepts the legitimacy of the Roman Empire almost uncritically. The book of Revelation views it very negatively. For many years the passage in Rom. 13 about respecting "the powers that be" was interpreted as a sacral legitimation of state power and sometimes even as a Christian metaphysic of the state. This frequently led to an ultraconservative view of the state. Some Christians see the state as an "order of creation" (*see* **Orders**). More recent exegesis, however, generally agrees that Rom. 13 contains no theology or metaphysics of state power. In it the apostle Paul merely answers a specific question of the church in Rome, using the understanding of state power available to him at the time. Current theological ethics tends to view the state, like other institutions for exercising power, as strictly instrumental to human justice and devoid of metaphysical substance or supernatural grounding in divine creation. This allows for a much more pragmatic view of institutions* and suggests the possibility of altering them when they no longer serve a humanizing purpose.

A more recent issue in theological ethics is the problem of revolution*, the seizure of power through extralegal means. Although Thomas Münzer raised this question in the early 16th century in connection with the German Peasants' Revolt, Christian theology has usually denied the legitimacy of the revolutionary exercise of power. Calvin taught that when the sovereign is unjust, the lesser magistrates should assume responsibility for replacing him. Luther rejected the right of revolution, insisting that even an unjust ruler does preserve that order without which political life is impossible. During the Puritan period in England, the revolutionary reorganization of the state according to the demands of God was seen to be the duty of Christian people. Thus the use of power to alter political institutions to serve moral purposes became not just a right but an obligation (*see* **Resistance**).

Some years ago the ideal of the "responsible society" was used to suggest that power should be utilized in response to the legitimate needs of those governed. Though the term "responsible society" is now used less frequently, the idea that people should control and participate in the institutions that exert power over them continues to find wide support. Power is not always responsible. It is exercised in various ways and with varying degrees of legitimacy. It can take the form of (1) coercion*, in which people are forced by extrinsic means to act contrary to their will; (2) authority*, in which power is exercised by agencies in some way answerable to those ruled; (3) manipulation, by which people are made to act against their will without realizing it. Only when power is controlled and exercised by legitimate authority can it be called responsible.

The subject of power occupies a central place in the sociological study of communities and therefore is crucial to social ethics. Some sociologists speak of a "power elite," that is, a relatively closed circle of influential decision makers only peripherally responsive to those outside. Others see power distributed much more widely and diffusely, with "decision-making centers" emerging and disappearing from issue to issue. All agree that the sources of power in a community include wealth, property, holding elective or appointive office, reputation, control of information and media, and organizational skill.

Recent studies have emphasized the increasing importance of technical skills and scientific knowledge as sources of power in advanced industrial societies whose dependence on technology steadily grows. Some have even compared the role of scientific technologists today with the role of bourgeois capitalists at the close of the age of feudalism. Both were used at first by the predominant groups of their time with little recognition of how this might affect the distribution of power. Both began to exercise their power to change the structure of the society itself, the capitalists demanding mercantilist measures that eventually subverted feudal economies, the scientists requiring a type of planning and resource allocation that will eventually undermine capitalism*. If the values of scientific technologists influence the coming society as much as those of the capitalists have influenced the present one, then respect for empirical verification, unlimited research, free exchange of information, and the thrust toward quantification may become more pervasive as the power of science grows.

In international relations, power is organized in nation-states limited only marginally by international organizations and world opinion (see **International Order**). Before the First World War, the concept of the "balance of power," that is, not concentrating too much power in any single nation or group of nations as opposed to any other, was relied on to maintain peace. After the First World War the balance of power theory fell into disfavor, with such diverse figures as Woodrow Wilson and V. I. Lenin opposing it. The idea of collective security organized through the League of Nations was introduced as a substitute. America's decision not to join the League and the failure of the League to prevent aggression resulted, after the Second World War, both in a strengthening of the idea of collective security* in the United Nations and in the return of a de facto balance of power between the USA and its allies on one side and the USSR and its allies on the other. The introduction of nuclear weapons (see **Nuclear Warfare**) and the theory of deterrence* in international affairs led some to refer to the new situation as a "balance of

terror." This balance of power was disrupted both by the weakening of the two coalitions, mainly through the independence of France vis-à-vis the USA and China vis-à-vis the USSR, and by the emergence of the "Third World" of Africa, Asia, and South America, often uncommitted in the power struggle between the USA and the USSR. A recent dilemma for the large powers has been posed by so-called "wars of national liberation" in formerly colonial areas. Strategies of massive deterrence built on nuclear weaponry seem unable to quell guerrilla uprisings in territory where the insurgency has widespread popular support, forcing a serious redefinition of the nature and limits of military power.

Future theological research on power will have to clarify how Christ's defeat of the dehumanizing powers and the gospel's call to humankind to subdue the earth and exercise responsible stewardship* can illuminate such obdurate ethical problems as the legitimacy of revolution*, the alienation of large segments of the population in industrial countries from effective participation in governing, the growing influence of technology*, and the awful hazards of nuclear deterrence* as a method of securing peace*.

HARVEY G. COX

Practical Ethics see Applied Ethics

Practical Reason

By this is understood usually reason as controlling action. The term is specially associated with Kant who contrasted it very sharply with theoretical reason. The latter tells us what is in fact the case and is limited to the realm of experience (or the world of appearances), but practical reason which lays down moral laws is conceived by him as *a priori*, and therefore it can serve as the ground of arguments in metaphysics for God, freedom, and immortality which quite transcend experience.

See **Kantian Ethics.**

A. C. EWING

Practical Wisdom see Prudence

Pragmatism

Pragmatism, a movement considered by many to be America's most important contribution to philosophy, made its greatest impact in the first four decades of the 20th century. It arose in reaction to idealist philosophies, drew heavily on empirical, scientific, and evolutionary thought, and tended not to build philosophical systems but to address specific problems of philosophy and life. It has had considerable general influence in many areas, including education, ethics, and religion. As a philosophical movement, pragmatism was dominated by two brilliant and prolific thinkers, William James and John Dewey.

William James (1842–1910) was educated at Harvard University, where he studied first at the Lawrence Scientific School and then at the Medical School (M.D., 1869). Three years later he began his lifetime of teaching at Harvard, serving successively in the fields of physiology, psychology, and philosophy. In his definitional work, *Pragmatism* (1907), James indicated that the general background for the movement was British empiricism associated with such names as Locke, Hume, and Mill; appropriately, James subtitled the book "a new name for some old ways of thinking" and dedicated it to the memory of John Stuart Mill. The work of Charles Sanders Peirce (1839–1914) provided the specific point of departure for pragmatism. Peirce also had divided his time between between science and philosophy, and was devoted to the mood and method of the laboratory. His seminal article, "How to Make Our Ideas Clear," was popularized by James twenty years after its first appearance in 1878. Peirce affirmed that beliefs are really rules for action that establish habits. Different beliefs are to be distinguished by the different modes of action to which they give rise. To develop a thought's meaning, then, we need only to determine what conduct it is fitted to produce; to attain clearness in our thoughts of an object, we need to consider what practical effects the object may involve.

James developed this principle of pragmatism in his own way, especially applying it as a test of truth. In *Pragmatism* he declared with emphasis: *"True ideas are those that we can assimilate, validate, corroborate and verify. False ideas are those that we can not."* The truth of an idea is not some stagnant property inherent in it, he insisted, but rather: "Truth *happens* to an idea. It *becomes* true, is *made* true by events." The meaning and value of all our conceptions and terms must be evaluated in a radically empirical way by attention to their practical consequences in use. James rejected any fixed or static interpretations of the universe to insist on the changing and evolutionary character of reality, especially in *A Pluralistic Universe* (1909). All theories, including metaphysical and theological theories, are to be considered as instruments to be tested in their working.

James made much use of the distinction between the "tender-minded" (who tend to be rationalistic, idealistic, religious, monistic) and the "tough-minded" (empiricist, materialistic, irreligious, pluralistic). He classified himself among the latter, yet he continued to be fascinated by the religious question. He found that religion is always a live hypothesis, and that the choice for or against it is momentous and cannot really be evaded, for evasion itself is a denial in practice. In *The Will to Believe* (1897), James showed the part played by inner or emotional evidence in determining one's world view, and justified the appeal to purpose and will as an unavoidable element in the process. In his famous Gifford Lectures, published in 1902 as *The Varieties of Religious Experience,* James affirmed that there is a certain empirical justification for religious experience in the way that it enriches life and shapes conduct. He demonstrated a willingness to be open to all kinds of experience in the search for new truth. His understanding of religion was open and searching but certainly not traditional; the study of experience led him to suggest a finite God in the pluralistic universe.

James was deeply concerned with the moral life. Though he never developed his ethical views systematically, he discussed them often. For him, ethics admits no transempirical basis, rejects all intellectualistic demands that it be based on reasoning only (for the emotions and the will must be consulted and respected), and denies that any one individual or any group has the final word in ethical questions. Ethics is, however, more than mere description of the actual concrete behavior of humans; it does provide standards of conduct. But they are those which have grown up within human experience; they are to be verified pragmatically by seeing if they help people to deal successfully with their practical problems. On pragmatic considerations, James frankly based ethics on the will to believe those concepts which answer human cravings for moral order and which direct people fruitfully in organizing their experiences. Though not unaware of the importance of social factors in individual moral choice, James stressed the importance of the individual's decision and the freedom to make it. Once made, however, a decision is open to revision as it is tested by results.

John Dewey (1859–1952) drew much from James, but in a long and influential career gave pragmatism an interpretation often called "instrumentalism" or "experimentalism" and became the acknowledged leader of the later pragmatists. Educated at the University of Vermont and at Johns Hopkins (Ph.D., 1884), he taught at the universities of Michigan, Minnesota, and Chicago before coming in 1904 to Columbia University, where he taught until retirement a quarter century later. A man of broad interests, he wrote in the fields of philosophy, logic, ethics, education, religion, art, and politics. Much of his philosophical work centered on the epistemological problem and on the relationship of thinking to conduct. As he put it in an important work of 1903, *Studies in Logical Theory:* "Thinking is adapation *to* an end *through* the adjustment of particular objective contents." Mind is thus a tool of the organism to guide action; the function of mind is to redirect activities by an anticipation of their consequences. Dewey later defined instrumentalism as "an attempt to constitute a precise logical theory of concepts, of judgments and inferences through their various forms, by considering primarily how thought functions in the experimental determinations of future consequences." His development of pragmatism was along more naturalistic and less individualistic lines than that of James; he devoted much more attention to the social dimensions of personality. In his Chicago years, Dewey was associated with George Herbert Mead (1863–1931), a pragmatist who did much of his work on the social nature of the self. In *Experience and Nature* (1925), Dewey explained that acts are of both the organism and its environment, natural and social. The world cannot be called a whole or given a meaning as a whole; meanings, purposes, ideas, and minds are being generated continually. Experience is not seen as subjective, but as a process of undergoing, of doing and suffering, as a relationship between various types of objects. Thus the human and the mental are seen to be in continuity with natural processes—all of them subject to modification. "Ideas are worthless," wrote Dewey in *The Quest for Certainty*, "except as they pass into actions which rearrange and reconstruct in some way, be it small or large, the world in which we live."

Dewey was more critical of traditional religion than James had been. He rejected any association of ideas about value with Antecedent Being, arguing that they should be associated always with practical activity. He himself espoused a position of religious humanism, signing the "Humanist Manifesto" of 1933 and the next year publishing *A Common Faith,* in which he urged the separation of religious values from organized religion, in order that the values might be focused on the actual possibilities of life.

Concern for ethics marked Dewey's entire career. One of his very early books, *Outlines of a Critical Theory of Ethics* (1891), was based on dynamic idealism, but as his pragmatic philosophy developed, his ethical approach was largely recast. The new style shows in many of his later books, as, for example, *Ethics,* written jointly with James H. Tufts in 1908. Ethics became for him an examination of the norms that actual conditions continually generate for the adaptation of habitual conduct to new circumstance. In *Human Nature and Conduct* (1922), Dewey affirmed that "morals is the most humane of all subjects. It is that which is closest to human nature; it is ineradicably empirical, not theological nor metaphysical nor mathematical." All conduct is interaction between elements of human nature and the total environment. Hence behavior is controllable through the modification of the physical and social setting. Ethics always looks ahead, not back; punishments are not ends in themselves but are instruments for the development of responsibility in persons. Ethics for Dewey involves a never-ending search for actual interests and values; through the making public of various and often hidden factors a truly open, democratic society in which continuous reform is always possible can be maintained. Thus ethics is not normative or merely descriptive, but always prospective, studying the total range of individual and social behavior in the quest for ways of living that lead to more enriching, satisfying, and freeing relationships of persons to others and to the world about them.

The impact of pragmatism on Protestant theological and ethical thought and practice was strong, especially on liberalism. Centered at the University of Chicago, efforts were made to reinterpret Christian faith in terms of pragmatic and empirical philosophy. The religious education movement, immensely influential in American Protestantism in the earlier decades of the century, drew heavily on progressive and pragmatically based educational theories and practices. Ethical thought of conspicuously different orientations from pragmatism nevertheless had to take account of its emphases. Outside the United States, the leading exponent of pragmatism was F. C. S. Schiller (1864–1937), though he preferred the term "humanism." Pragmatism also had some impact on the Catholic Modernist movement in Europe. With the rise of realistic and neo-orthodox trends in Protestant theology and ethics in the 1930s, the influence of pragmatism began to wane.

B. P. Brennan, *The Ethics of William James,* 1961; J. J. McDermott (ed.), *The Writings of William James: A Comprehensive Edition,* 1967, ²1977; J. E. Smith, *Purpose and Thought: The Meaning of Pragmatism,* 1978; H. S. Thayer, *Meaning and Action: A Critical History of Pragmatism,* 1968.

ROBERT T. HANDY

Praxis *see* **Conscientization; Counseling, Ethical Problems in; Ecumenical Movement, Ethics in the; Liberation Theology; Marxist Ethics; Political Theology; Revolution; Socialism**

Pregnancy, Termination of
see **Abortion**

Prejudice
The OED's first three definitions of the word "prejudice" state the essential elements for a moral understanding of the concept: Prejudice is an injury, detriment, or damage caused to a person by judgments or actions that disregard his rights; prejudice is a previous judgment, especially a judgment formed before due examination or consideration; prejudice is a favorable or unfavorable preconceived opinion, bias, or leaning. The third definition is the generic meaning of the concept, but the first definition is crucial for religious and philosophical ethics.

Prejudgments are normal and common because perception and cognition require the placing of particular items into more general categories. As long as the prejudgment is ad-

justed to correspond with reality no harm is done, and the process of thinking may be made more efficient. Quite frequently, however, the judgments of individuals or groups are not corrected by reference to the facts of the situation, and a favorable or unfavorable bias, often based on stereotypes, enters into moral evaluation and action. If the bias is favorable and does not result in harm to any individual or group, it may lead to positive moral acts, such as love, charity, or mercy. There is a tendency, however, to restrict the term "prejudice" to attitudes and actions with an unfavorable bias that has been formed without due consideration, is resistant to correction when the facts upon which it is based are disclosed to be erroneous, and results in harm or injury to some individual or group. Prejudice is most often manifested toward individuals or groups because of their racial, religious, national, or gender identity. Such prejudices are commonly called racism*, anti-Semitism*, ethnocentrism, or sexism (*see* **Sex Discrimination**).

Attitudes of prejudice are frequently expressed in acts of discrimination*, particularly when prejudiced individuals or groups feel that their self-interest and advantages are threatened by others. The term "prejudice" is often used to denote this practice of discrimination.

Attitudes and actions of unfavorable prejudice clearly violate standards of fairness*, justice*, impartiality, and universalizability* affirmed in both philosophical and religious ethics and of love* affirmed in Christian ethics. Even favorable prejudice is ambiguous because, by implication, it tends to assert the superiority of one individual or group and the inferiority of another. Loyalty* to a group, association, or cause may reflect favorable prejudice, but it usually implies unfavorable prejudice toward outsiders. Even if such favorable prejudice is acceptable in some intimate relationships, such as love or marriage, it is not acceptable in most interactions in the society and is acceptable only in a qualified sense when there is a conflict between loyalties to intimate relationships and other associations. In addition, both unfavorable and favorable prejudice stand under the moral requirement to have all judgments examined and tested by reference to the relevant facts in the situation. But various psychological and sociological theories, as well as most theological interpretations of sin, all suggest that the eradication of prejudice cannot be accomplished merely by appeal to moral principles and to the facts of the situation, however indispensable and helpful such appeals may be.

See **Race Relations; Women, Status of.**

G. W. Allport, *The Nature of Prejudice,* 1954.

PRESTON N. WILLIAMS

Prenatal Diagnosis *see* **Abortion; Genetics**

Prescriptivism

Prescriptivism is a name commonly given to views which hold that moral judgments are in some strong and special sense action-guiding, and that this forms part of their meaning, in addition to any descriptive meaning which they may have (thesis (1) of **Ethics**). It is to be distinguished from emotivism*, relativism*, subjectivism*.

R. M. HARE

Price, Just *see* **Just Price and Just Wage; Justice**

Pride

An unattractive sin, pride is not only "inordinate self-esteem" but the "contempt for others" to which it gives rise (OED). It is more nearly synonymous with arrogance than with mere vanity and conceit. People are glad to think that it "goes before a fall."

Yet there is a strong human tradition that admires pride. To Aristotle, the pride that is "magnanimity,"* "greatness of soul," is the desirable mean between "empty vanity" and "groveling humility." He expatiated upon its nobility, its concern with "honor on the grand scale." He offers an ethic for the great on the assumption that it is a good thing to be great. More impishly, in reaction against centuries of Christian teaching against pride, David Hume stated as a fact that "pride is a pleasant sensation, and humility a painful," and invited his readers' agreement that "the most rigid morality allows us to feel a pleasure from reflecting on a generous action" (*A Treatise of Human Nature,* bks. 2.1; 5; 7). Later, in *An Enquiry Concerning the Principles of Morals* (9.1), he called humility "a monkish virtue," almost a vice.

The characteristic Christian horror of pride develops well beyond commonsense

disapproval of overweening presumption into a reversal of the world's values. Alan Richardson describes the biblical teaching as "unparalleled in other religious and ethical systems" ("Pride," *A Theological Word Book of the Bible,* 1950). In both OT and NT, prophets and saints bear witness that it is not the great and the proud who matter most to God, and that human pride really is due for a fall; though eventually what is to topple it is not to be the pride of God but his undefeatable gentleness. In the NT, though there is a good deal about boasting, especially in Paul's epistles, there is not very much talk of pride and proudness in so many words. There is an essential and pervasive emphasis expressed by different people in many different ways on Christian humbleness rather than pretension (even, indeed especially, religious pretension). This whole way of thinking is summarized by Paul, not a man to whom humility came easily: "Far be it from me to glory except in the cross of our Lord Jesus Christ" (Gal. 6:14).

This reversal of values is more than the establishment of a different set of people to be the esteemed and important ones. What it involves is a diagnosis of the human condition as such. We have to understand that pride besets us all, not only the mighty. "No people," said William Law, "have more occasion to be afraid of the approaches of pride than those who have made some advances in a pious life," and "You can have no greater sign of a confirmed pride than when you think you are humble enough" (*A Serious Call to a Devout and Holy Life,* ch. 16).

That is easy enough to understand, but notoriously hard to abide by. Besides the practical corruptibility of human beings, who are as quick to thank God that they are not Pharisees as the Pharisee was confident of his superiority over the publican (Luke 18:11), there is a more subtle difficulty that creeps up slowly. With every good intent it is possible to lose one's grasp of the specific sin of pride by expanding it to mean anything or nothing.

In Christian teaching pride includes more than the kind of obvious presumption that shows itself in arrogance, more even than the insensitive worldliness that shows itself in snobbery (cf. Law, *Serious Call,* ch. 17). It is the more fundamental presumption by which any human creature or group, large or small-scale, constantly puts itself in the place of God. The biblical teaching has been unfolded over the centuries to explain this. "This then," said Augustine, "is the original evil: man regards himself as his own light" (*City of God* 14.13). That is why pride has been regarded as the root of all sin, the sin of angels and of the first human beings. Understood in this way, pride becomes a technical term for human rebellion against God. To belittle the wisdom of this understanding could itself be an example of rebellion.

But when pride is allowed to colonize the whole country of sin there comes a time when it cannot hold down its territories. Human beings are not prepared to believe that all sin is pride, or even that all pride is sin. If it is taken for granted that sin is practically synonymous with self-centeredness and that self-centeredness simply is the same thing as pride, this lumping of possibly distinguishable ideas together will tend to revive a kind of discontent, a feeling that there is more to be said for the "great-souled" virtues than Christians like to admit. To talk grudgingly about "proper pride" does not quite meet the case. There is dignity; there is magnanimity; there is even nobility; there is greatheartedness; and on the other hand there is the petty small-mindedness which is a persistent caricature of humility. If Christianity means a reversal of values in favor of the latter, it is not morally obvious that Christianity has got it entirely right. "It is as though there were two moral universes: the Promethean and the religious. In one a chief virtue is a properly measured pride. In the other a chief virtue is faith . . . the virtue of one is the vice of the other" (J. Kellenberger, "Religious Faith and Prometheus," *Philosophy,* Oct. 1980, pp. 500–501).

From a Christian point of view it is no answer to arrange a head-on confrontation of Augustine with Aristotle, nor to parcel out the territory between their rival concepts of pride, nor to belittle the difference of emphasis between their accounts. An answer could begin by distinguishing two senses of pride, but not as one sinful and one virtuous: they can both be sinful in different ways.

The first sense puts pride at one end of a spectrum with its contrary sin, small-mindedness, at the other end. To condemn pride as overweening grandeur could be to condemn it, not as an Aristotelian mean, but as an extreme. Both arrogance and the petty "umbleness" of Uriah Heep are wrong. If one is looking for magnanimity one will not find

it at either end of this spectrum. The emphasis of the moralist, Christian or otherwise, will not be static but likely to shift along the line, constantly trying to redress falsity of emphasis; though Christian moralists have been especially alert to dangers at the arrogant end.

Second, there is pride not as *a* sin but as the root of sin. It is the self-centeredness that shuts out other people and God, the turning upon oneself that makes love impossible. Instead of a spectrum here there is a precipice, the fall from the innocent self-love of a child of God to rebellion against God. There is a real cliff-edge here. To recognize one's own "lovability" ought to be gratitude not pride, the model not the rival for Christian love. The easy slip, both in theory and in practice, from the best to the worst is the clearest indication of human sinfulness.

This is the main point. The worst is, precisely, the corruption of the best, the spoiling of a splendid creature. It is no wonder that the sin of pride is so near, not just to amiable weaknesses but to great virtues. Christian theology, said G. R. Dunstan, "fearful (and with good cause fearful) of naughty pride, . . . has all too often played man down; but in its fulness Christian theology can only warn man against his pride because it ranks him as a creature so high. We do not preach humility to the worm" (*Not Yet the Epitaph,* 1968, p. 13). What really matters about pride, considered as the heart of sinfulness, is not just any selfishness but the corruption of *glory.*

See **Humility; Hybris.**

Aristotle, *Nicomachean Ethics* 4.3; Augustine, *City of God* 12.6; 14.13–14; D. Hume, *A Treatise of Human Nature* 2.1; A. Kolnai, "Dignity," *Philosophy,* July 1976, pp. 266–271; D. L. Sayers, "The Other Six Deadly Sins," *Creed or Chaos,* 1947, pp. 85–88.

HELEN OPPENHEIMER

Prima Facie Duties, Rules, etc.
see **Conflict of Duties; Dilemma; Norms**

Primitive Ethics
All peoples distinguish in various ways between good and bad behavior, and have ways of transmitting these values to their growing children. The content of this morality, its goals and ideals, the personality characteristics selected for approval or disapproval, the

rules and expectations, sanctions and justifications, however, all differ widely among "primitive" peoples.

The study of the ethics of preliterate groups is not very advanced. Few anthropologists have been primarily interested in this phase of the culture of the groups they were studying, and few philosophers have entered the complex field of the cross-cultural study of cultures. Ethical values, of course, are a part of many aspects of the life of groups, and most of the information about primitive ethics is thus buried in other contexts in anthropological descriptions.

The psychological undergirding of morality varies widely in primitive groups. Guilt* is not widespread. Shame* at being caught, at the ridicule of members of the community, is more nearly universal. Pride* sustains many peoples in their support of the moral code, as the Plains Indian undergoes torture rather than betray the community. Fears of illness, of spirits, of mana, of ancestors are often very powerful forces.

Morality in primitive societies may be taught or expressed in a variety of ways. There are injunctions to children, moralism, proverbs; the fear, horror, or revulsion of relatives is transmitted to children, as when they learn to feel disgust and revulsion over the idea of sexual contact with their mother's sister's child but not their father's sister's child in a society where cross-cousin marriage but not parallel cousin marriage is permitted. Laughter, approval, scolding, punishment, threats, are many of the devices of society to instill its moral values in the young learning member.

Some preliterate societies have developed highly specialized sanctions for the enforcement of proper behavior. Among some Plains Indian groups the infant learns not to cry by having water poured down its nostrils every time it starts. The gods periodically come in the form of masked men to Hopi children, whipping them for their misdeeds. Some kinship systems have a "joking" relationship, allowing considerable sexual license and the right to tease and ridicule the joking relative with impunity. The whole community shares in the laughter and keeps the deviant in line. In the Eskimo drum contest one man challenges someone who has wronged him to a rhyming contest, and the community, through its laughter and ridicule, supports the cleverer verse maker of the two, regardless of who is at fault. The skill shown in reciting appropriate proverbs will often win an African legal case rather than the evidence shown in court. Armed force, ambushes, and raids may be a principal institution for retribution.

Variety in the content of morality is also very wide. The Pueblo Indian must not be competitive. It is shameful to seek to do better than one's neighbors. The neighboring Plains Indian is highly competitive and aggressive in war and trade, seeking an individual vision from the gods to set him apart from his fellows. In some groups an individual has the rights to the fruits of a tree he inherited no matter how long ago his ancestors sold the land to someone else. In others no crop is private. All produce is communal property. For a man to eat a deer may be the most shameful of acts, causing him to become ill and die, whereas his wife may eat it with impunity. He belongs to the Deer clan and she does not.

As wide as the variety of good and bad behavior may be, some kinds of action are universally condemned. Incest* is one such well-known universal prohibition. Relations with mother or sister are almost always included within the incest restriction, but beyond that cultures differ widely in the size and scope of the incest group. It may include all the mother's relatives, in an extended family comprising scores of people who would not be counted in our kinship system, or a multitude of other relationships, large and small. It may be ritually broken on special highly charged emotional occasions for religious purposes. But whatever the variety, the incest prohibition is there.

In-group aggressions are limited or controlled in all societies to some degree. The degree of limitation may be the Zuni extreme of eliminating all competition, or it may allow a large amount of friction, tension, fighting and ill will, but there are always limits. Some kind of reciprocity in the group, some requirement of telling the truth, at least under certain circumstances, is universally required.

The size of the world of a primitive group is smaller than that of industrialized society. The world to which ethical behavior is required may also be much smaller. The outsider, the stranger, may often and without compunction be treated far differently from "people," as primitives often call their own group in distinction to others. The rights of humanity in the abstract are not likely to be a part of the morality, but interpersonal relationships in the community or family may be sharply defined.

Real behavior and ideal behavior often differ. The very fact of ideal behavior among a people, however, is evidence of moral values. This ideal behavior among primitives is not formally coded. When people have it called to their attention it is justified in the terms that "our fathers did so formerly," "the gods have commanded it," "the ancestors would be displeased if it were not done," or "the consequences of infringement would be terrible." In the actual structure of the society, however, ideal behavior is tied in with the rest of the culture in its prevalent themes and value system, its economics, its social structure and religion, deriving its strength from its functional relationship to them.

See **Anthropology and Ethics; Comparative Religious Ethics; Taboo.**

R. B. Brandt, *Hopi Ethics,* 1945; M. and A. Edel, *Anthropology and Ethics,* 1959; J. Ladd, *The Structure of a Moral Code,* 1957.
WILLIAM A. SMALLEY

Principles
See **Love; Middle Axioms; Norms; Situation Ethics,** as well as such principles as **Equality; Justice;** and **Respect for Persons.**

Prison Reform *see* **Penology; Social Service of the Church**

Privacy
As a moral and legal category privacy received little explicit attention until late in the 19th century when J. F. Stephen defended the right of privacy in a brief passage and two legal scholars argued for a right of privacy in an influential article in the *Harvard Law Review* (1890). In 1965 the US Supreme Court explicitly invoked the right of privacy to overturn legislation that prohibited the use or dissemination of contraceptives, and in 1973 it appealed to this right to overturn restrictive abortion* legislation.

There are controversies about the definition of privacy, in part because some definitions seem to focus on the right of privacy rather than privacy itself. According to F. Schoeman, privacy is "a state or condition of limited access to a person." Persons have a right of privacy if they can control others' access to them, including access through touching, observing, or obtaining information about them. Much of the modern debate about privacy has focused on access to information about a person. The right of privacy is valued in part because personal control over access to information about oneself is essential for important human relationships. In Alan Westin's image of concentric circles, the core self with its secrets (*see* **Secrecy**) is at the center, and it chooses to grant others access to information in accord with the relationships it wants to establish. The outer circles represent less intense and less personal relationships that require less personal information. We grant others access to information about ourselves in order to create, maintain, and symbolize such relationships as love, friendship, and trust. In addition, there are specific reasons in health care and elsewhere to share personal information with other people. In therapeutic contexts, confidentiality becomes important because it is a mode of control over others' access to information disclosed in that relationship. But the rule of confidentiality* is not absolute and others may—and sometimes should—disclose information in order to protect other persons.

The right to privacy has been criticized as excessively individualistic (*see* **Individualism**); disruptive of community*, and protective of wrongdoing. Yet privacy, as the right to be let alone, has also been praised as a bulwark against unwarranted intrusion by the state* and others. The critical question is the appropriate balance between individual and community. It is not clear that any information as such is intrinsically private; definitions of what is private and unavailable for public scrutiny are socially relative. But if nothing is private and protected as private, the self and its relations surely suffer. Some forms of privacy result from human neglect; for example, F. Schoeman has observed that the industrial revolution* and its associated urbanization* increased anonymity, the kind of "privacy that results from the indifference of others." However, in modern society with the development of computer* technologies in the hands of the state and others, many are concerned about the threat to privacy.

See **Autonomy; Computers; Confidentiality; Freedom; Human Dignity; Individual-**

ism; Liberalism; Morality, Legal Enforcement of; Persons and Personality; Respect for Persons; Secrecy; Totalitarian State.

S. I. Benn and G. F. Gaus (eds.), *Public and Private in Social Life,* 1983; F. Schoeman (ed.), *Philosophical Dimensions of Privacy: An Anthology,* 1984.

JAMES F. CHILDRESS

Private Morality *see* Censorship; Morality, Legal Enforcement of; Privacy

Probabiliorism

As a method of resolving practical doubts, probabiliorism requires one to act on the assumption that the law (moral principle, or rule) in question obliges when the argument in its favor is more probable than that on the side of liberty or is at least equally probable. Only when the argument in favor of liberty is clearly the *more* probable can one safely conclude that a supposed obligation does not exist. Its proponents urge that, just as in matters of belief the more probable view is the more likely to be true, so also in matters of conduct the more probable opinion is the more likely to indicate right action and save us from sin. Its critics complain that most people have neither time nor ability to undertake the sifting and weighing of conflicting probable opinions that probabiliorism requires.

See **Probabilism.**

THOMAS WOOD

Probabilism

Probabilism holds that, in a case of practical doubt, a probable opinion in favor of liberty may be followed even when the contrary opinion is more probable. It relies upon the principle that a doubtful law does not oblige and remains uncertain even when it has more probable opinions on its side. Probabilism was precisely articulated by Bartolomeo Medina in 1577, taught by many fellow Dominicans during the next eighty years, and enthusiastically propagated by many Jesuits. But experience quickly revealed how easily an unqualified probabilism could promote moral laxity; and, during a long period of unedifying controversy, successive popes had good reason to condemn laxism in 1665, 1666, and 1679. From 1656 the Dominican reaction had been to adopt probabiliorism*, and probabilism remained under a cloud

until its rehabilitation toward the end of the 18th century in a modified form. This soon became official Jesuit teaching and, with its well-understood safeguards, is the casuistical method most commonly practiced throughout the Roman Catholic Church: it will not allow any opinion in favor of liberty which a truly prudent man would not consider to be "*solidly* probable"; nor is it to be applied to those special cases in which tutiorism* is the correct procedure.

See **Equiprobabilism; Casuistry.** *See also* **Anglican Moral Theology; Counter-Reformation Moral Theology; Moral Theology.**

THOMAS WOOD

Procreation

"Be fruitful and multiply." This biblical injunction occurs first in the context of a divine word of the Creator to the newly created human beings (Gen. 1:27–28). The same injunction, in the context of the divine rescue of creation, is addressed to Noah and his family as they set foot on dry land again. Having offspring carries on and supports the work of creation. Procreating, as its Latin roots denote, is acting on behalf of (*pro*) creation (*creare,* to create). Procreation is good from the perspective of Christian ethics, both as divinely sanctioned and as a participation in creation. Also viewed as good, as divinely sanctioned and created, is the companionship of male and female, described biblically as destined toward a "one flesh" union as wife and husband (Gen. 2:18–24; Eph. 5:31). These two purposes of marriage* and sexual intercourse, the procreative and unitive, are generally affirmed in Christian thought and action, now, as in the past. Historically, procreation has been regarded as the primary purpose of marriage and a major justification for sexual intercourse. During the Reformation, the growing emphasis on companionship was accelerated and procreation was less emphasized—a continuing tendency. (For the history of the shifting weight given to procreation, *see* **Sexual Ethics.**)

Another generally accepted understanding of procreation is that it involves the responsibility of rearing one's children*. Being a parent has invariably included educating and disciplining one's children. Indeed, Calvin, commenting on 1 Tim. 2:15, where it is said that "woman shall be saved through bearing children," expects women who have no children of their own to be saved by participating in the education of children. In Eph. 6:4, fathers are warned not to provoke their children to anger but rather to "bring them up in the discipline and instruction of the Lord." Giving moral instruction to their children is an obligation of all fathers and mothers (Deut. 6:4–8).

There is a broad consensus that the responsibility for nurture may limit the number of children a given couple should plan to have. Regard for the health of the wife and the welfare of the children already born has extended as well to consideration of the economic and physical circumstances that circumscribe the couple's ability to provide nurture. Responsible parenthood* means that a couple planning to have children should take into account the needs of society as they plan the size of their family. However, the whole idea of choosing if and when to procreate has raised a number of questions on which 20th-century Christian ethical thought and practice have diverged as never before. Each procreative theme discussed below is one such question or set of questions.

Procreation: divine imperative or personal preference? During and in the Reformation, sexual intercourse within marriage was deemed not to require procreation as a justification; companionship was seen as a sufficient, divinely ordained purpose for such an expression of love. At the same time, procreation, the other divinely ordained purpose of marriage, continued to be viewed as a responsibility within marriage. Indeed, Protestants and Roman Catholics were united in their rejection of birth control throughout the 17th, 18th, and 19th centuries and in their acceptance of both the unitive and the procreative purposes of marriage (*see* **Contraception**).

The view that having children, where possible, is an explicit divine expectation of married couples is held today, not only by the Roman Catholic and Greek Orthodox churches, but also by some churches of Reformation ancestry, such as the Christian Reformed Church, the Reformed Church in America, and the Lutheran Church—Missouri Synod. All of these churches admonish Christian married couples not to refrain from having children for selfish reasons, but they agree with Christians generally that couples should, under some circumstances, voluntarily limit the number of their children. But doing so is never for these churches a matter of purely personal preference or convenience. Nor is abortion a method for limiting family size.

But, for some churches and Christians, procreative choices have come to be viewed as a matter of individual freedom*. The clearest espousal of this outlook is found in the current materials of the Episcopal Church, the Lutheran Church in America, the United Methodist Church, the Unitarian Universalist Association, and the Presbyterian Church (U.S.A.): few legal restrictions of abortion are justifiable; in general, decisions as to whether to abort are for individual women to make on grounds of their choosing. Furthermore, in view of what these groups perceive as a continuous and problematic population growth in the world, couples may responsibly decide not to have any children, irrespective of their personal socioeconomic circumstances. Indeed, the Lutheran Church in America speaks of a *right* not to have children and not to be accused of selfishness or of thwarting divine design.

All of this is very recent. It is possible quickly to observe this historical development within Christian thinking and action by a brief look at how this happened in the United Presbyterian Church U.S.A. In 1930 the (then) Presbyterian Church U.S.A. did not condemn the use of contraceptives (as it had in 1862) but warned Christians not to "fly in the face of God's decree" by avoiding the responsibilities and care of having children. Not until 1959 did the United Presbyterian Church U.S.A. officially approve contraceptives and emphasize that procreation of children was not as such necessary to justify sexual life within marriage, doing so without any of the qualifications voiced in 1930, and with no reference to an obligation to bear or rear children. The "Special Committee on Responsible Marriage and Parenthood," authorized in 1959, reported in 1962. (The history immediately above is taken from their report.) They claimed to offer a new perspective based on a new historical situation exhibiting the following three factors: (1) a serious problem of "overpopulation" to which the alternate solution is in population limitation—preferably by voluntary family planning"; (2) the call for reexamining sexuality in marriage from a theological perspective that will neither insist upon the full adequacy of the church's traditional teaching, nor simply react to Roman Catholic preoccupation with procreation and concentrate too exclusively on companion-ship as the primary good of marriage; and (3) an emerging ecumenical consensus about responsible parenthood, sparked in part by the 1958 Anglican report, *The Family in Contemporary Society.* That consensus included, for this committee, a notion of marriage as a covenant*. In 1970, the idea of covenant was used explicitly to reject the procreative imperative associated with some conceptions of the "orders of creation." That same report rejected all legal prohibitions of abortion. Among the reasons cited were the bodily rights of women and their right not to bear an unwanted child, and the claim that the majority of women seeking abortion had children and wished to limit family size. This view was adopted by the General Assembly of 1972: procreation became officially the choice of individuals exercising their rights in accord with their wishes, women having special bodily rights in these matters.

Feminism (*see* **Feminist Ethics**) and the growing voice of women in church decision-making, as well as in the academic pursuit of Christian ethics, are certainly in evidence in the development briefly reviewed in the above paragraph. However, it is a serious error to attribute a monolithic view to women and to feminists.

There are church bodies and Christian thinkers who depict procreation neither as a moral imperative nor as a completely individual preference. On the one hand, procreation is a blessing; on the other hand, limiting procreation is a marital decision, and abortion is not a method of birth control from a moral point of view. Among the churches with this general perspective are the American Lutheran Church, the Presbyterian Church in America, the Disciples of Christ, Assemblies of God, Brethren, Jehovah's Witnesses, and the Moravians.

Procreative and unitive sexual relations: separable or inseparable? One might argue that this question has been answered: Since sexual relations for the sake of companionship within marriage have been condoned by Christians generally, then have not sexual intercourse for the sake of procreation and sexual intercourse for the sake of nourishing the marital relation been separated, and are they not separable? They are separable in some respects, but not in every respect in the thinking and actions of some Christian groups and individuals.

Within official Roman Catholic teaching, *Humanae Vitae* (1968) advocates that every act of marital sexual intercourse remain open to its procreative biological potential. What that means is that no barriers to the possibility of procreation through sexual relations be used except the one naturally and biologically present during a woman's infertile period. For some Roman Catholics, only natural family planning is licit. Ruled out also is any recourse to artificial insemination, by a husband (AIH), or by a donor (AID): AIH and AID are both attempts to have children without the loving and unitive act of sexual intercourse with one's spouse (*see* **Reproductive Technologies**).

However, among some Roman Catholics, moral theologians and others, as reflected in Vatican Council II, it is marriage that is intended to be procreative, not every marital act. This is the generally held Protestant point of view. However, there are Protestants as well as Roman Catholics who see AID as a threat to the relation that should exist between wife and husband: they should both bodily and lovingly contribute to their offspring. Protestants who approve AIH and AID emphasize the spiritual, psychological, and physical bonds between the couple using artificial insemination and the child that results. In short, nurture, rather than the one-flesh bond between two people, is accented (*see* **Reproductive Technologies**).

Having children: a blessing received or selected? Christians are united on the goodness of procreation: becoming and being parents is a blessing of God. Scriptural references for this conviction include Gen. 1:28; Pss. 127:3; 128:3–4. Numerous church bodies are explicit about their belief that having children is a blessing. Though this consensus is genuine, it applies only to children who have been born and not to all of them. The concept of an unwanted child has been introduced into church statements. The Lutheran Church in America declared in 1970 that every child has a right to be a wanted child. An unwanted child is not being called a blessing by those who use this language, at least not prospectively.

In addition, abortion is also considered morally acceptable—for some, required—when a fetus has been diagnosed as defective. Here again the child in prospect is not viewed as a blessing, but as a possible burden to the parents or society, or as destined for a burdensome life. Among churches that single out abortion for the sake of avoiding the birth of a defective fetus are the Episcopal Church, the Lutheran Church in America, and the Presbyterian Church (U.S.A.).

What divides Christians is a different conception of marriage as a covenant*. The difference may be illustrated by comparing two current views; that of Pope John Paul II and that adopted by the 195th General Assembly (1983) of the Presbyterian Church (U.S.A.).

In his apostolic exhortation *Familiaris Consortio* (1981), Pope John Paul II portrays the marital covenant as a God-given capacity and vocation of each person to love and be loved. God's own love is exhibited in initiating a "personal loving communion," by creating and sustaining the human race in the divine image. Through these actions, God has "inscribed in the humanity of man and woman the vocation, and thus the capacity and responsibility, of love and communion." This love in marriage entails, then, at once a responsibility for sustaining the human race and personal communion. Human beings, without qualification, bear God's image (*see* **Image of God**). Each life is a blessing to be welcomed. Some Protestant bodies and individuals also portray the marital covenant in this way.

In "Covenant and Creation," a 1983 policy statement of the Presbyterian Church (U.S.A.) on contraception and abortion, marriage is also described as a covenant with God. Pope John Paul II would agree with these Presbyterians that courage, love, patience, and strength are called for in bearing children, as well as the economic and spiritual resources to nurture a human life. The parting of the ways comes when the termination of pregnancy is said to be "an affirmation of one's covenant responsibility." This may occur in two instances: when the fetus is diagnosed as defective; and when resources are considered inadequate to care for a child appropriately. From the papal perspective, any failure to welcome these pregnancies and subsequent births would be a break in a covenant established not solely by parental decision but by divine activity. Furthermore, the Presbyterian document "Covenant and Creation" states that making a decision about abortion is a woman's decision and should be a legal right. Once again there is a parting of the ways: the papacy regards men and women as equally responsible for procreation and protecting human life at every stage. Not all Catholics agree with the papal view; not all Protestants agree with the Presbyterian Church (U.S.A.).

Characteristically, church bodies and Christian ethicists are united, however, in calling for the churches, its members, and, to some extent, governmental agencies, to provide support, financial and spiritual, for pregnant women and families in need of it. Feminists have provided leadership in these matters, both in the churches and the literature of Christian ethics. Christians are agreed that human beings should work for a world in which each child is treated as befits a gift or blessing of God.

See **Abortion; Children; Contraception; Family; Feminist Ethics; Freedom; Life, Sacredness of; Marriage; Parenthood; Population Policy; Responsibility; Sex Discrimination; Sexual Ethics; Sterilization; Women, Status of.**

M. A. Farley, "Sexual Ethics," *EB*, 1978; B. W. Harrison, *Our Right to Choose*, 1983; J. T. McHugh, *A Theological Perspective on Natural Family Planning*, 1983; P. Ramsey, *Fabricated Man*, 1970; W. Yates, "Population Ethics: Protestant Perspectives," in *EB*, 1978.

VALERIE DEMARINIS/ARTHUR J. DYCK

Professional Associations
see **Trade Unions and Professional Associations;** *see also* **Codes of Ethics; Professional Ethics**

Professional Ethics
A profession is not only a way of making a living; it is the carrying out of an occupation to which standards of competence and responsibility are attached. Robert K. Merton has named the social values that make up the concept of a profession as: "First, the value placed upon systematic knowledge and the intellect: knowing. Second, the value placed upon technical skill and capacity: doing. And third, the value placed upon putting this conjoint knowledge and skill to work in the service of others: helping." A professional person is committed to maintaining standards. These are partly standards of competence; he or she will normally have been expected to have secured recognized qualifications for entry into the profession. They will also be standards of

"professional integrity." Professional ethics concern the particular kinds of conduct recognized as necessary to this integrity in the profession in question. In some cases, notably the medical profession, professional ethics form an explicit code, disregard of which can be a matter for disciplinary action on the part of the professional association. Social work in the UK, which is a grouping of various occupations, was given a professional code in 1975, based on an explicit value judgment: "the recognition of the value and dignity of every human being irrespective of origin, status, sex, sexual orientation, age, belief, or contribution to society," and it sets out consequential principles and conduct for the kinds of situation social workers are likely to meet. The National Association of Social Workers in the U.S.A. had formulated its professional code by 1960. The American Nurses' Association adopted its first code of ethics in 1950, and a comparison of that code with the 1976 revision reveals an altered conception of the profession, particularly in its movement away from obedience to the physician to responsibility to the patient.

The earliest known instance of a "professional code" is the Hippocratic Oath*, probably of the 4th century B.C.:

> I will look upon him who shall have taught me this Art even as one of my parents. I will share my substance with him, and I will supply his necessities, if he be in need. I will regard his offspring even as my own brethren, and I will teach them this Art, if they would learn it, without fee or covenant. I will impart this Art by precept, by lecture and by every mode of teaching, not only to my own sons but to the sons of him who has taught me, and to disciples bound by covenant and oath, according to the Law of Medicine.
>
> The regimen I adopt shall be for the benefit of my patients according to my ability and judgment, and not for their hurt or for any wrong. I will give no deadly drug to any, though it be asked of me, nor will I counsel such, and especially I will not aid a woman to procure abortion. Whatsoever house I enter, there will I go for the benefit of the sick, refraining from all wrongdoing or corruption, and especially from any act of seduction, of male or female, of bond or free. Whatso-

ever things I see or hear concerning the life of men, in my attendance on the sick or even apart therefrom, which ought not to be noised abroad, I will keep silence thereon, counting such things to be as sacred secrets.

The Hippocratic Oath is still read to medical students when they receive instruction in medical ethics in the course of their training. This code emphasizes the need to maintain a relationship of confidence between doctor and patient; the patient must be sure that the doctor will respect information given him or her in the course of professional service. This is analogous to the "seal of the confessional" between priest and penitent, whereby a priest is bound not to divulge what he hears in confession. (In this case there are sacramental as well as ethical reasons, since the priest is looked on as instrumental in the relation between the penitent and God.) In some countries these communications are "privileged," that is, the recipient is not bound to disclose them in a court of law under threat of contempt of court if he or she refuses. Communications between lawyers and their clients are privileged. The reasons for this were given by L. J. Knight-Bruce, in *Pearse* v. *Pearse* (1846), De Gex and Sm. 28.29:

> Truth, like all other good things, may be loved unwisely—may be pursued too keenly—may cost too much. And surely the meanness and the mischief of prying into a man's confidential consultations with his legal adviser, the general evil of infusing evil and dissimulation, uneasiness, suspicion and fear into those communications which must take place, and which, unless in a condition of perfect security, must take place uselessly or worse, are too great a price to pay for truth itself.

This pronouncement throws light on the general character of professional ethics. Professional ethics do not concern the general obligations of human beings to other human beings as such, but canalize certain of these obligations in relation to the functional requirements of carrying out a particular kind of service. They formulate the sort of conduct needed if the relation between the professional person and his or her client is to be such that the work in which they are both interested can be done. The relation between the professional person and the client is, however, only one of the role relationships in which the former is professionally concerned. There are also relationships to colleagues, and relations as a professional person to the lay public. Thus, though lawyers or barristers are under an obligation not to divulge communications between themselves and their clients, they also have a duty to the court and to the cause of justice. While their duty is to put the best interpretation on the evidence in the interest of the client, they must not deceive the court by making a statement they know to be false. Professional ethics as between colleagues are intended as means of maintaining mutual trust and collaboration within the profession. They often prescribe that professional persons shall not advertise their services, shall not entice clients from another practitioner, and shall be ready to help a colleague in case of need. Some of these matters are questions of "professional etiquette"; the borderline between etiquette and ethics is, however, not easy to draw.

An important part of professional ethics is concerned with the maintenance of what Talcott Parsons called "affective neutrality." Some personal relations are such that affections and emotion enter into them in a particular and intimate way. The relation between husband and wife is an outstanding case in point. Professional relationships are best served where professionals can achieve a certain emotional detachment while at the same time being genuinely concerned to help their clients. This does not mean they need be "cold fish"; it means they must avoid the kind of emotional involvement that could cloud their judgment; and while they may not be able to avoid liking some of their clients better than others, they must not let this be a reason for giving them preferential treatment. A sexual relationship between a doctor and a patient can be a matter for disciplinary action and for striking the doctor's name off the register. Psychoanalysts in particular have had to give careful thought to the ethical restraints necessary in the "transference" situation, where an emotional attitude on the patient's part has to be allowed temporarily for therapeutic reasons.

A professional code can therefore be presented as a form of functional role morality, designed to promote the kind of relationships within which a required service can best be carried out. Beyond this, the behavior so enjoined also becomes valued on its own account, as a matter of professional integrity, and adds to the respect with which professional persons are regarded in the community. Professional ethics are therefore concerned not only with relations with clients, colleagues, and members of the public but also with maintaining the public image of the profession. In the case of the established professions in particular, professional ethics are preeminently conservative in the nonparty sense of conserving the moral and intellectual traditions of the profession, and also in the sense of being administered by what tends to be a conservative hierarchy not always sensitive to new social conditions. Nevertheless, they can represent a tradition of careful thought and experience concerning certain specific problems that a practitioner is likely to meet in the course of his or her work. They thus protect against certain kinds of pressure—for instance, the pressure to use professional influence in a "nepotist" way to secure jobs for relations and friends whose qualifications may not be equal to those of other candidates, and above all, against the pressure to divulge confidential information. The work of a professional person, especially perhaps that of a doctor, gives rise to a large number of often very difficult problems for moral decisions. That the lines for guidance on some of the more typically recurrent of these problems have been laid down in a person's professional ethics is not likely to mean that the individual's own powers of moral judgment need go unexercised, or that he or she need not acquire skill and sensitivity in personal relationships.

See **Applied Ethics; Bioethics; Business Ethics; Codes of Ethics; Confidentiality; Hippocratic Oath; Medical Ethics.**

W. W. Boulton, *A Guide to Conduct and Etiquette at the Bar of England and Wales,* 1953; A. M. Carr-Saunders and P. A. Wilson, *The Professions,* 1933; *Code of Ethics for Social Work* (1975) by British Association of Social Workers; A. Etzioni, *The Semi-Professions,* 1969, ch. on "Social Work as a Semi-Profession"; A. Jameton, *Nursing Practice: The Ethical Issues,* 1984; R. K. Merton, *Some Thoughts on the Professions in American Society,* 1960; T. Parsons, *Essays on Sociological Theory,* 1949, ch. 8, "The Professions and Social Structure."

DOROTHY EMMET

Progress, Belief in

Progress—the view that both the ends of natural and human life and the means to those ends are improving and that desirable goals are being achieved—is a characteristically modern notion. Belief in progress was almost nonexistent in the Greek, Roman, and even Far Eastern world views, particularly as long as the dominating notion was that of fate. Even early Christian thought, holding that the end of the world was soon to come, looked forward to a better condition only in the next life and then only for those who are saved.

Belief in progress is based on the conjunction of two modern notions: (1) the view that *change* characterizes all existence, that this is a growing universe from the microscopic to the macroscopic levels; (2) the doctrine of *evolution*—the view that all existence is growing in complexity and longevity (*see* **Evolutionary Ethics**). Joining these two basic notions with certain historical considerations, 19th-century thought (Spencer) held that progress is not only possible but inevitable. In various theories of progress there are diversities of views concerning the *rate* and the *pattern*—that it proceeds in a straight line, that it is cyclical and embodies periods of regression, etc.

Believers in progress, along with believers in democracy, usually emphasize the increasing domination of matter by mind (Peirce) and the guidance of the mind by ever higher ends. As a consequence, there is little if any debate about what is usually called "outward progress"—control over environment, communication, relief of pain, and growth in health. Argument exists chiefly, if not solely, about the fact and degree of so-called "inward progress"—that is, the human being's capacity to become a free and responsible person in a world of free and responsible nations. Thus, from Will Durant to J. B. Bury, contemporary observers, while placing serious strictures on evolutionary naturalism's belief in the inevitability of progress, soundly reaffirm belief in the idea of progress, either within the naturalistic and humanistic context or within the framework of Christian theology. The latter emphasizes the possibilities of individuals' personal and collective growth when they are under the guidance of God. Indeed there is *a contemporary reassessment* of the whole doctrine of nature and grace which, employing both philosophical and biblical insights, stresses, though cautiously and critically, the redemptive and therefore improving character of a life under God.

With particular reference to religion, the last decades of the 20th century witness the appearance, at least among scholars, of efforts to develop, after centuries of conflict, a progressive spirit of mutual understanding and cooperation among the major religions of the world, with a cautious metaphysical thrust; it is argued that the deity will bring about an ultimate redemption of all human life.

See also **Hope; Optimism; Transcendence.**

J. Baillie, *The Belief in Progress,* 1951; C. L. Becker, *Progress and Power,* 1960; J. B. Bury, *The Idea of Progress,* 1920; K. W. Marek, *Yestermorrow: Notes on Man's Progress,* ET 1961.

CHARLES W. KEGLEY

Prolongation of Life *see* **Life, Prolongation of**

Promise

Jewish and Christian morality is largely founded on the biblical conception of God as one who makes promises and lives up to those promises, as reflected in his covenants* and his fidelity* to those covenants. God's righteousness* is reflected in his covenant-faithfulness, which grounds the Christian's faith* and hope* (*see* **Old Testament Ethics; Prophetic Ethics; New Testament Ethics; Eschatological Ethics**). "Promise" may be defined as a person's declaration that he or she will do or refrain from doing what has been specified. A promise is a self-imposed obligation. In promising, agents make a commitment and thus bind themselves to actions in the future. Through their promises, they transform what was morally optional, discretionary, or neutral into an obligation. Other moral principles and rules limit promises; promises to do what is morally wrong are generally held not to be obligatory.

There are various philosophical accounts of both the institution* or convention* of promising and an agent's obligation to keep his or her promises. The utilitarian or consequentialist account of the institution or convention of promising holds that it maximizes human welfare by facilitating interaction and trust. But this account does not adequately explain the individual's obligation of fidelity, particularly when it is advantageous to break a promise. According to one proposal (G. J. Warnock, *The Object of Morality,* 1971), promises are binding because of truthfulness* or veracity; agents are obligated to make the situation conform to their statements (*see also* **Honesty**). Although there are similarities between veracity and fidelity to promises, the major difference is that in making a promise, people create expectations on the part of others who trust them and rely on the promise. This difference suggests the relevance of the principle of fairness*, and according to another proposal, "the principle of fidelity is but a special case of the principle of fairness applied to the social practice of promising" (John Rawls, *A Theory of Justice,* 1971). The key moral element is the agent's commitment to do X in the future through the invocation of the institution of promising and the creation of expectations and trust* on the part of the promisees. There are often disputes about whether a particular promise was knowingly and freely made, as well as about justified exceptions to promise-keeping. Many interpreters hold that promise-keeping is the key moral ingredient in contracts*, which play an important role in modern societies. For promises made to God, *see* **Vows.**

JAMES F. CHILDRESS

Propaganda

It is embarrassing for the modern Christian to remember that as a matter of semantic history, propaganda has been used synonymously with evangelism. When the (Roman Catholic) Congregation for the Propagation of the Faith was instituted in 1622 or the (Anglican) Society for the Propagation of the Gospel in Foreign Parts in 1701, "propaganda" was clearly assumed to be a suitable word for evangelism or the mission of the church. Propaganda was appropriate when it meant persuading people to become Christians. The embarrassment for the modern Christian is that "propaganda" has now come to mean contriving conditions where people's critical resistances are so weakened and their freedom of choice so severely reduced as to make acquiescence all too likely. Such acquiescence is incompatible with the free responsible response of faith.

The biblical material and Christian practice suggest the necessity for clarifying the distinction between education, propaganda, and evangelism. In Christian history "religious instruction" has frequently amounted to propaganda in the same way that in Marxist thought Communist propaganda is equated with education. The object of education, however, is to increase the understanding of knowledge and the ability to handle it with humility, patience, and a critical appreciation. It seeks to enlarge the range of experience and to nurture independence of judgment. In propaganda as it has now developed, on the other hand, there is a systematic attempt to influence people by reducing the amount of information available for discussion and encouraging them to act on impulse. Those to be persuaded are led to believe that only one line of action in a particular situation is possible.

Christian evangelism may be defined as a way of handling the gospel in a style that is appropriate to the manner of Christ. This manner is that of the "sign" which is at the same time a *skandalon* ("a stumbling block"). Jesus did not engage in propaganda about himself or about God. He spoke and acted in a signful, parabolic way which suggested that he believed that not he but God would do the revealing. His vocation was not to preach himself or explain himself but to do the task God had given him. This explains what Kierkegaard calls the indirect communication of Jesus, and it has as a corollary a certain indirectness in the manner of Christian evangelism. This is necessary to safeguard the freedom* and autonomy* of the decision* of faith* and to eschew the kind of language which assumes, for instance, that the divinity of Christ is logically demonstrable or that faith is simply another word for ability to follow an argument.

In what ways, then, would propaganda, as presented above, be inappropriate for the activity of Christian evangelism? Propaganda would violate the "signful" character of communication which the NT shows to be normative to Christians. Christ's method of parable, allegory, and irony needs to be reflected in the manner of those who seek to act and speak in his name. In the words of C. S. Lewis: "Christian evangelism should by its very means convey the gospel which heals the wounds of individuality without undermining the privilege of it" (*An Experiment in Criticism,* 1961, p. 140). Propaganda is as inimical to Christianity as it is to the arts and for the same reason: it destroys the economy which is the feature of both modes of communication by saying too much and leaving too little margin for the free response of the person addressed.

See **Human Dignity; Persons and Personality; Respect for Persons**.

S. Kierkegaard, *The Point of View for My Work as an Author* (1851), ET 1962; *Training in Christianity* (1850), ET 1941.

E. J. TINSLEY

Property

Property is that which one owns, one's wealth or goods. It presupposes the right to possession, use, or disposal of anything. Whereas in the past it was land and material goods that were important, in our day such intangibles as insurance policies, copyrights, trademarks, professional rights of tenure, and trade secrets are also significant.

Property is of great interest for Christian ethics. Inequality in the distribution of property stratifies society and gives rise to considerable differences in social status, political power, and well-being. Christians must discern how they should respond to the dominical commandment to love the neighbor in their use and distribution of property.

The essence of Christian thinking about property is that the goods of the earth are given by God so that all humankind may use them in the pursuit of self-realization*. Property rights are subordinate to the common right to use property, but there is a right to own property.

An important OT teaching was that the land belonged to God. The people were tenants. Legitimate and appropriate possession was protected by the Decalogue, but the Torah protected the weak and underprivileged, and the prophets denounced exploitation of the poor and excessive concentrations of wealth in the hands of the rich.

In the NT Christ proclaimed the primary importance of the kingdom*. He pronounced the poor blessed, taught that wealth was an obstacle to the kingdom, and required of his followers that they be radically detached. Although he did not condemn private property he taught that possessions were to be used for those in need.

The Acts of the Apostles witnesses to a primitive love-communion, but this did not persist. New Testament writings offer no plan for the betterment of society but rather emphasize the obligation to help the poor and avoid avarice.

In the patristic period there was no single attitude to property. Some renounced it completely and chose monasticism, but the church accepted rich members, who had, however, to help the poor. It also ran efficient welfare organizations.

Thomas Aquinas (ST II-II.66) taught that private property was of positive law, not natural law, but was legitimate because it offered certain advantages. Property must be rightly used. Temperance*, liberality, munificence, and almsgiving* are virtues, and avarice* and prodigality vices (see **Covetousness**).

Until recently manuals of moral theology concentrated on defining justice in the acquisition and exchange of property and in almsgiving. The modern concern is more for social justice (see **Justice**). The modern economy is characterized by science and technology. Much economic activity is concentrated in large organizations and, recently, automation has enabled a few managers and workers to produce great quantities of goods. Desire for social justice encourages concern about how the economy should be controlled and how wealth and income should be distributed.

Early liberal capitalism exalted the freedom of individuals to pursue their own interest in a free market in goods and labor. It was believed that, as if by the workings of an unseen hand, the pursuit of private self-interest would best achieve the prosperity of all. There was resistance to all groupings and to government intervention in the economy. The essential institution of capitalism is the private ownership of the means of production. Ownership is separate from labor. The right to profit goes with capital, and ownership does not imply social obligations.

Capitalist economies are much altered by the growth of government intervention and the welfare state*, by nationalization, the rise of trade unions*, the shift of control from capital to management, and the control of the market by large retail chains. But companies still operate more freely in the international market, and the ideology* of capitalism* still has its defenders.

Socialism* cannot be identified with Marxism, but that is its most important form today. Whether its economic and political theory can be separated from its philosophy of dialectical materialism is a moot point. Essential features include centralized control and planning of the economy, and communal ownership of the means of production. Economic and political theory is allied to a theory and practice of revolution*, and predictions are made about the inevitable downfall of capitalism and the advent of a socialist society. Socialist economic systems, like capitalist, have altered with the increased scale of modern industry, and the two systems now have many common features.

The churches, in response to these economic systems and the ideologies that accompany them, have stressed a number of principles of economic morality, notably in a series of papal encyclicals and in the work of the World Council of Churches: There is a right to private property, particularly because it is a defense for freedom*. But there are social obligations attached to ownership. Capital must have regard for the dignity of the workers, the social character of the economic regime, social justice and the common good*. Both capital and labor have rights to a share in the profits. Workers have a right to form free trade unions, to participate in the running of enterprises, and to receive a just wage. The state should coordinate economic activities for the common good and has a right to assume ownership or some other form of control of productive property when the common good requires it.

In recent years the churches have expressed concern about the gross inequalities that exist between nations and have urged economic coordination and aid to developing countries, while rejecting economic liberalism in world trade. The basic principle, that economic activity must serve humankind in all its phases and that all have a right to benefit from it, must be applied at the international level too.

Recent writings have stressed that no single aim—for example, freedom* of the individual or equality*—should alone guide work for social reconstruction. Integral human development and personal and communal excellence are more comprehensive goals. Policies must be pragmatic and realistic, and must result in a just and sustainable society. New forms of ownership may facilitate social cohesion. The church is urged to make a preferential but not exclusive option for the poor.

See **Capitalism; Collectivism; Common Good; Communism; Covetousness; Ecumenical Movement; Equality; Freedom; Individualism; Liberation Theology; Libertarianism; Justice; Mammon; Official Roman Catholic Social Teaching; Oppression; Poverty; Socialism; Usury and Interest; Wealth; Welfare State.**

D. Dorr, *Option for the Poor,* 1983; M. Hengel, *Property and Riches in the Early Church,* ET 1974; Pastoral Constitution on the Church in the Modern World, pt. I, ch. 3, *The Documents of Vatican II,* ed. W. M. Abbott, S.J., 1966.

BRENDAN SOANE

Prophetic Ethics

The ethics of Israel's prophetic tradition is grounded in religious faith. What God requires of Israel and of its individual members —that is by definition what is good. But like other elements of the teaching of the prophets, what is revealed is also to be explained, tested, refined, and continually related to the changing circumstances of the community's life. What God requires, therefore, is both revealed and discovered, or rediscovered.

The language of the book of Deuteronomy puts this view before the people clearly: God sets before them the choice of life or death, but urges them to choose life (Deut. 30:15–20). The demands that God discloses through Moses on the sacred mountain are not far away, obscure, ambiguous; rather, they are near at hand, knowable, doable (Deut. 30:11–14). This understanding, from the 7th or the 6th century B.C., is in full accord with Israel's prophetic heritage.

The book of Deuteronomy also lays down the fundamental motive of ethical action: responsive love to the God who loved Israel and chose its forebears to be the people of God (Deut. 7:6–11; 10:12–22). This understanding also derives from the great prophets of Israel, especially from Amos, Hosea, Isaiah, and Jeremiah. We can therefore define prophetic ethics as human conduct stemming from God's demands, placed upon the people out of love for them, and to be fulfilled out of love for God. The kind of human conduct demanded is the heart of prophetic teaching; fundamentally, it involves establishing and maintaining in the structures of the society the justice (*mishpat*) and righteousness (*sedaqah*) that God demands in the people's dealings with one another, with other peoples, and with God. These two terms are relational terms; the first points to the public structures of the common life and of religion; the second has in view the inward quality of this relation between God and people, and among the members of the society. The specific content of the terms shows up in the concrete teaching of the great prophets.

Origins. Like Israel, the neighboring peoples had their prophets. These prophets had the task of discerning the will of God or the gods for the public life of the community. They were especially important in times of public danger or at the launching of major new undertakings, for they received the word from the transcendent realm as to whether or not the proposed public act was propitious and in line with the deity's will. Prophets were messengers of the deity, bringing, in a form of speech recognizable and familiar to the people, the message they had received. Various means for the reception of such a message were practiced: examination of natural phenomena, study of portions of animals offered as sacrifices, dreams, ecstatic seizure, the sacred dance, isolation and silence. The prophet had the task of *interpreting* what was disclosed, making available to rulers and to the people at large God's answer to particular questions or issues brought to the deity. But in the ancient world as well as within the Israelite community, prophets also received messages from the deity that they had not asked for: God took the initiative to communicate words that king, people, and prophet might very well not care to hear. But the society had to find ways to let such messages come, and to respond to them as best it could. The story of the prophet Micaiah ben Imlah of the 9th century B.C. (1 Kings 22) is an excellent example of how kings might take the initiative in a time of proposed military engagement to discover the will of God, only to receive from one prophet a message differing from that of the majority of the prophets, and much out of line with what the king and the people wished to hear.

By the time of the prophet Amos, around 750 B.C., prophets were an essential part of Israelite society. They had ground on which to stand, were expected to deliver God's messages, and were accustomed as well as required to explain and to defend such messages before king and people. They clearly drew upon what they understood to be the Israelite religious heritage, going back to Moses and to the other ancestors. They were, in their own view, reformers of a religious understanding and practice that had grown corrupt and dangerous, even though the society was prospering, and religious observances were flourishing too. Yet we know that they were persons of great originality of thought and of immense literary talent. Form and content combine to provide a revolutionary ethical and religious message that has endured to the present day.

Essential teaching. Amos, Hosea, Isaiah, and Micah appear at the time of the crisis posed by the westward movements of the Assyrians shortly after the middle of the 8th century B.C. These prophets saw the crisis not in military terms but as one arising from Israel's apostasy from God. Israel had forsaken God's demands so thoroughly and utterly that only death to the society seemed the sure result. "The end has come upon my people Israel; I will never again pass by them" (Amos 8:2). Preparations for defense against one or another enemy in such a time as that would count for nothing (Isa. 7:1–7; 30:1–5). Israel's only course of conduct in such a crisis was to place its entire life faithfully before God. To practice righteousness might not mean deliverance—but it just might. At all events, Israel could meet the crisis, these prophets say, in only one way: by turning from evil and practicing justice and righteousness. The prophets make it entirely clear just what such practice entails: it means the end of corrupt economic practices, of the perversion of justice in the courts, of the abuse of family members and of the poor and the defenseless. It also means, on the larger scale, the end of viciousness and cruelty in dealing with one's neighbors. Amos begins his message with a picture of the cruelty and viciousness rampant among Israel's neighbors and also within Israel (Amos 1–2). Isaiah vividly portrays the corruption in Jerusalem, a virtual "harlot city" (Isa. 1:21). Hosea shows that the corruption includes priest and prophet alike; indeed, there can be found "no faithfulness or kindness, and no knowledge of God in the land." Wherever he looks, the prophet finds only "swearing, lying, killing, stealing, and committing adultery." All the structures of the society are in a state of collapse, as "murder follows murder" (Hos. 4:1–3). Since priest and prophet have responsibility for "knowledge of God," their failure is most serious, even more serious than the failures and the corruption of king and prince and judge and business operator. For without these interpretations of the divine will, how is anyone within the community to know what true justice and righteousness and faithfulness are? (Hos. 4:4–10).

The first fundamental point in prophetic ethics is thus before us: The prophets of Israel threaten the entire community with imminent destruction from the God who loved and chose it, a death that is the virtually certain consequence of its failure to be a just and faithful community, living in accordance with God's will. God's demands are a life-or-death matter. Israel can choose life or can enter into death (Deut. 30:15–20, as noted above), and the evidence of its choice is to be seen in the quality and character of its dealings with God, with the neighboring peoples, and within the community itself.

Did these prophets offer hope for Israel's future? The question is often put in the wrong way. These prophets clearly believed that God remained Lord even over the divine judgments that were pronounced. The prophets called upon Israel to turn from evil and to God, to the good (Amos 5:4, 6, 14–15), that they might live and not die. The important question is not whether the prophets as individuals may have had hope for Israel's future. The question is whether they gave a message to the community that was intended to drive them only to despair in their contrition; or whether they delivered a message from God that invited the people to turn to God and either find forgiveness and a new possibility for faithfulness, or at least die with the awareness that they had "given God glory"—a term that seems to mean to acknowledge that God is in the right and one is oneself in the wrong (see Josh. 7:19 and Acts 12:23). The prophets may well have believed that there was no hope for Israel beyond the coming destruction God would visit upon the people. But the prophets were confident that there was hope in God, and that the people were to repent and turn to God, whether or not the result was a positive one for the then-existing generation.

The second element in the prophetic teaching that stands out everywhere is God's concern for those who seem most frequently to be without adequate protection within the existing social structures: slaves, widows, orphans, persons under heavy debt, the landless, the stranger within the community. There is not, according to the law (Ex. 23:3; Lev. 19:15; Deut. 16:19–20), to be any bias in favor even of the poor and the needy, for the community is charged to show no partiality at all. But God is especially the champion of those who have no other; God hears the outcry of the suffering and the oppressed, and God acts to bring aid, even when the people fail to do so.

Prophetic ethics not only offers denunciations of the mistreatment of these needy ones; it portrays the evildoers in such gripping terms that the outrage and pathos of evil are powerfully evident to any hearer or reader. Isaiah speaks of those who grab up available land, joining house to house, field to field, until they are left alone in the land. The very process of enlarging landholdings beyond any possible need ends with isolation, the loss of any meaningful human community (Isa. 5:8). Amos pictures those who live in incredible luxury while around them misery increases to desperate proportions; and yet such prosperous ones idle their lives away uncaring. They do not even grieve over the ruin of Joseph. They could at least grieve over the fate of their victims (Amos 6:4–6).

A third element seems to derive from the traditions connected with Moses: God's exclusive claim upon the people, which relativizes all other claims, including the claim of religious practices. The prophets probably did not wish to see the entire system of sacrifices and cultic offerings abandoned, for religious practice without sacrifice is difficult to imagine in the ancient world. But they clearly did see sacrifices and offerings as secondary to public justice and to the practice of right dealings in home and community. Indeed, they saw that religious practices could very easily become a substitute for the practice of public justice, and they went so far as to say that God did not really demand sacrifices and offerings in earlier times; rather, God called for obedience (see Isa. 1:10–20; Jer. 7:21–26; Hos. 6:6; Amos 5:21–27; Micah 6:1–8).

But not only was religious practice secondary to the full range of God's demands; God alone was Israel's true king. God gave kings and God took away kings, entirely at the divine pleasure (Hos. 8:4; 9:15; 10:3–4). Zion was the symbol of God's presence with the people and a glorious mark of God's purpose to fulfill the promise made to Israel's forebears and to David. But not even Zion was sacrosanct; it could be plowed like a field (Micah 3:12), its temple brought to ruin and abandoned (Jer. 7:1–15; see Jer. 26). And the people of God was itself not so sacred in God's sight that it was indispensable to God; if need be, God could raise up another people (Amos 9:7–8).

This extraordinary relativizing of all the structures of the common life, including the religious structures that provided a place for the prophets to speak and that also maintained their messages over the decades and the centuries, is of immense import for ethics. It assured a critical dimension to Israel's religious ethics, requiring that the prophets defend with passion and with argument the radical positions they often took. This in turn means that prophetic ethics, like the ethics of the wisdom tradition, was under continuing review, challenge, and elaboration, and was kept relevant to changing times and circumstances. It also preserved the community and its members from authoritarian ethical pronouncements and systems, or at least offered the leverage for such freedom. It is a democratizing principle—this relativizing of all the structures and figures of the society—and the community of Israel and the Christian community have taken advantage of it abundantly. The Pharisaic movement of later times, a lay movement against the Jerusalem priesthood, and Jesus' bold and sweeping eschatological ethic were heirs to this prophetic principle.

A last special feature of prophetic ethics is found in its use of prophetic eschatology. The prophets used a variety of images to portray the coming fulfillment of God's purposes on earth. At its heart, prophetic eschatology is an affirmation that God will not finally be defeated in the divine purpose for the creation. Though the people fail God, and though evil spreads, this world will not slip from the divine control, not finally. God will bring to consummation the promises made to Israel. Peace, righteousness, and a full life on a transformed earth await, despite the vast evidence to the contrary. Whether the prophets speak of a new and righteous king, a newly transformed people delivered from bondage and brought to the land of promise afresh, a new Zion that has been transformed and made into the city of righteousness, a people with a new heart, a new covenant made with the two houses of Israel, or even a new

heaven and earth, all such images of consummation carry with them an ethical demand and produce fresh energy for ethical activity. They judge the community not just for its sins against the God of Israel's past and present, but also for its sin against God's future plans and purposes. They offer an undergirding hope and support for the people in times of despair. Most important, they provide the lure and the beckoning light that draw the people toward the time awaiting, and toward the quality of life appropriate for the consummation. The ethical power and creativity of the prophetic heritage, which have continued to inspire and guide Judaism and Christianity, derive in large measure from this prophetic eschatology and the continuing drawing power that it exercises.

The prophets promised more than found realization. Were they therefore failures? Did prophecy come to an end because the people finally saw that what the prophets promised was not credible, and therefore turned away from them? So it has been claimed. Here too, the question may be put in the wrong way.

On one level, prophecy does not fail when the impulses that led prophets to prophesy also produced hearers and preservers of their messages, to such an extent that we have the massive collections of prophetic materials in the books of Isaiah, Jeremiah, Ezekiel, and the twelve Minor Prophets, as well as the other books dominated by the influence of the prophets, Deuteronomy in particular. The messages of the prophets became a part of the living heritage of faith of Israel and of Christianity, and their message claims the attention and offers guidance to these communities throughout the centuries.

Secondly, the prophets demanded so much of Israel, and promised so much to Israel, that on one level it is evident that they failed. But what sort of failure was theirs? It was the kind of failure that has accompanied religious revolutions throughout the centuries. They demanded nothing short of a world marked by peace with justice, a community that was an example to the nations of earth, a demonstration of devotion to God, reflecting God's own love for the community, the world, the cosmos. They called upon the community to believe that, with all the failures of humankind, God would at the last triumph, so that what God demanded, God also provided. That was much to promise, much to hold to, much to accept. Small wonder that the prophetic heritage daunts and overwhelms those who seek to embody its demands and live in the power of its promises.

But who would doubt that many have done so, and continue to do so, living as sons and daughters of the world that in faith they know is coming into realization, upon an earth that God is transforming and making fit for its transformed citizens, even as God acts to fit these citizens for it.

See also **Mosaic Law; Old Testament Ethics.**

A. Heschel, *The Prophets,* 1969; J. Lindblom, *Prophecy in Ancient Israel,* 1962; G. von Rad, *Theology of the Old Testament,* vol. 2, ET 1962; R. Smend, "Ethik, III," *Theologische Realenzyklopädie,* ed. G. Krause and G. Müller, vol. 10, 1982.

WALTER HARRELSON

Proportionalism *see* **Proportionality;** *see also* **Double Effect; Modern Roman Catholic Moral Theology**

Proportionality, Principle of

This principle is invoked in several contexts. For example, it is one of the two main principles of the *jus in bello* (right conduct in war), along with the principle of discrimination* (noncombatant immunity from direct attack). (*See* **Just War.**) It also appears in debates about withholding or withdrawing life-sustaining medical treatment, where the language of "proportionate" and "disproportionate" means of medical treatment has to some extent replaced the earlier language of "ordinary" and "extraordinary" means (*see* **Life, Prolongation of**). Two senses of proportionality are particularly important. One is the proportion (fittingness, appropriateness) of specific means in relation to specific ends of action (*see* **Ends and Means**). In a discussion of killing in self-defense Thomas Aquinas (*ST* II-II.64.7) argues that "though proceeding from a good intention, an act may be rendered unlawful, if it be out of proportion to the end" and that "if a man, in self-defense, uses more than necessary violence, it will be unlawful." A second sense is broader —the proportion or balance among the various immediate and long-term consequences of actions. A major debate in Christian ethics and moral theology is whether proportional-

ity is the only or the dominant moral consideration and whether it may be invoked to resolve "hard" cases. In particular, the question is whether some moral rules identify actions that are intrinsically and absolutely wrong and thus cannot be justified whatever their consequences (*see* **Absolutes, Ethical; Situation Ethics**). In Catholic moral theology in recent years, this debate has focused on the rule of double effect* (*see* **Modern Roman Catholic Moral Theology**). There are parallel philosophical debates over consequentialism* and utilitarianism* and also over cost-effectiveness, cost-benefit*, and risk*-benefit analysis. There is little dispute about the moral relevance of judgments of proportionality; the dispute concerns their limits.

See also **Deontology; Teleological Ethics.**

A. Donagan, *A Theory of Morality,* 1977; J. Finnis, *Fundamentals of Ethics,* 1983; P. Ramsey and R. A. McCormick, S.J. (eds.), *Doing Evil to Achieve Good,* 1978.

JAMES F. CHILDRESS

Prostitution

The practice of engaging in sexual activity for immediate compensation in money or other valuables, in which affection and emotional investment are minimal or absent, and in which the selection of sexual partners is relatively indiscriminate. For a variety of reasons, the largest numbers of prostitutes are women serving male customers. However, there are also sizable numbers of young male prostitutes (hustlers) serving the homosexual desires of male (often married) clients, other male prostitutes (gigolos) who sell their services to women usually older than they, and a relatively small number of female prostitutes serving the homosexual interests of other women.

Historically, prostitution has existed in most societies since ancient times, in some instances associated with religious practice and ritual. In the OT there is evidence of some tolerance of female prostitution in spite of its general condemnation. From its beginnings the Christian church also has condemned prostitution in all forms and yet at various times has tolerated it as "the lesser of the evils." Augustine and Thomas Aquinas laid the ethical foundations for medieval toleration, believing that if prostitution were abolished, greater evils—rampant lust, rape, adultery, and homosexual practices—would result. As Aquinas said, "Even the palace must have its sewers." During the Protestant Reformation, however, church leaders unqualifiedly attacked prostitution and urged the state to suppress it. About the same time the growing fear of venereal disease led to severe punishments for prostitutes in many societies. The phenomenon persisted, however, and during the 18th and 19th centuries efforts at its civil regulation were largely unsuccessful. At present, prostitution has been legalized or decriminalized in a number of countries but remains outlawed in all US states with the exception of several counties in Nevada. In recent decades in the USA, the development of more effective birth control and the greater acceptance of nonmarital sex has resulted in some decline in female prostitution, though little change in male prostitution, and, overall, prostitution remains a major phenomenon especially in urban areas. In Great Britain the sociological factors are similar. While British law deals with soliciting and with offenses against public decency, most legislation is directed neither at the prostitute nor at the client but against third parties involved, e.g., brothel keepers, procurers, and pimps.

Christian ethics has widely condemned prostitution on the grounds that an appropriate understanding of sexuality calls for the investment of the total person in acts of sexual intimacy in relationships marked by fidelity* and commitment to the wholeness of the partner—qualities that are absent in the typical prostitute-client activity. There are, however, additional grounds for ethical concern.

Christian ethics must also challenge the male sexism and double standards which have so long supported female prostitution. It has been widely assumed that men have a different sexual nature which demands release and which justifies treating women as sexual objects. Further, sexist assumptions lead to prosecution of female prostitutes but rarely of their male customers. And, such assumptions shape the situation of most female prostitutes who keep a fraction of their earnings, the larger share going to male managers (pimps) and male owners of the various facilities that profit from prostitution.

Further, Christian ethics must address the conditions that give rise to prostitution. For females these conditions frequently include childhood sexual abuse by males, disrupted family relationships, and economic discrimination. Among male prostitutes drugs, inadequate education, parental apathy or abuse, and repressive juvenile correction systems are frequent contributors. For both sexes poor sexuality education and low self-esteem are typical. But since the overwhelming percentage of prostitution customers are male, a fundamental contributor is a social system and a pattern of sexual socialization encouraging males to regard sex as a commodity to be purchased.

Nevertheless, controversial ethical issues remain. The question of decriminalization or legalization is one. While antiprostitution laws are often seen as an effort to prevent the exploitation of women, evidence from some societies suggests that the legalization of prostitution decreases the exploitation of prostitutes themselves and reduces crime associated with prostitution. Further, some people argue that government ought not to impose penalties on private, consensual sexual behavior by adults, and that antiprostitution laws are ineffective, selectively applied, and expensive to enforce. Others, however, view the maintenance of antiprostitution laws as an important symbol of the majority's understanding of sexual ethics and the good society (see also Morality, Legal Enforcement of).

Another difficult issue is the use of sexual surrogates in certain forms of sex therapy. Surrogates, most of whom are women, engage in sexual activity for compensation, but with clients referred by sex therapists. The surrogate's purpose is to contribute to the relief of a diagnosed sexual dysfunction in the client (usually an unmarried male). While some believe that the use of sexual surrogates is simply another form of prostitution, others point to the different motives, intentions, and consequences involved.

However, about another issue there is little controversy: the alarming rise of childhood prostitution, typically among teenagers who are runaways from disintegrating families. This phenomenon underscores the importance of dramatically improved services to victims of incest and child abuse, day-care programs, appropriate and sound sexuality education in the schools, and equal economic and sexual treatment of all people. An adequate Christian ethical approach to prostitution must always address underlying causes as well as the phenomenon itself.

See also **Children; Sexual Ethics.**

V. L. Bullough, *Sexual Variance in Society and History,* 1976; G. D. Nass, R. W. Libby, and M. P. Fisher, *Sexual Choices,* 1981.

JAMES B. NELSON

Protest *see* **Boycott; Civil Disobedience; Conscientious Objection; Dissent; Resistance; Strikes; Whistle-blowing**

Protestant Ethics *see* **Modern Protestant Ethics;** *see also* **Anabaptist Ethics; Anglican Moral Theology; Calvinist Ethics; Ecumenical Movement, Ethics in the; Evangelical Ethics; Fundamentalist Ethics; Lutheran Ethics; Mennonite Ethics; Pietism, Ethics of; Puritan Ethics; Quaker Ethics; Wesleyan Ethics**

Protestant Work Ethic *see* **Business Ethics; Calvinist Ethics; Sociology of Ethics; Vocation; Work, Doctrine of**

Prudence

Prudence is understood in two different ways in the Western moral tradition. For Augustine and Aquinas, it is a virtue which is closely linked to justice* and charity*. Thus Augustine, in accordance with his understanding of virtue as true love of God, defines prudence as "love distinguishing with sagacity between what hinders it and what helps it" (*On the Morals of the Catholic Church* 15). Aquinas regards prudence as an intellectual virtue which directs the human person to the choice of right means for an end (*ST* I-II.57.5); but the proper working of prudence also requires the presence of moral virtue in the will, directing the will to right ends (*ST* I-II.65.1). Aquinas here follows a distinction originally drawn by Aristotle between practical wisdom (which presupposes moral virtue) and cleverness (which does not). For Aristotle, *phronēsis* or practical wisdom differs from political wisdom by reason of its concern for the good of the individual (*Nicomachean Ethics* 6.8). It is distinguished from the knowledge of universals which constitutes science because of its concern with the particulars of action. While Ar-

istotle discusses practical wisdom as an intellectual virtue, Aquinas explicitly says that it has the character of both an intellectual virtue and a moral virtue (*ST* II-II.47.4c). (*See also* **Aristotelian Ethics; Augustinian Ethics; Thomistic Ethics.**)

Thomas Hobbes conceives of it as an intellectual ability ordering a plurality of things to an end, an ability which is dependent on experience and memory. The 18th-century Anglican bishop Joseph Butler defines prudence as "a due concern about our own interest or happiness, and a reasonable endeavor to secure and promote it" and argues that we regard it as a virtue (*Dissertation on the Nature of Virtue*). As the traditional Western framework of divinely established teleology was replaced by efforts to argue for the distinction and ultimate reconciliation of self-love and benevolence, and as the moral life came to be seen as based either on altruistic feelings or on universal norms of reason, prudence came to be regarded as interested calculation, not as moral virtue. Thus Francis Hutcheson and David Hume separate prudence and morality; though, like nearly all moral and psychological theorists prior to the Romantic period, they acknowledge a certain convergence between the demands of morality and the requirements of prudence and welcome the contribution of prudence or rational self-interest in curbing the passions. But Immanuel Kant insists that prudence or "skill in the choice of means to one's own greatest well-being" deals only with hypothetical imperatives, not with the categorical imperative of morality (*Groundwork of the Metaphysic of Morals,* ch. 2). The view of prudence as a rational guide to self-interested action rather than as a moral virtue is dominant in contemporary Anglo-American moral philosophy. It is quite common, especially in social contract* theories, for the central problem in establishing ethical principles is the transition from individual prudence to social morality.

Scripture does not offer a clear resolution of this conceptual conflict. In the wisdom literature, in the theological framework of the Deuteronomic history, in formulations of God's promises, and in certain NT parables (Matt. 7:24–27; 10:16; 25:1–30; Luke 16:1–9) we can find advice and commands to act on the basis of rational self-interest and to exhibit prudence in decisions and actions. We can also find denunciations of false prudence and injunctions to act on principles that contradict self-interest as normally understood (Matt. 5:43–48; 6:19–34; 10:37–39; 16:24–27).

In particular, the example of the self-sacrificial love of Jesus crucified challenges the hypothesis of an assured harmony between interest and duty, or between prudence and discipleship (see 1 Cor. 1:17–31). Prudence, or a capacity for reasonable judgments about the means needed to attain our ends in complex situations, seems both necessary and inadequate as a guide to Christian life. For Christian theologians, including Augustine and Aquinas, prudence does not serve as an independent action guide but as an intelligent application of Christian love*. It is viewed with suspicion by those who regard it as hindering the expression of *agapē* and as blunting the impact of the gospel challenge to human selfishness.

See **Cardinal Virtues; Virtue.**

D. Gauthier, *Practical Reasoning,* 1963; J. Pieper, *Prudence,* ET 1959; H. Sidgwick, *The Methods of Ethics* (1874), 1907, bk. III, chs. 3 and 9.

JOHN LANGAN, S.J.

Psychoanalysis

Psychoanalysis is the name Sigmund Freud (1856–1939) gave to his method of psychological investigation and therapy. It primarily refers to a method of understanding the unconscious meaning of conscious forms of speech, especially self-referential speech about one's own feelings, thoughts, and intentions. The term also refers to the body of psychological propositions and theory that Freud gradually elaborated through the use of psychoanalytic methods and their employment as an aid to psychotherapy. Hence, it is a word referring to Freud's method of psychological investigation, his approach to psychotherapy, and the body of knowledge that these procedures generated.

It is important to distinguish the term "psychoanalysis" from the preferred way of referring to other psychological therapies and systems associated with some of Freud's early associates and followers. Psychoanalysis must be distinguished from both "analytical psychology," which refers to the psychotherapeutic psychology of Carl Jung, and "individual psychology," which refers to the work of Alfred Adler. "Neo-Freudian" psy-

chology, associated with the names of Karen Horney, Erich Fromm, and Harry Stack Sullivan, is often thought to be still within the general psychoanalytic tradition but stretching its outer limits. On the other hand, the movement called "ego psychology," associated primarily with American psychiatrists such as Heinz Hartmann, David Rapaport, and Erik Erikson, usually is thought to be well within the general tradition of psychoanalysis. This is a status generally granted also to the English tradition of "object relations" theory associated with the names of W. R. D. Fairbairn, Donald Winnicott, and Harry Guntrip, as well as the newly developing American tradition of "self psychology" associated with the name of Heinz Kohut. Yet the term "psychoanalysis" is still primarily associated with Freud's own theories and practice or those of some of his earliest and most orthodox followers. Yet when used to refer specifically to Freud and some of his early faithful followers, the phrase "orthodox psychoanalysis" is frequently used to distinguish Freud and his more conservative followers from the later movements which are, however, still considered broadly psychoanalytic.

A psychology of the unconscious. Freud considered his psychology to be primarily a psychology of the unconscious causes of certain symptoms such as hysteria, obsessional neurosis, or the various phobias which he frequently encountered in his clinical practice (*see also* **Unconscious**). Although first a neurologist, Freud turned to the study of medical psychology in his early work on hysteria done in collaboration with Josef Breuer (1842–1925). In this work Freud frequently employed hydraulic and electrical models to order his observations and inferences about how the unconscious works. At one point (1895) he tried to write a book now referred to as *Project for a Scientific Psychology,* which would base psychology on strictly physical and chemical models and terms. However, he abandoned this project and began taking a more introspective approach to psychology.

His masterpiece is commonly thought to be *The Interpretation of Dreams* (1900). In addition to the analysis of the dreams of many of his patients, Freud frequently used his own dreams. This is often thought to be the true beginning of psychoanalysis. It is out of his work with dreams that Freud began to develop his insights into the defensive, protective, and distorting maneuvers of the unconscious. In relation to these observations, he developed the technique of free association as an aid to psychotherapy. The patient was invited to recall, in as unguarded a way as possible, all memories associated with a particular life experience or dream fragment. Through this it was hoped that dimensions of the patient's unconscious wishes and defenses would begin to become conscious. This procedure is the very essence of psychoanalysis.

Freud and religion. Freud had strong personal and scientific interests in religion, although he did not consider himself a believer and indeed argued in his *The Future of an Illusion* (1927) that religion would play a declining role in the future of the human race. In his formative essay entitled "Obsessive Actions and Religious Practices" (1907) he contended that there was an analogy between the repetitive and rigid practices of obsessive neurotics and the ritual repetition to be found in all religions. In *Totem and Taboo* (1913), *Civilization and Its Discontents* (1930), and *Moses and Monotheism* (1939) he carried these themes forward, and what was first of all presented as a rather loose analogy between religion and obsessive-compulsive neurosis gradually became a hard identity. Freud believed that religion was built primarily on the repression and internalization of the ambivalent relation that all humans have early in life with their fathers. On the one hand, all young children, especially young boys, love and are emotionally dependent upon their fathers; at the same time, they fear their father's prohibitions and have anger and repressed hostility toward their father's restrictions, especially his sexual restrictions pertaining to the mother. Religion is built upon the repression* of these mixed feelings and the subsequent projection of them upon an imagined god who is the source of both consolation and renunciation.

Ethics and religion. It is easily seen, then, why Freud thought religion had so much to do with ethics. Religion was the source of the basic instinctual renunciations that make civilized life possible. But the kind of ethics that Freud had in mind was superego ethics built around the Oedipal conflict and its resolution. Freud thought that every child around the fifth or sixth year falls in love with the parent of the opposite sex. This parent's

prohibitions become the ground upon which the child learns to regulate his or her own instinctual wishes. This internal process of self-regulation Freud called the superego*. But the ethics of the superego is largely unconscious, prohibitive, and uncritically conforming to the values of parents and inherited traditions. It is difficult to imagine the grounds for a critical, self-reflective, and autonomous ethic within the terms of the Freudian understanding of either ethics or religion.

Freud's psychology and theory of religion cannot provide a full account of either religion or ethics in human life. Yet in the area of ethics, it is doubtless necessary developmentally for all humans to pass through a period of life when their ethics is grounded on an unconscious identification with the values of admired and feared adults within their environment. But at least some individuals grow to higher levels of critical and autonomous ethical thinking and acting. It is not clear that Freud's understanding of the relation of religion to ethics is adequate to understand these more mature expressions of ethical thought and action.

See also **Ego; Id.**

S. Freud, "Obsessive Actions and Religious Practices" (1907), *Standard Edition of the Complete Psychological Works of Sigmund Freud* (1953–64), 9:116–127; *Totem and Taboo* (1913), *Standard Edition* 13:1–161; *The Future of an Illusion* (1927), *Standard Edition* 21:3–56; *New Introductory Lectures on Psycho-Analysis* (1932), *Standard Edition* 22:3–182.

DON S. BROWNING

Psychology and Ethics

There are two approaches to the question of the relevance of psychology to the field of ethics. One approach deals with the question of how moral capacities develop and what goes into our psychological readiness to act morally (*see* **Moral Development**). The second is more directly concerned with the question of how our psychological feelings or scientific knowledge about human psychological regularities may or may not inform normative ethical judgments about the morally right action to pursue. The first question deals with the area of moral psychology. On the whole, moral philosophers and moral theologians have only a secondary interest in issues pertaining to the psychological development or formation of our capacity for moral action. They generally prefer to leave this question to the field of psychology. But whether or not a moral philosopher or theologian will be interested in the second question—the relevance of psychological feelings or knowledge to normative moral judgments—depends upon the style or method of ethical thinking that he or she prefers to use in ethical deliberations.

Teleological ethics and psychology. Philosophers and theologians who accept teleological ethics* are often thought to be able to make direct use of psychology in their normative ethical work. Teleologists believe that the morally correct action can be found in attempting to actualize the greatest amount of nonmoral good over evil that is possible. The distinction between the moral and the nonmoral good is crucial to understanding this position. The nonmoral good refers to all the ways that we use the word "good" in the specifically nonmoral sense of the term. For instance, we are using the word "good" in the nonmoral sense when we say that this is a good car, a good steak, a good hammer, or a good piano player. In none of these cases are we saying that the car, steak, hammer, or piano player is morally good. We do not assign moral qualities to cars, steaks, or hammers, and in the case of the piano player, we are referring in this sentence to the player's technical and artistic abilities and not to his or her moral qualities.

Hence, it is often argued that teleological ethicists require some kind of value theory pertaining to the nonmoral good and that psychology, as one of a variety of disciplines, can make a contribution to such a theory (*see* **Values and Value Judgment**). This would be true, according to some thinkers, no matter what kind of teleologist one is. Hence, it would be true for ethical egoists who argue that the moral thing to do is to maximize as much nonmoral good as possible for oneself. Or it would be true for those ethicists who hold some variety of utilitarianism*. The utilitarian attempts to actualize as much good (in the nonmoral sense) over evil as is possible, not just for himself or herself, but for the community as a whole, or, more specifically, for the largest number of individuals. In both cases, however, knowledge of what humans feel they want and desire, or what an objective scientific discipline such as

psychology indicates they truly and regularly want and desire, may make a contribution to the theory of the nonmoral good that the teleologist requires.

Of course, different psychological views about what humans truly want and desire will make a difference in the way any position in teleological ethics actually works. If a teleologist's psychology sees the nonmoral good in terms of a narrow theory of pleasure*, as it is often said of the utilitarian positions of both Jeremy Bentham and John Stuart Mill, then this will certainly affect the final practical outcome of this ethic. If, however, a teleologist's psychology describes humans as pursuing a great number of nonmoral goods—such as the actualization of one's potentials, the need for attachment, the need for self-esteem, identity, or intimacy—this too will affect the final outcome of this ethic (*see* **Self-Realization**).

Psychology can influence teleological forms of ethics in both philosophical and theological contexts. Catholic Thomistic ethics* is often seen as an older form of teleological ethics and it is frequently open to the use of psychological or psychobiological knowledge. Thomism's interest in the natural law* leads it to use a variety of disciplines, including psychology and psychobiology, to discover the natural inclinations and structures of human beings. Psychology has also had a direct or indirect influence on those contemporary theologians, such as Joseph Fletcher or John Giles Milhaven, who have been influenced by utilitarian thinking—especially act utilitarianism—in their understanding of Christian love.

Sociobiology, psychology, and ethics. The recent discussion of the relevance of sociobiology to ethics has great implications for the topic of the relation of psychology and ethics. Sociobiology, a term made popular by E. O. Wilson in his *Sociobiology* (1975), is a new discipline which attempts to discern the regularities of adaptive patterns of the various species, including the human species (*see* **Evolutionary Ethics**). The line between sociobiology and a biologically oriented psychology is difficult to draw. This is especially true in view of the fact that Darwin's own biological theories have had enormous influence on a great deal of modern psychology. Although Wilson's own argument for the relevance of sociobiological and psychological knowledge for ethics is confused, recent statements by

Mary Midgley in *Beast and Man* (1978) and Peter Singer in *The Expanding Circle* (1981) have developed more adequate statements. In brief, both positions seem to suggest that sociobiology and psychobiology can provide information into the nonmoral good for humans, information that must be further refined by more specifically moral theories of obligation.

Psychology and deontological ethics. It is often thought that psychology can make no contribution to the other great method in ethics that is often referred to as deontological ethics (*see* **Deontology**). Deontologists claim to proceed with discerning moral obligation without reference to maximizing the nonmoral good. The deontologist believes that ethics is grounded on some principle of obligation that can be seen as intrinsically moral without reference to consequences in promoting the nonmoral good. Immanuel Kant (1724–1804) is considered the foremost proponent of this position (*see* **Kantian Ethics**). In his thought the highest good (the moral good) depends necessarily upon a principle independent of our psychological inclinations and their drive toward satisfaction and happiness. Such a principle is his categorical imperative*, which says, "I should never act in such a way that I could not also will that my maxim should be a universal law." Here the appeal is to consistency and to universalizability* and not to the maximization of psychological-experienced wants or goods, even if they include those of the other person.

But William Frankena in his *Ethics* (²1973) has argued that one can still be a deontologist and need some theory of the nonmoral good (and thereby need psychological knowledge). Frankena does this by first arriving at a theory of justice on more strictly deontological grounds and then turning to psychology and other such disciplines for determining the theory of the nonmoral good that should be justly and fairly divided among all persons relevant to the moral issue at hand.

See also **Persons and Personality.**

DON S. BROWNING

Public Opinion

The precise meaning of the term "public opinion" is difficult to determine. It does not necessarily imply a general consensus because public opinion can contain both majority and minority elements. Again, it is not to be equated with public taste since it is a socially significant attitude capable of influencing national policy. It can exist without being articulated; some particular major issue will have to arise before it achieves public expression.

Serious interest in and study of public opinion is a comparatively recent phenomenon. Greek and Roman writers generally express contempt for the opinion of the public, and this attitude was common until the 18th century, when it came to be assumed that public opinion is formed according to rational processes, and that public opinion is sufficient as a sanction for moral codes (cf. D. Hume's *An Enquiry Concerning the Principles of Morals,* 1751): *Vox populi, vox Dei.* The 20th century has seen a sharp decline of confidence in the idea that the formation of public opinion follows the laws of human reasoning. This is due to increased awareness, especially as the result of researches in psychology and social investigation, of the part played by subconscious and irrational fears and prejudices. This is particularly the case where changes are proposed in the laws relating to contentious issues, for example, homosexuality, race relations, or capital punishment. On these issues it cannot be argued that public opinion is inevitably in the right. It may be the case that an enlightened minority will succeed in moving a government to legislate on such matters long before the majority of the people would themselves have wished to take action. But while changes may thus be brought about which are in advance of public opinion, they stand very little chance of success if they are too far ahead of it.

See **Democracy; Politics; Media, Ethical Issues in; Morality, Legal Enforcement of.**

E. J. TINSLEY

Public Ownership *see* **Capitalism; Communism, Ethics of; Property; Socialism**

Public Policy

Public policies, defined by Thomas Dye as "whatever governments choose to do or not to do," include both procedural policies (how decisions are reached) and substantive policies (what decisions are reached). Common substantive policies authorize, permit, regulate, or prohibit activities and allocate or distribute goods (e.g., health care) and burdens (e.g., taxation). Policy analysis is an applied social science. The role of ethical considerations in public policy is a subset of the question of ethics and politics, particularly in a democratic state in a pluralistic society.

See **Democracy; Morality, Legal Enforcement of; Pluralism; Politics; State.**

T. Dye, *Understanding Public Policy*, ²1975; S. Nagel (ed.), *Encyclopedia of Policy Studies*, 1983.

JAMES F. CHILDRESS

Punishment see **Capital Punishment; Corporal Punishment; Penology; Rewards and Punishments; Sanction**

Puritan Ethics

Major figures and systematic themes. Puritanism as a religious and political movement in English history extended from the later years of the reign of Henry VIII for more than a century until the time of Charles II. Six monarchs—Henry, Edward I, Mary, Elizabeth I, James I, and Charles I—had to deal with Puritan efforts at ecclesiastical and social reform, efforts that came to a head in England during the period of the Commonwealth (1649–1660). While Puritanism as a major theme in English life quickly disappeared after this, it continued as a significant religious, moral, and political force in the New England Puritan commonwealth considerably longer, until it dissipated into the newly emerging American culture in the early 18th century.

In general the major Puritan thinkers up through the 1640s were to be found in England, and these were the ones who first defined the character of the movement theologically. The principal theological personalities of the later stages of the movement's history were, by contrast, New Englanders; there is no English Puritan theologian or ethical writer of stature after the 1640s, while New England Puritanism reached its own theological peak in the reflections of the second generation of American Puritans published in the 1660s and 1670s. A complicating factor is that in England the social and political reforms of the Puritans may be regarded as having been tested and having failed in the experiment that was the Commonwealth, while in New England, Puritan ideals of government and social organization succeeded and eventually became part of a developing larger sense of American identity as a people. Discussion of these broader implications of Puritan ethics is, however, beyond the reach of this article.

There were two main types of Puritan ethical writings, the sermon and the treatise; sometimes these overlapped, producing treatises in the form of extremely long sermons. Much of the literature on major ethical topics such as marriage, government, and community generally is in the form of published sermons, though authors from the Puritan party who were not divines wrote treatises on such individual issues; Thomas Barnes's *Vox Belli, or An alarme to Warre* (1626) and Milton's writings on marriage and divorce from the 1640s are significant examples of the latter.

This article will treat only the major definitional period in Puritan ethical thought, which begins in the late 1590s and ends in the late 1640s, coincident with the effects of the Revolution. Three stages in this development can be identified and connected with the thought of specific Puritan writers.

Without doubt the most significant Puritan theologian from the beginning of this period is William Perkins, Cambridge don as well as Puritan divine, a prolific and wide-ranging author. In Perkins's time Puritans coexisted with classical Anglicans in the Church of England and fought for control over the church itself and over the spheres of English life it controlled. Perkins's published *Works* (1609) include discussions of domestic and national government, jurisprudence, war, medicine, and individual moral life along with scriptural commentary and a thorough and systematic rewriting of Christian theology from a Puritan perspective. The central theme in Perkins's ethical thought is the liberty given to the Christian individual through grace. Though he employs language and concepts inherited from scholastic theology, this emphasis makes his conception of Christian ethical life much more Augustinian than Thomistic, centered on motivation rather than on acts.

For Perkins charity is the form of grace that connects God and man. God manifests himself through charity, and the proper human response is through acts in accord with charity. These acts are largely set out in the scriptures, but biblical law is not externally binding; rather, charity causes it to be internally ratified. In "indifferent" matters (not covered in scripture) charity provides direct guidance for the Christian (*see* **Adia-phora**). Thus, in general the Christian will follow scriptural discipline, but only because charity inspires this discipline in the heart; going beyond the scriptures is possible where charity leads (cf. Johnson, 1970). We shall see below how this conception of ethics works out in a particular case.

In Perkins's conception, only persons with charity can act in a manner pleasing to God, but they do so largely in scripturally defined ways; in the next stage of Puritan ethics, authoritative thought inverts this so that a discipline based in following scriptural law is defined as itself the working out of charity and the only form of behavior pleasing to God. Here the category of "indifferent" matters diminishes to nothing, while the scope covered by biblical law becomes comprehensive. Exemplifying this shift toward conservatism is William Gouge, like Perkins a Cambridge divine and a prolific author on a range of significant issues, who flourished in the 1620s and 1630s. In Gouge's thought, Christian duty emerges as the primary ethical category; grace still supplies the Christian's motivations, but these are experienced as duties to act according to divine law as set forth biblically. Gouge's writings well represent the morally conservative Puritan orthodoxy that developed in the 1620s, partly in response to a new atmosphere of repression of Puritanism in the English church, and that became normative in American Puritan ethics.

In England the liberal side of Perkins's charity-based ethic continued alongside the growing conservatism, being developed most fully in debate over the ethics of marriage and divorce. Since public law on this was determined by church law, and since the debate on the "commonwealth" of marriage held implications for the larger commonwealth of England, the outcome was of great significance. Perkins had accepted the traditional antidivorce teaching of the church, but he had so revised the undergirding reasoning for the conception of marriage on which this teaching was based that later generations could take quite different directions on this topic. In Gouge (1622), representing the trend toward social and individual conservatism in Puritan ethics, marriage becomes nothing beyond a complex matrix of mutual duties of the partners within their scripturally defined roles. In New England the whole of society came to be conceived on such a

model (see Miller, 1939; Wertenbaker). The opposite position is illustrated by Thomas Gataker, a Puritan divine contemporary with Gouge, and by John Milton some twenty years later. Gataker, though employing the same language of duty as Gouge, yet emphasizes (1620 and 1624) that the whole relationship of Christian marriage must be based in a special providence of God. The moral quality of acts in this relationship is determined by the depth of response to this providence, and the term "duty" is always employed by Gataker to refer to this response, not, as in Gouge, to the imposition of biblical precepts. Milton takes this liberalizing line of reasoning to its climax in his divorce tracts (see Johnson, 1970). For him, where there is no evidence of divine charity in the marital relationship (that is, where the marriage duties cannot be fulfilled), this implies that God never established this relation through his special love in the first place. Hence the external relationship does not exist, he argues, since there is no internal one.

The close of the definitional period is exemplified by the major ethical work of William Ames, *Conscience, with the Power and Cases Thereof* (1639). Ames, who had been a pupil of Perkins at Cambridge, was a separatist and thus belonged to the most ethically conservative wing of Puritanism. In his thought the earlier concept of the divine-human relation as based on divine gift and human response is regularized into a concept of covenant, whereby the patterns of behavior on both sides can be defined systematically. In this covenant theology, duty is established as the essential category of ethics: the scriptures and natural law interpreted through them define in legal form the divine-human covenant; in this partnership God always does his part, and it is the duty of all Christians to do theirs, according to the terms of the covenant agreement. The interesting thing in Ames's ethics, apart from his carrying forward systematically the line of thinking exemplified in Gouge, is his incorporation of natural law into a Puritan framework. This paralleled currents in scientific thought in Puritan circles, according to which a new beginning or "instauration" of knowledge about the world was being given to those who possessed grace (Webster). The result was to restore the possibility of a Christian interpretation of natural law as distinct from interpretations unaided by divine grace.

This Puritan conception of natural law, while not identical with that of scholastic tradition, was close enough to allow some conversation; significant in Ames's *Conscience* is his use of Thomistic categories and conventions of thought, unheard of in earlier Puritan generations.

The covenant idea and applied ethics in Puritanism. The most pervasive theme of applied ethics in Puritan thought is what the Puritans called "government" but what would most likely today be termed "community." "Government" in Puritan usage meant not only the activities of monarchs, members of Parliament, or local officials; like God's government of the world, it referred to the entire nexus of human relationships, their proper ordering, and the use of the resources of the world by humans. Of course, this term had a special use in referring to the governing persons and associated institutions of the nation; yet it is crucial that this special meaning was implicitly connected to the broader sense of the term. The fullest expression of this conception, present already in Perkins, was in covenant theology as developed by Ames, William Preston, and others (Miller, 1939). On this view all human relationships were to be understood as "common-mutual covenants," binding the parties together by mutual agreement made with respect to the natural order and the special circumstances of the relation. Marriage, discussed above, was one such covenant; so was friendship; so also were business partnerships; and so also the relationships that defined the church, the nation, and the local community (Johnson, 1970). Christians participated in all of these; yet each Christian also was a partner in a "covenant of grace" with God, and this relationship was understood as helping to define the terms of all the other relations. The failure of Charles I to live up to his responsibilities in the covenant of national government thus became cause for revolution and the establishment of Parliament at the head of the state (Prall); similarly, the theocratic form of magistracy established in New England was an attempt to ensure that the divine-human relationship had force in all forms of human "government" or community (Miller, 1956; Morgan; Wertenbaker). The rapid growth of new economic relationships (cf. Tawney) and parallel changes in the field of law (cf. Little) provide further examples of the application of the covenant understanding of "government" in other arenas of human relationship (*see also* **Covenant**).

By contrast with this broad area of applied ethical thought, worked out in particular debates such as that on marriage, an ability to focus much more narrowly when circumstances dictated is exemplified by Puritan writings on war. These writings were generated by the fact of religious war on the Continent and continuing Protestant-Catholic conflict at home, and they revolved around the dual themes of the biblical concept of holy war and the inherited just war tradition. Played out in Puritan debate on war was a larger movement found generally in the Reformation period among Catholics and Protestants alike: an initial flirtation with apocalyptic holy war concepts (paralleled by an equally eschatological pacifism), followed by a synthesis between these and just war ideas and an eventual rejection of the earlier extremes in a renewed just war theory (Johnson, 1975). Gouge's arguments, published (1631) during the intermediate period of synthesis, provide a window on Puritan thought on war and also point to another significant thematic factor in Puritan ethics: the use of the OT as a source for model understanding of human life in the world. Gouge works well within inherited just war categories; yet he is one of the last writers to argue seriously for a concept of war "commanded" by God and thus obligatory for Christians. In such war Christian soldiers are not only to fight fiercely for their cause; since God is fighting too, the end is not in doubt, and therefore the Christian can show mercy toward the enemy in battle. The *jus in bello* of just war tradition becomes in this representative Puritan theorist an implication of the personal righteousness necessary for Christians living in covenant with God and to be maintained even under the stress of war. The later development of the New Model Army, with its strict internal discipline maintained in part by religious sanctions, illustrates the implications of this concept of the Christian soldier.

W. Ames, *Conscience, with the Power and Cases Thereof,* 1639; T. Barnes, *Vox Belli, or An alarme to Warre,* 1626; T. Gataker, *Marriage Duties,* 1620; and *A Marriage Prayer,* 1624; W. Gouge, *Gods Three Arrowes,* 1631; and *Of Domesticall Duties,* 1622; J. Milton, *The Complete Prose Works,* vol. 2, 1959.
S. E. Ahlstrom, *A Religious History of the*

American People, 1972; J. T. Johnson, A Society Ordained by God, 1970; and Ideology, Reason, and the Limitation of War, 1975; D. Little, Religion, Order, and Law, 1969; P. Miller, The New England Mind: The Seventeenth Century, 1939; and Errand Into the Wilderness, 1956; E. S. Morgan, The Puritan Family, 1966; S. E. Prall, The Puritan Revolution: A Documentary History, 1968; R. H. Tawney, Religion and the Rise of Capitalism, 1954; C. Webster, The Great Instauration, 1975; T. J. Wertenbaker, The Puritan Oligarchy, 1947.

JAMES TURNER JOHNSON

Quadragesimo Anno see **Business Ethics; Official Roman Catholic Social Teaching; Subsidiarity, Principle of**

Quaker Ethics

The message of the Quakers can be called the appeal to the enlightened conscience*. At every stage of the history of the Society of Friends and of each Quaker's life, they have expected to encounter a spirit or Light within themselves and others, usually known as the Spirit of Christ or of God, and have identified as Truth what they were shown by that Light, both as to their own "inner states" and as to ethical norms for society. Lifelong effort to obey the daily "leadings" of that Light, in all actions and speaking, and even in prayer, was expected to shape Friends' characters, conduct, and careers. Quakers insisted on the possibility and duty of perfect inner obedience; their ethic thus stands between the "perfect faith" of radical Pietists, the Wesleyans' inner holiness, and the Anabaptist code of total obedience to the NT commandments, with each of which Quaker perfectionism* has at times been confused, even by Friends.

In their movement's first decade, the 1650s under the Puritan Commonwealths in England and its colonies, George Fox and the other "publishers of Truth" expected not only their own lives but those of all nations to be taken over in the cosmic conquest of "the Lamb's War." Early norms of Quaker conduct, which echoed the calls in the Bible or radical Puritanism to renounce oaths* and all dishonesty, war and all violence, and titles and all inequalities, also were rooted in what Friends saw as "truth," for instance in a truly grammatical use of "thee" and "thou" to individuals. Each Quaker work or action such as refusing "hat honor" was also a challenge

to their hearers' pride, hence a blow within "the Lamb's War" aimed at total "convincement" by arousing "the witness of God" within each hearer. But the conscientious refusal of individual Quakers to bear arms and to pay "tithe"-taxes for the support of the parish clergy of the Church of England came to be seen by 1660 in the face of political challenge as permanent and universal truths, "Testimonies" to which all Friends were called to witness.

The religious persecutions and indifference of Restoration England, 1660–1678, tamed Quaker hopes of the Spirit's world victory and turned their ethical "Testimonies" into badges of loyalty to "the children of Light," to be maintained even after changes in the larger society had outdated many Quaker customs. Quakers developed networks of mutual aid* based on local, regional, and national "Meetings for Business" without hierarchies or clergy and with almost equal roles for men and women. Imprisonment and public scorn also led Friends to "disown" all individual acts that caused scandal or were "contrary to Truth," and like a sect to "disown" members who performed such acts if they would not "condemn their own conduct." But William Penn reinterpreted the universality of the Light as humanism and reshaped the Quaker prophetic ethic into Protestant liberalism in support of toleration and reform by political consensus in England and Pennsylvania.

The rationalism of "the Augustan Age" in 18th-century England drove the Quakers, as an alternative to sectarian isolation, into quietism* as a way to preserve the purity of their "leadings" from human impulses. John Woolman, to keep his own purity and that of Philadelphia Friends in a time of wealth and war (and also of the Great Awakening), led Quakers into new collective acts against owning slaves, as they had earlier acted against slave-trading and would less unanimously act in the 1840s to help escaped slaves. Friends partially reached a similar consensus about war taxes: hence Friends suffered from both sides in the War of 1756–63, in the American Revolution, and in the Irish uprisings around 1798.

When Quakers reentered the social mainstream in both England and America in the 19th century, their shared concern for social evils took the form of programs and committees for service, notably adult education, work for the insane by the Tukes of "York Retreat" (a pioneer mental hospital in the UK) and the Philadelphia founders of the Friends Hospital, Elizabeth Fry's work for women prisoners, antislavery work by many Friends, and Lucretia Mott's struggle for women's rights. These widely supported programs arose from personal "leadings" but never became shared Testimonies of all Quakers. From the Civil War onward even service in war and marriage to non-Quakers ceased to be grounds for "disownment." In the 20th century, Quaker service became channeled through the American Friends Service Committee and British equivalents, but the motivation became increasingly a humane response to "that of God in every person"—a phrase that appears in Fox's writings but is used now in a more humanistic sense.

Since the 19th century, Friends in touch with Protestant evangelicalism have felt led to couple with their service programs an evangelistic outreach at home and abroad. In modern social crises many liberal Quakers now turn to Jungian, Marxist, or other secular patterns for analyzing the roots of personal and social evils.

See **Pacifism.**

H. Barbour, *The Quakers in Puritan England,* 1964; H. Barbour and A. O. Roberts (eds.), *Early Quaker Writings,* 1973.

HUGH BARBOUR

Quietism

The attitude of passivity and receptivity before God, as opposed to activism.

See **Contemplation; Mysticism and Ethics.**

JOHN MACQUARRIE

Race Relations

The term "race relations" refers to the interaction between any two or more groups which are defined culturally as races. While such relations existed in the ancient and medieval world, modern race relations are generally thought to have originated in the overseas expansion and discovery of new land by European people from the 15th century onward. The classification of humankind into races varies widely, from two to two hundred, but generally three races or racial stocks are named. These are the Mongoloid or Asian, Negroid or African, and the Caucasoid or European, frequently called the yellow, black, and white races. The classification is arbitrary and generally based upon biological and cultural characteristics related to the scientific and popular way in which Europeans and their descendants have perceived their differences from other members of the human family. Racial classificatory systems tend also to reflect a hierarchical ordering establishing the superiority of one racial group above that of others. The relations between racial groups are rarely mutual or reciprocal and reflect the power advantage possessed by the dominant group. The goal of race relations may be the increased dominance of one group over another, the maintenance of the status quo, or the amelioration of the inequalities among the groups.

In the period prior to and following World War I the inability of scientists to establish with certainty the concept of race and the attack upon the concept by social scientists such as Franz Boas led to the use of terms other than "race relations" to designate interactions between groups. "Intergroup relations" became the generic term, and intercultural, national, interfaith, religious, ethnic, sex, and class relations were some of the many other categories used because they were felt to be more precise and less odious. The racist ideology adopted by the Hitler regime, 1933–1945, led, however, to a revival of the terms "race" and "race relations." Following World War II, theories and strategies were devised to deny the validity of the concepts of race, to diffuse racial classifications, and to steer race relations in the direction of tension and conflict resolution. Race relations became prominent in order to destroy racism. The Charter and the Universal Declaration of Human Rights of the United Nations was devised in part to forward this development. The emergence of new nations in Asia and Africa as well as the quest for civil and economic rights by minority populations within the nations of the free world and the USSR also helped to make relations between races a matter of explicit concern. The goal was to create a universal standard of human relations that would render race relations myopic and obsolete. E. Franklin Frazier, Gordon W. Allport, and Gunnar Myrdal devised theories and practices to reduce exploitation and to facilitate integration in democratic societies. Success in the modification of belief in white racial superiority, the elimination of certain forms of racial dominance, and the reduction of discrimination based upon race further awakened people's interest in their rights. Race relations became less paternalistic and more mutual in character, and Asians and Africans or subgroups of these racial stocks such as Afro-Americans in the USA sought to participate actively in the definition of the norms and perceptions that determine intergroup relations.

The altered dynamic of race relations led to a clearer recognition of the imbalance in power, especially economic and political power, that contributes to tensions and conflict among the racial groups; at the same time it suggested that moral suasion is not always an effective means of securing justice because the dominant racial groups experience less moral guilt than had been believed and more interest in preserving their power than had been acknowledged by their values and legal systems. The new analysis was related to an appreciation of Marxian theory (Reinhold Niebuhr and O. C. Cox) as well as the improved status and power of the less powerful racial groups in society. Thus, greater emphasis was placed upon the concepts of power, class, and ethnicity. Racial groups frequently described themselves as ethnic groups and saw race as a disguised conception of class. Nevertheless, race relations theory and practice remain useful because race is a popular way for individuals to classify themselves and intergroup contacts can be improved by correcting the errors and misjudgments made as a result of these classificatory systems. Race relations can best be viewed as a form of intergroup interaction that cannot be reduced to or explained by such variables as class, sex, nationality, culture, ethnicity, and religion or comprehended easily in more general classifications such as human rights* and liberation. Since racial classification has affected and will continue to affect the most basic and fundamental structures in which persons live, a science of race relations is necessary to provide theories, practices, policies, and strategies that will enable groups and individuals to live together with a minimum of conflict, coercion, and violence.

From its inception Christianity has stressed the individual and his or her equality with all other persons irrespective of their membership in any particular group. It affirms that all individuals are of equal worth because they are of supreme worth to God

(*see* **Image of God; Human Dignity; Persons and Personality; Respect for Persons**). Group relations are thereby transcended because individuals not groups are the foundational unit of relationship, even of the new community, the church. The new community was not seen as coterminous with any natural association or group: family, tribe, clan, nation, religion, language, sex, or culture. To evaluate an individual by his or her group membership was to commit a sin against God and to violate the norms of love and justice. (The word "race" is not part of the lexicon of the NT.) The Christian community attached no significance to breeding populations (John 1:3) or cultural orientations (Acts 2:7–13; 8: 26–39; 10:9–35; 13:43–46; 15:14; Rom. 12: 5–10; Gal. 3:28–29; Col. 3:11–15). With its stress upon inclusiveness, the new community, the church, becomes then a prototype for the world society (*see* **Ecclesiology and Ethics**).

The new community did not possess the power to rid the external society of group loyalties and determinations. It chose then the strategy of keeping itself pure until the end of the world or of seeking to transform society through the preaching of the gospel, conversion, and moral suasion. Its goal was to actualize, by focusing on interpersonal relations and universalism, its vision of a society free from hostile feelings, evil acts, and separation. Race relations was not an explicit concern, but implicitly the church recognized only one race and sought a universal community of the one family of God and of all humankind.

In the expansion of Christianity from a sect within Judaism to a religion dominant in the West a portion of this dream was realized. In the process of expansion, however, Christianity adopted the Greek notion of an organic society with fixed conceptions of inequality (Plato and Aristotle). The fruition of this way of thinking was set forth by Thomas Aquinas and in the medieval synthesis of the church. Theologically and metaphysically persons were equal, but on earth they were unequal. Their inequalities were grounded in both nature and God. Society now not only included but required persons of low birth, inferior class, and diminished rights, and also persons of superior intelligence, power, and wealth. Although the concept of race was not prominent, the ground was prepared for acceptance of classification schemes based on hereditary physical or cultural characteristics. The Protestant conception of society could also be accommodated to group differences based upon race. Protestantism strengthened the focus on the individual, but weakened universalism by creating its religious communities on national, language, city-state, dogmatic, or class groupings.

Even though the Christian ethic did not contain explicit teachings regarding race and race relations prior to the European expansion in the 15th century, it had developed conceptions that made it possible to affirm the religious equality of individuals while at the same time asserting their inequality in social, economic, and political spheres or in groups (see **Equality**). Christians employed these ideas both to justify and to reject the new racial myths and classificatory schemes. Most of these myths were the creation of the dominant European races and taught white superiority. Race relations was a method of applying their beliefs to behavior. Seldom did any scheme of race relations advocate full social, economic, or political equality. Christians tended to accept the racial teachings of the general society in respect to social, economic, and political institutions and differed from the society only in the acceptance of the idea of the equality of all individuals in the presence of God. From c. 1840 to 1860, Christians began to affirm that an equality before God entailed an equality in citizenship. The resistance to this idea was so great that Christian communities even took up arms to oppose it, and the Protestant religious community was split along racial lines, creating independent African and Afro-American churches and congregations. Race and race relations became a matter not only for individuals and groups but also for religious associations to adjudicate. The norms of love* and justice* remained central in these relationships, but they were not capable of destroying the belief in white supremacy and the use of race relations as a mechanism for maintaining white control over nonwhite persons. In the Roman Catholic community a similar outcome was achieved by the subordination of race relations to groupings based upon ideas of status and class, language, natural and national groupings, and an organic society.

Because of the atrocities committed in the name of race during World War II, Christians and others sought to rid the world of these evils by using other classifications than race for the divisions among humankind and using race relations as a way to achieve equality among different human groups (see **Anti-Semitism; Genocide**). Recognizing the limitations of persuasion, Christians sanctioned power, coercion, and even violence as a last resort. World War II, for example, was justified by some Christians because it helped rid the world of a particularly virulent form of racism*.

In the quarter century following World War II race relations received considerable emphasis in the churches. Following the secular models of decolonization, overseas mission churches were transformed into independent denominations. Often more energy was expended in making these churches multiracial than was expended in making the parent church multiracial. In some denominations and world church bodies, nonwhite persons were occasionally elevated to positions that enabled them to participate more fully and to represent previously disenfranchised racial groups. In liturgy, theologies, and other ways, symbols and institutions were modified to indicate that group interaction between socially defined races must be based on the belief that equality before God entails equality of persons and groups on earth. The churches continued debating whether equality entails equal distribution of economic and political resources or merely recognition of an individual's personhood. Nevertheless, the increased recognition of the need for equal dignity, opportunity, and political freedom did enable the several racial groups to assert their claims to equal treatment in all areas of life. Beyond the destruction of the racial mythology of the Nazi regime, the greatest gain in race relations was not the destruction of white feelings of superiority but rather the insistence by nonwhite racial groups that their grievances must be heard and that they must be free to fight for a new religious and world order. The substantive and procedural gains have led to a proliferation of groups other than racial groups seeking liberation from injustice. Consequently, there has been a decline in the last decade in the attention paid to race relations. In the long run this may lead to new definitions of what significantly divides the human family and to new coalitions.

The pattern of progress that has marked race relations since World War II has been notably absent in South Africa, where the Nazi racial ideology has been continued by the Afrikaner Nationalist Party, which came to power in 1948. The policy of apartheid* separates the population on the basis of race and color and enforces white supremacy. South Africa proclaims itself a Christian state, and its racial policies are supported by the Dutch Reformed Church of South Africa but sharply criticized by most other Christian churches and organizations.

As the South African case suggests, "racism" depends upon cultural beliefs rather than scientific facts. These beliefs gain more allegiance when a breeding population feels itself threatened. In 1982, for example, Great Britain established immigration laws among its commonwealth nations that confirm this view, and the USA proposed such rules with respect to the citizens of other American nations (*see* **Refugees**). Whatever its limitations, the Christian ethic remains a major resource for criticizing and altering attitudes, policies, and actions that violate the norms of love, equality, and justice.

See **Afro-American Religious Ethics; Anti-Semitism; Apartheid; Civil Rights; Colonialism; Discrimination; Prejudice; Racism; Segregation; Slavery.**

G. W. Allport, *The Nature of Prejudice,* 1954; O. C. Cox, *Caste, Class, and Race,* 1948; E. F. Frazier, *On Race Relations,* 1968; G. Myrdal, *An American Dilemma,* 1944, repr. 1962; H. R. Niebuhr, *The Social Sources of Denominationalism,* 1927; R. Niebuhr, *Moral Man and Immoral Society,* 1932; J. H. Oldham, *Christianity and the Race Problem,* 1924.

PRESTON N. WILLIAMS

Racism

Racism is a modern concept that characterizes certain dominant-subordinate behavioral practices among different groups within the human family. The concept gained wide currency among Europeans following their overseas expansion from the 15th century onward as a way to explain their military and technological hegemony over and enslavement of largely nonwhite peoples. Racism continues as a societal and cultural system of dominant-subordinate relationships among white and nonwhite people. In racist ideologies, these relationships are alleged to be the conse-

quences of innate physical and biological differences, intellectual and cultural hierarchies, and ethnic and class differences. The crux of racism is the institutionalization of unequal treatment based upon perceived or real physical, biological, and cultural characteristics and the classification of individuals according to whether they possess or lack these characteristics. Racist practices involve not only differential treatment but also harmful and unjust treatment. Racism thus refers to institutional practices, such as colonialism*, slavery*, segregation*, and discrimination*, and to the complex of beliefs, attitudes, and values that support such institutional practices. Since World War II racism has declined in significance, even though it remains important, in most areas of the world. An exception is South Africa, where a constitutional and governmental policy of apartheid* has sought to preserve and strengthen racism.

Western philosophical and Christian moral systems have both supported and condemned racism. Since World War II these moral systems have tended to condemn racist classificatory schemes because the concept of race has become increasingly problematic and the conclusions drawn from it have been deemed to be unjust and unchristian. Most Western ethical systems seek to establish impartial standards that apply to all groups and individuals irrespective of race, and in its main lines of development, the Christian ethic has stressed the oneness of humankind as created in the image of God*, the equality* of persons*, and the impartial nature of God's love and judgment. But this almost universal condemnation of racism has resulted not only from greater clarity about the demands of Western ethics; it has also been influenced by the relative increase in power, participation, and self-determination on the part of nonwhite people, for example, in international organizations such as the United Nations and the World Council of Churches (*see* **Ecumenical Movement**).

See also **Prejudice; Race Relations.**

J. R. Feagin, *Racial and Ethnic Relations,* [2]1984; C. Hamilton and S. Carmichael, *Black Power,* 1967; L. L. Knowles and K. Prewitt, *Institutional Racism in America,* 1969; D. C. Maguire, *A New American Justice,* 1980.

PRESTON N. WILLIAMS

Rape

Rape involves sexual intercourse with a person without his or her consent*. Women are the most frequent victims, though it sometimes happens that men are subjected to homosexual assault. Rape is a violation of the victim's body, dignity, and self-determination. Whether or not accompanied by other physical violence, it causes considerable distress. Rape victims may sometimes become pregnant or be infected by venereal disease, and rape may well have negative consequences for the person's self-confidence and interpersonal relationships. Unfortunately, victim treatment may be impersonal and unsupportive, if not frankly disbelieving and hostile. A common myth is that the victim somehow encouraged the assailant. Successful prosecution of rapists can be difficult, and in addition many cases of rape simply go unreported. In recent years, growing concern for rape victims has led to the proliferation of rape crisis centers, to provide support and advice for the victims and their relatives and friends. Apart from rape as such, there are various forms of indecent assault, and it is also important to note the far wider problem of sexual harassment. Women frequently receive unwanted sexual attention at their places of employment or elsewhere. The quest for sexual respect is in effect a major social concern.

See **Respect for Persons; Women, Status of.**

___

S. Brownmiller, *Against Our Will,* 1975; S. L. McCombie (ed.), *The Rape Crisis Intervention Handbook,* 1980; S. Read, *Sexual Harassment at Work,* 1982.

ELIZABETH R. MOBERLY

Rationalization

In ethics this term usually suggests efforts to justify actions by appealing to reasons that are not in fact the agent's actual motives (*see* **Justification; Motives and Motivation**). It presupposes a distinction between justifying reasons and motivating reasons (or other causal factors). In Freudian theory (*see* **Psychoanalysis**), rationalization involves appealing to conscious in contrast to unconscious* motives in actions. Marxist theories (*see* **Marxist Ethics**) of false consciousness and ideology* view rationalizations as systematic, rather than ad hoc, and locate them in determinative socioeconomic structures.

Rationalization may involve conscious deception of others (*see* **Honesty; Truthfulness**), hypocrisy*, or self-deception*. In any event, it is possible to criticize rationalization by pointing to discrepancies between stated and actual reasons, as well as to deficiencies in both. However, motives for action are often mixed (*see* **Mixed Motives**), and it may be difficult to determine for oneself or for others which motives were necessary and/or sufficient to motivate the action.

Rationalization is sometimes viewed as a more general social phenomenon, such as systematization of life and thought, means-ends reasoning, etc. According to Max Weber, rationalization is part of the process of secularization* in the West, particularly in its disenchantment (*Entzauberung*) of the world through the elimination of spirits in and awe before nature (*see* **Environmental Ethics**).

JAMES F. CHILDRESS

Rationing *see* **Justice; Triage**

Realism

The term "realism" is used of several metaphysical, epistemological, and aesthetic as well as moral and political ideas, methods, and attitudes. For example, "realism" designates opponents of nominalism in medieval controversies and opponents of idealism (*see* **Idealist Ethics**) in the last two centuries; in art it designates a method or perspective of accurate representation of reality. In contemporary philosophical ethics* (*see also* **Metaethics**), "realism" often designates a cognitivist theory that affirms the existence of moral facts. The term has a different meaning in modern Christian ethics. According to Reinhold Niebuhr (1892–1968), whose Christian realism was very influential in the USA from the late 1930s through the 1960s, "realism" in moral and political thought "denotes the disposition to take all factors in a social and political situation, which offer resistance to established norms, into account, particularly the factors of self-interest and power." Without repudiating the moral standards emphasized by idealists, including the social gospel*, Niebuhr and other realists such as John C. Bennett (b. 1902) emphasized that it is impossible fully to realize norms and ideals because sin is present in every person and every act, particularly self-interest and the desire to dominate and control others. It is often necessary to choose "the lesser of two evils," and God's grace* as forgiveness frees us to act responsibly in situations of conflict, for example, by using violence when necessary. Niebuhr appealed to Augustine as "the first great 'realist' " in Western thought, and he tried to avoid the cynicism of such realists as Machiavelli by emphasizing the relevance of (even impossible) ethical ideals and norms as a source of both indiscriminate judgment (identifying the sin in all actions) and discriminate judgment (indicating which actions are better and which worse than others). Cynicism and even nihilism results when the normal (what is) is construed as normative (what ought to be); Niebuhr attempted to hold them in a dialectical relation. He influenced such political realists as Hans Morgenthau, George Kennan, and Kenneth Thompson, all of whom acknowledged their indebtedness to him. Theological movements since the late 1960s, such as the theology of hope and liberation theology*, have challenged realism's concentration on limits, its ideological adjustment to existing arrangements, its emphasis on the sin of pride* in transgressing limits rather than the sin of sloth* in accepting limits, its focus on the cross instead of the resurrection, and its modest attention to the utopian values, to the virtue of hope, and to the transformative power of grace, the Holy Spirit, and the Christian community.

See **Hope; Modern Protestant Ethics; Utopian Thought.**

D. McCann, *Christian Realism and Liberation Theology,* 1981; D. Meyer, *The Protestant Search for Political Realism, 1919–1941,* 1973; R. Niebuhr, *Moral Man and Immoral Society,* 1932; *The Nature and Destiny of Man,* 2 vols., 1941–43; and *Christian Realism and Political Problems,* 1953.

JAMES F. CHILDRESS

Reason in Ethics *see* **Christian Ethics; Ethics; Modern Protestant Ethics; Modern Roman Catholic Moral Theology; Moral Theology; Natural Law**

Rebellion *see* **Resistance; Revolution; State**

Reciprocity *see* **Fairness/Fair Play**

Reconciliation

The Vulgate uses Latin *reconciliare* and its cognates to translate variants of the Greek *katalassein* (e.g., 2 Cor. 5:18–20), which has the root-meaning "change" and refers to a change of attitude from hostility to amity, of God toward humanity, of humanity toward God, and of individuals toward each other. This concept, primarily relational, is enlarged from its use in discussion of sin and atonement and acquires moral and theological overtones of conversion and forgiveness. It is central to Jesus' teaching about divine forgiveness* that our reconciliation with God must depend upon our openness to reconciliation with those who have offended us or whom we have offended (e.g., Matt. 5:23f.). Partly under the influence of the Stoic doctrine of *oikeiōsis* (Latin *conciliatio*), the term has sometimes assumed a metaphysical implication and been extended to include the idea of an eschatological cosmic reintegration (cf. Col. 1:20). The patristic church assigned a special importance to the formal reconciliation to the church of a penitent after grave postbaptismal sin. In the 3rd and 4th centuries this was effected, after a long period of penitential exclusion from Communion, by a rite involving the imposition of the bishop's hand. It was conceded to any individual only once in his or her life. Episcopal control over reconciliation was asserted, somewhat controversially, in the 3rd century, displacing an earlier practice which allowed discretion to the church's confessors, who were thought to have special intercessory power with God by virtue of their faithful endurance in persecution. The medieval substitution of private penance* for public reconciliation originated in the monastic communities of the early Celtic church. For reconciliation in other settings, *see* **Peace; War.**

OLIVER O'DONOVAN

Recreation *see* **Amusements**

Redemption *see* **Forgiveness; Grace; Justification by Faith; Kingdom of God; Law and Gospel**

Refugees

"A wandering Aramean was my father," begins the credo of OT faith that remembered Israel as a refugee people, uprooted by human tyranny, finally secure only because

Yahweh's "mighty hand and outstretched arm" brought them to "this place" and "this land" (Deut. 26:5–9). The NT reports that the people of faith "acknowledged that they were strangers and exiles on the earth" (Heb. 11:13).

That sacred history created obligations toward other wanderers and strangers. Other peoples, like Israel, remembered obligations to the widow and the orphan, but in addition, Yahweh's people were told that "the stranger who sojourns with you shall be to you as the native among you, and you shall love him as yourself; for you were strangers in the land of Egypt" (Lev. 19:34). The sabbatical freedom and renewal Jesus evokes always drew the stranger into the heart of Israel's life and ritual (Luke 4:18–21; cf. Ex. 23:12; Lev. 25:6; Deut. 5:14). At the great eschatological Day of the Lord, according to the Gospel of Matthew, the king declares that a reason he invites them to enter his kingdom is that "I was a stranger and you welcomed me" (Matt. 25: 35).

Although millions of immigrants moved from Europe to North and South America in the 19th century, some of the greatest challenges to biblical faith's commitment to the stranger have come in the 20th century. After World War II ten million displaced persons were repatriated or settled in new nations. From 1947 to 1952 ten million exiles from Eastern Europe and the USSR moved into other countries, particularly Britain, Western Europe, and the USA. In 1982 ten million people qualified as refugees, according to the United Nations definition of a refugee as one who "owing to well-founded fear of being persecuted for reasons of race, religion, nationality, membership of a particular social group or political opinion, is outside the country of his nationality and is unable or, owing to such fear, is unwilling to avail himself of the protection of that country." In addition to refugees, the stranger includes millions of people who have entered countries illegally; as of 1980, an estimated three and a half million to six million in the USA alone.

Today those committed to loving and respecting the stranger face complex ethical issues. Are quotas governing the number of immigrants from the various regions of the world morally permissible, and if so, on what grounds? Are there morally permissible limits to the protection refugees should receive? If greater safety would encourage a larger flow of refugees, is it justified to provide boat people no effective protection against piracy? Once aliens without legal entry documents have been discovered, should their dependents no longer receive benefits, such as public education, available to the children of citizens? Is it just for guest workers to be excluded from voting in countries where for many years they have lived and been employed?

However, the fundamental ethical dilemma is the clash between those who claim that strangers, particularly refugees, should be free to enter a nation and become citizens and those who insist a nation has not only a right but a duty to control its borders, even if it means excluding victims of oppression.

Hallowed in numerous instruments of international law is the statement of the Universal Declaration of Human Rights (1948) that "everyone has the right to leave any country including his own." Not so widely acknowledged is the next sentence: "Everyone has the right to seek and enjoy in other countries asylum from persecution."

The tension between asserting the rights of refugees on the one hand and protecting national sovereignty on the other can be seen in the two parts of the UN Convention Relating to the Status of Refugees. Its promulgation of the fundamental principles of *non-refoulement* begins with a ringing defense of refugees.

1. No Contracting State shall expel or return (*refouler*) a refugee in any manner whatsoever to the frontiers of territories where his life or freedom would be threatened on account of his race, religion, nationality, membership of a particular social group or political opinion.

That is quickly followed by a statement protecting national sovereignty*.

2. The benefit of of the present provision may not, however, be claimed by a refugee whom there are reasonable grounds for regarding as a danger to the security of the country in which he is, or who, having been convicted by a final judgment of a particularly serious crime, constitutes a danger to the community of that country.

Refugees wander in a moral no-man's-land: They have the right to leave one country but no right to enter another.

However, during the last fifteen years of

massive movements of refugees, countries have increasingly emphasized the first provision protecting refugees. The result is what Goodwin-Gill calls "*non-refoulement* through time," the presumption that refugees will be admitted to the country to which they seek entrance, while the international community finds a long-term solution: resettlement in third countries, permanent residence, or eventually repatriation to the country of origin.

Of course, thoroughgoing liberal theory would assert that not only refugees have the right to leave a country and enter another. Everyone does. Individual free choice is supreme. Individuals should be free to come and go, to choose their attachments, to change their political loyalties. Nations are basically contrivances to serve individual interest. "In a truly liberal polity, it would be difficult to justify a restrictive immigration law or perhaps any immigration law at all. National barriers to movement would be anomalous" (Schuck, p. 85).

These political and moral assumptions of the British and European Enlightenment led George Washington to declare in 1783 that "the bosom of America is open to receive . . . the oppressed and persecuted of all Nations and religions." Interpretation of the US constitution extended that perspective for a hundred years. Indeed, 19th-century liberal theorists of free trade in Britain, Europe, and the USA advocated unrestricted immigration. However, from the 1880s on, legislative and judicial decisions in the USA reflected a very different set of moral assumptions, assumptions still widely shared.

Arguments that exclusion of immigrants or refugees is a legitimate exercise of national sovereignty rest on the moral significance of community*. Memories and emotions shared by people within a geographical territory establish mutual bonds and commitments, what Michael Walzer calls "communities of character, historically stable, ongoing associations of men and women with some special commitment to one another and some special sense of their common life" (*Spheres of Justice*, 1983, p. 62). If it is inherently appropriate to preserve a distinctive, shared past, communities must be able to exclude immigrants, even refugees and asylum seekers.

Furthermore, according to this view, national communities are useful, indeed neces-

sary, to protect the human rights of individuals. There must be an effective government primarily responsible for protecting and implementing the rights of people living in a given territory. In the contemporary world, governments are expected not only to protect people's rights to noninterference but to respond actively to people's demands to receive minimal levels of welfare. If a large influx of aliens threatens the ability of a nation to protect its citizens' human rights, that nation has the right, indeed the responsibility, to refuse them entry (Nickel, p. 42).

Particularly since World War II Christians and Jews have emphasized the rights of the stranger. They have urged governments of Western Europe and the USA to reform immigration laws, expand quotas for refugees, and extend the civil rights of guest workers. Since 1982 churches in the USA have led efforts to grant sanctuary to Salvadorans and Hondurans whom the government calls illegal aliens. By 1985 over two hundred churches had declared their determination to provide refuge to these strangers, even if members of the congregations are prosecuted and sent to jail.

The power of the stranger and pilgrim to elicit commitment from Christians emerges from the heart of biblical faith. What has traditionally been described as grace or redemption (drawing on the language of law and commerce) can also be called the return of the exile. Biblical faith not only proclaims forgiveness to the criminal and offers freedom to the captive; it welcomes the stranger home.

While Christianity affirms the importance of the individual stranger, it also values community. The sanctuary movement not only draws attention to the exile but also to the cities of refuge. As in designated OT towns, and in British and European cathedrals into the 16th century, security from retaliation and injustice must be provided. Now, as before, the sanctuary movement argues, barriers must be honored. It must be clear that those on the inside are different from those on the outside. Boundaries setting a group apart are to be respected.

As the emphasis on sanctuary and refuge highlights, fellowship, memory, community are of surpassing importance to biblical religion. What must persist is the covenant people, the body of Christ. Without community where is the stranger to go? The history of

Christianity is the record of survival through preservation of community.

The theme of exiles and pilgrims as the chosen of God, who must in turn welcome the stranger, is so strong a theme in biblical faith that it creates a presumption in favor of admitting the immigrant, granting asylum to the refugee, and treating the alien as an equal. At least in its Pauline form, Christianity could not override that presumption in order to maintain wealth or racial purity. However, the presumption can be overcome if continued admission of strangers threatens the survival of the community.

See also **Hospitality; Human Rights; Nationalism; Persecution and Toleration; Race Relations.**

P. G. Brown and H. Shue (eds.), *Boundaries: National Autonomy and Its Limits,* 1981; G. S. Goodwin-Gill, *The Refugee in International Law,* 1983; A. Grahl-Madsen, *The Status of Refugees in International Law,* 1966; J. W. Nickel, "Human Rights and the Rights of Aliens," in *The Border That Joins,* ed. P. G. Brown and H. Shue, 1983; P. H. Schuck, "The Transformation of Immigration Law," *Columbia Law Review* 84, no. 1, Jan. 1984, pp. 1–90.

ROY BRANSON

Refusal of Medical Treatment
see **Autonomy; Consent; Euthanasia; Life, Prolongation of; Omission, Sin of; Paternalism; Respect for Persons; Suicide**

Relativism
Relativism is the view that the morality of actions, etc., depends upon the attitudes taken to them by particular societies or individuals. It is to be distinguished from emotivism*, prescriptivism*, subjectivism*.
See also **Relativism in Ethics.**

R. M. HARE

Relativism in Ethics
Relativism in ethics can take a number of forms. As a popular doctrine, it is the thesis that what is right or wrong, good or bad, for a person varies in relation to the cultural group to which he or she belongs. This may be called "cultural relativism." It involves the denial that there is a standard or objective morality in principle applicable to all human beings; and it rests on the empirical premise that in fact values and mores differ between

one culture and time and another. This premise may be called "descriptive relativism." It is not so much a thesis in ethics as in comparative anthropology (its truth has been, in a qualified way, questioned by one or two anthropologists, notably Ralph Linton). Cultural relativism, as a moral doctrine, holds not merely that what is believed to be right differs, but that what actually *is* right differs, even though relevant circumstances are similar. Thus polygamy can be right for the people of one culture; monogamy for those of another.

The term "relativism" can also be used to signify a theory about ethical concepts, namely, that they are relational. This theory may be called "analytic relativism." Thus "X is right" is interpreted in some such way as this: "X is approved by——" ("valued," "commended," etc.), the blank being capable of being filled up in various ways. Since feelings and emotions seem to play an important role in morality, such relativism commonly takes the form of a subjectivist theory. Since relativism in this sense raises problems about the justification of moral judgments, relativism is also used in a wider way to mean the theory that there is no rational or objective way of justifying basic ethical judgments, so that different basic judgments can be equally valid ("metaethical relativism").

The thesis that ethical terms are relational does not by itself entail a recognition of equally valid moral systems or judgments, since the analysis of "right" as "commanded by God" would, given faith in God as described in a certain way, uniquely determine a single morality as the only valid one. However, one ground for a relational analysis of moral terms is the fact of moral disagreement, and thus analytic relativism is usually stated in such a way that it has pluralistic consequences.

The plausibility of cultural relativism rests not merely on the fact of moral disagreements and variations between culture, but also on two aspects of moral thinking. First, it is generally held that a person should obey conscience and should not be blamed for ignorance (normally). If people act according to their lights, what they do is in a sense right, or at least not wrong, even if "objectively" their acts conflict with what we believe to be the true morality. From this point of view, what is right for a polygamous Muslim differs from what is right for a monogamous humanist. Second, a person's duty depends on circumstances; it can be thought that cultural differences themselves constitute relevantly different circumstances, so that a person has a duty A in culture I, but a duty B in culture II.

Neither of these points (about intentionality and about the situational aspect of morality) in fact entails cultural relativism, and once they have been understood they are seen to constitute all that is confusedly valuable in the thesis of cultural relativism. First, the fact that a person should act according to his or her conscience* does not entail that all consciences are equally valuable. Integrity, etc., are relevant to judgments about a person's character, but are only indirectly relevant to the worth of the morality he or she professes or acts upon. It remains important to know what moral rules are best for society. Of course, cultural *milieu* can be important when it comes to trying to apply the best rules. It may be that imposing monogamy on a polygamous society may have side effects much more disastrous than the institution of polygamy itself. This is a problem in social engineering, rather than about moral ends as such. Second, the situational aspect of morality only entails that duties differ where circumstances are different in morally relevant ways. It is quite another thing to hold, as cultural relativism implies, that there can be different moral duties in relevantly similar circumstances. It may of course be held that as a matter of contingent fact circumstances are never relevantly similar as between one person and another. This would be compatible with holding that *if* they were, then the same duty would apply. It would be a puzzling belief, however, as it would fail to explain how general terms in morality ("lying," "stealing," etc.) have come to be used.

Analytic relativism, in its subjectivist form, encounters the difficulty that moral arguments ought to evaporate. For if "A is wrong" means "A is disapproved of by Henry"; and if George disagrees, so that "A is not wrong" means "A is not disapproved of by George," there is no incompatibility between "A is wrong" and "A is not wrong." There is no incompatibility between the propositions that Henry disapproves of A and that George does not. Thus analytic relativism is not a good reflection of the way

moral concepts actually work, since people take moral disagreements to be genuine disagreements. Further, Henry's disapproval of A is a biographical fact, not a moral assertion, and analytic relativism, even in its nonpluralistic forms, does not take account of the gap between "is" and "ought" (that is, it commits the so-called naturalistic fallacy). Emotivism, or an expressive analysis of moral terms, does not fall under this objection, since on this analysis, when Henry says "A is wrong," he is expressing his emotions, attitude, etc., and not (strictly) making a statement. However, emotivism seems to imply metaethical relativism. The latter, however, remains quite unproven, since it is not clear that differences in supposedly basic ethical judgments do not themselves depend on differences of belief about empirical facts (for example, Western and Indian attitudes to animals differ, but so do Western and Indian beliefs about the nature of animals). Nor is it clear that there is no unique set of moral reactions to other people without which a person would not be capable of using moral concepts.

The chief value of relativism is that, by drawing attention to cultural diversity, it has brought philosophers to distinguish between moral rules, etc., and laws of nature, and has encouraged a critical appraisal of the grounds offered for divergent moral judgments.

See **Relativism; Subjectivism, Ethical; Anthropology and Ethics; Sociology of Ethics.**

W. K. Frankena, *Ethics,* ²1973, ch. 6; A. Macbeath, *Experiments in Living,* 1952; C. L. Stevenson, *Facts and Values,* 1963, ch. 5; E. Westermarck, *Ethical Relativity,* 1932; B. R. Wilson (ed.), *Rationality,* 1970.

NINIAN SMART

Religion and Morality, Relations of *see* **Morality and Religion, Relations of**

Religious Ethics *see* **Comparative Religious Ethics;** *see also* **Afro-American Religious Ethics; Buddhist Ethics; Christian Ethics; Confucian Ethics; Eastern Orthodox Christian Ethics; Hindu Ethics; Islamic Ethics; Jewish Ethics; Manichean Ethics; Modern Protestant Ethics; Modern Roman Catholic Moral Theology; Taoist Ethics; Zoroastrian Ethics**

Remarriage *see* **Divorce; Marriage**

Remorse

Stronger than mere regret, remorse is heavy
sorrow over the guilt* one has incurred
through actions that harm or wrong others or
that violate religious requirements. It may be
appropriate or inappropriate, depending on
the circumstances. At any rate, it is not identical with, but may and should lead to, repentance* that may involve acts of reparation or restitution* where possible. Through
confession* the Christian seeks God's forgiveness* as well as the neighbor's forgiveness. Unresolved remorse may, of course,
have detrimental psychological consequences
for the agent.

See **Absolution; Penance; Reconciliation.**
                                    JAMES F. CHILDRESS

Renaissance, The

While it produced nothing new in philosophical ethics, the Renaissance introduced a
change of general perspective that helps to
explain the differences of method and criteria
between the medieval and the modern views
about morality. The recoil from the medieval
outlook and way of living had undoubtedly a
variety of causes (e.g., natural reaction, mental maturing, commercial advance, and political events), but the usual reference to the
recovery of the knowledge of the ancient
Greeks and Romans has still to be stressed.
The broad effect of that recovery was an excited recognition of the width and height of
the achievements of the classical age. These
smote astonished minds with the force of a
revelation; and the vision of the past became
an apocalypse of the future, for what two
Western peoples had done might be done
again. The ancient philosophy and science
showed that the structure of the physical
world and the laws of its processes could be
investigated; the ancient literature showed
that it could be admired, honored, and loved;
and the ancient ways of living showed that
the human lot could be handsomely alleviated by hygiene, self-respect, and grace-
fulness (there were Renaissance manuals of
good manners). The contrast with the medieval outlook, temper, and manner of life was
immense. Human beings, it now seemed,
were not merely sinners, in need of little but
a postmortem salvation. Their present life
was not just a testing for the next, a testing
in which the material and temporal were to
be despised as corruptible and corrupting. It
had much value of its own, human nature

being instinct with high and versatile possibilities that could and should be realized
here. The classical world was indeed being
pictured too rosily; nevertheless what the
Renaissance scholars saw in it really was in
it. They caught the force and fragrance of
forgotten ideals, and revived them in letters,
conversation, and to some extent in conduct.
They became a new aristocracy, and some of
the ruling aristocrats welcomed them, the
most remarkable instance being the close association of the Medici dukes with the Flor-
entine Academy, the noble firstfruit of the
Renaissance.

The changed attitude was called in a later
period "humanism," intended as a term of
praise (*see* **Humanistic Ethics**). In its very
recent disparaging use it would not be applicable generally. True, the attitude could, and
here and there did, contract into a purely
this-worldly one. Its original basis was certainly the sense, evoked by the intellectual
and artistic greatness of the Greeks and the
moral heroism and political magnanimity of
the best Romans, of the wrongness of a low
view of human nature. A low view had been
propagated by the church's doctrine of original sin*; but a high view could be grounded
on other church doctrines, or in the Platonic
theory of the supremacy of the Good, or in
the Stoic conviction that every human is a
part of the divine Reason. Although, then, in
some persons and groups humanism took a
very earthy form (for a while even in papal
circles), largely under the ideal of *virtu* (viril-
ity as proved by powerful action, sometimes
splendid, sometimes merely gross), it was not
in general antireligious. On the whole it had
in the writers a high tone, varying from aesthetic idealism and cosmic emotion to Platonism pure or christianized, or to a Christianity inwardly liberalized. It gave us, among
other things, the NT in Greek and the Greek
fathers.

So far as philosophy was concerned, one
feature was an exchange of ecclesiastical authority for the authority of the ancient pagan
thinkers, whose systems were revived rather
than rethought, one consequence being that
Plato's *Republic,* Aristotle's *Ethics,* Cicero's
On Duties, and Epictetus's *Manual* came to
be the favorite ethical books of the 17th and
18th centuries. In another respect philoso-
phizing came to mean an escape from the
medieval kind that served the church to the
Greek kind that stood on its own rational and

empirical feet. The very few relatively independent philosophers let themselves go, unclassically, in riotously imaginative speculation about nature as a whole. For them the problem of the place and rightful life of human beings does not seem to have been central. Rather than being interested in humans as particular living beings with problems of conduct daily facing them, they were thrilled at the discovery of how much (and how well) humans were able to think and feel about; that is, their attention was directed more on the universe than on themselves. This objective interest ran also into the groove that led to modern astronomical physics, that is, to Galileo and Newton, but before it reached these the largely medieval priest Copernicus (d. 1543) had pushed the earth from the center of the solar system, and the unmedieval monk Bruno (d. 1600), a pantheist of passion and genius, had announced, entranced, an infinity of worlds beyond the solar system. This reduction of humanity's abode by the former to a peripheral and by the latter to a minute status in the physical universe embarrassed orthodox Christians and delighted sophisticated libertines, but hardly became formative of an antireligious and wholly this-worldly morality until the new science had proceeded to something like proof, and even then the effect was ambiguous, for a vaster and more marvelous universe was seen by many as resounding to the greater glory of God, and the spatial pettiness of the earth as leaving untouched either the humanist's conviction of humanity's spiritual greatness or the Christian conviction of human responsibility, immortality, and privilege under God.

The few works of moral reflection that are remembered from this period do not support the common view that the Renaissance was wholly a wave of individualism, for they are about social and political morality. Machiavelli's *The Prince* belongs to political science, and More's *Utopia* to serious imaginative literature rather than to ethics. Campanella's *City of the Sun* is an adaptation of Plato's *Republic*. The one weighty ethical treatise was late, Grotius's *On the Law of War and Peace* (1625) in which the Stoic and Roman concept, familiar to the medievals, of natural law* as the rational (though God-given) criterion of right human laws was applied to the changed situation of emerged and emerging nation-states. This work virtually created international law as a subject of modern technical juristic study. It is more than an addendum to note the controversy (1524–27) between Erasmus, prince of Renaissance scholars, and Luther, on the subject of moral responsibility. The former argued for it with restraint, acknowledging the mystery of God's sovereignty; the latter could think only of sin and unmerited grace. The issue was that of Pelagius and Augustine again (to be renewed a century later by Arminius). The clash is a reminder that the Reformation was contemporary with the Renaissance. The relation between these two reactions against ecclesiastical authority was neither simple nor constant: felt affinity and felt hostility varied with the personalities involved. The one was intellectual and aesthetic, the other a practical passion for religious and moral righteousness; yet both were liberating, and both, in shifts of harmony and conflict, shaped the modern era—with the difference that the Reformation reached much more quickly the common people.

J. Burckhardt, *Civilization of the Renaissance in Italy* (ET 3rd ed., rev., 1951), is still invaluable as a general survey, though confined to the first home. On the philosophical and scientific ideas, see H. Höffding, *History of Modern Philosophy* (ET 1900, repr. 1955). See also W. J. Bousma, *The Culture of Renaissance Humanism*, 1973; P. O. Kristeller, *Renaissance Thought and Its Sources*, 1979; C. Trinkaus, *The Scope of Renaissance Humanism*, 1983.

T. E. JESSOP

Reparation see Reconciliation; Repentance; Restitution

Repentance

Jesus called the people to "repent, for the kingdom of heaven is at hand" (Matt. 4:17). Repentance (*metanoia*, a change of mind) presupposes regret, remorse*, sorrow and contrition* for one's unrighteousness, and it involves turning to God and changing one's ways. Explications of repentance depend on various anthropological and theological convictions, particularly ideas of faith*, forgiveness*, grace*, justification* and salvation, and conceptions about the respective roles played by God and human beings. In general, Roman Catholics have had a larger place for acts of penance*, while Protestants have emphasized the personal relationship between God and humans, but these differences are no longer so pronounced. There is wide agreement that repentance involves the whole person and not simply mind, will, emotion, or action.

J. Haroutunian, "Repentance," *A Handbook of Christian Theology,* ed. M. Halverson and A. A. Cohen, 1958.

JAMES F. CHILDRESS

Repression

Repression has the root meaning of checking or holding something back and hence has been used in social and political contexts in areas as diverse as the putting down of sedition, on the one hand, and, on the other, of overstrict control of children which has an inhibiting effect on their development. In more recent usage it has tended to imply the denial, often by fear or by force, of the legitimate rights and aspirations of others.

Modern political repression is commonly based on ideological, racial, tribal, or ethnic rivalries or is shaped by economic considerations. It is as much a feature of the post-colonial era as of colonial days and may be present within all political systems, although more obvious in dictatorships of both the left and the right. It is a weapon of power* and may be exercised both by minorities over majorities (as in colonialism*) and by majorities over minorities (as, e.g., in the treatment of many aboriginal peoples). Serious ethical issues arise in the use and abuse of power and the denial of rights*. Contemporary social liberation movements, including women's liberation and gay liberation, are responses to perceived repression. (*See also* **Oppression; State; Totalitarian State.**)

Repression may be the result of deliberate policy or the unintended result of actions and forces that are not necessarily evil in themselves. In either event, it usually requires the active or passive acquiescence of other people. Organizations such as Amnesty International have demonstrated the power of public opinion to correct or mitigate some instances of repression, particularly of individuals.

In dynamic psychology the term "repression" is used to express the exclusion from consciousness of impulses, ideas, wishes, attitudes, feelings, etc., which would result in intolerable threat or pain if openly acknowledged. Repression is regarded as the most important of all the defense mechanisms* and is carried out in such a manner that the person concerned remains unaware of the threatening material and of the steps taken to prevent its intrusion into consciousness. Repression can be effective against even the most powerful instinctual impulses, but since it involves a refusal to recognize and accept whole tracts of psychic life, it can also result in the destruction of the integrity of the personality. Even when not pathological in degree, repression can rob life of much of its richness for the person. If, for any reason, the repression ceases to be effective, the consequences can be explosively disruptive.

The psychic phenomenon of repression is often discussed in relation to sexual ethics*, and there has been a popular misunderstanding that any regulation or disciplining of sexual impulses and desires could have the unfortunate effects of repression. The distinctive thing about repression, however, is that it is not within the conscious control of the subject and its negative effects are directly related to its unconscious nature. An understanding of repression and other defense mechanisms is important to an understanding of neurotic behavior, including neurotic sexual reactions. Genuine repression may be overcome constructively through psychotherapy.

P. Freire, *Pedagogy of the Oppressed,* ET 1970; A. Freud, *The Ego and the Mechanisms of Defence,* 1937.

GRAEME M. GRIFFIN

Reproductive Technologies

Researchers in embryology, obstetrics, and medicine have developed procedures that alter or replace altogether human fertilization by heterosexual intercourse and initial gestation *in utero.* Two of these procedures are: (1) artificial insemination by husband (AIH) or by sperm donor (AID), and (2) *in vitro* (outside the human body) fertilization (IVF) using sperm of husband or donor, and egg of wife or surrogate mother. These procedures, and especially the many possibilities and ramifications of IVF, were occasions for recent conflict in religious ethics. Key issues were that these techniques involved a third party in the sexual relationship, posed possible social and physical risks to offspring, and displaced the traditional mode of conception and childbearing. Disputes still exist about the validity of the moral arguments for and against these methods.

Other aspects of reproduction such as banking sperm, ova, and zygotes are also controversial. The potential of cloning (asexual reproduction of) a human being was widely discussed in the early 1970s, but no arguments for cloning have yet been made on any ethical grounds that appeal to religious views of life and its meaning. This article will not discuss cloning but will concentrate on AID and IVF, practices that actually affect growing numbers of persons, and briefly refer to ancillary techniques. Each year, perhaps as many as 10,000 infants in the USA and 1,000 in the UK are born as a result of AID. Since the birth of the first child following IVF in 1978, approximately 800 have been so conceived and delivered.

Married couples mainly request AID or IVF to overcome involuntary infertility. The extent of infertility in the USA is estimated to be between 10 and 15 percent of all married couples. Problems with the female oviductal system cause 30 to 35 percent of cases of infertility. Male infertility is largely due to various forms of sperm incapacitation or low sperm production. Some couples request AID to avoid transmission of a genetic disorder, especially when both parents are carriers of a recessive gene. Such practices are now totally voluntary, although some people would favor more control over selective reproduction. AID with selected sperm from supposed highly fit donors figured strongly in the thought of some eugenicists who desired to improve hereditary qualities with social control of human reproduction by selection. No contemporary religious ethicist has supported "positive eugenics," and the weight of Catholic, Protestant, and Jewish moral traditions remains firmly against the loss of freedom and equality such practices would entail (*see* **Eugenics**).

Artificial insemination by donor (AID). AID's growing use in recent decades prompted a significant ethical debate about its validity and effects on the ethics of sexuality and parenthood. This older debate partly conditioned the positions currently taken by Christian ethicists about IVF.

Roman Catholic ethical teaching and warnings against AID have dominated the contrary position, but significant opposition also arose from some Protestant and Jewish sources. Some arguments against AID also apply to AIH, e.g., objection to masturbation* and departure from natural processes. But the theologically based opposition to AID rests primarily upon views of human sexuality and parenthood* shaped by the belief that the unity in God as Creator is the foundational unity for the various goods and goals of sexuality (*see* **Sexual Ethics**). Without this deeper unity, according to these views, these goods and goals fragment, become competitive, and result in alienation of human beings from their Creator and themselves. The separation of marital love and procreation by acts of AID was considered to be harmful to the fidelity of the couple and probably harmful to offspring and family. Additionally, the promises of marital fidelity* and monogamous marital bonds were understood to be violated by the use of semen obtained from a man other than the husband. By the nature of the AID procedure, the unity that is supposed to be cherished between the husband, wife, and child was disrupted.

Paul Ramsey, a Protestant ethicist, proceeded from a Christocentric interpretation of the meaning of creation, based on the Prologue of John's Gospel and Ephesians 5, to oppose AID either to overcome infertility or for genetic reasons. In his view, the love out of which God created the world found its ultimate expression in Christ. Accordingly, Christians should tell their own creation story rooted in the belief that their one Lord and the unity he represents presides over "procreation as well . . . as all marital covenants." The proper end of sexuality and parenthood is the indivisible unity between Christ and his love for the church, which is the prevailing symbol in a Christian marriage. Ramsey found AID theologically objectionable because it "means a refusal of the image of God's creation in our own." Sexuality and procreation in the sole context of the marital bond was thus the only way to remain faithful to God who in creation established the unity between love and procreation.

The argument of Richard McCormick, a leading Roman Catholic moral theologian, rests primarily on ethical rather than explicit theological categories. He argues that AID disrupts the continuity of love necessary for the optimal expression of sexuality and parenthood. If the foundation of procreation in marriage has been violated, in McCormick's view, this violation probably will also undermine the parental obligation to love and care for children. There is little evidence to suggest that these negative consequences are highly probable, much less inevitable, in most cases.

It is also difficult to find evidence to support two other consequentialist arguments that have been used against AID: (1) it might encourage adultery if women once granted the right to AID began to prefer receiving the sperm by intercourse, and (2) AID's widespread use in animal husbandry and breeding experiments could be used as a pretext for a "stud-farming" attitude toward marriage.

Opposition to AID does not necessarily imply opposition to all control of fertility or to all alternatives to infertility. For example, Ramsey supports voluntary contraception* and sterilization* to avoid transmission of genetic disorders. Although official Roman Catholic teaching opposes both means, some Catholic moral theologians have also accepted them. McCormick supports adoption* as an alternative to AID as a way to overcome infertility, but he indicates that it is not as desirable as genetic parenthood from an ethical standpoint.

Joseph Fletcher was an early challenger of the prevailing negative view of AID in religious ethics, basing his challenge on Christian personalism*. By placing higher values on the personal relationship of husband and wife than their sexual generativity and on the moral relationship between parents and children than their biological relationship, Fletcher supported AID as a morally valid means to overcome infertility. He viewed the practice of levirate marriage (Deut. 25:5–6) as a clear biblical exception to an exclusive claim of husband-wife reproduction. Further, he stressed that AID emancipated human beings from natural causality and determinism, therefore providing more humanly satisfying goals and relief of the emotional deprivation of childlessness. Indeed, for Fletcher we are more human in artificial reproduction than in natural reproduction. (*See* **Genetics** for a discussion of attitudes toward control of natural processes.)

Another key element in Fletcher's support of AID was that the protection of anonymity of the donor by physicians effectively discounted the idea that a third person was personally involved in the sexual relationship. The outcome of a desired pregnancy outweighed, in Fletcher's view, the minimal chance that anonymously donated sperm would be wrongly interpreted by husband and wife as a real intrusion in their sexual relationship. The present writer and others also generally supported AID as a morally acceptable exception for fertilization of a desired child provided there is informed consent by the husband and safeguards for the recipient and the donor.

Informed consent of recipients of AID ought to include information about genetic history and genetic screening of donors, especially when the woman is at a higher risk to transmit a genetic disorder. AID is not without genetic risk, and some recent studies suggest that the procedure may be linked to a higher risk of malformations. The President's Commission (1983) recommended genetic history-taking on all sperm donors, new laws to permit informing recipients of genetic facts about donors without violating confidentiality, and more safeguards for the use of AID. The Committee of Inquiry Into Human Fertilisation and Embryology, chaired by Dame Mary Warnock, a philosopher, made similar recommendations for the UK in 1984 and also proposed changes in the law to deny the semen or egg donor any rights or duties in relation to the child and to grant the child at age eighteen access to genetic information about the donor.

In vitro *fertilization (IVF) and embryo transfer (ET).* Early and sharp debate between proponents and opponents of IVF showed some continuity with the AIH and AID issues but also raised several new ethical questions, including the moral status of the human embryo, the unnaturalness of tampering with the mystery of nature, risks of IVF to the transferred embryo and surgery (laparoscopy) to the mother, allocation of health resources, social-psychological effects on the identity of the child and family, and the precedent IVF may set for eugenic measures. Only the first three of these issues will be discussed here.

Does the moral status of the new zygote demand the same respect due to a newborn or to an adult? When does the developing human being *begin* to have claims on society for the protection deserved by persons? In IVF, this question becomes important in the cases of the embryos that may never be transferred, since two or more ova may be fertilized after superovulation in order to spare the mother more surgery. For those who confer personhood at the time of biological fertilization, to waste embryos is equivalent to killing. Reflection on the biological evidence lent support to the idea that the rudiments of self are truly present at about eight weeks of gestation. The integral oneness of self is absent at fertilization and even at implantation, for twinning may yet occur or cell differentiation may result in a tumor rather than an eventual fetus. The possibility of sentience is probably not present until electrical brain activity and nerve cells mature at six weeks. In recognition of biological development and the controverted nature of the discussion, an Ethics Advisory Board (1979) to US federal health authorities, among whose members was Richard McCormick, concluded that "the human embryo is entitled to profound respect; but this respect does not necessarily encompass the full legal and moral rights attributed to persons." This stance allowed, with the previous consent of egg and sperm donors, the disposal of excess or maldeveloping embryos. Similarly, the Warnock Committee in the UK concluded that "the embryo of the human species should be afforded *some protection* in law," though not the full protection accorded to persons. It recommended that "no live human embryo," which has not been transferred to a woman, be kept alive or used for research purposes beyond fourteen days after fertilization (excluding any time during which the embryo may have been frozen).

The US Ethics Advisory Board approved IVF only if done with consenting *married* couples, but the Warnock Committee recognized the legitimacy of infertility treatment for stable, nonmarried heterosexual couples. The restriction to consenting married couples may accord more closely with the traditions of sexuality and procreation in Christian ethics, but it may be difficult to defend in a pluralistic society. Even the broader standard favored by the Warnock Committee will be subject to pressures from homosexual couples or other individuals who want to have a child.

Does IVF interfere with the mystery of our human existence in the name of an inordinate desire to have children? It has been objected that biological parenting has been unfairly made a measure of personal human worth. The force of this objection to IVF is limited. Because some infertile couples may devalue themselves as persons, it does not follow that they ought to be deprived of a chance to have a child.

Ramsey and Hans Tiefel challenged IVF as fundamentally unethical because of the unknown degree of risk of chromosomal damage to the embryo and subsequent child, and because consent of the child-to-be is impossible. Normally, investigators would seek consent especially from those who are most directly affected by research, including new therapeutic measures. The lack of the child's consent became, in their view, a door to examine the wrongs that may be justified by the moral reasoning of those who defend IVF.

Scientifically, little is known about the risks of IVF. Too few births and no significant follow-up studies of children have occurred to make a valid estimate of risk. In terms of the animal and human results to date, some researchers place the risk at an additional 3 percent that an IVF child may be born with an abnormality. Ramsey held that even a 1 percent chance of error in any procedure surrounding the unborn child is not negligible, and that such a possibility creates a "conclusive argument" against any attempt at IVF. Tiefel agreed with Ramsey and claimed that most arguments for a low risk rate began with calculations on the high rate of spontaneous abortion in the earliest weeks of pregnancy—a fact that does not address the question of whether the procedure leads to an initial increase in those abnormal embryos. The upshot of the conflict about the unknown risks of IVF left the burden of proof and caution clearly on the side of those who would do IVF in the name of relieving the suffering of involuntary infertility.

The Warnock Committee's recommendations also encompassed two of the most ethically controversial ancillary developments of new reproductive technologies, surrogate mother arrangements and freezing human embryos (or ova) for future use. Surrogacy means, in the most usual case, that one woman carries a pregnancy for a man whose wife is infertile. She becomes pregnant by AID using the commissioning father's sperm and by request of the infertile mother. The intent is that the surrogate will give the child to the commissioning parents after birth. Payment of the surrogate is usually involved, sometimes mediated by an organization created for the purpose of facilitating surrogate arrangements. In response to arguments for surrogacy that it may be the only chance to remedy infertility, the Warnock Committee did not recommend that the *act* of surrogate gestation be made illegal. However, out of concern to protect vulnerable surrogates and parents from exploitation and to avoid the dehumanizing effects of commercialization of substitute gestation, the British government was requested to (1) ban agencies that recruit or arrange for women to be surrogates, (2) make such organizational activity punishable as a crime, and (3) enact legislation to render surrogacy agreements illegal contracts unenforceable in the courts. The Committee also recommended that no use of frozen ova for therapy in infertility be allowed until research shows no risk of abnormalities to the subsequent embryo. The use of frozen embryos, which avoids repeated attempts to obtain ova, was allowed, with the provision that observation be made after thawing that the embryo is developing normally. A number of other provisions sought to reduce conflict and disputes over "ownership" in eventual disposition of frozen and stored embryos. The paths opened by the Warnock Committee have yet to be officially explored in the USA, since no governmental body designated for this task has yet been appointed to succeed the expired President's Commission. Cultural differences will likely result in a less prohibitory stance toward surrogacy in the USA, although efforts to restrict commercialization of gestation would fit ethically with the intent behind restrictions on sales of organs for transplantation. Taking unfair advantage of human suffering for financial reasons is an undesirable but controllable aspect of technological development.

See **Children; Eugenics; Marriage; Parenthood; Procreation; Sexual Ethics; Technology.**

Ethics Advisory Board, U.S. Department of Health, Education, and Welfare, *Report and Conclusions: HEW Support of Research Involving Human In Vitro Fertilization and Embryo Transfer,* May 4, 1979; J. Fletcher, *The Ethics of Genetic Control,* 1974; C. Grobstein, *From Chance to Purpose: An Appraisal of External Human Fertilization,* 1981; R. A. McCormick, "Reproductive Technologies: Ethical Issues," *EB,* 1978; and *How Brave a New World?* 1981; O. O'-Donovan, *Begotten or Made?* 1984; P. Ram-

sey, *Fabricated Man,* 1970; and "Manufacturing Our Offspring: Weighing the Risks," *HCR* 8, 1978; H. O. Tiefel, "Human In Vitro Fertilization: A Conservative View," *Journal of the American Medical Association* 247, 1982; W. Walters and P. Singer, *Test-Tube Babies,* 1982; M. Warnock (chairman), *Report of the Committee of Inquiry Into Human Fertilisation and Embryology,* July 1984; and the relevant articles in *DME.*

JOHN C. FLETCHER

Rerum Novarum *see* **Business Ethics; Laissez-faire; Official Roman Catholic Social Teaching; Wages and Salaries**

Research with Human Subjects
see **Experimentation with Human Subjects**

Resistance
Resistance is standing against or opposing other persons, groups, or institutions, especially the state*—for example, the resistance movements in various countries in World War II. In the Sermon on the Mount (Matt. 5) Jesus admonished his followers, "Do not resist one who is evil," specifying "nonresistance" with the hard sayings about turning the other cheek, going the second mile, etc., in the context of the demand to love one's enemies. In Romans 13, Paul noted that "he who resists the authorities resists what God has appointed, and those who resist will incur judgment." Nevertheless there has been debate, especially in the last twenty years, about whether Jesus accepted and even participated in more resistance than Christians have usually admitted. On the one hand, there are suggestions of connections between Jesus and the Zealots, who led the abortive violent rebellion against Roman occupation in A.D. 66–70. It has been argued that some of Jesus' followers participated in the Zealot movement; the temptation* story (Luke 4:1–13) may include the temptation to use violence to obtain the kingdoms of the world; Jesus' use of "force" in cleansing the temple, his entry into Jerusalem, the response of the people, the response of Jewish and Roman authorities, the mode of his execution, and the sign over the cross all have political overtones. On the other hand, Jesus clearly distinguished his message from the Zealot position at important points, particularly in his call to practice "nonresistance" and to "render to

Caesar the things that are Caesar's, and to God the things that are God's" (Mark 12:17).

Despite the terminology of "nonresistance," the practice of most Christians who have taken these NT passages with utmost seriousness can be described as "passive resistance." But if the term "resistance" implies efforts to effect or prevent social and political change, their actions might better be viewed as noncompliance or conscientious objection*. Instead of passively obeying rulers, Christians have refused to comply with laws, orders, or demands that conflict with God's will, usually accepting the consequences of their noncompliance. Thus, when Christians were ordered to commit idolatry*, for example, they were willing to suffer martyrdom* rather than violate their duty to God (see **Patristic Ethics**). Noncompliance is consistent with the division of loyalties between God and Caesar and also with the statement attributed to Peter and the apostles: "We must obey God rather than men" (Acts 5:29). However, Christians have frequently disagreed about where to draw the line between what is God's and what is Caesar's. It is not possible to limit God's sphere to the inner life, since faith always requires some actions such as worshiping God and avoiding idolatry. But there has been vigorous debate about whether loyalty to God precludes military service, taking an oath*, etc.

The distinction between "passive" and "active" resistance is not always clear. For example, "active" could mean (*a*) violent actions, or (*b*) vigorous, but nonviolent actions. It is thus more instructive to consider a continuum of Christian responses to evil and injustice: (1) nonresistance; (2) nonviolent resistance; (3) violent resistance limited by a principle of discrimination* among targets (as in just war* theories); (4) violent resistance limited by a principle of proportionality* or a calculus of probable good and bad effects; and (5) unlimited violent resistance.

Christians stop at different points on the continuum, but their arguments for stopping at those points are strikingly similar: they usually contend that the end of reduced evil or injustice will not justify the next means on the continuum, and that God is in control of history so that humans do not have to take the next step to ensure that goodness and justice will prevail. For most Christians, (1) is morally irresponsible when others are suffering evil and injustice. Thus, resistance to

evil is widely accepted, often in distinction from resistance to "one who is evil." However, this distinction is subject to the criticism that evil is embodied and that institutions consist of individual acts. Position (5), unlimited violence, often appears in crusades* or holy wars to destroy the forces of evil and injustice; it is usually rejected because it equates human and divine responses to evil, neglects the ambiguity of all human actions, and justifies inhumane actions. Most of the Christian debate about responses to evil concerns the legitimacy of positions (2) through (4). The justification for moving from one position to the next one, for example, from nonviolent to violent resistance, usually focuses on the Christian's responsibility for the outcomes of action and inaction.

For many Christians, the critical dividing line is between (2) and (3). Such defenders of the moral priority of nonviolence as Martin Luther King, Jr., argue that there is an intrinsic distinction between nonviolence and violence in resistance to the evil deed rather than the evil doer. They affirm nonviolence as a way of life, not merely as a tactic to be adopted as the circumstances dictate. Nonviolence and violence are not two alternative ways to reach the same end; because of the interpenetration of means and ends, they achieve different ends (see **Ends and Means**). Many proponents of nonviolence in social conflict contend that it is both *right* and *effective* to assume rather than to inflict physical harm*. Their claims about the effectiveness of nonviolent actions often rest on religious convictions about the efficacy of love and suffering, about the human capacity for and propensity to goodness, or about God's actions in the world—for example, the Quaker belief in "that of God in every person," King's belief that "unmerited suffering is redemptive," and Gandhi's claim that "the law of suffering will work, just as the law of gravitation will work, whether we accept it or not" (see **Quaker Ethics; Afro-American Religious Ethics**). These claims are challenged by realists who argue that human beings are sinful and that coercion is necessary in social interactions (see **Realism**). In *Moral Man and Immoral Society* (1932) Reinhold Niebuhr contended that the differences between nonviolence and violence are extrinsic rather than intrinsic; they are differences in degree rather than in kind because both often involve coercion, that is, forcing people to act against their will. Thus, Niebuhr insisted that the choice between nonviolent and violent means is mainly pragmatic; he recognized that nonviolence could be an important tactic in some conflicts (e.g., the black struggle for equality in the USA), but he insisted that it would be ineffective in many other conflicts. Studies suggest that nonviolent resistance sometimes works because it stimulates the sense of injustice in third parties who then bring moral, economic, and political pressures to bear on oppressors. It is possible, however, to combine an affirmation of the moral priority of nonviolence with a realistic recognition of its limitations, especially in some contexts, and of the role of coercion in its effectiveness.

Not all nonviolent resistance is justified merely because it is nonviolent and potentially effective. It is important to examine the mechanisms of various nonviolent actions; since nonviolence often involves coercion* it cannot be assessed merely as persuasion or conversion. It is also important to consider particular forms of nonviolent resistance, such as economic boycotts* and civil disobedience*, because they raise distinct moral issues. Finally, Paul Ramsey (*Christian Ethics and the Sit-In*, 1961) has proposed limitations on the targets of nonviolent actions, claiming that it is not right to attack innocent persons, even nonviolently, in order to oppose other persons or groups.

In part because of a recognition of the need for order in a fallen world, Christians have generally justified violence for the state more readily than violence against the state. This general tendency is evident in Augustine's interpretation of Jesus' statement that "all who take the sword will perish by the sword." According to Augustine, "To take the sword is to use weapons against a man's life, without the sanction of the constituted authority." Liberation theologians* and others have argued that it is also necessary to consider "structural" or "systemic" violence. Otherwise it is easy to condemn revolutionary violence while overlooking the violence of the system it opposes. From this perspective, the violence of the oppressed is counterviolence.

The criteria for justifying violent resistance are similar to those for justifying war—for example, just cause, last resort, reasonable chance of success, and proportionality (*see* **Just War**). One major difference is that the criterion of legitimate or right authority is reinterpreted, usually to refer to the people. A major debate about violence concerns positions (3) and (4)—whether violence is limited by the principle of discrimination*, which requires that innocent persons not be direct targets of violence, or only by the principle of proportionality*, which balances the probable good and bad effects of violence. Some forms of violence, such as terrorism*, clearly violate the principle of discrimination. Then the question is whether they can ever be justified by their ends and consequences. Defenders of position (4) may accept such forms of violence in some cases; defenders of position (3) repudiate them as immoral.

See **Coercion; Just War; Law; Pacifism; Power; Revolution; State; Terrorism; Tyrannicide.** For a discussion of the causes of violence, such as homocide*, *see* **Aggression; Crime.**

J. F. Childress, *Moral Responsibility in Conflicts*, 1982, ch. 1; J. Douglass, *The Non-violent Cross*, 1969; J. Ellul, *Violence*, ET 1969, M. K. Gandhi, *Non-violent Resistance*, ed. B. Kumarappa, 1961; M. L. King, Jr., *Stride Toward Freedom*, 1958; T. Merton, *Faith and Violence*, 1968; W. R. Miller, *Nonviolence: A Christian Interpretation*, 1964; R. Niebuhr, *Moral Man and Immoral Society*, 1932; G. Sharp, *The Politics of Nonviolent Action*, 1973.

JAMES F. CHILDRESS

Respect for Persons

The phrase commonly refers to a moral principle expressed most influentially by Kant in his second formulation of the Categorical Imperative* (in *Groundwork of the Metaphysic of Morals*, p. 96): "Act in such a way that you always treat humanity, whether in your own person or in the person of any other, never simply as a means, but always at the same time as an end." Some regard the principle as important and inspiring; others judge it to be vacuous or unintelligible. Claims for alliance and overlap between the principle of respect for persons and the scriptural commandment to love your neighbor as yourself recur throughout the philosophical literature (*see* **Love**). A. Donagan in his own restatement of the principle purports to draw more closely together Kant's second formulation and this commandment. And Kant himself incorporates the love commandment into his account when he treats duties to other persons (*The Doctrine, of Virtue*, pp. 118–119). Finally, W. G. Maclagan and also R. S. Downie and E. Telfer insist that their depiction of respect for persons converges with the Christian notion of *agapē*. Such claims make the philosophical literature on respect for persons especially important for Christian ethics.

We may ask the following questions about the principle: (1) what content it possesses; (2) how it applies to specific moral problems; (3) what status it occupies in ethical theory; (4) how it may be justified.

1. Content. Modern interpreters often treat Kant's Categorical Imperative as substantive and not merely formal or abstract by pointing to the importance of the second formulation. They call attention to two salient features of "humanity" that prove basic to the meaning of our principle: humanity is not itself a goal to be produced or a value to be traded off. (*a*) Kant writes that human beings "are called *persons* because their nature already marks them off as ends in themselves" (*Groundwork*, p. 96). His statement assumes his distinction between subjective and objective ends. Subjective ends are objects of our free choice and remain relative to our inclinations. They do not exist and must be produced (*bewirkender*), i.e., we pursue them only insofar as we endeavor to bring about some prospective situation or state of affairs. Objective ends, on the other hand, are self-existent (*selbständiger*). They are not relative to our inclinations, but are prescribed by pure practical reason. Just so, persons qualify as ends by virtue of what they are, i.e., rational creatures. An "end" in this sense is not a goal to achieve or a quantity to increase. Rather than produce something valuable, we cherish persons as already existent beings *"for whose sake"* we act or refrain from acting (Donagan). (*b*) Absolute value is attributed to human beings as rational creatures. Here Kant invokes another distinction: between *price* (either a market or a fancy price), which allows something else to serve as a substitute, and *dignity* (*Würde*). Dignity has "unconditioned and incomparable worth" (*Groundwork*, p. 103); human beings as rational creatures are "exalted above all price" and admit "of no equivalent" (p. 102). The absolute value of each person is thus (*a*) incommensurable with the value of contingent desires satisfied or profits secured; (*b*)

noninterchangeable, both in the sense that it is unquantifiable and so can never be measured or traded, and irreplaceable in that its loss cannot be compensated (the presence of one person cannot make good the loss of another); (*c*) permanent in that in no circumstances can someone cease to matter (see also Maclagan).

Though humanity is not a producible or quantifiable end, it still, *qua* end in itself, ought to be maintained and promoted. We are to combine negative restraint (duties of omission) and positive furtherance (duties of commission). In his discussion of duties to others, Kant restricts respect (*Achtung*) to a refusal to abase any other person to a mere means to my (subjective) ends, and construes love (as a maxim of benevolence or practical love, not as feeling) as making others' ends my own (provided these ends are morally permissible) (*The Doctrine of Virtue*, pp. 115–117). The concept of respect in modern usage typically encompasses both: we should treat the subject as inviolable, and cultivate his or her subjective ends (e.g., Downie and Telfer).

Now in many cases respect involves an impersonal concern for oneself and all others. We are to regard ourselves and others impartially or at least similarly, and never make an arbitrary exception on our own behalf. "In a sense, the requirement is that you love your neighbor as yourself: but only as much as you love yourself when you look at yourself from outside, with fair detachment" (T. Nagel, *Mortal Questions*, 1979, p. 126). Since each is an end in itself, beyond all price, the points of view of self and others alike are to receive separate and equivalent weight.

Yet the general notion of respect must likewise accommodate structural and fixed differences between my relation to myself and my relation to another. Kant specifies these differences in *The Doctrine of Virtue*. Here we are told that we are not required to maintain and promote happiness and perfection in general, for this is impossible. Instead, I have a duty to develop my own natural and moral perfection, but my happiness cannot be a duty since I necessarily desire it. I have a duty to promote the happiness of others, but not their perfection. I contradict myself if I say that it is my duty to promote the perfection of others, because each agent's perfection is, again necessarily, the work of his or her own freedom. So in my own case, "another person can indeed compel me to perform actions which are means to his end, but he cannot compel me to have an end; only I myself can make something my end" (*Doctrine*, p. 38).

This claim about structural differences and the restrictions they impose concerns sheer capabilities, particularly what we can and cannot effect in others. It should not be conflated with another claim voiced by Donagan: "One does not fail to respect another as a rational creature by declining to procure a good for him, if that good can be procured only by relinquishing an equal or greater good for oneself" (*The Theory of Morality*, p. 86). The second claim returns us to questions of impartiality and receives rival assessments by different writers, some of whom prefer a riskier standard where one's own good is concerned. All of the discussants in this second case assume, however, that the courses they commend are realizable ones.

2. Application. What follows practically from the principle that persons are to be respected as ends in themselves? For Kant and Donagan in particular the single fundamental principle yields a comprehensive set of duties or precepts. Both appeal overall to our rationality and capacity to set ends, and they acknowledge the structural differences noted above by dividing the duties of each person between those one has to oneself and those one has to other human beings as such. Kant adds duties to other human beings regarding their circumstances ("differences in rank, age, sex, health, prosperity or poverty"; *Doctrine of Virtue*, p. 139), which he maintains cannot be classified completely; Donagan adds duties that arise from participation in human institutions (institutions of purely voluntary contract, and civil or noncivil societies of which individuals are members). Kant distinguishes further under duties to oneself between (*a*) limiting or negative or perfect duties which forbid certain actions for the sake of preserving the self-existent end (and which always take precedence), and (*b*) widening or positive or imperfect duties which promote certain actions for the sake of perfecting the self-existent end; and under duties to other human beings as such, between duties of love which are meritorious and duties of respect which are due others. And Donagan includes in his moral system three classes of specificatory premises—the permissible, the forbidden, and the obliga-

tory—each of which identifies "a species of action as falling or not falling under the fundamental generic concept of action in which every human being is respected as a rational creature" (*Theory of Morality*, p. 68).

To judge seriously the success of these efforts would require us to evaluate case by case how convincingly specific duties are derived from the principle. It is only feasible to give examples of Kant's duties to oneself and Donagan's duties to others. Kant's list of negative duties includes the following. To the human person as an "animal being," the actions of suicide, carnal self-defilement, and immoderate consumption of food and drink are all forbidden (the latter, for instance, weaken one's capacity to use one's powers purposefully); and as a "moral being," the actions of lying, avarice, and servility are also forbidden because they rob one of the prerogative to act in accordance with inner freedom and make one instead "a plaything of the mere inclinations and hence a thing." Moreover, Kant in places recognizes that attitudes and gestures are significant, e.g., when he discusses the vices of pride, calumny, and mockery. Donagan considers, under duties to other human beings as such, the use of force at will on another (killing, bodily injury or hurt, and slavery), injuries such as loss of property, honor, and reputation, veracity, the principle of beneficence; and under institutional duties, promising, the prohibition of robbery and theft, marriage and divorce, the conception and rearing of children, obedience and disobedience to laws in a civil society, and military conscription.

Such attempts at systematic application must answer certain standard questions. (*a*) Do the actual lists of duties which the principle yields remain incomplete? If so, can those not identified also be derived from the principle? If they cannot, is the principle no longer fundamental? (*b*) Are the actual lists of duties as we have them pulled in large part out of a given cultural or traditional hat? (*c*) Does the normative universalism governing so much of the discussion (i.e., duties outside stations and roles, applicable to human beings as such)—however formidably opposed to various forms of tribalism and hierarchy—skew badly the moral claims we ordinarily must weigh? Donagan attends at greater length than Kant to duties tied to institutional arrangements, but does even he misleadingly downplay communal and role-related claims? Is there a viable place for respect due to persons as defined by social roles? Do these roles not effectively determine the distribution of moral attention and energy, to an extent that goes unrecognized? (*d*) If both negative and positive duties derive from the same principle, should the former always take precedence? Does the effort to avoid a conflict of duties in this way fail to give complexity in the moral life its due?

3. Status. One's answers to the questions just posed doubtless connect directly with the status one ascribes to the principle of respect for persons in ethical theory. We can envisage three claims. (*a*) Respect for persons is *one* among several principles (e.g., beneficence) all of which are equally basic. To accord any one principle fundamental status provides no determinate guidance in specific situations of moral choice. The putatively basic principle is either so vague and general that it contains its own internal conflicts without resolving them, or so delimited that extraneous considerations intrude to influence or determine conclusions reached. Embedded in our moral judgments are diverse considerations that require a range of basic principles to articulate adequately, and clarity is served if we opt formally for such pluralism. (*b*) Respect for persons stands as the most *general* substantive principle, not of morality as such, but of a *distinctive* scheme of morality. This claim has two versions. (i) All moral judgments commonly made in our (Western) society *presuppose* the principle, or can be explained in terms of it. Downie and Telfer, for example, argue that the principles of both social morality (utility, equality, and liberty) and private morality presuppose it as their ultimate justification. (ii) All moral judgments may be traced to the principle as a final or irreducible normative reference point. It is not the originating source of all other principles, rules, and particular judgments in the sense that they must be self-consciously deduced from it, or explained in terms of it. A more dialectical relation obtains in which respect for persons both summarizes and adjudicates. On the one side, it *generalizes* those features of our specific rules and judgments which are not tied to their immediate surroundings but perdure over a range of cases and historical periods; and it *conveys* in *abridged* form the distinctive "spirit" of the particular scheme in question. On the other side, it locates the *point* and

rationale of specific rules and judgments; it *organizes* and *integrates* them (thus the moral life is not a "mere heap" of unrelated obligations); it *resolves conflicts* among them; and it furnishes a criterion for assessing critically new problems and changed circumstances. (*c*) Respect for persons is *the* fundamental principle of morality as such: it serves as the basis or originating source of all other principles, rules, and particular judgments, and does not depend on them for its own binding power (see Kant and Donagan). Foundationalist versions of this claim maintain that to acquire genuine moral knowledge and to avoid an infinite regress, a first principle must be (i) relatively context-free, allowing for a strictly deductive order of epistemic dependence; (ii) exceptionless and thus never rightly overridden; (iii) substantive, in the sense that it provides answers to specific questions about conduct and character.

4. Justification. In the famous passage that exemplifies why Kant believes human beings possess incomparable worth, he writes: "Two things fill the mind with ever new and increasing admiration and awe, the oftener and more steadily we reflect on them: the starry heavens above me and the moral law within me" (*Critique of Practical Reason,* p. 166). Kant goes on to say (and this is usually ignored) that the moral law within me "reveals a life independent of all animality and even of the whole world of sense . . . , a [purposive] destination which is not restricted to the conditions and limits of this life but reaches into the infinite" (p. 166). Here is the point perhaps at which Kant comes closest to a doctrine of the *imago Dei* *. No wonder then that the autonomy of the will, so bound up with the moral law and making one "free of all laws of nature," constitutes "the ground of the dignity of human nature" (*Groundwork,* p. 103). Modern exponents such as Downie and Telfer similarly contend that human beings differ from animals by virtue of two abilities: each of us can be self-determining, and each can adopt rules one accepts as binding on oneself and on all rational beings. Donagan interprets the Kantian justification of the principle of respect for persons as less than an *a priori* demonstration or a matter whose force is intuitively self-evident. Rather, Kant "drew attention to certain characteristics implicit in being a rational creature, with regard to which he claimed to have sufficient insight into the nature of practical reason confidently to affirm that it must prescribe that rational creatures be unconditionally respected" (*Theory of Morality*, p. 237). These characteristics include a negative freedom requiring us to distinguish agent causation from event causation, and so an absence of determination to any end by our physical or biological nature; and it is this former type of causality which marks us as creatures of a different and higher kind than others in nature. In brief, our own rational nature is already an end which is not producible, but rather itself generates action, and accordingly warrants respect.

Two criticisms of this Kantian justification regularly surface. (*a*) Rational self-determination serves as the too-restricted basis not only of human distinctiveness but of human dignity* Neglected (at least relatively) as candidates for our respect are features of sentience, as found in both human beings and nonhuman animals, especially a liability to pain and suffering. Moreover, those sympathetic to the Kantian interpretation face the problem of what to say about beings who by mental or physical impairment appear to lack rational self-determination. Does this lack compromise their claim to dignity? (*b*) Exponents of the principle prove unpersuasive when they claim to give it a purely secular meaning and defense. Maclagan (as well as Donagan, and Downie and Telfer) is firm in his rejection of a theological answer to the question of justification: the principle can sustain the absence and survive the loss of the theistic faith so frequently cited in support of it ("Respect for Persons," p. 208). Some philosophers, however, express doubts that Kant, Donagan, and others convincingly extract a notion of respect for persons from the entire web of Hebrew-Christian belief. For example, some critics hold that Donagan's arguments lose much of their force when they are separated from a theistic framework and that even a Kantian ethics needs a religious foundation. Such doubts find specific illustration in Donagan's acknowledgment that the common morality of the Hebrew-Christian tradition to which he appeals rests on a view of human persons as autonomous and responsible, and as living in a natural world governed by morally neutral laws. These presuppositions are at odds, he admits, with those found in other "venerable cultures" (e.g., Hinduism) and in some post-Christian theories of human nature (e.g., B.

F. Skinner's radical behaviorism). His critics to date often conclude that to cite traditional presuppositions which by no obvious reckoning are universally shared jeopardizes his own attempt to seek moral foundations for the principle of respect that are ascertainable at any period, and permanently valid.

Any comprehensive assessment of the claims for alliance and overlap between respect for persons and the scriptural commandment to love your neighbor as yourself should consider all four questions canvassed here. And even if one finds the claims exaggerated or otherwise mistaken, the work of comparing this philosophical literature on each of the questions with materials in Christian ethics yields important clarificatory benefits and sets one promising agenda for the future.

See **Autonomy; Categorical Imperative; Honor; Human Dignity; Image of God; Kantian Ethics; Love; Persons and Personality; Reverence.**

A. Donagan, *The Theory of Morality*, 1977; R. S. Downie and E. Telfer, *Respect for Persons*, 1969; O. H. Green (ed.), *Respect for Persons*, 1982; I. Kant, *Critique of Practical Reason*, tr. L. Beck, 1962; *The Doctrine of Virtue* (pt. 2 of *The Metaphysic of Morals*), tr. M. Gregor, 1964; and *Groundwork of the Metaphysic of Morals*, tr. H. J. Paton, 1964; W. G. Maclagan, "Respect for Persons as a Moral Principle," *Philosophy*, 1960.

GENE OUTKA

Responsibility

Responsibility, now so familiar a word in moral discourse, came into general use in the languages of Western culture only in the 17th century. In the late 19th century, two works gave the term a central place in the lexicon of morality: F. H. Bradley's essay "The Vulgar Notion of Responsibility and Its Connection with the Theories of Freewill and Determinism" (1876) and Lucien Lévy-Bruhl's study of the problem of freedom, *L'idée de responsabilité* (1883). As its etymology suggests (from Latin *respondere*, "to answer"), the most obvious meaning of the term is accountability, being answerable for one's behavior. Thus, it is within discussions of the conditions requisite for moral liability to praise and blame, punishment and reward, that the term is most frequently encountered. However, a deeper etymology reveals another dimension: within the word for response is hidden the Greek word for "promise,"* recalling the practice of reliably performing one's part in a common undertaking. In this sense, responsibility refers, not merely to the conditions for imputability, but to the trustworthiness and dependability of the agent in some enterprise. This meaning has been explored by theologians rather than by philosophers. In this article, the concept of responsibility will be explained in terms of these two notions, accountability and commitment.

1. Responsibility as accountability. The classical discussion of accountability is found in the first chapter of book 3 of Aristotle's *Nicomachean Ethics.* The student of virtue and the lawmaker, says Aristotle, should understand the distinction between voluntary and involuntary action, in order properly to distribute rewards and punishments. He proposes that actions are involuntary when performed under coercion or in ignorance* and defines voluntary action as "one in which the initiative lies with the agent who knows the particular circumstances in which the action is performed" (3.1, 1111a21). In this brief chapter, Aristotle sets the terms in which discussions of accountability will be carried on throughout the history of Western thought. Subsequent thinkers will specify various sorts of coercion: physical violence, fear, passion, habit, psychological and social influence, pathological conditions; and they will distinguish various sorts of ignorance: of fact and of law, vincible and invincible, antecedent and consequent, etc. In all these discussions, the basic question is, Under what conditions of the agent and the action can it be said that the agent deserves to be praised or blamed, rewarded or punished, for the action he or she performed?

This question is exceedingly complex. An answer depends on what an action is understood to be, how action is distinguished from consequences, what it means for a person to be the cause of an action and, in particular, a "moral" cause of a "moral action." All these matters are controverted; this article can only refer to two issues raised by the final question, What is it to be a moral cause? During most of the Western cultural tradition, "moral causation" was identified as action resulting from the unique property of human beings, "freedom." Freedom, explained in various ways by Stoics, Neoplatonists, and various Christian thinkers, was

the necessary presupposition for responsible action, that is, action for which moral praise and blame was appropriate. Aquinas begins his article on whether there is free choice, "Man has free choice, otherwise counsels, exhortations, commands, prohibitions, rewards and punishments would be in vain" (*ST* I. 83.1). Kant's elaborate argument for freedom as a postulate of practical reason asserts that the unconditioned *ought* of the law requires a *can* on the part of the rational will (*Critique of Practical Reason* 1.2.2). Responsibility, then, in the sense of being subject to praise or blame for one's actions, requires, in some sense, the existence of a free cause, a being that is self-determining and capable of choosing otherwise than one actually does choose.

However, since the 18th century, another position has developed that denies the necessary logical association between freedom and responsibility. This position, championed by Hume (*Enquiry Concerning the Principles of Morals,* sec. VIII) and Mill, requires not a "free cause," but only the absence of impediments to the realization of one's wishes and desires, which themselves are caused by many determinants. In fact, moral responsibility, far from presupposing freedom, presupposes determinism, since properly to associate agent and act, the rational desires of the agent must be the determining cause of consequences; praise and blame, punishment and reward are themselves causes that modify the character of the agent. This "soft determinism," as William James called it, seems the dominant view today, although the debate continues (*see* **Free Will and Determinism**).

The second issue concerns certain characteristics of moral action itself, such as intention*, motive*, deliberation*. While it is commonly believed that judgments about praise and blame must take into account the motives, intentions, understanding, and reasoning of the agent, it is extremely difficult to do so. All of these can be known only on the report of the agent or by inference: both sources may be deceptive or faulty. Also, repeated philosophical analysis of these concepts has never succeeded in making them very clear.

Responsibility as accountability is as important in the law as it is in morality. Legal judgments must assign fault to individuals; the validity of legal instruments, such as contracts and wills, requires capacity on the part of the agent. Thus, both in criminal and civil law, conditions for designation of responsibility have been developed. Categories of intentional wrongdoing, recklessness, and negligence* specify the sorts of action or nonaction for which persons can be held legally responsible or blameworthy; similarly, responsibility can be excluded or diminished by such factors as threats, mistakes, accident, provocation, duress, and insanity. In civil matters, incapacity to perform certain legal acts can be ascribed to duress, undue influence, minority, etc. Centuries of analysis, in legal judgments and in legal theory, have brought these concepts to a high degree of specificity and technical refinement. Philosophers have been attracted by this feature of the legal doctrines about responsibility and have, in recent years, drawn analogies between these and the questions of moral responsibility (Hart, 1955; Feinberg, 1970).

Despite suggestive similarities, important differences must be recognized. The courts are concerned with claims that can be sustained by evidence about events in the public world of spoken words, observed actions, manifest consequences; moral judgments evoke, as well, the private world of intentions, motivations, attitudes. The former is *in foro externo;* the latter *in foro interno.* While legal responsibility cannot avoid looking toward the inner forum, it must eventually move in the external forum of provable acts and relationships. Thus, concepts such as "intentional," "voluntary," "foreseen," and "unforeseen" must be translated, for legal purposes, into pragmatic concepts susceptible of demonstration. The long dispute in the criminal law about the ancient term *mens rea* (guilty mind) bears witness to the law's need to remain in the realm of the demonstrable. Further, law serves practical objectives of public order; morality serves, as well, the ideal objectives of personal integrity. Thus definitions and standards of responsibility in the law will often be framed to meet the ends of policy or the need to conclude some business expeditiously. Questions of moral responsibility, although often pressed by the urgency of a public or social resolution, remain largely matters of conscience for individuals. They can be debated perennially and can tolerate ambiguities and paradoxes. Thus, legal and moral responsibility, while similar in many ways (particularly in the root question whether *this* act can properly be

attributed to *this* person), differ significantly.

2. Responsibility as commitment. The second meaning of responsibility, as a description of the character of a person. This meaning reflects the deeper etymology of performing one's promised part in a solemn engagement. In this sense, responsible persons are not only those who are uncoerced and aware of the nature of their action and its consequences; they are also persons who demonstrate certain stable or habitual attitudes to their relationships with other persons. In this sense responsibility describes the character of a person.

Responsible persons conscientiously and consciously commit themselves to a task or form of life and readily accept accountability for its success and failure. They enter into the task, aware of its potential and its risks, willing to be blamed if it is performed faultily and rightfully claiming credit for its probity. In addition, the moral quality of a person grows out of the commitments made and stood by: persons form their lives in certain ways and come to be identified by others as responsible for themselves and their actions. Responsibility is, as Nicolai Hartmann stated, "the basic ethical capacity of a person . . . assuming the moral quality of the value and disvalue of his mode of action" (*Ethics,* 1926; ET 1932, vol. 3, p. 162). Modern moral philosophy has showed little interest in analyzing these dimensions, although some discussion about the nature of assuming or accepting a role (e.g., the professional responsibility of being a physician or a lawyer, or the social responsibility of parenthood), as well as a renewed interest in the traditional subject of virtue, may stimulate more careful analysis.

Theologians have been attracted to this dimension of responsibility. Judeo-Christianity has always stressed responsibility in the sense of accountability: God as creator dictates a law and will judge accordingly; human beings must know God's law and freely obey it. They are responsible, that is, accountable before God's judgment. In modern theology, however, the etymological relationship between response and responsibility has appealed to theologians as a fundamental metaphor for the relationship between God and humanity: humanity must *respond* to God's call and intention for the world. The Calvinist theologian Karl Barth writes, "It is the idea of responsibility which gives us the most exact definition of the human situation in face of the absolute transcendence of the divine judgment" (*Church Dogmatics* II/2, ET 1957, p. 641). The Jewish thinker Martin Buber, the Lutheran Dietrich Bonhoeffer, the Catholic Bernard Häring, and H. Richard Niebuhr from mainstream American Protestantism all identify their ethics as an ethic of responsibility. Each of these authors gives profound theological meaning to the term, setting it within the theological doctrines of creation, redemption, and eschatological reconciliation. Common to the ethics of responsibility is the Judeo-Christian belief that God speaks to human beings in the words of created nature, of sacred scripture and, above all (for Christians), in the Word incarnate, Jesus Christ. Central to this message is the announcement that humans are made responsible for self, for society, and for creation. Human moral life consists in the dedicated effort to discern the word of God in the situations of life and to respond to that word by faithful, loving, and hopeful action. Moral life is not passive obedience to an immobile law. It requires initiative, interpretation, revision. It reveals both stability of commitment and the attentive readiness to change.

This interest in an "ethic of responsibility" reflects the concern of contemporary theologians that the church has historically fostered an ethic of withdrawal and defensiveness in the face of the realities of personal and social life. The extent to which this is so is controversial, both as a matter of history and of doctrine, yet certain trends and teachings, such as the concentration on individual holiness, justification by faith alone, preservation of a pure conscience by retreat from an evil world seem to draw believers away from the political and social world to a world of private religious experience or, at best, into a closed community of the "saved." The ethic of responsibility repudiates this trend. God calls individuals to himself, not by calling them away from the urgent needs of social and civic life, but by summoning them to work within the world, redeeming and reforming its structures so that all persons might live freely and responsibly. The moral life is not merely a life of accountability to God's preordained law. It is a response to God's invitation to live in the world and, in the deeper etymological sense of the term "response," to enter into the solemn undertaking of redeeming the world in concert with its creator (*see* **Ecclesiology and Ethics**).

This concern to promote a morality of vital involvement reflects the distinction made by the German sociologist Max Weber. He was the first to use the expression "ethic of responsibility" in contrast to an "ethic of ultimate ends." The latter describes a morality of absolute injunctions; it forbids adoption of any means that would compromise these absolutes. It is concerned principally with purity of intention and necessitates a withdrawal from the ambiguities and contamination of worldly affairs. The former engages in a search for the best available means to attain worthy ends within a highly imperfect world. It is principally concerned with the consequences of actions that will always be a manipulation and balancing of the good and evil in every decision. In "Politics as a Vocation," Weber proposed that the morality governing the vocation of politics must be an ethic of responsibility pursued by responsible persons, "with a trained relentlessness in viewing the realities of life and the ability to face such realities and to measure up to them inwardly." Lutheran Pastor Bonhoeffer shaped a theological version of Weber's ethic of responsibility in his revulsion at the reluctance of German Christians to condemn Nazism. He was repelled particularly by their theological justification for this reluctance: the avoidance of the moral contamination of political activity. The Christian must engage in politics and seek realistic means of reaching goals suitable to the gospel of God's grace.

Authors espousing an ethic of responsibility reveal differences stemming from their theological traditions and from their view of the problems facing the church and persons who profess religious belief in an unbelieving world. One problem they share is how to express the content of such an ethic. Since the notion of responsibility, either as accountability or as commitment, refers primarily to the subjective state of the agent, it implies nothing in itself about the standards, norms, or principles against which the value of a moral action must be assessed. For some authors, such as Häring, the normative content of an ethic of responsibility differs but little from the traditional natural law* ethic of Roman Catholicism. The responsible person heeds the values revealed in nature, particularly the nature of persons. For others, such as H. Richard Niebuhr, the normative content is designed by viewing moral action as "fitting action," that is, as acts that fit into the ongoing creation of integrity of the self within the human community and the universe. Authors differ also about how the word of God's invitation and command is communicated: in the scripture, through the created order of nature, in the structured yet evolving relationships between human beings. They differ about how that word is discerned: in personal inspiration, by faith alone, by reasoned affectivity, in historical and personal experience.

Two simplifications plague the ethic of responsibility: "situationism" and "activism." In the first, the responsible persons are described as those who are "responsive" to the demands and needs of the situation in which they find themselves; the context of moral values, principles, and structures is depreciated in favor of immediacy (see **Situation Ethics**). In the second, immersion in activities to reform social structures becomes so deep as to stifle the perennial warning of Judeo-Christianity: all persons are marred by sin and are in need of divine grace to bring about the good.

Apart from theological ethics, a pervasive concern for responsibility, in the sense of conscientious commitment, appears in discussions of the ethics of professional and public life. The "responsibility" of government leaders, physicians, journalists, scientists, business people, and others is constantly debated. Their personal integrity in dealing with the demands of their task is examined; the relationship between personal integrity and the needs of society is explored. Philosophers and other scholars have only begun to analyze this widespread concern in ways that would bring greater conceptual clarity and more vivid empirical description to the discussion. In addition, the ways in which responsibility is imparted to individuals in their upbringing and education and how it is endorsed and supported (and subverted) by the structures of professional and social life require further explanation.

J. Feinberg, *Doing and Deserving: Essays in the Theory of Responsibility,* 1970; J. Glover, *Responsibility,* 1970; J. M. Gustafson and J. Laney (eds.), *On Being Responsible,* 1968; H.

L. A. Hart, "The Ascription of Responsibility," in A. Flew (ed.), *Logic and Language* I, 1955; H. L. A. Hart and A. M. Honore, *Causation in the Law,* 1959; A. R. Jonsen, *Responsibility in Modern Religious Ethics,* 1968; H. R. Niebuhr, *The Responsible Self,* 1963.

ALBERT R. JONSEN

Restitution

Genuine sorrow for a sin implies not only the desire for future amendment of life but the desire to repair or minimize the injuries inflicted by the sin or sins already committed and now repented of. Restitution is the making good of whatever injury has been inflicted. Of course, it may sometimes be impossible to make restitution. Wherever possible, however, an act of restitution or the sincere intention of performing such an act must be regarded as a necessary part of repentance*, and as a condition for receiving absolution*.

JOHN MACQUARRIE

Retribution

The *lex talionis*—"An eye for an eye, and a tooth for a tooth"—is often regarded as the core concept of retribution. However, it prohibits unlimited revenge, and any mature understanding of punishment must likewise seek to discard crude concepts of retribution. The problem is particularly acute for Christians. How may one balance the ethical seriousness of sin with the possibilities of mercy*, forgiveness*, and redemption, which are so central and crucial to the Christian gospel?

On a historical perspective, the retributive approach has been championed by some major modern philosophers, such as Kant, Hegel, and the Hegelian school of British idealists. The concept of desert is of central importance here, and at the same time it is combined with an emphasis on annulment or reformation. Unfortunately, contemporary criminology has divorced retribution and reformation. The reformative ideal of recent decades is now declining, and there is a renewed call either for a "justice model" or for measures of increased severity. Historically, the latter have generally proved ineffective, and their ethical justification is questionable. The current agenda for secular and Christian criminologists must be the reintegration of retributive and reformative ideals, to prevent further oscillation from one extreme to another.

See also **Capital Punishment; Corporal Punishment; Penology; Rewards and Punishments.**

H. B. Acton (ed.), *The Philosophy of Punishment,* 1969; E. R. Moberly, *Suffering, Innocent and Guilty,* 1978.

ELIZABETH R. MOBERLY

Reverence

The attitude of respectful attentiveness toward God and things divine or consecrated to God, which can focus in praise and worship, and whose absence can take extreme forms in expressions of blasphemy or acts of sacrilege. The Latin *revereor* has a root meaning of "fear," but theology, influenced by Rom. 8:15, has distinguished between "servile fear," as a self-regarding attitude, and a "filial fear of the Lord," expressing a proper respect for the majesty of God, which is a delight and gift of the Spirit (Isa. 11:2–3) and is consonant with love of the heavenly Father and the friendship of Christ (John 15:15). The attitude of reverence to God has been considered to extend to those deriving their function from God, notably parents (cf. Eph. 6:1–4) and civil authorities (cf. Rom. 13:1–5). Reverence for rulers has frequently made more acute for Christians the difficulties of resisting unjust forms or exercise of government (*see* **Resistance**). Reverence for the sacredness of human life, of which God is the author, is often appealed to by Christians in contemporary discussions on such matters as abortion* and euthanasia*.

See **Blasphemy; Human Dignity; Persons and Personality; Respect for Persons; Sacrilege.**

J. MAHONEY

Revolution

In its plainest sense revolution refers to radical political and social change, yet the incapacity of the social sciences to give it clear definition and its widespread use in nonpolitical contexts suggest that revolution is as much a normative idea in modern consciousness as it is an empirical reality. Modern social theory and social science are deeply intertwined with the first modern revolutions in the 17th and 18th centuries, and critical divisions in social science and other contemporary disciplines often have roots in differing interpretations of revolution. On the religious side, the fact that the first edition of this dictionary had no article on revolution not only lends credence to the revolutionary criticism that religion is inherently conservative but also displays the difficulty that modern consciousness has posed for Christian ethics.

Revolution in its modern meaning must be kept distinct from traditional ideas of resistance* to tyranny or of civil disobedience*. The latter notions may be treated ethically along lines parallel to "just war"* analysis: these all have in common the assumption of a universal ground for moral argument, the notion of the normal legitimacy of political institutions* measured against this universal moral ground, and the idea that political strife and violence, whether war, civil disobedience, or resistance to tyranny, are exceptions to the norm, requiring careful ethical grounding and limitation. In all cases, the purpose of political conflict or violence is to restore a previously established but temporarily lost or abrogated situation of legitimacy (*see also* **Tyrannicide**).

The modern notion of revolution denies all these premises. The term was first used in its modern sense during the French Revolution (the American Revolution was so named only in retrospect) and its distinctiveness lay in the revolutionaries' sense that they were creating something genuinely new in history, not restoring, or correcting a violation of, a previous legitimate regime. All the previous errors and evils of the human race were to be swept away and a new social order established in the name of liberty and under the canons of reason. As the religious rhetoric of the French Revolution displayed, and as Tocqueville later noted, such utter transformation of both individual consciousness and the social order was akin to religious conversion.

Such ideas have clear roots in the eschatological and apocalyptic ideas of Judeo-Christianity and clear predecessor movements in millenarian politics (see Cohn, Hobsbawm) as well as in developments of Calvinism and Puritanism (see Hill, Walzer). But *the* theory of modern revolution is provided by Karl Marx and the Marxist tradition with its distinctive interpretation of human action and history: that all previous forms of human society and consciousness have been alienated modes (*see* **Alienation**) because human activity has been subjugated to the forces of nature and constrained by the particularistic and religious consciousness connected to specific forms of production and class domination; that the advent of capitalism* has made possible the emancipation of the human species from nature and the release of consciousness from the particularistic horizons of previous modes of production; and that capitalism has produced a class, the proletariat, which is potentially (but only that) a universal class in a very specific sense. The proletariat is, negatively, the first class not to have familial, tribal, national, or even class identity (therefore, Marx says, it is not genuinely a class); it is the first class to have at its command the technical capacity (in the double sense of knowledge and accomplished productive technology) to produce abundantly and thereby to release humans from the necessity of condemning certain of its members to the perpetual drudgery of production on behalf of others; and it is thus potentially the first class able to transcend the unconsciously evolved forms of particularistic human association (class, nation state, religion, etc.) with consciously created universal forms that serve human ends (*see also* **Marxist Ethics; Social Class**).

This conscious creation of human institutions* is revolutionary praxis. Its power as an idea lies not only in the promise that such historical transformation is possible but also in the special historical role accorded revolutionary agents, a role that holds great fascination for peoples who have been politically powerless and exploited. Even when revolutions fall far short of their goals (as they always do), they can help transform politically passive peoples into active political participants, so being vehicles of modernization.

Virtually all modern revolutions, European or non-European, have been waged under the banner of either Christian millenarian thought or a version of Marxism. (Islamic revolutions, hostile to both Marxism and modernization, probably fall into a different category altogether.) And many have argued that the Marxist tradition, in spite of its criticism of religion, has kept alive the eschatological dimension of the Christian religion while the Christian mainstream has served mainly to legitimate existing social patterns and various forms of political and economic injustice (*see also* **Eschatological Ethics; Utopian Thought**).

The conservatism* of much of the Chris-

tian tradition is undeniable, although that history is far more complex than any generalization admits, and Christian movements have contributed to profound social change far more often than critics recognize. But modern revolutionary ideas have significantly affected Christian thought, drawing attention to the political and economic sources of much human misery, pointing to the churches' complicity in some of this misery, reminding Christians of their own radical beginnings and their radical and critical resources. The response has been a host of new theological modes: liberation theology*, political theology*, theology of hope*, theology of revolution. These "theologies" are by no means alike but they have several key points in common. (1) they all take the eschatological dimension of Christianity as normative for understanding the whole; (2) they all make positive use of Marxist language and analysis; (3) they all understand Christian life and action in terms of the Marxist notion of praxis, a deeply ambiguous notion that embraces both the conversion aspects of revolutionary change and the idea of critically self-conscious historical transformation.

Any assessment of this modern theological proclivity must attend to these features and any moral analysis of revolution is dependent on this assessment. The following issues and problems are critical.

1. Any attempt to make one part of Christian faith and doctrine normative for the whole (a canon within the theological canon) is always open to internal theological criticism. Two points are particularly relevant: First, while the eschatological theme certainly can and should help correct the institutional rigidity of the church and its unconscious social captivity, it carries its own deep ambiguities to the task. Chief among these is the tension between the emphasis on God's miraculous transformation (conversion) of persons and the world, and the emphasis on human freedom and social action. This ancient tension is newly translated but not resolved simply by substituting the idea of praxis. The second point is connected. The emphasis on radical conversion and the transformation of consciousness betrays a deep kinship with a long ethical tradition that includes not only millenarian thought but also the Lutheran emphasis on justification, the Barthian ethics of divine command, the

Bultmannian ethics of radical obedience. As this brief list indicates, the kinship system as a whole is not inherently revolutionary and it is open to the criticism of those ethical positions that emphasize sanctification, the importance of virtue, the institutional dimensions of ethics, and the creative aspects of law*.

2. Some may well argue, as this writer would, that Marxist thought must be appropriated by theology (generally as a significant interpretation of the institutional dimensions of sin, specifically as a powerful critique of capitalism), but it would be ironic if theology came to embrace Marxism as its chief social translation just as we are witnessing Marxism's decomposition. The theological use of Marx is often facile and chiefly rhetorical (e.g., when all oppressed persons are identified as the universal class) and serves more for political motivation than for theological or ethical direction. What is at stake is the interpretation of evil* in the world, and even careful Marxist class analysis has not been adequate to the complexity of modern society and to the immense variety of human oppression*, wrongdoing, and suffering*. An adequate Christian ethical analysis of revolution must attend to this variety. It may be helped in this by more sophisticated versions of neo-Marxist thought, but even this must be subject to theological control.

3. It is not at all clear that programs which make radical transformation the paradigm for all human action can sustain a consistently ethical interpretation of human life. As implied in the first point above, such theological programs often are not revolutionary in their social effect and those that are often fail. In fact, successful revolutionary programs (successful in the sense of being able to give ethical shape to human life) have often been carried out by those for whom the language of sanctification* and institution* take precedence over, or at least balance, the language of radical transformation (as, e.g., in Puritanism). More often, the disillusionment that comes from the failure to eradicate evil, and the absence of an adequate institutional ethic for the continued ambiguities of human existence, motivate the desperate attempts to root out persisting evil ("revolutionary terror"), and thus prepare the ground for new forms of tyranny.

From this it is evident that revolution is a peculiar kind of ethical problem: it presents the Christian not with a contemplated action requiring justification but with religious conversion. To the extent that this conversion represents a move from political passivity to political activity, and a fighting against domination and injustice, the Christian will find much to support. To the extent that revolution is committed to the eradication of evil, Christian involvement in it must be deeply ambiguous and precarious, and this precariousness requires the whole art of Christian ethics. On the critical and hermeneutical side it requires the analysis of moral failure, injustice, and wrongdoing, particularly under the circumstances of modern social life, within the structure of the Christian narrative. Its positive normative task is to articulate institutions for "after the revolution," when evil persists in spite of genuine social transformations.

At the center of this problem is the relation of ethics to both evil and redemption, the way in which faithful Christian character, intention, and action are related to moral failure as well as to unintended social consequences. The moment one moves from this center through any sustained analysis, one encounters the deepest perplexities of modern consciousness, involving inquiries as diverse as philosophy, economics, social theory, linguistics, and science: the problem of rational agency and unintended social effect, of language and world, of continuity and discontinuity, of personal identity and political legitimacy, of reason and historical consciousness. If Christian ethics comes to understand social revolution, it may come also to a theological understanding and construal of these intellectual features of modernity. They are, after all, theological problems.

Classical texts: F. Fanon, *The Wretched of the Earth,* ET 1963; K. Marx, *Critique of Hegel's "Philosophy of Right"* (1843), ET 1970; "A Contribution to the Critique of Hegel's "Philosophy of Right": Introduction" (1843–44); and other writings; K. Marx and F. Engels, *The German Ideology* (1846), ET 1970; *The Communist Manifesto* (1848); A. de Tocqueville, *The Old Regime and the French Revolution* (1856), ET 1955.

Religion and revolution: N. Cohn, *The Pursuit of the Millennium,* rev. ed. 1970; C. Hill, *Puritanism and Revolution,* 1958; E. J. Hobsbawm, *Primitive Rebels,* 1959; M. Walzer, *The Revolution of the Saints,* 1969.

Revolution, modernity, and rationality: P. Berger, *The Sacred Canopy,* 1969; J. Habermas, *The Legitimation Crisis,* ET 1975; T. Kuhn, *The Structure of Scientific Revolutions,* ²1970; H. Marcuse, *Reason and Revolution,* 1960.

Revolution and theology: J. P. Gunnemann, *The Moral Meaning of Revolution,* 1979; G. Gutiérrez, *A Theology of Liberation,* ET 1972; P. Lehmann, *The Transfiguration of Politics,* 1975; J. Moltmann, *Theology of Hope,* ET 1967; R. Niebuhr, *Moral Man and Immoral Society,* 1932.

JON P. GUNNEMANN

Rewards and Punishments

The modern approach to the problem of rewards and punishments must be governed by an understanding of its roots in history. Rewards represent the workers' hire, the exchange received for goods, and the fair price paid in normal conditions. Honor, wealth, and a long life are a sign of divine favor. Punishments, however, belong to the abnormal sphere of offences. The Judeo-Christian tradition reflects the long process of taming the instinct of vengeance for wrongs suffered. The law decrees that justice be administered impartially and that punishments are inflicted on evildoers for the protection of the good life, that is, of life and property. The principle of the *lex talionis* is to restrict the destructive effect of penal consequences and to secure a measure of restitution proportionate to the victim's loss. Punishment is not meant to be reformatory and there is no system of imprisonment to deprive the offender of liberty. The purpose of retribution is to secure, as far as is possible, a state of normality by eliminating the consequence of the offense. The conditional laws of the Torah and of subsequent legislations, Jewish and Christian, determine in advance the steps to be taken to establish the equilibrium of society (*see* **Penology**).

Owing to the peculiar development of Jewish apocalyptic this legal tradition became enshrined in a far wider setting of distinctly otherworldly proportions, so that both rewards and punishments were seen to be appropriate to an eternal existence. The martyrs' struggle against fearful odds postulated a moral necessity that heroic endurance be rewarded with compensations which this life cannot afford. The apocalyptic writers developed a veritable dialectic of such compensa-

tions, making the poor rich, the weak victorious, etc. Above all, those who resist to the point of giving their own lives are rewarded with eternal life, while those who betray the fight are "rewarded" with everlasting shame. The Christian dialectic mirrors this conviction in the NT and early Christian writings, where Christian mortifications and sacrifices are not considered abnormal but the normal way of life. Thus the poor own the kingdom of heaven, the mourners are consoled, the meek inherit the earth; the martyrs for truth, mercy, and righteousness receive their stake back a hundredfold in the regeneration of the world. The eschatological future is thus called in as the turning point when at the point of judgment the "sheep and goats" receive their "due reward." No one is exempt from the eternal tribunal and there is no sentence except life or death. Moreover, the mythological setting of the Last Judgment surrounds heavenly rewards and punishments with a supernatural setting, in which good and evil angels minister to fulfill the will of God and in which Christ consummates his work as the Judge.

The power of the ecclesiastical institutions had the effect of imparting to the apocalyptic portrayal of rewards and punishments a forensic rigidity which extended not only to heroes and renegades but to all ordinary Christians and non-Christians. Assuming the existence of a Book of Life, as evidence produced in the divine court, the doctors of the church taught that salvation and condemnation were the alternate destinies awaiting humans. The unbaptized as well as the wicked could only qualify for the eternal torment, and the pessimism of the Dark Ages made it appear probable that even the just stood in need of mercy. The popular doctrine of rewards and punishments can best be appreciated by a study of the typical Judgment scene over medieval cathedral porches: the blessed mount to pleasures which are heightened by the spectacle of the miseries of the damned. This symmetrical representation knows of no qualifications, except that the doctrine of purgatory and good works (Masses, intercessions, alms) provided some mitigation of the severity of the system of retribution. Similarly the postulate of degrees of hell and heaven acknowledges a differentiation in the stages of individual destinies. But the essential and hard core of the retributive character of humanity's final state remained unaltered even when the political life of Europe required perhaps a less drastic eschatology and when the Reformation shifted the general interest away from a primary concern with death and the fate of the departed. Indeed, the doctrine of predestination only accentuated the moral problem, for how can a just and loving God predestine humans to any reward except a good one?

The tension inherent in the whole complex of retribution, which must be accentuated by the fears of the community, has never failed to evoke protests, most of which converge upon the teaching of Origen. This 3rd-century scholar and martyr propounded a doctrine of universal restoration in which even the hardest punishments were interpreted as remedial. Origen also held that "we punish ourselves" and that our conscience is our own executioner. In all similar schemes rewards and punishments are no more final than death itself. Or, if death be considered final, immortality itself is considered conditional and thus a loophole for liberal feeling remains open, inasmuch as immortality itself is the reward for a good life, and death the natural punishment of life abused.

Although the execration of Origen and his followers on the part of orthodox Christianity will find no approval among modern moralists and a liberal view of punishment is apt to prevail among most theologians—leaving the judgment to God—the fundamental thesis that the life on earth causes incontrovertible consequences after death is not so easily disposed of. Even if punishment be considered essentially immoral if it has an element of vindictiveness in it, and admitting that human beings cannot simply be divided into sheep and goats, the respect for human personality and the high regard for freedom and responsibility suggest that the future of human beings in eternity cannot be separated from belief and conduct on earth. A sentimental attitude can only lead to indifferentism, that is, a very low estimate of humanity and a type of disinterested religion which is incapable of making passionate and rational discriminations between good and evil. The sin of indifference, branded as infernal by Dante, is hardly a commendable prop for the doctrine of the love of God which underlies the postulates of future rewards.

The problem is indeed not as new as some moderns allege. Thomas Aquinas, for example, discusses at length the proposition whether the pangs of conscience cannot be equated with eternal punishment or whether evildoers may not escape the dire consequences of their misdeeds by death. It is difficult to see how his moral logic can be faulted when he points out that the identity of personality demands strict continuity of existence and that the very perversion of evil states the moral need for objective judgment. It is of the nature of demonic criminals that they deem themselves in the right and that they would change the whole moral structure of the universe in order to be found in the right. Moreover, for the wicked eternal life would mean on their own terms the free indulgence of immeasurable evil. Therefore, argues Aquinas, their privation of freedom is punishment, for they can no longer do as they would.

The correctness of this view needs to be qualified, however, with the tentative insight that all humans share the demonic nature. Hence a psychological light may be thrown upon the moral calculus of crime and punishment by our insisting upon the reality of self-exposure as a necessary and ultimately healing form of punishment. But this therapeutic estimate cannot operate beyond certain limits, for healing is not apposite in cases of resistance. The freedom of personality is such that it can decree its own dissolution into the nothing of a God-less existence.

Since God is the end of all life, and the source from which rewards and punishments flow, we must be prepared for an ineffable mystery which transcends all earthly conceptions of recompense. As in all Christian discourse, the earthly analogies prepare us for the "how much more" of the heavenly reality. A purely legal framework which results in convictions and acquittals can hardly do justice to the God-centered eschatology of Christian love. To the souls in God, rewards do not ultimately come by way of privilege and position—which they despised on earth—but by the mystical union with God in which love itself is the reward and seeks for none other. Similarly the final punishment of the devils is not to be found in fire and decomposition, valid though the pictures may be, but in the separation from God and eternal loss. If the latter, however, be deemed to be a mitigation of torment—"the wicked suffer *only* separation from God"—such a view, though perhaps satisfying to those who are sensible of the impossibility of eternal punishment, suffers from an inadequate conception of God.

A religious ethic, such as the Christian, is bound to decline in vigor as it forsakes its original mainspring. The Christian doctrine of judgment, involving the difficulties of rewards and punishments, is unthinkable without eternal incentives and warnings which provide the spur to Christian behavior. The dismissal of these final realities would undermine the Christian ethic for most ordinary people. At the same time it is equally intolerable for so transcendent a theme to be contained in the narrow confines of the weighing up of merits on the one hand, and sins on the other. The reality of God and the infinite complexity of the whole universe in all its vastness must never fail to impinge upon and interpret our belief in retribution.

See also **Blessedness; Discipline; Excommunication; Heaven; Hell; Sanctions.**

Thomas Aquinas, *Compendium Theologiae,* ET 1952, chs. 149–184, 241–245. J. A. Beet, *The Last Things,* 1897; T. D. Kendrick, *The Lisbon Earthquake,* 1956; H. Quistorp, *Calvin's Doctrine of the Last Things,* ET 1955; U. E. Simon, *The End Is Not Yet,* 1964.

ULRICH SIMON

Riches *see* **Covetousness; Mammon; Poverty; Property; Wealth**

Right and Wrong

It has been common in ethical writing to distinguish between moralities expressed in terms of the words "right" and "wrong" and those expressed in terms of "good" and "bad." Both sets of terms, however, share certain characteristics: they seem to have some sort of "action-guiding" or "prescriptive" function, and are applied to acts, etc., in virtue of something about the act in question which is the reason for applying the word (*see* **Ethics**).

The following differences between the "right" group of words and the "good" group are to be noted, among others. (1) "Good" has a comparative, "right" normally has not. (2) An act can be neither good nor bad; but it cannot be neither right (in the sense of "all right") nor wrong. (3) There is, however, another sense of "right," normally only in the phrase "the right . . . ," in which an act can be neither wrong nor yet "the right act" (in the circumstances). On the other hand, we cannot normally speak of "the good act"; we say, rather, "the best act." (4) It is sometimes said that an act is called right solely in virtue of its own qualities and the circumstances in which it is done, whereas an act is called good in virtue of being the sort of act that a good man would do in these circumstances— that is, "good" carries, and right does not, some allusion to the character of agents. (5) Except for the use mentioned in (3) above, the word "wrong" rather than "right" (to use the late J. L. Austin's expression) "wears the trousers." That is to say, we normally, in deciding whether an act is right, ask first whether there is anything to make it wrong, and if not call it right. This procedure will not work with "good" and "bad," for reasons connected with (2) above.

These logical features of the words account for the above-mentioned difference between the characters of moralities expressed in terms of them. A morality of right and wrong is likely to have a clear-cut character; there will be definite prohibitions against certain types of action, and actions not so prohibited will be all equally permitted. Such a morality can be very strict or very lax, depending on how many kinds of acts are prohibited. A morality of good and bad, on the other hand, will set out certain positive ideals which we are to try to realize; there will be infinite gradations between complete success and complete failure, both humanly impossible.

Christian morality has at various times and in various societies combined elements of both types—as must any satisfactory morality. There are, however, logical difficulties and dangers in seeking to combine them. An example of these is the problem of giving an adequate account of "works of supererogation."* Perhaps the simplest account of these is that they are acts which are good but whose omission would not be wrong; that is, they are approaches to the ideal set forth by one type of morality, but are not specifically required by the other.

This account of the matter, however, is ruled out if we take the command "Be ye therefore perfect" as implying that it is always wrong to fail to do what the best of men would do; this interpretation of the command implies that there are no works of supererogation but only a comprehensive series of duties, in which we all fail; that is, the "right-wrong" morality is screwed up to the limit, so as to enjoin the complete fulfillment of the ideals of the "good-bad" morality. This is done at the cost of making all men sinners, not to be saved except by redemption.

The latter view is no doubt more typical of Christians than the former. Nevertheless, the word "wrong" is not, like "sinful," tied specifically to religious moralities; and therefore Christians must expect to find atheists—and indeed their fellow Christians at times—using it in the former, less exacting way.

See also **Duty; Good Works; Goodness; Sin(s); Virtue.**

R. M. HARE

Righteousness

The most general meaning is uprightness, rectitude, or justice, and the word may be applied to God or to humans. In the OT God's righteousness (*sedeq/sedaqah*) is seen in his covenant* relations with his people; it involves both justice and compassion as expressed in God's concern for the weak and vulnerable (*see* **Old Testament Ethics**). In the NT God's righteousness (*dikaiosunē*) is directed toward human salvation, but theologians have long debated the relation between God's righteousness and justification (*dikaiōsis*). According to Lutheran theologians (*see* **Justification by Faith; Law and Gospel; Lutheran Ethics**) God's righteousness is not abstract justice but rather his grace* and forgiveness* by which he justifies sinful humans and accepts them as righteous. Hence human good works* are not efficacious, and humans must rely instead on God's righteousness, which is imputed to them. By contrast, Roman Catholics, joined by some Protestants, hold that sinners do become righteous to some extent, through God's grace as well as their own actions.

These theological disputes obviously shape whether and how divine righteousness functions as a norm for human conduct and how human righteousness is to be understood. Jesus pronounces blessed (*see* **Blessedness**) those who "hunger and thirst for righteousness" (Matt. 5:6), but Christian moral theologians and ethicists have debated the nature of human righteousness or uprightness: for example, whether it can be defined through the law* without becoming legalistic (*see* **Formalism; Legalism; Moralism**); whether it is best construed in terms of actions in accord with norms*, creative judgments in situations (*see* **Situation Ethics**), or traits of character* (*see* **Virtue**) and what

content it has in any of these; whether there are minimal and maximal standards of righteousness so that people may be righteous and act righteously without being good or perfect (*see* **Good Works; Goodness; Excellence; Holiness; Perfectionism; Supererogation**); and how moral categories of right and wrong* relate to religious categories (*see* **Morality and Religion, Relations of; Sin(s)**). For further discussion of the relation between divine justice and human justice, see **Justice.**

JAMES F. CHILDRESS

Rights

Rights can be characterized as powers or privileges to which an individual has a just claim such that he or she can demand that they not be infringed or suspended. Rights involve a mutual recognition on the part of each individual of the claims or rights of others; rights are thus correlative with duties. Rights have usually been divided into two classes, political rights and civil rights, although the two are likely to overlap in many cases. The former have to do with the voice the individual has in determining the form, operation, and powers of the government under which he or she lives, including the right to vote and to hold public office. Civil rights embrace a variety of freedoms and entitlements for individuals within the body politic such as equality before the law, religious freedom, the right to property, to work, to privacy, to education, to information, to counsel, and to be secure from arbitrary arrest.

Both forms of rights are rooted in some theory of the status of right as such; such a theory is at the foundation of political life in all its forms. Among the major theories of rights we may mention the theory of divine or natural right, according to which every individual is endowed by either God or nature with certain rights that should never be violated. Second, there are various forms of the contract theory (*see* **Social Contract**), according to which individuals join together in mutually limiting their freedom in return for the guarantee of a secure political order, each individual retaining such rights as could not conceivably be contracted away. Third, there are utilitarian theories according to which individual rights are made to depend on the general welfare. Fourth, there are the prima facie theories of rights. Finally, there are the totalitarian theories according to which the individual has no rights save those granted by the civil power which is the sole source of rights.

One of the most perplexing questions in the theory of rights concerns the extent to which it is possible to maintain absolutely universal rights for all individuals (see **Human Rights; Natural Rights**). The fact that every right for an individual must be correlative with a duty or obligation on the part of all the other individuals seems to make any guarantee of absolutely universal rights virtually impossible to maintain. Sometimes the problem has been approached by interpreting universal rights in a purely formal way, as when we say that every individual has an absolute right to equal treatment or consideration under all circumstances. Some philosophers and political theorists have held that the right to self-realization or to at least a minimum development of one's own capacities and potentialities is the one universal and absolute right, and indeed the liberal democracies of the West have made this right absolutely basic.

In the sphere of political rights the continuing debate is between forms of government based on "consent"* and operating through representative persons and offices, and states governed by an imposed dictatorial power where there is little or no machinery through which the individual can be represented or the governmental power criticized in the light of the diverse interests existing in the state.

Three major developments stemming from the intensified concern during the 1960s for the cause of securing civil rights* have had the effect of extending their scope to include rights for blacks and other minority groups, equal rights for women, for the handicapped and the elderly. The first is the heroic effort of Martin Luther King, Jr., in appealing to the gospel and the Christian conscience as the basis for the recognition and enforcement of civil and political rights for blacks and other victims of discrimination and violations of human dignity*. The second development is the movement for the liberation of women and for equal rights in social, economic, and religious relations; this movement has its religious counterpart in the aims of feminist theology—the attack on the retention of sexist language in religious doctrine and literature and the cause of securing equal rights for women in the churches (see **Feminist Ethics; Sex Discrimination; Women, Status of**). The third is the movement known as liberation theology*, dedicated to the defense of the rights of those facing poverty* and oppression* in the developing nations of the Third World, with the emphasis falling largely on nations in Africa and Latin America.

The extensive development of communication, transportation, and international trade in recent decades has served to bring the nations of the world into closer, more complex and competitive relations to each other than in the past; as a result, attention has been focused on the need for an acknowledged international law for determining the rights of sovereign nations vis à vis each other.

See **Human Dignity; Persons and Personality; Respect for Persons**.

R. M. Brown, *Theology in a New Key*, 1978; M. L. King, Jr., "Letter from Birmingham Jail," in *Why We Can't Wait*, 1964; and *The Trumpet of Conscience*, 1968, John Rawls, *A Theory of Justice*, 1971; G. H. Sabine, *A History of Political Theory in the West*, 1938.

JOHN E. SMITH

Rigorism *see* Casuistry; Tutiorism

Risk

The term "risk" may refer to the probability of loss, to the amount of that loss, or to both. According to Nicholas Rescher, risk is "the chancing of negativity—of some loss or harm." Risks can be analyzed according to the amount of potential loss or harm and the degree of probability of that outcome. The phrase "magnitude of risk" encompasses both the degree of probability and the severity of loss or harm. Losses or harms may be viewed as damages to interests, such as life, health, property, and reputation (see **Harm**).

Life is a risky business and cannot be made totally safe and free of risk. We take risks when we are aware of them and choose to accept them, but we are also at risk or run risks without being aware of them. It is important to distinguish taking risks for ourselves from imposing risks on others. A related distinction is between voluntary and involuntary risks, the former being assumed by the actor, the latter being imposed by others or created by a situation for which no one is responsible.

Taking or assuming risks presupposes an individual's voluntary choice in awareness of the probability and amount of potential harm. Risk-taking varies according to life plans with their dominant ends and goals. As Charles Fried notes, "a person's life plan establishes the magnitudes of risk which he will accept for his various ends at various times in his life." In effect, a person's life plan includes what Fried calls a "risk budget," which allots risks of death (and other harms and losses) in relation to ends and times in life as well as to the plan as a whole. A person's style of life is determined to a great extent by the risks he or she will accept for such ends as success, friendship, and salvation. Studies of the psychology of risk-taking show that people are more willing to take risks that are familiar, avoidable, voluntary, controllable, etc. It is also easy to discount remote or distant harms, such as lung cancer from cigarette smoking, however probable they may be. Even though a liberal society will tend not to override an individual's choices as long as others are not harmed, the Christian community has standards of risk-taking correlative to its conception of a good life that transcend mere prudence. Thus, it can make judgments about individual risk-taking (see **Paternalism**).

Imposing risks on others raises important moral questions from both religious and secular viewpoints. There is a generally recognized duty of nonmaleficence*—not to harm or injure others—and this duty encompasses the prima facie (but not absolute) requirement not to impose risks of harm on others, especially when they do not consent* to those risks. Moral negligence, parallel to legal negligence*, is a careless or deliberate violation of the standard of "due care" in action. The standard of due care is met when the goals the agent pursues are significant enough to justify the risks imposed on others. Grave risks require very important ends for their justification, and an emergency, such as a major fire, may justify risks, such as a rescue vehicle's breach of the speed limit, that ordinary ends would not.

The previous example suggests the use of risk-benefit analysis, however informal it may be. Risk-benefit analysis is a subset of cost-benefit* analysis, with risk being viewed as one kind of cost. It balances the probability and amount of potential harm against the probability and amount of potential benefit. The whole process of risk-benefit analysis, widely used in societal debates about safety standards for the workplace and technologies such as drugs and nuclear energy, includes identification and measurement of risks (the probability and amount of harm) and assessment of risks (determining their acceptability in relation to benefits), which may lead to risk management. Such analysis is not and cannot be value-free because values determine what will count as harms and benefits and how much various harms and benefits will count. Even though the determination of probability is more value-free and objective, how the society responds to that probability, and particularly to any uncertainties, will reflect its values. Douglas and Wildavsky have suggested a cultural theory of risk perception to account for the selection of some risks, rather than others, for attention at certain times. In particular, they are interested in why technological risks (e.g., dangers of environmental pollution) have been emphasized in recent years over other risks such as violence (war, terrorism, and crime) and economic failure. Their argument is that "the selection of dangers and the choice of social organization run hand in hand"; thus, risk-benefit analysis is always political. In determining whether some risks are acceptable, it is always necessary to ask, "Acceptable to whom?" as well as "For what ends?" The assessment of technologies through risk-benefit analysis can be morally acceptable only if there is public participation, including participation by all affected parties.

Since risk-benefit analysis is a subset of cost-benefit analysis, many of the objections to the latter also apply to the former, including the tendency to ignore soft variables in favor of hard variables that can be quantified. In particular, the utilitarian* (see **Utilitarianism**) perspective back of both modes of analysis sometimes considers only aggregate risks and benefits without attention to the justice* of their distribution, i.e., who will gain the benefits and who will bear the risks. Several patterns of distribution are possible: (1) the risks and benefits may fall on the same party (e.g., in most medical treatments); (2) one party may bear the risks, while another party gains the benefits (e.g., the current generation may gain the benefits of nuclear energy while imposing the major risks of nuclear waste on future generations); (3) both parties may bear the risks, while one party gains the benefits (e.g., a nuclear-powered artificial heart would benefit the user but would create risks for others as well as himself or herself); (4) one party may bear the risks, while both parties gain the benefits (e.g., persons in the vicinity of a nuclear power plant may bear significantly greater risks than other persons while all of them benefit from the plant). It is not sufficient from a moral standpoint merely to consider the sum of risks and benefits. Justice in distribution is always important, and it is particularly complicated when future generations are involved.

See also **Accidents; Energy; Environmental Ethics; Future Generations, Obligations to; Technology.**

J. F. Childress, "Risk," EB; and Priorities in Biomedical Ethics, 1981, ch. 5; M. Douglas and A. Wildavsky, Risk and Culture, 1982; G. R. Dunstan, "The Ethics of Risk," in Explorations in Ethics and International Relations, ed. N. A. Sims, 1981; B. Fischoff et al., Acceptable Risk, 1981; C. Fried, An Anatomy of Values, 1970; N. Rescher, Risk: A Philosophical Introduction to the Theory of Risk Evaluation and Management, 1983; R. Wilson and E. Crouch, Risk/Benefit Analysis, 1982.

JAMES F. CHILDRESS

Ritschlian Ethics

Albrecht Ritschl (1822–1889) was professor of theology successively at Bonn and Göttingen and ranks as one of the leading representatives of 19th-century German liberal Protestantism. He began his career under Hegelian influences but was affected by the reawakened interest in Kant in the middle of the century. This neo-Kantianism revived two emphases that had been prominent in Kant's own thinking—the distrust of metaphysics, carried almost to the length of positivism, and the recognition of the ultimacy of moral values, which then become the foundation for religion. Thus Ritschl was dissatisfied with the Christological dogma of Chalcedon, for such a dogma is an illicit mixture of faith and metaphysics. He believed that the historical Jesus, prior to all dogmatic speculation, has a compelling moral stature that demands from us the recognition of his

ultimacy. So when we ascribe divinity to Jesus, we are not making a metaphysical assertion. There may indeed be a mystery about Jesus, but Ritschl's positivist leanings made him leave mysteries alone. When we say Jesus is divine, we are making a value judgment, that is to say, we are assigning to Jesus an absolute moral worth so that we honor him as God. The moral figure of Jesus supplies for the Christian the meaning of the word "God." We should note, however, that Ritschl was opposed to any individualism* in religion. "Justification . . . is related in the first instance to the whole of the religious community founded by Christ, and to individuals only as they attach themselves to this community." Thus the kingdom of God*, understood in ethical terms, becomes a focal concept in his theology. "The Christian idea of the kingdom of God denotes the association of mankind—an association both extensively and intensively the most comprehensive possible—through the reciprocal moral action of its members." The state he understood as an institution ancillary to the kingdom of God.

This version of Christianity, built on history and ethics and free from dogma and metaphysics, made a strong appeal in the later 19th century and early 20th century. Among distinguished disciples of Ritschl were Wilhelm Herrmann (1846–1922); Theodor Haering (1848–1928), a pioneer in attempting the detailed application of Christian ethics to the society of his day; and Adolf Harnack (1851–1930), who carried the rationalist tendencies of Ritschlianism to their furthest point. The Ritschlian influence was felt also in the USA, where Ritschl's teaching was known and approved by such leaders of the social gospel* as Henry Churchill King (1858–1934) and Walter Rauschenbusch (1861–1918).

Ritschlianism declined very rapidly in the early part of the 20th century. Biblical studies called in question its picture of the historical Jesus, and Ritschl's own son-in-law, Johannes Weiss, struck at the NT roots of Ritschlianism by claiming that Jesus' understanding of the kingdom of God was an apocalyptic one, while Ritschl's own conception of the kingdom was merely a revised version of Kant. But the main cause for the decline was the discrediting of liberal 19th-century optimism* by such theologians as

Barth and Niebuhr (*see* **Modern Protestant Ethics**).

A. E. Garvie, *The Ritschlian Theology*, 1899; T. Haering, *Ethics of the Christian Life*, ET 1909; W. Herrmann, *Communion with God*, ET 1909; J. K. Mozley, *Ritschlianism*, 1909; J. Richmond, *Ritschl: A Reappraisal*, 1978; A. Ritschl, *The Christian Doctrine of Justification and Reconciliation* (1874), ET 1900.

JOHN MACQUARRIE

Robbery *see* **Property; Theft**

Robots

Robots, mechanical devices that carry out a predetermined sequence of actions, have been in use in manufacturing industry for over a decade.

Basic robots are relatively simple machines that repeat a series of movements taught them by expert human operators. They can perform routine, repetitive jobs such as spot welding and paint-spraying. More advanced robots contain rudimentary senses of sight and touch and are programmed to alter their actions according to changed circumstances. The next step in their development is the creation of "artificial intelligence." For example, a robotic welding system with adaptive control would make possible a constant alteration of the production process. Robots offer a number of advantages to employers. They do not arrive at work late, go off sick, go on strike, take holidays, or in other ways disturb the regular production process. They offer more accurate and more predictable results. On the other hand, employees can benefit too. Robots can relieve them of much work that is monotonous, repetitive, unpleasant and unsafe.

Although the development and installation of robots may be expensive, they offer increased efficiency and savings in costs to manufacturing industry and hence contribute to economic growth and the more effective meeting of human need.

See also **Automation; Computers; Technology; Unemployment.**

R. U. Ayres and S. M. Miller, *Robotics: Applications and Social Implications*, 1982.

PAUL BRETT

Roman Catholic Moral Theology

see **Counter-Reformation Moral Theol-** ogy; **Modern Roman Catholic Moral Theology; Moral Theology; Thomistic Ethics**

Romanticism

This is a term used so vaguely that its usefulness has been much questioned. In its original use it was a name for a mood and movement excitedly and powerfully operative around 1800, which may be characterized generally as an assertion of high sentiment and intuition against cool and standardized rules in all the main spheres of culture, and a reaching out toward the Infinite: for example, in poetry, a rebellion against the constrictions of perfect form, and a claim that aesthetic sensibility can give insight into moral and religious truth, to which intellect should not claim a monopoly; in theology, a return to the immediacies of religious experience, to which abstract constructions should be evidently related; in philosophy, a revolt led by Fichte, Schelling, and Hegel against the old tight logic of a persisting scholasticism, against the empiricism, commonsense reasonableness, and utilitarian temper of the Enlightenment (*see* **Enlightenment**), and against Kant's agnosticism. In ethics, Schiller's ideal of the "lovely soul" was an aesthetic protest against Kant's moral rigorism of the "good will" (from which Fichte did not break loose). A demand arose for an ideal that would engage a person's entire nature: so, for example, Hegel, but more attractively in Schleiermacher, in the special form that the possibilities of the spiritual factor in the universe are so vast and many-sided that they can be realized and brought together only through the use by each of us of our individual gifts. The Romantic movement was not predominantly individualistic: it was standing for a social solidarity that cannot be contrived by rationalist planners but has to grow through community of interest and spiritual affinity in an expanding tradition. One expression of this respect for tradition was a love of things medieval, another a gathering up for the first time of Germanic and Indian lore and an admiring use of them in literature and philosophy. European culture was at last breaking its local bounds.

J. J. McGann, *The Romantic Ideology: A Critical Investigation*, 1983; H. Peyre, *What Is Romanticism?* ET 1977; S. Prickett, *Romanticism and Religion*, 1976; J. R. Talmon, *Romanticism and Revolt*, 1979; C. Thacker,

The Wildness Pleases: The Origins of Romanticism, 1983.

T. E. JESSOP

Rules *see* Anglican Moral Theology; Casuistry; Christian Ethics; Love; Modern Protestant Ethics; Modern Roman Catholic Moral Theology; Moral Theology; Natural Law; Norms; Situation Ethics

Sabbatarianism

The term properly refers to the understanding of the Christian Lord's Day as a Sabbath, applying to it the Fourth Commandment. In particular it refers to the attempt to impose this understanding on the community as a whole through legislation.
See Sunday Observance.

JAMES A. WHYTE

Sacrifice *see* Love

Sacrilege

An extreme lack of reverence manifested in deliberate violation of religious places, persons, or objects. Local sacrilege includes desecration of churches and cemeteries. Personal sacrilege refers to sinful actions performed against, or sometimes by, ecclesiastical or religious persons as such. "Real" (Latin *res*) sacrilege involves deliberate irreverence toward sacramental rites or the Bible and profanation or theft of sacred vessels, statues, etc.
See Reverence.

J. MAHONEY

Saintliness

To say that saintliness is the quality saints have is somewhat like saying that humanity is the quality human beings have. The saints are, according to biblical usage, the holy people of God. One would expect their diversity to be as great as the good diversity of people. Yet, just as we tend to pick out certain characteristics and call these "humane," so we tend to pick out other characteristics and call these "saintly." Because "saint" came to mean, not any member, nor even any faithful member, of God's people, but a hero or heroine of the faith, it has been the heroic virtues that have been singled out as notably saintly; and in practice the virtues of asceticism and austerity.

So it is even said anxiously of some beloved person whom we deeply believe has been acceptable to God, "Of course, he was no saint," lest anyone should imagine a narrow personality. Christians must reckon with this usage, not imagine mere counteraffirmation will end it. They may concentrate on praising certain characteristics agreed to be both "saintly" and attractive: serenity, patience, loyalty, integrity, wisdom. Yet these excellencies are still preconceived and in a way selective. Saintliness looks like a character someone is either born with, or not, rather than everyone's goal. It might be better to define saintliness as "fitness for heaven": not a particular set of qualities but the maturity of a whole personality, nature perfected by grace. Then, for instance, the witty as well as the patient, the eager as well as the calm, can aspire to fulfillment.
See Sanctification; Holiness; Perfectionism.

W. Beach and H. R. Niebuhr (eds.), *Christian Ethics: Sources of the Living Tradition,* 1955, e.g., ch. 5; K. E. Kirk, *The Vision of God,* 1931; J. Macquarrie, *Paths in Spirituality,* 1972, p. 5; J. Urmson, "Saints and Heroes," in *Essays in Moral Philosophy,* ed. A. Melden, 1958.

HELEN OPPENHEIMER

Salaries *see* Wages and Salaries; *see also* Just Price and Just Wage

Sanctification

The idea of sanctification is rooted in the idea of setting someone or something apart for ritual purposes. In the NT the Greek *hagiazō* is used for "sanctify," "consecrate," and "make sacred," from the heights of John 17 to the technicality of Matt. 23:17, 19. In Christian history the ethical sense of the word, having to do with the attaining of moral perfection, has been both dominant and controversial. The great question has been, In what sense is *holiness**, given or earned, within the reach of God's people in this life? Is "You shall be perfect" command, promise, or hyperbole?

Sanctification cannot be considered optional; but to treat it as compulsory can be just as misleading. There are plenty of available heresies, Catholic or Protestant, mostly brandishing proof-texts. Compulsory sanctification develops the rigorism that requires Christians to be sinless on pain of rejection, or the superstition that supposes that grace works like magic. Optional sanctification allows the antinomianism* that justifies sinners and stops there (as in the famous satire of James Hogg), or the worldliness that asks only for decent behavior and hardly cares for holiness.

Perfectionism* is easily attacked as arrogant, its denial as defeatist. There is always the safety net, or snare, of a doctrine of two standards, a minimum for all and a better way for some: an understandable expedient to avoid legalistic rigorism*, but desperately unsatisfactory as a self-sufficient theory, as K. E. Kirk pointed out (*The Vision of God,* 1931, ch. 4). It is essential to hold on to the understanding that sanctity is for everyone (cf. A. M. Allchin in *Man's Concern with Holiness,* ed. M. Chavchavadze, 1972, p. 38), and that somehow, explain it as we may, "morals constitute a preamble to beatitude" (Tranøy on Aquinas in *A Critical History of Western Philosophy,* ed. D. J. O'Connor, 1964, p. 116). What matters is to set no limits upon the ultimate capacity of God's creatures to glorify God: to take seriously the idea that "You are holy, for I am holy" is meant to be fulfilled (Lev. 11:44; 1 Peter 1: 16). To stop short with justified sinners is no more adequate than to celebrate an aristocracy of blessed ones.

Are we driven by a process of elimination to a Wesleyan doctrine of perfection? One need not call such a view proud or priggish; but its precise application is not easy to determine; and it has a tendency to lose itself in a dispute about words. Without denying anyone's assurance, one may sit loose to such a decided formulation (*see* **Wesleyan Ethics**).

Three things need to be said about sanctification.

1. Whatever it is, sanctification is a *harvest,* the fruit of the spirit (Gal. 5:22–23). Our hope of becoming our true selves does not lie in making an effort but in *response,* in being taken out of ourselves. "The Gospel preceded the demand" (J. Jeremias, *The Sermon on the Mount,* ET 1961, p. 29, and see pp. 32–33). "To follow Christ is not to go in pursuit of an ideal but to share in the results of an achievement" (T. W. Manson, *Ethics and the Gospel,* 1960, p. 59). Augustine loved to quote, "What have you that you did not receive?" (1 Cor. 4:7), and summed the matter up: "When God crowns our merits, he crowns nothing but his own gifts" (*Epistle* 194.19; see J. Burnaby, *Amor Dei,* 1938, ch. 8). In this context,

even the Eastern Orthodox emphasis on *deification,* so alarming to Western propriety, is safe and salutory. People made in the image of God* are to shine with reflected but real light.

2. The holiness to which we are to aspire is not a static concept. "The perfection of human nature," suggested Gregory of Nyssa, "consists perhaps in its very growth in goodness" (*Life of Moses* 10). "The continual development of life to what is better is the soul's way to perfection" (ibid., 306). The idea of maturity, and a developing maturity at that, is more promising than an emphasis upon attained sinlessness, for this world or the next.

3. It could be the case that the most profound understanding of sanctification is after all the nearest to its primitive roots. "Holy in the Bible does not mean devout or virtuous but separated by God" (K. Barth, *Ethics,* ET 1981, p. 112). Such an idea could be crudely superstitious, with fear uppermost and ethics lost. But the consecration of a sacrificial offering can mean more than the propitiation of incomprehensible powers. When the human impulse to consecrate a sacrifice is allowed to develop in the context of *sacrament* and indeed of *eucharist,* the ethical meaning of "sanctification" can be removed from the optional/compulsory trap and associated with grace, gift, and thanksgiving (cf. E. McDonagh, *Invitation and Response,* 1972, p. 25). To be sanctified is to be offered like the elements of a sacrament, to be blessed and given back to nourish other people.

R. N. Flew, *The Idea of Perfection in Christian Theology,* 1934; B. Häring, *Christian Maturity,* ET 1967, pt. 3; W. Law, *A Serious Call to a Devout and Holy Life,* 1728, chs. 2–3; V. Taylor, *Forgiveness and Reconciliation,* 1952, ch. 5; J. Wesley, *A Plain Account of Christian Perfection,* ²1766.

HELEN OPPENHEIMER

Sanction

Although the term "sanction" sometimes denotes the authority* for an action, it most often denotes the penalties that ensure compliance with formal or informal rules in morality, law, religion, etc. For example, in religion, whatever the authority for some modes of conduct, such as God's will, some sanctions may make compliance more likely (*see* **Rewards and Punishments; Heaven; Hell**).

Even conscience* itself is sometimes viewed more as a sanction than an authority when its threat of disunity and disharmony motivates the agent to perform actions that he or she otherwise would have had difficulty undertaking (*see also* **Mixed Motives**). Some philosophers distinguish morality and law* in part according to the nature of their sanctions: Morality often involves sanctions of praise and blame, while law often involves sanctions of force. The term "sanction" frequently refers to coercive measures such as criminal punishment or embargoes. Hence the major ethical questions focus on when it is justifiable to use coercion* and what sort of coercion is justifiable. Views about the necessity and importance of sanctions as motivating reasons for actions often depend on doctrines of human nature, particularly its disposition to sin* (*see* **Original Sin; Realism**).

See also **Behavior Control; Coercion; International Order; Law; Morality, Legal Enforcement of; Penology; Power; Resistance; State.**

JAMES F. CHILDRESS

Sanctity of Life *see* **Life, Prolongation of; Life, Sacredness of**

Sanctuary *see* **Refugees**

Satyagraha

Gandhi's designation for his movement of nonviolent resistance against the British in India. It means firm and steadfast adherence to the truth. *See* **Civil Disobedience; Resistance.**

Scandal

Scandal arises when a member of the Christian community, by action or opinions, goes against the commonly accepted standards of the community and causes distress to the other members, perhaps even bringing the whole community into disrepute. From the earliest times, the church has had to exercise discipline* in order to deal with erring members and to maintain its standards. The really difficult case, however, is the one in which the person who gives rise to the scandal is acting not from carelessness or rebellion against the church, but from conscience*, sincerely believing that he or she has a right or a duty to declare the opinion or perform the actions that are scandalizing the others. In such cases

we should remember the advice given by Paul in 1 Cor. 10. Things that are lawful may not be expedient, and even where individuals are passionately convinced of the rightness of their acts or opinions, they ought to act with charity* toward their brethren. It may become a very difficult matter to decide between the prompting of the individual conscience and the distress caused to the community. Conscience cannot be coerced, but before causing scandal by some unilateral act, a member of the community should consider very carefully whether he or she is acting with charity to the others, and whether really impelled by conscience or by less worthy motives, such as pride and the desire for notoriety.

JOHN MACQUARRIE

Science and Ethics

The word "science" covers a wide range of meanings: (1) a system of knowledge, split up into a number of distinct "sciences," which together constitute a more or less coherent scientific world view; (2) a method of investigation characterized by a rational empirical, objective, and critical approach to natural phenomena; (3) applied science (technology*)—the ability to manipulate the natural world predictably. "Science" in all these senses is of concern to ethics, though in different ways that need to be carefully distinguished.

1. Science as a source of factual information. Moral judgments are not made *in vacuo*, but require a knowledge of facts and an ability to predict the probable consequences of actions. Scientists are concerned with both. The general scientific understanding of the world is therefore an important part of the background of moral choice, and many traditional moral issues have been seen in a different light as scientific knowledge has increased. Sexual morality, for example, has been affected by advances in physiology and psychology, even among those who would claim that there has been no change in the fundamental principles that should govern sexual behavior. Homosexuality remains for many an area of moral uncertainty, partly for the reason that there is not as yet any scientific agreement about its causes. A soundly based concern about the moral dimensions of animal welfare needs to pay proper attention to biology. Sociologists offer interpretations of human behavior that, by revealing the character and extent of social constraints, can enlarge the area of choice. To know that one is conforming to type is to be given the freedom not to do so. Psychology can create similar areas of freedom, as well as enlarge perceptions of the consequences of behavior on other people.

In addition to these countless general ways in which scientific knowledge has ethical implications, there are also examples of particular discoveries that relate to particular moral choices. The link between cigarette smoking and lung cancer has created new moral problems for smokers and tobacco manufacturers. Work on the deleterious effects of bottle-feeding infants in Third World countries has opened up a new moral dimension in the promotion and export of dried milk. Once again, the list is endless (see **Risk**).

There are also less direct ways in which scientific information has influenced ethical thinking. Anthropology* has weakened the appeal of authoritarian ethical systems by its disclosure of the enormous variety of social patterns and of the extent to which morality is socially conditioned. The moral sense itself has become an object of scientific study. Research on the social behavior of animals, developmental psychology, and the evolutionary origins of altruism have led some scientists to conclude that there are certain moral norms or tendencies, discoverable by science, built into human nature. The new, and controversial, science of sociobiology attempts to explore this field from an evolutionary perspective.

2. Science as a source of values. Since G. E. Moore's description of the naturalistic fallacy (see **Naturalistic Ethics**), it has been customary to hold that statements of value cannot be derived exclusively from statements of fact; in other words, science by itself cannot prescribe what is right or wrong. In most practical contexts this is obviously true. Sound factual information is a necessary but not a sufficient basis for moral choice. Judgment about the facts goes beyond the facts themselves.

This neat distinction, however, ignores the extent to which facts and values are interrelated. It can be questioned whether any facts are totally value-free. Thus it is possible for moral judgments to appear to be made on strictly factual grounds by overlooking the element of evaluation already built into them.

The various systems of evolutionary ethics*, of which T. H. Huxley, Julian Huxley, and, from a Christian perspective, Walter Rauschenbusch were notable exponents, made use of the idea of evolutionary "progress"* as a moral guide, as if it could somehow be read directly from the biological facts themselves. Sociobiology provides the most modern attempt to perform the same operation, but has difficulty in producing convincing evidence of evolutionary traits in human nature strong enough to be treated as ethically normative. Psychology has been a fruitful source of hidden norms, as expressed in such concepts as abnormality or maturity, both of which are extremely hard to detach from their cultural contexts.

The most powerful claim that science provides a source of values is made, not on the basis of any particular discoveries or theories, but by extrapolation from the scientific method itself. Science "works," runs this claim, and intrinsic to it are certain values and attitudes that are validated by this success. Jacques Monod (*Chance and Necessity,* ET 1972) proposed what he called "an ethic of knowledge" in which the main value is objective knowledge itself.

Monod's proposal was criticized for its arbitrariness and restrictiveness. There is, however, a more general and acceptable sense in which the values inherent in scientific activity spill over into ordinary life. Scientists form a community with its own professional code concerned with such matters as honesty in reporting facts, the publication of unfavorable as well as favorable evidence, the acknowledgment of sources and the safeguarding of original discoveries, and cooperation with colleagues irrespective of nationality. In addition the successful scientist depends on personal moral qualities such as open-mindedness, a readiness to accept criticism, patience, persistence, love of the truth for its own sake, even an element of passion. Some have described science as an adventure of faith. Scientific progress would not be possible unless by and large scientists could trust one another, and this is why in professional terms the penalties for fraud are high.

In its beginnings modern science depended on the moral and philosophical assumptions of Christian Europe. Nowadays, in the light of its practical achievements, the values that sustain it have come to be regarded by many as self-authenticating. Science is its own justification, and what makes for good science must itself be good. Misplaced trust is eventually exposed, and the overwhelming weight of scientific opinion acts to reinforce the values of the scientific community. In this very general sense, therefore, it can be argued that science operates as a moral force. Critics of this argument point out that in practice the main characteristic of science is power rather than disinterested knowledge. And scientific power can suffer the same corruptions as any other kind of power.

3. Science as a source of new ethical problems. Applied science has given humanity increasing power to control and adapt its environment, and to manipulate some of the most fundamental characteristics of human life and society. New powers always create ethical problems of peculiar difficulty, since there are no precedents to act as guides. Nevertheless certain general principles seem to apply. Broadly speaking, answers to questions about the use of new powers reflect differing views about the place of human beings in nature. At one extreme are those who stress the "givenness" of the natural world and the dangers of upsetting the existing order of things (*see* **Natural Law**). At the other extreme are those who doubt whether "givenness" means much in an evolving universe, and who see every new advance as increasing the range of human choice, and hence the possibilities of human freedom and personal fulfillment. Both extremes are found among Christians, some emphasizing human creatureliness and others human creativeness. The weight of Christian opinion, however, has generally been on the side of conservatism*, and there is a long history of opposition to new techniques, not least in medicine (*see* **Bioethics**).

Technical power tends to be morally ambiguous. The new freedoms it brings often have hidden costs. The automobile is a classic example of a technological advance that has enormously increased the range of human experience, but has also created new forms of enslavement as well as huge environmental damage. Nuclear energy contains both a promise and a threat. New understandings of human psychology open the way to new forms of human manipulation. Perhaps the biggest source of moral ambiguity today is the extent to which almost any discovery can be made to serve military purposes (*see also* **Energy; Environmental Ethics; Nuclear Warfare**).

Advances in the biological sciences closely affecting human life itself already pose some intractable problems that are likely to become even more difficult as research continues. The ethics of research on human embryos, for example, must depend in part on the length of time for which it is possible to keep an isolated embryo alive; and all the evidence suggests that this is likely to increase. The possibilities of genetic manipulation pose in an especially acute form questions about the extent to which the "givenness" of human nature should be regarded as inviolable. Even such a relatively simple operation as choosing the sex of one's children has deep personal and social implications (*see also* **Experimentation with Human Subjects; Genetics; Reproductive Technologies**).

The abuse of psychiatry for penal purposes in the USSR is a particularly striking example of the way therapeutic insights can be used to serve evil ends. Fears that some genetic studies might act as a basis for racial discrimination have led to acrimonious controversy both in Britain and in the USA. And at the more trivial end of the scale, there are those who regard public opinion polls, a very modest instance of scientific data collection, as a threat to electoral integrity.

"Big science," of a size that has to be funded directly by government or some major industry, presents special problems of control and assessment, not least when most of the available expertise is engaged in, and therefore has a vested interest in, the particular project in question. The preliminary work on atomic energy suffered this kind of isolation, with the result that its moral and political implications came to the surface too late to influence the course of research.

It is an open question whether some research may or may not be inherently immoral. Clearly there are, or ought to be, moral limits to the methods used in research, especially insofar as these apply to human beings or animals*. But are there some things that it is better not to know? Most scientists would deny this, even though Pandora's box once opened proves impossible to close.

R. Attfield, *The Ethics of Environmental Concern,* 1983; J. Habgood, *A Working Faith,* 1980; J. Mahoney, *Bioethics and Belief,* 1984; J. R. Ravetz, *Scientific Knowledge and Its Social Problems,* 1971; R. Trigg, *The*

Shaping of Man, 1982; World Council of Churches, *Faith and Science in an Unjust World,* 1979.

JOHN HABGOOD

Scrupulosity

A term used in Catholic moral theology to denote the overuse of the confessional for the confession* of trivial and diminutive sins. Though absolution* is eagerly sought, it is never fully satisfying to scrupulous persons in this sense of "overscrupulous," who fear they may have forgotten something, and who will soon return to confess many of the same offenses.

From the standpoint of psychology, scrupulosity is closely related to an obsessive-compulsive neurotic pattern of behavior. Persons afflicted with this disorder are obsessed with certain ideas which they can only put out of their minds by repeating certain actions, such as a hand-washing compulsion, which is associated with the need to assuage guilt feelings. In such cases the thing for which guilt is consciously felt (dirty hands) is a disguised representation of unconscious guilt too painful to bear in conscious awareness. This is the reason that the confessions of scrupulous persons deal with such trivial matters. The trivia cloak unconscious guilt feelings which usually relate to childhood experiences with parents and the fantasies about these, such as the wish to kill the father, though they often have associations with adult life as well.

Though Protestants who do not have formal confession do not use the term, the phenomenon is present in overzealous church workers who seemingly cannot find enough to do in the church, and also frequently seek the pastor out to pour out their troubles and get advice, which is seldom taken. In such cases psychiatric help may be indicated, though such help may be unwanted, since the symptoms are partly intended to keep such persons unaware of their disturbing unconscious guilt feelings as well as providing a degree of release from them.

See also **Guilt; Defense Mechanisms.**

JAMES N. LAPSLEY

Secrecy

Secrecy may be defined as "intentional concealment" (Bok). There are several conceptual and moral questions about its links to autonomy*, privacy*, and confidentiality*, as well as to deception and truthfulness*. The question of the ethical justification of intentional concealment, or intentional nondisclosure of information, is not reducible to the ethics of lying, even though they may overlap where there are affirmative duties to disclose information. As Bok notes, secrets do not stand in need of justification in the same way as lies, because secrets are morally neutral rather than prima facie wrong. And secrets are frequently legally protected, e.g., in confidential relations between physicians and patients and between priests and penitents (*see* **Codes of Ethics; Confidentiality; Professional Ethics**). However, in several areas of life, such as government, business (e.g., trade secrets), and science, there is significant debate about which secrets, if any, are justified, particularly in view of the interests of others in the concealed information. In a democracy*, the public is presumed to have a right to relevant information, but secrets are often alleged to be justified, at least temporarily, by political or military necessity* in foreign policy and military actions. Such secrets are sometimes disclosed to the public through whistle-blowing*. In the USA the Freedom of Information Act (1966, strengthened in 1974) granted citizens broader access to government information, within certain limits, including national security and crime prevention.

<hr style="width:30%;margin:0">

S. Bok, *Secrets: On the Ethics of Concealment and Revelation,* 1983; I. Galnoor (ed.), *Government Secrecy in Democracies,* 1977; K. G. Robertson, *Public Secrets: A Study of the Development of Government Secrecy,* 1982; R. B. Stevenson, Jr., *Corporations and Information—Secrecy, Access, and Disclosure,* 1980.

JAMES F. CHILDRESS

Sect

In theology and much ordinary usage, "sect" refers to a body of believers who follow a particular practice, doctrine, or leader distinct from that of the majority or "orthodox" norm, but within the same religion. Until recently, established churches in Europe referred to all nonestablished churches as sects and lumped "free churches," cults, and denominations in this category.

A sect may be schismatic, heterodox, or

heretical. That is, it may break communion with the representatives of orthodoxy, remain in fellowship but insist on unusual beliefs, or be judged to present such a dangerous perspective on faith and morals that it must be condemned and excluded. Adherents of a sect, of course, often claim that it is the majority that has fallen away from orthodoxy or has failed to recognize new truth.

Since the work of Ernst Troeltsch and Max Weber in the early part of this century, however, the term has taken on a meaning in ethics that is less doctrinally oriented. In religious social ethics a sect is understood to be a particular type of religious organization which, by combining and applying in a distinctive way theological doctrines that in themselves may be quite orthodox, forms small, intimate, exclusive, voluntary societies based on explicit faith; resistance to compromise with "the world"; participatory, protodemocratic, or populist leadership; and a normative metaphysical-moral vision, demanding rigorous ethical standards. This is understood to be in contrast to a church-type religious organization, which is large and based on implicit faith, adjustment to the world, a hierarchical priesthood, and modulation of ethical rigor. The sect attempts to embody "pure" ideals in a new society of believers. This attempt can be either withdrawing, i.e., by disengagement from the world (in monastic or communal enclaves), or aggressive, i.e., by energetic action to transform the world by universal proselytism, or by political and military action to enforce perfectionist standards. Sects can, in these terms, be centers of prophetic change or reactionary resistance to change. (Elaborate typologies of sects have been developed by sociologists of religion, such as Bryan Wilson.)

This idea of sect has been taken over from Christian history and applied to other religions (e.g., Druze Islam, Hare Krishna Hinduism, or Jōdo Buddhism). The idea is also now commonly used in reference to schools of philosophical, scientific, or social thought as well as to various branches of "unorthodox" secular political organization —as in forms of pacifism or socialism— where radical ethical commitments become organized in intentional alternative or change-oriented groups.

See **Church; Cults; Ecclesiology and Ethics; Institution/Institutionalization.**

MAX L. STACKHOUSE

Secularism

The shift in the meaning of secularism is one of the most significant developments in modern religious thought. Traditionally the word "secular" has been the antonym of "religious." It has been taken to mean a way of life pursued without reference to religious realities. Where the functions of religious institutions are taken over by the state, secularization* is said to have occurred, as in programs of education and social amelioration. Understandings of life without reference to the idea of God and his alleged intervention in the process of the world are called secular views.

The inception of secularism in Western culture is usually dated at the Renaissance and ascribed to the afflatus of human pride*. Human beings at that epoch put themselves at the center of reality and arrogated to themselves authority over life and responsibility for it. Christendom since the Renaissance has been hard pressed to justify its theocentric universe and its traditional conceptions of a God who is all-powerful, a human creature who is abased and weakened by finitude and sin, and a system of things which is contingent upon the sustaining power of God as expressed in miraculous interventions in history and nature.

Friedrich Schleiermacher was the first theologian to attempt to express the Christian faith in terms of the new understandings of the modern world which the Renaissance* introduced. Protestant theology following the First World War made Schleiermacher its primary target. The situation after the Second World War is quite different, even though the experiential grounds for the despair of humanity over its secular adequacy have seemed even more obvious than after the First World War. Now it is being seen that secularism, far from being the enemy of the church, as theology in the medieval and orthodox Protestant orientation has tended to hold, is the product of the Christian faith. The Protestant Reformation is held to be the only major attempt since the apostolic age to reintroduce the meaning of the Christian movement as the secularizing of the world.

In modern Christianity two theologians,

mainly, have contended for this view. Dietrich Bonhoeffer, in fragmentary suggestions through his prison correspondence prior to his death, conceded that modern man had "come of age." That is to say, human beings are capable of handling their affairs without invoking a god. That is secularism. Bonhoeffer was probably unique in the conclusions he drew for this description of modern life, a description already patent in the Renaissance period. His conclusion for Christianity was that the church ought not force these modern, mature humans to become weak in the world in order to convert them to faith. It might rather call them to discipleship at the point of their strength. For Bonhoeffer this was no simple compromise* with modern humanity. It was the nub of the Christian revelation. The meaning of the faith is that God has allowed himself to be edged out of the world onto the cross. Because of the cross, therefore, humans can know that the world is now left to them as their responsibility.

Friedrich Gogarten gave this theme its most systematic and comprehensive treatment. The major text for Gogarten's explication is Gal. 4:1–7. The significance of Jesus of Nazareth is that in him God has called the world to obedience. The call to obedience is given in the context of God's gift of the world to human beings as their responsibility. In Jesus of Nazareth humankind is delivered from the time of its childhood and slavery where the world had become the vehicle by which humanity was required to justify its life before God. In the cross, it is God who justifies human beings. They no longer need to justify themselves. That means that the world no longer needs to be exploited for religious purposes. To say it positively, that means God has given humanity the world as its responsibility, as a father gives his heritage to his son.

Nietzsche and Kierkegaard had both addressed themselves to the situation of secularism in the modern world. Both saw that secularism was a Christian outcome. Kierkegaard regarded the outcome as bad, and believed it was his responsibility to reintroduce a purer Christianity into the secularized Christendom. Nietzsche regarded it as good, but doubted that Christianity was an adequate basis for supporting the secularism it had inaugurated. Gogarten, on the other hand, believes Christianity is indispensable to

the conservation of secularism. His reasoning is as follows: God has turned the world over to humans as that for which they are responsible. If they do not continually receive the world from God as the one *to* whom they are responsible, they may make the world itself their new object of responsibility—as Judaism and Hellenism did before the time of Jesus, worshiping the creature rather than the creator and thus converting law and wisdom into demonic powers which thereby lost their status as instruments of responsibility. If humans become responsible *to* the world, they will lose their capacity to be responsible *for* it. In the Christian proclamation through which humanity learns to receive the world from God, responsibility *to* God is kept alive, and with it, responsibility *for* the world, which is the condition we know in the modern world as secularism.

See **Responsibility; Secularization; Stewardship; Technology; Worldliness.**

D. Bonhoeffer, *Letters and Papers from Prison,* ET 3rd ed., rev. and enl., 1971; F. Gogarten, *The Reality of Faith,* ET 1959; *Despair and Hope for Our Time* (²1958), ET 1970.

CARL MICHALSON

Secularization

Derived from the Latin word *saeculum* (world), the term "secularization" was first used to refer to the transfer of property from the church to the civil princes by the Treaty of Westphalia (1648). It now denotes the process by which religion loses some or all of its authority, power, and dominance. The contemporary debate about secularization involves conceptual, empirical, explanatory, and normative questions: What does "secularization" mean, has it been occurring, how can it be explained, and how should it be evaluated?

Adapting a framework developed by Larry Shiner, we can distinguish several conceptions of secularization: (1) Decline of religion. This decline might be considered from an objective standpoint (such as institutions, membership, or participation in worship and activities) or from a subjective standpoint (religious consciousness). From each standpoint there is debate about the norm by which decline is measured. It is not always clear what is central to and what is peripheral to religion in general or to particular religious traditions, and the line between the religious and the secular is controversial. Although there are shifts from time to time, some religions still flourish in the modern age; indeed, the recent revival of evangelical and fundamentalist traditions surprised many analysts (*see* **Evangelical Ethics; Fundamentalist Ethics**). (2) Disengagement or differentiation of institutions, practices, and activities from religion. Such a process has occurred in the West and in much of the world; for example, the welfare state* now performs several functions formerly performed by the churches, such as education and many social services (*see* **Social Service of the Church**). It can be argued that societies advance morally when they move from charity* to justice* in meeting human needs. However, there is debate about whether secularization in this sense tends to drive religion out of the public sphere, resulting in the "privatization" of religion. (3) Transposition of norms from religion to the world. Despite or even through the process of differentiation some religious norms may have been institutionalized in social practices (*see* **Institution/Institutionalization**). Thus, Talcott Parsons has argued that society has been Christianized in some respects—e.g., through the institutionalization of the norm of equality*. (4) Desacralization of the world—approaching the world through rational explanation and manipulation rather than through awe and a sense of mystery. According to Max Weber, rationalization* involves disenchantment (*Entzauberung*) of the world. But even though instrumental rationality dominates much of society, including science* and technology*, it does not necessarily exclude religious consciousness, and religious consciousness still persists even though some theories of secularization had predicted its disappearance. For example, Robert Bellah and others have identified a "civil religion" in such putatively secular societies as the USA; such a "civil religion" may serve both priestly and prophetic functions, legitimating but also criticizing and directing institutions, practices, and policies. (5) Conformity of religion to the world. Over time some religions do become more accommodationist toward the world, adopting the world's standards and losing their distinctiveness. But this process is not universal or inevitable. For example, sects* do not always become churches* in the sociological sense (*see* **Ecclesiology and Ethics**).

Analyses of religion in the modern world often flounder because of a lack of clarity about the meaning of secularization. This brief survey suggests that there is no single process of secularization and that secularization is occurring in some senses but not in others. Furthermore, causation is complex: along with such sociological factors as industrialization* and urbanization*, some beliefs and practices in Judaism and Christianity may have fostered some forms of secularization. Secularization is not necessarily inimical to religion; it does not necessarily produce secularism*, an ideology* that opposes, or is indifferent to, religion. In the 1960s several theologians, in part under the influence of Dietrich Bonhoeffer, defended what they called worldly, secular, and religionless Christianity (*see* **Worldliness**). That movement lost its momentum largely because of the recognition that Christianity is a religion and that some tension between Christian ethics and the world is important, even though it should not be exaggerated.

From the standpoint of Christian ethics, one of the most important features of secularization in the modern world is the increasing autonomy* of social institutions* (see the second conception of secularization). Such institutions earlier resided under a "sacred canopy" (Peter Berger, *The Sacred Canopy*, 1967), but they now tend to operate according to the functional logic of their own particular domains (*see* **Social Ethics**). However, in some cases, the values embedded in those institutions are defensible—some of them may even have originated in Christianity (see the third conception)—and it may be possible to appeal to those values to criticize and direct policies.

J. F. Childress and D. B. Harned (eds.), *Secularization and the Protestant Prospect*, 1970 (includes essays by Bellah, Parsons, and Shiner, among others); R. K. Fenn, *Toward a Theory of Secularization*, 1978; A. MacIntyre, *Secularization and Moral Change*, 1967; D. Martin, *A General Theory of Secularization*, 1978; B. Wilson, *Religion in Sociological Perspective*, 1982.

                                    JAMES F. CHILDRESS

Security

Security has a theological meaning in the OT and the NT. In its contemporary meaning in international politics, security is a condition in which the territorial integrity, political independence, and constitutional processes of a state are not threatened or harmed by internal or external forces. Internal security is preserved by three elements: an independent judicial system, impartial police forces, and a responsible citizenry. External security is the task of national armed forces, occasionally of international peacekeeping contingents, together with whatever protection is afforded by the United Nations system, regional agencies, or military alliances. Although the UN does not provide a reliable system of collective security*, it has developed institutions of parliamentary diplomacy, judicial and other means for the peaceful settlement of international disputes, peacekeeping with the consent of the host country, and forums for the negotiation of disarmament*.

K. Lonsdale, *Security and Responsibility,* 1954; Working Party Reporting to the British Council of Churches, *The Search for Security,* 1973.

SYDNEY D. BAILEY

Segregation

The exclusion of an identifiable group from the right and opportunity to participate in social institutions and the common life. Exclusion may be based on gender, religion, occupation, social class, race, or color. Segregation may be systematically enforced throughout a society by government action; or it may be practiced on a smaller scale by employers, trade unions, schools, stores, hotels, owners of real estate, clubs, and churches.

Segregation rests upon a claim to superiority by a dominant group, who feel themselves tainted or annoyed by association with "inferiors." It is most effectively practiced against a group who are visually recognizable, so that segregation is easily implemented. Color segregation has been frequent in history; for example, Hindu caste segregation apparently originated in differences of race and color, which led to occupational distinctions.

Modern segregation has been most prevalent in three areas: (1) in regions where white colonial powers have excluded colored natives from social institutions; (2) in South Africa, where a white minority has enforced apartheid*; (3) in the USA, where as an after-

math of slavery* "Jim Crow" laws and customs have enforced segregation against the former slaves and their descendants.

In the USA, although the Fourteenth Amendment to the Constitution (1868) guaranteed full rights to all citizens, legal segregation continued under a Supreme Court decision authorizing "separate but equal" treatment (1896). Religious and political groups protested against segregation, as did black people. In 1946 the National Council of Churches advocated "a non-segregated church and a non-segregated society." In 1954 the Supreme Court, in effect reversing the decision of 1896, determined that compulsory segregation was a denial of equality in education. Later rulings and legislation have extended the principle to include other spheres of life, including housing and employment.

Ethical opposition to segregation has usually appealed, whether on theological or rational grounds, to a common humanity that makes irrelevant the distinctions upon which segregation rests. In the USA that has often meant the "melting pot," in which those distinctions are dissolved. Or it has meant an aspiration for a "color-blind" society. In practice these ideas often meant that minorities were asked to lose their historical and cultural identity. More recent thinking has led to revised policies in two ways: (1) the search for a pluralistic society that treasures the distinctive contributions of various groups; (2) affirmative action programs that temporarily call attention to color and sex, especially in employment and education, in order to overcome the persisting legacy of segregation.

See **Human Dignity; Discrimination; Equality; Justice; Race Relations; Racism; Respect for Persons.**

J. Williamson, *The Crucible of Race: Black-White Relations in the American South Since Emancipation,* 1984; C. V. Woodward, *The Strange Career of Jim Crow,* rev. ed. 1957.

ROGER L. SHINN

Self and Selfhood see **Persons and Personality; Self-Realization**

Self-Actualization *see* **Counseling, Ethical Issues in; Self-Realization**

Self-Deception

At a commonsense level, it might be thought that self-deception was similar to deceiving others. To deceive others, one must knowingly make them believe something one does not believe oneself. Similarly, self-deception would consist in knowingly getting oneself to believe something one does not believe. Several philosophical difficulties can at once be raised. If self-deception is possible, must it therefore be possible for someone to know (or believe) that *p* is false while at the same time believing *p* to be true? Or to believe that *p* and also not to believe that *p?* Or is "deception" a misnomer, and self-deception rather a case of attending to the reasons in favor of *p* (for instance, because one wishes to act as if *p* were true) without in fact believing that *p?* A useful summary of recent literature is to be found in Jeffrey Foss, "Rethinking Self-Deception," *American Philosophical Quarterly* 17, 1980, pp. 237–244.

See also **Ideology; Rationalization.**

GERARD J. HUGHES

Self-Denial

This term is likely to be used by Protestants where Catholics would speak of mortification*, but its meaning should not be reduced to particular acts of discipline or renunciation. As Gregory the Great observed, it is easier to give up what one has than to renounce what one is (*Homilies on the Gospels* 32, on Luke 9:24). But it is to this renunciation that Jesus calls us—cf. Luke 14:26; and Paul adds, when urging a particular form of self-denial, that even Christ did not please himself (Rom. 15:3). We are here confronted with the paradox of Christian ethics, that the gospel presents us with an ethic of fulfillment (cf. John 10:10—"life more abundantly") as well as of sacrifice, indeed with an ethic of fulfillment in and by sacrifice (cf. Mark 8:35 and parallels—"whoever loses his life for my sake and the gospel's will save it"). One modern writer like Kierkegaard may find in the teaching of Jesus a call to utter renunciation; another may comment with equal truth, though not as the whole story, that "the Gospel is a message of joyous eudaemonism" (P. E. More, *The Christ of the New Testament,* 1924, p. 121). As Augustine observes in commenting on John 12:25, to love one's life "in this world" is in fact to lose it, and to lose one's life is in fact to save it. We are not indeed called on to renounce desire for our own true welfare, but to find it in self-sacrificing love—and the NT does after all accept the OT precept to love one's neighbor "as oneself" (Mark 12:31 and parallels, from Lev. 19:18; cf. Rom. 13:9). This is presumably the answer to the doctrine of "pure love" maintained by Fénelon against Bossuet in a famous 17th-century controversy—or the idea popularized by Nygren's *Agape and Eros* (ET 1953) that Christian love is wholly free from self-regarding aspects. Yet it remains that in an ethic of love, selfishness disappears; as Augustine points out, two cities are formed by two loves, the earthly by love of self even to contempt of God, the heavenly by love of God even to contempt of self (*City of God* 14.28) (*see* **Augustinian Ethics**).

See **Love; Self-Love; Self-Realization.**

E. R. HARDY

Self-Determination *see* Autonomy

Self-Examination

Critical reflection upon one's own conduct and character, in relation to the standards that one has accepted. While indeed there is the danger of falling into a morbid introspective brooding or into scrupulosity*, conscience* will scarcely develop unless there are honest attempts at self-assessment. The examination may be given a systematic framework by basing it, for example, on the Ten Commandments. Paul enjoins self-examination, especially before receiving Holy Communion (1 Cor. 11:28). In the same connection, the *Book of Common Prayer* urges that we should "examine our lives and conversations by the rule of God's commandments," seeking God's forgiveness and making restitution to any persons wronged; and it adds that anyone who "cannot quiet his own conscience" by these means should resort to the sacrament of penance*.

JOHN MACQUARRIE

Self-Love

The OT (Lev. 19:18) injunction to love one's neighbor as oneself is reiterated in the NT in Matt. 19:19; 22:39; Rom. 13:9; Gal. 5:14; James 2:8. Taken by itself the injunction can be read as a vindication as well as a limitation of self-love. There seems little merit simply in making oneself miserable and some, though not all, asceticism would probably now be ascribed by psychiatrists to the pathology of the self rather than to Christian living. In an age where psychological categories are widely known, it is well to make it clear that masochism is a counterfeit of Christian discipleship, even if at times it has succeeded in passing itself off as the real thing.

On the other hand, Luke 14:26, "If any one . . . does not hate . . . his own life," set as it is in the midst of references to martyrdom, is a reminder of the sterner side of Christianity. Martyrdom is a possibility of the Christian life and the path of the martyr from Stephen to Bonhoeffer is not that of those who put self-love unduly high in their scheme of things.

In view of this dialectical attitude to self-love, it is not surprising that the references of theologians to it have sometimes appeared ambiguous. Augustine, for instance, sometimes speaks of self-love as a good and sometimes as an evil. But in the former case he is probably simply referring to the fact that all our desires are conditioned by the structure of the self, which has in turn been created by God. In the latter he is referring to the fact that sometimes the soul puts itself before God.

Of all theologians, perhaps Joseph Butler has given the clearest and most rational defense of self-love, pointing out its superiority as a principle of action to the particular passions (such as hunger and sex). Surrender to any one of the latter at a particular time may be as imprudent as it is wrong and thus self-love is established as a principle second only to conscience.

Butler, however, though a great theologian, was a figure of the 18th century with all its distrust of enthusiasm*, and one wonders if his enthusiasm for cool self-love is compatible with the kind of reckless behavior that is sometimes praised in the Bible. The three valiant men (2 Sam. 23:13–17) who fetched the water of Bethlehem for King David were obviously little concerned for their expectation of life. Nor was the widow (Mark 12: 42–44) who put her last coin into the collection plate paying much heed to her calorie intake.

See **Love; Self-Denial; Self-Realization.**

IAN HENDERSON

Self-Realization

As a subject for moral reflection, self-realization usually centers on the injunction to be-

come the person one "potentially" or "truly" is. Many critics dismiss this entire subject as too murky to warrant sustained attention. This judgment is not without point, for the injunction encompasses a wide and heterogeneous range of normative proposals and beliefs about human nature. Any snap dismissal nevertheless ignores the pivotal role the subject plays in both philosophical and cultural traditions with which Christianity has had a long and complicated history, and in modern movements that have influenced theological literature and ecclesiastical practice. Versions of the injunction occupy a central place, for example, in the traditions of Platonism, Aristotelianism, romanticism, and idealism (see **Aristotelian Ethics; Platonic Ethics; Romantic Ethics; Idealist Ethics**). Other versions approximate philosophical defenses of ethical and psychological egoism*. Still others appear in modern psychological and psychoanalytic literature; here the term "self-realization" occurs along with others used more or less interchangeably with it, such as self-development, self-fulfillment, self-actualization, and individuation (see **Psychology and Ethics**). Three traditions especially important for Christian ethics may be distinguished as follows.

1. Classical self-development. An early tradition extols the quasi-moral, quasi-aesthetic Greek ideal of *eudaimonia* as the best possible life (see **Eudaemonism**). Proponents assume that human beings, like all other species, are endowed with a specific nature, a proper *ergon* that distinguishes us, a *telos* toward which we naturally move. We may flourish in varying degrees, according to our kind. It is with respect to what is incumbent on us as human beings that excellence is measured and virtues are specified. In short, we ought to "realize" our "essence" by developing a given capacity to act in a specifically human way.

Specifically human action is linked above all to our capacity to act on reasons or intentionally. Aristotle says that "he who exercises his reason and cultivates it seems to be both in the best state of mind and most dear to the gods." Yet on the question of how far reason should dominate, interpreters debate between two possible answers they find in Aristotle, in the form of two distinguishable accounts of *eudaimonia*. The first account is intellectualist. Theoretical contemplation, *theōria* (finally, the contemplation of God) is that activity which attests to the divine element in our human nature, and thus represents the highest attainment of our rational function. *Theōria* should serve not only as our single dominant aim but also as the sole criterion for evaluating actions of every kind: actions are good and admirable if and only if they promote this aim. The second account is inclusive. *Eudaimonia* consists in an interplay between the rational function that distinguishes us from other animals and the nonrational functions we share with them. We are a kind of compound or an ensouled body in which reason interacts with emotion, perception, and action. *Theōria* remains the most valuable human activity, but it cannot furnish complete guidance, for a life consisting only of contemplation surpasses what is humanly possible. Reason must guide practical life as well, and excellence here includes virtuous activities that are good and admirable in themselves. *Theōria* and virtuous action thus combine to constitute the best possible life.

Despite this difference between the two accounts of *eudaimonia,* they share a view of self-development as more than a haphazard aggregate of goods. Some objective organization obtains; to realize the best possible life, superior and subordinate goods must be rightly ordered.

2. Autonomous self-direction. Another tradition, articulated in modern liberal and existentialist writings, shifts what predominantly distinguishes human nature from rationality to choice*.

Liberal writers are more moderate than existentialists in that they defend choice as part of a wider depiction of human nature and human excellence. They are inclined to grant a given potential, or pregiven potential, to human beings, and to link the idea of autonomy* expressly to rationality. Indeed, J. S. Mill in *On Liberty* praises the Greek ideal of self-development. And he observes in a similar vein that religious faith in "a good Being" most consistently holds "that this Being gave all human faculties that they might be cultivated and unfolded . . . and that he takes delight in . . . every increase in any of their capabilities of comprehension, of action, or of enjoyment." Some think that Mill in such a passage presupposes, albeit hesitantly, a conception of human flourishing grounded in what is incumbent on us as human beings.

After we allow for these complexities and areas of overlap with classical self-development, two claims nevertheless set liberal self-direction apart. (*a*) I am *most myself* if and only if I choose, and do not have my choices made for me. The great enemy of this conviction is conformity to existing social roles and conventions*. Mill dwells repeatedly on the dullness, mediocrity, and threats to individual well-being that unquestioning adherence to "custom merely *as* custom" produces. (*b*) Human nature is perpetually incomplete and capable of unpredictable, inexhaustible self-transformations. No single universal goal, or pattern of goals, can be discerned. Any acceptable account of human flourishing must remain in principle open-ended. Because we may be altered both by our own actions and by new experiences, "experiments in living" (Mill) constitute the only permanently viable strategy. To extol choice is precisely to acknowledge an absence of final closure (*see* **Liberalism**).

Existentialist writers are more radical. They are disinclined to grant any inherent teleological potential or to forge links between will and rationality. On their account, to realize oneself simply means to exercise one's capacity to choose. At the start one is not "truly" anything distinctive beyond a being who remains free to set and pursue objectives which are united solely by being self-imposed. Such views are summarized by J.-P. Sartre in the formula, "Existence precedes essence" (*see* **Existentialist Ethics**).

3. Romantic self-discovery. Three features mark a final tradition, in which the accent falls on becoming the self one "truly" is. (*a*) Uniqueness (*Einzigkeit*) rather than singleness (*Einzelheit*) defines the self to be realized. To quote F. Schleiermacher: "It became clear to me that each man ought to represent humanity in himself in his own different way, by his own special blending of its elements, so that it should reveal itself in each special manner, and, in the fulness of space and time, should become everything that can emerge as something individual out of the depths of itself." This differentiation thwarts all attempts to characterize the best possible life in general terms, for no single goal, the same for everyone, exists. Yet the absence of a single goal derives not from humanity's alleged open-endedness as such, but rather from the originality or incomparable image each person possesses. (*b*) *Emergence* implies that an *innate* plan or *telos* inscribed in one's existence waits to be realized. Emergence also connotes discovery, not self-creation or self-constitution as in autonomous self-direction. For some writers, one must more or less passively *accept* a given trajectory and destination. At most one *follows* inner instructions; one does not actively posit what one will become. (*c*) The process by which one discovers and accepts one's own *telos* is preeminently *affective*. At stake is a "vital design" (Ortega y Gasset). The personal insight required is too suffused with emotion to be called rational, and too instinctive and spontaneous to be deemed a choice.

Uniqueness and emergence are expressed in altered but recognizable form in influential modern psychological and psychoanalytic writings. C. G. Jung, for example, finds uniqueness in the process of "individuation" or self-differentiation from collective values and definitions. Here too self-differentiation, while a generally desirable goal, cannot be characterized in general terms, for paths to self-realization may vary from person to person. Furthermore, one discovers and accepts one's personal, inner *daimōn* or destiny; choice is restricted to whether or not one lives in accordance with the destiny one innately has (*see* **Destiny; Psychoanalysis; Psychology and Ethics**).

Assessment. To focus as the three traditions do on the self's *own* flourishing generates complex responses in Christian ethics, responses that reflect in part varying and sometimes rival judgments about the propriety of "self-love."* At a minimum all responses assume that any such focus remains (*a*) incomplete in theory if it neglects a test of consistency or omits norms for social responsibility that limit self-aggrandizement; and (*b*) corruptible in practice whenever it encourages patterns of self-absorption that exclude as a matter of psychological fact serious concern for other persons. Beyond this, however, difficult issues arise:

1. The eudaemonist structure of classical ethics is at once perpetuated and transformed in Augustinian and Thomistic thought (*see* **Augustinian Ethics; Thomistic Ethics**). In this thought the best possible life consists in communion with God. Our quest for such a life reflects a teleological orientation toward our supreme good which characterizes our humanity as such (*see* **Teleological Ethics**). A realist interpretation is given to this account: we do not choose our supreme good but are necessarily oriented to it by virtue of the creatures we are. Many Protestants in particular hold that eudaemonist ethics cannot be transformed sufficiently to serve as model for Christian ethics: no immanent teleology, however circumscribed, does justice to the priority that revelation and grace must always retain. These well-known controversies bequeath uncertainty at two key points. (*a*) To the extent that eudaemonist ethics requires concern about neighbors to be *derived from* concern about the self's own flourishing, it will not do. This conclusion, however, leaves unanswered another question often conflated with it: Is concern about the self's own flourishing a substantive moral claim *along with* concern about neighbors? (*b*) Accounts of Christian ethics that take as their point of departure the priority of revelation and grace* confront this question: If they jettison immanent teleology together with the objective ordering of human goods internal to it, can they specify such an ordering on another basis?

2. In the modern period Roman Catholic as well as Protestant writers stress the importance of freedom* in a life of communion with God, and so explicit affinities with autonomous self-direction have arguably increased. This stress disposes them to insist energetically that we cannot regard a person's conscious relation to God as a mere "case" of the highest human activity; and we cannot prevent by coercion all that is morally evil in the world. And if we could bring about optimal material prosperity without freedom, something essential would be lost. How can such insistence be harmonized with an ongoing commitment to some objective moral order knowable by human reason? And religiously, can freedom be more than passive acceptance but never "absolutely creative," so that it continues to reside in appropriating or resisting a call?

3. In many Christian accounts of human flourishing, no one of the distinctive human capacities—reason, freedom, and affectivity—is banished as irrelevant or given total sway. All interact and mutually influence each other. This inclusiveness certainly affords legitimacy to a romantic emphasis on personal insight suffused with emotion. Affirmed as well is a stress on the self's unique relation to God, and a place for a passive ingredient in one's response to grace.

Nevertheless, a traditional belief that our human nature is "fallen" casts a permanent shadow over all one's own efforts at self-discovery (*see* **Original Sin**). To ascribe primal self-transparency (either noetic or conative) to any person is a sinful conceit. This belief does not rule out all insight into our "deepest" desires, only that insight which claims total or absolute knowledge. The self "sees through a glass, darkly," plagued always by the possibility of self-deception* and rationalization*. And thus many orthodox thinkers fix a sequence from religious awareness to "true" self-discovery.

Aristotle, *Nicomachean Ethics,* tr. D. Ross, rev. ed. 1980; I. Berlin, *Four Essays on Liberty,* 1977; C. G. Jung, *Memories, Dreams, Reflections,* ET 1961; S. Lukes, *Individualism,* 1973; J. S. Mill, *On Liberty,* 1859; D. L. Norton, *Personal Destinies: A Philosophy of Ethical Individualism,* 1976; O. O'Donovan, *The Problem of Self-Love in St. Augustine,* 1980; P. Rieff, *The Triumph of the Therapeutic,* 1968.

GENE OUTKA

Sermon on the Mount

Most interpretations of the Sermon on the Mount throughout Christian history fall into one of three categories: (*a*) The demands of the Sermon are to be interpreted literally and applied absolutely in all times and situations; (*b*) the Sermon's demands are to be interpreted literally but were intended to apply only to certain limited times—such as the brief interim that Jesus expected between his ministry and the end of the world; (*c*) the demands of the Sermon must be adapted to the realities of ongoing historical existence.

We will approach the Sermon here as an integral part of the Gospel of Matthew, probably written by a Hellenistic-Jewish Christian. Though the Sermon is a discourse and not a narrative, a simple narrative structure of process underlies it, the three constituent parts of which are potentiality, process actualized, and consequence. Viewing the Sermon in relation to its narrative substructure shows that this discourse is not an abstraction but teaches a way of life.

1. Potentiality. Employing three different motifs, the Sermon begins by portraying how human beings are given the potentiality to achieve the kind of righteousness necessary to enter the kingdom of heaven (Matt. 5:20).

The Beatitudes (Matt. 5:3–12). The beatitude (pronouncement of blessedness or happiness) is a traditional literary wisdom form (Ps. 1:1), here transformed by eschatology. The principle governing Matt. 5:3–6 is that spiritual-moral emptiness is blessed. "The poor in spirit" might refer to the pious in spirit, but it can refer as well to those who *lack* spiritual resources. This interpretation is supported by the fact that these same people hunger and thirst for—and therefore lack —righteousness, Matthew's inclusive term for what God requires of human beings. It is not a general principle that those who lack righteousness are blessed, but rather a matter of the eschatological situation: emptiness is fortunate when filling is near and when emptiness is the potentiality for being filled (5:3b, 6b). Matthew 5:7–12 then suggests that *potentiality* for being filled with righteousness is already in some sense the *actuality* of moral achievement. For in these verses it is the merciful, the peacemakers, the pure in heart, the righteous achievers, who are pronounced blessed.

If both the empty and the filled are blessed, those who are not are the self-deceived, who are empty without knowing it. With these people the eye, the source of light, the angle of vision from which the self sees, is unsound (6:22–23). They do not see the truth of their own moral fault (7:3–5) and thus cannot interpret with understanding what confronts them in their history (16:1–4). This leads to the recognition that those who are empty in 5:3–6 are those who do know their lack. Matthew seems to envision two fundamental human situations: spiritual-moral lack concealed by self-deception, which is the condition of the lost; and the simultaneity of acknowledged emptiness and achieved fullness, which defines the condition of the saved.

This paradox, implied by the first clauses of the Beatitudes, is underscored by the eschatological statements that follow immediately. The kingdom that fills with righteousness and makes disciples children of God (5:6, 9) is both present (5:3, 10) and future (5:4–9). Realized eschatology frames futuristic eschatology. In the framing verses (5:3, 10) the kingdom is specifically referred to in the abstract and is *present*. In the framed verses (5:4–9) concrete manifestations of the kingdom (filling, seeing God, etc.) are projected into the *future*.

Identity. Jesus confers identity or moral

character (a continuing disposition) upon the disciples by pronouncing them the salt (purification, preservation, flavoring) of the earth and the light of the world (5:13–16). Since light is an image both of who the disciples are (5:14) and of the works they perform (5:16), works are seen to flow from being. Character is potentiality for action. Here we have the Sermon's first clear statement of ethical intention (a forward-looking reason for acting). The disciple is to perform good works for the purpose of leading others to acknowledge the glory of God. If the works attest to the reality of God, then grace as power for action must underlie them.

Jesus' fulfillment of the law. Potentiality for righteousness is further provided by Jesus' clarification of what is required: he fulfills the law in that he legitimates it by bringing out its true meaning (5:17–20). In 5:18–19 Matthew's Jesus affirms the validity of the law of Moses in every detail. But Matthew also interprets the law by love (5:43–48; 9:13; 12:7; 19:19; 22:34–40) and in various ways criticizes and abrogates the law (see below). Therefore, whatever may have been the intention of the historical narrator (or his source) in 5:18–19, the contextualized meaning is that the reinterpreted and radicalized law is still law—a condition for salvation— even though not all the details of the law are upheld.

2. *Process actualized (5:21–7:12).* The teaching that comprises the center of the Sermon implies two conflicting narrative processes. The statements of norms defining the new righteousness that qualifies a person for the kingdom suggest a process of redemption, while references to various manifestations of unrighteousness and hypocrisy imply a process of opposition or dissolution. These will be selectively considered.

The antitheses (5:21–48). Jesus says, "You have heard . . . But I say . . . ." If Jesus' word is placed against the Word of God in the law, then what qualifies as the Word of God, the content of righteousness, must be open to reformulation.

The law forbids murder and adultery, but Jesus also forbids anger or contempt, and the lust that is already adultery in the heart. Jesus claims for God not only one's action but the obedience of one's inner, hidden core. The law is not here set aside; rather, its claims are intensified. To whom is the inner disposition (anger or lust) the equivalent of the act (murder or adultery)? Since it is surely not the ethical object or other, it must be the subject. (This could be viewed as an intuitive anticipation of Freud's claim that the punitive action of the superego does not distinguish between intentions and actions.)

The command to remove an offending eye or hand (5:29–30) points to the reciprocal interaction between act and character. An act oriented to hand or eye can involve the whole self, the character, in sin. But the self has power to reverse such an action, to remove the hand or eye.

The law allows divorce generally, but Jesus allows it only on the ground of unchastity. Here Jesus is made to agree with the rabbi Shammai and is less radical than in the absolute prohibition in Mark 10:1–12. The law is limited but not set aside.

The law requires that oaths be kept, but Jesus forbids oaths altogether because a disciple always has the obligation to speak the truth. If the law is not here abrogated, it is nevertheless made superfluous.

The law allows an eye for an eye, but Jesus forbids all retaliation and resistance to evil. Thus the principle of equal retaliation, to which the law gives voice, is set aside.

Jesus requires love for the enemy rather than hatred. The law did not require hatred of enemies, but some interpretations of it did (e.g., the Qumran Manual of Discipline, 1QS 1.3–4, 9–10; 9.16, 21–22; 10.20–21). Such interpretations may be what is being opposed here. The disciples' concern for the well-being of the other is to be as boundless and inclusive as God's care for the just and the unjust. In this context we have the second major statement of intention: in order that they (the disciples) might be children of God, they must love their enemies.

It cannot be said in an unqualified way that the antitheses shift interest totally from self to other. The norms do concern themselves radically with the other person: the other is not to be the object of anger, lust, neglect, untruth, or vengeance, but is to be cared for. With regard to intentionality, however, the generating purposes for action are that the subject might enhance the glory of God (Matt. 5:16) and might be his child (5:45). Additional intentions are to inherit eternal life (6:19–21) and to avoid earthly suffering (5:23–26). Self-interest is also expressed in warnings to avoid such consequences of lovelessness as judgment, hell, guilt, and evil.

Against hypocrisy. Matthew 6:1–18 attacks the hypocrisy of practicing righteousness (6:1)—almsgiving, prayer, and fasting—for human praise rather than for secret divine reward. Whether the public pious role is a conscious pretense or is based on the self-deceived belief that it is true righteousness is not clear. In 7:1–3 the hypocrisy involved in judging others is definitely self-deception rather than pretense. The guilty judge actually does not see his or her own fault.

3. *Consequence (7:13–27).* The way of righteousness is a hard way that leads to life, while the easy way of unrighteousness leads to destruction (7:13–14). Matthew warns against the false prophets who do not produce the fruits of ethical works. He comprehends human wholeness, a correspondence between tree (heart) and fruit (works) (7:15–20). Either both are bad or both are good. This raises a question that cannot be pursued here: Do deeds, qualified as good or bad on the basis of rules, determine the condition of the heart, or does the heart, independently of rules, determine the quality of deeds? Perhaps it is both in Matthew.

The confession of Jesus as Lord when based on prophesying and miracle-working is empty and even evil (7:21–23). This is in striking contrast to the parallel in Luke 13:26–27, where those who are rejected performed no deeds at all. Matthew is perhaps combating a form of Christian enthusiasm that emphasized prophecy and miracles. Against this he wants to affirm that only words from the heart (Matt. 12:33–37) and deeds from the heart (7:15–20) count as doing the will of God (7:21).

At the very end (7:24–27) the consequences of following the two ways are imaged as the house that stands and the house that falls. The house that stands in the flood is the wholeness of hearing (understanding) and doing that Matthew calls wisdom. The house that falls in the time of crisis is the foolishness of hearing alone. The Sermon ends on the note of fall and therefore needs the rest of the Gospel narrative to reverse the declining movement.

However extreme the demands may be, Matthew regards acts of radical obedience as the necessary condition for salvation (6:14–15; 7:13–14, 19, 23–27; 16:27; 18:35), and he regards them as possible (7:24–27; 11:28–30; 19:17–19; 23:23) just as the law regarded itself as fulfillable and within human reach

(Deut. 30:11–14). We might agree that this obedience is possible to the extent that the kingdom is present as *enabling power* (Matt. 5:3, 6; 7:15–20; 13:16–17). But to the extent that the kingdom is future and beyond, the ethic is problematical and less possible. When Matthew deals thematically with radical obedience as a necessary condition for salvation, he does not really take cognizance of the impossibility and ambiguity. Yet there is an undercurrent in tension with this legal strain. Salvation is also by grace as *forgiveness* (1:21; 20:28; 26:28). And ethical acts do retain a dimension of ambiguity if the one who performs them has difficulty grasping their full significance, as in 25:34–40: "When did we see thee hungry and feed thee?"

See also **Eschatological Ethics; Jesus, Ethical Teaching of; New Testament Ethics.**

H. D. Betz, *Essays on the Sermon on the Mount,* 1985; W. D. Davies, *The Setting of the Sermon on the Mount,* 1964; M. Dibelius, *The Sermon on the Mount,* ET 1940; R. A. Guelich, *The Sermon on the Mount,* 1982; W. S. Kissinger, *The Sermon on the Mount,* 1975 (history of interpretation and bibliography); H. Windisch, *The Meaning of the Sermon on the Mount,* ET 1950.

DAN O. VIA

Seven Capital Sins *see* **Seven Deadly Sins**

Seven Deadly Sins

Although the phrase "seven deadly sins" is commonly used, the Christian tradition has often referred to the sins in question as "capital" rather than "deadly" sins. The word "capital" is derived from the Latin *caput* (head). In this context "capital" does not imply "mortal" sins worthy of death or capital punishment. Rather, as Thomas Aquinas suggested (*ST* I-II.84.3–4), its sense is "principle, leader, director," and the capital sins are sources or fountains of other sins, largely because their ends such as wealth are so attractive and require other sins for their realization. Aquinas also used the terms "capital sins" and "capital vices" interchangeably, "sin" suggesting acts and "vice" suggesting habits. Contemporary usage includes both acts and habits under the "seven deadly sins." There is no list of seven deadly or capital sins in scripture, even though there are several other lists of sins. Gregory the Great presented an early list of seven capital sins that was modified over the centuries. The following sins are now most often recognized: pride*; covetousness* (avarice or greed); lust*; gluttony*; envy*; anger*; and sloth*.

JAMES F. CHILDRESS

Seven Gifts of the Holy Spirit

These are the gifts enumerated in the Septuagint version of Isa. 11:2. They are wisdom, understanding, counsel, fortitude, knowledge, piety, and the fear of the Lord (godly fear). Augustine considers them in reverse order as "seven steps" in the development of the Christian life.

JOHN MACQUARRIE

Sex Discrimination

References to "sex" are ambiguous because this English term may denote a broad spectrum of human reality, from specific genital activity to numerous aspects of ancient and modern social, cultural systems that shape the meaning of femaleness and maleness. In spite of ambiguity, sex discrimination most commonly refers to acts, practices, or policies that disadvantage persons on the basis of gender, whether as female or as male (see **Discrimination**). Because of widespread historical-cultural patterns of male supremacy (see **Women, Status of**), most expressions of sex discrimination, or "sexism"—as practices that express sex discrimination have come to be called—involve unfairness to females. Claims of sex discrimination against males are increasing, however, as awareness of the conditioning effects of gender spread. Specifications of what constitutes sex discrimination and evaluations of its legal, moral, and religious significance vary. Such disagreements are always ideological because all human beings have interests and perceptions of self-interest related to gender.

Because law reflects the interests of dominant social groups, male-dominated societies have been slow to adopt legal constraints against sex discrimination. Laws aimed to proscribe or limit it are of recent origin. Much initial legislation aimed to remedy the disadvantaged status of women actually further legitimated separate and distinctive treatment of women under law. As a result, compensatory laws have become sources of contemporary men's claims that they are victims of sex discrimination.

The current legal status of sex discrimination in the USA is difficult to summarize. The absence of basic constitutional provision mandating gender equality before the law (what is now referred to as the Equal Rights Amendment) means that no consistent, clear line of constitutional interpretation about women's rights has emerged. Constitutional provisions for the rights of citizenship have been applied to women erratically because gender fairness is not mandated. Furthermore, the few pieces of federal civil rights legislation prohibiting sex discrimination have been casually enforced, or rendered null and void by subsequent judiciary interpretation. In addition, many of the laws which most conspicuously disadvantage women are shaped by civil or criminal codes that are the province of the separate states or local communities. In spite of weak legal provisions against sex discrimination, the accelerating moral and theological debate about it is certain to increase challenges to its legality. (In the UK the 1975 Sex Discrimination Act has been somewhat effective in reducing discrimination against women in the workplace.)

The range of ethical and religious assessments of sex discrimination is also difficult to summarize. A complex variety of positions is the result of intricate sets of assumptions rooted in divergent interpretations of human and divine nature, including varied theories of society and conceptions of justice implicit in these. Such differences appear not chiefly as moral disagreement in the narrow sense—that is, differences over moral principles—but as more inclusive philosophical and/or theological presumptions. Normative evaluative opinions about sex discrimination run the gamut of the ideological spectrum, from beliefs that most differing treatment of women and men is "natural" or "divinely ordained" and has positive moral and theological significance, to convictions that such differences are deeply suspect morally and religiously. At the former end of the spectrum, any gender role shifts are themselves wrong because they violate natural and/or divine order, while at the latter end, the common humanity of men and women is presumed to require active effort to minimize the differential social advantages of being born male or female.

It is important to observe that unless some common ontic ground between male and female being is presumed, the existence of "sex discrimination" itself will not be acknowledged. To speak of such discrimination already presumes such a negative moral judgment and affirms the belief that males and females ought to be considered members of the same species so that the most basic universalizing criteria of morality apply. It is widely agreed that we should treat like cases alike, so rights and obligations predicated of one gender must be applicable to both if species commonality is assumed. Not all agree that the universalizability* intrinsic to the moral point of view applies to gender.

This normative diversity is paralleled by a range of empirical disagreements about the scope and manifestation of sex discrimination. Those whose normative convictions incline them to accept a broad range of difference in the treatment accorded men and women usually presume that manifestations of sex discrimination are rare. The burden of proof as to its existence falls on the claimant, since sex discrimination, in this view, exists only in infrequent situations where a woman of demonstrated equal or superior competence to a given male can be shown to have been the victim of conscious prejudice*. Those at the other end of the evaluative spectrum, who believe differential patterns of gender treatment are ethically and/or theologically dubious, see a different empirical reality. They believe that sex discrimination is widespread, and that its manifestations are subtle and self-perpetuating. They assume that justifications about gender difference as "natural," or divinely decreed, are ideological myths designed to perpetuate gender injustice, and that such rationales, when critically scrutinized, reveal assumptions of male supremacy.

Explicit ethical and theological debates about gender have become widespread only in the last two decades. In vast areas of the world this issue is now being raised for the first time. As a result, we may predict that ethical controversy regarding sex discrimination will escalate.

See **Equality; Fairness; Feminist Ethics; Justice; Liberation Theology; Oppression; Respect for Persons; Women, Status of.**

___

B. A. Babcock, A. E. Freedman, E. H. Norton, and S. C. Ross, *Sexual Discrimination and the Law,* Law School Case Book Series, 1975 (new edition forthcoming); B. A. Brown, A. E. Freedman, H. Katz, and A. M. Price, *Women's Rights and the Law,* 1977; B. Chiplin and P. J. Sloane, *Tackling Discrimination at the Workplace: An Analysis of Sex Discrimination in Britain,* 1983; M. Cohen, T. Nagel, and T. Scanlon (eds.), *Equality and Preferential Treatment,* 1977; L. Kanowitz, *Equal Rights: The Male Stake,* 1981; D. Maguire, *A New American Justice: Ending the White Male Monopoly,* 1980; J. Pleck, *The Myth of Masculinity,* 1981; A. Sargent (ed.), *Beyond Sex Roles,* 1977; R. A. Wasserstrom, *Philosophy and Social Issues: Five Studies,* 1980.

BEVERLY WILDUNG HARRISON

Sexual Ethics

The traditional Judeo-Christian framework for evaluating sexual acts and relations is marriage*. The central purpose associated with sexual intercourse has been procreation*; procreation, sexuality, and marriage have been understood largely in terms of the welfare of societies rather than individuals, i.e., of familial, tribal, national, and religious communities. The ideal sexual act has been defined as heterosexual, potentially procreative, and expressive of the permanent, monogamous relationship which facilitates nurture of children and domestic and social stability.

Post-Reformation, especially post-Enlightenment, Western Christianity stresses the value and subjective experience of the individual, and construes the importance of individuals as on a par with that of society. The consequences for ethics, especially sexual ethics, have been significant. Personal fulfillment and interpersonal relationship have become preeminent criteria of sexual morality; marriage and procreation are evaluated in relation to these goals. The extent of this shift may be gauged by the degree to which the influence of five norms of sexual activity has varied in Christian tradition and its biblical precedents. Three of these norms regard the normative *purposes* of sexual activity: (1) procreation; (2) satisfaction of sexual desire or drives; (3) expression of a positive affective relation between the partners (love). Two additional criteria regard the normative *relation* within which these purposes may be met: (4) marital commitment, usually permanent and exclusive; (5) heterosexuality. The partnership of persons of opposite sex is an implicit precondition of procreative marriage; the heterosexual norm comes into question in proportion to a decline in emphasis on procreation and a rise in emphasis on interpersonal sexual communion and pleasure.

The Bible is the universal and fundamental source of specifically *Christian* ethics. The OT (Hebrew Bible) presents procreative marriage as the norm (*see* **Old Testament Ethics**). The accounts of the creation of humanity in Gen. 1–3 construe sexual differentiation as part of God's design, as good, and as ordained not only to reproduction (1:26–28) but also to personal and social partnership (2:18–25). They portray an original equality of male and female, ruined by disobedience and sin (Gen. 3, esp. vs. 16–19). The egalitarian thrust of Gen. 1–3, however, is reflected consistently neither by the patriarchal social organization of ancient Israel nor by the biblical materials as a body, in which most central figures are male. Marriage in Israel occasionally was polygamous (polygynous) until about the time of the monarchy in the 10th century B.C. (Gen. 29:21–30; 2 Sam. 5:13–16; 1 Kings 11:1, 3); it was accompanied by concubinage (Gen. 16:1–4; 30:1–13) and levirate marriage (Gen. 38:8; Deut. 25:5–10), which augmented the production of heirs; and marriage could be dissolved by divorce at the husband's initiative (Deut. 24:1–4; but cf. Mal. 2:14–16). Sex outside of marriage was prohibited, more stringently for women. Females were regarded as under the absolute authority of, if not as the property of, husband or (if unmarried) father. The penalty for adultery was death for both partners (Lev. 20:10; Deut. 22:22; cf. Ex. 20:14; Lev. 18:20; Deut. 5:18). A betrothed virgin was considered as a wife; if convicted of intercourse, she escaped death only if the act took place in a rural area where demonstrably she would have been unable to call for help (Deut. 22:23–27). If a man had intercourse with an unbetrothed virgin, he was required to marry her and pay the bride price to her father (Deut. 22:28–29). Although prostitution* was not punishable by law, the man was warned against it (Prov. 5; 7:5, 25–27). Homosexual acts were forbidden (Lev. 18:22; 20:13), and bestiality was punishable by death for both men and women (Ex. 22:19; Lev. 18:23; 20:15–16). Also prohibited were incest*, nakedness, and sexual intercourse during menstruation (Lev. 20:11–12, 14, 17–21). Despite this generally patriarchal framework, prominent women are commemorated

in the biblical literature, e.g., Rebekah, Sarah, Rachel, Leah, Zipporah, Deborah, Naomi, Ruth, Abigail, and Judith (cf. Prov. 31:3–31). A counterpoint to the procreative focus is the Song of Solomon (Song of Songs), in which the tender, passionate eroticism of lovers is portrayed with no reference to procreation or even to marriage.

In the NT the importance of kinship, marriage, and the production of children is relativized by the eschatological horizon and gospel universality of primitive Christianity. In neither Testament is specific sexual morality a major concern; sexuality always is seen in relation to the nature and call of the people of God, and to the sort of faith and obedience that ought to characterize its members. Marriage is by no means forbidden; but one's relation to God and to the community of believers no longer depends on marital, familial, or racial ties (Matt. 10:37, 12:46–50; Mark 3:31–35; 10:29–30; Luke 8:19–21; 14:26). Marriage and family are background to many of Jesus' teachings and deeds, and he evidently concurs that adultery is wrong (Matt. 5:27–28; John 8:3–11). He repudiates the Jewish practice of divorce (Matt. 5:31–32; 19:9; Mark 10:11–12; Luke 16:18; 1 Cor. 7:10–11) in the name of the "one flesh" unity of man and woman established at the creation (Matt. 19:3–8; Mark 10:2–9), and insists that both wife and husband are obligated to fidelity*. The major theme of Jesus' teaching, however, is not morality, but conversion to the kingdom through repentance (Mark 1:14–15).

The only extended discussion of sexual ethics in the NT occurs in 1 Cor. 7. There Paul (*see* **Pauline Ethics**) sees the primary purpose of marriage as the legitimate satisfaction of sexual passion (vs. 2, 9, 36–37). Procreation is not a particular objective of the Christian community, not only because membership is not dependent on it, but also because the end of the world and the fulfillment of the reign of God are anticipated in the present generation (vs. 26, 29, 31b). As far as Paul is concerned, sexual activity and marriage only distract from preparation for the kingdom (vs. 32–35). Nor is the cultivation of one-to-one interpersonal affective relationships a priority for Paul, since, like the Hebrew tradition, he gauges all aspects of human life by their contribution to the community of faith. In the NT this means enhancement of cooperation in worship, service, and witness (1 Cor. 12–14).

One striking dissimilarity to the Hebrew view is Paul's clear preference for celibacy* over marriage (1 Cor. 7:7–8, 38–40) since the unmarried state better facilitates "undivided devotion to the Lord" (v. 35). Paul rejects all "sexual immorality" (*porneia*), including fornication (1 Cor. 5:19; Eph. 5:3–5), prostitution (1 Cor. 6:15–16), adultery (6:9), incest (5:1), and homosexual acts (Rom. 1:26–27; 1 Cor. 6:9). One reason for exclusion of sexual communication and shared enjoyment as positive reasons for sexual intercourse in the NT and early Christianity (in contrast to the Song of Solomon) is the influence of Greek and Roman Stoic philosophy. The Stoic aim was to subordinate emotions and passions to rational ends, or even to rise above passion completely. Primitive Christianity appropriated Stoic themes while trying to counteract the Hellenistic Gnostic view that the material world is evil, that the body is the prison of the soul, and that procreation merely perpetuates imprisonment of souls. Christianity affirmed, against the Gnostics, the created goodness of the body, sex, marriage, and the bearing of children; but, with Stoicism, it set procreation as the only end that justifies sexual passion (*see* **Gnosticism, Ethics of; Stoic Ethics**).

In the patristic period, in medieval Christianity, and up to the Reformation, the central sexual norms remain constant: celibacy is valued highly as a witness to the coming kingdom, but is not mandatory; sexual activity, a secondary good, is justified completely only by intending procreation, and should be carried out in a heterosexual, monogamous, and permanent relationship. To seek marital intercourse to release sexual tension or to experience pleasure was not commended but tolerated; the petitioned spouse was enjoined to comply, i.e., to "render the debt" (cf. 1 Cor. 7:3–4). Early Christian views of the positive value of marriage seem to vary in inverse proportion to the urgency of eschatological expectation (*see* **Patristic Ethics**). The Latin father Tertullian (c. 160–c. 225), who looks for an imminent second coming of Christ, exalts virginity* and celibacy within marriage, counseling the avoidance of second marriages (*To His Wife*). An extreme form of this ascetic, rigorist strain was Montanism, defined by the church as heretical, but with which Tertullian eventually identified himself, renouncing marriage entirely for all Christians. On the other hand, Tertullian's Greek contemporary Clement of Alexandria (c. 150–c. 215) agrees that continence* is better than sexual relations, but much more decisively affirms that marriage is instituted by God as part of the good of creation (*On Marriage*). Certainly the patristic figure who most set the parameters of Christian sexual ethics was Augustine (354–430), bishop of Hippo in North Africa (*see* **Augustinian Ethics**). Although he, too, sees virginity or continence as higher, he resists the Manichean doctrine (*see* **Manichean Ethics**) that matter is evil, and defines the purpose of sexual union as procreation. Marriage, the context of legitimate sex, has three purposes: children (*proles*), fidelity and the avoidance of fornication (*fides*), and the indissoluble and sacramental bond of Christian spouses (*sacramentum*). Augustine also speaks of companionship between the sexes. Although sexual intercourse was created good, Augustine seems convinced that after the fall of Adam and Eve it always is tainted by sin. He believes that the rational faculty ought to dominate the passions and control the body. Since intercourse does not take place by a sheer act of the rational will but involves involuntary bodily sensations and movements, Augustine thinks that it inevitably occasions the disordered ascendency of passion over rational volition, and therefore is concupiscent (*see* **Concupiscence**). His ambivalence toward sexuality is demonstrated particularly in his occasional suggestions that original sin* is transmitted physically through intercourse to offspring (see especially *On the Good of Marriage*).

Thomas Aquinas (c. 1225–1274), the medieval Dominican, synthesized Christian teaching (including Augustine's) with Aristotle's philosophy (*see* **Thomistic Ethics**). His ethics rests on the premise that God has created a hierarchy of beings with distinct "natures" or intrinsic principles of existence and activity. Human nature is distinguished by intelligence and free will; these faculties as well as the physical structure of the human person form the criteria of moral responsibility. Thomas's view of sexual acts is informed both by the traditional enumeration of Augustine's three "goods" and by the Roman jurist Ulpian's emphasis on the moral implications of aspects of human nature shared with other animals, e.g., the procreative design of copulation. While Thomas concurs with the tradition that permanent, monogamous, procreative, and patriarchal marriage realizes the natural and normative meaning of sexual acts and relations, he expands Augustine's perspective by drawing attention to the friendship and intensity of love that should exist between spouses. He nowhere suggests that the passions or sexual desire are intrinsically sinful, or that they need override rational ends (*ST* II-II.26.11; 151–154; and *Supplement to the ST* 41–68).

The Protestant Reformation challenged the medieval tradition in sexual ethics. Most radically, Martin Luther (1483–1546) insists that marriage is an "estate" to which God has ordained most Christians (*see* **Lutheran Ethics; Orders**). Because the gift of celibacy is given rarely, mandating it for clergy and religious had resulted, observed Luther, in widespread abuse. Resolving to test all doctrine by Scripture, Luther grounds the meaning of sexuality in the Bible. On his reading of Genesis, he teaches that although male and female were created equal, through sin woman has fallen into submission, and man into debilitating toil. Woman, he claims, regains some of her original status through motherhood. Augustine's influence on Luther is strong; Luther retains procreation as the sole complete justification of sexual intercourse, and he manifests ambivalence regarding sexual desire, even when directed to procreation. In general, however, Luther has high praise for the vocations of marriage and parenthood. He also denies that marriage, one of the earthly callings, is a sacrament and he permits divorce in extreme cases. (See *Lectures on Genesis* and *On the Estate of Marriage.*) Appreciation of the companionship of wife and husband is more evident in the writings of John Calvin (1509–1564). (*See* **Calvinist Ethics.**) Procreation remains the purpose of sexual intercourse, but since Calvin emphasizes human sociality, he identifies the sacredness of the conjugal bond with the unity of husband and wife in body and soul. Marital intercourse is in itself holy and is no sin for married believers. Inability to remain continent becomes a motive for marriage only after the Fall. Although the woman is partner and helper, she always is subordinate to her husband. Even before their sin, Eve was subject to Adam; but subjection is compounded as a penalty for sin (see Calvin's *Commentaries* on Genesis 3 and 1 Corinthians 7; and *Institutes* 2.7). In general, the Re-

formers elevate marriage to a vocation* of service to God, church, and society. This is particularly clear in Anglicanism (*see* **Anglican Moral Theology**) and in manifestations of the Reformed (Calvinist) tradition such as Puritanism (*see* **Puritan Ethics**). By taking away the sacramental status of matrimony, thus removing it from the purview of ecclesiastical regulation, they make its institutionalization a civil affair and tend to make its morality more private.

Twentieth-century Protestant ethics has reinforced biblical origins, lifting up the norm of love and generally relying on individuals' perceptions of the sorts of acts which embody that norm. The most obvious exception is fundamentalist biblicism, which sees scripture as the source of definite and absolute moral rules. Mainstream Protestant bodies have guided believers with the reports of church-sponsored committees, usually not promulgated as law. The Roman Catholic Church differs by virtue both of its commitment to the natural law* and of its univocal teaching office (the magisterium*). (*See* **Modern Roman Catholic Moral Theology.**) Protestantism places less emphasis on procreation and more on acceptance of nonmarital sexual acts; Catholicism continues to insist, at least officially, that sex take place within marriage, undeterred from procreation by artificial contraception*. Orthodox Christianity, premised on Scripture and the church fathers, affirms marriage as the sole legitimate context of sex, but some authorities permit the contraceptive spacing of births (*see* **Eastern Orthodox Christian Ethics**). Christianity recently has been the object of feminist critiques of its support of the patriarchal institutionalization of sexuality and procreation. In response, growing attention has been directed in the churches to past bases of subordination of women and sexist interpretations of sexuality; to recovering biblical warrants for the equality of men and women; and to fostering reciprocal and egalitarian views of sexuality and male-female cooperation (*see* **Feminist Ethics; Women, Status of**).

Contemporary Christian sexual ethics in general gives more emphasis to love as a norm, and less to procreation. In the light of post-Freudian psychology, sexuality is seen as a profound stratum of the personality, not to be equated with genital activity. The ability to experience sexual desire and pleasure is seen as a positive good and an avenue of love and commitment. This emphasis on the affective and enjoyable aspects of sex has had implications for moral criteria. Procreation is widely seen as valuable but not essential. Marriage continues to be affirmed as the normative or ideal context for sex, and certainly for procreation, by most Christian bodies and authors, but some justify pre- or extramarital sex that expresses love. Sexual interactions previously considered deviant or unnatural because not apt for procreation are judged by the same criteria of love and mutual pleasure. To the extent that the affective and interpersonal dimensions of sex have replaced procreation and marriage as its morally definitive criteria, it has become possible to reevaluate previously condemned sexual expressions, e.g., homosexual relations. Since recent empirical research suggests that the bases of sexual orientation lie beyond individual choice, both Catholicism and major Protestant denominations have ceased to define the homosexual orientation (same-sex preference) as in itself sinful, though some (including the Catholic Church) view it as abnormal or as a "sickness." Catholicism encourages the homosexual person to remain celibate, though with pastoral understanding of the difficulty. Some revisionist thinkers see loving homosexual relations and acts as intrinsically no less valuable than heterosexual ones.

Warrants supporting an affective norm in sexual ethics are the centrality of love in the NT, the inclusivity and personalism of the teaching of Jesus, and the influence of cultural presuppositions on biblical texts condemning adultery, fornication, and homosexuality. Natural law revisionists argue that *human* "nature" is rational, affective, and volitional, i.e., *personal,* not merely biological. Concrete acts must be placed in the context of personal relations before their morality can be evaluated. Countercritiques of these modifications see in them the pursuit of individual fulfillment to the denigration of moral continuity and of social responsibility; a new dualism that separates the personal, affective dimension from the physical dimension of sex (which is reproductive as well as physically pleasurable); insufficient attention to the fundamental heterosexual and monogamous ideal of Bible and tradition; and neglect, in interpreting sexual experience, of the Christian understanding of original sin's radical effects on the good creation.

See **Abortion; Asceticism; Body; Celibacy; Chastity; Children; Continence; Contraception; Divorce; Embodiment; Family; Fidelity; Homosexuality; Lesbianism; Lust; Marriage; Masturbation; Monogamy; Morality, Legal Enforcement of; Original Sin; Polygamy; Procreation; Prostitution; Rape; Reproductive Technologies; Self-Realization; Temperance; Virginity; Vocation.**

O. J. Babb, "Marriage," "Sex," "Woman," *IDB* III, IV, 1962; D. S. Bailey, *Sexual Relation in Christian Thought,* 1959 (also titled *Man-Woman Relation in Christian Thought*); J. Dominian, *Proposals for a New Sexual Ethic,* 1977; M. A. Farley, "Sexual Ethics," *EB,* 1978; H. Thielicke, *The Ethics of Sex,* ET 1964.

LISA SOWLE CAHILL

Shame

The word "shame" denotes a feeling or emotion that agents sometimes experience after wrong or bad actions. According to John Rawls's valuable analysis of shame, it is the feeling that a person has when experiencing damage to his or her self-respect or self-esteem. How is shame distinguished from and related to guilt*? The distinction is not found in sensations but in the types of explanations offered for the feelings. If we distinguish natural shame from moral shame, the latter is explained by moral concepts. The moral concepts that explain shame and guilt come, roughly, from different parts of morality. As Rawls notes, "In general, guilt, resentment, and indignation invoke the concept of right, whereas shame, contempt, and derision appeal to the concept of goodness." In short, moral shame involves aspiration*, ideals, and supererogation*—forms of moral excellence* and goodness* that the agent attempts to attain. People who feel guilty invoke moral concepts of right and wrong* and expect their victims to be resentful and observers to be indignant; their "guilt is relieved by reparation, and the forgiveness* that permits reconciliation*." People who feel shame, or are ashamed, invoke an ideal, such as self-control, expect others to feel contempt for their shortcomings, and overcome the feeling of shame for their failures by improving in the future. Of course, the same act may evoke feelings of both guilt and shame; for example, a person may feel ashamed of a failure to control his or her anger* and guilty for hurting a friend by the outburst. In the Jewish and Christian traditions, which emphasize the commands of a personal God, guilt tends to be primary, in contrast to some Eastern traditions in which shame is primary, for example, in the "loss of face."

H. Morris (ed.), *Shame and Guilt,* 1971; G. Piers and M. Singer, *Shame and Guilt,* 1953; J. Rawls, *A Theory of Justice,* 1971; D. A. J. Richards, *A Theory of Reasons for Action,* 1971.

JAMES F. CHILDRESS

Sick, Care of the

The foundation of a Christian responsibility to care for the sick lies in the teaching and example of Jesus as portrayed in the Gospels. Among the important aspects of that healing activity are a rejection of the idea of sin as the sufficient cause of illness (John 9:1–5), an association of healing with faith or trust in God, and an affirmation that healing affects body and mind. The healing affirmed is more than a change in attitude.

Responsibility to care for the sick was focused for a time on bishops, and found institutional expression in hospices and hospitals. Priest and healer were one. Over the centuries, a clear differentiation between medical practice and religious ministry evolved. In the past century various ways of integrating the two kinds of healing have been proposed, and two kinds of bridges have been constructed.

Some have suggested that Christian life and ministry should involve medical care as a central component, and that argument has led them to suggest reforms in theological education. The importance of providing care for the sick and the idea of the physician as counselor to the patient are associated with the Clinical Pastoral Care movement, which remains influential in hospital chaplaincies and other institutional ministries in the USA. In a contrasting vein, Robert Lambourne and Michael Wilson in the UK have insisted that the churches should include persons who are ill and those who care for them as central actors in their services of worship: Medical healing should be related to the communal wholeness renewed in the eucharist. The church should be a community of healing in both a social and a medical sense.

The other tactic to bridge the gap between medicine and religion is to push for a kind of moral ethos in medicine that will be compatible with a Christian moral vision. Here, of course, there have been different interpretations of what the "Christian moral vision" involves, but the general tactic remains one of urging reforms on medicine so that dissonance between the two worlds will be minimized.

Some important stages in the American evolution of this strategy include: Joseph Fletcher's defense of personal rights* and later of utilitarianism* in *Morals and Medicine* (1954) and subsequent writings, and Paul Ramsey's insistence on "covenant fidelity" as the appropriate norm for the relationship between physician and patient. Ramsey's analysis, especially in *The Patient as Person* (1970), has been particularly influential. Two themes of note are: First, covenant* fidelity* always requires care, but care must be distinguished from cure. At the end of life care requires company and comfort; there comes a point when attempts to cure are no longer caring. Second, care is directed to the "person"* of the patient whose choices, loyalties, and integrity must be respected. Consent* can never be presumed for nontherapeutic experimentation*. Exploitation* of persons for the sake of medical progress cannot be condoned, and paternalism* becomes a major issue, logically pursued by many influenced by Ramsey.

An interesting recent discussion of the relation of Christian faith to care for the sick appears in John C. Fletcher's *Coping with Genetic Disorders* (1983). Fletcher argues that ministry to those in distress should be understood as "faithful companionship," which involves honestly being present with someone who is suffering. Care for the sick is not best described either as advocacy (for patients' rights or a course of treatment) or as being an intermediary between professional and patient. Rather, the companion shares the patient's pain.

See **Bioethics; Body; Codes of Ethics; Health and Disease, Values in Defining; Health Care, Right to; Hippocratic Oath; Hospice; Life, Prolongation of; Love; Medical Ethics; Mental Health; Mental Illness; Social Service of the Church; Suffering.**

P. Laín Entralgo, *Doctor and Patient,* ET 1969; R. Lambourne, *Community, Church and Healing,* 1963; M. Wilson, *The Church Is Healing,* 1966.

DAVID H. SMITH

Simony

The practice of buying or selling ecclesiastical preferment.

JOHN MACQUARRIE

Sin(s)

Most theological discussions of sin have concentrated on original sin*, the causal connection between Adam's first actual sin and our subsequent sin or sins; this article focuses on intentional, concrete, historical actions of individuals and groups in violation of God's will as expressed in natural law* or revealed law. "Sin is any word or deed or thought against the eternal law" (Augustine); hence sin is a religious category, however much it overlaps moral categories (*see* **Morality and Religion, Relations of**). In addition to moral transgressions, sin includes violations of God's will that do not count as moral offenses (e.g., idolatry, which is prohibited in the first table of the Decalogue*). Sin thus encompasses more than immorality. Among the several NT metaphors for sin, the terms related to *hamartia*—missing the mark or goal, especially a target or road—are the most common. The mark or goal is defined by righteousness*, expressive of and expressed by God. Various actions such as lying, murder, and adultery have been viewed as sinful.

In general, Roman Catholic moral theology has concentrated on sins, while Protestant ethics has concentrated on sin, emphasizing the broken relationship with God in mistrust and a lack of faith*. Building on the NT distinction between sins that "exclude from the kingdom of God" (e.g., 1 Cor. 6: 9–10; Gal. 5:19–21; Eph. 5:5) and sins that do not (James 3:2; 1 John 1:8; 5:16), traditional moral theology developed various classifications of sins, particularly as a guide in casuistry*, confession*, and penance*. The Council of Trent (*see* **Counter-Reformation Moral Theology**) required that all mortal sins committed after baptism be confessed according to their kind and number. Mortal sins contravene the love of God and merit eternal damnation, while venial sins, which are not necessarily trivial, do not contravene the love of God and do not merit damnation. Tradition-

ally there have been three necessary and sufficient conditions for mortal sins: agents perform gravely sinful actions with sufficient reflection and consent*. As Van Harvey (*A Handbook of Theological Terms,* 1964) notes, "the Protestant Reformers rejected the distinction between mortal and venial sins, largely because they tended to view sin as opposite to faith, not to virtue. They acknowledged that certain sins were, humanly speaking, more serious than others, but they argued that all transgressions of the law were equally damnable in the sight of God, the difference being that God pardoned the sins of believers." In recent Roman Catholic moral theology (*see* **Modern Roman Catholic Moral Theology**) the categories of mortal and venial sins have been reinterpreted in terms of the fundamental option. From this perspective the focus is on the tendency of the self in its exercise of freedom, i.e., its commitment to the life of grace or the life of sin, rather than on particular acts. Mortal sin is a state or condition, rather than a sin, and a good person may commit a serious sin without being mortally sinful. This approach fits with the effort to recapture the Thomistic emphasis (*see* **Thomistic Ethics**) on character*, virtue*, and vice*). Actual sin is distinguished from habitual sin (*see* **Habit**) or vices as settled dispositions to sin; however, the language of sins sometimes encompasses the vices, e.g., the seven deadly sins*.

Moral theology has also recognized a distinction between formal and material sin. In formal sin, the act must be deliberate and voluntary. An act may be materially wrong from an objective standpoint, but the agent may not have satisfied the conditions of responsibility* required by formal sin. Whatever language is employed, this kind of distinction is common in the analysis of immoral actions and sins, both of which violate norms (*see* **Act, Action, Agent; Deliberation; Intention**).

There are several other important issues in modern Christian discussions of sin. First, how is it possible to affirm both the universality of sin, that is, its presence in each person and act, and human responsibility for sin? (*See* **Original Sin.**) Second, what is the relation between sinful individuals, actions, and social structures? According to most interpretations of the doctrine of original sin*, sin is located in the human self rather than exclusively or even primarily in social institutions and practices. However, as liberation theology* and political theology* emphasize, social institutions and practices may make a major difference in the extent and kind of sin, even if their radical transformation will not eradicate sin. Third, what is the fundamental or root sin? Traditionally, theologians have viewed pride* as the root sin, but other sins such as sloth* have also been proposed, particularly in order to account for what Hannah Arendt described as the modern "banality of evil" and what others view as serious indifference to the plight of others. Fourth, the distinctions and relations between sins of commission and sins of omission* continue to require attention in moral theology and ethics, as does cooperation with evil*. Fifth, the theological doctrines of forgiveness* and grace*, of justification* and sanctification*, play a major role in what Christian moral theologians and ethicists say about reducing sins or sin and about diminishing their effects. Luther's emphasis on *simul justus et peccator* (simultaneously righteous and a sinner) is countered by those who recognize greater progress in the Christian life on the way to holiness* (*see* **Perfectionism**).

See **Act, Action, Agent; Confession; Evil; Free Will and Determinism; Goodness; Guilt; Innocence; Law and Gospel; Morality and Religion, Relations of; Norms; Original Sin; Remorse; Repentance; Right and Wrong; Righteousness; Sanctification; Shame; Temptation.**

G. C. Berkouwer, *Sin,* 1971; E. Brunner, *Man in Revolt,* ET 1939; J. Gaffney, *Sin Reconsidered,* 1983; B. Häring, *Sin in the Secular Age,* 1974; R. Niebuhr, *The Nature and Destiny of Man,* 2 vols., 1941–43.

                                    JAMES F. CHILDRESS

Sin of Omission *see* **Omission, Sin of**

Situation *see* **Norms; Situation Ethics**

Situation Ethics

In Protestant ethics and Roman Catholic moral theology over the last forty years, there has been widespread and vigorous debate about the place of the situation, context, or circumstances of moral actions, in relation to moral principles and rules (*see* **Norms**). This debate has often centered on proposals for "situation ethics" and "contextual ethics,"

which clearly reject legalism* and sometimes seem, at least to their critics, to reject law* too. In 1952 Pius XII condemned "situation ethics" as an individualistic and subjective appeal to the concrete circumstances of actions to justify decisions in opposition to the natural law* or God's revealed will. However, most proposals of "situation ethics" or "contextual ethics" represent serious attempts to shape moral responsibility*.

Although there are many different versions of "situation ethics," or "contextual ethics," many of its proponents hold that there is a single fundamental principle of morality such as free choice, love, obedience to the divine will, or response to divine actions, and that the agent has to discern what should be done in the immediate situation without relying on intermediate rules to connect that principle to the situation. Following are a few of the main types of "situation ethics," or "contextual ethics"; their diversity suggests the inadequacy of such general labels because they conceal major differences among these positions and their warrants.

First, existentialist ethics has sometimes concentrated on the agent's free choice* and defended antinomianism* because principles and rules lead to an inauthentic existence (*see* **Authenticity**); some of these themes appear in writings by Rudolf Bultmann and Paul Tillich (*see also* **Existentialist Ethics; Kierkegaardian Ethics**).

Second, the popularizer of the phrase "situation ethics," Joseph Fletcher, presents situation ethics as a third way between antinomianism and legalism, emphasizes the primacy of the principle of love*, and recognizes other principles and rules as mere advisers without any veto power. Principles and rules other than love are illuminative rather than prescriptive. Fletcher also translates the principle of love into the principle of utility and develops a form of act-utilitarianism that applies love (utility) directly to judgments in situations rather than to rules (*see* **Utilitarianism**). The moral quality of actions derives from their consequences (*see* **Consequentialism**); it is extrinsic rather than intrinsic. Fletcher's method of situation ethics thus involves the rational calculation of consequences rather than free choice, intuition*, conscience*, or God's command and action.

A third approach, usually discussed as a form of "contextual ethics" rather than "situation ethics" (though many use the phrases interchangeably) and defended, for different reasons, by such theologians as H. R. Niebuhr and Paul Lehmann, focuses on responding to what God is doing in the world. For example, in analyzing and recommending "contextual ethics" in the first edition of this dictionary, Lehmann sharply distinguished it from ethical relativism*, situation ethics, and ethical absolutism (*see* **Absolutes, Ethical**): "The point of departure for Christian thinking about ethics is the concrete reality in the world of a community, a koinonia*, called into being and action by Jesus of Nazareth. In this community, what God is doing in the world is clearly discerned (*see* **Discernment**) as exposing the human meaning of behavior by giving a human shape to action. God is doing in the world what it takes to make and keep human life human. . . . Thus, the koinonia is a kind of laboratory of humanization in the world." While Lehmann's contextualism concentrates on humanization as the direction of God's activity, some contextualists emphasize other directions of divine activity —e.g., God's creating, governing, and redeeming actions (H. R. Niebuhr).

A fourth approach, evident in the writings of Karl Barth, among others, also begins with God's will but focuses on his concrete commands rather than on his actions in the world (*see* **Divine Command Morality**). (For further discussion of contextualism interpreted as "relationalism," *see* **Modern Protestant Ethics**.)

These approaches to situation ethics or contextual ethics have helpfully directed attention to aspects of ethical decision-making that are sometimes neglected or downplayed. However, these approaches have been sharply criticized for overlooking other aspects that are equally important. The presuppositions and implications of their positions have been challenged on grounds of scripture, tradition, and moral experience. Although some of these criticisms and challenges apply more to some approaches than to others, they can only be stated in general terms in this article. First, whether the central category is love (as for Fletcher) or humanization (as for Lehmann), there are arguments that it requires more specific rules, such as the prohibitions of the Decalogue* (for a discussion of love and the authority of moral rules, *see* **Love**). It is inappropriate to set love or persons over against rules, since, for example, many rules are designed to pro-

tect persons* (*see* **Respect for Persons**) by establishing their rights* over against others, including rights not to be harmed or killed. Second, if principles and rules are merely illuminative and never prescriptive, the agent in the situation can never rely on them; hence, Ramsey and others argue, situation ethics tends to slip into antinomianism*. Third, some forms of situation ethics or contextual ethics presuppose human capacities of intuition*, or rational calculation of the consequences, or discernment* that may not be present or sufficient. For example, it is not clear that people can calculate, predict, or control the consequences of action as Fletcher presupposes or that Christians are transformed to discern and follow God's action as Lehmann presupposes. Some Christian doctrines about human finitude, the universality and effects of sin* (*see* **Original Sin**), and the limited effects of grace* could lead to a greater appreciation of the role of principles and rules. Furthermore, several consequentialists and utilitarians ask not which acts but which rules will probably produce the best consequences, because of the necessity of coordinating actions, developing and maintaining trust*, and reducing the dangers of self-deception* and rationalization* (*see* **Utilitarianism**). Human tendencies to interpret situations from their own standpoint and to pursue their own interests must be included in any assessment of the need for binding principles and rules. Fourth, the situation itself requires interpretation*; its boundaries in time, space, and relationships are by no means clearly defined. This interpretation or definition will involve moral principles and rules as well as theological, anthropological, and other perspectives. Fifth, actions, including their various circumstances, are not as discontinuous or as unique as some situationists suggest. They are often relevantly similar from a moral standpoint, and the principle of universalizability* requires that similar cases be treated similarly. Recognizing such similarities involves the formulation or application of a rule. Sixth, the Christian tradition has not been uniformly legalistic, and it has resources for the interpretation and application of principles and rules in situations (*see*, for example, **Casuistry; Conscience; Discernment; Prudence**).

For many Christian ethicists and moral theologians, the question is not whether there are moral principles and rules, but rather, which principles and rules apply and with what weight or strength. Many situationists and contextualists rightly criticized the limitations of a pure rule-ethics; helpfully focused on the significant differences among situations that are often inadequately captured in principles and rules; and properly challenged the content, weight, and application of some moral principles and rules. But it is one matter to reject a rule prohibiting contraception*, for example, and another to reject rules altogether.

The debate about situation or contextual ethics still persists in somewhat different language; it is now focused largely on deontological (*see* **Deontology**) versus consequentialist or teleological considerations (*see* **Consequentialism; Teleological Ethics**), or on exceptionless moral norms versus proportionate moral judgments (*see* **Proportionality**; *see also* **Double Effect; Modern Roman Catholic Moral Theology**), and it appears in discussions about applied ethics* and casuistry*. These debates frequently involve larger philosophical and theological questions about authority*, such as the role of reason (*see* **Natural Law**), scripture (*see* **Bible in Christian Ethics**), tradition (*see* **Tradition in Ethics**), and the church (*see* **Magisterium**).

See also **Christian Ethics; Love; Modern Protestant Ethics; Norms.**

H. Cox (ed.), *The Situation Ethics Debate,* 1968; R. L. Cunningham (ed.), *Situationism and the New Morality,* 1970; C. E. Curran and R. McCormick (eds.), *Readings in Moral Theology, No. 1: Moral Norms and Catholic Tradition,* 1979; J. Fletcher, *Situation Ethics,* 1966; J. M. Gustafson, *Christian Ethics and the Community,* 1971, esp. chs. 1–4; G. H. Outka and P. Ramsey (eds.), *Norms and Context in Christian Ethics,* 1968; P. Ramsey, *Deeds and Rules in Christian Ethics,* 1968; J. A. T. Robinson, *Christian Morals Today,* 1964.

JAMES F. CHILDRESS

Skeptics

Like all the Hellenistic philosophers the Skeptics sought for *ataraxia,* serenity, the untroubled mind. They found it in "a state of mental rest in which we neither deny nor affirm anything" (Sextus Empiricus, *Outlines of Pyrrhonism* 1.10).

The Skeptics held that there is absolutely nothing which is certain. A tower may look one shape from one angle, and another from another. A thing will taste sweet or bitter according to what one has eaten immediately before it. To every argument there is an equal and opposite argument (Sextus Empiricus, *Outlines* 1.12, 202). Peace will come when a person realizes this and completely suspends judgment, and is content not to know. It is, of course, true that the Skeptics held even this undogmatically, for quite clearly on this view it is not even certain that nothing is certain. The Skeptics found their peace in consenting not to know.

So the Skeptics had a series of catch phrases: "Not this more than that"; "Perhaps and perhaps not"; "Possibly, possibly not"; "Maybe and maybe not." This uncertainty issues in suspension of judgment (*epochē*), which in turn issues in *arrepsia,* equipoise, which in turn issues in *aphasia,* nonassertion. "I determine nothing," said the Skeptic (Sextus Empiricus, *Outlines* 1.188–200).

This obviously paralyzes action because the mind is never made up. To solve this, Arcesilaus held that the Skeptic acts on what is reasonable in the light of wisdom (Sextus Empiricus, *Against the Logicians* 1.158). Carneades worked out the degrees of probability that anything may have (Sextus Empiricus, *Outlines* 1.227), and formed a theory of graduated probability.

All this seems to abolish all standards and to abolish all possibility of ethics. Carneades in a notorious speech in 156 B.C. argued that there is no such thing as natural right, that law and justice are merely expedient agreements for mutual protection, and that self-interest is the real end of life. An intelligent man, he said, despises justice (Lactantius, *Institutes* 5.15, 16; Cicero, *De Republica* 3. 4.8–12; Quintilian, *Institutio Oratoria* 12. 1.35). But in point of fact the Skeptics did recognize a fourfold standard in life (Sextus Empiricus, *Outlines* 1.24). There is the guidance of nature, which makes us capable of sensation and thought. There is the tradition of custom and laws, whereby we regard piety as good and impiety as evil. There is the constraint of the appetites, which makes us eat and drink. There is the instruction of the arts. The real ethic of the Skeptics was simply convention. They lived "in accordance with the rules of life," but "quite undogmatically" (Sextus Empiricus, *Outlines* 1.21). The Skeptics practiced conventional virtue because it seemed to them that in all probability there was no other way to be happy.

We may add one more odd idea of the Skeptics. They held that God cannot possess virtue, because virtue presupposes a fault to be overcome. He alone is continent who could be incontinent. And further, virtue is something *above* its possessor, and there can be nothing above God (Sextus Empiricus, *Against the Physicists* 1.152–175).

In the end Skepticism perished because an individual cannot always remain suspended in mental space. Skepticism broke down before "the exigencies of life . . . before the fact that man is not only a spectator of reality, but a maker of it" (E. R. Bevan, *Stoics and Sceptics,* 1931, p. 141).

WILLIAM BARCLAY

Slander

Slander is the utterance or dissemination of false statements or reports concerning a person, or malicious misrepresentation of his or her actions in order to defraud or injure the person. It is evil both in its origin, since it springs from envy*, hatred*, malice*, and uncharitableness, and in its effects on those defrauded and those who listen to or read it. Sometimes slander is decided on rationally and coolly, sometimes on the spur of the moment, and both are equally blameworthy. At a lesser level there is gossip, which can easily move from a genuine interest in other people and in talking about them, through harmless curiosity about them, into a reprehensible and prying spirit that can quickly turn into the grave sin of slander. A certain self-control in talking is the chief safeguard against being led away in our speech into these evils.

See **False Witness; Lying; Truthfulness.**

RONALD PRESTON

Slavery

The form of human servitude in which persons become the property of others. The function of slavery has been to serve the economic advantage, the vanity, and the sexual lust of slave owners. It began probably when victors in battle enslaved the losers. It developed into a commercial institution in which slaves were bought and sold in local and international markets.

Slavery was practiced in many ancient societies, including those of the Bible. Biblical records include many allusions to slavery and many laws governing it (*see* **Mosaic Law**). Masters had few legal responsibilities toward their slaves and could punish them severely. Yet Israel, remembering its own slavery in Egypt, recognized moral responsibility to slaves. The slave was part of the master's household, sharing in the Sabbath rest (Ex. 20:10; 23:12) and in the religious feasts (e.g., Deut. 12:12). If the master destroyed an eye or a tooth, the slave was entitled to freedom (Ex. 21:26–27). A slave could become the heir of the master or on occasion marry the master's daughter. Sometimes a strong moral sensitivity entered into the system (Job 31:13ff.).

The NT begins with the proclamation of the kingdom of God*, which brings judgment on all human institutions*. God's kingdom is a blessing upon the poor; it means that the meek shall inherit the earth. Jesus declares the good news of release for captives and liberty for the oppressed (Luke 4:18). Thus he offers a fundamental criticism of slavery and of the whole social order in which persons are subjected to others. But in heralding the kingdom, Jesus does not prescribe new social institutions for the age that is passing.

For Paul the whole inherited meaning of slavery has been shattered by Christ. In Christ there is no distinction between bond and free (Gal. 3:28). Slave and master become brothers in Christ (Philemon). But in the expectancy of the new age, there is no effort to overthrow the public institutions of the old age, including slavery.

As the church developed within the Roman Empire, it took for granted the persistence of slavery. But a slave might become a leader, even a bishop, within the church; legal and economic status did not modify the value of persons in the community of faith.

In its early life the church was powerless to change the institutions of the Empire and, in view of its eschatological expectations, scarcely thought of doing so. When the church became established, it transferred its revolutionary impulses to otherworldly expectations and sought to ameliorate rather than overturn prevailing social institutions. The church itself, inheriting pagan properties, became a slaveholder. Augustine declared that slavery was a consequence of sin —a radical departure from Aristotle's teaching that some people were born to be slaves. But this doctrine had the effect of conditioning Christians to expect the persistence of slavery until the distant consummation of the kingdom of God.

In European history slavery gradually gave way, partly under the influence of Christianity, to serfdom. The feudal order established inequality as inherent in the natural and divine order, but it departed from slavery by affirming moral obligations on all levels of the hierarchy. However, the exploration of Africa and the colonizing of America produced a huge slave trade, commercializing the institution on a scale never known before. Increasingly the humanitarian spirit, both in Christianity and in the Enlightenment, became critical of slavery. The Congress of Vienna (1814–15) brought an end to the slave trade among the European powers. Slavery itself then declined.

In the USA, where slavery remained economically profitable in the South, a struggle of conscience ensued. The ethos of the Declaration of Independence, with its affirmations of liberty and equality, conflicted with the institution of slavery, creating what Gunnar Myrdal called "the American dilemma." Christians used the Bible both to attack and to defend slavery. It is no defense of slavery to point out that recent scholarship has shown the remarkable cultural and religious strength that emerged among the slaves. The Civil War ended slavery (Emancipation Proclamation, 1863; Thirteenth Amendment, 1865), but the nation still suffers its bitter legacy.

In the following years slavery ended throughout most of the world. But in parts of Africa and Asia it has persisted well into the 20th century.

Both moral and economic impulses have contributed to the obsolescence of slavery. Morally the idea of liberty* and human dignity* has undermined the traditional ideologies that justified slavery. Economically, the drudgery once performed by people is increasingly the work of machines, which have become for many purposes the slaves in industrial societies.

See **Colonialism; Equality; Freedom; Human Rights; Justice; Race Relations; Racism; Respect for Persons.**

D. B. Davis, *The Problem of Slavery in Western Culture,* 1966; I. Mendelsohn, *Slavery in the Ancient Near East,* 1949; A. J. Raboteau, *Slave Religion: The "Invisible Institution" in*

the Antebellum South, 1978; E. Troeltsch, *The Social Teaching of the Christian Churches* (1912), 2 vols., ET 1931.

ROGER L. SHINN

Slippery Slope Argument *see* Wedge Argument, Slippery Slope Argument, etc.

Sloth

Traditionally one of the seven deadly sins*, sloth is indeed an isolating condition, cutting people off from receptiveness. Moralists have emphasized it variously in different centuries. Proverbs (e.g., 6:6–11) is eloquent against the sluggard. The NT has a recurring theme of wakefulness (e.g., Mark 13:35–37; Rom. 12: 11; Eph. 5:14; 1 Thess. 5:4–8).

Aquinas took up the concept of accidie (torpor), analyzing it as spiritual apathy, contrary to joy in God. Since the Reformation, sloth has been deplored as the opposite of zeal. "I take it for granted," declared William Law, "that every Christian that is in health is up early in the morning" (*A Serious Call to a Devout and Holy Life,* ch. 14). Puritans denounced laziness; the virtues of "industry" came into their own. Today the wider idea of accidie* is revived, emphasizing rather the attitude of "couldn't care less" as truly a deadly sin.

Thomas Aquinas, *ST* II-II.35; W. Beach and H. R. Niebuhr (eds.), *Christian Ethics: Sources of the Living Tradition,* 1955, ch. 10.

HELEN OPPENHEIMER

Smoking *see* Tobacco, Use of

Social Class

A multidimensional concept that is usually measured in terms of the following indexes: occupation, income, style of life, prestige (status), interaction patterns, and power. Confusion often arises from the fact that these dimensions of social placement are relatively autonomous and sometimes even contradictory. A change in occupation may mean a rise in status but not in income, and power may be exercised by individuals whose prestige, life-style, and social interaction pattern is not at all "high." Nevertheless the concept of social class is a conceptual device that enables analysts to make useful generalizations about identifiable groups and the attitudinal or behavioral characteristics they are likely to exhibit.

We might think of social class as a constellation of attributes that can be contained in a circle drawn around points on several continua representing the six indexes referred to above.

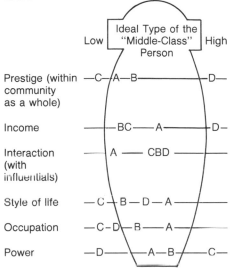

	Low	Ideal Type of the "Middle-Class" Person	High
Prestige (within community as a whole)	—C—A—B——————D—
Income	——BC——A————D—
Interaction (with influentials)	—— A —— CBD ——————
Style of life	—C—B—D—A————
Occupation	—C-D—B——A————
Power	—D——————A—B——C—

A An apolitical lawyer who deals mainly with low-income clients.
B Son of a highly respected pillar of the community who runs the once-important family business that is now in decline.
C A blue-collar worker who plays a leadership role in a strong union.
D A farm boy who is a popular country and western singer.

A class would be composed of the individuals (indicated by letters) who fall within the circle on the above diagram. Since it can be shown that many persons do in fact fall within this circle, it can logically be claimed that there is such a thing as a "middle class" in the sense that it may be useful to refer to the individuals sharing the indicated characteristics under one rubric. So long as the circumscribed meaning of the ideal type is explained, it can be asserted that A and B are middle-class, but it would be misleading to say that of C and D, except "in regard to."

Normative thought is usually concerned with social class in one of two ways: the concept is employed to justify economic and status inequalities (and to persuade people not to be troubled by them), or it is utilized to identify and criticize injustices that are regarded as remediable. W. Lloyd Warner (whose six-category typology of upper-upper through lower-lower classes dominated popular literature on the subject in America for many years) and Robert Ardrey are exemplars of the first tendency. Warner emphasizes subjective community opinion about relative prestige and offers his theory as "a corrective instrument which will permit men and women better to evaluate their social situations and thereby adapt themselves to social reality and fit their dreams and aspirations to what is possible." Ardrey declares that the social contract is nothing more nor less than acceptance of one's place in the pecking order of the society in which one lives.

Social philosophers of both Marxist and liberal persuasion usually fall into the other camp. Marxists view class stratification as an objective economic and political condition which ought to impel the lower orders to revolt in the name of justice and humanity (but which is hidden from them by false consciousness). John Rawls is willing to tolerate absolute inequality (and the sense of relative deprivation that accompanies it) so long as the least advantaged citizens are better off than they would otherwise be, and so long as equality of opportunity prevails.

See **Marxist Ethics.**

R. Bendix and S. M. Lipset (eds.), *Class, Status and Power*, 1966; E. Burns (ed.), *A Handbook of Marxism*, 1970; R. Dahrendorf, *Class and Class Conflict in Industrial Society*, 1959; H. Gans, *More Equality*, 1973; R. K. Merton, *Social Theory and Social Structure*, 1968.

HENRY CLARK

Social Contract

This has been a recurring conception in the history of philosophy, to account for the origins of society and for the fundamental nature of obligation. The theory of a social contract has taken many forms. All of them begin from the idea of an original individualism*, in which each human being lived for himself or herself, though some writers (Rousseau) thought of this primitive state as a happy one, while others (Hobbes) regarded the primeval anarchy as a miserable existence. In any case, the individuals agreed to surrender some of their "natural rights," and thus society and social obligation were born. One should not press the question of his-

toricity too much here, for, like the story of the fall of humanity, this is a parable rather than a historical account. It is open to various objections. Can one properly speak of "natural rights"* or of any kind of rights without corresponding duties? But if rights and duties are correlative, there is no presocial condition of humanity, either chronologically or logically. This points to the main weakness of the theory, namely, that it thinks of human beings as "naturally" individualistic. A modern version of something like the social contract theory was put forward by Freud to account for the origins of religion and morality. In *A Theory of Justice* (1971) John Rawls draws on the contractarian tradition to develop principles of justice*.
See **Contract.**

JOHN MACQUARRIE

Social Ethics

The term usually refers to normative ethical reflection that focuses upon social structures, processes, and communities, especially those that are large and complex, such as government, economic life, or international politics. It can also refer descriptively to socially shared patterns of moral judgment and behavior. In a fundamental sense all ethics are social, because human beings are by nature social. The discipline of Christian ethics stresses people's mutual belongingness under God and their responsibility for one another in society. Any effort to establish boundary lines between social ethics and what one might call individual or interpersonal ethics is artificial. Sexual ethics, for example, might appear to be interpersonal rather than social, yet sexual life is strongly influenced by its sociocultural context and in turn has a significant impact upon that context. If one avoids the suggestion that any dimension of morality is nonsocial, the term "social ethics" represents a valuable focus within the field of ethics (*see* **Personal Ethics**).

That focus requires attention to much more than how individuals should respond to social institutions and processes, though that is part of its concern. For one thing, it necessitates inquiry into how given social contexts shape and direct moral selfhood and moral action. This is partly a question of what one can reasonably expect to happen. A social context influences the perspectives and incentives of individuals acting within it, so that,

for example, one would not ordinarily be surprised if a corporate executive, labor union officer, or government leader supported the policies of his or her institution.

How social contexts shape morality is also partly a question of the range of one's moral responsibility. The occupants of any institutional office have special responsibility to and for those who will be especially affected by their decisions, whether it be the responsibility of a school principal in relation to teachers, students, and the wider community, or of a prime minister in relation to the populace of a nation and closely affected nations.

It is, furthermore, a question of what constitutes right action. In Christian ethics this is shaped not only by one's identity as a member of the Christian community but also to some extent by the circumstances within which one acts. Moral judgments about the policies of nation-states, for example, need to take into account the absence of any overarching governmental authority in international politics. Similarly, the moral significance of saving money varies, depending upon whether the relevant context is a family, a corporation, or a nation-state.

For such reasons, special attention is given in social ethics to what policies and practices institutions should follow, and not only to how individuals should behave within the framework of existing policies and practices. If one wishes to help the poor and the hungry, the economic behavior of large institutions is far more likely to affect them for good or ill than the uncoordinated efforts of individuals acting on their own. From such concerns as these, Christian ethicists have traditionally given attention to questions of an institution's proper purposes in society, right means in the pursuit of these purposes, and the nature of the common good (*see* **Institution**).

Christian moral teachings have always included concern about moral responsibility in political, economic, and other social relationships. In recent times, with the aid of advances in the social sciences, Christian theologians have given far more attention to such socioethical subjects and have tended to become more specialized within that inquiry.

E. Brunner, *The Divine Imperative,* ET 1937, bk. III; S. Hauerwas, *A Community of Character: Toward a Constructive Christian Social*

Ethic, 1981; R. Niebuhr, *Faith and Politics,* ed. R. H. Stone, 1968; R. L. Shinn, *Forced Options: Social Decisions for the Twenty-first Century,* 1982.

                                    JOSEPH L. ALLEN

Social Gospel

Nineteenth-century American Protestant social ethics* were deeply influenced by the theories and practices of individualism*, which often made it difficult for the churches to come to terms with the consequences of the Industrial Revolution. As some of the unfortunate human consequences of the concentration of economic power, of the unequal distribution of wealth, and of the growth of vast cities became clearer, certain Christians challenged the widely accepted identification of Christian faith with individualistic philosophies. In the late 19th and early 20th centuries, social Christian movements that based their approach on the message of the prophets and the teachings of Jesus, and that also drew on the insights of the developing historical and social sciences, appeared in most Western countries. In the USA, the social Christian movement developed conservative, progressive, and radical forms. Of these the progressive, mildly reformist, moderate, and generally middle-class wing was the most significant in its time, and to this movement the name "social gospel" is generally given. The social gospel was shaped in the closing decades of the 19th century, mostly by those of evangelical liberal theological premises who had accepted biblical criticism and evolutionary theories, and who were informed religiously by Ritschlian "kingdom of God" theology and socially by the progressive movement. The social gospel had wide influence in American Protestantism from about 1890 to the 1940s.

Washington Gladden (1836–1918), for over thirty years liberal Congregational pastor in Columbus, Ohio, and author of many books on social themes, has often been called the father of the social gospel. The leading prophet of the movement was Walter Rauschenbusch (1861–1918), who first confronted the social question in a forceful way as pastor of a German Baptist church on the edge of New York's "Hell's Kitchen." The social gospel gained a considerable following in Congregational, Baptist, Methodist, Episcopal, and Presbyterian churches, especially in the North, and was conspicuous in the movement for cooperative Christianity, particularly as seen in the formation of the Federal Council of Churches in 1908.

Certain key ideas, rooted in liberal theology, were characteristic of the social gospel. For their authority its leaders looked to the historical Jesus as they believed he could be known through scholarly methods. The principles of Jesus were put forward as reliable guides for personal and social life in any age. Preachers of the social gospel explained that at the very center of Jesus' message was the doctrine of the kingdom of God*, which they understood to be a historical possibility that would soon come on earth in some fullness and bring with it social harmony and the elimination of gross injustices. Though some proclaimers of the coming kingdom were more cautious than others, the high sense of expectancy in the early arrival of a more ideal social order gave the social gospel movement a utopian cast. There was also great stress on the immanence of God, though the divine transcendence was not denied. God was seen to be at work in the regular processes of nature and history, progressively working out the divine purposes. Thus the social gospel believed heartily in *progress*, but did not usually refer to it as inevitable or automatic, for it was seen as conditional upon human response to divine leading. The social gospel estimate of human potentialities was high, however; in most cases it was affirmed that humans could be educated to make the right choices and so contribute to the coming of God's kingdom on earth.

The social gospel's "ethics of the kingdom of God" put great emphasis on the law of love*. God who is love works in and through persons toward the kingdom of love, a cooperative commonwealth in which socialized and enlightened humanity will work for the good of all. Sin was considered primarily to be selfishness, but humans can be educated to prefer social good to private advantage. The social gospel was sensitive to the facts of the corporate transmission of sin through human institutions*, yet believed that social salvation would come as both institutions and individuals came under the law of love. Through determined moral effort, people can hasten the day of the kingdom's coming; through self-sacrifice, the Christian can be a hero of the coming dawn.

The practical ethical concerns of the social gospel focused around economic issues, especially on the relations between capital and labor. The right of labor to organize in the struggle for recognition and justice was forthrightly upheld, but as democracy was extended into the industrial order it was affirmed that cooperation would replace competition and strife. The "Social Creed of the Churches," as affirmed by the Federal Council of Churches in 1912, declared that the churches must stand for the principles of conciliation and arbitration in industrial dissension, for the abolition of child labor, for the reduction of the hours of labor, for a living wage as a minimum standard in every industry, for the most equitable division of the products of industry as can ultimately be devised, and for the abatement of poverty.

Much social gospel thought was pacifistic, especially in its later phases between the two world wars. In the 1930s and 1940s the movement was sharply criticized by Reinhold Niebuhr and others who challenged its view of human nature as being overoptimistic and its strategy of preaching and pronouncement as naive. The social gospel era passed, but a deeper awareness of social realities and a lasting concern for social justice persisted in Protestant social ethics.
See also **Realism.**

R. T. Handy (ed.), *The Social Gospel in America, 1870–1920,* 1966; H. F. May, *Protestant Churches and Industrial America,* 1949; R. C. White, Jr., and C. H. Hopkins, *The Social Gospel: Religion and Reform in Changing America,* 1976.

ROBERT T. HANDY

Social Justice *see* Justice; Official Roman Catholic Social Teaching

Social Service of the Church

The basis of individual and corporate Christian social service appears in part in Jesus' depiction (Matt. 25:31–46) of the King's welcome to the righteous as "blessed"* inheritors of the kingdom: "For I was hungry and you gave me food, I was thirsty and you gave me drink, I was a stranger and you welcomed me, I was naked and you clothed me, I was sick and you visited me, I was in prison and you came to me." In response to their question about when they did all this to him, the King will answer, "Truly, I say to you, as you did it to one of the least of these my brethren, you did it to me." This theme also appears in the parable of the good Samaritan (Luke 10:29–37) and in James's interpretation of the relation of faith and works (James 1:27; 2:14–17; see also Heb. 13:1–3). Much of this social service has aimed at the needs of Christians (see Acts 4:32), but it has also involved individual and corporate actions to benefit others, for example, in the monastic movement (*see* **Neighbor; New Testament Ethics; Johannine Ethics; Monastic Ethics; Patristic Ethics**).

Churches have been involved in many different patterns of social service. When the state, society, and church have been intertwined, the church has sometimes been the state's agent in social welfare. As Martin Marty has noted, "For centuries, Catholics and Protestants had built, run and financed the hospitals and charitable institutions—but usually through their alliance with the state, as most churches were governmentally subsidized." The process of differentiation between state and society and within the society between the church and other social institutions changed the nature of the problem, as did the disaffection of large numbers of people from the church. Both of these processes can be viewed as part of the secularization* of society. With the Industrial Revolution* and urbanization*, major human problems emerged and were often discussed under the heading of the "social question." Out of compassion* religious groups, both directly and indirectly, attempted to meet these new and urgent needs.

Although the process of secularization reduced the churches' control over some social services, Talcott Parsons and others have argued that society was "Christianized" insofar as it institutionalized certain norms of Christian action in the welfare state*. According to D. D. Raphael, "the gradual extension of the scope of rights means that the concept of justice gradually takes over what formerly came under the concept of charity." The decline in the use of the phrase "social question" suggests that an "answer" was found. In fact, debates still continue about the appropriate answer, especially about the appropriate lines between justice* and claims of rights*, on the one hand, and compassion* and charity* as expressions of voluntary individual and corporate activity, on the other (*see also* **Capitalism; Laissez-faire; Socialism**).

Where the welfare state does not exist or is severely limited, the role for the churches' social services is correspondingly greater. But however the line is drawn, it is doubtful that the state could meet all fundamental human needs. Not only will there be holes in the social safety net, but some needs may not be covered adequately or at all. Furthermore, churches and various voluntary associations* are often able to respond in ways not open to state bureaucracies. Various mixes of private and public social services can coexist in the same society. In some social services, the private sector is primary or exclusive; in others, it plays a major role, sometimes with public funds and subsidies; in still others, its role is minor (e.g., corrections). The public share comes from taxes, while the rest comes mainly from private charity* and philanthropy*, especially by religious bodies, communities, and foundations.

Both ethical and practical questions emerge. (1) What is the appropriate mix of public and private? Charity sometimes demeans recipients, who prefer to assert their rights. (2) What is the proper balance between two legitimate concerns of love*: aiding victims and reforming structures? (See **Liberation Theology; Revolution.**) (3) How can *instrumental* actions be combined with *expressive* actions? Sometimes victims are viewed mainly as occasions for the expression of love, and the effectiveness of different responses is not adequately assessed. Thus, critics contend that the churches' social services are simplistic and, in some instances, even counterproductive (see **Compassion; Philanthropy**). (4) When should churches adopt bureaucratic approaches to social services? It is not possible to equate bureaucratic and personalistic approaches with public and private approaches respectively, for the church itself must sometimes develop bureaucratic structures in order to increase its effectiveness and efficiency in loving actions. (5) What is the proper balance of responses to material needs and to spiritual needs? Evangelicals (see **Evangelical Ethics**) insist on a major spiritual component in their social service, while some other groups neglect or shun it. This question also connects with questions about whether to provide services directly or indirectly and about modes of cooperation with secular groups that do not share Christian beliefs. (6) Which human needs should receive priority when resources

are scarce? (7) What are the best mechanisms for participation by recipients in identifying and weighing their needs? (8) When there are disputes between givers and receivers about the relevant needs and their priorities, whose interpretation and evaluation should prevail? When should love become paternalistic (see **Paternalism**) and override the *wishes* of "victims" in order to meet their *needs*?

See several other articles on specific social services: **Aging, Care of the; Almsgiving; Care; Children; Counseling; Handicapped, Care of the; Health Care, Right to; Hospice; Hospitality; Hunger, World; Orphans; Poverty; Sick, Care of the; Race Relations; Refugees; Widows.** *See also* **Charity; Ecclesiology and Ethics; Ecumenical Movement; Institution/Institutionalization; Liberation Theology; Love; Official Roman Catholic Social Teaching; Philanthropy; Voluntary Associations.**

JAMES F. CHILDRESS

Socialism

It is no easier to give an objective account of the essence of socialism than to do the same for Christianity. Neither is amenable to neat definition. On the one hand, socialism is an ideal, a vision of a day when equality, justice, fraternity, and liberty will all find full expression in society. On the other hand, socialism is a set of policies or institutions calculated to initiate and maintain such a society. In particular there is usually an emphasis on the common control or ownership of the means of production, distribution, and exchange. There is much disagreement as to whether ownership is necessary for control, whether control or ownership of only one sector of the economy is enough, and whether the common interest can best be expressed through the state or in other ways. The term socialism is often used interchangeably with communism*; or, in some types of Marxist thought, as a stage on the way to a Communist society.

Among early instances of socialist experiments, the so-called "apostolic communism" of the Jerusalem church (Acts 2:44–47; 4:32–5:11), the monastic life-style of Plato's Guardians, and the Levellers and Diggers in 17th-century England are often mentioned. These suggest that there is a perennial attractiveness in the socialist vision, particularly for Christians, but they have no contribution to make to the framing of socialist policies or institutions in the modern world. Indeed, although one may trace socialist ideas from roots in classical philosophy and the Judeo-Christian tradition, and much modern socialist thought stems from Rousseau, the term itself first came into common use referring to the "utopian socialists" of the early 19th century such as Robert Owen (1771–1858), Charles Fourier (1772–1837), and Henri de Saint-Simon (1760–1825). Through writings and experiments in community living they maintained and developed a socialist vision and made a significant protest against the injustices of their society. But they were politically and economically marginal, and did not engage with the structures of political power. With some justice Engels said of them: "To one and all socialism is the expression of absolute truth, reason and justice; it needs but to be discovered in order to conquer the world by the virtue of its own strength." Their socialism had a timeless quality and was not rooted in detailed and careful economic analysis.

What has been called "scientific" socialism began to emerge in the work of Saint-Simon, but Marx and Engels claimed to have made a science out of socialism by placing it on solid ground rather than dreams and speculations. The key idea is expressed neatly by Durkheim: "Society cannot become industrial unless industry is socialized. This is how industrialism logically ends in socialism." Marx's great work was a minutely detailed analysis and critique of capitalist society, in which he saw the seeds of the future socialist society germinating and sprouting. There is today a vigorous debate under way about the interpretation of Marx's thought (see **Marxist Ethics**). One school sees in Marx's early humanistic and moral writings the key to the understanding of his thought; the other regards these writings as a false start and regards Marx's real contribution as his mature writings in which he "established a new *science:* the science of the history of 'social formations' " (Althusser). Of the many variants of Marxist thought three deserve mention here: Stalinism was a simplified, rigid, and dogmatic version of Marxism which became the ruling ideology of the USSR and its satellites under Stalin's regime; Maoism, which emphasized the role of the peasantry as the agents of revolution and asserted that contradictions and thus change will continue even in a Communist society; and the visionary Marxism of Ernst Bloch (1885–1977), with its strong emphasis on a secular eschatological hope, which has had considerable influence on theologians.

The alternative, non-Marxist, strand of socialist thought is often called social democracy and sees socialism as compatible with liberal democracy*. It often has close historical and present links with Christianity—British socialism has been said to owe more to Methodism than to Marxism. A characteristic form of social democracy is Fabianism (the Fabian Society was founded in 1884), which has little systematic theory but seeks a range of detailed reforms ("gas and water socialism"), is nonrevolutionary ("the necessity of gradualness"), and attempted to effect change constitutionally by influencing the administrative and political elites. Social democracy believes that capitalism has changed and that socialist values may be substantially realized within a mixed economy in which the market is regulated in the public interest and there is provision for hardship and progress toward a more equal form of society in some form of welfare state*. The influence of John Maynard Keynes (1883–1946) upon modern social democracy is profound, and the collapse of the Keynesian consensus in the Western nations has led to a major crisis for social democracy. Many contemporary social democratic thinkers like C. A. R. Crosland (1918–1977) eschew Marxist theory and see socialism as essentially the pursuit of equality*, although there is considerable ambiguity in their understanding of that term.

There is a long history of interaction between Christianity and socialism. English Christian Socialism was founded in the mid-19th century by F. D. Maurice, J. M. Ludlow, and Charles Kingsley and has been carried on in a variety of groups and societies until today. Some of these Christian Socialists mainly opposed capitalism's emphasis on self-interest and competition. On the continent of Europe there has been an ongoing dialogue between theology and socialist ideas which profoundly influenced the thought of many major theologians, most notably Karl Barth and Paul Tillich. Since the death of Stalin and the rediscovery of the thought of the young Marx, more open discussion has been possible between Christianity and Marxism, and a greater awareness on both sides that, despite Marxism's explicit atheism, there are many common concerns. Thus, much recent theology has seen Marxism as an essential and challenging dialogue partner. The influence of Marxism upon Latin American liberation theology* is profound, and many liberation theologians adopt Marxist social analysis and see Marxism as a constructive corrective to distortions in Christian understanding and praxis.

See **Capitalism; Collectivism; Property.**

J. Bentley, *Between Marx and Christ,* 1982; R. N. Berki, *Socialism,* 1975; L. Kolakowski, *Main Currents of Marxism,* 3 vols., ET 1978; J. Miguez-Bonino, *Christians and Marxists,* ET 1976; R. H. Preston, *Church and Society in the Late Twentieth Century,* 1983.

DUNCAN B. FORRESTER

Society

In Ferdinand Tönnies's famous discussion of *Gemeinschaft* (community*) and *Gesellschaft* (society), society is the type of associational organization and impersonal human contact characteristic of the modern industrial world. Society "is conceived as mere coexistence of people independent of each other," who relate to one another only because it is in their interest to relate segmentally in particular areas of life where they are, for utilitarian reasons, interdependent. Apart from "transactions" there would be no "common values," and the latter would disappear when the former had been concluded. Max Weber stressed society's rationalization of all productive energies in the laws and regularized procedures that make bureaucratic institutions so different from traditional collectivities and legal-rational authority so different from traditional or charismatic authority.

Social analysis rooted in the ideal typification of "community" and "society" yielded an abundance of insights, but both concepts were never more than heuristic devices that could mislead as well as guide. The unprecedented pace of technological, social, and cultural change in the 20th century soon led to the development of more highly differentiated typologies. One of the most important is that of William Kornhauser, whose discussion of the distinguishing characteristics of totalitarian, pluralistic, and mass societies (in addition to traditional society, which is roughly equivalent to Tönnies's *Gemeinschaft*) has achieved widespread acceptance. In a *totalitarian* society (see **Totalitarian State**) the state employs propaganda, infor-

mants, the secret police, the courts, and even the health care system to suppress deviance of all kinds. A *pluralistic* society (see **Pluralism**) has many intermediate groups (such as labor unions, voluntary associations, and political parties or relatively independent coalitions of constituencies with mobile allegiances) that give vital expression to the interests of all major segments of the population and inspire a sense of legitimacy among the citizens. *Mass* society contains atomized masses who no longer feel adequately represented by intermediate groups and no longer acknowledge the authority of stable elites; therefore, the health of the body politic is endangered by apathy and attendant vulnerability to manipulation by demagogues who know how to use the mass media to exploit the anxieties, prejudices, and frustrated aspirations of the citizenry.

Establishment social analysts usually maintain that contemporary America is a healthy pluralistic society in which representative democracy functions reasonably well under the protection of a relatively free press. Critics such as Herbert Marcuse or Bertram Gross are less sanguine: they contend that it is already a "one dimensional society" in which various forms of surplus-repression and oppression are masked by modern forms of "bread and circuses," or that we are clearly headed toward a "friendly fascism" that will be justified by propaganda and made palatable by the distraction of "mass culture." Neoconservatives distinguish between totalitarian societies and those which are merely *authoritarian* (i.e., those which snuff out political dissent while allowing economic and cultural freedom), but this distinction is regarded as an ideological ploy by most observers.

Typologies that are advanced as purely analytical usually have, or are given, a normative thrust. Thus the *Gemeinschaft-Gesellschaft* schema is frequently used as a means to bemoan the anonymity, rootlessness, and anomie* of modern urban life. Yet admirers of the benefits of technological abundance and pluralism have not been bashful about pointing out the advantages of the "secular city" and the "I-You" relationships which it fosters, the argument being that *"Stadt Luft macht frei"*—that urban life is liberating in a very pervasive and profoundly humanizing sense. Daniel Bell even went so far as to assert that the concept of "mass society" serves as a romantic ideology of protest against modernity that is second only to Marxism as a sentimental illusion of intellectuals.

But the most important normative use of the concept of "society" is in opposition to "individual," and in that connection what Emile Durkheim said long ago about a misconceived and excessive individualism as "the great sickness of the modern age" may be more pertinent than ever before. Many contemporary ethicists would agree with Robert Bellah and William Sullivan in their contention that liberal social philosophy as propounded by John Locke and Adam Smith is bankrupt. So long as the political community is viewed as nothing more than an artificial construct designed to serve the interests of individuals, so long as covenant bonds are neglected and demeaned by exclusive reliance on contract, and so long as the acquisitive instrumentalism of individuals is not restrained and guided by a sense of civic virtue, justice cannot flourish and even order may disintegrate into something akin to a war of all against all.

P. Blau, *The Dynamics of Bureaucracy,* 1953; J. Habermas, *Legitimation Crisis,* ET 1975; W. Kornhauser, *The Politics of Mass Society,* 1959; M. Olson, *The Logic of Collective Action,* rev. ed. 1971; F. Tönnies, *Community and Society* (1887), ET 1957; M. Weber, *The Theory of Social and Economic Organization* (1922), ET 1947.

HENRY CLARK

Sociobiology *see* **Aggression; Evolutionary Ethics; Psychology and Ethics; Science and Ethics**

Sociology of Ethics

This discipline is concerned with analyzing ethics and the processes of moral decision-making as social phenomena. The priorities given to particular ethical notions, approaches, and legitimations differ from one age to another and from one culture to another. A perspective based on the sociology of knowledge would suggest that these changes can be analyzed in terms of changing social contexts. Viewed in these terms, ethics, like any other cognitive enterprise or human activity, can be analyzed in terms of the social factors that have shaped it. Alternatively, ethical notions, approaches, or legitimations can be analyzed in terms of their

own possible influence upon particular societies. In either instance, ethics is regarded as a "social reality," as a phenomenon shaped by social determinants or itself shaping other social realities. Of course it is not necessary to assume from this that ethics is "only a social reality" or that it is to be understood only in wholly relativist or nominalist terms. It is sufficient to make a connection between social structures and ethics, either at the level of individual moral decision-making or at that of overall ethical notions. This applies equally to ethics in general, to religious ethics, or to specifically Christian ethics.

It has been a commonplace of polemics to claim that moral viewpoints that differ from one's own result from distorting social factors. And, indeed, there is nothing unfamiliar about the observation of ethical pluralism and its connection with cultural pluralism (*see* **Pluralism**). Much Greek philosophy was fully aware of this. But Marx and Engels's *The German Ideology* of 1846 (ET 1965) is often regarded as the first systematic modern attempt to make a serious connection between social structures and cognitive realms, such as that of ethics, and thus to propose the social determinants of the latter. Reacting sharply against contemporary Hegelianism, they argued that "morality, religion and metaphysics" were merely socially structured forms of ideology*, reflecting a wrongly conceived division between mental and material behavior and, in turn, a division between the privileged rulers over and against the disprivileged ruled. Using these insights in a less value-laden manner, others since have sought to show that a sociology of knowledge can be successfully applied to ethics as a cognitive discipline.

Cultural anthropologists, in particular, have attempted to demonstrate various connections between particular cultures and social structures and the ethical notions present in them. Malinowski's pioneer work is particularly important in this respect (see further, Max Gluckman's *On the Diversity of Morals,* 1956). Among recent sociologists, the Polish sociologist Maria Ossowska has drawn heavily upon them and upon the pioneer sociological work of Weber and Durkheim, to map out the social determinants of moral ideas. She points out, for example, that at the beginning of the Industrial Revolution in Britain, lifelong, monogamous marriage would entail, on the average, a couple being together for some seventeen years, whereas today it would entail some forty years: "The present duration of marriage is a function not only of longevity but also of the fact that people marry earlier. Both these factors make the requirement of strict fidelity much more demanding" (*Social Determinants of Moral Ideas*, p. 36). Among the social determinants that she examines are demographic factors, such as age, sex, and mobility, urban-rural factors, industrialization, economic and social-class factors, political and personal factors, and even "the mutual knowledge at the disposal of the group" within which the moral agent lives. The British sociologist John H. Barnsley uses, in addition, more statistically based data. He concludes his study with a discussion of ethical relativism*, which he believes is not a unified phenomenon, but which does itself have moral consequences: for example, "it might reasonably be thought that the evidence of cultural relativism invites us to treat undeveloped societies in less cavalier, or exploitative, a fashion than was once common, and which in certain areas still persists, and to recognize that these societies comprise distinct ways of life, and ways of thought, *sui generis,* and not merely inferior versions of our own" (*The Social Reality of Ethics*, p. 357). The exploration of the moral consequences of sociological methods and of values actually implicit within sociology itself is forming a growing, but distinct, field of study.

Within both comparative religious ethics* and Christian ethics there is a growing interest in sociological methods. The work of Little and Twiss in comparative religious ethics ably demonstrates that sociological analysis can help to distinguish empirically between various types of argument—moral, religious, and legal—that might otherwise be conflated. And in Christian ethics Gustafson, in particular, has shown that he is well aware of the various social determinants that have contributed to the evident pluralism within the discipline and within differing ecclesiastical responses to moral issues. The dilemmas over contraception and abortion within Roman Catholicism in the 1960s and over nuclear weapons within many churches in the 1980s have highlighted this pluralism.

However, it is the seminal work of Max Weber which has proved to be one of the most fruitful resources in this discipline. It was he *par excellence* who suggested that ethical notions might be socially influential as well as socially determined. His work on the social significance of ethical notions is dominated by his so-called Protestant-ethic thesis, which he developed first in his *The Protestant Ethic and the Spirit of Capitalism* in 1905 (ET 1930) and subsequently in a number of studies on world religions, culminating in his posthumously published *The Sociology of Religion* (1922; ET 1963). In these works he sought to show that certain ethical notions such as thrift, hard work, and honesty were instrumental in the rise of Western capitalism and had particular roots in popularly perceived Calvinism. More specifically, he believed that (whatever other social factors were also responsible) the shift in religious consciousness that occurred at the Reformation had indirect repercussions upon people's attitudes toward "asceticism"* (becoming more this-worldly rather than merely a monastic virtue) and toward the morality of work (rigid predestinarianism forced individuals to search for signs of their salvation, both in their work and in their lives generally) (*see* **Calvinist Ethics**). Without claiming that this shift in moral consciousness was either intended by Calvin or Luther or necessarily religiously based in the continued maintenance of capitalism, he did regard it as an important means for understanding the social function of ethical and religious notions. It has continued to interest sociologists of religion in particular, and has inspired considerable research into continuing differences between Catholic and Protestant attitudes toward work and, more recently, toward unemployment. Whatever its merits or demerits as an explanation of the rise of capitalism, it does still provide a startling and intriguing possibility that ethical notions can be socially significant. It is a suggestion that might be applied fruitfully to the social function of ethical notions in present-day communism or those in Western laissez-faire liberalism.

See also **Anthropology and Ethics; Comparative Religious Ethics.**

J. H. Barnsley, *The Social Reality of Ethics,* 1972; R. Gill, *The Social Context of Theology,* 1975; and *Theology and Social Structure,* 1977; J. A. Gustafson, *Protestant and Roman Catholic Ethics,* 1979; D. Little and S. B. Twiss, *Comparative Religious Ethics,* 1978; A. C. MacIntyre, *Secularization and*

Moral Change, 1967; M. Ossowska, *Social Determinants of Moral Ideas,* 1970.

ROBIN GILL

Socratic Ethics

The question of the historical Socrates is only a little more complex than that of the historical Jesus. And even if we refuse (against the views of the late Professors Burnet and Taylor) to allow that the "theory of ideas" developed in Plato's middle dialogues is part of Socrates' teaching, we have still to face the issue of the contradiction between the likeness of Socrates discernible in Plato's earlier dialogues, including the *Apology,* and that presented by Xenophon in his *Memorabilia.* In the latter work Socrates is represented as virtually identifying the good with the useful, and although we must not underestimate the utilitarian element in Plato's earlier dialogues, it is hard to reconcile such a presentation of Socrates' central emphasis with, for instance, the figure in the *Apology* who, at his trial, defends himself against the suggestion that he is a Sophist by insisting that while the Sophists taught rhetoric for money, he engaged in dialogue with his fellow citizens under a religious imperative. It was Apollo whose oracle at Delphi had declared Socrates to be the wisest man in Greece, and it was because he found the deliverance incredible that Socrates had felt it necessary, out of respect for the god, to put it to the test, learning in consequence that in this alone he was superior to his fellows, that he knew his own ignorance.

It is in the *Charmides* that Socrates distinguishes his conception of self-knowledge from that of the Sophists, with whom he indeed was frequently confused (compare also Aristophanes' savage caricature in the *Clouds*). The reader is also advised to compare Socrates' attitude to self-knowledge with that displayed in the tragic treatment of the theme by Sophocles in the *Oedipus Tyrannus.* For Socrates the ultimate evil was the "unexamined life," and by his interrogations, often conducted with a playful irony illuminating to compare with that of the tragedians and of the Fourth Evangelist, he forced upon people a recognition of their own ignorance. It would seem that there was in his temper, as Plato portrays it, a combination of the profoundly reverent with the profoundly skeptical. The eminent Platonic scholar, the late Léon Robin, conjectures an element of attachment to the Orphic tradition in his mentioning, in particular, his reliance in moments of crisis upon the guidance of his *daimonion.* Yet among his intimates his example encouraged a skepticism far more searching than that of the Sophists. In the supreme crisis of the Peloponnesian War, when the survival of the whole Athenian culture and civilization was at issue in a power struggle with another Greek society, whose military strength on land was at least as great as Athens' maritime resources, and whose social and political system morally revolted Pericles by its prodigal wastage of excellent human material in the perpetuating of a fantastic order of conquest and subordination, Socrates' views seemed inevitably to encourage *apragmosynē,* a scrupulosity destructive of human energy. Again there was the figure of Alcibiades, who loved Socrates but whose profligacy and radical instability played its part in the disasters that led to Aegospotami, even as his impiety was attested by his suspected involvement in the mutilation of the Hermae on the eve of the Athenian fleet's departure for Sicily. "Do men gather grapes of thorns or figs of thistles?" If the Socratic *elenchus* was irrefutable, the Socratic *paideia* seemed to result in disintegration; so Socrates' history issued inevitably in condemnation and death with his refusal to flee or to see in his drinking the hemlock anything other than a duty owed in part to the community which nurtured him, a last manifestation of his surprising spirit.

For Plato he is the type of the "perfectly just man" in *Republic* 2, portrayed with subtle admission of the justification of his reputation for injustice, even as it is arguable that the lineaments of the "perfectly unjust man" are suggested by Pericles. It is the Socratic *elenchus* that Plato may have had in mind when he described the forceful conversion of the prisoners in their cave to the light, when bewildered they would fain return to the familiar environment they have hitherto known in their place of radical *apaideusia.* It is with the ontological validation of the Socratic way that Plato is obsessively concerned in the ethical and metaphysical sections of the *Republic,* and it is one of the most illuminating ironies of the history of philosophy that the enterprise involved suggesting as a metaphysically final form of human association a closed, nonhereditary aristocratic paternalism in which the rigorous and disciplined loyalty of its civil service and police would have crushed at birth the slightest manifestation of the quizzical Socratic temper.

In the work of Kierkegaard a valuable contribution to Christology has been achieved through comparison of the work of Socrates with that of Christ. According to Plato, Socrates described himself as a midwife, bringing to consciousness what human beings already innately (viz., dispositionally) knew; a *locus classicus* here is the *entretien* with the slave boy in the *Meno*. But as Kierkegaard saw, Christ faced the task of communicating himself and therefore required an indirection quite other than that caught in those of the Platonic dialogues which would seem to echo most faithfully Plato's recollection of the words and methods of his master.

See **Platonic Ethics; Sophists.**

A. F. Blum, *Socrates: The Original and Its Image,* 1978; W. K. Guthrie, *Socrates,* 1971; A. E. Taylor, *Socrates* (1932), 1975 (repr. of 1951 ed.); L. Versenyi, *Socratic Humanism,* 1963.

D. M. MACKINNON

Sodomy

Strictly, sodomy (from Sodom) denotes coition, either homosexual or heterosexual, by anal penetration, but it is loosely used for male homosexual intercourse in general.

See **Homosexuality.**

SHERWIN BAILEY

Solidarity *see* **Community; Ecumenical Movement, Ethics in the; Liberation Theology; Marxist Ethics; Political Theology**

Sophists

The title is given to the itinerant teachers in 5th-century Greece who offered, for a fee, to instruct young men on the threshold of public life in the skills of rhetoric. Because they were itinerant they were familiar with the variety of moral and political traditions to be met with in Hellas, and became in consequence sympathetic with relativistic as distinct from absolutist conceptions of morality. In recent appraisals of their work there has been sharp reaction against supposing them fairly presented in Plato's vivid but damning portrayals of Callicles in the *Gorgias* and Thrasymachus in the first book of the *Republic.* Thus the teaching of Protagoras that man

is the measure of all things has been construed as the principle of a genuine humanism, and the role played by the Sophists' work in dissolving the power of traditional ties of blood and family in the Athens of Cleisthenes, Ephialtes, and Pericles, and substituting more rationally conceived bonds of human association, has been stressed. In the concluding speech set by Thucydides in the mouth of Pericles, when the latter is weakened by the plague which killed him, and when he was aware that the willingness of Athens to continue the war with Sparta was flagging, we find in the statesman's *Realpolitik* a clear example of the Sophists' refusal to ignore the foundations on which the often-quoted political idealism of Pericles' earlier speech in praise of the Athenian dead in the war actually rested. He was not afraid to speak of the Athenian *archē* as a tyranny which maybe it had been wrong in the first instance to take, but whose power had now to be defended; for with the loss of that power went everything that differentiated Athens from Sparta, and that rendered her the cultural superior of the two rival contenders for Greek hegemony.

We find examples of the Sophists' influence in Euripides' handling of the ancient myths in his tragedies, and we cannot, for instance, withhold our admiration for the way in which, in his *Electra,* he displays Orestes and his implacably dedicated sister as alike devastated in the climax of the play by experiencing at first hand the actuality of matricide. If the killing of Clytemnestra can, in primitive penal theory, be justified as an action of retributive justice, its execution reveals itself as a human outrage, involving its perpetrators in a sense of guilt that no traditional casuistry can expel. A question mark is here set against an appalling moral convention, and we must admire those whose teaching made it possible.

If Plato is always the relentless critic of the Sophists, quick to bring out the extent to which their relativism encouraged *in the end* an indifference to the distinction between what is and what is not the case, and if, further, a study of the political commentary embodied in the speeches of Thucydides' *History* and in such sections of his text as the discussion of civil war following the account of its outbreak in Corcyra, the Mytilenean debate and the Melian dialogue must to some extent confirm his unfavorable view of their influence, we must not forget the speech of Pericles with its classical analysis of the relations of power and culture as expressive of a more subtle variant of the Sophists' understanding of human life mentioned above. It is often said of them that they tore apart *nomos* and *physis,* custom-based ethics and a morality based on human nature. But the latter frequently took for granted conditions of life that came near contradicting its supposed norms; whereas the former, although inclined to encourage relativist judgments, nonetheless faced the empirical realities of human existence as men and women were constrained to live it. Again it is commonplace that Plato sought to overcome the sharp diremption of *nomos* and *physis,* and to provide an understanding of human nature that would acknowledge the critical self-consciousness with respect to its moral foundations to which the Sophists had drastically alerted their hearers.

Plato's presentation of the democratic state in *Republic* 8 identifies democracy with a morally permissive society, and the democratic citizen with the one whose moral tolerance is indistinguishable from a complete indifferentism. Yet the presentation shows the depth of his attachment to Athens, for all his tendency sometimes to romanticize Sparta. At some level of his being he realized that it was only in the context of an Athens where Periclean political institutions and the cultural style partly represented by the Sophists combined to make radical questions concerning the foundations of human life possible, that Socrates' and his own work could have been done.

See **Absolutes, Ethical; Conventional Morality; Conventions; Natural Law; Platonic Ethics; Relativism; Socratic Ethics.**

W. K. Guthrie, *Sophists,* 1971; G. B. Kerferd, *The Sophistic Movement,* 1981.

D. M. MACKINNON

Sovereignty, National *see* **National Sovereignty; Nationalism**

Speciesism *see* **Animals**

Standards *see* **Norms; Situation Ethics**

State

The state is the institution in which the ultimate social authority and power are located, authority* and power* which are necessary to maintain order* and to give conscious direction to the life of a society. The distinction between the state and society* is the starting point for all discussion of the limits of the state. In the modern world we think of the state as being an essential structure of the nation, as being the expression of its sovereignty and the source of its government (*see* **National Sovereignty**). The modern nation has given to the state a much clearer form than was the case with ancient empires or the fluid feudal order of the Middle Ages. Christian thinking about the state developed in response to those earlier conditions of political life. It was colored by the descriptions in the OT of the political kingdoms of Israel and Judah, and these were seen against the background of a theocratic ideal which in principle limited the authority and power of kings (see the stories of Nathan and David, and Elijah and Ahab).

The passages in the NT which refer to government (especially Rom. 13:1–7; 1 Peter 2: 13–17; and Rev. 13) naturally refer to the authorities of the Roman Empire. It is not possible to derive from these passages adequate guidance for Christian ethics in relation to the state as the political structure of a nation in which Christians have the rights and responsibilities of citizens. The first two passages assume a positive attitude toward the political authorities as God-given instruments of order in society. The passage in Revelation recognizes that the Roman Empire had become an idolatrous power, for its demand for worship of the emperor exceeded its authority and therefore Christians were bound to resist it by suffering. No form of political resistance* could have been considered at the time. (See Oscar Cullmann, *The State in the New Testament,* 1956.)

The NT teaching about the state sets the outside limits within which Christian political ethics has moved. It warns at the same time against anarchism* and against the unlimited state. The great words of Peter in Acts, "We must obey God rather than men" (Acts 5:29) have had great force in Christian history, but in relation to the state there has been a tendency for them to be nullified by the words in Rom. 13:1: "Let every person be subject to the governing authorities." It has often seemed possible to harmonize these two passages even in the face of the most difficult historical circumstances by assuming that in spite of appearances God was expressing his will through the governing authorities of the moment. Since the recognition of the church by the Roman Empire at the time of Constantine this readiness to harmonize these two principles has usually dominated Christendom. There has, however, been a contrary tendency which was present especially in the Protestant sects and on Calvinistic soil in spite of the main tendency in Calvin's thought. In Roman Catholic thought there have been resources for the independence of the church and even for the sanctioning of political resistance against the state—the proclamation of natural law* as being above the state and the authority of the pope over against that of emperor or king—but there has also been a strong presumption in favor of political authorities with some claim to legitimacy. This latter tendency was especially prominent in the 19th century when the church was controlled by fear of the influences from the French Revolution. The modern experience of totalitarianism on the part of both Catholics and Protestants has brought about a shift of emphasis, and theological sanction for political resistance to tyranny in extreme cases is now more widely held among Christians than ever before.

One pervasive contrast in Christian attitudes toward the state is the difference between those who think of the state as having chiefly the negative function of providing a dike against sin and those who see the state as a natural consequence of the social nature of humanity. The Roman Catholic teaching about the state, which has been influenced by Aristotle's positive attitude toward the political order of the city, is the clearest case of the view of the state as the expression of humanity's social nature, as belonging to creation rather than to the Fall. (See H. Rommen, *The State in Catholic Thought,* 1947, and the pastoral constitution *Gaudium et Spes* of Vatican Council II, chs. IV and V.)

The negative view of the state is most characteristic of Luther and even more of some strains in traditional Lutheranism. Since the struggle against National Socialism there has been a widespread movement in Lutheranism against the dualistic interpretation of the "two kingdoms"* which had been one result of the negative view of the state. (See Karl H. Hertz, ed., *Two Kingdoms and One World,* 1976.) Lutherans, in common with Roman Catholic and Reformed churches, generally emphasize the responsibility of Christians to bring Christian influence to bear on the state for the sake of justice and peace and humane policies, while they may often allow more for the moral limitations of the state than those of other traditions. Calvinism has always held a more positive view of the state than traditional Lutheranism in spite of its dark view of sin.

The development of the welfare state* in most industrialized societies has also led to recognition of the positive functions of the state. While it is generally recognized that the state should have a monopoly of police power and military power, the assumption that this is the essence of the state is naturally modified or displaced by the experience of the state's positive functions. There is, however, coercion* in the background in the case of the enforcement of laws prescribing and raising taxes for those positive functions, including education, the provision of medical care, and social security. Also, the negative view of the state has often been accompanied by uncritical support of its war-making function, and while pacifism* is a minority movement in the churches, there is today general emphasis on the need to limit the military activities of the state based on criteria for "the just war"* and motivated by the threats to human survival in a nuclear war*. Today the traditional differences between Catholicism, Lutheranism, and Calvinism have little influence on the broadly ecumenical teaching on political and social issues that is developing in the churches.

The experience of totalitarian states*, especially Stalinist communism and National Socialism, has had a shock effect on Christian thinking about the state. Churches have experienced and even sanctioned despotisms in earlier periods, but totalitarianism, inspired by ideological commitments and enabled to control all aspects of culture by modern technology, has been in some ways a new experience for churches. This has been the more so when the totalitarian state has been antireligious in its ideology or has attacked forms of religion that it found to be threats to its policies and power. This experience has rightly caused the churches to emphasize the need to limit the state (*see* **Church and State**). The distinction is made between totalitarian and authoritarian states. The latter may be dictatorships or oligarchies that are relatively relaxed or inefficient, or they may be aggressive dictatorships controlled by their opposition to leftist or revolutionary movements. In the latter case they may not seek to control all aspects of culture in line with the totalitarian tendency, but they may be as cruelly oppressive, through arbitrary arrests, torture, kidnaping, and disappearances, of the most feared forms of dissent as totalitarian states. Christians often find themselves in confrontation with both totalitarian and authoritarian states and in both cases seek limitations on the state for the sake of religious freedom that involves ethical action.

The problem of limiting the state will always be present, but Christian ethics does have to balance the danger that the state may become unlimited and even demonic over against the danger that the state may be too weak to deal with the problems of modern society. Sometimes the primary issue is the preservation of social order where society is vulnerable to tribal or economic or political conflict. Sometimes there is a tendency toward stalemate as between management and labor in industrial societies, and the state must be strong enough to bring about a decision. In a complicated technological society the state inevitably acquires many economic functions. It alone has the authority or the resources to deal with many national problems that require large-scale action. There is no one Christian pattern that is relevant to the needs of all societies for the relating of the function of the state to that of private bodies of all kinds. But there is a Christian emphasis on the needs of the people who are neglected or exploited, of the poor who have no private economic power. This emphasis does often call for united action by the society working through government to direct the use of the resources of the society for the sake of all the people, especially the weak and neglected ones. Christian ethics offers no sanction to a consistent capitalism* or a consistent socialism*, but it should encourage openness to the most varied combinations of public and private action for the sake of justice* and welfare. The teachings of the encyclicals of the popes since Leo XIII, recently the social encyclicals by John XXIII, Paul VI, and John Paul II, transcend the current contrast between economic systems. The letter entitled *Octogesima Adveniens* by Paul VI comes closest to providing permission for Catholics to support democratic socialist movements. *Pacem in Terris* by John XXIII had opened

the door to cooperation between Catholics and Marxist movements in case they were no longer in practice dominated by ideological positions contradicting Catholic teaching (*see* **Official Roman Catholic Social Teaching**). The social teachings of the World Council of Churches as expressed in reports of all six Assemblies from Amsterdam through Vancouver are quite similar in the way in which doctrinaire forms of capitalism or socialism are transcended (*see* **Ecumenical Movement**).

One major controversy in the churches has to do with the ethics of political revolution*. The theological veto on all resistance* to the state that has often obtained was overcome by the need to resist National Socialism in many branches of the church, though pacifist opposition to violent resistance remains as a minority witness. The debate today has to do chiefly with the struggles against political and economic oppression* in the Third World and especially in Latin America. Christians influenced by liberation theology* assume that revolutionary violence against oppressive regimes is justifiable as a last resort. (See Gustavo Gutiérrez, *A Theology of Liberation,* 1973; Robert McAfee Brown, *Theology in a New Key,* 1978, as a guide to this literature; and Dennis P. McCann, *Christian Realism and Liberation Theology,* 1981, as a warning against illusions that often accompany revolutionary theology.) Much of the opposition to theological and ethical support for revolution as a last resort comes from those who oppose particular revolutions and who for their own interests seek to preserve the status quo, or those who assume that moderate and incremental reforms may be sufficient and would be preferable to illegal or violent revolutionary change.

Just as there is no one Christian pattern for the relating of government to economic institutions, so there is no one Christian form of government. The church has had to live with many forms of government but this does not mean that all are of equal merit. Christian ethics is favorable to the trend associated with political democracy* so long as it includes both lawful limits on the power of the majority and political channels for the expression of dissent*. (See Jacques Maritain, *Man and the State,* 1951; also Reinhold Niebuhr, *The Children of Light and the Children of Darkness,* 1944.)

The role of the national state in the international sphere raises another dimension. All that has ever been said by theologians about the state as the providential instrument for preserving order applies to the need for political structures to preserve order* amid the near anarchy* of nations (see **International Order**). No national state should regard itself as ultimate. The serving of the welfare of humanity as a whole, the breaking down of barriers between peoples, the prevention of fratricidal war, even of mutual annihilation in the nuclear age, call for the development of the institutions of world order which will limit the power of national states. Christian teaching always points beyond the national state to God's love for all humanity, and the church by its very nature is a community that transcends all nations and is under the authority of no national state.

See also **Church and State; Civil Disobedience; Conscientious Objection; Democracy; Freedom; International Order; National Sovereignty; Orders; Politics; Resistance; Revolution; Totalitarian State; Tyrannicide.**

JOHN C. BENNETT

Sterilization

The procedure by means of which a human being or an animal is rendered permanently incapable of reproduction. Until the end of the 19th century, sterilization, especially of males, was accomplished through castration. However, in 1897 a Swiss surgeon developed the technique of cutting the Fallopian tubes to sterilize women; two years later an American surgeon performed the first recorded vasectomy on a man.

The two primary subtypes of sterilization, when one considers the goal of the procedure, are to protect the health of the person being sterilized (therapeutic sterilization) and to prevent reproduction (contraceptive sterilization). Sterilization can also be categorized as either voluntary or nonvoluntary.

Voluntary sterilization.

Contraceptive sterilization. As noted above, the contraceptive use of vasectomy in males and tubal sterilization in females is a 20th-century phenomenon. Voluntary sterilization has been promoted as a safe and effective means of birth control in the USA and the UK, as well as in Asia, where India has a major sterilization program.

During the 1970s and early 1980s, the use of sterilization as a means of contraception increased at an exponential rate in the USA.

In 1970, approximately 3 million Americans had been sterilized. By the end of 1982, this number had grown to 15.8 million. In 1971 the number of tubal sterilizations greatly exceeded the number of vasectomies (72 percent vs. 28 percent). By 1982 the percentage figures for male and female sterilizations in the USA were almost completely reversed (31 percent female, 69 percent male).

According to data collected in the third US National Survey of Family Growth, sterilization of either the husband or the wife was relied upon for contraception by 27 percent of married women in 1982, while 14 percent used oral contraceptives. A majority of married couples using birth control and not intending to have more children also chose sterilization as their contraceptive method.

The ethical appraisal of voluntary contraceptive sterilization varies among Christian groups (see **Contraception**). In this context one should recall that birth control methods in general were first accepted by a Christian body, the Anglican Church, in 1930. Sterilization, a permanent and usually irreversible method of contraception, would seem to be even more difficult to justify from an ethical point of view.

Protestant Christians generally accept sterilization as a legitimate method of contraception; however, some Protestant theologians, including Bonhoeffer and Thielicke, emphasize that the willingness to have children before sterilization is performed is essential to marital fellowship. Official Catholic teaching has condemned all types of contraception except the rhythm method; contraceptive sterilization is opposed, in addition, because it is a mutilating act not required to save one's life or to preserve bodily integrity (see **Totality, Principle of**). However, some Catholic theologians, including Curran and Häring, accept contraceptive sterilization as a morally justifiable act of conscience if it is chosen for sufficiently serious reasons. Eastern Orthodoxy has not taken an official position on contraceptive sterilization. Some Orthodox theologians do accept nonpermanent methods of contraception for the purpose of spacing and limiting the number of children.

Therapeutic sterilization. Catholic commentators have devoted the most detailed attention to the problem of sterilization for reasons of health. The official view is that therapeutic sterilization is permissible only as an unintended, indirect effect of a procedure whose primary goal is to remove a pathological organ, for example, a cancerous uterus (*see* **Double Effect**). Still under discussion is the question whether therapeutic sterilization must be corrective or whether it can also be preventive. The early Joseph Fletcher explicitly and other Protestant theologians implicitly accept therapeutic sterilizations.

Nonvoluntary sterilization.

Persons of diminished competence. During the 1970s a much-debated issue in both the USA and the UK was the moral justifiability of sterilizing mentally retarded individuals. Such proposed sterilizations are difficult to categorize because they are often voluntarily accepted by the parents and because they are not involuntary in the sense of being performed against the will of a competent person.

This recent debate had its background in ill-conceived and often discriminatory policies of the early 20th century (*see* **Eugenics**). In the USA from 1905 to the early 1930s and in Nazi Germany during the 1930s, there was a strong interest in preventing "feeble-minded" persons from reproducing. By 1931, thirty states in the USA had passed compulsory sterilization laws, which applied to a wide variety of "hereditary defectives." In 1933 Adolf Hitler promulgated the Eugenic Sterilization Law in Germany.

Because of the excesses committed in the name of eugenics during the early decades of the 20th century, most Christian thinkers have been reluctant to support nonvoluntary sterilization of the mentally retarded. Only Joseph Fletcher continues to advocate such a policy. Other Christian commentators have been willing to support hysterectomy for the benefit of some retarded teenagers (see Curran) or the review of individual cases to determine whether sterilization fulfills the formal requirements of just cause, last resort, and due process (see Walters and Gaylin).

Competent persons. The classic instance in which competent persons were sterilized against their will was punitive sterilization, especially in the case of sexual offenders. More recent cases involve (1) pressure on women who have already borne several children to be sterilized, and (2) the requirement by some employers that applicants for certain types of potentially hazardous jobs be sterilized as a precondition for employment.

Most Christian theologians oppose punitive sterilization, although a few have approved it in limited circumstances (see Lebacqz). Although few Christian thinkers have explicitly discussed sterilization for excessive childbearing or as a prerequisite for certain kinds of employment, the general tendency of the Christian ethical tradition is diametrically opposed to such coercive measures.

See **Contraception; Eugenics; Population Policy; Procreation.**

———

C. Curran, "Sterilization: Roman Catholic Theory and Practice," *Linacre Quarterly* 40, no. 2, May 1973, pp. 97–108; J. Fletcher, *Morals and Medicine,* 1954; K. Lebacqz, "Sterilization: Ethical Aspects," *EB,* 1978; K. M. Ludmerer, *Genetics and American Society: A Historical Appraisal,* 1972; "NSFG [National Survey of Family Growth] 1982: Sterilization Use Up, Pill Use Down Among Married Women," *Family Planning Perspectives* 16, no. 1, Jan./Feb. 1984, pp. 40–41; J. T. Noonan, Jr., *Contraception: A History of Its Treatment by the Catholic Theologians and Canonists,* 1965; "Sterilizations Off Sharply in 1982," *Family Planning Perspectives* 16, no. 1, Jan./Feb. 1984, pp. 37–38; L. Walters and W. Gaylin, "Sterilizing the Retarded Child," *HCR* 6, no. 2, April 1976, pp. 13–15.

LEROY WALTERS

Stewardship *see* **Energy; Environmental Ethics; Image of God**

Stoic Ethics

For the Greek, philosophy was divided into three parts, logic, physics, and ethics (Cicero, *On the Chief Good and Evil* 4.2.4), but for the Stoic the other departments of learning existed solely for the sake of ethics. If the Stoic speculated, it was in order to live (Diogenes Laertius 7.84; Epictetus, *Discourses* 3.2).

Basic to the Stoic idea of ethics is the Stoic idea of God. God is everywhere and in every human being. "God is near you, with you, within you. I say it, Lucilius, a holy spirit sits within us, spectator of our evil and our good, our guardian" (Seneca, *Letters* 41.12). But not only is God everywhere present. Everything is settled and arranged by God. Thus the Stoic has two allied conceptions. There is the conception of *heimarmenē,* which is fate.

This in itself might be detached and mechanical. But to it there is joined the conception of *pronoia,* which is providence. The control of God is carried out in care for all living things (Cicero, *On the Nature of the Gods* 2.53.132; 2.56.164). Fate and providence are one, and literally nothing happens but by the will of God.

An obvious question emerges. If everything is settled and arranged, how do human beings come into it at all? How can there be such a thing as ethics? To us there is left one thing, and it is all-important—the power of assent.

This then gives us the key to Stoic ethics. Goodness is willingly to accept the will of God, or, to put it in another way, to live according to Nature. If everything is the will of God, then the secret is to learn to want what we have (Epictetus, *Manual* 8). Seneca says: "To obey God is liberty" (*On the Happy Life* 15.7). "He does not will it," says Epictetus, "I do not wish it" (*Discourses* 4.1.89). We can either accept the will of God willingly or we can struggle against it. Accept it we must. This has certain consequences. (1) Virtue is a thing of the mind. It comes by putting one's mind to it, and, like walking in a child, it comes by practice. (2) Virtue may therefore be learned, and in the end virtue is knowledge and vice is ignorance. (3) Virtue itself is all-sufficient; nothing else matters. Everything else is *adiaphoros,* indifferent. But if everything is indifferent, then action is paralyzed. So the things that are indifferent are divided into things to be sought, like health and beauty and honor and good birth, and things that are to be rejected. (4) The Stoic draws a distinction between things in our power and things not in our power. Only one thing is in our power—the assent of the will. Here we come to the most characteristic aspect of Stoicism. If the will is everything, then the supreme evil is emotion. To have emotion is to be diseased (Cicero, *Tusculan Disputations* 3.10.23). The wise must become *apathēs,* not apathetic, but cleansed of all emotion, so that they can endure the greatest pain, and see even the death of their nearest and dearest, and say only that this is the will of God (Epictetus, *Discourses* 1.4.111, 112).

Stoic ethics consist of the remembrance that life is lived in the presence of God, that humanity is a sacred thing and the resting place of the Divine (Seneca, *Letters* 92.13; 120.14), and that goodness means the total acceptance of the will of God, which is expressed in events.

E. R. Bevan, *Stoics and Sceptics,* 1931; L. Edelstein, *The Meaning of Stoicism,* 1966; J. M. Rist, *Stoic Philosophy,* 1969; J. M. Rist (ed.), *The Stoics,* 1978.

WILLIAM BARCLAY

Strikes

The ultimate weapon of trade unions* and professional associations to induce managements to agree to acceptable terms in wages and conditions (*see* **Collective Bargaining**). Less extreme forms of pressure include the "go slow" or "work-to-rule." Many lightning (or wildcat) strikes are a quick way of getting grievances at work settled. Others are a more serious and prolonged trial of strength whose success or failure depends upon a mixture of the cogency of the cause, the extent of unionization, the financial strength of the corporation or public authority, the basic importance of the product, and the extent of available alternative sources of supply of the good or service in question. Strikes are meant to hurt the employers, and through them the consumers of the product. To what extent strikes should be regulated by public law, civil or criminal, is much discussed, and it varies from country to country. A major question is how far any such law is enforceable against determined collective opposition. Another question is what occupations are considered so sensitive that strikes in them are forbidden, and how the community which forbids them is to provide for grievances in those occupations to be dealt with.

Efforts have been made to produce criteria for the just strike akin to those for the just war*. (1) Is there a just cause? (2) Have all forms of negotiation been exhausted? (3) Will the good achieved outweigh the damage caused? (4) Is there a reasonable chance of success? (5) How much harm will be done to innocent parties? (6) Will the strike be carried out by legitimate means? If these criteria are seen not as fixed rules but as considerations to be borne in mind, there is the possibility of useful developments along these lines; they are an instance of traditional Christian wisdom in handling conflicts by criteria of prudence* and proportion (*see also* **Proportionality, Principle of; Ends and Means**).

Attempts are made to distinguish between industrial and political strikes, with the latter frowned on by many as illegitimate, but there is no clear distinction between the two, especially when in all advanced industrial countries local and national political authorities are substantial employers. Using industrial action to bring down the entire political order is another matter and has to be treated under the heading of civil disobedience*, its nature and justification. As to strikes, Christians have collective responsibilities in their jobs; they must stand by their informed conscientious judgment (as in the case of conscientious objection* to war), but they are likely to be very careful before going against collective decisions in the case of a strike, and becoming blacklegs (or scabs).

R. H. Preston (ed.), *Perspectives on Strikes,* 1975.

RONALD PRESTON

Subjectivism, Ethical

Ethical subjectivism is the view that moral judgments are equivalent to statements about the psychological states or attitudes of those who utter them. It is to be distinguished from emotivism*, relativism*, prescriptivism*.

R. M. HARE

Sublimation *see* Defense Mechanisms

Subsidiarity, Principle of

The term comes from Latin *subsidium,* meaning "help." The principle of subsidiarity spells out the limited but positive role of the state in the light of a social theory that insists on the dignity and the social nature of the human person, the rights of the family, the need for intermediate associations, and a limited state with the positive function of seeking the common good. The content of this principle is found in Thomas Aquinas and in the Roman Catholic ethical tradition. However, the term was first used and defined by Pope Pius XI in *Quadragesimo Anno* (1931): "Just as it is gravely wrong to take from individuals what they can accomplish by their own initiative and industry and give it to the community, so also is it an injustice and at the same time a grave evil and disturbance of right order to assign to a greater and higher association

what lesser and subordinate organizations can do." In *Mater et Magistra* (1961), Pope John XXIII cautioned against a too restrictive interpretation of the principle, especially in view of the greater complexity existing in social relationships in the modern world.

See also **Official Roman Catholic Social Teaching.**

CHARLES E. CURRAN

Suffering

Suffering is the opposite of action*. In action, a person freely initiates a series of events in order to bring about some desired state of affairs. In suffering, a person undergoes a series of events initiated from outside and leading to a state of affairs which is not desired. The "problem of suffering" is part of the wider problem of evil*, and that is a metaphysical or a theological problem rather than an ethical one. There are, however, at least two points where suffering impinges on ethics.

There still lingers a widespread and ancient idea that suffering befalls a person as a punishment for sins and wrongdoings. This belief was already contested in the OT drama of Job, and was explicitly denied by Jesus (Luke 13:1–5, etc.). It is true, of course, that some sins, especially sins of indulgence, may bring suffering on the sinner, e.g., by undermining health. But this is not a divine judgment, and though the world today is full of suffering people, there is no correlation between their suffering and their sinfulness (*see* **Theodicy**).

The other point is that in many cases suffering contributes to the development of moral character*. This would certainly seem to be an implication of the Christian ethic, for insofar as it is understood as a conformation to Christ, it is a conformation to the crucified One (*see* **Imitation of Christ**). It is hard to imagine how there could be any depth of sympathy* and love* in a person who had never known suffering at first hand. But while some suffering has this morally educative character, there is much more that is so severe and apparently pointless that it is as likely to embitter as to ennoble the sufferer. Because so much suffering has this apparently senseless character, it is generally regarded as a duty to relieve suffering whenever possible.

C. S. Lewis, *The Problem of Pain,* 1940.

JOHN MACQUARRIE

Suicide

Discussions on the morality of suicide are often confused by a failure to distinguish between the willing surrender of one's life and the deliberate taking of it. Traditional Christian teaching affirms that in certain circumstances a person may innocently relinquish his or her life. They are occasions which call for self-sacrifice—for example, in the performance of one's duty while on military service, in the defense of a friend unjustly attacked, in ministering to the infectious sick, in witnessing to one's faith in time of persecution. In all instances of this kind the persons concerned do not primarily or directly will their own death, but they are prepared to accept it as the unavoidable consequence of their performing some act of charity, justice, mercy, or piety to which they believe God has called them. If the same acts could be performed without their death they would not choose to die. But the act that can properly be called suicide, namely, the direct and deliberate taking of one's life (with or without assistance) for any self-regarding motive, is another matter. In antiquity and in modern times it has been defended as permissible or even virtuous and honorable, on the ground that, as a human being, one's life is one's own, and that in the last resort an individual must therefore be allowed to terminate it at his or her discretion. Some Christians have also attempted to justify it in cases of painful and wasting incurable disease especially when there are major burdens on others (*see* **Euthanasia**). But (notwithstanding those instances of suicide in the Bible which are not expressly condemned) the overwhelming weight of traditional Christian opinion has held that suicide (as defined above) is a grave sin.

A human being is not the author of his or her own life nor its absolute owner. Life is entrusted to us by God that it may begin to find its fulfillment in the loving service of God and our fellow humans here in this world, and it is not for us to decide for how long it shall be so used. Directly and deliberately to destroy one's own life is therefore said to be (1) a sin against God its creator and redeemer, a rejection of his love and a denial of his sovereignty; (2) an offense against the proper love of one's own person as a creature made in God's image to share his glory, a violation of the Sixth Commandment, and an act of despair which precludes repentance;

and (3) an offense against humankind in that it both deprives society and one's own family of a member prematurely and also denies them any opportunity of ministering to one's needs. (Richard Fox, in the DME, 1981, p. 426, has noted that suicide "is the most significant of all deaths in its impact on survivors, causing long-lasting grief and guilt and a high suicide-expectancy.")

It is in accord with this teaching that many codes of criminal law have imposed penalties for suicide and attempted suicide, and that over long periods ecclesiastical law has withheld Christian burial from one who has "laid violent hands" on himself or herself. It has long been recognized, however, that acts of suicide (though always "materially" or "objectively" sinful) may vary from the coldly premeditated to the utterly compulsive, that they can be related to a great variety of adverse personal, social, and environmental circumstances, and that in any particular case the degree of culpability depends upon the state of mind in which the act is done. In the present century increasing attention has been paid to the psychopathology of suicide, and it seems clear that suicide is very often a less voluntary act than was hitherto assumed. Thus, without conceding either that one has the right to take one's own life or that all who make the attempt must be presumed insane, a growing number of Christians support the view that neither suicide nor attempted suicide should be regarded as a crime, since medical and sociological studies have shown the irrelevance of the criminal law to the solution of the problem. In some countries this is now being recognized. In the UK, for example, suicide ceased to be a felony in 1961, though to aid or abet suicide remains an offense. How great is the need for befriending ministries specifically for the suicidal is shown by the enormous worldwide use of them since the foundation of The Samaritans in London in 1953.

See also **Autonomy; Involuntary Hospitalization; Life, Sacredness of; Mental Illness; Morality, Legal Enforcement of; Paternalism; Responsibility.**

M. P. Battin, *Ethical Issues in Suicide,* 1982; M. P. Battin and D. J. Mayo (eds.), *Suicide: The Philosophical Issues,* 1980; E. Durkheim, *Suicide: A Study in Sociology,* ET 1952; S. E. Sprott, *The English Debate on Suicide,* 1961; E. Stengel, *Suicide and Attempted Suicide,*

1970; E. (Chad) Varah (ed.), *Samaritans in the 80's,* 1980.

THOMAS WOOD

Summum Bonum *see* **Agathology; Axiology; Finality; Goodness; Teleological Ethics; Thomistic Ethics**

Sumptuary Laws

Laws intended to restrain extravagant expenditure and to prevent the spread of habits of luxury. Such laws were being passed as long ago as the days of ancient Rome, and they may be compared with the "credit squeezes" of modern times.

JOHN MACQUARRIE

Sunday Observance

The word "Sunday" first occurs in Christian writing in Justin Martyr. In the NT the day is known by the Jewish term "the first day of the week" (Acts 20:7; 1 Cor. 16:2), and once as "the Lord's day" (Rev. 1:10; cf. *Didache* 14). This, the day of resurrection (Mark 16:2; etc.), was chosen for Christian gatherings, which were held either in the evening or very early in the morning, since the day was a normal working day.

There is nothing in the NT to associate this day with the Sabbath. Jewish Christians continued to observe the Sabbath, and problems arose between Jewish and Gentile groups. Although this issue is not mentioned in Acts 15, for Paul any insistence on holy days, like the insistence on circumcision, contradicts the freedom and sufficiency of faith (Gal. 4:9ff.; cf. Col. 2); but otherwise he commends mutual respect and tolerance (Rom. 14).

The Gospels recount the free attitude of Jesus to the Sabbath, and the conflict that this aroused. The saying "The sabbath was made for man, not man for the sabbath; so the Son of man is lord even of the sabbath" (Mark 2:27–28) seems to be not a general principle, but a messianic claim. The Sabbath finds its fulfillment in the liberating activity of Jesus, just as does the year of jubilee (Luke 4:21).

In 321, a law of Constantine proclaimed Sunday as a day of rest, but the church was slow to interpret Sunday in a Sabbatarian way. Augustine can write, "Well, now, I should like to be told, what there is in these ten commandments, except that on the observance of the Sabbath, which ought not to

be kept by a Christian?" (*On the Spirit and the Letter* 23).

The view that the Sabbath command was transferred to the Lord's Day is first found in the late 8th to the 9th century, in Rabanus Maurus and Alcuin. It received definitive form from Thomas Aquinas (*see* **Thomistic Ethics**). On his view, the moral precepts of the Decalogue* correspond to natural law* and are binding on all men; the ceremonial precepts are abrogated. The moral precept in the Sabbath commandment is "to give some time to the things of God"; with respect to "the fixing of the time" (i.e., the seventh day) it is a ceremonial precept (*ST* I-II.100.3). To Aquinas we owe the distinction between works of necessity and mercy (which are permissible) and servile work (which is not).

Luther stays close to Aquinas, but stresses the humanitarian reasons for a day of rest and repudiates a holy day or Sabbath imposed on religious grounds, which would be bondage. Calvin also distinguishes moral and ceremonial law, but identifies only the second table of the Decalogue with natural law (as did some early Christian writers). The Sabbath commandment is interpreted spiritually by Calvin as a "type of the spiritual rest by which believers were to cease from their own works and allow God to work in them" (*Institutes* 2.8.28). This accords with his view of the Christian life as self-denial* (*see* **Calvinist Ethics**), and is not confined to one day in the week. Like Luther he sees the provision of a day for rest and worship as humane and convenient, and abhors a "superstitious observance of days." He even says, "I do not cling so to the number seven as to bring the church under bondage to it."

Yet in Reformed churches and countries Sabbatarianism* revived. The Westminster Confession of Faith states it with utter clarity. "As it is of the law of nature that, in general, a due proportion of time be set apart for the worship of God; so, in his Word, by a positive, moral, and perpetual commandment, binding all men in all ages, he hath particularly appointed one day in seven for a Sabbath, to be kept holy unto him: which, from the beginning of the world to the resurrection of Christ, was the last day of the week; and, from the resurrection of Christ, was changed into the first day of the week, which in Scripture is called the Lord's Day, and is to be continued to the end of the world as the Christian Sabbath" (XXI.7). Here the Sabbath is simply transferred to the first day of the week. This owes more to Thomas than to Calvin or the NT. Yet for centuries this view held almost unquestioned influence in Protestantism. In Scotland and England, from the 17th century, the Sabbatarian assumption was accepted. The only difference was over the strictness of the observance. In the Evangelical revival strict Sabbath observance, and action for its enforcement, became a mark of evangelical seriousness. In 1831 the Lord's Day Observance Society was formed.

Though the foundation of Christian Sabbatarianism was the belief that Sabbath rest was a divine command, the arguments that found widest support were those of Luther and Calvin—the convenience of a day free for worship and the humane requirement to ensure rest for servants and laborers. Changing technology and social conditions have been more powerful to alter attitudes than theological reflection. By the 1830s, proposals to run railway trains on Sundays occasioned much controversy. Improved travel, increased leisure (the five-day week, the "weekend"), television, and the pluralism* of modern society have contributed to the erosion of Sabbath legislation and have made what remains seem like a relic from the past. The blessings of a quiet Sunday are less appreciated than its restrictions.

The churches have been reconsidering their position. Reports, such as "The Christian Use of Sunday" (Church of Scotland, 1962) and others, distinguish the Lord's Day from the Sabbath, stress the duty of Christians to worship, and point to opportunities of rest, family life, and healthful recreation.

The convenience of a day on which people are free for worship is obvious, but it is questionable how far the church can insist on Sabbath legislation on this ground. More important, perhaps, is the need to interpret rest and leisure. Much of the "recreation" of the modern world only continues the anxious competitiveness that mars the rest of the week. Men and women need more than ever to learn how "to cease from their own works and allow God to work in them." But such a rest cannot be made binding on all people, however much they need it. It is the fruit of faith.

See **Morality, Legal Enforcement of; Paternalism.**

D. A. Carson (ed.), *From Sabbath to Lord's Day,* 1982; A. A. McArthur, *The Evolution of the Christian Year,* 1953; W. Rordorf, *Sunday,* ET 1968.

JAMES A. WHYTE

Superego

The term "superego" was introduced by Sigmund Freud in 1923 to describe the way the ego* appears to be able to observe and judge itself. In this sense superego is a similar concept to conscience*, but there are many aspects of conscience that are not included in the idea of a superego.

Freud believed that the superego develops between the ages of three and five years when a child works through the strongly ambivalent feelings he or she has toward parents, and particularly toward the parent of the same sex. The superego reflects the child's understanding, or misunderstanding, of what parents approve or disapprove, and hence of what they are likely to reward or punish. These judgments become part of the way the child sees the world for himself or herself and are capable of bringing considerable pressure to bear on the ego to inhibit or prevent ideas or actions of which the superego disapproves. Associated with the superego is the *ego-ideal,* a conception of an ideal or perfect self modeled on the parental standards. It is as if there is a faculty in the ego which stands off and constantly watches and criticizes by comparing the actual performance of the ego against this ideal.

Both superego and ego-ideal are, then, forms of internal censorship based not so much on intelligent appraisal of evidence as on unexamined acceptance of what the child believed about the parents' wishes. The superego has the positive function of helping the child develop some moral criteria for living in society. These criteria are inadequate, however, as a basis for adult decision-making, in which the ego ought to be the dominant psychic structure. The superego is commonly too severe and limiting. Sustained conflict between ego and superego can produce deep psychic distress and strong feelings of guilt even when the person concerned can see nothing wrong or immoral in his or her actions.

Some psychologists have dismissed religion as nothing more than a product of the superego. While it is clear that some religious belief and practice is an unreflective adoption of parental views or is dependent upon experiences with the earthly parents, this is a totally insufficient explanation for all religious experience and phenomena. There is no agreement among psychologists as to the roots of religion in human life.

S. Freud, *The Ego and the Id* (1923), ET 1927; G. Peterson, *Conscience and Caring,* 1982.

GRAEME M. GRIFFIN

Supererogation, Works of

In the traditional moral theology, these were deeds going beyond what could be regarded as of strict obligation. For instance, to obey the counsels* of perfection was to go beyond what is demanded by duty. Protestants have tended to reject the whole notion of works of supererogation, and of course it is surely the case that nothing humans can do could be more than they owe to God. Yet it is equally true that one can distinguish between acts that are obligatory on all and acts that arise from a distinterested and wholehearted pursuit of the good. To give a concrete illustration, one could hardly say that it was Albert Schweitzer's *duty* * to give up his career and train as a doctor. It may well be that he himself saw it as a duty, once he had pondered it; but no one would have dreamed of blaming him had he continued his earlier activities. Perhaps we could say that in such cases there is unusual sensitivity to what constitutes one's duty. But judged by the common level of human and even Christian conduct, one might well call such extraordinary acts "works of supererogation."

JOHN MACQUARRIE

Superior Orders

In Shakespeare's *Henry V* one of the soldiers says, "We know enough if we know we are the king's subjects. If his cause be wrong, our obedience to the king wipes the crime of it out of us." This doctrine of *respondent superior,* of a soldier's plea of superior orders as an excuse for and a denial of his responsibility* for his illegal or immoral actions, such as killing innocent civilians, was rejected in the Nuremberg Trials after World War II. The United Nations War Crimes Commission ac-

cepted the following rule: "The fact that the Defendant acted pursuant to the order of his Government or of a superior shall not free him from responsibility but may be considered in mitigation of punishment if the Tribunal determines that justice so requires." The plea of superior orders could serve to excuse conduct under some circumstances, or at least mitigate the blame, even when it cannot justify the conduct. But, Michael Walzer argues, "only a man with a gun at his head is not responsible" because people can still choose not to do what is illegal or immoral even if they are ordered to do so under the threat of severe sanctions*.

See **Civil Disobedience; Coercion; Conscience; Conscientious Objection; Conscription; Just War; Military Service; Pacifism; Resistance; Responsibility; Sanction.**

G. Lewy, "Superior Orders, Nuclear Warfare, and the Dictates of Conscience," in *War and Morality,* ed. R. A. Wasserstrom, 1971; M. Walzer, *Just and Unjust Wars,* 1977.

JAMES F. CHILDRESS

Surrogate Motherhood *see* **Reproductive Technologies**

Swearing *see* **Cursing/Swearing; Oaths; Vows**

Sympathy

Sympathy relates primarily to the human ability to understand and to share the feelings of other human beings. One common form it may take is the arousal of, for example, compassion* and pity in one person by the sufferings of another. By extension, sympathy is also used in a social or political context to describe a sense of approval and support of ideologies or activities in which one is not oneself directly engaged.

Sympathy may also take the form of awareness of the feelings of another in such a way that the person concerned experiences those same feelings within his or her own being. When sympathy in this sense is distinguished from empathy*, attention is commonly drawn to the danger of overinvolvement in the feelings of others.

Ethically, sympathy is important for its capacity to motivate action in relation to the situation of other people. It is, therefore, open to manipulation, and strong feelings of sympathy are not always reliable guides to appropriate action. People are said to play on the sympathy of others when they attempt deliberately to influence decision-making by arousing feelings of pity or of involvement.

GRAEME M. GRIFFIN

Synderesis

Synderesis (or synteresis) is a term used by medieval theologians for our knowledge of the first principles of moral action. The word is generally supposed to be a corruption of the Greek *syneidēsis,* "conscience"*.

JOHN MACQUARRIE

Synergism

Synergism (derived from Greek *synergein,* "work together") is the teaching that the human person cooperates with the divine grace*, even if such co-working is no more than a response or acceptance of the gift of God. If there were no such co-working, the human recipient of grace would seem to be only a puppet. The term was used for the view of Melanchthon, who held that the human will works with the divine grace, though priority belongs to grace. This was in opposition to Luther's view, sometimes called "monergism," according to which it is God's working alone that effects salvation and good works in human life.

JOHN MACQUARRIE

Systems, Moral
see **Moral Systems, The**

Taboo

Taboo refers to prohibition such that supernaturally caused danger will result from infringement of the prohibition. By extension it also refers to anything forbidden by general cultural sanctions or mores (rather than legal ones).

The term "taboo" came into the English language from Polynesian languages. The concept is most fully developed and explicitly elaborated in the cultures of the Pacific region. In this area it is always associated very closely with the concept of *mana,* nonpersonal extraordinary power. Whatever has powerful mana is taboo to the person who is not protected from that mana, or whose mana is not itself stronger. Thus mana at work in one person's garden makes it taboo to another person, who therefore cannot steal from the garden because of the danger of calamity resulting from contact with mana

from which he or she has no protection. Unusual mana, which by definition goes with high status in Polynesian society, made it impossible for a king and a commoner to come in physical contact because of the danger to the commoner, thus forcing the most powerful of kings into lonely, isolated lives.

In less elaborately defined fashion, taboo can be seen on all levels of ancient and modern life. The Ark of the Covenant and the Holy of Holies were taboo to the ancient Israelites. Here danger stemmed partly from inherent mana and partly from the wrath of God, depending perhaps on the sophistication of the observer. The caste system of India is an extraordinary complex of taboos, as are the attitudes of many racists for whom calamity runs in the form of the degeneration of the "pure" race in some undefined but deeply feared manner.

Incest* is taboo for all societies, although not all societies define incestuous relationships in the same way, and some provide occasional ritualized rites for breaking the incest taboo with impunity. These are emotionally highly charged religious occasions.

Where taboos are strong they support the ethical system peculiar to the culture because of their built-in sanctions. Like any other custom* a taboo may eventually lose its force, be broken with impunity, or become a perfunctory relic to which lip service only is given. Shortly before the arrival of missionaries in Hawaii, the people, led by the king and an important priest, suddenly gave up an extremely complex taboo system. The king publicly broke the taboos by way of demonstration, and much of the population followed. The system had become so onerous that its repudiation was a great relief. More typically, however, taboos disintegrate under the impact of culture contact, urbanization, education, skepticism, etc., because people gradually cease to believe in some of the forms of danger and calamity ascribed to them.

See **Anthropology and Ethics; Primitive Ethics.**

WILLIAM A. SMALLEY

Taoist Ethics

This term is highly misleading in at least two respects. As a name for philosophical Taoism (*tao-chia*) associated with the works *Lao Tzu* (also called *Tao-te Ching*) and *Chuang Tzu,* the term may mistakenly suggest that these works embody a normative ethical system. For in these works, particularly in *Chuang Tzu*, one finds a radical critique of ethical systems, particularly of Mohism and Confucianism (*see* **Confucian Ethics**). Furthermore, the term is apt to suggest a confusion of philosophical Taoism with Taoist religion (*tao-chiao*), which is a corruption of the basic thought of *Lao Tzu* and preaches some form of divination, astrology, faith healing, witchcraft, etc., and the existence of living immortals. The term, however, with these qualifications, is a convenient way to refer to the ethical significance of the ideas in *Lao Tzu* and *Chuang Tzu*. It must be noted that in spite of the similarities in these works (which have been influential throughout the history of Chinese philosophy), there are important differences. *Lao Tzu,* on the whole, tends to be this-worldly; *Chuang Tzu,* otherworldly. Moreover, some of the inchoate ideas in *Lao Tzu* are more explicit in *Chuang Tzu,* e.g., the ethical significance of the notion of transcendence and the unity and harmony of opposites.

Characteristic of Taoist ethics is its emphasis on *wu-wei,* or taking no action. From the individual point of view, *wu-wei* has the force of "letting things be." In *Lao Tzu,* there is an exaltation of weakness and submissiveness. The good human life is viewed as one that conforms to the natural order, alternatively, a life of *tao* (Way), or heaven, where events occur spontaneously and yet with a constancy, though *tao* is said to be unutterable, nameless, and mysterious but amenable to "makeshift descriptions" such as "the great." In *Lao Tzu,* one also finds a statement on "three treasures" such as compassion, frugality, and "not getting ahead in the world." On the whole, the good life recommended is one that follows nature, i.e., a life of nonassertiveness and adeptness in coping with unforeseen circumstances of human life. An ideal society is depicted as one of contentment and tranquillity, with no knowledge of or concern for peoples of other societies, and a small state with a small population, equipped with defensive weapons but no occasion to use them.

From the philosophical point of view, the *Chuang Tzu* is a work of greater significance. First, we have here an explicit argumentative critique of all ethical systems that purport to offer guidance to resolving perplexities. The principal argument points to the absence of consensual standards for resolving disputes. Every normative system, moreover, presupposes values that are disparately at odds with other systems. There is and can be no value-neutral standard for resolving ethical disagreements. Secondly, because of these value presuppositions, each ethical system may be viewed as a product of the obscuration of the human mind, which inevitably fails to respond to changing circumstances. The key point in resolving perplexities is to cultivate a clear mind, much like a clear mirror, that can reflect and respond to things as they come. This feature of *Chuang Tzu* has influenced Hsün Tzu and the Neo-Confucians of the Sung and Ming dynasties, particularly Chu Hsi and Wang Yang-Ming. While *Lao Tzu* and *Chuang Tzu* are critical of conventional morality and ethical systems, they are an important challenge to any ethical philosopher concerned with the problems of ethical skepticism or relativism.

Wing-tsit Chan, *The Way of Lao Tzu,* 1963; Wing-tsit Chan (tr.), *A Source Book in Chinese Philosophy,* 1963; Chen Ku-ying, *Lao Tzu: Text, Notes, and Comments,* 1977; D. C. Lau (tr.), *Lao Tzu: Tao Te Ching,* 1963; T. Merton, *The Way of Chuang Tzu,* 1965; B. Watson (tr.), *The Complete Works of Chuang Tzu,* 1968; Kuang-ming Wu, *Chuang Tzu: World Philosopher at Play,* 1982.

A. S. CUA

Technology

The relationship between Christian belief and practice and the development of technology is complex. On the one hand, it may be argued that Christianity and the cultural world it has influenced have done as much or more than any of the other major world religions or the civilizations associated with them to sustain an ethos in which the purposive control of the natural environment for the attainment of better health, greater comfort, increased prosperity, additional mechanical power, and productive knowledge has been considered an appropriate human activity. On the other hand, Christians have frequently expressed negative concerns about the consequences that flow from the pursuit of technological agendas and even at times have tried to resist them.

Western technology has developed in several patterns, each of which has been most characteristic of a particular period of its history. The first pattern began in the ancient world and existed up through the fifth century of the Christian era. During this long time span, technology took the form of manual and artistic techniques that aided the making of pottery, cloth, furniture, aqueducts, paved highways, and masonry buildings. J. David Bolter calls this "the elegant technology of the hand rather than of the machine," since mass production was not yet imagined. In the Greco-Roman world, technology was more akin to the contemporary crafting of artifacts than to the widespread manufacture of standardized goods. Military weaponry, consisting of the sword and spear, basically extended the arm and fist of the individual warrior.

The medieval world, which saw the development of the stirrup and moldboard plow, made a great effort to harness first animal and then inanimate power for the doing of work. The development of the weight-driven clock made possible the invention of machines that would run mechanically and without the constant guidance of human operators. The development of the clock also tremendously increased the importance of chronological regularity in the ordering of human affairs. Even the workings of the cosmos came to be interpreted as a pattern of inflexible regularity.

The Industrial Revolution* was characterized primarily by the effort to harness the power of nature to do work on a hitherto unprecedented scale. First the steam engine and later the internal-combustion engine (both impossible without accurate means of timing) were developed and put to use in a variety of applications. These engines depended upon the transformation of heat into mechanical motion and were driven by the consumption of fuels that could be burned but once.

The technology of the Industrial Revolution provided exhilaration with power, since the belief was widespread that harnessing large amounts of power for the creation of material goods would be an unprecedented boon to humankind. But industrialization subordinated many human sensibilities to the achievement of growth and to the mastery of nature, and it posed the first versions of those practices that later would lead to the ecological crisis. One of the features of the later industrial age that remains with us even today is a compulsion for speed, made feasible by the internal-combustion engine and the extraction of petroleum from the earth on a massive scale. Occasional Christian voices appeared throughout this period to protest or to resist these trends, but such voices were but whimpers as the majority in the Western world poured psychic and material resources into the development of a technology marked by escalating amounts of mechanical power. Warfare was transformed by these developments from contact battle to massive destruction by mechanical means, and architecture came to depend more on steel than on masonry for structural strength.

The advent of nuclear power is sometimes looked upon as bringing a new age because it provided the prospects of obtaining energy, not from the burning of fossil fuels, but by the direct transformation of matter into energy. This seemed at first to promise to overcome the limits inherent in a technology of power dependent upon nonrenewable resources. This age was ushered in with a military action that was as stunning in the amount of power unleashed as it was troublesome in the indiscriminate killing involved. While regretting the military action which announced this age, most Western nations placed a great initial hope in the peaceful use of the atom for the production of power, but the path to that end has proved to be both more expensive and more dangerous than anyone at first supposed it would be. The eventual possibilities of this technology are still matters of intense debate—not least in ecumenical circles.

Not only mechanical devices but also chemical processes have been part of the industrial age. Chemical engineering has furnished fertilizers and pesticides used in agriculture, the plastics that have significantly replaced the use of metals, the medicines used in the healing arts, and the explosives used mainly in warfare. Interestingly, chemical warfare, while it threatens at any time to crawl out of the bottle like a malignant genie, has not as yet been used to a major extent. Some of the most severe ecological problems are associated with the chemical industry— which produces many toxic wastes.

The discovery of means to use electricity to run motors and light lamps has made possible many technological innovations of an industrial nature. Indeed, it is the medium of electricity for the transmission of power that makes energy more widely useful than it could be if used only at the source of its generation. Electricity, used in a different way, has made communication possible over long distances, it has changed the habits of the culture by providing illumination for the doing of work at night, and—more recently —it has made possible a whole new kind of technology. The computer*, which depends upon highly reliable electrical service, extends the working orbit of the human mind rather than the power of human hands or limbs. Perhaps we stand too close to this new technology to know all its possible impacts, but it poses somewhat distinctive, if not utterly different, kinds of issues. If computers were to be utilized only to control the machines of the industrial period, their implications would be momentous enough. In that application the computer makes possible automated manufacturing, space flight, incredibly sophisticated diagnostic devices in medicine, and new forms of conflict that enable military personnel to destroy others at great distances. But electronic technology is momentous because it promises to channel and control information, not merely extend mechanical power. This opens up entirely new kinds of technological achievements and ethical issues, the scope and consequences of which we are just beginning to explore.

Over the years Christians have been concerned about certain problems and issues raised by these technological developments. However, those concerned in this way have generally constituted but a minority within the Christian tradition, and there has seldom, if ever, been an instance in which a religiously expressed reservation about a particular technological process has stunted its development or decisively curtailed its use. The craft technology in existence when Christianity arose did not create too much concern. Monasticism (see **Monastic Ethics**) was a protest against the use of such technology as a means of amassing riches, but not against it as a way of doing things. Indeed, monasticism has probably done a good deal to preserve the craft tradition for its inherent values against the pressures of industrialization and commercialism*. But the technology of the machine, the advent of industrialization, and the coming of the nuclear age have posed issues of great concern to certain groups of Christians.

Some groups, like the Luddites, destroyed machines because they were fearful they would put craftspeople out of work. Others have complained that machines, the consummate exemplifiers of chronological rigidity, dehumanize individuals and seriously affect the cultural ethos in which all of us live. They argue that as a result the Western way of life has experienced an increasing disconnectedness with nature that has cut the human species off from the authentic ground of its creaturely existence, has intensified a mind/body dualism, and has made social and political life harsh, manipulative, and obsessed with power and productivity to the detriment of more humane values. Jacques Ellul, the French lay lawyer-theologian, has expressed this charge in perhaps its most forceful and extensive contemporary form.

Another criticism of technology and its impact has come from those, including many Christians, who have recognized that the industrialization of the West has brought about tremendous damage to the environment. Those who are concerned for the care of the earth (or, in the case of nuclear weapons, for its very preservation) offer different suggestions for guarding against the ecological consequences of technology. Some advocate a return to a less exploitative kind of life-style and a social system of greater decentralization and slower growth. Others believe that serious cultivation of greater scientific knowledge will provide the know-how for overcoming present difficulties. Still others argue that only as social, legal, and political systems are changed so as to make the illegitimate exploitation of nature either unprofitable or illegal will the ecologically destructive consequences of technology be overcome.

Some of the most important and the most vexing ethical considerations raised by technology arise in connection with the transfer of technology from industrially developed nations to other parts of the globe. Many people believe that the Christian faith calls us to understand technology as something that intensifies the inequities that exist in the world and widens the gulf between the haves and the have-nots. This way of thinking about the role played by technology in the contemporary world was especially evident in the discussions at the World Conference on Faith, Science and the Future sponsored by the World Council of Churches at the Massachusetts Institute of Technology in the summer of 1979. In the eyes of these critics, science and technology must be understood as instruments to be used to liberate people from oppression*, to serve the cause of justice, and to facilitate widespread participation in the making of decisions that affect their lives.

Moral and ethical decisions relating to technology figure significantly in a new process of cost-benefit and risk-benefit analysis (*see* **Cost-Benefit Analysis; Risk**) known as "technology assessment" (a phrase and process dating from the 1960s). Technology assessment considers all the possible and probable effects on society of introducing or expanding particular technologies. Thus it must entail a broad and imaginative exploration of many issues. If the assessment of technology's impact and decisions about the transfer of technology are monopolized by the holders of technological and political power, then they can easily see things from the standpoint of their privilege. As Langdon Winner argues, it may be necessary to supplement "technology assessment" with "technology criticism"—looking at long-term trends in technological and social developments as well as at particular technologies and how they operate. It is also crucial to hear from all affected, or potentially affected, parties before technology is transferred into different geographical locations or put to use in different social circumstances.

See also **Automation; Bioethics; Computers; Deterrence; Energy; Environmental Ethics; Future Generations, Obligations to; Genetics; Nuclear Warfare; Reproductive Technologies; Risk; Robots; Science and Ethics; Urbanization; War.**

I. Barbour, *Science and Secularity,* 1970; J. D. Bolter, *Turing's Man: Western Culture in the Computer Age,* 1984; T. S. Derr, *Ecology and Human Need,* 1975; F. Elder, *Crisis in Eden,* 1970; J. Ellul, *The Technological Society,* ET 1964; W. Kuhns, *The Post-Industrial Prophets: Interpretations of Technology,* 1971; L. Mumford, *The Myth of the Machine,* 1967; E. F. Schumacher, *Small Is Beautiful,* 1973; M. L. Stackhouse, *Ethics and the Urban Ethos,* 1972; L. Winner, *Autonomous Technology,* 1977.

EDWARD LEROY LONG, JR.

Teleological Ethics

The contrast between teleological (from *telos,* end, and *logos,* discourse or study) and deontological ethical theories (*see* **Deontology**) has become quite common since being proposed by C. D. Broad in *Five Types of Ethical Theory* in 1930. Like all such classifications, it must be used with caution, but it can illuminate major tendencies of ethical theories. Whereas deontological theories hold that right and wrong actions are not determined simply by their ends and consequences, teleological theories focus exclusively on ends and/or consequences of acts. One major example is Utilitarianism*, which holds that the criterion of right and wrong actions is whether they maximize welfare. Teleologists may disagree sharply about the nonmoral values* that determine good and bad ends and consequences, for example, whether those values are subjective or objective. Critics of teleological theories contend that some features of acts other than or in addition to their ends and consequences are morally relevant—for example, patterns of just distribution of goods—and that the ends do not always justify the means (*see also* **Ends and Means; Consequentialism; Agathology; Axiology**).

There is another important interpretation of teleology in ethics: sometimes the foundations of ethical principles and rules are located in the ends of nature, of human life, of organs of reproduction, of marriage, etc. Such a teleology was common in classical thought and is prominent in natural law* thought, which holds that some acts are wrong because they are not in accord with the ends of nature (*see* **Thomistic Ethics**). Most moral theology* has been teleological in this sense. Major questions arise about whether nature exhibits such ends, how they can be known, and what they imply for ethics.

See **Ethics; Finality; Natural Law; Naturalistic Ethics; Virtue.**

W. Frankena, *Ethics,* ²1973; L. Cahill, "Teleology, Utilitarianism, and Christian Ethics," *Theological Studies* 42, Dec. 1981.

JAMES F. CHILDRESS

Temperance

I. The Virtue of Temperance

Although the virtue of temperance now refers primarily to moderation in the use of alcoholic beverages, it was broader and richer in classical thought. For Plato (*see* **Platonic Ethics**), *sōphrosunē,* which literally means "soundness of mind," was one of the four cardinal virtues*, but it tended to expand and to become virtually identical with wisdom and justice. Aristotle (see **Aristotelian Ethics**) offered more precise definitions of the virtues and, using the doctrine of the mean*, interpreted *sōphrosunē* as a mean between self-indulgence and insensibility, noting that the latter is very rare. Thus, as self-control, *sōphrosunē* suggested both restraint and mastery of passions and desires. Translated into Latin as *temperantia, sōphrosunē* was common in other classical ethical systems. It was also praised in the NT (Titus 2:2, 6) along with *egkrateia,* another term meaning self-control (Gal. 5:23; 2 Peter 1:6). According to Paul self-control is not only a matter of effort but a gift of the Spirit (Gal. 5:23).

In his major synthesis of Aristotelian ethics and Christian ethics, Thomas Aquinas (*ST* II-II.141–189) viewed temperance as both a general virtue and a specific virtue (see **Thomistic Ethics**). As a general virtue, it "signifies a certain temperateness or moderation" common to all the moral virtues; as a special virtue, its matter is the desires and pleasures of the sense of touch, particularly eating, drinking, and sexual intercourse, which, according to Aristotle, are the pleasures we share with other animals. Aquinas also noted that temperance may secondarily concern the pleasures of taste, smell, or sight insofar as the sensible objects of these senses increase the pleasurable use of objects of touch (e.g., the smell and taste of food). The specific virtue of temperance is a cardinal virtue, according to Aquinas, because the objects of the sense of touch are necessary for human life, the pleasures of touch are natural, and yet it is difficult to control desires for them. However, temperance is unique among the cardinal virtues because it concerns only the agent. It is also the lowest of the cardinal virtues: "justice and fortitude are more excellent virtues than temperance: while prudence and the theological virtues are more excellent still." The virtues annexed to temperance lack any direct connection to the love of God or neighbor, but the effects of departing from such virtues as sobriety and chastity* may violate love. Hence, the Decalogue* identifies and prohibits "the effects of the vices opposed to the parts of temperance."

The general theme of temperance and moderation is also prominent in Protestant ethics. For example, John Calvin (see **Calvinist Ethics**) found in scripture a "rule of temperance" and a "rule of moderation" and in Jesus a "remarkable example of temperance" (see R. S. Wallace, *Calvin's Doctrine of the Christian Life,* 1959, pt. III, ch. 6). For Calvin moderation requires avoidance of all excess and requires modesty, contentment with one's lot, patience, and prudence.

Even though the virtue of temperance or moderation should pervade the whole Christian life, it is difficult to specify the actions that express this virtue or the actions that are intemperate. Over against world-denying forms of asceticism, the virtue of temperance reflects an appreciation of the pleasures of touch, as part of God's creation, as well as the necessity of constraining them. Some forms of asceticism*, self-denial*, and mortification* may even be intemperate. The difficulty of specifying the virtue of temperance emerges in the debates about the use of alcohol, the major context for discussions of temperance in the last two centuries.

JAMES F. CHILDRESS

II. Temperance in the Use of Alcohol

It is obvious enough why the word "temperance" has come to be associated almost exclusively with the use of alcohol. The abuse of alcohol and the prevalence of drunkenness have long been a source of human misery and degradation. There are indeed many references to strong drink in the Bible, and its capacity to make mischief if taken to excess is the subject of stern warnings. Parents who have a drunkard for a son "shall say to the elders of the town, 'This son of ours . . . is a wastrel and a drunkard.' Then all the men of the town shall stone him to death" (Deut. 21:20–21). Happily there are less brutal ways of dealing with an intractable problem!

For some people the Christian obligation of temperance in relation to the use of alcohol means moderation, for others total abstinence. There is certainly no general prohibition on the use of wine in the Bible and indeed it is described as a good gift of God. An ancient blessing was "God give you dew from heaven . . . corn and new wine in plenty!" (Gen. 27:28). There are references to two sects that practiced total abstinence, the Rechabites and the Nazirites, but their example is not enjoined on the rest. Jesus himself was not a total abstainer. John the Baptist, being a Nazirite, was an abstainer, but Jesus significantly comments on the inconsistency of the Pharisees in condemning both John and himself: "For John came, neither eating nor drinking, and they say 'He is possessed.' The Son of Man came eating and drinking, and they say, 'Look at him! a glutton and a drinker!' " (Matt. 11:18–19).

There is, however, one place in the NT where total abstinence is commended—Romans 14. Paul is concerned mainly with the question of meat, and the background is the fact that some are in danger of being enticed away from Christianity by having set before them meat which has been offered up sacrificially in heathen worship. Drink is brought in almost as an afterthought: "It is a fine thing to abstain from eating meat or drinking wine, or doing anything which causes your brother's downfall" (Rom. 14:21).

There is here the enunciation of an important principle of Christian caring. In applying it to the very different conditions of today, the Christian must weigh a number of factors. In Paul's time there was no problem caused by the association of drinking and driving resulting in the slaughter of thousands on the roads. There was no high-powered vested interest spending millions on drinking advertising*. The technique of distilling spirits had not been invented. The alcohol content of wine was not above 14 percent and its use was restricted by the comparative poverty of most people.

In this dramatically changed situation the question which many ask is, What would Paul, applying the same principle of Christian concern, be saying today? It is understandable that considerable numbers have concluded that total abstinence is a valuable witness and a positive contribution to the solution of an increasingly serious problem. There has also been debate among Christians about the use of wine in Communion.

The temperance movement. The history of the temperance movement and its many organizations during the 19th century is full of interest. Among other things, the temperance movement helped to channel religious energies into party politics, particularly as several Protestant groups such as the Methodists and the Baptists opposed alcohol (*see* **Nonconformist Conscience**). The diverse organizations included the Woman's Christian Temperance Union, which was founded in 1874 in the USA and spread around the world. The opposition to alcohol was not only religious and moral; for example, in the USA it included such factors as suspicion of industrial cities and immigrants.

The main debate in the temperance movement was between those who believed that the only way to attack the drink evil was through education or "moral suasion" and those who espoused the cause of legal prohibition. In 1846 Maine became the first state in the USA to introduce prohibition. The visits of O. W. Kellogg and Harriet Beecher Stowe to Britain led to the founding in 1853 of the United Kingdom Alliance dedicated to the suppression by law of the drink trade. It differed significantly from "The Reform," founded twenty-one years earlier by Joseph Livesey and "the seven men of Preston": for them moral suasion was primary and legislative action secondary and contributory.

Both aspects of the temperance movement have registered success and failure. The moral suasionists have not solved the drink problem, but they have saved many from the catastrophe of overindulgence and have permeated public opinion with knowledge of alcohol and its effects. The suppressionist movement's major triumph was the 18th Amendment to the US Constitution (ratified in 1919), which prohibited the manufacture, sale, and transportation of alcoholic beverages. However, this amendment was repealed in 1933 because of public opposition, problems of enforcement, and other social problems. Ultimately, the suppressionist movement failed because intemperance cannot be eliminated by mere legal enactments, but through its activities the public was alerted to the need for legislative controls of alcohol. Most legislation now concentrates on the regulation of the use of alcohol, operating automobiles while under the influence of alcohol, advertising*, etc.

Temperance in the use of alcohol has declined as a live political issue. Attempts to isolate the drink problem from other social questions have increasingly been seen as unprofitable. Many temperance organizations have now extended their brief, especially to take account of the menace of other types of drug addiction*. For a discussion of the medical factors, *see* **Alcoholism.**

See also **Health and Disease, Values in Defining; Morality, Legal Enforcement of; Paternalism.**

J. S. Blocker, Jr., *Retreat from Reform: The Prohibition Movement in the United States,*

1890–1913, 1976; H. Carter, *The English Temperance Movement: A Study in Objectives,* 1933; J. Gusfield, *Symbolic Crusade: Status Politics and the American Temperance Movement,* 1963; B. Harrison, *Drink and the Victorians,* 1971.

KENNETH G. GREET

Temptation

The situation where we are attracted to a course of action incompatible with our proper relation to God is well known to the Bible. From Gen. 3, which describes the first temptation of humans, to Rev. 3:10, which hints at a great final trial at the end of time, the theme of temptation, coming in its varied forms to a Jacob, a David, and a Peter, is worked out in detail. And it is clear not only from the temptation narratives but from Luke 22:28 and Heb. 2:18 that the life of Jesus was not exempt from temptation. Indeed the first lesson to be drawn from the Bible on the subject is that almost anything —the ambition of a Jacob, the sexual desire of a David, the cowardice of a Peter, the sufferings of the writer of Ps. 42, the prosperity of the rich fool of the parable (Luke 12: 18), the rectitude of the Pharisees, and the sense of divine mission of Jesus himself—can provide material for temptation.

Genesis 3 contains a penetrating study of temptation. By giving the woman the chance to put him right (Gen. 3:1) the serpent induces in her that state of complacency which is so often a prelude to wrong action. By assuring the couple that they will be as gods (3:5) the serpent appeals to the urge to escape from the limitations of finite existence which is a feature even of innocence* and which we have learned, since Kierkegaard, to call dread or *Angst.* By stressing that to be as God is the primal temptation, the Bible makes it clear that sin* is not, as the evolutionists thought, a relic of the brute. For to be as God is not a temptation primarily of those most at the mercy of their animal passions (though they may seek in surrender to these a temporary release from the uncertainties of human existence). It is rather a temptation of the competent and the well disciplined, the follower of a good cause and the ecclesiastic.

If the Bible is unambiguous about the prevalence and diverse character of temptation, it is less so about its origin. In the OT in particular there is found the thought that temptation is really trial and comes ultimately from God (cf. Deut. 13:3). Abraham and Job are outstanding examples of those whose temptations are interpreted in this way, and trial of this kind can even be sought after in Ps. 139:23–24. It should be noted that to the writer of Gen. 3 the serpent was simply the serpent and not the devil of popular theology, a much later conception. Even in the book of Job, Satan is not a proper name, but the name of a functionary, the satan, who has his proper place in the heavenly court.

In the NT the thought is rather that God does not himself bring about temptation (James 1:13). His part consists in not letting the temptation go too far (1 Cor. 10:13). The temptation, if not from the person himself or herself (James 1:14) or from others (1 Cor. 15:33), proceeds from Satan, conceived now as an evil personal superhuman being (Mark 1:13; Luke 22:31). This raises the question whether the Christian view of temptation implies belief in a more than human tempter. Such a figure appears in the teaching of Jesus and belief in him plays a leading part in the religious life, for example, of Luther, though by the 18th century he is no longer taken so seriously (Burns, in his "Address to the Deil," thinks of him not without humor and compassion). It is interesting that the 20th century, which in its third and fourth decades saw something like an apocalypse of evil, shows little sign of revived belief in a personal devil. This is perhaps in some measure due to realization that in the history of the church belief in evil spirits has played an unhappy part in witchcraft hunts and in the cruel and improper treatment of mental illness. The rise of modern psychiatry coincides with abandonment of belief in demonic possession. This does not mean that the concept of a devil is devoid of content. On the contrary, it is, so to speak, a limiting concept, bringing out the fact that humans need to be tempted before they sin, whereas the mythological figure of the devil is that of a being who, as it were, sins spontaneously.

The only account we have of Jesus being tempted is the scene in the wilderness, and perhaps also that laid in the Garden of Gethsemane. But Luke 22:28 speaks of temptation as a continuing feature in his life and Heb. 2:18 links it with his sufferings. As McLeod Campbell reminds us, not the least of these sufferings must have sprung from the fact that loving both God and humanity with a perfect love, he found the two estranged from each other. To love two parties at variance with one another inevitably involves suffering in proportion to the purity of the love. Did the temptation then lie for Jesus in reducing the suffering by loving God or humanity with a love less perfect? It may not be irreverent to find in the two words from the cross, "Father into thy hands I commit my spirit" (Luke 23:46) and "Father, forgive them; for they know not what they do" (Luke 23:34), the triumphal outcome of the supreme trial of Jesus' love of God and humanity.

See **Temptations of Jesus.**

IAN HENDERSON

Temptations of Jesus

The temptation narrative is found only in Matt. 4:1–11 and Luke 4:1–13, although Mark 1:12–13 also refers briefly to a period of testing following Jesus' baptism. Except for a reversal in the order of the second and third temptations, variations between the Matthean and Lucan accounts are minor.

While the details of the story represent the work of early Christians, it seems probable that the narrative had its origin in Jesus' own account of an inward, spiritual struggle that he faced shortly after his baptism and reflects in dramatic and symbolic language his wrestling with the implications of his vocation. Whatever his own conception of his vocation may have been at the beginning of his ministry, the early church acclaimed Jesus as the Messiah, and it interpreted his decision about his vocation as essentially a decision concerning the manner in which he should fulfill the messianic role.

The first temptation, according to both Matthew and Luke, took place while Jesus was in a state of intense hunger, resulting from a long period of fasting. Under such circumstances the devil urged him to use his miraculous power to turn stones into bread, thus enabling him to satisfy his own immediate need and also to gain a popular following by giving the hungry masses bread. Jesus rejected this prompting of the devil as a temptation to use his power selfishly and also to confuse humanity's true good with the satisfaction of physical hunger alone.

According to Matthew, the second temptation consisted of the subtle suggestion that Jesus demand a sign that he was indeed the Son of God by casting himself down from the pinnacle of the temple, thus compelling God to intervene with a miracle in his behalf. As proof that God would not permit the Messiah to be harmed, the devil cited the Septuagint text of Ps. 90:11–12 (91:11–12 Eng.), interpreting the latter as a messianic prediction. Not only would such a dramatic rescue remove any lurking doubt which he might have concerning his own mission, but it would likewise cause the crowds to accept him as the Messiah. But Jesus answered Satan with the reply that humankind is forbidden to put God to such a test; human beings are summoned to trust God unconditionally and to obey him without first demanding proof of God's power and providence.

Finally, again following the order in Matthew, Jesus was tempted in the third place to be a political messiah. The devil, who was believed in rabbinic and early Christian circles to have the kingdoms of this earth in his power, promised to deliver them to Jesus if the latter would only bow down and worship him. If Jesus would use his power and divine favor as the Messiah to overthrow the Roman rule and restore Israel to national independence and glory, he would quickly gain a popular following. But Jesus rejected this temptation to seek an easy, popular way to fulfill his messiahship as a form of self-will and idolatry. In his reply to Satan he singled out the central requirement of Judaism, namely, that humanity shall worship and serve the God of Israel and him alone.

E. CLINTON GARDNER

Ten Commandments see **Decalogue; Mosaic Law; Old Testament Ethics**

Terrorism

While difficult to define, terrorism in practice is often a smear word applied indiscriminately to military opponents, especially nongovernment ones. But three useful definitions of the word are possible: (1) Indiscriminate military violence. This violates the principle of noncombatant immunity (see **Discrimination**) and many theorists of just war* regard it as absolutely wrong. On this definition, the British bombing campaign against German cities in World War II stands condemned as an instance of terrorism. (2) Indiscriminate military violence by non-state organizations such as resistance and revolutionary movements (see **Resistance; Revolution**). This definition is closer to normal practice in excluding by definition the possibility of state terrorism. In this definition also, terrorism offends against noncombatant immunity. The trouble is that it suggests one standard for states and another for rebels, contrary to the spirit of the just war idea, as applied to resistance and revolution. (3) The use of terror as a military/political instrument. This is rather wide, since all military operations rely for at least part of their effect on instilling fear in the opponent. But it is useful to have a word for the type of operations that seek to avoid the arduous task of defeating the enemy's armed forces by demoralizing the opponent instead. Some theorists of air power in the period between the two world wars thought that bombing could win a war in this "indirect" way, especially the Italian Douhet, and at the level of guerrilla war there is often a strong incentive to seek anti-morale alternatives to taking on the full strength of the organized military power arrayed against one. Terrorism in this sense may be indiscriminate, as the terror bombing of World War II was. But it need not be so. For example, a resistance movement might confine the application of terror to leading representatives of the occupying power against whom it is embattled. This might call down atrocious reprisals upon compatriots, and so offend against the principle of proportionality*, but this depends on the circumstances.

In common parlance, "terrorism" is such a lazily deployed pejorative that one needs to ask for a clear explanation of what is meant whenever the word is used.

B. Paskins and M. Dockrill, *The Ethics of War,* 1978; P. Wilkinson, *Political Terrorism,* 1974.

BARRIE PASKINS

Test-Tube Babies *see* Reproductive Technologies

Theft

Theft is the secret appropriation of another's property with the intention of using or disposing of it and against the reasonable will of the owner. When it is violent and open it is called robbery. It includes other actions that have the same effect, such as fraud, nonpayment of debts, and keeping what one finds. Economic change occasions new types of theft.

The definition requires that the owner be reasonably unwilling because moral theology has traditionally recognized the right to take from an owner who ought in justice or piety to be willing to part with the property. Someone in extreme necessity might take enough for his or her immediate needs or those of dependents from an owner who had more than enough. This is because the goods of the earth are given by God for the well-being of all his children, and the right to own is subsidiary to this purpose. Similarly a wife might take what she needed from a husband who withheld it unreasonably. Persons who had been robbed or defrauded might compensate themselves occultly, though one should be cautious about recommending this.

Scripture refers both to occasional theft and to those who live by theft. Theft is condemned unconditionally in both Old and New Testaments (Ex. 20:15; Deut. 5:19). In the OT it is listed with murder, adultery, and false witness as one of the chief sins. It may be of things, animals, or persons. It is a sin against God and dishonors God even when motivated by need (Prov. 30:9). In the NT the thief is told to steal no more but rather to work and earn enough to help those in need (Eph. 4:28). Romans 13:9–10 says theft violates the commandment to love. Theft disrupts fellowship. In the new dispensation of love, thieves are enabled and called to live usefully.

The gravity of theft depends in part on the harm done to the victim, but larger thefts, even from the rich or big organizations, harm society and are always grave faults. The malice of theft depends on the conscience of the thief. Some thefts may be symptoms of psychological distress. Whoever steals is obliged to make restitution to the owner insofar as that is possible.

See **Property.**

Art. *"kleptō,"* *TDNT* III, 1965, pp. 754–756; C. Peschke, *Christian Ethics,* 1978, vol. 2, pp. 551–563.

BRENDAN SOANE

Theocracy

Domination of the civil power by the ecclesiastical.

See **Church and State.**

JOHN MACQUARRIE

Theodicy

Compounded of two Greek words *theos* (God) and *dikē* (justice), the term "theodicy" denotes attempts to explain evil or, more specifically, to vindicate God in the face of evil in the world, including both non-moral evil, such as pain, suffering, and premature death not brought about or preventable by human agency, and moral evil inflicted by human beings, such as the Holocaust. In a Christian context special problems are created by two claims that are made about God: goodness and omnipotence. If God is both good and omnipotent, why evil? The significance of various theodicies for ethics was emphasized in Max Weber's classic studies, particularly of the role of the doctrine of predestination in the contribution of the Protestant ethic to the spirit of capitalism.

See **Evil; Fate and Fatalism; Free Will and Determinism.**

J. P. Gunnemann, *The Moral Meaning of Revolution,* 1979; M. Weber, *The Protestant Ethic and the Spirit of Capitalism,* ET 1930, and *Sociology of Religion,* ET 1964.

JAMES F. CHILDRESS

Theological Ethics *see* **Christian Ethics; Moral Theology; Morality and Religion, Relations of**

Theological Virtues

The three theological virtues are faith, hope, and love (or charity). These three are, of course, mentioned by Paul in 1 Cor. 13:13. Strictly speaking, they are not virtues in the narrower sense, but may be thought of as introducing a new dimension into the moral life with its natural virtues—the dimension of grace*, based on God's action on human life.

See **Cardinal Virtues; Faith; Hope; Love; Virtue.**

JOHN MACQUARRIE

Third Use of the Law *see* **Calvinist Ethics; Law and Gospel**

Third World

This term is commonly used for countries or areas that have not developed either capitalist or socialist economic systems; the appropriateness of the term is also widely disputed. Earlier these countries or areas were often referred to as underdeveloped or developing.

See **Business Ethics; Colonialism; Economic Development; Hunger, World; Imperialism; Liberation Theology.**

Thomistic Ethics

All Thomistic ethics (and moral theology) is based on the writings of Thomas Aquinas (c. 1225–1274), a Dominican friar who taught theology and commented on Aristotle's works at the University of Paris and various study centers in Italy. His *Commentary on the Nicomachean Ethics,* along with the moral sections of the *Disputed Questions,* the *Commentary on Lombard's Sentences,* the third book of the *Summa Contra Gentiles,* and the second part of the *Summa Theologiae* constitute the original ethical corpus. Aquinas's moral views stem from a rethinking of biblical teachings (chiefly the Decalogue and the two NT precepts of love) in the light of the philosophy of Aristotle, Plato, and the Stoics.

In general, Thomistic ethics is teleological, stressing the natural desire of human beings for the perfect good (God) as their ultimate end, to which all morally good acts must be reasonably conformed (*see* **Teleological Ethics**). Since the human soul is immortal, the attainment of a loving vision of God in a future life is the culmination of good moral living on earth. A good life consists in the best possible use of one's rational powers (intellect and will) and of one's lower capacities (sense cognition, sense appetites, and bodily activities) under the control of right reason. The guidelines for such rightness stem from the principles of natural law*, of which the first (good should be sought after and done, evil avoided) is known through synderesis* (an intellectual intuition of practical precepts of moral behavior).

Aquinas organized his moral teaching around a highly developed theory of many virtues. Skill in directing one's own life and counseling others depends on good habits (acquired by practice or instilled by God). These virtuous habits of *prudentia* (right practical reasoning), *temperantia* (moderation of emotions), *fortitudo* (courageous facing of troubles), and *justitia* (willing and doing good to other persons) are natural virtues complemented by the supernaturally infused virtues of faith, hope, and charity (*see* **Cardinal Virtues; Theological Virtues**). Evils to be avoided are treated in terms of numerous bad habits (vices) opposed to the virtues.

This theory of moral habituation leading to character excellence somewhat resembles later ethics of self-perfection, but the Thomistic stress on justice and charity (love animated by God) also emphasizes altruistic duties. Moreover, Aquinas devoted much thought to the inner activities of will, understanding, and emotions (passions of the soul) and gave great importance to practical judgment, the intention of appropriate ends, the selection of right means, and reasonable choice of external (commanded) actions.

This view, that human activities derive their moral quality from the agent's thinking, feelings, and willing, somewhat anticipates later deontological ethics: our moral duties are known through our best practical judgment on what is required for any particular personal problem. This practical judgment is called moral conscience: it is not a separate power but an action of judging. Such judging is guided by rules of action known by careful reasoning on one's life experiences. This leads to certain general practical precepts (such as, be moderate and avoid extremes, stand firm against adversities, do no harm to others) which are conclusions of natural right reason. These precepts constitute what human beings can know naturally about moral laws with their ordinary powers of observation and reflection. Since natural law is but a partial sharing in God's eternal law, humans may be more fully informed by divine revelation about additional requirements of good conduct as found in scripture and Christian tradition. Since love (divine charity) gives the highest moral quality to all inner thoughts and intentions, as well as to external actions, mercy and forgiveness are features of Aquinas's ethics unknown to his predecessors in classical Greek ethics (*see also* **Medieval Ethics**).

The seven centuries since Aquinas's death have witnessed many different interpretations of his moral teachings. Latin commentators up to the late Renaissance adapted Aquinas's views to the changed circumstances of their times. Antoninus of Florence stressed social ethics; Francis Suarez and other Spanish Scholastics developed elaborate theories of legal ethics. But in recent times a larger number of "schools" of Thomistic ethics have appeared. (No up-to-date monograph covers recent Thomistic ethics adequately, but R. McCormick's "Notes on Moral Theology" in *Theological Studies* offered an annual survey from 1965 to 1984; it is now being co-authored by McCormick and others.)

Traditionalists continue to study textual and historical problems and to adhere to expositions that are close to the views of Aquinas (M. Wittmann, A. B. Sertillanges, I. T. Eschmann, R. A. Gauthier, R. McInerny). Teleologists stress the consideration of man's natural and supernatural ends and they investigate the correspondence of proposed actions with a human being's rational nature and its ultimate end. A growing group of consequentialists (P. Knauer, R. McCormick) see many ethical problems as soluble in terms of the theory of double effect*, in which one result is good and the other bad. For them much depends on the intention of the agent facing such dubious choices. Still other Thomists (G. Grisez, J. Finnis, J. Boyle) vigorously oppose all forms of consequentialism* (particularly utilitarianism) and espouse certain basic goods or duties as the determinants of ethical action. Where traditional Thomists taught that certain general types of action are absolutely wrong (murder, fornication, theft, lying, etc.) but admitted that particular actions in these categories may not appear immoral to the individual conscience, a recent school argues that such absolutes* are of little importance in practical living: each proposed action has to be judged in its own peculiar circumstances (J. Fuchs, C. Curran).

Cultural differences have resulted in some diversity in recent Thomism. Spanish, Italian, and Japanese thinkers stress natural law ethics. In the USA, John Dewey has had some impact. The result has ranged from critical appraisals of pragmatic ethics (J. Dougherty) to a partial adoption of a modified empiricism (G. Klubertanz, V. Punzo). British and Irish Thomists sometimes use analytic procedures in their studies of natural law (J. Finnis), practical judgment (P. McGrath), and moral action (E. D'Arcy). Continental European Thomists often combine phenomenological methods with their ethical thinking.

Since a teleological ethics is necessarily concerned with the sort of goods at which persons should aim, a controversy among Thomists dating back to mid-century should be noted. Some ethicists (C. De Koninck) have argued that Thomism values the common good* more than the private good.

Other thinkers (J. Maritain) have stressed the opposite: the individual's good is more important than that of the community. The problem is not resolved in more recent Thomism, for some (P. Knauer) focus on individual choice in terms of private goods, where others (P. S. Rossi) shift the ethical emphasis to the good of the community. This is not a complete bifurcation: both sides admit to some overlapping of common and private good.

In recent decades there has been some challenge to the apparent absolutism of earlier Thomism (C. Curran, ed., *Absolutes in Moral Theology?* 1968). Most Thomists insist on the difference between universal ethical judgments and particular personal judgments on doing or omitting this particular action (judgments of conscience). While many universal judgments are thought to impose absolute obligations, it is usually held that judgments of conscience may differ in regard to much the same particular problems. In other words, while I am obliged to follow my own best judgment in governing my own action, such judgments do not have the character of absolute rules for others. (See E. D'Arcy, *Conscience and Its Right to Freedom,* 1961.)

The 1979 publication of Karol Wojtyla's *The Acting Person* in English drew widespread attention, partly because of his elevation to the papacy as John Paul II. His combination of Thomistic ethics with the personalism* of European phenomenology* has directed attention to the importance of the moral agent and his development. There have even been attempts to work out a complete phenomenology of moral law (W. A. Luijpen, *Phenomenology of Natural Law,* ET 1967).

Distinctive positions have been taken recently by Thomists on special ethical problems. While the earlier tradition was never entirely pacifist, today's world conditions have moved many to question the propriety of any present war. J. K. Ryan (*Modern War and Basic Ethics,* 1940) was one of the first to take this position. The older rules for justifying going to war (declaration by legitimate authority, for a just cause, and with a proper intention) no longer seem adequate. One must now also consider the character of the weapons to be used, the distinction between combatants and noncombatants, and the proportion between the good and bad features of the total results of any war (*see* **Just War**). A

good many Thomists now think that nuclear war* can never be justified.

Problems in sexual ethics* and marriage* find most Thomists still conservative, opposing adultery, fornication, artificial contraception*, and abortion*. Divorce* in its perfect form is condemned, but there is some tendency toward a less strict handling of marriage annulment. (J. E. Biechler, ed., *Law for Liberty,* 1967.) In legal ethics traditional Thomism supported the use of capital punishment*, where needed to protect the common good. But recent thinking has tended to reject such killing, as opposed to the sacredness of human life, and as open to many abuses in the application of such extreme and irreversible punishment.

See also **Modern Roman Catholic Moral Theology.**

V. Bourke, *Ethics in Crisis,* 1966; W. Kluxen, *Philosophische Ethik bei Thomas von Aquin,* 1964; R. McInerny, *Ethica Thomistica: The Moral Philosophy of Thomas Aquinas,* 1982; J. Maritain, *Moral Philosophy,* ET 1964; T. Miethe and V. Bourke, *Thomistic Bibliography: 1940–1978,* 1980; J. Pieper, *The Four Cardinal Virtues,* ET 1966.

                                    VERNON J. BOURKE

Tissue Transplant *see* **Organ Transplantation**

Tobacco, Use of

Tobacco, which was used by American Indians, became very important in the trade between Europe and the New World. At first tobacco was valued primarily as a medicinal herb and occasionally as an ornamental plant. After Sir Walter Raleigh introduced smoking to England in the latter part of the 16th century, it soon became widely used for pleasure as well as for its alleged medicinal value. *A Counterblaste to Tobacco* (1604), by King James I, opposed "tobacco taking" as "a custome loathsome to the eye, hatefull to the Nose, harmfull to the braine, dangerous to the Lungs." Disputing the claim that "tobacco taking" had medicinal value, King James opposed it mainly for medical and moral but also for religious and aesthetic reasons. Medical and moral arguments also supported the prohibition measures adopted by several European and other countries in the 17th century, but the use of tobacco continued to spread. His own arguments having failed to deter tobacco use, King James I imposed a stiff import tax on tobacco a year later.

Although chewing tobacco and using snuff are not insignificant, most of the current controversy focuses on smoking, particularly of cigarettes, which are more popular and more dangerous than either cigars or pipes. When cigarettes became widely available in the 19th century, they were associated with undesirable social groups, and at the turn of the century their sale was banned by fourteen states on moral rather than health grounds: Smoking cigarettes was corrupting and would lead to other immoral activities. This restrictive legislation was overturned in the 1920s, and by the 1950s and 1960s smoking had acquired positive symbolic significance, especially under the impact of massive advertising campaigns. When concern about cancer emerged in the early 1950s, the cigarette companies responded with filter cigarettes. The US Surgeon General's report in 1964 associated smoking with cancer of the lung and larynx, and various studies in the USA, the UK, and elsewhere have established that smokers are at increased risk for such diseases as coronary heart disease, chronic bronchitis, pulmonary emphysema, and peptic ulcer, as well as various cancers, particularly lung cancer, the subject of primary concern. It is estimated that 300,000–350,000 people in the USA and over 90,000 in the UK die each year because of diseases brought on by cigarette smoking. Of course, the incidence of morbidity and disability is also tremendous. The evidence for the risks of cigarette smoking is substantial, despite attacks by the tobacco industry. Various private and governmental actions in the UK and in the USA—for example, banning advertising of tobacco on television and requiring health warnings on packs of cigarettes—have contributed to a substantial decline in the last two decades in the percentage of adults who smoke. For example, in the USA this percentage has dropped from 42 percent to 33 percent, with a sharper decline occurring among male smokers. Nevertheless, it is appropriate to describe smoking as a major health problem, even an epidemic, in both the UK and the USA, as well as in many other parts of the world (e.g., China).

Opposition to smoking has been strong among some religious groups, particularly the Mormons and Seventh-day Adventists, but also some Mennonites, Brethren, and Quakers as well as the Salvation Army. However, most religious groups view smoking as a matter of individual discretion, perhaps in deference to Jesus' principle that "not what goes into the mouth defiles a man, but what comes out of the mouth, this defiles a man" (Matt. 15:11). Nevertheless, there are grounds for urging people not to commit what has been called "slow-motion suicide," in part to fulfill their responsibilities to others (e.g., parents to children). People find it easy to discount the risks because smoking is so familiar and the harm occurs in the future rather than immediately. It is unclear whether temperance* or moderation rather than abstinence* is acceptable because there is debate about whether there is a safe level of consumption (see Risk).

Several factors militate against vigorous policies to reduce smoking. First, there are the vested interests of tobacco farmers (in the USA tobacco is the sixth largest cash crop, with $2.5 billion in cash receipts in 1978 and 600,000 families involved), of tobacco companies, and of the government in tax revenues and balance of trade. The US government policy is ambivalent—the federal government maintains a price support system that restricts the production of tobacco in an effort to maintain its price and the income of tobacco farmers, and yet it prohibits some advertising and promotes education of the public about the dangers of smoking. (It has been suggested that the removal of the price-support program might actually lead to the overproduction of tobacco, a decline in the price of cigarettes, and an increase in consumption.)

Second, there are claims about personal autonomy* and liberty* that resist various paternalistic policies (see also Paternalism; Morality, Legal Enforcement of). Smoking is clearly dangerous and addictive, but proponents of autonomy and liberty contend that government intervention should be limited to education and warnings rather than extended to the prohibition of production, sale, or use, except for sale to minors.

In recent years, public concern about the rights and interests of nonsmokers has greatly increased, in part because of the rise in nonsmoker militancy. Many people find cigarette smoke unpleasant and offensive and assert their right not to be exposed to it. There is also mounting evidence of the harm of so-called "passive smoking," exposure to smoking by others. One possible compromise is the provision of "zones," for example, segregation of smokers and nonsmokers in transportation and many public facilities. More complicated is smoking in the workplace, but it might be argued that the right of nonsmokers not to be put at risk should outweigh the right of smokers to smoke. Another difficult question concerns the pregnant smoker's imposition of risks on the fetus, including the risks of spontaneous abortion, neonatal death, malnutrition, and low birth weight.

Finally, there is controversy about the economic costs of smoking to nonsmokers and to the society. Prudence*, as suggested by King James I, might dictate a different allocation of personal resources, but justice* also becomes an issue when there are identifiable costs to nonsmokers, through increased premiums in health plans or increased taxes. Opposition to paying for the avoidable afflictions of others can be expected not only on grounds of self-interest but also on grounds of fairness* in the distribution of burdens. In some settings, it is possible to pass the additional costs of health care on to smokers, for example, through increased premiums or increased taxes on cigarettes. However, it would be difficult to defend the denial of medical care to smokers or other risk-takers, in part because of the difficulty of determining, for example, whether a person's lung cancer resulted from cigarette smoking, environmental pollution, work conditions, or heredity (see **Health Care, Right to; Sick, Care of the**). In addition, the prospect of "health police" violating privacy* and keeping detailed records of risky conduct is morally offensive. Several studies indicate that the cigarette smokers create additional and heavy costs for the society, particularly in medical care, but when a broad cost-benefit analysis* (including social security and retirement programs) is used, the argument for government intervention may be weakened. Howard Leichter argues that "over the long run, under public or private health and retirement systems, one can expect an increase rather than decrease in social expenditures as a result of avoiding health risks." Risk-takers may actually save the society money by dying early and, even if they consume more health care, they may relieve the system of other burdens later. Obviously, other moral and

religious considerations are important and suggest the limitations, perhaps even the callousness, of cost-benefit analysis. Nevertheless, if cost-benefit analysis is invoked for restricting cigarette consumption, critics argue that the full range of costs and benefits should be considered.

Public policies must be examined for their effectiveness and efficiency as well as for their consistency with principles of justice and autonomy. For example, increasing the tax on cigarettes and thus raising their price might reduce the number of cigarettes smoked while inducing smokers to smoke each cigarette longer and farther down, thereby increasing the health risks. Similarly, studies about the use of safer cigarettes, with lower tar and nicotine, indicate that smokers may smoke more or smoke them differently in order to compensate for the decline in tar and nicotine.

See **Behavior Control; Drug Addiction.**

H. Leichter, "Public Policy and the British Experience," *HCR* 11, Oct. 1981, pp. 32–39; H. M. Sapolsky, "The Political Obstacles to the Control of Cigarette Smoking in the U.S.," *Journal of Health Politics, Policy and Law* 5, Summer 1980; R. J. Troyer and G. E. Markle, *Cigarettes: The Battle Over Smoking,* 1983.

JAMES F. CHILDRESS

Tolerance, Toleration *see* **Church and State; Persecution and Toleration**

Torah *see* **Jewish Ethics; Mosaic Law; Old Testament Ethics; Paul, Ethical Teaching of**

Torture

Torture is one of the very few things that are absolutely prohibited in international law, but in practice it is rampant and may well be on the increase. In many countries it is a standard way of intimidating opponents, though no state admits to engaging in it, and some of the offenders can be shamed into curbing some excesses by the concerted human rights* campaigning of such organizations as Amnesty International. Liberation movements, too, make shamefaced use of torture, though some leading theorists of guerrilla warfare, e.g., Mao Tse-tung, argue that it is counterproductive. Why should torture be absolutely prohibited? What about the textbook problem of the terrorist who can be forced to reveal the whereabouts of a nuclear bomb only by torture? In theory, one could apply something like just war* criteria to argue that torture would be licit in such a case, but in practice legalizing any exceptions would be exploited to legitimize practices going far beyond the hypothetical extreme case.

Amnesty International, *Report on Torture,* 1975; E. Peters, *Torture,* 1985.

BARRIE PASKINS

Total Abstinence *see* Abstinence; Asceticism; Mortification; Temperance

Total Depravity

The confidence in reason which was a feature of the Renaissance has been undermined by Freud and Marx as well as by some elements in the teaching of Barth. Reason, so far from being what Platonism took it to be, something uncorrupted by evil, can deteriorate into rationalization. If the doctrine of total depravity simply meant that every part of the human being is affected by sin, it would be accepted in fairly wide circles today. But the doctrine goes much further and holds that there is no good in humans at all, that every part of them is *entirely* corrupted. As the Westminster Confession puts it (ch. VI), Adam and Eve at the Fall became "wholly defiled in all the faculties and parts of soul and body" and from this original corruption we are "utterly indisposed, disabled, and made opposite to all good, and wholly inclined to all evil."

How did such a doctrine come to be held? One reason is that the Bible says some fairly pungent things about the depravity of the human heart. "The heart is deceitful above all things, and desperately corrupt" (Jer. 17: 9). "Behold, I was brought forth in iniquity, and in sin did my mother conceive me" (Ps. 51:5). "For I know that nothing good dwells within me" (Rom. 7:18). But it is one thing to take a realistic and even a dark view of human nature and another to hold the doctrine of *total* depravity. If all people are totally bad, then there is no difference between the good and the bad. Jesus, however, draws such a distinction in at least three places, Matt. 5:45; 13:49; 25:37, 46. Paul does the

same in Rom. 13. It should be noted also that even when Jesus and Paul are emphasizing the basic evil in life, they do not hold that it excludes manifestations of good (cf. Matt. 7:11 and Rom. 7:18). Another reason for acceptance of the doctrine has been the evangelical emphasis that we are saved by the grace of God and not by our own merits. But to say that our good actions are irrelevant for our salvation is not to say that we do not do any good actions.

See **Original Sin; Sin(s).**

IAN HENDERSON

Totalitarian State

The concept is derived from Mussolini's description of the Fascist state as a *stato totalitario,* a state that had total control. After the Second World War political scientists developed the theory to describe both Fascist and Communist dictatorships, of which the paradigms were Nazi Germany and Stalinist Russia. Their common features were held to constitute a new type of state. These features were the unlimited demands of a pseudo-religious ideology (whether world revolution or the master race) which claimed to be the agent of history in transforming society and the world, and the institutional methods of giving effect to these revolutionary creeds, including a single mass party under centralized leadership, state control of the economy, a state monopoly of information and education, mobilization of the entire population, condemnation of opposition (real or imaginary) as enemies of the state, restriction on any independent social activity such as religious societies unless under state control, obedience ensured by the instruments of terror, secret police, state-controlled courts, show trials, and concentration camps. The concept of totalitarian dictatorship is distinguished both from its antithesis, pluralist democracy*, and from traditional dictatorships which it is held lacked either comparable ambitions for the total control of society or comparable instruments with which to achieve them.

There are major difficulties in the concept including the differences between Fascist and Communist dictatorships and the evolution of the Soviet system since the death of Stalin. However, the theory marks an important attempt to explain the phenomenon of the combination of dictatorship and mass politics peculiar to the 20th century.

See **Dictatorship; State; Tyrannicide.**

H. Arendt, *The Origins of Totalitarianism,* new ed. 1967; C. J. Friedrich and Z. K. Brzezinski, *Totalitarian Dictatorship and Autocracy,* ²1965; C. J. Friedrich, M. Curtis, and B. R. Barber, *Totalitarianism in Perspective: Three Views,* 1969.

                                         J. R. C. WRIGHT

Totalitarianism *see* **Fascism; Totalitarian State**

Totality, Principle of

The most general form of the principle of totality states that the good of the part may legitimately be sacrificed for the good of the whole. The principle finds its most natural application in the case of organisms, such as human beings, but it has also been applied by analogy to nonorganic wholes such as the family, the state, or society at large. The principle has been invoked especially in medical ethics, as part of an argument to justify, e.g., sterilization as a method of contraception where childbearing might prove injurious to health. A healthy reproductive system is sacrificed for the sake of the human being as a whole. This principle might also serve to establish the conclusion that it is right for soldiers to give their lives to ensure the safety of their country.

The principle of totality has proved highly controversial. In some applications it might seem quite unobjectionable, whereas in others it has been regarded as tantamount to the equally controversial view that the ends justify the means (*see also* **Ends and Means**). In general, it seems that the principle is too vague to support the weight of argument that has been laid upon it.

                                         GERARD J. HUGHES

Trade Unions and Professional Associations

In Western-type economies, trade unions and professional associations are organs through which those who earn their living in a job or a profession join together to exercise some control over the terms and conditions under which they work as against the power of the employer or management, whether public or private. In centralized collective economies they are bodies through which certain government policies in work, social, and health matters are propagated, but they do not form an independent power base. Professional associations have other functions, such as guaranteeing standards of work and protecting the consumer against possible idiosyncracies of a practitioner (*see* **Professional Ethics**). Trade unions share these functions to a lesser extent in social and educational roles and sometimes in apprenticeship regulations. Some unions are for a specific occupation; some are general or industrial unions. Interunion disunity and rivalries can sometimes cause trouble and be as difficult to mend as disunity among the Christian churches. How far unions should participate in management problems is much debated in general and within unions, and opinions and practices are divided, some seeing it as a desirable extention of democratic procedures to industry, others as a confusion of roles. In Western-type economies West Germany has gone farthest in this direction; in collectivist economies Hungary and Yugoslavia.

An ethical issue often raised is that of the closed shop. The *pre*-entry form of it precludes the employment of anyone not already in a union, the *post*-entry form requires all workers once employed to join. The former is open to the objection of being too restrictive, the latter is often favored by managements as simplifying industrial relations*. Trouble arises when there is a conscientious objector, sometimes a Christian, with a very individualist outlook. In proportion to the strength of the union it may be urged on it to agree that union dues might in this case be given to a nominated charity instead. Unions of course need to see that their internal procedures conform to principles of natural justice.

See **Collective Bargaining; Labor Movements; Strikes.**

                                         RONALD PRESTON

Tradition in Ethics

The term "tradition" can refer either to something handed down from generation to generation (*traditum*) or to the mode of transmission itself (*traditio*). No one doubts that there are ethical traditions in both senses, but there is no consensus among students of morality concerning the nature and significance of tradition in ethics. Several major movements in modern ethical thought portray tradition as inessential to ethics or even as morally dangerous, though each has met with serious opposition.

Some Protestants have argued that scripture, interpreted by human reason in light of the Holy Spirit, should serve as the sole rule of faith and morals. Their point has been to deny tradition the essential role ascribed to it in Catholicism, where the living magisterium* functions not only as the definitive interpreter of scriptural revelation but also as the official organ of nonscriptural divine traditions. Against the doctrine of *sola scriptura,* Catholics have maintained that scripture cannot operate independently as a rule of faith and morals, for scripture is silent on some important matters, requires interpretation disciplined by tradition, and does not provide a criterion for determining which writings are genuinely scriptural. Without denying the authority of scripture, Catholics have therefore insisted upon the necessity of acknowledging tradition as a source of authority as well. On the other hand, Protestants have often seen tradition as too inconsistent and corruptible to be a genuine source of moral authority. Not all Protestants, however, have taken such a dim view of tradition, and Protestant theologians like James Gustafson and Stanley Hauerwas are among those now assigning tradition a central role in ethics.

Many modern moral philosophers have viewed tradition as, at best, an ultimately dispensable aid to fallible human reason and, at worst, a repository of superstition and a threat to autonomy*. They have therefore attempted to ground moral knowledge and action in something not essentially dependent upon tradition. For intuitionists, moral knowledge is derived from a foundation of certitudes accessible in principle to all rational persons. For followers of Immanuel Kant (1724–1804), morality is a set of rules required by pure reason, rules we legislate for ourselves out of respect for free rational agency (*see* **Kantian Ethics**). Even the received moral teachings of Christ, according to Kant, must be subjected to scrutiny by autonomous reason before being accepted as authoritative.

Intuitionists and Kantians face a common difficulty—that of how to square moral variety or disagreement with the idea that moral knowledge derives from foundational certitudes or from the requirements of pure reason. Why, if moral knowledge is what intuitionists and Kantians have said it is, do some ethical traditions differ significantly from others? One answer, Kant's own, is that some traditions are simply more fully rational than others. They are further along the road to moral perfection. Kant, who took a more favorable view of tradition than many of his followers have, interpreted religious traditions as "vehicles" of perfect moral rationality, vehicles that help fallible human beings make progress toward pure rational faith. Religious traditions, while dispensable in the long run, are suited to the failings of sensuous humanity, but some represent relatively little progress toward perfection, others more. Kant thus explains moral variety by judging some traditions less rational than others and then endeavoring to show how nonrational factors enter in. His successors, however, have been reluctant to declare alien traditions irrational without closer examination. Some have tried to show that much of the putative evidence of moral diversity is merely apparent. Others, agreeing that Kant's ascriptions of irrationality cannot be supported but remaining unpersuaded that moral diversity can simply be explained away, have suggested that practical reason makes use of tradition-bound presuppositions and that variation in such presuppositions explains variation in moral conclusions.

This last option in effect grants what the proponents of tradition have insisted upon all along—that tradition is essential to moral reasoning, that the rational acceptability of a moral conclusion can be determined only relative to a context of inherited assumptions, and that "pure reason" does not suffice to generate a uniquely rational moral system. Once this much has been granted, however, it becomes hard to avoid the further conclusion that pure reason is an empty abstraction lacking any explanatory power whatsoever. This was the conclusion G. W. F. Hegel (1770–1831) drew in his critique of Kant, and recent defenses of tradition as an essential dimension of the moral life continue to show Hegel's influence. Those most deeply influenced by Hegel—philosophers like Hans-Georg Gadamer and Alasdair MacIntyre, theologians like David Tracy—have taken pains to dissociate themselves from a picture of tradition as basically continuous and conservative. For such thinkers, traditions are ongoing conversations or arguments subject to dramatic reversal and, at times, revolutionary innovation. Tradition, for them, far from being opposed to critical reason, is its necessary embodiment (*see* **Hegelian Ethics**).

See also **Authority; Bible in Christian Ethics.**

J. M. Gustafson, *Ethics from a Theocentric Perspective,* vol. 1: *Theology and Ethics,* 1981, ch. 3; A. MacIntyre, *After Virtue,* 1981, ch. 15.

JEFFREY STOUT

Tranquilizers *see* Drug Addiction

Transcendence

To transcend is to go beyond or surpass something. Human beings are peculiarly able to transcend what they receive from nature, environment, and society. This self-transcendence or creative freedom is recognized as being of central ethical significance in existentialism. Furthermore, it informs Marx's conviction of humanity's ability, collectively, to transcend socioeconomic alienation. The way of transcendence, in which the natural self is transcended in other-directed action and concern, has also been commended as the essence of a secular Christianity. But a theological anthropology sees in human "openness to the future" (Pannenberg) or in "transcendental experience" (Rahner) an indication of what makes such human transcendence possible, namely, an "all-encompassing reality," an ultimate supernatural transcendence, that calls us out of nature and makes possible human transcendence. This divine transcendence, which for Christian theology differentiates the Creator from the creature, for Christian ethics constitutes the absolute ground of all goodness, beauty, and truth. Just because it is the ground and resource of all human transcendence, this divine transcendence cannot be thought of apart from divine immanence, whereby the Spirit of God is present and active in and through the creature.

Modern Christianity has felt the force of the criticism that traditional conceptions of divine transcendence inhibit and threaten human freedom, and has sought to develop a nonalienating conception of divine transcendence that can be seen as liberating rather than oppressive (Macquarrie). An increasingly influential way of doing this has been in terms of "the future as a new paradigm of transcendence" (Moltmann). But this emphasis is in danger of obscuring the equally liberating immanence of divine incarnation and presence.

J. Macquarrie, *In Search of Humanity,* 1982; J. Moltmann, *The Future of Creation,* ET 1979.

BRIAN HEBBLETHWAITE

Transcendentalism
see **New England Transcendentalism**

Transplants, Transplantation
see **Organ Transplantation**

Transsexualism

The transsexual is a normal male or female according to physiological criteria, but experiences himself or herself as a member of the opposite sex, and may seek hormonal and surgical reassignment—a so-called "sex-change." The specific medical and social recognition of transsexualism is very recent—essentially since 1952 when former American GI Christine Jorgensen made world headlines by undergoing sex-change surgery. However, the historical and cross-cultural evidence suggests that transsexualism has been known from early antiquity and within a variety of cultures.

Transsexualism is to be distinguished from several other conditions: physiological intersexuality (hermaphroditism), where the person has some actual physiological characteristics of the opposite sex; transvestism, where a male experiences erotic arousal from dressing in female clothing, but is generally heterosexual in practice and does not seek surgical reassignment; and homosexuality, where there may be little or no sense of cross-gender identity.

A number of legal and ethical questions are raised by transsexualism. It may be possible to change most personal documents after reassignment, but often not the birth certificate.

Another question is the status of marriage and sexual relationships for the postoperative transsexual. The transsexual may regard the relationship as heterosexual, but he or she was formerly classified as a member of the same sex as his or her partner, and is still genetically a member of that sex.

Stoller suggests that the male-to-female

transsexual acquires his abnormal gender identity through a nonconflictual learning process based on imprinting and conditioning. In Moberly, *Homosexuality* (1983), it is proposed that transsexualism in both sexes has a conflictual origin, stemming from disruption in attachment to the parent of the same sex. This radical disidentification, which is present in a lesser degree in the homosexual, checks the acquisition of a same-sex identity. Ethically, the evaluation of transsexualism is seen as comparable to that of homosexuality. The underlying desire for a same-sex attachment marks the persistence from early years of a legitimate developmental need. Its fulfillment, together with the resolution of an underlying ambivalence toward members of the same sex, may further the developmental process. However, as a preadult need, it is considered more appropriate to fulfill this nonsexually.

E. R. Moberly, *Homosexuality: A New Christian Ethic,* 1983; and *Psychogenesis: Early Development of Gender Identity,* 1983; R. J. Stoller, *The Transsexual Experiment,* 1975.

ELIZABETH R. MOBERLY

Triage

The process of deciding which medical patients should receive priority in treatment. When medical resources are scarce, patients are "sorted" in order to use the resources in ways deemed most effective.

Medical triage developed first in military medicine with the need to treat large numbers of casualties quickly and efficiently. Baron Larrey, Napoleon's chief medical officer, generally is credited with the first organized plan for the classification of casualties. It was not, however, until World War I that triage (both the word and the practice) became a standard part of modern warfare. Later, triage became a common feature of emergency medicine as well as disaster and civil defense planning.

The triage plan which has gradually become customary in military and emergency medicine includes three categories: (1) the slightly injured who will probably survive even if not treated immediately; (2) the hopelessly injured who cannot be expected to survive even if treated immediately; and (3) the priority group of those who probably will survive only if treated immediately. The most obvious moral justifications for such triage

are utilitarian—saving the greatest number of lives and, in the case of military medicine, preserving military strength.

In recent years, the metaphor of triage has been employed in rationing scarce new medical technologies, such as the artificial kidney. Patient selection based on utilitarian criteria, especially estimations of each patient's worth relative to society, has touched off a debate about the morality of such triage. While some ethicists (e.g., Joseph Fletcher) have defended utilitarian selection, other ethicists (e.g., Paul Ramsey) have argued instead for selection by chance or randomization (lottery, queuing, or "first-come, first-served") among medically suitable candidates, contending that only such a procedure can preserve equality* of opportunity, fairness*, and justice* and avoid reducing persons* to their social roles and functions. Ramsey also argues that random selection avoids "godlike judgments of human worth" and is an extension into human affairs of God's indiscriminate care. As medical research continues to result in new and often costly therapies, it is likely that the debate about the justness of various schemes of patient selection will continue (*see* **Health Care, Right to; Sick, Care of the**). (The metaphor of triage is also used in discussions of world hunger; *see* **Hunger, World**).

J. F. Childress, "Who Shall Live When Not All Can Live?" *Soundings* 53, 1970; and "Rationing of Medical Treatment," *EB,* 1978; P. Ramsey, *The Patient as Person,* 1970; G. R. Winslow, *Triage and Justice,* 1982.

GERALD R. WINSLOW

Trust

Pervasive in human interactions and prominent in the Christian's relation to God (*see* **Faith; Justification by Faith**), trust is confidence in and/or reliance upon another. In Løgstrup's language, to trust is "to deliver oneself over into the hands of another." Trust cannot exist where there is absolute control over the other, but many acts are mixtures of trust and control. In its broad sense, trust is the expectation that the other will act in accord with his or her public presentation of self; in its narrow sense, it is the expectation that the other will act morally. If the other has given signals of untrustworthiness, the truster may not be able to complain of a breach of trust. There is no moral duty to express trust if the other person is utterly untrustworthy. Yet Horsburgh has argued that we cannot express generalized, systematic, absolute, and incorrigible distrust of another person without denying his or her nature as a moral agent or person. Sometimes acts of trust may be "therapeutic" and even "redemptive" to the trustee, contributing significantly to his or her moral development (e.g., parents trusting their children). Various beliefs about human nature undergird attitudes and actions of trust or distrust and mistrust in interpersonal and institutional settings. For example, proponents of nonviolent resistance* often believe that their attitudes and acts of trust can lead their opponents to respect moral principles and to become trustworthy, while their critics contend that control, through coercion* or violence, is often necessary (see **Realism**). Even though trust is essential to human community*, there is disagreement about when and where trust is appropriate, particularly in such contexts as international relations.

B. Barber, *The Logic and Limits of Trust*, 1983; J. F. Childress, *Moral Responsibility in Conflicts*, 1982, ch. 1; H. J. N. Horsburgh, "The Ethics of Trust," *Philosophical Quarterly* 10, Oct. 1960, pp. 343–354; K. Løgstrup, *The Ethical Demand*, ET 1974; N. Luhmann, *Trust and Power*, ET 1980.

JAMES F. CHILDRESS

Truth see **Lying; Truthfulness**

Truthfulness

The heart of the matter is found in Eph. 4:15, where Christians are told to speak the truth *in love**. Truthfulness is the proper use before God of his gift of speech; but it must be in love. We are not called upon to utter the whole truth at all times and to all and sundry. There are truths better left unsaid; not to speak is not necessarily to sin against the truth. Or on occasion part of the truth may be better withheld. Only those who are devoted to the truth will have the sensitivity to discern how and how much of the truth to speak. Otherwise we become sly. In the NT it is the epistle of James which stresses most fully the right use of the tongue and condemns most strongly its misuse (cf. 3:2, 6) and in doing so echoes Matt. 12:36f. (see **Lying; False Witness; Slander**).

The question of professional secrets is involved in the question of truthfulness. Put briefly, what is known in a professional capacity should not be revealed without the consent* of the person concerned. The supreme example of this is the confessional, and for a fuller treatment of this, works on pastoral theology should be consulted. It also applies to lawyers, doctors, and more and more to social workers. At the same time teamwork and group practices and the secretarial work involved in them are leading to greater access to files and making issues of confidentiality prominent. The extent to which professional secrecy is safeguarded by law varies from country to country; where it is not it may in fact be respected. Except in an extreme situation professional confidentiality should be maintained (see **Confidentiality; Secrecy**).

RONALD PRESTON

Tutiorism

In cases of practical doubt, tutiorism says that one must always follow the "safer opinion" (*opinio tutior*), in the sense of always assuming that the law (moral principle, or rule) in question obliges unless the opinion in favor of liberty is so exceedingly probable as to be morally certain. A broadly tutiorist approach was generally characteristic of the early church fathers, adopted by many medieval theologians, and reaffirmed by the Jansenists. It is criticized on the grounds that, if *invariably* practiced (when it is known as rigorism), it undermines moral initiative and panders to scrupulosity*: on some occasions it will impose intolerable hardships and on others justify actions that are patently absurd. Rigorism was condemned by Pope Alexander VIII in 1690. Nevertheless, there are occasions when tutiorism is the correct procedure: when the practical doubt relates either to the *validity* of an action (e.g., the sacraments) or to some especially *vital interest* whether of the agent or of someone else.

See **Casuistry; Compensationism; Counter-Reformation Moral Theology; Equiprobabilism; Probabiliorism; Probabilism.**

THOMAS WOOD

Two Realms

Luther's social ethic tries to reestablish the theological coordination of civil and religious authority which had been advocated in Augustine's *City of God* prior to the late medieval church's program of subordinating the civil to the ecclesiastical realm.

The uniqueness of Luther's formulation lies in his rejection of any kind of biblical-philosophical synthesis, as with Plato in Augustine or with Aristotle in Aquinas. Instead he interprets the totality of human experience within the strictly biblical categories of God's twofold rule of humanity through his law as Creator and through his gospel as Redeemer (*see* **Law and Gospel**). Ultimately, Luther's doctrine of the "two realms" is grounded firmly in the Pauline eschatology of the "two ages" (*aeons*) in Adam and in Christ (Rom. 5).

Luther wrote in *Secular Authority: To What Extent It Ought to Be Obeyed* (1523, *WA* 11, pp. 249f.):

> We must divide all the children of Adam into two classes; the first belong to the kingdom of God, the second to the kingdom of the world. Those belonging to the kingdom of God are all true believers in Christ and are subject to Christ and the gospel of the kingdom. . . . All who are not Christians belong to the kingdom of the world and are under the law. Since few believe and still fewer live a Christian life, do not resist evil, and themselves do no evil, God has provided for non-Christians a different government outside the Christian estate and God's kingdom, and has subjected them to the sword. . . . For this reason the two kingdoms must be sharply distinguished, and both permitted to remain; the one to produce piety, the other to bring about external peace and prevent evil deeds; neither is sufficient in the world without the other.

The key points in Luther's position are these: (1) God is the Lord of both kingdoms, although he rules each by different means (law and gospel) for different ends (peace and piety); (2) all Christians live in both kingdoms simultaneously—in the kingdom of God insofar as they are righteous, and in the kingdom of the world insofar as they are sinful; (3) the two kingdoms are to be sharply distinguished from one another, which means that the realms of law and gospel are to be neither separated (in secularism) nor equated (in clericalism). Both kingdoms should be permitted to coexist in harmonious interaction and coordination as complementary expressions of the triune God's creative and redemptive activity among humans.

Through this doctrine of God's "two realms," or better, "twofold reign," Luther reaffirmed the "sacred secularity" of the ordinary tasks of the common life as those which best meet our neighbors' needs in the service of Christ.

See **Justification by Faith; Law and Gospel; Lutheran Ethics; Orders.**

WILLIAM H. LAZARETH

Tyrannicide

Violent resistance* in which a private person or a subordinate within the government takes the life of a tyrant. Traditionally identified as one who pursues his or her own ends rather than the ends of the community, the tyrant may be (1) a usurper of power without title or legitimate authority, or (2) a legitimate holder of power who becomes tyrannical through the abuse of power. Without extensive discussion of the arguments for and against tyrannicide, such Greek thinkers as Plato and Aristotle assumed that tyrannicide was normal and the perpetrator honorable, and such Roman thinkers as Cicero approved the assassination of Julius Caesar. In view of NT passages that call for nonresistance and political submission and the OT's recognition that even wicked rulers could be God's instruments to chastise the people, it is not surprising that early Christian writers did not support tyrannicide, even though the OT also records stories of heroic tyrannicide, in which God raised up a "deliverer"—for example, Ehud (Judg. 3:15–30) and Jehu (2 Kings 9:22–35). When a distinction is drawn between God's ordination of the office of the ruler and his ordination of a particular ruler, it is possible to justify tyrannicide without contravening Romans 13. According to Thomas Aquinas, revolt against a tyrant is not sedition, which is a mortal sin, because the tyrant himself is guilty of sedition (*ST* II-II.42 and 104.6). Sometimes, however, subjects ought to obey "for the sake of avoiding scandal* or danger." Approving only the private assassination of tyrant (1), Aquinas emphasized the dangers of justifying tyrannicide—for example, if it is unsuccessful it may lead to greater cruelty; if it is successful, the successor may become tyrannical, and especially, bad people may take advantage of this moral license to kill good rulers (*see De Regimine Principum*). Nevertheless, Aquinas and others justified community removal of tyrant (2). Luther and Calvin agreed that one fundamental recourse against a tyrant is prayer. Luther also recognized that God might raise up heroes to overthrow the tyrant, and Calvin recognized the possibility of resistance by the lesser magistrates. With the ruler's attitudes and policies toward "true religion" becoming a test of tyranny, several arguments for tyrannicide appeared in subsequent Protestant and Catholic writings, for example, during the Wars of Religion in France in the 16th century. They were also prominent in England in the 17th century (e.g., the justification of regicide by John Milton in *The Tenure of Kings and Magistrates*, 1649). The development of public, legal, and constitutional means of controlling the ruler's exercise of power tended to reduce the importance of private, illegal resistance, including tyrannicide, but the question of tyrannicide became important again with the emergence of Hitler. For example, Dietrich Bonhoeffer, formerly a pacifist, decided to participate in the abortive July 20, 1944, plot to assassinate Hitler. Although Bonhoeffer's theological-ethical method appeared to exclude principles and rules, his "operative guidelines" included the requirements of clear evidence of serious misrule; respect for the scale of political responsibility and authority (those lower or outside the political hierarchy should act only after others have failed); reasonable assurances of successful execution; minimal necessary force; tyrannicide as a last resort. In view of various assassination attempts in the USA, the UK, and elsewhere in the world in the last thirty years, the dangers of the justification of private "tyrannicide" are evident.

See **Resistance; Revolution; Homicide; Capital Punishment; Dictatorship; Fascism; State; Totalitarian State.**

O. Jaszi and J. D. Lewis, *Against the Tyrant: The Tradition and Theory of Tyrannicide,* 1957; L. Rasmussen, *Dietrich Bonhoeffer: Reality and Resistance,* 1972.

JAMES F. CHILDRESS

Tyranny *see* **Tyrannicide;** *see also* **Dictatorship; Fascism; Resistance; Totalitarian State**

Tyranny, Resistance to *see* **Resistance; Tyrannicide**

Unconscious

Because of the work of Sigmund Freud it is now widely accepted that there are within the person unconscious mental processes of which the individual person is not aware and which cannot be consciously controlled. These unconscious processes are nevertheless potent factors in determining attitudes, feelings, and behavior. They are thus important for ethics. Unconscious thoughts, wishes, desires, and impulses may thwart or frustrate conscious actions or intentions, may produce "irrational" feelings of guilt*, ambivalence, dissatisfaction, etc., and may precipitate conflicts leading to mental illness*.

In Freud's view, the contents of the unconscious consist of repressed material (*see* **Repression**) and material relating to the original, instinctual, primitive, and infantile elements of psychic life (*see* **Id**). These contents obey their own laws and adopt their own modes of expression. The unconscious contents cannot voluntarily be brought into consciousness—the acknowledgment of their presence would conflict too painfully with the individual's socially learned ideas of what is good, proper, or acceptable. Contents temporarily forgotten, but which can be recalled into consciousness, are called preconscious. The unconscious repressed contents may only enter (or reenter) consciousness either with the sort of assistance available in psychotherapy, or in disguised or distorted form either in pathological symptoms or in the more normal phenomena of dreams, wit, slips of the tongue, etc. The two basic mechanisms that operate in the unconscious are condensation and displacement.

Most, but not all, contemporary theories of the unconscious are based on the Freudian model with modifications in detail. One significant addition has been suggested by Carl Jung, who claims that, as well as those contents which derive from the personal life-experience of the individual, there is also a stratum of the unconscious which is held in common by persons of the same tribe, race, or culture. This "collective unconscious" forms part of a living deposit of all human experience right back to the remotest beginnings. The powerful images that arise from the collective unconscious (called archetypal images) recur widely in religions, mythologies, folklore, and in individual dreams. These images tend to cluster around a limited number of themes concerning the basic power of life, the development of wholeness, salvation, etc. In Jung's view, the unconscious tends to act as a corrective to one-sidedness or imbalance in conscious psychic life.

S. Freud, *The Psychopathology of Everyday Life* (1904), ET 1914; *A General Introduction to Psychoanalysis* (1910), ET 1920; rev. ed. 1938; C. G. Jung, *Two Essays on Analytical Psychology,* (1928), ET 1953; *Psychology and Religion: West and East* (1939), ET 1958.

GRAEME M. GRIFFIN

Unemployment

A characteristic of modern Western industrial societies. Preindustrial societies in different ways give some basic communal role to their inhabitants; so do modern centralized collective economies in principle, and in reality for the most part, though there is some unemployment within them, especially if they have elements of Western economies in their system. These latter, based on the theory of the free market, in which labor is one factor of production responding to changes in market conditions, moved from a theory of basic status for a citizen to one of free contract. The reality was never totally like that and, because workers felt unprotected against changes over which they had no control, various collective provisions were made in these societies against the worst consequences of them (*see* **Welfare State**). The reason was that Western economies in the last century developed in roughly ten-year cycles of booms and slumps, the slumps producing large-scale unemployment. In this century it has been rather different with smaller movements of shorter duration, combined with a major slump beginning with the Wall Street crash of 1929 and another following in the wake of the OPEC price rises after 1973. When the economy is working well there will always be some unemployment as people change jobs (and some who are unemployable), so that in practice an unemployment rate of not more than 3 percent of the working population is almost a state of "full employment," and this was achieved for some twenty years or more in the West from about 1948.

However, in addition to cyclical unem-

ployment there is long-term structural unemployment, as technical innovation makes types of jobs obsolete. We are seeing this happen through the development of computers and microprocessors. In particular, routine mental and physical jobs in which many semiskilled and unskilled workers have earned their living are rapidly disappearing. Advanced industrial societies are all moving more and more into service economies, and it seems that they need to do so more consciously, and to devise a society that will utilize and pay for personal services from those displaced from routine manufacturing jobs. There are plenty of service jobs which are needed. These societies tend to define people's place in the community by the work they do, and they cannot tell a large section of the working population that there are no jobs for it and are not likely to be, without an inhumanity that courts disaster. As it is, many school leavers, and those thrown out of work in middle life, face a serious prospect. Western societies have forms of unemployment benefits, usually related in some way to insurance payments made when in work; and they also have to make some basic provision for maintenance when insurance benefits run out. The case is beginning to be made for a basic citizens' wage as of right, and at a sufficient personal and family level to reduce the traumas of losing a job and the defensiveness which because of this clings to obsolete jobs. A further element in the contemporary unemployment situation is its bad effect on racial relations, for ethnic minorities are nearly always at the bottom of the struggle for jobs.

See also **Vocation; Work, Doctrine of.**

RONALD PRESTON

United Nations *see* **International Order; Internationalism; National Sovereignty; World Government**

Universalizability of Moral Judgments

The name given to the commonly accepted but sometimes disputed thesis that a moral judgment, if it applies to a case, must equally apply to any exactly or relevantly similar case. For example, if I judge that my act in this situation would be right, I must acknowledge that were anybody else just like me to do the same in a situation just like this (say where I were the victim, and had all the characteristics of my present victim, including his preferences), that would be right too. The thesis has obvious affinities with the Golden Rule*, with utilitarianism*, and with Kantian ethics*. For if we have to apply the same principles to ourselves and to others in similar situations, this will lead us to do to others as we wish them to do to us, to act (as Kant said) so that we can will the maxim of our action to be a universal law, and treat human nature in ourselves and others never merely as a means but also as an end, and, in conformity to all these precepts, to seek the good of all impartially, counting everybody for one and nobody for more than one, as Bentham and J. S. Mill enjoined.

In order to understand the thesis, we must distinguish carefully between generality and universality. "General" and "universal" each have many different uses in philosophical writing, and many writers use them as if they meant the same. But it is best to reserve "general" for terms and propositions which are unspecific; that is to say, they characterize acts in simple terms without entering into specific details. "Universal" can then be used of terms and propositions which, however highly specific, nevertheless apply to *any* act of a given (perhaps minutely specified) kind. Universalizability, properly understood, has nothing to do with generality. The thesis does not maintain that acts similar in their broad features have to be similarly judged, for small differences might all the same make a difference. This is the important truth emphasized by situation ethics*, which, nevertheless, commits an equally important error if it holds that it is not possible, by making universal moral principles sufficiently specific, to find one which suits any individual situation, and which will then apply to any exactly similar situation.

The objection that no two actual situations are ever exactly similar misses the point. It is to be answered by first understanding the difference between generality and universality, and then that between different levels of moral thinking (*see* **Utilitarianism**). To have general moral principles is useful for general guidance in our day-to-day intuitive moral thinking. For example, we normally observe a principle not to tell lies, and observe it without thinking about the specific details of a particular case. However, unusual cases may arise in which two sound general principles conflict. In such cases we need a higher, critical level of thinking to adjudicate between the principles, and this has to address itself to the details of the case, as situation ethicists demand. But in doing this we shall still arrive at universal, though highly specific, principles applicable to this case and to others just like it.

It is extremely important in this kind of thinking to be able to consider *hypothetical* cases exactly like the actual one (which can always be conceived, even if no two actual cases are ever precisely similar). This enables us to ask, in the way Nathan asked David, what we judge right for someone to do in a similar case where we are not involved, or where we are involved in the role of victim instead of agent. This will force the Kantian principle upon us and make our critical thinking impartial. This use of universalizability survives the passage from more general to more specific principles. It has the same effect as John Rawls's requirement that principles of justice be selected in imagined ignorance of our own role in the world; it prevents us tailoring our moral principles to suit that role in disregard of the occupants of other roles.

Problems have been raised about the status of the thesis of universalizability: is it a logical thesis about the rules governing our use of the moral words or of the word "moral," or is it a substantial moral principle, as the Golden Rule is usually taken to be? One answer might be that it is a thesis which *now* holds true of our uses of these words, but has come to hold because ways of thought have come to prevail (above all, owing to Christian teaching) in which such a use best expresses what we want to say. All words must have come into use at some time; language as a whole is a relatively recent invention, and uses of particular words change from one period to another. For example, the word "ten" has not always been in use, and some tribes still do not have an equivalent, not being able to count above four or five. Nevertheless the restriction which forbids us to say that ten is a prime number is a logical restriction. Similarly, the universalizability restriction which forbids us to say of two identical acts that one is wrong and the other not wrong may be a logical restriction which came into being when we adopted this word or this use of the word. *Any* words which had the same meanings as "ten" and "wrong" would be subject to these restrictions. Just as, if we wanted to assert that ten was a prime number, we should have to change the use of "ten" or of "prime," so if we wanted to be free of the universalizability restriction and of its potent use in moral argument, we should have to start using "wrong" in some different way.

It is unlikely that we would be willing, on reflection, to do this, simply because most of the dealings we have with one another—the "negotiations" whose upshot, if they go well, is a more tolerable life for all than would have been possible without them—depend crucially on having a language in which they can be conducted. And the universalizable moral language is the most suitable for this purpose, because it alone can express the prescriptions which all are looking for, namely, those which all can agree on as binding on all. Morality, thus understood, is what enables society to cohere.

The society in question may not embrace the whole of mankind, let alone all the animal kingdom. It is therefore perfectly possible to confine the benefits of a universalizable prescriptive language to a limited society or even a tribe, though we should not then call the resulting mores a morality. However, the reasoning that operates universally within a tribe naturally extends itself beyond its original borders, as Christ extended the range of the word "neighbor" to include Samaritans. Just as, once we have learned to count, we get led on by degrees into the differential calculus and beyond, so, once we have grasped the idea of universalizable prescriptive reasoning, it is hard to stop within our own borders, as both Stoics and Christians found. As the world gets smaller, we find that more and more people are our neighbors, in that we affect one another by our actions, and so a truly universal moral language becomes a necessity if we are to learn to live with one another. And perhaps all sensitive creatures will in the end get included, as both the utilitarian Jeremy Bentham and Kant's disciple Leonard Nelson (unlike Kant himself) wished to include them.

Christians are likely to come to believe that this is God's will, and that he has fashioned the world in such a way that by following the law of love we shall do the best, not only for those we love but for ourselves.

R. M. Hare, *Freedom and Reason,* 1963, ch. 2; *Moral Thinking,* 1981, ch. 6; J. L. Mackie, *Ethics: Inventing Right and Wrong,* 1977.

R. M. HARE

Urbanization

In sociometrics and in ordinary language, urbanization refers to the movement of rural populations into high-density city environments and the increased ratio of people living in metropolitan areas to those living in villages or on farms. In this usage, urbanization is associated with higher crime rates, greater discrepancies of wealth and poverty, and intense politicization of all issues. Historical and cross-cultural studies show, however, that population density is not a reliable indicator of urbanization or its primary cause. Specific social transformations of religion, life-styles, mores, dominant values, and of economic, political, educational, and legal institutions are more significant. These produce an "urban ethos" to which immigrants must adapt to avoid severe disadvantages and which, in modern urbanized societies, spills over the boundaries of any city, bringing dramatic social change to farm and village and sometimes producing urbanized nations and regions. In this sense, urbanization means adopting cosmopolitan values, accepting religious, ethnic, and often political diversity, increasing autonomy and anonymity, and developing rationalized, professionalized, and bureaucratically organized institutions in economy, culture, and government.

Traditional stereotypes of race, class, sex role, nationality, clan, or caste, often allied with religion, are in principle reduced in importance by urbanization, although they continue to play a debilitating role among those prevented from or incapable of acculturating to the urban ethos. Traditional bonds based on these factors are modified into "voluntary associational groupings" or "family tradition" among those who try to preserve them. Ascribed status based on these distinctions, considered "natural" in traditional societies, is often considered immoral in a society more urbanized, and discrimination on these grounds is usually proscribed by law.

Christian ethics has focused on urbanization in three distinct ways, although various ethicists draw these foci together in divergent ways.

1. Pastoral concern has prompted personal care of, advocacy action for, and social engagement with populations caught in the travails of transition. From the settlement houses, city mission societies, and Christian labor organizations of the 19th century, through much of the social gospel and

worker-priest movements in the early 20th, to contemporary urban priority programs and liberation churches of the present, church professionals have been involved in meeting the immediate needs of people who are not full participants in the urbanization process, who need a sense of cultural identity amid the acids of change, and who are marginalized by the lack of educational, organizational, and political skills or access. The black churches in the USA are a remarkable example of this; comparable stories are now being written in Asia, Africa, and Latin America, sometimes with the aid of quasi-Marxist analyses of social change.

2. Christian social ethics has been deeply influenced by "classical" sociological theorists who saw the pending urbanization of the Western world in the late 19th and early 20th centuries as involving fundamental transformations of religious ethics—sometimes as cause, sometimes as effect. The tools of social analysis forged by Ferdinand Tönnies, Emile Durkheim, Max Weber, Charles Cooley, Robert Redfield, and others continue to provide the categorical links between Christian ethics as it bears on urbanization and the disciplines of sociology, anthropology, urban planning, and social history.

3. Theological ethicists have attempted to show that while urbanization often involves a process of secularization entailing the displacement or collapse of many traditional beliefs and practices, it is compatible with basic Christian doctrines. Indeed, some argue that certain aspects of the Christian faith support urbanization, encourage the formation of an urban ethos, and give normative guidance to urban peoples and institutions in contrast to both rustic "pagan" world views and modernist technocratic pretenses. Historical and systematic arguments about the formation of the Christian scriptures in the Mediterranean cities and the development of Christian ethics in the most urbanized centers of the Roman Empire and later among the urbanizing populations of the late medieval and Reformation cities are cited as prologue to the contemporary reconstruction of doctrine and morals in urbanizing contexts around the world on Christian grounds.

What is not clear in any of these efforts, however, is whether the modern directions of urbanization, now often cut off from theological concerns, can become so ethically guided as to prevent permanent damage to the eco-sphere, to provide care for those marginalized by massive, modern urban institutions, and to provide a livable, safe, and humane habitat.

C. Cooley, *Social Organization,* 1909; H. Cox, *The Secular City,* 1965; E. Durkheim, *The Division of Labor in Society* (1894), ET 1933; J. Ellul, *The Meaning of the City,* ET 1970; M. McKelvey, *The Urbanization of America,* 1963; D. W. Shriver and K. Ostrom, *Is There Hope for the City?* 1977; M. L. Stackhouse, *Ethics and the Urban Ethos,* 1973; F. Tönnies, *Community and Society* (1887), ET 1957; M. Weber, *Economy and Society* (1911–13), ET 1968 (esp. vol. 3).

MAX L. STACKHOUSE

Usury and Interest

The charging of interest by the Jews to their own people was forbidden by the law (Ex. 22:25; Deut. 23:19–20). In the early church it gradually came to be regarded as unlawful, largely on the basis of Aristotle's argument about the barren nature of money. It was formally condemned by the Third Lateran Council (1179). The medieval attitude to usury was related to the doctrine of the just price*. The essence of this was that in any transaction justice demanded an equivalent return by the buyer to the seller. In the contract of mutuum, or loan, where the money lent became the property of the borrower, subject to the obligation to return an equal amount, it was held that the mere passage of time did not reduce the value of the money and hence gave rise to no claim for more than repayment of the principal. Interest could, however, be justified where the lender forwent a gain or suffered a loss through the loan, for which compensation should fairly be paid. The possible advantage to the borrower in making a profit through the loan was not, however, considered.

In practice, as commerce developed in later medieval and early modern times, most actual forms of interest payment in business came to be justified, but the formal condemnation of usury survived into the 17th and 18th centuries, often being held to exclude excessive interest rates.

Modern economic thinking sees the reason for interest both in the greater productive power which can be achieved when resources are diverted from consumption and used for investment, and in the need to provide an inducement to income receivers to abstain from consumption and forgo control of liquid resources, to make them available to investors. It is also seen as an essential price, allocating a limited supply of capital between alternative uses. An investment can be regarded as worth making if it promises a return that exceeds the market rate of interest, and some equivalent to a notional interest rate is used in investment calculations even in Communist economies.

Interest is so much a part of modern life that Christian thinking nowadays generally accepts these pragmatic justifications, as in other features of the working of the market system. In some circles, however, the influence of the traditional fear of usury can still be seen, in the guise of a fear that the financial interests will exploit the producers. The attraction of "social credit" theories some years ago for certain schools of Christian thought was an example of this.

B. W. Dempsey, *Interest and Usury,* 1948; B. Nelson, *The Idea of Usury,* 2nd enl. ed., 1969; J. Viner, *Religious Thought and Economic Society,* 1980.

JOHN F. SLEEMAN

Utilitarianism

Utilitarianism is the extension into philosophy of the Christian doctrine of agape (*see* **Love**), which has counterparts in the various formulations of the Golden Rule* that have been preached within all the higher religions. If we are to love our neighbors *as* ourselves, this requires us to love all equally. And if to love someone involves seeking his good, this in turn requires us to seek equally the good of all. Where the good of one conflicts with the good of another, a balance has to be found; and the obvious way of doing this is to seek always to do as much good as we can to all, treated impartially, diminishing the good of one only when this is necessary in order to secure the greater good of others.

Similarly, if we are to do to others as we wish should be done to us (sc. in like circumstances, including the preferences which *they* have in those circumstances), this requires us to ask, "What do I prefer should happen to me were I placed in the same position as that other person, with his or her preferences?" The obvious answer is that I prefer that the preferences which I then had should be

fulfilled. And if I try to do this with regard to a great many other people whose interests my actions affect, then I shall be led, as before, to try to maximize the satisfaction of the preferences of all, or for short the good of all, treated impartially.

The relation of the love of our neighbor, so expressed, to the love of God demanded in the "first and great commandment" (Matt. 22:38) is not hard to state summarily, though obviously there is more to be said. If God, as many Christians believe, loves all people equally, and commands us to do the same, the precept "If ye love me, keep my commandments" (John 14:15) requires us to obey the second commandment, to love our neighbor, as a consequence of the first, to love God. In other words, if God wills the good of all his children impartially, and we are required, in loving him, to try to do his will, we too must seek this good.

A similar result comes from the application of the thesis of the universalizability* of moral judgments. Such formulations of utilitarianism in terms of preferences are better than the traditional one which bids us seek the greatest happiness of the greatest number, since that is quite indeterminate (what are we to do when we can either increase the number of those benefited, or increase the benefits accruing to the existing number?).

In its traditional religious formulations, the Golden Rule appears as a substantial principle of conduct. Many, though not all, formulations of the thesis of universalizability treat this as a logical feature of the moral concepts. Since utilitarianism is so closely related to these two doctrines, we need to ask of it too whether it is a substantial moral principle or a purely formal doctrine, logical or methodological; and how, if it is purely formal, it can have any practical implications for our moral thinking and moral life. Certainly formal and methodological principles can have practical implications in other fields: mathematics, for example, which is a purely formal discipline, is indispensable for science, including applied science. Utilitarianism has been claimed to be formal in the sense that it can be established by formal arguments alone, resting on the meaning and logic of the moral concepts. It is also formal in another sense, that it only tells us to maximize the satisfaction of preferences; it does not tell people what they are to prefer. The substance of the precepts comes from the content of their preferences.

It is a mistake to treat utilitarianism as a form of naturalism (*see* **Ethics; Naturalistic Ethics**). J. S. Mill in particular has been misinterpreted as holding that "right" *means* "productive of maximum happiness"; the last chapter of his *System of Logic* makes clear that he was not a naturalist but an adherent of prescriptivism* with a heavy debt to Hume.

Utilitarianism has been expressed in a bewildering variety of forms, by no means equivalent to one another, and some of them are open to obvious objections to which others are immune. The principal distinctions are the following:

1. *Positive* utilitarianism enjoins us to seek to maximize the good of those affected by our actions; *negative* utilitarianism to minimize the harm. It has been objected to the latter that its precept could be obeyed by minimizing the number of those affected, and this in turn by seeing to it that there were as few people as possible. But it is better to dissolve this dispute by treating the deprivation of good as a harm and the avoidance of harm as a good; the two versions then become identical.

2. The good or utility to be maximized can be defined in different ways. For Bentham and J. S. Mill it was happiness, defined as pleasure and the absence of pain. More generally, it has been seen as the enjoyment of certain states of feeling. Such formulations are not now so popular as those in terms of desires or preferences. The reason is that we desire, prefer, and think good for ourselves many other things besides pleasure or even happiness. It has been objected to utilitarianism that it narrows too much the aims of beneficence by pretending that there is only one good thing to aim at, happiness, whereas there are many (*bonum est multiplex*). The "preference" version avoids this objection because it enjoins us to seek the satisfaction of preferences, which may be for many different kinds of things. But this invites a further objection, to be considered below, that not all preferences *ought* to be satisfied, as in this version utilitarianism seems to require.

3. Utilitarianism is a combination of *consequentialism** (the doctrine that acts are to be judged in the light of their consequences,

what is judged being the total difference made to the history of the world by doing the act; the act itself is the bringing about of this difference) and *welfarism* (the view that what counts in assessing consequences is the good that they bring to those affected) (see Sen, 1979). The simplest form of consequentialism is act-consequentialism, engendering *act-utilitarianism,* which enjoins us to do that act, out of all the alternatives, which has at least as good consequences as any of the others. Intuitive objections (to be considered below) to this simple version have led utilitarians, including, on one interpretation, J. S. Mill, to advocate instead various forms of *rule-utilitarianism,* according to the most attractive of which "an act is right if and only if it conforms with that learnable set of rules, the adoption of which by everyone would maximize intrinsic value," i.e., utility (Brandt, 1963). Such versions are designed to avoid the criticism that according to simple act-utilitarianism we ought sometimes to do acts which seem contrary to common moral convictions (for example, execute an innocent man if that would do the most good). Rule-utilitarianism says in answer to this that the rule or principle forbidding execution of the innocent is one having a higher acceptance-utility than any alternative rule, and that therefore it ought to be obeyed.

The dispute between rule- and act-utilitarians cannot be understood, let alone resolved, without a grasp of the distinction, almost always blurred in these discussions, between generality and universality (*see* **Universalizability**). Although the rules or principles of the rule-utilitarian have to be universal, it is obviously going to make a difference whether he allows them to be very specific, or insists on their being highly general (like the rules that we ought never to tell lies, or break promises, or punish the innocent). A general rule-utilitarian would insist on conformity to simple general rules of the latter kind because their general adoption (in another sense of "general") has a high utility. On the other hand a more specific rule-utilitarian might say that we ought to conform instead to more detailed rules such as "You ought never to tell lies, except that you may tell them in order to preserve innocent lives." Clearly such exceptions could be proliferated, making the rules more and more specific, though still universal, until they were specific enough to cater for any particular minutely described situation, and for any other situation *exactly* like it. At this point the precepts yielded by act-utilitarianism and rule-utilitarianism for particular situations would have come to coincide; the distinction would thus have lost its practical and theoretical usefulness, and its effectiveness as an answer to the objection raised earlier that utilitarianism runs counter to our common convictions. For we could again justify the execution of an innocent man if the circumstances of this precise situation made it most conducive to good to accept a rule that in situations just like this he should be executed.

If specific rule-utilitarianism thus collapses into act-utilitarianism, is general rule-utilitarianism any better? It is open to the objection that in cases where a specific rule-utilitarian would want to write exceptions into his rule, the general rule-utilitarian would find it hard plausibly to forbid this. If (to adapt an example that was used against Kant) a maniac comes into my shop in pursuit of his victim and asks me where he is hiding, most people would say (unlike Kant) that I ought to make an exception to the rule against lying. And the same will happen in all such difficult cases. So the general rule-utilitarian will not, after all, be able to square his view with our common moral convictions, as was his aim in devising his theory. Is there then no middle way between an unbending rigorism* and the extremes of situation ethics*?

The dispute is better understood by distinguishing between different levels of moral thinking. At the everyday or intuitive level at which we operate most of the time, we need rules or principles that are at least general enough to be learnable (as Brandt says). Such is the rule forbidding lying, or lying in circumstances which can be described without going into too much detail. However, this level is not self-sufficient. It yields no way of telling *which* are the good general principles that ought to be our guides at this level; and when they conflict with one another in particular cases, it has no means of telling which ought to override the other. For these two purposes we need a higher level of thinking that does not rely on the principles of the intuitive level, but subjects them to critical scrutiny. A utilitarian will maintain that, although the intuitive level of thinking may not operate in a utilitarian way at all, the correct method of critical thinking is wholly utilitarian. At this higher level we select for use at the intuitive level those principles whose general acceptance or adoption is for the best, and in cases of conflict prefer those whose observance in the particular case will be for the best.

On such a view, intuitive thinking will be of a fairly general rule-utilitarian sort, and will, as the rule-utilitarian wished, yield practical precepts in ordinary cases which are the same as those yielded by our common moral convictions, provided that they are sound. On the other hand, critical thinking will be at liberty to consider cases in much more (indeed, in principle in unlimited) detail, formulating to suit each case a highly specific principle, which, however, will still be universal in the sense that it would apply to *any* precisely similar case. So the critical thinker will be the kind of highly specific rule-utilitarian who is indistinguishable in practice from an act-utilitarian.

This view also has implications for the practice of moral education which seem to be in accordance with some commonly accepted ideas. We normally bring up children initially to observe some fairly general principles like that against lying; and even when we grow up we continue to attach very great importance to these principles, and in all ordinary cases treat breaches of them as unthinkable. They are for us far more than "mere rules of thumb" (an expression that in this context has caused nothing but confusion). As Bishop Butler said, "As we are not competent judges, what is upon the whole for the good of the world, there may be other immediate ends appointed to us to pursue, besides that of doing good, or producing happiness. Though the good of the creation be the only end of the Author of it, yet he may have laid us under particular obligations, which we may discern and feel ourselves under, quite distinct from a perception that the observance or violation of them is for the happiness or misery of our fellow-creatures."

But since we have no direct and reliable access to the divine intelligence, it may be necessary, if our consciences give us unclear or conflicting guidance, to do our best to determine what such a perfect critical thinker would say. This is so, not only in particular "hard cases," but when we are trying to decide in general what is the content of the principles that a sound moral education would seek to inculcate. Conscience*, properly understood, is not just the childlike adherence to unquestioned traditional rules, but the critical ability to assess such rules and adjudicate between them when they conflict. The Spirit has to guide us, in different ways, at both these levels. At the intuitive level, his voice is that of the Ten Commandments, with their stringent insistence on obedience to very general rules; at the critical level, it is that of the two commandments to love God, and our neighbor as ourself. All this is in accord with a properly understood utilitarianism.

Such a fully developed utilitarian doctrine can overcome fairly easily the objections commonly made to earlier and cruder versions. To the objection that its precepts conflict with commonly received opinions, it can answer that received opinion is sometimes rightly discarded, and that when it is not, this is because it can be justified by critical thinking, as is indeed the case with most of the hallowed moral principles. For example, if it be objected that common opinion bids us satisfy not all desires impartially, but only good ones, it can answer that this is true of the principles for intuitive thinking that a sound critical thinker would select; for the acceptance-utility of principles bidding us restrain evil desires in ourselves and others is high. If it be objected that impartial benevolence would require us to neglect our own children if we could do more good to the children of strangers, it can answer that the principle bidding us look after our own children first has, in general, the best consequences if accepted, for there is more chance then that children will get looked after. But it can add that this principle is probably observed to excess, and that a more universal benevolence should have at least some say in our decisions.

To the objection that the impartial universal beneficence which utilitarianism enjoins is an ideal impossible for humans to achieve, it can answer that the same is true of agape itself; this "impossible possibility" (Niebuhr, 1936, p. 129) is what we should be aiming at, but we are more likely to get as near it as our natures allow if we submit ourselves to less demanding, though still demanding, principles. How demanding, may depend on our vocation*.

R. B. Brandt, "Towards a Credible Form of Utilitarianism," in H.-N. Castañeda and G.

Nakhnikian (eds.), *Morality and the Language of Conduct,* 1963; Joseph Butler, *Fifteen Sermons,* 1726, sermon 12; J. P. Griffin, "Modern Utilitarianism," *Revue Internationale de Philosophie* 141, 1982; R. M. Hare, *Moral Thinking,* 1981; D. Lyons, *Forms and Limits of Utilitarianism,* 1965; R. Niebuhr, *An Interpretation of Christian Ethics,* 1936; A. M. Quinton, *Utilitarian Ethics,* 1973; A. Sen, "Utilitarianism and Welfarism," *Journal of Philosophy* 76, 1979.

R. M. HARE

Utopian Thought

Recent controversy regarding the role of utopian thought in Christian ethics is largely an ideological struggle over the relationship between religious faith and radical politics. As a strategic weapon in that struggle, as well as a hotly contested piece of theological turf, the category of utopian thought has been used both to denounce and to defend the methodological pragmatism of the so-called "Christian realism" (*see* **Realism**) of Reinhold Niebuhr and his disciples, as well as the uncompromisingly prophetic demands for various programs of revolutionary social change advocated by the disciples of the broad spectrum of political and liberation theologians. Contested in this struggle is the political significance of that central symbol of NT Christianity: the kingdom of God*. Must it be read as an indictment of, or as an inducement to, utopian thought and the revolutionary changes that it envisions?

No doubt this controversy is a far cry from what one might expect from a familiarity with only the literary tradition of utopian thought, epitomized by that minor classic, Sir Thomas More's *Utopia.* The current participants, by contrast, are arrayed along the lines drawn long ago between political Augustinians and the Franciscan spirituals inspired by Joachim of Fiore. In a typically modern fashion, these lines manage to unite both Protestants and Catholics on either side, under the overarching presuppositions of the sociology of knowledge.

Intellectual history aside, the theological issue is of central concern: How is religious transcendence*, or God's action in history, to be discerned and responded to in concrete political terms? While the partisans on neither side have a fully satisfactory answer to this question, their attempts to address it in terms of utopian thought are illuminating.

Common to both is the assumption that utopian thought functions hermeneutically in relation to the symbols of Christian eschatology, especially the kingdom of God (*see* **Eschatological Ethics**). Among Christian realists utopian thought serves to clarify what the eschatological promise is *not:* it is *not* an imperative to institutionalize the vain imaginings of Christian perfectionists who expect to remodel society in the image of the kingdom. Hence, utopian thought stands repudiated as a false absolute, a demonic distortion of the meaning of eschatology. Christian hope*, by contrast, renounces such false absolutes. Among political and liberation theologians, however, utopian thought is embraced as an imaginative breakthrough that enables the eschatological promise to become incarnate in history. Without utopian thought eschatology remains inarticulate. Christian hope thus consists in continually creating a synthesis of faith and social action bent on hastening the fulfillment of the kingdom. Utopian thought, in this view, is not a false absolute, but a faithful response to the enabling—precisely because absolutizing—power of Christian hope.

As diverse as these perspectives may seem, both appeal to the sociology of knowledge for vindication (*see* **Sociology of Ethics**). Karl Mannheim's seminal work, *Ideology and Utopia,* distinguished the two by their concrete political tendencies. Ideologies defend the social status quo; utopias envision a radical alternative. On the basis of this definition, many political and liberation theologians construct their positive correlation between eschatology and utopia and denounce Christian realism's negative view as ideological. Christian realists argue that Mannheim's intention was not to canonize utopian thought but to overcome both ideology and utopia in a new kind of social science. His proposal, however, does not go far enough: eschatological faith, and not the scientific pretensions of the intelligentsia, provides the transcendent perspective necessary for a truly critical approach to political thought and action. While Christian realists may have a more insightful reading of Mannheim, they seem to have forgotten that even a negative formulation of the meaning of eschatology, willy-nilly, must unfold in ideological and/or utopian terms. The sociology of knowledge, beset by problems of its own, grants a hermeneutic privilege to neither eschatological perspective.

Perhaps this impasse can be resolved by setting aside Mannheim's distinction between ideology* and utopia. If both forms of political thought are considered as part of a cultural system, then it becomes a question of how this polarity of legitimating and critical tendencies within a culture's collective representations is to be related to the claims of Christian faith, which itself is always already part of the cultural system. In other words, how does utopian thought help to interpret the political meaning of the kingdom of God, assuming that utopian thought functionally is an ideology, and that all ideologies contain utopian elements? If David Tracy is right about the limit-character of religious experience and language, it may be that both Christian realists and political and liberation theologians have grasped an indispensable dynamic of utopian thought: The finite character of concrete utopias inevitably testifies to the meaning of eschatology as symbolizing the "limit-to" any historical promise and fulfillment; by the same token, the imaginative leap of finite transcendence involved in any attempt to envision a radical alternative inevitably arouses a sense of ultimate possibility symbolized by eschatological hope as a "limit-of" these same historical processes. In short, Christian eschatology remains both constraining ("limit-to") and liberating ("limit-of"), and utopian thought allows us to understand both dynamics better as they pertain to the broad agenda of Christian social action.

If this is the case, then two conclusions may be drawn for Christian ethics: (1) Christian realists are wrong to denounce utopian thought as such as a distortion of Christian eschatology. The problem of false absolutes is real; but it is endemic to all forms of social thought that take transcendence seriously, including Christian realism. (2) Nevertheless, political and liberation theologians are not thereby entitled to assume that utopian thought effectively substitutes for specifically ethical reflection. While utopian thought has a positive role to play in theological hermeneutics, any concrete proposals for Christian social action that stem from such a hermeneutic process still take us only to the threshold of ethical reflection. Assuming the vision, we are still faced with difficult and unforeseeable moral choices attendant upon our struggle to embody it historically.

See **Eschatological Ethics; Hope; Inter-**

pretation; Kingdom of God; Liberation Theology; Marxist Ethics; Perfectionism; Political Theology; Progress, Belief in; Realism; Revolution; Transcendence.

E. Bloch, *Das Prinzip Hoffnung,* 3 vols., 1954–59; U. Eco, *The Name of the Rose,* 1983; C. Geertz, *The Interpretation of Cultures,* 1973; K. Mannheim, *Ideology and Utopia* (1929), ET 1936; J. Miguez-Bonino, *Toward a Christian Political Ethics,* 1983; T. More, *Utopia,* 1516; R. Niebuhr, *Faith and History,* 1949; J. L. Segundo, *The Liberation of Theology,* ET 1976; P. Tillich, *Political Expectation,* 1971; D. Tracy, *Blessed Rage for Order,* 1975.

DENNIS P. McCANN

Values and Value Judgment

"Value" is a modern term used to indicate what traditionally has gone by the name of "good" or "the good." While for some the new term is taken to have a basically subjective connotation because it is believed to imply the identification of what is good with human interest and desire*, not all philosophers hold this view. At one end of the spectrum there is the subjectivist view that asserts an essential connection between value and human interest, as in Ralph Barton Perry's thesis: "That which is an object of interest is *eo ipso* invested with value. Any object, whatever it be, acquires value when any interest, whatever it be, is taken in it." At the opposite end of the spectrum stands the objectivist view, running through Western thought from Socrates and Plato to Nicolai Hartmann, according to which value is an intrinsic part or aspect of whatever has value; since value is taken to be independent of the observers it is their task to develop the necessary sensitivity for perceiving the values presented to them.

Despite a long tradition that identified all questions concerning the good for humankind as a goal, or individual goods involved in particular situations as "ethical" questions, the aim behind the development of a general theory of value is to characterize value in its *generic* sense. This means that moral value represents a special form of value with its own distinctive characteristics and is not coextensive with value as such. The way is then open for recognizing values in the religious, aesthetic, legal, economic, and political domains. In each case a proper understanding of the values involved is to be gained

only by combining the generic meaning of value with the special features that define each context in which value figures. In economics, for example, we are interested in the values of commodities in exchange, whereas in ethics we may be concerned instead for the intrinsic worth of persons in a sense that takes us entirely beyond the idea of an exchange value.

One of the central questions about the nature of value has already been indicated—the issue about "subjectivity" and "objectivity" —and it concerns the status of value in existence. The topic is endlessly complex, involving the subtle distinctions characteristic of contemporary "metaethics"*; only the main positions can be marked out. The subjectivist position asserts that "good" and any synonymous value term means no more than the human response—interest, desire, or expression of approval—that is made by a person when confronted with the object or when considering it for the purpose of evaluation or appraisal (*see* **Subjectivism, Ethical**) On this view the value term is *constituted* by the feelings aroused in the person. It is sometimes said that the one making the judgment is *expressing* his or her feelings—the most extreme form of the so-called emotive theory of values—but generally it is claimed that the individual is *asserting the existence* of the appropriate feelings in relation to the object when using a value term in referring to it. In either case value does not reside in the object as something antecedent to the mind that judges, but depends instead on the subjective response.

The main criticism urged against this view by proponents of one or another of the various objectivist positions is twofold: On the one hand, it is held that while we may discover the value of something by attending to it and responding, the value does not thereby come into existence on this occasion. On the other hand, it is claimed that many of the things and actions that have attracted human interest or called forth desire are not in fact good but represent instead something bad or evil and hence something to be avoided. Over against the attempts of subjectivists to show that value terms like "esteemed," "coveted," "admirable," etc., are one and all translatable into responses made by judging persons, objectivists are concerned to show that the value terms denote instead characteristics of objects, either simple qualities or complex rational properties, that belong to the objects themselves and are discovered by the mind sensitive to their existence. Frequently the objectivist appeal is to intuition or direct insight as the appropriate means of apprehension, and most intuitionists have laid down the condition that only a trained mind, sensitive and sincerely attending to the relevant features of value situations, will be in a position to grasp the values presented (*see* **Intuitionism**).

The objectivist approach is significantly represented by two Catholic interpreters of Christian ethics, Dietrich von Hildebrand and Bernard Häring. Both were influenced by the thought of Max Scheler and, indirectly, by the Platonic realism of the ethics of Nicolai Hartmann. Von Hildebrand developed a thoroughly objectivist conception of value rooted in the immediate datum of "importance" as manifested in the lives of saintly figures. Häring reinterpreted the substance of Christian morality through the fundamental concept of the law of Christ. Both directed their belief in the objectivity and universality of value and law against relativism* and situation ethics*.

The attempt to pass beyond the opposition of subjective and objective in value theory was made by the instrumentalists, whose major spokesman was John Dewey. For him value considerations are relevant wherever there are alternative courses of action. Distinguishing between "prizing" and "appraising," Dewey held that while the basic materials of value must be acknowledged to be human desires and preferences, we cannot remain content merely with the reports of what people actually prize or find satisfying. Instead we must appraise our immediate desires, which means subjecting them to a test. Instead of taking such desires for final values, we must use them as starting points for ethical inquiry. To know that some object or situation has been deemed satisfying is to have but a subjective report; the next step is to see whether the claim made on behalf of the object can be sustained in a critical test. The aim is to discover whether the objects in question really are satisfactory or have the capacity claimed for them. It is important to notice that whereas the starting point of this approach is in the desires and satisfactions of persons, the outcome of critical inquiry is meant to refer to the capacities of objects. To the thirst-crazed person, the immediate de-

sire is for liquid; drinking sea water, however, though it may be immediately satisfying, can never be satisfactory because the constitution of the water itself is inadequate for meeting the demand that is put upon it. Our prizings themselves must be appraised, and we must weed out short-run and immediate satisfactions in favor of values "approved on reflection," by which Dewey meant longer-range satisfactions arrived at through a knowledge of the natures of things and by considering the means required to obtain them.

Value judgments have to be considered as special cases of the general function of judgment. Judgment of value embraces not only the basic assertion of values or goods as values, but also the application of the standards implied to individual situations, actions, and objects. Judgment presupposes standard or leading principle whether it is made fully explicit or not. Even if we interpret judgment as merely a report of individual preferences, the fact that a priority is established indicates that some standard is involved. Explicitly expressed judgment belongs to the sphere of reflection. In actual deliberation*, or in the process of deciding what we are to do, we may not be aware of making judgments of the fully explicit sort that are to be found in books on ethics, but this does not alter the fact that judgment is present. In the sphere of moral judgment, "conscience"* is the name for the judging activity. Dictates of conscience are properly understood as judgments involving a comparison between an acknowledged norm and some feature of behavior, actual or contemplated. The judgmental character of conscience has often been obscured by the metaphor of the "voice" supposedly declaring immediately and infallibly what is to be done or avoided. This conception is misleading, since conscience is not immediate but embraces knowledge—*scientia*—of ourselves, the situation, the action in question, plus an apprehension of the norm or standard to which appeal is made. Accordingly, conscience cannot be infallible but shares the limitations of all human judgments. The peculiarity of the judgment is that the one who makes it is also the one whom the judgment is about; an affective element thus enters in the form of, for example, the "bad" conscience or painful sense of the gap existing between what was done and what should have been done.

In addition to the logical problems that

arise in connection with the interpretation of value judgments, there are also moral considerations attached to judging in this sphere. The ancient injunction "Judge not!" leads to a distinction between judgments passed by a person on his or her own conduct and judgment passed by another on that same conduct. The moral quality of a person is revealed not only through the conduct dictated by his or her own judgments, but also through his or her understanding and forbearance in passing judgment on others.

B. Blanshard, *Reason and Goodness,* 1961; W. K. Frankena, *Ethics,* ²1973; B. Häring, *Christian Renewal in a Changing World,* tr. M. Lucida Häring, 1964; D. von Hildebrand, *Christian Ethics,* 1953; R. O. Johann (ed.), *Freedom and Value,* 1976; A. MacIntyre, *After Virtue,* 1981; J. Macquarrie, *Three Issues in Ethics,* 1970.

JOHN E. SMITH

Vatican Council II *see* Modern Roman Catholic Moral Theology; Official Roman Catholic Social Teaching

Vegetarianism

Vegetarianism is the belief that people should refrain from eating the flesh of animals. Some vegetarians (now sometimes called "vegans") omit all animal products from their diets. Others refuse only to eat the flesh of mammals, or "red meat." Another common form is lacto-ovo-vegetarianism, which accepts for food such animal products as milk and eggs but omits all animal flesh, including fish and poultry.

The moral arguments in favor of vegetarianism can be grouped in four divisions:

1. Raising and killing animals for food is wrongful treatment of animals. All animal life is considered, by some, to be sacred. Since it is known that human beings can live healthfully without eating animal flesh, the needless killing of animals is morally wrong. Additionally, it is argued that animals are sentient creatures who have interests and rights because they can experience pain and pleasure. The process of killing animals for meat causes suffering that cannot be outweighed by the pleasure humans may derive from eating flesh.

2. Eating animal flesh is detrimental to human health. It is contended that most human beings would be healthier and live longer without a meat diet. Some point out that, according to the biblical account (Gen. 1:29), the original and thus ideal human diet was vegetarian. Moreover, since there is some scientific evidence that a properly balanced vegetarian diet is the most healthful, people have a duty, insofar as possible, to choose such a diet. The preservation of the best possible health is viewed both as a duty to oneself and as a means to maintaining the capacity to serve others.

3. The use of animal flesh for food is harmful to human character. The needless killing of animals undermines character by cheapening life and making people insensitive to suffering. Further, it is sometimes argued that eating animal flesh harms character directly by fostering undesirable behavior.

4. Raising animals for their flesh is an inefficient use of scarce resources. It is well-established that the use of land and agricultural products such as feed grains to produce meat is extremely inefficient when compared to the production of vegetable protein. At a time when many people are starving, it is argued, the change to a vegetarian diet is the morally responsible choice.

According to the biblical account, God's permission to use animals for food was granted only after the Flood (Gen. 9:1–4), perhaps as a concession to human sinfulness, but the legitimacy of the use of animals for food is usually assumed rather than argued for in Christian theology and ethics. For some of the arguments, *see* **Animals.**

See also **Environmental Ethics.**

P. Singer, *Animal Liberation,* 1975.

GERALD R. WINSLOW

Venial Sins *see* Sin(s)

Vice

As the opposite of virtue*, vice is a settled disposition to do what is wrong, bad, or sinful. Vices are habits* acquired by repeated actions (sins). Often the term "sin"* refers to dispositions or habits along with acts, as in the seven deadly, or capital, sins*, which are more accurately viewed as vices. Grace* is indispensable for overcoming vice and developing virtues, particularly the theological virtues*. Although Protestant theologians use the language of "virtue" and "vice," many of them have objected to Roman Catholic moral theology's* concentration on vices and virtues, holding that it tends to emphasize human actions, habits, and merit*, rather than God's forgiveness*.

JAMES F. CHILDRESS

Violence see Aggression; Coercion; Crime; Harm; Homicide; Just War; Pacifism; Power; Resistance; Terrorism; War

Virginity

Virginity, as a physical state, is innocence of physical intercourse, and may be predicated of either sex; hence the apostle John is often referred to by the fathers as John the Virgin. The Bible assumes virginity as the proper state of one about to be married (cf. Deut. 22:13–21). Hence it may be used as a metaphor for the proper relation of Israel to God, or of the church to Christ (2 Cor. 11:2). Physically a woman is *virgo intacta* when the hymen (or maidenhead) has not been broken, whether by intercourse or accident. But as a moral quality virginity is not lost by involuntary violation—a point developed by Augustine in connection with the Gothic sack of Rome in 410 (*City of God* 1.15–17).

As a spiritual quality or virtue virginity is no mere negative condition. It is the state of one who has not wasted or misdirected his or her deepest forces of body and soul, but either reserves them for due fulfillment in marriage or dedicates them in obedience to God according to God's call. The virgin state dedicated to God was highly esteemed by the early church, in accordance with the example of Christ and the counsel of Paul (1 Cor. 7:8ff.)—although the virgin martyrs who figure prominently in the accounts of the persecutions are often simply young girls, as are also the bridesmaids of Matt. 25:1–13. The dedicated virgin became so by her own vow, as noted by Hippolytus of Rome c. 200 (*Apostolic Tradition* 13), without separation from society. But since there was little place in the ancient world for the unmarried adult woman—though there was some (for example, the virgin who is said to have concealed Athanasius in her family vault was obviously an old maid)—the protection of virgins became the responsibility of the church in default of family, and hence one of the problems faced by the bishop (cf. Chrysostom, *On the Priesthood* 3.17). A natural solution was to bring them together under the guidance of older women such as the widows whom the church also supported. Hence monastic or conventual communities of women are somewhat older than those of men (cf. Athanasius, *Life of Anthony* 3).

Tertullian (*On the Veiling of Virgins*) discusses a rather amusing practical problem: Should dedicated virgins assume the matron's veil, as brides of Christ, or in token of innocence continue to go bareheaded, which might imply that they were marriageable? The former custom prevailed, and by the mid-4th century Rome developed a ceremony of the "veiling of virgins," along the lines of an ordination—first referred to by Ambrose with reference to the veiling of his sister by Pope Liberius, c. 360. By the Middle Ages, however, dedicated virgins were normally members of monastic communities, and the liturgical *velatio* became obsolete, being succeeded by the taking of vows* and the blessing of abbesses. In the later Middle Ages the older institution reappears in the form of the recluse, who lived in a cell attached to a church. The most famous is the mystical writer Dame Julian of Norwich, at St. Julian's Church in the city c. 1380–1410.
See **Celibacy; Monastic Ethics.**

E. R. HARDY

Virtue

"Virtue" is the translation of the Greek *aretē*, which simply means any kind of excellence. Thus a knife's *aretē* would be its sharpness, that of a horse its speed, and that of an athlete his or her skill. As these examples suggest, virtue was also thought to enhance or bestow power either by building on potential or by creating habits. Thus, as a moral category the virtues are dispositions that form passions and/or create habits. As Aristotle suggested, virtues are a "kind of second nature" that dispose us not only to do the right thing rightly but also to gain pleasure from what we do (*see* **Aristotelian Ethics**).

In heroic societies a virtue was determined by roles or functions. The virtue of the soldier is therefore not the same as the virtue of the statesman. Alasdair MacIntyre has argued that this is not just an oddity of heroic societies, but any account of the virtues requires display by a society's tradition. Attempts to depict the virtues in the more general sense as the means to, as well as the constituents of, the good, such as that of Plato and Aristotle, presuppose the importance of a society and tradition for the material content of the virtues. An account of the virtues therefore requires a sense of the *telos* of human existence, of some good, to which the virtues contribute, that gains its intelligibility from a community's concrete life.

The particularity of the virtues is often overlooked because *virtue* and the *virtues* are not distinguished. The former is sometimes, especially in modern society, used as a commendation for someone being generally upright. The virtues, however, are not equivalent to virtue even when virtue is understood in the sense of strength of character. The virtues are specific dispositions determined by the need to correct certain deficiencies (Foot), for the formation of the passions (Thomas Aquinas), as skills internal to activities or practices (MacIntyre), or as necessary for the performance of certain roles or offices. Virtue, on the other hand, is the stance of the self that coordinates or embodies the virtues in a manner that makes them virtues.

The relation between virtue and the virtues is complex and differs from one account to another. But the distinction is necessary in order to make clear that it is not enough simply to have a disposition to be courageous, but that such a disposition must be of the kind not easily lost. Thus Aristotle insisted that it is not sufficient to do what a just person does; to be virtuous we must do it in the manner that the just person does it. For Aristotle *phronēsis* (practical wisdom) is that virtue most needed for any individual virtue to be rightly formed (*see* **Prudence**). Yet the issue is complex, for he also maintained that practical wisdom cannot function rightly unless it is directed by the moral virtues. This circularity is but a reminder that virtue as well as the virtues entails a teleological account of human existence (*see also* **Teleological Ethics**).

It is one thing to recommend the virtues but it is quite another to know which virtues should be recommended. Plato's account (*see* **Platonic Ethics**) of the centrality of temperance*, courage*, prudence*, and justice*, which were later to be called the cardinal virtues*, has been misleading in this respect. For his list makes it appear that there was general agreement, even among the Greeks, about which virtues were central. But in fact that was not the case. Aristotle gives quite another account of the virtues, making no attempt to determine a central list but instead naming the virtues that were so identified

because they were the mean between two extremes. He lists temperance, liberality, magnificence, pride, good temper, and even an unnamed virtue between boastfulness and self-depreciation. His use of the mean to determine the ideal virtue has often been criticized as arbitrary.

This lack of agreement about which virtues were essential is only confirmed by later developments. Thus with the advent of Christianity a different set of virtues was emphasized. Charity, patience, and humility* were assumed to be as important as prudence and courage. Aquinas attempted to bridge the two traditions, suggesting that the "natural" or "acquired" virtues needed to be formed by the supernatural or theological virtues* of faith*, hope*, and charity*. Hence his famous formula: "Charity is the form of all the virtues."

Yet Aquinas's analysis of how charity is the form of the virtues is a good deal more complex than the formula itself suggests. For it is not that charity simply supplements the "natural" virtues, but rather that it must essentially transform the natural virtues to direct them to their proper end. Therefore Aquinas maintained that along with "infused supernatural virtues" come "infused natural virtues," which are not the same as the natural virtues in themselves. While the idea of infused natural virtues may be puzzling, it at least denotes Aquinas's clear view that Christian presuppositions about the *telos* of our lives change not only the status but also the content of the virtues emphasized by the Greeks. At the very least the language of "infusion" is an attempt to suggest that the virtues are as much a gift as an achievement.

How the virtues are individuated also involves the question of their interrelation. Plato and Aristotle maintained that the virtues were unified; that is, if a person were rightly formed by all the virtues in the right manner, there could be no possibility of a conflict between the virtues. Correlative with this view is the assumption that if a person is to be virtuous in one way, he or she must have all the virtues; for example, it is not enough to be temperate but we must be temperate as a person of courage or justice is temperate. In the light of such a claim many have wondered if it is possible for anyone to be virtuous. Such a view, moreover, seems to deny the temporal character of moral development, for it appears that people become virtuous by developing one virtue at a time.

The question of the interrelation of the virtues is connected with the issue of how virtue and the virtues are related. For it may be that the assertion of the unity of the virtues is an attempt to try to account for the virtue necessary for the virtues to be rightly formed. Yet Aristotle knew that virtue was not simply the result of the individual virtues added to one another. That he knew this may indicate his intuitive grasp of the possibility of conflict between the virtues and the necessity of virtue as the means to provide continuity to the self. In this respect Aquinas's claim that charity is the form of the virtues may perhaps be understood as his attempt to suggest the kind of life necessary to coordinate the many virtues we need to live as finite creatures destined for a life with God.

Various accounts of the moral life will emphasize some virtues as more primary than others. It has been the characteristic of modern moral philosophy, insofar as it has used the language of virtue and the virtues at all, to stress the virtues of sincerity, conscientiousness, and fairness* as primary. In the past these virtues have been considered secondary to more substantive virtues of courage, temperance, love, and, in particular, wisdom. Thus a commander of a death camp might be quite conscientious, but we resist calling such a person virtuous. Obviously other virtues are needed to inform our understanding of what it means to be conscientious.

A further issue is whether some virtues should be more prominent in certain stages of life than in others. For example, we almost think it unseemly for children to be wise, but think it important for them to be obedient. Of course it can be objected that such obedience is not a true virtue as children have not developed the capacity for virtue. However it remains the case that we do associate certain virtues with stages and functions in life that make it difficult for any one account of the virtues and their interrelation to be satisfactory. Thus, MacIntyre argues that it is a mistake to try, as Aquinas did, to provide an exhaustive and consistent classification of the virtues (see **Thomistic Ethics**). Too much of our knowledge of the virtues—both as to their kind and interrelation—is empirical to make such a scheme reasonable.

But it is just such "untidiness" that makes many concerned with moral theory suspicious of an emphasis on the virtues. Virtues seem to invite a subjective arbitrariness into moral considerations that it has been the purpose of modern moral philosophy to avoid. Thus the virtues have largely been treated as morally secondary to an ethics of obligation that emphasizes the centrality of rules and principles. The latter, it is assumed, are more likely candidates to ensure widespread agreement. Yet defenders of the stress on the virtues argue that rules and principles in fact involve the same kind of problems.

There has been a renewed interest in the virtues in contemporary Christian ethics. Some claim that an emphasis on "What ought we to be?" is more amenable to the display of how theological convictions work morally. Moreover, an emphasis on the virtues is said to offer a constructive alternative to the situation ethics* debate which seemed to require that we choose between situationalism and a rule-determined ethic. Most practitioners of Christian ethics, however, feel it is as yet too early to assess the success of this development for theological ethics.

See **Character; Habit; Cardinal Virtues; Theological Virtues.**

Thomas Aquinas, *Summa Theologiae;* Aristotle, *Nicomachean Ethics*; P. Foot, *Virtues and Vices,* 1978; P. Geach, *The Virtues,* 1977; J. Gustafson, *Can Ethics Be Christian?* 1975; S. Hauerwas, *Truthfulness and Tragedy,* 1977; A. MacIntyre, *After Virtue,* 1981; J. Wallace, *Virtues and Vices,* 1978.

STANLEY HAUERWAS

Virtues *see* **Cardinal Virtues; Virtue**

Virtues, Cardinal *see* **Cardinal Virtues**

Virtues, Infused *see* **Thomistic Ethics; Virtue**

Virtues, Theological *see* **Theological Virtues**

Vivisection *see* **Animals**

Vocation

The AV uses "vocation" only at Eph. 4:1, to translate *klēsis.* In the other nine places where this Greek word occurs the AV uses "calling." The RSV is consistent in using "calling" at Eph. 4:1 as well. Closely related is *klētos* (called), which occurs ten times.

Both primarily refer to the call of God through Christ to be a member of the community of his people and to show the qualities of Christian life that this implies, i.e., the call is to be a "saint," which is the NT term for every Christian. But in 1 Cor. 7:20 Paul also applies the term to the daily work of the Christian. The AV brings out this double use by translating this verse, "Let every man abide in the same calling [i.e., job] wherein he was called [i.e., when he became a Christian]." This was to have momentous consequences at the Reformation. In the intervening centuries the doctrine of the double standard had grown up. According to this, life in the world is a second best and follows the *precepts* that are binding on all; but a minority are *called* to follow the *counsels* of perfection* (poverty, chastity, and obedience). To them the term "religious" is given, and this remains a technical term for monks and nuns in the Roman Catholic Church, though since the Second Vatican Council the religious life is not seen as a superior vocation, though still a vocation; and so celibacy is not a superior vocation to marriage—both are vocations.

Luther rebelled against the doctrine of the double standard, and developed on the basis of 1 Cor. 7:20 a theology of the Christian's calling in the world (the German term is *Beruf*). The idea of vocation was brought from the monastery to the marketplace. The Christian's calling is to carry on the world's work to the best of his or her ability. If one is a cobbler, one's vocation is to cobble shoes well and thus to be a Christ to one's neighbor; there can be no higher vocation than that (cf. G. Wingren, *The Christian's Calling: Luther on Vocation,* 1957).

Paul's view was static. He did not envisage the Christian changing jobs. "So, brethren, in whatever state each was called, there let him remain with God" (1 Cor. 7:24 RSV). The reason is the same as for the grudging permission he gave to an unmarried person to marry; he thought the time would be very short before the Parousia (v. 29). Luther likewise had a static view, thinking it was far on in the history of the world. The Catechism of the Church of England in the 1662 Prayer Book, on which many children were brought up until into this century, was more dynamic where it refers to getting one's living "in that state of life unto which it *shall* please God to call me." In this it reflects a more dynamic

Calvinist emphasis. Out of elements of Calvinism have developed what is known as the Protestant work ethic, an ethic of hard work and thrift, which fitted in well with the requirements of capitalism. Max Weber's classic study *The Protestant Ethic and the Spirit of Capitalism,* ET 1930, showed this. It has produced an immense discussion that has tended to obscure the force of what Weber actually said (*see also* **Sociology of Ethics; Business Ethics**). However, in advanced industrial societies the adequacy of the ethic is being questioned; not that work should not be well done, as a Christian vocation, but whether contemplative elements from the Christian tradition are not also needed (*see* **Contemplation**).

See **Calvinist Ethics; Lutheran Ethics; Puritan Ethics; Work, Doctrine of.**

RONALD PRESTON

Voluntarism

In ethics and in theodicy*, voluntarism is a view closely (though not inseparably) associated with the nominalist philosophy. In answer to the question whether a thing is good because God wills it or whether God wills it because it is good, voluntarism chooses the first alternative. Voluntarist ethics is thus based on revelation, an ethic of the divine command rather than of natural law; and, similarly, God's dealings with humans are known in the mandates of his inscrutable will (the divine decrees) rather than in the effects of the divine intelligence discerned in the nature and purpose of things. From the first Reformers (and especially Calvin) until today, voluntarism has been a recurrent strain in Protestant thought. In spite of the crudities in which it has sometimes been expressed, the view has sought to safeguard the sovereignty of God, and the personal nature of his dealings and his commands.

See **Divine Command Morality; Morality and Religion, Relations of.**

JAMES A. WHYTE

Voluntary Associations

Voluntary associations are generally said to be of two types. If the association is concerned with the immediate satisfactions of leisure-time activities of the participants, it is spoken of as an *expressive association,* e.g., for the improvement of gardens or photography, the enjoyment of literature and the arts, the cultivation of hobbies. If the association is concerned to affect nonmembers as well as members for public goals with satisfactions immediate or deferred, it is called an *instrumental association;* usually, the intention is to engender or affect public opinion as a social force, and thus to resist or promote social change. Neither kind of association exists for the making of monetary profits. Both kinds of association are voluntary in the sense that a member is free to join or to sever membership. Although a church as a voluntary organization shares some of the characteristics of these associations, its self-understanding is different, especially because of its transcendent orientation, its sense of being called of God.

In federalist theory instrumental associations are to be understood in terms of a separation of powers, separation in that these associations provide intermediary "spaces," middle structures, between the relatively involuntary associations, the family* and the state*. These associations claim the constitutional right to freedom of association, a freedom that has had to be fought for, not without dust and heat. They provide the opportunity for the dispersion of power, the freedom of the individual or the group to participate in the making of social decisions affecting public policy. The voluntary and involuntary associations interact with each other in conflict or cooperation; when in conflict the voluntary association amounts to the institutionalization of dissent—in contrast to merely individual (relatively ineffective) dissent*. The open society is not willing to say, *"L'État c'est moi!"* The *moi* is larger. The voluntary association is not the creature of the state; moreover, the state itself is the creature of the community, which in turn is limited by a bill of rights preventing the sovereignty of the majority; democracy is *not* the rule of the majority.

The separation of powers may be traced far back in history. Max Weber observed that the Hebrew prophets by reason of their independence anticipated the modern free press. These prophets found sanction for dissent in numinous, charismatic authority. Likewise, the primitive Christian churches were associations independent of the establishment. The maxim "Render therefore to Caesar the things that are Caesar's, and to God the things that are God's" expresses this independence. Alfred North Whitehead speaks of it as a new principle of social organization. In

Roman law the young churches were in principle outlawed.

In the Middle Ages heretical groups were conspicuous dissenting associations. Taking the primitive church as its model, the covenanted "voluntary church" of left-wing Puritanism had to struggle through exile for its freedom of association, an important element of "the Protestant ethic" (overlooked by Weber). For Thomas Hobbes free associations were "worms in the entrails of the sovereign," necessarily to be "wormed." The demand for freedom of religious association opened the way for the demand for freedom of other associations to be actively concerned with public affairs. The demand for freedom of religious association brought about the separation of church and state; the voluntary church, the church of believers, thus relied upon voluntary financial support and not upon coercive taxation at the hands of the state. The collection plate almost became a sacrament. But more than independence was at stake. By the middle of the 18th century sectarians like the Quakers had devised the major strategies of the modern pressure group.

Already, then, the modern "organizational revolution" was taking place, manifest in the changing structure of the state, the separation of powers. With this revolution came also the antislavery movements, the organization of dissenting minorities, ethnic groups and women, neighborhood associations, scientific and professional societies, missionary societies, communitarian groups proposing models of an alternative society, socialists looking toward fundamental structural change, the promotion of civil rights or civil disobedience, or of liberation theology, private academies, libraries, and so on.

Church members have formed or have participated in these groups, and thereby have entered into association with members of other denominations and with nonchurch people. Vatican Council II promoted voluntary associations for the lay apostolate. In this way new conceptions of social responsibility, new types of leadership, new skills of organization appear, expanding the concept of the consent of the governed.

The voluntary association has become the characteristic and indispensable institution of a democratic, pluralistic polity—in contrast to an authoritarian or overintegrated (totalitarian) polity. Inevitably, associations compete with each other for support. Moreover, racist and other "antisocial" or antidemocratic groups enter into the competition. The availability of a variety of voluntary associations makes it possible for an individual to cooperate in concert with others of similar mind on a particular issue, and yet to participate also in other associations bringing together people quite unwilling to support the particular concern of the former group. This is the organizational meaning of pluralism*. Thus individuals do not need to agree on everything in a differentiated society where they presuppose a basic principle of freedom and order and at the same time agree to disagree on penultimate issues. Here we see the multiple relatedness of the individual in an open society.

At times the citizenry can find itself in the situation where voluntary-association theory becomes an ideology* for reducing the responsibilities of the state in face of the deprived. Voluntary associations often serve as watchdogs exposing the government as a violator of the law (also as refusing to enforce the law). They also attempt to expose lobbies and coalitions of lobbies supported by ample expense accounts from major economic "special interests" and geographical groupings, cotton, dairy products, lumber, corn and wheat, etc. Because of these coalitions the legislature has been called the "clearinghouse" for the lobbies. Of peculiar significance in the present era of nuclear weaponry is the opposition of increasingly international voluntary associations to the industrial-military-university complex.

See **Democracy; Ecclesiology and Ethics; Freedom; Pluralism; Politics; Society; State; Totalitarian State.**

J. L. Adams, "Mediating Structures and the Separation of Powers," *Democracy and Mediating Structures: A Theological Inquiry,* ed. M. Novak, 1980; F. I. Gamwell, *Beyond Preference: Liberal Theories of Independent Associations,* 1985; D. B. Robertson (ed.), *Voluntary Associations: A Study of Groups in Free Societies,* 1966; C. Smith and A. Freedman, *Voluntary Associations,* 1972.

JAMES LUTHER ADAMS

Vows

A vow is a definite promise* made to God. It differs therefore from an aspiration* or an intention*, or even a resolution. It is a definite undertaking whereby a person binds himself or herself to do or not to do, or to give something by a promise to God. A vow therefore is not something to be undertaken lightly or carelessly, but only after full deliberation* and recognition of all that is involved (*see also* **Oaths**).

Vows may be private or public. A public vow is one that is accepted in the name of the church by a legitimate ecclesiastical superior. A private vow is one made without seeking such acceptance. There is a further distinction within public vows, between simple and solemn vows. The distinction is not nowadays of much importance and concerns certain juridical effects attaching to solemn vows. Simple and solemn vows, public and private vows all create the same obligation.

Any person who has the full use of reason is competent to make a vow. For the vow to be valid, there must be (1) a clear intention to make a vow; (2) adequate deliberation, that is, a person must understand what burden of obligation it is that he or she is undertaking; and (3) free choice, that is, the vow must not be taken as a result of fear. The object of a vow, or what is promised to God, must be (1) something that is possible; (2) something pleasing to God—you cannot make a vow to do something that you know to be wrong, or make a vow about some triviality; and (3) something that effects an improvement in the present moral or spiritual state of the one who makes the vow. For example, chastity is an improvement on unchastity. A vow of chastity therefore is a valid vow.

Every valid vow creates a moral and religious obligation. Unless the vow itself specifies a time at which it is to be discharged, it should be discharged as soon as possible. A negative vow, i.e., a vow *not* to do something, becomes obligatory at once. Because a vow is a restriction on liberty, it is to be interpreted strictly.

A private vow ceases automatically to bind if there is such a radical change in the situation of the person who made it or in the thing vowed that had things been so at the time, the vow would not have been made. For example, a rich man vows to give a large sum annually to charity, but later loses his money and becomes poor. Or a person vows to build a church on a given site, but then cannot get planning permission. Public vows cease by dispensation granted by the appropriate authority. For a valid dispensation a just and sufficient cause is required. Such a cause is either the general good of the church or the private necessity or advantage of the person under the vow. A monk who is dismissed by his community because of his scandalous conduct may be dispensed from his vows for the good of the church. A monk who, convinced that he has mistaken his vocation, is finding it increasingly difficult to live in the spirit of his vows and is under constant grave temptation to break them may rightly be dispensed for the sake of his own good. Indeed, in the case of life vows, though a dispensation may often be delayed in order to give the person who asks for it time for further reflection, it is seldom, if ever, finally refused.

A vow may be commuted; that is, something else may be substituted in place of the original vow. If the thing substituted is something better than or at least not worse than the original vow, no just cause is required and it may be done by the person who made the vow. If something less than the original vow is to be substituted, there must be an adequate reason and also recourse to superior authority.

The Reformers frowned on vows, both public and private, and especially on the life vows of poverty*, chastity*, and obedience* taken by the religious. Their main objection was that vows restrict future liberty of action, and changing circumstances may and often do create altered duties. A vow may prevent or seem to excuse a person from discharging these new duties. Yet vows are of value both as affording strength and determination to the will, and as an expression of devotion and obedience to the will of God. The objections are met if care is always taken to prevent rash and ill-considered vows, and if wise and charitable use is made by those in authority of their dispensing and commuting powers.

Thomas Aquinas, *ST* II-II.88; J. Calvin, *Institutes* 4.13.

R. C. MORTIMER

Wage, Just *see* **Just Price and Just Wage**; *see also* **Wages and Salaries**

Wages and Salaries

There is no clear distinction between wages and salaries, though there is a tendency to call weekly payments for labor wages and monthly ones salaries, and these latter are often quoted on a yearly basis (*see* **Collective Bargaining**). In economic terms labor is one of the basic factors of production, the other two being land and capital. Because in industrial society labor considered as a unit by itself is in a weak position, as compared with the other two factors of production, there has been a tendency in Christian social ethics in the last century to say that a "living wage" must be the first charge on any enterprise, whereas the pure theory of laissez-faire competition would put the residual profit to the shareholders (owners of capital) first. The living wage in Roman Catholic thinking, where this demand has been strong since the first modern papal social encyclical, *Rerum Novarum* (1891), has meant sufficient to support a family of unrestricted size at a standard of life appropriate to the level of a particular state. This thinking goes back to the concept of the just wage (*see* **Just Price and Just Wage**) in medieval society, which was relatively stable; it was held to be that which would enable a family to maintain itself at whatever status and economic level it had. When this is applied to a dynamic economy there are many problems to be faced, not least how many essentials of a "reasonable" standard of life should be provided collectively and not by each family separately. Even allowing for this there is the challenge to see that disproportions of power do not allow some to be employed as "sweated labor" at wages and conditions which a humane society should not tolerate, because of the absence of collective provision. Also the difference between the highest and the lowest paid needs scrutiny; it is, for instance, much less in Sweden than in the USA or the USSR.

See also **Official Roman Catholic Social Teaching; Unemployment.**

RONALD PRESTON

War

The term has the principal meaning of armed conflict between or among nations or groups of people; by extension it also can refer to an intense, protracted struggle not involving arms. In this latter sense Christianity since the early centuries has encouraged the idea of the "soldier of Christ" (*miles Christi*) and the "army of Christ" (*militia Christi*) engaged in spiritual combat with evil as an alternative calling to that of military service on behalf of the state. Taking this seriously implies the moral rejection of war as armed conflict among peoples. Yet the majority of Christians over history have accepted such armed conflict as characteristic of life in a yet unredeemed world and have sought to define the limits of their participation in it. A "crusade" or "holy war" theme has recurred occasionally: in such wars God has been represented as calling Christians to take up arms and as fighting along with them. A more continuous tradition has defined the idea of "just war," in which Christians may morally participate according to the guidelines laid down in the tradition; by contrast, Christians must not take part in unjust wars.

In practice, Christian thought on war in any age has focused on the problems posed by war in that historical context. The attitudes of the early church were shaped in part by the character of imperial Roman military service, those of the Middle Ages by chivalric warfare and by the threat of militant Islam. In the context of the 20th century, discussion has focused chiefly on the destructiveness of contemporary warfare and the heavy economic burden imposed by military spending. Most recently these two concerns have been raised more specifically in connection with nuclear weaponry. A secondary contemporary issue has been argued sharply in some quarters: how far "wars of liberation" may be just and how far a Christian can or must participate in them.

See **Aggression; Conscription; Crusade; Deterrence; Just War; Militarism; Nuclear Warfare; Pacifism; Peace; Resistance; Revolution.**

JAMES TURNER JOHNSON

Weakness, Moral

The earliest extended discussions of moral weakness occur in Plato's *Protagoras* 352b–356c and Aristotle's *Nicomachean Ethics* 7. 2–3. Plato suggests that it is in some way impossible for human beings knowingly to do wrong. Aristotle admits that we do frequently speak of moral weakness as if it were a case of knowing what we ought to do and failing to do it, and he tries to explain how this paradoxical state of affairs can possibly come about. The shortest way with the problem of moral weakness is to assert roundly that there is nothing here that *requires* explanation. It is simply a fact about ourselves that we are able to act against our sincerely held moral principles, with full knowledge and full deliberateness. Romans 7 is the *locus*

classicus for the theological treatment of moral weakness, where it is seen as a consequence of sin, but not as in itself paradoxical or philosophically puzzling.

Many philosophers, however, follow Plato and Aristotle in believing that there is something paradoxical about moral weakness that does need to be explained, and various different types of explanation have been proposed. It has been suggested, for example, that moral weakness occurs when our knowledge of right and wrong is clouded by desire; or when our desire to do what is right is less strong than some other, perhaps more immediate, desire; or when, although we do in one sense know why we ought not to act in a certain manner, we do not properly attend to this knowledge in deciding how to act. Alternatively, it has been suggested that, despite appearances, we never in fact act contrary to a moral principle to which we *sincerely* subscribe at the time of acting. This line of approach, unlike the others, sees the issue as *conceptual* rather than psychological. No clear solution to the problem has won general acceptance.

G. W. Mortimore (ed.), *Weakness of Will*, 1971.

GERARD J. HUGHES

Wealth

Contrasting attitudes to wealth are to be found in the Christian tradition. These range from qualified approval to absolute rejection. Approval is found in stories about the patriarchs in Genesis, and among those in all ages who have emphasized the existing order as divinely ordained. In this regard Paul has often been misinterpreted and other central elements in the tradition ignored. That wealth is a gift and a blessing, especially when not sought, is part of the tradition (1 Kings 3:13). Hard work and diligence are certainly commended (Prov. 10:4; 1 Thess. 4:11). Whether the emphasis on this theme and the qualified permission of usury* at the Reformation led to the rise of capitalism* is much debated. Inequalities were certainly seen as necessary to the functioning of the worldly kingdom by Luther, and the need for differentials has been emphasized in modern times as a realistic way of encouraging the development of skills of value to the whole community (*see* **Just Price and Just Wage**).

The dangers of riches are stressed in various ways. Religions, and especially Christianity, teach that the true wealth is spiritual. Acquisitiveness, covetousness*, and the love of money are emphatically condemned throughout the tradition (Ex. 20:17; Isa. 5:8; 1 Tim. 6:10) as is trust in wealth (Ps. 49:6; Luke 12:19) (see also **Mammon**). These vices can render people insensitive to spiritual values and callous about the harm done to others. Where fraud, injustice, or oppression are linked with wealth, the prophets offer the sharpest condemnation (Micah 6:10ff.) as does James 5:4. Luxury is condemned by prophets (Isa. 3:18ff.), the fathers, medieval moralists, and the Reformers alike. Calvin was critical of commercial cities such as Venice and Antwerp.

Generosity as a positive obligation is emphasized both in the Bible and in the subsequent tradition. This has inspired the establishment of charitable foundations, and also campaigns to remedy grievous disadvantages, and to lessen the gulf between rich and poor societies (see **Charity; Philanthropy**). Equality* is seen by some (e.g., D. L. Munby) as the only ultimate standard. This motif certainly is found at 2 Cor. 8:14, and in biblical passages critical of great inequalities. For others community of goods is the goal. In Acts 4 this latter is probably a literary ideal used to describe and encourage a generous system of mutual aid* in earliest Christianity. The outright renunciation of property and wealth is urged in many passages in the Gospels. The story of the rich man's refusal in Mark 10 is only one instance of a wider motif in which discipleship was held to require renunciation of property* (Luke 9:57ff.; 14:33). Early Christian itinerants traveled without resources (Mark 6:8), and life without care was commended. This was a more significant feature of primitive Christianity than many will admit, but it was modified even within the NT period. Asceticism*, however, was the hallmark of the hermits and of the early monks and friars. Simplicity of life survived as a virtue also among Quakers, early Methodists, and others. The ideals of equality and community have been upheld by monastic orders, in the Radical Reformation, and by modern Christian social reformers in varying ways.

Among liberation theologians José P. Miranda condemns *differentiating* ownership. Gustavo Gutiérrez distinguishes liberation from revolution but is highly critical of a system in which there is wealth for the minority at the expense of poverty for the majority (see **Liberation Theology**). This echoes biblical passages such as Luke 1:53; 6:20–26; 16:19ff. There is urgent need to correct the injustice of gross maldistribution within and between societies while preserving or indeed enhancing basic values such as freedom. Attempts at the solution of unrestrained economic growth for all have drained scarce resources and caused pollution. However, the careful proposals of the Brandt Commission deserve attention. Also, technically advanced and disproportionately affluent societies may still have something to learn from those traditional societies which achieve a balance between their members and a balance with their environment.

See also **Poverty.**

G. W. Forell (ed.), *Christian Social Teachings,* 1966; G. Gutiérrez, *The Power of the Poor in History,* ET 1983; D. L. Munby, *God in the Rich Society,* 1961; J. F. Sleeman, *Economic Crisis: A Christian Perspective,* 1976; J. V. Taylor, *Enough Is Enough,* 1975.

DAVID L. MEALAND

Wedge Argument, Slippery Slope Argument, etc.

Often in disputes about such matters as abortion or euthanasia, someone will object to an act by saying that it is "the leading, entering, or thin edge of the wedge," "the first step on the slippery slope," or "the camel's nose under the tent." All of these metaphors express the conviction that the act in question —for example, abortion* or voluntary euthanasia*—will lead to other acts or practices that are recognized as morally objectionable and that, therefore, the act itself should not be performed. Accepting the act in question would cross a line that has already been drawn, and once that line has been crossed, it will not be possible logically or practically to draw it again to preclude terrible acts or practices. What will follow from the first act is alleged to be inevitable, perhaps irreversible, and certainly bad. For example, abortion may be held to lead to infanticide*, voluntary euthanasia may be held to lead to nonvoluntary or involuntary euthanasia, and letting terminally ill patients die may be held to lead to killing such patients (see **Life, Prolongation of**).

Although wedge arguments and similar arguments frequently appear in moral disputes, they are rarely analyzed and are usually dismissed out of hand. Such arguments are often more rhetorical than serious, and they are often invoked in ideological defenses of the status quo against proposed changes. Nevertheless, it would be a mistake to conclude that these arguments are always mistaken. They may be quite defensible in some cases.

It is essential to distinguish two major versions of wedge arguments and similar arguments. One version focuses on the logic of moral reasoning, noting that a justification of act X (e.g., abortion) implies a justification of act Y (e.g., infanticide) if there are no morally relevant differences between the acts. This version of the wedge argument appeals to the principle of universalizability*, which commits us to making the same moral judgment about relevantly similar cases. This first version of the wedge argument is sometimes used to support changes in moral practices; for example, a proponent of active euthanasia may argue that if a society accepts passive euthanasia, it ought to accept active euthanasia because there are no morally relevant differences between them. While the first version of the wedge argument focuses on the logic of moral reasoning—the hammer back of the wedge—the second version focuses on the actual historical, social, and cultural setting of the act—what the thin edge of the wedge is driven into. According to this second version, even if acts X and Y can be morally distinguished in principle, act X will practically lead to Y because of various social forces, such as scarcity of resources or racism*. For example, it might be argued that in a racist society, a policy of letting some patients die because of their anticipated quality of life will be applied to some races. Obviously this second version of the wedge argument hinges on an analysis, not of the logic of moral reasoning, but of various social forces, and on a judgment about the probability of those forces leading to act Y if act X is accepted. Frequently invoked in the wedge argument, especially the second version, is the specter of Nazi Germany, particularly its euthanasia program. An assessment of the second version of the wedge argument is in part empirical—what can be expected to happen in the society if act X is accepted? But an assessment of the first version depends mainly on the logic of moral reasoning— what does act X imply about other acts such

as Y? The ideological use of such arguments in many cases should not obscure their legitimacy in other cases.

S. Bok, "The Leading Edge of the Wedge," and P. Ramsey, "The Wedge: Not So Simple," *HCR,* Dec. 1971; P. Ramsey, *Ethics at the Edges of Life,* 1978.

JAMES F. CHILDRESS

Welfare State

The term "welfare state" seems first to have been used by Archbishop William Temple in his *Citizen and Churchman* (1941, p. 35). It is a reaction against the laissez-faire* theory of the state which goes with a belief in a free market economy, not only as a convenient mechanism by which many basic economic problems of production and distribution can be solved automatically without the complications of political decisions, but also as expressive of a philosophy of possessive individualism*. This holds that the best available way of running society is to leave it to the personal responsibility of self and family interest, the upshot being the maximum common good. Adam Smith was the main inspirer of this view. Many held it to be a powerful weapon against effete privilege, and it was the inspiration of the enormous economic growth brought about by the Industrial Revolution*. Along with it went the view that poverty* was probably one's own fault; where it was not, the appeal was if at all possible to private benevolence*, and to the state only as a last resort. If state relief was involved, it should be under conditions stringent enough to induce the recipient to get out of it if at all possible. Accordingly the 19th century spent much time in discriminating between the "deserving" and "undeserving" poor.

The foundations of the welfare state were laid in the UK by the minority report of a Royal Commission on the Poor Law in 1909. It was written by Sidney and Beatrice Webb, who were to devote their lives to social research. (No one remembers the majority report.) The view of the minority report underlay many of the social reforms of the pre 1914 Liberal government, and the social policies that followed the 1914–18 war. In the course of the 1939–45 war William Beveridge produced a report on social insurance and allied services, in which he identified what he called the "five giants" of want, disease, ignorance, squalor, and unemployment which government social policy should deal with. This in turn underlay the social policies of the Labour government from 1945, when the welfare state can be said to have arrived. It carried a good deal of conservative agreement, too, for there is a strong element among conservatives which is not so enthusiastic about laissez-faire, and feels a sense of public responsibility by the privileged for the underprivileged. Bismarck, for instance, arrived at many of the institutions of a welfare state in Germany in the late 19th century. In practice all advanced industrial societies have many welfare features, whatever their philosophy.

A welfare state means that the community makes corporate provisions for its citizens by guaranteeing them a minimum standard of life as of right, below which they will not be allowed to fall. It is not a matter of merit or desert. It is likely to include a guaranteed subsistence in the case of unemployment*, as well as access to education and health care, and some housing provision (see **Health Care, Right to**). It can be financed by elements of compulsory weekly insurance contributions, direct and indirect taxation on income, and wealth taxes. It is a recovery of a more organic view of human society and of the role of the state. The free market theory dissolves social relationships into individual contracts, and the view of the state that goes with it stresses its duty to provide law and order, security against aggression, the maintenance of contracts, and little else. It is suspicious of any political or government activity in the economic realm.

Laissez-faire* never worked out in practice very close to the theory. At the height of its influence cholera undermined one key feature of it; the disease could not be confined to the poor areas of cities but spread to the rich, and only public health measures could stop it. Also on the employers or management side there has been continued recourse to trusts and cartels and pressures on governments for protective tariffs and quotas; while the individual worker has felt unprotected and has organized defensive trade unions*, especially as Western economies have not developed smoothly, but in booms and slumps. The hardships the latter produced are beyond the bounds of the uncertainties of private benevolence to deal with. These modifications have made Western societies hard to

govern, and since the difficulties following the OPEC price rises from 1973 there has been a reaction by a radical Right in some countries against the welfare state, and renewed arguments for a free market economy. They are not, however, new arguments, and the public debate is repeating arguments from the past. Collectivist economies are centralized welfare states but lack the political freedom of the Western ones.

A welfare state may be said to translate into public terms Paul's words to the church in Gal. 6:2, "Bear one another's burdens, and so fulfil the law of Christ." Note that it requires an uncorrupt civil service and a lot of supplementary voluntary action by citizens if it is to work well.

See also **Capitalism; Philanthropy; Social Service of the Church; Socialism; State.**

RONALD PRESTON

Wesleyan Ethics

The life and thought of John Wesley (1703–1791) provide the inspiration for and the shape of Wesleyan ethics. Brought up in an atmosphere of piety in a high-church Anglican home, Wesley began to study at Oxford such works as Jeremy Taylor, *Holy Living and Holy Dying,* Thomas à Kempis, *The Imitation of Christ,* and William Law, *Christian Perfection.* These works instilled in him the conviction that one could not be "half a Christian," that "through grace" one must devote the whole of one's life to love of God and neighbor, and that discipline is crucial in cultivating such devotion. Wesley pursued this discipline by making a commitment to the priestly ministry and later by participating in a special group, which was gathered by his brother Charles for the study of scripture and the church fathers, for common worship, including frequent Communion, and for doing good works*. Its detractors called this group the "Holy Club" or the "Methodists." After several significant experiences, Wesley devoted himself to the proclamation of the gospel in the streets and fields of England and to the administration of the Methodist "societies" that arose in the wake of this proclamation. Although he did not produce a systematic work in Christian theology and ethics, an analysis of his sermons and other occasional writings reveals a clear and organic unity in his theological and ethical thought.

The proper foundation of Christian belief

and behavior for Wesley, as for Martin Luther and John Calvin before him, is God's action in and through Jesus Christ to justify sinful human persons. Human beings cannot merit God's "gracious" action, which must be accepted as a gift "by faith." God's grace* is thus prevenient, i.e., it comes before all human action. Wesley parted company with the classical Reformation, especially with Calvin and his followers, the Puritans, in holding that God's saving grace is offered to all, not only to the few who are the "elect." In addition, Wesley held that God's grace is "co-operant" rather than "irresistible": it works together with the free will* of the human person for his or her salvation. These controversial theological moves were dictated, Wesley believed, by scripture and by the requirements of moral responsibility*.

In contrast to Luther (see **Lutheran Ethics**), Wesley held that the fullness of faith* and the final aim of justification are achieved only when Christians are made righteous, that is, when righteousness* is imparted and not only imputed to them. This righteousness actually transforms Christians so that they are able to bear the fruits of faith in the form of love* of God and neighbor. While the transformation begins with the act of justification itself, it must continue in the ongoing and lifelong process of sanctification*, the completion and crown of which is Christian perfection (see **Holiness; Perfectionism**). Developed in response to such NT passages as Heb. 10:14 and Matt. 5:48 as well as to writings by the church fathers and by Taylor, Law, and others, Wesley's conception of perfection was distinctively Christian because perfection, like faith, is finally a gift of God in and through Christ. There is, however, nothing automatic about human progress toward perfection: Sanctification* is accomplished by the Holy Spirit but human discipline is also required for this growth. Here as elsewhere Wesley combined distinctively Protestant and Catholic motifs. Perfection in no way delivers one from ignorance*, mistaken judgment, bodily infirmity, or threat of temptation*. And Wesley insisted that perfection does not obviate the need to " 'grow in grace' and daily to advance in the knowledge and love of God." Christians may become perfect, not in the sense that they are not able to sin, but in the sense that they are privileged "not to commit sin." Wesley further qualified this claim by limiting it to sin* that is willful or "deliberate." Wesley not only spoke of Christian perfection in terms of the privilege "not to commit sin," but he also referred to it—perhaps more characteristically—as purity of, and perfection in, love of God and neighbor. Wesley did not believe that he had attained such a state, but he insisted on such a possiblity in this life as one important way to affirm and to celebrate the sovereignty of God's grace.

Wesley was concerned about "social holiness" as well as the salvation of individual souls: "The Gospel of Christ knows of no religion, but social; no holiness, but social holiness." This conviction led to efforts to meet the needs and promote the welfare of those around him—e.g., efforts to set up a loan society, to found a school for poor children, to establish a free medical dispensary, and to oppose the practice of slavery.

Wesley was a loyal Tory in politics, never wavering in his support for the Crown and for the established church, and he instructed his ministers not to preach on politics, except when they might express support for the government. There were, however, seeds in Wesley's thought that could develop in other ways, especially his emphasis on the rational and responsible conduct of individual moral agents. The essence of Wesley's economic message is contained in the sermon "On the Use of Money," which admonished "gain all you can," "save all you can," and "give all you can," maxims that appeared to accord closely with the philosophy of unlimited free enterprise. But since this message was intended for the lower classes as well as for the wealthy entrepreneurs, its aim was to inspire and encourage workers, many of whom made their way into the ranks of the middle class. In addition, Wesley sought to remind all persons that they are stewards of their earthly possessions, and thus should gain all they can and save all they can, so that they may give all they can.

There is debate among social historians about the character of Wesleyan ethics in England in the late 18th and early 19th centuries. Some have seen Methodism as a conservative movement opposed to all change, others as a liberal sect of almost revolutionary power, still others as a moderate force to stabilize and then bring progressive reform to society. Some have even claimed that the Methodist movement saved England from the revolution that swept over France. It is plausible to argue that the movement's political conservatism* served to check any revolutionary impulses that its participants might have had because of their social, economic, and political conditions. And the impact of Wesley's economic message along with the galvanizing effect of his religious message may have mitigated some of the social alienation* of the lower classes. Whether the net effect was beneficial or harmful is still debated.

The twofold objective of Methodism in the USA as in England was "to reform the nation . . . and to spread scriptural holiness over the land." Often, the emphasis in American Methodism fell on only one side of this commitment. For instance, in the latter half of the 19th century, more attention was given to the gospel of individual salvation and less to "social holiness." The typical practitioner of Wesleyan ethics in this period was often more concerned about whether or not to smoke, drink, swear, gamble, or go to the theater than about what could and should be done to alleviate continuing racial tensions, social inequalities, or threats to civil liberties. This imbalance between personal and social ethics, between individual piety and "social holiness," was redressed in part with the rise of the social gospel* in the late 19th and early 20th centuries. However, the social gospel did not always retain the concern for personal sanctification that had earlier characterized Wesleyan ethics.

One major direction of Methodist ethics in the 20th century has come from the influential writings of the "Boston personalists," including E. S. Brightman, A. Knudson, and Walter Muelder, among others (see **Personalism**). This movement is but one part of an ongoing attempt to recapture all aspects of Wesley's ethical outlook—his emphasis on grace* and good works*, on the God who is good enough to offer salvation to sinful human beings and who is great enough to bring about a large measure of this salvation here and now, and on personal sanctification and "social holiness."

See **Enthusiasm; Holiness; Nonconformist Conscience; Perfectionism; Sanctification; Social Gospel.**

R. M. Cameron, *Methodism and Society in Historical Perspective,* 1961; D. Hempton, *Methodism and Politics in British Society,* *1750–1850,* 1984; T. A. Langford, *Practical Divinity; Theology in the Wesleyan Tradition,* 1983; H. Lindstrom, *Wesley and Sanctification: A Study in the Doctrine of Salvation,* 1950; W. Muelder, *Methodism and Society in the Twentieth Century,* 1961; A. C. Outler (ed.), *John Wesley,* 1964; W. J. Warner, *The Wesleyan Movement in the Industrial Revolution,* 1967; J. Wesley, *The Works of John Wesley,* ed. F. Baker, 26 vols., 1974–.

WILLIAM H. BOLEY

Whistle-blowing

A relatively new term for an old activity, perhaps first appearing in print in the USA in the early 1970s. Whistle-blowing refers to actions intended to sound an alarm about a serious problem that needs correction, such as corruption on the police force, abuse of governmental power, a physician's incompetence, or the illegal or unethical practices of a business. Whistle-blowing is a metaphor drawn from the policeman's use of the whistle to stop traffic and from the official's use of the whistle to interrupt play in a game. While the policeman and the official in a game have institutional authority and sanction, whistle-blowers in government, business, or health care generally go beyond established channels. Whistle-blowing usually occurs when an insider, often a subordinate, dissents from policies and actions and, through the provision of information to the public, accuses his or her colleagues of wrongdoing. The whistle-blower decides that silence or withdrawal is not sufficient and seeks to direct public attention to the problem in question, often incurring a charge of disloyalty to the institution and colleagues.

Whistle-blowing may be justified when serious problems cannot be corrected through established channels; the whistle-blower should very carefully examine the facts, weigh the seriousness of the matter, and consider the effectiveness of alternative courses of action as well as the side effects of whistle-blowing. As Sissela Bok notes, "the ideal case of whistleblowing—where the cause is a just one, where all the less dramatic alternatives have been exhausted, where responsibility is openly accepted, and the whistleblower is above reproach is rare. The motives may be partly self-serving, the method questionable, and still we may judge that the act was in the public interest." The moral issues are similar to other modes of dissent*, such as civil disobedience*, but whistle-blowing is generally not illegal and is sometimes protected and even encouraged by the law. One major moral issue concerns the anonymity of some whistle-blowing (e.g., "Deep Throat" in the Watergate scandal). Public responsibility* is morally preferable to anonymity, but in some cases the risks to the identified whistle-blower may be significant. While whistle-blowing received favorable attention during and after the Watergate era in the USA, its dangers include mistaken or malicious actions, irreversible damage to reputations, invasions of privacy*, and subversion of trust* among colleagues. These dangers must be balanced against its probable benefits in particular cases. While whistle-blowing is morally right and even obligatory in some cases, one major task is to develop institutional structures of accountability to reduce the need for it.

See **Secrecy.**

S. Bok, "Whistleblowing and Professional Responsibilities," in *Ethics Teaching in Higher Education,* ed. D. Callahan and S. Bok, 1980; M. Glazer, "Ten Whistleblowers and How They Fared," *HCR* 13, Dec. 1983, pp. 33–41; A. Westin (ed.), *Whistle Blowing? Loyalty and Dissent in the Corporation,* 1981.

JAMES F. CHILDRESS

Widows

Widows are women whose husbands have died and who have not remarried. Among the Hebrews the practice known to anthropologists as the levirate was laid down in Deut. 25:5ff., wherein a widow had a definite claim to be treated as a wife by her husband's brother. There was, in fact, a reproach attached to permanent widowhood (cf. Isa. 54:4), based on the assumption that the brother would not have her. Nevertheless widows and orphans had a special call on the protection of God (Ex. 22:22). A widow, particularly one with young children, is in a position of great weakness, for the breadwinner and traditional protector of the family has gone. In English law this frailty was made more acute by the fact that before the Married Woman's Property Act of 1882 the property of a woman became the property of her husband on marriage and she had no prescribed

right to any part of his estate on death, and the husband could, in fact, will the estate away from his relict. This was further altered by an act of 1938 which gave a wife certain claims on the estate.

Most husbands left little or no property and widows were cared for either by relatives or by some form of public assistance. In most cases the English Poor Law was more generous to widows than to most other applicants for relief, but at certain times even they were forced to take institutional aid. England introduced a system of widow's pensions in 1925. This lasted for the rest of the widow's days. In the postwar recasting of social insurance the pension was substantially increased but was receivable only while the children were at school and not earning. In the USA since 1939 widows who have dependent children or who are past retirement age and are eligible for social security as widowed mothers or as older widows receive government support. There is debate about whether the level of support is adequate for those who are covered and about whether others should be covered.

See **Aged, Care of the; Children; Family; Poverty; Sex Discrimination; Social Service of the Church; Welfare State; Women, Status of.**

H. P. Brehm (ed.), *Widowhood,* 1983; H. P. Brehm and H. Z. Lopata, *Widowhood: From Social Problem to Social Program,* 1983; P. Morris, *Widows and Their Families,* 1958; H. Z. Lopata, *Women as Widows: Support Systems,* 1979.

BRIAN RODGERS

Will

Both ethicists and psychologists seem reluctant nowadays to talk about the will. Perhaps the word savors too much of the old faculty psychology, as if the will were some kind of mental organ, or a department of the mind or personality. The will is not thinglike or departmental. Will is rather the whole person behaving in a certain way, namely, striving to bring about some state of affairs. The will is not a "ghost in the machine" behind our actions, but is inseparable from and manifested in those actions. Perhaps one might say that the will inaugurates the action, but it also continues in the action. Sometimes too there may be an interval before an action, already willed and therefore inaugurated, manifests itself.

The word "will" has been used in very different senses. When one speaks of the "will to live," what is meant is something like an instinctive determination to survive; but when one says, "I deliberately willed this," one has in mind a kind of behavior in which calculation and reason play a major role. These examples from common speech are reflected at the philosophical level.

Schopenhauer and Nietzsche are examples of philosophers for whom the notion of will was very important, but who understood it in the first of the two senses, as an irrational instinctive drive. For Schopenhauer there is a universal will that is blind and aimless. In human beings, this universal blind will has attained consciousness. Schopenhauer associates it with the bodily instincts. Human life can never be happy when driven by this insatiable urge. So Schopenhauer was attracted by the Buddhist ethic* and its attempt to eliminate desire*. Will cannot indeed be extinguished, but cultivation of the mind and a life of contemplation* can help to diminish the tyranny of will. Nietzsche followed Schopenhauer in recognizing the fundamental importance of will. He spoke of the "will to po\., :," a will that is in everything, including the human being. But he differed from Schopenhauer's view that the will is to be subjected to reason. As against the Apollinian or rational ideal, Nietzsche sought to find a place for the Dionysian, symbolizing will and ecstasy. The human being must realize himself or herself in the will to power and create new moral values reflecting the will to power. The goal is a new order in which human power will achieve absolute dominance over the world, replacing the illusory divine power. (Some commentators have seen in this teaching the philosophical charter of technology*.) Will to power and transvaluation of values are thus closely related.

A quite different and perhaps ethically more orthodox understanding of will is found in Kant (see **Kantian Ethics**). For him, will is "nothing but practical reason*," and this reason, in turn, is the ability to act in accordance with laws. The essence of morality is the exercise of the "good will," the will that performs for their own sake the duties that reason deduces from universal laws. Kant does in fact acknowledge that the human will is sometimes weak and sometimes even cor-

rupt, and he acknowledges the value of religion to the extent that it educates and supports the will, but he has great difficulty with the idea that God might somehow supplement the strength of the will (see **Weakness, Moral**).

See also **Free Will and Determinism**.

J. N. Lapsley, *The Concept of Willing*, 1967; F. Nietzsche, *The Will to Power*, 2 vols., ET 1909; A. Schopenhauer, *The World as Will and Idea*, 3 vols., ET 1883.

JOHN MACQUARRIE

Wisdom Literature, Ethics in

Much of the wisdom literature of the Bible offers moral guidance to the community's youth. This guidance can be for quite practical purposes: the training of governmental personnel, the education of youth generally, or the passing on of the wisdom heritage to one's most gifted students. It can also be for the edification and entertainment of the community at large, as the sages practice their profession, just as priests and prophets practice theirs (see Jer. 18:18). In addition, the wisdom tradition, with its orientation to life as actually experienced, often plumbs the depths of human experience, showing how elusive wisdom can be as the search for her proceeds (Baruch 3:8–4:4 and esp. Job 28), how questionable is the proposition that in wisdom God created, sustains, and directs the universe (Job and Ecclesiastes), and yet how challenging and rewarding is the search for wisdom (see esp. Proverbs and the apocryphal books of Sirach [Ecclesiasticus] and the Wisdom of Solomon).

Kinds of ethical emphasis. The ethics of the wisdom traditions of the Bible are of several kinds. Best known is the pragmatic counsel offered by the proverb, the balanced, pithy utterance, known to most cultures in world history, by which a society passes on its experience in memorable, entertaining, and often ironic sayings. The ethics of the proverb is essentially prudential, hortatory, conservative. It commends diligence and care in one's labors, respect for elders and for those in authority, prudence in speech, sobriety, frugality, and especially the diligent pursuit of wisdom. But the proverb can also point to the depth dimensions of experience, and to life's essential mystery, thereby preserving this genre from banality. "The rich and the poor meet together; the LORD is the maker of them all" (Prov. 22:2). Such a proverb vividly reminds hearers that rich and poor alike stand mute before the power and the mystery of the divine creation.

Parables, fables, and extended personifications or self-representations also are prominent in the wisdom tradition; their ethical power is immense. Nathan's parable of the rich man who prepares a meal for his guest by using the poor man's pet lamb (2 Sam. 12:1-6) is well known. So is Jotham's fable about the trees' decision to choose a king for themselves, which ends with the acceptance of kingship only by the bramblebush (Judg. 9:7-15). Jesus' parables also derive from the world of wisdom. Parables offer guidance for ethics while they also give fundamental orientation for life as such. And many of the parables, like some proverbs, also challenge existing ways of understanding and action, beckoning the community to look more deeply and to ponder conventional moral action (see, among the many NT parables, that of the unjust judge, Luke 18:1-8).

Personifications are especially important for ethics because they give models of a compelling sort by which members of the community should or should not shape their lives. The model wife of Prov. 31:10-31 and the temptress of Prov. 7:5-27 are vivid examples —both, by the way, showing much independence on the part of women in ancient Israel —even if the conduct portrayed comes from the male-dominated viewpoint. The personification of wisdom in Prov. 1:20-33 and 8:1-36 also serves to encourage not only the pupils of the sages to devote themselves to learning; it urges the whole community to recognize the power, the truth, and the beauty of a life lived in pursuit of conduct that is in harmony with the divine wisdom itself.

Wisdom collections of special value for ethics are found in Job 29-31 (esp. ch. 31) and Sirach 44-50. But the fact is that the ethics of wisdom pervades all parts of the Bible: narratives, prophecy, the Psalms, the Gospels, the letters of the apostles, and the apocalypses.

Dangers and Values. The wisdom tradition can easily become tasteless and flat to sensitive members of the community, as is evident in Job and Ecclesiastes. It can also seem to be denied by the very experience of life that it purports to sum up (note the prosperity of the wicked as portrayed in Ps. 73, a wisdom psalm). Even so, the wisdom tradition outside the Bible and within it includes elements of skepticism and agnosticism that hold under criticism the flat assertions that the good life always is rewarded in this world by divine blessing. Wisdom ethics thus provides self-correction. Conversely, the skeptical wisdom carries its corrections as well: even Ecclesiastes includes much positive ethical counsel, invites the joyous living of one's life, and perhaps insists that vanity too—if pushed too grimly—would be vanity (Eccl. 3:1-15).

J. L. Crenshaw, *Old Testament Wisdom: An Introduction,* 1982; J. L. Crenshaw (ed.), *Studies in Ancient Israelite Wisdom,* 1976; G. von Rad, *Wisdom in Israel,* ET 1972.

WALTER HARRELSON

Wisdom, Practical *see* Prudence

Women, Status of

Discussion regarding the status of women in society has become widespread in academic settings only in the last decade. In earlier periods only a few, chiefly women, pondered this question. As with all matters related intimately to social change—and therefore to social conflict—factual or descriptive assessments of what the status of women in society *is* or *has been,* on the one hand, and morally normative evaluations of what the status of women in society *ought to be,* on the other hand, are intimately interconnected.

Those who favor traditional sex roles— that is, who believe that both women's and men's status should remain as it has been— also usually presume, at the descriptive level, that women's lives have been characterized by a constancy across cultures and through time that is conditioned by the biological reality of women's capacity to bear children. Whether the division of labor between men and women in society is understood to be dictated "by nature" or by "divine decree," the traditional view presumes that all women's lives are relatively homogeneous, repetitive with respect to social function, and characterized by minimal change. Here the assumption operates that men have been the active agents of historical change while women provided the stability of cultural continuity, chiefly within the domestic sphere or household. Until recently, such views were challenged infrequently at either the factual or the moral level.

Movements aimed at changing public policy with respect to women's lives began to develop in the middle of the 19th century, but the social conditions for such pressure greatly accelerated after World War II. As a result of this social pressure, acknowledgment that sex discrimination* exists has become widespread. Along with this moral reevaluation has come a new factual interest in the status of women historically and through social-scientific inquiry aimed at contemporary understanding. A protocol for historical scholarship is emerging that requires any characterization of the past to address gender relations explicitly. More and more, it is recognized that theories of gender relations can be developed only in cross-cultural perspective. Lively scientific, ethical, and religious debates have ensued.

On the descriptive level, rising skepticism about traditionalist assumptions regarding the status of women has produced unprecedented amounts of new historical research and social-scientific investigation. While the massive number of new studies has not resulted in simple consensus, historians and other social scientists who investigate the past, or work cross-culturally, have laid to rest all assumptions about either the cross-cultural uniformity or historical constancy of women's lives. Sex roles are reciprocally embedded in the social structure and all macrosocial change impacts males and females equally. The social roles of women as a group have varied widely from society to society. Household arrangements, divisions of labor between genders, child-raising patterns, etc., are far more diverse than traditionalists imagine. Conflicting conclusions have been reached as to whether there have ever been female supremacist, or matriarchal, societies in which both women's political power and their symbolic standing have been superior to men's. If matriarchies existed, they have been both rare and ancient. Matrilineal and matrilocal societies—i.e., those that designate kinship lines or residence rules through the mother—are not rare, and there are definite examples of matrifocal societies, societies where primary solidarity relations are sustained by women. However, most societies have had one of three forms. Some premodern simple societies have exhibited relative equality between the male gender system as a whole and the female gender system as a whole. Others were or are characterized ei-ther by "mythical" male dominance (Sanday) or by actual male dominance, sometimes viciously enforced. The latter is, overall, the most frequent form of social gender relation, and invariably characterizes politically powerful and highly differentiated societies.

As cross-cultural comparisons based upon this recognition of diversity accelerate, the question more and more asked by social scientists is: Why are some societies so much more disposed to male supremacy and role domination than others? We are far from having uncontroversial answers to this question. It appears that the frequency of natural disasters that threaten food supplies and warfare are variables closely related to male supremacist systems, and that a centralized, institutionalized religion and priest-centered cult is a major variable in sustaining male supremacist social systems over time. Furthermore, women's cross-cultural capacity for reproducing the species no longer appears to justify notions that homogeneous patterns of child care and child-raising prevail. Fear of women's reproductive power is recognized as a major factor in men's control of women, but when examined cross-culturally, patterns of socialization of children differ widely. In fact, the child-centered family or domestic unit is by no means a cross-cultural constant, and patterns of domestic divisions of labor also turn on one's location in the social strata. Upper-class women in complex societies rarely nurture the children they bear, and women in slave or indentured and/or poverty groups often are forced to raise other people's children but are prevented from nurturing their own.

What has become clear is that modern capitalist political economies (and perhaps, post-capitalist ones as well) have dramatically altered and reshaped gender relations and the status of women. Most premodern societies with traditionalist political economies pattern male and female gender roles in ways that publicly constitute and sustain gender roles as a social system. Both men and women *as groups* exercise important symbolic, productive, and consumptive functions in society, however. Even in male-dominated societies men's and women's collective social roles were grounded in and sustained by discrete female or male cultures. Neither gender had a monopoly on public impact because the collective functions of production and reproduc-

tion were interrelated so that all were necessary to communal well-being. The development of capitalist centralized production accelerated the splitting off of these productive
functions from the household unit (*see* **Capitalism**). This destroyed the social value of
work in the household because the domicile
ceased to be the basic unit where income-
producing activity took place. This "privatization" of the family* slowly but surely
eroded the collective power of women within
society. The modern perception of women is
that their lives are to be lived out in this
private sphere. The (fairly recent) advent of
the nuclear, child-centered family and urban
migration weakened traditional women's cultures. Women became more isolated from
their mothers, sisters, and women friends,
and the social value of their culture declined.
The personal and political disempowerment
of women was the consequence. Because
these structural changes are now pervasive
and touch the lives of women globally, movements seeking justice for women have
emerged within and across various cultures.

One dramatic side effect of the deluge of
new historical and cross-cultural research on
women's lives is methodological. It is recognized that previous social-scientific, including historical, inquiry has deeply distorted
human self-understanding by rendering half
the species invisible. Acknowledging the bias
against women's reality in established modes
of inquiry has also exposed other biases in
historical and cross-cultural description. Prevailing views of "the history of mankind"
appear now as a "view from the top," an
account of our social past rendered from the
perspectives of social elites and their hired
literati. To better grasp the status of women
in the past, it has been necessary to reorient
the focus of historical investigation from the
activities of political, economic, and intellectual elites, to concentrate upon those sociocultural relations of everyday life neglected
in dominant historiography. This "feminist"
or "liberation" hermeneutic, or principle of
interpretation*, requires intense skepticism
about generalizations regarding the past
drawn from data taken from the cultural
repositories of social elites. Since there is an
indisputable connection between dominant
moral and religious ideologies, on the one
hand, and institutions and systems of male
supremacy, on the other, this hermeneutic
also requires a new rigor and intellectual ma-

turity among religious ethicists and theologians. We must ask, for example, about
whether religious systems that emphasize
male blood sacrifice and salvation from
"earthly" sinful existence are not male supremacist religious legitimations developed
to transcend the earthy "once-bornness" of
women. It remains to be seen whether the
mainstream of so-called orthodox Christianity, and also Judaism, can deal candidly with
the mounting evidence of the connection between male supremacy and the salient characteristics of Western religious systems, as
presented, for example, in the scriptures.

The normative moral debate regarding the
status of women does not logically depend
upon these factual disputes about what is the
case. These normative differences do not follow scientific debates precisely, because ideology*, or one's contemporary political and/
or symbolic interests, provides an intervening
variable that conditions the judgment as to
the seriousness of sex discrimination*.
Nevertheless when moral and theological
difference exists, it is because our disposition
toward truth claims and our religious vision
are intimately related. Whether, or to what
extent, one concedes the disadvantaged status of women to be an urgent moral issue
depends upon how one assesses one's interests in relation to the status quo, and upon
one's conception of what sort of world is divinely intended or makes for human well-
being. Male supremacist visions of society are
best sustained by images of the historical past
in which women's role and place were at least
relatively fixed by nature or God. By contrast, those who believe change is morally
desirable will be drawn to pluralistic charac-
terizations of the past that incorporate
human diversity.

At the descriptive level, it is clear that the
material and emotional pressures on women
are dramatically on the increase. "The femin-
ization of poverty*" is a recently coined
phrase to characterize the discovery that well
over three fourths of the very poorest people
in the world are women and their dependent
children. The phrase also identifies a long-
term trend in the global political economy
that ensures that women and their children
will make up an even larger proportion of the
poor in the future. Hence, it is certain that
whatever the outcome of scholarly debates at
the scientific level, the status of women as a
normative moral question in social ethics re-

quires urgent attention in Christian ethics now and in the future.

See **Feminist Ethics; Liberation Theology; Oppression; Sex Discrimination.**

A. Y. Davis, *Women, Race and Class,* 1981; S. Dowell and L. Hurcombe, *Dispossessed Daughters of Eve,* 1981; J. L. Flandarin, *Families in Former Times,* 1979; B. W. Harrison, *Making the Connections: Essays in Feminist Social Ethics,* 1985; N. C. M. Hartsock, *Money, Sex and Power: Toward a Feminist Historical Materialism,* 1983; G. T. Hull, P. B. Scott, and B. Smith (eds.), *But Some of Us are Brave: Black Women's Studies,* 1982; N. Jay, *Throughout Your Generations Forever: A Sociology of Blood Sacrifice,* Ph.D. dissertation, Brandeis University, 1981; J. Kelly, *Women, History and Theory,* 1984; R. P. Petchesky, *Abortion and Woman's Choice: The State, Sexuality and Reproductive Freedom,* 1984; P. R. Sanday, *Female Power and Male Dominance: On the Origins of Sexual Inequality,* 1981; E. Schüssler Fiorenza, *In Memory of Her: A Feminist Reconstruction of Christian Origins,* 1983; A. Swerdlow and H. Lessinger (eds.), *Class, Race, and Sex: The Dynamics of Control,* 1983; E. Zaretsky, *Capitalism, the Family and Personal Life,* 1978.

BEVERLY WILDUNG HARRISON

Work, Doctrine of

Work is a central reality of existence; and as soon as there is any division of labor (we cannot imagine any society without it) work is a basic social reality. It can be both a brute necessity and drudgery and also a joy, either because of the creativeness involved in some jobs or because of the social significance work brings, or both. This double aspect of work as toil and a joy is brought out in the biblical "parables" of Creation and Fall in Genesis. The Bible has a realistic attitude to work and is not at all fastidious, unlike the Greeks. The educated Greek thought ordinary work degrading for a free man; it was for slaves; and a touch of this attitude can be seen in Ecclesiasticus 38, which comes significantly from hellenized Judaism. The Bible may not do enough justice to creative art, but it certainly sees the vast bulk of the world's work positively under God. The NT stresses the need to work and not to be idle, to work well and cheerfully (cf. 1 and 2 Thess., passim; Col. 3:23). Work is a vocation.

The doctrine of vocation* has been cor-rupted in the Christian tradition to refer especially to the work of the ordained ministry (not more than 1 percent of the church) or paid church work; and to spill over from that to work with a high personal content, such as nursing, teaching, or social work, but not to manufacture; so that a Christian in industry is more likely to regard personnel management as a vocation and not the job of works manager. In particular semiskilled or unskilled work has not been thought of within a doctrine of work. There has also been a bias to think of work in agriculture as more of a vocation than work in industry, an indication of the slowness with which Christians have come to terms with the new kind of society produced by industrialism. However, agriculture is so mechanized in Western countries that it makes this attitude increasingly absurd.

The Christian doctrine of work sees it as a means of loving God by serving human needs. Needs are interpreted in a broad sense, but not as broad as wants. There are some wants which it is hard to please God by supplying, but in general we should not be too fastidious. If gambling, for instance, is within bounds a legitimate activity, so is the supplying of facilities for it. The church has never excommunicated bookmakers. As to choice of jobs, those who have the longest and most specialized training will expect to exercise it, but they usually have a fair choice where to do so, and what life-style they will adopt. Those with the least differentiated skills will find it easiest to change jobs. However, while there may well be a "right to work" if one lives in a society that evaluates people by their work, there cannot be a right to a particular job if the needs of society change. At the same time the state should so arrange its economic affairs that there is no long-term unemployment. A wise society moves younger rather than older men to new jobs, and provides generous adjustment allowances and retraining facilities when a change of type of job requires this.

See **Unemployment; Vocation.**

RONALD PRESTON

World Council of Churches
see **Ecumenical Movement**

World Government
A proposal to create a world authority with full powers of government over a limited

range of functions. These functions would include external affairs and control of military forces, and perhaps also certain aspects of trade, taxation, and international transport and communications. Remaining functions of government would be the responsibility of a second tier of national governments, and of any lower tiers. A world court would interpret the legal instrument setting out the distribution of functions among different parts of the international authority or between international and national authorities, and would adjudicate in disputes between different authorities. This arrangement would be to elevate the federal idea from the national to the international level. Proposals for world federal government enjoyed some popularity in the West in the years immediately before and after the Second World War. In Western Europe, the movements for world government tended to split in the 1960s between those advocating regional unity in part or all of Europe, as a step toward world government, and those who feared that regional unity or unification might prove an obstacle to world government. Some proponents of world government see the UN and its agencies as an embryonic world authority, while others favor the establishment of a completely new international authority with limited executive, legislative, and coercive powers. World government, like all federal systems, confronts problems arising from divided sovereignty, dual allegiance, and the need for appropriate checks and balances. It has been criticized as utopian.

See **International Order; Internationalism; National Sovereignty; State.**

E. Culbertson, *Summary of the World Federation Plan,* 1944; R. Hutchins et al., *Preliminary Draft of a World Constitution,* 1948; S. H. Mendlovitz (ed.), *On the Creation of a Just World Order: Preferred Worlds for the 1990s,* 1975; C. K. Streit, *Union Now,* 1939, ²1949.

SYDNEY D. BAILEY

Worldliness

The ambiguity of the concept of the "world" in Christian thought is present from the beginning. In the NT the world is the world of humans, in opposition to God, but it is also the world which God loves and which he has reconciled to himself in Christ.

The history of Christianity may be seen in terms of the dialectic which arises from this ambiguity. Sometimes the world-denying ascetic element has prevailed, as in the early monastic movement, sometimes the assertion of the world and its claims, as in Luther's words to the German nobility: "The sphere of faith's work is worldly society and its order." Yet even in the great periods of world denial, or the periods of greatest insight into the necessity of world affirmation, there has never been established a final resting point for Christian thought: no direct or simple solution, either simply in the world or simply out of it, has been found. The tension which has consequently been maintained has been immensely fruitful for all spheres of Christian thought and enterprise. In the realm of ethics there has thus been a long-drawn-out struggle with classic views, especially with the Stoic view. At this point the recognition of the reality of the intramundane ethical demand has worked powerfully to save Christianity from simple denial of the world. Yet even here the issue has not been resolved. For how may the Christian speak of harmony with the rational order, in face of his or her belief in the revelatory reality both of evil and of suffering as historically focused in Christ? On the other hand, the Christian cannot take refuge in total resignation either. Worldliness, even "holy worldliness," is often thought of today (the terminology is usually influenced by the later thought of Dietrich Bonhoeffer) as the necessary form of Christian life. But since this conception flows primarily from a specific though not always articulate Christology, it is not possible to identify it with any straightforward naturalistic ethic. Christians, though recognizing that they are entirely within this world, and have their duties and claims alongside all people, are still not simply "of" this world. Their "worldliness" is thoroughly dialectical. This dialectic arises out of their faith that the absolute demand upon them is simultaneously the demand of a Demander: They acknowledge God as a personal will active in history. This absolute will, acknowledged as concentrated in the historical person of Jesus Christ, asks for their total commitment in an ultimate relation. At the same time, this absolute claim upon them puts them back into the world, where they must be engaged, in the penultimate sphere, with the same problems and demands as everybody else. The problem of a Christian secularism arises here, and the unfinished discussion on this and related points is an indication of the continuing vitality of Christian faith in relation to the world.

See **Dialectic; Secularism; Secularization.**

D. Bonhoeffer, *Letters and Papers from Prison,* ET 3rd ed., rev. and enl., 1971; W. G. Maclagan, *The Theological Frontier of Ethics,* 1961; H. R. Niebuhr, *Christ and Culture,* 1952; R. Gregor Smith, *Secular Christianity,* 1966; A. R. Vidler, "Holy Worldliness," *Essays in Liberality,* 1957.

R. GREGOR SMITH

Wrong *see* **Norms; Right and Wrong; Sin(s)**

Zeal

Not a common word now, "zeal" in its positive sense has been replaced by "enthusiasm"* and in its negative sense by "fanaticism." In the NT, praiseworthy zeal is distinguished from blameworthy zeal according to their goals and their effects. Christ's redemption was to purify a people who "are zealous for good deeds" (Titus 2:14), and Christians are exhorted to be zealous for "higher gifts" (1 Cor. 12:31). But zeal may also be misguided; for example, before his conversion Paul was "as to zeal a persecutor of the church" (Phil. 3:6). In Jesus' time the Zealots actively sought to overthrow Roman occupation by violent means; one of Jesus' disciples, Simon, had been a Zealot (Luke 6:5; Acts 1:13), and Jesus was probably viewed by the authorities as a rebel even though he did not endorse the Zealots' use of violence or refusal of taxes (*see* **Resistance**).

JAMES F. CHILDRESS

Zoroastrian Ethics

Schwerer Dienste tägliche Bewahrung,
Sonst bedarf es keiner Offenbarung.

In the years 1814 and 1815, Goethe gave expression to his deep interest in Eastern religion, history, and literature in a cycle of poems to which he gave the title *West-östlicher Divan.* His study of the religion of Zoroaster (Zarathushtra), the prophet of ancient Iran, and his desire to achieve a synthesis of Eastern and Western thought and philosophy resulted in a lengthy poem, written in 1815, to which he gave the title *Vermächtnis* (Heritage). In the two pithy lines quoted above, Goethe seems to indicate that the Zoroastrian mind has no need for a revelation other than the daily performance of one's burdensome duties.

In Goethe's day little precise knowledge of Zoroastrianism had reached the Western world. In addition, Goethe's summary statement gives as much an insight into his own mind as a reflection of Zoroastrian philosophy. Yet, diligence in the performance of one's daily duties is truly one of the essential tenets of the Zoroastrian way of practical behavior. As it is put by Zarathushtra himself, it is "dawn, noon, and evening that remind the 'faithful' of his [daily] obligation[s]."

In the 2,500 years that lie between the first half of the 6th century B.C., the most likely period of Zarathushtra's activities, and the present-day Parsees (or Parsis) in India, who profess Zoroastrianism as their creed, important changes, if not complete reversals, in ideology, beliefs, and practices have taken place. Indeed, as Zaehner has pointedly observed: "The history of [the Zoroastrian] religion, even in its heyday, has been so checkered that a Parsee would have no difficulty in finding scriptural evidence to justify a total monotheism, an uncompromising dualism, or even a barely disguised polytheism." But perhaps the relative validity of statements based on the nonhomogeneous materials contained in the Avesta and in the Pahlavi books, which date from Sassanian times (A.D. 250–650), is in no need of further emphasis.

A case in point is the often-mentioned practice of good thought(s) (*humata*), good word(s)(*hūkhta*), and good deed(s)(*hvarshta*), which, according to Parsee and Western interpreters alike, is "the fundamental principle of the Zoroastrian creed" (Masani) and "the quintessence of the moral and ethical teachings of Zoroaster" (Jackson). A recommendation of this practice as such, however, is not included in any one passage of the *Gāthās,* those portions of the Avesta that are supposed to be the true reflection of Zarathushtra's own thoughts. On the other hand, the three terms occur frequently in other Zoroastrian texts. For instance, they are part of a well-known prayer ("We are praisers of good thoughts, good words, good deeds [that are being thought, spoken, and] done and [have] been [thought, spoken, and] done . . ."); they are used at several important moments in the Zoroastrian liturgy and they symbolize the three steps by which the soul of the true Zoroastrian approaches paradise after death. The Zoroastrian devotee makes a pledge to "well-thought thought, the well-spoken word, the well-performed act"; the three coils of the girdle (kustī) worn around the middle by the Parsees are thought to symbolize the trifold ethic of thought, word, and act.

Cases like this are not rare; in fact, they are the rule rather than the exception. It is not until later, particularly Sassanian, times that a systematic code of Zoroastrian ethics was developed. This code was in part derived from the original teachings contained in the ancient writings; other parts of it were based on more recent ingredients. The mainspring of this code lies in the Zoroastrian assumption of the original and complete separation of the principles of good and of evil. The triple injunction implied in the (Sassanian) terms humat, hūkht, and huvarsht is the practical conclusion drawn from this view. It is also part of the consequence of the well-known Zoroastrian premise that man by his origin belongs to Ahura Mazdā ("I belong to Ohrmazd") and as such is in a position to choose for the good on his own.

Statements on ethics abound in the Sassanian texts. The old virtues, already recommended or suggested by Zarathushtra, of husbandry and agriculture ("Till the earth . . . for all men live and are nourished by the tilling of . . . the land"); of truthful and righteous behavior in accordance with the nature of Asha (truth) ("Speak the truth so that you may be trusted"); and the obligation to keep earth, water, and fire free from contact with impure matter, are repeatedly mentioned. Other passages refer to such virtues as generosity ("Be as generous with your property as you can"); hospitality ("Make the traveler welcome so that you yourself may receive a warmer welcome in this world and the next; for he who gives, receives and [receives] more abundantly"); industry ("Rise before dawn so that your work may prosper"); education ("Be zealous in the acquisition of education, for education is the seed of knowledge and its fruit is wisdom"); moderation ("Show restraint in your eating [and drinking] so that you may live long"); contentment with one's lot ("Do not be unduly glad when good fortune attends you, do not be unduly sad when misfortune befalls you"); tact ("All actions depend on the proper time and place"— "Speak sharply only after much reflection,

for there are times when it is better to speak out and times when it is better to hold your peace"—"So far as you possibly can, do not bore your fellowmen"). Still other passages provide bits of popular wisdom ("Put out of your mind what is past and do not fret and worry about what has not yet come to pass" —"Do not make a new friend out of an old enemy, for an old enemy is like a black snake which does not forget old injuries for a hundred years"). In short, "Live a good and useful life, be considerate to others, fulfill your religious duties, cultivate the land, rear a family, and bring up your children to be literate and educated," while keeping in mind that "men are like a water skin full of air; when punctured nothing remains; men are like suckling babies, creatures of habit who cling to their habits."

Without going into the complex problem of the relationship between Zoroastrianism and Plato's philosophy (see, e.g., J. Bidez, Eos, ou Platon et l'Orient, 1945), it may be of interest to quote the generally correct echo of Zoroaster's way of thinking in Plato's view (Alcibiades 1.121): "When a boy reaches fourteen years, he is entrusted to four royal tutors, the most wise, the most just, the most temperate and the most brave [among men]. . . . The first of these teaches . . . the Magian wisdom of Zoroaster . . . , that is, the worship of the gods . . . , also what pertains to a king; the most just . . . , to be truthful all his life; the most temperate . . . , not to be subject to even a single pleasure in order that one may be . . . a free man, not a slave; the most brave . . . , to be fearless and bold."

These quotations show that on the basis of the old ideas of Zarathushtra a set of new values was developed. On the one hand, these values reflect the polished standards of behavior characteristic for Sassanian civilization; on the other, they are the outcome of the acceptance, for theological as well as secular purposes, of the doctrine of the avoidance of extremes. "Neither too much nor too little" has become the favorite theme of both theologians and the laity. In this connection, it is worth noticing that theological speculation developed a list of vices to be avoided as opposites of each virtue to be pursued. This systematization is, in part, the consequence of the basic Zoroastrian distinction between the separation of good and evil as symbolized by Ahura Mazdā (Ohrmazd) and Angra Manyu (Ahriman). Falsehood became the standard opposite of truthfulness, stinginess of charity, greed of contentment, sloth of industry, bad manners of education, and so forth.

The controversial matter of the next-of-kin or consanguineous marriage can only be mentioned. Its occurrence is actually attested in Achaemenian and Sassanian times, it is critically mentioned by Syriac authors and not infrequently recommended in Sassanian texts. The evidence has been contested by modern Parsee authorities, and Western interpreters have looked upon the custom as being of foreign (Median) origin (Zaehner).

Since the arrival of Zoroastrianism in India in about the 8th century, the Parsee community in Bombay and other places in northwestern India has striven to live up to the ancient ethical values in its religious and social behavior. In the words of one of its distinguished members: "Some of the sterling qualities of the Parsi community . . . are its vitality . . . , its adaptability to changing circumstances . . . , its industry and spirit of citizenship; and above all, its philanthropy."

M. Boyce, *A History of Zoroastrianism,* 2 vols., 1975, 1982; J. Duchesne-Guillemin, *La religion de l'Iran ancien,* 1962; *Symbolik des Parsismus,* 1962; A. V. Williams Jackson, *Zoroastrian Studies,* 1928; F. M. Kotwal and J. W. Boyd (eds.), *A Guide to the Zoroastrian Religion,* 1982; R. Masani, *The Religion of the Good Life: Zoroastrianism,* 1938; J. J. Modi, *The Religious Ceremonies and Customs of the Parsees,* [2]1937; M. Molé, *Culte, mythe et cosmologie dans l'Iran ancien,* 1963; J. M. Unvala, "Die religiösen und sozialen Sitten und Gebräuche der Parsen," *Wörter und Sachen* 17, 1936, pp. 174–192; and vol. 18, 1937, pp. 145–163; G. Widengren, *Iranische Geisteswelt,* 1961; and *Die Religionen Irans,* 1965; R. C. Zaehner, *The Teachings of the Magi,* 1956; and *The Dawn and Twilight of Zoroastrianism,* 1961.

MARK J. DRESDEN

INDEX OF NAMES